The Gemäldegalerie, Berlin

ECCE ANCNVS DEI

THE GEMÄLDEGALERIE, BERLIN

A History of the Collection and Selected Masterworks

Weidenfeld and Nicolson, London

The publication of this book has been made possible by the generosity of the Kaiser-Friedrich-Museums-Verein, the association of friends of the Gemäldegalerie and the Sculpture Gallery.

Compiled by Henning Bock, Rainald Grosshans, Jan Kelch, Wilhelm H. Köhler and Erich Schleier

Jacket: Gerard ter Borch, *The Parental Admonition* (p. 239)
Frontispiece: Fra Filippo Lippi, *The Adoration in the Forest* (p. 293)

© 1985, 1990 Staatliche Museen Preussischer Kulturbesitz
English translation © 1986 George Weidenfeld and Nicolson Limited

Photos: Jorg P. Anders, Berlin; Gerald Schultz, Berlin; Bildarchiv Preussischer Kulturbesitz, Berlin; Museum Archives

All rights reserved. No part of this publication may be reproduced, stored in a retrieval system, or transmitted, in any form or by any means, electronic, mechanical, photocopying, recording or otherwise, without the prior permission of the copyright holder.

First published in Great Britain in 1986 by
George Weidenfeld and Nicolson Limited
91 Clapham High Street, London SW4

Translated from the German by John Gabriel
Designed by Simon Bell
Jacket designed by Regelindis Westphal, Berlin
Typeset by Keyspools Ltd, Golborne, Lancashire
Colour separations by Newsele Litho Ltd
Printed and bound by L.E.G.O., Vicenza

CONTENTS

PREFACE

When you come upon it in the residential and university suburb of Dahlem, the Berlin Gemäldegalerie might well seem very grand – a Neo-Classical edifice with three wings, built in 1912 along the lines of the Baroque county seats that once dotted the plains of Brandenburg, a lone reminder of Prussian history among the modern functional buildings of the Free University. Seven museums are housed in this building complex and its new additions: the Museums of Ethnology, Far Eastern, Indian and Islamic Art; the Department of Prints and Drawings; and the Galleries of Sculpture and Painting (the Gemäldegalerie). Collections of immense contrasts – Polynesian outriggers, splendid works by Riemenschneider and Rembrandt, statues of Buddha and Chinese scroll painting – vie for the visitor's attention. Yet it is just this variety that best characterizes the Berlin Museums' purpose. Ever since their founding in 1830 they have been devoted to collecting, studying and exhibiting the art and artefacts of all the world's cultures.

The Gemäldegalerie has its exhibition rooms in the 'old building', with about 650 paintings that illustrate the development of European art from the thirteenth to the eighteenth centuries. The collection, as you will see, is not large, and in sheer number certainly cannot match the great museums of Munich, London, or Paris. Yet a fine selection of masterpieces from van Eyck to Rembrandt, from Giotto to Tiepolo, from altarpieces of the Hohenstauffen period to paintings by Watteau and Gainsborough, puts our museum among the few in the world whose treasures are familiar to everyone seriously interested in art.

The tradition-conscious atmosphere of the gallery's rooms, however, is misleading. It tends to make one forget the long and often ugly history this collection has had to weather. One of the best public museums of painting even before the First World War, it was threatened by total destruction in 1945; and it would seem almost a miracle that despite irreparable losses – of over four hundred superb paintings – so much was saved from the ruins.

The inauguration of the Gemäldegalerie in 1830 was one result of the idealistic, cosmopolitan thinking of the generation around Wilhelm von Humboldt. After the Second World War the gallery was incorporated in the Prussian Cultural Heritage Foundation (Stiftung Preussischer Kulturbesitz) with its headquarters in the Western Sector of Berlin. This was also a far-sighted political decision, for in 1947 the State of Prussia, to which the museums owe their existence, was abolished. Its art treasures survive as a testimony to the great spiritual achievements of a troubled nation.

The present volume contains a selection of major works from the gallery which gives an impression of the scope and quality of the collection and its high-points. Let me say two things about the arrangement of this book. First, you may find that some of the commentaries, particularly those on Italian art, have a flavour of the history of ideas. What we wished to show, by example, is that research in art history must often negotiate a rocky road in order to explain the significance of a work in terms of its historical milieu. Much of our knowledge is still in the hypothesis stage and a great deal of further study is required. Secondly, we decided not to combine our small groups of French and Spanish paintings into national sections. Instead, we have classified them according to era and school. Thus you will find Fouquet and Marmion among the Old Netherlands artists; Poussin and Claude Lorrain, and also Velasquez and Murillo, in the Italian Baroque section; and Watteau and Chardin among German and English painters of the eighteenth century. Rigorous historians might object, but this arrangement corresponds to the system by which the collection was traditionally organized, as well as reflecting the emphases and departments of today's museum. This volume of reproductions and notes, in other words, mirrors the collection's history. To supplement it, we are planning a complete catalogue of the museum's holdings, the first of its kind since the 1931 edition of our *Descriptive Catalogue*. That catalogue will contain an index of artists together with an illustrated section arranged by nation and school.

In retrospect, the post-war history of the Gemäldegalerie sometimes seems to have been a long series of East-West quarrels over its priceless contents. Yet we should not forget the tenacious and selfless efforts made by its members and employees, in public and behind the scenes, without which the gallery would never have been able to continue its work for the public good, nor have become the fine member-institution of the Prussian Foundation Museums it is today. It is to them, therefore, that I gratefully dedicate this book. My cordial thanks are also due to the Supporters' Association for the Galleries of Painting and Sculpture, the Kaiser-Friedrich-Museums-Verein, whose generosity has made the publication of this volume possible.

Henning Bock
Director, Gemäldegalerie
Staatliche Museen
Preussischer Kulturbesitz

Bruno Paul (architect)
The former Asiatic Museum, 1912
Today the Gemäldegalerie, Dahlem

THE HISTORY OF THE COLLECTION

BY HENNING BOCK

Our collection originally began with the seventeenth-century princes of Brandenburg and kings of Prussia. Of course they had begun decorating their residences with art before that time, in the sixteenth century; but apart from a few works by Lucas Cranach, purchased during a trip to Berlin in 1529 and over the following years by Prince Joachim III for his palace and the Protestant Cathedral, little of significance is recorded. Art collecting in the serious sense, indeed a considered taste in art, developed only later.

The Thirty Years' War of 1618–48 laid waste any modest prosperity which Brandenburg's rulers may have achieved – and it was certainly modest by comparison with the pomp and glory of the great towns and residences of south and central Germany. Not until 1640, when Frederick William, the Great Elector (1640–88), took the throne, did Brandenburg's rise to European rank begin. His relations with the House of Orange in Holland, the years he spent at the court of Governor Frederik Hendrik, and his studies at the University of Leyden (1634–6), had been an education in taste for the gifted statesman. On his maternal grandmother's side Frederick William was a great grandson of William I of Orange, and his marriage to Luise Henrietta in 1646 consolidated this tie. In Holland he experienced a country that had been largely spared the devastation of war and which enjoyed unparalleled economic and cultural prosperity.

In addition to his familiarity with Dutch painting, Frederick William also had a great interest in Italian art. His humanist education had been broad enough to take him beyond the Dutch masters, whose intimate world was basically like his own, on to the idealistic world of antiquity. He expanded the Kunstkammer at Berlin Palace, acquiring coins, cameos, bronzes and vases, and Greek and Roman sculpture. Later, Frederick William also organized excavations within his own territories to unearth ancient relics, and began collecting Far Eastern porcelain and rarities from Africa.

S.Blesendorff after A.Clerck
Frederick William, the Great Elector
Etching

On the death of the Dutch Governor's wife, Amalie von Solms, Frederick William's kinship with the House of Orange brought a bequest of forty-two (or forty-three) paintings to Berlin, among them works by Rubens, van Dyck, Roelant Savery, and Jan Brueghel the Elder. These were exhibited at Berlin Palace, in a small room known as the *Schildereien-galerie*. The only painting in the present collection which can be traced back to this bequest is Titian's *Portrait of a Young Man*. When William III, King of England and grandson of Amalie von Solms, died in 1702, another portion of the Heritage of Orange, as it was known, fell to Brandenburg-Prussia. Besides a number of minor Dutch masterpieces, two fine early works by Rembrandt have come down to us from this bequest, the *Rape of Proserpina* and the canvas known as *Minerva*.

After the political, military and economic rise of Prussia to become a kingdom under Frederick I (1688–1713) and his puritanical, even bigoted successor, Frederick William I (1713–40), there began an epoch that more than any other shaped Prussia's image for better or worse. Frederick II, the Great, was a lifelong and uncritical admirer of everything French, even when political alliances among the great powers of Europe, which now included Prussia, made France an enemy. He spoke, wrote and thought in French, and had no high opinion of his native language and literature. His active interest in contemporary French painting, however, lasted only twenty years or so, up to the Seven Years' War (1756–63), the period in which he commissioned most of the elaborate new buildings or additions to his personal apartments at Potsdam, Charlottenburg and Berlin Palace – and at Rheinsberg, which had been rebuilt while he was still Crown Prince.

Frederick's acquisitions began in 1734, when his father, Frederick William I, gave him the small castle at Rheinsberg and a stipend which allowed him to live as befitted his rank. At last the young, musically gifted Crown Prince could escape his father's tyranny and associate with friends of his own choosing. His life at Rheinsberg to 1740 was a continuous round of conversation and debate on French and classical literature, philosophy and science, concerts, theatre and masquerades. At the regular dinner parties of about fifteen select guests, the prince was surrounded by such gifted contemporaries as the architect and painter Georg Wenzeslaus von Knobelsdorff, Antoine Pesne, artist and director of the Berlin Academy, the renowned Kapellmeister and composer Johann Gottlieb Graun, the flautist Johann Joachim Quantz, and, at the harpsichord, Carl Philipp Emanuel Bach.

Suitable surroundings for Frederick's short-lived idyll were created by von Knobelsdorff, who rebuilt the castle on Grienerick Lake and landscaped its park. The dreams of his Spartan youth seemed to have come true in its carefully composed vistas and seem to be reflected in the paintings by Watteau, Lancret and Pater which he now began to collect enthusiastically. The carefree Regency and Rococo art lifted Frederick and his 'Court of the Muses' far above the pomp and parades of the capital. With the rebuilding of Rheinsberg, with his new paintings, the wit and intelligence of his companions, the joy of music, and his own poetry inspired by Roman idylls, Frederick created an Arcadia in the midst of the Brandenburg sands. Painting was only one facet of this ideal world; yet a year before reality asserted itself, he could report proudly to his sister, Wilhelmine, Margravine of Bayreuth, that he had already filled two rooms with pictures, most of them by Watteau and Lancret.

On 31 May 1740, Frederick was crowned, and all the power and wealth of the Prussian State stood at his disposal. He moved from his beloved Rheinsberg to the royal residences at Berlin, Charlottenburg, and, most importantly, Potsdam. At all these places, impatient and peremptory, Frederick had new apartments built or the old ones refurnished in *Le style moderne*. The exquisite décor required pictures to match, and these he ordered, often with precise requirements, from Paris. Helping to arrange purchases were Count Rothenburg, Prussian attaché in Paris; Marquis d'Argens; Francesco Algarotti, a Venetian who also served as middleman to the Dresden Court; and Antoine Pesne, official painter to the Prussian Court. Gradually the collection grew to several hundred works. Watteau, master of *fêtes galantes*, was represented by nineteen paintings, among them his *Signboard for the Art Dealer Gersaint* (acquired in 1745) and *Embarkation for Cythera* (documented at Potsdam since 1765).

But Frederick could not be long without a refuge from his official duties, so he designed a small Palace for the park at Sanssouci which was built under von Knobelsdorff's supervision in 1745–7. Except for paintings and a few sculptures from the recently acquired Polignac collection, installed at the existing Small Gallery on the north side of the park. Frederick's paintings were again exhibited as part of the elaborate decoration.

Art historians characterize this epoch in Prussia as 'Frederician Rococo', but this really touches on only one aspect of Frederick's collecting activity. The *fêtes galantes* period was certainly a happy time in the King's life, full of projects and ideas which a circle of superb artists transformed into reality; but the period was short. In the early 1750s Frederick's requirements changed, and with them his view of art. More than a mere change of taste, his turn to the great and lasting art of van Dyck, Rubens, Rembrandt, Poussin and Correggio grew out of the monarch's realization that the duties of his high office must be taken seriously and that among the demands they placed on him was the need for outward show. Though he still sometimes made an exception, he struck Watteau, Lancret and Pater from his purchasing list and replaced them with the classical masters.

For this new collection Frederick took nothing from the old one at Berlin Palace, but built it up exclusively from new acquisitions. Whether he was led more by personal preference or by reasons of state, with an eye to the great collections at Dresden, Kassel or Salzdahlum in Brunswick, we can only conjecture. At any rate, Frederick commissioned his Chief Architect, Johann Gottfried Büring, to add a gallery to the east side of Sanssouci Palace. Begun in spring 1755, work was soon interrupted by the outbreak of the Seven Years' War, and not until 1764 was the gallery completed. It was a long, single-storey building with a central bay and tower, its façade design based on that of the Orangery. A square of massive central columns was the sole interior division, and at the east end a chamber was set aside for the smaller paintings. An exquisite, if rather austere, colour scheme of gold, white and green provided a noble setting for the great classical works on which Frederick had now set his eye – all of them, characteristically, large compositions

Georg Friedrich Schmidt
after Antoine Pesne
Frederick the Great, 1764
Engraving

Sanssouci
The Picture Gallery, 1755–64
Interior

with figures; no still lifes, landscapes, or genre subjects found their way into the great hall.

This independent gallery-building, the first at any of the royal residences in Germany, was widely acclaimed by Frederick's contemporaries. Even the exacting Gottfried Schadow recalled in his memoirs of 1849 that the Potsdam Painting Gallery was 'the most glorious hall of pictures in Europe'.

The hanging of the pictures still followed the late Baroque style of covering the walls with hardly a gap between the frames. Nevertheless, an attempt – the first of its kind – was made to arrange the works historically, with Dutch art in the east wing and Italian in the west wing. Compared with the collection of August III in Dresden, however, the Potsdam gallery remained a modest endeavour, particularly as Frederick refused to pay what were even then horrendous prices for masterpieces of the first order, which would have completely overtaxed Prussia's budget. He also invariably trusted his own judgement above anyone else's, with the result that errors and mistaken attributions to great and renowned artists could hardly be avoided. There remained, none the less, an impressive body of major works which left the collection's rank undiminished. The catalogue prepared by Matthias Oesterreich, Gallery Inspector, listed in its second edition of 1770 a total of 168 paintings, sixty-five of them Italian, ninety-six of the Flemish and Dutch schools, and seven of the French school.

*

The more conservative Frederick grew during his final years at Sanssouci, the more fiercely his policies were resisted, particularly among the progressive artists of Berlin. The first condition of any meaningful change, they knew, would have to be a fundamental reform of the Academy of Fine Arts and Mechanical Sciences, which during the eighteenth century had sunk to insignificance. No revival of contemporary art was possible without a reform of the Academy, insisted Berlin's artists, with Daniel Chodowiecki foremost among them. And Frederick, perhaps surprisingly, listened to them and found their proposals convincing. Shortly before his death in 1786, he nominated a new curator, the capable and circumspect Minister of State von Heinitz, who immediately took the necessary steps.

Von Heinitz's most important decision was to establish annual exhibitions at the Academy along French, English (and also Dresden) lines, where recent work of German and foreign artists could be seen. These made contemporary art accessible to a bourgeois public for the first time (and later, under Frederick William III and IV, provided a source of paintings and sculptures for the royal residences). At the same time, there was a plan to open the royal collections to the public. The Minister of State managed to obtain permission for a limited number of artists to study and copy the paintings in the collection, arguing that like the treasures in the royal libraries, these classical masterworks should gradually be made accessible to all in the name of public education.

Frederick the Great's successor, Frederick William II (ruled 1786–97), devoted much energy to furthering this aim. He had the royal collections placed under the jurisdiction of the Academy, and in 1787 named an artist, Johann Gottlieb Puhlmann (1751–1826) as Inspector of Galleries in Berlin and Potsdam – this despite Frederick the Great's declaration that, since no further purchases need be made, the collection would not require an inspector after Matthias Oesterreich died. Frederick William II also established prizes for the best works in each genre at the annual Academy shows. And though these and other measures represented only a small part of a wider programme of administrative and judicial reform, they spurred and decisively shaped later developments.

As far as museum planning was concerned, the nomination of Alois Hirt, an archaeologist, to the chair of Art Theory at the Academy proved to have far-reaching consequences. Hirt (1759–1837) had lived in Italy from 1782, and was familiar with progressive tendencies in European thought which attributed a key role to fine art in the public sphere. In an address to the Academy on the occasion of Frederick William II's birthday in 1797, Hirt explained his plans for a great public museum. The best works in sculpture, painting and craftsmanship from all the royal Prussian collections, he said, should be brought to Berlin, where they would serve as a school of good taste for the entire nation. Not only were the works selected to be of high artistic quality, but they were to be

Sanssouci
The Picture Gallery, 1755–64
Exterior

exhibited in a way that illustrated the historical development of the arts, school by school and epoch by epoch. The unique character of each period, each country, and every artist, must be made manifest, Hirt explained. His idealistic aim, in short, was to enlist the fine arts in a programme that combined an appreciation of beauty with a general, historical education.

This dual task of a public museum – to show fine and beautiful works of art which had been collected and arranged according to scholarly, historical criteria – remained the keynote of every discussion about the Berlin museums from that point on and has shaped their character and purpose down to the present day.

The King was impressed by Hirt's suggestions. To him, art was not a mere decorative adjunct to the royal palaces and apartments, not a treasure to be hoarded but to be shared with people generally. Though he realized that the troubled times were not conducive to the building of a new museum, the King requested Hirt to outline a provisional scheme. Working rapidly, Hirt had finished his project by September 1798; but it was too late for Frederick William II's approval. The plans presented to his successor, Frederick William III, foresaw a massive square edifice at the most prominent site in central Berlin, the Forum Fridericianum, next to the Arsenal and across from Knobelsdorff's Opera House. The ground floor was to house the department of antiquities, and the upper floor the collection of paintings. The rooms were to be fitted with tall windows whose lower sections could be closed by means of wooden shutters, which, as Hirt assured, would 'create lighting conditions of the kind artists have in their studios'. And as to the purpose of the new museum, its designer again stressed that 'a gallery ought to be an education in good taste, which means that the first principle of any gallery should be logical order in the arrangement of its works of art'.

Anonymous artist
Alois Hirt

The museum idea was beginning to find support in other quarters as well. The Chairman of the Royal Kunstkammer, Jean Henry, had developed his own conception of a general, public museum of art by 1804, a scheme which continued the universal approach of the old *Kunstkammer* collection – natural sciences, fine art, and cultural history under one roof.

The vicissitudes of politics, however, put an end to both of these ambitious projects. All the effort invested in them came to nothing when Prussia was totally defeated on the battlefield in 1806. Worse still, as Napoleon's armies were decimating the Prussians at Jena and Auerstädt on 14 October, preparations were under way to bring the art treasures from Berlin and Potsdam to safety in Küstrin. The crates, some containing valuable paintings from Potsdam, fell into French hands and were immediately transported to Paris. A short time later, a French Trophies of War Commission under Vivant Denon, whom his own officers mockingly called '*voleur à la suite de la Grande Armée*', requisitioned some of the finest things in the royal palaces for the new Musée Napoléon in Paris. A highly knowledgeable connoisseur, Denon chose 123 paintings, most of them Old German and Old Netherlandish, including sixteen by Cranach (his *Fountain of Youth* among them) and a number by Baldung Grien and Altdorfer. He also chose Correggio's famous *Leda*, Rembrandt's *Samson Threatening His Father-in-Law* and *Samson and Delilah*.

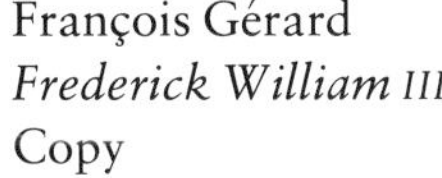

François Gérard
Frederick William III
Copy

In spite of these serious losses, the notion of establishing a public museum in Berlin continued to be discussed, if with a shift of emphasis. Prussia's defeat had set off a wave of reform proposals which aimed at nothing less than reshaping the state and its administration from top to bottom and infusing new life into moribund institutions. Wilhelm von Humboldt projected far-reaching educational reforms in which both the museum and the newly founded university (1809) had their place, for, in his eyes, the humanities and natural sciences had an equal contribution to make to the education of liberal-thinking, well-rounded individuals.

Yet though the university was able to open its doors by 1810, plans for the museum made little headway. The first task at hand was to take stock of the remaining royal collections. Christian von Mecheln (1737–1817), a Swiss publisher and etcher, and librarian to Queen Luise, undertook a complete inventory which revealed that despite losses, the collections still contained a total of 80 statues, 133 busts, 29 vases and 2,244 paintings. The King ordered that a selection of these works be put on temporary exhibition in the university building, entrusting Minister of State von Dohna and Privy Counsellor Wilhelm von Humboldt with the task of choosing suitable items.

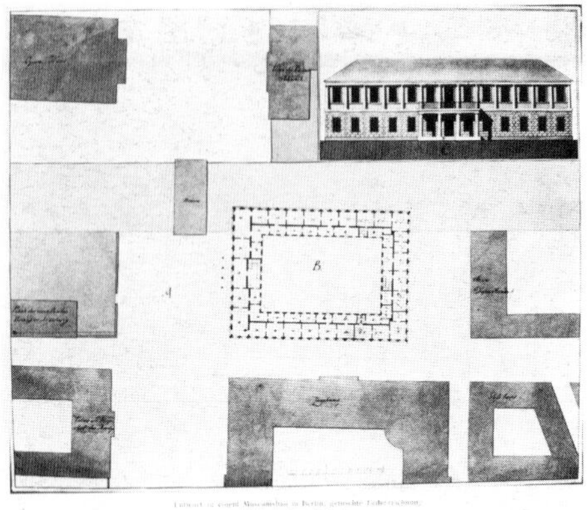

Alois Hirt
Plans for the museum building in Berlin, 1798
Pen and wash

Again political events intervened, but this time for the better. Following Prussia's victory in 1814, Frederick William III went to Paris and saw the erstwhile Musée Napoléon. He was deeply impressed, not only by its opulence, but also by the systematic arrangement of its collections. In 1815, the Napoleonic Era definitely over, the King ordered the stable buildings of the Academy on Unter den Linden to be rebuilt to house a museum. Its inaugural exhibition was to consist of the art treasures brought back from Paris.

*

The idea of creating a public museum, however, had another consequence: the systematic purchase of individual works and entire collections with the ambitious aim of comprehensively illustrating the history of art. The first spectacular acquisition was made before the year 1815 ended. While in Paris in 1814, the King had seen a collection amassed by the brothers Vincenzo and Benedetto Giustiniani, principally during the early seventeenth century, which had been on view in Paris since 1812. Prominent among its 158 paintings were masterpieces of the early Roman Baroque, including Caravaggio's *Doubting Thomas*, *Amor Victorious*, *Christ on the Mount of Olives*, and *St Matthew, Evangelist*. The Giustiniani collection also contained fine examples of the work of Baglione, Baburen, Terbrugghen, Honthorst and Vouet, Claude Lorrain and Guido Reni. Now, these artists certainly did not conform to the Neo-Classical taste then prevalent in Prussia, which epitomized Raphael and the late Italian Renaissance; nevertheless, the Prussian government decided to buy the Giustiniani Collection for a price of 500,000 francs. Not surprisingly, when it went on exhibition in 1826, no one praised it very highly, and we have little means of knowing today how significant the collection actually was: too many of its major works were destroyed by fire in 1945 at the Friedrichshain shelter where they were stored during the war. Of the five Caravaggios only *Amor Victorious* and (at Sanssouci) *Doubting Thomas* survived the catastrophe.

Another attempt to purchase a whole collection for the projected museum went awry. In 1815, von Altenstein, Prussian Minister of Culture, saw the famous collection of early German and Dutch paintings which the brothers Sulpiz and Melchior Boisserée had brought together at Heidelberg. Very much taken by it, he asked Karl Friedrich Schinkel if he could make some arrangement with the Boisserées to sell their collection to Prussia. Thanks to his negotiating skill, Schinkel drafted a contract acceptable to all before the year was out, which involved a payment of 200,000 guilders, a life pension for the collectors, and the transfer of their treasures to Berlin. Yet though the Boisserées had refused tempting offers from other countries and reached a basic agreement with the Prussian government, the contract was never signed. The Minister of Finance withheld his approval, arguing that the quality of the collection did not justify the expense. The Old German school, he maintained, was no model for the art of the present or the future and therefore did not deserve inclusion in the new museum. This triumph of the fiscal arm spoiled a unique opportunity. Ten years later King Ludwig of Bavaria bought the Boisserée Collection, which has been a mainstay of the Old Pinakothek in Munich ever since.

Wilhelm Hensel
Edward Solly
Drawing
Berlin, Nationalgalerie SMPK

While medieval German art found slow acceptance in Prussia, a hesitation due partly to the enthusiasm shown for it by the Romantic school, Italian art became a key facet of the new collection with the purchase of the Solly Collection in 1821. Edward Solly (1776–1848), an English merchant, was the younger partner in the London firm of Isaac Solly & Sons. Specializing in the Baltic Sea trade during the Napoleonic Period, the Sollys had prospered immensely. Edward lived in Berlin, where he brought together a collection of over 3,000 paintings with the help of agents scattered all over Europe. His main interest was Italian art, the development of which he hoped to illustrate from its beginnings to its apogee in Raphael and the High Renaissance. After Napoleon's demise and the lifting of the blockade, however, business slackened and Solly's firm came into difficulties. Though he had received 200,000 thalers from the Prussian government in settlement of old claims, he was forced in 1819 to put up his collection as security on a further 200,000-thaler loan. His situation did not improve, however, and Solly finally made over his collection to Prussia on 21 November 1821, against compensation to the sum of 500,000 thalers.

Thus it was that the Prussian state collections, their new museum still pending, were enriched at one fell swoop by works of truly inestimable value. The old, rather haphazard royal collection, increased first by purchases in Paris and then by the Giustiniani Collection, had now been placed on a broad and solid foundation. When in 1823 the unfortunate Solly was compelled to relinquish his house on Wilhelmsstrasse, 677 pictures were selected for the museum, another 538 went to decorate the royal palaces, and the remainder were put in storage. The Trecento was represented by Giotto, Taddeo Gaddi, Bernardo Daddi, Lorenzetti, Lippo Memmi, Allegretto Nuzi, and others. Of the much more comprehensive Quattrocento group, Filippo Lippi's *Madonna in the Wood*, Botticelli's *St Sebastian*, Mantegna's *Presentation in the Temple*, and Carpaccio's *St Stephen* deserve special mention, as do, from the early sixteenth century, an early Raphael Madonna, Titian's *Self-portrait*, Lotto's *Christ Taking Leave of Mary*, and Savoldo's *Lady of Venice*. The Solly Collection also contained such superb examples of early Netherlandish and German painting as two wings of the Ghent Altar by the van Eyck brothers (demanded as war reparation by the Belgian government in 1918, though Solly had purchased them from the dealer Nieuwenhuys), Holbein's *The Merchant Gisze*, and the delightful little *Portrait of a Lady* by Petrus Christus.

Friedrich Tieck
Karl Friedrich Schinkel, 1819
Marble
Berlin, Nationalgalerie SMPK

*

The problem of housing these new collections, however, still had to be solved. To save money, the government initially intended to convert the former royal stables at the Academy, Unter den Linden, and Hirt and Schinkel drew up a plan for this in 1815 (it was Schinkel's first involvement in the museum). The considerable sum of 200,000 thalers was finally granted for conversion work in 1822; but a few months later a quite different project made all previous planning obsolete.

On 8 January 1823, Karl Friedrich Schinkel, architect, High Privy Counsellor for Building, and Professor of Architecture at the Academy, showed his plans for an autonomous new museum to the King. Schinkel's project revealed not only architectural skill but a brilliant mind for city planning. Siting the new museum at the Lustgarten north of the palace, he envisaged a spacious square flanked by Arsenal, Schlüter's Baroque palace façade, and a cathedral, which would provide a noble introduction to Berlin's most magnificent thoroughfare, Unter den Linden. The museum's façade, an imposing colonnade fronting the square, conformed to the scale of the surrounding structures yet set a contrasting aspect which emphasized the high moral aspirations of this first public museum in Prussia.

The superb solution to the protracted debates seems to have convinced the administration immediately, particularly Frederick William III, who approved the project on 30 April. Due to unfavourable site conditions, the cornerstone could not be laid until 9 July 1825, but by 10 November 1826, rough construction was finished and the traditional *Richtfest* could be celebrated. The new building was inaugurated on 3 August 1830, the King's sixtieth birthday, after what was even by today's standards an astonishingly short construction time of five years.

Oldermann, after F. Krüger
Wilhelm von Humboldt
Lithograph

In 1828, Schinkel and Gustav Waagen, later Director of the Gemäldegalerie, wrote a paper in which they stated their aims so succinctly that it deserves to be quoted. After pointing out that the Berlin collections were still the only ones in Europe to be compiled and shown according to systematic, scholarly criteria, the two authors concluded that the museum's 'first and true purpose consists in awakening in the public mind a sense of visual art as one of the most important branches of human culture, and when this has been awakened, to nourish and develop it to an ever finer sense. All the various interests of individual classes in society must be subordinated to this general purpose. By far the most pressing need is to give artists ample opportunity for study. Only then can the interests of art scholars be taken into consideration. Thirdly and finally, knowledge of art history should be generally encouraged and the dissemination of this knowledge be made as wide as possible ... However, this is not to say that aesthetic interests may not be combined to a certain extent with historical interests, if only this first and fundamental principle is kept in mind: enjoyment first, then edification.'

What was it about Schinkel's museum plan that immediately convinced his con-

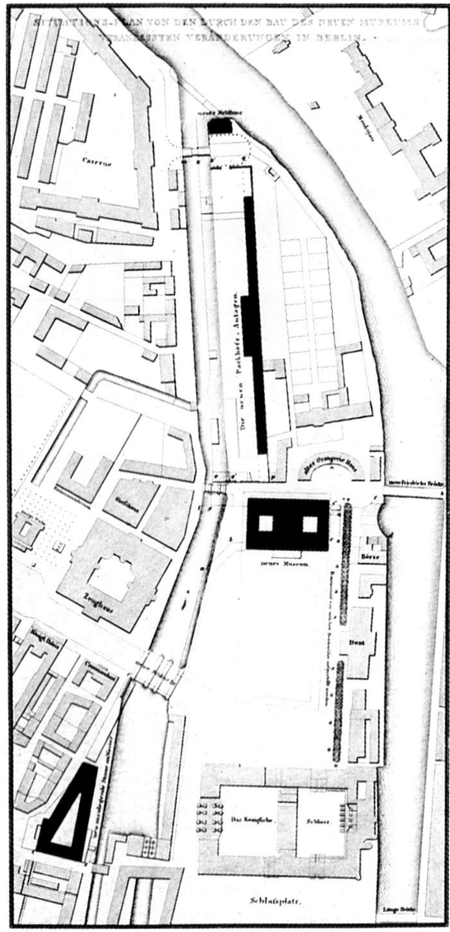

Site plan of the old museum between palace, cathedral and customs buildings

temporaries? He succeeded, I think, in combining outer display with inherent nobility in a building that perfectly symbolized the meaning of Prussia's historic collections. The row of columns which his imposing temple presented to the square completely concealed the two storeys within. A broad flight of steps led up to the entrance and into a spacious rotunda, which served as the entrance hall and hub of the exhibition rooms grouped around it. Before visitors went on to the halls of sculpture on the ground floor and painting on the first, this awesomely solemn domed room, as Schinkel wrote, was to 'put them into a receptive mood, ready to enjoy, appreciate and find insight into all that the building harbours'. Based on the Pantheon in Rome, this hall was intended for meditation not exhibition: it was to be a space consecrated to the experience of art.

The arrangement of the exhibition rooms that opened out from this domed hall reflected the museum's dual aim of providing enjoyment and edification. The first floor was divided into forty small rooms which contained a total of 1,198 paintings, selected from the original collection by a museum commission under Wilhelm von Humboldt; their authenticity and attribution were carefully investigated by Gustav Waagen in a critical catalogue. Schinkel's spacious halls were divided by wooden partitions that extended only part of the way to the ceiling, allowing diffuse light from the high windows – skylights had not yet been added – to fall on the paintings on the side walls. These were reserved for major works, while associated paintings of more historical than aesthetic interest hung close together on the rear walls. Each section was devoted to a certain school or group and was captioned accordingly. The colour scheme of the exhibition spaces was wonderfully festive, dominated by red and gold. We have since become so accustomed to monochrome, usually pale-toned, walls that Schinkel's conception may strike us as garish. But it had a deeper purpose, that of integrating the paintings – in their famous, standard Schinkel frames – completely with their architectural surroundings. Art, architecture and ornament had yet to be strictly separated, which is why Schinkel's colour scheme and the furnishings of the gallery represent a fascinating chapter in the history of museum design and artistic taste. Sabine Spiro has attempted to reconstruct the original scheme. 'Schinkel,' she writes, 'chose a dark red wallpaper with a shaded pattern in dark greyish-blue, and, for the smaller rooms, paper with large flower décor. The twenty-six pine partitions were also covered with this paper, which was pasted over burlap; walls and doors were framed with gilded mouldings and the plinth marbled in greenish encaustic. Between the ceiling beams, which were decorated with plaited bands and meanders in red, yellow stars gleamed on a white ground. The cornice above the partitions and along the rear wall was gilded, as were the hanging arrangements for the pictures. The protective railings in front of the pictures made do with black enamel ... Contributing to the brightness of the rooms was the tone of the window casings, which were marbled in very light hues.'

It was an opulent yet a rational and quite thrifty scheme, though as construction proceeded Schinkel made every attempt to convince the authorities that costlier materials should be used. However, they were not willing to grant the necessary funds.

*

No one person, of course, deserves all the credit for making Berlin's long-awaited museum a reality. It was the result of dedicated and persistent effort by many. Though it was Alois Hirt who gave the sign in 1797 and incessantly bombarded the King and ministers with suggestions and memoranda, the museum idea was gradually taken up by a younger generation who had the enthusiastic support of Crown Prince Frederick William. Besides Hirt, Schinkel was involved as architect in all the planning stages, later assisted by the sculptor Rauch, the painters Dähling and Wach, the restorer Schlesinger, and, as consulting art historian, by Dr Gustav Waagen. Wilhelm von Humboldt, an idealist philosopher who was also eminently efficient in practical matters, certainly provided great and possibly decisive inspiration, though his official duties allowed him to concentrate on the project only twice – in 1809, during his sixteen months as Chief of the Prussian Ministry of Culture, and in 1829, when he headed the Museum Furnishing Commission.

A man who devoted himself to the collection and museum like no other was Freiherr Karl Friedrich von Rumohr (1785–1843). Rumohr was a universally gifted, financially

The Palace Bridge with the old museum, cathedral and palace, 1855
Steel engraving

independent connoisseur of Italian art rare in Germany at that time. His important *Italienische Forschungen* appeared in 1827–32, and when in Italy he was able to acquire several paintings for the museum, among them such significant works as Botticelli's large *Madonna* from Santo Spirito in Florence, Piero di Cosimo's *Mars and Venus*, the *Portrait of a Girl* by Lorenzo di Credi, and Franciabigio's *Portrait of a Young Man.* A critical philosopher, historian, and essayist who even wrote a book on *The Spirit of Cooking* (1822), Rumohr was a friend of von Humboldt, Hegel, Schlegel, Tieck, and Goethe, and belonged to the intimate circle of Crown Prince Frederick William. Although he never held public office, his practical and moral support for the museum was invaluable. He modified and clarified Hirt's systematic exhibition scheme, and it was probably as much at his as at Wilhelm von Humboldt's instigation that Hirt's predominantly antiquarian (that is, historical) approach was tempered by an appreciation of the aesthetic qualities of art.

The artistic quality of a painting is more important to a museum than its historical interest; in Wilhelm von Humboldt's words, only the beautiful in art can educate, and it is this which places art and science on the same level. This fundamental assumption of von Humboldt's philosophy was central in the intellectual optimism that pervaded nineteenth-century Berlin, and it was the museum founders' main justification for their conception of a public museum.

A special place in this inspired and high-minded circle of artists, universal historians, and connoisseurs was held by Gustav Waagen. His career may perhaps stand as a typical example of the scholarly life in nineteenth-century Prussia, a life devoted completely to education and service to a state whose ingrained thrift was only matched by the high demands it placed on itself. Waagen was born in Hamburg in 1794, the son of a minor painter, and studied art history at Breslau (1812) and Heidelberg (1818). While in the army

Karl Friedrich Schinkel
The old museum, 1823–30

Karl Friedrich Schinkel
Floor-plans of the old museum, 1825

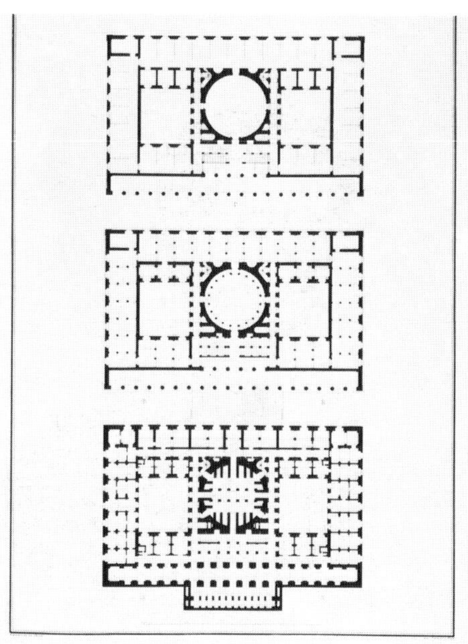

he saw and marvelled at the Musée Napoléon in 1814. In 1818 he met the Boisserée brothers in Heidelberg, who at the time were still negotiating with Berlin about the transfer of their collection. When Waagen's dissertation on Hubert and Jan van Eyck was published as a book in 1823, Rumohr tracked the author down and persuaded him to come to Berlin. Waagen's great knowledge of European and world art, his infallible critical eye, and his connoisseurship of medieval painting in particular, made him a leading candidate for the commission which ordered the Solly Collection in 1823. The critical catalogue of the Gemäldegalerie that he edited in 1830 caused a furore as he did not shrink from attacking the accepted attributions which were often lavish with great names; nor was he afraid of public controversy if that was what a scholarly justification of systematic cataloguing and organization of the collections entailed. Though he was initially overshadowed by Rumohr, and Wilhelm von Humboldt tried in vain to make the museum directorship attractive to his brother Alexander, Gustav Waagen was none the less nominated to the post because the King refused to countenance any suggestion that Rumohr deserved it.

Waagen's career as a Prussian civil servant in Berlin was not successful in a material sense. Continually plagued by money worries, he regularly put in for special leave to travel, returning again and again to England where he made a lasting name for himself as one of the leading experts on European painting. His *Works of Art and Artists in England*, published in 1838, and his three-volume *Art Treasures in Great Britain* (1854) are still astonishingly erudite, accurate, and well-written accounts of the great English art collections of the day. In 1857 he was even commissioned by Prince Albert to oversee the planning of the great Manchester Exhibition. This exhibition, which reflected Waagen's profound knowledge of early Italian art, proved significant for England in helping to set the stage for the Pre-Raphaelite movement. Waagen died in 1868 while on a journey to Copenhagen.

*

With the inauguration of its new home in 1830, the Gemäldegalerie had a firm base on which to begin a considered expansion of the collection. Initially, Gustav Waagen was able to make a number of fine acquisitions, among them Titian's *Girl with Fruitbowl* (in 1832), Rogier van der Weyden's *Bladelin Altar* (in 1834), Spanish paintings from the collection of Baron Matthieu de Favier, Paris (in 1835), and Cornelis de Vos's charming portrait of his two children (in 1837).

The idealism and fervour of the founders' generation, however, had begun to ebb, and different interests now came to the fore. The issue of Enjoyment versus Edification began increasingly to be decided in favour of the latter. Perhaps most symptomatic of this emphasis on scholarship and expertise was the naming of Dr Ignaz von Olfers, in 1839, as Director General of Museums. Though Olfers devoted all his energy to expanding the collections, his policy diverged ever further from the idealistic aims formulated by Wilhelm von Humboldt and Schinkel. In his view, the museums were to serve mainly as repositories of expert knowledge, institutes which in the academic discipline of the visual arts must hold their own against the concentrated scholarship of Berlin University. He found particular support for his ideas among leading archaeologists, who thought that the museums' educational task could be performed best by exhibiting plaster casts of the finest classical sculpture alongside the museums' few originals, and indeed by making these the focus of the entire museum group.

What may have suited the archaeological department was bound to be more than harmful to the Gemäldegalerie and the Department of Prints and Drawings. It is said that Director General von Olfers prevented the purchase of Michelangelo and Raphael drawings from the estate of Sir Thomas Lawrence by arguing that with the 40,000 reichsthaler he would save, he could buy plaster replicas of the *Horsetamers* at the Roman Quirinal! This kind of thinking was to prove fateful to the Gemäldegalerie and its acquisition policy, though its full effects were not immediately felt.

In the meantime, a quite different event had given everyone reason for optimism. In 1840, Crown Prince Frederick William (IV), art-lover and talented historian, became King of Prussia, exactly a hundred years after the predecessor he most admired, Frederick II. The middle classes placed great hope in this liberal monarch who seemed one of their own, and they expected long-overdue reforms which initially, at least, were almost realized.

The years until the March 1848 Rising abounded with projects, whose political significance may still be perceived today from plans and the few buildings that have survived. They give an idea of the broad intellectual and political stream in which the Royal Museums could prosper and expand; this included such different projects as the completion and restoration of Cologne Cathedral (from 1842, after the Church Schism had been overcome) to fantastic plans for a Protestant cathedral between palace and museum in Berlin; and the great hospital complex at Bethanien to the *Krollsche Oper* at the edge of the Tiergarten. The old eighteenth-century Protestant cathedral, which Schinkel had already restored and integrated in his museum ensemble, was particularly close to Frederick William IV's heart. The church, he thought, needed yet another refurbishment to symbolize a renascence of Christian faith and to create a national Protestant cathedral as a counterpart to the Catholic cathedral at Cologne. 'I am building my cathedral not for its Protestant congregation in Berlin,' admitted the monarch, 'but in my capacity as Protestant leader of the Protestant Church of Germany; and seeing that I hope to complete Cologne Cathedral, I should be granted the right if not actually to execute such a gigantic project, then at least to plan it.' This project gave birth throughout the remainder of the century to innumerable plans, from the fantastic to the merely outsized, which also had their effect on museum planning. Finally, on 17 June 1894, the cornerstone of the new cathedral, which still stands in East Berlin, was laid.

Frederick William IV, after establishing his summer residence at Sanssouci in Potsdam, began expanding the park in 1844 to include the Church of Peace and Marly Garden. He and Schinkel, in the 1830s, had already conceived a grand Via Triumphalis behind the palace, probably the largest and most ambitious project of the Romantic period in Germany. Work on the avenue was begun under Persius in 1842, but it was never completed. The King's desire to restore Sanssouci Palace to its original state even led him to attempt to nullify a democratic decision made by his predecessor, Frederick William III. A cabinet order signed on 30 June 1840 declared that all works that had been at Sanssouci before the Gemäldegalerie had opened were to be returned there.

Ludwig Knaus
Friedrich Gustav Waagen
Berlin, Nationalgalerie SMPK

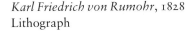

Karl Friedrich von Rumohr, 1828
Lithograph

Franz Krüger
Frederick William IV

This order might well have been carried out had it not been for the negotiating skills of the Director General, who managed to convince the King that copies of the paintings would suffice. Potsdam nevertheless remained his dream. 'The entire enclave of Potsdam and beyond, over the shoreline hills on the Havel River, transformed into a most glorious, grandiose, mile-wide landscape painting that has come to life,' mused the Romantic on the throne; and traces of this vision are still visible in the countryside around Potsdam, scarred by the Second World War and Germany's partition.

In this larger context were also plans to expand the museum which got underway immediately the Crown Prince had taken the throne. These aimed not only at providing space for a continually growing collection but at establishing 'a refuge for the arts and sciences' on Spree River Island in central Berlin. This vision, and the Monarch's own architectural ideas for its realization, led to plans drawn up by the architect Friedrich Stüler (1800–65), which retained their validity for generations to come.

Stüler's project foresaw a shifting of the planning focus from the Lustgarten adjoined by palace, cathedral and museum, to the northern end of the large island that divided the River Spree. He envisaged the new museum as a complex of great halls, colonnades, two- and three-storey exhibition buildings, all crowned by a temple of the arts. His designs were visionary and sensible, and also charged with political symbolism. This is his own description: 'If we are to satisfy, with a great building complex, the ever-growing need for facilities devoted to the arts and sciences and, as far as humanly possible, to unite everything that belongs together there, then efforts must be made to secure a spacious site at the city centre yet away from the noise of traffic. This complex should be linked with the reconstructed Cathedral and its cemetery hall, the whole thus gathering into itself the highest spiritual emotions of the populace and forming a focus of a kind which probably no other capital city can boast.'

After Stüler had drawn up a general plan for the gigantic undertaking based on the King's sketches, work got underway on a New Museum behind Schinkel's original building. Though construction was begun in 1843, various delays prevented its completion until 1859. With the New Museum, the royal contractor and his architect created a decorative unity of museum architecture and contents which was quite opposed to the austere, Neo-Classical style of the Schinkel period in Berlin. In fact, the new building had been earmarked for the Egyptian collection and Department of Prints and Drawings. But thanks to the intervention of the Director General, the collection of plaster casts was given a prominent place there which continual acquisitions strengthened. Then, in 1861, Consul Wagner's collection of contemporary German art came to Prussia as a bequest, and the last bastion against modern art in the museums fell. Despite the great Wilhelm von Humboldt and his injunctions, a modern museum, the National Gallery, was established to house the new collection in 1864, and an imposing new building was erected between 1866 and 1876.

This general development of the Berlin Museums – their physical expansion, increasing comprehensiveness, and primarily scholarly orientation – should be kept in mind to understand the role played by the Gemäldegalerie during the thirty eventful years to 1872. At first, all signs were propitious. In 1840 the King put a 100,000-thaler stipend at Gustav Waagen's disposal for a protracted buying trip through Italy. Waagen managed to acquire about seventy paintings in Florence and Venice during 1841 and 1842; these included two large altarpieces by Moretto, several mythological subjects by Tintoretto and Veronese, and also a number of fine sculptures. On his return the following year, Waagen succeeded in securing the collection of Reimer, the Berlin book-dealer, which consisted mostly of Dutch genre paintings. Other significant purchases of the period were the *Deidesheimer Altar* from Nuremberg in 1844, the *St John Altar* and *Mary Altar* from the collection of King William II of Holland in 1850, Raphael's *Madonna Terranuova* in 1854, and the two unique *Hohenstauffen Altar Panels* in 1862. Yet not even these acquisitions could hide the fact that interest had shifted to other departments, or that financial subsidies, not only to the Gemäldegalerie, were continually shrinking. By 1865 the funds available to all of the museums totalled only 15,000 thalers.

*

The period between the wars of 1870–1 and 1914–18 was a time of unprecedented expansion for Berlin, which rose to be the political centre of Germany and the industrial, business and scientific capital of the new empire. The city's population tripled from 774,452 in 1870 to 2,071,257 in 1910. Berlin's museums also prospered, becoming the unique repositories of world art and culture we know today. The founders' generation had dedicated them to the ideal of liberally educated people; now, Berlin's economic improvement and financial resources, unknown to other German museums, led to an almost total triumph of faith in historically oriented museum science. The Berlin museums led in every field. Famous scholars and researchers in the history of art, archaeology, and the various branches of world art, brought a systematic collecting activity and scholarly evaluation which remained without parallel.

As regards the historical departments of the museums and the Gemäldegalerie in particular, this period is indissolubly linked with two names, men who established the gallery's ranks as largest and most important division of the entire museum group: the museums' protector, Frederick William, Crown Prince and later – too late – Frederick III, German Kaiser for ninety-nine days (with his English wife, Crown Princess Victoria), and second, Wilhelm von Bode. On 16 June 1871, the Franco-Prussian War at an end, Kaiser William I named the Crown Prince Protector of Royal Museums (royal they remained because they were Prussian rather than national or imperial, though they certainly could claim to represent the German nation abroad). Thanks to Frederick William's understanding, to his untiring aid and innovative thinking, the true *spiritus rector* of the museums, Wilhelm von Bode, was able to give free rein to his inexhaustible energy and ideas.

At no other period could a man like Bode have been so eminently successful as in the decades between 1871 and 1914. Born in Calvörde (Brunswick) in 1845, Bode briefly studied law before turning to art history, in which he took his Ph.D. at Leipzig in 1870. In 1872, a junior barrister, he asked for leave to become an assistant in the sculpture department with permission to work in the Gemäldegalerie as well. In 1883 he advanced to director of the Gallery of Sculpture, becoming Head of the Gemäldegalerie in 1890 and finally Director General of Museums in 1905. Not until 1920 did he retire from his other posts to devote himself exclusively to the Gemäldegalerie, which he headed until his death in 1929.

These dry dates, of course, say very little about Wilhelm von Bode's fascinating, always controversial personality – that of a man who was highly respected and greatly feared both in his own country and abroad. The best character study of Bode came from the pen of one of his most outspoken opponents, the Berlin art critic and writer Karl Scheffler. 'Bode is actually a leftover from the previous generation,' wrote Scheffler, 'that race of strong-willed, not yet weak-nerved, and quite unsentimental parvenus who shaped the aspect of the New Germany after 1870. He is a practical organizer among art historians, a *realpolitiker* of art, something on the order of a Bismarck of museums ... Much of the imperial, boom-year mood still hovers about him, and his thinking and feeling blend Prussian method with American enterprise. A new breed of gallery manager was born with Bode. Yes, perhaps even a sensational one. He is also a worker in the grand manner, who achieves in a matter of decades what others would need centuries to do. This man with the hawk's profile has without doubt imposed his personal regime and demanded his own way so self-righteously that he has managed to get his hand in really every German museum ... Never has there existed a Right Honourable more remarkable than he.'

Bode's independent means assured him a lifelong freedom of movement and even enabled him to give paintings to his museum when State funds reached one of their periodical low ebbs. Despite continual illness, he placed the highest demands on himself relentlessly. He was a brilliant universal historian who took a passionate interest in all fields of museum research, and he was also a specialist and leading authority on fifteenth- and sixteenth-century Italian painting and sculpture, and on Dutch and Flemish Baroque painting. Bode was equally a connoisseur of sculpture, bronzes, furniture, and even of historic picture frames, to which he attached great importance in the presentation of the gallery's works. His memory for pictures was infallible and precise, his judgement incorruptible. His scholarly works, published in bulky volumes, were so pioneering and fundamental that their results have since become part of general knowledge. He knew every collector and art dealer in Europe, and there were only a few rare pieces, including

Emperor Frederick III as Crown Prince, c.1880

those purchased by his sharpest competitor, the National Gallery in London, that escaped his attention or, if at all possible, incorporation into the Berlin collection.

But to return to the early years of Bode's career. Director General von Usedom was making one last attempt to rescue the old notion of an edifying collection of plaster replicas extending from antiquity to the present. He even considered building, on the Museum Island site behind the New Museum, a great structure largely reserved for this collection; but the project never came to fruition.

In 1874, thanks to years of effort on the part of Julius Meyer, the gallery succeeded in acquiring the collection of Bartholdt Suermondt, an Aachen industrialist. The Crown Prince had used all his influence to convince the Prussian parliament that the collector's price, one million gold marks, was not too high. Extraordinary funds like this were repeatedly made available by the Ministry of Finance when it was a question of acquiring masterpieces for the museums – for example, a sum of two million gold marks in 1884 exclusively for buying painting and sculpture of the Christian era. To give just one comparison, during the same period the old Pinakothek in Munich had an annual purchasing fund of no more than 10,000 marks.

With the Suermondt Collection, which Waagen had already catalogued in 1859, first-rate works of the early German and Netherlandish schools entered the gallery. Jan van Eyck's *Church Madonna*, paintings by Altdorfer, Holbein, and Baldung set new accents in a still modest department of German art. The increase of famous names in the Dutch rooms was even greater – five paintings by Frans Hals alone, including *Boy Singing with Flute* and *Malle Babbe*, which Courbet had shortly before copied in Aachen (and which is now in the Kunsthalle, Hamburg); then five works by Ter Borch, Vermeer's *Lady with Pearl Necklace*, and paintings by Steen, Brouwer, Rubens, Ruisdael and others.

No wonder the exhibition rooms on the top floor of the Old Museum had become hopelessly overcrowded, despite conversion work between 1872 and 1878 which improved lighting conditions by replacing the side windows with skylights.

Julius Meyer, now frequently aided by the young Bode, took advantage of the favourable economic situation to purchase many fine works, particularly in England, where more and more masterpieces from the superb private collections were now for sale. Among Bode's acquisitions was Rembrandt's famous *Portrait of the Mennonite Preacher Anslo and his Wife*, from the collection of Lord Ashburnham – who, however, would not agree to sell until Bode proved the seriousness of his intentions by purchasing Pollaiuolo's *Portrait of a Young Woman* (1894).

The Amsterdam master probably fascinated and moved Bode more deeply than any other artist. He was able to add thirteen paintings to the gallery's Rembrandt collection, of which *Man in a Golden Helmet*, acquired in 1897, soon achieved almost legendary fame. This painting, from an English private collection, came to be identified with certain Pan-Germanic tendencies then in flower, which found their most popular expression in a book called *Rembrandt als Erzieher* – as teacher and guide. Published anonymously ('by a German'), the tract quickly went through an incredible number of editions. Later, its author Julius Langbehn revealed his identity and his countrymen honoured him with the title of 'the Rembrandt German'.

Bode's contribution to Rembrandt research, by contrast, consisted of a five-volume book in which he reviewed and summed up current knowledge of the Dutch master. In spite of the rigorous gleaning-out of over-generous attributions which has since reduced Rembrandt's accepted œuvre to a fraction of its former size, Bode's acumen and connoisseurship remain impressive.

His almost uncanny sense for the favourable opportunity led to similar increases in the Flemish department. Fifteen paintings by Rubens were acquired by Bode (eight of which, large compositions with figures, were lost in 1945 when fire destroyed the stocks that had been evacuated to Friedrichshain bomb shelter). For the German department, which had not a single Dürer, Bode purchased seven paintings by that artist in the short time between 1882 and 1889, four of them from British collections. The Italian collection profited no less by his expertise, with significant new acquisitions such as the predella panels by Masaccio (in 1880) and paintings by Botticelli, Signorelli, Titian, Bellini and Carpaccio.

It would lead too far afield to describe Bode's almost obsessive purchasing activity in detail. Suffice it to say that by 1914 he had succeeded in making the Berlin collection a complete record of European painting from the thirteenth to the eighteenth centuries which in terms of quality and systematic arrangement was unique in the world at that time. The only definitely under-represented fields were eighteenth-century English and French painting. A handful of English works had come to the gallery, largely as gifts, on the inauguration of the new Kaiser Friedrich Museum in 1904; French painting was slighted because, still associated with Frederick the Great, it was considered of more historical than aesthetic interest. Frederick's collection of Watteau, Pater and Lacret remained in the royal residences at Berlin and Potsdam.

Wilhelm von Bode, c.1890

Bode did not rely exclusively on departmental goodwill and government money for his purchases. He also approached those industrialists, businessmen and bankers who, during Germany's boom years, had built up collections that could match, or even surpass, public ones. Not surprisingly, the largest private collections amassed in Germany during the few decades between 1880 and 1914 were to be found in Berlin. They must have been superb, judging by the opulent volumes which are all that remains in witness. These were often written by Bode himself, who admittedly did not expect his services to go unrewarded in the way of gifts or financial support for the royal museums. Among these potential patrons were men of such stature as James Simon, M. Kappel, Oscar Huldschinsky, Carl Hollitscher, von Kaufmann, Carstanjen, Beckerath, Hainauer, Oppenheim, and many more.

Only James Simon, however, showed his gratitude more than abundantly for Bode's efforts, becoming probably the greatest private supporter and patron of the Berlin Museums ever. He was Jewish, and like many Jews in Berlin he was dedicated to German national unity and had a strong sense of the obligations attached to his position in society. Owner of Germany's largest textile firm with an annual turnover of more than 600 million marks, Simon began collecting art in 1882 with Bode's assistance and advice. His collection was beautifully exhibited in his house on Tiergartenstrasse (almost next to the present site of the new Museum of Applied Arts). He also financed the museum's archeological expeditions – *Nofretete* was unearthed on one; Simon co-founded the Museum of German Ethnology, he established orphanages, and, indeed, was philanthropically active in many areas. On the opening of the Kaiser Friedrich Museum in 1904 he donated the larger part of his Italian Renaissance collection, with works by Mantegna and Bronzino, sculptures and finely crafted objects – a total of 350 pieces. A special room in a private house was reserved for Simon's collection, bearing witness respectfully and impressively to his generosity.

Private initiatives of this kind, Bode realized, would benefit the museums most if channelled through a supporters' association. In 1897, the Kaiser-Friedrich-Museums-Verein, named in honour of Emperor Frederick, who had died in 1888, was established to further the Painting and Sculpture Galleries. Its list of members was headed by Emperor William II and included such prominent men as Karl von der Heydt, F.A.Krupp, Max Liebermann, Rudolf Mosse, Friedrich Sarre, Leo Bernstein, Arnold Guilleaume, Walter Rathenau, and Louis Ullstein – names that stand for a key phase in the economic and cultural development of Berlin. This association of private supporters enabled Bode to act quickly, without bureaucracy, when government endeavours to buy some fine work of art proved insufficient. Some of the most valuable and beautiful pieces in today's gallery still belong to the Kaiser-Friedrich-Museums-Verein, whose activities on behalf of the museum have continued unabated to this day.

*

Hardly had its new building been inaugurated than the Gemäldegalerie was pressed for space, and during the 1870s the need to expand grew increasingly obvious. The exhibition rooms on the top floor of the Old Museum were hopelessly overcrowded; not even conversion work and a complete reorganization of the collection could alleviate matters more than temporarily. Frederick William IV's grandiose vision of Museum Island as a 'refuge for the arts and sciences' in downtown Berlin – capital of the Empire since 1871 – had not been forgotten. When the Berlin Society of Architects and Engineers sponsored a competition for an expansion of the museums in 1882, the response was overwhelming.

James Simon,
*c.*1915

The number and variety of entries showed how seriously this project was taken in the new imperial capital, particularly by Bode, who was out to create a new type of museum. Besides more space, what he really wanted was to re-order and thus re-interpret the museum's collection. Previously, the art of each period had been divided by the medium, but Bode thought in terms of historical epochs. This is why the final project for a new gallery at the northern end of Museum Island was expressly conceived as a Renaissance museum where painting and sculpture would be exhibited together, in surroundings decorated and furnished in the Renaissance style.

However, there were many obstacles in the way of its realization. A branch of the new inter-urban railway, crossing Museum Island, left only a narrow triangular site for the museum at the island's northern point, and this posed great architectural difficulties. The death of Kaiser Frederick III in 1888 brought all progress to a halt, until Bode finally intervened with his successor, William II. The Kaiser issued an imperial order, and Ernest Eberhard von Ihne, court architect, was commissioned in 1898 to complete the building. The Kaiser Friedrich Museum, named in memory of its former protector and containing the Gemäldegalerie and Sculpture Gallery and the numismatic collection, was officially inaugurated by William II on 19 October 1904. Today it lies in the Eastern sector of the city and bears the name Bode Museum.

The museum was an architecturally impressive terminus for Museum Island, although its location between the railway line, Spree River and Kupfergraben canal, with barracks and clinics on the opposite shore, was rather prosaic, and its main entrance was at some distance from the square where palace, cathedral and other museums were concentrated. Its long rows of pilasters above a massive Neo-Renaissance foundation and the soaring dome over its rounded façade lent the building a monumental dignity quite in keeping with its purpose of a repository of Renaissance art.

The Gemäldegalerie moved into the rooms on the upper floor. Bode, as obstinate with his architects and building authorities as he was sensitive to the harmony of decoration, colour schemes, antique furnishings and picture frames, apparently succeeded in creating an atmosphere that tremendously heightened the effect of the collection. 'By no means did we intend to imitate the model of other museums of arts and crafts,' he summed up in his memoirs. 'On the contrary, we conceived these monumental settings as placing the works of art in surroundings that suited their period and character and which would enhance their effect and be as faithful as possible to their original intention. Had we gone so far as to copy old rooms, we should have impaired the nobility and calm of the paintings, and done harm to the nature and significance of the museum.'

Yet Bode's plans went still further. In February 1907 he wrote a memorandum projecting the development of the entire museum group as he saw it. Since the Kaiser Friedrich Museum was already overcrowded and much of importance had to remain in storage, he wrote, the next step would have to be the construction of another new museum – a Museum of German Art, in which art of all the northern European countries could be brought together under one roof. Germany did not yet possess a museum of this kind, neither at Nuremberg nor at Munich, wrote Bode. 'A German Museum would present an abundance of beautiful individual pieces which, taken together, would give the first true and correct picture of the German style in the arts. A recognition of this uniquely Germanic quality would in turn contribute to the refinement and development of modern German art, and would help stimulate and improve it.'

Ernst Eberhard von Ihne
Ground-floor plan of the Kaiser Friedrich Museum, 1904

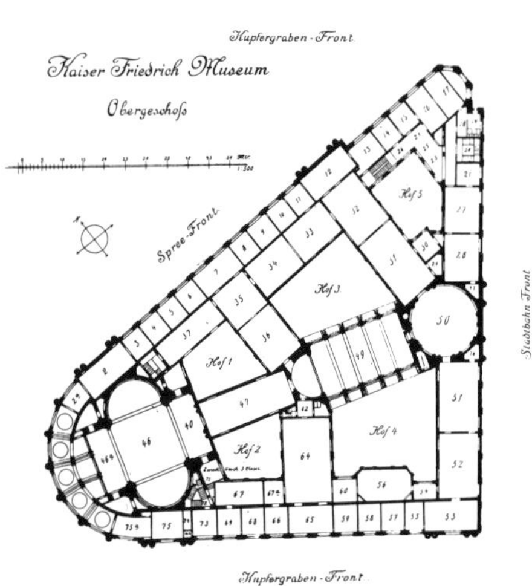

Bode's ideas found rapid acceptance, and he engaged the brilliant architect, Alfred Messel, to plan the new building. Messel (1853–1909) had already designed the Landesmuseum in Darmstadt and a series of department stores and office buildings that put him in the first rank of modern German architects. His plans called for a great U-shaped structure of three wings, with a courtyard open to the canal side and a Doric colonnade connecting the two projecting wings. Art of three civilizations was to find a home here: late antiquity and Pergamon Altar in the central tract, Oriental art with a Near Eastern Department in the south wing, and Germanic art in the north wing, the German Museum proper. After Messel's death in 1909, Ludwig Hoffman became supervisor of the project. But technical and financial problems delayed its completion until after the First World War, and Bode did not experience the realization of his idea. The new building was

The Kaiser Friedrich Museum, 1904

opened to the public in 1930, on the occasion of the Berlin Museum Centennial.

Bode's comprehensive plans also included the far-sighted suggestion to relocate a portion of the non-European collections in the suburb of Dahlem, this making more space available in the central museum buildings. Since Dahlem, a former state demesne, had already become the home of several scientific institutes attached to the university, among them the Kaiser-Wilhelm-Gesellschaft (later Max-Planck-Gesellschaft), Bode's idea amounted to creating a new combined centre of the arts and sciences in Berlin. Construction of a new Museum of Asian Art, designed by Bruno Paul (1874–1968), began in 1913.

*

The outbreak of war brought all these ambitious projects to an end. Work in Dahlem ceased in 1915. By 1921 it was decided to abandon Bode's general plan and temporarily use the unfinished Museum of Asian Art to store the ethnological collection.

The First World War and its consequences also critically weakened the Gemäldegalerie. Article 247 of the Versailles Treaty stipulated the return to Belgium of the panels of van Eyck's *Ghent Altar* which had been in Berlin since Solly purchased them in 1818, and also the two wings of the *Löwen Altar* by Dieric Bouts, acquired for the museum by Waagen in 1834. The great Berlin private collections, built up with Bode's help and advice, were dispersed or left Germany altogether during the inflation. Only James Simon again, in 1919, donated a large group of sculptures, paintings and applied art to the museums, a gesture intended as a sign of warning to his country that it was in dire need of moral and spiritual renewal.

Bode's original museum conception celebrated one last triumph. To commemorate the

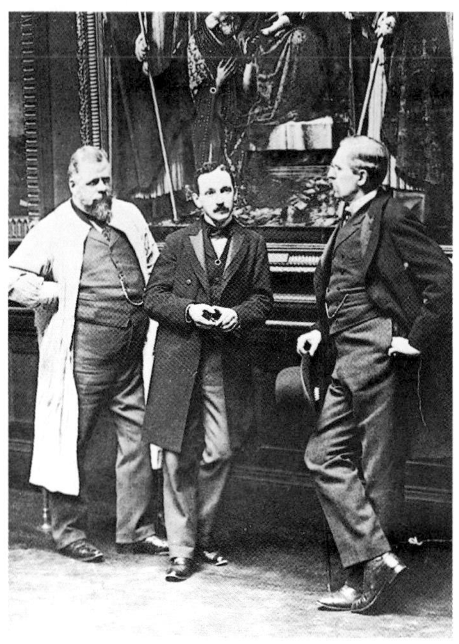

Wilhelm von Bode, Max J. Friedländer and the restorer Mr Hauser
(From right to left)

hundredth anniversary of the Berlin Museums, the Messel Building (with the German Museum, the Pergamon Museum and the Near Eastern Department) was inaugurated on 2 October 1930. The installation of the German Museum still faithfully reflected Bode's ideas. Medieval Christian art was on the ground floor and art of the Post-Renaissance period upstairs, the paintings and sculptures together: in this way Bode's vision of a Renaissance museum, equally compelling for its art of the Germanic nations, was realized.

As reorganization of the Kaiser Friedrich Museum became necessary during the 1930s, however, a new generation of museum curators gradually prevailed. They looked askance on Bode's notion of presenting all the arts of each epoch together, and believed that what really counted was the individual work of art in its aesthetic autonomy. The Berlin Revival Style in museum installation – 'historicism' – had had its day. Up to the 1936 Olympic Games, sculptures and paintings were exhibited separately, against light-coloured walls, and a puristic narrowing-down replaced Bode's expansive historical approach. The results can still be seen in the structure of Berlin's museums to this day, for the generation who pioneered this reorientation stipulated the same strict division of the artistic genres when the city's museums were rebuilt after the Second World War.

When the Nazis came to power in 1933 there were changes of an incomparably more injurious kind. Their inhuman racial policy led to the dismissal, emigration or demotion to inferior posts of many of the museums' finest scholars. The Director of the Gemäldegalerie, Max J. Friedländer, was relieved of his office and emigrated to Holland. Hermann Voss, unrivalled connoisseur of Baroque painting, was transferred to Wiesbaden. The Nazis' propaganda exhibition, *Degenerate Art*, and subsequent pillaging of the museums struck a blow at the National Gallery and its modern collection from which it never completely recovered.

On the outbreak of war in 1939, the museums were immediately closed and their collections temporarily put in storage in the basement of the Kaiser Friedrich Museum. In 1942 and 1943, as the air raids on Berlin grew increasingly threatening, the paintings and sculptures were taken to massive anti-aircraft shelters which seemed to offer the best protection imaginable. They were indeed safe – until after the capitulation.

By late January 1945 the Red Army had reached the Oder River. The Nazi regime declared Berlin a fortress to be defended to the last. At this point, the Director General of Museums managed to convince Hitler to order the evacuation of the most valuable portions of the collections from the Berlin shelters to depots which were made ready in

Kaiser Friedrich Museum
James Simon Room, 1904

Western Germany. This happened on 8 March 1945; three days later the first shipment left Berlin. A total of six shipments were made, the last on 7 April, just before the Russian armies sealed off the city. Sixty-two cases containing 1,225 paintings reached Thuringia by road, where they were stored at Kaiseroda-Merkers Salt Mine, on the Werra River near Eisenach. Several hundred authentic old frames and about four hundred paintings, most of which were too large to fit into the pit cages at the mine, remained behind in the Friedrichshain shelter. Another thousand paintings were left in the Kaiser Friedrich Museum basement.

Berlin capitulated on 2 May and Germany on 8 May. A week later several serious fires broke out in the shelter at Friedrichshain, which in the meantime had been occupied by Russian troops and was hermetically sealed. Though what caused the fires has never been adequately determined, they very probably destroyed all the State Museum treasures in the shelter. The Gemäldegalerie apparently lost all the paintings it had stored at Friedrichshain, among them such irreplaceable works as Signorelli's *Pan as God of Nature*, three major paintings by Caravaggio, monumental altar panels by Fra Bartolommeo, Francia, Moretto, and Sarto; eight works by Rubens, four by van Dyck, all of the Jordaens paintings, and many by Murillo, Zurbarán, Vouet, and Lebrun. Russian troops confiscated about 230 paintings from the basement of the Kaiser Friedrich Museum, which had suffered serious bomb damage. By 17 May, despite the chaotic circumstances, a new City Council for Greater Berlin had been established. One of its tasks was the supervision of the former State Museums, and work began to recover and secure what was left.

American troops occupied the evacuation point at Kaiseroda Mine on 4 April. A week later, General Eisenhower and his staff came to inspect the mine, which in addition to art treasures contained the gold reserves of the German Imperial Bank. On 15 April, the U.S. Monuments and Fine Arts Section removed all the paintings to Frankfurt, then to Wiesbaden, where a central art collecting point had been established at the Landesmuseum under the supervision of the U.S. military government. As a consequence of the Yalta Agreement, Thuringia and Saxony were relinquished to the Soviets on 1 July. In November 1945, 202 major works belonging to the Berlin Gemäldegalerie were taken finally from Wiesbaden to Washington DC and deposited at the National Gallery of Art.

Though evacuation saved the gallery's collection, in the nick of time, from the total destruction which certainly awaited it in Berlin, it was now dispersed and divided among the Allied powers, mainly the United States and Russia. Whatever the future held in store,

Kaiser Friedrich Museum
Cinquecento Room, 1904

Alfred Messel
Project for extensions on Museum Island
(German Museum in left wing), 1908

the existence and structure of the Berlin Museums were now inextricably involved in world politics and the East-West confrontation. Their home city of Berlin, like Germany itself, had been divided.

On 25 February 1947, the Allied Control Commission formally abolished the State of Prussia. The Berlin Museums became collections without a country.

*

Those few museum employees who stayed in Berlin during the final days of the Third Reich did what they could to secure the damaged museum buildings and what works of art remained. Yet since the greater part of the Gemäldegalerie's stocks were in Wiesbaden, their fate was largely in the hands of the American art officer there, though he had German museum staff to assist and advise him. Shortly after Ernst Holzinger, Director of the Städel Institute in Frankfurt, joined this group as expert adviser, an exhibition of part of the gallery's collection was arranged for February 1946, and further exhibitions followed.

Finally, in February 1948 President Truman agreed to return the paintings stored in Washington. A bill to this effect was passed in Congress, but it included a rider by Senator Fulbright that before the collection returned to Germany it was to be shown in thirteen American cities because it had been kept from the public eye for years in the National Gallery depots. This travelling exhibition proved a spectacular success, and by the time it ended in Toledo in March 1949, over two-and-a-half million people had seen it. The net proceeds of $300,000 went to the Emergency Assistance Fund for German Children. The paintings arrived back in Wiesbaden in May, and were placed under German jurisdiction. The responsible authority was now the Regional Government of Hessia at Wiesbaden.

In the meantime, however, political developments dashed all hopes that the collection might be returned to Museum Island in Berlin. A monetary reform carried out in the three Western zones of occupation on 20 June 1948, was joined by the three Western sectors of Berlin. A few days later the Russians blocked the access routes to the city, and the heroic airlift began that insured Berlin's survival until the blockade was lifted on 11 May 1949. The previous autumn, two separate city councils had convened in Berlin, and on 23 May 1949 Western Germany received a new constitution, the *Grundgesetz*, establishing the German Federal Republic with provisional capital in Bonn. October 7, 1949, saw the formation of the German Democratic Republic to the East, with the Eastern sector of Berlin as its capital. The division of the city – and its museums – was sealed for the unforeseeable future.

This brief review of key dates in four years of German post-war history might serve to

German Museum *Room with early German painting and sculpture*, 1930

Bruno Paul
Design for the Asiastic Museum in Dahlem, 1913

give some idea of the often dramatic difficulties faced by the Berlin Museums as a result of the Cold War. Nothing less was at stake than their continued existence and coherence. To anyone who is interested in more information on this period, I recommend Irene Kühnel-Kunze's first-hand account of the Berlin Museums from 1939–59, a vivid record of troubled and often bizarre times.

*

The West Berlin City Council began laying the groundwork for a return of the museums' collections soon after its inception; and the unfinished Asian Museum in Dahlem, which had survived the war in comparatively good shape, was repaired to house them. It opened in December 1949 with an exhibition of part of the ethnological collection.

The fate of the Gemäldegalerie stocks, however, was still uncertain. The Hessian government hesitatingly agreed to lend a small number of paintings to Berlin for a series of eleven temporary exhibitions. They were reluctant to do more because the legal status of property, formerly belonging to Prussia, had yet to be determined among the new federal and regional German administrations. A first exhibition of 149 paintings from Wiesbaden none the less went on view in the Dahlem museum buildings on 2 October 1950. The exhibition was opened with a moving address by Ernst Reuter, Mayor of Berlin, who pointed out that the harsh political struggles over Berlin lent the exhibition the character of a dramatic testimony to the city's link with the Western world.

Yet the Hessian government remained adamant against returning the Gemäldegalerie collection. It was at this critical point that private initiative again tipped the scales. The Kaiser-Friedrich-Museums-Verein, founded in 1897 to support the gallery, lodged a suit against the State of Hessia in 1951 for the restitution of works of art belonging to them – and won. The significance of these legal proceedings was increased still more by the fact that such world-famous paintings as van Eyck's *Christ Crucified* and Rembrandt's (?) *Man in a Golden Helmet* were among the works at issue. Then, on 7 July 1955, the state governments of Baden-Württemberg, Berlin, Hessia, Lower Saxony, Northrhine-Westphalia, Rhineland-Pfalz, and Schleswig-Holstein signed an administrative agreement which stipulated the return to Berlin (West) of the former Prussian art treasures. This was followed on 25 July 1957 by a federal bill establishing the *Stiftung Preussischer Kulturbesitz* or Prussian Cultural Heritage Foundation, placing under its sole administration all the cultural assets that had formerly belonged to the Prussian State and which were now within the jurisdiction of the federal constitution. The foundation was to function solely as trustee, expressly emphasized in the bill, which defined its purpose as follows: 'To keep, maintain and enlarge the Prussian cultural heritage assigned to its care for the German nation, until other arrangements are made after reunification.'

Although legal difficulties prevented the foundation from beginning work until 1961, all the evacuated paintings had been returned to Berlin by May 1957, and as far as space permitted, were exhibited at the old Dahlem Museum. By the end of 1958 the Soviet Union

Bruno Paul
Site Plan of Museum Buildings in Dahlem, 1913

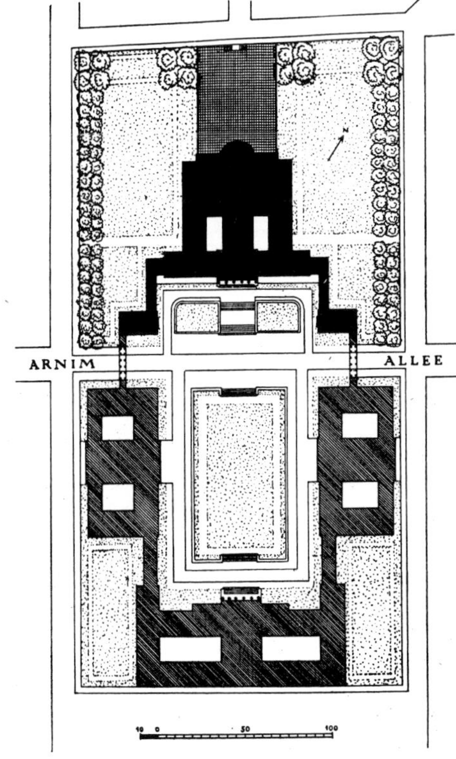

1

2

3

4

5

6

7

8

9

10

11

12

13

14

16

15

Figs 1–16 During the war it proved impossible to evacuate the gallery's entire collection to places outside Berlin. A considerable part was stored in an anti-aircraft bunker there, and in May 1945, over four hundred paintings were destroyed by fire, including these sixteen:
1 Giacomo Francia, *The Virgin as Queen of Heaven*
2 Cosma Tura, *The Virgin Enthroned*
3 Alvise Vivarini, *The Virgin Enthroned*
4 Domenico Ghirlandaio, *The Virgin and Child in a Gloriole, Worshipped by Four Saints*
5 Luca Signorelli, *Pan as God of Nature*
6 Caravaggio, *St Matthew with the Angel*
7 Caravaggio, *Christ in the Garden*
8 Charles Lebrun, *Portrait of the Cologne Banker Everhard Jabach with his Family*
9 Anthony van Dyck, *John the Baptist and John the Evangelist*
10 Anthony van Dyck, *The Mocking of Christ*
11 Anthony van Dyck, *The Lamentation of Christ*
12 Peter Paul Rubens, *The Conversion of Paul*
13 Bartolomé Esteban Murillo, *St Anthony of Padua with the Christ Child*
14 Peter Paul Rubens, *Neptune and Amphitrite*
15 Francisco de Zurbaran, *St Bonaventura and St Thomas Aquinas*
16 Francisco Goya, *Portrait of a Monk*

General Dwight D. Eisenhower (centre) inspecting the evacuated paintings in the Kaiseroda Mine

had also returned, to East Berlin, the works of art confiscated in 1945. Since then a portion of this collection, about nine hundred items, has been on view in the Bode Museum, formerly Kaiser Friedrich Museum.

And from then, too, the old Asian Museum in Dahlem has been the home of the Gemäldegalerie – a provisional solution not robbed of its charm by the years. Set among the new scientific institutes of the Free University, this Neo-Baroque structure under a wide-spreading cornice still exudes a quiet if rather heavy sense of dignity much in keeping with the traditions it represents. About 650 paintings on view from the original stocks, supplemented by new acquisitions, provide a lucid and impressive overview of European painting from the thirteenth to the eighteenth centuries. Those who recall the old Kaiser Friedrich Museum will naturally feel the painful absence in Dahlem of the large canvases that lent the former collection such nobility; but they have gone up in flames, a loss which not even an unlimited purchasing budget could repair. Now the small and medium-sized paintings predominate, filling the rooms with an atmosphere of intimacy very conducive to the enjoyment of fine works of art.

Some of the gaps torn in the collection by war, particularly in the Flemish and Italian departments, have of course been closed by new acquisitions. The previously quite small collection of eighteenth-century art has also grown in recent years, with additions ranging from Longhi, Tiepolo and Panini to Boucher, Restout, Largillierre, Vigée-Lebrun, and Vernet. And a group of English paintings has at last added the names Reynolds, Gainsborough, Raeburn, Lawrence, and Hoppner to our lists, all now represented by major portraits.

The old problem of insufficient space began to plague us again, but no further expansion of the Dahlem Museum was possible. Only a new building that fulfilled all the technical and conservational conditions would insure the gallery's undisturbed future growth. The provision of new facilities has been discussed continually since the early 1960s, yet as I write this twenty years later, none of the many suggestions has got beyond the planning stage.

*

The Senate of West Berlin started to develop plans as to how to enlarge the Dahlem Museum as early as 1949, but the land in the immediate vicinity had been handed over to the Free University (founded in 1948) and was no longer available. Finally, in 1961, the Stiftung Preußischer Kulturbesitz took responsibility for the museum. The following year the foundation decided to re-organise the existing museum in West Berlin and embark, at the same time, on a new, large-scale building programme. Preserving the cultural inheritance of Prussia for a unified Germany in the distant future and establishing an organised structure for research, presentations and collections was a national task which, politically, called for more than simply money.

The Committee set up by the Foundation decided to reconstruct the State Museum in three separate locations. The Ethnographical Museum and the three Asiatic Departments would stay in Dahlem, as Wilhelm von Bode had planned before the First World War; Pre- and Early History, the Antique Museum and the Egyptian Museum were to be housed in Schloß Charlottenburg; and all the Museums of Western Art would be installed around the Tiergarten, in what had once been the Diplomatic Quarter. These, standing together with the State Library (1967),the Philharmonic by Hans Scharoun (1963) and the new National Gallery – constructed between 1964 and 1968 after a Mies van der Rohe design, right in the heart of Berlin – would create a new cultural forum that would resemble, as closely as possible, the old Museum Island in the eastern sector of the city. It would be in keeping with the traditions of the Prussian State museums and, were the two German states ultimately to be re-unified, it would become the necessary mirror image of the buildings on the Museum Island.

Steeped in the optimism of the sixties, people were very conscious of the need to create a work which embodied the mood of the time. In 1965 a two-stage competition was announced, the aim of which was to resolve the total concept of the museum. It was suggested that the museum be divided up according to genres, so that there would be

Botticelli's *Madonna with Singing Angels* in the National Gallery of Art, Washington D.C., its condition being checked before its return to Germany in 1948 by a War Department representative, a National Gallery restorer and Dr Irene Kühnel-Kunze, the German representive

The Gemäldegalerie, Dahlem
The Rubens Room, 1983

The Gemäldegalerie, Dahlem
The Multscher Room, 1984

independent museums for painting, sculpture and arts and crafts, together with the prints and drawings collection and the art library, but that they should form a large complex. Formal architectural elements would link the separate buildings together to form a cohesive whole, while the interior of each museum would present itself as a multiplicity of individual units.

Architect Rolf Gutbrod, from Stuttgart, produced a blueprint which met with this requirement, so in 1968 he was commissioned to propose a final building plan. The basic idea of his design remains the firm foundation, even after decades of extremely changeable planning. A central, asymmetrical and gently sloping square opens on to the Matthäi-Kirchplatz and forms the heart of the museum complex. The architect described his first design as an open architecture, incorporating as much as possible the more widespread surroundings of the Tiergarten – a huge problem, bearing in mind the great density of buildings. 'The component structures of the four collections group in a three-quarter circle around this (square) as if around their Megaron and proceed, ray-like, to the outer edge of the site. Between these, respectively, are two green courtyards, which strongly reinforce the green of the Tiergarten, and link the buildings of the surrounding area and the adjoining open spaces to pleasant open expanses' (Gutbrod). In the sloping 'Piazzetta' the visitor would be able to relax and gradually remove himself from the workaday, before proceeding through a broad entrance hall in the art precinct, into the museum itself.

This was to be an 'architectural landscape' – a concept with precedents in the fifties and sixties. The first plan of the Gemäldegalerie itself saw a loose succession of open rooms on different levels. Although this was clearly an extremely successful architectural invention which would have created exciting architecture on its own, with surprising vistas, open and closed rooms, the practical demands of a museum had not been taken into account sufficiently. What may perhaps work well for a museum of modern art is not necessarily the most suitable setting for classical painting produced in the thirteenth to eighteenth centuries; highly demarcated, clearly defined spaces are required here, giving the paintings some form of correctly proportioned and appropriate environment. Indeed, the great paintings of the Baroque and the eighteenth century need the visitor to be reminded of a ceremonious palace in order to look 'correct'.

The more the technical demands of the museum influenced the building plan, the more strongly the design was simplified and regularised. The exhibition rooms – lit by skylights – were to be grouped around two inner courtyards in two wings situated opposite each other, in order to offer the visitor a relaxed tour through the history of European painting. A guideline through the collections was to be discernible, but cross-connections would allow the visitor to proceed easily from one part of the collection to another.

Years passed and plans were continually being reworked. Finally, in 1985, the first part of the museum centre was opened – the Kunstbewerbemuseum. Public reaction was negative: people no longer wanted to understand or accept the basic principles of Gutbrod's design. Wolf-Dieter Dube replaced Stephan Waetzoldt as Director General, all then-current plans were suspended, and a new, more limited invitation to tender for the Gemäldegalerie was issued.

Five designs were submitted, and the judges decided to award first prize to the ingenious, simple idea produced by Heinz Hilmer and Christoph Sattler, a team of young architects from Munich. Their proposal conformed to traditional nineteenth-century principles of museum architecture. A simple, right-angled block would adjoin the entrance hall. Inside there were to be two rows of galleries lit by skylights, around a large three-aisled hall; inside there would be large rooms, and outside smaller ante-rooms. It seems appropriate to note Leo von Klenze's Alte Pinakothek in Munich – the groundplan simply being doubled here; it seems that Klenze's design established a basic blueprint for all the museum architecture that would eventually be constructed. The new Gemäldegalerie was designed to exhibit the Gemäldegalerie collection properly, in a space of 8000 square metres, in fifty-three rooms.

But on 9th November 1989 something happened that nobody could have foreseen: the partition between the two sovereign states of divided Germany – previously jealous neighbours – began to dissolve at a rate no one could have expected. The Berlin Wall, taken as a symbol of the Iron Curtain, was literally broken down in the peaceful revolution in East Germany. And East was allowed through to West. The deep-reaching and radical

Rolf Gutbrod
Schematic plan of the Gemäldegalerie in the new Tiergarten museum complex, 1981

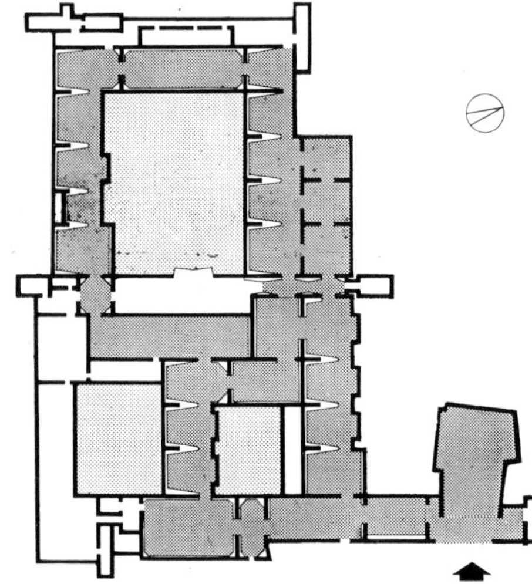

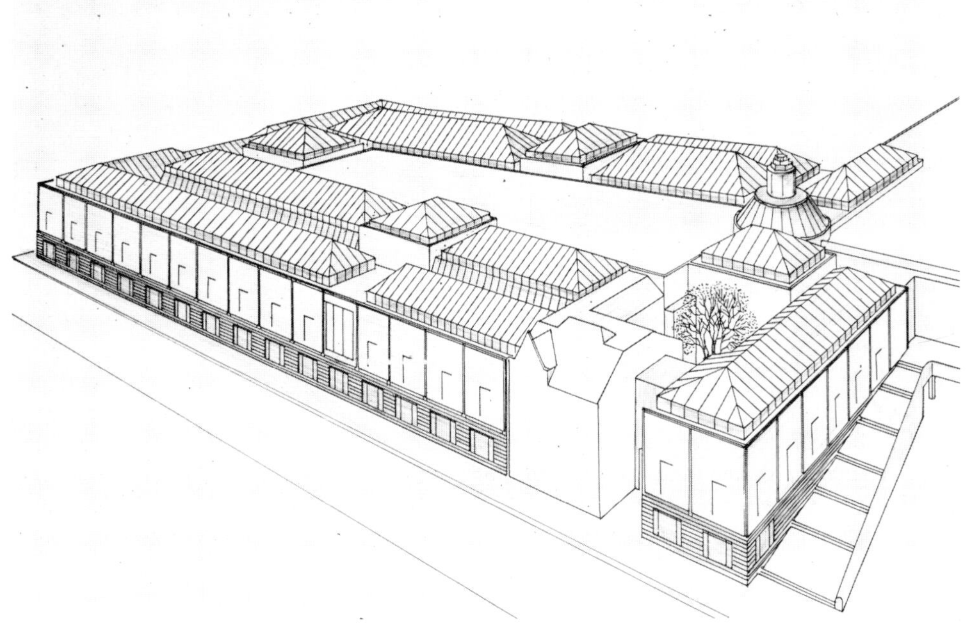

Heinz Hilmer, Christoph Sattler
Design for the Gemäldegalerie,
General view 1989

change this effected in the political landscape – going so far towards German unity, and at such a breathtaking pace – naturally affected Berlin's museums too.

At this stage, the consequences may still not be conclusively stated. For the museums of the Preußischer Kulturbesitz and for the State Museum in the eastern sector of Berlin, there is the question of how the institutions – now in duplicate – can be united. What can be abandoned and how can the demands for exhibition space, administration rooms, depots and workshops be answered?

The old buildings on the Museum Island are in 1990 in such a bad state of repair that first of all a fundamental reconstruction of the fabric of the building has to be effected. Moving the Gemäldegalerie from Dahlem into the old Kaiser-Friedrich-Museum is not, then, in the long-term, feasible. First of all, the new Gemäldegalerie will have to be built at the Kemperplatz – the best location because other collections of European art are in close proximity. Wilhelm von Bode's original idea of expanding the Museum Island will be revived at the Kemperplatz and finally realized after long decades of planning. And when the museum of European sculpture is also housed in a new building there, Berlin will have a new and great museum centre. The Gemäldegalerie will be its highlight.

Heinz Hilmer, Christoph Sattler
Design for the Gemäldegalerie,
Ground plan 1989

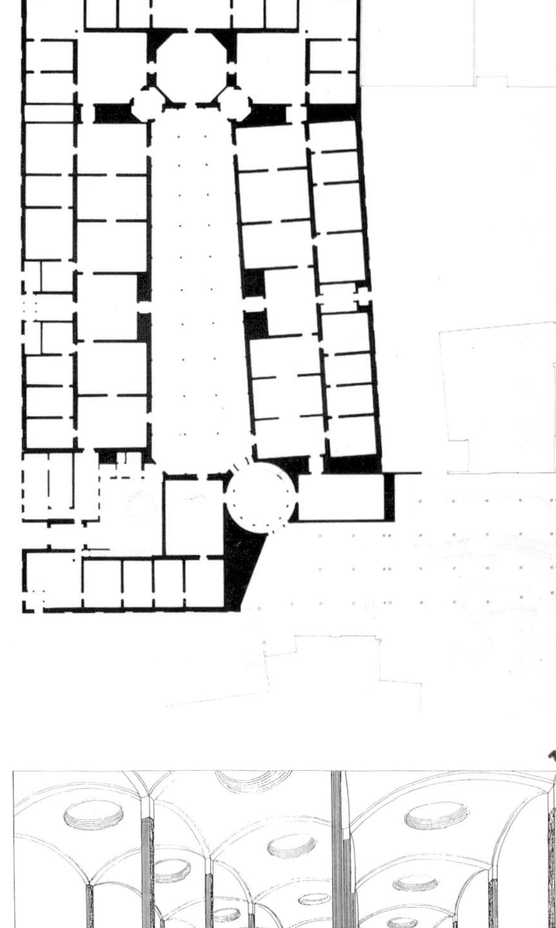

Heinz Hilmer, Christoph Sattler
Design for the Gemäldegalerie,
Great Hall 1989

GERMAN PAINTING OF THE THIRTEENTH TO THE SIXTEENTH CENTURY

BY WILHELM H. KÖHLER

Westphalian (first third of the thirteenth century)
Altarpiece with Three Fields

Oak, 81 × 194 cm ($31\frac{7}{8} \times 76\frac{3}{8}$ in)
Acquired from the Wiesenkirche, Soest, 1862
Cat. no. 1216 A

In 1858, concealed behind fourteenth-century altarpieces in the Wiesenkirche at Soest, Westphalia, two thirteenth-century altarpieces were discovered which have since come to be classified among the incunabula of German altar painting. Since both antedate the church they were found in, they must have been installed in an earlier building, perhaps even on the same site. Recognizing their great significance for the history of art, the Royal Museum in Berlin purchased them without delay. The older of the two paintings, one of the earliest painted altar retables anywhere in Germany, was executed about 1230; the other presumably twenty to thirty years later.

The earlier painting, an irregular rectangular panel divided into three fields, illustrates the meaning of Christ's sacrifice. In the centre field, dominated by an image of the Crucifixion, Christ's figure has been made larger than the others to emphasize its importance. Only a few witnesses are present: Mary and John and Mary's faithful attendants at the left, on the side of the good, where Jesus turns his head; and at the right, the Roman captain with soldiers and figures representing Jews, from whom the Saviour averts his face. Above these groups, on a parapet symbolizing a higher plane of existence, Ecclesia, a personification of the Christian church, appears at the left accompanied by an angel. With the blood of Christ flowing into her goblet, the Church symbolically receives sacrament and means of grace. On the same level at the right, an angel castigates a figure representing the synagogue, an embodiment of the Old Testament, Old Covenant and Judaism, who is divested of her crown and with it her former power. Above the arms of the cross is a third, heavenly realm in which angelic choirs rejoice.

On the left-hand panel, we see Christ bound and led before the high priests. Caiphas, seated with another priest behind the table, asks him, 'How long do you intend to keep us waiting? If you are the Saviour, then admit it openly.' Behind the group, evoked with a few eloquent lines, rise the walls and battlements of Jerusalem. The blue cloth draped over them may symbolize the city's mourning, or perhaps only the lateness of the hour.

The image at the right shows Mary and her attendants at the mouth of the cave where Christ was buried, which is empty except for his shroud. The angel seated on the sarcophagus (which very much resembles an altar) points triumphantly to the empty tomb, as if to proclaim that Christ has arisen. And at the right, asleep, are the Roman soldiers who were set to guard the grave.

The essence of Christian salvation has been rendered here with the utmost simplicity of means. The story begins with the inquisition of Christ, who faces his accusers alone, abandoned by his followers. This scene may be taken to introduce the Passion, which reaches its climax in the central depiction. Here the cross is flanked by Ecclesia and Synagogue, with the victory of the former over the latter symbolically heightening the redemption which Christ's sacrifice brings to man. In the corners of the two fields to right and left, are images of the prophets with inscribed scrolls. These are citations from Scripture prophesying the coming of a Messiah, a prophecy fulfilled with the life and death of Jesus. Thus the figures of the prophets, with those of Ecclesia and Synagogue, give visible form to the agreement of the Old and New Testaments in assuring that man's covenant with God will continue unbroken. The truth of Holy Scripture stands confirmed. The scene at Christ's empty grave, finally, by illustrating his resurrection, affirms the Christian promise that death will be overcome. The separate images and their elements form a meaningful whole, emphasizing Christ's sacrifice as the central event in the story of salvation, an event symbolically repeated in celebrations of the mass at the altar.

The outward form of this retable reveals much about the origin of painted altarpieces of this kind. In the late Middle Ages shrines containing relics of saints were frequently exhibited above the mensa. These shrines were often made of gold and silver, and

Westphalian, after 1250
Altar Superstructure in Three Compartments, with Mercy Seat
Berlin, Gemäldegalerie SMPK

encrusted with precious stones, pearls, and enamels. The early retables that superseded such shrines apparently adopted certain features of their form and decoration. The peaked curves along the top of the present altarpiece, whose central division recalls the triptych form, may be an example of this derivation. The panel and its fields have frames ornamented in relief, recalling goldsmiths' work, as does the convexity of the two round fields, which heightens the effect of their gilded grounds. The painting technique itself, in clear, brilliant colours applied in rather broad, flat areas, was apparently influenced by enamelwork. Borrowings such as this from other techniques indicate that the altarpiece is a very early example of its genre.

Stylistically speaking, the treatment of the figures reveals certain transitional traits. Some of them still have garments draped in parallel folds that describe ovals or arcs around the figures' limbs or the objects they hold: soft, flowing curves that derive from an earlier style. Other draperies show the sharp, angular, crystalline forms typical of a more modern approach which entered thirteenth-century painting from the Byzantine tradition. Art historians have coined a vivid term to characterize it: the angular style.

While the earlier of the two altarpieces stands at the beginning of this stylistic phase, the second, later one (illustrated above) reveals the angular style in its full maturity. The Holy Trinity is represented – God the Father, Son and Holy Ghost – interlinked in the centre to form what is known as a throne of mercy, while on the flanking panels Mary and John the Evangelist appear as intercessors. Everything in the image has been resolved into sharp, angular, prismatic shapes which seem to jostle one another in continual, agitated motion, giving the impression of profound inner feeling and contained energy. This semi-abstract heightening of the pictorial elements suggests a date shortly before this stylistic phase ended, about 1265–70.

Master of Cologne (*c.*1320–30)

The Cologne Diptych

The Virgin Enthroned with Child – Crucifixion

Oak with frames, each panel 49.5 × 34 cm (19½ × 13⅜ in), each image 40.5 × 25 cm (16 × 9⅞)
Acquired 1902
Cat. no. 1627

This painting, named after its town of origin – it was kept during the last century at St George's Church in Cologne – is a rare example of a type of liturgical implement. It was made, as its small size indicates, not as a retable for a church but as a miniature altar for private, domestic use. A diptych or double panel, it is hinged to permit the wings to be opened and closed like a book. This arrangement derived from the writing tablets of antiquity, which were often made of costly materials and served as gifts, a primarily ecclesiastical tradition to which our diptych also belongs. Its versatility, allowing it to be viewed from different sides, reflects the traditional custom of celebrating religious holidays with greater display while reserving plainer imagery for daily worship.

This less ornate aspect of the altar is visible when the two panels are closed. On the back right-hand panel Christ's monogram IHS, an abbreviation of IEHUS, is inscribed in black on a red ground. Above and below it appear a cross and three nails, the instruments of torment that symbolize Christ's passion. The outside left panel bears a depiction of the Annunciation, with the Angel Gabriel and Mary against a simple, monochrome background in red. Both the symbolic image and the figurative one are characterized by a modest simplicity that suggests they were used in daily religious services throughout the year.

The interior depictions are much more richly ornamented by comparison. The tendrils filling their gold-leaf grounds are crafted in relief like fine jewellery, and their frames beautifully coloured. The frames also have two different types of hollows. Those at the corners are round and shallow, and apparently contained droplets of glass in imitation of precious stones; the other cavities, twice as deep, probably held sacred relics under pieces of crystal or glass. The private altar, in other words, doubled as a reliquary, a dual function seen in several other examples from the Cologne region.

On the main display side of the altar, the left panel depicts Mary as Queen of Heaven, seated on a throne with the Child on her lap. The rose-branch she holds is part of the multifarious symbolism of the rose traditionally associated with the Virgin. Like the bride in the Song of Solomon, Mary was compared to a thornless rose, a woman without sin. On the right panel, we see Christ on the cross, lamented by angels. Beneath the cross stand the Apostle John and the Prophet Isaiah, with a scroll which reads 'IPSE VULNERAT[US] EST PROPT[ER] INIQUITATES N[OST]RA[S]' ('But he was wounded for our transgressions'. Isaiah 53:5), a passage from the Old Testament thought to prophesy Christ's sacrifice. The Crucifixion, combined with an image of the Virgin and Child, invites the faithful to meditate on the fundamental symbols of Christianity.

The dating of this triptych varies from 1300 to 1350. Comparisons with illuminated manuscripts from the Cologne area place it between 1320 and 1330.

Cologne Master, *c.*1320–30
The Cologne Diptych
Exterior: *The Annunciation*

Bohemian School (*c.*1350)
The Virgin Enthroned with Child
(Madonna of Glatz)

Canvas over poplar, 186 × 95 cm
($73\frac{1}{4} \times 37\frac{1}{2}$ in)
Acquired from the Gymnasium in Glatz by the Kaiser-Friedrich-Museums-Verein, 1902; received by the gallery, 1905
Cat. no. 1624

This major altar painting of the Bohemian School was acquired by the gallery's supporters' association in 1902 from the Gymnasium in Glatz, a town near the border between Silesia and northern Bohemia. Called the *Madonna of Glatz* after its place of origin, it eloquently testifies to the flowering of art which took place at the court of Charles IV in Prague at that period. The image shows the Virgin with the infant Jesus, seated on a throne constructed of elaborate architectural motifs; she receives a crown from the angel hovering above her. The orb in her lap, her sceptre with fleurs-de-lis, and the second orb presented to her by the kneeling angel at the right, are attributes characterizing Mary as Queen of Heaven, *regina coeli.* The Child grasps a scroll symbolizing Holy Writ, whose prophecies have been fulfilled by his birth. At the top of the image, two angels spread a beautifully embroidered canopy while below them two others lean from windows, swinging censers. The gesture of the angel at the left centre was probably meant to call attention to the painting's donor, who kneels devoutly at the foot of the throne.

The complex shape of the throne and its exquisite materials were chosen to symbolize a divine edifice. Yet much in contrast to its marble wings and jewel-encrusted sides, the back of the throne is made of plain boards, perhaps in allusion to the cedarwood used to build the Temple of Solomon. The two lions crouching in the little temple-like structures at the top likewise recall Biblical descriptions of King Solomon's throne and temple. This Old Testament reference characterizes the Christ Child as a New Solomon, seated on the throne of His mother's lap; with Jesus, Solomon's wisdom is reborn, and Mary becomes the seat of divine wisdom. The image abounds with symbolic allusions of this kind, including a star in the gilding above the throne, which is a reference to one of the names by which Mary was known: *stella maris*, 'star of the sea'.

Though complete in itself, the surviving panel is a fragment. It was originally framed with smaller images in the manner of Italian devotional paintings. From a seventeenth-century manuscript we know that the small pictures surrounding the main panel at that period included a Nativity, Circumcision, Flight into Egypt, and Jesus in the Temple – in short, a series of scenes from the life of the Virgin (*Depictae in parvis imaginibus curae Divae Virginis ut* . . .).

The donor kneeling at the lower left, in an archbishop's vestments with a patriarchal cross, has laid his insignia at Mary's feet in humble offering. Based on these attributes, he has been identified as Ernst von Pardubitz, first Archbishop of Prague. He went to school in Glatz, studied in Italy and Paris, and was consecrated bishop in 1343. Only a year later, he convinced Pope Clement VI in Avignon to raise Prague to the rank of an Archbishopric, which made the city autonomous of the Archbishopric of Mainz. About 1350, Archbishop von Pardubitz founded an Augustinian monastery in Glatz, to whose chapel he presumably donated the altarpiece in our collection. This event would place its date of execution at no later than 1350.

Bohemian School (*c.*1360)
The Crucifixion
(The Kaufmann Crucifixion)

Canvas over panel, transferred to canvas, top in gable form, 67 × 29.5 cm ($26\frac{3}{8}$ × $11\frac{1}{2}$ in)
Collection of Richard von Kaufmann, Berlin
Acquired as a gift from P. Cassirer, F.W. Lippmann (Berlin) and H. Helbing (Munich), 1918
Cat. no. 1833

This tall, narrow panel, whose original frame has not survived, was probably the centre section of a small domestic altar with folding wings which presumably contained further events of the Passion. Their climax on Golgotha is depicted here in a composition dominated by the looming Crucifix and the writhing bodies of the two thieves. The three crosses dramatically divide the picture plane, the flanking ones repeating the austere yet decorative horizontals and verticals of the Crucifix. As angels descend to lament Christ's sufferings, a crowd mills below, a tumultuous scene which the artist has rendered lucid by choosing a view from above. The mourners are gathered in the left foreground: St John, supporting Mary; Mary Magdalene embracing the cross; and a third woman, mournfully averting her face. Behind and above them is Longinus, the blind man who opened Jesus's wound with a lance and was cured of his infirmity by the blood that fell on his eyes. To the right of the cross, the executioner's henchmen fight over Christ's robe, and behind them are Roman legionaries, with the figure of the Good Captain rising above them. He has recognized the Saviour, and declares with a gesture towards him that he is verily the Son of God. Behind him, another henchman raises the vinegar-soaked sponge to Christ. His lance, with that of Longinus, forms an almost symmetrical triangle.

The crowded, jostling figures with their excited faces, troubled glances and agitated gestures, reveal the deep emotions that this event has awakened in its witnesses. Even the folds of their garments seem fraught with tension. The drawing and modelling of the forms are precise and lucid, the line has calligraphic sharpness. The colours, light and brilliant yet strangely veiled in effect, subtly underscore the significance and symbolism of each figure in the scene. In its acuity and detail the treatment seems closer to a miniature illumination than to an easel work. The gold background was unfortunately restored at a later date.

Some authors believe this *Crucifixion* was modelled on a Bologne miniature of 1346–50, the canon page from a missal now in the Archivio di S. Pietro, Rome (*L'Arte*, 1907, p. 108). This image may indeed have inspired certain passages in the composition, and the fact that it is a miniature would seem to corroborate the link.

The regional origin of this small altar panel is still a matter for conjecture. It is traditionally attributed to the circle of Bohemian artists active at the Court of Charles IV, and many good reasons exist in support of this assumption. However, a stylistic connection with Austrian altarpieces has also been pointed out, especially with the painted panels of the *Verdun Altar* in Klosterneuburg (*c.*1330–1). Nor should similarities with such later works as the canon page of a missal at St Pölten be overlooked (Hs. 56; left). Since there was much cross-fertilization between Bohemia and Austria at that period, and both regions were subject to the same artistic influences, it is difficult to draw a hard and fast line between them.

Missal, St Pölten (?), *c.*1360
Canon page: *The Crucifixion*
St Pölten, Diözensanbibliothek, Hs. 56

INRI

Master of the Older Holy Kinship

Triptych with the Virgin and Child

St Elizabeth (left) – *The Virgin and Child in Paradise* (centre) – *St Agnes* (right)

First third of the fifteenth century

Oak, centre section with original frame, 40 × 35.5 cm ($15\frac{3}{4}$ × 14 in), each wing with frame, 40 × 17.5 cm ($15\frac{3}{4} \times 6\frac{7}{8}$ in)
Acquired with the Solly Collection, 1821
Cat. no. 1238

This domestic altarpiece is a miniature version of the large, three-part church retables known as triptychs. Like them, its central panel is flanked by two wings of half its width, which are hinged to close over it. Yet unlike larger altars, whose wings usually have scenes on both sides, the backs of all three panels here are painted plain red.

The middle panel of our triptych shows Mary with the Christ Child on her lap, accompanied by four saintly virgins. They are resting in a meadow dotted with many varieties and colours of flowers, a garden sequestered from the outside world. While Mary's crown characterizes her as *regina coeli*, Queen of Heaven, her attendants have names inscribed in their haloes and attributes to identify them. St Dorothy, the maiden in blue next to Mary, wears a wreath of red and white roses in her hair, and is presenting a basket full of rose petals to the Infant. From Caesarea in Cappadocia, St Dorothy suffered martyrdom during the persecution of Christians under Emperor Diocletian; her roses allude to a miracle that occurred during her torments. She was also among the Fourteen Holy Helpers, and with Saints Margaret, Barbara, and Catherine, belonged to the *virgines capitales*.

St Margaret, in a red dress and green mantle at Mary's right, holds out the cross with which she banished the devil who, during her martyrdom, appeared to her in the guise of a dragon. Seated in the left foreground, clad in a shimmering cloak of yellow and red, is St Catherine, who was of an Alexandrian royal house. Caesar Maxentius, enraged by her profession of Christianity, tried to force her to sacrifice to the heathen gods; she refused and was condemned to be broken on the wheel. Though spared by the intercession of an angel, she was fated to die by the sword. This weapon and a fragment of the wheel appear here as St Catherine's attributes.

St Barbara, seated in the right foreground and wearing a red mantle, holds a miniature tower in her lap that signifies the tower to which her father banished her. She, too, chose death rather than abjure her faith.

The garden with its surrounding arbour where Mary rests with her attendants (a *hortus conclusus*) recalls a metaphor in the Song of Solomon, the bride as an enclosed garden (4:12). This was one of the names by which the Virgin was known. The garden symbolizes her purity and the Immaculate Conception, but it also identifies Mary with this Old Testament bride and pictures her among flowers that perpetually bloom – in the Garden of Eden, Paradise. This symbol of divine and everlasting peace, often associated with the Virgin in medieval painting from about 1400 on through the fifteenth century, was a devotional image marked by mystical faith which visualized the bliss that the Mother of God and the saints enjoyed in Heaven.

The two panels flanking the main image represent individual saints. At the left we see St Elizabeth, Countess of Thüringia, a German noblewoman who lived in Marburg and devoted herself to the care of the needy and infirm. Here she is shown with a poor cripple to whom she hands a warming cloak. On the right is St Agnes with a lamb. St Agnes died a martyr's death rather than relinquish her virginity, and the white lamb is an attribute alluding to her vow. At the same time, the similarity of her name to the Latin for lamb (*agnus*) links her with Christ, the Lamb of God, who took the sins of the world upon himself.

The images of this altar are identified with femininity throughout. While in the centre Mary is united with her *virgines capitales*, St Elizabeth at the left embodies charity, and St Agnes at the right the self-denial of chastity. The consistency of these allusions suggests that the altar may well have been commissioned by a woman, perhaps by a nun.

Its style is characterized by colours of a flower-like delicacy, principally in combinations of contrasting and iridescent tones, and even with some complementary contrasts. The draperies have the gentle, clinging curves typical of the International Gothic style known as the supple or soft style, which predominated around 1400. The figures' heads, small, rather doll-like, and lacking in profound expression, their elongated limbs and torsos, and their mannered gestures and poses, all reflect an ideal of beauty current in the courtly society of the period. The tendency to miniaturize things – the attributes, for example, and even the instruments of torture – to the point of making them resemble toys, also reveals a love of delicacy at all costs. Though a gentle, lyrical, even sentimental and precious mood was not uncommon in late Gothic art in general, it was particularly marked in the painting of the Cologne region.

In terms of style, our *Triptych with the Virgin and Child* is closely related to an altarpiece representing the Holy Kinship from the Church of St Herbert in Cologne. Several other, stylistically similar paintings have been associated with this work, and the presumed artist was given the pseudonym of Master of the Holy Kinship. To distinguish him from another anonymous artist who painted a Holy Kinship towards the end of the century, he has also been called Master of the Older Holy Kinship. He was active during the first third of the fifteenth century.

Martin Schongauer (*c*.1445/50–91)
The Nativity
c.1480

Oak, 37.5 × 28 cm (14¾ × 11 in)
Acquired 1902
Property of the
Kaiser-Friedrich-Museums-Verein
Cat. no. 1629

Martin Schongauer of Colmar, an artist of unsurpassed power and a man of great gentleness, brought late Gothic painting in Germany to perfection. His lyrical style earned him the nickname 'Hipsch Martin' or 'Martin Schön' (Pretty Martin) during his lifetime, and after his death he was celebrated as *pictorium gloria*, the glory of all artists. His influence on German and Netherlandish art at the close of the fifteenth and far into the sixteenth century cannot be estimated highly enough. Known to us today primarily as a printmaker, he made great numbers of engravings, 116 of which have survived. They were widely known throughout Europe and continued to inspire artists long after his death. Among those who went to Colmar in the hope of working with Schongauer was Albrecht Dürer; though he arrived too late to meet him personally, Dürer's art was decisively shaped by the traditions of Schongauer's workshop. Most of Schongauer's paintings were destroyed by iconoclasts or fell prey to the vicissitudes of time. The handful which have come down to us, however, leave no doubt of his superb gifts. One of the most mature and beautiful of these is surely *The Nativity*, executed in about 1480 and now in Berlin.

Here, Schongauer recounts the Christmas story, how Joseph and Mary found shelter in a stable near a cave at the side of the road where Jesus was born. But to the familiar Bible account he has added certain legendary elements which derive partly from artistic tradition, partly from mystical writings – diverse sources which he has none the less lucidly arranged and welded into a meaningful whole. The infant Jesus lies on the ground in swaddling clothes, whose white colour, the lightest in the entire picture, symbolizes the unearthly radiance which legends say emanated from the Child. He is indeed the centre of interest around which everything in the painting is grouped. All the other figures face or glance towards him in adoration. Mary, closest to Jesus in every sense, is moreover visually linked with him by the folds of her mantle. Though Joseph stands at some distance, the same kind of visual link is provided by his stick and bag in the left foreground. Even the animals in the manger turn towards the Child. The fact that the ox is nearer to him than the ass may signify, as one interpretation suggests, that they stand for the Old and New Testaments.

While the Holy Family and the animals are sheltered in the stable as in a sanctified sphere, the shepherds who have come to worship the new-born King remain outside. The relationship of each of the figures to Christ is simply and unmistakably expressed in terms of physical proximity or distance. We as observers are also made to feel very much a part of the events, as if we were actually standing in the stable ourselves. And the shepherds at its entrance, a young, a middle-aged, and an old man, seem to signify that the worship of Christ knows no age barriers.

The posts and beams of the stable divide the picture plane, lend the composition solidity, and lead the eye by their perspective lines back into the distance, where shepherds tend their flocks in a broad, sunny valley. Yet the dark of night can still be sensed over the stable, as in the Christmas story, where the Star of Bethlehem shone so brightly that it turned night to day. This is a good example of the ease with which Schongauer combined features of Christian legend with symbolic allusion. His glowing, jewel-like colours further heighten the clarity of the composition.

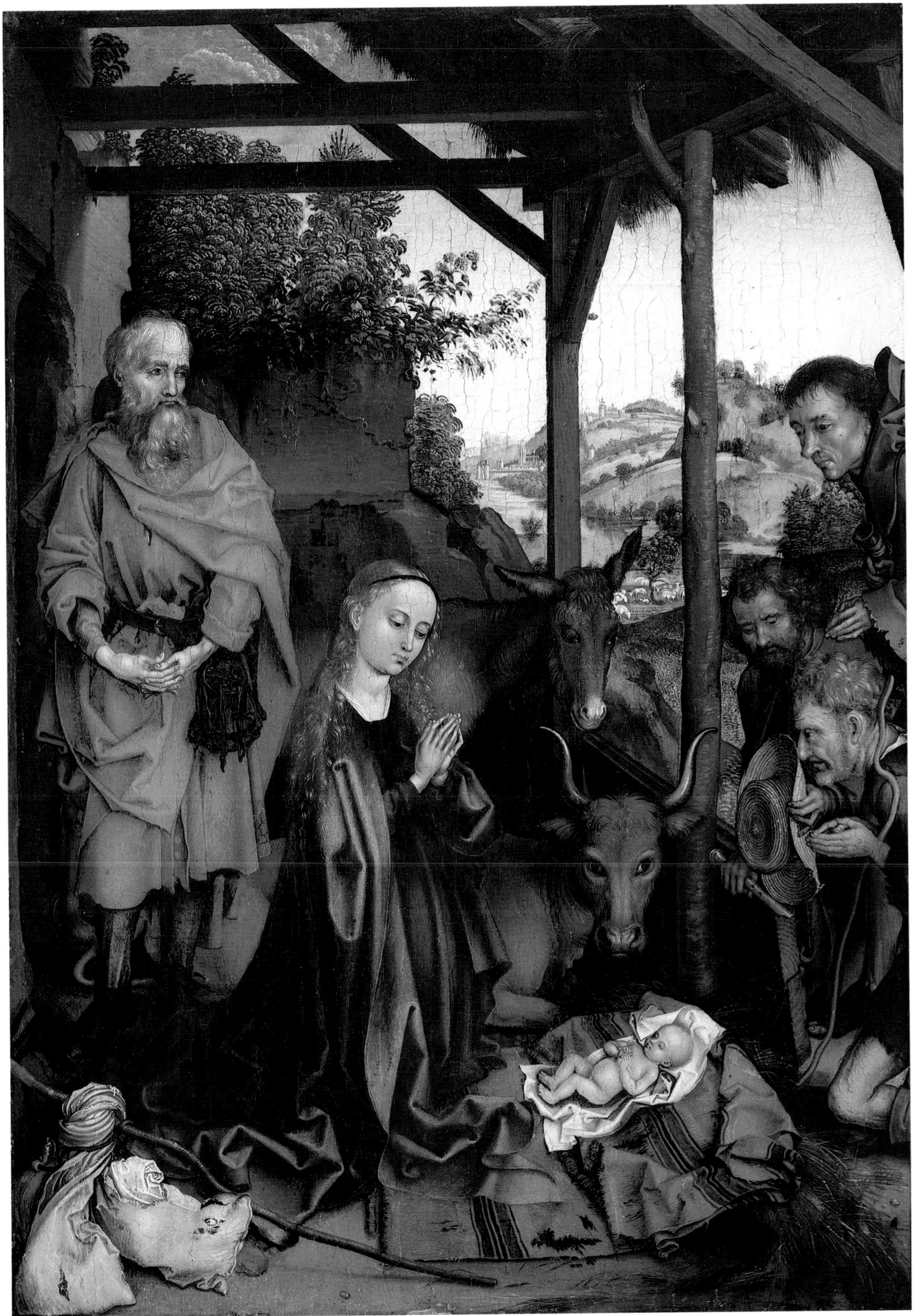

Konrad Witz (*c.*1400–pre-1446)

The Queen of Sheba before Solomon

*c.*1435–7

Oak, 84.5 × 79 cm ($33\frac{1}{4} \times 31\frac{1}{8}$ in)
Gold background renewed at a later date
Acquired 1913
Cat. no. 1701

Konrad Witz was born in Rottweil on the Neckar, in about 1400. History first records his name in 1434, the date of his joining the Guild in Basel, where he obtained civic rights in 1435. He apparently spent the next two years working on a large altarpiece devoted to themes from the *Speculum humanae salvationis* or *Mirror of Human Salvation*, presumably for St Leonhard Church, Basel. Very few other works by Witz have come down to us. His recorded frescoes have vanished, and most of his other paintings were damaged by the iconoclasts who stripped churches and chapels on the Upper Rhine with particular thoroughness. Sections of a later altarpiece may still be seen in Geneva. A short time after completing it in 1444, but before 1446, Witz died.

Witz was one of the great artistic innovators of the Upper Rhine region. Realism had begun to emerge in Netherlandish painting in the early fifteenth century, exemplified by the van Eycks and Robert Campin, and Witz's very personal version supplanted the courtly, transcendental style of International Gothic. The figures in his paintings have a stocky, square-built look about them as if they had been constructed of cubes and prisms. The drapery falls in sharp angular folds whose edges catch the light, and glow against the deep adjacent shadow. This stark modelling creates a wonderful effect of volume and depth. The same preoccupation is evident in the pictorial space, which Witz attempted to depict in its true size and depth. He also took great pains to reproduce the appearence of things, the surface qualities of different types of cloth and metal, of wood and masonry. Fidelity to reality was his credo.

The audience of the Queen of Sheba with King Solomon (1 Kings 10: 1 ff.) is one of eight images on the inside wings of the altar known as the *Heilsspiegel* or *Mirror of Salvation Altar*. The centre panel has been lost, and we know nothing about its subject-matter. The surviving inside wings depict themes from the *Speculum humanae salvationis*, a devotional book of fourteenth-century Dominican mysticism in which Old Testament and historical events were related to the life and sufferings of Christ. These connecting themes grew out of the idea that the incarnation of Christ and his sacrifice to redeem mankind were predestined from the beginning of the world by a plan of salvation. Past events, it was believed, repeatedly prophesied events to come.

The Queen of Sheba's meeting with Solomon, to whom she brought offerings of gold and spices, found various interpretations in the Middle Ages. Some believed it prefigured the Three Kings, who also came from the East to worship the Christ Child, a reading which lent Jesus the aspect of a New Solomon. Others thought that just as the Queen of Sheba went to Solomon to receive his wisdom, so the Church went out from all nations of the earth to receive the word of God. The *Mirror of Salvation* gives still another interpretation: the Queen's joy at experiencing Solomon's wisdom corresponds to the bliss of saved souls as they contemplate the face of Christ in heaven.

The wisdom illuminating Solomon's face and the reverential aspect of his visitor are superbly rendered in Witz's painting. The composition has been reduced to essentials. The two figures are linked by a single but eloquent gesture, the offering of a gift. Seated regally on a bench, Solomon receives the Queen's humble adoration as she kneels before him. The other scenes on the inside panels of the altar are painted with similar reserve and noble conciseness.

Attributed to Konrad Witz

The Crucifixion

*c.*1445–50

Panel, transferred to canvas, 34 × 26 cm
(13⅜ × 10¼ in)
Acquired 1908
Cat. no. 1656

Near a path worn into the meadows by wagons passing on their way to town, the cross has been raised, solitary on a grassy knoll. Mary with two attendants, and John are gathered in mourning, and John wrings his hands in silent appeal. To their left a clergyman, probably the painting's donor, kneels in prayer. (It was common practice for donors of altars or devotional images to have themselves included in sacred scenes, perpetuating their piety in the timelessness of art.) Three other figures are visible to the right, in the middle ground, perhaps on their way home, last stragglers from the crowd that had come to see the spectacle. The day is almost over; the mourners remain alone beneath the cross, which stands starkly against the brilliant glow of the evening sky. This composition makes the sadness of the scene immediate and tangible.

We as spectators are made to feel that the Golgotha of legend is no longer distant in space and time but is present here and now, in a stretch of countryside that somehow seems familiar. The bays and rocky promontories in the background have been identified as those of Lake Constance, Lake Geneva or Lake Annecy; but whether this assumption is correct or not, the city of Jerusalem that the town on the shore certainly represents, and the martyrdom that takes place before it, have been brought home to us. The temperate, European surroundings contribute to an emotional heightening of the scene, and the realism of the depiction gives it immediacy and encourages empathy. The cross, slightly inclined and foreshortened, the wheel-rutted path winding into the background, the cliffs projecting one behind the other into the lake, and the cloud strata against the setting sun, all lead the eye gradually into the distance, and evoke great depth. In a landscape we can experience, or re-experience, in this way, the climax of Christ's sufferings takes on a degree of reality which no hieratic crucifix against a numinous gold ground could ever attain. Seen in this light, the artist's striving to reproduce things as they are might signify a new kind of faith, a new way of illustrating the meaning of Christ's sacrifice and making Christian tenets manifest.

It was this realistic approach to landscape, the light flooding the scene, modelling the forms, and throwing everything into sharp contrast, the effect of atmosphere and space, and not least the profound melancholy with which the figures are infused, that led historians to attribute this painting to Konrad Witz. Instrumental in helping Netherlandish realism to its breakthrough on the Upper Rhine, Witz, in his late *St Peter Altarpiece* of 1444 in Geneva, set the story of St Peter fishing for souls in a real landscape – the shores of Lake Geneva – thus creating probably the first landscape portrait in the history of German painting. The present lakeside scene with Crucifixion follows models of this kind. However, the painting has certain traits which are difficult to reconcile with Konrad Witz's accepted œuvre: the facial types, the comparative softness and suppleness of form, and the striated, often parallel vertical folds of the drapery. Idiosyncrasies in the treatment of the landscape and the singularly magical effect of the evening twilight place the painting among a group of works associated with a *Lamentation (Pietà)* in the Frick Collection, New York. These are assumed to have been executed in Savoy or Provence, and most commentators agree in dating them about 1445–50.

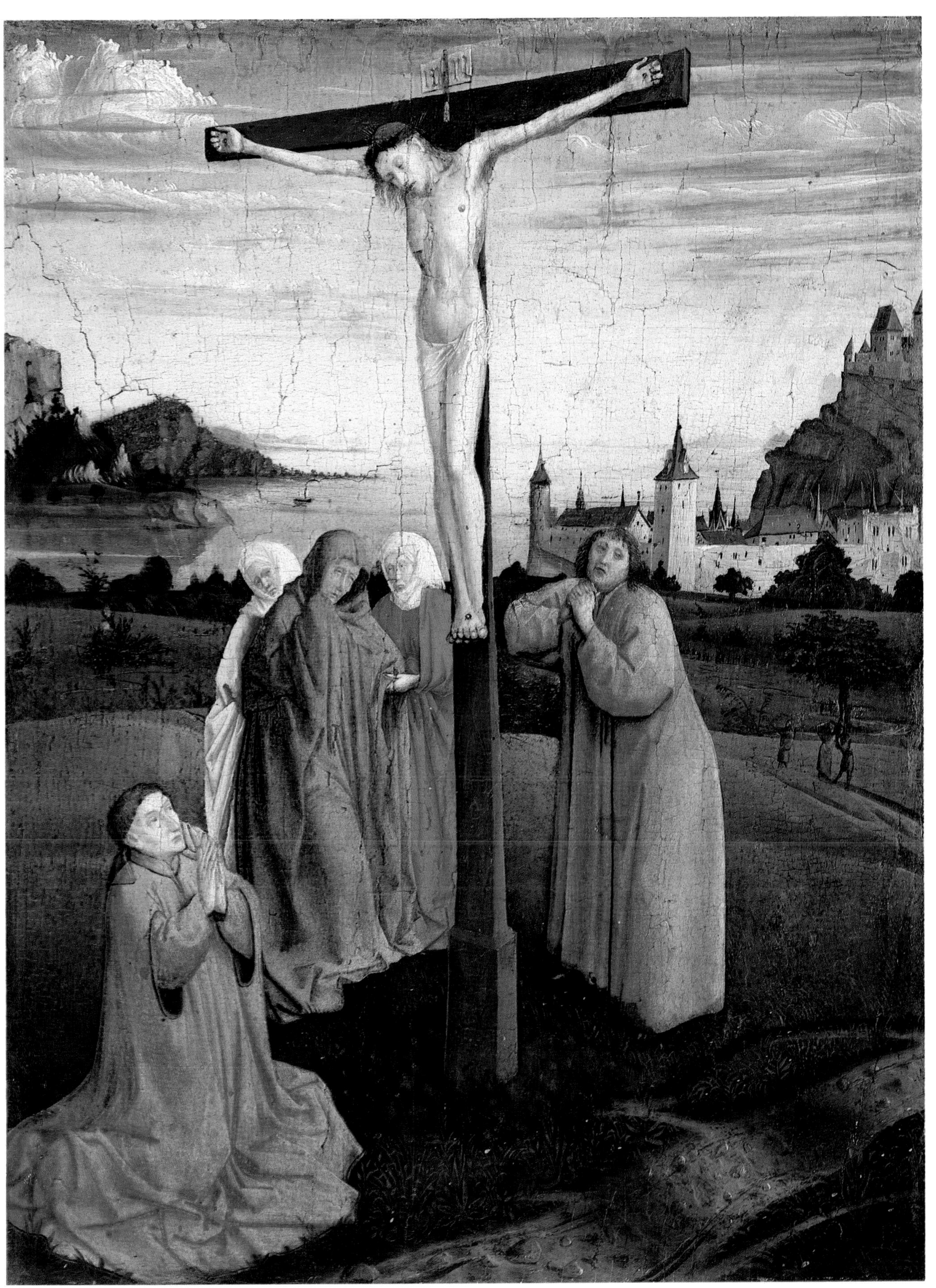

Master Lcz (active *c.*1480–1500)

Christ before Pilate

*c.*1500

Pine, 77.5 × 60 cm ($30\frac{1}{2}$ × $23\frac{5}{8}$ in)
Formerly in the Strache Collection, Dornbach near Vienna
Acquired as a gift, 1917
Cat. no. 1847

This panel was once part of an altarpiece which was dismantled, and its paintings were dispersed after having been in the collection of Dr Strache, of Dornbach near Vienna. The other side panels included a *Flagellation* (Paris, Louvre), *Christ Crowned with Thorns* (Nuremberg, Germanisches Nationalmuseum), and a *Crucifixion* (private collection). The centre panel of the original altarpiece was an image of *Christ Praying on the Mount of Olives* or *The Agony in the Garden* (Darmstadt, Hessisches Landesmuseum). Two wings depicting individual saints – a *St Jacob* (at Sigmaringen) and a *St Lawrence* (at Darmstadt) – were apparently also part of the original group. The latter, at any rate, has the same provenance as the central panel. The anonymous artist was long known, after the owner of the panels, as the Master of the Strache Altar, but subsequently stylistic similarities were detected with engravings of 1492–7, signed 'Lcz'. This signature still poses a riddle. Judging by other works of the artist's hand, including a painted *Crucifixion* dated 1485 with a view of Bamberg in the background (Nuremberg, Germanisches Nationalmuseum), 'Lcz' must have been active in that city. Attempts have been made to associate him, on stylistic grounds, with the Bamberg artists' family of Katzheimer. Some authors have even suggested that Lucas Cranach's father may be the mysterious 'Lcz'. About one thing, however, there can be little doubt – that our anonymous master was trained in Nuremberg. His firm drawing and delineation of character, and the striking intensity of his colour, make him one of the most original painters in Franconia before Dürer.

Master Lcz
Reconstruction of the *Strache Altar*
*c.*1500

Bernhard Strigel (1460–1528)

Christ Taking Leave of his Mother

(Part of an altarpiece formerly at Isny)

Fir, 86.5 × 71.5 cm (34 × 28⅛ in)
Hirscher Collection, Freiburg
Acquired 1850
Cat. no. 1197 A

Mary, having awaited her son before the gates of a walled town, sinks disconsolate into his arms. Her attendants look on from the right, while St Peter and other apostles approach from a copse of trees in the middle ground at the left. Behind them is a broad landscape vista with woods, a castle, and a mountain chain on the distant horizon.

This panel was once part of a disassembled altarpiece, another of whose sections, *The Disrobing of Christ*, is also in the gallery's collection. It shows the executioner's henchmen roughly tearing off Jesus's clothes as Mary attempts to cover his nakedness. Stylistically speaking, the two groups confront each other on the same pictorial plane, and their principal movements and gestures also describe planes parallel with the canvas surface. The structure of the composition is basically linear; the violence being done to Christ pulls his upper body towards the central axis of the painting, bringing his head to the centre and forcing him to look straight out at the viewer. This frontality transforms a dramatic narrative into a devotional image of Jesus as the Redeemer, a picture within the picture.

Both these paintings reveal certain characteristic features of Strigel's art, which grew out of the late Gothic style of the Swabian region. His figures are very slender and mannered, and their gestures and facial expressions tend to the extremes of sweetness and brutality. His compositions seem built up of a number of separate, clearly defined planes which overlap one another from foreground to background. Line and place are Strigel's primary means of expression, as can also be seen from his preference for profile views.

Two further panels from the dismantled altar – *The Annunciation* and *Christ Washing the Apostles' Feet* – may be seen today in the Karlsruhe Kunsthalle. Four of the original panels, each bearing depictions of two saints, were destroyed by fire in Berlin in 1945. Judging by these subjects, the original altarpiece must have contained a comprehensive Passion cycle and would have been extremely large, with multiple wings. However, it is almost impossible to say how it looked, since not enough panels have survived to permit a reconstruction. The lucid articulation of the scenes, the relation of their monumental figures to the background landscape, and a certain generosity in the application of luminous colour, would suggest a date about 1520, when Strigel's late style began. Though these paintings are believed to have come from Isny in the Allgäu region, their provenance remains uncertain.

Bernhard Strigel
The Disrobing of Christ
Berlin, Gemäldegalerie SMPK

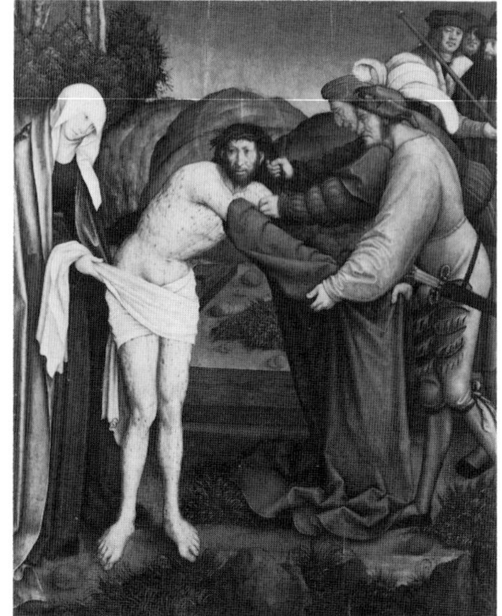

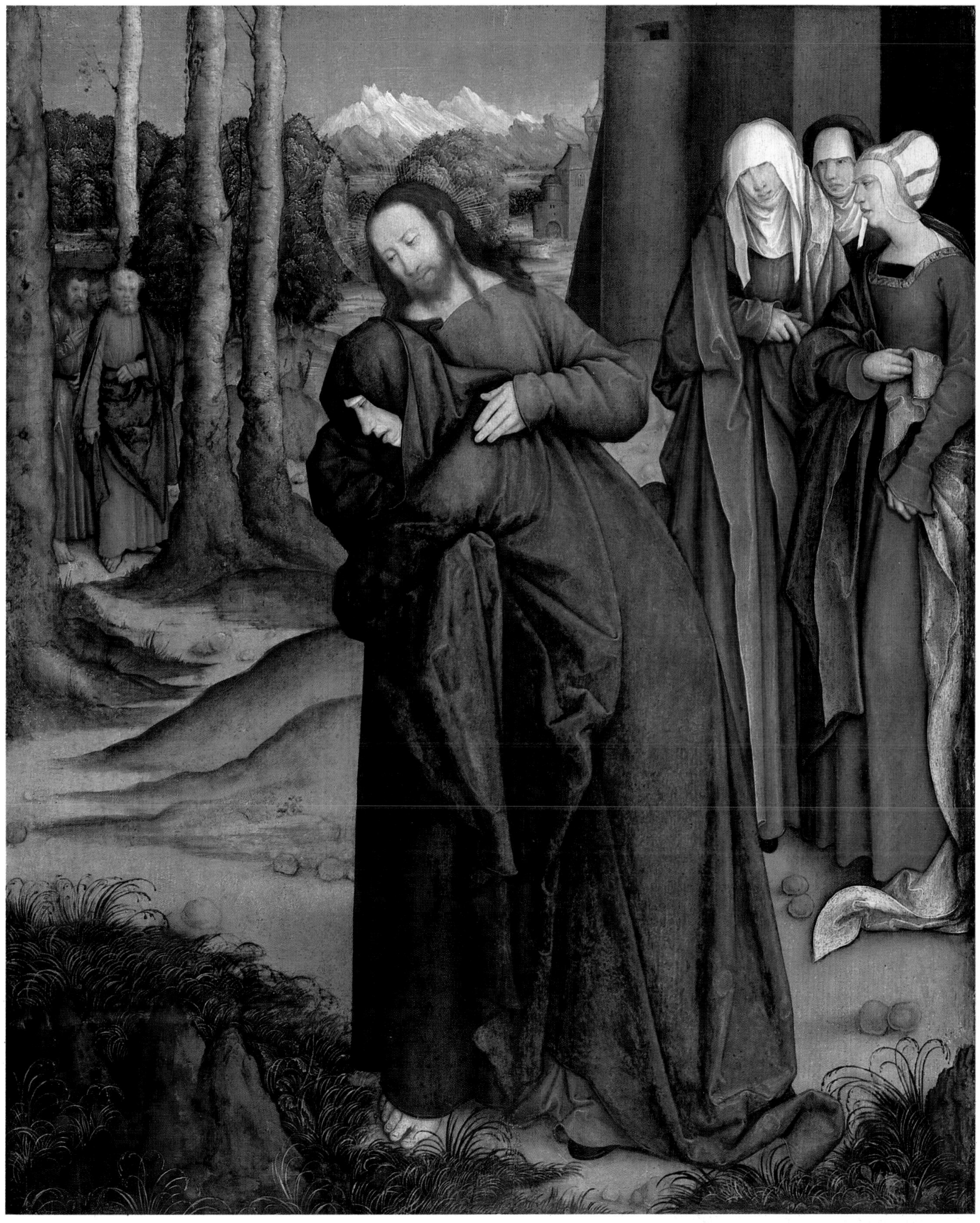

Hans Multscher (*c.*1400–67)
Wings of the 'Wurzacher Altar'
1437

Fir, each panel 150 × 140 cm (59 × 55 in)
Collection of The Truchsess of Waldburg-Zeil, Wurzach Castle
Acquired as a gift from Sir Julius Wernher, London
Cat. no. 1621 A–G

Hans Multscher, sculptor and wood-carver, was head of a workshop in Ulm. We know of his existence from several contemporary documents and a number of surviving sculptural pieces, though whether he ever worked in the painting medium remains uncertain. Signed with his name are the eight panels of a destroyed altarpiece of 1437 illustrated opposite, four scenes from the Life of the Virgin, and four from Christ's Passion. Their subjects, composition, and certain technical features suggest that they were originally arranged as follows:

Scenes from the Life of the Virgin (see p. 62):

The Nativity	*The Adoration of the Magi*
The Descent of the Holy Spirit – Pentecost	*The Death of the Virgin*

Scenes from the Passion (see p. 63):

The Agony in the Garden	*Christ before Pilate*
The Bearing of the Cross	*The Resurrection*

Along the bottom edge of *The Death of the Virgin* is a master's device and an inscription reading: 'bitte[n] got für hanssen muoltscheren vo[n] riche[n]hofe[n] burg[er] ze ulm haut d[a]ß werk gemacht do man zalt MCCCCXXXVII [1437].' A shorter inscription above the chapel arches in the *Pentecost* panel contains basically the same information – the name of the master of the workshop combined with a prayer for intercession. This was the common form of signature in the fifteenth century. Further lettering is found on the background tower in the *Adoration* panel – a tablet with a coat of arms bearing the inscription 'Roma'. The coat of arms itself is not that of the town of Landsberg, as some have assumed, but bears the letters 'SPQR' (*senatus populusque romanus*), a reference to the fact that Christ's birthplace was located in Roman territory. Another interesting detail is the hospital coat of arms held by a monkey above the column in *The Death of the Virgin*. Since it contains no tinctures of any kind, it cannot have been meant to stand for any particular hospital. By including it, the artist probably wished to identify the building in which the Virgin died as a hospital or infirmary.

These eight panels, arranged in pairs one above the other, originally formed the inside and outside of the altar wings. The arrangement illustrated derives from the architectural elements which continue from one panel to the next in the Life of the Virgin series. Which scenes were on the front and which on the back of the wings has been established from certain technical features of the wooden panels themselves, and these corroborate the sequence of events depicted. The four scenes from the Life of the Virgin form an integral composition, and they were no doubt originally on the outside of the altarpiece. This is confirmed by their inscriptions, which during the fifteenth century were almost always painted on the outside of such retables. The scenes from Christ's Life and Suffering, moreover, have a white pattern painted over the gilded ground which marks them as the costlier, more opulent inside of the altar reserved for special religious holidays. In short, the original altarpiece contained a sequence devoted to Mary on the outside of its wings and one devoted to Christ's Passion on the interior. The central panel, which has not survived, probably represented a Calvary or Crucifixion group. Though attempts have been made to reconstruct the central shrine using a statue of the Virgin by Multscher from Landsberg, they are misleading because they are based on false assumptions.

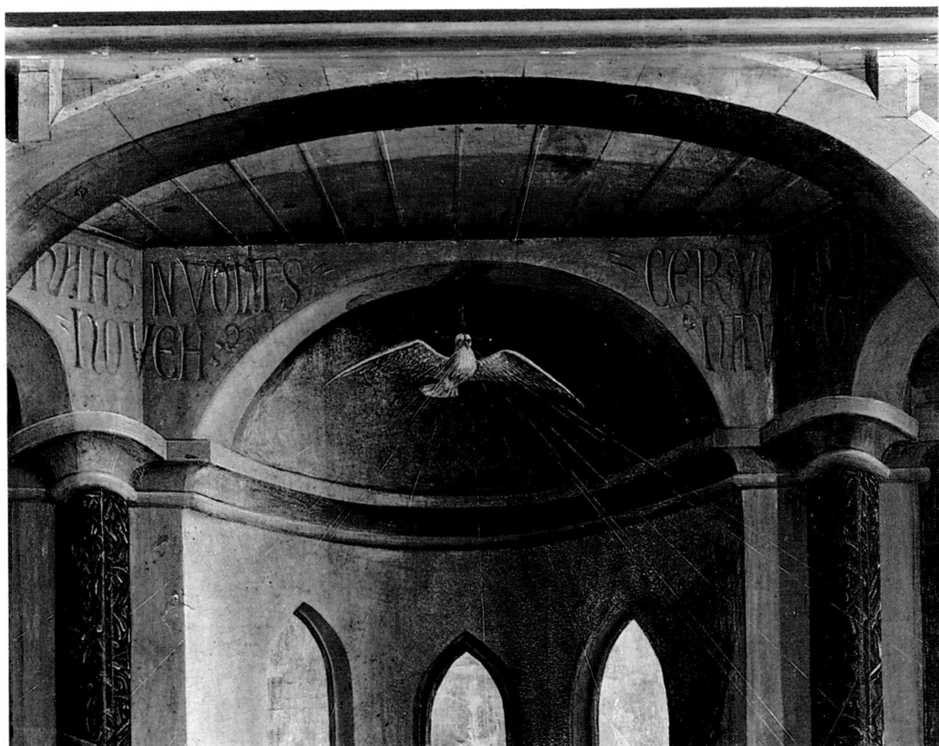

Hans Multscher
Wurzacher Altar
Detail: Second inscription in the Pentecost panel

The images are characterized by drastic realism, the artist having portrayed sacred figures and other participants alike as rough and rustic, sometimes positively ugly, and occasionally even brutal. This realism, seeing the Holy Family not as ideal figures but as real people, representatives of the life of the time, and giving Biblical events the appearance of everyday scenes, reveals a new understanding of the Scriptures. Perhaps influenced by contemporary Passion Plays, this approach brought Christianity closer to the daily lives and experiences of the faithful than ever before in Christian art. In this regard the stylistic influence of Netherlandish-Burgundian art also makes itself apparent.

According to the earliest written record, these panels were once in the collection of the Truchsess of Waldburg-Zeil in Wurzach, which is why they were collectively called the *Wurzacher Altar*. Though some authors believe they originated from Landsberg, there is no definite proof for this assumption. Nor has recent research been able to turn up evidence that the church at Landsberg, to which reconstruction attempts would assign the altar, ever existed in that city.

Albrecht Dürer (1471–1528)
The Madonna with the Siskin
1506

Poplar, 91 × 76 cm ($35\frac{7}{8}$ × 30 in)
Signed lower left: 'Albertus durer germanus faciebat post virginis partum 1506', and monogrammed 'AD' (interlocked)
Imhoff Collection, Nuremberg; Emperor Rudolf II, Prague; The Marquis of Lothian, Edinburgh
Acquired 1893
Cat. no. 557 F

The Virgin, clothed in blue, is seated on a throne in the midst of a spacious landscape, holding the Child on a red cushion in her lap. The boy at her feet, giving her a bunch of lilies-of-the-valley, is John the Baptist, recognizable from his cloak of camel's hair and the cross of staves held by the angel accompanying him. Mary's right hand rests on a book, while Jesus, his thin shirt slipping from his shoulders, plays with a sucking-bag, the medieval version of a pacifier. A siskin has settled on his raised left arm, and he inclines his head as if to listen to its song. Mary's head and shoulders are set off by the brilliant red canopy of the throne, the rest of which is hidden; to the right and left we look out over a broad valley with farmhouses and ruins set among trees. Two cherubim hover above the Virgin's head, about to crown her with a wreath of red and white roses. On the table at the lower left lies a slip of paper with Dürer's inscription: *Albertus durer germanus faciebat post virginis partum 1506 AD* (his interlocked monogram).

This date of 1506 places the painting in Dürer's Venice period. From other sources we may infer that he executed it at about the same time as his large *Feast of the Rosary* (Prague), painted for German merchants in Venice. In fact, his *Madonna with the Siskin* is a Virgin with rosary too – the garland of roses above her head. This crown of roses held by angels symbolizes the eternal bliss promised to Mary, and the red and white of their blossoms represents the mysteries of the rosary, the sufferings and joys of the Virgin's life. Other symbolic allusions include the lilies-of-the-valley, which are among the first flowers to bloom in spring; a sign of regeneration which stands here for the advent of Christ. They have also been traditionally associated with the Virgin and the Immaculate Conception because of their perfume and the chaste whiteness of their blossoms. And their name – *convallaria* – recalls a passage in the Song of Solomon which was often applied to Mary: 'I am the rose of Sharon, and the lily of the valleys.' As for the siskin, this bird is reputed to feed on thistles and thorny seeds, making its appearance here a reference to the crown of thorns and the Passion. The message it is whispering in the Child's ear, then, may be understood to presage his mission and the suffering it will entail. The bird becomes a symbol of the inexorable link between Christ's incarnation and his fate on the cross. The book so prominently displayed stands for the Scriptures, whose prophecy that a new King would be born is now fulfilled. Nor are the ruins in the background mere picturesque additions. In the iconography of the period they signified the ruins of King David's palace, where according to Christian legend the stable stood. The palace both alludes to Jesus's royal origins in the House of David, and symbolizes decline, the demise of the old covenant. Through Christ, God entered a new covenant with mankind.

The motif of the Christ Child with siskin apparently has a long tradition in art, as can be seen from a *Virgin* from the town of Most in Bohemia, painted before 1350. Dürer's inclusion of the young John in his *Madonna* suggests Italian compositions, which he probably saw during his stay in Venice. Presumably Dürer brought the picture back with him to Nuremberg, since only if he did so can a number of sources be interpreted as referring to it. It entered our collection at a late date, in 1893.

Albrecht Dürer
The Infant Christ
Preliminary drawing for *The Madonna with the Siskin*
Formerly Bremen, Kunsthalle

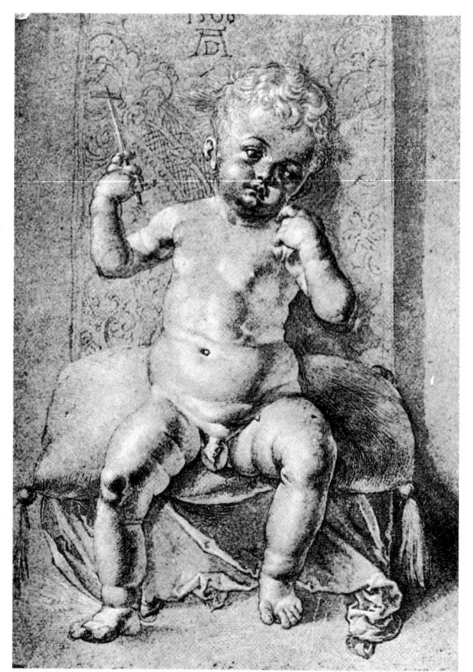

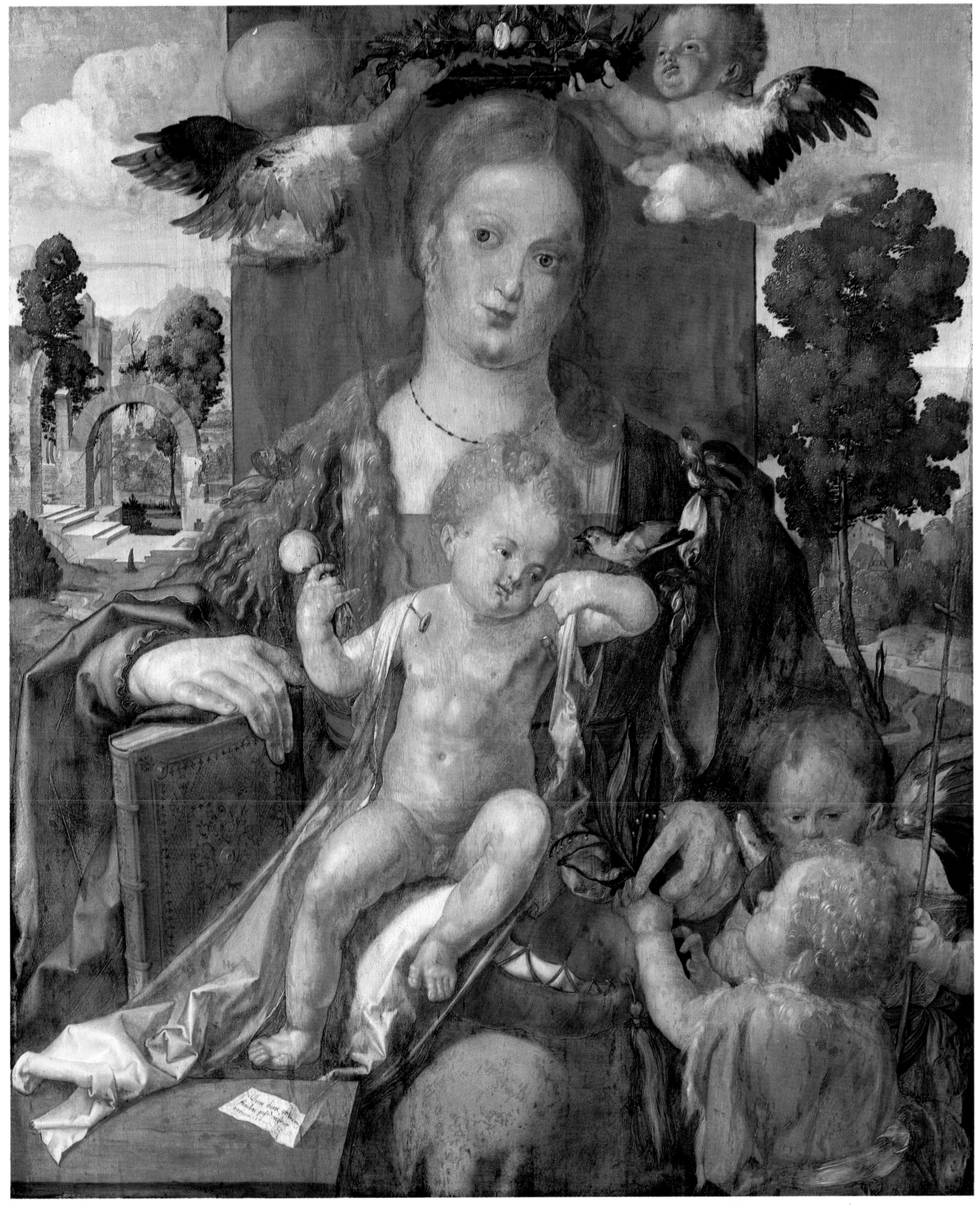

Albrecht Dürer

Portrait of a Girl in a Red Barett

1507

Parchment mounted on panel,
30.4 × 20 cm (12 × 7⅞ in)
Signed upper left: '1507 AD' (interlocked)
Imhoff Collection, Nuremberg
Acquired as a gift from P.D.Colnaghi, London, 1899
Property of the Kaiser-Friedrich-Museums-Verein
Cat. no. 5571

Here the head and shoulders of a young girl appear against a dark background, as if in close-up, almost entirely filling the picture plane. The girl, her head slightly inclined, has a pensive look; her light blonde curls billow out from beneath the red barett, framing the delicate rosy blush of her face. Decorating her barett is an exquisite piece of jewellery, a mounted ruby with dependent pearl.

Though the girl's head is depicted frontally, her strangely absent gaze is directed past the observer. Her dress of carmine red has a wide green band bordering the low, square-cut *décolleté*. In the upper left corner Dürer has inscribed the date 1507 and his monogram, AD.

There has been some debate about whether the painting was done in Venice, where Dürer worked from 1505 to the late autumn of 1507, or after his return to Nuremberg. Judging by the model's evidently German costume, the latter is probably the case. The girl's identity is not known, nor indeed whether this is a portrait in the strict sense at all. Some commentators think it may be an invented head of the kind Dürer frequently executed. The slight asymmetries of the features, however, would suggest that he worked from life. Old inventories mention the painting several times, and one mistakenly calls it a portrait of a boy – perhaps on account of the barett. Though the cut of the dress really leaves no doubt as to the model's sex, later critics have continued to detect an androgynous expression in her face.

The painting has had no lack of admirers through the centuries, and two copies show that artists were among them. The first of these, mentioned in seventeenth-century Vienna, has been lost. A second copy was executed by Peter Corduer, a Dürer specialist of Nuremberg. During the first half of the seventeenth century Corduer made several copies of the master's paintings, frankly marking his authorship by placing a 'C' above Dürer's monogram. His imitation of the present painting was in the collection of the Ebner Cabinet in Nuremberg until after 1800, when sometime during the early nineteenth century the 'C' was deleted in the hope of transforming the copy into an original. After that episode, the painting was lost to sight until just a few years ago, when it was acquired by the Vienna Academy.

Copy after Albrecht Dürer
by Peter Corduer
Nuremberg, *c.*1630–5
Vienna, Akademie der Bildenden Künste

Albrecht Dürer

Portrait of Hieronymus Holzschuher

1526

Linden in original frame with sliding cover embellished with arms of Holzschuher and Müntzer families, 51 × 37 cm (20 × 14½ in)
Inscribed upper left: 'HIERONIM[VS] HOLTZSCHVER ANNO DO[MI]NI 1526. ETATIS SVE. 57'; monogrammed upper right: AD (interlocked)
Acquired from the Holzschuher Collection, Nuremberg, 1882
Cat. no. 557 E

Dürer's *Portrait of Hieronymus Holzschuher* was preserved at Nuremberg until late in the last century, apparently largely forgotten for long periods. First rediscovered with the early nineteenth-century revival of interest in the German Renaissance, about 1812, the portrait became the talk of the town. So astonishingly new and modern did it seem that Sulpiz Boisserée, a great connoisseur and collector of old art, thought it was a fake. 'A rogue of the first order,' he wrote to his brother, 'has had his hand in this.' The idiosyncracies of Dürer's style were present in such concentration here that Boisserée thought he detected the exaggeration of a forger's hand. He was mistaken, for the painting was not unknown to earlier periods and many records of it existed; and today it is considered one of the finest of Dürer's late portraits. The inscription at the upper left names its sitter: 'HIERONIM[VS] HOLTZSCHVER ANNO DO[MI]NI 1526. ETATIS SVE. 57' (that is, painted in the sitter's fifty-seventh year). Herr Holzschuher belonged to one of the powerful Nuremberg families involved in municipal government. After advancing in 1499 to the Inner Council, he became Junior Mayor in 1500 and Senior Mayor in 1509. In 1514 he was elected as *Septemvir* to the High Council, in whose hands the affairs of the town rested. Holzschuher was also among Dürer's personal friends.

The artist has concentrated here on Holzschuher's massive head and shoulders. Unlike the sitters in many of Dürer's portraits, he turns towards us, fixing us with his brilliant eyes, in which the lights and reflections of the room shimmer. Judging by the mixture of kindness and scepticism in his gaze, Holzschuher must have been a man of frank and fearless character. For all the softness of the modelling, which follows every surface, furrow and protuberance of the face, its forms are sharply, even mercilessly delineated. The slight asymmetry of the features, and the furrowed forehead, are carefully observed. The sitter's rather austere expression is mitigated by gently arched, sensitive lips and by silvery hair encompassing his high-complexioned, ageing face like a wreath. The hair in itself is a masterpiece of variety and interest. From the long, flowing curves of locks and strands above, to the tranquil lines in the moustache emphasizing the shape of the mouth, to the thickly intertwined beard, Dürer's brush has traced a silvery weave that has a fascination all its own.

For all the undoubted realism of this portrait, Dürer clearly intended to do more than reproduce the appearance of an individual. His close study of character leads us to believe that we know more about the sitter than a face can be expected to divulge. And this characterization is so heightened as to transcend the individual to become a general type. This was no official portrait, however. The old frame in which it is still mounted has a sliding wooden cover, decorated with the allied arms of the families of Holzschuher and Müntzer, from which Holzschuher's wife came. This cover, inserted between the dark-stained inner frame and an outer frame of light ashwood, was meant to protect the portrait, which was presumbably kept in the family and rarely exposed. Perhaps it owes its excellent condition to this very circumstance.

Albrecht Dürer
Sliding cover of *Portrait of Hieronymus Holzschuher*
Berlin, Gemäldegalerie SMPK

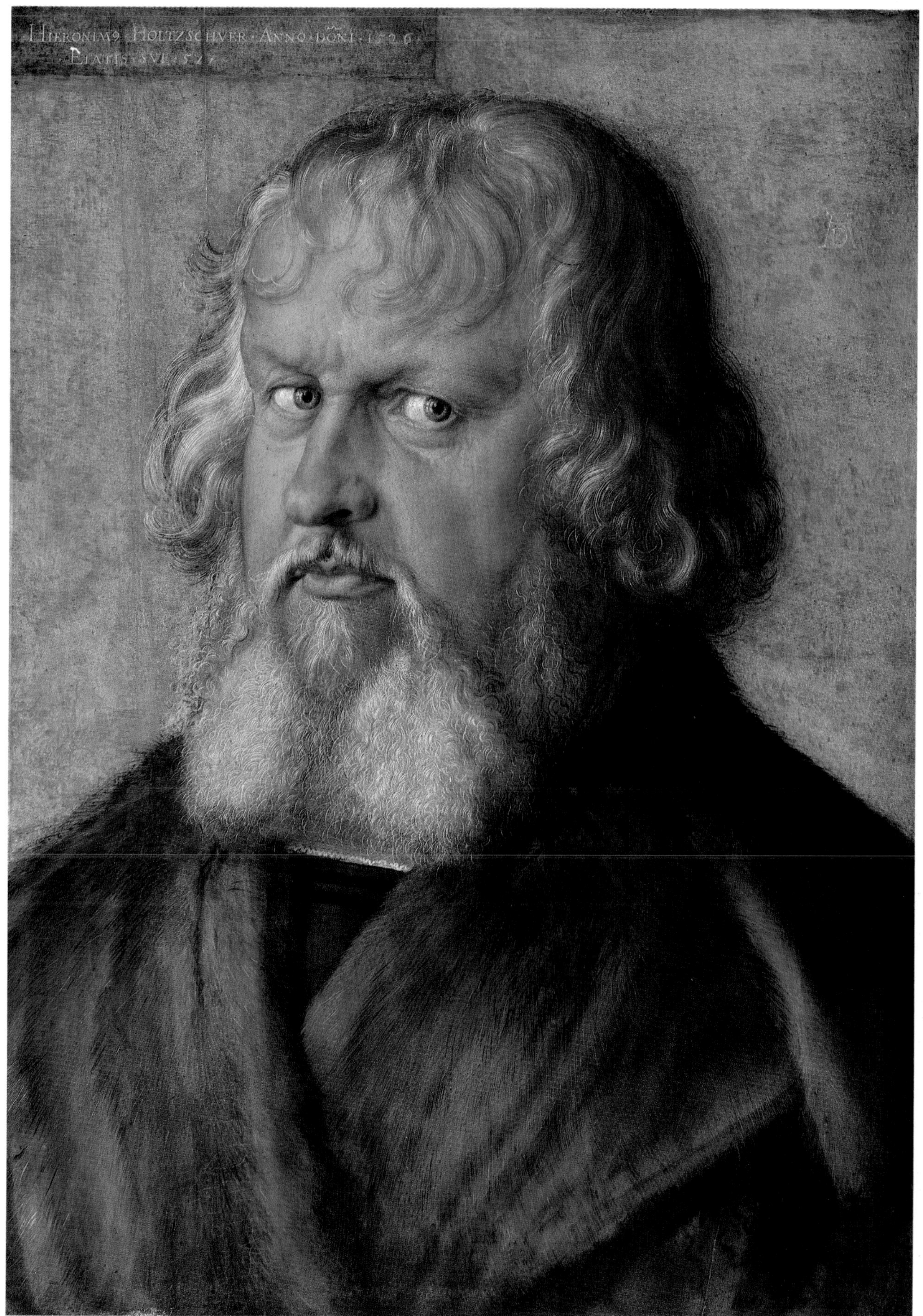
HIERONIMVS HOLTZSCHVER · ANNO · DÕNI · 1526 ·
ETATIS · SVE · 57 ·

Hans Suess von Kulmbach (*c.*1480–1522)

Adoration of the Magi

1511

Linden, 153 × 110 cm ($60\frac{1}{4} \times 43\frac{1}{4}$ in)
Signed left, on the post: '1511 HK' (interlocked)
Acquired from the Fr. v. Lippmann Collection, Vienna, 1876
Cat. no. 596 A

The Adoration scene is set in the ruins of an ancient palace, with the Virgin and Child seated before a column of greenish marble. The three wise men from the East and their retinue have followed the star to Bethlehem, and give obeisance to the new-born King. Two of them kneel before the Christ Child, offering gifts. The young African king at the left brings a covered chalice made of chased gold. Opposite him, an old monarch in a red robe trimmed with ermine kneels before the Virgin, presenting a bowl of gold coins for which the Infant stretches out his hands. A third monarch, an exquisitely clad Oriental in a turban, approaches with his attendants from the rear. His gaze seeking the Child, he takes from his servant a pear-shaped, chased silver goblet. Through the arch behind him is a spacious landscape with men approaching on horseback, some of them in Polish costumes, and one leading a camel. At the left edge of the painting is the stable; on its corner-post is a slip of paper with the date 1511, and below it Kulmbach's interwoven monogram HK. Behind Mary, Joseph talks with two noblemen from the king's retinue. A night sky over-arches the ruined walls, illuminated by the Star of Bethlehem, while in the distant valley, bright daylight still suffuses fields and woods.

According to legends, the ancient ruin where Christ was born was all that remained of the once glorious Palace of David. Here it symbolizes Christ's origin from the tribe of David, and at the same time graphically illustrates that the era of David and the Old Covenant is over. The column behind the group, recalling the column against which Christ was scourged, anticipates the Child's destiny and future suffering. The Three Kings are distinguished from one another both by age and by race. While the African king is young, the Oriental is middle-aged and the third, whose costume seems European, has reached venerable old age, signifying that every generation has come to worship the new-born King. And the three races to which the Magi belong show that all three continents of the known world – Africa, Asia and Europe – are present at the great event. Among the attendants is one whose features are strikingly individual: the man in a black cap beneath the archway. This is presumably a portrait of the donor.

The *Adoration of the Magi* is the middle panel of a disassembled folding altar. Two other panels, *The Presentation in the Temple* and *Flight into Egypt*, are still at the Na Skalce Monastery in Cracow, as is a copy of the *Adoration*. We may conclude that the original Altar of the Virgin was executed for a Cracow church – perhaps that of the Na Skalce Monastery – and was long located there. Two preparatory drawings for the heads of Mary and Joseph are now in the collection of the Erlangen University Library.

Hans Suess von Kulmbach
Head of Joseph
Drawing
Erlangen, Universitätsbibliothek

Hans Baldung, called Grien (1484/5–1545)

Three Magi Altarpiece

1507

Linden, central panel 121 × 70 cm ($47\frac{5}{8} \times 27\frac{1}{2}$ in), wings each 121 × 28 cm ($47\frac{5}{8} \times 11$ in)
Domkirche Halle an der Saale, 1838
Acquired 1872
Cat. no. 603 A

Shortly after leaving Dürer's workshop, Hans Baldung Grien executed two alterpieces for a church in Halle, traditionally thought to be St Liebfrauen, the Church of the Blessed Virgin. One of these was the *Three Magi Altarpiece*, a three-part folding altar with hinged wings which can be closed over the central panel to conceal the main display side. When the wings are closed, images of two female saints are visible, St Catherine and St Agnes. St Catherine, on the left, was an Alexandrian noblewoman who resisted Caesar Maxentius's attempts to make her renounce her Christian faith and suffered martyrdom by the wheel and sword. St Agnes, depicted on the outside of the right-hand panel, was a Roman martyr of about AD 300. The lamb she is leading refers to the consonance of her name with *agnus* ('lamb') and also alludes to her faith in Christ, the Lamb of God.

The middle panel represents the three Wise Men from the East who have come to worship and present their gifts to the Christ Child. Their different ages suggest that reverence for the new-born King knows no age barriers, while the African and Oriental monarchs symbolize the continents which join with Europe in bringing their offerings. An embodiment of Europe may be seen in the standing figure in the centre, whose penetrating gaze and individual features suggest that he may represent the painting's donor. A portrait of this man also appears – as Emperor Diocletian – on the related *St Sebastian Altar* in Nuremberg, which also includes a self-portrait by Baldung. In all probability, the donor was a member of the Wettin family, the princely house of Saxony. Several of its members have been suggested, among them Ernst von Wettin, Archbishop of Magdeburg and Bishop of Halle at the time the altar was executed. Other authors believe it was commissioned by his brother, Frederick the Wise, Elector of Saxony. The figure's cap, worn aslant and topped by a floral wreath, has many key features in common with the lozenged chaplet of the Saxon arms, and may be an allusion to them.

Depictions of two saints in knightly armour are on the interior of the wings. St George, on the left, was a legendary Cappadocian soldier who served the Emperor Diocletian. Most renowned for freeing a princess from the clutches of a dragon, St George was patron saint of all knights and soldiers. Opposite him on the right wing is St Mauritius or Maurice, leader of the Theban Legion, who suffered a martyr's death. As patron of the Archbishopric, he was also of great importance to the town of Halle. The Moritzburg citadel on the heights above the town was erected in his name by Archbishop Ernst of Magdeburg, one of the presumed donors of the present altar.

The *Three Magi Altar* is a companion work to the *St Sebastian Altar* in Nuremberg, which is dated 1507. It is not known for which church these retables were created. At the beginning of the last century they were both at Nuremberg Cathedral, possibly commissioned for that Cathedral by Archbishop Ernst in 1507. A comparison of styles indicates that the altar now in our collection must have preceded the one at Nuremberg, though both were among the first works Baldung executed after leaving Dürer's workshop. The emphasis on the figures, which dominate the composition, is new for him and quite foreign to the art of Dürer. Brilliant colours and a joy in representing shimmering textiles and highly polished metal are also characteristic of Baldung's style. These features have suggested Cranach's influence, some of whose paintings Baldung probably saw in Saxony.

Hans Baldung, called Grien
Altarpiece of the Three Magi
Exterior of wings. Left: *St Catherine*
Right: *St Agnes*
Berlin, Gemäldegalerie SMPK

Hans Baldung, called Grien

Portrait of Count Löwenstein

1513

Linden, 46 × 33 cm ($18\frac{1}{8}$ × 13 in)
Inscribed along top edge: '· LVDWIC · GRAF · ZVO · LEWENSTEIN · HB [interlocked] 1513' (behind Löwenstein a further, unexplained symbol)
Acquired 1918
Property of the Kaiser-Friedrich-Museums-Verein
Cat. no. 1842

Baldung has concentrated here on the head, shoulders and left arm of the sitter, whose long, determined-looking face is surmounted by a red barett tied under the chin with a black cord. His locks billow out from beneath the cap, which is adorned with a golden bangle; at his throat is a similar one, a figure formed of the letters ANA or AHA. His shirt is trimmed at the neck with a border embroidered with a pattern of lozenges, each filled with a 'B' in pearls. Below this hangs a heavy golden chain. The Count's black coat, a *houppelande*, is elaborately trimmed with gold brocade strips and with fur at the seams and collar. His firm grip on the collar with a beringed hand was apparently meant to evoke force and tenacity of character, traits certainly evident in Löwenstein's masculine features. The background is green, without much suggestion of depth. Along the upper edge of the painting Baldung has inscribed '· LVDWIC · GRAF · ZVO · LEWENSTEIN ·' with his interlocked monogram HB and the date 1513.

Louis, Count of Löwenstein, born in 1463, was a natural son of the reigning Elector Frederick I, the Victorious, and Clara Tott, daughter of a citizen of Augsburg. Administrating the Pfalz in the name of his infant nephew, Frederick I avoided making a marriage of rank for dynastic reasons. His marriage with Clara Tott was later made legitimate (1471?) and with it his son, Ludwig, who received territories which included the County of Löwenstein in the Neckar region from his cousin, Philip the Good. In 1494, Louis was granted the rank and title of Count of Löwenstein by Emperor Maximilian. He later served as Imperial War Counsellor and was entrusted with diplomatic missions. He died at the hand of an assassin in 1524.

The present portrait was presumably executed during a journey Baldung made to the Neckar region, which is also documented by drawings in an album known as the Karlsruhe Sketchbook.

LVDWIC · GRAF · ZVO · LEWENSTEIN
1513

Hans Baldung, called Grien
Pyramus and Thisbe
*c.*1530

Linden, 93 × 67 cm ($36\frac{5}{8} \times 26\frac{3}{8}$ in)
Acquired 1920
Cat. no. 1875

Here an ancient story (Ovid, *Metamorphoses IV*, 55 ff.) is recounted in contemporary costume. Pyramus and Thisbe, children of neighbouring families in Babylon, loved each other against their fathers' wills. They agreed to meet one night at a spring outside the city. Thisbe arrived first, but only to confront a lioness which had come to slake its thirst at the spring after a kill. Thisbe fled, leaving her veil behind; the wild beast tore it, sullying it with blood. All Pyramus found when he came on the scene were the lioness's tracks and the bloody veil. Distraught at the apparent death of his loved one, he killed himself. Thisbe, returning to find Pyramus dying, realized what had happend and turned her lover's sword against herself.

In the painting, Pyramus lies prostrate on the ground in his blood, a dagger in his breast, his red cloak spread out beneath him. He is clad in a blue doublet and yellow hose; his blue, plume-trimmed hat has slipped from his head. The pose of the figure, depicted diagonally from below and extremely foreshortened, lends it decorative grace even in death. Thisbe, in a red gown with a pale skirt, has apparently just come upon her lover's body and wrings her hands in despair. Behind the couple rises a fountain and two pools; Pyramus's head has sunk on to the pools' steps. The central column of the upper trough is crowned by a winged *putto* that may signify Cupid, symbol of the couple's love. In the background, the buildings of a town or castle grounds are visible. The scene is set in a glowering, blue-black night; the clouds part at the upper right to reveal a whitish-yellow glare of moonlight that tinges the clouds and suffuses the landscape with dim, cold illumination.

Ovid's tale, a variant of which also appeared in the *Gesta Romanorum*, one of the widest-read narratives of the Middle Ages, tells of the love of two young people and how they died for its sake. Their sacrifice for love and mutual faithfulness was frequently cited as an example of great virtue. As such the Pyramus and Thisbe story often appeared together with similar themes in cycles of paintings representing the virtues.

Baldung executed the present painting about 1530, and at the same time three other subjects from classical antiquity: *Hercules and Antaeus*, *The Sacrifice of Marcus Curtius*, and *Mucius Scaevola at Porsenna*, stories similarly illustrating exemplary virtue.

Such mythological themes were often infused with a Christian message during the Middle Ages, Pyramus's death, for instance, being treated as a symbol of Christ's sacrifice. However, certain differences among the four paintings just mentioned would seem to indicate that they were not meant as an integral sequence. The assumption that they were is a shaky one at best.

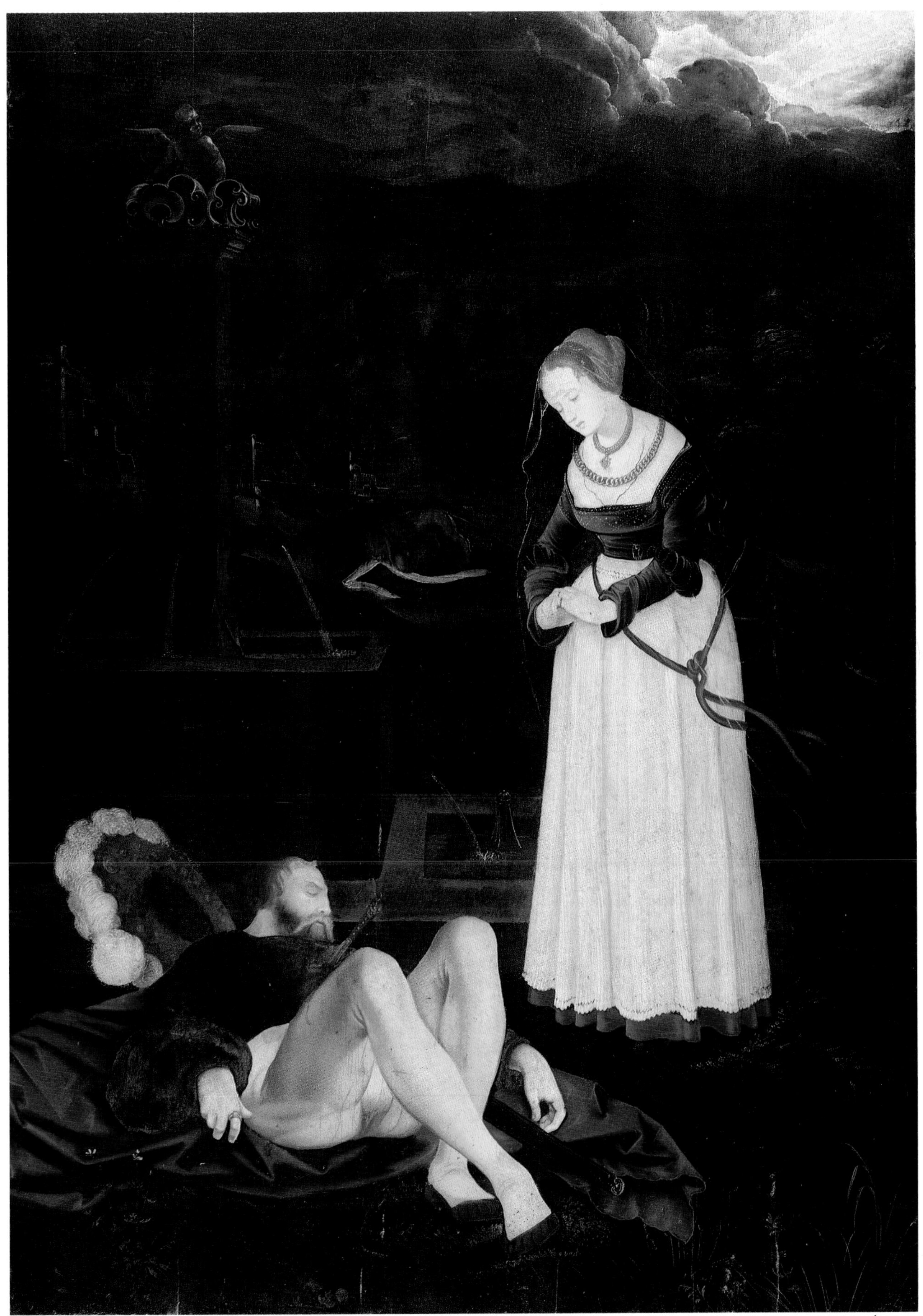

Lucas Cranach the Elder (1472–1553)
Portrait of a Law Scholar's Wife
1503

Conifer, 52.5 × 36.2 cm ($20\frac{5}{8} \times 14\frac{1}{4}$ in)
Collection of
Prince Schwarzburg-Rudolstadt
Acquired 1923
Cat. no. 1907

Cranach has placed his sitter before rugged mountain scenery much in contrast to her red gown with its elaborate gold embroidery. Her hair is wrapped in a kerchief, a sign that she is a married woman. An elaborate belt and the many rings on her fingers underline the impression of prosperity which the artist evidently wished to give here.

Behind the sitter's shoulders, two trees are silhouetted against the sky on the right and left, linking the foreground figure with the background mountains, human being with environment. But the trees are more than a formal device. While the tree on the left is in full, green leaf, the other is almost bare – a contrast that visually evokes the course of the seasons, indeed the transience of all life. The idea of birth and death, growth and decay, is translated into visual symbolism which enriches the significance of the portrait image.

Never intended to stand alone, the picture was originally half of a double portrait or perhaps even the right wing of a portrait diptych. Its counterpart represents the lady's husband, a lawyer clad in rich, red robes (Nuremberg, Germanisches Nationalmuseum). This portrait is dated 1503. According to a later pencil note on the back (which has since become illegible) the sitter was a certain Stephen Reuss of Constance, member of the law faculty and Rector of Vienna University. Based on this information, the Berlin painting was long known as *Portrait of Frau Reuss*. Subsequent investigation, however, has revealed that the office of university rector was incompatible with marriage during the period in question. This makes the identification of the portrait with Stephen Reuss doubtful. The sitter's costume and attributes nevertheless characterize him as a jurist of Vienna University.

Though Cranach did work in Vienna in 1503, it proved difficult to attribute this portrait to him, since his work from 1500 to 1505, when he becomes court artist in Wittenberg, long remained in obscurity. Not much more is known even today about the early œuvre of this artist, who was almost contemporaneous with Dürer and who was active presumably from about 1490. Our portrait of a woman was classed as a Dürer in the nineteenth century probably because of its high quality. Later it was attributed to Albrecht Altdorfer, then to Hans von Kulmbach. Not until the 1890s were those paintings gradually associated with Cranach and they are now classified as belonging to his early œuvre. In 1903, the Nuremberg *Portrait of a Law Scholar* and our female portrait were exhibited side by side for the first time, and since then no one has doubted that they belong together. The dating of our portrait is based on this perception.

Lucas Cranach the Elder
Portrait of a Law Scholar, 1503
Nuremberg, Germanisches
Nationalmuseum

Lucas Cranach the Elder

Rest on the Flight into Egypt

1504

Red beech, 70.5 × 53 cm (27¾ × 20⅞in)
Signed bottom on two slips: 'LC' (interlocked) and '1504'
Galleria Sciarra, Rome, 1873; K. Fiedler Collection, Munich
Acquired 1902
Cat. no. 564 A

The Holy family rests on a grassy slope, Mary at the edge of a path leading up from the right, with the Child standing in her lap. Behind her is Joseph, hat in hand and leaning on his staff. Three young and beautifully clad angels in the centre sing and play the flute, surrounded by five *putti*. As one listens, another sleeps with his head resting on a mossy boulder behind the group. At a spring coming from the rock a third infant angel fills a pilgrim's flask opened at the side. Two others are bringing gifts to the Child – a strawberry plant with blossoms and fruit, and a live bird, a goldfinch, struggling in the grasp of the *putto* at the left. An abundance of plants and flowers, among them primroses, thistles, columbine and fumitory, lend the wild spot the appearance of a garden in bloom. The scene is set off by a middle ground consisting of a bluff at the left, where a young spruce grows among other trees both green and bare, a yellowing old fir in the middle, and a birch at the right. In the background ranges of steep hills lead back to the mountains on the horizon.

This depiction of *The Flight into Egypt* is unusual, and it is interspersed with many symbolic and legendary allusions. The flowering garden sequestered among hills surely represents a haven of peace; many of its plants refer symbolically to Mary and Jesus and the events of their lives. While the strawberry was considered a fruit of paradise, columbine and primrose were often symbolically associated with the Virgin and Child as well as with Christ's Passion. The thistle, too, being a thorny plant, recalls his Crown of Thorns and his agony. Underlying the tranquil peace of the scene is a foreboding of torment to come. The spring derives from the legend where Jesus made the rock give water to refresh a weary pilgrim, water that transformed the waste into a garden. The angels singing and playing enhance the other symbolic references and contribute to the paradisal aspect of Mary's and Joseph's resting place, where worldly cares give way to divine joy.

Cranach's composition was apparently influenced by some of Dürer's prints. Several motifs in Dürer's *Holy Family with Rabbits* of 1496–7, for instance, anticipate those in the painting. Cranach himself later, in 1509, repeated the composition in a series of woodcuts, and a quite faithful copy of this painting is still to be seen in Vienna. Its existence suggests that Cranach must have executed his *Rest on the Flight* before leaving Vienna for Wittenberg.

This is Cranach's earliest signed and dated work (1504). Before it became known, art historians had great difficulty reconstructing the years before the artist's Wittenberg period and establishing convincing attributions. Very few had ever seen the painting, and had to rely on descriptions. Not until 1892 was it publicly exhibited for the first time, in Munich, a crucial event for research on Cranach's early period. His *Rest on the Flight* is certainly one of the most charming and aesthetically significant paintings he ever executed.

Albrecht Dürer
The Holy Family with Rabbits, *c.*1496–7
Woodcut

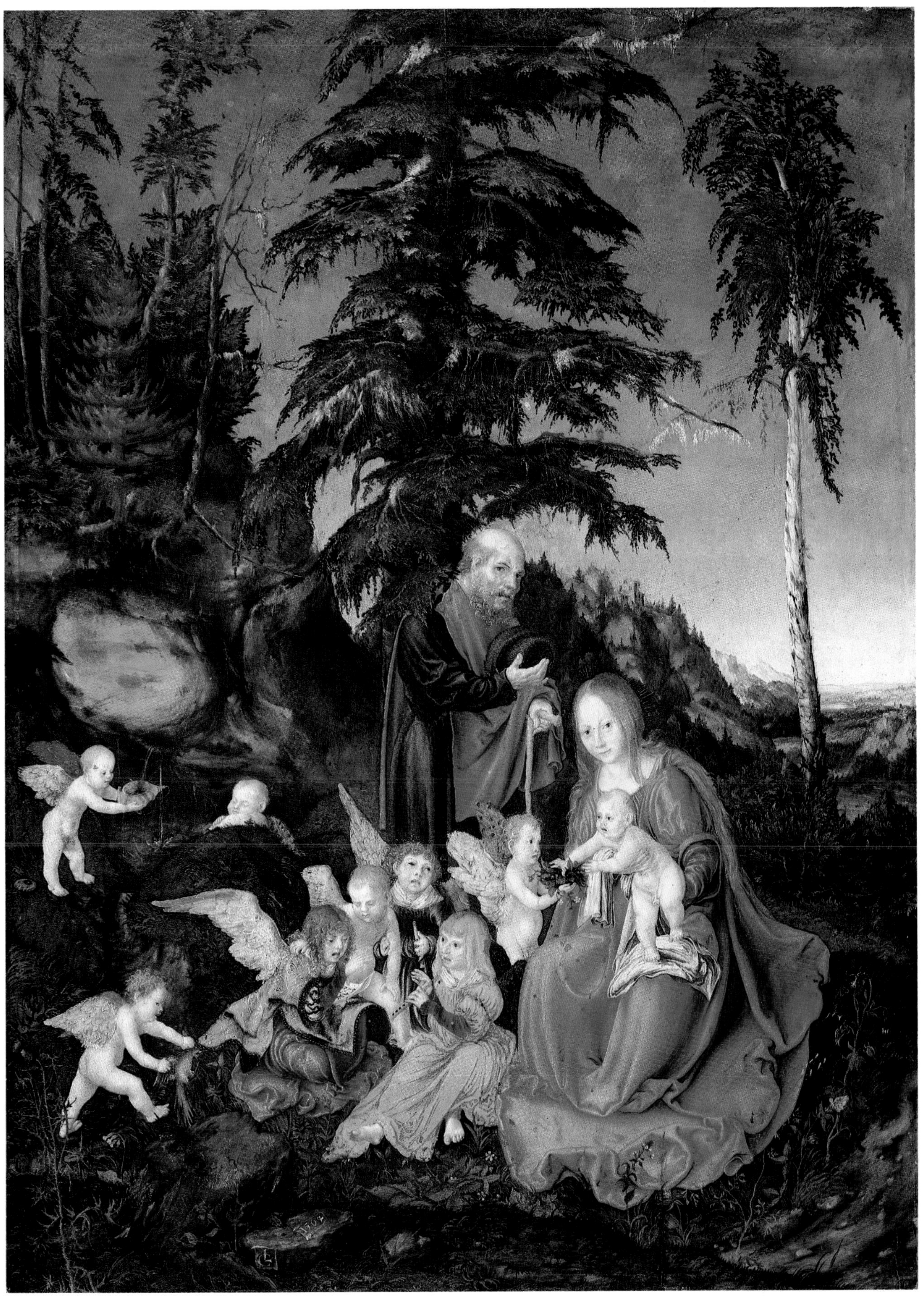

Lucas Cranach the Elder
David and Bathsheba
1526

Red beech, 36 × 24 cm ($14\frac{1}{8} \times 9\frac{1}{2}$ in)
Inscribed on the wall with sign of the snake and date, 1526
Acquired 1890
Cat. no. 567 B

One evening, as the Bible relates (2 Samuel 11:2), David went up onto the roof of his house and saw 'a woman very beautiful to look upon', washing herself. Through a messenger he asked her to come to him; it was Bathsheba, wife of Uriah, one of David's hired soldiers. He slept with her, and she became pregnant. To be rid of Uriah, David sent him into battle, putting him in the front rank where he was sure to die. Bathsheba became David's wife. 'But the thing that David had done displeased the Lord' and, in expiation of this sin, the couple's first-born son fell sick and died.

During the Middle Ages, the story of David's adultery and blood-guilt was often interpreted as an example of women's cunning and power over men. For their beauty and love, men would become treacherous – the just unjust, the brave callow, and wise men fools. David and Solomon, Hercules and Aristotle were continually held up as men blinded by female charms, men who consequently fell into disgrace and dishonour. The story of David's temptation by Bathsheba, in medieval eyes, was just such an *exemplum malum*, an instance of immorality cited in the hope of deterring others from doing the same. The subject duly appeared in this moral light in many sequences of paintings contrasting good and bad deeds, such as the so-called 'justice pictures' exhibited in German town halls and courtrooms to admonish judges and jury.

Our small panel, however, does not really belong to this category. It was probably intended for private rooms, those of a connoisseur schooled in courtly manners on whom the effect of the scene, as with many other moralizing subjects of the time, may well have derived from its rather equivocal character. Cranach tells the story in the present tense and in courtly costume. Bathsheba, accompanied by three ladies-in-waiting, is seated on the bank of a brook, having her feet washed by a maid. This motif of the washing of feet occurs with great frequency in illustrations of the story; perhaps it had an erotic significance which now eludes us. Immediately behind this group rises a massive wall, and on its parapet King David plays a lyre, with an audience of three courtiers. The composition is by no means realistic, since instead of adhering to the laws of perspective Cranach has compressed distances, telescoping foreground and background planes as if to distil the plot to essentials and bring the protagonists into the kind of proximity they would have on a theatre stage.

Cranach depicted the subject several times, each time evidently placing different weight on the symbolic meaning involved. Drawings also exist, one of which is very similar in key respects to the painting and also chronologically close to it, though its composition differs in important points (Berlin, Department of Prints and Drawings SMPK). Its relation to Cranach's *David and Bathsheba* of 1526 was apparently not direct. A later drawing presumably from Cranach's workshop (now in Leipzig), varies the composition by opening out the pictorial space. Interestingly, this theme strongly attracted Picasso, who based many studies on Cranach's various compositions.

Lucas Cranach the Elder
David and Bathsheba,
*c.*1526
Drawing
Berlin, Kupferstichkabinett SMPK

Lucas Cranach the Elder

The Fountain of Youth

1546

Linden, 122.5 × 186.5 cm ($48\frac{1}{4} \times 73\frac{3}{8}$ in)
Inscribed lower centre with the sign of the winged snake and date, 1546
From the Royal Palaces, Berlin
Cat. no. 593

A longing for immortality, for perpetual youth, can give rise to visions of being born anew, of sloughing off the pains and weariness of age. In the past, rejuvenating powers were attributed to the four elements – earth, water, fire and air – which were thought to embody magical, procreative and purifying forces. Everyone had seen how nature refreshes herself in the course of the seasons – awakening in spring, maturing in summer, bearing fruit in autumn, and wasting in winter only to revive again. This power to create new life continually from the old, it was believed, could also help the ageing to recover their youth. A miraculous rejuvenating force was attributed especially to fire and water. The legendary phoenix, consumed in flame and emerging from the ashes in new glory and youth, is only one instance of human longing for reincarnation, expressed in many and varied myths, legends, and fairy-tales. Somewhere in the wilderness, in unexplored territories far from the habitations of man, existed a fabled source, a spring or lake whose water had the power to wash away the traces of old age. Whoever bathed there would emerge transformed. The story and the belief were widespread in Cranach's times.

By the late Middle Ages the Fountain of Youth legend had already entered literature. A poem on the subject by the Nuremberg poet Hans Rosenplüt enjoyed wide popularity in fifteenth-century Germany. Two years after Cranach painted his *Fountain of Youth*, Hans Sachs wrote a poem whose motifs recall those in Cranach's image. And though it is unique in being the only known large easel-painting on the theme, Cranach's *Fountain of Youth* by no means stands alone. Representations in the graphic arts are not rare, and frescoes also exist. There were many variations of the fable, from the traditional fountain where pilgrims of both sexes gathered, to some where only women bathed.

A belief in the purifying powers of water also underlay the ritual washings common in many religions. Christian baptism, one such ritual cleansing from sins, provided a parallel with the ancient fable and brought it into the religious sphere. In a book entitled *Badenfahrt* (Strasbourg, 1514) Thomas Murner, a humanist philosopher of Alsace, described baptism as a fountain of youth for the soul. This idea inspired many artists, among them Jean Bellegambes, who in a painting now at Lille depicted a baptismal font filled with the blood of Christ, a crucifix emerging from the font like the shaft of a fountain. Personifications of the virtues, Caritas and Spes, help the faithful to the font where their sins will be washed away.

Cranach's *Fountain of Youth* is rather more secular by comparison. Far from the town, whose roofs and towers are visible on the horizon, a rectangular basin, with steps leading down into it, lies among gentle hills and meadows. This fountain is apparently reserved for women, who approach from a rugged and parched mountain region that evokes the infirmities of old age. Unable to help themselves, the women are being brought by carts or waggons, on stretchers, even pick-a-back, to the edge of the pool, where girls help them to undress. One submits to her doctor's last sceptical inspection before taking the plunge. Their different personalities are well characterized, their poses and gestures contributing to reveal expectant hope, doubts, even fears. While some of them descend resolutely into the basin, others sit vacillating on its edge, waiting to be convinced, by force if need be. They enter the water infirm, helpless, deformed by age, and as they pass through it the women's wrinkles are magically smoothed, their sallow skins take on tone, until on the other side they emerge girlish and desirable. There a gallant gentleman receives them, pointing the way to a tent where they may dress. Adorned in new gowns and jewellery they enter a round dance, consort with cavaliers, take their places at table. It is a courtly group spending a pleasant day in the country with dancing, feasting and flirting, a joy in life and youth revived that are symbolically echoed in the sylvan surroundings. Here are the green fields and verdant vegetation of a pleasure-garden while behind, dry precipices symbolize old age.

The nature of the fountain's rejuvenating power is suggested by the figures presiding from the column in its centre: Cupid, god of love, and Venus, goddess of love and beauty. The revivifying forces are in them, and through love these forces take effect. But why is it that only women experience the magical metamorphosis in Cranach's fountain? A contemporary of his, Rabelais, gives the answer in *Gargantua and Pantagruel* (Book 5, chapter 21). Here we read how Pantagruel, among countless other incredible happenings in the 'Realm of Quintessence', sees old crones melted down and recast into girls of fifteen and sixteen. Asking whether old men were not similarly transmuted, he is told, no – only the society of young women can rejuvenate *them*.

Cranach's *Fountain of Youth*, in other words, is a fountain of love. He has reinterpreted this ancient theme and given it a new and ironic twist to accommodate the sophisticated tastes of his noble patrons.

The painting, signed and dated 1546, has traditionally been classified as a work of Lucas Cranach the Elder. However, it was twice attributed to his son, Lucas, once erroneously and again wrongly. The disposition of the landscape elements as pictorial symbols; the drawing of the figures, varied and assured yet fluent; and the thin, transparent paint application, are sure signs of Cranach the Elder's mature style.

Hans Burgkmair (1473–1531)
Wings of an Altarpiece
St Ulrich – St Barbara
*c.*1518

(*St Ulrich*)
Conifer, 105.2 × 41.2 cm ($41\frac{1}{2} \times 16\frac{1}{4}$ in)
Acquired 1843
Cat. no. 569

(*St Barbara*)
Conifer, 105.3 × 41.3 cm ($41\frac{1}{2} \times 16\frac{1}{4}$ in)
Acquired 1843
Cat. no. 572

These depictions of St Ulrich and St Barbara are fragments of an altar retable which was destroyed and for the most part lost, apparently all except for the two present panels. That they were originally juxtaposed may be gathered from such formal characteristics as the way the figures face each other, the related colour schemes, the treatment of the foreground, and from the hills and mountains in the background, which evidently form a continuous panorama. That is to say, the compositions must have stood next to one another in the original altar, as here, and accordingly must have formed the outside of its hinged wings. They give an idea of how the retable probably looked in a closed position. The size of the panels, however, is not that of the original wings. Their compositions, together with certain technical findings, clearly indicate that they have been cut down considerably. Traces of the original image boundary are detectable only along their vertical edges. The imagery also shows that the panels were once larger. The sword at St Barbara's feet, the weapon with which she was put to death, was probably completely visible in the original state of the image. And what are we to make of the mysterious dark object resembling a stone at the lower right of the St Ulrich panel? On closer observation, it seems more like a shoe. An entire figure might conceivably have been cut away here. Further inferences about the original proportions of the panels may be drawn from comparisons with other altars by Burgkmair. Apparently the Berlin panels have been considerably reduced in height, causing a noticeable constriction of the figures, altering and disturbing the relation of figure to landscape. Nevertheless, the two saints in their exquisite and gloriously coloured garments are monumentally conceived, and their poses are both dignified and highly expressive.

On the left panel, St Ulrich appears in the vestments of a bishop, grasping the symbol of his office, a crozier. His garb is very elaborate and ornate, with red and gold brocade set off by green velvet and shot silk taffeta shimmering in blue and red. The fish in his hands, a pike, is his personal attribute. St Ulrich was born in 890 and Bishop of Augsburg from 923 to 973. He later became patron saint of the Swabian city. Wishing to reward a messenger, the bishop gave him a cut of meat, having forgotten that it was a day on which meat-eating was a sin. The messenger was about to denounce him for it when the meat was transformed into a fish. A miracle had saved the bishop from the charge of breaking ecclesiastical law.

The right-hand panel shows St Barbara, who is also beautifully and elaborately costumed, wearing a crown set with pearls. She holds a communion chalice, and a palm frond that symbolizes her martyrdom. St Barbara lived during the third century, when persecution of Christians was at its height; she was the lovely daughter of a rich unbeliever who locked her up in a tower to keep her from temptation. Yet even here Christ's message reached her and she was converted to the faith. When her father heard of this, 'his love turned to hate' and he delivered her over to the authorities. Seeing that she remained steadfast, he himself demanded her execution, and she was beheaded. The sword at the bottom of the painting alludes to her martyrdom. And as a sign of her fearlessness in the face of death, for which the condemned traditionally invoke her saintly patronage, she bears the attribute of the chalice of the last communion.

The identity of the two saints depicted here suggests that the retable of which they were part was originally intended for the town of Augsburg. Stylistically, the panels are closely related to the images of saints on the *St John Altar* of 1518, now at the Old Pinakothek in Munich. Their dating, *c.*1518, is based on this similarity.

Albrecht Altdorfer (*c.*1480–1538)
Rest on the Flight to Egypt
1510

Linden, 57 × 38 cm ($22\frac{1}{2}$ × 15 in)
Signed lower left, on the tablet: 'A[l]b[er]tu[s] Altorffer pictor Ratis ponen[sis] in salutem a[n]i[ma]e hoc tibi munus diua maria sacrauit corde fideli 1510. AA' (interlocked)
Fr.v.Lippmann Collection, Vienna
Acquired 1876
Cat. no. 638 B

Dominating the foreground of this image is a great fountain, with a wide, shallow bowl and a central column richly ornamented with figures. Mary, seated beside it in a throne-like chair, lets the Christ Child down to dabble in the water and marvel at the playful antics of the *putti*. From the right Joseph enters, bringing a handful of cherries to his wife. An unusually intimate and personal mood pervades this rendering of the flight into Egypt, which is charged moreover with Scriptural and symbolic allusions.

The fountain itself recalls the spring in the Bible story that began to flow when the weary travellers desired refreshment. Another reference to this passage may be seen in the cherries Joseph holds, which are like the fruit on the palm tree that bent down to the Holy Family. The legends also record that when the young Jesus entered the town of Sotina its graven idols and temples fell to the ground. Altdorfer evokes this event by ruins of old Romanesque churches which in his day stood for the past in general and the Old Covenant and Judaism in particular. The broken statues also allude to this passage, as probably do the figures surmounting the fountain like raised idols – a Cupid with bow and two arrows, and a bearded man holding a winged object. What this object represents and who its bearer may be, cannot be said with any certainty. Graphically clear, though, is the significance of the gradual metamorphosis from pale, cold stone at the top of the column to pulsating life and colour in the figures closest to the water and the Christ Child. The Virgin and Child become 'a well of living waters', 'the fountain of life' (Song of Solomon 4:15; Psalm 36:9). Behind the devastated town at the right, rugged, mountainous countryside extends along the shore of a lake into the distance. Altdorfer later used a similar landscape in another painting, a *Crucifixion* (at Kassel). Some authors believe the artist modelled it on real scenery, a stretch of countryside near Wörth, on the Danube. True or not, Altdorfer certainly transformed the scenes he knew and adapted them to the story he wished to tell. The rather gentle mountains along the Danube have shot up into rugged precipices and seemingly impassable ranges. The drama of this landscape, a visual evocation of Mary and Joseph's arduous journey, serves also to counterpoint the idyllic scene at the fountain.

In the dedicatory inscription on the base of the fountain, Altdorfer consecrates his picture, with pious heart, as an offering to the Blessed Mary. The painting is certainly a very personal and moving profession of faith.

Albrecht Altdorfer
The Rest on the Flight into Egypt
Detail: Dedicatory inscription

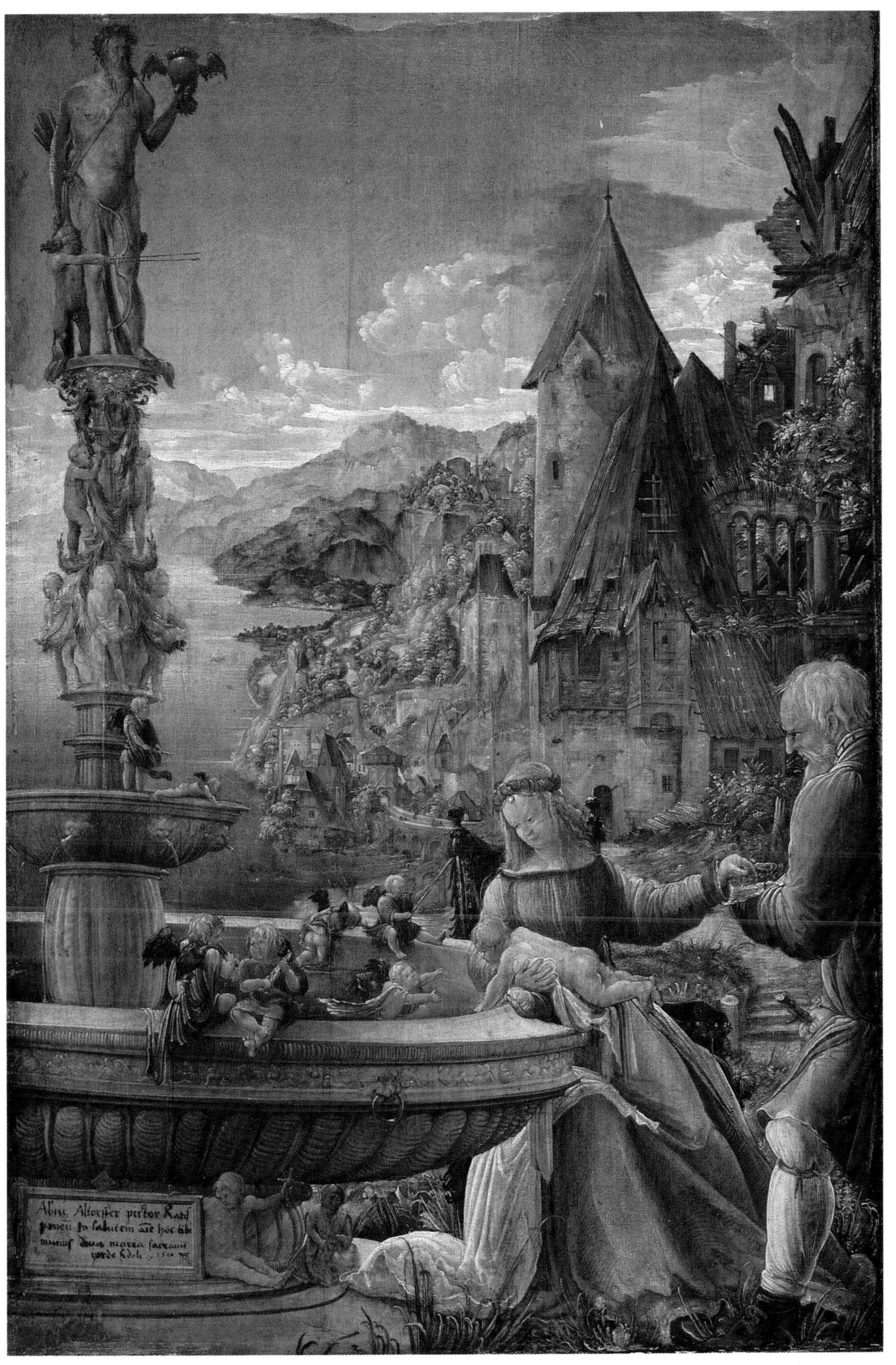
Albrts Altorffer pictor Ratis
ponen in salutem aie hoc tibi
munus diva maria sacravit
corde fideli 1510

Albrecht Altdorfer

Allegory

Paupers Come in the Train of Pomp

1531

Linden, 28.7 × 41 cm
Signed lower right: 'AA [interlocked] 1531'
Fr. v. Lippmann Collection, Vienna
Acquired 1876
Cat. no. 638 C

A palace of many towers rises in the left foreground of an expansive valley vista. A broad, curving stairway leads up to its forecourt, which has seats along the parapet like those of an arena. There is something very strange about the architecture of this edifice, with its massive corner towers each built in a different style and linked by wings and colonnades. The lower part of the building resembles a fortress, its rough-hewn walls buttressed and pierced by openings like embrasures. Yet above this formidable foundation it presents a quite different aspect: balconies with balustrades, vaulted spaces resembling loggias, and rows of round-arched windows bracketed by larger arches. Topping the towers are temple-like cupolas with lantern turrets. These upper storeys of the building seem to open out to their surroundings, like a country seat, a pleasure dome amidst bucolic scenery. This comparison is partly borne out by the events depicted.

An elegantly dressed couple are approaching the palace stairway, where a gentleman waits to receive them, hospitably offering refreshment in a great goblet known as a *Willkomm*. Another nobleman leans against the parapet, looking on. The cloaks or capes of the distinguished arrivals apparently merge behind into a single and exaggeratedly long train, spread like a carpet along the path. On its end, a group or family of beggars or vagabonds have made themselves comfortable. The difference in rank between the two groups is emphasized – rather against the laws of perspective – by the figures' differing scales. Trees frame the vista on the right. The eye is led back into the landscape by fascinating details – castles on the hills, and, farther down the valley, spreading towns with mansions and towers. A river is visible in the distance, spanned by the arches of a bridge and flanked by buildings. On the horizon is a chain of blue mountains with castles and villages nestling in its foothills. The shores of a lake lose themselves on the right in a misty blue distance.

This is a charming vista, bright and serene. But what it and the figures signify have never been adequately explained. Obviously its allegorical meaning lies in the contrast between the conspicuous wealth of the couple on their way to the pleasure dome and the evident poverty of the family seated on their train. Poverty rides in the wake of wealth; need begins at the palace door. Or, as the word-play of the proverbial title later attached to this painting has it, *Paupers Come in the Train of Pomp*.

An essential feature of the image is its atmosphere of serene, almost fairy-tale unreality. Even the palatial edifice is more an architectural vision than a real structure, as becomes clear when one tries to imagine how it was built. This is strange when one considers that Altdorfer was himself an architect, a master builder. Yet as the records indicate, he took his inspiration for such composite images from architectural engravings, transforming their rather prosaic depictions into fantastic scenes. And if his architecture is dreamlike, so is the world he projects. Its charm derives above all from his rendering of the landscape, soaked in sunlight and enlivened by bushes and trees in full leaf and flower. Against them the figures glow like precious gems, yet in spite of their brilliant colours they remain integrated with their surroundings. The couple's cloaks and train continue the curve of the terrace and stairs; figures and environment merge into a unity. Yet for all the radiant calm of the landscape spread out before us, timeless and unchanging, it seems somehow to tremble, to pulse mysteriously with life.

Albrecht Altdorfer
Christ on the Cross between the Two Thieves
*c.*1526

Linden, 28.7 × 20.8 cm ($11\frac{1}{4} \times 8\frac{1}{8}$ in)
Signed bottom: 'AA' (interlocked); on the reverse, allied arms, largely effaced
Acquired as bequest of M. Weber, Berlin, 1886
Cat. no. 638 D

Here Altdorfer depicts the Crucifixion in open country, the three crosses on a low rise, stark against the sky. Behind them extends a rolling plain dotted with bushes and trees, with paths winding through the fields to villages and castles in the distance. Just right of centre is a group of farm buildings on a hill, at the foot of which a town spreads along the shore of a lake or ocean bay. Ranges of mountains, rugged and icy, grow increasingly dim in the blue haze towards the horizon. The clouds glow pink in the sun, whose light breaks through with white-gold brilliance for the last time before the storm-clouds close.

The three victims are dead, the execution over. The onlookers have left the scene; a few people are still visible in the background on their way home. The mourners, too, are preparing to go, John supporting Mary and accompanied by an attendant and by Joseph of Arimathaea, pleading and gesticulating. Nicodemus and a yeoman raise the ladder to recover Christ's body. In the foreground, ignored by the others, Mary Magdalene sits on a mound with her back turned, before her a jar of ointment and linen bandages. Head in hand, abandoned and disconsolate, her pose reflects the day's terrible events, the horror of the last hour. These are echoed again in the livid illumination and glowering clouds. The darkness that engulfed the land in the hour of Jesus's death is symbolized here by clouds of night gathering while twilight is still in the sky. This dramatic illumination reflects and recapitulates the events of the day.

Altdorfer relates the Crucifixion story in a personal way unlike most representations. The true theme of his devotional image is the melancholy and mourning that followed the Saviour's death. As numerous copies show, his painting found many emulators and admirers. It is signed at the lower centre with the monogram AA, but not dated. Stylistic similarities with another *Crucifixion* dated 1526 in the Germanisches Nationalmuseum, Nuremberg, indicate that it may have been executed the same year, or perhaps slightly later.

Albrecht Altdorfer
The Mount of Calvary, 1526
Nuremberg, Germanisches Nationalmuseum

Wolf Huber (1480/5–1553)

The Flight into Egypt

*c.*1525–30

Linden, 56.2 × 56.6 cm ($22\frac{1}{8} \times 22\frac{1}{4}$ in)
On loan from the Lipperheide Collection, Kunstbibliothek SMPK, Berlin

The Holy Family fleeing into Egypt, after Joseph had been warned by an angel in a dream that Herod's soldiers were abroad – that is the story Huber depicts here. Mary cradles Jesus in her arms as Joseph leads the ass; and Joseph, staff and sack across his shoulder, searches Mary's face with a look of tender concern. An ox, there to provide sustenance on the journey, trots on a lead in the family's wake. Their path takes them through rough country which evokes the desert waste of the story; the rocky promontory they are crossing symbolizes the harshness of their exodus. In the background, icy peaks recall the solitude and the dangers that await the travellers in unknown territory far from human habitations – represented here by the town in the distant river valley far below.

To emphasize the family's closeness and to give visual coherence to the group, Huber has turned them to gaze towards one another, and disposed the figures and animals in a circular configuration. Back-lighting from the left lends them monumental presence. The forbidding aspect of the countryside is softened by fir trees with fresh green shoots, magically illuminated by morning light that makes the crisp air of dawn almost palpable. The shaggy trunk on the left represents a palm tree, a motif inspired by an engraving of *The Flight into Egypt* by Dürer. It served many artists as a model, and Huber has freely adapted it here. This palm tree, as the Bible story relates, bent its boughs down to the travellers so that they might pick its fruit.

The present panel is a fragment of an altar retable. Only one other panel has survived, a *Visitation of St Elizabeth by the Virgin*, now in the Bavarian National Museum at Munich. Investigations of the two panels and their stylistic features have shown that they came from an altar to the Virgin, executed some time between 1525 and 1530.

Wolf Huber
The Visitation of St Elizabeth
Munich, Bayerisches Nationalmuseum

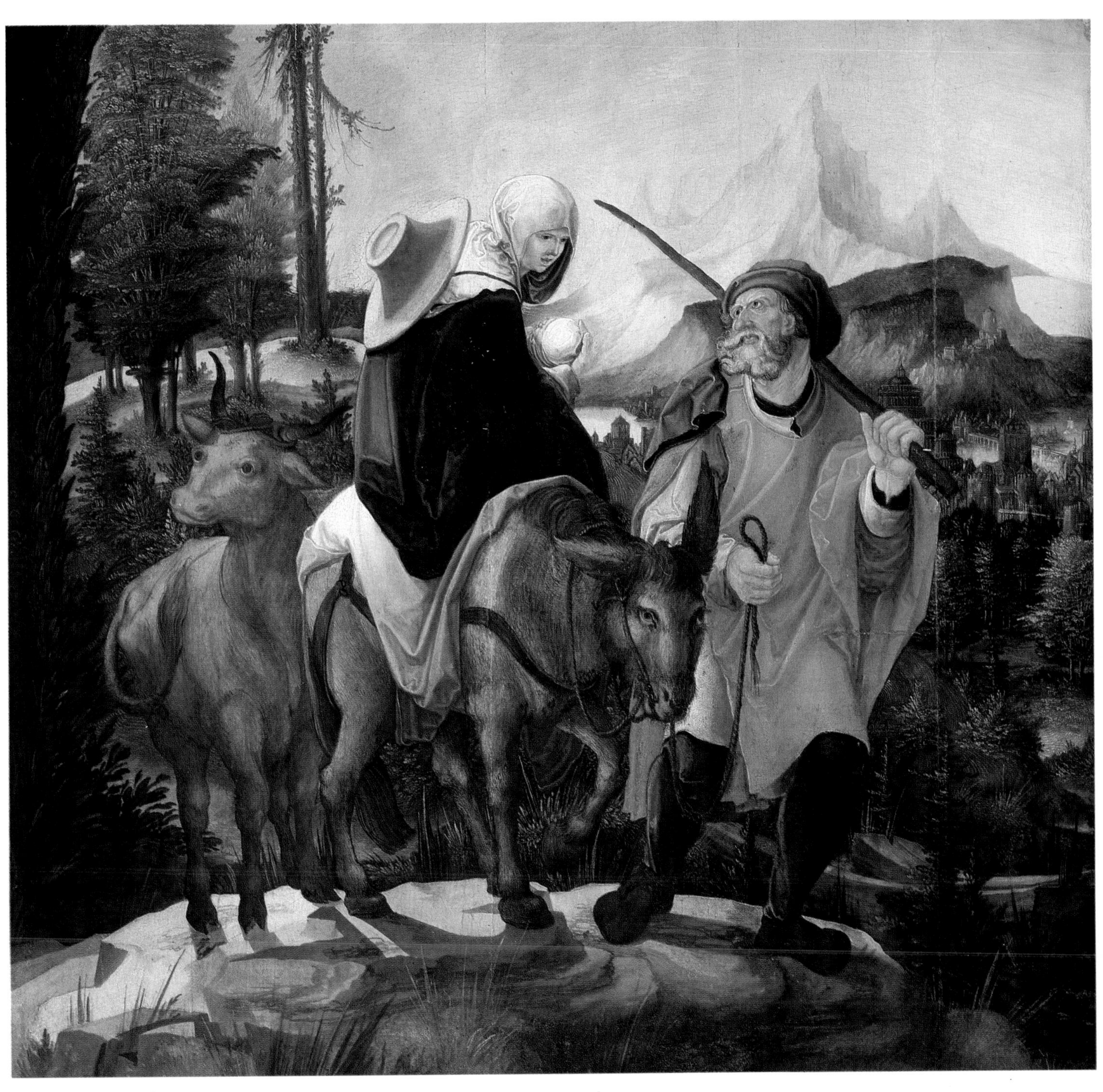

Christoph Amberger (*c.*1500–61/2)

Portrait of Sebastian Münster, Cosmographer

*c.*1552

Linden, 54 × 42 cm ($21\frac{1}{4} \times 16\frac{1}{2}$ in)
Inscribed verso in a sixteenth-century hand: 'Sebastian Münster Cosmographus. Seines Alters 65 gemalt Ao 1552'
From the von Praun Cabinet, Nuremberg
Acquired for the King of Prussia together with *Portrait of Emperor Charles V* through the dealer Frauenholzer, 1819
Cat. no. 583

The portrait is of an ageing man with ruddy complexion and sprouting beard which casts a silvery shimmer over his gentle, resolute features. White hair shows beneath the broad, black barett, and the embroidered collar of his white shirt is delicately pleated and ruffled at the neck. Over it he wears a red doublet and black coat, a *houppelande*, trimmed with greyish-white, light-brown tipped fur. A table or parapet covered in red velvet, on which his fingers rest, is before him. This red band along the bottom of the painting, together with the background, to which shadows lend depth, frames the figure in a unified pictorial space. The painting's effect derives largely from a colour harmony in green, two shades of red, and black. The lighting is also unique: it is frontal and strikingly brings out the thoughtful, even pensive cast of the sitter's features.

According to an inscription on the back of the painting, this sitter was Sebastian Münster, a great scholar of the sixteenth century. He was born on 20 January 1488, in the town of Ingelheim in Rhine-Hesse. Destined by his parents for the clergy, he entered the Franciscan Order at eighteen, then attended university at Heidelberg, Löwen and Tübingen. In 1509 he began to learn Hebrew from a fellow monk, Konrad Pellikan of Ruffach, Alsace, which was to prove decisive for his scholarly career. After studying mathematics, astronomy, cartography and geography at Tübingen in the years 1514–18, he followed Pellikan to Basle, where he became acquainted with the writings of Martin Luther. At the University of Heidelberg, as Professor of Hebrew from 1524 to 1529, Münster presumably began to fall away from the Old Church. An appointment to the Chair of Hebrew formerly held by his mentor at Basle, which had just been reformed, eased his conversion to Protestantism. Subsequently, Münster devoted himself to ancient languages and to geography. Among his many writings and the volumes he edited, two stand out: the first Bible in Hebrew to be printed in Germany, of which he was editor, and a six-volume description of the entire known world at that time. This *Cosmographia*, as its short title runs, summed up the geographical knowledge of the period, was translated into many languages, and continued to be reprinted far into the seventeenth century (twenty-one editions by 1628). In 1547 Münster was elected Rector of the University of Basle and had reached the apex of his career. He died in Basle on 23 May 1552. The present day has paid its own tribute to his memory by reproducing this portrait, reversed, on the 100 Deutsche Mark banknote.

Amberger's portrait bears an inscription on its reverse side which, though not by the artist himself, does show traits of a sixteenth-century hand. It translates, 'Sebastian Münster, Cosmographer. Painted in his 65th year of age, anno 1552.' He must have sat to Amberger only a few months before his death.

Amberger, a master in the Augsburg Guild since 1530, was one of the major German painters of the second third of the century. During his lifetime he was renowned primarily for his portraits. He had been to Italy, and had met Titian in Augsburg, so he was well acquainted with Italian painting of the period. The gallery possesses another work by his hand: a portrait of Emperor Charles V in delicate tones of silver-grey and violet, equally compelling in its psychological penetration and assured technique. This painting dates from about 1532, the beginning of Amberger's master period. His portrait of Sebastian Münster, with its frontal lighting and deep, luminous palette, is characteristic of his late style.

Christoph Amberger
Portrait of Emperor Charles V, *c.*1532
Berlin, Gemäldegalerie SMPK

Hans Holbein the Younger (1497/8–1543)
Portrait of Duke Anton the Good of Lorraine
*c.*1543

Oak, 51 × 37 cm (20 × $14\frac{1}{2}$ in)
Inscribed: 'AETATIS SVAE 54'
Collection of Sir I.E.Millais, London
Acquired 1897
Cat. no. 586 D

As the inscription says, the bearded gentleman who sat to Holbein for this portrait was fifty-four years old at the time. Shown in three-quarter profile, he wears a voluminous black coat over a doublet with red sleeves and a barett ornamented with golden tags. This costume marks him as a man of high rank.

The sitter's identity is uncertain, and there are many conjectures. Perhaps the most plausible, based on comparisons with other portraits, identifies him as Duke Anton the Good of Lorraine (1489–1544). Duke Anton spent most of his active life serving in the armies of Francis I of France. His nickname, 'the Good', alludes to the benevolence with which he ruled his territories. Yet though Duke Anton's age tallies with that given in the portrait, difficulties arise when we try to imagine when and where he could have met Holbein in order to sit for him. That he could have travelled to England at that period is doubtful, since he was in ill health; and it is not recorded that Holbein was in France at the time. The evidence for this interpretation, then, is rather tenuous, but still it remains more plausible than any other that has been advanced.

The portrait is memorable in its simplicity of form and the expressive poignancy of the sitter's composed features. The hands, so often present in Holbein's portraits, are not visible here; indeed there is nothing to distract from the countenance with its tight-pressed lips, and its pensively lowered gaze clouded with a touch of melancholy. This expression is at once determined, thoughtful and impassively noble.

The reduction of the composition to essentials and its focus on the expressive force of the sitter's features suggest Holbein's late period. Presumably the painting was finished, one of the last by his hand, in 1543.

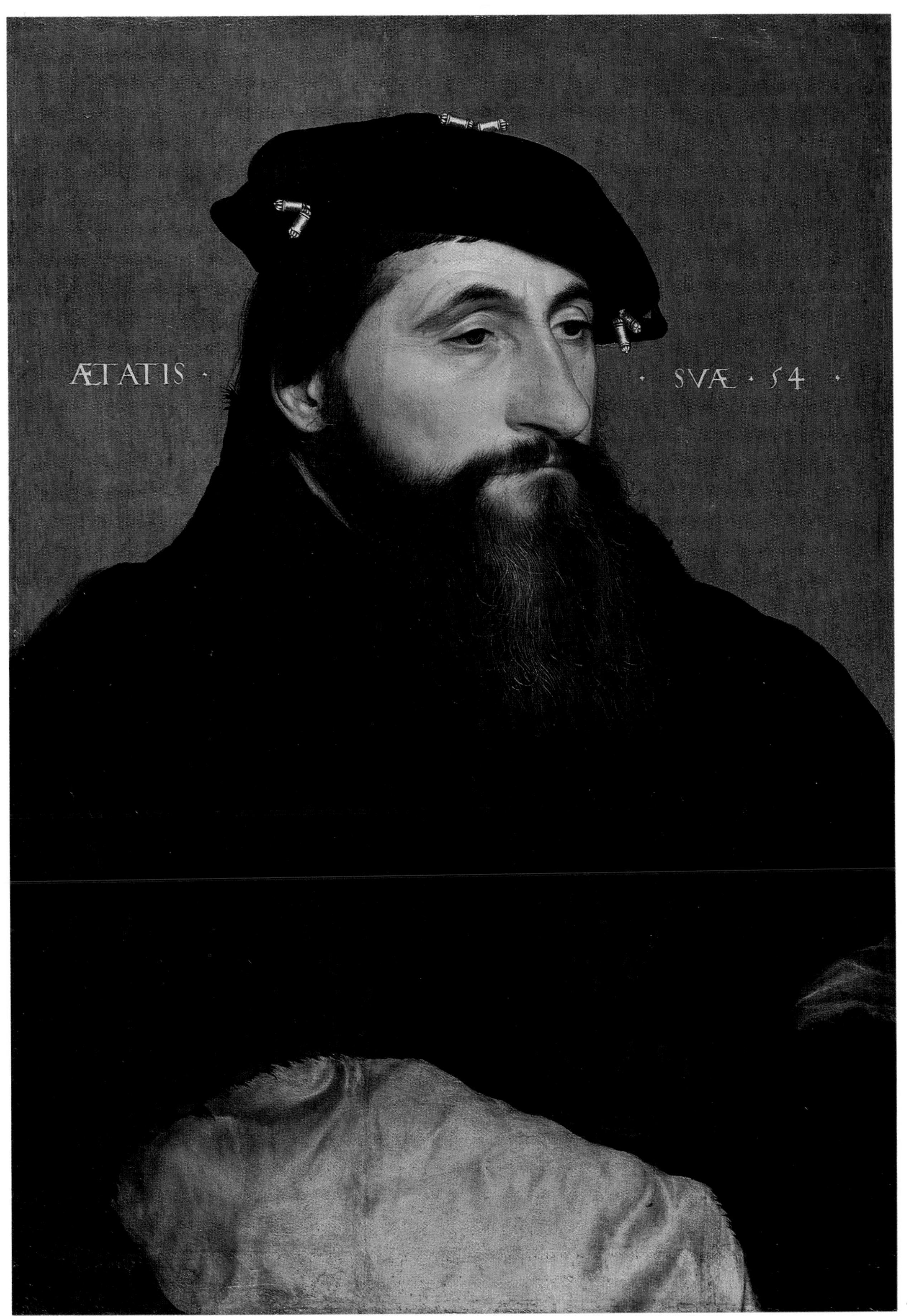
ÆTATIS ·
· SVÆ · 54 ·

Hans Holbein the Younger

Portrait of Georg Gisze, Merchant

1532

Oak, 96.3 × 85.7 cm (38 × 33¾ in)
Inscribed on slip upper left centre: (see text)
Collection of Duc d'Orleans, Paris
Acquired with the Solly Collection, 1821
Cat. no. 586

Hans Holbein came from a family of Augsburg artists, and learned his trade from his father, one of Germany's finest painters in the years before and after 1500. From 1515 he worked in Basle, and later in Lucerne for a time (1517–19). He spent the years 1526–8 in the Netherlands and England, then returned for a short period to Basle. Back in England in 1532, he became court artist to Henry VIII in 1537, a position from which he exerted a lasting influence on sixteenth-century English art. Holbein died of the plague in London, in 1543.

It was probably at the outset of his second stay in London, in 1532, that he executed this portrait of Georg Gisze, a merchant of Danzig. It is a true and evocative likeness, with everything in the painting – inscriptions and letters, tools of trade, decorations, even the room itself – contributing to the characterization of the sitter. In the midst of these eloquent surroundings is a young man, superbly dressed, a finely wrought dagger in his belt. Everything about his appearance suggests prosperity. His work-table, covered with a costly Oriental rug, is in a panelled office whose walls are painted green and fitted with shelves for books and utensils. On a slip pinned to the wall is an inscription in Greek and Latin which translates, 'Distich on the portrait of Georg Gisze. What you see here depicts Georg's features and aspect; thus is the quickness of his eye, thus have his cheeks rounded. In his thirty-fourth year, this Year of Our Lord 1532.'

Judging by the languages of this inscription, Herr Gisze must have enjoyed a humanistic education. This is confirmed by his Latin motto, written on the wall at the left: 'No pleasure unearned'. The letter he is opening, and others on the wall, reveal his address: the *Stahlhof* or Steel Yard in London, seat of the influential merchants of the German *Hansa* there. The sample seals and return addresses on the letters show that Gisze maintained a wide correspondence. Books, boxes and implements are scattered on the shelves and a book, a pair of scissors, writing utensils, a seal, and a signet ring lie on the table. A gilded brass clock and a Venetian glass vase complete the still life. The clock, showing time and measuring it in regular intervals, evokes both the virtue of moderation and the transience of all earthly things. In a similarly dual way, the glass vase is transparent, lucid and pure, and yet fragile and transient, like the flowers it contains – carnations, rosemary, hyssop, perhaps charlock. The blossoms are still fresh, but will have wilted by tomorrow. And they also convey symbolic allusions to love, fidelity, purity and humility, virtues and qualities attributed to the man portrayed. The counting-room we see him in is an attribute that characterizes his station in life, his profession and status.

This room is by no means as realistically depicted as might appear at first sight. When you try to imagine how the figure, table, and walls are related in space, you quickly realize that there is hardly enough room behind the table for someone to stand. To emphasize the figure's importance Holbein has purposely enlarged it in relation to its surroundings. He has also brought the back wall forward, perhaps to ensure the clarity of the many symbols and inscriptions. These proportional and spatial discrepancies are deliberate, yet skilfully veiled so as to ensure verisimilitude. That Holbein worked at this impression may be seen from textural traces on the painting's surface and in underlying paint layers, visible in X-rays. He made many changes during the painting process. Originally the model seems to have been depicted frontally, and the corner of the room lay to the left. The composition may have been similar to the *Portrait of a Banker* by Jan Gossaert in Washington, which also shows the sitter frontally, surrounded in his office by the tools of his trade. Netherlandish portraits of this kind very likely inspired Holbein; perhaps his patrons even suggested he emulate them. By altering his original composition, however, he gave the image a different perspective, and the resulting structure makes it difficult for spatial inconsistencies to be detected. The room surrounds the man like a shell, close and intimate.

Jan Gossaert
Portrait of a Banker,
*c.*1530
Washington, National Gallery of Art

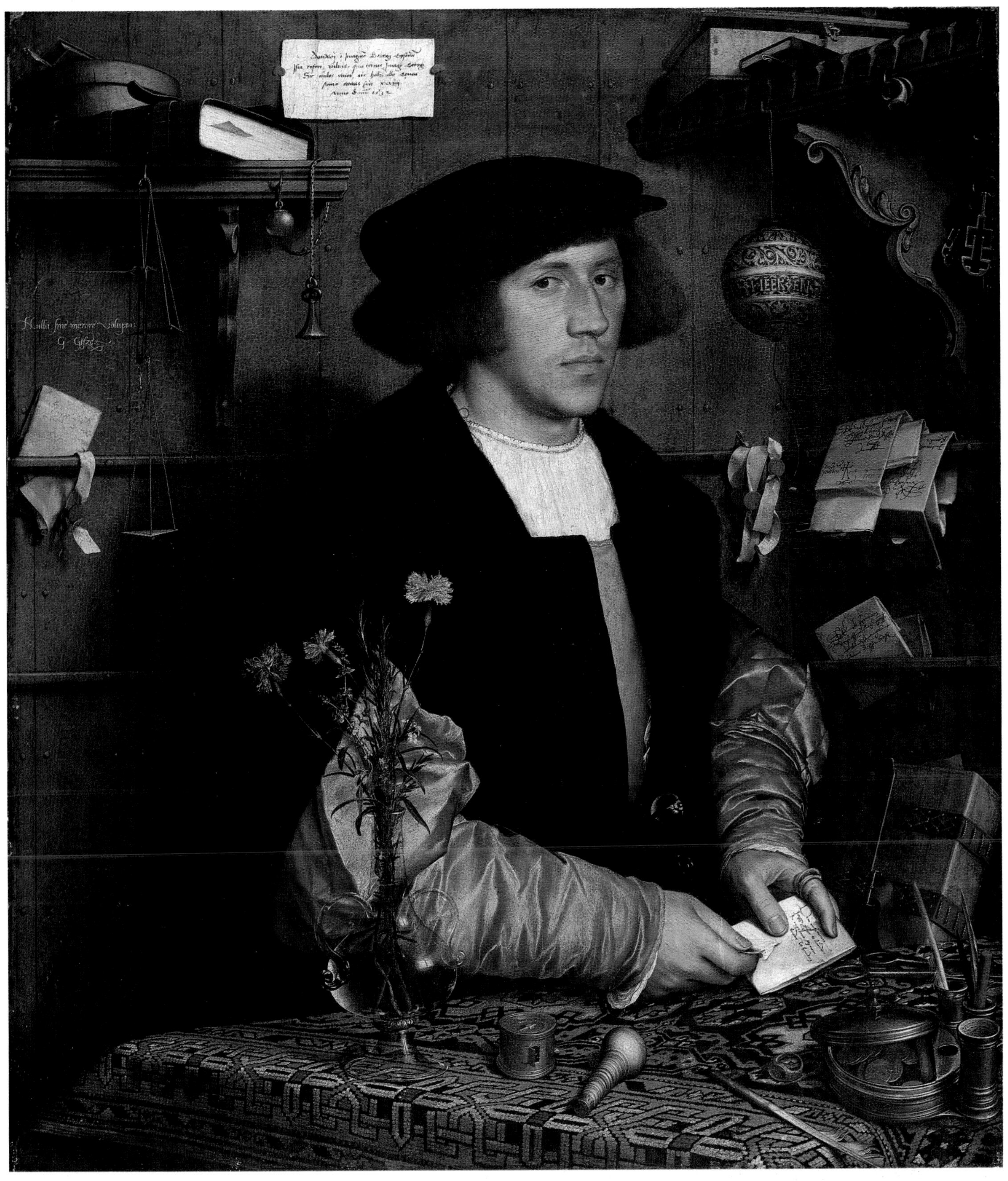
Nulla sine merore voluptas
G Gysze

The many and varied objects in it are rendered with the immediacy of a still life, yet remain subordinate to the essential theme, the portrait itself. The seemingly random arrangement of the things in the room and their owner's simple activity give an impression of vital, immediate presence, a slice of life. This multiplicity of surfaces, textures, materials is nevertheless carefully ordered and contributes to a feeling of comfortable intimacy.

The artist's intention might be described as recording an individual's appearance, elucidating the nature of his activity and status, and surrounding him with typical attributes that evoke his personality and character. It is conceivable that the erotic allusions conveyed by carnations refer to Gisze's engagement to Christine Krüger, on which occasion this portrait of her fiancé may have been commissioned. The elaborateness of the composition and its sumptuous paint handling make it one of the finest portraits of Holbein's London period.

NETHERLANDISH AND FRENCH PAINTING OF THE FIFTEENTH AND SIXTEENTH CENTURIES

BY RAINALD GROSSHANS

Jan van Eyck (*c.*1390–1441)
The Madonna in the Church

Oak with semicircular top, 31 × 14 cm
($12\frac{1}{4} \times 5\frac{1}{2}$ in)
Acquired with the Suermondt Collection
1874
Cat. no. 525 C

The art of Jan van Eyck, court artist and chamberlain to the powerful Duke of Burgundy, Philip the Good (1396–1467), aroused the astonished admiration of his contemporaries. Albrecht Dürer was deeply moved when he saw his monumental altarpiece in the Church of St Bavo in Ghent: that 'supremely charming, supremely intelligent painting' which Jan's brother Hubert had begun and which Jan himself finished in 1432. His motto, '*als ich can*', or 'as well as I can do', inscribed with his signature on many works, reveals diffidence as well as pride in his own skill. Another contemporary, the Italian Bartolomeo Facio, wrote in 1454–5 that Jan van Eyck '. . . is considered the greatest painter of our time; he is also learned in letters, and, most of all, skilled in geometry and in the disciplines connected with painting.' It was perhaps these talents, and certainly his wide learning, that won van Eyck the favour of the Duke of Burgundy. He served him for sixteen years, even being entrusted with diplomatic missions that took him as far as Spain and Portugal.

Jan van Eyck is generally described in histories of art as the inventor of oil-painting. Though this is a legend, it testifies to the great admiration his work has always inspired. His artistic exploration of the visible world, coupled with a fine feeling for the effects of colour and atmospheric light in all their subtle gradations, and heightened by an incomparable sensibility for the appearance and material qualities of things, made him the father of 'modern' painting in the Netherlands. Viewing his pictures one feels that a curtain has risen to reveal a new world, highly reminiscent of the real world yet strangely transcending it.

The Madonna in the Church is perhaps one of the finest, most exquisite works Jan van Eyck ever conceived. Copies made in the fifteenth and sixteenth centuries show that the superb quality of this small panel was recognized early. It depicts the high domed space of a Gothic cathedral, a nave with lectern and, a few steps higher, the choir. Aisle, transept, the pier and columns rising to the vaulted roof are all delineated precisely and with a great love of detail. The gallery above the arches in choir and transept is more elaborate than in the nave, indicating that it was built later – which often happened in great cathedrals whose construction took decades. This strengthens the impression that the artist must have been inspired by a real building, but though many attempts have been made to identify it, none is convincing. We can only conclude that van Eyck imaginatively adapted his memories of Gothic church architecture to create the semblance of reality which conformed to his vision.

The detailed architecture and the subtle gradations of light possess such immediacy and atmosphere that it is almost as if we are privileged to look on a timeless world. The bright daylight shining through the clerestory windows and side portal, reflecting from buttresses and arches to sparkle on the floor of the nave, suggests the inexorable passage of time, which none the less seems to stand still. The artist has placed the Virgin and Child of supernatural stature in these evocative surroundings. The figure of Mary, taller than the soaring Gothic arches, truly transcends the human. This suggests that van Eyck was concerned to do more than merely depict a realistic Madonna in a realistic church, and no strictly aesthetic discussion of the image can do justice to his intention. It is characteristic of Jan van Eyck's art that it combines an unprecedented fidelity to the visible world with medieval symbolism in all its multiplicity. Much in his work that at first sight appears no more than real may contain hidden allusions and references to deeper meaning. His *Madonna in the Church* is no exception, being suffused by an underlying belief that the beauty of the external world reveals a divine order. Closer scrutiny of the image reveals many covert references of this kind.

The Mother of God stands solitary and imposing in a space which encompasses her like a precious shrine. Dressed in a dark-blue mantle and red gown, she holds the Child in swaddling clothes in her arms. As he reaches up to touch his mother's breast, with his other

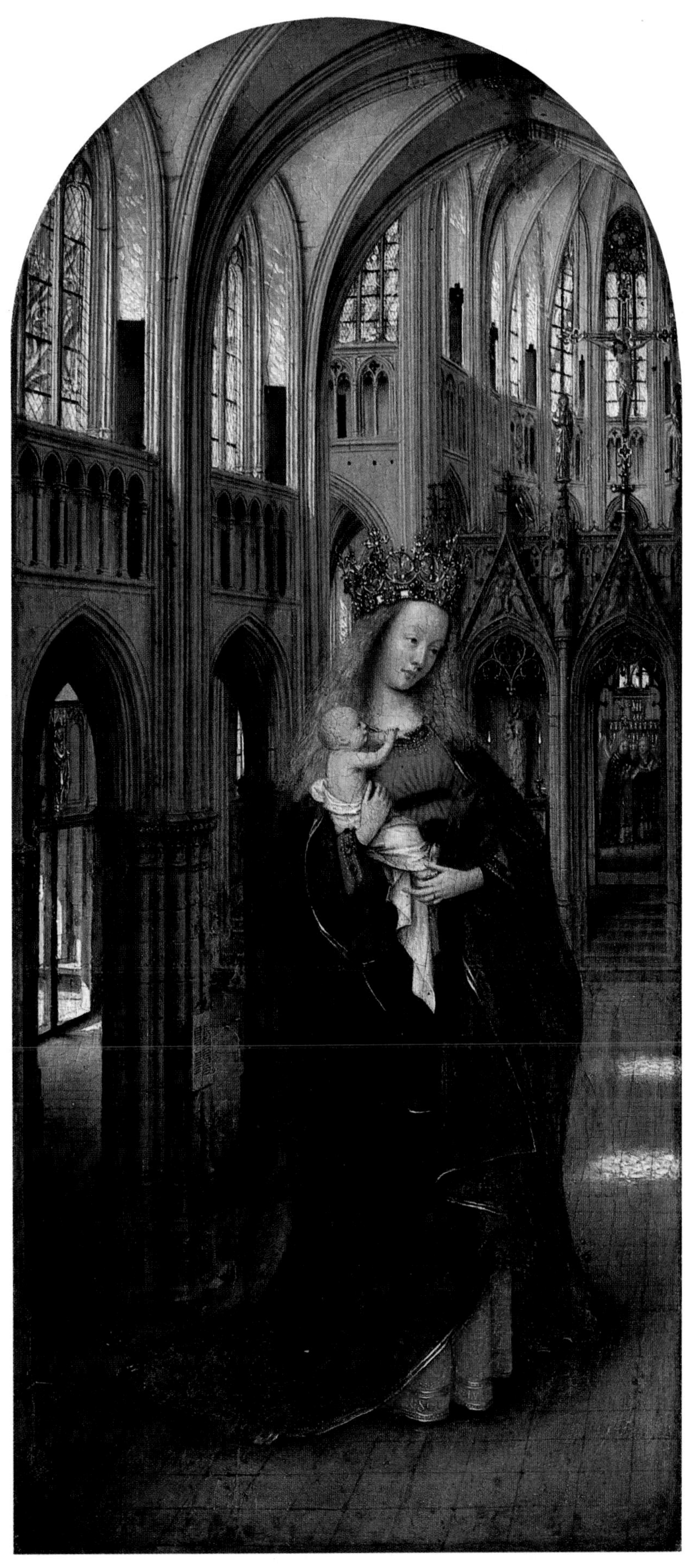

hand he grasps her left wrist, a gesture that in the Middle Ages signified respect, but also mourning. The golden crown Mary wears, and the splendid jewels and pearls encrusting her gown, are badges of her distinction and exaltation as Queen of Heaven. Each shimmering stone, in colour and in the qualities attributed to it, was symbolically associated with the Virgin Mary during medieval times. Even church interiors such as this possessed that symbolism. From the early Christian period, Mary was often compared to the house or temple of the Lord, since Christ lived in her womb as in a temple. Obvious references to Mary's elect position are found in the reliefs of the Annunciation and Coronation which van Eyck has represented in the tympana on the choir screen. These images stand for the beginning of the work of redemption and the climax of the Virgin's life. At the top of a spire on the screen is a sculpture of Mary mourning beneath a cross suspended from the vault above. This juxtaposition recalls that Mary, by sharing in the sorrows of her son, contributed to his work of salvation.

An angel and a priest sing from an antiphonary in front of the high altar in the choir. Their garments characterize them as deacons, and they represent the close link between sacrament and redemption, as well as the everlasting mass of the millennium. The clearest hint towards an explanation of this image was given by van Eyck himself in the inscription he made on the original frame, which has not survived. Its text was taken from a medieval hymn in praise of the miraculous birth and Mary's purity. In one of its verses she is compared to sunlight which can penetrate a window without breaking it, a simile for the woman who conceived yet remained a virgin. No wonder van Eyck devoted such care to the rendering of light in this image – light as a symbol of God and the Virgin Mary. That this allusion was conscious is verified by the letters embroidered on the seam of Mary's dress, part of a longer inscription taken from the Wisdom of Solomon, Apocrypha (7:29 and 26): 'She is more beautiful than the sun and excels every constellation of the stars, and compared to the light, she is found to be superior. For she is a reflection of eternal light and a mirror of the working of God and an image of his goodness.' Remembering that the choir of every Gothic church pointed east, it might seem odd that the sunlight in this painting, instead of shining from the south as it would in reality, falls into the church from the north. In other words, the light represented here is not natural but eternal, a light independent of the course of the sun and stars. This symbolism of light finds its most complex expression in the burning candles that flank the statue of the Virgin in a niche of the screen. There is a striking similarity in the pose of this cold statue and that of Mary, who confronts us with such a semblance of life. One is tempted to speak of a miraculous awakening, an incarnation. Visions of this kind are found again and again in the various legends of the saints. The most famous of these is probably the vision of the Virgin experienced by St Bernard of Clairvaux, which fundamentally shaped his life and the Cistercian Order of which he was founder.

Because two copies of Jan van Eyck's *Madonna in the Church* have been combined with portraits of donors to form diptychs, it is safe to assume that our panel was originally the left wing of a small, two-part altar. The copy made by the Bruges Master of 1499 (Antwerp, Koninklijk Museum voor Schone Kunsten) is probably a faithful facsimile of van Eyck's lost composition. It was commissioned by Christiaan de Hondt, who from 1495 to 1509 presided as abbot over the renowned Ter Duinen Cistercian monastery near Veurne. One of his successors also had himself portrayed on the exterior of this small altar. This replica certainly testifies to the high regard in which Jan van Eyck's work stood long after his death.

Bruges Master of 1499 (after van Eyck)
The Diptych of Christiaan de Hondt
Antwerp, Koninklijk Museum voor Schone Kunsten

Jan van Eyck
Portrait of Giovanni Arnolfini

Oak, 29 × 20 cm ($11\frac{1}{2} \times 7\frac{7}{8}$ in)
Collection of the Earl of Shrewsbury, Alton Towers
Acquired 1886
Cat. no. 523 A

The portraits created by Jan van Eyck introduced a new phase in the history of painting. They rested on precise observation, a dispassionate and highly objective recording of his sitters' features which gave their likenesses great presence and immediacy. This is especially true of his *Portrait of Giovanni Arnolfini*, which recent research has dated *c.*1440, that is to say, from the last years of his active career.

Arnolfini is depicted from the waist up before a monochrome black background, his arms crossed in front of him. In his right hand he holds a folded piece of parchment with an inscription that is no longer legible. The collar and sleeves of his green robe are edged in reddish-brown fur; a red turban with dangling flaps sets a strong note of colour which makes Arnolfini's brownish complexion appear paler than it may have been. This is the face of a sharp-featured and, at first glance, rather foreign-looking middle-aged man who exudes great self-confidence and aplomb. Thin-lipped mouth and long nose, protuberant cheekbones and heavy-lidded eyes, the hair shaved over the ears, the slight turn of the head to the side, and a gaze that takes no account of the observer, all contribute to the unique presence of this remarkable man. It is as though the artist's inexorable eye had seen to the depths of his sitter's nature, with a penetration that no verbal description could match.

What distinguishes this portrait from the summary and non-individual characterizations of medieval portraiture is its realism and immediacy. While almost all earlier portraits were idealized images of rulers, this is a unique human being in all his individuality. Van Eyck worked during a period when Dutch society was growing increasingly aware of its political significance and power. The history of Dutch cities was closely linked with a burgeoning of trade and industry which, since the late Middle Ages, had put the Netherlands among the most highly developed regions in Europe. Bruges and Ghent advanced to being centres of textile manufacture and international trade, with the representatives of banking and business houses in the Netherlands playing a key role.

One of these businessmen was Giovanni Arnolfini, of Lucca, Italy. From 1420 he represented the powerful commercial firm of Marco Guidecon in Bruges, where he was knighted by Philip the Good, Duke of Burgundy, and where he died in 1472. His wife, Giovanna Cenami, was the daughter of Guglielmo Cenami, also a merchant from Lucca, who settled in Paris in 1403. The Arnolfini couple enjoyed high social standing in Bruges, where they spent most of their lives. In 1434 Arnolfini commissioned Jan van Eyck to do a portrait of him and his wife. This famous marriage or engagement portrait, now in the National Gallery, London, shows a younger man than the one in our portrait, and has been associated with Arnolfini's name since the sixteenth century. The London picture of the Arnolfini couple in a room came from the collection of Don Diego de Guevara to Margaret of Austria. The inventory of her collection lists the model's name as 'Arnoult Fin'. So there can be no doubt that the traditional identification with a member of the Arnolfini family is correct, though some critics suggest that not Giovanni, but his brother Michele (d.1473 in Bruges) may be the man represented in the London portrait and our panel.

Jan van Eyck
The Arnolfini Couple, 1434
London, National Gallery

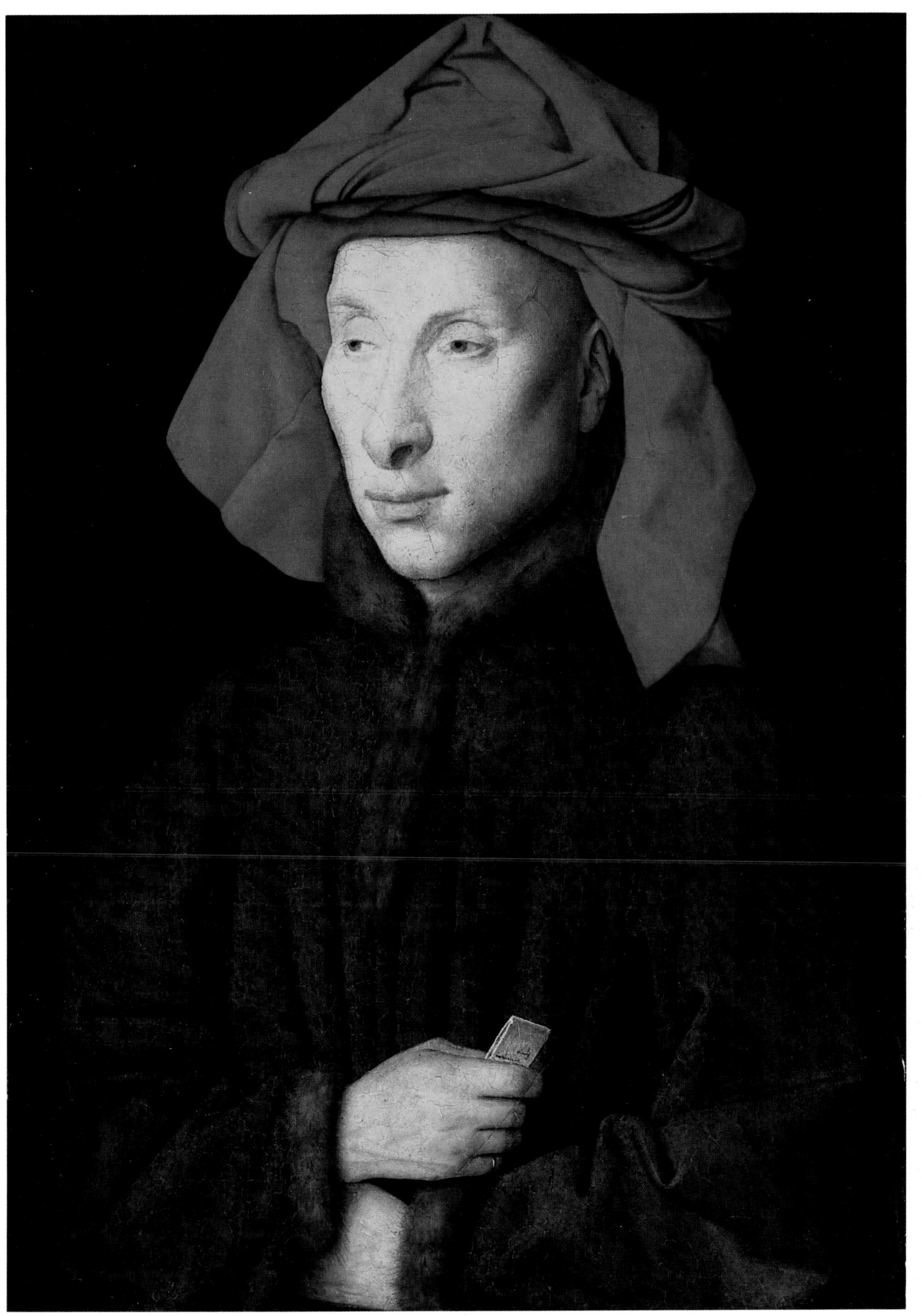

Robert Campin (c.1375–1444)
Portrait of Robert de Masmines

Oak, 28.5 × 17.7 cm (11¼ × 7 in)
Acquired 1901
Property of the
Kaiser-Friedrich-Museums-Verein
Cat. no. 537 A

This portrait is among the most impressive achievements of early Netherlandish portraiture. And though it owes its effect to such artistic factors as great immediacy and merciless fidelity to life, the personal appearance of the sitter certainly contributes to it. When he saw the portrait at the London auction of Sir Hope Edwards's collection in 1901, Max J. Friedländer, the great connoisseur of Netherlandish art, attributed it to the Master of Flémalle. This attribution is still valid, though the anonymous master is now generally associated with Robert Campin, a painter of Tournai. Campin headed a workshop from which artists of the rank of Jacques Daret and Rogier van der Weyden came. Even more importantly, with Jan van Eyck he was one of the first artists in the Netherlands to achieve a transition from the late phase of the European Gothic style to a new realism. An expansion and deepening of the pictorial space, realistic detail, and the plastic conception of the figures are among the essential factors in the monumental quality and the immediacy that is characteristic of his best work. These qualities are strikingly present even in the fragment which is all that remains of Campin's triptych with *Deposition*, and which has a section of the right sidepiece showing *The Thief on the Cross with Two Onlookers* (Frankfurt am Main, Städelsches Kunstinstitut).

An equally monumental presence and fidelity to appearances mark Campin's work in portraiture, particularly his likeness of Robert de Masmines. The constricted format, the white background, and the incomparable verisimilitude in the treatment of the flesh, all contribute to the sitter's vitality. His heavy face and double chin, curly hair and deeply lined forehead suggest a dominating personality, strong-willed and fond of life, a man whose worldliness borders on the carnal. The portrait is so astonishingly true to life that only on a second look does a lack of psychological penetration become evident.

The question of this fascinating personality's identity has often been asked. Robert de Masmines is the most plausible of the various names advanced: he was counsellor and military commander under the Burgundian Dukes John the Fearless (d.1419) and Philip the Good (d.1467). De Masmines was knighted during the siege of Rheims in 1420, and in January 1430 was accepted into the Order of the Golden Fleece. Before the year was out, he died in battle with the armies of Liège, near Bouvignes, in the service of Philip the Good. What adds to the convincing identification of de Masmines is not so much the other few portraits of him, but the fact that a second version of this picture has come down to us. Formerly owned by the Counts of van de Straten-Ponthoz, whose ancestors were related to de Masmines, the second version is now in the Thyssen-Bornemisza Collection (Castagnola-Lugano). If we assume that the sitter was indeed de Masmines, and remember that the Order of the Golden Fleece was to be worn at all times, then the fact that it is missing from the present portrait (right) would date it to before January 1430. If all these considerations hold, this portrait could have one of the earliest reliable dates in the history of Netherlandish painting.

Robert Campin
The Thief on the Cross with Two Onlookers
Fragment of the right wing of a triptych
Frankfurt am Main, Städelsches Kunstinstitut

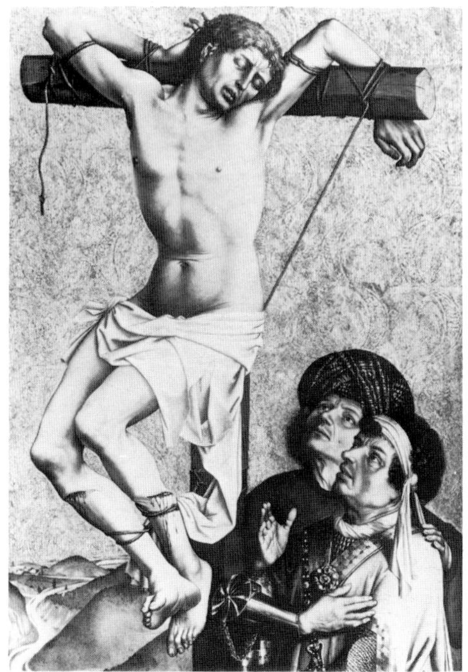

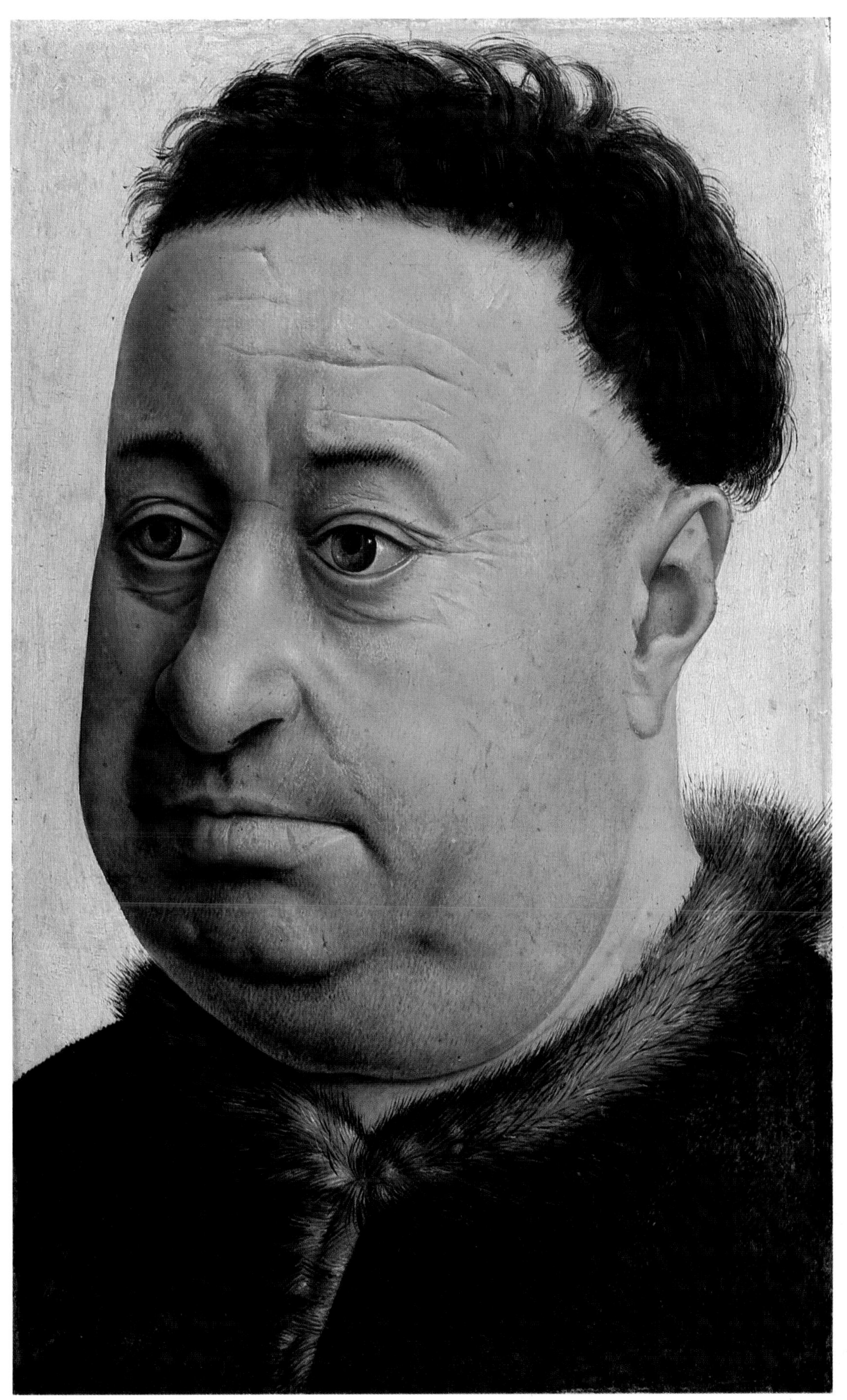

Petrus Christus (*c.*1410–72/3)

The Virgin and Child with St Barbara and a Carthusian Monk

(Exeter Madonna)

Oak, 19 × 14 cm ($7\frac{1}{2} \times 5\frac{1}{2}$ in)
Collection of the Marquis of Exeter, Burleigh House
Acquired 1888
Cat. no. 523 B

In 1444, three years after the death of Jan van Eyck, Petrus Christus, independent Master of his art, became a citizen of Bruges, where he lived and worked for about the next three decades. There is much to indicate that he had been a pupil of van Eyck, for he did not hesitate to base his compositions on his Master's, apparently even finishing works van Eyck had left uncompleted. This led many to call him an imitator who was unable to shake off his predecessor's tremendous influence. Yet, though he undeniably never achieved van Eyck's diversity, nor perhaps wished to, Christus enriched his work with innovations that have led to a more positive evaluation. His special strength was a lucid and logical pictorial structure that aimed at integrating figures and surroundings. Petrus Christus was the first Netherlandish artist to reconceive traditional laws of perspective, a pioneering exploration which paved the way for such artists as Dieric Bouts, Aelbert van Ouwater and Geertgen tot Sint Jans.

In about 1450, Christus painted the present *Virgin and Child*, a miniature-like panel in which he freely reinterpreted Jan van Eyck's *Madonna with a Carthusian Monk between St Barbara and St Elizabeth* (New York, Frick Collection). Van Eyck had died before finishing this painting, and it was completed by a pupil, perhaps by Christus himself. The donor of this much larger painting was Jan Vos, Prior of the Genadedal Carthusian Monastery near Bruges from 1441–50. When he left to become Prior of the Nieuwlicht Monastery outside Utrecht, Vos took the large panel with him, apparently commissioning Petrus Christus to do a facsimile to replace it.

That, in brief, is the rather unusual story of the origin of our small panel, a story that of course leaves many questions unanswered. The image includes a portrait of its priestly donor in the white Carthusian habit, which is tied with a cord at his waist and covered by a cape-like scapulary and cowl. He kneels in prayer before the Virgin and Child, who raises his right hand in blessing and in the left holds a crystal globe symbolizing his universal sovereignty. Behind the donor stands St Barbara, with her symbol, a tower, beside her. A palm frond, representing martyrdom, in her right hand, she respectfully touches the donor's shoulder, beseeching the Virgin for her good grace and protection for him. The scene is set in an open hall with leaded windows above arcades. A broad valley with hills, woods, fields, and a riverside town, lies beyond.

The houses, streets and inhabitants are lovingly rendered in great detail. Puddles from the rain gleam on the paths; smoke rises from chimneys. A woman is spreading laundry out to bleach in her garden, while a maid fills a bucket at a well. The streets are filled with people promenading, watching the boats on the river, or going about their everyday errands. This view of a well-populated country town with its countless little events invites the eye to linger and gives the painting a special charm. At the same time, it conveys a deeper meaning – that the Blessed Virgin and Child have entered the earthly world, bringing a promise of redemption to mankind.

Jan van Eyck and follower
The Madonna with a Carthusian Monk between St Barbara and St Elizabeth
New York, Frick Collection

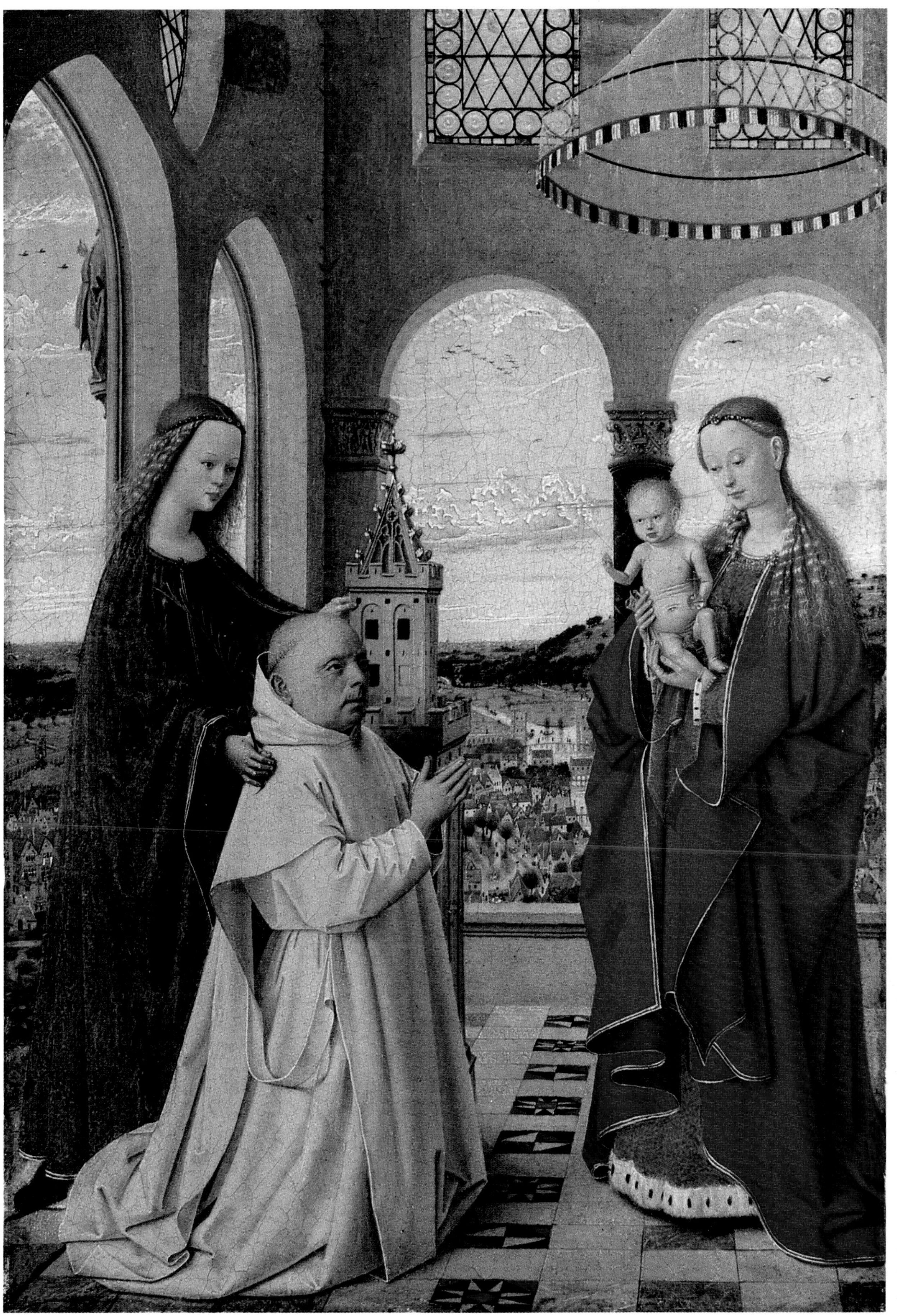

Petrus Christus

Portrait of a Young Woman

Oak, 29 × 22.5 cm ($11\frac{1}{2} \times 8\frac{7}{8}$ in)
Acquired with the Solly Collection, 1821
Cat. no. 532

This artist and his contribution to the development of portraiture as an independent genre have been widely underestimated. For the first time in Netherlandish painting, Petrus Christus represented people in real settings which gave his portraits great immediacy and presence. It was a means of heightening individuality of which neither Robert Campin (Master of Flémalle) nor Jan van Eyck took advantage. Christus's step from empty, neutrally coloured backgrounds to interiors representing the natural ambience of the sitters changed portraiture profoundly.

The portrait of a young woman in our collection, the only one of its type known to be from Petrus Christus's hand, shows the model in an interior before a greyish-brown wall with brown wainscot. Light shining diagonally from the left front defines spatial relationships, and creates a tension between figure and surroundings that evokes great emotional immediacy. It is almost as if we were meeting this young woman personally, were somehow admitted to her private world.

The model gazes out attentively towards the viewer. She wears a tall cap of black velvet edged with gold braid and tiny pearls, and tied under her chin with a broad band. Her three-tiered golden necklace is set with pearls, and her blue dress trimmed with ermine. A transparent veil, gathered in front with a pin, covers her shoulders and *décolleté*. The velvet loop on the headdress emphasizes her high forehead, as does her hair combed back in the fashion of the period, which also brings out the lovely clear contours of her face. Slanting almond eyes gaze out inquiringly from beneath carefully plucked brows. These eyes, and a seemingly overlarge ear, convey an impression of concentrated attention. The girl's pale face, with its dark eyes and finely chiselled lips, is strangely fascinating. Despite her aristocratic dignity, the narrow shoulders, slender neck, and delicate body make her appear incredibly fragile. All these traits contribute to her enigmatic child-woman air.

Who she is we do not know, though there have been endless attempts to find out. None of the identities suggested, including that of the wife of Edward Grymeston, whom Petrus Christus portrayed in 1446 (London, National Gallery), has more than circumstantial evidence. The model's costume seems to indicate that she lived in France, not the Netherlands, as it is similar to those in a number of pictures including a miniature in the *Livre de cur d'amour épris* by René d'Anjou (*c.*1465; Vienna, Österreichische Nationalbibliothek). Though the painting was acquired in a frame inscribed 'Opus Petri Christophori', no precise records of its provenance exist. It may nevertheless be assumed that the portrait was once in Florence, in the collection of Lorenzo de' Medici (1449–92). The inventory of this collection mentions a portrait of a French lady (*una testa di dama franzese*) and expressly names its author as Petrus Christus (*Pietro Cresti da Bruggia*).

Embarkation to the Island of Love
Detail of miniature from the *Livre du cœur d'amour épris* of René d'Anjou
Vienna, Österreichische Nationalbibliothek

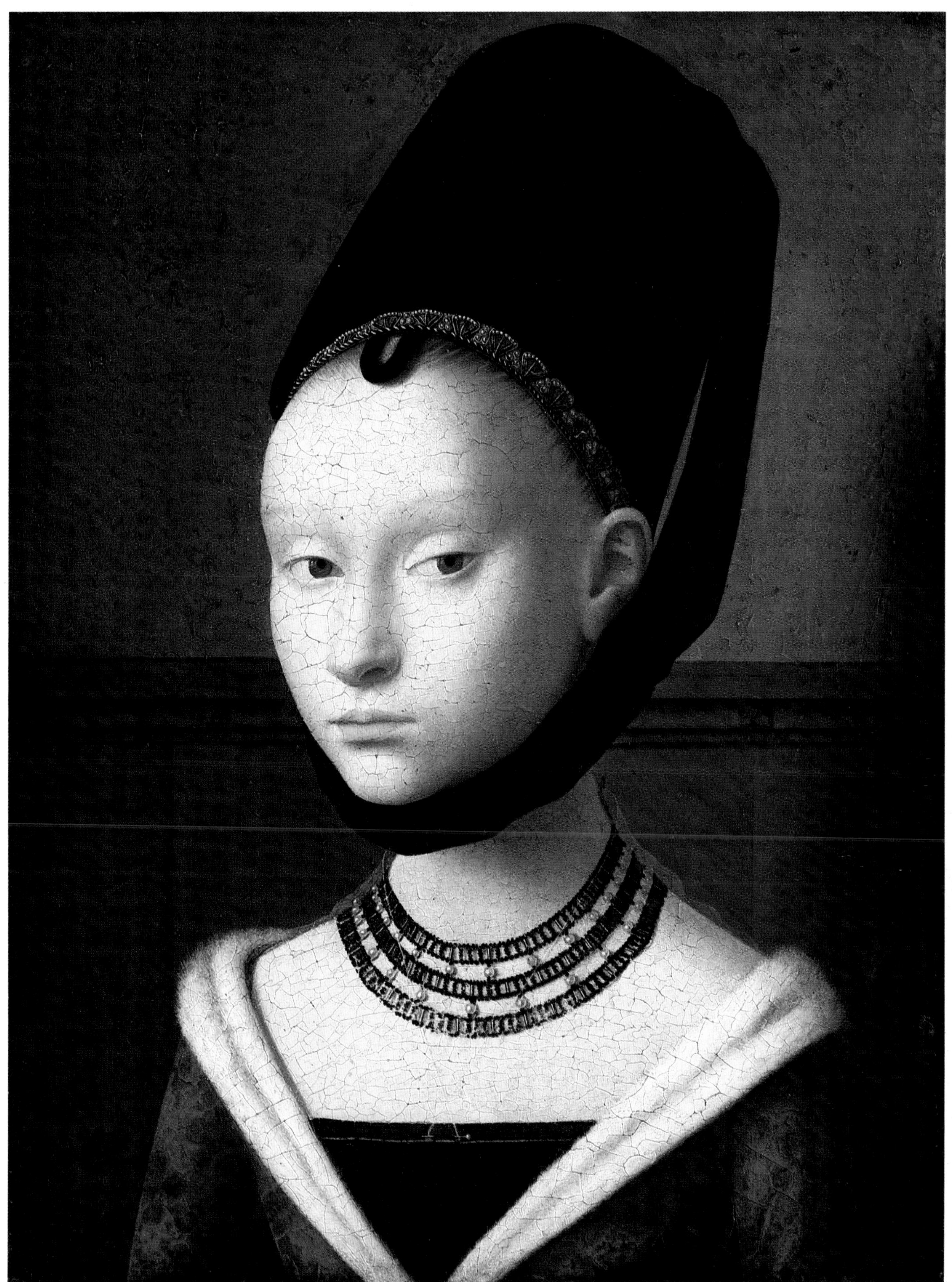

Rogier van der Weyden (1399/1400–64)

The Middelburg Altarpiece

(Bladelin Altarpiece)

*c.*1450

Oak, central panel 91 × 89 cm
($35\frac{7}{8}$ × 35 in),
each wing 91 × 40 cm ($35\frac{7}{8}$ × $15\frac{3}{4}$ in)
Purchased by the dealer Nieuwenhuys in 1833 in Mecheln, from the family of Baron Snoy
Acquired 1834
Cat. no. 535

Rogier van der Weyden, whose contemporary fame rivalled that of Jan van Eyck, worked in a compellingly austere pictorial form and in a tactile, realistic style which decisively shaped northern European art. He was the central figure in Netherlandish painting during the second half of the fifteenth century.

The first name by which this altar is known derives from the town for which it is traditionally said to have been made; the second name is from its donor, Pieter Bladelin (*c.*1410–72). Bladelin advanced from being a tax-collector of his birthplace, Bruges, to omnipotent Minister of Finance in Burgundy and Treasurer of the Order of the Golden Fleece. He was an outstanding personality in a period rich in extraordinary men. The power of the state of Burgundy was in its natural wealth and in the riches of its first representatives whom the reigning dukes won to their side with gifts and protection. Life at court with its fêtes and tournaments and chivalric ideals, set the tone of Burgundian society, in which Bladelin – knight, high financier, and influential adviser to Philip the Good – played a leading role. Among the tasks entrusted to him was the raising of funds for a crusade against the Turks. In 1440 he was given the important mission of ransoming Charles of Orléans from the English prison where he was kept since the defeat of the French knights at the Battle of Agincourt in 1415.

Bladelin's rapid rise, his political influence and wealth were astonishing even by contemporary standards. Among the uses to which he put his seemingly inexhaustible fortune was the building of a new town – Middelburg, in a stretch of open land north-east of Bruges. Bladelin moved in to his castle there, one of the first buildings to be finished, in 1450. In 1460 there was the consecration of the town church for which Rogier van der Weyden's altarpiece was made.

This altar is among the works that represent Rogier's perfect art. Not surprisingly, it soon came to be regarded as a model achievement and was often copied. One of these copies, still on view today in the Middelburg church, together with an illustration of Bladelin's castle in *Flandria Illustrata* (1641) – which is based on the town architecture in the *Bladelin Altarpiece* – provides convincing arguments for the origin of the altar and its donor's name.

The Birth of Christ, the focus of the work's form and content, is represented on the central panel. The Child lies on the floor of the stable beneath its ruined roof, worshipped by Mary and Joseph, three angels, and Pieter Bladelin, the donor. Another group of three angels approaches from above, while in the distant landscape to the left the Annunciation to the Shepherds is shown. In the background right a town's inhabitants go about their daily tasks.

Continuing old traditions, Rogier's depiction of the Birth of Christ is enriched with allusive motifs. The Romanesque architecture of the stable stands for a past age whose end was marked by the birth of the Redeemer and His promise of a coming age of grace. The massive column supporting the roof was associated in the Middle Ages with the miraculous birth and, as a reference to the column of the Flagellation, with the sufferings Jesus would later undergo. The candle Joseph holds, its dim light outshone by the Child's divine aura, is a motif apparently taken from the *Revelations* of St Birgit of Sweden (1303–73). All these symbols refer to a new era of salvation for mankind.

Accompanying the Holy Family is a figure representing Pieter Bladelin, who kneels reverently in prayer. He is dressed in the black robe trimmed with fur that was worn by the dukes of Burgundy and their courtiers. Another sign of Bladelin's high social position are the pointed shoes, whose length indicated the wearer's rank and title. As compellingly as in his other (independent) portraits, Rogier has caught the donor's energetic and sharply cut features, recording them for posterity with great penetration.

The altar's central painting is supplemented by the images on its flanking wings. On the left is a version of the heavenly vision seen by Caesar Augustus, as told in the *Legenda aurea*. Augustus, pressed by his senators to show proof of his divine origin, asked a sibyl if a more powerful sovereign than he had ever been born. Suddenly at noon on the day of Christ's birth, the Madonna and Child on an altar appeared to him in the sky. Told by the oracle that this Child was all-powerful, Augustus made an offering of incense to the vision and from then stopped demanding to be worshipped as divine. In the left painting, Augustus, the Western emperor, kneels before the vision, making his sacrifice with his crown held humbly in his hand. Next to him is the sibyl prophesying the significance of the heavenly omen, which is witnessed by three men from the emperor's retinue.

As counterpoint, the right-hand panel depicts the Annunciation to the Kings of the East. The Three Magi kneel at the foot of a hill, looking up in devout astonishment at the Star of Bethlehem, in whose centre the Christ Child shines. This is another instance of the artist's reliance on the *Legenda aurea*, which tells how the star-child told the monarchs to go to Judea and proclaim the miraculous birth of the Redeemer to all the world. This legend also says that the Magi washed themselves – symbolic purification – to prepare for the vision they would see. Rogier shows them bathing in the river that winds through the landscape in the distance.

The painting on the altar, therefore, was meant above all to represent Christ's incarnation, His birth among men, and its Annunciation to the Orient and the West. The harmonious palette and masterly composition, with its realistic landscape vistas, help communicate the underlying significance of this work with an immediacy of appeal which could be felt by the faithful.

The great verisimilitude of Rogier van der Weyden's art astonished his contemporaries, as may be gathered from the words of Cyriaco d'Ancona, an Italian antiquarian, who said in 1449, '... one sees the faces he wished to depict living and breathing ... and one might say especially that the many garments and mantles of various colours ... have been fashioned excellently, and the vivid fields, flowers, trees, the cultivated and shadowed hills, the ornamented halls and forecourts, the gilding like true gold, the pearls, gems and everything else have been made by all-creating Nature herself rather than by the hand of a human artist.'

Bladelin's Castle in Middelburg
From Antonius Sanderus, *Flandria Illustrata*, 1641

Rogier van der Weyden

Portrait of a Young Woman with a White Headdress

*c.*1435

Oak, 47 × 32 cm ($18\frac{1}{2}$ × $12\frac{1}{2}$ in)
Soltikoff Collection, St Petersburg
Acquired 1908
Cat. no. 545 D

Among the highest praise Rogier van der Weyden received was a mention, during his lifetime, by the great theologian and philosopher Nicolaus von Cues (1401–64). His self-portrait in the Brussels Town Hall moved von Cues so deeply that in his *De visione dei* (1452) he called its painter *'maximus pictor'* and compared his eloquent gaze with that of an 'all-seeing God'. The motif of eye-contact and face-to-face dialogue with the spectator was an innovation in portraiture, pioneered in the Netherlands by Jan van Eyck and Rogier van der Weyden. However, only one portrait by Rogier with a direct gaze has come down to us. This is his *Portrait of a Young Woman with a White Headdress*, and its human warmth and revelation of soul is unmatched by any other work he did in this genre.

Unlike most portraits of the period, in which the models appear reserved and introverted, or gaze off into the distance, or in the votive diptychs turn reverently towards the Virgin, this young woman's eyes seek and meet our own; they have an expression seemingly full of interest and sympathy. Of the type known as half-figure, the portrait shows the model from the waist up, turned slightly to the right. Her youthful, vivacious face is framed by a two-piece Flemish headdress of white linen, secured by a few skilfully placed pins. Beneath the finely woven, translucent cloth her high forehead is visible, conforming with the ideal of feminine beauty at that time; a more elaborate *hennin* headdress was also worn by ladies of the court. Rogier's model wears a much plainer and less exalted version of this bonnet which shows she belonged to the upper-middle class rather than to the more fashionably dressed aristocracy. The white cloth with its starched folds brings out the delicate complexion of the sitter's face and the lovely lines of its contours. Her simply cut dress, made of grey woollen material, has ample folds in the sleeves and is gathered together in close pleats over her breast. Her hands, ornamented with rings, rest one over the other on an imaginary parapet at the bottom edge of the painting. The background is treated in a dark, neutral colour. The figure is composed to fill the pictorial plane almost entirely, with arms and hands intersected by the image borders.

This *Portrait of a Young Woman* is generally attributed to Rogier's early period. It was probably painted in about 1435, the year he was named Town Artist in Brussels. Obvious similarities to the portraits of his teacher, Robert Campin, are still detectable here, as may be seen from a comparison with Campin's portrait of a lady in the National Gallery, London. Another portrait worth recalling to gauge the true significance of Rogier's innovation is Jan van Eyck's famous portrait of his wife (1439; Bruges, Groeningemuseum). A common feature of the two portraits is the direct way in which the women meet the spectator's eye. Yet while the gaze in van Eyck's work seems reserved and detached, that in Rogier's has a much more immediate and intimate character. Both, of course, reveal a new and psychologically acute perception of the sitters' personalities, and their similarities have raised the question of whether Rogier, like van Eyck, had not recorded his own wife's features in *Young Woman with a White Headdress*.

However, verifiable clues to her identity are missing, and the young woman Rogier painted so vividly and without any trace of official pomp must remain anonymous.

Jan van Eyck
Margareta van Eyck, 1439
Bruges, Groeningemuseum

Rogier van der Weyden

The St John Altarpiece

Oak, each panel 77 × 48 cm ($30\frac{3}{8} \times 18\frac{7}{8}$ in)
Acquired 1850 from the collection of King William II of Holland (left and central panels) and in England (right panel)
Cat. no. 534 B

The *St John Altarpiece*, which belongs to Rogier's late period, follows the same basic arrangement as his early *Miraflores Altarpiece*, also in our collection – three equally sized, fixed panels with each scene set in a portal of elaborately rendered architectural motifs.

The scheme of the retable begins on the left panel with the birth and naming of John the Baptist. Beneath the arch in the foreground stands Mary with the infant John in her arms. She looks towards Zacharias, who sits opposite her on a stool, recording the name of his son revealed to him by an angel. Not believing that a son would be born to him, Zacharias had been struck dumb by the Lord. But when he wrote down John's name, 'his mouth was opened immediately, and his tongue loosed, and he spoke, and praised God' (Luke 1:64). The Virgin's presentation of the infant John to Zacharias, however, is recounted not in the Gospels but in the widely read *Legenda aurea*, which Rogier follows here. Behind Mary and Zacharias the lying-in room is visible – coffered ceiling, tile floor, hearth and sideboard – where Zacharias's wife Elisabeth rests in a canopied bed. A maid smoothes the bedclothes while expecting a visit from a woman and girl who enter the house in the background, through the door in the rear wall of the room. The Apostles James the Less, Philip (left), and Thomas and Matthew (right) are represented on the portal frame. The reliefs above them show the angel appearing to Zacharias; Zacharias struck dumb, leaving the temple; the marriage of Joseph and Mary; and the Annunciation, Visitation and Nativity. The juxtaposition of these scenes unmistakably illustrates the close ties between Christ's life and that of John the Baptist, who prepared the way for him.

The central image is devoted to Christ's baptism as the most significant event in the story of salvation. Christ is represented frontally, standing up to his knees in the water of the River Jordan, which flows through a broad valley in the distance. John stands next to him, his right arm raised to perform the baptismal rite. In the right foreground an angel kneels, gazing up at Christ and holding his garment. Over Jesus's head hovers the dove of the Holy Spirit, as the heavens open behind to reveal God the Father, who utters the words: '*hic est filius meus dilectus in quo michi bene complacui ipsum audite*' ('This is my beloved Son, in whom I am well pleased; hear ye him'). Besides relating the historical event, van der Weyden clearly emphasizes the sacramental meaning of the baptism of Christ by placing it in a central position. On the columns of the portal are figures of the Apostles Peter and Andrew (left) and James the Great and John the Evangelist (right). The hollow moulding above contains a series of reliefs consecutively depiciting Zacharias's prophecy of John's mission; John praying in the wilderness, and baptizing the Pharisees and Sadducees; and Christ being tempted three times by Satan.

The third panel of the altarpiece represents the beheading of John the Baptist. In the foreground Salome, exquisitely dressed, receives John's head on a salver from the executioner. The way this man has tied his skirts up behind and rolled up his sleeves graphically emphasizes the horror of the proceedings. He and Salome, finding it impossible to look each other in the face, turn away demonstratively, as if realizing the heinousness of the deed. Beneath the executioner's sword, on the steps leading down to his subterranean dungeon, lies the body of John the Baptist, hands bound, blood gushing from his neck. To the right is a walled palace courtyard, where two witnesses mourn the victim. As the Gospels record (Matthew 14:2–12 and Mark 6:17–29), John publicly accused Herod of having committed adultery with Herodias, his brother Philip's wife; Herod took John prisoner without, however, daring to put him to death. Then Herodias's daughter, Salome, danced for Herod, and he was so enthralled that he promised to grant her every wish. Goaded by her mother, the girl demanded John's head. Herod was unable to recant, and ordered him killed.

Behind the execution scene beneath the portal, a wide passageway extends over two low

Rogier van der Weyden
Miraflores Altarpiece
Berlin, Gemäldegalerie SMPK

tiers of steps to a hall in the background, where Herod and Herodias are seated at a banquet. Salome kneels to present the Baptist's head to her mother, who, guilty of his death, stabs at the head in uncontrollable rage.

In the vertical mouldings Rogier has placed statues of the Apostles Paul and Bartholomew (left) and Thaddeus and Matthias (right). The reliefs along the arch represent John being questioned by priests and Levites; revealing Christ as the Messiah; warning Herod; being cast into prison; visited by disciples; and finally, Salome dancing before Herod. This last scene immediately precedes the beheading of John the Baptist. In this way, the three central events of the altar panels are placed in a larger context and, through renderings of simultaneous events from the life of Christ, are vividly and concretely linked with the story of salvation.

Jacques Daret (1400/3–68)
The Visitation

Oak, 57 × 52 cm ($22\frac{1}{2} \times 20\frac{1}{2}$ in)
Acquired with the Solly Collection, 1821
Cat. no. 542

Daret is first recorded in 1418, as 'being present at the house' of Robert Campin, who was earlier called the Master of Flémalle. After receiving his training there, he was officially apprenticed in 1427 with Rogier van der Weyden, and in 1432, earned the title of independent master. Daret's achievement was recognized and honoured early, as can be seen from commissions for extensive decoration work for a court festivity arranged by Philip the Good in Lille (1454), and for the marriage of Charles the Bold with Margaret of York, celebrated at Bruges in 1468. In the years 1434–5, 1441, and 1452, Daret worked for the St Vaast Abbey in Arras. The few pictures of his that have survived the intervening centuries stem from his first years of activity for that monastery. These are a total of four paintings which once formed the outside wings of an altarpiece executed in 1434–5 for the Lady Chapel in the monastery church. The donor was Jean du Clercq (b.1376), Abbot of St Vaast from 1428–62. Installed in the chapel in July 1435, Daret's altarpiece, as a contemporary witness records, was greatly admired by the participants at the congress then taking place in Arras, which led to a reconciliation between Philip the Good of Burgundy and Charles VII of France, and which has been recorded in history as the Peace of Arras.

A further report, from the year 1651, contains a precise description of the altarpiece with its wings painted by Daret. The central shrine was carved, with a representation of the Coronation of the Virgin in the middle, flanked on both sides by statues of the Twelve Apostles. To this shrine were attached two small wings, at the sides of its high, pinnacled superstructure, as well as two larger wings flanking the central shrine itself. The interiors of all four wings carried golden fleurs-de-lis on an azure ground, visible at both sides of the carved shrine when the altar was open. In a closed position, the exteriors of the wings with Daret's paintings of the life of the Virgin could be seen. These were originally crowned, on the two smaller panels, by an Annunciation scene which has not survived. Below it, in chronological order from the left, appeared *The Visitation* (Berlin, Gemäldegalerie SMPK), *The Nativity* (Lugano, Thyssen-Bornemisza Collection), *The Adoration of the Magi* (Berlin, Gemäldegalerie SMPK), and *The Presentation in the Temple* (Paris, Musée du Petit Palais).

The Visitation, based on the Gospel of St Luke (1 : 39–56), depicts the encounter of Mary and Elisabeth, wife of Zacharias and mother of John the Baptist. Jean du Clercq, the altar's donor, kneels in the left foreground, a devout witness to the event. His coat of arms hangs behind him on a tree; St Vaast Abbey is in the background in the middle of a flat lowlands landscape.

Jacques Daret
Altarpiece from St Vaast Abbey, Arras: exterior of wings
The Visitation
Berlin, Gemäldegalerie SMPK
The Nativity
Lugano, Thyssen-Bornemisza Collection
The Adoration of the Magi
Berlin, Gemäldegalerie SMPK
The Presentation in the Temple
Paris, Musée du Petit Palais

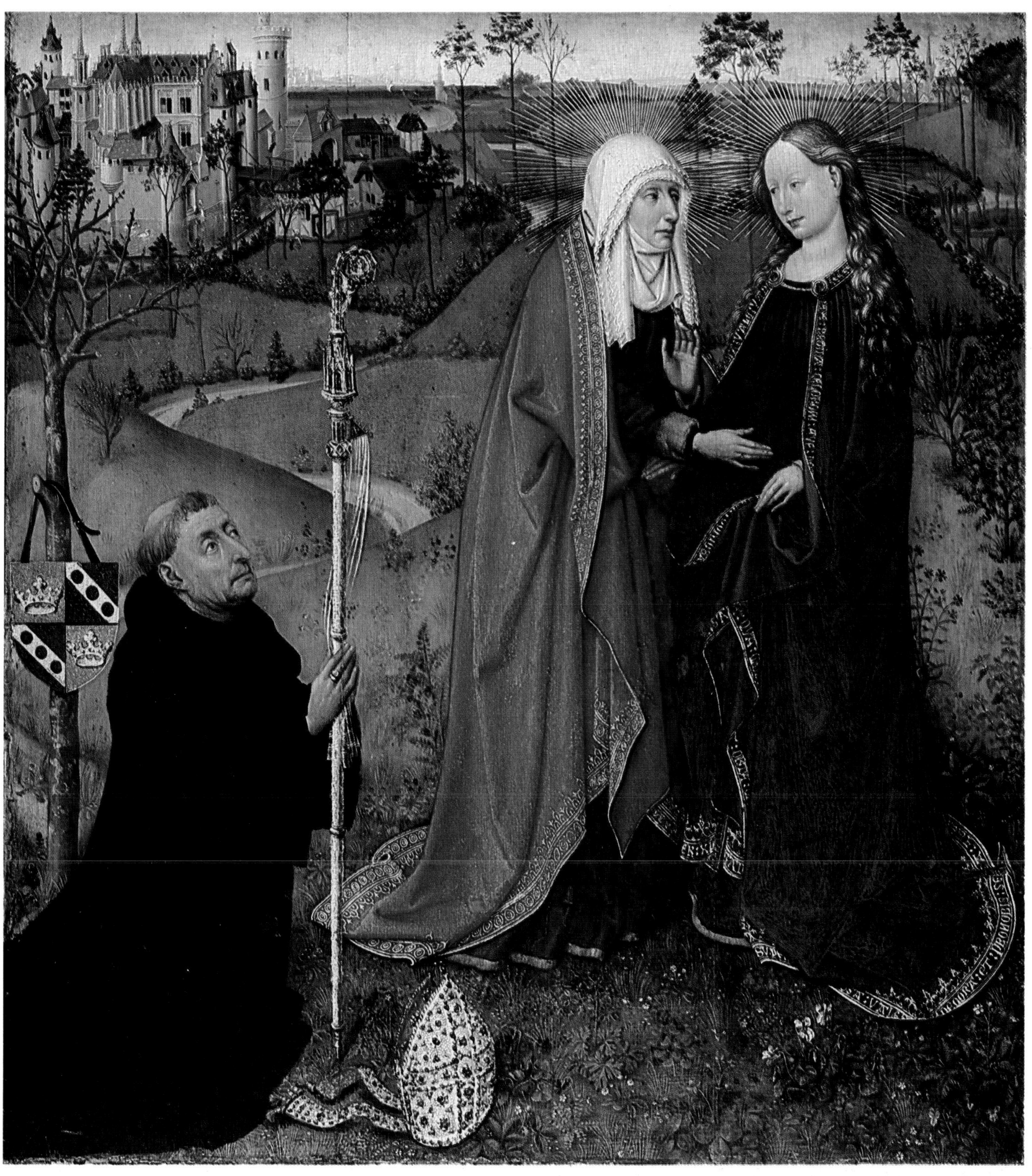

Jean Fouquet (*c.*1420–*c.*1480)

Estienne Chevalier with St Stephen

Oak, 98 × 86 cm ($38\frac{1}{2} \times 33\frac{7}{8}$ in)
Acquired 1896
Cat. no. 1617

Fouquet, the first French painter of international significance, was widely admired during his lifetime for the versatility of his talent. His portrait of Pope Eugene IV, painted in Rome from 1443 to 1447 and hung in the sacristy of S. Maria sopra Minerva, found a place of honour in the *Trattato d'architettura* (1460/4) written by the Florentine sculptor and architect, Filarete. It was also highly praised by Francesco Florio, an Italian traveller. When he saw it with other works by Fouquet in 1477, Florio remarked: 'I compare the old depictions of saints with modern ones, and think how Jean Fouquet surpasses other painters of every century with his art.'

Fouquet worked in Tours, the most important intellectual and cultural centre in France at the time, and the residence of Charles VII (1403–61) and Louis XI (1423–83). Though Fouquet did not become royal court artist until 1475, numerous paintings and book miniatures established his reputation early. The rarified taste of the Tours court and of his patrons, Mary of Cleve, the powerful Chancellor Guillaume Jouvénal des Ursins, and the influential Treasurer Estienne Chevalier, found its perfect expression in Fouquet's art. His priceless and richly illuminated *Book of Hours*, created for Estienne Chevalier, testifies just as eloquently to this as the painting here of Chevalier with St Stephen. The panel once formed the left half of a diptych that hung over Chevalier's grave in the choir of Notre-Dame in Melun, outside Paris. Originally, the panels had an elaborate frame, covered in blue velvet and ornamented with gilded medallions with Biblical scenes; these were interspersed with the first letters of the donor's Christian name in pearl embroidery. Some time after 1775, the diptych was taken down, its frame removed, and the panels sold separately. Fortunately the donor panel came into the possession of the poet Clemens Brentano and his brother Georg, who at that time owned a large portion of the famous Fouquet miniatures now at Chantilly. The panel was acquired for the museum in 1896, from the Brentano family; its counterpart with an image of the Virgin had entered the Antwerp Museum in 1840.

Estienne Chevalier, a native of Melun, rapidly advanced in the course of his career from *Secrétaire du roi* to *Trésorier de la France*. Under Charles VII and Louis XI he was entrusted with important diplomatic missions and amassed a considerable fortune. Fouquet's depiction of his determined features gives some idea of the great power and influence Chevalier must have wielded. Beside him is his name-saint, Stephen, his right hand resting on Chevalier's shoulder; in St Stephen's left hand, a book and sharp-edged stone symbolize his martyrdom. The rendering of St Stephen's spiritualized features is impressive. In the background, a wall in the Renaissance style, divided by pilasters and with inlays of coloured marble, recedes in sharp perspective. The donor's names are engraved on the plinth.

The saint and donor are turned towards the Virgin whose image appears on the panel that once formed the right part of the diptych. Angels in red and blue surround the Virgin's throne, which is richly encrusted with pearls and gems. She herself is a slender young woman whose dignified yet challenging pose seems strangely lascivious. Long tradition has it that Mary's features are those of Agnes Sorel (*c.*1422–50), the influential mistress of Charles VII, whose last will and testament Chevalier was appointed to execute. An eighteenth-century inscription on the back of the Madonna panel states that Chevalier donated the diptych in memory of Agnes Sorel. This sort of profanation was certainly not foreign to the bizarre, contradictory spirit of the era, which has been so aptly termed the 'autumn of the Middle Ages'.

Jean Fouquet
The Virgin and Child
Antwerp, Koninklijk Museum voor Schone Kunsten

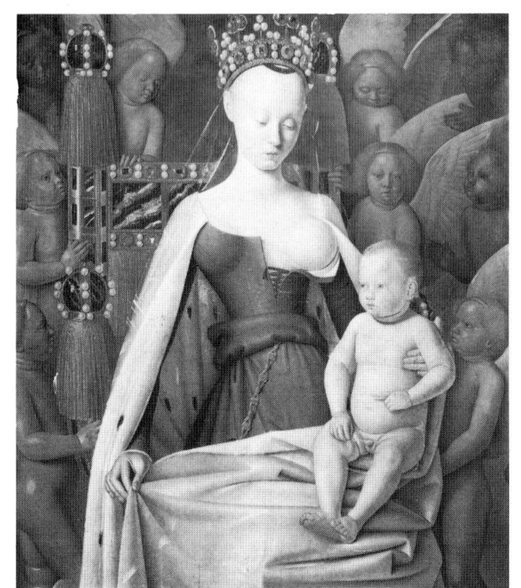

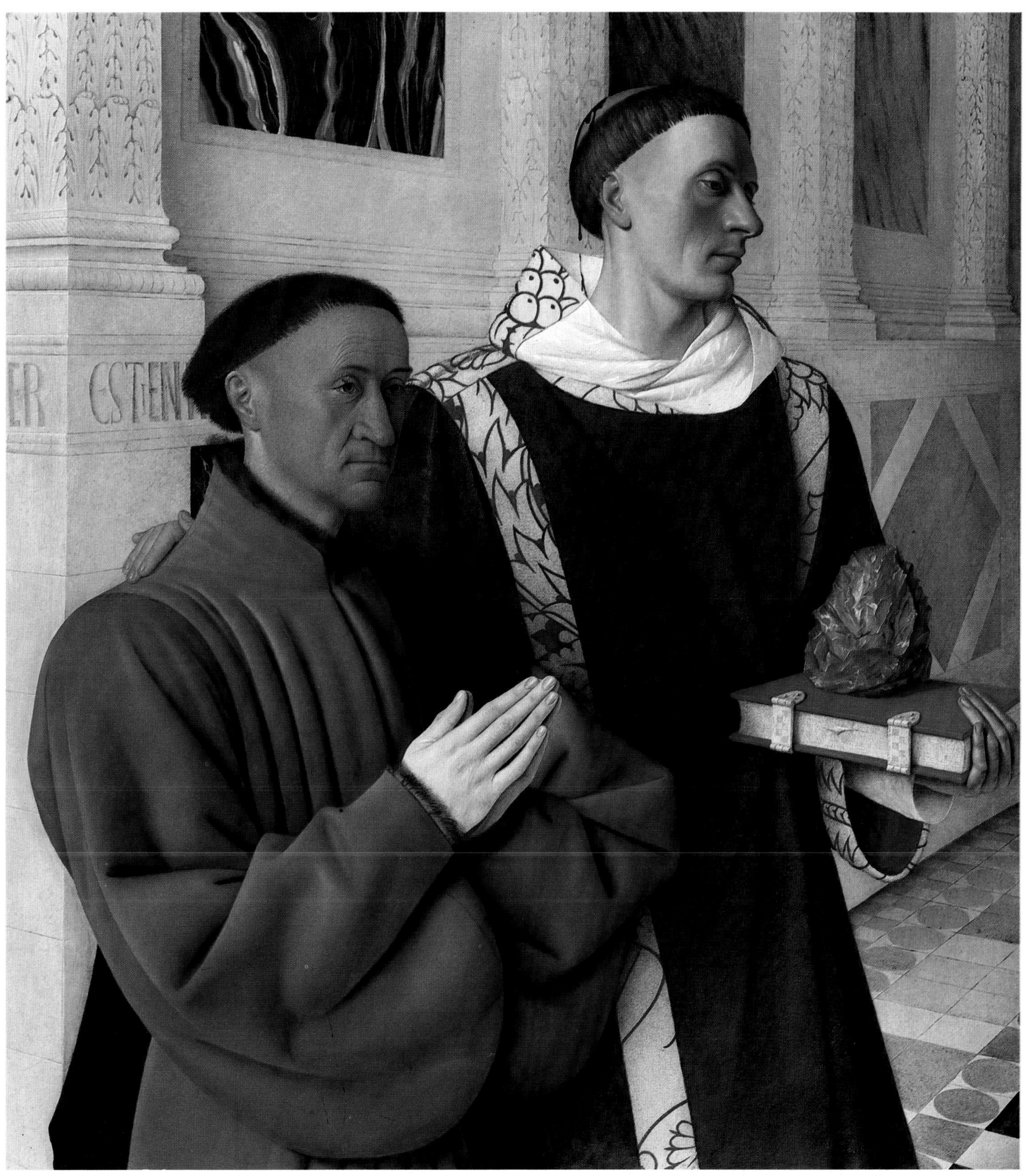

Simon Marmion (*c.*1425–89)
The Wings of the St Omer Retable: The Life of St Bertin

Oak, each wing 56 × 147 cm (22 × 57⅞ in)
Acquired 1905
Cat. nos. 1645 and 1645 A

Simon Marmion, who worked in Amiens, Valenciennes and for a time in Tournai, was among the greatest French artists of the later half of the fifteenth century. Even the earliest records praise him as a *Prince d'enluminure* and attest to the wonder with which the abundant and superbly rendered natural detail of his miniatures was received.

Marmion's major work and the point of departure for a reconstruction of his œuvre, which combined inspiration from French and Netherlandish art, is the altarpiece he did for the St Bertin Benedictine Abbey at St Omer in northern France.

The donor of this retable, which was installed in 1459 on the high altar of the abbey church, was Guillaume Fillastre, Bishop of Verdun (1437–9), Bishop of Toul (1449–60), Abbot of St Bertin (1450–73), Bishop of Tournai (1460–73), Chancellor of the Order of the Golden Fleece, and confidant of Philip the Good, the powerful Duke of Burgundy. Though the exquisite altarpiece remained in the abbey until 1791, like so many other ecclesiastical treasures it was damaged in the French Revolution. The central shrine, richly ornamented with sculptures in fine goldsmith work, was destroyed and melted down. All that survived were the wings by Marmion. After entering the collection of William II of Holland in the early nineteenth century, they came into the possession of the Prince of Wied, from whom they were acquired for the Berlin Museums. Originally, the ends of both wings were capped by pinnacled superstructures, but these were removed in the early nineteenth century and are now in the National Gallery, London. The two altar wings and associated fragments really cannot give more than a slight idea of the elaborate original retable and its monumental effect. In its open position, it was over 6 m (19 ft 8 in) wide.

The backs of the two wings are painted in *grisaille*. These exterior sides were visible when the altarpiece was closed and represented its 'everyday' aspect. At the left are Mark and Micah, John and Solomon, and the Archangel Gabriel, who is associated with the Virgin of the Annunciation on the right wing. The figures of David, Matthew, Isaiah, and Luke appear on her right. The kings, prophets, and four Evangelists, who carry banderoles

Simon Marmion
Saint-Omer Retable
Exterior of wings

and are identified by names inscribed beneath them, are arranged in pairs in painted niches flanking the Annunciation scene. These figures also refer to the painting on the original altar shrine, which bore an image of the Crucifixion at its centre with a gilded Tree of Life above it to symbolize Christ's work of salvation and its passing on to men through the wine of the Eucharistic blood.

The images on the inside of the wings that once flanked the gilded shrine are particularly striking for their colour scheme of great brilliancy and crystal clarity, and for their extraordinary abundance of detail. Together these images form a comprehensive cycle of five scenes, separated by elaborate architectural motifs, that record events from the life of St Bertin, the founder and titular saint of the monastery.

St Bertin was born in about 615 near Coutances (Manche) and died on 5 September 698. He entered the monastic order in Luxeuil (Haute Saône), became bishop of Thérouanne (Pas-de-Calais), and founded the Sithiu Monastery – renamed St Bertin in 1100 – whose abbot he was from 670 to his death. From the year 745 he was revered as a saint.

The sequence begins in the left corner of the left altar wing, with a depiction of the donor, Guillaume Fillastre, dressed in a bishop's vestments and kneeling before an open missal. A chaplain stands behind him. An angel hovering above him carries his coat of arms. Other angels, singing and playing, are represented on the superstructure of the image (now in London). The donor's gaze is directed towards the adjacent scenes from the life of St Bertin – his birth, then his investiture in the monastery of Luxeuil, where he is shown once in the foreground, humbly kneeling beneath the church portal, and again in the background, praying before the choir screen. The following scene, devoted to St Bertin's pilgrimage, shows him being received, with the monks Ebertramne and Momelin, by St Omer in Thérouanne. Next comes a rendering of the dedication and construction of the new monastery, with St Bertin accepting the gift of land from the rulers of the demesne, the knight Adrowald, whose castle is in the background near the River Aa. On the water is a boat with the saint and his attendants, who are being guided by an angel of the Lord to the place destined for the monastery.

The story continues on the right wing with the Miracle of the Wine. This legend recounts how the knight Waldbert, having neglected to receive the monastery's blessing, is thrown from his horse while hunting. Waldbert send his page to St Bertin for a consecrated drink, and when he arrives at the monastery, an empty cask miraculously fills with wine. Here, the monk Duodon kneels before the cask as the page and St Bertin witness the miracle. The next scene shows the knight, healed and converted, renouncing the world to enter the

monastery with his son. Their example is followed by four other Breton noblemen in the next image. The walls of the Gothic cloister in the background of these two scenes have a continuous frieze of the Dance of Death, a symbol of the transience of all earthly things, which strikes awe into the hearts of the young noblemen looking at it. Nor was St Bertin himself spared the temptations of the flesh, for in the following compartment we see him confronted with the apparition of a lovely woman finely dressed but the claws for feet – a demon of the underworld, being exorcised by St Martin of Tours. In the final scene of the sequence, St Bertin lies on his deathbed, mourned by a noble patron of the monastery and by monks who administer the last sacraments. The superstructure that once capped this scene, now in London, shows St Bertin's soul ascending to heaven.

The brilliance of the palette and the detail of the rendering prove Marmion's extraordinary talent as a miniaturist. The handling of light is also remarkable; it plays across the architectural motifs in subtle nuances and lends an atmosphere of unprecedented intimacy to the rooms. From the dimly lighted donor's cell and saint's death-room, the illumination gradually strengthens into the brilliant sunlight flooding the landscape, which served as a transition to the shimmering, gold-encrusted sculptures of the original central shrine.

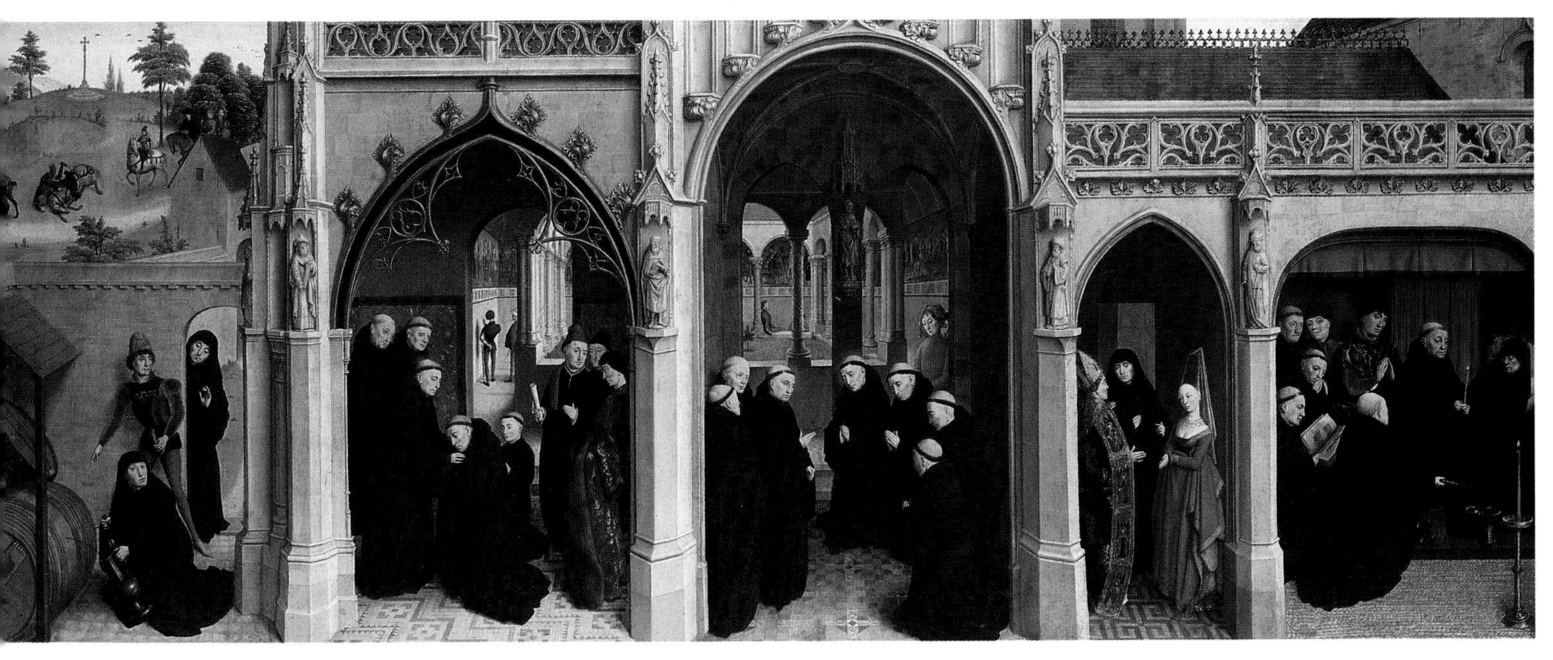

Dieric Bouts (1410/20–75)

Christ in the House of Simon the Pharisee

Oak, 40.5 × 61 cm (16 × 24 in)
Acquired from the Collection of A. Thiem, 1904
Cat. no. 533 A

The event pictured here goes back to the story in St Luke's Gospel (7:36–50) where Simon the Pharisee invites Jesus to eat with him. During the meal a woman of the town appears, a sinner not named by the Evangelist but who later came to be identified with Mary Magdalene, the sister of Lazarus. She kneels before Jesus, washes his feet with her tears, dries them with her hair, kisses and anoints them with oil. The Pharisee is scandalized and reproves Christ under his breath, 'This man, if he were a prophet, would have known who and what manner of woman this is that toucheth him: for she is a sinner.' Jesus replies with a parable, explaining his behaviour to Simon in a form he can understand. There was once a creditor, Jesus begins, who had two debtors, one of whom owed five hundred pence and the other fifty, and both of whose debts he forgave. Which of these would love him more? 'I suppose that he, to whom he forgave most.' replies Simon without hesitation. Then Jesus recalls that Simon had neither kissed nor anointed him when he entered the house and that he had received more abundant gifts from the outcast woman at his feet than from the rich Pharisee. For that reason, many sins would be forgiven her, 'for she loved much: but to whom little is forgiven, the same loveth little'. And to the sinner, 'Thy faith hath saved thee; go in peace.'

According to the *Legende aurea* of Jacobus de Voragine (1230–98/9), it was Mary Magdalene 'who in the time of grace first did penitence; who chose the best part; who at the feet of the Lord heard His word and anointed His head; who stood next to the cross at the death of the Lord; who there prepared ointment, to anoint His body; who did not forsake the grave when the apostles went away; to whom Christ first appeared after His Resurrection; and whom He made Apostle of the Apostles.'

The scene is set in the shallow space of a room with a wooden, barrel-vaulted ceiling. Two side-entrances lead to another room on the right, and to a colonnaded forecourt on the left through which a distant landscape is visible. In the centre of the room is a table set with plates of smoked fish, earthen jars, glasses, knives and bread – a beautifully composed still life in its own right. Simon is seated behind the table in the middle, bending forward at the unwelcome interruption of his meal; his mouth is slightly open as if he were about to express his disapprobation of the scene. Christ, seated as a guest of the house at his host's right, looks down calmly at the woman kneeling before him, blessing her act with his raised right hand. Astonishment and discomfiture also characterize the pose and gesture of Peter, seated to the left of the Pharisee, while John turns to the priest kneeling beside him as if to explain. This figure at the right is a portrait of the painting's donor. In the white robes of a Carthusian monk, he kneels reverentially at the side of the table, hands folded in prayer, his distinguished face turned aside, looking into the indeterminable distance.

Dieric Bouts, a native of Haarlem, received his first artistic training there before emigrating to the southern Netherlands. He settled in Louvain in about 1445, married in 1448, and soon had achieved great renown and considerable prosperity. In 1468 he was elevated to the prestigious position of Town Artist of Louvain. Bouts's major works were painted on commissions from the Municipal Council and the religious orders of this famous university town. Sint Pieterskerk in Louvain still preserves his famous triptych with *The Last Supper*, painted from 1464 to 1467 for the Brethren of the Holy Sacrament.

Though the painting in our collection antedates his major works, it already contains all the essential traits of Bouts's art – a lovingly delineated interior with carefully planned and balanced illumination, shimmering intense colours, and figures who appear self-engrossed, as if withdrawn into themselves. The compelling and memorable simplicity of this image has struck many later observers. Besides the artist's son, Aelbrecht Bouts, a number of other masters have taken this treatment of the theme as a model and a point of departure for their own compositions.

Aelbrecht Bouts (after Dieric Bouts)
Christ in the House of Simon the Pharisee
Brussels, Koninklijke Musea voor Schone Kunsten

The fascination of Dieric Bouts's work derives largely from a superb sense of interior space, developed during his training in the northern Netherlands and through profound study of the work of Petrus Christus and Rogier van der Weyden. The role of space is so dominating in solidly positioning the figures, which appear so static and immutable, that the time factor seems eliminated. This is the key to the timeless and often enigmatic sublimity of Dieric Bouts's art.

Hugo van der Goes (1440/5–82)

The Adoration of the Magi
(Monforte Altarpiece)
*c.*1470

Oak, 147 × 242 cm ($57\frac{7}{8} \times 95\frac{1}{4}$ in); centre raised 9 × 76.3 cm ($3\frac{1}{2} \times 30$ in), originally higher but cut down by about 70 cm ($27\frac{1}{2}$ in) at an unknown later date. Acquired from the Monforte de Lemos Monastery, northern Spain, 1914
Cat. no. 1718

By the time Hugo van der Goes became an independent master in his home town of Ghent in 1467, Petrus Christus and Dieric Bouts in Bruges and Louvain had reached artistic maturity, and Hans Memling had just received citizen's rights in Bruges two years before. Van der Goes's advance to become the leading artist in Ghent, which was the site of the van Eyck brothers' magnificent altarpiece, led to the renascence of that city as a centre of art.

Van der Goes's achievement is even more remarkable because of the fact that all the works by him known today were done in only fifteen years. His major work was created for Tommaso Portinari, a representative in Bruges of the Medici Florentine banking house. This altarpiece, now in the Uffizi in Florence, attributed to van der Goes on the basis of Vasari's reports, formed the point of departure for a reconstruction of the artist's œuvre.

In 1473 van der Goes was nominated Dean of the Ghent Artists' Guild, but only held this office for a short time. In the spring of 1477, at the height of his fame, he entered the 'Rode Klooster' near Brussels as a lay brother. Despite a serious mental illness he remained active there until his death in 1482. Albrecht Dürer, who travelled through the Netherlands in 1520–1, noted in his diary the names of those artists he considered the greatest: Jan van Eyck, Rogier van der Weyden, and Hugo van der Goes.

The present altarpiece, named after its place of origin, the remote Monforte de Lemos Monastery in northern Spain, belongs among the artist's first major achievements. It is not known how the work came into the possession of this monastery, which was founded in 1593. Nor has it been determined who commissioned it, or the church for which it was originally intended.

The Adoration of the Magi was once the central panel of a large triptych. The intricate moulding of the old frame still bears iron hinges on its sides where movable wings were originally mounted. Replicas of the altarpiece (particularly of the middle panel) by contemporaries and followers of the artist, indicate that the composition was soon regarded as exemplary. This, however, was no insurance against the damage inflicted on it and on so many fine works of art in later centuries. Among other things, the wings of the altar were lost, and the rectangular top extension of the central panel truncated. Of the angels descending from above, only the hems of their garments remain.

This huge and imposing altar, which with opened wings measured almost 6 m (19 ft 6 in) wide, takes us into a new sphere of early Netherlandish art. It is a mature work that shows van der Goes at the zenith of his powers. The figures, unusual in their physical monumentality and inner grandeur, are convincingly integrated in the surrounding space, and possess a presence and dignity previously unknown in Netherlandish art. It is highly indicative that at the Monforte Monastery, this painting was ascribed to Rubens.

Probably no second Biblical event challenged the imagination of the faithful as much as the story of the Adoration of the Magi. So strikingly different from the Nativity, this story is recounted only in the Gospel of St Matthew (2:1–12). Seeing a new star in the sky and interpreting it as a sign that the King of the Jews had been born, three wise men from the East went to Jerusalem where they asked Herod how to find the birthplace of the new king. Troubled by this question, Herod gathered his chief priests and scribes in counsel, and they pointed the way to Bethlehem. Led by the star, the three Magi found the Child, whom they worshipped and to whom they made offerings of gifts.

This simple story was later embroidered by theology and popular faith. Tertullian decided the wise men were kings, and Origines then said there were three because of the three gifts mentioned in St Matthew. The names they are still popularly known by today, Caspar, Melchior and Balthasar, first occurred in the ninth century. During the High Middle Ages the three kings were regarded as emissaries from the three then-known kingdoms of the world: Europe, Africa and Asia. This explains why one of them was so often depicted as a Negro or Ethiopian.

In front of a ruined wall of a once magnificent palace, Mary is seated in tranquil dignity looking down at the naked Child, whom she gently supports in her lap with both hands. The Infant's attention is not so much captured by the great men who have come to pay obeisance to him as directed towards the spectator, at whom he looks. Joseph kneels in the foreground, having bared his head to greet the three kings. The eldest, kneeling in prayer before the Infant, has humbly removed his ornate crown. Before him on a stone is his gift, a chalice full of coins. The second king also kneels and with a gesture of his hand expresses deep reverence as his page beside him presents his offering. At the right, as if completely lost in wondering adoration, stands the African king, holding an exquisite vessel. The three kings are compellingly characterized, among other things by their different ages – a motif that arose in the fourteenth century and symbolizes the three ages of man. Behind the third king near the right edge of the painting, and behind the low barrier in the centre, are the royal retinues, who are involved in the event in various ways. The shepherds in the distance, according to a fourteenth-century tale by Johannes von Hildesheim, told the kings about the miracle they had witnessed and showed them the way to the stable. These shepherds were considered the elect among the Jews, just as the kings were the elect among heathens. Their combined appearance in this painting may be understood as a reference to the unifying force of the church established by Christ. To the left is an opening view of a village street, where the villagers watch as the kings' knights cross a bridge and dismount to lead their horses.

Hugo van der Goes
The Adoration of the Magi (Monforte Altarpiece)
Reconstruction of original state of central panel

The iris blossoms next to the ruined wall in the foreground were associated at that period with the sword which, as Simeon predicted (Luke 2:35), would pierce Mary's heart at the sight of her son's suffering. According to the *Revelations* of St Birgitta of Sweden, written in the late fourteenth century, 'Like the leaf of the iris, Mary had two very sharp edges: her heartrending pain over the agony of her son, and her steadfast defence against all the cunning of the Devil. So, truly, Simeon had prophesied that a sword would pierce her soul. For she was compelled to feel at her heart this sword's sharp blade as often as she foresaw in her mind's eye the wounds and torments of her son, whose witness she became at the Passion.' The columbine growing in the right foreground, venerated for its miraculous healing powers during the Middle Ages, belongs in the same symbolic context, being frequently used as a reference to the Virgin.

The stately calm and extraordinary monumentality of the realistic figures far transcend anything achieved in Netherlandish art until then. The worship of the future Monarch of the World has rarely been so memorably embodied as in the contrast between the newborn Infant, unconscious of his mission, and the venerable aspect of the eldest king with his worn, heavy hands folded in prayer. Here the mystery of salvation is given devout and compelling expression, whose truth to life does not detract at all from the formal sublimity of the composition.

Hugo van der Goes
The Lamentation of Christ

Canvas, 53.5 × 38.5 cm (21 × 15⅛ in)
Acquired as gift from O. Huldschinsky, 1900
Cat. no. 1622

Painted in tempera on canvas, this work is among the few of its kind – once known as '*Tüchlein*' or 'little cloths' – which have survived from the fifteenth century. The fragile paint surface, the canvas material, and the damp climate north of the Alps, have taken their toll on these paintings, and the surviving ones are often in poor condition. Hugo van der Goes's *Lamentation* is interesting for this reason, but also because it is an early example of the compositional form of a group with half-figures.

The painting shows Christ's next of kin mourning his death. They are drawn together and united in their shared sorrow, expressed by the artist with great subtlety. In the foreground, a youthful Mary, head inclined, crosses her hands over her breast in a gesture of profound submission. Supporting her is John, Christ's favourite disciple, his hand on her shoulder in an attempt to console her. To their right, Mary Magdalene expresses her sorrow, wringing her hands and turning her tear-stained face aside. The group is completed by the two other Marys, Mary Salome and Mary Jacobi, one with hands raised in lament and the other dabbing the tears from her eyes. Golgotha beneath a strip of blue sky is visible in the background. The painting's colour scheme, once accented by John's brilliant red mantle and Mary's blue gown, now appears faded and subdued.

The composition and its story are of course incomplete without the focus of the group's lamentation – the image of the dead Christ which once formed the companion-piece. Though numerous copies of the two canvases, especially a remarkable reinterpretation by Hans Memling (Granada, Capilla Real), conveyed an impression of the original, the companion-piece to the *Lamentation* was not discovered until 1950. Now in the Wildenstein Gallery, New York, *The Deposition* focuses entirely on the presentation of Christ's body by three men who hold it up frontally towards the spectator. The lifeless body with the wound in its side and its dangling arms forms the centre of interest; a shadowy Golgotha and the ladder on which Christ was taken from the cross are the only suggestions of the place and time of the event.

The two companion paintings are now generally referred to as *The Small Deposition*, to distinguish them from van der Goes's *Large Deposition*, a horizontal composition that has not survived though it has been recorded in over forty copies made in the sixteenth century.

The lasting admiration these compositions have inspired surely owes much to the adaptation of the half-figure to a subject full of action and involving many figures. This enrichment in form and content shaped the development of the 'narrative half-figure image' in Netherlandish painting far into the sixteenth century. Van der Goes's *Lamentation* proves how very well suited this genre was to concentrating interest solely on the figures' emotions and moods, and to achieving a corresponding concentration of pictorial content.

Hugo van der Goes
The Deposition
New York, Wildenstein Gallery

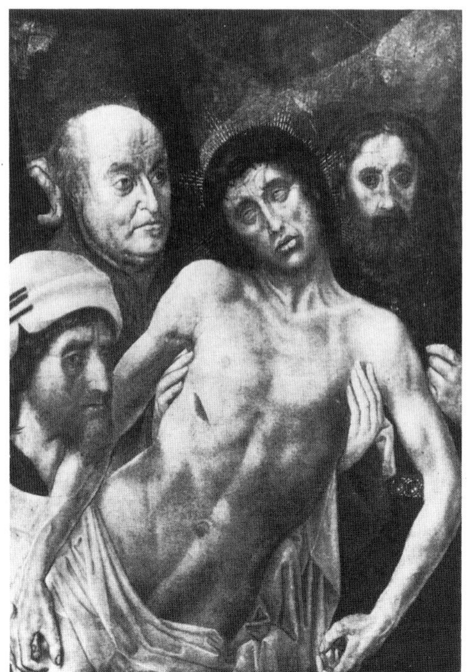

Hugo van der Goes

The Adoration of the Shepherds

*c.*1480

Oak, 97 × 245 cm ($38\frac{1}{8}$ × $96\frac{1}{2}$ in)
Collection of the Infante, Don Sebastian, Pau Castle (southern France)
Acquired from the estate of Christina of Bourbon, Madrid, 1903
Cat. no. 1622 A

This painting was probably done in about 1480, during the artist's last productive years. By that time van der Goes had gone into retreat as a lay brother of the 'Rode Klooster', in Soignies Forest near Brussels, where his step-brother Nikolaus also lived as a monk. Terrible bouts of depression had moved the artist to renounce the world and submit himself to a severe, monastic regime. According to the monastery chronicles of 1509–13, the prior of 'Rode Klooster' was a lover of art who granted van der Goes many favours and privileges. Travels to Louvain and Cologne are mentioned, as well as visits from such high-ranking men as Archduke Maximilian, who later became Emperor Maximilian I. The artist spent the last years of his life in constant worry that he would not be able to finish the commissions that reached him even in his monastic isolation.

Due to its unusual size, *The Adoration of the Shepherds* has sometimes been considered a predella, that is, the substructure of an altarpiece. This is unlikely for a number of reasons. The most important is its striking difference from his *Adoration of the Magi* of Monforte – its completely new approach in drawing, modelling and palette. The colours have a comparatively subdued character, corresponding to a simplification of line in the drapery and contours of the figures. The change might be summed up as an increase in the dynamic quality of pictorial form.

Mary and the Child in the manger are worshipped by angels while, from the left, shepherds approach hurriedly, falling to their knees or apparently halting in mid-stride with astonished wonder at the miracle before their eyes. Details such as the half-open mouth of the man panting with the exertion of his run, are rendered with great virtuosity. The image is framed on the left and right by two half-figures whose exaggerated size clearly distinguishes them from the smaller figures of the Adoration scene. These figures, identified as prophets, have opened the curtains concealing the great event of salvation, the birth of Christ. They stand aside to proclaim the incarnation of God and its profound significance to the observer. Though the theme of Old Testament prophets revealing the truth of the New Testament was familiar in medieval art, van der Goes's rendering of it is quite original. He may have been inspired by the popular liturgical Christmas plays that were performed near the altar and whose characters included prophets announcing the incarnation. Whatever the case, he has translated the theological message into a humanly moving one which speaks directly to the feelings of the faithful.

A striking detail is the open curtain hanging from a very realistic rod along the top edge of the painting. Old inventories and traditional iconography show that altar curtains of this type were in use from the early Middle Ages and became a common feature of altars in the fourteenth and fifteenth centuries. These curtains were fastened to movable arms or to rods mounted on columns at both sides of the altar. They had a decorative function too, as shown by the variety of materials and colours used; green cloth such as that in the painting is expressly mentioned in an entry in the 1479 inventories of the Bruges Tanners' Guild. The main purpose of such curtains, however, was to prevent the priest from being disturbed by the many people gathered around the altar during mass, and at the same time to emphasize the sanctity of the sacramental ceremony. This special task of altar curtains, and the priest's role, were wonderfully described by Berthold von Chiemsee, who in 1535 wrote: 'The priest at the altar must not turn around; for whoever lays his hand on the plough and looks behind him, is unfitted for the Kingdom of God. Therefore, there are usually two curtains on both sides, so as to signify that the altar is the inner, most Holy tabernacle behind the curtain.'

The sacramental symbolism of the image is underlined by the sheaf of grain lying in front of the manger. It conveys a reference to Christ's words, 'I am the bread which came down from heaven' (John 6:41). The Church understood this passage to refer both to the incarnation and to the Sacrament of the Last Supper. The parallels between the Child in the manger and the bread on the altar are central to van der Goes's painting. Not only does he narrate the unprecedented event of Christ's birth and the shepherds' adoration; beyond that, he points to the coming sacrifice of Christ and to its continual, symbolic renewal in mass and communion.

The plants in the foreground also deserve closer inspection. These are herbs used in medieval medicine to whose healing qualities were attributed specific symbolic meanings. At the far left is herb-robert (*Geranium robertianum*) with its pink blossoms, reddish tinged, feathered leaves, and beak-shaped seeds. Then speedwell (*Veronica officinalis*) and black nightshade (*Solanum nigrum*), recognizable from its black berries and white flowers. Herb-robert was highly valued throughout the Middle Ages and was used to cure many illnesses. The names by which it was popularly known in Germany, God's Gift and God's Grace Herb, emphasize its great therapeutic powers. According to Paracelsus (1493–1541), the drug distilled from herb-robert strengthened the heart and was also effective in relieving symptoms of depression. Speedwell was a frequently used herb in medieval medicine known popularly in Germany as 'cure of all ills' and 'all-heal'. In Hieronymus Bock's *Kreutterbuch*, speedwell is recommended among other things as a cure for dizziness, failing memory, and stomach ailments.

Hugo van der Goes
Portinari Altarpiece
Central panel
Florence, Uffizi

Black or deadly nightshade, a poisonous plant, yields a drug with a pain-killing and soporific effect. It has been known as a reliable sedative since ancient times. Not surprisingly, deadly nightshade was also popularly believed to be good against witchcraft. It used to be placed in babies' cradles to drive away demons. Tradition has it that nightshade was much esteemed by shepherds, who used it to cure various animal diseases. These notions were so familiar to the artist and his contemporaries that he has represented the Christ Child holding a blossoming sprig of deadly nightshade in his right hand. This suggests that the Child is protected from all evil, and that the demons of the underworld are powerless against him. In his *Portinari Altarpiece* (Florence, Uffizi), van der Goes depicted the Devil incarnate concealed in the shadows of the stall, to show that with Christ's birth, his power was broken. The same idea echoes in the *Legenda aurea*, where we read, 'The birth of Our Lord was also munificent in great good. The first good is protection against the Devil. For now the Evil One may not injure us so gravely as he formerly did.'

The multiple symbolism of the image is combined with an equally compelling composition, symmetrically arranged and yet extremely dynamic. This, with the timeless immediacy of its content and feeling, reveals Hugo van der Goes's extraordinary artistic stature.

Aelbert van Ouwater (*c.*1415–*c.*1475)
The Raising of Lazarus
*c.*1450–60

Oak, 122 × 92 cm (48 × 36¼ in)
Acquired from the collection of the Marchese Mamelli, Genoa, 1889
Cat. no. 532 A

The only knowledge we have of Ouwater, a highly significant figure in the development of northern Netherlandish art in the fifteenth century, is based on a report by Carel van Mander, painter, poet and art writer of Haarlem. In his *Schilderboeck*, van Mander maintains that prior to Ouwater, the northern Netherlands produced no artist to match Jan van Eyck (*c.*1390–1441) or Rogier van der Weyden (1399/1400–64). Thanks to Ouwater, who lived at about the same time as van Eyck, the county of Holland was able to join the powerful cities of Flanders and Brabant in contributing to the glorious tradition of Netherlandish art.

Van Mander's book is particularly important for its description of two works by Ouwater which were in the Grote Kerk in Haarlem before the Spanish invaders took them as booty in 1573. Speaking of his *Altarpiece of the Roman Pilgrims* with *The Apostles Taking Leave of Jesus* (which has not survived), van Mander praises Ouwater's superb skill in painting landscape. He then goes on to give a detailed account of *The Raising of Lazarus*: 'There was a quite large vertical panel by Ouwater there, an under-painted copy of which I have seen, namely *The Raising of Lazarus*. The original, along with other beautiful works of art, was removed under false pretences by the Spanish after the siege and surrender of Haarlem, and taken to Spain. The Lazarus was a very fine and extremely lucidly treated nude by the standards of the time. The painting also showed temple architecture which was lovely though its columns and other elements were a bit small. On one side stood Apostles, on the other were Jews. A few pretty ladies were also present, and in the background a crowd of people peered through the little columns of the choir. Heemskerck [Haarlem artist, 1498–1574] often used to pore over this painting insatiably, and once he said to its owner, who was his pupil, "My son, what can these people have eaten?" which was as much as to say that these masters must have spent incredible time and effort to achieve this type of thing.' This report by van Mander led to the rediscovery and purchase of the panel. Reputedly once in the possession of King Philip II of Spain, it is the only known work by Ouwater to have survived.

The traditional theme of Christ raising Lazarus is treated in a new and unusual way, and the design and composition of figures and space are also new. Every nuance of the light shining through the windows of the ambulatory has remarkable clarity. In the play of light and shadow, the columns of the choir, the window embrasures, arcades and ambulatory columns take on great sculptural relief. By contrast, the wall separating the choir from the passage is held in a neutral tone to provide a suitable background for the figures in front of it.

The story of the miracle performed by Christ in Bethany near Jerusalem is told in the Gospel of St John (11:1–45). Lazarus lay ill in the house of his sisters, Martha and Mary, who went to Jesus and asked him to come quickly. Jesus, knowing that Lazarus had died, delayed to explain to his disciples that this sickness was for the Glory of God. When they finally arrived in Bethany, his disciples heard that Lazarus had been in the grave for four days. After meeting Martha and telling her that he is the resurrection and the life, Jesus raised Lazarus: 'And when he thus had spoken, he cried with a loud voice, Lazarus, come forth. And he that was dead came forth, bound hand and foot with graveclothes: and his face was bound about with a napkin' (John 11:43–4).

This is the dramatic climax of the events in the painting. Lazarus, arisen from the open grave in the floor, sits on the stone facing the viewer, the shroud across his legs. His hands are thrown up in astonishment as he looks, dazed, into the distance. Christ stands next to him at the left, blessing him with a raised hand. At Christ's side, Mary faces her brother, kneeling in prayer. Martha and three disciples complete the group around Jesus. Standing opposite them is a group of Jews in rich clothes who had come to console Mary. Now,

Aelbert van Ouwater
The Raising of Lazarus
Detail: *The Sacrifice of Isaac*

shocked and incredulous, they turn away from the grave and its former inhabitant, and they hold handkerchiefs to their mouths and noses to ward off the smell of decay. Between these two groups with their different reactions stands Peter who, gesturing eloquently, tries to convince the Jews of the profound significance of what they have seen. Peter holds an unusually prominent place in the centre of the composition. Ouwater depicts him as the leader of the Church, using a missionary's eloquence towards the disbelief of the Jews there – the people who would later call for the death of Christ.

Diverging from the Bible story in which Lazarus arose from a cave in the rock closed by a stone, Ouwater sets the scene in the choir of a Romanesque church. A milling crowd looks on through a barred door in the wall between choir and ambulatory. On the capitals of the columns between the choir windows are reliefs of Old Testament scenes: on the left, the Flight of Hagar and Ishmael (Genesis 21:9–21) and the Sacrifice of Isaac (Genesis 22:1–19). And on the right, Moses and the Burning Bush (Exodus 3:1 ff.) and Moses receiving, then proclaiming the Ten Commandments to the Israelites (Exodus 31:18 and 34:29). Like the old Romanesque architecture, these Old Testament scenes signify that with Christ's advent a new era has begun, an era promising redemption to the faithful. The prophesies of the Old Testament, it was thought, envisaged Christ and his works, just as Abraham's sacrifice was long associated with Christ, the innocent, sacrificial Lamb of God, and understood as a symbol of the Holy Communion.

But belief in Christ's divine mission was probably fed most by his miraculous healings and resurrections. Already in the early Christian period, the raising of Lazarus was a symbol of the resurrection of all men after death. Ambrosius, one of the three great Western church teachers in the fifth century, stated that Christ had not only raised Lazarus but through this miracle had fortified the hearts of all Christians in the belief that their souls would be saved at the Last Judgement. It cannot be a coincidence that Ouwater represents Lazarus here in a pose like that of the saved souls in many depictions of the Last Judgement, nor that the separate groups of believers and unbelievers resemble the division between good and evil in the visions of Doomsday.

All this indicates that Ouwater, depicting the historical event, was also concerned to illustrate its consequences to the faithful and unfaithful for all time to come. In truth, what he created was a doctrinal image whose subject is the power of faith. Central to the message of Ouwater's *Raising of Lazarus* are the words Christ spoke to Mary: 'I am the resurrection, and the life: he that believeth in me, though he were dead, yet shall he live: And whosoever liveth and believeth in me shall never die' (John 11:25–6).

Hieronymus Bosch (*c.*1450–1516)

St John on Patmos

*c.*1490

Oak, 63 × 43.3 cm ($24\frac{3}{4}$ × 17 in)
Signed lower right: 'Jheronimus b[osch]'
Collection of W. Fuller Maitland, Stanstead House, London
Acquired 1907
Cat. no. 1647 A

Born in s'Hertogenbosch, which was chartered in 1184 and at that time belonged to the Duchy of Brabant, Hieronymus van Aken (his family originated in Aachen) later adopted the name of his home town, which he never left. Among the greatest Netherlandish artists, he gave provincial s'Hertogenbosch a lasting place in the history of art. Bosch came of humble origins, but marriage brought him a considerable fortune; judging by his income tax returns, he was one of the richest men in town. He was also a member of the distinguished 'Our Blessed Virgin' fraternity, and his name appears frequently in its registers in connection with artistic commissions, among other things. His paintings, so obviously different in approach from the works of his contemporaries, brought him great fame even during his lifetime. Among the admirers of his art were Philip the Handsome, Duke of Burgundy and Brabant; Margaret of Austria, Governess of the Netherlands; Cardinal Grimani of Venice; Diego de Guevara, Treasurer to Margaret of Austria; and King Philip II of Spain. Philip II especially found Bosch's art profoundly fascinating, and decorated his private chambers in the Escorial Palace with much of his work. A table-top with a painting of the Seven Deadly Sins and the Four Last Things (Madrid, Prado) was a continual source of inspiration for the orthodox King's meditations. Even in his hour of death he had this *memento mori* in front of him.

Bosch stands alone in the way he translated his themes and visions into imagery. Artists have rarely addressed the observer so directly, or illustrated so poignantly the foolishness and depravity of the world and the consequences of sin. In many of his works, Bosch seems a moralist in the Christian sense. His depictions of human fallibility reflect the beliefs of a period when the end of the world and the terrors of the Last Judgement seemed imminent: it was a time concerned with why men did not repent instead of wallowing in temporal pleasures. In this respect, Bosch's work is one of the most compelling records extant of the attitudes of mind that prevailed at the close of the fifteenth century shortly before the Reformation.

In the traditional subjects from the life and Passion of Christ and from the lives of the saints that Bosch painted with great penetration, he largely depended on the iconographic tradition. But even here he introduced an aspect that was unprecedented. He pictured the divine realm surrounded by a world whose elements, both organic and inorganic, were infused with evil. His earth abounds with demons composed of human, animal, and inorganic parts which, despite their lack of resemblance to all known forms of life, could not be more vital. Hemmed around by these creatures, even a saint seems powerless to do more than endure them with steadfast patience.

This is the mood of *St John on Patmos*, an image whose meaning would appear to be relatively straightforward. Its main figure, St John, was thought during the Middle Ages to be the author of the Book of the Apocalypse, which describes the end of mankind. He is seated on a grassy mound, which is apparently the foothill of a mountain, a book open on his knee and a quill in hand. His youthful face, given in profile, is turned upwards as he gazes into the sky. Behind him extends a wide landscape whose details gradually blur in the distant haze, and whose depth is underlined by a slender tree in the middleground. The abundant details of the scene include a broad river with undulating shoreline, low hills, woods, meadows, a farmstead, and a town on the horizon. It is a peaceful landscape that recalls less the island of Patmos than the plains of the Lower Rhine, somewhere near Arnhem or Nijmegen. On closer scrutiny, however, this tranquillity proves deceptive. Stranded ships burn and sink within hailing distance of the mainland, where the gallows tree of the Last Judgement looms.

The saint seems quite oblivious of all this, seeing only the heavenly vision revealed to him by an angel. This angel, standing on the mountain in the middleground, has large,

Hieronymus Bosch
St John on Patmos
Reverse: Scenes of Christ's Passion in circular arrangement

fantastically shaped wings which, like its clothes, hands and face are suffused with a whitish blue tone that merges with the sky. In the pale sun-disc surrounded by clouds is the apparition of the apocalyptic woman who from the twelfth century was identified with the Virgin Mary. She holds the Child in her lap, wears a starry crown, and is seated on a crescent moon (Apocalypse 12:1). Transfixed by the vision, St John prepares to record it in his book. Next to him is his symbolic animal, the eagle, which Bosch has pictured as a falcon, a bird more familiar to him. It keeps a sharp eye on the writing implements at his master's feet as at the right, a demon with an iron hook, afraid to steal them, retreats, throwing up his arms in fright. This is one of the strange hybrid creatures familiar from many of Bosch's paintings. Above a spherical abdomen pierced by an arrow, its pale human face perches with emaciated features and a bespectacled nose. A burning sphere on its head, its pointed wings, the tail, and the legs of a gecko (a nocturnal lizard), characterize the creature as an emissary of Realms of Darkness.

The painted reverse of the panel is similarly populated by demons, dim and shadowy forms against the dark background. There are suggestions of a figure riding on a fish, of a man in a helmet carrying a ladder, of a huge jug, a bell, a harp, and a flock of birds emerging from a huge fish with a gaping mouth. It is like gazing into the eternal night of outer space – were it not for the flowers scattered here and there, a sign that what Bosch has depicted in this picture is the earth plunged in darkness and overrun by demons.

In the centre of the pictorial field hovers a round disc in monochrome hues and suffused with light, whose outer ring shows the Stations of the Cross in rapid succession. Beginning with the Agony in the Garden, the sequence runs clockwise through Christ's Arrest, His appearance before Pilate, the Flagellation, the Crowning with Thorns, the Carrying of the Cross and the Crucifixion, and closes with the Entombment. Finally the Crosses on Golgotha appear, raised above a broad plain. While Mary and John remain alone beneath the Cross, a woman holding a child by the hand rushes away from the scene. The darkness behind the city on the far horizon gradually lightens until, at the Entombment, the glorious light of Easter morning dawns. The Resurrection scene is missing; yet its consolation is symbolized, in the centre of the disc, by a steep cliff rising out of still waters on a broad landscape plain. A fire burns in a cave as a huge bird spreads its wings on the peak. This is a pelican, tearing its breast to feed its young with its own blood – a legend symbolizing the blood sacrifice of Christ and the salvation of mankind.

Bosch leads the eye in three stages from the darkness dominated by demonic forces on earth, through the dawning light of Christ's sufferings, to the brilliance at the centre which promises hope of salvation. In this way he gives concrete form to the dualism between the Christian doctrine of salvation and the threat of infernal intervention. It would seem as though the artist had consciously illustrated the passage from St John, 'And the light shineth in darkness; and the darkness comprehended it not' (John 1:5).

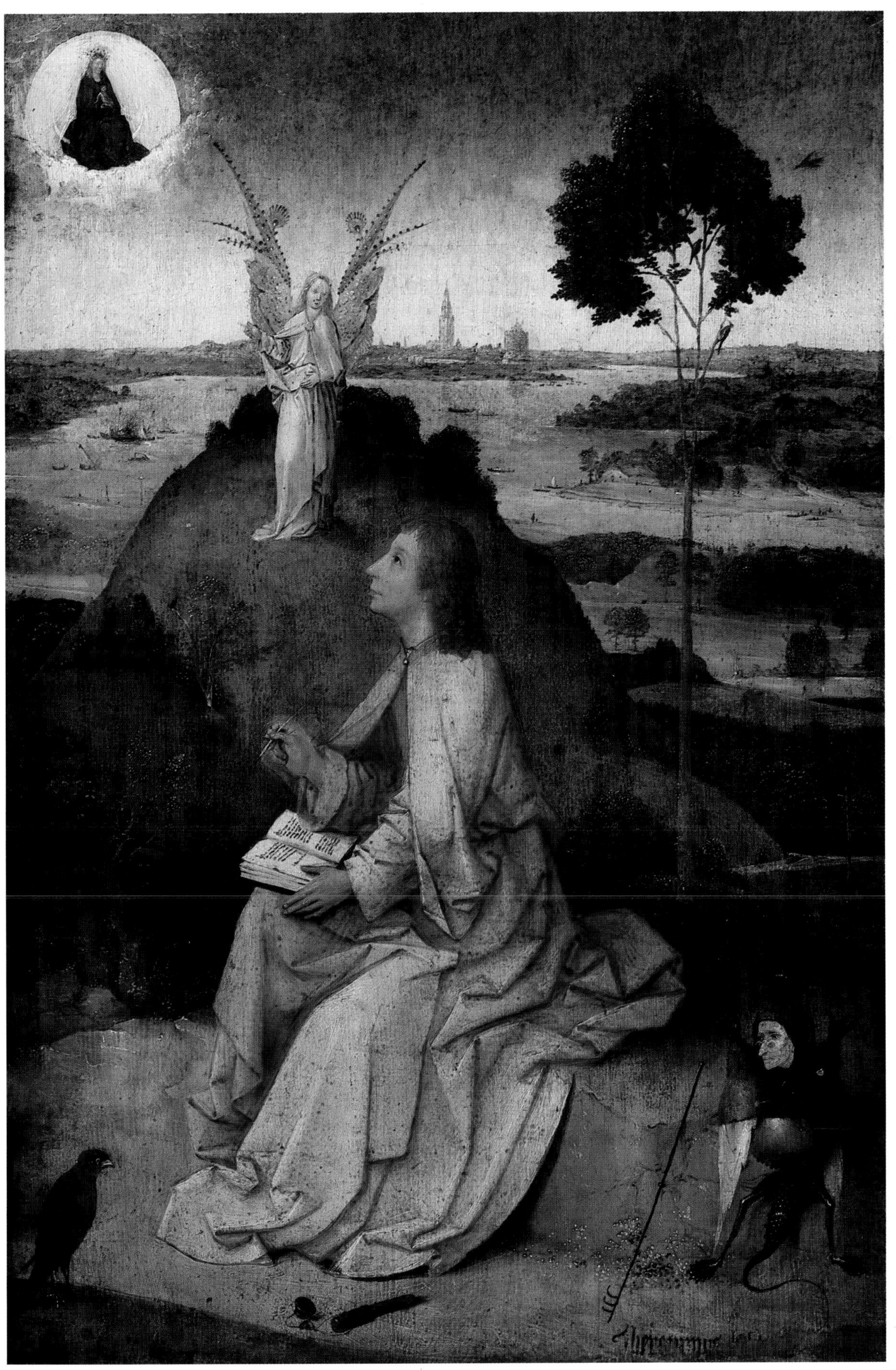

Geertgen tot Sint Jans (1460/5–before 1495)
John the Baptist in the Wilderness

Oak, 42 × 28 cm ($16\frac{1}{2}$ × 11 in)
Acquired from the Percy Macquoid Collection, London, 1902
Cat. no. 1631

Like Aelbert van Ouwater, Geertgen tot Sint Jans was active in Haarlem and decisively influenced the development of painting in the northern Netherlands. His name, which means 'Little Gerrit who lives among the Knights of St John', points to his close ties with this religious order, for whom he created many fine works of art. The intimate character of this image of their patron saint suggests that it once served the pious devotion of one of the St John brethren.

The saint has sat down to rest on a grassy outcrop in the middle of a wood. Thoughtful, his chin resting in his hand, he gazes wide-eyed into the distance. Over a cloak of dark brown camel-hair he wears, draped over his shoulders, a blue mantle that falls to the ground in abundant folds. His head is surrounded by an aureole of golden rays; his bare feet, which he absent-mindedly rubs together, show that he has walked strenuously, far from human habitation. His tranquil melancholy contrasts strangely with the profusion of the countryside. It is summer, the season of vital growth and awakened life. Swifts cleave the air, rabbits nibble the fresh leaves, a hare frolics; we see a magpie hopping through the grass, pheasants shooting out of the bushes, deer browsing beneath shady trees, and a heron exploring the swampy banks of a pond for food. Our eye is gradually led over the rolling meadows, a meandering brook, the pool reflecting the sky, and clumps of trees into the distance, where the roofs and towers of a town, symbolizing human habitation, shimmer before the blue mists of a far mountain range. All this contributes to the feeling of St John's seclusion, his profound solitude.

At the holy man's side rests a white lamb, rays of gold emanating from its head. The lamb symbolizes Christ, of whom St John said, 'Behold the Lamb of God, which taketh away the sin of the world' (John 1:29). The object of his tragic meditation, then, is the agony which Jesus was destined to suffer for the sake of divine mercy and forgiveness of sins, a theme also evoked symbolically by the blue columbine growing at his feet and the thorn-studded thistle at the right.

This is no arid waste in which John prepares himself for his task of Christ's precursor, but a wooded wilderness devoid of human life which Geertgen, like many northern European artists, equated with the deserts of the Christian legend. And it was from the contrast between tranquil countryside and the bitter thoughts troubling the man that the artist derived his enigmatic image, which is both lyrical and dramatic. Since the early Christian years, the births of Christ and of John the Baptist had been associated with great seasonal changes and celebrated at the winter and summer solstices. John's moving words, '*Illum oportet crescere, me autem minui*' ('He must increase, but I must decrease': John 3:30) were always related to the changing length of days. It seems that the artist, too, has alluded to this custom of placing St John's birth in summer's green abundance in order to link indissolubly his tragic end with the death of Christ.

Yet regardless of the multifarious meanings in this devotional image, its landscape represents an innovation that no artist before Geertgen had achieved – a contrast and a mutual heightening of mood with landscape and figure.

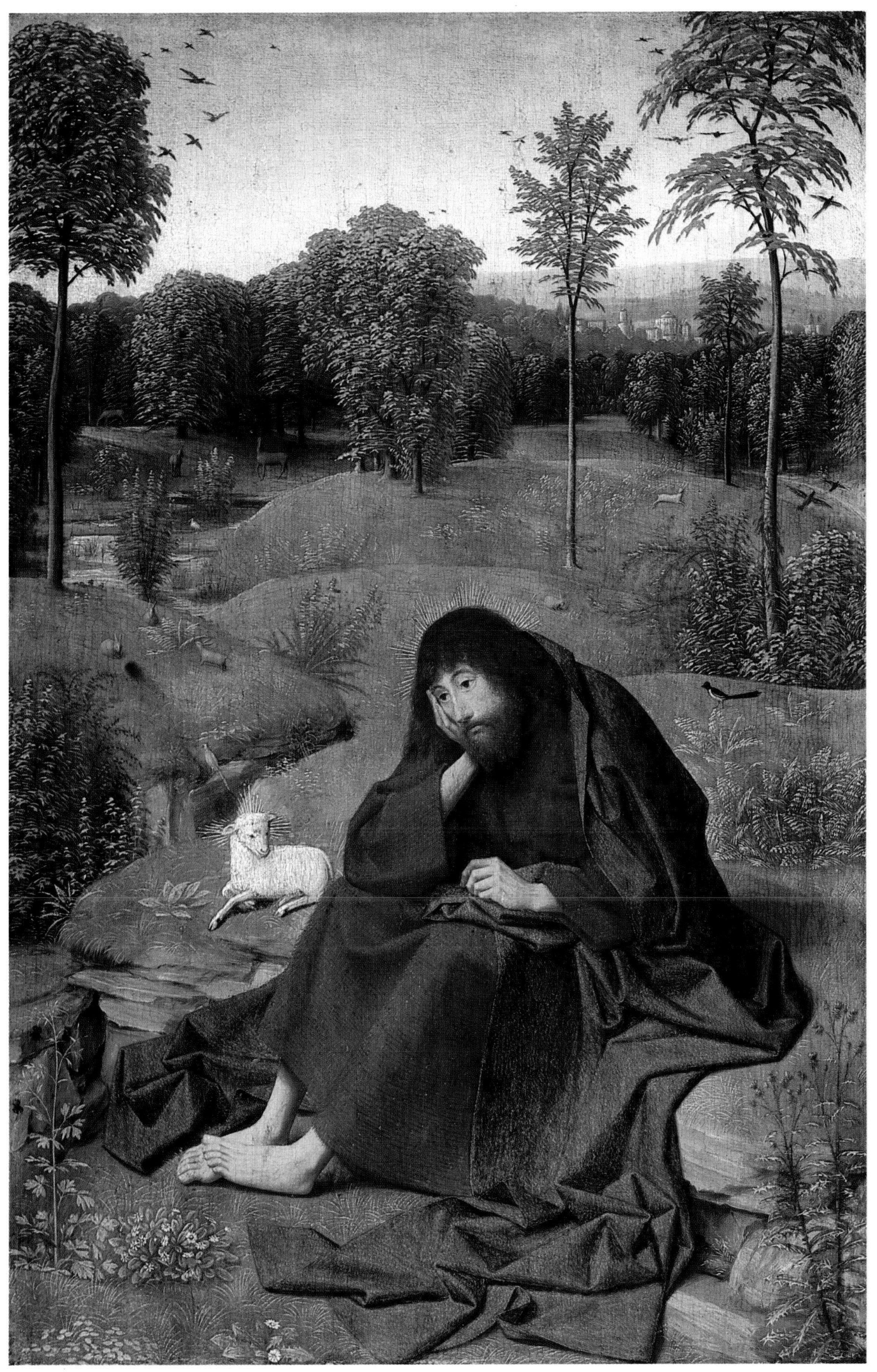

Hans Memling (*c.*1435–94)

The Virgin with Child

1487

Oak, cut on all sides and subsequently enlarged on all four sides, dimensions of original panel 41.5 × 31.5 cm ($16\frac{3}{8} \times 12\frac{3}{8}$ in)
Acquired 1862
Cat. no. 528 B

Memling's merit was to sum up in an inimitable way the achievements of his great predecessors, from the van Eycks through Rogier van der Weyden to Hugo van der Goes. The last major Netherlandish master of the fifteenth century, he put the final touches to this resplendent epoch of painting. His extraordinary technical skill, his superb execution, and the absolute harmony of his rich colour schemes, gave the spirit of Netherlandish art its most lucid expression. Memling's images are joyful and unconcerned in mood, and elegantly decorative in effect; they are more narrative than dramatic in character. The tranquil beauty of his Madonnas, his meditative saints, and his landscapes like parks in the freshness of summer, come very close to the sensibility and outlook of Romanticism. It is not surprising that the nineteenth-century rediscovery of old Netherlandish art began with Memling.

A characteristic equilibrium of pictorial structure and a palette based on a harmony of blues, reds and greens are seen in this *Virgin and Child*, which belongs to the artist's late period. A bright yet mild light suffuses everything in the image – figures, the gently rolling summer landscape, and the undisturbed plane of a brilliant blue sky that is almost cloudless. Mary, oblivious of her suffering, faces the observer in tranquil, composed beauty, her eyes cast down. Everything in her vicinity has a charm that is difficult to describe but which culminates in the gentle way she cherishes the Child and hands Him an apple.

From the early Middle Ages, the apple signified the forbidden fruit of the Tree of Knowledge which Eve picked for Adam. The old antithesis between Mary and Eve reverberates here. As St Birgit of Sweden (d.1373) recorded, the Virgin herself once told her in a vision that 'Just as Adam and Eve forsook the world for an apple, we, my Son and I, have recovered the world with a heart.' For Memling, the presentation of an apple conveyed the additional significance of Christ's taking the sins of the world upon himself to redeem mankind.

All the many images of the Madonna created by Memling are infused with the profound reverence felt for the Virgin at that time. The painting in our collection was most likely commissioned by Benedetto Portinari (b.1466) as the central panel of a small triptych whose wings, a portrait of Portinari and an image of his patron saint, St Benedict, are now in the Uffizi in Florence.

Hans Memling
The Portinari Triptych 1487
St Benedict
Florence, Uffizi
The Virgin and Child
Berlin, Gemäldegalerie SMPK
Portrait of Benedetto Portinari
Florence, Uffizi

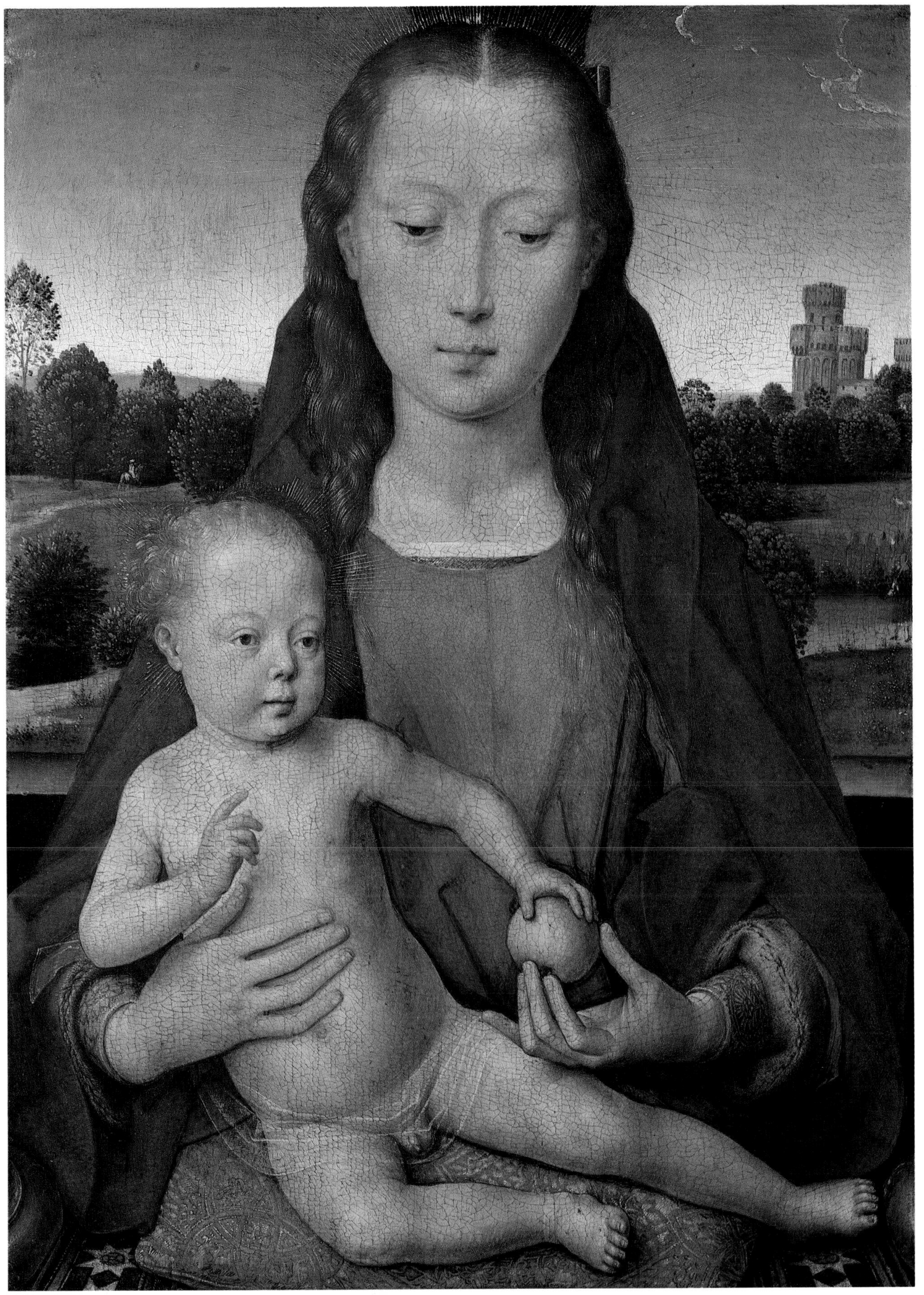

Michel Sittow (*c.*1469–1525)

The Virgin and Child

*c.*1515

Oak, 32 × 24.5 cm ($12\frac{1}{2} \times 9\frac{5}{8}$ in)
Acquired 1914
Property of the
Kaiser-Friedrich-Museums-Verein
Cat. no. 1722

Sittow came from Reval, which at that time belonged to the Teutonic Order in Livonia, but he was also a member of the German Hanse and maintained widespread commercial and political ties. Like many other artists of the period, Sittow travelled to the Netherlands to seek out the leading masters and to learn from them. He settled in Bruges in 1484, where he was formatively inspired by Hans Memling. Memling's influence is frequently seen in his images of the Virgin and in his portraits. In spite of his extraordinary technical mastery, Sittow consciously remained aloof from the great contemporary developments in art. Perhaps he owed his success to this devotion to maintaining artistic tradition.

After his apprenticeship in Bruges, Sittow went to Spain, where in 1492 he entered the service of Isabella of Castile as court artist. Under Philip the Handsome he returned to the Netherlands in 1502, but by 1506 he was back in Reval again. In 1514 he went to the court of King Christian II of Denmark in Copenhagen, and the following year was active in Mecheln for Governess Margaret of Austria. Another journey took him to Valladolid in Spain before he again returned to the Netherlands in 1516, to enter the service of Charles V, later Emperor. In 1518, finally, he settled in his home town, where he was highly esteemed by the time he died. The great respect in which this widely-travelled artist was held by his patrons is shown by the fact that Charles V, after his abdication, took works by Sittow with him to St Juste, where he hung them in his chambers alongside paintings by Titian.

The Berlin *Virgin and Child* is one of the loveliest and most characteristic of Sittow's paintings. Though its half-figure was obviously modelled on Memling Madonnas, Sittow's approach reveals more physical emphasis: a more tactile treatment of figures and materials, and a heightened individuality of the Virgin's features. The brilliance of the colours is augmented by the dark background, which contrasts strongly with the flesh tones and the reds of the mantle. On a parapet covered with an Oriental carpet, the nude Infant lies cradled in Mary's hands as she presents him to view. With one hand he caresses his mother's chin; in the other he holds a finch symbolizing the Passion he is destined to endure.

This panel once formed the left wing of a diptych. Its counterpart, now in the National Gallery in Washington, shows the donor of the diptych, Don Diego de Guevara (d.1520). Guevara, Treasurer to Margaret of Austria and Knight of the Calatrava Order, owned one of the most superb collections of Netherlandish art of the period, whose masterpieces included Jan van Eyck's famous portrait of the Arnolfini couple.

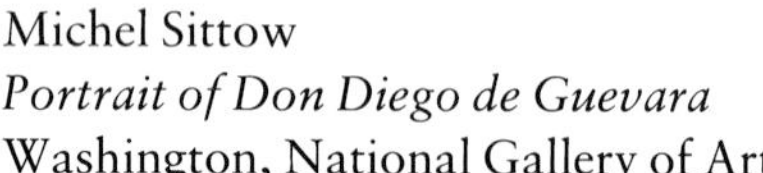

Michel Sittow
Portrait of Don Diego de Guevara
Washington, National Gallery of Art

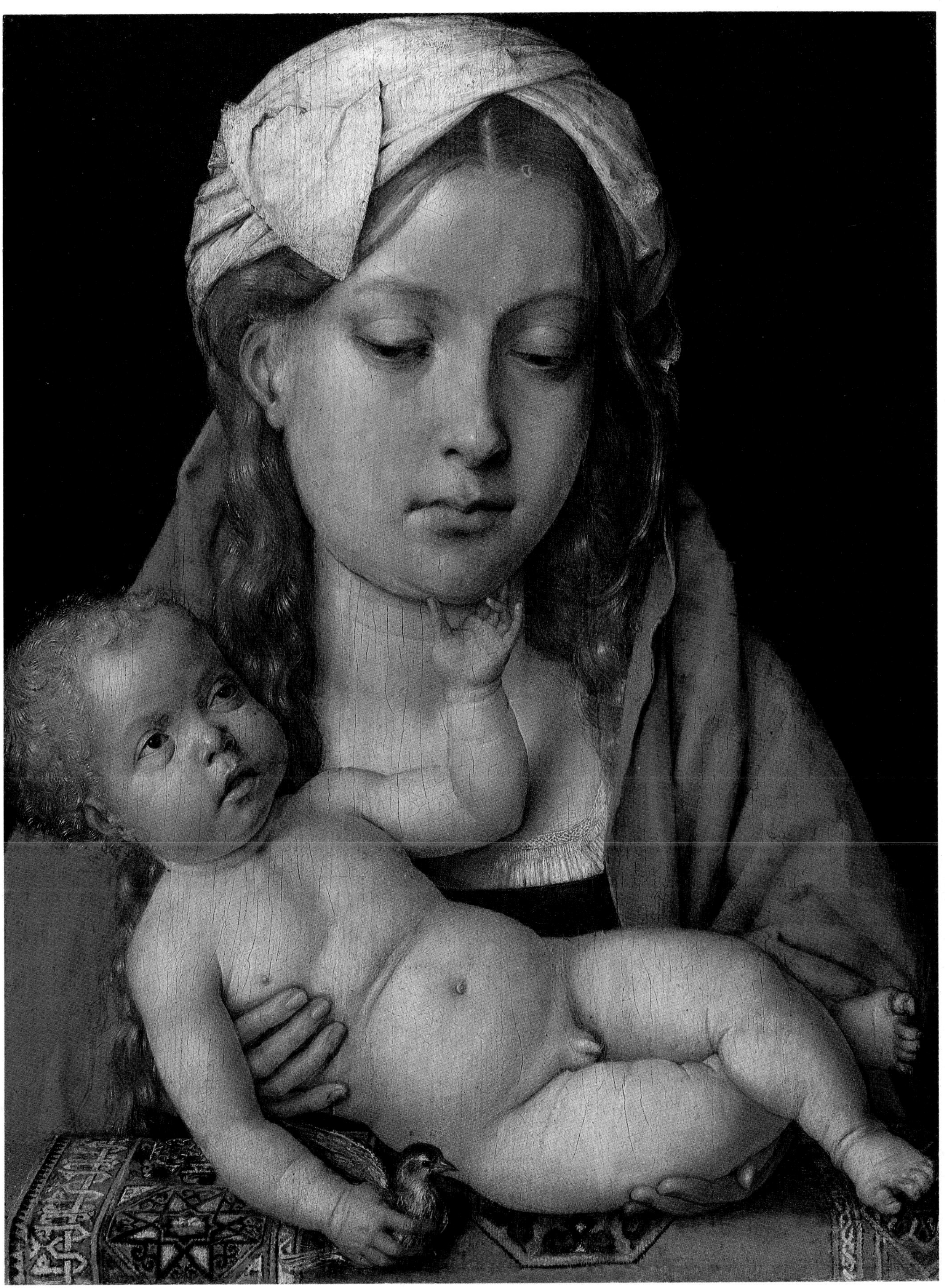

Gerard David (*c.*1460–1523)
Christ on the Cross
*c.*1515

Oak with rounded top, 141 × 100 cm
($55\frac{1}{2} \times 39\frac{3}{8}$ in)
Acquired with the Solly Collection, 1821
Cat. no. 573

Gerard David was born in the northern Netherlands, in the town of Oudewater, Holland. As the influence of Geertgen tot Sint Jans in David's early work suggests, he probably received his first training in Haarlem. In 1484 he emigrated to Bruges, where Hans Memling was a leading master. Here he became a member and later the head of the artists' guild and received many commissions from the town council. David painted his major works in Bruges where, apart from short interruptions, he lived and worked for the rest of his life. He seems to have spent some time in Antwerp, since an entry of 1515 in the register of the Antwerp Artists' Guild records the acceptance of a 'Gheraet van Brugghe, scildere'. At that period, Bruges had lost its importance as a harbour due to the silting up of the Swijn, the city's connection to the sea, while Antwerp was beginning to establish itself as a new trade centre. Though this meant new artistic opportunities, David may have found the changing climate uncongenial. In any event, he returned to Bruges, where as the last major representative of its great tradition he enjoyed a high reputation.

Gerard David's achievement links the best in fifteenth-century Netherlandish art with the new concerns of the Renaissance. His imagery is characterized by a tranquil monumentality and a lucid organization of the figures, which are modelled in great relief and integrated with their surroundings in an unprecedented way. In this regard, David's art marked a decisive step forward in the development of a unified pictorial space. Indicatively, the first pure landscapes known in the history of art are by his hand – on the wings of an altarpiece now at The Hague, Mauritshuis. *Christ on the Cross* stems from the artist's late period. Its palette, dominated by harmonies of green and blue, is strangely cool and reserved, and yet, thanks to a great range of nuance, is extremely subtle. This consistent simplification of colour, which creates a strong atmospheric effect, corresponds to a rendering of the events that is both poignant and moving in its simplicity. These traits are particularly marked in David's later work.

The Crucifix on the heights of Golgotha stands at a slight angle, pointing into the distance. Christ looks down at the mourners beneath Him – Mary Magdalene nearest the cross, then the Virgin Mary, supported by John, and finally Mary Salome and Mary Jacobi. With the words '*mulier ecce filius tuus*' (Woman, behold thy son. St John 19:26) Christ entrusts his mother to the care of his favourite disciple. The reserved sadness of the mourners seems to have communicated itself to the centurion and his men, who stand aside to deliberate. Other troops are visible in the background, returning to Jerusalem. This detail indicates that, instead of representing a particular moment of the happenings, the artist wished to illustrate their timeless significance, anticipating his later extreme reduction of the motif (Genoa, Palazzo Bianco). The impression of timelessness is increased by the ragged clouds scudding across the sky, and by the spacious landscape with its low mountains that shimmer in the blue twilight and converge behind the vertical of the cross.

Gerard David
Christ on the Cross
Genoa, Palazzo Bianco

Quinten Massys (1465/6–1530)
The Virgin Enthroned with Child
*c.*1520

Oak with fluted top, 135 × 90 cm
($53\frac{1}{8} \times 35\frac{1}{2}$ in)
Acquired 1823
Cat. no. 561

Massys, born in Louvain, was the son of a blacksmith, and legend has it that he learned his father's trade. His artistic training must have been thorough, because it enabled him to hold his own among the 'Mannerists of Antwerp', where he settled and became a free master in 1491. Massys built on the achievements of fifteenth-century Netherlandish painting, particularly those of Dieric Bouts and Hans Memling, who were active in Louvain and Bruges. He developed a personal idiom in which fifteenth-century Dutch tradition and Italian Late Renaissance art, above all that of Leonardo da Vinci, blended into a harmonious unity. Important commissions from the guilds and fraternities of the prosperous trading town made him Antwerp's foremost master, and his style influenced many later artists. Besides devotional images, altarpieces and genre scenes, Massys also created medals and portraits. In 1517, Erasmus and his friend Petrus Aegidius sat to Massys for a double portrait which they sent as a memento to their common acquaintance, Thomas More. In his letter of thanks, the great statesman and humanist praised Massys as the rejuvenator of ancient art, perfectly characterizing his special role in the transition to a new epoch.

The present panel, dated about 1520 from Massys's late period, is one of the finest of the many works he devoted to the theme of the Virgin enthroned. Mary is depicted full figure and almost life-size, seated on a carved stone throne whose sideposts are ornamented with columns of polished reddish marble. Its back consists of an open arch with Gothic tracery whose curve follows the semicircular top edge of the panel. Mary is dressed in a blue gown with silk sleeves in opalescent pink and bluish grey; a brilliant red mantle falls in soft folds over the base of the throne to the coloured tiles of the floor. A delicate translucent veil covers her hair, spreading over her shoulders and around the Child kneeling in her lap.

The motif of the kiss, which lends this solemn image of the Virgin a touch of intimacy, derives from Italian art – more precisely from Leonardo da Vinci and his followers. The treatment of the faces, delicate and with barely perceptible transitions from light to shade, similarly shows Massys' knowledge of Leonardo's paintings. A debt to Netherlandish realism, by contrast, is evident in the treatment of the landscape and the superbly rendered still life on the small table before the throne. The distant background vistas show the influence of Joachim Patenier's approach, for whose landscapes Massys sometimes supplied the figures. Incidentally, this collaboration between specialists set a precedent for what later became a widespread practice.

Central to the symbolic content of the image is the fenced garden with its rose-hedge and fountain behind the throne. This element evokes the 'enclosed garden' in the Song of Solomon, a simile associated with the virginity and purity of the Mother of God. The foreground still life also possesses symbolic meaning. Cherries represent the fruits of Heaven, and the apple symbolizes the original sin which Christ's advent overcame; bread and wine refer to the sacrifice and redemption symbolically renewed in celebrations of the mass.

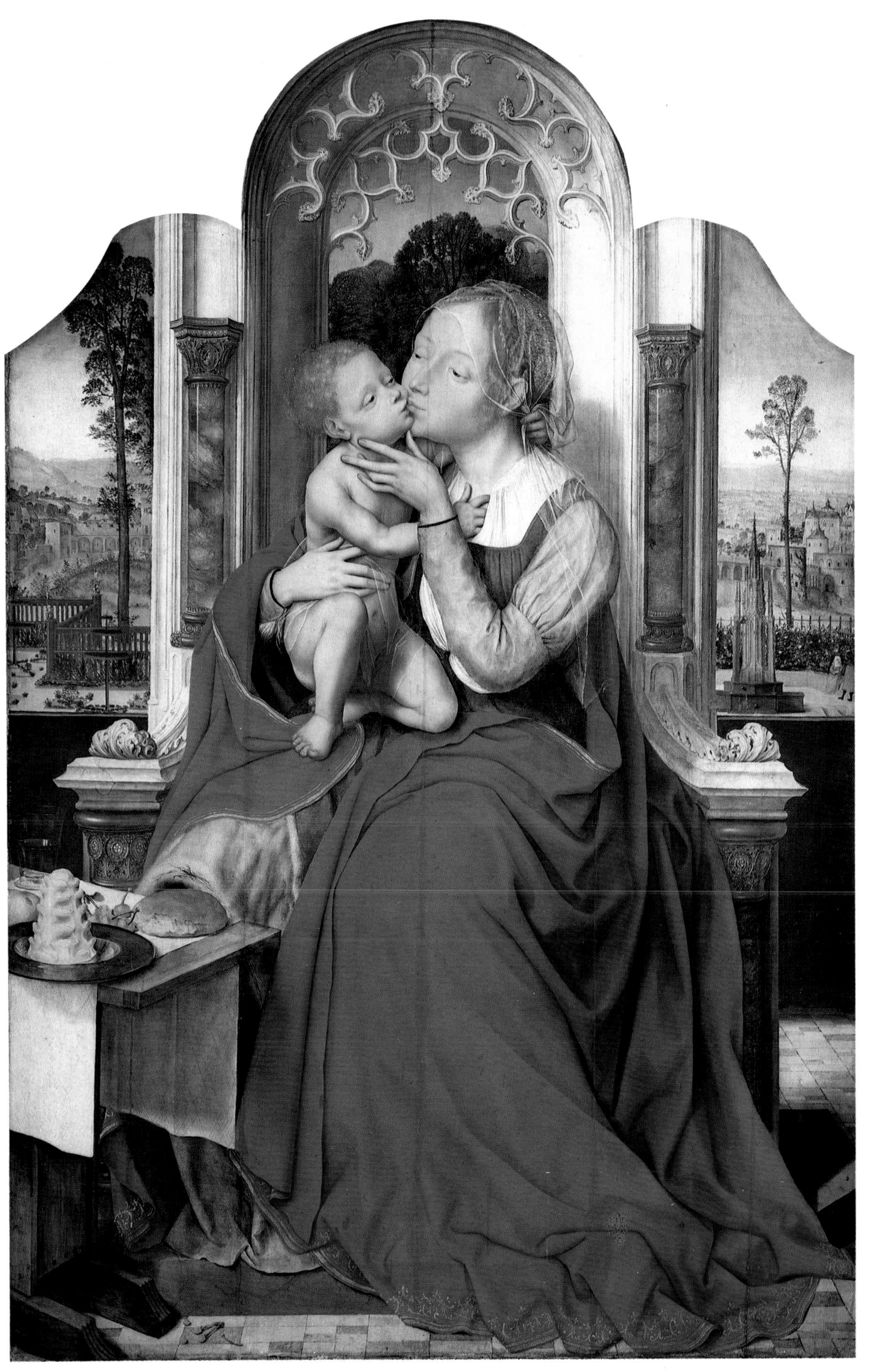

Joos van Cleve (1480/5–1540)
Triptych with the Adoration of the Magi
*c.*1515

Oak, central panel 72 × 52 cm ($28\frac{3}{8} \times 20\frac{1}{2}$ in), each wing 69 × 22 cm ($27\frac{1}{8} \times 8\frac{5}{8}$ in)
Acquired from the Reimer Collection, Berlin, 1843
Cat. no. 578

Few artists thought it necessary to sign their works until well into the sixteenth century. This put art historians in the paradoxical position of having to invent makeshift names for the creators of major groups of paintings, while not being able to associate any of these with the names of the numerous active artists recorded in contemporary sources. The creator of the present triptych was long known only as Master of the Death of the Virgin, a pseudonym derived from two altarpieces on this theme at Cologne and Munich. In all probability, however, he is identical with the 'Joos van Cleve alias van der Beke' mentioned in the Antwerp records, an artist who became an independent master there in 1511 and served as Dean of the Artists' Guild in 1519 and 1525. Joos van Cleve, a native of the Lower Rhine region and probably a pupil of Jan Joest van Kalkar, was decisively influenced in Bruges, through the art of Hans Memling and Gerard David. In Antwerp, he was impressed with Patenier, Massys and the 'Antwerp Mannerists'. A trip to Italy appears to have acquainted him with the art of Leonardo da Vinci. Joos van Cleve's altarpieces and portraits were known and admired far beyond the borders of the Netherlands; he worked for a time as court artist to Francis I of France, and travelled to England to paint a portrait of Henry VIII.

It was during his early period that van Cleve created the present small altarpiece with *The Adoration of the Magi*, which once served private devotion. In its closed position, the wings show St Christopher and St Sebastian, figures in *grisaille* dramatically set off by the reddish-brown painted niches in which they stand. By contrast, the interior of the altar glows in brilliant colours. The central panel and wings are linked by a landscape vista beneath a blue sky growing lighter towards the horizon, which extends across the entire width of the altar. Dominating the centre panel are imposing palatial ruins with arches, columns, pilasters, and a gilded statue. Mary is seated in the foreground with the Child on her lap, his hands extended towards the kings who have come to present their gifts. Their clothes and features evoke the three regions of the then-known world – Europe, Africa and Asia. Kneeling before Christ, the Western monarch is identified by the chain of the Order of the Golden Fleece. Behind them Joseph looks on reverentially, hat in hand; at the left are an ox and ass at the feeding trough. In the distance, near a group of strangely-shaped rocks, the arrival of the three kings' retinues is depicted. The spacious landscape with its abundant and carefully observed details still owes much to the landscape style of Joachim Patenier, with whom van Cleve occasionally collaborated.

The right side-panel shows St Barbara with a book and pen in hand, identified by her symbol, a massive tower, looming behind her. On the left side-piece is St Catherine, dressed in elaborate robes and a crown which signify her royal origins. She holds a sword whose point rests on a wheel studded with iron teeth. According to the legend, St Catherine was condemned to be broken on the wheel, but her prayers were answered, and fire fell from heaven to consume the wheel. Nevertheless, she was executed by the sword, and her body borne by angels to Mount Sinai. The artist has rendered the miraculous burning wheel in the distant landscape, with the same fond fidelity to detail that characterizes the altar as a whole.

Joos van Cleve
Triptych
Exterior of wings
St Christopher and St Sebastian
Berlin, Gemäldegalerie SMPK

Joachim Patenier (c.1480–1524)

The Rest on the Flight into Egypt

c.1520

Oak, 78 × 62 cm (30¾ × 24⅜ in)
Acquired with the Solly Collection, 1821
Cat. no. 608

Patenier worked in Antwerp, becoming a free master there in 1515. About 1520–1, Dürer visited the cosmopolitan town and, meeting Patenier, recorded in his travel diary that he was a 'good landscape painter' – the first use of this term in the history of art. Influenced by Bosch, David and Massys, Patenier's landscapes combined a fine observation of detail with a sense of universal order which paved the way for Pieter Bruegel the Elder, and consequently formed the point of departure for late sixteenth-century landscape art in the Netherlands. His overview or universal landscapes were unique, and they were widely distributed and admired far beyond the borders of his country.

The Virgin and Child in the foreground of his *Rest on the Flight into Egypt* were not painted by Patenier himself but by an artist from the studio of Joos van Cleve. In his conception of the figures, this anonymous artist relied on the great Netherlandish tradition, basing their pose on the *Madonna at the Fireplace* by Robert Campin (Leningrad, the Hermitage).

As if seen from the air, a vast landscape with mountains and fields, plains and watercourses, trees and buildings, extends to the far horizon. The eye roams over this expanse of countryside as over an intricate tapestry, a natural scene infused with human order and expressing the divine order of the universe. The unity of the image derives from the masterly way in which the artist has evoked depth and atmosphere. An abundance of carefully observed details forms and reforms kaleidoscopically into a comprehensive yet ever-changing image. Led into the distance, the eye rests first on bizarre cliffs raised against the clouds, then moves unhindered to the horizon where seemingly endless forests spread and ships sail from the harbour onto the plain of the sea. The impression of depth and expanse is remarkable, and it is created by the use of only a few local colours, but in many nuances that extend from warm greens and browns to a cool, crystalline, pastel blue.

Robert Campin
The Madonna at the Fireplace
Leningrad, Hermitage

Combined with this superb colour handling and detailed reportage is an equally conscientious description of the happenings associated with the Holy Family's flight into Egypt. These many and strange events are not described in the Bible but in the books of the Apocrypha, particularly the Gospel of Pseudo-Matthew, which influenced literature and art from the Middle Ages to the Renaissance more than the Scriptures themselves. This book tells how the Holy Family came to the town of Sotina near Hermopolis, and how, when they entered the temple, the heathen idols disintegrated and crashed to the ground. In the painting, this temple appears high on the flank of the cliff, and beside the path leading to it is an idol toppling off its column. The spring emerging at the roots of a tree in the foreground alludes to another miracle described in the legend. And the birds fearlessly approaching Mary and the Infant signify that the animal realm, too, recognizes the Lord, as in the story, where lions, leopards, and all variations of wild beasts meekly accompany the Holy Family on their journey.

The humble village on the right, near the mouth of the river, represents Bethlehem, where Herod's soldiers slaughter innocent children as their mothers vainly attempt to protect them. The artist depicts successive events simultaneously, to illustrate that the significance of the Flight became apparent only in its consequences. Among these were also the Miracle of the Harvest, a legend frequently recounted in Netherlandish art. When the Holy Family left Bethlehem to escape Herod's vengeance, they met peasants sowing grain in the fields. Joseph implored them to tell their pursuers that they had passed while the wheat was being sown. Then, miraculously, the wheat ripened overnight, and by morning it was ready for harvest. Herod's men, misled by the peasants information although it was quite true, gave up the chase. The artist symbolically illustrates this miracle in the two adjacent fields outside the town, one freshly sown and the other ready for cutting.

Not only the scenes set in the landscape, but also the flowers and plants growing there

contribute to a deeper understanding of the events related: the iris (*Gladiolus*) blossoming at the spring in the foreground, like the thorns of the thistle, allude to Christ's Passion and the redemption it promises to mankind. This symbolic reference is only one of the many aspects of Patenier's imaginative landscape, which abounds in wonders and surprises.

Antwerp Master (*c.*1520)
The Beheading of John the Baptist

Oak, 48 × 35 cm ($18\frac{7}{8} \times 13\frac{3}{4}$ in)
Acquired as gift from Frau Hainauer, Berlin, 1906
Cat. no. 630 C

Thanks to a liberal trade policy, Antwerp had become a serious competitor to Bruges and Ghent by the fifteenth century, and during the sixteenth century it advanced to be the largest harbour and commercial city in northern Europe. An international crossroads, Antwerp exerted a great attraction to artists. Its prosperity and wide mercantile relations created ideal conditions for the export of works of art throughout the world. As the guild lists indicate, artists from everywhere in Europe flocked to Antwerp, and the number of studios burgeoned. The exchange of artistic and workshop information at that period must have reached proportions previously unknown in the Netherlands. The wishes of individual patrons now began to count less than the tastes of a broad sector of purchasers for whom works of art were created *en masse*. This stockpiling against future demand also facilitated export trade in art on an unprecedented scale.

Antwerp's many workshops, most of whose masters are known today only by the pseudonyms later given them, turned out devotional images and altarpieces decorated with sculptures and painting for export throughout the Continent, from Scandinavia to Portugal. Among the anonymous artists active in early sixteenth-century Antwerp who painted numerous variations of some subjects – as illustrated by their pseudonyms – were the Master of the von Groote Adoration, the Master of the Antwerp Adoration, the Master of the St John Martyrdom, the Master of 1518, and the Master of the Munich Adoration, who is also known by the name of Pseudo-Bles. This last artist, who painted *The Adoration of the Magi* in Munich (Alte Pinakothek) with its spurious signature 'Henricus Blesius', stands out from the large group of anonymous artists collectively known as the 'Antwerp Mannerists'. The present panel, *The Beheading of John the Baptist*, can also be attributed to him; it is a characteristic work, and much finer in quality than the average productions of this group.

An open square partly bordered at the left and back by high façades with round towers, columns, pilasters and narrow windows, forms the imaginative setting for the execution scene. Still gripping his sword, the executioner places John's head on a platter held out by Salome, who is accompanied by two ladies-in-waiting. The body lies on the ground, blood gushing from the severed neck. Next to it stands an elaborately dressed soldier, his back turned to us – and to the execution; he is talking with two other men, one of whom has a falcon perched on his hand. In the background, John, his hands tied, is being led to the block by the executioner and his henchmen. In the open hall of the palace, Salome dances for Herod and as a reward she has demanded John's head. On the far right is a view of mountainous country with men around a fire. Apparently this scene was meant to represent the immolation of John's remains, which took place later by order of Emperor Julian the Apostate.

The lucid and brilliant palette of this masterfully composed image, its elaborate architecture, and the fantastic costumes show the hand of a skilled craftsman. These features, together with the artist's penchant for elegantly artificial poses and gestures, elongated figures, and a certain calculated picturesqueness in the way the figures overlap, are characteristic traits of 'Antwerp Mannerism', a style in which late Gothic and Renaissance approaches were combined to achieve new and unexpected visual effects.

Antwerp Master, *c.*1520
The Adoration of the Magi
Munich, Alte Pinakothek

Lucas van Leyden (1489–1533)
The Game of Chess
*c.*1508

Oak, 27 × 35 cm ($10\frac{5}{8} \times 13\frac{3}{4}$ in)
Collection of Ambassador Baron Werther, Vienna
Acquired with the Suermondt Collection, 1874
Cat. no. 574 A

Meeting Lucas van Leyden in Antwerp in 1521, Albrecht Dürer noted in his diary, 'I was the guest of Master Lucas, who engraves on copper; he's a little manikin and comes from Leyden in Holland.' Dürer took the opportunity to make a portrait sketch of the artist and to exchange engravings with him. For van Leyden, this personal encounter proved extremely important because Dürer's graphic art stimulated his own much more lastingly than the late-Gothic mannerism of his teacher, Cornelis Engebrechtsz.

Carel van Mander, biographer of the Netherlandish artists, praised van Leyden, who died young, as a precocious talent. At nine years of age he already had a sure hand with an engraving tool, and painted his first picture a few years later. Assuming the year of birth given by van Mander to be correct, the young artist must have painted his *Game of Chess* at fourteen. The panel is indeed remarkable in every respect. It is among the first genre paintings in the history of Dutch art, one of the *incunabula* of a new field which was to enjoy such great popularity during the seventeenth century.

The scene gives the impression of a slice of everyday life. Yet in fact it is as carefully composed as an elaborately staged play and, like a play, is meant to convey a message to its audience. The small panel contains twelve people, ten men and two women, represented in half-figure and crowded together beside and behind one another. The room is reduced to a dark foil against which the faces, each highly individual and looking in different directions, stand out in dramatic contrast. The centre of interest is the game being played by a young woman and a man. Some of the onlookers follow the game closely, particularly the elderly man who seems to be advising the woman on a decisive move. Her opponent's face reveals a mixture of incredulity and superiority as he turns away from the board to remove his cap and to scratch his head. This chessboard, twelve squares across and eight down, belongs to a game popular from the thirteenth century – courier chess – in which each side has an additional four pawns and, as new figures, two couriers, one adviser, and one straggler (*Courier, Mann-Rath, Schleich*).

As to the meaning of the game and therefore of the painting, the strict rules of chess have from ancient times been associated with a social hierarchy extending from an all-powerful king down to powerless vassals; also, the game was a common metaphor for love and courting, an erotic aspect illustrated by many representations of young couples playing chess in a garden of love. Winning the game was not so important, since it was the loser who could expect to be lucky in love. In a painting with a similar composition, *Woman Telling Fortunes by the Cards* (*c.*1509; Paris, the Louvre), van Leyden pictures a young woman predicting a boy's future and giving him a flower as a sign of her admiration. The fool standing behind her is intended as a rash young fellow who has lost his head and succumbed to female charms. *The Game of Chess* can also be interpreted in this way, since its message is closely related to the theme of 'petticoat government' to which van Leyden devoted two great graphic sequences in his œuvre that proved him to be one of the most gifted artists of his time.

Master E.S.
Garden of Love with Chess Players, *c.*1460
Engraving

Jan Gossaert (1470/80–1532)
The Agony in the Garden
*c.*1510

Oak, 85 × 63 cm ($33\frac{1}{2} \times 24\frac{7}{8}$ in)
In the Gottfried Winkler Collection, Leipzig, during the eighteenth century
Acquired 1848
Cat. no. 551 A

Jan Gossaert was admitted in 1503, as 'Jennyn van Hennegouwe', to the artists' guild in Antwerp, where he lived and worked as an independent master until 1507. In the retinue of Philip of Burgundy (1465–1524) he undertook an Italian journey in 1508–9 which profoundly influenced his later work. While in Rome, Gossaert made drawings of antique sculptures and buildings for his influential patron, and later painted mythological subjects for Philip's castle at Walcheren. After following Philip to Utrecht when he was named bishop there in 1517, Gossaert worked for Philip's nephew, Adolf of Burgundy, in Middelburg. In addition he was active at the courts of Margaret of Austria and Christian II of Denmark, and served the Marquise Mencia de Mendoza, the third wife of Henry III of Nassau. Gossaert's many talents, his profound knowledge of the great fifteenth-century masters, his study of Dürer's prints, and his exhaustive work on the monuments of antiquity established his unique position in Netherlandish art. Besides devotional paintings and altarpieces, he concentrated on portraits and mythological subjects which compellingly presaged the release of art from ecclesiastical strictures.

Gossaert's *Agony in the Garden* was probably executed about 1510, shortly after his Italian journey, though the impressions he gained at Rome were yet to become apparent. As the Gospels relate, on the evening after the Last Supper, Christ went with his disciples to the Mount of Olives. Asking them to watch with him, he withdrew to kneel down and pray: 'Father, if thou be willing, remove this cup from me: nevertheless not my will, but thine, be done. And there appeared an angel unto him from heaven, strengthening him. And being in an agony he prayed more earnestly: and his sweat was as it were great drops of blood falling down to the ground. And when he rose up from prayer, and was come to his disciples, he found them sleeping for sorrow' (Luke 22:42–5). Then Judas Iscariot, leading the priests and elders of the temple, entered the garden of Gethsemane to greet Christ with the kiss which was the pre-arranged sign of his betrayal.

Gossaert's subject is Christ's agonized soul-searching in the face of inevitable death, not the dramatic moment of his arrest. These are the last hours of the night Jesus had to endure alone, 'grieved unto death', as his disciples slept. A waning crescent moon casts pale unreal light on the clouds, the rocky wooded hill, and the distant towers of Jerusalem. Light gleams on the youthful face of Christ, streaming with sweat and tears, and touches the upturned face of Peter, asleep in the foreground with his sword beside him. Next to him, overcome by weariness, John and James rest with their heads in their hands. An angel descends from heaven to Christ, who has placed the chalice and host before him on a rock. Approaching from the open city gates in the background, Judas leads the search party to the garden, their weapon and armour gleaming in the moonlight, torches held high to light their way through the gloom.

This work, one of the earliest and most compelling nocturnal scenes in art, proves Gossaert a painter of extraordinary virtuosity. The illumination, striking yet astonishingly subtle, points up the inner drama of the Biblical event.

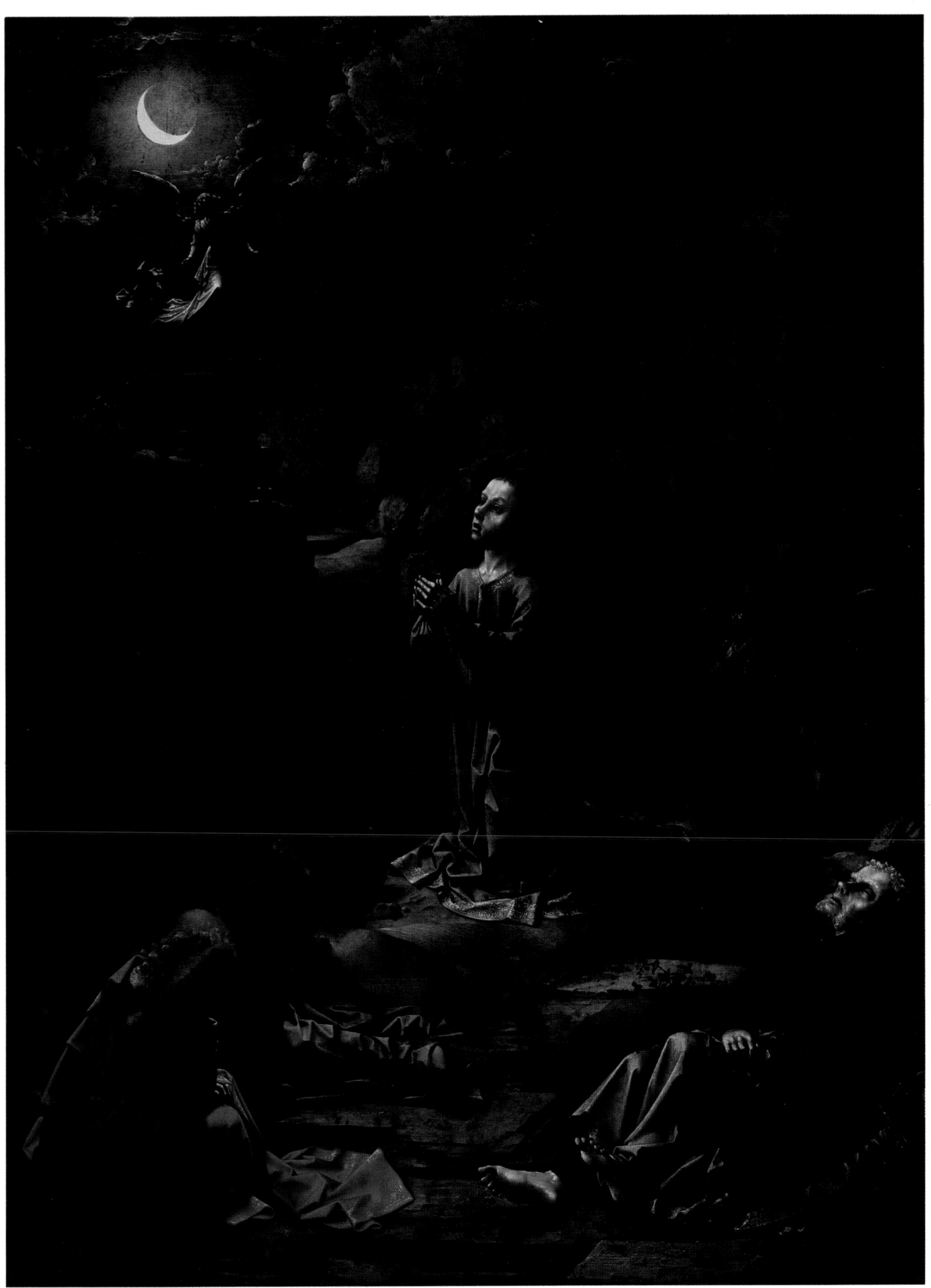

Jan Gossaert
The Virgin and Child
*c.*1530

Oak, 44.7 × 38.2 cm ($17\frac{1}{2}$ × 15 in)
Acquired with the Solly Collection, 1821
Cat. no. 650

Gossaert's images of the Virgin are among the finest paintings in his œuvre. When we trace the development of this time-honoured theme in Netherlandish painting from van Eyck through Memling, Sittow and Massys, and on to Gossaert, it becomes apparent that for all their adherence to tradition, these artists enriched it by many innovations. None but the greatest talents of the time, of course, managed to incorporate the new realism of the Italian High Renaissance without sacrificing spiritual and religious depth. The combination required a high degree of self-insight and a confidence in the use of artistic means, both of which are impressively evident in Gossaert's late *Virgin and Child*.

The shallow pictorial space, for which the figures seem almost too bulky, is a device intended to underline their three-dimensional quality. Mary and the Child appear before a richly profiled, greyish-brown painted frame which the figures overlap at several points and out of which they emerge as if in high relief. The reddish-brown back plate of the frame provides a perfect background foil to Mary's lovely features. The subtle chiaroscuro modelling is just as impressive as the painterly treatment of the Virgin's curls, her hands, and the agitated folds of the garments. Gossaert's mastery of illusionistic effects becomes particularly obvious in the lettering in the groove of the frame, which looks as though it were cut out of metal and bowed slightly outwards. This sequential inscription reads, 'VERVS DEVS ET HOMO · CASTA MATER ET VIRGO' ('A True God and Man, a Pure Mother and Virgin').

Her head slightly inclined, Mary gazes down at the Child seated on a carpet-covered parapet before her. She wears a red mantle and a blue dress which is open over her right breast. From beneath a white scarf her long, reddish-blonde hair falls in curls over her shoulders. In her left hand Mary holds a bunch of grapes for which the Child reaches out eagerly, a gesture which seems to cloud Mary's thoughts with a premonition of her son's fate. His wide, intelligent eyes seem to gaze into the future. The lively Child is dressed in a thin chemise that reveals the lines of his sturdy body. In his right hand is an apple, the fruit that once sealed Adam and Eve's fall from grace, now transmuted into a warranty of salvation.

This symbol of the apple brings together the many strands of meaning associated with the Incarnation and Christ's death on the Cross. The notion that an apple brought mankind's downfall but also promised its redemption, is an aspect of the ancient idea that past history was repeated in the re-creation of the world through Christ. A contrast between the old Adam and the new, represented by Christ, and between the first Eve and the second, identified with the Virgin, was part of the same association of ideas. Just as Mary was praised as the vine that bore the grapes which gave mankind the wine of the Eucharistic blood, the bunch of grapes she holds here represents a symbolic promise that the blood Christ is to shed will erase the curse Eve brought to men when she picked the forbidden apple. All these associations were real and present to the faithful who worshipped at images of this kind.

Jan Gossaert
The Virgin and Child
Chicago, The Art Institute of Chicago

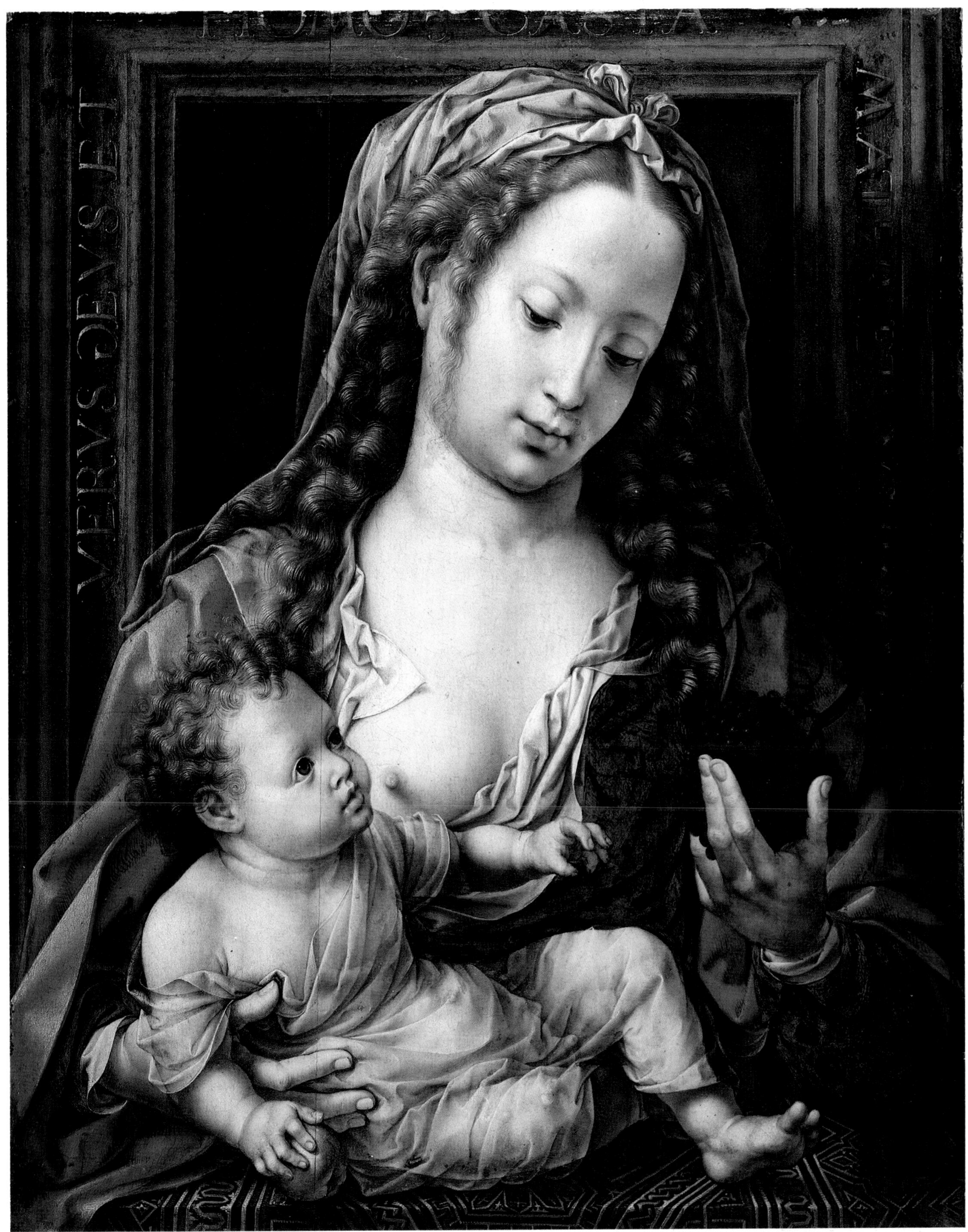
VERBVS DEVS EST

Anthonis Mor (1517/20–1576/7)
Portrait of Two Canons
1544

Oak, 74 × 96 cm (29⅛ × 37¾ in)
Signed: 'Anthonis mor fecit 1544'
Acquired 1859
Cat. no. 585 A

Apart from a very few religious subjects, Anthonis Mor devoted himself almost exclusively to portraiture. In this field he is justifiably considered the greatest Netherlandish artist of his period. His impressive portraits of Habsburg Spanish court society brought him international renown. Some of the most powerful personalities of the time vied for the privilege of sitting to Mor, among them Philip II of Spain, Cardinal Granvella, Margaret of Parma, the Duke of Alba, William of Orange and Mary Tudor.

Anthonis Mor came from Utrecht, where he began his career as a pupil and an assistant of Jan van Scorel (1495–1562). In 1547 he settled in Antwerp as an independent master. A short time later he went to Brussels to enter the service of Antoine de Granvella (1517–86), then Bishop of Arras, later Cardinal and Minister under Charles V, Philip II, and Margaret of Parma. Granvella, who played a key role in Habsburg politics, considered the artist 'his own man'. Thanks to his protection, Mor obtained numerous commissions from important people of the highest ranking nobility. In 1548, he is said to have travelled in Granvella's retinue to the Imperial Diet at Augsburg, where he met Titian. Whether or not this is true, Titian's portraiture decidedly influenced Mor's own approach and contributed to his unique style. In 1550 Mor went to Spain and Portugal, where he worked at the courts in Valladolid, Lisbon and Madrid. He returned to the Netherlands in 1553, and the following year, as court artist of Philip II, he went to London for the Spanish King's marriage to Mary Tudor, Queen of England. After another journey to Spain he lived and worked in Utrecht and Antwerp, where he strongly influenced such artists as Frans Pourbus (*c.*1540–81) and Adriaen Thomasz. Key (*c.*1544–84), just as earlier he had influenced the Spanish court painters Alonso Sánchez Coëllo (1531/2–88) and Juan Pantoja de la Cruz (1553–1608). Mor's *Self-portrait* of 1558 (Florence, Uffizi), very much in the manner of his aristocratic portraits and containing a reference to the Greek painter Apelles, testifies to an awareness of his high social position and the considerable freedom he enjoyed at the royal courts he served.

Anthonis Mor
Self-portrait, 1558
Florence, Uffizi

Portrait of Two Canons of Utrecht Cathedral of 1544 is the earliest known work by Mor. Still very much indebted to the art of his teacher, Jan van Scorel, it recalls that artist's groups of Jerusalem pilgrims at Utrecht and Haarlem. Its most striking feature is perhaps the incredibly tangible presence of the two figures, who emerge bodily from the dark grey background. Their white gowns seem to glow, and the treatment of the folds and delicately graduated modelling reveal an artist of great sensibility. Even greater emphasis is placed on the faces of the two men, with heightened colour in what is otherwise a very reserved, almost monochrome palette. Every contour of their faces, whether brightly illuminated or cast in shadow, is defined with short, fine brushstrokes in a manner extremely unusual for the period and verging almost on pointillism. This vivacious play of light and shade lends the faces immediacy, which not even the austere profile pose of the one can mitigate. In this regard, Mor had already clearly begun to surpass his teacher, Jan van Scorel.

The obvious discrepancies between this portrait and his later works are surely due to the demands of his patrons, who cannot have allowed him a great deal of freedom here. They stipulated the half-figure portrait type, the procession of figures, and the detailed personal information which was to be included in the picture. Beneath the two clergymen is a painted inscription tablet with their family arms and two quatrains which record for posterity their names, ranks, and the date of their pilgrimage to Jerusalem. The red cross of Jerusalem appears at the centre of the white field.

The figures portrayed are Cornelis van Horn and Anthonis Taets van Ameronghen, canons of Utrecht Cathedral who, as members of the Jerusalem Brethren, had made a pilgrimage to the Holy Land and Jerusalem. The date of van Horn's journey is given as 1520 – over twenty years before this commemorative portrait was painted. The men's

piously folded hands, the palm fronds over their shoulders, and the inscription itself, all testify to a devout faith that their pilgrimage has helped them attain redemption and eternal peace.

Like the sequential portraits of Jan van Scorel, Anthonis Mor's double portrait marks an important stage in the development of group portraiture in the Netherlands, which was to culminate in the seventeenth century with Frans Hals's and Rembrandt's images of regents and guilds.

Pieter Bruegel the Elder (1525/30–69)
The Netherlandish Proverbs
1559

Oak, 117 × 163 cm (46 × 64⅛ in)
Signed lower right: 'BRVEGEL 1559'
First mentioned in the inventory of Peter Stevens, official of the Antwerp Poor Relief, 1668
Acquired 1914
Cat. no. 1720

Lodovico Guicciardini, in his 1567 description of the Netherlands, called this artist 'Pietro Brueghel di Breda', indicating that he may well have been born and brought up in the town environment of Breda rather than in the country. His date of birth was probably some time between 1525 and 1530. Emperor Charles V (1500–58), monarch of the Netherlands, was about thirty years old at the time, and Philip II (1527–98) had just been born. The Netherlands enjoyed unprecedented prosperity in that period, yet by the time Bruegel died, the country had been laid waste by the Duke of Alba's armies and the population had taken up arms in defence. During these turbulent historical changes, Bruegel's work developed into the most brilliant and significant contribution made by any artist of his time.

Shortly after being admitted as independent master to the Antwerp Artists' Guild in 1515, Bruegel went to live in Italy for several years. What impressed him there was not so much the art of antiquity or contemporary Italian painters but the sublime vistas of the Alps, the Tessin Valley and the region around St Gotthard, which had a lasting effect on his conception of landscape. In 1555 Bruegel was back in Antwerp, where he made drawings for the publisher Hieronymus Cock which were engraved and found wide distribution. In Brussels in 1563 he married the daughter of Pieter Coecke van Aelst, the artist who according to Carel van Mander's report (1604) was Bruegel's teacher. Bruegel left many friends behind in Antwerp, among them the humanist and geographer Abraham Ortelius (1527–98). Ortelius introduced him to a circle of Catholics who, infused with Erasmus's philosophy, condemned the intolerance of State and Church. The sense of tolerance and humaneness that informs Bruegel's work and still moves us so deeply today, certainly owed much to his Antwerp friends. Yet he soon found appreciative patrons in Brussels as well. Among them was no lesser figure than Cardinal Antoine Perrenot de Granvella (1517–86), confidant of Philip II of Spain and adviser to Margaret of Parma.

The connoisseurs of the period thought of Bruegel as a congenial successor to Hieronymus Bosch, who had died ten years before Bruegel's birth. Yet Bruegel himself was destined to die young. In a Latin obituary of about 1573, his friend Ortelius wrote, 'Revered by the manes, Pieter Bruegel was doubtless the greatest painter of his time. No one would dare to deny this, except an envious man, a rival, or someone to whom this master's art was completely foreign. To fell the whole truth, I would repeat that not only was he the greatest painter, but he contained within himself the entire universe of painting. And this Bruegel I extol painted many things that cannot be painted, as Pliny once said when speaking of Apelles. In all his works he continually strove to reveal more than could be seen on the surface of his pictures.'

In the year 1559, a watershed in Bruegel's career, he painted *The Netherlandish Proverbs* and *The Battle between Lent and Carnival* (Vienna, Kunsthistorisches Museum). These, the first of his large paintings, introduced a highly productive period that established his reputation and for which he is still admired today.

The Dutch language of Bruegel's time was richer in proverbs than it is now, and interest in vernacular speech was widespread, as may be seen from the *Adagiorum Collectanea*, a famous compendium of idiomatic Latin proverbs by Erasmus of Rotterdam. This interest developed veritably encyclopaedic proportions in Bruegel's mind.

Shortly before completing his *The Netherlandish Proverbs*, Bruegel made a drawing of the *elck*, the proverbial everyman who, armed with a lantern, rummages through a pile of barrels, baskets and sacks. Like the man beside him, shown tugging at the corners of a blanket, he thinks only of his personal advantage. The caption to the engraving based on the drawing says, 'All over the world, everyone sees only himself, and hopes to find himself in all things. But how can anyone find himself when everyone is looking? We all fight for an advantage (the longer straw), some from above, others from below. Almost nobody knows himself. Those who realize this will see wonders.' This insight is surely central to an understanding of Bruegel's painting.

The first visual compendium ever made of over one hundred proverbs and idioms, its images are as realistic as the concise characterization it gives of typical human behaviour. Each scene can stand alone; though they take place simultaneously, the events illustrated have all the incidental and random character of everyday life. A village on a river near the sea forms a spacious stage for the seemingly mundane activities of its inhabitants. They play against a backdrop of a farmhouse, dilapidated huts, a stony bridge with a pillory and tower, a marketplace – the focus of events – and a farmstead among wheatfields near a wood. The plain of the open sea spreads into the distance, shimmering in the brilliant sunlight of a late-summer day.

The various scenes are linked by subtle colour combinations, with salient points in the composition marked by strong reds and blues. Dominating the centre is the blue of a cloak which a young woman in a bright red dress hangs over the shoulders of her old, infirm husband. One of the painting's early titles derives from this motif of a blue cloak, a common symbol of deception. The same title appears on an engraving published in Antwerp in 1558, which may have been one source of inspiration for Bruegel's image. Its caption reads in part, 'Most call this the cloak of blue, but worldly folly would better do.' The notion that folly and self-deception were the source of all unhappiness found its most poignant contemporary expression in Erasmus of Rotterdam's *Praise of Folly* (1511).

The other early title of our painting, *Topsy-turvy World*, goes back to the reversed globe prominently displayed on the house at the left of the picture, a symbol of the absurdity of human existence. The figures in the painting are accordingly characterized not as individuals but as typical representatives of their social class, strutting across the stage like mindless marionettes, oblivious of their surroundings. The *mise en scène* of this play recalls Rabelais's description of Pantagruel's journey to the Kingdom of Quintessence (1564), whose inhabitants' strange antics embody proverbial human absurdities.

Bruegel, too, following this *leitmotiv* of a topsy-turvy world, pillories every variety of the illogicality, absurdity and foolishness in human behaviour. People fill in a well after the calf has drowned, and carry lights under bushels in broad daylight. Other scenes allude to the Seven Deadly Sins, supplemented by such other negative qualities as deception, lying and cant. This is a world that pays obeisance not to God but to the devil. Even the clergy decorate the face of the Lord with a false beard of flax.

Obviously, Bruegel's painting contains a great deal of acid criticism, and its basic tenor is pessimistic. Yet it is more than a depiction of human life as a farce destined to play itself out no matter how much we should wish to change it. By helping people realize and understand the absurdity of their actions, Bruegel hoped to improve people, and in this regard his message is as apt today as ever.

Franz Hogenberg
The Blue Mantle, 1558
Engraving (detail)

The Proverbs

1 Their roof is tiled with tarts (they live in a land of plenty; a fool's paradise)
2 They were married over a broomstick (without going to the trouble of obtaining a church blessing)
3 The broom is sticking out there (the master's away; when the cat's away, the mice will play)
4 He looks through his fingers (can afford to be indulgent, or never look a gift horse in the mouth)
5 Now the knife's out (an open challenge)
6 There stand the wooden shoes (to wait in vain)
7 They've got each other by the nose (trying to trick each other)
8 The die is cast
9 Fools are always dealt the best cards
10 It depends on the fall of the cards
11 Shitting on the world (in utter disgust)
12 Topsy-turvy world (the opposite of the way it should be)
13 To pull something through the eye (between the blades) of a pair of scissors (to make a dishonest profit)
14 Keep at least *one* egg in your nest (a nest egg; something for a rainy day)
15 To have a toothache (possibly: to fool others by malingering)
16 a) He's pissing at the moon (attempting the impossible, or barking at the moon)
b) He has pissed at the moon (his enterprise has failed)
17 He's got a hole in his roof
18 An old roof needs a lot of patching
19 The roof has laths (there are eavesdroppers)
20 An inn at the sign of the chamber-pot (instead of a tankard; it's a crazy world)
21 To shave a fool without lather (give him the bum's rush; take him for a ride)
22 Something growing out of the window (an open secret, or truth will out)
23 Two fools under one cap (like to like; folly loves company)
24 a) A fellow shooting a second arrow to find the first (foolish misdirected perseverance)
b) Shooting all his arrows at once (and having none left when he really needs one)
25 She could tie the devil himself to a pillow (spiteful obstinacy overpowers the devil himself)
26 He's a pillar-biter (a hypocrite)
27 She carries fire in one hand and water in the other (is two-faced, deceitful)
28 a) He's frying a herring for the roe (throwing a sprat to catch a herring, that is, to sacrifice a trifle to gain something substantial)
b) His herring's not frying this time (his plans are going awry)
c) The lid fell in on him (he's been left holding the bag)
29 a) There's more in it than a gutted herring (more to it than meets the eye)
b) The herring will hang by its own gills (everyone must bear the consequences of his own mistakes)
30 He's sitting in the ashes between two stools (having missed his opportunity, failed through indecisiveness)
31 What good is smoke against iron? (why fight the inevitable?)

32 The spindles are falling in the ashes (something is failing, going on the rocks)
33 Let the dog in, and he'll go into the larder (a loss that might have been expected, or give him an inch and he'll take a mile)
34 The sow pulls the bung in this house (it's poorly managed; negligence will be punished)
35 He's banging his head against a brick wall
36 He's in armour (up in arms; fighting mad)
37 He's belling the cat (attempting a difficult task, or letting the world know what he's up to, usually with dire results)
38 Armed to the teeth
39 He's an iron-eater (a bully, tough customer, eats nails for breakfast)
40 He's feeling the hens (counting his chickens before they are hatched)
41 He's always gnawing the same bone (involved in a thankless, futile task, or continually harping on something)
42 The sign of the shears (the pickpocket's symbol; a clip joint)
43 He speaks with two mouths (out of both sides of his mouth; with a forked tongue)
44 One shears sheep, the other pigs (rich man, poor man, or some people have all the luck)
45 All that bleating and so little wool (much ado about nothing)
46 Shear them but don't skin them (do not pursue your advantage at any price)
47 Patient as a lamb
49 a) One winds that the other spins (to spread rumours, gossip)
b) Don't let the black dog interfere (because he could ruin everything, or with gossips in the house, the watchdog may sleep)
49 To carry a bushel of light to the sun (waste one's time)
50 To light candles for the devil (make friends in all camps because they might come in useful)
51 Confessing to the devil (telling one's secrets to one's worst enemy)
52 An ear-blower (putting a flea in someone's ear; scandal-mongering)
53 The crane entertaining the fox (from Aesop's *Fables*: two deceivers conniving, whereby one will be deceived)
54 What good is a pretty plate when it's empty?
55 He's a skimming ladle (a flatterer, sycophant)
56 It's chalked up (a debt or unkindess that will not be forgotten)
57 He's filling in the well after the calf drowned (shutting the door after the horse has bolted)
58 He's got the world spinning on his thumb (on a string; everything is going his own way)
59 To put a spoke in someone's wheel (put an obstacle in his path)
60 One must stoop to get on in the world (stoop to conquer)
61 He's tied a flaxen beard on God (His excessive piety probably conceals a selfish motive)
62 He's casting roses (pearls) before swine (Matthew 7:6)
63 She's putting the blue mantle on her husband (deceiving him)
64 The pig's been stuck in the belly (the matter is clinched; there's no going back now)
65 Two dogs over one bone (to fight bitterly over a thing; symbol of envy, strife, malice)
66 Sitting on hot coals (to be anxious and extremely impatient)
67 a) A roast must be basted
b) It's good luck to piss on the fire
c) His fire is pissed out (he's completely discouraged)
68 There is no turning a spit with him (he's uncooperative, a spoil-sport)
69 a) He catches fish with his bare hands (by taking them out of other people's nets; i.e. lazy but clever)
b) To throw a smelt to catch a cod (same meaning as 28a)
70 He's fallen through the basket (been given the cold shoulder by a woman, or otherwise failed)
71 He's hanging between heaven and earth (between the devil and the deep blue sea; an insoluble situation)
72 She's taken the hen's egg and let the goose egg go (made a bad choice out of greediness)
73 He's yawning at the stove, or You have to yawn a long time to out yawn the oven (to bite off more than you can chew, overestimate your own abilities, or fight a losing battle)
74 He can't make it from one load to the next (cannot live within his budget)
75 He's looking for the hatchet (for an excuse), and, He can use his lantern at last (let his light shine)
76 It's a hatchet with a handle (a good proposition? The meaning is uncertain)
77 It's a hoe without a handle (perhaps a doubtful proposition or unripe plan)
78 Spilled porridge cannot be scraped up again (there's no use crying over spilled milk; what's done is done)
79 They're pulling for the longer end (each concerned only for his own advantage)
80 He's hanging on tight (or: love is on the side where the money bag hangs)
81 a) He's standing in his own light
b) If you look for someone in the oven, you must have been there yourself (only he who is wicked himself thinks badly of others)
82 He's playing in the pillory (drawing attention to his own shame, or People who live in glass houses should not throw stones)
83 He's fallen from the ox to the ass (made a bad bargain)
84 One beggar pities the other outside the door
85 Anybody can see through a plank with a hole in it
86 a) To rub one's bottom on the door (to make light of one's own misfortune)
b) To have one's burden to bear
87 He's kissing the ring (showing insincere respect, ingratiating himself)
88 He's fishing behind his net (expending useless effort)
89 Big fish eat little fish
90 He can't bear to see the sun shine on the water (envy of one's neighbour)
91 He's throwing money into the water (squandering it, throwing it out of the window)
92 They shit through the same hole (being bosom friends)
93 Something is like an outhouse over a ditch (obvious, a clear-cut matter)
94 He's trying to kill two flies with one blow (and being too ambitious, will probably miss them both)
95 She's watching the stork (daydreaming, wasting her time)
96 You can tell a bird by its feathers (or a man by his acts)
97 He hangs his cloak to the wind (is an opportunist)
98 He tosses feathers to the wind (all his effort has been in vain; to work unsystemmatically)
99 The best straps are cut from someone else's leather (it's easy to be generous with others' property)
100 The pitcher goes to water until it breaks (everything has its limit)
101 He's got an eel by the tail (is involved in a difficult and probably futile undertaking)
102 It's hard to swim upstream (to oppose custom or generally accepted opinion)
103 He's hanging his habit on the fence (forsaking his familiar life without knowing what the new one will bring)
104 This proverb has not been identified with certainty, but it may be either:
a) He sees bears dancing before his eyes (as a result of hunger)
b) Wild bears prefer each other's company (in the derogatory sense of birds of a feather flock together)
105 a) He's running like his arse was on fire
b) If you eat fire, you'll fart sparks (if you court danger, don't wonder at the results)
106 a) Leave the gate open, and the pigs will get into the corn
b) Where the corn decreases, the pigs increase (i.e. get fatter. You don't get something for nothing; or, One man's loss is another man's gain)
107 He doesn't care whose house burns down as long as he can warm himself at the coals (he profits by others' misfortune)
108 A cracked wall will soon fall
109 It is easy to sail before the wind
110 He keeps an eye on the sail (is alert, knows which way the wind blows)
111 a) Who knows why geese go barefoot? (there is sure to be some reason)
b) If the Lord didn't intend me to keep geese, I'll let them be geese (mind my own business)
112 Horse droppings are not figs (beware of swindlers)
113 Dragging the log (a jilted suitor, or slaving at a senseless task)
114 Fear makes an old woman trot (brings out unexpected qualities, or necessity is the mother if invention)
115 He shits on the gallows (is fearless and incorrigible and will likely come to a bad end)
116 Where there is carrion, there are crows
117 When the blind lead the blind, they both fall in a ditch
118 The journey is not yet over when one can discern church and tower (the goal is reached only when one has finally completed one's task)

One final proverb relates to the sun in the sky: Every plot, however finely spun, finally comes to the sun (nothing remains hidden)

(Based on the translation by Haijo and Monique Westra)

Pieter Bruegel the Elder

Two Chained Monkeys

1562

Oak, 20 × 23 cm ($7\frac{7}{8}$ × 9 in)
Signed lower left: 'BRVEGEL MDLXII'
First mentioned in the inventory of Peter Stevens, official of the Antwerp Poor Relief, 1668
Acquired 1931 (Friedländer Foundation Fund)
Cat. no. 2077

This unusual painting was executed in 1562, shortly before Bruegel moved from Antwerp to Brussels. It represents two monkeys chained to an iron ring in an arched window opening. The heavy chains, the massive masonry, and the low opening increase the impression of inescapable captivity. The animals are apparently resigned to their lot. While one cowers with a bent back, staring absently in front of him, the other fixes us with an unmoving, wide-eyed stare that seems almost human. This gaze and the nutshells scattered on the ledge are the only signs that the animals have not been completely abandoned. The attitudes of creatures sapped of vitality by captivity are characterized with great empathy.

As though seen from a high tower, a spacious plain suffused with light opens out beyond the dungeon window. In the mist, Antwerp lies with its harbour and the jutting tower of the Onze Lieve Vrouwekatedraal; in front of it, the broad River Schelde flows into the distance, where water and sky merge. The contrast between the depressing closeness of the dim room and the bright sunshine outside, with birds in the sky and ships evoking the freedom of distant shores, heightens the feeling of captivity within.

The simple yet carefully considered composition of the small panel and its limited colour range of nuances in grey and brown, suggest an equally straightforward and poignant meaning. Yet perhaps because of this concentration in form and content, interpretations of the image diverge widely.

In terms of composition, Bruegel may well have taken hints from such engravings as *Four Monkeys* by Israhel van Meckenem or *Madonna with the Long-tailed Monkey* by Dürer. Studies from life, however, were more important. The animals depicted belong to the family of long-tailed monkeys, a species called *Cercocebus torquatus* whose natural habitat reaches from Cape Verde, West Africa, to the southern parts of what was then the Congo and is now Zaire. Monkeys of this type were imported as curiosities into the Netherlands by Portuguese Indiamen who picked them up on the west coast of Africa. They were popular pets, and drew high prices. 'I paid 4 golden guilders for little monkeys,' noted Dürer in 1520, during his stay in Antwerp.

Though Bruegel's depiction shows evidence of minute observation, he cannot have intended it merely as a realistic animal study. Associations with the artist's life – his imminent move to Brussels, his marriage, and his loss of independence – would also seem rather unlikely. It is more plausible that the tiny panel was meant as a going-away present for a friend left behind in Antwerp. Some observers see a bitter allusion to the town's inhabitants here, while others advance the quite different political interpretation that the chained monkeys represent the Dutch population suffering under the yoke of Spanish tyranny.

In short, the painting has inspired many explanations. Those based on the symbolic or allegorical meanings associated with monkeys throughout the history of art are the most plausible: man is seen as enslaved by his instincts, prisoner of his own carnal, animal desires. Bruegel's monkeys in chains, then, would allude metaphorically to human beings who for the sake of dubious pleasures – symbolized here by broken, empty nutshells – are willing to sacrifice their freedom. The animals' captivity suggests the self-enslavement of people who, ignoring the Christian virtues, play havoc with destiny and can expect to meet a sad end. This captivity is self-chosen, Bruegel seems to say, since no one need succumb to it who has enough strength of will to recognize that moderation and sense are the best guides to a meaningful life. This critical view of human nature underlies many of the enigmatic allegories of the artist who later was all too unthinkingly labelled 'Peasant Bruegel'.

Albrecht Dürer
The Madonna with the Long-tailed Monkey
*c.*1498
Engraving

BRVEGEL · MDLXII

Pieter Aertsen (1507/8–75)
Marketwoman at a Vegetable Stand
1567

Oak, 111 × 110 cm ($43\frac{3}{4} \times 43\frac{1}{4}$ in)
Signed top: '1567 · 16 · AVG P.A.'
(with trident, Aertsen's device, between the initials)
Acquired 1961
Cat. no. 3/61

Still life did not become a subject thought worthy of art until quite late in its history, largely because of the tenacious notion that artists were called to higher things than depicting trivial, everyday objects. Artists of the Netherlands, however, made an immense contribution to the development of the still-life genre, with Pieter Aertsen and his nephew, Joachim Beuckelaer, doing the groundwork. Their paintings represent the point of departure from which the artists of the seventeenth century, increasingly specializing in particular aspects of still life, went on to superb achievements.

After an apprenticeship in Amsterdam, Aertsen settled in Antwerp in about 1530. Though he became well known and prosperous there, he nevertheless returned to Amsterdam in 1555. His work was much in demand, particularly the still lifes, which are said to have gained him a commission for an altarpiece for the Oude Kerk in Amsterdam. He had established his reputation with religious subjects, but it was the realism of Aersten's still lifes that fascinated and impressed his contemporaries most. In his book *Den grondt der Edel Vry Schilderconst* Carel van Mander marvelled, 'For you imagine you see things of every variety, and yet they are all nothing but paint, which he knew how to mix so that they seem to become robustly alive, the surface to take on sculptural relief qualities, and mute objects seem to speak, dead ones to live.'

The painting in our collection, from the artist's late period, is dominated by a peerless still life of fruit and vegetables. A deluge of harvest produce and kitchen and table ware, painted in intense, glowing colours, is displayed on an inclining stand. The sensual appeal is stressed by the inviting gesture of the young farmwoman seated among this plenty. Wearing a large straw hat, a red dress with a black bodice and white collar, and a grey-blue apron, she offers baskets of cucumbers, pumpkins and parsnips, radishes, cabbages, grapes, apples and peaches, walnuts and chestnuts. Waffles, bread and baked delicacies are also on display, as well as butter, exotic lemons, and a salted herring.

The produce indicates that the season is autumn, a time of preparations for winter; but its formal, still-life presentation points beyond this to symbolize nature as experienced by man. Underlying much of Aertsen's imagery are notions associated with the four Seasons, the four Elements, or the five Senses, though this last reference, as in the present painting, is often only indirect. Aertsen frequently included in the backgrounds of his paintings some religious scene, such as Christ's visit to Mary and Martha, the disciples at Emmaeus, or Jesus with the woman caught in adultery. Yet far from being merely an excuse to paint still life, such religious scenes refer to other human needs beside the sensual side of their nature. As in so many of Aertsen's works, the figures in the background here, a couple embracing, warn that the pleasures of the flesh, *voluptas carnis*, can threaten spiritual welfare, a message clearly emphasized by the empty wagon and the idle horse. By contrast, the vendor among her wares and the peasant driving his ox to market, can be measured, both literally and figuratively, by the fruits of their industry.

Yet the products of physical labour spread out so convincingly before our eyes are not the measure of all things. The lemon, in art a traditional emblem for superficial beauty, has bitter flesh. It evokes the doubtfulness of pleasures whose consequences can be equally bitter, since they entail a loss of peace of mind, even of one's soul. The herring, which strikes a seemingly strange note in the still life, was a traditional Lenten dish. It brings fasting to mind, a practice meant to help human beings resist sensual temptation and lead them on the path of righteousness. Seen in this light, Aertsen's image indeed contains a message. Illustrating the dualism of life, it reminds us that for the sake of spiritual welfare, earthly possessions must be used well.

Pieter Aertsen
The Cook
Brussels, Koninklijke Musea voor Schone Kunsten

FLEMISH AND DUTCH PAINTING OF THE SEVENTEENTH CENTURY

BY JAN KELCH

Peter Paul Rubens (1577–1640)
St Sebastian
*c.*1618

Canvas, 200 × 128 cm (78¾ × 50⅜ in)
Acquired 1878
Cat. no. 798 H

Sebastian, a Roman officer during the reign of Diocletian, was condemned to be executed for his Christian faith. By a miracle he survived the archers' arrows; yet when he publicly accused the Emperor of persecuting Christians, Diocletian had him clubbed to death.

Rubens shows St Sebastian, his body pierced by arrows, bound to a tree trunk in the foreground of a landscape. The bow and quiver at the lower left symbolize his martyrdom. Clad only in a loincloth, the almost life-sized nude figure nearly fills the entire height of the pictorial field. It is illuminated by light falling from the upper left, and stands out in strong contrast to the dark trees and overcast sky.

The crucifixion of Christ was depicted in similar terms. According to traditional doctrine, the sufferings of Christian martyrs, who were revered as contributing to the work of salvation, mirrored the agony of Christ. This concordance was particularly close with St Sebastian, whose martyrdom by arrows and miraculous survival clearly paralleled Christ's crucifixion and resurrection. This is one reason why Sebastian's sufferings at the hands of Roman archers, rather than his death by clubbing, entered pictorial tradition as the motif most often associated with the St Sebastian legend.

Rubens has concentrated the meaning of the event in a single figure of great emotional force. The herculean limbs bound and pressed into passivity, and the tortured body looming far above the low horizon, are pictorial examples of the counter-reformation with which the Catholic Church in the southern Netherlands challenged the spread of Calvinism in neighbouring Holland, and which included a demonstration, in religious imagery, of its superior doctrine.

Rubens's *St Sebastian* is a highly individual expression of his experience in Italy. The pose is almost a mirror-image of that in Mantegna's version of the subject (Vienna, Kunsthistorisches Museum), whose small figure Rubens enlarged to life-size, giving it a sculptural massiveness. In force of design, the image compares to the monumental figures of Michelangelo, even to the famous statue of *Laocoön*, whose configuration is recalled here by the motif of the torso swelling outwards from a slight turn of the hips. The saint's expressive features are similar to those of the *Dying Alexander*, a Hellenistic marble head (Florence, Uffizi) which was included in pictorial and literary tradition as an *exemplum doloris*, a rendering of the death agony worthy of emulation. The realism of the still life composed of a bow, a quiver and arrows, like the pronounced chiaroscuro, suggests the influence of Caravaggio. In the treatment of the landscape, by contrast, Rubens follows the northern tradition, conceiving it as the place of action and allowing it to convey its own meaning. As if to mirror the drama of the event, the foreground illumination skimmers again in the cool yellow twilight on the far horizon.

In the lucidity and balance of its pictorial means, this image of *St Sebastian* is among the works with which the Flemish master set lasting standards for the Late Baroque style, bringing it to full fruition. Rubens himself spoke of 'the flower of my things' when together with other paintings he offered this one, in 1618, to Sir Dudley Carleton, English Ambassador at The Hague, in exchange for his collection of antiquities.

The Dying Alexander
Florence, Uffizi

Peter Paul Rubens

Perseus and Andromeda

*c.*1622

Oak, 100 × 138.5 cm ($39\frac{3}{8} \times 54\frac{1}{2}$ in)
Pasquier Collection, Paris, 1755; in the Picture Gallery, Sanssouci, from 1764
Acquired from the Royal Palaces, Berlin, 1830
Cat. no. 785

It was the Roman poet Ovid who, in his *Metamorphoses*, transmitted and popularized the ancient story of Perseus and Andromeda. Andromeda, daughter of King Cepheus of Ethiopia, was bound to a cliff to be sacrificed to a terrible sea-monster. This fate was ordained by Poseidon to punish the pride of the king's wife, Cassiopeia, who compared her own and her daughter's beauty with that of the Nereids. Perseus, returning on Pegasus from his victory over Medusa, saw the captive princess and, entranced by her loveliness, approached her, saying, 'Not chains like these do you deserve/But the bands that unite ardent lovers./Now the maiden cannot speak, does not dare/To address a man, and were her hands not tied,/She would hide her innocent face in them.'

In Ovid's version of the story, the encounter between Perseus and Andromeda precedes the hero's battle with the sea-monster. Rubens, whose narrative skill lives up to the highest Homeric standards, combines the two scenes. The monster already lies dead in the water as Perseus, in the red mantle of the victor, loosens Andromeda's fetters. Two *putti* assist him, while three others romp around Pegasus, one helping another up on the horse's back as a third holds the reins. Set on an outcrop at some distance from the spectator, the story unfolds chronologically from left to right, to the triumphant meeting of the two protagonists. Their complementary poses, one active, the other passive, and the contrast of shining armour next to delicately modelled flash, emphasizes the awakening love described in Ovid's poetry. Never at a loss for apt quotations from classical art to underline his message, Rubens has modelled the figures of Andromeda and the *putto* who is helping to untie her on the *Venus felix* (Rome, Vatican Collection). The artist may have seen this sculpture while he was in Rome, or perhaps Hendrick Goltzius introduced him to it.

Rubens painted several variations of the Andromeda myth, interpreting it slightly differently each time. Among these are a late work, also in the Berlin Gallery, and an almost identical version in the Hermitage, Leningrad, which was done immediately before the painting discussed here. In the Hermitage composition, Perseus, holding the weapon of a Medusa shield, dominates at the centre. The sea-monster at his feet, Pegasus reined in by *putti*, and Andromeda being released by other infant angels, are arranged around him concentrically like symbols of his valour; and a figure of Fama crowns him with a wreath to signify his heroic victory. This treatment of the theme could be interpreted as a political allegory. There are, in fact, paintings in which Andromeda personifies a city, a nation, or a religion which, threatened by the monster of an enemy power, internal division, or heresy, is saved by a soldier or king in the guise of Perseus.

The Berlin painting, however, does not seem to contain allusions of this kind. Rather, it is as if the artist took the Horatian principle '*ut pictura poesis*' ('let poetry be like painting') literally, and, vying with the poet's art, tried to create a visual narrative whose lucid form and feeling could stand beside the great verses of Ovid.

Hendrick Goltzius
Venus Felix
Drawing
Haarlem, Stichting Teyler

Peter Paul Rubens
Child with a Bird
(Philipp Rubens?)
c.1624–5

Oak, 50.8 × 40.5 cm (20 × 16 in)
In the Picture Gallery, Sanssouci, 1770
Acquired from the Royal Palaces, Berlin
Cat. no. 763

Here Rubens has captured that mixture of excitement and trepidation with which children play with animals, in this case a startled bird fluttering on a short string. The colour accents are distributed with great subtlety, the delicate reddish heightenings of the flesh colours rising to brilliance in the coral necklace, and complemented by the green tones of the bird's feathers and the golden blonde of the child's hair. These colours, by being set against a contrast between the dark background and bluish white chemise, are made to shine out.

The allegorical significance of the bird motif is thought by some authors to be connected with the *Reductorium morale* of Petrus Berchorius (mid-fourteenth century). There, the goldfinch, which is easily tamed and can be trained to sing in captivity, is compared with men who, in the familiar confines of religion or church sing praises of God. A reference to the efficacy of religious training in producing good Christians would certainly not be out of place in this portrait of a child. Another implication might be seen in the coral necklace. In the emblematic literature of the seventeenth century, coral, which grows hard and takes on its beautiful colour only when it is removed from the water – its home, so to speak – is seen as a symbol of early training in courage to resist the world's temptations and dangers.

The combined motifs of child and bird, however, may have no deeper meaning than the artist's desire to enliven his composition by introducing a contrast and a bit of drama. Songbirds were popular pets at that time, and necklaces of coral, thought to be good charms against evil influences, were worn by many children.

Though Rubens's portraits were as highly regarded as his other works, he does not seem to have received commissions to portray individual children. The children he painted were his own, from his two marriages; he may also have painted children from his wider family circle, if the recent identification of this portrait with Philipp, Rubens's nephew, is correct. Philipp, born in 1611, became his charge when Rubens's brother died at an early age. Rubens has rendered the charm of childhood compellingly; the countless possibilities of the child's later development are contained as if in suspension – a universal reference that might speak against the suggested identification of Philipp. Behind the unique individuality of all his young sitters, Rubens perceived the sublime beauty of angels or *putti*, which was how he often depicted his own children in religious or mythological pictures. The boy in our portrait, too, has been cast as an angel elsewhere, for instance in *Madonna with Flower Wreath* (Munich, Alte Pinakothek). This was his first role in the present painting as well. Originally larger, the panel had a horizontal format that must have shown the boy in an expanded narrative and with further motifs respectively. Why Rubens rejected this first version, painted about 1613–14, cannot be determined. At any rate, he had the original panel cut diagonally along the child's profile and through his shoulder and chest, and on the new piece joined on at the left, added hands and a bird. In the process of integrating this motif with the existing figure he repainted the entire image, including a vestige of angel's wings on the shoulders, which X-ray analysis has revealed beneath the paint layer of the dark background.

The present, definitive version, most likely executed about 1624–5, might indeed be classed in the portrait genre, were it not that the artist's original intentions remain quite clear. What other reason can he have had for making the child's locks so angelically lovely?

Peter Paul Rubens

Landscape with Cows and Duck Hunters

*c.*1635–8

Oak, 113 × 176 cm (44½ × 69¼ in)
Collections of the Duc de Richelieu, Paris, 1677; Lord Cavendish, London, 1815; Earl of Burlington, Holker Hall, Lancaster; Duke of Devonshire, Leeds, 1868
Acquired 1927
Cat. no. 2013

In the foreground of heavily wooded meadowland, a herd of cows grazes on the bank of a stream. Women from the nearby farm are occupied in milking and filling jugs, while another, with upstretched arms, balances a wooden tub of milk on her head. Rays of the setting sun filter through the leaves and cast deepening shadows of a warm brown. The mild light of dusk lends shimmering brilliance to the tones of the women's skin, a red blouse, a deep blue dress, or the ochre and rust-brown hues of the animals' coats; yellow highlights on the vessels evoke a more precious metal than brass. Thanks to illumination and colours, the landscape has the character of an idyll, which not even a sudden shotgun blast can disturb for long. This interruption caused by a hunter crouching to the right of the stream only heightens the tranquil mood of the scene.

Though Rubens was primarily a historical painter and made only guest appearances among the landscape specialists, his work in this genre brought seventeenth-century Flemish landscape art to culmination. He mastered a great range of natural imagery, from fantastically rugged mountain vistas and violent storms to sun-drenched southern fields and motifs from his own, familiar lowlands. These last images are very much in evidence here, in a landscape whose essential elements – arrangement of figures, narrative, and composition – go back to such paintings of about two decades before as *The Farm at Laeken* (London, Buckingham Palace) and *Polder Landscape with Cows* (Munich, Alte Pinakothek).

Connections with the Munich painting are particularly close, since the three cows and central group of two seated women were derived from it. Other self-citations are the motif of the cow relieving itself near the stream, and the animal at the far left edge (which is cut off in the Munich version). The pasture setting with the milking scene, the land that slopes down to the foremost pictorial plane, and the distant vista opening out at the left are also comparable. Besides these visible analogies, invisible ones have also been detected. X-rays have revealed, in places corresponding to the Munich piece, gnarled willow trunks in the right foreground, a dark-coloured cow in profile at the centre of the composition, and a cowherd with a milk jug. These findings indicate that the genesis of the Berlin landscape must have been a second version of the Munich painting by Rubens's own hand.

It is characteristic of the artist's working method that pictorial solutions, once found, were retained and often repeated. In the present case, by leaving out elements or painting over them, by adding or shifting them in the composition, even by changing the picture format (which he made considerably wider and higher than the Munich version), and by modifying colour and illumination, Rubens created an entirely new landscape.

Elaborating the straightforward approach of the Munich piece, the artist enriched the composition and correspondingly enlivened his palette, developing a chiaroscuro that captured both the objective appearance and atmospheric essence of the landscape. This chiaroscuro, based on subtle and harmonious colour nuances, not on a monochrome scale, enabled him to use a variety of motifs without jeopardizing the continuity of the whole. Besides the splendid effect of the design, it is above all to its emotional content, its view of nature as the embodiment of human ideas or sentiments, that this late work, like all Rubens's later landscapes, owes its rank.

Peter Paul Rubens
Polder Landscape with Cows
Munich, Alte Pinakothek

Peter Paul Rubens
Portrait of Isabella Brant(?)
*c.*1626

Oak, 97.3 × 71.5 cm ($38\frac{1}{4} \times 28\frac{1}{8}$ in)
Acquired 1903
Cat. no. 762 A

The seated subject, holding a fan and turned slightly to the right, is portrayed life-size and three-quarter length. She gazes directly at the observer. Her face, neck and hands, brilliantly illuminated, shine against the deep red of the background and the dark, primarily blue tones of her dress. This concentration of light corresponds to brushwork that, smooth and controlled in the blushing glazes of the flesh, becomes looser in the background, and finally grows tentatively sketchy in the rendering of the various textures of the gown. This differentiation in touch lends each part great objective realism while emphasizing its autonomous value-qualities which, together with the rich palette and illumination, create an effect of fascinating and festive variety. The model's pose is correspondingly informal and her social status apparently incidental. Portrayed in strictly personal terms, she faces the observer with unaffected frankness. This naturalness of expression is heightened by a composition that flows, as if organically and with gradual shifts of axis from the sleeves, circumscribing the figure through hands, torso, head and gaze.

The immediacy of the sitter's presence and the fact that her rank is not emphasized, would place her among the artist's relatives, a consideration that has led to her identification as Isabella Brant (1591–1626), Rubens's first wife. However, this assumption is still questioned for various reasons. Some details of her features and her youthful appearance diverge from the almost contemporaneous *Portrait of Isabella Brant* of 1626 (Florence, Uffizi) which shows her considerably aged and perhaps marked by illness. This work, probably intended as a memorial, was executed shortly after Isabella died on 20 June 1626, presumably of weakness after an attack of the plague.

The Berlin panel, which as X-rays have shown, consists of two chronologically separate versions, has also been called a posthumous portrait. On the original paint layer of the first version, done some time around 1622, is a portrait sketch resembling the *Isabella* in the Cleveland Museum. In both her right hand grasps the folds of a pleated bodice, pressing it towards her. Other similarities revealed by X-ray are a scalloped bodice seam and a starched, turned-up lace collar. The same gesture and costume are present, in modified form, as in the Florence portrait. What seems decisive for the identification of the first Berlin version, however, is how some facial details are read. The eyebrows, just visible in the X-ray, appear originally to have been more highly arched, while in the final version, unlike the securely identified portraits of Isabella, they are turned up towards her temples. The hypothesis that this is a posthumous portrait, which attempts to reconcile these obvious facial differences with a desire to retain the portrait's present title, assumes that Rubens may have developed it from an existing portrait that was in his studio. The different appearance of the model – or, if you will, the entirely new personality in the definitive version of the Berlin portrait – may have resulted from the artist's desire to create a youthful and idealized image of his dead wife.

Peter Paul Rubens
Portrait of Isabella Brant
Cleveland, The Cleveland Museum of Art, Mr and Mrs William H. Marlatt Fund

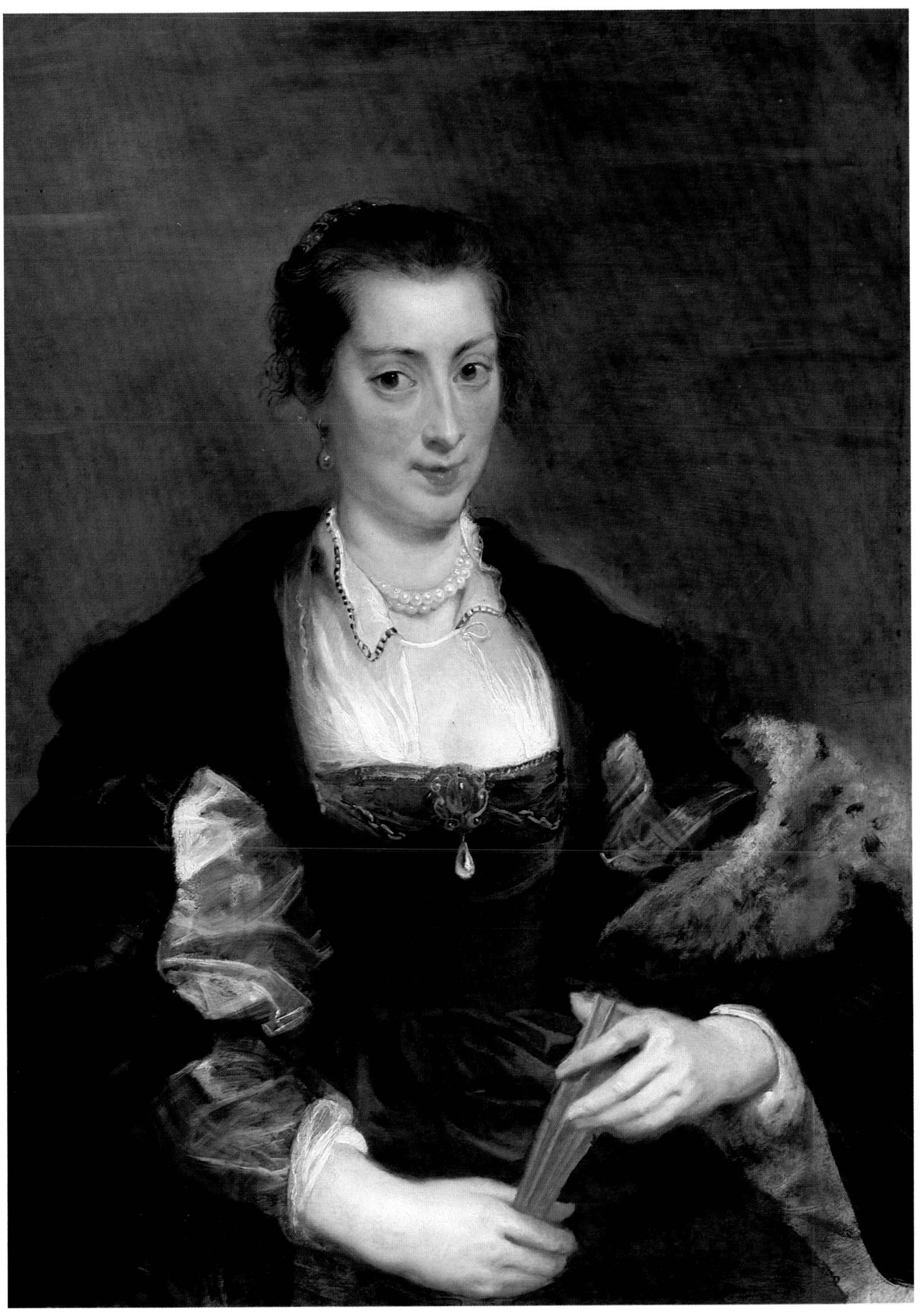

Peter Paul Rubens
St Cecilia
*c.*1639–40

Oak, 177 × 139 cm ($69\frac{5}{8}$ × $54\frac{3}{4}$ in)
From the Royal Palaces, Berlin, 1830
Cat. no. 781

This life-sized figure dominating the picture represents St Cecilia, patron saint of music. She sits slightly inclined to the left and the back, singing and playing the virginal. With greatly contained emotion she gazes heavenward, inclining her head as if to catch strains of the celestial music which inspires her. Angels cavort around her: one clambers up the instrument as if to immerse himself physically in the melody, while behind the open score two other angels watch and listen. The scene is set in opulent, columned architecture, with a view across the distant plains of Flanders.

Symbolic motifs enrich the composition. At the upper right, a *putto* draws a curtain aside and brings a wreath of roses, the emblem of St Cecilia's virginity and chastity. Her steadfast faith is symbolized by the massive column at whose base she sits. The little dog asleep at the lower right, often found in depictions of the saint, was a symbol of marital faithfulness. It probably alludes to Cecilia's unconsummated marriage to husband Valerian, whom, on their wedding day, she converted both to Catholicism and to a physically pure, Christian love. Husband and wife, as the *Legenda aurea* relates, suffered martyrs' deaths during the reign of Caesar Alexander Severus or Marcus Aurelius.

Some commentators have been prompted by the picture's rich palette to speak of synaesthesia, a principle followed by many Baroque artists. The colour combinations do seem to echo harmonies of sound. Translucent, cool, whitish flesh tones with blushes of red on cheeks and lips; brilliant emerald green in the gold-trimmed velvet gown, complemented by a carmine red in the drapery at the upper right; the soft black of the cape whose lining shimmers golden yellow at the wrist; and finally, the countless shades of ochre and dull red suffusing the skirt – all these colour accents are so consciously developed that, beyond their descriptive character, they must have significance in a larger context. The differentiation achieved through the multiple colours softens the monumental quality of the figure and architecture, giving the sacred image its intimacy and individuality that reveal her origins in the artist's personal life. The model for this saint, who has negligently slipped off her shoe and let her hair down, was Helene Fourment, Rubens's second wife.

The painting undoubtedly belongs among the artist's last works. An impetuous handling of some parts of it has, I think wrongly, been attributed to Rubens's poor health. From about 1626 he began to suffer from attacks of gout, which became more violent during his final years until in March 1640 they led to a partial paralysis of his hands. However, to blame sketchy passages, such as the *putto* with drapery, on the artist's weakened physical condition, is to ignore the care with which, for example, the capitals of the columns or the ornament band on the instrument are rendered. The mixture of summary and finely articulated forms more likely resulted from a principle of design, in which primary elements were distinguished from secondary ones. This, moreover, heightened the variety of an already bursting composition, transforming it from an unpretentious record of chamber music at home into a Baroque performance of great refinement and sensibility.

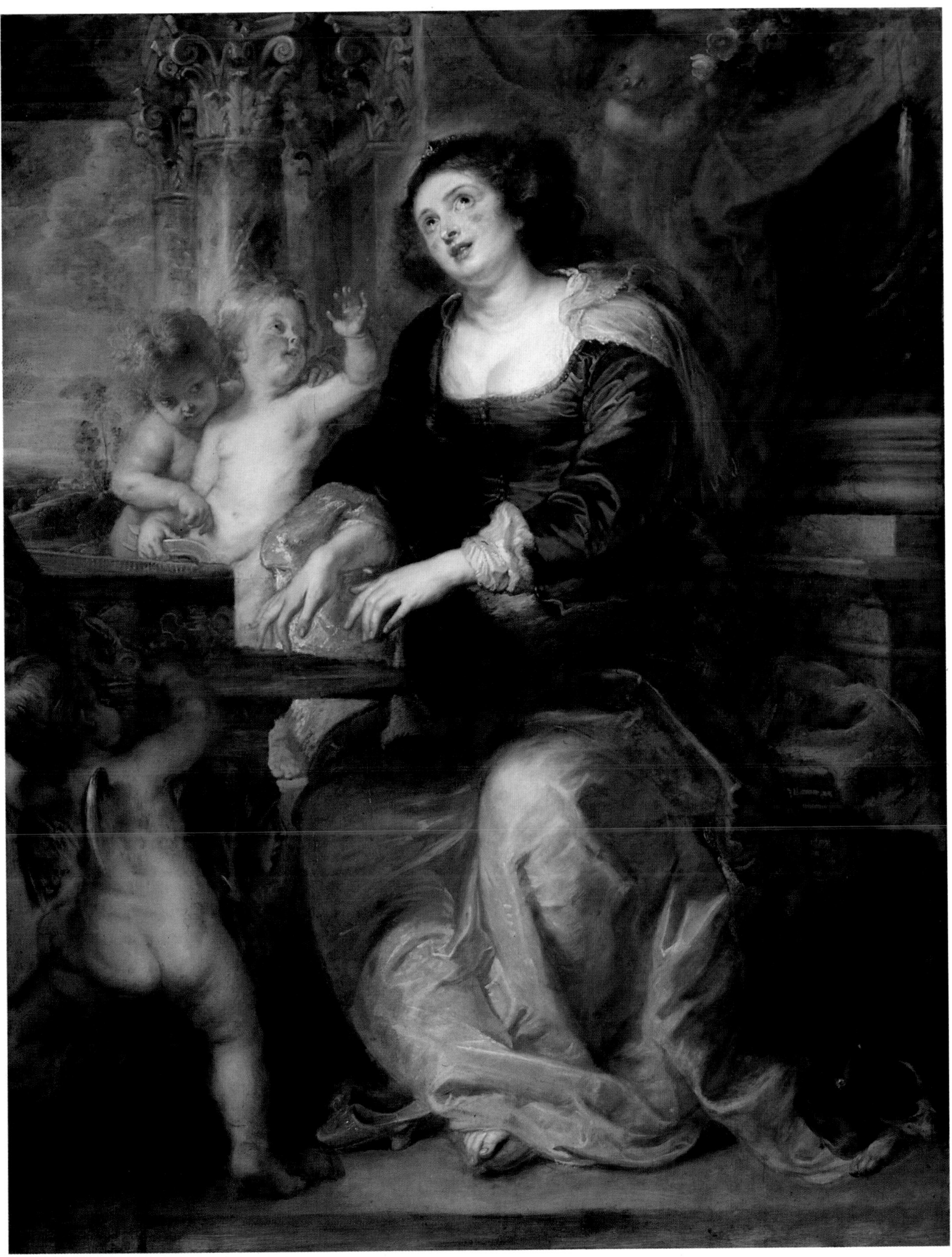

Jan Brueghel (1568–1625)

Bouquet of Flowers

*c.*1619–20

Oak, 64 × 59 cm ($25\frac{1}{4} \times 23\frac{1}{4}$ in)
Acquired 1862
Cat. no. 688 A

Flowers of all varieties and seasons, rendered with extreme naturalism, are gathered here into a single opulent bouquet. The composition's unity is ensured by the almost concentric arrangement of the flowers, the balance of a wreath and currant sprig on the table, and finally by the strict symmetry of the reliefs on the terracotta vase with their personifications of water and earth, elements crucial to the life of plants. Subtle gradings of light also contribute to the harmony of the whole. While the blossoms in the front of the picture catch the light and shine in brilliant, purposely variegated colours, those immediately behind recede into half-light and take on greyed colours that mark a transition to the darkness of the background.

Jan Brueghel's *tour de force* was probably intended first of all to celebrate the advanced cultivation of flowering plants in the Netherlands. At the time of this painting, exotic imports and new hybrids were introducing a tremendous variety of flowers which, though we now take them for granted, were then still rare and valuable. This explains how they came to be in still-life painting, and also why so many early flower pieces have the character of a botanical record. Botany had long before detached itself from herb-medicine to become an exact science, and the geographical discoveries of the sixteenth century had spurred an interest in exotic flowers, which were cultivated by royalty and prosperous patricians. Besides being lovely, these flowers had a market value that increased in direct proportion to their rarity. In the northern Netherlands during the early seventeenth century, some varieties of tulip bulbs were bought for incredible sums of money.

As we know from Jan Brueghel's letters, he had the opportunity to study rare flowers in Brussels, in the gardens of the Grand Duke and Duchess. His letters also contain references to his working methods. Painting flowers, he repeatedly complains, was tedious work because he did it '*alla prima*', without preparatory drawings or oil sketches. And since all the flowers grew within a period of four months, he was forced to paint them unimaginatively and painstakingly as they blossomed. From this it would appear that Brueghel worked directly from life. Since the flowers bloomed at different times, he could not finish a bouquet until the season was over. This time-consuming procedure, however, must have been used only for his earliest works, one of which he seems to have kept in his studio. It is likely that as his repertoire of motifs expanded, he could develop variations to match any problems or ideas.

The question remains whether Jan's still lifes exhaust themselves in the superficial significance of 'painted flower catalogues'. This aspect is surely there in his portrait-like precision. On the other hand, the emphasis he places on the flowers' beauty – as if some higher essence were distilled in their gemlike colours – would point beyond mere botanical intentions. To the thinking of the age, the short-lived beauty of flowers signified the transience of earthly life. A small flower piece Brueghel painted on copper (now in the art trade) has verses that translate:

> Why regard these blossoms so lovely to the eye
> When the sun's force wilts them so rapidly.
> Behold God's word alone, that eternal blooms,
> While all the world becomes – nothingness.

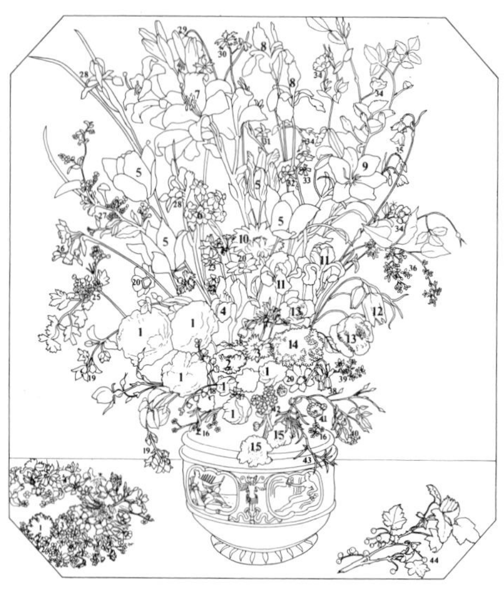

Bouquet of Flowers
Diagram by Marina Heilmeyer

Botanical Key by Marina Heilmeyer and Bernhard Zepernick

No.	Name	Latin name	Flowers in	Cultivated in Europe since
1	Moss-rose	Rosa certifolia	June–July	1573
2	Marigold	Calendula officinalis	June–Autumn	Filled variety since late 16th cent.
3	Ragged-lady	Nigella hispanica	June–August	1596
4	Iris	Iris pseudacorus	May–July	Native
5	Tulip	Tulipa	April–May	Mid-16th cent.
6	Narcissus	Narcissus tazetta	May	1557
7	Madonna lily	Lilium candidum	June–July	One of the oldest cultivated flowers
8	Iris	Iris xiphioides	June	1568
9	Tiger-lily	Lilium bulbiferum	May–June	1596
10	Peacock anemone	Anemone pavonina	May–June	Late 16th cent.
11	Iris	Iris germanica	May–July	Native
12	Fritillary	Fritillaria meleagris	April–May	1572
13	Peony	Paeonia officinalis	May– June	Before 1500
14	Guelder-rose	Viburnum opulus	May–June	Native
15	Marsh marigold (double)	Caltha palustris 'multiplex'	March–May	Native
16	Forget-me-not	Myosotis alpestris	May–July	Native
17	Dog-violet	Viola canina	April–June	Native
18	Lily of the valley	Convallaria majalis	May–June	Native
19	Mock jasmine	Philadelphus coronarius	June–July	Native
20	Crown anemone	Anemone coronaria	April–May	1596
21	Cornflower	Centaurea cyanus	May–July	Native
22	Gillyflower	Matthiola longipetala	May–June	16th cent.
23	White narcissus	Narcissus poeticus	April–May	*c.*1600
24	Sweet-william	Dianthus barbatus	June–August	1554
25	Hawthorn	Crataegus monogyna	May–June	Native
26	Daffodil	Narcissus pseudo-narcissus	April	*c.*1600
27	Bird cherry	Prunus padus	May	Native
28	Siberian iris	Iris sibirica	June	Native
29	Turk's cap	Lilium martagon	May–June	Native
30	Pink	Dianthus superbus	July–August	1583
31	Pyramid bellflower	Campanula pyramidalis	July–August	1569
32	Jonquil	Narcissus jonquilla	April– May	1565
33	Cross of Jerusalem	Lychnis chalcedonica	June–July	1561
34	Dog-rose	Rosa canina	June	Native
35	Snowdrop	Leucojum vernum	March–April	1420
36	Lilac	Syringa vulgaris	May	Mid 16th cent.
37	Ramson	Allium ursinum	May	1561
38	Narcissus	Narcissus triandrus	April–May	1579
39	Squill scilla	Scilla bifolia	March–April	1568
40	Jasmine	Jasminum officinale	June– August	1548
41	Immortelle	Helichrysum arenarium	July–September	Native
42	Auricula	Primula auricula	April–June	Native
43	Rosemary	Rosmarinus officinalis		Old medicinal herb
44	Currant	Ribes rubrum		Native

The flowers in the wreath:

No.	Name	Latin name	Flowers in	Cultivated in Europe since
1	Carnation	Dianthus	June–August	Mid 16th cent.
2	Borage	Borago officinalis	May–July	Very old cultivated plant
3	Primula	Primula clusiana	April	1583
4	Nasturtium	Tropaeolum minus	July–September	1573
5	Cyclamen	Cyclamen purpurascens	June–September	1600

Anthony van Dyck (1599–1641)

Portraits of a Genoese Nobleman and his Wife

*c.*1622–6

These two companion-pieces, with seated models in life-size and full figure, were painted during van Dyck's visit to Italy (1621–7), the happiest period of his career, which he spent in the harbour town of Genoa in Liguria.

Though the couple has not yet been identified, the man's black cap and the paper in his right hand at least indicate that he was a high official. The same objects appear in van Dyck's *Portrait of Gian Vincenzo Imperiale*, a Genoese procurator (Washington, Widener Collection). This similarity suggests that the nobleman in our painting also held the position of procurator, a financial official next in power only to the doge in the aristocratic ruling hierarchy of the Genoese city-state. That he and his wife belonged to the highest circles may be inferred from their distinguished and rather distant manner, the simple elegance of their dress, which was modelled on that of the Spanish Court, and finally from the architectural setting, whose pilasters and columns on high pedestals increase the imposing effect of figures seen from a low vantage point. Yet the pomp of their surroundings pales before the personalities themselves, who need not show their awareness of rank. Bolstered by this self-confidence, the kindly indifference of the lady and the man's imperious yet mistrustful gaze seem like extreme expressions of the same attitude.

Portraits of this kind brought van Dyck wide recognition and well-rewarded commissions from noble families, for whom most of his work was done. Relying first on Rubens, whose Antwerp studio he entered as a precociously talented young man of seventeen, and then taking cues from the courtly portrait style of Titian, van Dyck developed those nonchalantly distinguished portrayals which even today are regarded as the quintessence of nobility. Although his late portraits sometimes slipped into a rather dry and facile elegance – partly because of the great number of commissions he had to fulfil in his influential position of Court Artist to Charles I of England (from 1632) – his reputation as the greatest of Rubens's successors and one of the major portraitists of his age remains secure.

Canvas, each 200 × 116 cm ($78\frac{3}{4} \times 45\frac{5}{8}$ in)
Palazzo G. Balbi Collection, Genoa, 1773; purchased 1828 in Genoa for David Peel, London, by the English artist David Wilkie
Acquired 1900
Cat. nos 782 B, 782 C

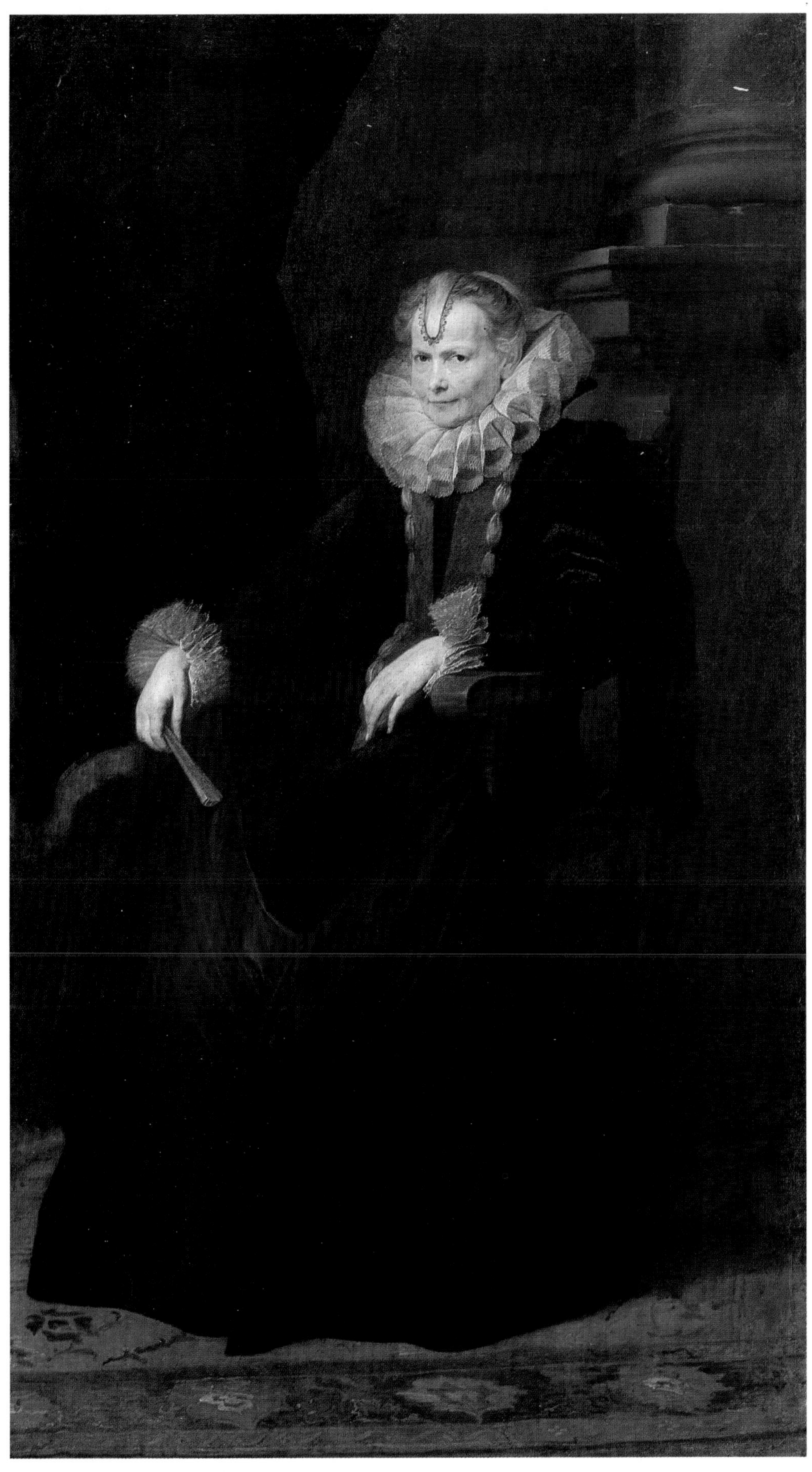

Jacob Jordaens (1593–1678)
The Rape of Europa
*c.*1615–16

Canvas, 173 × 235 cm ($68\frac{1}{8} \times 92\frac{1}{2}$ in)
Acquired 1981
Cat. no. 2/81

Ovid records the classical tale of Jupiter's abduction of Europa in the second book of his *Metamorphoses*. 'Sovereignty and love do not mix well,' he ironically says when the god transforms himself into a steer to mingle with the herds of King Agenor of Phoenicia; these Mercury had driven to the very place on the seashore frequented by Europa, the king's daughter. Drawn by the beauty and gentleness of the animal, 'that strutted so grandly, with no sign of threatening attack', and urged on by her companions, Europa mounts the snow-white steer whose head she has garlanded with flowers. 'Yet slowly the god, stepping deceptively, left dry land/Gradually behind, forsook the shore for the water, and/Moving deeper and deeper, abducted his prize through the sea.'

This is a scene that invites staging with a full cast. Jordaens has assembled sixteen actresses in front whose life-sized figures reach far above the low horizon. On the left is Europe on the steer of Jupiter, to whom a garland is proffered by Mercury in the guise of an old woman; at the right are the maidens of Tyre, the companions of Europa's youth. The seaside setting does not appear, Jordaens having illustrated the events solely through the figures' poses and gestures. Nor is 'illustrated' quite the right word. The figures are very close together in shallow space, each interlocked and superimposed like strata. Their attitudes correspond. Resting on the ground, crouching and kneeling, or standing, some bent slightly forward and others at their full height, with arms outstretched – nude bodies observed in many attitudes and complex, foreshortened twists and turns fill the picture more from bottom to top than from front to back.

The palette heightens a composition already effective in itself. The lively colours of the clothes, harmonizing with flesh tones that alternate between suntan and cool paleness, give the painting an opulently festive character. Like a skilled decorator, Jordaens derives strengths from this basic design and focuses the illumination to bring out well-placed ornamental forms – blossoms with the brilliance of gems, exquisite jewellery, the straw-blonde of modishly dressed coiffures, even the shine of a wide-open eye.

Palette and design point to a date during the artist's earliest phase, which began after he finished his training with Adam van Noort in Antwerp and earned the title of Master in 1615. Jordaens's early style was shaped above all by his knowledge of Rubens. A vigorous, suggestive plasticity of form clearly indicates that his high standard was that of Rubens's sculpturally classical figures. Among his most direct adaptations is the central figure of the present painting. Jordaens's Europa, in appearance and pose, is similar to the Rubens sketch, *Silenus and Aegle* of about 1611–13 (Windsor Castle). Other links might be shown, but without prejudice to the quite unique talent of an artist who expressed Flemish tradition with an almost primitive freshness of conception. If Rubens relied on an extreme range of noble, classical and classically derived figures to achieve an ideal of sublime humanity, Jordaens remained rooted to a much greater extent in local soil. His choir of maidens has a rustic look, with something of the insouciant freshness and raciness of Flemish countrywomen. It was above all this aspect of his achievement that earned Jordaens recognition as having been 'the truest Fleming' among the Flemish artists of his times.

Peter Paul Rubens
Silenus and Aegle and other Figures
Drawing
Her Majesty Queen Elizabeth II,
Windsor Castle

Cornelis de Vos (1585–1651)
Magdalena and Jan-Baptist de Vos
*c.*1622

Canvas, 78 × 92 cm ($30\frac{3}{4}$ × $36\frac{1}{4}$ in)
Acquired 1837
Cat. no. 832

With a touch of just noticeable surprise at the interruption, these two children look out at the observer with great candour from large, dark, brilliant eyes, while the cherries and peach that had their undivided attention a moment ago seem forgotten. This motif of fruit held in a child's hand would appear to have significance. Ripe in form, colour, and by implication taste, the fruit suggests the freshness and sweetness of children's nature, though the comparison need not have been conscious. The vivaciously modelled faces, cheeks heightened with a touch of rose, have so much natural charm that they speak for themselves, and they speak of a close and loving relationship between the artist and his models.

These are Magdalena (baptized 19 September 1618) and Jan-Baptist (baptized 6 December 1619), the artist's two eldest children. Their features also appear in the large group portrait in the Brussels Museum, which shows the artist with his family.

Like most parents who see their own social prestige reflected if not in the behaviour then at least in the outward appearance of their offspring, Cornelis de Vos has depicted his two children for his and our sake and not for their own. Their exquisite clothes, trimmed with an abundance of fine lace, evoke the really quite honourable parental maxim that for one's own progeny, only the best is good enough; yet it also reveals some of the complacency of high position.

De Vos indeed earned a reputation and prosperity by his craft. No less an artist than Rubens later asked his co-operation on large commissions, though de Vos's rather sober approach cannot have harmonized well with Rubens's Baroque exuberance of form. Nor was he able, with his historical pictures, to make notable contributions to Flemish painting, which was superb in this genre. His gift of lucid observation found a more suitable expression in portraiture, which demands more objectivity. This quality, together with the basical conservativeness of his art, soon made de Vos the leading portrait painter of the Antwerp bourgeoisie, whose sense of self-importance he infused with a dignified gravity matched by no other artist. He allowed himself more freedom in his children's portraits, which were much admired by his contemporaries and whose vivacity and harmonious colour come closer to Rubens than any other of de Vos's works. Why he chose to portray his own two children against the background of a gloomy twilit landscape, is difficult to say. The afterglow in the sky contrasts strangely with the youthful bloom of his models. Perhaps the mood of pathos that suffuses the landscape was meant to evoke, by contrast, a father's pride and hopes in his children.

Cornelis de Vos
The Artist and his family
Brussels, Koninklijke Musea voor Schone Kunsten

David Teniers the Younger (1610–90)
The Artist with his Family
*c.*1645–6

Oak, 38 × 58 cm (15 × 22⅞ in)
Monogrammed on the leg of the table: 'DTF'
Collection of the Duc de la Vallière; Neues Palais, Potsdam, 1773
From the Royal Palaces, Berlin, 1830
Cat. no. 857

An ornamented stone door-frame with balustrade where a monkey perches, not unlike a heraldic animal, is behind the group of figures in the left foreground; to their right, calm water flows to the far shore with a village church among trees. These motifs are carefully poised in a composition whose balance is enhanced by an alternation of nearness and distance: a terrace with some of the good things in life, and a landscape view that gives the impression of a desirable idyll. This is a refined setting in which Teniers has pictured himself and his family. He is seated at a table playing the viola da gamba, with his wife, Anna Brueghel, and his son David, both holding songbooks. The pageboy bringing a glass of wine may be a portrait of the artist's younger brother, Abraham, and the man standing in the doorway and looking on probably also belongs to the family.

Judging by the ages of the two boys, the painting must have been executed in about 1645 or 1646. Another authentic version in an upright format (English art trade, 1975) may be associated with it. In that version, the almost identical ensemble of figures is expanded by the motif of a standing woman playing a lute in front of the table with her back turned to the spectator. As X-ray analysis has revealed, the Berlin panel originally included a similar figure, which the artist painted out, or rather, for whom he substituted the drapery spread over the balustrade, the '*Trumscheit*' leaning against the door frame, and the still life with a musical instrument and musical score on the table. Perhaps what disturbed him was the anonymity of this averted figure, which would have heightened the genre character of the group portrait still more; or perhaps the figure's assertive upright pose was felt to shift the balance of the lateral composition too far to one side.

Teniers's penchant for music, especially for playing the viola da gamba, at which he is said to have been a virtuoso, is well documented. It is not surprising that he chose to represent himself and his family performing music at home, a motif that certainly suggests the congeniality and harmony of his domestic life. Beyond that, this painting may very well contain an allusion to the theory of art. The hierarchy of the arts was still a great subject of debate during Teniers's times. While music had long enjoyed the rank of an intellectual discipline, painters still had to struggle up from the depths of mere artisans. The main point of contention was an improvement of the professional and social status of painters, who were subject to the strict rules of guilds devoted primarily to the interests of craftsmen. Grouped together with house-painters, decorators of carriages and ships, with gilders, bookbinders and embroiderers, artists had begun to feel that their interests were definitely under-represented. Teniers was Dean of the Antwerp Lucas Guild from 1644 and later, having resigned from this institution, became a founding member of the town's first art academy. So he was certainly aware of this problem, and his self-portrayal as a musician probably reflects this awareness. The assurance and poise with which he assumes the musician's role here reflect on his real profession and confirm its worth.

David Teniers the Younger
The Artist and his Family
English art trade, 1975

Frans Hals (1582/3–1666)
'Malle Babbe'
*c.*1629–30

Canvas, 75 × 64 cm (29½ × 25⅛ in)
Acquired with the Suermondt Collection, 1874
Cat. no. 801 C

A slip with the words *'Malle Babbe van Haarlem ...'* (roughly, 'Crazy Babette of Haarlem'), is attached to the back of this canvas. Though this title was a later addition, it seems to reflect the artist's intention faithfully, which was to shed light on a doubtful aspect of human behaviour rather than to create a traditional portrait.

The vivacity of the life-size half-figure comes from its abrupt counter-movement. Though the model glances aside with a raucous laugh, her upper body remains turned to the right, the line of her shoulders leading the spectator's eye back – and to the open pewter tankard in front of her. This tankard sets a vertical line, which is repeated in the owl perched on the woman's shoulder – two perpendiculars which set off and augment the oblique, opposing movements of her head and torso. Loose brushwork that only condenses in her face into descriptive modelling, and is otherwise limited to summary indications of form in slashing strokes, increases the impression of a spontaneous and seemingly random slice of life. It is no wonder that the nineteenth century admired Dutch paintings in the *'Malle Babbe'* style as prototypes of realistic art. Gustave Courbet's 1869 copy of the painting is a case in point (Hamburg, Kunsthalle). Yet as much as Hals anticipated a later approach in his virtuoso yet invariably objective rendering, the content of his works remained just as exclusively rooted in Baroque thinking, with its penchant for a didactic and moral message.

Malle Babbe's attribute, the owl, is an ancient symbol of wisdom. Yet being a nocturnal bird that avoids the light of day, it also embodies such darker aspects of human behaviour as stupidity, foolishness, and drunkenness. Which of these traits is alluded to here may be seen from the arrangement, along a diagonal from lower left to upper right, of the motifs of tankard, grimacing laugh, and immobile owl. The saying, *'zoo beschonken als een uil'* ('drunk as an owl'), which by Hals's time was in common usage, would be a fitting caption for a personification of the vice of alcohol abuse. Not without humour and empathy, Hals seems to have recommended moderation by negative example here.

The assumption that *'Malle Babbe'* has a companion-piece in *'Pickled Herring'* (the so-called *Mulatto*; Leipzig Museum), a stock type in contemporary Dutch farces, would seem unlikely on stylistic grounds. Nevertheless, just such a pair of paintings – Hals in miniature, so to speak – has been traced in the background of Jan Steen's *Baptizing a Child* (also in the Berlin Gallery). Here, *Malle Babbe Smoking* (present whereabouts unknown) and *Pickled Herring Drinking* (Kassell, Staatliche Gemäldesammlungen) are cited quite obviously for their moral significance. It is not by accident that the two pictures hang on the wall above a group of people carousing around a table, surrounded by children who eagerly imitate the adults' bad habits, already learning to enjoy the taste of wine (right) and of tobacco (left).

Jan Steen
Baptizing a Child
Berlin, Gemäldegalerie SMPK

Frans Hals
Catharina Hooft with her Nurse
*c.*1619–20

Canvas, 86 × 65 cm ($33\frac{7}{8}$ × $25\frac{1}{2}$ in)
Acquired with the Suermondt Collection, 1874
Cat. no. 801 G

The child dressed in Italian brocade and fine Brussels lace has been identified from recently discovered documents. Catharina Hooft, born in 1618 and the daughter of Pieter Hooft, a jurist of Amsterdam, was living with her parents in Haarlem when this portrait was done. In 1635 she married Cornelis de Graeff, later mayor of Amsterdam. In keeping with her rank as one of the country's first ladies, towards the end of the 1640s she and her husband sat for a life-size, very dignified portrait by the Amsterdam artist Nicolaes Elias (East Berlin, Bodemuseum). She never parted with the portrait Hals made of her as a child. After her death in 1691 at Ilpenstein Castle, it passed to her son; in the records of his estate, it was listed under the title, '*Een Minne met een Kindje*' ('A Nurse with a Little Child').

It is not likely that Hals thought of Catharina as a 'little child' when he portrayed her with such regal sovereignty. The contrast between her brocade gown, painted with old-masterly precision, and the plain dress of her attendant, sufficiently indicates the social difference between them. There may be the same significance in the way she extends her arm to the nursemaid's breast and the bell-rattle she holds like a sceptre.

Whether its decorous composition evokes rank or not, the decisive message of the painting is certainly conveyed by the models themselves, whose features have been captured with great penetration. A grasp of personal uniqueness and its dependence on a real environment – that was the new and fundamental discovery of Dutch portraiture, which, before Rembrandt, was largely shaped by Frans Hals. In the present portrait, too, differences in social status are mitigated by an emphasis on individual worth. The nursemaid's diffident smile reveals an awareness of her role. Like a mother, and performing a mother's office, she voluntarily subordinates herself to the little girl's self-confident gesture and follows her gaze to look towards the observer. The apple, on which they focused their attention a moment ago, is now forgotten. This effect of instantaneousness contributes a great deal to the individuality of the people portrayed. Instead of looking down at us from disdainful heights like the figures in aristocratic portraits, they face us eye to eye, on the same level, as if frankly seeking contact. In short, we feel them to be people like ourselves. And thanks to the superb illusionism of Hals's portrayal, their presence remains vital beyond the limitations of one period and the strictures of a portrait commission.

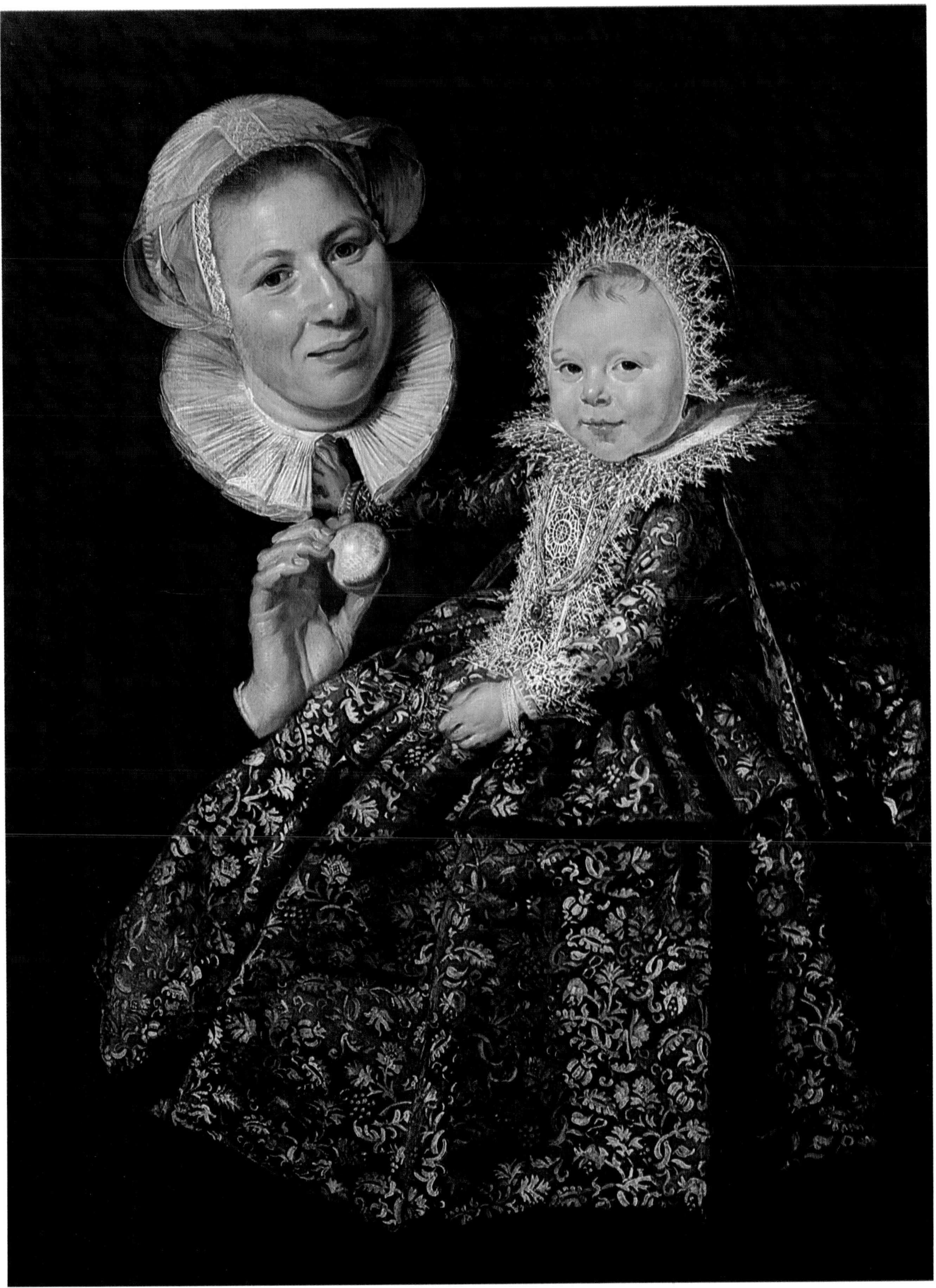

Thomas de Keyser (1596/7–1667)
Portrait of a Lady
1632

Oak, 79.1 × 52.4 cm ($31\frac{1}{8}$ × $20\frac{5}{8}$ in)
Monogrammed top, on the door: 'TDK' (interlocked) '1632'
Acquired 1982
Cat. no. 1/82

Though the subject of this portrait (whose counterpart, *Portrait of a Gentleman*, hangs in the Louvre) has not yet been identified, there can be little doubt about her social status. Her superb and festive dress, the fine Oriental carpet on the table, the patterned inlay of the floor tiles, even the mouldings of the door, in the most tasteful of Neo-Classical styles, are all unmistakable signs of her prosperity and rank. Yet she herself, of course, embodies these qualities best. Seated erect and stately, she looks out as though, just having suppressed a start of surprise at the interruption, she were quite prepared to receive us.

This delicate nuance of expression corresponds, in terms of style, with the careful brushwork and subdued, shimmering palette. The noble black of the satin dress acts as a foil to heighten the warm flesh tones, and also effectively brings out such accessories as the wide latticed collar and matching lace gauntlets, and the exquisite gold brocade trimming of the bodice, whose colour and shield-like shape are charmingly repeated and softened in the more evanescent gold of the bows on the sleeves. Rings, an abundance of pearls, golden chains, and an egret feather complete her toilette, which was obviously intended for a festive occasion. In view of the model's age, this occasion can only have been her marriage, and the gown her bridal dress. The portrait was probably made to commemorate this, which would justify its association with the Parisian *Portrait of a Gentleman*.

A decorous composition that sublimated the model's real world was characteristic of portraiture in Amsterdam. In Holland's largest and richest town, art invariably had an undercurrent of ostentation. Thomas de Keyser, being the son and pupil of Hendrick de Keyser, a highly regarded architect and master of courtly portrait sculpture, grew up surrounded by art intended for official use. And he would probably have cleaved to traditional conventions had Frans Hals, in nearby Haarlem, not confronted him with innovations. Hals's glimpses of spontaneous emotion and gesture helped him loosen the strictures of a set formula, and, thanks to other inspiration from Haarlem, he developed a predilection for the cabinet piece. De Keyser later owed his ability to employ this genre to superb effect to the courtly portrait style of Antwerp. In the figurative compositions of van Dyck he found that *grandezza* of presence in which the tension between personality and official role was resolved and synthesized. And it is just this vital combination of individual worth and social claim which de Keyser developed into the main expressive trait in his *Portrait of a Lady*.

Thomas de Keyser
Portrait of a Gentleman
Paris, Musée du Louvre

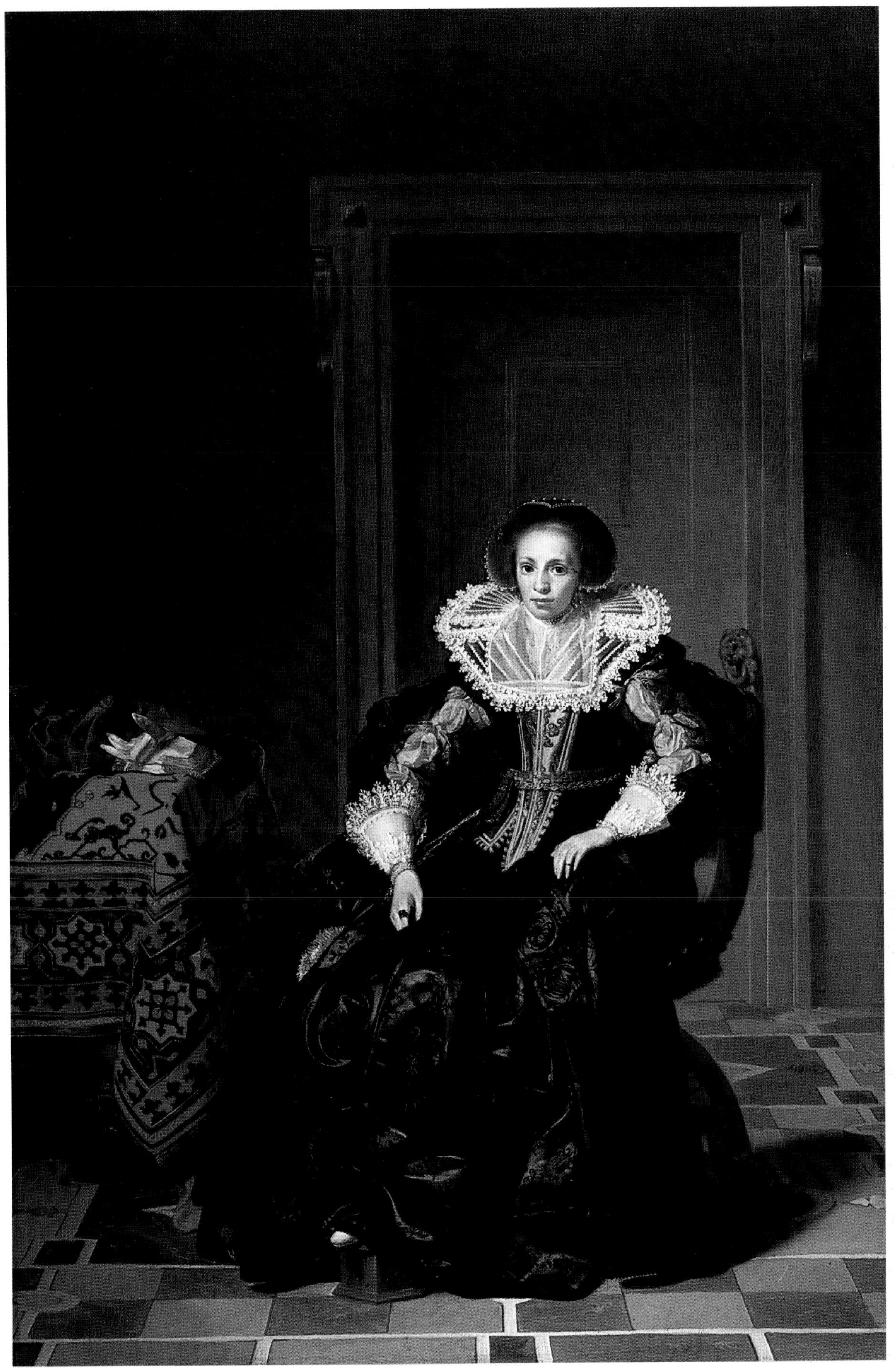

Rembrandt (1606–69)

Self-portrait with Velvet Barett

1634

Oak, 58.3 × 47.5 cm (23 × 18¾ in)
Signed lower right: 'Rembrandt f. 1634'
In the Picture Gallery, Sanssouci, 1764
From the Royal Palaces, Berlin, 1830
Cat. no. 810

Unlike any other artist before him, Rembrandt applied himself to the study of his own face, and in painting, drawing and engraving created an autobiographical record that extended from his early youth to the final years of his life.

A deep fissure in his life and his artistic development, seen particularly in his self-portraits, came with Rembrandt's move from Leyden to cosmopolitan Amsterdam in 1631. He decided on this change mostly because he expected profitable portrait commissions. Though he always considered himself as primarily a history painter, it was above all the many commissioned portraits he painted during his early years in Amsterdam that laid the basis for his financial and social advancement. Professional success was followed by private happiness when in 1634 he married Saskia van Uylenburgh, daughter of a prosperous lawyer of Friesland.

This painting, which dates from the year of Rembrandt's marriage, is a life-sized bust that shows the artist looking out at the spectator with an abrupt turn of his head. While one shoulder is met at about chin height by the left edge of the painting, the other dips diagonally in a gentle curve to the lower right corner. The asymmetry of these outlines heightens the aggressive effect of the way he turns his deeply shadowed, narrowed and penetrating eyes on his spectator, as though the artist intended to meet the exacting demands of an environment he himself has invested with profundity and pathos. The way his face is divided vertically by a sharp contrast of light and shade reveals a desire to idealize the naturally rather heavy and irregular features. Unlike the self-portraits of his early Leyden period, in which Rembrandt depicted himself without social reference, as if in spiritual and spatial isolation, he represents himself here as a successful artist whose gentlemanly elegance attests to his frank enjoyment of prosperity and social recognition.

Rembrandt
Saskia
1643

Mahogany, 75.2 × 60 cm ($29\frac{1}{2} \times 23\frac{1}{2}$ in)
Signed right, above the shoulder:
'Rembrandt f. 1643'
From the Royal Palaces, Berlin 1830
Cat. no. 812

This is a full-size bust of Saskia van Uylenburgh, Rembrandt's wife; turned slightly to the left, her face, throat and left hand are brightly illuminated, and their softly modelled forms shimmer against the warm brown tones of the background. The subdued golden yellow of her dress and the carmine red in the mantle increase the luminous flesh colours. The colour scheme is enlivened by delicately glowing highlights in the heavy golden chain across her bodice and the clasp at her shoulder, and in the pearls of the necklace, on the fur cap, and at her ear. The decorative sweep of the line of this jewellery enhances the planar effect of the treatment of the figure.

Saskia came of a respected family of Friesland. Her father, Rombertus van Uylenburgh, was mayor of Leeuwarden and the Frisian ambassador at The Hague. Saskia's parents, however, had no chance to pass on to her much more than a good name and considerable material security. They had both died by the time she was ten years old, and she went to live with relatives in Amsterdam. Saskia and Rembrandt met in 1633 at the latest, as may be gathered from the portraits he did of her that year. These were presumably done in the home of Hendrick van Uylenburgh, Saskia's uncle, where Rembrandt lived and had his studio at the time. Their marriage, publicly announced on 10 June 1634, took place on 2 July in the reformed church of St Anna. This relationship opened the doors of patrician Amsterdam to Rembrandt and contributed much to his professional and social success, not to speak of the private happiness it brought him. He subsequently made more than twenty portraits of his wife, frequently in the elaborate, imaginative costumes of roles such as Flora, the Roman goddess of flowers and spring (Leningrad, Hermitage), testifying to their mutual love and admiration. Yet Saskia, perhaps weakened by the quick succession of her pregnancies, became ill after the birth of her son, Titus, on 22 September 1640. On 5 June 1642, '*ziek te bedde leggende*', she made her last will and testament. She died a short time later and was buried on 19 June in the Oude Kerk in Amsterdam. Of the couple's four children, only Titus survived his mother. Rembrandt never recovered from Saskia's death. The blow came at the height of his career, as he was finishing what was to become his most famous painting, *The Night Watch* (Amsterdam, Rijksmuseum).

Of all the portraits of Saskia, that in Berlin remains unique for the strangely indeterminate quality of the rendering of her features and expression. As if tentatively feeling his way, the artist applied stroke after fine stroke in the face, changing and correcting. The date of 1643 inscribed on the panel indicates that it was not finished until after Saskia's death. It is even conceivable that Rembrandt painted the portrait entirely from memory, and that in the process, he was not able to recall the uniquely personal quality he had always seen in his wife. What he created is an image of a reserved, even shadowy physical presence, the apparition of a yearning love. It is a moving memorial not only to his wife but to his own bereavement.

Rembrandt

The Mennonite Preacher Anslo and his Wife

1641

Canvas, 176 × 210 cm ($69\frac{1}{4} \times 82\frac{5}{8}$ in; upper corners rounded)
Signed lower left: 'Rembrandt f. 1641'
Collections of Cornelis van der Vliet, Amsterdam, 1767; Sir Thomas Dundas, London, 1794; Lord Ashburnham, London, 1894
Acquired 1894
Cat. no. 828 L

Cornelis Claesz Anslo (1592–1646) was both a prosperous entrepreneur and one of the leading Dutch Mennonite ministers, pastor of the Waterland parish in Amsterdam. Though Rembrandt's choice of a huge format with life-size figures suggests a prosperous businessman's commission, his portrait is devoted solely to Anslo's personality and religious calling. Looking up from the Bible that lies open on his work-table, the clergyman turns to speak to his wife, Aeltje Gerrittse Schouten (1589–1657). He lends weight to his words by a gesture of his left hand, which marks the centre of the composition and whose suddenness is so vividly rendered that the hand seems to emerge bodily from the picture plane. His wife's humble attention would seem to indicate that the pastor seeks a dialogue by 'brotherly admonition': the central importance of this in Mennonite doctrine was based on Matthew 18: 15–20. That Anslo indeed fulfilled his minister's office with 'churchly rigour' at home as well as among his flock, is shown by the notes which Cornelis van Vliet, a descendant of Anslo, transcribed in 1767.

Rembrandt had depicted Anslo once before, alone, in an etching also dated 1641. This slightly earlier work prompted Joost van den Vondel, the most famous Dutch poet of the seventeenth century, to compose a quatrain that roughly translates, 'Oh, Rembrandt, paint Cornelis's voice/ The visible is his least important aspect/ The invisible is perceptible only through the ear/ Whoever would see Anslo must hear him.' Expressed here is above all the widespread Protestant belief that in communicating the Christian faith, the word definitely took precedence over the image. Though the seventeenth century found the Mennonites more liberal and less opposed to the painted image than at the close of the sixteenth century, the theological dispute over word and image, hearing and seeing, spirit and body, was still very much alive. A case in point is Rembrandt's portrait etching itself, in which the motif of a picture turned against the wall, standing on the floor next to Anslo, beneath its empty nail, quite unambiguously decides the primacy of word over image.

But Vondel's verses might be construed with equal justification as a criticism of Rembrandt, or rather, of the capacity of visual art in general to convey sounds, including the utterances of a great preacher. Now if this were true, then the artist might have taken the quatrain as a challenge to show what he could do, replying to it in an extremely convincing way with this painting. By expanding a portrait to a double portrait, Rembrandt provided an audience for the minister's words and gave direction to his gesture. The meaning and effect of his words become clear in the attentive and empathetic attitude of his wife. The true subject of the image, then, is the spoken word, which is both embodied in the juxtaposition of two figures and unites them in a visually dramatic dialogue.

Rembrandt
The Mennonite Preacher Anslo, 1641
Etching

Rembrandt
Susanna and the Two Elders
1647

Mahogany, 76.6 × 92.7 cm
Signed lower right: 'Rembrandt f. 1647'
Collections of E. Burk, London, 1769; Sir Ed. Lechmere in the Rydd
Acquired 1883
Cat. no. 828 E

Seeing Susanna, lovely wife of the rich Joachim of Babylon, two elders grow 'foolish and set their eyes so fixedly on her that they could not gaze heavenwards nor think either of God's word or of punishment'. As they know she bathes in her garden at about noon, they wait for her there. 'No one can see us, and we are inflamed with love for you; so grant us our will. If you refuse, we shall testify that we discovered you alone with a young man.' But Susanna fearfully replies, 'If I should do such a thing, it would mean my death; but if I do not, I will never escape your grasp. But I would rather fall innocent into the grasp of men than sin against the Lord.' Susanna is brought to trial, the two elders give false evidence against her, and she is condemned to death. As she is being led to her execution, young Daniel recognizes her innocence in a vision and exposes the elders, who are put to death in her place.

With its erotic overtones and a moral exemplifying marital virtue bolstered by Christian faith, the story of Susanna surprised in her bath became one of the most popular subjects of Baroque painting. Rembrandt chose to represent its dramatic climax. Susanna has left her clothes on a parapet and is just walking down the curved stone steps into the water when one of the elders comes up behind her and grasps the remaining cloth around her hips. Bent forward in fright, she turns her face to the viewer as if appealing for help. The other intruder, propped on a cane, passes through the garden gate without taking his eyes off Susanna's nakedness for a moment.

The composition is based on an initial version executed in the mid-1630s, which the artist reworked into the present version of 1647. This finding is confirmed by X-ray analysis, as well as by a number of drawings by Rembrandt and his studio which relate to the first and final versions. The alterations made in the original composition, involving a deletion or at least dampening of over-violent movements, faithfully reflect the artist's stylistic development during the 1640s. After the great Baroque compositions that characterized his work of the previous decade and culminated in *The Night Watch* of 1642 (Amsterdam, Rijksmuseum), a serenity of expression, and simplicity and lucidity of design, now predominated. In the final version of *Susanna*, the picture is divided into two contrasting halves: the left recedes through twilit 'empty' space to the shadowy architecture of a castle in the background, while the right, with its overgrown, arching cliff emerging in the foreground, is reserved for the closely grouped figures and the narrative itself. The illumination reaches its highest intensity here on Susanna's body and the exquisite red of her clothes, beside which she has demurely placed her shoes. A sensitively toned atmospheric chiaroscuro unites these two very different parts of the composition into a single, shimmering, light-suffused whole.

The two versions developed in this painting, and another *Susanna* of 1634 (The Hague, Mauritshuis), go back to a work of 1614 by Rembrandt's teacher, Pieter Lastman (also in the Berlin Gallery). In about 1633, Rembrandt made a drawing after this composition, which he must have admired, already re-forming it in terms of the paintings named above (Berlin, Kupferstichkabinett SMPK).

Pieter Lastman
Susanna and the Two Elders, 1614
Berlin, Gemäldegalerie SMPK

Rembrandt

Rembrandt

Portrait of Hendrickje Stoffels

*c.*1659

Canvas, 88.5 × 67 cm ($34\frac{7}{8} \times 26\frac{3}{8}$ in)
Acquired 1879
Cat. no. 828 B

Hendrickje Stoffelsdr. Jaeger (*c.*1625/7–63) began to keep house for Rembrandt in about 1649. Their relationship was a marriage in all but name. When Hendrickje became pregnant in 1654, she was called before the church council, required to do penitence, and excluded from Holy Communion. Rembrandt was in no position to legalize the bond because if he remarried, he would have been obliged by his first wife's will to repay half of her inheritance to her family; and the money had been spent long before. By the close of the 1640s his financial position was so dire that he could not have raised a sum of this size. He had debts on the great house he had arranged to buy in 1639 by instalments; a passion for collecting continually led him to buy objects of art and exotic curiosities at high prices, bringing him to bankruptcy in 1656 and, over the next two years, to the compulsory sale of his house and collection. To protect his income from creditors, he began in 1660 to work *pro forma* as an employee of an art dealing firm founded by Hendrickje and his son Titus. What little we know about this period indicates that Hendrickje stood by Rembrandt faithfully through all his difficulties. It is not surprising that their neighbours considered her his wife.

Rembrandt's portrait here, a life-size half-figure, shows Hendrickje turned slightly to the left, leaning against the upper frame of a Dutch door. As if by an unconscious movement of her shoulders, the key or ring on the cord around her neck has slightly shifted. Rembrandt apparently attached just as much significance to this simple adornment as to the fine pearl bracelet, for whether it is a ring or key, both symbolized marital or housewifely virtue. Though Hendrickje looks directly out of the picture, she seems to take little notice of the spectator. Rather, her casual pose and devoted attention suggest the presence of Rembrandt, whom she watches at work. The relationship between artist and model here becomes extremely intimate, so much so that we almost seem to be intruding.

The loose, free paint handling corresponds with the model's relaxed attitude. The glowing reds of her dress and the white of her chemise, laid on in broad swaths of impasto, emerge boldly from depths of shadow. Only her face and throat are rendered in compact strokes and modelled in full sculptural relief, which is heightened by the luminosity of their colours in a mild reflected light. Rembrandt derived two key elements of his late style from his penchant for Venetian painting – chiaroscuro as a means to unified design, and increasingly, design through colour. His involvement with Venice shows again here. The configuration of the motifs suggesting movement – torso turned, head slightly inclined, one arm across the breast and the other raised – are found in essence in a half-figure *Portrait of a Young Woman* by Palma Vecchio.

Palma Vecchio
Portrait of a Young Woman
Berlin, Gemäldegalerie SMPK

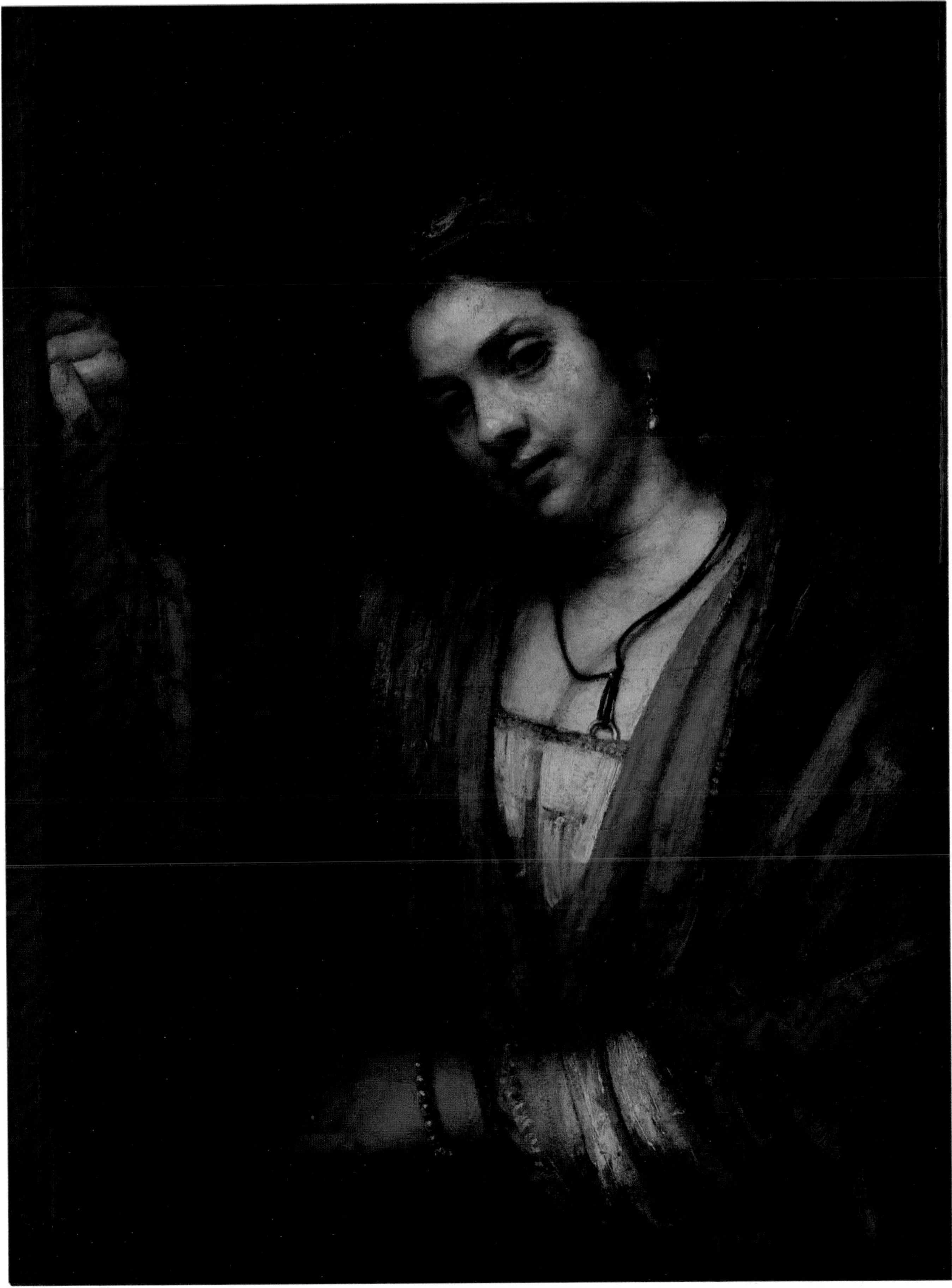

Rembrandt

Head of Christ

c.1655

Oak, 25 × 21.5 cm ($9\frac{7}{8} \times 8\frac{1}{2}$ in)
Collection of R. Kann, Paris, 1907
Acquired as a gift from M. Bromberg, Hamburg, 1907
Cat. no. 811 C

The brushwork of this panel is thin and transparent in the shaded areas, but condenses in the brightly illuminated face into descriptive modelling which evokes Christ's expressive contemplation. The small format and spontaneity of paint handling establish it as a study. Rembrandt created a number of essentially comparable works, all revealing a pursuit, through variation after slight variation, of a 'truthful' image of Christ.

A few of these studies of heads are listed in Rembrandt's inventory made in 1656, when he was forced to declare bankruptcy. One of them has the inscription, '*Een Christus tronie nae 't leven*' ('A picture of Christ from life'). These words perfectly describe the present image. Rembrandt was probably the first artist to paint Christ's face from life, that is, from a model. And it was fitting that an artist who strove for historical truth and life-like presence should have chosen a young Jew as model. Rembrandt was a close neighbour in Amsterdam of the community of Spanish and Portuguese Jews, among whom he found models as well as friends and patrons. Nevertheless, to interpret his heads of Christ only in terms of their relation to men he knew, would be to belittle his wide artistic and intellectual interests. He continually kept an eye on traditional art, and its countless images of Christ inspired him with a generally accepted model which the Italian Renaissance had imbued with the sublime beauty of the classic image of man. In this painting, too, the regular features and the decorative way the face is framed with softly flowing hair, point to the classical tradition, which merges imperceptibly with what was then a startlingly innovative idea – to model Christ's image on the face of a young Jew.

The essence of Rembrandt's art, after all, was that beyond a record of the physical facts he captured the 'inner' human phenomenon and gave it vital presence. Christ's expression here shares in a deep, and deeply moving, humanity. And it is this characterization that unmistakably identifies the Son of God and Saviour of mankind.

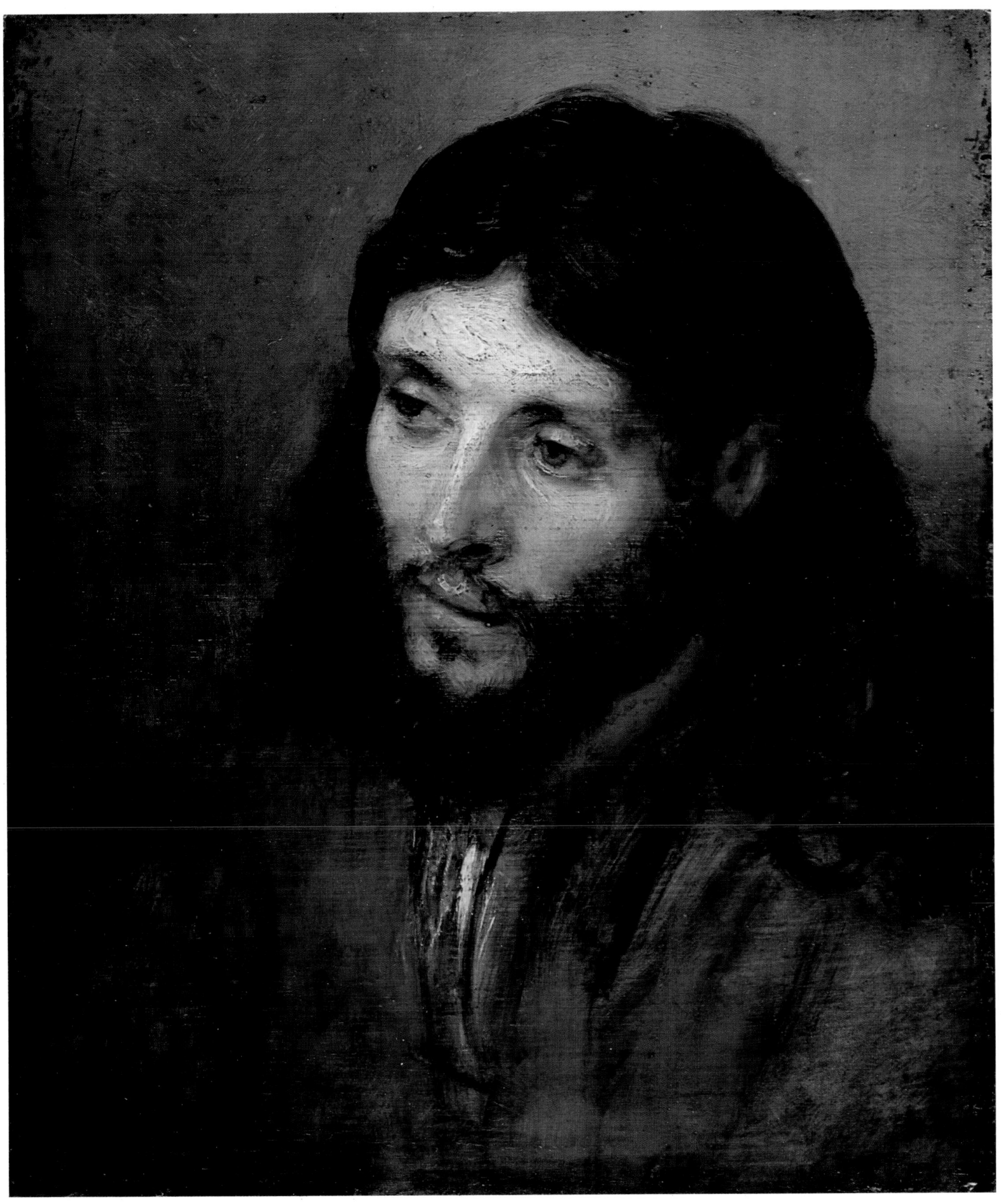

Rembrandt

Moses Breaking the Tablets of the Law

1659

Canvas, 168.5 × 136.5 cm ($66\frac{3}{8} \times 53\frac{3}{4}$ in)
Signed lower right: 'Rembrandt f. 1659'
In the Picture Gallery, Sanssouci, 1764
From the Royal Palaces, Berlin, 1830
Cat. no. 811

When Moses descended from Mount Sinai to bring the Israelites the tablets of the Law he had received from the Lord, he found his people dancing around the golden calf. 'And it came to pass, as soon as he came nigh unto the camp, that he saw the calf, and the dancing; and Moses' anger waxed hot, and he cast the tables out of his hands, and brake them beneath the mount' (Exodus 32: 19). In Rembrandt's image the figure of Moses, three-quarter length and life-size, dominates the plane. Above his head he holds the two tablets of the Law, the front one inscribed with the last five of the Ten Commandments in Hebrew: he is about to throw and break both tablets. Framed at the centre of the composition by his upraised arms and the dark tablets, Moses' head seems to glow with divine light. This alludes to a later event in the Bible story, where Moses shows his people the new tablets he had hewn from rock at God's behest. 'And it came to pass, when Moses came down from Mount Sinai with the two tables of testimony in Moses' hand . . . that Moses wist not that the skin of his face shone while he talked with him. . . . And afterward all the children of Israel came nigh; and he gave them in commandment all that the Lord had spoken with him in mount Sinai' (Exodus 34: 29, 32).

In combining the two events into a single, simultaneous breaking of the old tablets and the presentation of the new, Rembrandt followed pictorial tradition. Francesco Parmigianino, in his fresco for the Madonna della Steccata church in Parma, had established a composition of the same subject with a formally related figure, and Rembrandt may have known this from an engraved reproduction made by D. Fontana in 1644.

It has been assumed that the painting was originally much larger in size, having been conceived to hang over the fireplace in the jury room of the Amsterdam Town Hall, and that the artist reduced its dimensions after his patrons had rejected it. Though this cannot be confirmed, there is no doubt that the looming figure of Moses, rendered from an extremely low vantage point, was meant to be viewed from a distance, and that therefore the painting must have been intended for a room of considerable size. In any event, here as in another late work in the Berlin Gallery, *Jacob Wrestling with the Angel*, Rembrandt approaches the planarity and emphasis on contour of the main style of his period, Neo-Classicism. The elemental force of his message and conception, however, are undiminished.

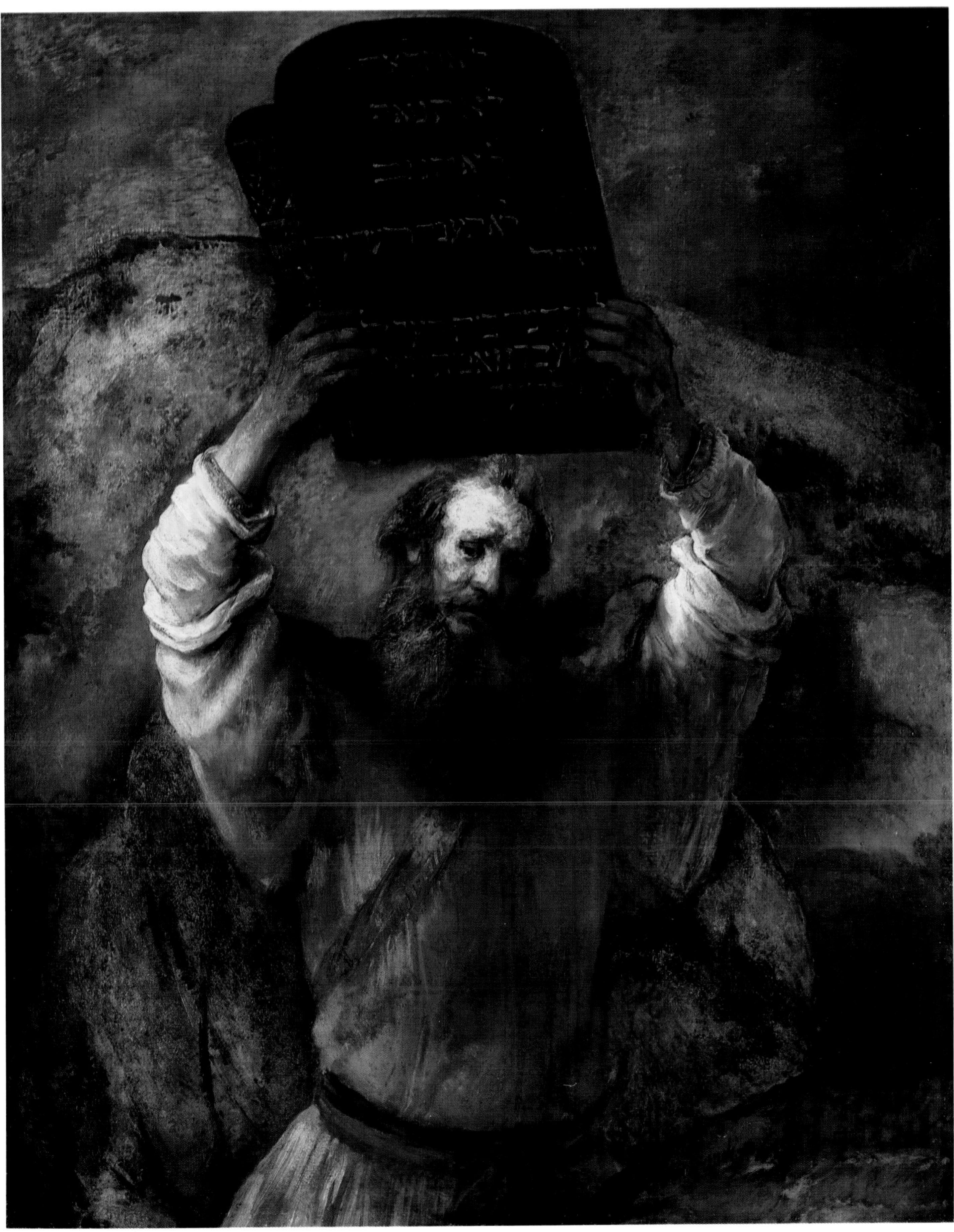

Follower of Rembrandt

The Man with the Golden Helmet

*c.*1650–5

Canvas, 67.5 × 50.7 cm (26½ × 20 in)
Property of the
Kaiser-Friedrich-Museums-Verein
Cat. no. 811 A

The splendid dress helmet and iron collarpiece perfectly suit the stern, weather-beaten face they frame; all, apparently, are meant to characterize a type not an individual. This life-size, half-length figure cannot have been intended as a portrait in the traditional sense: the pose of the isolated figure, the composition, and especially the treatment of the helmet could well be a reference to the god of war, Mars. Reflecting the light shining from the left in a golden glow, the helmet's rich ornament is made tactile by heavy impasto, while the face, painted in flat, scumbled strokes, recedes into shadow. The handling of light and paint has given the helmet predominance in the composition, and the artist might have attached corresponding significance to it. This piece of armour, known as a Spanish helmet, was not in use at the time, but originated from the late sixteenth century. The artist's contemporaries could have thought that its wearer embodied some heroic figure of the past – a warrior whose costly regalia marked him as an officer of the highest rank.

Recently, highly sophisticated research methods and a considered respect for Rembrandt's achievement, have led to a 'purge' of over-generous attributions from his œuvre. *The Man with the Golden Helmet* is one of the works whose authenticity is questioned. It is not signed or dated, and though its style does have a strong resemblance to Rembrandt's from 1650–5, instead of being a perfect match, its touch has a clearly formalized or heightened character by comparison. This is especially true of that much-admired helmet, which because of its colouring and illumination, and particularly its impasto layer built up in low relief, is the formally isolated centre of interest. Technically daring as Rembrandt certainly was, he never used oil paint like clay, to model in three dimensions. His effects were created solely through light and colour, even in paintings executed in full, sweeping impasto strokes. In *Man in Armour* (Glasgow Art Gallery) the rich decoration and brilliant sheen of the metal are illusionary, evoked by painterly means only. Being above all a historical painter, Rembrandt invariably attempted to make his models' clothes as historically accurate as he could, yet this concern never become an end in itself. Though in the *Man in Armour* he gave free reign to his love of materials and their qualities, the armour, with its delicate balance of painterly values, does not overwhelm its wearer.

The claim that Rembrandt did not paint *Man with the Golden Helmet*, however, leaves much to be said. Art historians generally agree that such reversals of opinion are convincing only when the true painter can be found. In this case, our growing knowledge of Rembrandt's work, of his school, and the artists who came under his influence, does make it possible that the question of attribution may be answered. There is evidence of a quite personal touch in *Man with the Golden Helmet*, for instance in the treatment of the face, which is articulated section by section, in brief linear strokes interwoven like cross-hatching. This manner, a graphic, additive approach that diverges from Rembrandt's characteristic concern for the continuity of larger forms, might be a key clue to the artist.

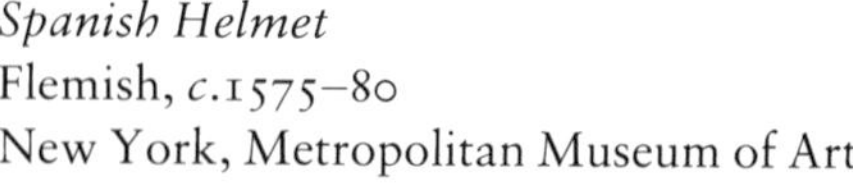

Spanish Helmet
Flemish, *c.*1575–80
New York, Metropolitan Museum of Art

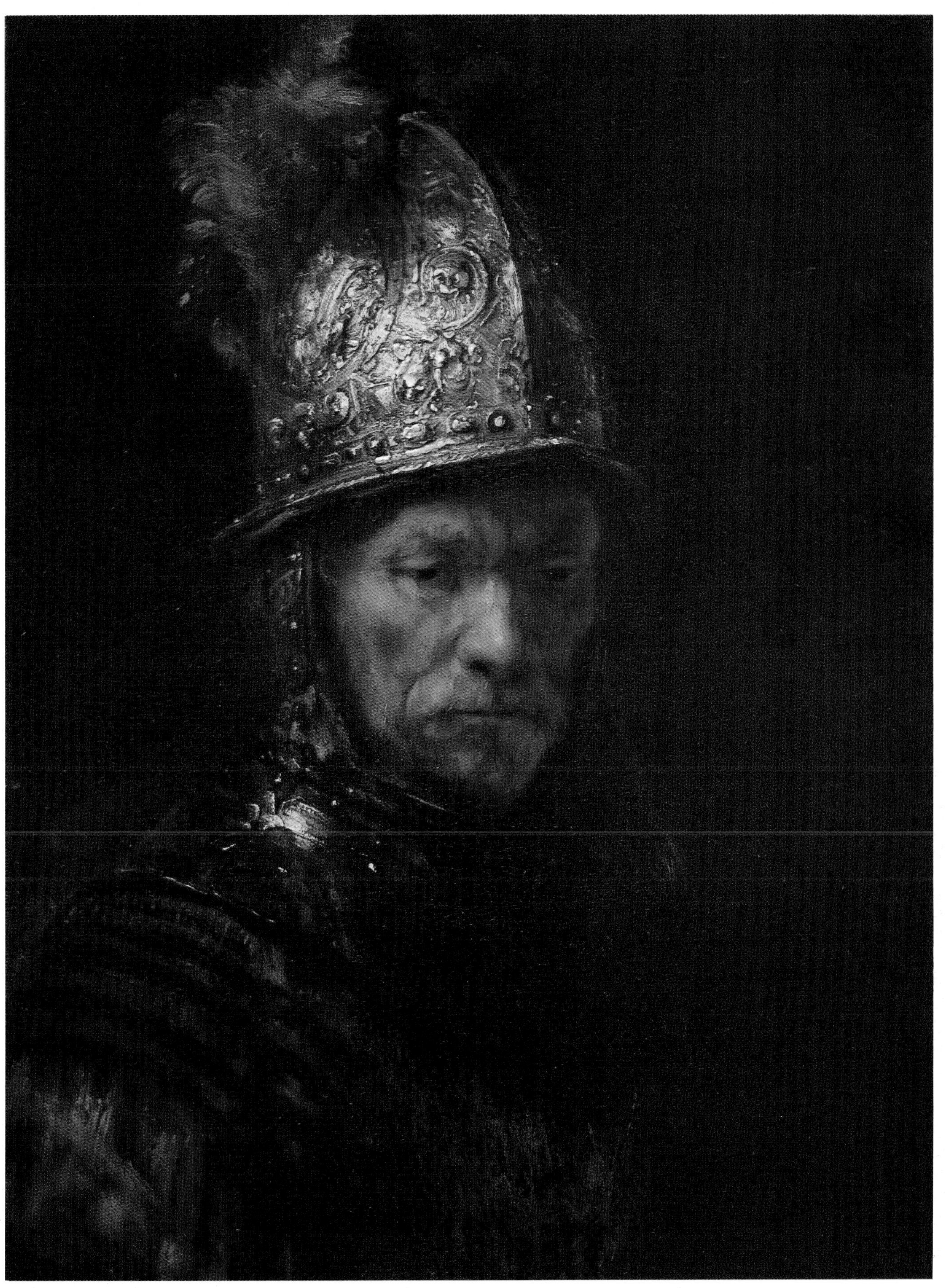

Gerard Dou (1613–75)
The Young Mother
*c.*1660

Oak, top rounded, 49.1 × 36.5 cm
(19⅜ × 14⅜ in)
Collections of the Duc de Choiseul, Paris, 1787; the Duc de Praslin, Paris, 1793; Mr de la Hante, London, 1814; the Earl of Grosvenor, London, *c.*1829; the Duke of Westminster, London
Acquired 1974
Property of the Kaiser-Friedrich-Museums-Verein
KFMV 269

A young mother preparing to nurse her baby is interrupted by a little girl who comes from behind and distracts the baby with the merry sound of a bell-rattle. This delightful scene is set in an elegantly furnished bourgeois interior with an adjacent room visible in the left background.

The painting is one of the finest examples of Gerard Dou's mature style. Using colours applied so smoothly as to leave almost no visible trace of a brushstroke, Dou brought the form and the feel of each object and material to perfection – not by delineating them with graphic precision but by immersing them in atmospheric tones of light and shade. The brass of the chandelier, whose ornamental shape literally crowns the scene, reflects the light in a warmer shimmer than the cool silver of the candlestick. The mother's velvet house-jacket seems palpably different in texture from the rough weave of the tapestry draped in Baroque curves in the foreground. As Joachim van Sandrart reported, the artist worked '*mit Hülf der Augengläser*' (with the aid of a magnifying glass), which might well explain the unmatched precision in the rendering of the grain of the floorboards or the wickerwork of the cradle.

The point of departure for Dou's subtle technique and chiaroscuro was the early work of his teacher, Rembrandt. Yet what was for Rembrandt only a transition to a sweeping, painterly style, became the guiding principle of his student's œuvre. With tenacious independence Dou developed the style to perfection, and his efforts were widely admired and imitated. They brought him recognition as the founder and most significant representative of the Leyden school of 'fine painting'.

So much exactitude astonished his contemporaries. Mayor Orlers of Leyden, for example, wrote that 'No one who saw him work could help marvelling at his care and remarkable execution.' Among the exquisite gifts that official Holland sent to Charles II of England in 1660, were pictures by Dou, including his *Young Mother* of 1658 (The Hague, Mauritshuis) and presumably also the Berlin panel. The general high regard in which Dou was held far surpassed Rembrandt's reputation. And this remained unchanged during the subsequent, classicizing period. Not until the second half of the nineteenth century, with the spontaneous, painterly approach of Realism and Impressionism, did a reaction against Dou's 'smooth manner' set in. In 1901, his renowned *Woman with Dropsy* of 1663 was removed from the Salon Carré, the gallery of honour in the Louvre – an outward sign that Dou had been demoted from the ranks of masters of the first order. But he remained a major representative of Dutch genre painting.

During the period to which this painting belongs, Dou's technical finesse could compare to that of Gerard ter Borch or Jan Vermeer, though he was not able to achieve their concentration of design or emotional force. He remained in the first instance an artist of surfaces, in the positive sense of the term. In the Berlin panel, the rich interrelations of form, colour, light and atmosphere are treated with the devoted care of a still-life painter, celebrated with precision, if you like. Thus the normal intimacy of mother and child is raised to a special realm revealed to the spectator's eye by the swept-up curtain – a common device in Dou's work.

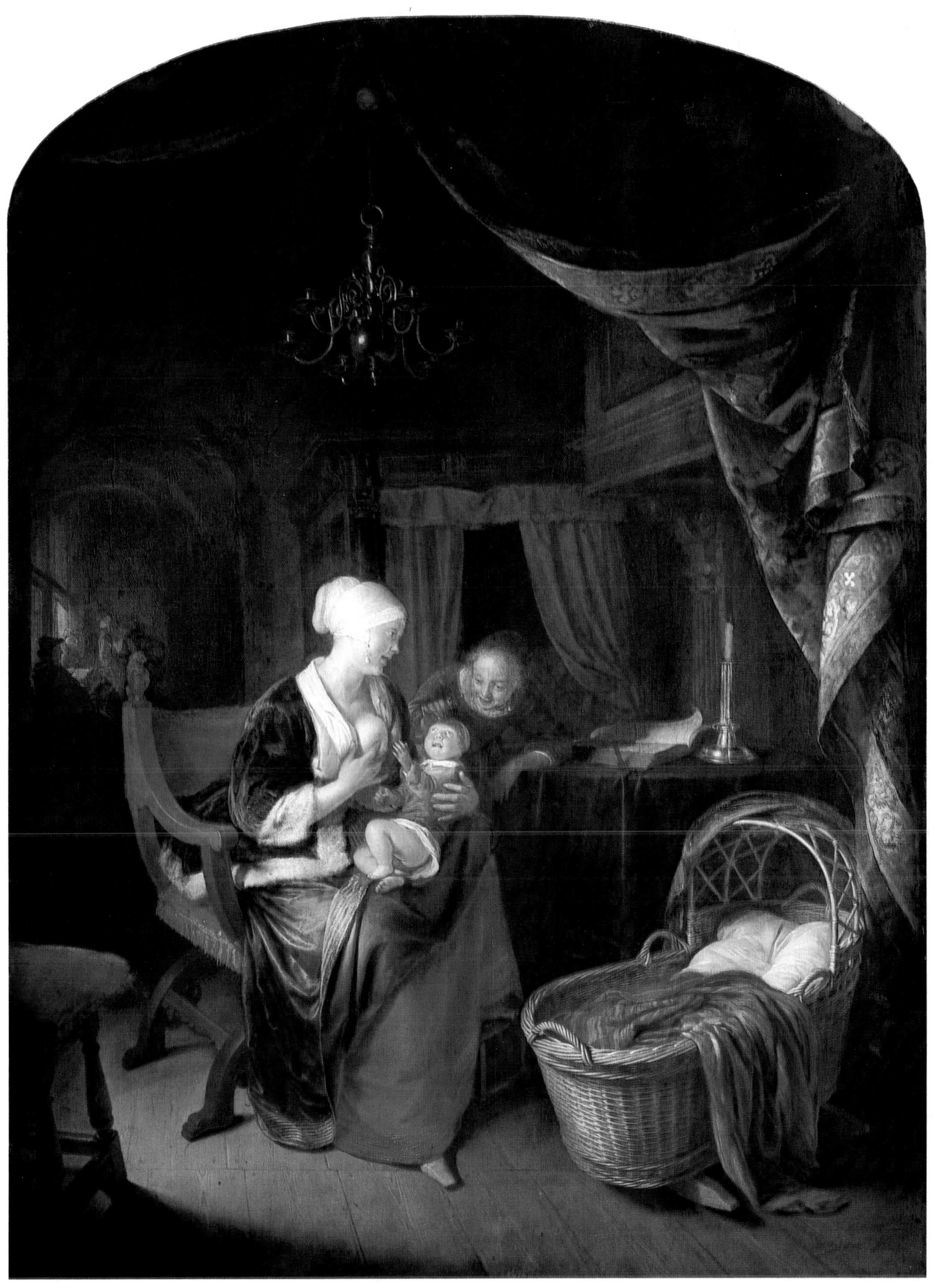

Gerard ter Borch (1617–81)
'The Parental Admonition'
*c.*1654–5

Canvas, 70 × 60 cm ($27\frac{1}{2} \times 23\frac{5}{8}$ in)
Acquired 1815
Cat. no. 791

An engraving of this painting, made in 1765 by J.G. Wille, has the caption, 'Instruction Paternelle'. It was under this title, accepted by no less a connoisseur than Goethe, that the painting became famous. Yet it does not appear to represent a domestic scene after all, judging by the youthfulness of the persons depicted, and also by the somewhat blasé attitude of the supposed father, whose uniform shows he is a military man. And this gentleman's true intention is by no means moral, as may be seen from the coin in his raised right hand.

The subject here is love for sale, and the room where the transaction takes place, with its curtained four-poster bed and dressing table, is well furnished for the purpose. If the gentleman, who believes that '*Auro conciliator Amor*' (money smooths the path of love), is making his offer for the lady Goethe called that 'glorious figure in the richly draped white satin gown', then the woman beside him has probably arranged the match. Nor can the decorous way in which she raises the wine glass to her lips clear her of this dubious role.

Ter Borch treated the theme of prostitution several times – shortly before 1650, in *Gallant Proposal* (Moscow, Pushkin Museum), and in about 1662–3, in *Young Couple Drinking Wine* (Berlin, Gemäldegalerie SMPK). In both works the amorous encounter is reduced to its main protagonists, who appear as three-quarter length figures facing one another in front of a neutral background. The masters of the Utrecht School devoted themselves much earlier to this type of genre scene, though in large-format compositions with vigorous chiaroscuro in the style of Caravaggio. Ter Borch's approach is much more reserved by comparison. Serenity and emotional moderation are the predominant traits of his art, and he refined them throughout his career. The works just mentioned illustrate this development, and particularly *The Parental Admonition*, which belongs among the finest accomplishments of his mature style.

A clue to the dating of the painting to the period shortly before 1655 is provided by a copy from the hand of Casper Netscher, a pupil of ter Borch, which is dated 1655 (Gotha Museum). No less than twenty-four repetitions, partial copies, and replicas of the Berlin painting exist, which shows how much it set an example. The slightly earlier version in the Amsterdam Rijksmuseum gives the scene in a broader format. There, the pictorial field is extended to the right, and the motif of a dog is included – a rather mongrelly looking one who slinks with his tail between his legs behind the gentleman's chair. Perhaps the animal was meant to allude to his master's unrestrained instincts. That the gentleman seriously intends a proposal of marriage, as has recently been suggested, would seem unlikely because of the 'negative motif' of the dog, if for nothing else. And though ter Borch omitted the dog from the Berlin version, it was surely not to show the scene in a more positive light but to increase the noble effect of the Amsterdam composition by freeing it of disturbingly obvious references. His choice of a narrower format eliminated the dog in any case, and more importantly, brought a narrowing down of the field of vision that gives the group of figures greater formal cohesion and heightens the compositional value of the standing woman. This figure, seen from behind, her head slightly bowed, leaves the spectator very much in suspense about her decision. But in all ter Borch's genre scenes, the story's end remains a tantalizing, open question.

Gerard ter Borch
'The Parental Admonition'
Amsterdam, Rijksmuseum

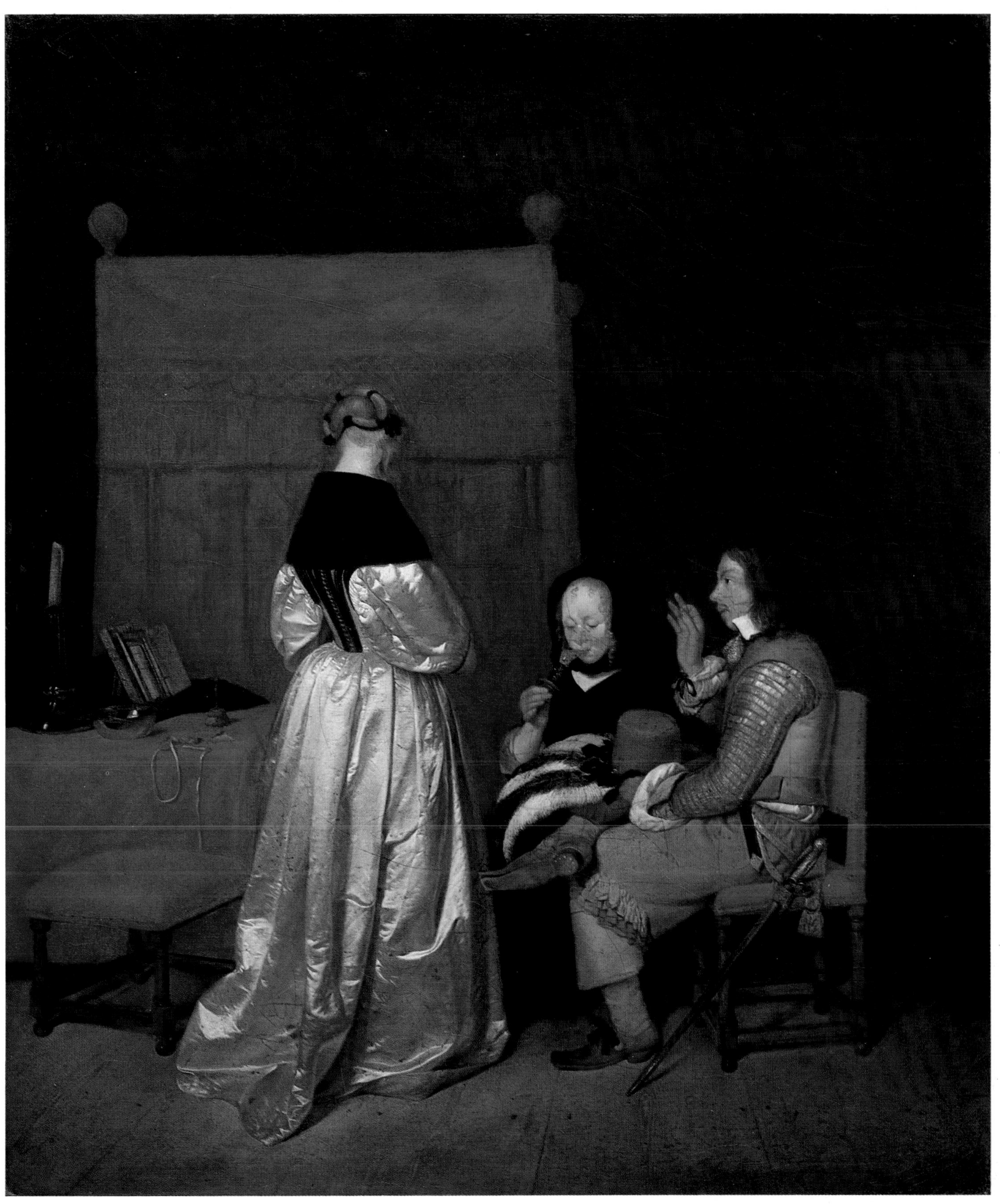

Pieter de Hooch (1629–84)
The Mother
*c.*1661–3

Canvas, 92 × 100 cm ($36\frac{1}{4} \times 39\frac{3}{8}$ in)
Acquired 1876
Cat. no. 820 B

Smiling down into the wicker cradle beside her, a woman laces her bodice. The intimate scene, which speaks of a mother's care for her child, is set in a comfortably furnished middle-class interior. An alcove bed with striped curtains is in the background and there are Delft tiles on the rear wall. Through the living-room door at the right, a little girl stands in the front entrance, the door open to the bright sunshine. A simple contrast between the dim room in the foreground and the light-filled foyer behind gives a compelling effect of spaciousness to the interior, which is divided into two almost equal halves that cover two planes parallel to the picture surface but at different depths. The architecture of interiors was indeed the point of departure for all de Hooch's paintings of domestic life. As early as 1658 he conceived spaces that had a referential quality previously unknown. Constructed by exact perspective, amply dimensioned and comfortably furnished, his rooms took on autonomous pictorial value, that is, their effect no longer depended exclusively on the figures that inhabit them. No less an artist than Jan Vermeer, a colleague of de Hooch's in Delft and three years younger, was inspired by de Hooch's 'architectural' gift. But Vermeer also narrowed the focus of his compositions and brought the human figure more strongly into play and, thanks to his ability to design in colour and light, created images that far transcend mere objectivity. Not that de Hooch's means were limited to the description of objective appearances. Cases in point here are the delicately shimmering highlights on the brass warming pan and candlestick, or the intense red of the cradle blanket, bodice and skirt – colour stresses that lead the eye in premeditated steps over the mirror-smooth floor tiles and towards the sunny entrance. This harmony of colour and light evokes an intimate atmosphere which not only suits the scene represented but seems to raise it to a more sublime world.

Mothers themselves did not necessarily nurse their infants in early seventeenth-century Holland; those in better circumstances, at least, usually employed a nursemaid. And accordingly, voices were raised to remind mothers of their natural duty. In 1625, the poet Jacob Cats moralized, '*Een die haer Kinders baert, is moeder voor een deel,/Maar die haer Kinders sooght, is moeder in 't geheel*' ('A woman who bears children is mother only in part, but one who nurses them herself is a complete mother'). And Johan van Beverwijk, a doctor, wrote in 1651 that the mother who breastfeeds her baby not only gives it nutrition but instils moral and intellectual capacities as well. With this as background, de Hooch's contemporaries must have attached a special significance to his painting, for what he depicted was the positive example of a mother who has nursed her baby and remains seated beside the cradle with affectionate care. In addition to maternal virtues, he also alludes to those of a housewife who in the place of activity which society has allotted her, the home, ensures that everything is spotlessly clean and orderly.

Jan Vermeer van Delft (1632–75)

The Glass of Wine

*c.*1660–1

Canvas, 66.3 × 76.5 cm ($26\frac{1}{8}$ × $30\frac{1}{8}$ in)
Acquired 1901
Cat. no. 912 C

From the two windows at the left – particularly the nearest one – cool daylight illuminates a young woman seated at a table drinking wine, and an elegantly dressed gentleman standing beside her. She holds the emptied glass up to her face as if to avoid his expectant eyes, for though he has no glass himself he is ready to refill hers from the jug in his hand. There seem to be amorous possibilities although the scene has nothing indelicate or blatantly erotic about it. The zither may also be significant. This instrument was a common symbol of harmony, but it also conveyed dissolute living.

The contained serenity in the attitudes of the two figures is matched in the structural clarity of the interior. A corner of the room is represented, in simple one-point perspective, a right-angled projection. The lines of the bench and table recede to the same vanishing point as the wall, as does, in more complex perspective, the diamond pattern of the floor tiles. A right angle is retained even with the figures: her profile with his frontal view. Only in the cavalier's glance and the placing of the chair with the instrument are divergent directional references given, likely to underscore the significance of these motifs. This is also true of the window, which is slightly ajar and has a coat of arms with a female figure holding intertwined ribands. A corresponding figure is among the emblems published by G. Rollenhagen in 1613. The ribands, it turns out, represent a harness, an attribute of temperance. '*Serva modum*' (preserve moderation) is this emblem's motto.

Previously, Vermeer rendered the domestic interior with an extremely narrow focus, giving a close-up view of the human figure and its immediate surroundings. Now, for the first time, he abandons this close view, allowing the observer to step back, gain distance on the scene, and widen his field of vision. The interior is no longer perceived as an auxiliary to the figure, but vice versa – the figures seem part of, as they are framed by, the expanded interior view.

Innovations of this kind point to the influence of Pieter de Hooch's first masterworks. De Hooch also worked in Delft and was three years older than Vermeer. His interiors of about 1658 were primarily conceived and designed in terms of the architecture of interior space. This in itself represented a great contribution to the development of art, for de Hooch was among the first Dutch genre painters to give his figures a 'natural environment'. Nor does it detract from his accomplishment that Vermeer, a talent of the very first rank, was immediately able to improve upon the de Hooch interior. This is particularly clear in the Berlin painting, whose precisely calculated construction is as impressive as an illusionistic technique that extends to different surface textures without ever succumbing to mere objective description. In the light-suffused atmosphere everything takes on a quality that transcends the real. The girl's silk dress shimmers with the cool and noble tones of fresh roses. Now, this admittedly makes it rather difficult to see an allusion in this figure to the dangers of intemperance. Aesthetic factors nevertheless do not preclude the artist's interest in content. The gloomy landscape on the wall, visually associated with the man, and the restless way in which the light plays over the figures, set tones of suspense that contrast with the cultivated order of the interior and suggest a corresponding emotional disquiet in the two people who meet there.

Emblem from *Selectorum Emblematum*
G. Rollenhagen (ed.)
Arnheim, 1617

Jan Vermeer van Delft

Young Lady with a Pearl Necklace

*c.*1660–5

Canvas, 55 × 45 cm ($21\frac{5}{8} \times 17\frac{3}{4}$ in)
Signed on the tabletop: IVMeer
Acquired with the Suermondt Collection, 1874
Cat. no. 912 B

In cool light filtering through a leaded window, a young woman stands at a table looking into a mirror on the wall opposite her to see how the string of pearls with its pale yellow ribbon suits her. Her tranquil pose and expression are in keeping with the careful way the things on the table are arranged, as if for a still life; among them are aids to beauty and vanity such as a powder puff, a comb and a jewellery box. The motif of a woman before a mirror can be traced in Netherlandish painting as far back as Hieronymus Bosch, and it was popularized in Holland shortly after 1650 by Gerard ter Borch. It was an allegory of pride and vanity, and, interpreted morally, an allusion to the emptiness and transience of all worldly concerns. A mirror flatters the lovely woman who looks into it; yet what she sees is an illusion, for just as no one can capture an image in a mirror, every human being's time on earth is momentary compared to the eternity of God.

Most of Vermeer's interiors – in contrast, say, to *The Glass of Wine* in Berlin – were conceived as narrowly framed close-ups of the human figure and the immediate surroundings. This idea may have been derived from comparable pictorial solutions by ter Borch or Frans van Mieris the Elder, yet it was Vermeer who concentrated its effect to the highest degree in formal composition and emotional message. Here, in keeping with the mood of calm evoked by the figure's pose, the image structure is predominantly horizontal and vertical. With the exception of the chair that, foreshortened, occupies the lower right corner and intervenes between the figure and spectator, the surrounding space is defined by motifs arranged at right angles to one another and in layers from the front to the back. And since the pale back wall of the room appears to come forward, the multicoloured foreground scene seems to occupy a very shallow space. If in Rembrandt's paintings the background invariably dissolves in shadow and the brightest light collects around the figures, with Vermeer the figures stand out in accentuated colour against light grounds. This is a reversal of the light-dark relation. In terms of colour scheme, too, Vermeer introduced significant innovations. While in Rembrandt's imagery the areas of deep shadow are sometimes completely colourless, even the darkest passages in Vermeer's paintings still have colour – such as the ultramarine of the Delft faience vase here, and the soft blue in the table drapery. The greatest intensity of colour is seen in half-light. While the yellow of the curtain pales because of its proximity to the source of light, that in the girl's fur-trimmed satin jacket shines with great brilliancy. These two passages of yellow are also a kind of frame within the frame for the back wall, which is painted with superbly delicate modulations of colour. Who but Vermeer would have dared to put this 'empty' plane in the centre of an image? Of course the wall motif has more than a strictly objective meaning; it also works as a force field across which the girl communes with her own image in the mirror.

Vermeer's optical discoveries were long overlooked. It was not until the nineteenth century that Realists and Impressionists achieved similar results from close observation of light. All the qualities of Vermeer's design in light and colour seem united in his *View of Delft* (The Hague, Mauritshuis), the painting that led to a Vermeer revival when the French politician and journalist Bürger-Thoré saw it in 1842 and described its genius. The collection of this sensitive connoisseur and friend of Corot also once contained *Young Lady with a Pearl Necklace*.

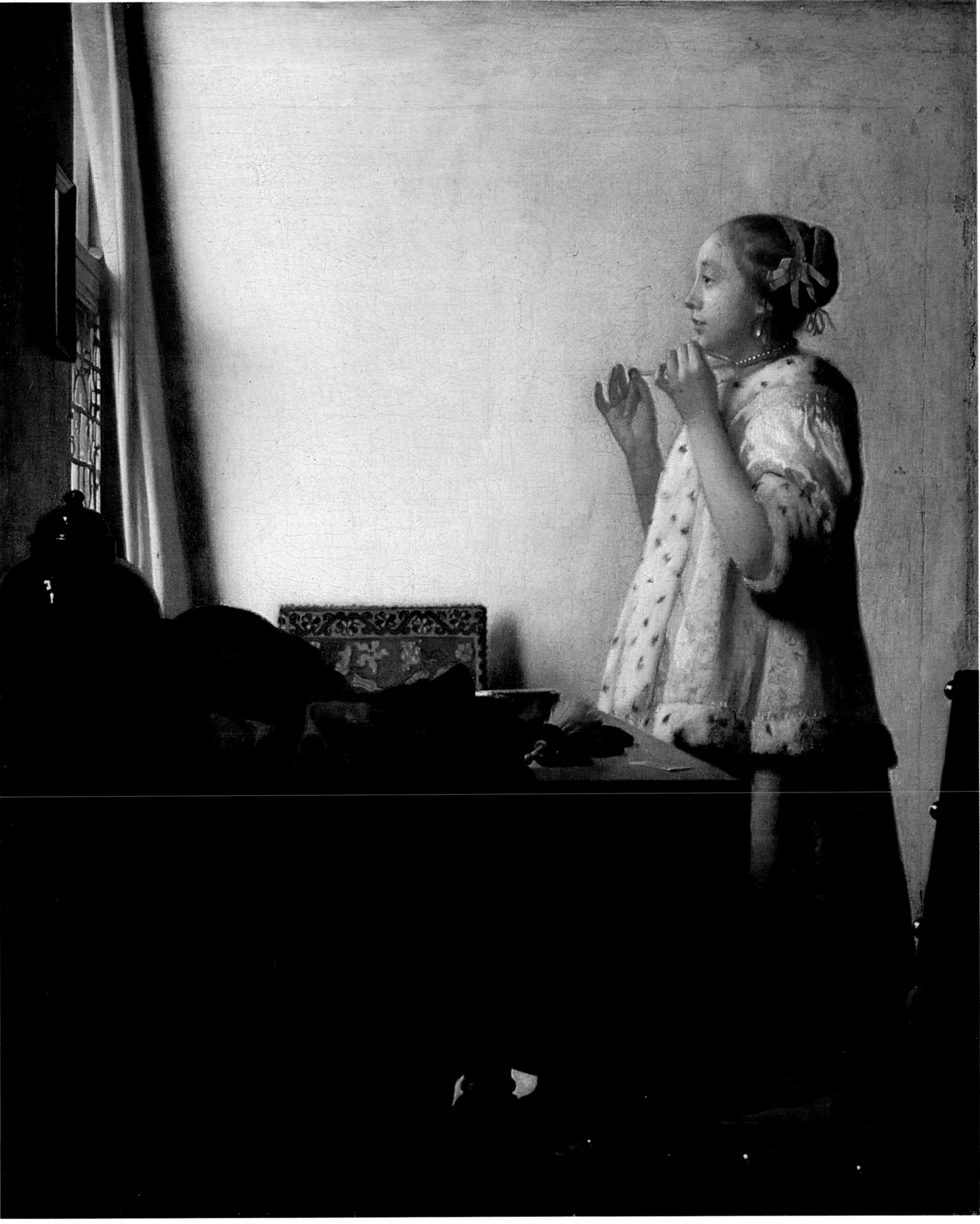

Gabriel Metsu (1629–67)
The Family of Dr Valckenier, Mayor of Amsterdam
*c.*1657

Canvas, 72 × 79 cm ($28\frac{3}{8}$ × 31 in)
Signed lower left: 'G. Metsu'
Tschiffeli Collection, Berne
Acquired 1832
Cat. no. 792

A large patrician family has gathered to be portrayed in their elaborately furnished living-room. In keeping with the family hierarchy the master of the house seated expansively at the table, and his son bringing in a falcon, dominate the left half of the picture, while his wife and three other children, the youngest held by a young woman, are slightly crowded in the same space opposite. Pride in prosperity, status and the honour of high social position – this was certainly what the artist's patron wished him to embody in his portrait with his family. And Metsu conformed to this wish by giving the figures an attitude of formal dignity, by emphasizing the fashionable elegance of their clothes and carefully evoking its variety of materials and colours, and finally by rendering with equal precision the luxury of the family's surroundings, which include gold-embossed leather wall-covering, paintings in elaborate frames, a great, columned fireplace, and a finely carved stone portal.

The painting was earlier in the possession of Maria Petronella Geelvinck (1769–1831), a native of Holland and wife of Frans Anton Tschiffeli, City Councillor of Berne. It was formerly called *Family of the Merchant Geelvinck*, because supposedly it never left Frau Tschiffeli-Geelvinck's family. Yet, although material recently discovered has confirmed this assumption, it has not confirmed the identification of the sitters as Geelvincks. In fact, they were close relatives of the family, the Valckeniers.

Dr Gillis Valckenier (1623–80), Mayor of Amsterdam, graduated from the University of Leyden and entered civic service there in 1647. He was first named alderman in 1649, and from 1665 served several terms as mayor of Amsterdam, an office his father had held before him. In 1648 he married Jacoba Ranst (1622–75). Their first child died, but their second, a son, Wouter, was baptized on 11 October 1650, in the Oude Kerk in Amsterdam. The boy in the painting, about six years old, is Wouter, and the falcon he so proudly has perched on his hand is the family emblem. Jacoba Ranst is represented with her daughter Eva Catharina, about two years old (she was baptized in March 1655), while Rebecca, about four (baptized in April 1653) plays with a puppy on the floor. The youngest child, Peteranna (baptized in July 1656) is held by a young woman whose plain dress has suggested to some commentators that she is a servant or nursemaid. However, she may very well be Anna Ranst (d.1679), the baby's aunt and sponsor, who remained unmarried and helped in her sister's household throughout her life.

Though the painting takes us into the cultivated world of patrician Amsterdam and the portraits may express more of their social status than their individuality, its dignified and serious mood is not at all tinged with pretention or pomp. Families like the Valckeniers owed their advancement and influence to bourgeois values, and it is to bourgeois concerns that the image is devoted. The grouping of the figures (and their small scale) creates an intimacy that, with the liveliness introduced by the children and the detailed painting of the domestic environment, lends the picture some of the character of a genre scene.

Jan Steen (1625/6–79)

The Garden of an Inn

*c.*1660

Canvas, 68 × 58 cm ($26\frac{3}{4} \times 22\frac{7}{8}$ in)
Signed on the table: 'JSteen'
From the Royal Palaces, Berlin, 1830
Cat. no. 795

Warm sunlight filters down through the canopy of leaves outside an inn, where pleasure seekers have gathered for refreshment. A woman seated in the foreground holds a goblet to her boy's lips, and she is ready to refill the goblet from the great pewter jug as if she were sure he wants more. The brilliant red of her jacket, and, behind her, the trellis post, which is a strong vertical accent, show that she is the main protagonist of the crowded scene. Nor is it by chance that the slate with the innkeeper's bill hangs on the post directly above her. Opposite her, a man relaxes with one foot on the bench, skinning a herring that he apparently has just bought from the fish dealer at the head of the table.

It was previously thought that the group represented the artist himself with his wife and children, and indeed Jan Steen ran a brewery for a time. His self-portraits, however, speak against this. It is not even clear whether the painting here is a family scene at all. The two men laughing at the spectator seem to owe their existence to a homily, '*Jemand een bokking verkopen*' ('to sell somebody a red herring'), which did not then mean to put people off the track but to put them sharply in their place. This reprimand could have been directed at mothers who bring their children to places where alcohol is consumed, and if so, then Steen's intention is to make parents pause to consider better ways to bring up their children – a subject that was already much debated in Steen's time and to which he devoted many works. Here, he has augmented his great storytelling talent by drawing the spectator into the debate, for the two men appeal directly to us for a decision.

Pithy phrases from the colloquial usage of the period, from emblematic literature, or from the theatre, are often found illustrated in Steen's versatile œuvre, which mostly consists of genre scenes from the life of the Dutch middle class and peasantry; these show the basically moral and educational purpose of his art. Though he did not initiate major stylistic developments like his more specialized colleague, Jan Vermeer van Delft, the imaginative variety of Steen's compositions, the humorous detachment of his narratives, and especially the virtuosity of his execution, made him one of the outstanding representatives of Dutch genre painting in the seventeenth century.

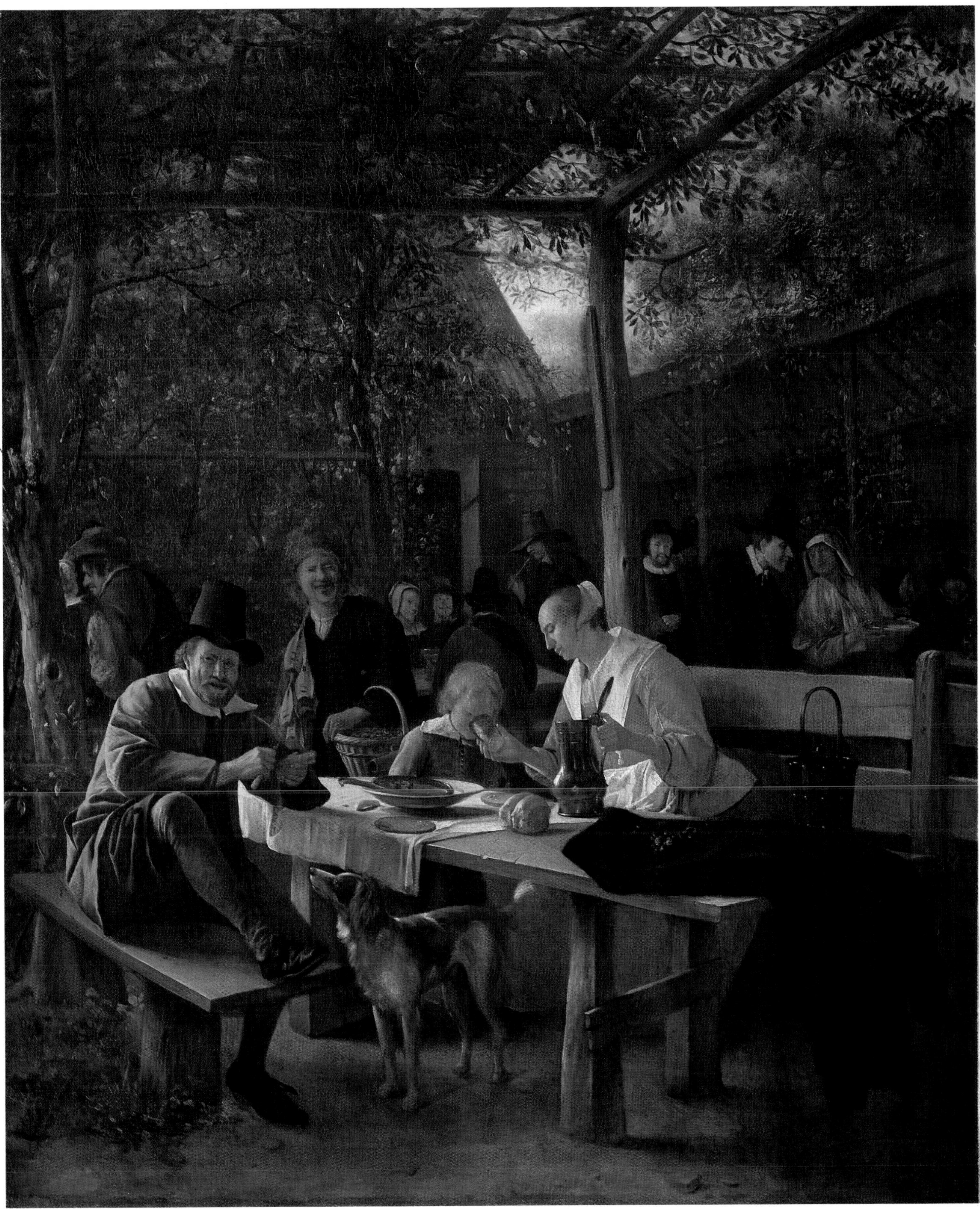

Jan Steen
Men Quarrelling over Cards
*c.*1664–5

Canvas, 90 × 119 cm ($35\frac{1}{2} \times 46\frac{7}{8}$ in)
Monogrammed lower left on carved stone: 'IS'
Acquired with the Suermondt Collection, 1874
Cat. no. 795 B

Men playing cards outside a country inn have become involved in a violent quarrel. Peasants on the right brandish knives and a pitchfork at a gentleman in doublet and knee-hose who is drawing his sword, while a little girl and a woman try to prevent him using it. The elderly man behind the table also seems to have kept calm despite the turbulence, and tries to pacify both sides. Slate, cards and the backgammon game on the ground suggest that the loser of the game has started the argument, and that one of the players has been accused of cheating. The disgruntled loser is probably the swordsman, because the small winnings are scraped together on the peasant's side of the table. The copious pewter jug in the foreground shows that alcohol has contributed to bringing events to a head. A man with a pilgrim's banner leaves the ugly scene without further trouble, while the peasants at the left, including one peering out at the inn door, seem – in the bleary-eyed way of most public house *habitués* – to find it rather comical.

Steen again proves himself an imaginative narrator here, a characteristic quality that is certainly matched by a skill in composing subjects rich in people. The many gestures and movements called for by the theme have been integrated into a carefully ordered whole, and what initially seems hopeless confusion turns out on second glance to follow a premeditated plan. The figures are arranged in the style of a relief across the wide format, not simply one next to the other but in alternations of more or less compact groupings at various depths, violent and calm attitudes, and in pronounced or subdued colour. This accentuates the dramatic climax of the plot, the encounter between peasant and gentleman, without detracting from the rhythmic expressiveness of the whole.

Human behaviour is pilloried here. The antagonists who lose all self-control when they have a weapon in their hand embody *Ira* (Anger), one of the seven deadly sins. And the reasons for their error – alcohol and gambling – are set directly before our eyes through the empty jug and the backgammon game.

A glance is enough for us to recognize, however, that Steen's grasp of human weaknesses has nothing bombastically moralistic about it. The peasant at the far right looks out at the spectator with a conniving laugh; indeed all the figures act theatrically and are characterized as comic types. Similarly the gentleman with the sword is not meant to represent a soldier. His clothes and the studied drama of his pose mark him as an actor – Capitano, the incorrigible braggart of the *Commedia dell'arte*, a figure who is absolutely harmless and whose histrionics are thus easily contained by a woman and a little girl. Steen often used stage characters and stage-like scenes in his pictorial narratives: and his personality was most attuned to comedy with its mixture of light entertainment and moral instruction.

Isack van Ostade (1621–49)

Frozen Canal with Sleds and Ships

*c.*1645

Oak, 21 × 24.5 cm ($8\frac{1}{4} \times 9\frac{5}{8}$ in)
Signed lower left: 'Isack Ostade'
Acquired as the gift of a Parisian art dealer, 1813
Cat. no. 1709

Across the frozen expanse of an inland waterway, framed by the bare branches of a tree and by the masts of boats caught in the ice, people walk and skate, push or let themselves be pushed in sledges, and guide horse-drawn sleighs that are heaped with goods. While in the foreground half-melted, caked snow, a filigree of grass on the bank, and the branches of the tree, are painted with a precision that throws them into high relief, the figures are treated as accessories whose contours dissolve in the misty winter air to indeterminate silhouettes. A few local colours in the front – the subdued carmine of a dress, a touch of lemon yellow under the dull blue of a cap, even the impasto white in the coat of a grey horse – become subdued in carefully graduated perspective, and then merge with the softly toned browns of the middle distance and the background. This treatment emphasizes the landscape at the expense of the figures. Instead of merely being a setting for the colourful narrative, the landscape itself becomes an image of winter.

This emphasis was untypical of Isack van Ostade, whose favourite subjects were figures and particularly genre scenes from the daily life of the peasantry. Inspired by his brother Adriaen, whose pupil he was, he observed rural people going about their daily tasks among the picturesque disarray of their cottages, or in the market-place, on a village road outside an inn where coachloads of travellers arrived and departed, or on the banks of a river, in scenes sometimes bathed in the warm colours of summer, sometimes suffused with cold, grey-blue winter light. Outdoor views of this kind interested the artist more and more as his career progressed; figures and accessories increasingly declined in compositional importance, and the landscape spread out unencumbered before the eye. Towards the end of his short life Isack finally accomplished a sensitive balance between figure and landscape, though he only occasionally crossed the borderline into pure landscape painting. Nevertheless, his works in this genre deserve to be considered achievements of an unusual kind. The present view of an icebound canal, arched over by a frosty blue sky and greyish-lilac clouds, does not exhaust itself in visual description of a familiar and quite undramatic slice of nature; its delicate nuances of light and colour raise it to the level of a poetic image of a mood. The subjectivity of the artist's interpretation comes through, and this frees the spectator of the need simply to register what he is shown: it stimulates his own subjective reaction. The great emotional appeal of this image, which recalls Rembrandt's *Winter Landscape* of 1647 (Kassel, Staatliche Kunstsammlungen), gives some idea of the grave loss to Dutch landscape painting when Isack van Ostade died at an early age.

Philips Wouwerman (1619–68)

Winter Landscape with Wooden Bridge

*c.*1660

Oak, 28.5 × 36.5 cm ($11\frac{1}{4} \times 14\frac{3}{8}$ in)
Acquired 1908
Cat. no. 900 F

A picturesque, rickety wooden footbridge over a frozen stream is the centre of interest here; it stops the eye in the middleground before it moves across the winter vista beyond. Though the flat land of Holland is evoked, it is only by means of this circumscribed foreground. And although this is populated, the tiny figures seem strangely lost, and their activities take up much less room than the great space given to them. In other words, the foreground, instead of serving merely as a setting for figures, remains an integral part of the landscape view.

Only when seen in this way does the image fully reveal its abundance of carefully observed natural details: the sensitively toned reflections on the ice sloping into dark, deep water beneath the bridge; the transitions between packed, crusted and fresh-fallen snow on the right bank; the rise at the left with its traces of old snow mingling with the brownish clumps of last autumn's grass; the masonry of the bridge, which decay has reduced to rounded shapes much like those of the surrounding countryside – indeed everything built by human hands seems weathered as if it had not been built at all but created by nature herself, and soon to be reclaimed.

It is, above all, this variety of superbly perceived detail that shows the artist's devotion to his Dutch homeland. Nor did his eye for detail make him lose the larger scene from view – the great dome of sky, whose cool light casts a subduing, atmospheric veil over the variegated colours of things, and whose stupendous cloud formations have been made, with an eye to unifying the composition, to repeat in softened form the angular contrasts of the bridge construction and of the bare tree. Nothing has been left to chance in this carefully arranged composition, which is why it cannot be explained simply as a record of natural appearances. Though it may give the impression of a straightforward description of a real place, the image is none the less mostly arranged consciously and is enriched with human ideas and emotional values. Take the ice-covered branches of the tree, shimmering pale against the gathering clouds of a snowstorm: this skeletal line evokes feelings that are slightly ominous, as if it were a sign for all to see that the forces of nature can imperil human existence.

Pure landscapes of this type, as profound and compelling as those by Jacob van Ruisdael, are found only occasionally in Wouwerman's prolific œuvre. He preferred subjects of equestrian scenes with thoroughbred animals and fashionably dressed figures. It was particularly to this genre, in which he created imagery of great variety and appeal, that Wouwerman owed his high reputation during his lifetime and posthumous fame during the Neo-Classically oriented eighteenth century.

Jacob van Ruisdael (1628/9–82)

Damrak Square in Amsterdam

*c.*1675–80

Canvas, 52 × 65 cm ($20\frac{1}{2} \times 25\frac{1}{2}$ in)
Signed lower left: 'JvRuisdael'
(JvR interlocked)
Acquired with the Suermondt Collection, 1874
Cat. no. 885 D

The building in the left middleground is the old Municipal Scales House in Amsterdam, a public institution to determine correct weights and ensure that buyers and sellers received what was due to them. Under its projecting roof lie bundles of goods waiting to be put on the scales in the entrance. To the right is a view of the Damrak, the town's inland harbour, crowded with boats, its far shore lined by warehouses; above the gabled roofs the tower of the Oude Kerk rises into the evening sky. The square is full of people out promenading, groups of elegantly dressed ladies and gentlemen, some stopping now and then to look at the wares offered by a fishmonger or vegetable seller. These people were not painted by Ruisdael, who was no figure specialist himself, but probably by Gerard van Battem, a skilled artist of Rotterdam.

Ruisdael was very familiar with the place he depicted here. After moving from Haarlem to Amsterdam in 1657, he lived near Damrak Square. In 1670 he found rooms on the south side of the square, where he spent the rest of his life. The view from his windows was probably very similar to that here, though it is not a *vedute* in the strict sense, that is, not a topographically precise delineation of one aspect of the town. Compared with the preliminary drawing in the Brussels Museum, the proportions of the buildings have been altered. To give the municipal scales more compositional weight, Ruisdael reduced the height of the buildings at the left and of the church tower. And while in the drawing, the Scales House is in the shade and the buildings to the right brightly illuminated, this distribution of dark and light is reversed in the painting. The Scales House emerges from the shadows of its architectural surroundings in a cool greyish-blue – a perfect foil for the elaborate town arms of Amsterdam on the upper façade, which glow in delectable colour in the twilight. Distinguished in this way, the building, a solid structure that is higher than everything else in the painting and projects into the square like a portico, takes on a monumental presence.

Primarily a painter of landscape, Ruisdael turned to the city rather late in his career, probably because it suited his growing penchant for ample form. Though architectural motifs might well have been thought to put strictures on his creative imagination, his townscapes by no means fall behind his compelling renderings of natural scenes. Just as in his landscapes Ruisdael visualized growth and decay in the many trees beneath heavily clouded skies, in his views of towns he transcended mere sober, straightforward description. They too were painted 'uyt den gheest' ('from the spirit'), and raised to poetic images of emotion and mood.

Jacob van Ruisdael
View of Damrak Square
Drawing
Brussels, Koninklijke Musea voor Schone Kunsten

Jacob van Ruisdael

Landscape with a View of Haarlem

*c.*1670–5

Canvas, 52 × 65 cm (20½ × 25½)
Signed lower right: 'JvRuisdael'
(JvR interlocked)
Acquired with the Suermondt Collection, 1874
Cat. no. 885 C

Ruisdael was born in Haarlem, where he also spent his apprenticeship and the first years of his career as an independent artist. Only much later – long after moving to Amsterdam – did he begin to use his home town as a subject for his art. Distant views of Haarlem as in this painting are among the finest examples of Ruisdael's fully mature landscape style. From about 1670 he began to include them in his rich and varied repertoire of themes.

From the high vantage point of the dunes north-west of Haarlem, near Bloemendaal, we look across the plain to the shimmering red roofs of the town and the huge bulk of Sint Bavo. To its left the Bakenesser Church, St Jans Kerk and the Klokhuis are visible, and to the right, the Town Hall, Nieuwe Kerk and, on the ramparts at the edge of the city, a line of windmills. The bands of sunlight and shadow that cross the plain reflect the great expanse of cloud and sky above the low horizon. In the foreground, set off by woods, long strips of linen have been spread out to bleach in the fields, a familiar sight in the environs of old Haarlem. The bleaching of linen – most of it Dutch, but some imported from Germany, England and Scandinavia – was among the town's most important commercial enterprises, and the clear water from the dunes was perfect for the purpose.

In almost all of his *Haarlempjes*, as this type of landscape created by Ruisdael and developed by Jan van Kessel and Jan Vermeer van Haarlem was then known, the artist gave particular prominence to the motif of linen bleaching. For him, it must have held a significance beyond the typical trait of a certain area. As the Dutch poet Jan Luiken once wrote, linen bleached in the sunshine was like snow and evoked the memory of saved souls. Then he quotes from the Bible: 'And to her was granted that she should be arrayed in fine linen, clean and white: for the fine linen is the righteousness of saints' (Revelation 19:8). In view of the penchant of Dutch painters for combining realism with transcendant meaning, it is certainly conceivable that Ruisdael intended the bleaching to be understood as an ethical allusion to the virtues of purity and innocence of soul. As early a commentator as Goethe, in his essay 'Ruisdael als Dichter' (1813), marvelled at the comprehensive symbolism of the artist's works. An interplay of natural appearances with deep allusions is indeed a prime trait of Ruisdael's œuvre, which brought seventeenth-century Dutch landscape painting to its most impressive heights.

Meindert Hobbema (1638–1709)
Village Road under Trees
*c.*1665

Canvas, 97 × 128.5 cm ($38\frac{1}{8} \times 50\frac{1}{2}$ in)
Formerly in the Royal Palaces, Berlin
Acquired 1926
Cat. no. 1984

A village road meanders from the foreground past trees and farmhouses to the deep middle ground, where it forks at a clump of trees, bringing the eye up short; the distant horizon is obscured. Instead of evoking the vast plains of Holland, the artist has chosen an intimate view enclosed by trees, whose variety he has organized in three symmetrical planes – gathered in groves around the houses on the right and left, and looming solitarily in the centre. Trunks, limbs and branches have sinuous, rhythmic curves against the leaves, into whose range of greens the light blue of the sky plays as much as the brown, ochre, and pale grey tones of the landscape.

Though Hobbema shared his preference for trees in full leaf with his teacher, Jacob van Ruisdael, he never emulated the latter's compact, dense groupings. The contours of his trees open out fan-like against the sky, and indeed wherever there are closed areas they are scattered, interspersed with spaces that reveal what lies beyond – slopes in the land, sometimes a section of open horizon, and always the shadowed, interior masses of the trees' foliage. Space in Hobbema seems transparent, expansive: it is evocative of a harmonious coexistence of nature with man and his works. For unlike Ruisdael's imagery, in which the force of the elements is everywhere, Hobbema's landscapes show nature in a state of calm. And he underscores this calm by the delicacy of his line, the sensitiveness of his handling of light and colour, giving the natural scene an appearance of singularity, of cultivation. The village street here seems suffused with the peace of Sunday. Though the furrows in the sandy soil show that much traffic passes through, there are only a few people to be seen, walking at their ease like promenaders in a park beneath the gentle blue sky and the clouds touched with warm tawny sunlight.

This approach to nature certainly conformed with the sophisticated tastes of Dutch middle-class society in the late seventeenth century. Yet surprisingly, Hobbema's work was not particularly well received. To improve his financial position he became a *wijnroier* or inspector of wines in 1668. After taking on this work, which ensured him a tolerable income for the rest of his life, his skill remained undiminished though he painted less. If it were not for his most famous and finest work, *The Avenue of Middelharnis* (1689; London, National Gallery), the late phase of Dutch landscape art, which had already begun to exhaust itself in decorative formulas, would have been shallow indeed.

Willem Kalf (1619–93)
Still Life with Chinese Porcelain Bowl
1662

Canvas, 64 × 53 cm ($25\frac{1}{8}$ × $20\frac{7}{8}$ in)
Signed lower left: 'W KALF 1662'
Acquired 1899
Cat. no. 948 F

Arranged here on a marble-topped table covered with an East Persian carpet gathered into rich folds, a few exquisite objects glow in dim half-light against a dark ground. The centre of interest, compositionally emphasized as the primary motif, is a Chinese sugar bowl of the Wanli period (1573–1619) with applied figures in relief. These figures, arranged in pairs, have been identified as Immortals of Taoism. The lid of the bowl is decorated with a figurine of a Fo dog. A lemon with a dangling arabesque of peel, a Seville orange, and a small knife with an agate handle complete the arrangement on a silver tray, presumably from an Amsterdam workshop. The sugar bowl and fruit are probably intended to flavour the red and white wine served in glasses of three beautiful shapes – a slim flute glass which marks the central axis of the composition, a Venetian-style glass at the left, and a large *roemer* at the right.

Kalf repeatedly depicted, in various arrangements, all the table ware here, which can still be found in exact or similar versions. From a collector's point of view, at least, his still lifes do seem like documents of exquisitely crafted objects whose form and aesthetic effect he thought worth recording. But few would deny that he saw beneath the surface of things. The pocket clock at the left, marking the passing of time, the peach stones on the plate, even the twilight of the room, seem to signify the uselessness of worldly ostentation and material possessions, which, like human life itself, are all too transient.

In the still lifes executed before 1653, the year he moved to Amsterdam, Kalf favoured precious metal objects whose extremely crowded arrangements evoke the irreverent notion of hastily piled booty. By contrast, the paintings of the Amsterdam period, to which this one belongs, show things carefully chosen for their variety of texture, form and colour and in continually new, pyramidal groups. And now the striking character of the objects as well as the beauty of the artist's painting come into full play. In the light shining into the dark room from the left, the rough yellow peel of a lemon or the subdued red of an orange appeal to the eye no less than the Chinese bowl, whose natural delicacy is almost magically heightened by sensitively modulated chiaroscuro. This perfect harmony of motif with design established Kalf as a major representative of the Classical phase of seventeenth-century Dutch still-life painting.

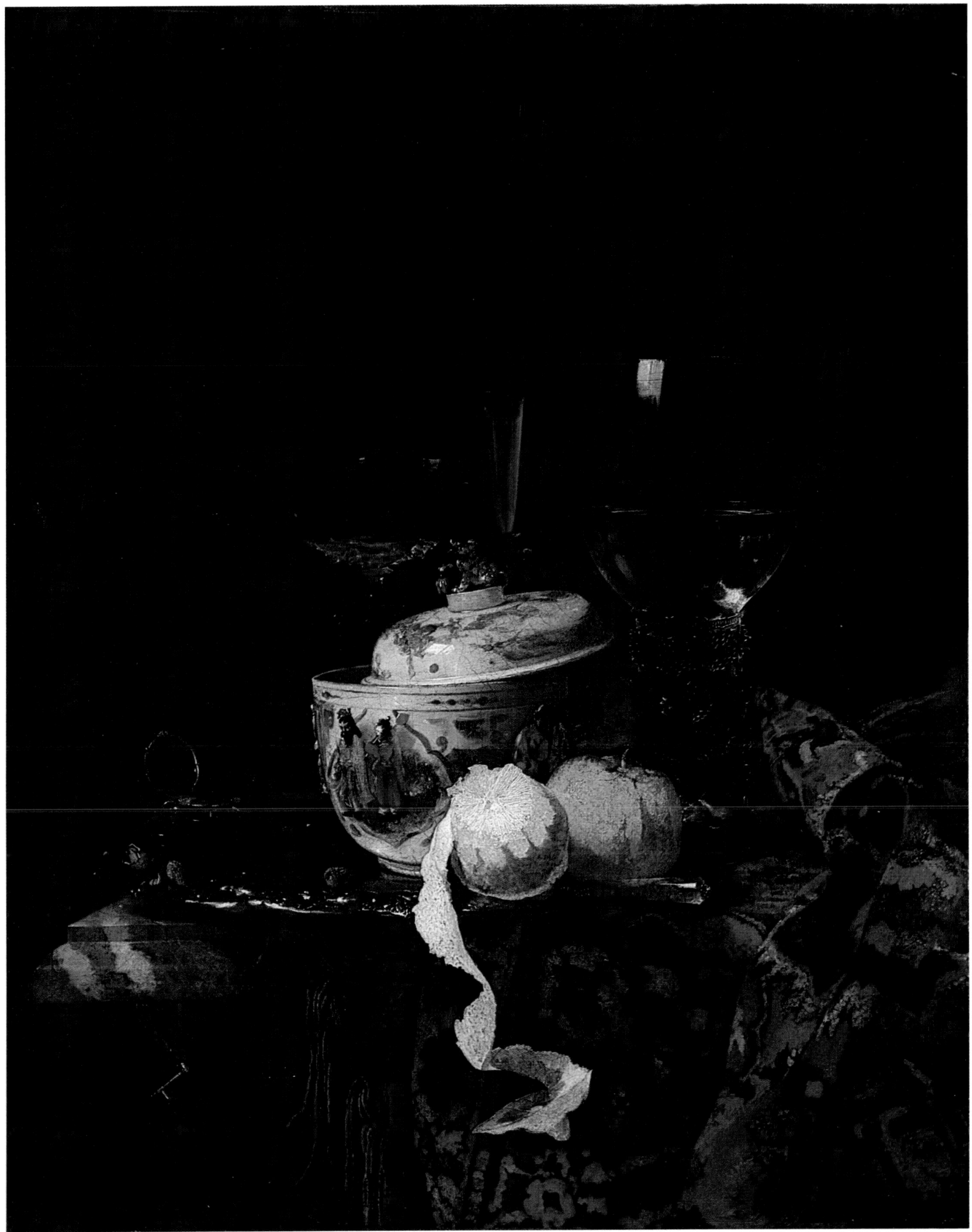

Jan Davidsz de Heem (1606–83)
Still Life with Fruit and Lobster
*c.*1648–9

Canvas, 95 × 120 cm ($37\frac{3}{8} \times 47\frac{1}{4}$ in)
Signed upper right: 'Jan de Heem f.'
Acquired 1975
Cat. no. 3/75

De Heem was born and trained in Holland. In keeping with his artistic environment in Utrecht and Leyden he first painted small-format still lifes with simple arrangements – in Utrecht, mostly flowers and fruit, to which he added Vanitas motifs in Leyden. De Heem's rendering is always objective and the pictorial structure strictly ordered and self-contained. The colours in his paintings appear subdued by soft light, and, particularly in the Vanitas motifs, the palette is often reduced to monochrome tones of greyish-brown in very delicate light-and-dark gradations. In 1636 he moved to Antwerp. There, in the cultural centre of the southern Netherlands and Rubens's sphere of influence, which extended to the leading Flemish still-life painters of the time, Frans Snyders, Adriaen van Utrecht, and the internationally recognized Daniel Seghers, de Heem's approach changed profoundly. It was a mark of his artistic and intellectual stature that he was able to adopt these new ideas frankly, without belying his origins in Dutch pictorial tradition. Consequently, he bridged the stylistic gap between Flemish and Dutch painting and synthesized the two.

Described as a combination of these opposites in a new pictorial unity, the present painting shows a great variety of objects on a large canvas, but rendered in fine detail: a decorative sweep of line which is none the less subordinated to the static, triangular composition; and a richness of palette in which the colours merge in the toned chiaroscuro of subdued illumination. What is the significance of the abundance of fine fruit, crustaceans, exotic shells and costly objects such as a prominently placed pitcher made of a nautilus shell in a gold-plated silver mount? The notion that these things have simply been represented without a motive, as the makings of a superb meal, would seem to be contradicted by the care with which they have been arranged into an ostentatious display. The pleasures of the table are not alluded to here, but the morally dubious aspect of exaggerated devotion to them. It is not even necessary to cite the motif of the clock, commonly used in Netherlandish still life to symbolize transience and the need for moderation, to realize that this super-abundance is a warning against gluttony and a reminder that the things of this world do not last. Doubtless the artist's contemporaries admired the skill with which he heightened the natural beauty of these things, but all the same, it is precisely the sumptuous and tactile quality of his painting that calls the luxury of the display into question.

Adam van Vianen
Pitcher, 1614
Gold-plated silver
Amsterdam, Rijksmuseum

ITALIAN PAINTING OF THE THIRTEENTH TO THE EIGHTEENTH CENTURY. GERMAN, FRENCH AND SPANISH PAINTING OF THE SEVENTEENTH CENTURY

BY ERICH SCHLEIER

Giotto di Bondone (1266/7 [or 1276]–1337)

The Death of the Virgin

*c.*1310

Poplar, top in the form of a low gable, height at centre 75 cm ($29\frac{1}{2}$ in), at sides 51 cm (20 in), width 179 cm ($70\frac{1}{2}$ in)
Acquired 1914
Property of the Kaiser-Friedrich-Museums-Verein
Cat. no. 1884

Giotto's *Death of the Virgin* was acquired through Langton Douglas in London for the Kaiser-Friedrich-Museums-Verein in 1914 shortly before the outbreak of war. It was the last of several important acquisitions in the field of Trecento painting which, since the turn of the century, Wilhelm von Bode was able to add to the remarkable group of early Italian paintings which had entered the gallery with the Solly Collection in 1821 (Ugolino da Siena, 1904–11; Simone Martini, 1901). Giotto's panel had been in the Davenport Bromley Collection since the mid-nineteenth century and earlier in that of Cardinal Fesch (d. 1839), which had been sold in 1841 and 1845. Nothing is known about its fate from the second half of the sixteenth to the eighteenth centuries.

This is one of the four panels by Giotto which Lorenzo Ghiberti, in the second of his *Commentarii* (1445/55), described as having been in the possession of the Frati Humiliati together with a chapel and a large crucifix. This order presided over the church and convent of Ognissanti in Florence at that period. As Ghiberti wrote about one of the panels, 'the death of Our Lady, around her angels and twelve Apostles and Our Lord, was rendered with great perfection'. Another was the great *Maestà* or *Ognissanti Madonna* (now in the Uffizi), which is stylistically closely related to *The Death of the Virgin*. Ghiberti does not specify the location of the 'Dormitio', but it is probably identical with the altarpiece by Giotto which, according to a document of 1417, was installed on the altar 'beside the door of the choir on the right side'. Vasari wrote in 1550 that it leaned (*'appoggiata'*) on the choir screen (*'tramezzo'*). He called it a *'tavolina'*, which would seem to indicate that he had not seen it for some time. He described it enthusiastically, quoting Michelangelo's praise: 'The uniqueness of this story could not have been represented more naturally or truly.' The citation appears in the second edition of Vasari's *Lives* of 1568, in which he notes that the painting was no longer in the Ognissanti church. Apparently he did not know what had become of it.

The elongated and low horizontal format of the panel with its flat gabled top, unusual in altarpieces, resembles the gabled *dossales* that were quite common in Tuscan painting of the last quarter of the thirteenth century but which were superseded, after 1300, by polyptychs and upright altarpieces. These were usually divided into five fields with arched tops. For his *Death of the Virgin*, in other words, Giotto used an already rather outmoded format, and to represent a subject that was not depicted on other *dossales*.

The Virgin's body is being gently lowered by one of the Apostles onto a shroud spread by two tall angels over a sarcophagus, decorated with inlay work. Behind the sarcophagus, invisible to the mourners, Christ cherishes Mary's soul in the guise of a newborn infant. A single Apostle kneels before the casket, seen from the back; at either end, two angels, smaller than the others, hold the death watch with candles in their hands. Among the mourners approaching from the left are two women and several Apostles, including Peter. Reading a prayer from a book, he occupies a place of prominence in the centre of the group. To his right is perhaps Barnabas, then perhaps Paul, in a red garment, bearded and already balding; then to his right, in a green mantle, John, shown in a frontal pose bending disconsolately over the body and wringing his hands. Other Apostles and angels approach the foot of the sarcophagus from the right. One of them holds a half-covered censer and blows on it mightily. The bearded, grey-haired Apostle (Matthew?) in the green robes immediately next to Christ sprinkles Holy Water on the corpse.

The composition is slightly asymmetrical. While the group of Apostles and angels rises from the right to the height of Christ's figure, paralleling the diagonal of the gable, the line of heads on the left rises at less of an angle; and behind Paul, in the contour of the figure of John, it declines again to the centre.

The question of authorship, that is, whether and to what extent Giotto painted the panel, as well as that of dating within his œuvre, has remained controversial to this day. At the time Bode purchased the painting in 1914, F.M. Perkins published it, identifying it with a work of Giotto's described in the sources, and dating it to the second decade of the fourteenth century. Berenson then immediately questioned Giotto's authorship, though he was later to recant. Most scholars have followed Perkins in recognizing the panel as a work primarily by Giotto's hand (for example, Sirén, Offner, Longhi, and the majority of younger Italian art historians). Friedrich Rintelen, on the other hand, denied Giotto's authorship in 1923, calling the panel a 'trivialization' of his art. Oertel agreed (1949, 1953, and in the Berlin Gallery of Painting Catalogues of 1975 and 1978), stating in 1953 that 'not even the design for the whole composition can possibly go back to Giotto himself'. He followed a hypothesis expressed by Marchini (1938) that the panel represented a scaled-down workshop version of a lost monumental fresco by Giotto that belonged to the cycle of frescoes depicting scenes of the Life of the Virgin in the Tosinghi Chapel in S. Croce. However, the surviving production of Giotto's workshop contains no examples of unaltered replicas of compositions previously produced there (M. Boskovits, Catalogue of the Gemäldegalerie, Berlin, 'Frühe Italienische Malerei', 1986). Suggested dates have ranged from the first years of the fourteenth century to Giotto's final years, about 1325–30 or even later. Most critics, however, follow Perkins's dating to the second decade, just as recent Italian scholars have commented on the panel's stylistic affinity to the frescoes in the Peruzzi Chapel, S. Croce. Though these were for a long time dated around or after 1320, more recent studies suggest 1310–13 (Previtali, 1967). The style of *The Death of the Virgin* is obviously more developed and advanced than the austere style of the Arena Chapel frescoes in Padua (1303–5); its lines are sharper and the rhythmic articulation of forms more agitated. Also, because of its stylistic closeness to the Uffizi *Maestà* or *Ognissanti Madonna*, which is generally placed in the first decade, the present panel probably dates to around or shortly before 1310 (Boskovits, 1986).

Simone Martini (*c.*1284–1344)
The Entombment of Christ
*c.*1340

Poplar, 23.3 × 16.6 cm ($9\frac{1}{8} \times 6\frac{1}{2}$ in)
Acquired 1901
Cat. no. 1070 A

After Duccio, who was presumably his teacher, and together with Pietro and Ambrogio Lorenzetti, Simone Martini was the leading Siennese painter of the fourteenth century, and in contrast to the Florentine oriented Lorenzetti brothers, he embodied Siennese art in its purest form. He was moreover one of the greatest Italian artists of the Gothic style. His art combined elegance of drawing, jewel-like brilliancy of colour, and great technical finesse with acute observation of nature and a narrative skill based on deep psychological penetration.

In 1315, already a renowned master, Martini executed a large *Maestà* in fresco for the Palazzo Pubblico in Sienna. In 1317, for the King of Naples, Robert of Anjou, he painted an altar panel with St Louis of Toulouse (Naples, Museo di Capodimonte), followed in 1319 by a large polyptych in Pisa. In the early 1320s he worked in Orvieto, and presumably was active in Assisi towards the end of the 1310s. Most of his work during the 1320s, however, was done in Sienna, where in 1333 he dated and signed, with Lippo Memmi, the altarpiece of the Annunciation to the Virgin for the cathedral there (now in Florence, Uffizi). In 1335–6 he moved to the Pope's court at Avignon, where he died in 1344. Among the works of his last period were frescoes for the vestibule of Notre-Dame-des-Doms; a small panel with the Holy Family dated 1342 (Liverpool); and a small portable altar with four scenes of the Passion, one of which is the Berlin *Entombment*.

According to the very convincing reconstruction by Van Os-Rinkleff Reinders (*Nederlands Kunsthistorisch Jaarboek*, 1972), the four Passion scenes were originally arranged in a row, side by side, of course in chronological order of the events, which runs from left to right as follows: *Christ Carrying the Cross* (Paris, Louvre), *The Crucifixion* (Antwerp), *The Deposition* (Antwerp), and *The Entombment* (Berlin). The two middle panels formed the fixed centre section of the altar, and *Christ Carrying the Cross* and *The Entombment* its left and right wings. Still visible today on the back (exterior) of the left wing are the arms of the Orsini family of Rome. Presumably the Berlin panel also once bore these arms on its reverse, but they were destroyed when the panel was thinned and afterwards cradled. Since there are no traces of hinges or framing, it cannot be said whether the altar could be folded, that is, whether its wings could be closed. In a closed position the Orsini arms would have been visible on the outside of the wings, while the two Antwerp panels of *The Annunciation* would have appeared on the back of the central section – the reverses of *The Crucifixion* and *The Deposition*. The artist's signature once extended across the lower frames of the four panels, and is still partly legible: HOC OPVS (on *Christ Carrying the Cross*, obscured by new gilding); PINXIT (on *The Crucifixion);* SYMON (on *The Deposition*); and on the lost frame of the Berlin *Entombment*, presumably SENENSIS or DE SENIS or the date.

In the foreground of *The Deposition*, there is the kneeling figure of the donor, a bishop or cardinal deacon. This is probably Cardinal Napoleone Orsini, who died in 1442 in Avignon and was known to have been associated with Martini. If he was truly the donor of the piece, Martini must have painted it in Avignon. It later came to Dijon, presumably in connection with the marriage of the two of the cardinal's nephews with ladies of the high Burgundian aristocracy. Later it was donated to the Carthusian monastery in Champmol near Dijon, where it was recorded in 1791. During the nineteenth century the four panels were dispersed. The altarpiece had considerable influence on artists of Provence and Burgundy.

Not only are the original frame and coat of arms on the back of the Berlin panel missing, but the image itself has been altered. The sky with its reddish sunset glow was added over the original gold background, possibly in the early fifteenth century.

The panel shows Christ's body lying on a shroud spread over an open marble

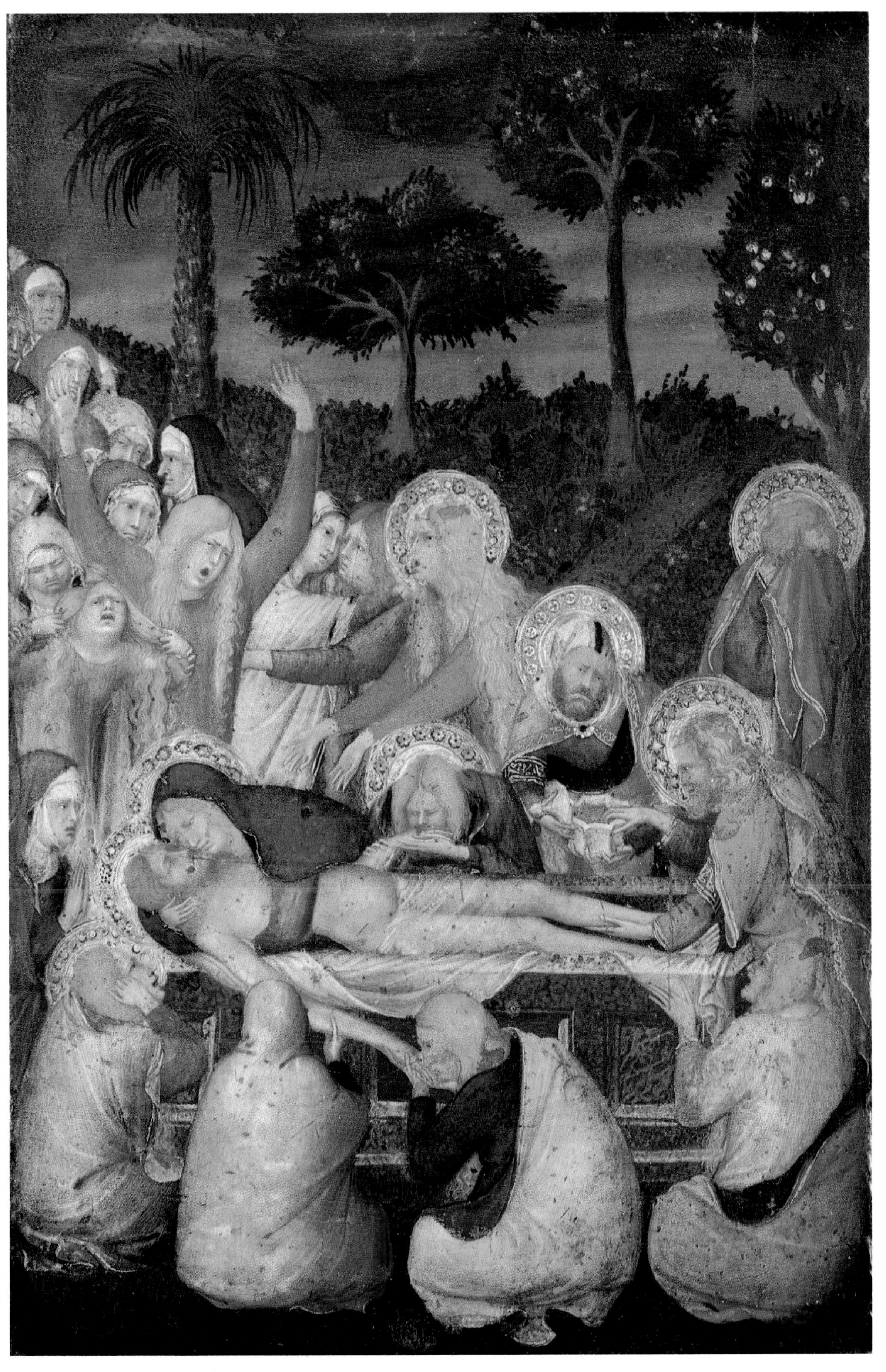

Simone Martini
Panels of the Orsini Altar:
1 *Angel of the Annunciation*
Antwerp, Koninklijk Museum voor Schone Kunsten
2 *The Annunciation*
Antwerp, Koninklijk Museum voor Schone Kunsten
3 *Christ Carrying the Cross*
Paris, Musée du Louvre
4 *The Crucifixion*
Antwerp, Koninklijk Museum voor Schone Kunsten
5 *The Deposition*
Antwerp, Koninklijk Museum voor Schone Kunsten
6 *The Entombment*
Berlin, Gemäldegalerie SMPK

sarcophagus. Mary embraces Christ as Nicodemus, on the right, brings a jar of spices and Joseph annoints Christ's feet. Behind them, on the far right, John averts his face from the scene to hide his tears. Mary Magdalene, the figure in the centre in a red gown, her long blonde hair in disarray, stretches out her arms to the dead Christ. On the left are two women in similar clothes and with similarly loosened hair, but without haloes, one of them throwing up her arms in desperation, the other tearing her hair. Around the sarcophagus, disciples and woman attendants sit or kneel. The haloed female figures probably represent Mary Jacobi and Mary Salome, who according to the Gospels (Matthew 27:55–6) were eye-witnesses to the death and burial of Jesus. Whether the old woman kneeling on the left of the grave represents St Claire of Montefalco, as Brink assumes (Paragone, 1977), remains uncertain.

1

2

3

4

5

6

Gentile da Fabriano (*c.*1370[?]–1427)

The Virgin Enthroned with Child, Two Saints, and a Donor

Around or shortly before 1400

Poplar, 131 × 113 cm ($51\frac{1}{2} \times 44\frac{1}{2}$ in), top rounded
Inscribed on a fragment of original frame, lost in 1945: 'gentilis de fabriano opus'
Presented by Frederick William III, 1837
Cat. no. 1130

Gentile da Fabriano is generally considered one of the leading Italian masters of the courtly style known as International Gothic, which originated in Burgundy and northern France and which he helped to spread in the key artistic centres of Italy. He was admitted to the Florence Artists' Guild in 1422, the same year as Masaccio, and worked in Florence from 1425–6 before going to nearby Sienna and to Orvieto. Gentile's fame was established by an altarpiece painted in 1423 for Palla Strozzi and intended for his family chapel in S. Trinita, and the high altarpiece for S. Niccolò Oltrarno (1425). For a time he was the most renowned painter in Florence, though his reputation was soon to be eclipsed by Masaccio. Gentile influenced such artists as Fra Angelico, and his pupils included Jacopo Bellini and Domenico Veneziano. In January 1427 he went to Rome to execute, on commission from Martin V, a cycle of frescoes in the Lateran Basilica; however, he died before he could finish them, in the autumn of the same year. Little is known about his early development; the origins of his art and its influences are still matters of conjecture. Gentile came of a well-to-do family of Fabriano in the Marches. The first established date in his career is 1408, when he received payment in Venice for an altarpiece (now lost). While in Venice he was commissioned to do fresco scenes in the Sala del Maggior Consiglio of the Doge's Palace, in connection with a general renovation of the interior decoration (1409, 1411, probably to 1414). The years 1414–19 he spent in Brescia, where he painted frescoes in the chapel of the Broletto for Pandolfo Malatesta. By the second half of the year 1420 he was already in Florence.

Gentile's date of birth has been set anywhere between 1360 and 1385. The year 1370 is generally accepted (Boskovits, 1986), though in his recent monograph of 1982, K. Christiansen suggests 1385. While those who propose the earlier date assume that Gentile was already active as an independent artist when his widowed father returned to a monastery in 1390, Christiansen believes that he was entrusted, barely five years old, to his grandfather's care. These questions are not without bearing on the Berlin panel, which is one of Gentile's earliest surviving works, if not the very first. It apparently comes from S. Niccolò in Gentile's birthplace, Fabriano. When the church was restored or rebuilt in 1630, the painting was removed. In 1660 it was in the possession of the Leopardi family in Osimo (the Marches), and in the early nineteenth century it was owned by a collector in Matelica (the Marches) who sold it in 1828. In 1829 it was in Rome where, according to Kugler, it was acquired by the Prussian Ambassador, Bunsen, apparently for the Crown Prince, who lent it in 1837 and later, as King Frederick William IV, donated it to the gallery.

Almost all commentators agree in associating the panel with a Madonna panel in Perugia and with the large polyptych from S. Maria di Valle Romita near Fabriano (now Milan, Brera). Controversy still reigns, however, with regard to the chronology and dating of these works, and recently even a new proposal for the original function of the Berlin panel has been made. Its dating varies from 1390–5 (as the earliest work done in Fabriano) to 1408–14, Gentile's Venetian period. The latter dating is proposed by only a minority of art historians. The proponents of a relatively early date, which would place the panel after the great Milan polyptych, conclude on a date of 1400 or shortly after on the basis of a correspondingly early dating of that work. Christiansen, by contrast, places the polyptych in the Venetian period, 1410–12. Though he agrees in this with those scholars who believe the Berlin panel to precede the Milan altarpiece, he dates it rather later than most, about 1406–8, shortly before Gentile's stay in Venice. Boskovits (1986) dates the panel a little before 1400 and the polyptych at about 1405.

The work's original function is a matter of some importance. Though it is generally considered an altar painting (Boskovits, 1986), Christiansen (1982) thinks it originally belonged to a sepulchral monument.

But to turn to the image itself. Mary is seated on a simple, bench-like throne with a red cushion, both hands supporting the Christ Child standing on her knee. The Child gazes down on and blesses the donor, who kneels in prayer on the lower left. This figure, seen in profile to the right, is represented on a smaller scale than the others. Behind the throne are two slender trees, each of which has seven angels concealed among the foliage, singing and playing. Turned towards the Virgin on the sides of the throne are two saints: on the left, St Nicolas of Bari (patron saint of the church from which the panel comes), in an exquisite vermilion cloak set with stars. He hold a crozier and three golden balls, his attributes, in his right hand, and with his left blesses the donor and presents him to the Virgin. At the right of the throne is St Catherine of Alexandria, princess and Christian martyr, in her right hand the palm frond of martyrdom and in her left a book. She is in a superb gown of plum colour over silver, with a pattern of flowering branches, and lined with white fur. Over her shoulders is a pale lilac-blue, fur-lined mantle which she gathers up with her left hand. The seams of her copious sleeve and the gathered mantle form soft, undulating lines similar to the hem of the Virgin's gold-embroidered mantle – traits of the style of International Gothic. The throne and figures are in front of a dark green, flower-studded meadow, above which the gilded background extends. The compositional type here is that of a *Sacra Conversazione*, for which parallels are found in altar paintings in the Veneto and the Marches.

Umbrian and Siennese painting of the late Trecento, as well as Venetian painting, and late-Trecento Lombardian miniatures have been named as possible influences on Gentile's early style. According to Christiansen, Gentile might well have seen Lombard miniatures even in the Marches, where they influenced other artists as well. It is not necessary to assume 'several years of work in Lombardy' before the Berlin panel was executed, as Oertel has done (1975). Boskovits (1986) sees precursors of Gentile's early work in the late-Trecento masters of Umbria and the Marches. The iconography of the *Madonna degli Alberetti* (that is, 'with little trees') is indeed Venetian or Veneto-Marchian, as is the shape of the panel with its unusual low-arched top (Boskovits). This author bases his dating to the years shortly before 1400 on considerations of fashion, among other things. Christiansen believes that the first decisive influence on Gentile came from Zanino di Pietro, who was in Bologna in 1389 and 1394–1405, and in Venice in 1407, and who also supplied paintings to the Marches but reviewers of his book have been sceptical about this hypothesis. Christiansen also sees the influence of Lombardian miniature painting. Despite these diverging opinions, it seems clear that Gentile did the Berlin panel at the start of his career, in his home town, and that he need not have travelled to other art centres to create it. Not until the subsequent large polyptych from S. Maria di Valle Romita near Fabriano, which Christiansen believes was painted in Venice, does Lombard influence make itself felt – through Michelino da Besozzo, a Lombard artist who worked for a time in Venice.

Tommaso di Ser Giovanni di Simone Cassai, called Masaccio (*c.*1401–28)

Two Panels of a Predella of an Altarpiece

The Adoration of the Magi – The Crucifixion of Peter/ The Beheading of John the Baptist

1426

Poplar, each panel 21 × 61 cm (8¼ × 24 in)
Acquired from the Gino Capponi Collection, Florence, 1880
Cat. nos. 58 A and 58 B

Masaccio was admitted in 1422 to the *Arte dei Medici e Speziali* in Florence. With the architect Brunelleschi and the sculptor Donatello he was one of the founders of Renaissance art. By applying in painting the system of one-point perspective developed by Brunelleschi and first used by Donatello in a marble relief, Masaccio transcended medieval methods of depicting depth in the two dimenions of the painted image. His imposing, forcefully modelled figures, conceived as forms in space and sculptural in effect, were influenced by Donatello. The unified pictorial space in which they appear is like a stage as seen by a spectator, and its effect of depth is heightened further by illumination from a constant source. Unlike medieval artists, Masaccio was able to render the effect of gravity on the human body in every movement and attitude. Masaccio's new realism also entailed an evocation of human emotion that was unprecedented in scope. His figures are infused with natural dignity, self-possession, and profound solemnity. In the simple, unadorned garments whose materials are depicted with great verisimilitude, Masaccio broke radically with the elaborate ornament and abstract line of the late-Gothic style of drapery.

Among the major works of his short, barely seven-year career are the frescoes executed with Masolino for the Brancacci Chapel in S. Maria del Carmine, and the Trinity fresco in S. Maria Novella, both in Florence. Another is his altarpiece for the Carmelite church of S. Maria del Carmine in Pisa, three of whose predella panels, and four figures of saints, which were originally mounted in the flanking pilasters, are now in the Berlin Gallery. Masaccio painted the altarpiece in 1426. It was commissioned by Ser Giuliano di Colino degli Scarsi da San Giusto, a Pisan notary, for his family chapel in the Gothic church, which was built some time after 1325. Ser Giuliano acquired rights to the chapel between 1414 and 1425, but since the church was rebuilt from 1560 to 1590, the chapel has not survived in its original state. C. Gardner von Teuffel (*Jahrbuch der Berliner Museen*, 1977) assumes that it was the right choir chapel. According to Vasari (1568) the altarpiece was installed '*dentro a una capella del tramezzo*'. Though this last term was earlier thought to mean transept, it is now generally interpreted as lectern or choir screen (cf. J. Beck, *Masaccio*, The Documents, 1978).

This 'chapel', built in 1425 by the Pisan mason Pippo di Giovanni di Gante, was apparently dedicated to St Julian, the donor's name saint. C. Gardner von Teuffel believed that work on the 'chapel' related to a kind of altar room within the Gothic chapel itself, consisting of a canopy resting on columns. The altarpiece proper was a polyptych in three tiers – predella, main and upper registers – that was probably dismantled and dispersed during the eighteenth century. The wooden structure and framework, now lost, were made by Antonio di Biagio of Sienna. Only a part of Masaccio's altar panels has survived. Vasari's cursory, incomplete description (1568) does give a few indications about the altar's original imagery, but says nothing about its appearance as a whole. The polyptych form, which originated in Trecento tradition, was probably determined by the donor together with the prior of the Carmelite monastery, Fra Antonio, a learned theologian who perhaps had taken note of the young Florentine artist's work in the Carmelite church in Florence. In executing this commission Masaccio did not enjoy the freedom to realize his pictorial ideas as he did in the Brancacci Chapel.

The predella, now in Berlin, has been completely preserved. It consists of a central panel with *The Adoration of the Magi* and two flanking panels, each divided into two fields by a band of gilding. Represented on the left panel are *The Crucifixion of St Peter* (left) and *The Beheading of John the Baptist* (right); and on the other, *St Julian Murdering his Parents* (left) and *The Miracle of St Nicholas* (right). These two last scenes were evidently not painted by Masaccio himself but by his assistant, Andrea di Giusto, after his master's design. In keeping with common practice in polyptychs of this type, the side panels of the

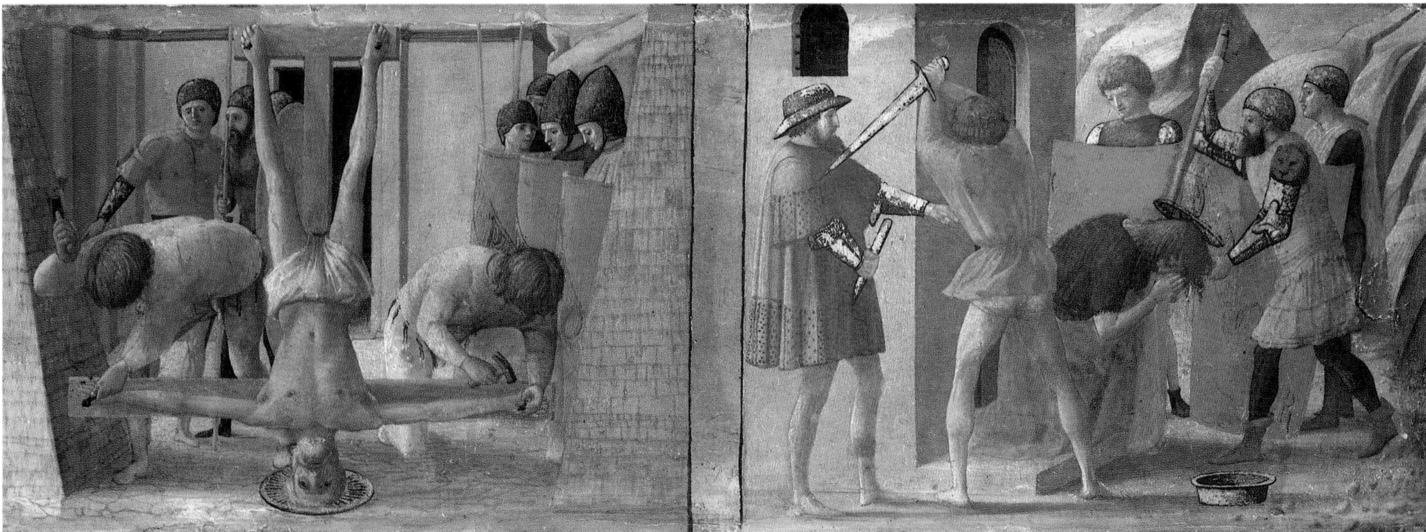

main tier flanking the Madonna in the centre were reserved for standing figures of those saints whose scenes appear in the predella below – Peter and John at the left, and Julian and Nicholas at the right. All four figures, which Vasari mentions, have been lost. Only *The Virgin Enthroned with Angels* (*Maestà*), which Vasari describes in detail and which is now in London, remains of the main tier. Above the Virgin, in the upper tier, was *The Crucifixion* (now in Naples), flanked on both sides by two half-figures of saints or Apostles, of which only two have survived (*St Paul* in Pisa, and *St Andrew* in Malibu, Getty Museum). These saints, like the Virgin, appear in front of a goldground. Goldground was a traditional compositional element whose pictorial effect must, however, have run counter to Masaccio's intentions, but apparently it was stipulated by the donor or the monastery. The fields of the upper tier are capped with pointed arches, though the panels themselves are rectangular, that is, have flat tops. They were probably originally surmounted by a further gable.

Just as St Julian was included as the name saint of the donor and patron of the chapel, the choice of St Nicholas most likely goes back to the names of the donor's parents, Colino and Cola, and the choice of the Apostle Peter to his grandfather's name, Piero.

There is some disagreement about the original horizontal division of the main tier. Salmi (1948) and Procacci (1952) postulated three sections divided by architectural elements, whereby the side compartments with their two saints each were presumably not completely subdivided as in the upper tier, but were divisions suggested by two pointed arches ending in a console. This would indeed seem likely, since the corresponding scenes of the predella are separated only by a narrow band of gilding. On the other hand, Shearman (1966), because of such features as the shadows cast on the steps of the throne in the Madonna panel, proposed a single, continuous scene on a unified panel across the entire width of the tier. However, C. Gardner von Teuffel (1977) has rightly returned to the tripartite division suggested by Salmi.

Masaccio was least hampered in developing his conception of space in the predella scenes, and here, too, he was able to forgo gilding in the landscape background and render the sky in a natural blue. In the agitated martyrdom scenes of the left flanking panel he gave the figures those 'beautiful poses, that movement, power and life' of which Vasari wrote. Peter is shown being nailed to the cross, head down, between two stone pyramids. The two henchmen are completely absorbed in their grisly task. The spatial stage has a backdrop of a light-coloured house wall with a dark door opening in the centre against which the cross stands out. To the right, in the opening between the pyramid and house, four soldiers with brilliant red shields watch the henchmen's actions closely but dispassionately; three more soldiers are visible in the left background. According to early Christian tradition, St Peter was martyred in Rome during the reign of Nero. The site was Nero's new Arena, between two chariot race pylons in the shape of cones or pyramids such as those in the painting. Depicted in the right compartment is the Beheading of John the Baptist, which was ordered by King Herod. According to the Gospels of St Matthew and St Mark, the execution took place 'in a prison'. Here it is set outside the prison, which is characterized by the bars in the high window. As a soldier at the right holds John by the hair and forces his neck against a lance, the executioner stands with his legs wide apart and his back to the spectator, raising his sword for the terrible blow.

The masterpiece among these images is undoubtedly the long, narrow central panel of the predella with its representation of the Three Magi presenting their gifts to the newborn Child. Like the others, this frieze-like scene is dominated by a colour combination of red and blue. The Three Magi and their retinues approach the stable from the right. The eldest king has removed his crown and kneels before the Virgin, who is depicted in full profile, seated on a gilded folding chair. The king kisses the foot of the Child on her lap, who gazes down at him and blesses him. Joseph looks on from behind, holding the king's gift, a golden vessel. The second king kneels farther to the right, obliquely behind the eldest king and near the central axis of the image. In the opening between him and Joseph is a deep canyon in the background hills, a vista that forms a division between the two main groups of figures. The second king, represented kneeling in three-quarter profile, looks attentively at Mary and the Child, his hands folded in prayer. A page has taken the king's crown. To his right is the third and youngest king, depicted in full profile and in the act of stepping forward as one of his retinue gently lifts the crown from his head. This attendant is largely obscured by the figures of two men in contemporary bourgeois clothes whose features have the individuality of portraits; evidently they represent the donor and a member of his family. They follow the happenings with some detachment. Behind them at the far right are more attendants leading the horses whose foreshortenings and overlappings aroused high praise from Vasari. The long shadows cast along the ground emphasize the perspective depth in the placing of the figures, who extend to almost the full height of the pictorial field.

Domenico di Bartolo da Venezia, called Domenico Veneziano (1405/10–61)

The Adoration of the Magi

*c.*1440

Poplar, diameter 84 cm (33 in)
Acquired 1880
Cat. no. 95 A

Domenico Veneziano was born between 1405 and 1410 in Venice. The first written record we have of him dates from 1438, the famous letter he wrote from Perugia to Piero de' Medici in Ferrara. In 1439 he began work on frescoes in the choir chapel of S. Egidio in Florence, assisted by the young Piero della Francesca. This project, one of the most important Florentine commissions since Masaccio's decoration of the Brancacci Chapel, occupied Domenico until 1445, the year of his major work, the altarpiece for S. Lucia dei Magnoli in Florence (1445–7). His development and activities up to the year 1438/9 have been the subject of much conjecture. According to the most recent monograph by H. Wohl (1980), Domenico came to Florence at a young age where, from about 1422–6, he was the pupil of Gentile da Fabriano. In early 1427, he followed him to Rome where Gentile began work on the Lateran Basilica frescoes, but died in October 1427 before he could finish them. The job was taken over by Pisanello, who had already completed Gentile's frescoes in the Doge's Palace, Venice, and was finished by about 1432. It was probably in Rome, therefore, and not in Northern Italy that Domenico Veneziano became acquainted with Pisanello's art (whose influence is so evident in the Berlin tondo) and where he saw Masolino's frescoes in S. Clemente as well. Probably when Pisanello left Rome to return to Verona, in 1432 after the death of Pope Martin V, Domenico went back to Florence, where he remained until 1437. There his work was influenced by the leading Florentine artist, Fra Angelico, and also by Paolo Uccello and Donatello. In 1437 he went to Perugia to decorate a room in the Baglioni Palace, probably on the occasion of a marriage (these decorations have not survived). It was from Perugia, on 1 April 1438, that he sent his famous letter to Piero de' Medici, one of Cosimo de' Medici's sons who had accompanied him to a church council in Ferrara. Domenico offered his services to Piero and asked him to speak to his father about an altarpiece that he had heard Cosimo wished to commission. Judging by the tone of the letter, Domenico had not yet worked for Piero de' Medici. Yet the Berlin *Adoration of the Magi* tondo almost certainly was in the Medici collections. F. Ames-Lewis (*Jahrbuch der Berliner Museen*, 1979) believes it was the work that Piero de' Medici ordered from Domenico in 1438 in reaction to his letter during the Council of Ferrara. Wohl (1980) thinks there was no direct relation, though his dating of 1439–41 does not significantly diverge from Ames-Lewis's.

The most obvious stylistic element of the tondo, which places it at the end of the artist's early period and sojourn in Umbria, is a strong influence by the courtly style of International Gothic. This style was passed on to Domenico by Pisanello, to whom indeed the tondo was earlier ascribed by von Bode. The tradition of International Gothic was widely followed in Umbria, though Domenico may well have seen Pisanello's work again at the 1438 Ferrara Council or the 1439 Florence Council, where Pisanello created a portrait medallion of the Byzantine Emperor Johannes VIII Palaeologus, who attended both Councils. Ames-Lewis sees a likeness of the emperor in the face of the man with a black, pointed beard and red cap in the king's retinue, exactly at the centre of the composition. Though the artist evidently concealed portraits in these attendant figures, their identification remains controversial. Wohl (1980) sees a portrait of Piero de' Medici in the man looking out of the picture behind the kneeling king, wearing a black doublet over a white shirt, whose face is marked by illness (Piero later suffered from gout and was called 'The Gouty') and who, though he wears no head-dress, is holding Piero's emblem of a falcon. This contention, convincingly supported by comparisons with known portraits, would invalidate Ames-Lewis's identification of Piero in the profile of the man in a red head-dress, standing to the left of the man on the white horse. The same author also sees, in the profile of a middle-aged man in a black head-dress to the horseman's right, a portrait of Cosimo, and the head to his right, a portrait of the young Giovanni de' Medici. The rider on the brown horse at the far left is apparently a falconer (H. Wohl, 1980) from whose extended arm the two falcons have climbed to bring down an egret.

The superb rendering of the exquisite, extravagant garments, the numerous animal motifs such as the peacock on the roof, hunting dogs, and a camel, betray the influence of Pisanello, though the clothes reflect the latest fashion of the day. The back view of the white horse and rider was anticipated by Pisanello's medallion roundel of the Byzantine emperor mentioned above; reflections of his art are also found in the juxtaposition of the foreshortened front and back views of horses. Pisanello's influence, of an intensity unusual in Domenico, may go back to the patron, who perhaps either intended to award the commission to Pisanello or did so, but who in any case requested Domenico to provide a work in his style. The elements of late medieval chivalry, including mottoes in Latin, Italian and French, are unusual in a picture of religious content, and have been traced back to the courtly International Gothic style prevalent in Northern Italy. However, they may also be associated with the Medici family and their patronage of the *Compagnia de' Magi* (from 1436), which organized annual festive processions in honour of the Three Magi from 1428. As Hatfield notes, the Magi in a sense became the 'heraldic representatives' of the Medici. Inscribed on the white horse's harness are the words HONIA. BO[N]A. IN. TENPO (*omnia bona in tempore*: 'all good things come in time'); on the hat of the rider in the background, TENPO; on the coat of the man facing right, near the white horse, ANSI VA LE ... (*ainsi va le monde*: 'so goes the world'); and on the coat of the man at the right, GRACE FAI[T] DIE[U], or 'God is merciful'. The meaning of these mottoes, that all good things will come in time by the Grace of God, may well refer to the reunification of the Christian world for which the Council of Florence strove (Wohl, 1980).

One final and special achievement of the Berlin tondo is the integration of figures arranged along a plateau (derived from Masolino's Crucifixion fresco in S. Clemente) into an expansive landscape projected in great depth. This goes back to Donatello's slightly earlier relief tondo of *St John on Patmos* in a landscape (San Lorenzo, Old Sacristy), which like Domenico's tondo is conceived as an *oculus*; it also probably reveals knowledge of Netherlandish prototypes.

Piero della Francesca (1420/2–92)
Landscape with St Jerome Penitent
1450

Chestnut, 51.5 × 38 cm (20¼ × 15 in); with original frame 59 × 45.7 cm (23¼ × 18 in)
Inscribed on *cartellino* lower right, on tree trunk, and dated 1450: 'PETRI DE BVRGO / OPVS . M°/CCCCL'
Acquired 1922
Cat. no. 1904

After the First World War, his life nearing its end, Wilhelm von Bode was able to acquire two further significant examples of Early Italian Renaissance painting: in 1924, a predella panel by Sassetta, and in 1922 this *Landscape with St Jerome Penitent* by Piero della Francesca, a master not then represented in the Berlin Gallery. Though the picture was fortunately signed and dated, the state in which von Bode acquired it and published it in 1924 revealed extensive parts by another hand. While Berenson (1932) declared that only the figure was authentic, Longhi (*Piero della Francesca*, 1942) rightly included the surrounding area, the bench with books, the cliff with its niche and books, and the inkwell and lion, though he said that Piero had left the painting unfinished and that it had been completed by someone else towards the end of the fifteenth century. The treatment of the compact foliage, uniform sky and the chain of hills with their awkward line, dull colours and thick impasto, obviously deviated from Piero's touch. In 1968 Robert Oertel, then director of the gallery, decided that the painting should be cleaned, and the gallery's then chief restorer, Hans Böhm, carefully removed the overpaint with a scalpel. When restoration was completed in 1972, it revealed that the original image was by no means unfinished. Piero's painting appeared for the most part intact, without significant gaps, and largely preserved, particularly in the parts with trees, sky, and landscape. What proved to have been most damaged by an earlier, too drastic cleaning was the figure, which until then had been considered the only element in the picture by Piero himself. The original, intense blue sky with its characteristic flat and sharply contoured white clouds came back to light – the same sky familiar from such works as *The Baptism of Christ* (London), *The Flagellation* (Urbino), Piero's frescoes in S. Francesco in Arezzo, and *The Resurrection* (San Sepolcro). The sky now extended down to the hill above the house, and the chain of higher hills disappeared. The trunks and crowns of the trees, whose contours had been extended over the sky blue, recovered the loose, transparent texture familiar from the Arezzo frescoes (*Adoration of the True Cross*), *The Baptism of Christ*, and *St Jerome with Donor* (Venice, Academy). As X-rays revealed, Piero had first blocked in the trees' basic structure, the trunk and limbs, and then added the foliage over them. His delicate, light green meadows had been concealed beneath a layer of dirty brownish-green. But most importantly, the stream meandering through the wood towards the ford in the foreground has recovered its original, light ivory colour. The reflections of the trees, which had been almost completely obscured, are now back in their full beauty – recalling those in *The Baptism*. Everything in the image has become lighter, more translucent, suffused with light. The penitent's robe, previously a dull blue, now shimmers in delicate lilac-grey heightened with white, and he has a light-green tendril of a plant around his waist.

In his right hand St Jerome hold a stone, and in his left (sadly very damaged) a rosary of oblong, white pearls. Lying on the ground beside him is his red cardinal's hat, the strongest accent of local colour apart from the green of the meadows and the blue of the sky. The books on the bench and in the rocky niche are arranged carefully like a still life. Their precise detail, the rendering of clasps and cords serving as place-markers, the brilliant colours of their bindings, edges, and fittings, suggest that Piero may have had Netherlandish models in mind – or before his eyes, since he could have seen a painting by Rogier van der Weyden at the Ferrara court where he was working at the time, or perhaps even a Jan van Eyck. A *St Jerome* commissioned from van Eyck by Cardinal Albergati and completed by Petrus Christus, was in the Medici collections in 1492 (and may be identical with the Detroit painting; cf. R. H. Oertel, *Studies ... in honor of Millard Meiss*, 1978). Bartolomeo Fazio, in his *De Viris Illustribus* (Naples, 1456), described a work by van Eyck that was apparently in Urbino at that period.

Piero della Francesca
Landscape with St Jerome
State before cleaning
Berlin, Gemäldegalerie SMPK

The results of cleaning not only disprove Longhi's hypothesis that the picture was

unfinished, but make his reservations about the signature and date superfluous. The date of 1450 suggests that Piero did the painting in Ferrara, where he was active at the court of Lionello d'Este from 1449 (or perhaps 1446–7). His *St Jerome Penitent* is a small devotional image that was surely kept out of the public eye. Salmi, in his *Piero della Francesca* (1979), writes that it may be one of the paintings Vasari mentions, those 'small pictures he painted for the Duke of Urbino' (Guid' Antonio da Montefeltro or his son, Duke Federico II). A direct derivation from Piero's original image in its state before it was painted over by another artist, which Oertel dates to the third decade of the sixteenth century, is seen in an altar lunette in the Gualino Collection, Galleria Sabauda, Turin. This image of St Jerome in the wilderness, measuring almost two metres in length, has been ascribed to Nicola di Maestro Antonio d'Ancona, who was active in the Marches in the second half of the fifteenth century. How this provincial artist could have had access to Piero's original image, however, remains uncertain.

A much more direct reference to Piero's *St Jerome* is found in a St Christopher fresco by Bono de Ferrara, presumably of 1451 and formerly in the Eremitani Church, Padua (destroyed in the Second World War), which also showed the meandering stream with reflections (Oertel, 1978; R. Cocke, *Burlington Magazine*, 1980). The fact that the river motif is a necessary ingredient of the St Christopher iconography but not of the St Jerome iconography, has led Oertel to assume a lost St Christopher landscape by Piero which might not only have inspired Bono's fresco but been Piero's own point of departure for his *St Jerome*. Similar links exist with Jacopo Bellini, who worked in Ferrara in 1441, and whom Piero may have visited on a journey from Ferrara to Venice, as Longhi already suggested in 1942 in connection with the Venice *St Jerome*. Piero might also have been inspired by the depictions of St Jerome penitent in a landscape which Sano di Pietro of Sienna repeatedly included in the predellas of altarpieces (1436, 1444; cf. Oertel, 1978). In none of his other works does the landscape play such a predominant role, nor is the figure constricted so tightly into a corner as in the Berlin painting. It is conceivable that while he was assisting Domenico Veneziano on the choir frescoes in S. Egidio, Florence (1439), Piero may have seen that artist's *Adoration of the Magi* tondo (Berlin), in which the landscape also holds such a significant place.

Nicola di Maestro Antonio D'Ancona (attributed to)
Landscape with St Jerome Penitent
Turin, Galleria Sabauda, Gualino Collection

Master of the Osservanza (active in Sienna *c.*1430–50)

St Anthony Abbot at Mass

*c.*1435

Poplar, 46.8 × 33.4 cm (18½ × 13⅛ in)
Acquired 1910
Cat. no. 63 D

In a side chapel of a Gothic church whose dark grey and white striped columns recall those of Sienna Cathedral, a priest reads mass, assisted by a choirboy. The young man listening in the foreground is St Anthony the Hermit, still in secular costume but his head already surrounded by a halo. He is represented again in the right background, kneeling down and probably in the act of taking his vows. St Anthony the Hermit (also known as the Great, or St Anthony Abbot) was born in about AD 250 in Egypt. As the *Legenda aurea* relates, at the age of twenty he was inspired by the words of Christ at a church service, '... go and sell that thou hast, and give to the poor' (St Matthew 19:21) and he gave away everything he owned and spent the rest of his life as an ascetic and penitent.

The Berlin painting belongs to a series of eight surviving panels with scenes from the saint's life, which used to be attributed to Sassetta. It was Longhi (*Critica d'Arte*, 1940) who recognized that they must have been done by an artist whose style resembled Sassetta's but was slightly more archaic, an artist he called, after a triptych dated 1436 in S. Bernardino dell' Osservanza in Sienna, the Master of the Osservanza – a name that soon found wide acceptance. The series consists of six upright panels (including the Berlin panel) and two of horizontal format. Graziani (*Proporzioni*, 1948) grouped these eight images around a fragmentary panel of *St Anthony Abbot* (Paris, Louvre) to reconstruct a presumed altarpiece devoted to the saint, arranging three upright panels one above the other at each side of the central image, and the two broader panels in the predella area. Oertel (1975), however, realized that the figure of the Saint in the Paris fragment was once a standing figure rather than a seated one as Graziani had believed. Laclotte (*Retables italiens du XIIIe au XVe siècle*, Paris, 1978) then determined that instead of a central panel, it must have been one of the side panels of a polyptych, and that therefore it did not belong to the eight St Anthony scenes after all but to a different polyptych. In other respects Laclotte agreed with Graziani's reconstruction, in which only the central predella panel was still missing.

As the scene represented in the Berlin panel indicates, it is the first in the sequence. The others are *St Anthony Gives His Possessions to the Poor* (Washington), *The Temptation of St Anthony by a Devil in the Guise of an Angel* (New Haven, Yale University Art Gallery; horizontal format), *St Anthony Harassed by Demons* (New Haven), *St Anthony in the Wilderness* (New York, Metropolitan Museum, Lehman Collection), *The Meeting of St Anthony and the Hermit Paul* (Washington), and *The Death of St Anthony* (Washington; horizontal format).

As P. Scapecchi recently pointed out (*Arte Cristiana*, 1983), in 1870 two of the eight panels were in the collection of Count Caccialupi, Macerata (the Marches), which included other fifteenth-century Siennese paintings. Moreover, a member of this family lived in Sienna during the fifteenth century. From this, as well as from the presence of Siennese works of the period in the Marches (S. Severino), Scapecchi concluded that the St Anthony altarpiece to which the eight scenes belonged was intended for a Franciscan church in the Marches. Accepting Laclotte's conclusions with regard to the Louvre panel, he assumed that it was the side panel on the extreme left of a five-part polyptych with the eight scenes from St Anthony's life arranged in the predella. This last assumption, however, would seem unlikely because of their different formats (six upright panels each about 47 cm high and two horizontal ones 36.5 and 37.7 cm high) and the narrow, upright format and corresponding vertical wood grain of six of the panels, which would certainly have been unusual in a predella. Laclotte (1978), noting this inconsistency, rejected the possibility of this arrangement.

In the forthcoming catalogue of Italian paintings in the Lehman Collection (Metropolitan Museum of Art, New York), J. Pope-Hennessy and L. Kanter reject Scapecchi's

1 *St Anthony at Mass*
Berlin, Gemäldegalerie SMPK
2 *St Anthony Gives his Possessions to the Poor*
Washington, National Gallery of Art, Kress Collection
3 *St Anthony Leaving the Monastery*
Washington, National Gallery of Art, Kress Collection
4 *The Temptation of St Anthony*
New Haven, Yale University Art Gallery
5 *St Anthony Harassed by Demons*
New Haven, Yale University Art Gallery
6 *St Anthony in the Wilderness*
New York, Metropolitan Museum of Art, Lehman Collection
7 *The Meeting of St Anthony and the Hermit Paul*
Washington, National Gallery of Art, Kress Collection
8 *The Death of St Anthony*
Washington, National Gallery of Art, Kress Collection

reconstruction. Returning to Graziani's view, they assume that the St Anthony scenes were once arranged in tiers of four each to flank a central St Anthony figure, perhaps a painted panel, perhaps a sculpture. Yet while Graziani's sequence began at the upper left with the Berlin panel and continued downwards to the predella, then ran from top right to bottom right, Pope-Hennessy and Kanter, on the basis of technical evidence, reverse the sequence, from lower left to upper left, and from lower right to upper right, making the two broad-format panels the concluding scenes at the top of the altar instead of assigning them to the predella, as Graziani did.

Some scholars distinguish two different hands within the group of eight panels. Pope-Hennessy, for instance, in 1956 reascribed those which seemed to him higher in quality to Sassetta. Carli (1957) retained these, including the Berlin panel, for the Master of the Osservanza, attributing the qualitatively weaker group to Sano di Pietro. Taking the opposite view, Oertel (*Katalog der Gemäldegalerie*, 1975), attributed the panels of higher quality to Sano di Pietro. Italian art historians tend to insist on the homogeneity of the group and its attribution to the Master of the Osservanza.

That the authorship of these panels has remained one of the most controversial problems of fifteenth-century Siennese art, in itself shows how closely the artist adhered to Sassetta – his ideal and possibly his teacher. This is particularly true of the Berlin panel, which except for *The Death of St Anthony* (Washington, National Gallery of Art), is the only one in the cycle to depict an interior. *St Anthony Abbot at Mass* is one of the finest of the eight panels. The light-suffused, crystal clarity of the spacious Gothic church interior, its perspective construction, which is empirically convincing if not fully precise, the geometric purity and elegance of form whether in architecture or figures, are all stylistic features which the author of the Berlin panel shares with Sassetta, indeed which he owes to his example.

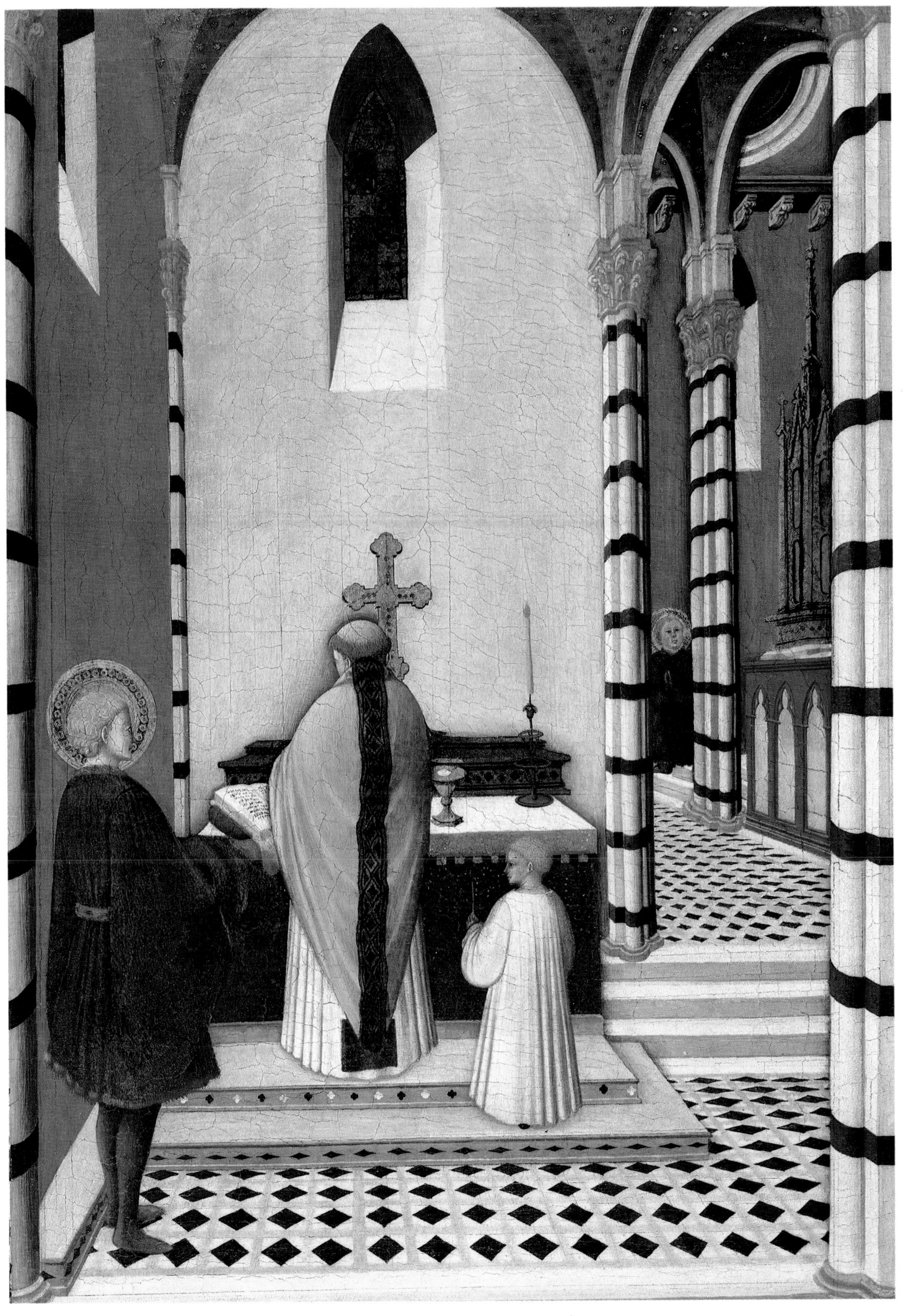

Andrea di Bartolo di Simone, called Andrea del Castagno (*c.*1419–57)

The Assumption of the Virgin

*c.*1449–50

Poplar, 131 × 150.5 cm (51½ × 59¼ in)
Presumably acquired with the Solly Collection, 1821
Cat. no. 47 A

As his pseudonym indicates, Andrea del Castagno came from the town of Castagno in the Mugello near Florence. His first documented work, now lost, was a fresco on the façade of the Palazzo del Podestà depicting the members of the Albizzi conspiracy of 1433, who were hanged in 1440 after the Battle of Anghiari. Soon after completing this political commission at the age of twenty-one, Castagno left Florence. In 1442 he was in Venice, where together with Francesco da Faenza he painted frescoes in the apse vault of a chapel in San Zaccaria. Back in Florence by 1444, he was paid for a cartoon for a stained-glass window in the cathedral there, and accepted into the Artists' Guild. In 1447 he created frescoes of the Last Supper and Stations of the Cross in the refectory of S. Appollonia, and in November 1449 was commissioned by Ser Lionardo di Francesco de' Falladanzi da Orte, the rector of a small church in the centre of town, S. Miniato fra le Torri, to paint the altarpiece which is now in Berlin. Castagno finished this work in April 1450, and by the summer, he was already engaged in the famous *Uomini Illustri* frescoes in the Villa Carducci, at Legnaia near Florence. Then, from 1451–3, he continued the fresco cycle begun in 1439–45 by Domenico Veneziano in the choir of S. Egidio (S. Maria Nuova), but broke off work because of disagreements with the monastery. In 1455–6 he executed the famous fresco of the equestrian monument of Niccolò da Tolentino in the cathedral, and in May 1457 completed his final work, *The Last Supper* fresco in the refectory of S. Maria Nuova. He died of the plague in the autumn of that year, at the age of only thirty-eight.

Castagno was influenced above all by Donatello's sculpture and Domenico Veneziano's painting. Vasari praised 'the force in the movements of [his] figures and male and female heads', his 'earnestness of expression', and good drawing, but he also noted that Castagno's forms and colours tended to be 'harsh and garish'. With his strong sculptural modelling and sharply contoured, harsh, even sometimes crude treatment of form, Castagno introduced a new style that influenced painters of the next generation such as Antonio and Piero del Pollaiuolo. In 1754 the altarpiece now in Berlin was still *in situ* in S. Miniato, which was demolished in 1785. It entered the Berlin Gallery in 1821, with the Solly Collection.

It shows the Virgin dressed as a nun, seated and gazing upwards in prayer, before a glory of fiery clouds shaped like a mandorla that merges from the sarcophagus and is borne heavenwards by four angels. In the sarcophagus are the roses and lilies which, as the *Legenda aurea* relates, surrounded the Apostles during the Assumption – the roses revealing the presence of martyrs, and the lilies that of angels and virgins. The boldness of the poses and movements of the flying angels – especially the one at the lower left, seen in three-quarter view from below – and their draperies fluttering in the wind, already struck Vasari, who commented on the angels of the *Annunciation* formerly in S. Egidio.

The central group is flanked by two standing figures in courtly costume, St Julian at the left, and St Minias at the right who looks up towards Mary. Minias was one of the patron saints of Florence and the titular saint of the church for which the altar panel was intended. According to legend, he was a soldier who in about AD 250 was beheaded on the outskirts of town, at the place now marked by the church of S. Miniato al Monte. Later he came to be considered an Armenian prince, which explains the sceptre and crown here, above which his foreshortened halo reflects the flaming clouds of the Virgin's aureole. St Minias is in a brilliant vermilion tunic and red hose, and gathers up his dark green, cape-like mantle in his left hand. Opposite him is St Julian (Hospitator), a young Christian knight and martyr. Poised with his left foot slightly raised, he looks out of the picture and presents a sword, a symbol of his inadvertent murder of his parents (a subject also represented in Masaccio's predella scene in Berlin). He is in a vermilion mantle lined with wine-red cloth patterned

like damask, over a dark green, gold embroidered tunic. St Julian was revered in Florence as patron saint of innkeepers.

The conception of the two youthful figures and their noble features reveals the influence of Castagno's ideal and friend, Domenico Veneziano. They also anticipate his own *Uomini Illustri*, in the way they are silhouetted against the glory – though where real and transcendent worlds meet, their contours overlap the angels in a rather confusing and jarring manner. Castagno had yet to master spatial relationships. His use of a gold background, perhaps by request of the patron, was certainly anachronistic by 1450. Yet he has consciously integrated it in the colour composition, which rests on a dual contrast of gold with red, and blue with dark green. Against these accents, the diverse nuances of red – vermilion, carmine, reddish brown, wine red, violet, lilac – shimmer with a strange tension.

The idea of the Assumption of the Virgin, in a *mandorla* of clouds, is derived from Donatello's marble relief in the Brancacci monument in Naples, executed in Pisa in 1427.

Fra Filippo Lippi (*c.*1406–69)

The Virgin Adoring the Child

(Adoration in the Forest)

*c.*1459

Poplar, 129.5 × 118.5 cm (51 × $46\frac{5}{8}$ in)
Signed: 'FRATER PHILIPPVS P[inxit]'
Acquired with the Solly Collection, 1821
Cat. no. 69

Fra Filippo Lippi was only about five years younger than Masaccio, whose works strongly influenced him, particularly the frescoes in the Brancacci chapel in S. Maria del Carmine which Masaccio executed while Fra Filippo was a Carmelite monk there. However, his artistic career did not begin until after Masaccio's untimely death. In 1434 Filippo was in Padua, then from 1452 to 1464 he worked in Prato near Florence, and finally, from 1466, in Spoleto. With Fra Angelico, Domenico Veneziano, and Paolo Uccello, Fra Filippo Lippi was one of the leading Florentine artists of the mid-fifteenth century. His pupils included his son, Filippino, and above all Sandro Botticelli.

The Berlin panel was commissioned in 1459 by the Medici family to grace the altar of the chapel in their Florentine palazzo, planned by Michelozzo and built in 1444. The chapel, originally completely windowless and illuminated only by candles, has frescoes on the walls by Benozzo Gozzoli representing a procession of the Three Magi moving towards the Virgin depicted in Lippi's altarpiece. This compositional feature suggests they were conceived in connection with Filippo's altarpiece. After the Medicis were expelled from Florence in 1494, the painting was taken to the Palazzo della Signoria, but in the mid-sixteenth century it seems again to have been in the Medici palace. In its place today is a contemporary copy by the Pseudo Pier Francesco Fiorentino (active *c.*1474–97).

The Adoration of the Child in the Forest is related compositionally and iconographically to two other altarpieces which Filippo Lippi executed during the 1450s and early 1460s – a panel for the altar of the Annalena Convent (Florence, Uffizi) done shortly after 1453; and a painting commissioned about 1463 by Piero de' Medici's wife for a cell in the convent of Camaldoli in the Casentino, east of Florence. All three paintings include a hermit in a monk's habit, witnessing the miraculous event deep in prayer. In the Berlin panel, this is St Bernard of Clairvaux, the founder of the Cistercian order. The two Medici panels have an additional figure representing the youthful John the Baptist, patron saint of Florence, but they do not include the figure of Joseph.

The motif of the Virgin kneeling to adore the Christ Child on the ground, was inspired by such mystical writings of the fourteenth century as the *Visions* of Johannes de Caulibus, a Franciscan monk, and the Revelations of St Birgit of Sweden (1303–73). Both saw visions in which the Christ Child lay not in the manger but naked on the ground, with Mary kneeling beside him. In the painting, this mystical element is combined with the idea of penitence, embodied by the infant St John. The axe plunged into the tree stump at the lower left alludes to John's preaching to the multitudes, 'And now also the axe is laid unto the root of the trees: every tree therefore which bringeth not forth good fruit is hewn down, and cast into the fire' (Luke 3:9; Matthew 3:10). 'The intimate mood of this scene and its use of medieval symbolism indicate a revival of mystical tendencies and a turn to deeper and more personal religious feeling both of which can also be discerned in mid-fifteenth-century Netherlandish painting' (R. Oertel).

View inside the chapel
Florence, Palazzo Medici-Riccardi

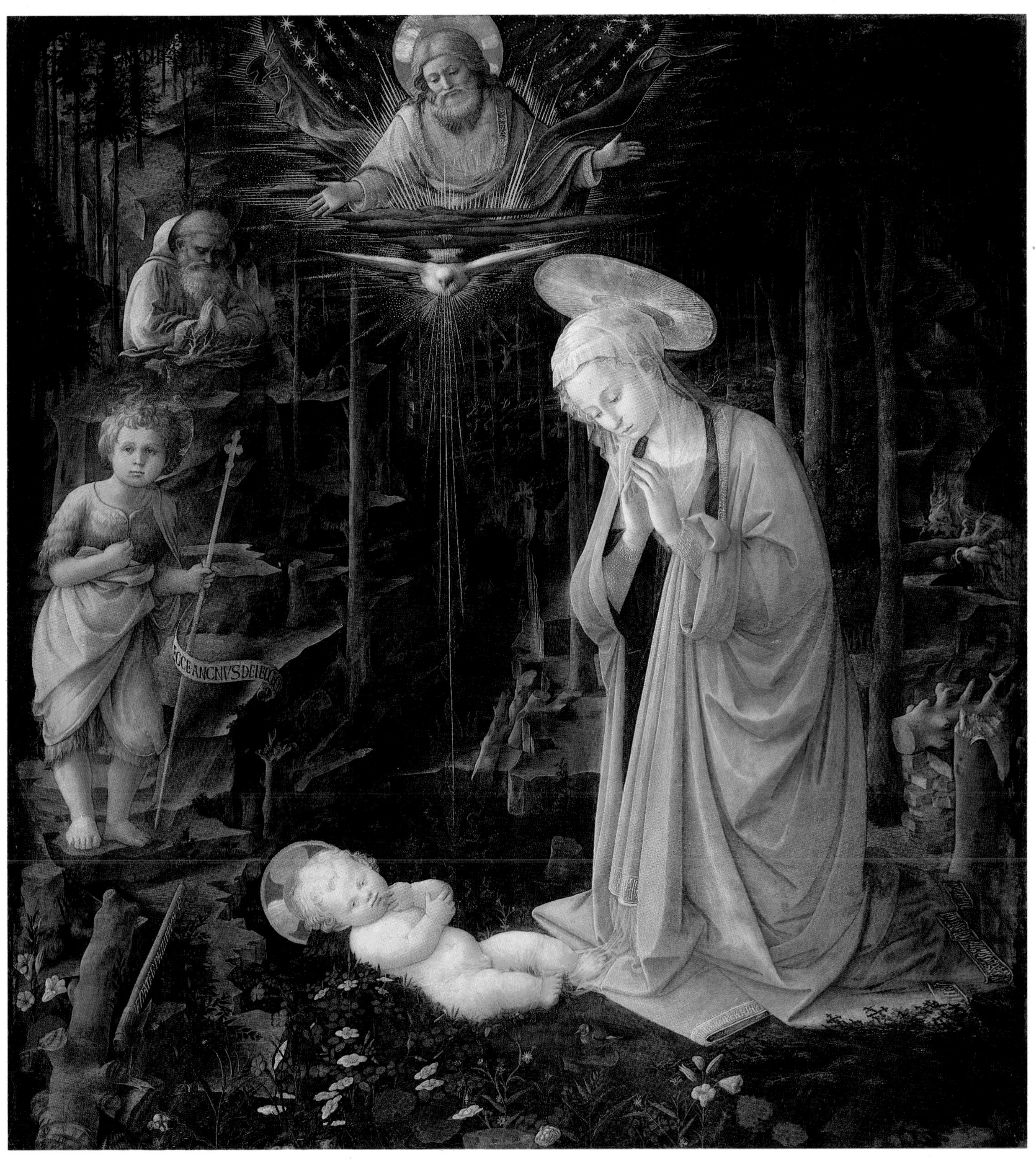
ECCE ANCNVS DEI

Antonio del Pollaiuolo (*c*.1431–98)
Portrait of a Young Woman in Profile
c.1465–70

Poplar, 52.5 × 36.5 cm ($20\frac{5}{8} \times 14\frac{3}{8}$ in)
Acquired 1894
Cat. no. 1614

This *Portrait of a Young Woman in Profile* is not only among the most popular paintings in the gallery, it is one of the most famous female portraits of the early Italian Renaissance. Yet nothing is known about its origin and history before 1800, and nothing certain about who painted it. After almost one hundred years of research since the painting came to light in 1894, art historians still disagree about its authorship. Initially it was considered to be a work by Piero della Francesca. Then, in 1897, recognizing its affinity to a profile portrait of a young woman in the Poldi Pezzoli Museum in Milan, also attributed to Piero della Francesca, Wilhelm von Bode ascribed both portraits to Domenico Veneziano. The gallery retained this attribution until 1972, though it had found little agreement from the beginning (Longhi, 1917; Van Marle, 1932) and today it must be considered invalid. After Berenson had given the portrait first to Verrocchio and then to Baldovinetti, in 1911 Adolfo Venturi attributed it to Antonio del Pollaiuolo. Though this has been accepted as sound by the majority of scholars, a considerable minority believe that Antonio's brother, Piero, painted the portrait. Over the past forty years, in other words, its authorship has been disputed only between the two brothers – despite L. Ettlinger's relegation of the portrait group back to anonymity in 1963 and in his recent book on Pollaiuolo (1978). It is true that among the principal works of the two Pollaiuolo brothers, no direct and convincing comparison with the female profile portraits can be found. The attribution to Antonio is based on a close scrutiny of certain stylistic elements that are not only characteristic but represent advances over earlier Florentine profile portraits. In the Berlin panel, these include the slight turn of the shoulders towards the spectator with the face remaining in strict profile, and the manner in which the contours are set off against a background of blue sky that covers almost the entire pictorial field, down to a narrow marble balustrade with encrusted discs (comparable to those in the altar panel in the chapel of the Cardinal of Portugal, S. Miniato al Monte). Also, the precise painting of the garment's ornamental pattern would seem to point to Antonio's experience as a goldsmith, a sculptor in bronze, and a designer of embroideries. In all events, in its purity of line, nobility of pose, and self-assured dignity of expression, this portrait is certainly one of the highest achievements in the field of portraiture of the Florentine early Renaissance.

Antonio del Pollaiuolo
Profile Portrait of a Young Woman
Milan, Museo Poldi Pezzoli

Piero del Pollaiuolo (1441–96)

The Annunciation

*c.*1470

Poplar, 150 × 174 cm (59 × 68½ in)
Acquired with the Solly Collection, 1821
Cat. no. 73

Piero del Pollaiuolo was ten years younger than his more gifted and renowned brother Antonio. And unlike Antonio, who was primarily a goldsmith, sculptor, and designer, he (at least according to the pre-Vasari sources) was foremost a painter. Vasari tells us that he was a pupil of Castagno, though he can only have been fifteen or sixteen years old when Castagno died in 1457. In 1466 Piero collaborated in the decoration of the chapel of the Cardinal of Portugal in S. Miniato al Monte, Florence, followed in 1469 by the important commission to paint six *Virtues* for the hall of the Arte della Mercanzia; in this project his brother Antonio managed the workshop and was responsible for the quality of the work and the punctuality of its execution. Membership in the Compagnia di San Luca, the artist's guild, followed in 1473, and in 1483, finally, Piero signed and dated his altar panel in S. Agostino at San Gimignano.

The *Annunciation* is generally regarded as a work of Piero's, and is dated about 1470 on the basis of its close similarities with his *Virtues* in the Mercanzia. Both main figures are in the foreground, very close to the picture plane, in an ante-room separated by a step from the room behind, which is divided into sleeping and dressing chambers. Each figure appears against the backdrop of one compartment of the partitioned room. The angel, powerfully winged and clad in a red mantle and a green gown trimmed with pearls and precious stones in golden settings, kneels before the Virgin with a long-stemmed lily in his left hand, raising his right in salutation. Mary, seated on a folding chair encrusted with precious stones, wears a light blue mantle lined in reddish-brown over a gold embroidered gown. A little book on her knee, she receives the angel's message with her hands devoutly put over her breast. The background is certainly the most brilliant rendering in any known painting of a noble interior in the Florentine Early Renaissance style. This partitioned room on the *piano nobile* of a villa on the hills north of Florence is a *tour de force* in one-point perspective. The right angles lead the eye past the exquisitely patterned walls, where in the room on the left an open arcaded window reveals a distant view of the Arno Valley and the walled town of Florence, with cathedral and Palazzo della Signoria. The vanishing point lies approximately on the horizon, near the blue mountains above the Palazzo Vecchio. Leading up to the villa is a curving path along which horsemen approach. The two chambers have geometrically patterned stone floors, coffered ceilings, and walls divided by pilasters, with red bays at the left and elaborately embossed leather wall-coverings in the sleeping chamber at the right. Next to its richly decorated bed, a door in the rear wall leads to a loggia-like room where three angels kneel, playing musical instruments. Visible through the window of this loggia room are other fine houses dotting the distant hills.

The original destination of this large panel is obscure. Cruttwell, in his *Antonio Pollaiuolo* (1907), wrote that Lorenzo de' Medici might have ordered it for the altar of his chapel in his villa at Careggi, since its view of Florence was taken from the same point as that from the villa. Though the figures are generally attributed to Piero, the elaborate interior has been thought to reveal Antonio's hand, and indeed Busignani (*Pollaiuolo*, 1970) attributes the landscape to him.

Andrea del Verrocchio (1435–88)

The Virgin and Child

*c.*1470

Poplar, 75.5 × 54.8 cm ($29\frac{3}{4} \times 21\frac{1}{2}$ in); original size of painted surface 68 × 51.5 cm ($26\frac{3}{4} \times 20\frac{1}{4}$ in), new strips of wood added at top, right, and bottom
Acquired 1873
Cat. no. 104 A

Though Verrocchio originally trained as a goldsmith, it was his sculptures, particularly bronzes, that made him famous. We are less well informed about his activity as a painter. In 1468 he is recorded as having executed a banner, now lost, for the Medici *Giostra* in honour of Lucretia de' Donati. Only two existing works can be associated with him through documents or other sources: an altarpiece of *The Madonna with Saints* in Pistoia Cathedral, ordered from him in 1479 but executed by his workshop, mainly by Lorenzo di Credi, and not finished until 1485; and a *Baptism of Christ* painted for S. Salvi in Florence (now Uffizi), which he began around 1470 and on which his pupil, Leonardo da Vinci, worked in about 1476, painting an angel in profile and also part of the landscape background. The figure of the Baptist in this work provides the basis for our evaluation of Verrocchio's activity as a painter. He had a large workshop, which besides Leonardo included Lorenzo di Credi and Perugino, and he influenced numerous Florentine artists, among them Domenico Ghirlandaio, Francesco Botticini, and Cosimo Rosselli. A group of Madonnas has survived that were previously attributed to him, but though some have been given back to him recently (Oberhuber, 1978), most of them are now attributed to Ghirlandaio and Perugino. These Madonnas are compositionally related to Verrocchio's marble and terracotta reliefs of the subject, and some similarities between individual paintings have led to their classification in sub-groups. Among the questioned Madonnas is a Berlin panel (Cat. no. 108) which, though generally attributed to Perugino or Ghirlandaio, has recently even been called a work of the young Botticelli. These attributions are still highly controversial. The only Madonna panel which by relatively wide consensus is now ascribed to Verrocchio himself, is the one illustrated here.

It shows Mary seated before a mountainous landscape, turned slightly to the left and visible to the knees: in her lap the Christ Child extends his arms to her with a vivacious gesture. Berenson (*Bollettino d'Arte*, 1933–4) considered it the earliest by Verrocchio and dated it between 1467 and 1470; Passavant (*Verrocchio*, 1969), agreeing on a date of 1468–70, maintained that it was the only piece by his hand in the entire group of similar Madonnas. Oberhuber (*Revue de l'Art*, 1978), whose attempt to expand the Verrocchio œuvre and return some of the Madonnas to him has not sparked much agreement, dated the panel to the 1470s and, in its rhythmic flux of line and strong modelling, detected the influence of Antonio del Pollaiuolo. This he explained by Verrocchio's contact with Polliauolo – in this case, Piero – during his work on the *Virtues* in the *Arte della Mercanzia* in Florence (1469). Oberhuber, noting a difference in quality between the heavy rendering of the Child and the more delicate modelling in the head of the Virgin, concluded that the artist's workshop may have participated in the execution. Also Shearman (*Burlington Magazine*, 1967) emphasized the uneven quality and attributed the execution to Botticini. Fahy (*The Legacy of Leonardo*, 1979), who accepts the work as authentic, has pointed out that Leonardo's Munich *Madonna* (*c.*1476) owes much in terms of motif and composition to his teacher's work of about six years before.

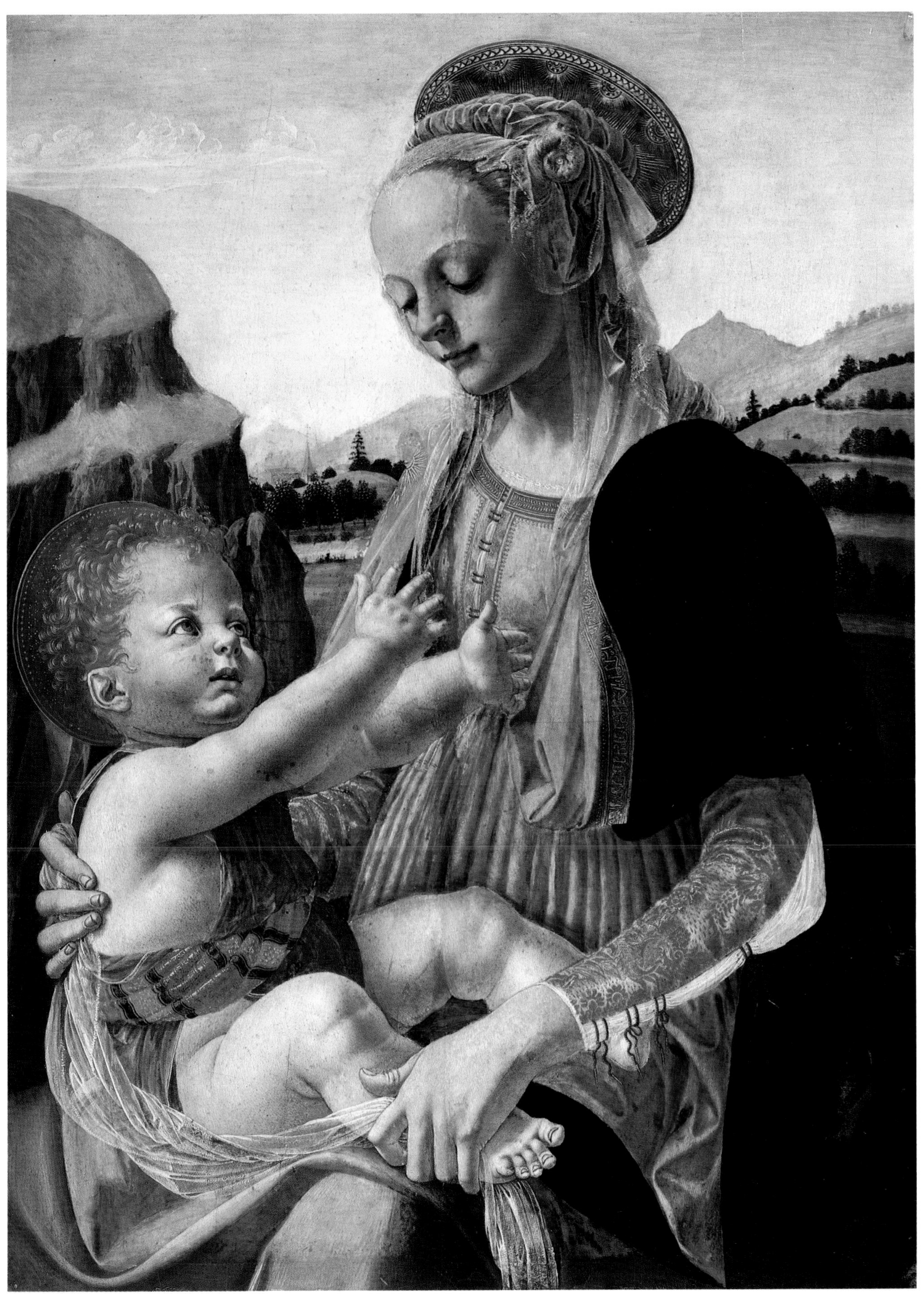

Sandro di Mariano Filipepi, called Botticelli (1445–1510)

The Virgin and Child Enthroned with the Two Johns

1484

Poplar, 185 × 180 cm ($72\frac{7}{8}$ × $70\frac{7}{8}$ in)
Acquired through Rumohr in Florence, 1829
Cat. no. 106

Botticelli, probably the most famous Florentine artist of the late fifteenth century, is represented in the Berlin Gallery by six works, though three of them are admittedly only workshop paintings or replicas. Of the three others, his *St Sebastian* from S. Maria Maggiore is perhaps the greatest masterpiece. The most splendid, best preserved and documented – and the one whose original context is still easily accessible today – is this altarpiece for the Bardi Chapel in S. Spirito, Florence. It was executed for the Florentine merchant Giovanni d'Agnolo de' Bardi, who lived in England for over twenty years, where he worked as the managing partner of the London branch of the Medici bank. Returning to Florence in 1483, he had a family chapel built in S. Spirito, on the back wall of the choir of this church which was designed by Brunelleschi.

The erection of the chapel and its altar owes its existence to a fire that ravaged the church in 1471, destroying most of its interior decoration. The families who owned patronage rights to individual chapels had no choice but to finance their complete refurbishment. By March 1484 the stone-masons had finished their work on the altars and orders for altar paintings could go out.

The Bardi Chapel altar in its tall and shallowly rounded niche beneath a high window – exactly at the far end of the left side-aisle extension and visible from there – was among the new chapels erected in the niches of the choir and the transept, most of which still exist and have their original tabernacle frames. Such renowned artists as Filippino Lippi, Raffaellino del Garbo, and Cosimo Rosselli, but also lesser known ones like the anonymous Master of S. Spirito, received commissions for altar paintings. Unlike the majority of chapels in the transept, whose original altars have survived, the four altars on the back wall of the choir, including that in the Bardi Chapel, had new, larger, upright rectangular altar structures built in the late sixteenth and on into the seventeenth centuries. Botticelli's altar painting was replaced by a new one, with a quite different theme, by the Florentine Baroque painter Jacopo Vignali (1592–1664). When the Bardi family reclaimed Botticelli's painting, its original carved frame, designed by Giuliano da Sangallo, was apparently lost. Only the original *paliotto* remained *in situ* on the front of the altar table, with a depiction of John the Baptist, patron saint of the chapel, in an octagonal field. In 1825 the Bardis sold Botticelli's altarpiece to the dealer F. Acciaj, from whom it was bought in 1829 for the Royal Museums by Karl Friedrich von Rumohr.

Botticelli has painted Mary enthroned with the Child on a stone bench faced with marble, flanked by the standing figures of John the Baptist and John the Evangelist, the saints most revered by the artist's patron. The place of honour at the Virgin's right is held by the Baptist, titular saint of the chapel, Bardi's name saint, and patron saint of Florence. In terms of composition, the image is a classical example of the *Sacra Conversazione*, the Madonna seated and 'conversing' with the saints beside her, who recommend the faithful into her protection. The figures stand out against a background of abundant and thick-grown vegetation – three arbours in the shape of niches made of intertwined palm fronds, cypress branches, and branches of myrtle, with roses, lilies and olive branches in vases on the parapet in front of them. Banderoles wound among the foliage, bearing Latin citations from the Book of Ecclesiasticus, refer to the medieval belief that the Virgin Mary was the seat of divine wisdom.

Florence, Santo Spirito
Choir gallery with the Bardi Chapel

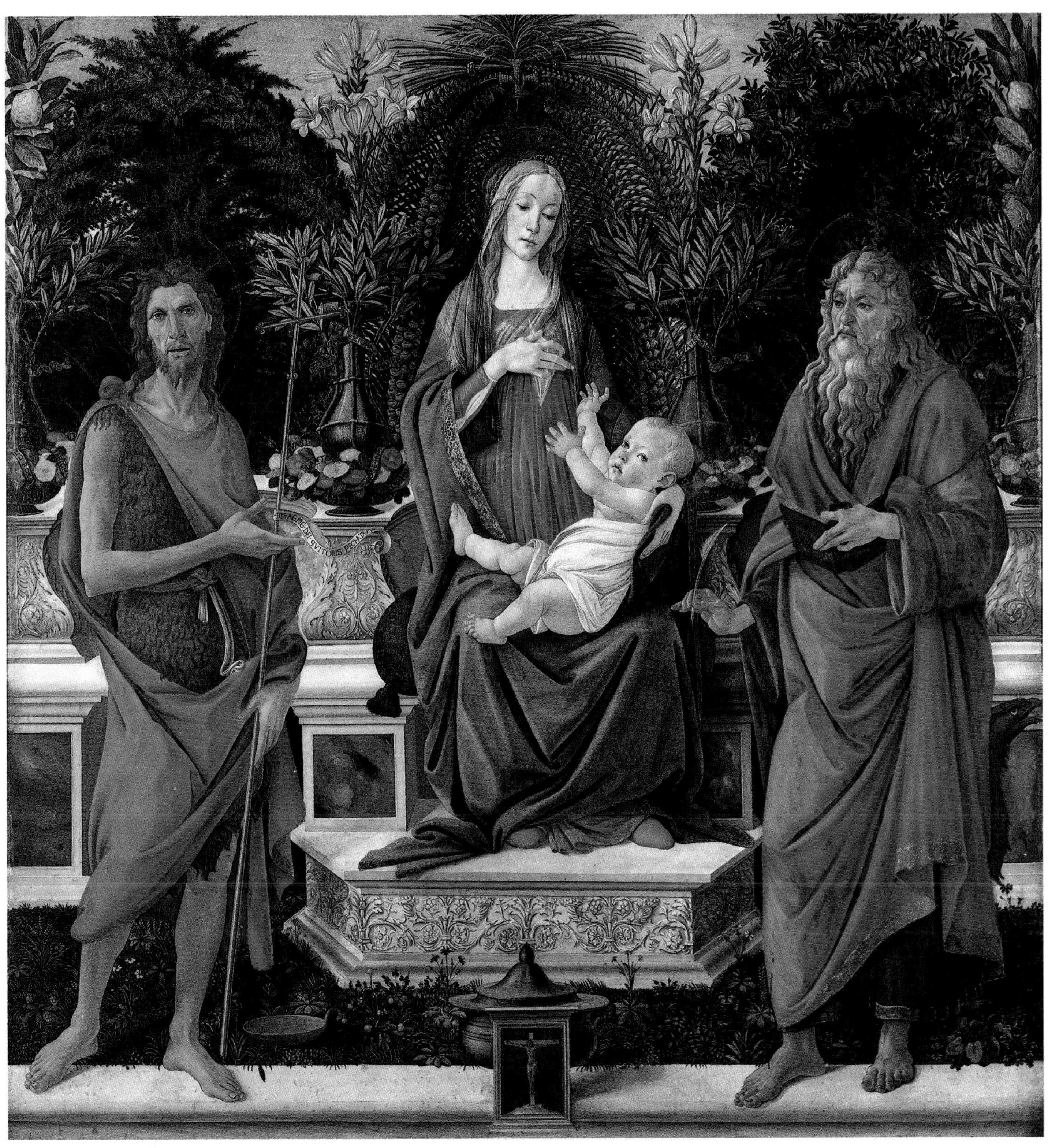
ECCE AGNUS DEI · QVI TOLLIS PECHATA

Piero di Lorenzo, called Piero di Cosimo (1461/2–1521)
Venus, Mars and Cupid
*c.*1505

Poplar, 72 × 182 cm ($28\frac{3}{8} \times 71\frac{5}{8}$ in)
Acquired through Rumohr, 1828
Cat. no. 107

Piero di Cosimo 'painted a picture in which Venus and Mars, undressed, are asleep in a flower-strewn meadow; around them are various little gods of love who carry away the war god's helmet, arm-guards, and other weapons; we see a myrtle bower and Cupid frightened by a rabbit, and the doves of Venus and other symbols of love have not been forgotten. This work is in the house of Giorgio Vasari in Florence, who preserves it in memory of Piero, as he has always found pleasure in his curious inventions.' This is Vasari's description in 1568 of the painting he once owned, which is now in Berlin. Though nothing is known about the work's original destination, its theme and composition were certainly inspired by Botticelli's painting in the National Gallery, London, which is almost identical in format and was presumably ordered on the occasion of a marriage in the Vespucci family. Piero's painting may well have been done for a similar occasion. However, there are obvious differences between the two compositions. In Botticelli's the figures are crowded with much overlapping into the front of the narrow horizontal format, almost as if in a relief, and the landscape background, the myrtle bushes to left and right, and the lake between them, have a flat, abstract character, like a foil or backdrop. Piero's composition is less tight, with a greater feeling of space. The figures, whose contours at no point overlap, are truly bedded in the foreground of a landscape that extends unimpeded past the *amoretti*, playing with Mars's weapons in the middle distance, to the shores of a bay on the far horizon. Botticelli, by contrast, shows satyrs at war games, very close up, and one of them blows on a conch in Mars's ear to rouse the exhausted god to new fervour, for which Venus seems to be waiting (C. Gould, review of Lightbown, *Botticelli*, *Apollo*, 1978). Piero leaves out the satyrs and tones down the rather dramatic erotic allusions, and has small Cupids playing with the weapons in the background instead. And he introduces the new motifs of a pair of doves (Venus's symbol) and Cupid with a rabbit nestling against his hand. The rabbit is a symbol of fertility that refers to Venus, and it also has specific sexual meaning (*cuniculus* – *cunnus*: rabbit – vulva; cf. P. Barolsky, *Infinite Jest*, 1978). Venus is not draped as in Botticelli's painting but is almost nude; her eyes are open, but she leans back in a more relaxed attitude, not watching over Mars and impatiently awaiting his revival as she does in the Botticelli version. The pose of the sleeping Mars, which Botticelli may have derived from a terracotta figure by Verrocchio (Berlin), is quite different in Piero's painting – more feminine, more closely related to that of Venus.

The theme goes back to classical antiquity. An association of the union of Mars and Venus with the harmony and fertility of nature is found in Reposianus's *De concubitu Martis et Veneris* of the third century AD, and it crops up again in the late fifteenth century, in Giovanni Pontano's *Eridanus*. These sources can in turn be traced back to Lucretius (d.55 BC) and his *De rerum natura* (Panofsky, *Studies in Iconology*, 1939). The key motif of the painting is the triumph of love over war, the calming, domesticating influence of Venus on the belligerent Mars. It has been associated with verses in the *Stanze per la Giostra* by the poet Angelo Poliziano, a friend of Lorenzo de' Medici, and its theme inspired Neo-Platonic philosophers of the Early Renaissance to far-reaching moral and cosmological speculations (E. Wind, *Pagan Mysteries in the Renaissance*, 1958). Peaceful Venus was said to love Mars because opposite temperaments attract each other: the daughter born of their union, called Harmony, represented *discordia concors*, discord brought to concord. Marsilio Ficino (1433–99), a member of the Platonic Academy in Florence, interpreted the theme from an astrological point of view, saying that Venus, the planet, watched over the planet Mars and overcame its destructive forces, but that Mars could never overcome Venus (Gombrich, *Journal of the Warburg and Courtauld Institutes*, 1945).

In 1480 Piero di Cosimo assisted in the workshop of Cosimo Rosselli, the artist from whom his working name derives. He is said to have accompanied Rosselli to Rome in

Sandro Botticelli
Mars and Venus
London, National Gallery

1481–2, and helped on his frescoes in the Sistine Chapel (1482–4). But much more important than the training he received from his teacher, an artist of limited talent, was the profound influence of Filippino Lippi's lively and highly expressive style. The penetrating realism of the figures in Hugo van der Goes's *Portinari Triptych*, which arrived in Florence in 1483 and was installed in S. Egidio, also made a lasting impression on the young Piero. Later he was also influenced by Ghirlandaio, Signorelli, and, as his biographer Vasari has written, by Leonardo da Vinci. Vasari describes Piero's eccentric, almost neurotic personality, which led to an increasing isolation from his contemporaries. He only belonged to the *Compagnia de San Luca* for a few years (1503–5), and though he applied for membership in the artists' guild *Arte dei Medici e Speziali* in 1504, he resigned the following year. The original, quite unacademic aspects of his art and the unorthodox and non-conformist style of his life have often been described. He was active in a period of political, intellectual, moral and religious crises marked by the expulsion of Piero de' Medici from Florence in 1494 and the rise of the Dominican monk Savonarola, who was convicted in 1497 and put to death in 1498. Evidently, Piero di Cosimo not only worked for the Medici and the families of their circle but also for the prosperous Del Pugliese, a family of rich merchants who opposed the Medici, supported Savonarola, and rose to public office towards the close of the century; he worked, too, for the Capponi, Vespucci and Strozzi families. Vasari emphasized Piero's imaginativeness and the bizarre character of his genius, which showed particularly in his secular imagery, and in his cycles with mythological themes as in this Berlin painting.

Luca Signorelli (*c.*1445/50–1523)

Portrait of an Elderly Man

*c.*1492

Poplar, 50 × 32 cm ($19\frac{5}{8}$ × $12\frac{5}{8}$ in)
Torrigiani Collection, Florence
Acquired 1894
Cat. no. 79 C

The Berlin Gallery is fortunate in having a large and varied collection of portraits. They record the development of Italian portraiture in the Early Renaissance from Filippo Lippi through Antonio del Pollaiuolo to Mainardi and Botticelli, Raffaellino del Garbo and the Master of S. Spirito. Signorelli's work in the genre was largely limited to donor figures on altarpieces and the collective portraits in his large frescoes (Rome, Sistine Chapel; Orvieto Cathedral). Autonomous portraits were the exception with him. His *Portrait of an Elderly Man*, which Mackowsky (*Zeitschrift für bildende Kunst*, 1900) interpreted as being of a jurist or lawyer, is a masterpiece in this field, and, since its acquisition from Florence in 1894, it has been one of the most famous pictures in the gallery. The model is portrayed bust-length, his shoulders slightly turned out of the picture plane, his face in three-quarter view to the left. He wears a red cap and a red gown closed at the neck, probably the long Florentine *lucco*, and over it a black stole. Seen from a relatively high vantage point, he gazes to the side and down, as if lost in thought, introspectively. His powerfully modelled features are heavy and determined, and deep creases frame his mouth, whose expression reveals energy and easy confidence. The humanitarian and antiquarian interests of the sitter are alluded to in a landscape background unusual in a portrait, where Signorelli has depicted two running female figures in classical costume in front of a Roman temple on the left and, on the right, two nude male figures in front of the ruin of a triumphal arch. These young men, the front one seen from his back, with the line of his legs intersecting the other's legs on the ground, recall a similar group in the background of the Florentine tondo depicting the Madonna and Child. They also recall the *ignudi* in the famous painting known as *Pan and the Gods* (formerly Berlin; destroyed by fire 1945), which was probably identical with the work Vasari mentions as having been painted for Lorenzo de' Medici.

Signorelli came from southern Tuscany, from the town of Cortona on the Umbrian border, and according to Vasari was a pupil of Piero della Francesca, whose influence is detectable in his earliest surviving documented work, a fresco of 1474 in Città di Castello, of which only fragments remain. In 1477–80 he worked in Loreto, and in 1482 in Rome, in the Sistine Chapel. While in Florence (1484–92) he was influenced above all by Antonio del Pollaiuolo. A major work of his late period are the frescoes in Orvieto Cathedral (1499–1503).

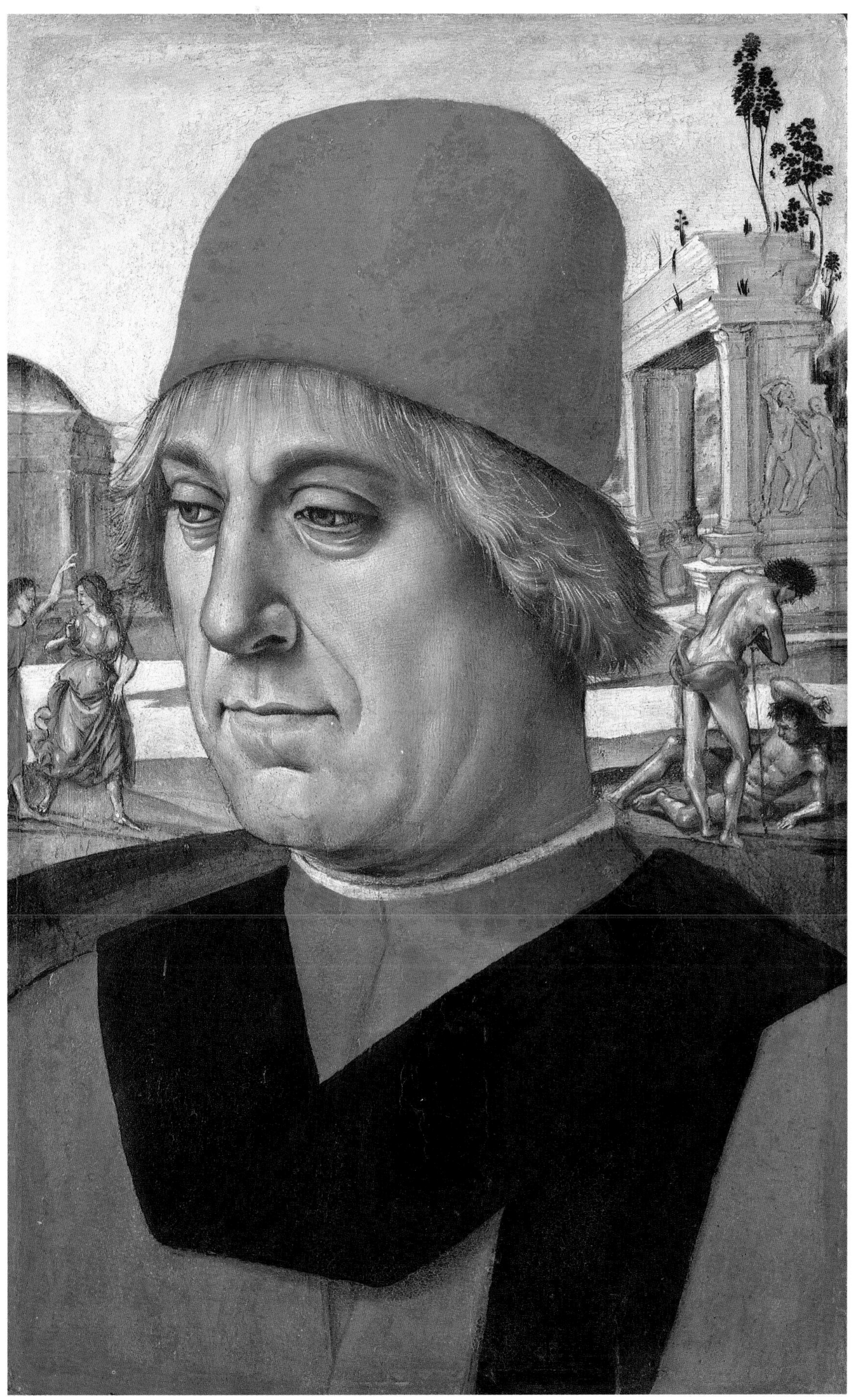

Raffaello Sanzio, called Raphael (1483–1520)
The Virgin and Child with the Infant St John
1505

Poplar, diameter 86 cm ($33\frac{7}{8}$ in)
Acquired from the Collection of the Dukes of Terranuova, 1854
Cat. no. 247 A

All five Raphael Madonnas in the Berlin Gallery were acquired in the first half of the nineteenth century, from 1821 to 1854. Almost all of them are early works. Three stem from Raphael's Umbrian period, and the *Madonna Terranuova* from the beginning of his Florentine period (about 1505). Only the *Madonna Colonna* dates from the end of the Florentine period (1508), shortly before Raphael left for Rome. By the time the Berlin Museum was founded and began building its collection, Raphael's mature works were no longer available, having long before entered princely, royal and imperial collections (in Florence, Paris, Dresden, Munich, Vienna, etc.). The Berlin Gallery shares its involuntary emphasis on the early œuvre with two other public collections that were not founded until the nineteenth century; the National Gallery in London, and the Metropolitan Museum in New York.

Of the Berlin Madonnas, the *Madonna Terranuova* (named after the collection from which it was acquired) is the largest, most imposing, and most important, besides being the only one in tondo form. Except for the slightly earlier *Madonna Connestabile* of 1504 (Leningrad), it is the artist's first circular painting, a format he was only later to master fully. Interestingly, the painting was based on a pen drawing (Lille) with a rectangular composition in which the Virgin and Child with the infant St John are flanked by two further background figures, an angel (Michael) and St Joseph. This left no room for a landscape. The drawing was later trimmed to a semicircular shape at the top; a large section of the original rendering with the Child's legs, the Virgin's left forearm, and Joseph's hand was missing and has been restored by another hand. Though a contemporary copy of the drawing in Berlin (KdZ 2358) is believed to record the Lille drawing's original state, there are certain obvious differences. In the Berlin drawing, the Madonna's left forearm and open hand emerge from beneath her mantle, as in the painting, while the Lille drawing shows her entire arm uncovered and no mantle. There are similar discrepancies with Joseph's hands. Since the Berlin copy diverges from the original, it would be misleading to draw conclusions from it about the missing corner of the drawing at Lille. In fact, the Berlin drawing represents a later stage of Raphael's development of the composition. The question remains whether he intended the Virgin's left hand in the Lille drawing to extend to the right, as in the painting, or to hold the Child, as the early copyist who restored the original drawing believed. A fragment of the full-size cartoon with the head of the Madonna is also in the Kupferstichkabinett (KdZ 11659).

Raphael
Composition Drawing
Lille, Musée des Beaux-Arts

after Raphael
Copy after *Composition Drawing* in Lille
Berlin, Kupferstichkabinett SMPK

The composition with the Virgin flanked by two saints corresponds to an Umbrian design of the late fifteenth century, which Raphael adopted from Perugino (painting in the Louvre, dated 1493) and used in modified form in his earlier painting of 1502 (Berlin, no. 245). After deciding on the tondo format for the *Madonna Terranuova*, he left out the flanking saints (which he must have thought antiquated), and divided the background exactly along its horizontal axis into a lower half occupied by a parapet and an upper half with landscape under an expanse of sky, against which the contours of the Madonna's head and shoulders stand out in sharp contrast. Then, by offsetting the figure of the infant John at the left with a second figure of a semi-nude boy with halo at the right, he created a pyramidal or triangular composition of a type he was later to use often. The identity of this new figure is still obscure, though some commentators have suggested James the Lesser (Mark 15:40).

The soft *sfumato*, the gestures, which are freer and more expanding than those in earlier Umbrian Madonnas, the increased sense of space, and the more elaborate landscape, in which northern elements have been detected, reveal the influence of Leonardo da Vinci, who returned to Florence from Milan in 1503. Raphael was deeply impressed by Leonardo's art. As E. Fahy has noted (1979), the Madonna's gracefully extended left hand here was inspired by Leonardo's *Madonna of the Yarnwinder* (1501, known from copies).

AGNIVS

Giovanni Battista di Jacopo, called Rosso Fiorentino (1495–1540)

Portrait of a Young Man

*c.*1517–18

Poplar, 82.4 × 59.9 cm ($32\frac{1}{2} \times 23\frac{1}{2}$ in; including later additions), original dimensions 75.7 × 57.1 cm ($29\frac{3}{4} \times 22\frac{1}{2}$ in)
Collection of the Marchese Patrizi, Rome
Acquired 1876
Cat. no. 245 A

Rosso Fiorentino was surely the most eccentric painter of early Florentine Mannerism. Like Pontormo, he was in conscious opposition to the classicizing art of Andrea del Sarto, who followed the tradition of Fra Bartolomeo. In this he had a particular affinity with Alonso Berruguete, a Spanish artist who worked in Florence from 1508–12 (perhaps to 1518) and who enjoyed Michelangelo's support. Rosso became a member of the Artists' Guild in 1517, and soon was working on the *Assunta* fresco in the forecourt of SS. Annunziata, and on an altarpiece for S. Maria Nuova (1518, now in the Uffizi). The Berlin *Portrait of a Young Man* also dates from his early period. Silhouetted against a background landscape, the seated model is in three-quarter view, his head turned back to face the viewer with what seems to be a scornful glance. His face is framed by long brown hair falling from beneath a flat, black barett. His angled left arm is supported by his hand at his waist, and his long slender fingers, emerging from the voluminous sleeve in greyish-black patterned damask, are parallel to the lower edge of the picture, stressing its horizontal line. His right hand, toying with the seam of the blackish-brown, fur-lined over-garment, has a large and very conspicuous ring on its index finger. Illuminated from the left, this hand forms a bright tone in the corner of the dark surface of the garment.

The painting was earlier attributed to Franciabigio. Its attribution to Rosso, suggested by Phillips in 1911, has since been widely accepted, with the exception of J. Shearman (*Andrea del Sarto*, 1965), who thinks it could be by Berruguete. In the pose and use of a landscape background, the artist uses a portrait type that was frequently employed in Florence by Andrea del Sarto and Franciabigio, and that goes back to Raphael's *Angelo Doni* (Florence, Galleria Palatina). Though the strange shift of the head out of the axis of the torso to the left is found in portraits by Franciabigio and Berruguete, it occurs in no other painting by Rosso. S. Freedberg writes that the sitter's expression gives '... no sense of a pacific and mutually interested inspection, as in Raphael's or Andrea's portraits, or of such deeply sympathetic interchange between sitter and spectator as in Pontormo's. Rosso's sitter inverts the normal relationship between spectator and the portrayed subject: he aggressively examines us, but does not permit us to examine him. We can look at him only with unease, and with the sense that association with him, even in this purely psychological world of art, might be dangerous: he is a male and anti-classical inversion of the *Mona Lisa*.'

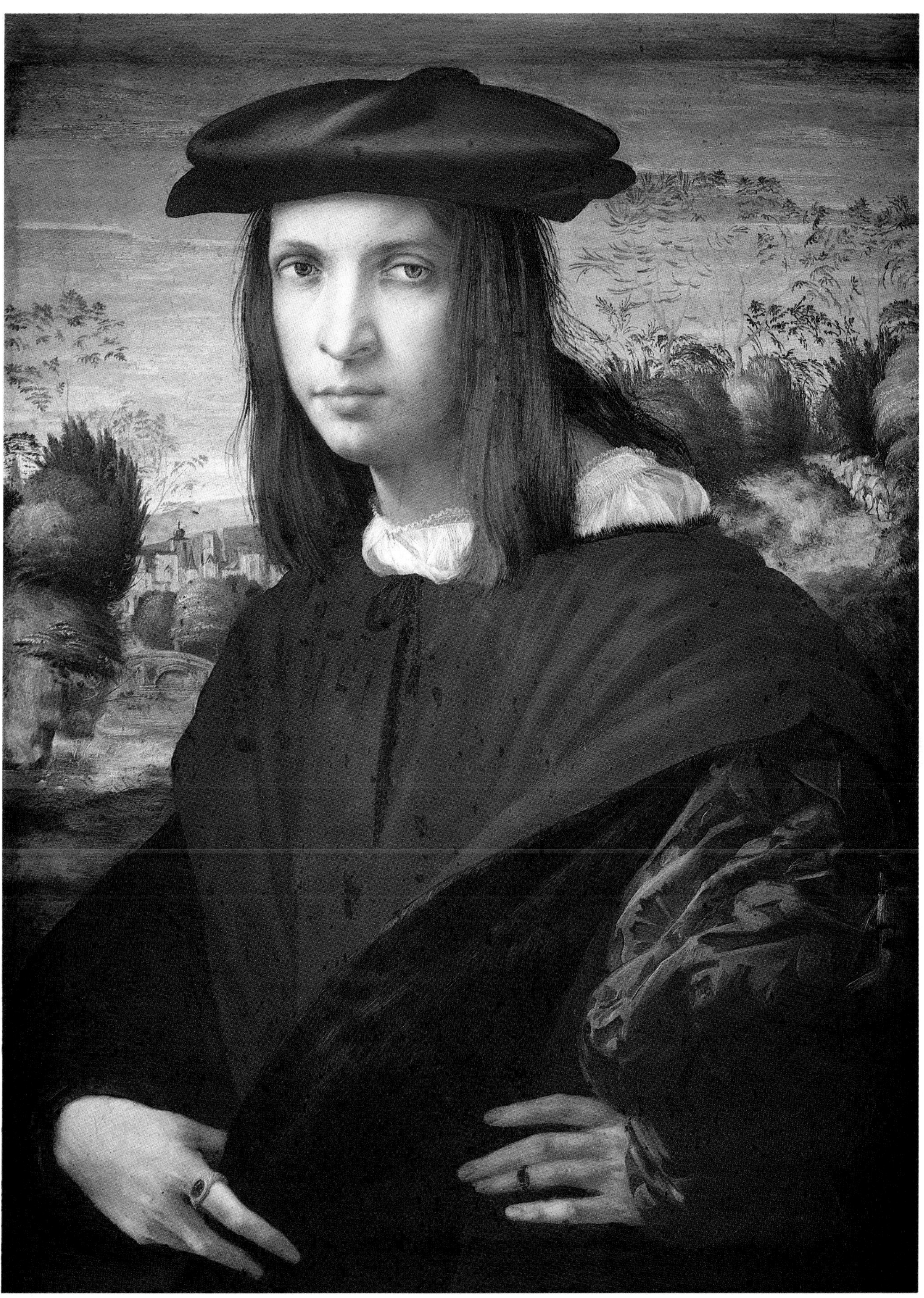

Agnolo di Cosimo di Mariano, called Bronzino (1503–72)
Ugolino Martelli
*c.*1535–6

Poplar, 102 × 85 cm (40⅛ × 33½ in)
Signed: 'BRONZO FIORENTINO'
Acquired in Florence, 1878
Cat. no. 338A

Pupil of Pontormo from 1522–6 and his assistant into the 1530s, court painter to Duke Cosimo I de' Medici from 1539–40, Bronzino became probably the most prominent portraitist of Florentine Mannerism, particularly under Cosimo. After the Siege of Florence, Bronzino went to the court of the Duke of Urbino, Francesco Maria della Rovere, where he worked from 1530–2. Between his return to Florence in 1532, and Cosimo's accession in 1537 and marriage with Eleonore of Toledo in 1539, Bronzino's art and career underwent transition and consolidation. By the latter half of the 1530s his portraits were more admired, and more in demand by the leading Florentine families, than those of any other artist. Yet of the long series of portraits of this period mentioned by Vasari, only a few have come down to us. Among the most important is that of the young *Ugolino Martelli* (1519–92), son of Luigi Martelli and Margherita Soderini, and a leading humanist and man of letters at the time.

Martelli is depicted among his books, at about the age of seventeen, which would date the portrait at about 1535–6. He is wearing a voluminous high-necked smock gathered at the waist and made of a dark olive-grey material that looks almost black, and close-fitting slashed trousers, and a flat, black barett. The scene is the courtyard of his father's palace, which was designed by Domenico d'Agnolo. A green cloth lies across the rose-coloured top of the stone table next to him, and on it is a volume of Homer's *Iliad*. The young man rests his hand on the open page, his finger at the ninth canto, which apparently he had just been reading when he was interrupted. At the far left edge of the painting is the corner of a volume of Virgil, marked with the letters [*Publius Vergilius*] MARO. Propped casually on Ugolino's knee is a book bound in blue, stamped with the name. M.P.BEMBO, the contemporary poet.

As in other Bronzino portraits of the period, the sitter is represented against an architectural background, whose perspective depth creates a tense contrast to the silhouette and static pose of the figure which is very close to the picture plane. And of these portraits, the background in his *Ugolino Martelli* is the richest and most logically constructed of all, a very accurate view of the Palazzo Martelli courtyard. Its perspective lines converge on a statue of David on the far wall at the left, a marble representing the *David Martelli* by Bernardo Rossellino after a wax modello by Donatello, to whom the marble was previously attributed. The marble is preserved in the National Gallery of Art in Washington. The perspective cone that opens out from the left background to the right foreground is, so to speak, capped by the sitter's figure, which interrupts the perspective lines and diverts them into the picture plane. This effect is heightened by the immobile calm of the sitter's pose and his cool, unapproachable expression and sidelong gaze, that might seem absent if it did not subtly reveal his awareness of the spectator's presence. The young man's attitude – seated at a table but with his legs stretching away from it and his upper body turned almost to face the front – is a highly artificial, stylized pose despite its apparent informality. It might well have been inspired by Michelangelo's seated figure of Giuliano de' Medici, a statue for the Medici Tombs in S. Lorenzo completed shortly before the present portrait.

Perhaps more compellingly than in any other portrait, Bronzino succeeded here in bringing his sitter to life, as John Pope-Hennessy has written, by portraying the individual 'in a physical setting . . . and in an intellectual setting, too'.

Bernardo Rossellino
David Martelli
Washington, National Gallery of Art

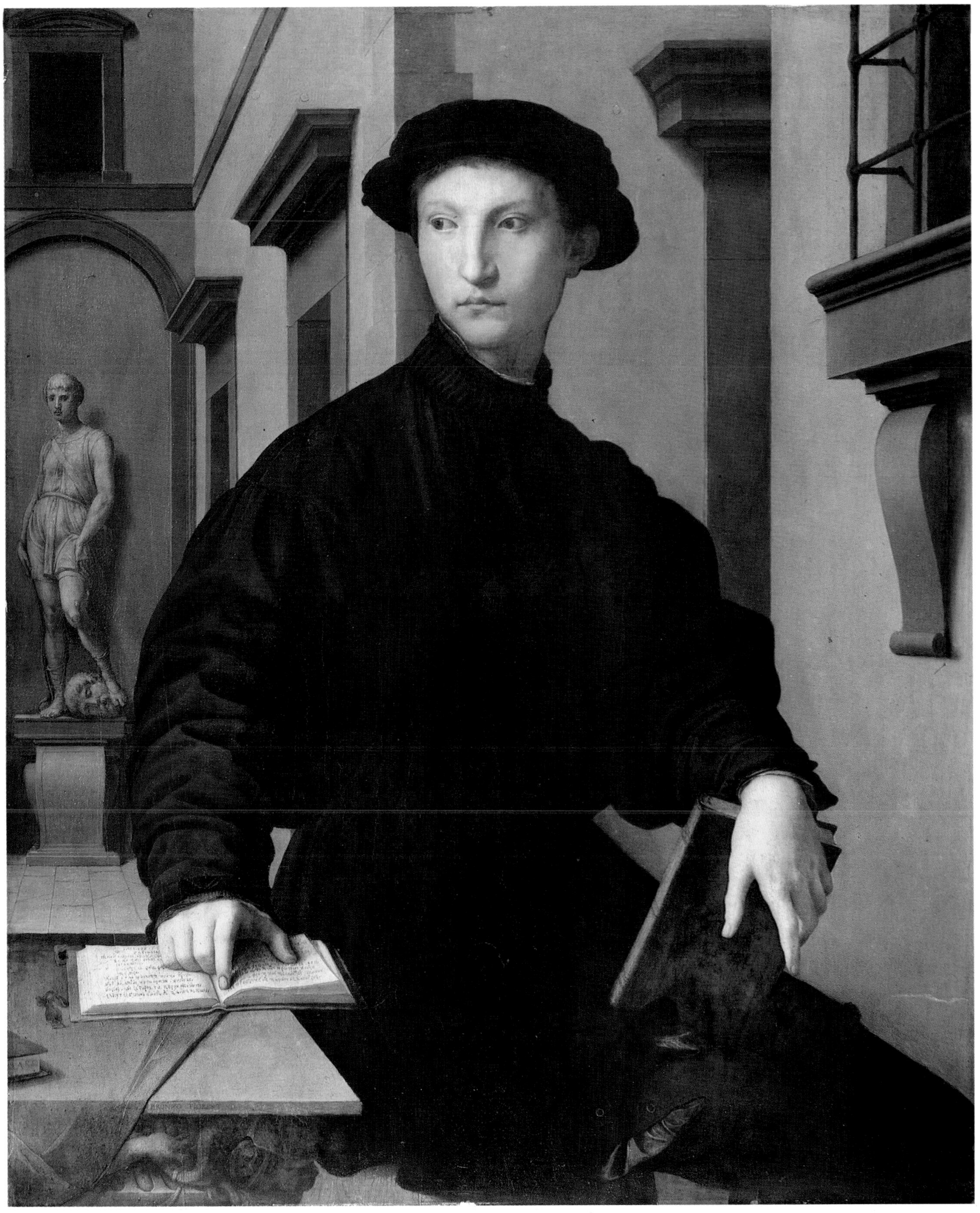

Ferrarese Master *c.*1450 (Angelo del Maccagnino?)

The Muse Polyhymnia as Inventor of Agriculture

Canvas (transferred from panel), 116.5 × 71 cm
Acquired 1894
Cat. no. 115 A

Though this panel is one of the most prominent paintings not only in the Berlin Gallery but of fifteenth-century Ferrarese art in general, its authorship is still uncertain, which is why it is illustrated here anonymously, as the work of a Ferrarese master of about 1450. Until recently, it was exhibited and catalogued (in 1978) as a Francesco del Cossa, but this attribution of Wilhelm von Bode's has been rejected by the majority of Italian as well as English art historians. The panel has also been ascribed by some to the almost mythical Galasso di Matteo Piva, an artist mentioned by Vasari who is recorded as having spent the years 1450–3 as a young painter in Ferrara and then worked in Bologna.

The young woman depicted here is a grape harvester, seen from a low vantage point against a hilly landscape with a low horizon and an expanse of pale blue sky. She stands with one foot on a stone step, shouldering a hoe and holding two ripe vines with her left hand while resting her right hand on a spade. Her statuesque pose and the pink gown with its twin girdles in the ancient Greek fashion point to the figure's allegorical significance. She was long thought to be a personification of Autumn or the month of October, when the vintage is gathered. Yet because of the plan for a cycle of the Muses outlined in 1447 by the great humanist philosopher, Guarino da Verona, in a letter to Margrave Leonello d'Este, she more probably represents Polyhymnia, the Muse celebrated as the inventor of agriculture. This interpretation is strengthened by the group of peasants threshing grain at the lower left.

Until recently, the work was thought to be among those associated with the decoration of a studio in Belfiore Castle outside Ferrara, which was owned by Margrave Leonello d'Este (who ruled in 1441–50) and his younger brother and successor, Duke Borso d'Este (who ruled 1450–71). These decorations were commissioned in 1447 from Angelo di Pietro of Sienna, called del Maccagnino, who did two paintings of the cycle. After his death in 1456, Cosmé Tura continued the project until about 1463. In 1483 the castle was demolished. According to contemporary sources (Cyriacus of Ancona, Lodovico Carbone), the sequence was devoted to the Muses, and was very probably based on the programme outlined in Guarino da Verona's letter.

Recent research has led to a division of the group of paintings associated with the Muse cycle for the Belfiore *studiolo*. The first group, comprising figures of the Muses seated on thrones, apparently once decorated the room. The second group differs in representing the Muses from a very low vantage point: they stand in a landscape against the sky. The Berlin *Polyhymnia* and two panels in the Budapest Museum, *Euterpe* and *Melpomene*, belong to this group. These three paintings apparently formed part of another cycle devoted to the Muses. Though their original purpose and circumstances remain obscure, they have been hypothetically attributed to Angelo del Maccagnino (M. Boskovits, *Burlington Magazine*, 1978).

Ferrarese Master (Angelo del Maccagnino?)
A Muse (Euterpe) and *A Muse (Melpomene)*
Budapest, Museum of Fine Arts

Andrea Mantegna (1431–1506)

The Virgin and Sleeping Child

1466–7

Canvas, 43 × 32 cm (17 × 12⅝ in)
Acquired as a donation from James Simon, 1904
Cat. no. s 5

Born in 1431 near Padua, Mantegna was the same age as Giovanni Bellini, who became his brother-in-law in 1453 or 1454. Of all the painters of his generation who came from Venice or the Veneto, Mantegna was surely the greatest Quattrocento master, beside Giovanni Bellini. His interest in classical antiquity was awakened by the humanism of Padua University. His work reveals a profound understanding of classical architecture, sculpture and epigraphy. Trained in Padua from 1441–8 by his adoptive father, Francesco Squarcione, Mantegna was influenced by Donatello, who was active in Padua from 1443–53, as well as by Antonio Vivarini, Jacopo Bellini, and Andrea del Castagno's Venetian frescoes (S. Zaccaria, 1442). In 1459 he moved to Mantua, where he became court painter to Margrave Lodovico Gonzaga and his successors. He travelled to Florence in 1466, and worked in Rome in 1488–90.

In the Berlin Gallery Mantegna is represented with three masterpieces. The most intimate, delicate, and poetic of these is certainly his *Simon Madonna*, which came to the gallery in 1904 as part of a generous donation from the Berlin collector, James Simon. It is painted in distemper on unprimed canvas, a technique used in Mantegna's time by few other artists, and the paint has been applied very thinly, leaving the fine texture of the canvas clearly visible.

Dressed in a simple, dark blue gown with a neckline cut low at the back, the Virgin gently holds the sleeping Child to her breast, supporting his head in her right hand and nestling it to her cheek; her face is turned so that it brings a diagonal into the composition. A mantle of exquisite gold brocade with a pattern of pomegranates surrounds her and the Child, who is wrapped tightly in swaddling clothes. A scarf of the same or similar material, perhaps part of the mantle, covers her hair, a few locks falling over her cheek. The sweeping contour of the sharply folded mantle continues without a break into her shoulder and neck, and on through the fold of the scarf. If the gesture of her hands expresses profound care for the Child's safety, the Virgin's features and meditative gaze show a melancholy anticipation of His sufferings to come.

Mantegna was inspired by many of Donatello's compositions, among them a plaster relief that was in the Berlin Museum before it was destroyed in 1945. The dating of the canvas is still debated, with most scholars placing it in the artist's early Padua period, while others see it as a work of the Mantua period, done in or after 1466–7. Yet others, Berenson for instance, considered it a late work of about 1490.

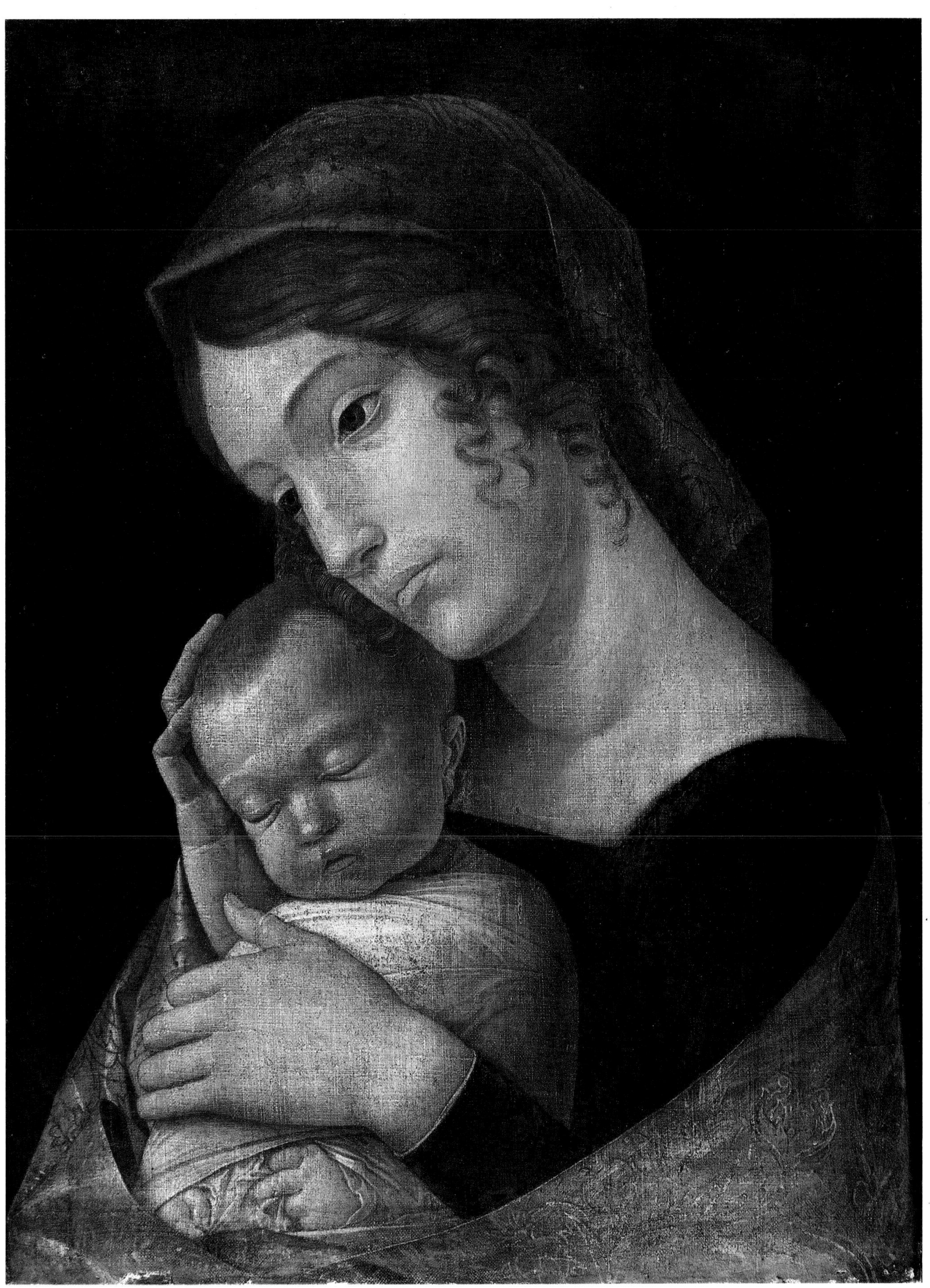

Giovanni Bellini (1430/1–1516)
The Dead Christ Supported by Two Mourning Angels
*c.*1480–5

Poplar, 83 × 67.5 cm ($32\frac{5}{8} \times 26\frac{1}{2}$ in)
Acquired with the Solly Collection, 1821
Cat. no. 28

Bellini was the most eminent painter in Venice in the second half of the fifteenth century. He became the leader of the Venetian school of painting, ran a large workshop and had many pupils; Giorgione and Titian were among the last, and their influence is reflected in the work of Bellini's final years. Born into a family of artists, his father and brother were both painters, and Andrea Mantegna was his brother-in-law. After an early period influenced by Mantegna and Donatello, Bellini began to develop his own personal style in about 1470, a style characterized by a completely unprecedented feeling for space, colour and light, a simplicity of composition and form, strong sculptural modelling, harmonious colour in mild, unifying light, and profound expression of human feelings.

The Dead Christ Supported by Two Mourning Angels is one of the most accomplished and classical works of his first mature period, which began in about 1480. The theme of a *pietà* with angels emerged in France in about 1400 and was used by Donatello before Bellini adopted it in several paintings that antedate the Berlin panel and are now in London, Rimini, and Venice (in the central compartment of the attic tier of the polyptych in SS. Giovanni e Paolo [1464]). The London work has sometimes been presumed to have held a similar position in another, unknown altarpiece, though both it and the more mature Berlin painting might have been intended as separate devotional images. In this rendering of *The Dead Christ*, Bellini at last achieved a figure of classical harmony and balance that could stand beside the sculpture of ancient Greece and Rome. The natural beauty of Christ's body even in death, the purity of line and the lucidity and force in the sculptural modelling, combine here with an unprecedented tenderness and depth of emotion into a perfect unity.

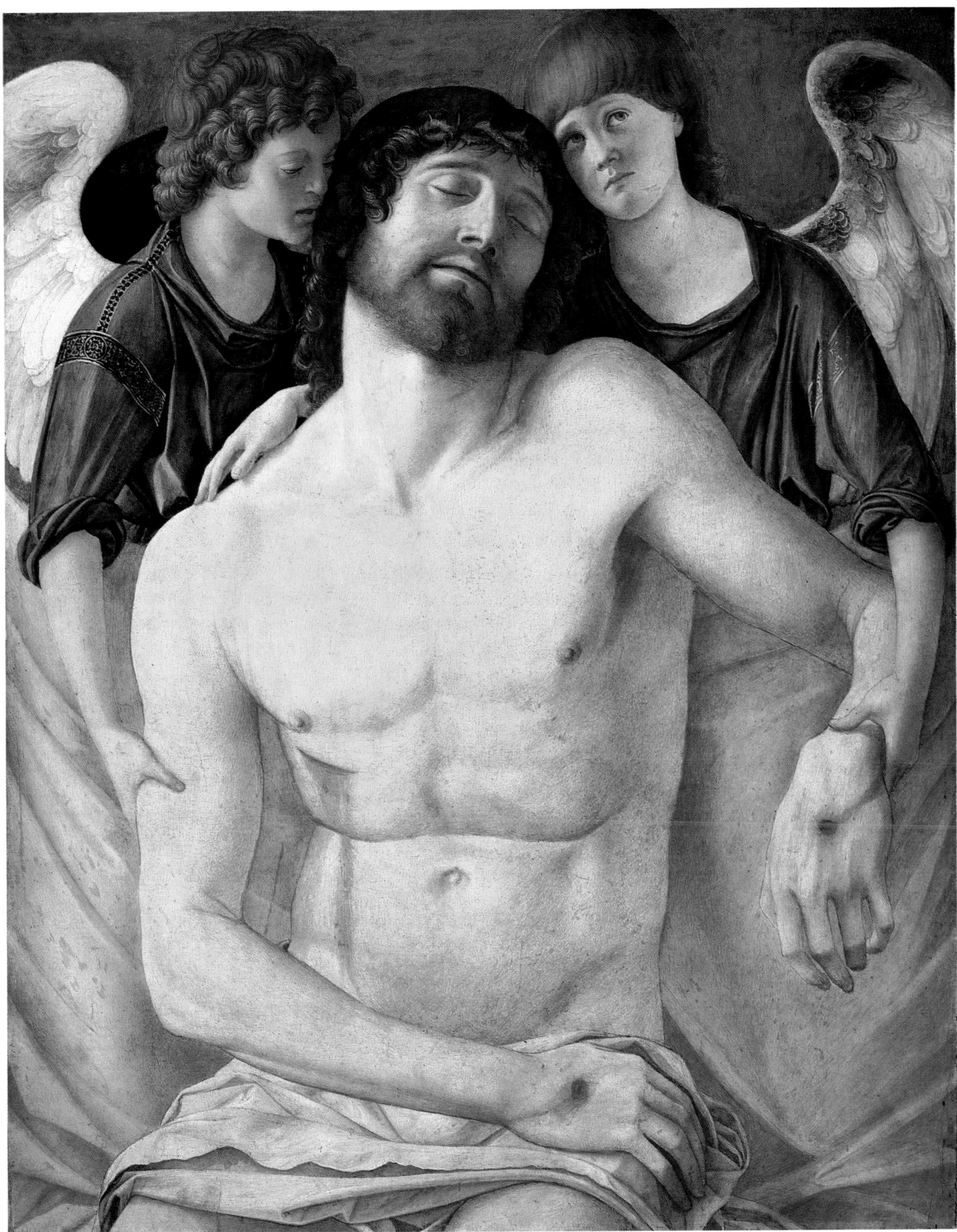

Giovanni Bellini
The Resurrection
1479

Poplar transferred to canvas, 148 × 128 cm
(58¼ × 50⅜ in)
Acquired 1903
Cat. no. 1177 A

The Resurrection was intended as an altar painting for the chapel built in 1475–8 by Marco Zorzi, a Venetian patrician, to the right of the choir in the Camaldoli church of S. Michele in Isola, on the island of S. Michele between Venice and Murano. Relatively small for an altar painting, it has justifiably been associated with others of similar format and date – *St Francis in a Landscape*, 1480–5 (New York, Frick Collection), and *St Jerome in a Landscape*, 1479 (Florence, Contini Bonacossi Bequest). In all these works Bellini was concerned with the relation of the figures to the landscape, or rather with the landscape as the true vehicle of the composition, and in which figures were integrated. Unlike Mantegna in his similar attempts, Bellini accomplished this on a stylistic level in which the painting of the rays of the rising sun, or the evocation of a spatial continuum by means of light and atmospheric perspective, took precedence. He may well have been influenced in this by some of Antonello da Messina's related Venetian works of 1475–6 such as the *Crucifixion* in Antwerp. Yet Bellini had essentially arrived at his new conception of landscape in the Pesaro altar (1471–4), even though there the landscape is limited to the background.

Instead of depicting Christ at the moment he rose from the grave, as Piero della Francesca and Donatello had done, Bellini shows him hovering in the air. In the foreground there is a rocky slope with the dark entrance to the tomb, and in front of that is the heavy slab which had sealed it. One of the soldiers (who some have identified as Longinus), seen in three-quarter view from behind, his right hand raised in astonishment, looks up at the resurrected Christ, who appears at an indeterminate distance above the hills, the banner of the Resurrection in his hand. A second soldier in full armour has fallen asleep, half sitting, half leaning against the rock, while a third has removed his armour and lies asleep on the ground. A path leads past the tomb to the right and into the middle distance, where the three Marys are approaching. In the far distance there is a town with a river and bridge, and behind it is a steep, conical hill with a castle on its peak – an imaginative view of the town of Monselice. Beyond the hilly horizon the sun is just about to rise, and tinges the sky a light yellow, almost a white colour that, interrupted by rose-coloured clouds, gradually becomes a deeper and deeper blue against which Christ's torso, head, hands and the banner stand out in great contrast. Here Bellini has consciously drawn an analogy between the natural phenomenon of the sunrise and Christ's resurrection.

The painting made a lasting impression on Venetian painters down to Titian (*The Resurrection*, Urbino), as copies by Filippo Mazzola and various borrowings of motifs by other artists prove. Cima in particular, to whom the work was ascribed from the seventeenth century onwards (Boschini, 1664), took it as the point of departure for the development of his style, not only in the rendering and proportioning of his figures and his treatment of landscape, but in the interrelation of these two. Landscape conceived as a unified spatial continuum evoked by grades of light – this was Bellini's innovation, which through Cima and Carpaccio reached its culmination in the landscape art of Giorgione.

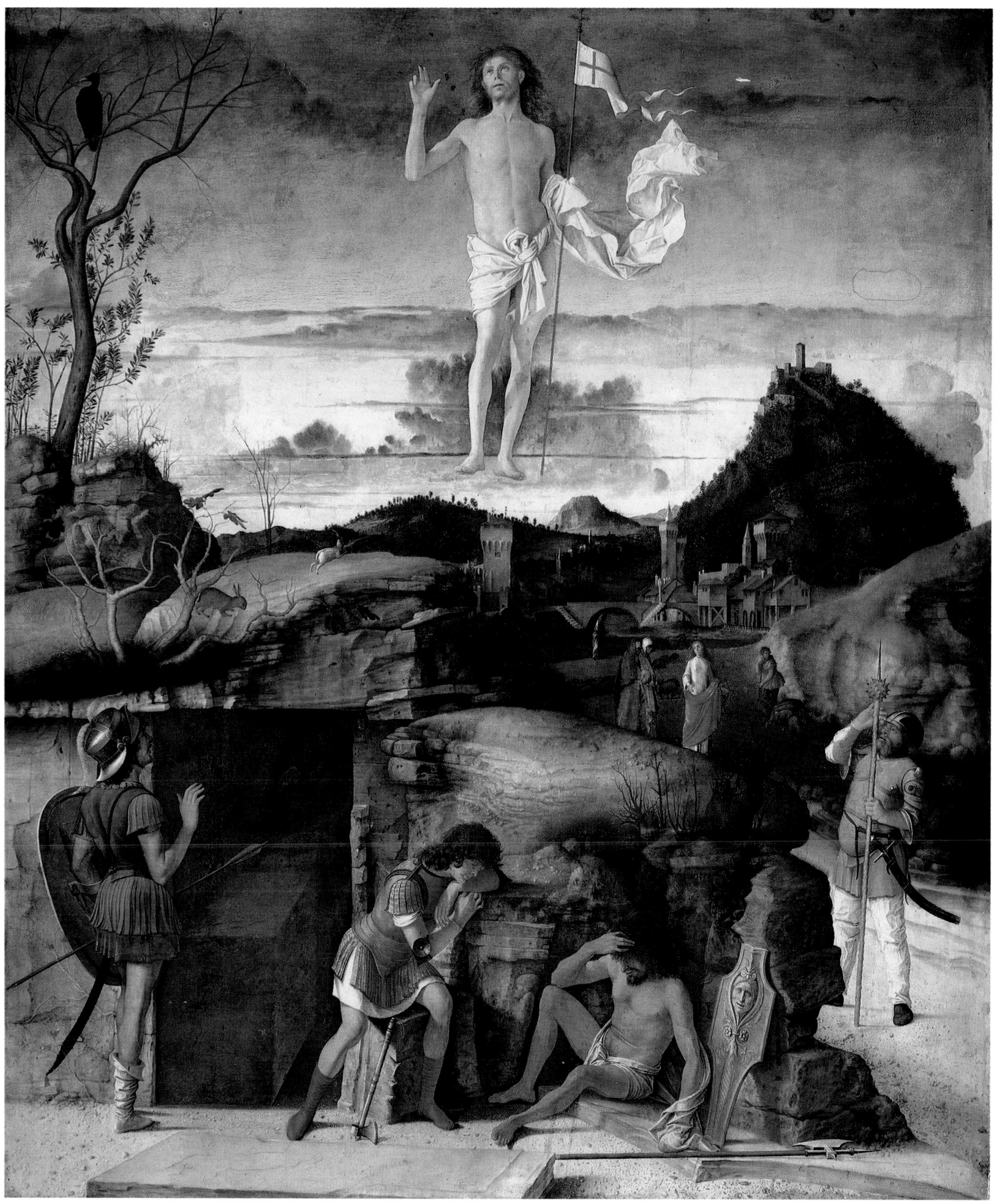

Giovanni Battista da Conegliano, called Cima (*c.*1459/60–1517/18)

St Mark Healing the Cobbler Anianus

1499

Poplar, 206 × 135 cm (81 × 53⅛ in), top rounded
Inscribed: 'Johannis Baptiste Coneglia/ nesis opus'
Acquired with the Solly Collection, 1821
Cat. no. 2

This painting belongs to a series depicting various scenes from the legend of St Mark, the patron saint of Venice. It once decorated the Chapel of the Annunciation that belonged to the silk-weavers of Lucca in S. Maria dei Crocicchieri, Venice. Other paintings in the sequence were *St Mark Preaching* by Lattanzio da Rimini (1499, lost), *The Arrest of St Mark* by Giovanni Mansueti (also 1499; Vaduz, Prince of Liechtenstein Collection), and a further work about which the sources give no precise information. Cima has illustrated the scene described in Jacobus de Voragine's *Legenda aurea*, where, on the marketplace in Alexandria, the Apostle Mark healed the hand of Anianus after he had injured it with an awl. The cobbler, seated here outside his shop surrounded by onlookers, was baptized and later became bishop of Alexandria. In the background is a temple in the style of the Venetian Early Renaissance, with a central cupola on whose balustrade men are conversing or enjoying the view.

Cima came from Conegliano in the Veneto. Though nothing is known about his early training, he was active primarily in Venice, where his name was registered for the first time in 1492. However, as an altarpiece dated 1489 indicates, he must have seen Giovanni Bellini's *Madonna* of 1488 in the Frari Church. In addition to the works of Bellini's middle period, the greatest influence on Cima was Alvise Vivarini, who was probably his teacher. Characteristic of Cima's style are the clarity of pictorial space and the lucid, light-filled atmosphere, logical perspective, the comparatively slender and classical proportions of his firmly, sometimes even dryly modelled figures, and a planar, almost metallically brittle treatment of drapery. His brilliant if cool colours underline the self-contained dignity of the figures, who are almost invariably far under lifesize; and his work reveals a poetic sensibility for landscape as a pictorial element. Cima retained his style almost unchanged to the end of his life, despite the advances made by Giorgione and Titian. When he died, a year or two after Bellini, Titian was already at work on his *Assunta* for the Frari Church.

Giovanni Mansueti
The Arrest of St Mark, 1499
Vaduz, Prince of Liechtenstein Collection

Vittore Carpaccio (1465/7–1525/6)
The Preparation of Christ's Tomb
*c.*1505

Canvas, 145 × 185 cm (57 × $72\frac{7}{8}$ in)
Inscription forged in an early hand:
'ANDREAS MANTINEA F.'
Acquired 1905
Cat. no. 23 A

With Cima and Montagna, Carpaccio belonged to a younger generation of artists from Giovanni Bellini's circle who were born between about 1450 and 1460. Carpaccio soon became known for his narrative talent, which he was able to use to full effect in the large pictorial cycles he did for the assembly halls of Venice's powerful lay brotherhoods. While relying on Gentile Bellini's history paintings with their abundance of figures, he overcame their rather dry, documentary character to create images that are characterized by subtle handling, harmonious colouring and poetic mood. His first major work was a cycle devoted to the legend of St Ursula, painted from 1490–96/8 for the Scuola di S. Orsola; later, in 1511–20, he created a cycle for the Scuola di S. Stefano with scenes from the life of St Stephen, to which the Berlin *Ordination of St Stephen*, dated 1511, belonged. Between these two works, Carpaccio executed another celebrated cycle, that for the Scuola di San Giorgio degli Schiavoni of about 1505. *The Preparation of Christ's Tomb* dates from about the same period as this cycle. It is in many respects an enigmatic image, and reveals a profound sensibility. Combining meditative calm with rich detail and narrative, its composition of auxiliary scenes distributed around the central figure indeed has much in common with the scenes of Carpaccio's cycles. There is no evidence, however, that it once formed part of a Passion sequence.

Christ's body lies on a low stone table in the foreground. The red pillar at the centre of the table represents the Anointing Stone, a relic greatly venerated in the Eastern Orthodox Church in Byzantium during the Early Middle Ages before being taken to the Church of the Holy Sepulchre in Jerusalem. Behind Christ, seated with his back against a tree in silent meditation, is Job, whose devout and patient suffering made him an Old Testament precursor of Christ. In Venice, Job was venerated as a saint, and in 1493 the church of S. Giobbe was consecrated to him there. From his figure the eye is led to the group behind him, representing the prostrate Virgin comforted by Mary Magdalene and St John. In the left background, two men in Oriental costumes carry the stone away from the tomb while a third, probably Joseph of Arimathia, prepares the cleansing of Christ's body. The combination of Christ's figure lying on a low table, with Job in mourning, is certainly unusual in Renaissance painting, occurring only once again in this form, with Carpaccio – in a painting in the Metropolitan Museum, New York: in fact this and the Berlin *Preparation of Christ's Tomb* were in the same early seventeenth century collection of Robert Canonici in Ferrara. Both paintings were considered works by Mantegna at that time, and had forged Mantegna signatures. The one on the New York painting was removed in 1945 to reveal Carpaccio's signature beneath it.

Among his special qualities, apart from his narrative talent, Carpaccio's sense of colour was remarkable. In contrast to Cima's penchant for local colours, he strived for colouristic unity, a tendency which he shared with Mantegna. Distributed throughout the entire image in *The Preparation of Christ's Tomb* is that reddish-brown colour, like copper, so typical of Carpaccio – from the Anointing Stone to Job's and Mary Magdalene's clothes, from the fragment of column and the garment of the bearded man shouldering the gravestone, to the most distant minor figures. This tone, with the cool blue of the sky, forms a dominating chord that reverberates above the modulated greens and browns of the landscape.

Carlo Crivelli (1430/5–*c.*1495)

The Virgin and Child Enthroned, with the Presentation of the Keys to St Peter, and Six Saints

1488

Poplar, 191 × 196 cm ($75\frac{1}{4} \times 77\frac{1}{8}$ in)
Signed lower centre:
'OPVS CAROLI CRIVELLI VENETI'
Acquired 1892
Cat. no. 1156 A

Carlo Crivelli, son of the Venetian painter Jacopo Crivelli, was first recorded in 1457 as an active master in Venice. In 1465 he was registered as a citizen of Zara, Dalmatia; soon afterwards he seems to have returned to Italy. In 1468 at the latest he settled in the Marches, first in Fermo, then in Ascoli Piceno, where he spent the remainder of his life. His last dated picture was painted in 1493. Initially influenced by Antonio Vivarini and the young Giovanni Bellini, his style was shaped most lastingly by the Paduan artist Francesco Squarcione and his student, Giorgio Schiavone, whom he may have met in Padua and later in Dalmatia. From them Crivelli derived that rigorous plasticity of form which he refined to a great linear precision and to modelling of metallic smoothness. Combined with brilliant local colour, a love of the surface qualities of precious materials, and a sense of the abstract, ornamental possibilities of pictorial elements, Crivelli developed these qualities with superb craftsmanship. His bizarre imagination sometimes led him to characterize his figures with almost expressionistic exaggeration. The consciously archaic style of his art was basically very much in the Late Gothic vein, and he remained aloof from such developments in contemporary Venetian painting during the 1470s and 1480s as those introduced by Giovanni Bellini. While Crivelli painted many two- or three-tiered Late Gothic polyptychs following the pattern of Antonio Vivarini, he also painted, in his late period, several large, unified, rectangular altarpieces (*pale*) with compositions of the *Sacra Conversazione* type. Among these is the Berlin panel of 1488, which unlike the London altarpiece with its Renaissance frame was, according to F. Zeri (*Arte Antica e Moderna*, 1961), originally framed in the Gothic style, with flanking pilasters and three narrow panels with standing figures of saints one above the other on each side. Two of these panels are now in Berlin; others are in the Colonna Collection, Rome; in the Museum of Fine Arts, Worcester, Massachusetts; and in the Dienst Verspreide Rijkscollecties, The Hague (formerly Lanz Collection, Amsterdam). These small panels were probably done with studio participation. In his book *The Early Venetian Paintings in Holland* (1978), I. Dragt thought it odd to imagine the Berlin panel, which one would expect to have a Renaissance frame (like that of the *Pala Odoni*), flanked by figures of saints in a Gothic frame. Though Zeri (*Antologia di Belli Arti*, 1978) countered this reservation by citing Signorelli's altar painting *The Baptism of Christ* in Arcevia, this work admittedly represents a rather different case.

The Berlin painting is probably identical with the altarpiece commissioned from Crivelli in 1488 for the Franciscan church of S. Pietro degli Osservanti in Camerino. The main panel represents the presentation of the keys to St Peter by the Christ Child seated in the Virgin's lap, and flanked on each side by three Saints and Blessed. The high throne in the centre of the image and the saints gathered around the Virgin to witness the ceremony, give it the character of a *Sacra Conversazione* of the kind introduced into Venetian art particularly by Antonello da Messina, in his altarpiece for S. Cassiano. That work's imposing architectural setting is missing here, however, and the Madonna, instead of being raised high above the saints, is seated with her head almost on a level with theirs. The tiara at St Peter's feet characterizes him as the first Pope; the papal 'power of the keys' (which he holds) symbolizes the power of the Church, as custodian of the sacred treasures, to bind its members and to absolve them. Of the six saints and immortals who witness the scene, four are members of the Franciscan order, the painting having been intended for a Franciscan church. In the left foreground is St Emidius, the first Bishop of Ascoli and its patron saint. Behind him to the right is St Francis of Assisi; and at the left edge, the Franciscan preacher and penitent, John of Capestrano from the Abruzzi (1386–1456), who miraculously turned the Battle of Belgrade against the Turks in 1456. Though not canonized until 1690, he is depicted here as beatified, with an aureole. Standing in the right foreground is St Louis of

Carlo Crivelli
St Bonaventura and *St Bernard*
Berlin, Gemäldegalerie SMPK

Toulouse (1274–97), Archbishop of Toulouse and a member of the House of Anjou, as signified by the fleurs-de-lis on his ornate bishop's cape, beneath which the Franciscan habit is visible. Behind him to the left are an unidentified bishop (Ambrosius?) and the Blessed Giacomo della Marca (1391–1474), a Franciscan monk who is identified by his attribute, a reliquary containing Christ's blood, and by the monogram of Christ suspended above him.

Antonello da Messina (*c.*1430–79)
Portrait of a Young Man
1478

Walnut, 20.4 × 14.5 cm (8 × 5¾ in)
Signed: '147(8)/Antonellus messaneus me pinxit'
Acquired from the Solly Collection in or before 1830
Cat. no. 18

Antonello da Messina received his training in Naples from Colantonio, a painter influenced by Netherlandish art, from about 1445 to 1455 (or to 1450, according to some accounts). At the court of the King of Naples, Alfons I of Aragon, he had the opportunity to study Jan van Eyck's work (*Lomellini Triptych, St George*), which helped him both stylistically and technically. According to a recently revived hypothesis that goes back to Vasari, Antonello is supposed to have travelled between 1450 and 1455 to Flanders, where he visited Petrus Christus's studio in Bruges (J. Wright, *Art History*, 1980; M.G. Paolini, *Storia dell' Arte*, 1980), but other scholars have rejected this assumption (J. Bruyn, *Oud Holland*, 1982). In 1456, Antonello settled in Messina, where he died in 1479. Associations with the art of Piero della Francesca and Fra Angelico suggest that he may have been to Rome in the 1460s, and presumably he made a first journey to Padua and Venice towards the end of that decade. At any rate, he did go to Venice, presumably by ship, in 1475 or late in 1474. During almost two years there he executed the large altarpiece for S. Cassiano, became a competitor of Giovanni Bellini, and lastingly influenced the development of Venetian painting.

Antonello was renowned for his portraits. Of the two in Berlin, one is dated 1474 (shortly before his journey to Venice), while the other has the date 147[8], the year before his death. This is his last surviving portrait. Antonello is credited with introducing the three-quarter view into Italian portraiture, a motif derived from such Netherlandish models as van Eyck and particularly Petrus Christus, from Rogier van der Weyden and Memling, examples of whose work could be seen in Italy at the time.

In all of Antonello's surviving portraits the sitter is depicted, without exception, at bust-length, without the hands, on extremely constricted formats. His sitters invariably face left, are illuminated from the left, and are given in striking chiaroscuro, looking out at us from the corner of their eyes. In some portraits, such as those in Berlin, they are seated behind a parapet which serves to create depth and distance, and to bear a *cartellino* with a signature; other portraits lack the balustrade, such as the early ones in Cefalù, Pavia and New York. All the portraits except the later of the two in Berlin depict the sitter in front of a dark, neutral background. Many of Antonello's portraits were painted in Venice, where they impressed Bellini in particular, despite his different approach. Bellini's models tend to look to the left out of the picture and past the spectator, which gives them an air of cool detachment. Also, from about 1480 Bellini began increasingly to use an open sky as background behind his parapets, though never with a landscape in his works to 1500.

While most of Antonello's portraits are between 27 and 36 cm high, the later Berlin portrait measures only 20 cm. This by no means reduces its inherent monumentality; the young man looks out, indeed down, on us with a coolly inspecting gaze. He has dark brown hair, and with his brown jacket wears a black cap with fine silk bands. Quite unusual are the dark blue evening sky, and especially the landscape visible in the angle between the sleeve contour and the left edge of the painting.

Longhi (*Paragone*, 1952) believed that this portrait was originally conceived with a dark background and that sky and landscape were added a few decades later by a northern (Netherlandish) artist, at the request of its owner. Yet as Oertel has pointed out (Berlin Gallery Catalogue, 1975), the technical examination does not corroborate this. Because the blue of the sky continues beneath the black of the silk bands and the brown coat, even showing between hair and cheek, and because strands of the young man's hair are painted over the sky colour, the sky is surely authentic. A rather large *pentimento* is visible at the right shoulder; its contour (or that of the sleeve) originally extended further to the left, leaving no space for a landscape view. Antonello corrected this part during the first phase of work – there is no other paint layer detectable between sky and the white gesso ground.

PROSPERANS MODESTVS ESTO INFORTVNATVS VERO PRVDENS

Giorgio da Castelfranco, called Giorgione (1477/8–1510)
Portrait of a Young Man

Canvas, 58 × 46 cm ($22\frac{7}{8}$ × $18\frac{1}{8}$ in)
Giustiniani Collection, Padua, until 1884
Acquired in Florence 1891
Cat. no. 12 A

Having been until 1884 in the Giustiniani Collection, Padua, this portrait came to be known as the *Giustiniani Portrait*. From 1884–91 it was in the possession of the art historian Jean Paul Richter, who attributed it to Giorgione and from whom Wilhelm von Bode bought it for the gallery in 1891. Though it is not among those works of Giorgione authenticated by inscriptions, sources or documents, it is one of a small group in which the experts almost unanimously see his hand. And of this small group, only a few are portraits – the *Laura* in Vienna (inscribed and dated 1506 on the reverse), a portrait of an elderly woman in Venice, the *Giustiniani Portrait*, and the rather less known male portrait *Terris*, in San Diego (Museum of Arts; formerly in the Terris Collection; inscribed and dated 15[1]0 on the back).

The sitter is depicted half-length against a dark background, his right hand resting on a parapet. His shoulders are turned slightly out of the frontal plane and his head is represented in three-quarter view, his eyes directed straight at the observer. The young man wears a pale violet, quilted garment with bows at the front, the top one untied to reveal a white shirt underneath. His self-confident expression, cool sidelong gaze, regular, almost classical features, and the touch of veiled melancholy, distinguish the image from all previous portraits of the late fifteenth century, such as those by Antonello da Messina and Giovanni Bellini. The motif of the hand resting on a parapet is not Venetian, and may have been derived from Netherlandish art, perhaps from portraits by Memling, which the artist could have seen in Venetian collections (T. Pignatti, *Giorgione*, 1978). Or it may have been inspired by Leonardo (G. Robertson, 'Giorgione', *Atti del Convegno*, Castelfranco, 1978–9). Giorgione accomplished the transition to the High Renaissance in this portrait, whose classical harmony is comparable to the work of Raphael. Giorgione's approach to portraiture became decisive for the young Titian, as well as for followers such as Cariani.

The inscription on the parapet, V V, has been repainted, but underneath are probably the original letters. It has been interpreted in many ways, most recently as '*Virtus Vincit*' or '*Vivo Vivus*': the last as in inscriptions on Roman portraits and sepulchral monuments. Though this opinion has had some acceptance, a number of art historians still question it.

The dating of the portrait is controversial. Pignatti (1978), Pallucchini (1981) and others date it about 1506, close to *Laura*. C. Hornig (1976) suggests 1500–1, and A. Ballarin proposes an even earlier date of 1497–8 (*Atti del Convegno*, 1978–9). D. Rosand (*Titian*, 1978) has wrongly attributed the portrait to the young Titian.

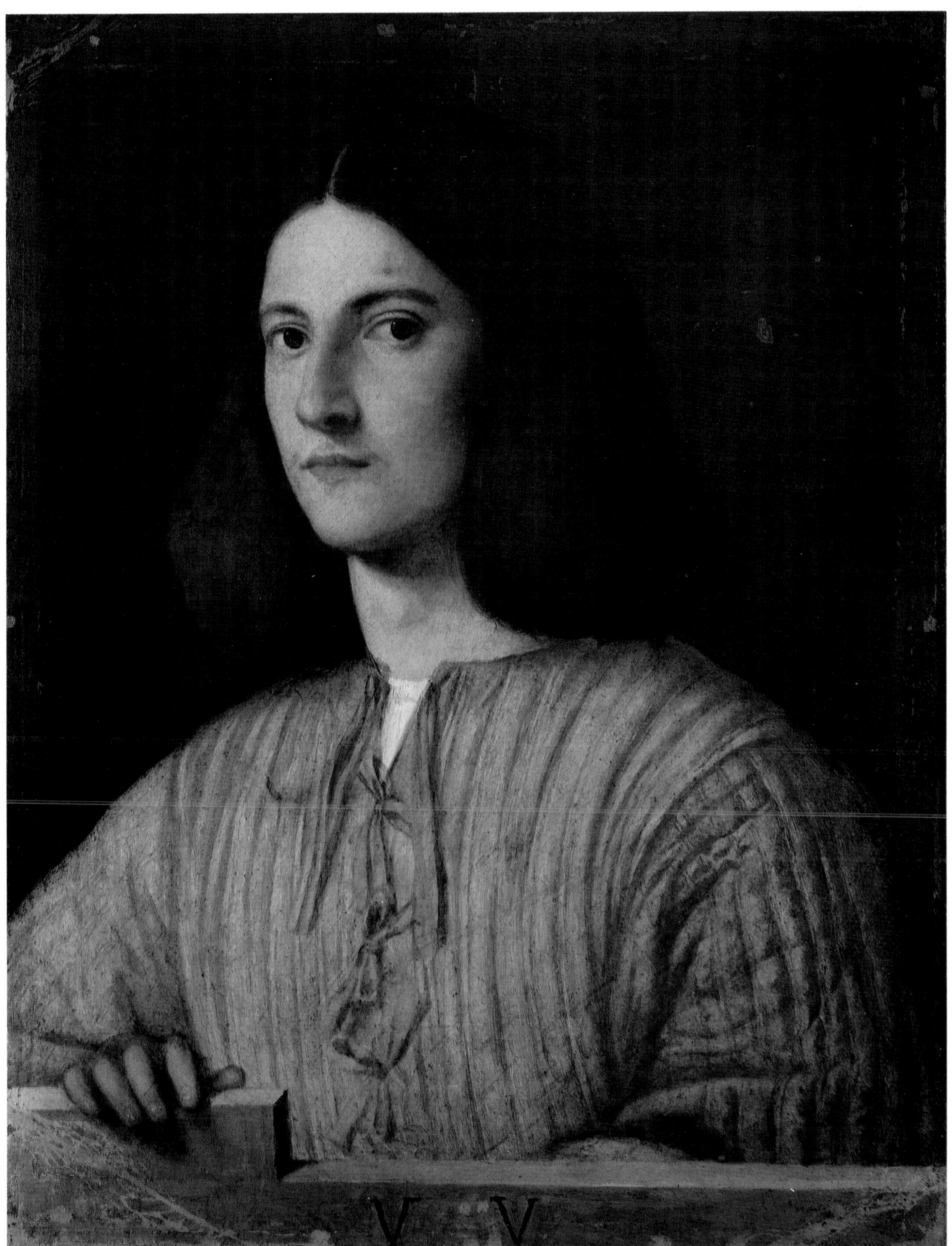
V V

Sebastiano Luciani, called del Piombo (*c.*1485–1547)

Portrait of a Young Roman Woman

*c.*1513

Poplar, 78 × 61 cm ($30\frac{3}{4}$ × 24 in)
Acquired 1885
Cat. no. 259 B

Sebastiano del Piombo first trained with Giovanni Bellini in his home town of Venice, and then, according to Vasari, turned to Giorgione, whose great influence on his early work is evident. In 1511, shortly after Giorgione's death, Sebastiano accepted the invitation of Agostino Chigi, a Roman banker then visiting Venice, to accompany him to Rome and help in the decoration of his villa on the Tiber (1511–12). Through Chigi, Sebastiano got to know Raphael, but this acquaintance was soon overshadowed by his friendship with Michelangelo, whose art had a deep impact on him and influenced his development from the mid-1510s.

The half-length portrait of a young Roman woman in Berlin, one of the most important works he produced during his first years in Rome, was probably painted in about 1513. Its composition is more accomplished, more formal than Sebastiano's portrait of a woman in Florence.

The sitter is represented in three-quarter view to the left, in front of a dark wall with a window on the left opening on a landscape vista with farms, mountains, and a sunset sky. She wears a superb, fur-lined mantle of ruby-red velvet, whose collar has slipped from her shoulder to reveal a dress whose light violet hue vibrates with a strange tension against the red. Her head thrown slightly back, she looks from the corner of her eye straight at the spectator, gathering the fur trim of her mantle to her breast with one hand; with the other she holds the handle of a basket of flowers and fruit. As this last is an attribute of St Dorothy, some have called the portrait an image of that saint, though the absence of a halo or palm fronds make this doubtful. All the same, a replica of the painting (Verona Museum) was called *St Dorothy* as early as 1657. The basket might well allude to the first name of the sitter, since the portrait is probably the same one Vasari saw in the home of Luca Torregiani in Rome in 1568. Later, when it was in the collection of the Dukes of Marlborough in England (1756–1885), it was attributed to Raphael, and thought to be a portrait of his woman-friend, 'La Fornarina'.

This is one of the last of del Piombo's Roman works containing Venetian elements. Recollections of Venice are seen in the conception of a half-length figure against an architectural background with a side window, in the palette, and in the cool, twilight mood of the landscape, shortly after sundown. Nevertheless, the pensive, musing expression typical of the Giorgione school has already given way to a tranquil dignity, even monumentality – characteristics of del Piombo's Roman style as it developed under Raphael's influence. The painting has often been compared to Raphael's *Donna Velata*, which may have been modelled on it. Though the architectural background is authentic, it was not in the original version of the composition, which showed the young woman in front of a laurel hedge, like Giorgione's *Laura* (Vienna). This suggests that it might have been intended as a portrait of a bride, which would explain why the young woman places her right hand over her heart; but this gesture can be traced with equal conviction to classical models.

Echoes of del Piombo's image are found in half-figures by Garofalo (formerly in the Duke of Northumberland Collection) and by a follower of Leonardo (private collection).

School of Leonardo
Portrait of a Young Woman
Private collection

Lorenzo Lotto (*c.*1480–1556)
Christ Taking Leave of His Mother
1521

Canvas, 126 × 99 cm (49⅝ × 39 in)
Signed and dated: 'mo Laurenttjo lotto pictor 1521'
Acquired with the Solly Collection, 1821
Cat. no. 325

After years of restless wandering from place to place – Venice, Treviso, Bergamo (1503–5), Recanati (1506–8), Rome (1509), the Marches – Lorenzo Lotto worked in Bergamo from 1513 to 1525 before returning to Venice. *Christ Taking Leave of His Mother* was painted in Bergamo, in 1521. According to Ridolfi's report (1648), the painting was kept in the Casa Tassi at the time; a century later, the biographer of Bergamasque artists, F.M. Tassi (*Vite de' Pittori* ..., Bergamaschi, 1793) noted that it was in the possession of Canon Giambattista Zanchi. According to Tassi, the woman donor in the painting represents Elisabetta Rota, the wife of Domenico Tassi. Domenico himself was depicted as the donor in a companion piece, an *Adoration of the Child*, which has not survived but whose composition some scholars believe is reflected in an early copy (Venice, Accademia). This is a *notturno* with almost the same dimensions as the Berlin canvas, and also includes a donor figure in profile, kneeling in a corner – in this case, the lower left corner.

The subject depicted here is relatively rare in Italian painting. After raising Lazarus and before entering Jerusalem, the event with which his sufferings began, Christ took leave of his mother in Bethany. The artist shows him accompanied by Peter and Thomas (?), kneeling before Mary and asking her blessing. She has fainted at her son's prediction of his fate, and sinks into the arms of his disciple, John, and Mary Magdalene. The scene is set in an arcaded hall with a barrel-vaulted ceiling. Between the columns at the far left there is open countryside and in the background the hall opens on a garden surrounded by high walls. Its pergola in the form of a cross with central dome is in turn surrounded by a fence with an open gate (an allusion to the *hortus conclusus* or enclosed garden, a metaphor from the Song of Solomon (4:12) applied to the Virgin and symbolizing the Immaculate Conception). The donor is kneeling in the right foreground, glancing up from her book to witness the leave-taking; she is seen in profile and is accompanied by a little dog. In the foreground at the bottom, darkly silhouetted against the floor and cut off by the picture edge, are a branch of cherries and an apple twig and leaf, allusions, respectively, to the Redeemer's blood and to his work of Salvation. Next to the apple is a *cartellino* with the artist's signature and the date.

Though this scene is not in the Gospels, it became a part of pictorial tradition in the late Middle Ages through the influence of the *Meditationes* of Pseudo Bonaventura; it was popularized through Passion Plays, and became associated with the cycle of the Seven Sorrows of the Virgin. In early renderings, particularly those by northern artists such as Dürer and Cranach, Christ stands before Mary and blesses her. The first depiction of him kneeling with his arms crossed submissively over his breast occurs in an early work by Correggio, executed before 1514 (London, National Gallery), a painting that evidently inspired Lotto. As X-rays of it have revealed, Correggio originally depicted Christ in a standing position, a direct reference to Dürer's woodcut from The Life of the Virgin sequence (1510). In an article on Lorenzo Lotto (*Atti del Convegno*, Asolo, 1980 [1981]), C. Gould says that on his return from Central Italy (Rome, the Marches) on the way to Bergamo Lotto may have met the young Correggio and seen the picture in his studio in Correggio, near Parma.

Correggio
Christ Taking Leave of His Mother
London, National Gallery

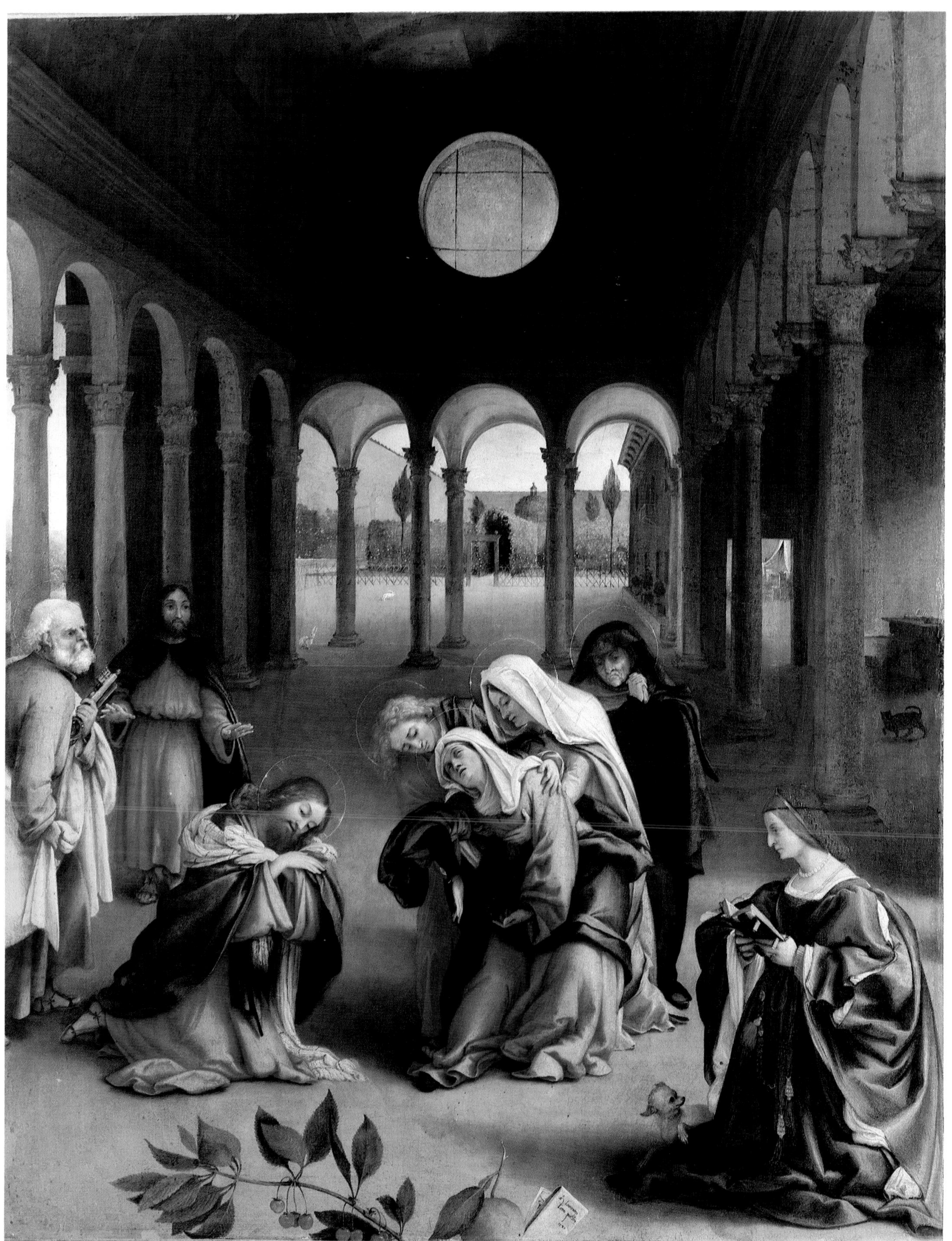

Antonio Allegri, called Il Correggio (*c.*1489–1534)

Leda and the Swan

*c.*1531–2

Canvas, 152 × 191 cm ($59\frac{7}{8} \times 75\frac{1}{4}$ in)
From the Royal Palaces, Berlin
Cat. no. 218

This painting belongs to a series of paintings depicting Jupiter's love affairs in various guises, commissioned by the Duke of Mantua, Federigo II Gonzaga, and painted in about 1530–2. Leda, the central figure in the Berlin painting, was the daughter of Thestios, King of Aetolia, and later wife of Tyndareos, King of Sparta. Of the very different versions of the Leda myth, Correggio has illustrated the best known, in which Leda, bathing on the banks of the Eurotas, is seduced by Jupiter in the guise of a swan. To the left of this central group, beside the grove of trees, two *putti* play wind instruments to accompany an adolescent, winged Cupid on the lyre, the instrument of Apollo's divine music.

Other paintings besides *Leda* have survived from Correggio's cycle – a *Danae* (Rome, Galleria Borghese) of almost the same dimensions, and two upright formats, *The Rape of Ganymede* and *Jupiter and Io* (Vienna, Kunsthistorisches Museum). Vasari, though he had not seen the pictures himself, was told of them by Giulio Romano, and reported (1550/68) that Correggio 'has made two paintings in Mantua for Duke Federigo II which were to be sent to the Emperor'. These were a *Leda* and a *Venus*, by which he may have meant the *Danae* though some details of his description suit the *Io* in Vienna better. Federigo might have ordered the four paintings for himself, as Verheyen believes and Gould thinks possible. However, as Gould suggests, he might also first have commissioned the two upright canvases (which Vasari does not expressly mention) for himself, and then, when Emperor Charles V saw and admired them, presented them to him with the promise to supply two more (*Leda* and *Danae*) which he then ordered from Correggio in order to present them to the Emperor.

Until recently, Vasari's information has been associated with the Coronation of Charles V in Bologna in 1530 (and with Federigo's accession to the Mantuan throne the same year). Gould thinks the events described by Vasari took place during one of the two visits the Emperor made to Mantua, probably the second, in November 1532. In September 1534, soon after Correggio's death, the Duke and the Governor of Parma began a correspondence about the artist's cartoons for the Jupiter cycle. Though Gould does not relate these cartoons to the four surviving paintings, Verheyen does, and, from the letters about them, he thinks the cycle must originally have contained more paintings. Verheyen supposes that the paintings were intended for the decoration of the Sala di Ovidio in the Palazzo del Té, the Duke's summer residence. This room belonged to an *'appartamento'* which perhaps was meant for the use of the Duke's official mistress, Isabella Boschetti. Gould, however, is sceptical about Verheyen's hypothesis and his reconstruction of the decoration of the room.

The subsequent history of the paintings was very chequered. According to Lomazzo (1584), the sculptor Leone Leoni owned two of the four (*Danae* and *Io*), which his son Pompeo had sent to Milan from Spain. Pompeo may have received them from Philip II's former secretary of state, Pérez, who fell out of favour in 1579 and who definitely owned the *Ganymede*, or he may have been given them by the King himself. In 1601, the Imperial Ambassador in Madrid bought the two paintings from Leoni for Emperor Rudolf II in Prague. He then, in 1603, bought the two others, *Leda* and *Ganymede*, from Philip III, the son of Philip II. The *Leda* is the only painting of the series to be listed in the inventory of Philip II's estate. Before shipping the paintings to Prague, Philip III had Eugenio Caxés copy them. While the two upright canvases were apparently taken from Prague to Vienna before 1621, the *Leda* and *Danae* were confiscated by the Swedish troops who captured Prague in 1648, and were taken to Stockholm. When Queen Christina of Sweden abdicated, she brought them with her to Rome in 1654. After her death in 1689, they passed through the hands of Cardinal Azzolino and Prince Livio Odescalchi, then in 1721 came into the collection of the French Regent, Duke Philippe d'Orléans (1674–1723). His son, Louis

Correggio
Danae
Rome, Galleria Borghese

Correggio
Ganymede
Vienna, Kunsthistorisches Museum

Correggio
Jupiter and Io
Vienna, Kunsthistorisches Museum

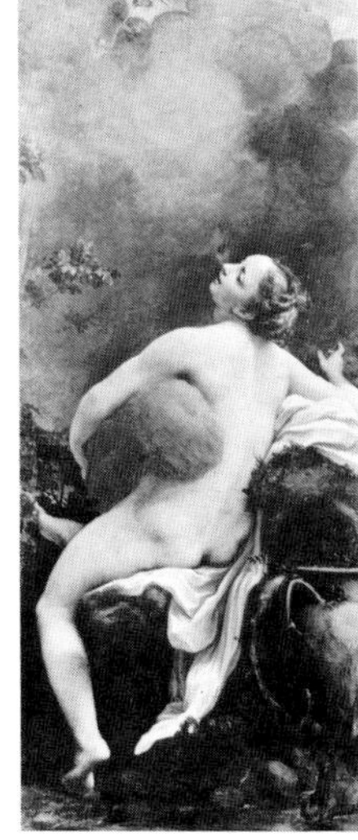

(1703–52), finding the depiction of Leda offensive, cut the canvas to pieces in a fit of religious fervour – probably between the death of his wife in 1726 and his entry into St Geneviève Abbey in 1731. He entrusted the pieces to his court artist and curator of his collection, Charles Coypel, who obtained permission to reassemble them and restore the painting. Coypel repainted the head of Leda, which had apparently been lost, and slightly altered the swan. Yet the canvas had evidently still not been reassembled when Coypel's collection was sold after his death in 1753. The remnants were bought by Pasquier, for whom the Widow Godefroi put them together again and Delyen painted the head of Leda for the second time. Pasquier died two years later, and at the auction of his collection, Count d'Epinaille bought the painting of *Leda* for Frederick the Great. It was hung in the Picture Gallery in Potsdam, where M.Oesterreich described it in 1770. When in 1806 Napoleon had it brought to Paris, Prudhon restored Leda's head for the third time. For the fourth and last time the head was painted in Berlin, by Jakob Schlesinger, in 1834–5, but not correctly. As the early copy by Caxés shows, Leda's head was originally inclined more to the right.

Tiziano Vecellio, called Titian (1488/90–1576)

Clarissa Strozzi at the Age of Two

1542

Canvas, 115 × 98 cm ($45\frac{1}{4}$ × $38\frac{1}{2}$ in)
Signed on the front edge of the tabletop: 'TITIANVS F.'; on the tablet, upper left: 'ANNOR. II. MDXLII.'
Acquired from the Palazzo Strozzi, Florence, 1878
Cat. no. 160 A

As the inscription on the tablet at the upper left records, Titian painted this portrait of Clarissa Strozzi in Venice, in 1542. It is one of the few pure children's portraits in the artist's œuvre, and, with Bronzino's almost contemporaneous portraits of the Medici children, one of the first autonomous portraits of a child in the history of Italian painting.

Clarissa Strozzi (1540–81), the eldest daughter of Roberto Strozzi and Magdalena de' Medici of Florence, was presumably named after her grandmother, Clarissa de' Medici. She was born in Venice, where her parents lived in exile from 1536 to 1542. In a letter dated 6 July 1542, Pietro Aretino, the famous writer and a friend of Titian, wrote to him when he had just finished the portrait and praised its beauty and truth to nature.

The little girl is pictured feeding a biscuit to her dog, standing at a stone table with a marble relief of dancing *putti* in the manner of classical antiquity. She wears a long satin dress, and dangling from her belt on a chain reaching almost to her feet is a scent box known as a musk-apple. Through a window above the table at the right is a view of a park with two swans on a lake and trees extending into the distance. The artist apparently painted over the mountains on the horizon, continuing the blue of the sky down to the trees.

The brightest light in the picture is concentrated in the girl's figure, in the flesh tones and the colours of her dress; the wine-red drapery spread over the table at the right represents the strongest colour tones, which with the dark green of the landscape and the blue of the sky forms a colour triad in the right half of the painting. Its left half, by contrast, is without colour accents, being painted in dark tones that are interrupted only by the tablet at the upper left, which balances the relief at the lower right. The girl's figure is oriented along the vertical axis of the image; her pose and gaze, directed past the spectator, betray self-assurance. The lower edge of the window and the tabletop mark the horizontal axis, and, integrated in this co-ordinated system, the girl's apparently informal, playful pose has extra dignity.

In the same year as the portrait was completed, the Strozzi family were forced to leave the Republic of Venice because their close ties with the French court made staying undesirable. They had settled in Rome by 1544, where Clarissa was married to Cristofano Savelli in 1557. After her death, the painting remained in the family *palazzo* in Rome. In 1641 it was shown in one of the annual exhibitions held in the atrium of St Giovanni Decollato. An engraving of it was made in 1770, by Domenico Cunego. In the early nineteenth century, it was taken from Rome to the Palazzo Strozzi in Florence, where Wilhelm von Bode bought it for the Berlin Gallery in 1878.

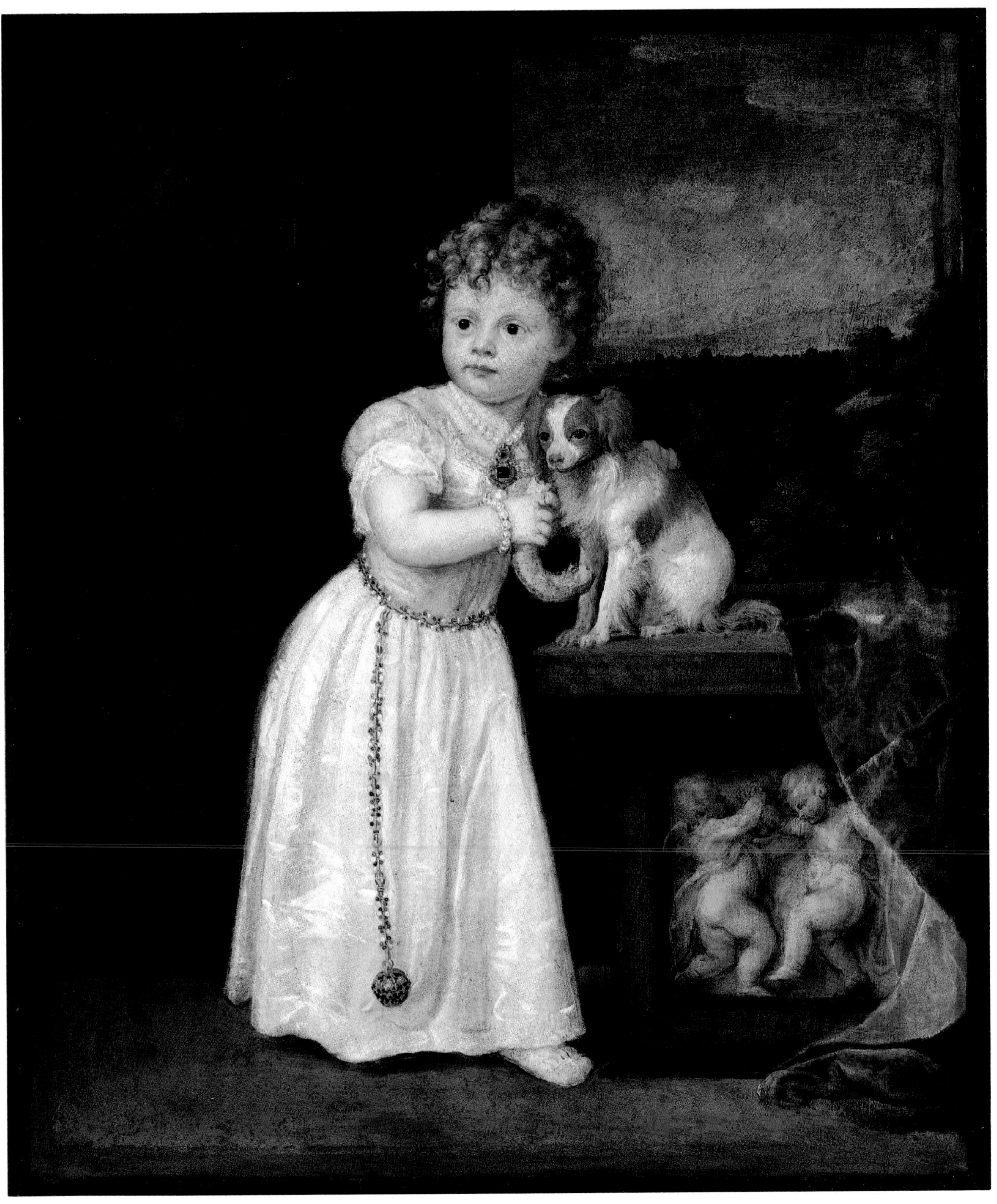

Titiano Vecellio, called Titian
Venus and the Organ Player
*c.*1550–2

Canvas, 115 × 210 cm ($45\frac{1}{4} \times 82\frac{5}{8}$ in)
Signed: 'TITIANVS. F.'
Acquired 1918
Cat. no. 1849

Particularly in his later years, Titian was not above repeating, varying, and developing his own earlier compositions, frequently with the assistance of his workshop, to meet the wishes of his patrons. His depictions of Danae, the *Girl with a Platter of Fruit* (Berlin), of Venus and Adonis, Diana and Callisto, the penitent Magdalene, and The Entombment of Christ, are only a few examples. Another is the series of *Venus* paintings he executed from about 1545 to 1565–70, which included the present canvas.

On 8 December 1545 Titian wrote to Emperor Charles V from Rome to say that he hoped soon to be able to present him personally with a *Venus* he had painted. In 1547, the Emperor invited Titian to the Imperial Diet in Augsburg. Titian travelled with his son, Orazio, from Venice to Augsburg in January 1548, and after the court had retired to Brussels on 12 August they returned to Venice in September. On 1 September, writing to Antoine Perrenot de Granvella, Bishop of Arras, son of the Chancellor of Charles V, and his adviser in Venice, Titian mentioned a *Venus* he had painted by order of the Emperor and had brought from Venice to Augsburg. This work he now apparently sent to Brussels. Subsequently, Titian spent another period in Augsburg in 1550–1, and created a number of other paintings of Venus, which evidently included this one in Berlin.

Recent Italian scholars and, with reservations, H. Wethey (*The Paintings of Titian*, II–III, London, 1971, 1975) assume that the 1545 Venus is identical with the painting Titian mentions in his 1548 letter to Granvella, and that it was given to Granvella by the Emperor. Though C. Hope (1980, see below) doubts this, the Granvella collection indeed contained a *Venus with Organ Player*, which is now in the Prado, Madrid (no. 421, signed). According to Italian scholars and Wethey, this painting is the earliest surviving version in the series and the direct precursor of the Berlin piece, which recent research generally dates about 1550–2. Wethey, however, gives the year 1548–9 on the assumption that it was done in connection with Titian's meeting in Milan with Prince Philip, future king of Spain, in late December 1548, and that it was among the 'certain portraits' for which he received a payment of 1,000 ducats on 29 January 1549. Wethey's hypothesis, and the identification of the organ player with Philip II, has been rejected by C. Hope (in 'Tiziano e Venezia', Venice, 1980).

The relationship of the different versions to one another, their chronological sequence, degree of authenticity, dating, and of course their meaning, have remained controversial to this day. The interpretation suggested by O. Brendel (*Art Bulletin*, 1946) and developed by Panofsky (*Problems in Titian*, 1969), explained the image in terms of the Neo-Platonic idea of rivalry between hearing and seeing beauty when under the spell of love. Most recently this hypothesis has been rejected by C. Hope (1980) and E. Goodman (*Storia dell' Arte*, 49, 1983), who interpret the image in the spirit of Petrarchian love poetry. Both authors believe that the nude female figure in the versions with a male partner (organ or lute player) does not represent Venus but a woman or courtesan whose charms have inspired the gentleman's ardour. Cupid, instead of being an emblem of Venus, becomes the man's messenger, whispering his words of love into the lady's willing ear. Hope thinks the Florence version, which shows Venus (with Cupid) but without a male partner, is a workshop copy of the lost original *Venus*, painted for Charles V in 1545. As this author notes, the folds in the precious, carpet-like drapery on which the female figure rests, are identical in the Florence, Madrid (no. 421, with Cupid), and Cambridge versions, while in each of the other versions (Madrid, no. 420; Berlin, New York) it is arranged differently. Hope concludes that the three first-named paintings are directly derived from the original as far as the drapery is concerned, and that they are much closer to it than the other three, in which he sees second-degree workshop derivations. This would mean that the Berlin version depends on the signed Granvella version in the Prado (no. 421), which according to

Titian (workshop)
Venus with Cupid
Florence, Uffizi

Titian
Woman with Organ Player
Madrid, Museo del Prado, no. 421

Hope is not the original version but a derivation of the first. In contrast to the Berlin painting, the background in the signed Madrid version (and in the other Madrid version) shows a beautifully planted garden with a fountain and poplar-lined avenues. The Berlin and all other versions (Florence, Cambridge, New York) have uncultivated, hilly landscape backgrounds with mountains on the horizon. Hope, like T.Hetzer before him (1940), considers the Berlin *Venus* to be merely a weak workshop product. Nevertheless, its painterly quality and the presence of *pentimenti* (particularly in the figure of the organ player) would tend to support the opinion of those scholars who see in it a product of Titian's own hand (H.Tietze, *Titian*, 1950; R.Pallucchini, *Tiziano*, 1969; Wethey, 1971, 1975).

The two paintings of Venus with a lute player in the Fitzwilliam Museum, Cambridge, and in the Metropolitan Museum, New York, were not done until the 1560s. According to Zeri (*Italian Paintings, Venetian School, The Metropolitan Museum of Art, New York*, 1973), the somewhat earlier Cambridge version is entirely by Titian's own hand, though Pallucchini (1969) and Wethey (1975) detect workshop assistance. The rather later New York painting is generally thought to be an authentic work that Titian left unfinished in his studio and that was later completed by another hand. It shares with the Berlin painting a provenance from the collection of the Princes Pio, Rome, and both are listed in an inventory of 1742 (as being in the Palazzo Falconieri). Wilhelm von Bode purchased the Berlin painting in Vienna, in 1917–18 – the last important Italian painting of the Cinquecento he was able to acquire. As Oskar Kokoschka reports in his memoirs, *Mein Leben* (Munich, 1971, pp. 131–4), the painting was in his studio for a time after it had been brought from Italy to Vienna by the artist Carl Moll before 1914. And before that it is said to have been in the possession of the Italian branch of the Bourbon family.

Giovanni Battista Moroni (1520/4–78)

Don Gabriel de la Cueva, Duke of Alburquerque

1560

Canvas, 114.5 × 90.8 cm (45 × 35¾ in)
Signed and dated: 'M. D. LX.
Io: Bap. Moronus. p.'
Above: 'AQVI ESTO SIN TEMOR
Y DELA MVERTE
NO HE PAVOR.'
Collections of Conte Teodoro Lecchi, Brescia, 1812–26; Sir William Forbes, London, 1827–42; King William II of the Netherlands, The Hague, to 1850; Earl of Warwick, Warwick Castle, 1850–1977
Acquired 1979
Cat. no. 1/79

After an apprenticeship with Moretto in Brescia, Moroni was active in his home town of Bergamo from 1554 to his death. He was, after Titian and Lorenzo Lotto, the most important and original portraitist in Northern Italy during the sixteenth century. While an artist like Tintoretto continued the detached and objective approach of Titian in his numerous official portraits, Moroni developed a portrait style of penetrating realism aimed at capturing the individual personality at its most vital and natural – an aim he shared with another artist who had worked, if temporarily in Bergamo, Lorenzo Lotto, though without emulating Lotto's underlying mood of troubled pessimism.

Bergamo, then part of the Republic of Venice, was an endangered and therefore fortified outpost in the immediate vicinity of Milan, which definitely succumbed to Spanish rule in 1559, at the Peace of Cateau-Cambrésis. Culturally, Bergamo had closer ties with Lombardy. It was in this climate of tense interplay of Venetian and Lombardian influence that Moroni portrayed the local aristocracy, clergy, prosperous citizens, scholars, poets, and tradesmen of many types. Though his sitters included supporters of Venice (G.G. Albani), more were leading representatives of the town's pro-Spanish party (Isotta Brembati, Gian Gerolamo Grumelli).

The clearest manifestation of the Spanish presence in Bergamo, at least as far as Moroni's art is concerned, is his portrait of Don Gabriel de la Cueva y Girón (1525–71). After the death of his older brother, the Fourth Duke of Alburquerque, Don Gabriel became Fifth Duke in 1563, and a year later was appointed Governor and Supreme Commander of Milan, a position he held until his untimely death in 1571, possibly by poisoning, at the age of forty-six. In Milan he represented the royal, civil legislature *vis-à-vis* the municipal government (the Senate) and the Church, whose new and powerful Archbishop, Carlo Borromeo, he had himself introduced into office in 1565. His relations with Borromeo were tense, for he saw the primacy of civil government threatened by the Church.

Moroni's portrait of the Governor is dated 1560, that is, a year after the Peace of Cateau-Cambrésis. At the time, Don Gabriel de la Cueva, Conde des Ledesma y de Huelma, First Marqués de Cuellar, was a Spanish grandee of the highest class, thirty-five years old, and, like his father before him, had just become Vice-Roy, Governor and Capitán General of the Kingdom of Navarra. His identity has been determined on the basis of inscriptions on the front and on the back of a contemporary variant of the portrait, not by Moroni's own hand (Solingen, Deutsches Klingenmuseum), and is corroborated by the sitter's similarity to the portrait medal of the Duke by Pietro Paolo Galeotti (active 1552–70).

Pietro Paolo Galeotti
The Duke of Alburquerque
Portrait medallion
Bologne, Museo Civico

Apart from Ludovico and Gian Federico Madruzzo, nephews of the Prince-Bishop of Trento to whom he devoted full-figure portraits, Alburquerque was by far the highest-ranking personality Moroni ever depicted. This is perhaps his most formal portrait, being based on portrayals of Philip II's court such as Titian's and Anthonis Mor's not only in pose and costume but in its *sosiego*, the calm and disdainfully casual attitude of the Spanish courtier. The figure is seemingly enclosed in the horizontal and vertical pattern of the almost abstract background, against whose cool light-grey the deep black, light brilliant red, and white of his clothes stand out. The high pedestal on which the Duke's hand rests, has, as in several other Moroni portraits, his sitter's motto: 'Here I stand, fearless, and death frightens me not.' This credo is emphasized by Albuquerque's reserved, even mistrustful expression and the icy coldness of his light blue eyes, which look directly past – if not through – the observer. The figure's pose corresponds to that in a portrait of a nobleman also dated 1560 (called *The Unknown Poet*) in Brescia, as well as that in Moroni's portrait of Gerolamo Vertova (Bergamo, private collection).

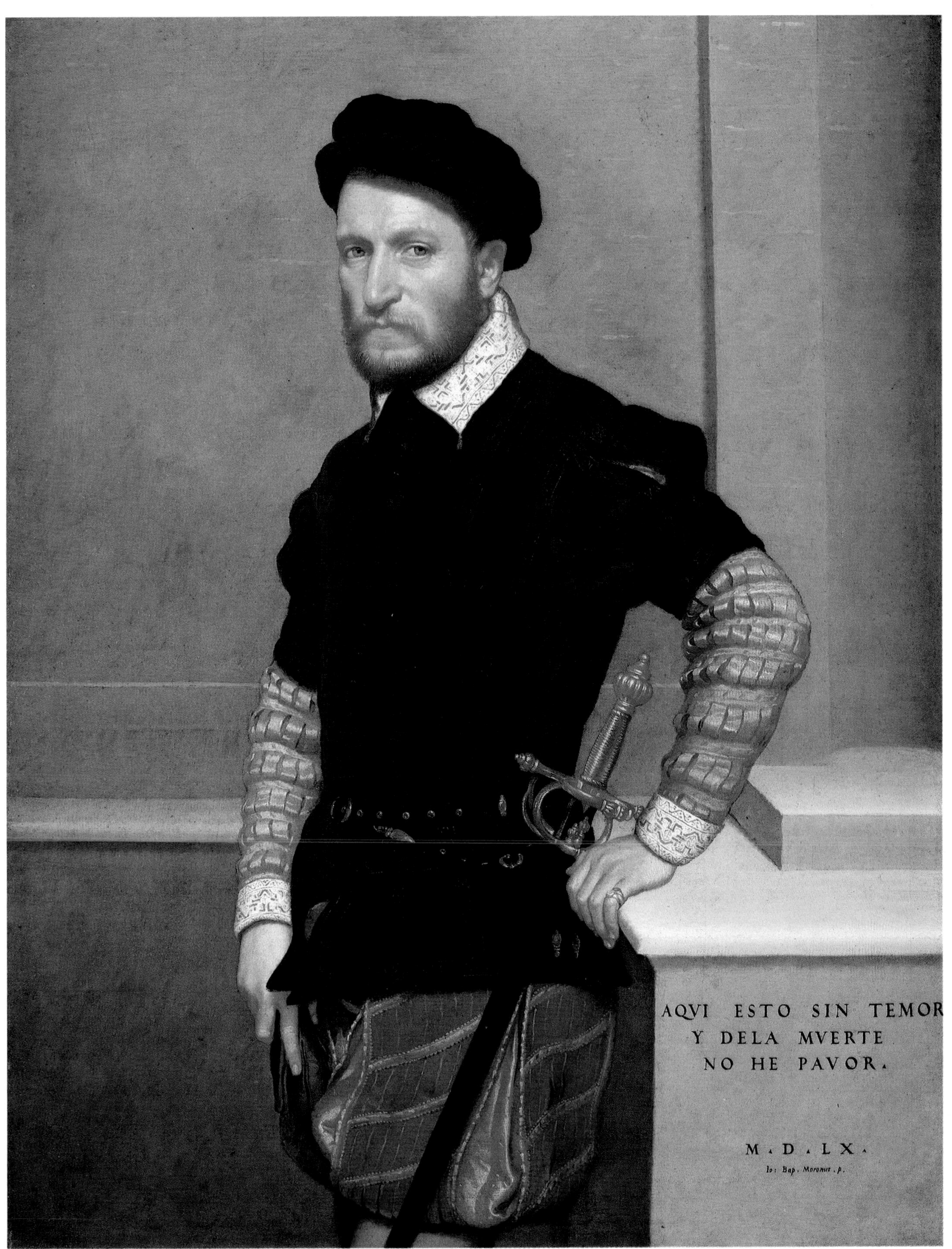
AQVI ESTO SIN TEMOR
Y DELA MVERTE
NO HE PAVOR.
M.D.LX.
Io: Bap. Moronus. p.

Jacopo Robusti, called Tintoretto (1518–94)

The Virgin and Child Adored by the Evangelists St Mark and St Luke

*c.*1570–5

Canvas, 228 × 160 cm ($89\frac{3}{4}$ × 63 in)
Acquired in Venice, 1841
Cat. no. 300

The present painting is one of the few large-format works of the Venetian Cinquecento which the museum was able to recover from the anti-air-raid tower in Berlin-Friedrichshain shortly before the end of the Second World War. It is an altarpiece, which dates *c.*1570–5, i.e. from Tintoretto's mature period, just before he began work on the canvases for the Sala Grande of the Scuola di S. Rocco. Unlike the other large Tintoretto in the Berlin Gallery, *Three Venetian Chamberlains (camerlenghi) before St Mark* from the Palazzo dei Camerlenghi, Venice (1571), which in our opinion was painted with workshop assistance, this altarpiece is entirely by his own hand. The *pentimenti* on the Evangelists' books and at St Luke's shoulder are visible even to the naked eye, and X-ray photographs fully reveal the master's sweeping brushstrokes. The Christ Child's arm, raised in blessing, was seemingly extended further out in the original version, and another figure was apparently planned to the right or behind St Luke. Perhaps the artist originally intended to depict all four Evangelists. It is not known for what chapel or church the paintings was intended.

In contrast to the sweeping brushwork of the preparatory stage visible in the X-ray photograph, the final version shows an unusually striking plasticity of form, particularly in the two figures of the Evangelists, which are modelled in powerful chiaroscuro. The Virgin's pose, as von der Bercken (1942) has said, may have been derived from Michelangelo's *Madonna* in the Medici Chapel, S. Lorenzo (Florence).

The crescent moon and crown of stars simultaneously characterize Mary as the Woman of the Apocalypse (Revelation 12:1–17) and as the *Immaculata.* Though the Immaculate Conception theme was widely included in visual art during the Counter Reformation in the sixteenth century, it did not become one of the principal subjects of Catholic imagery until the seventeenth century. After 1600, its diverse iconographic versions began to be recurrent stereotypes. Tintoretto more than once in the 1570s depicted the Virgin (and Child) with the attributes of the Woman of the Apocalypse and Immaculata, together with adoring saints on clouds – in *The Virgin with St Cosmas and Damian* (Venice, Accademia), and *The Virgin with St Catherine* (formerly Chrysler Collection, now in the art trade). Nevertheless, this combination remained unusual in Italian painting as a whole, and its consequences were few. The only exception seems to be Ludovico Carracci's *Madonna Scalzi* (with St Jerome and St Francis) in the Pinacoteca, Bologna, which appears to have been directly inspired by Tintoretto's Berlin painting.

Tintoretto
The Virgin with Two Evangelists
X-ray photograph
Berlin, Gemäldegalerie SMPK

Adam Elsheimer (1578–1610)

The Holy Family with Angels and the Infant John the Baptist

*c.*1599

Copper, 37.5 × 24.3 cm ($14\frac{3}{4} \times 9\frac{1}{2}$ in) top rounded
Acquired 1928
Cat. no. 2039

In 1598, twenty years old, Adam Elsheimer left his birthplace of Frankfurt, where he had studied with Philipp Uffenbach and associated with the Valckenborch family of painters (Martin I, Frederik and Gillis) and with the Frankenthal painters. The first stop on his way to Italy was Munich. If Frankfurt had brought an intensive involvement with Dürer's art (the *Heller Altar*, graphics), in Munich he came to know the work of Altdorfer. When exactly Elsheimer crossed the Alps and arrived in Venice is still debated, whether still in 1598, or the summer or early autumn of 1599 (K.Andrews, *Adam Elsheimer*, London, 1977; G.F.Koch, *Jahrbuch der Berliner Museen*, 1977). Nor can it be said whether an entry in the Munich Court Pay-Office register about the payment of half a guilder in 'the second half of 1599' to 'Adam Maller [painter] armen Studiosen' in fact refers to Elsheimer (Koch, 1977). If it does, he can have stayed in Venice only eight or nine months – no longer, presumably, than in Munich – for in April 1600 he is recorded as being in Rome, where he lived until his early death. In Venice, Elsheimer got to know the Augsburg painter Johann Rottenhammer (active there in 1589 and 1595–1606), who like him, worked primarily in cabinet format, usually on copper. He saw Dürer's *Madonna with the Rosary* and of course the works of the great sixteenth-century Venetian artists, among which Veronese's in particular made a deep impression on him. His *Holy Family with the Infant John the Baptist*, and the related *Baptism of Christ* in London, are among the few paintings which until recently were generally placed within Elsheimer's Venetian period. Both have similar dimensions, and a similar, upright format with semicircular top.

In the Berlin panel, the artist combines elements of two themes, the Rest on the Flight into Egypt, and the meeting between the Christ Child and the infant St John which legend has it took place on the Holy Family's return. Mary, in a traditional red gown and blue mantle, holds the Christ Child on her lap with her right hand, and with her left the infant John, who embraces Christ. The 'palm tree' she is seated under looks more like a gnarled old oak without much foliage, and without the dates that Veronese, for instance, often included in his depictions (London, art trade; formerly Milan, Borletti Collection), where angels pick the dates and present them on a platter. To the left of Mary, seen in profile, a large angel in a superbly coloured deacon's gown holds the sleeve of her mantle. Before him is the Baptist's symbol, the Lamb of the Lord, with cross and banderole inscribed *Ecce* [*Agnus Dei*]. Joseph, seated with his carpenter's axe on a tree stump at the right, seems lost in thought yet aware of the event taking place before him. His *repoussoir* pose might have been derived from the analogous figure in Altdorfer's *Rest on the Flight* (1510; Berlin). In the Veronese paintings just mentioned, Joseph is in a similar pose, viewed from slightly behind his shoulder, from the side or back. The twisted tree trunk grows obliquely upwards, to end abruptly with a few twigs that separate a heavenly area, the seat of divine effulgence, from the natural blue of the sky to the rugged chasms of the background landscape. A large angel peers over the treetop, pointing with a vigorous gesture, that recalls Tintoretto, to the scene below; and at the right, another angel, also rendered with a foreshortening worthy of Tintoretto, strews blossoms from his seat on an invisible cloud. A ray of divine light passes through his hand to illuminate the falling blossoms. Between the two large angels, who provide a compositional counterweight to the large figures below, a charming and vivacious chain of infant angels with garlands in their hair descends in gentle curves, the last in line presenting a garland to the Child and John in adoration. Just as this meandering line connects the far-distant heaven with the events at the foot of the tree in the foreground, shimmering light suffuses the space and combines figures and landscape into a harmonious unity. Recollections are strong here of Altdorfer and the fantastically delineated landscape details of the Danube school, and, as far as the figures are concerned, of Venetian painters like Veronese and Rottenhammer. The poetic mood of

Adam Elsheimer
The Baptism of Christ
London, National Gallery

the scene, the deep and tender emotions expressed in the figures' faces and gestures, the naturalness and truth to life of the landscape despite its fairy-tale touches, and the intimacy of the small format – these are inimitable characteristics of Elsheimer's art. This small painting, created when he was just over twenty, is one of his first masterworks, even if the stylistic components derived from the Roman art scene which were to become so important to him are not yet evident in this picture.

As the latest investigations have shown (E. Cropper and G. Panofsky-Soergel, *The Burlington Magazine*, 1984, pp. 473–88), both the Berlin painting and the London *Baptism of Christ* were once among the many works by Elsheimer owned by the Flemish painter Karel Oldrago, who settled in Rome in the 1590s, knew Elsheimer, and died in Rome in 1619. Elsheimer himself must have taken both the Berlin and London paintings with him to Rome. Or is it conceivable that he executed them at the very beginning of his stay there?

Annibale Carracci (1560–1609)

River Landscape with Citadel and Bridge

*c.*1600

Canvas, 73 × 143 cm ($28\frac{3}{4} \times 56\frac{1}{4}$ in)
Acquired 1815
Cat. no. 372

Working in Bologna in close collaboration with his cousin Ludovico and his younger brother Agostino, Annibale Carracci created a new figurative style in the 1580s that superseded the hollow formulas of Late Mannerism. By observing real appearances and the achievements of the great Venetian masters (Titian, Veronese, Tintoretto) the Carraccis reformed painting and established a point of departure for Italian Baroque.

In 1595 Cardinal Odoardo Farnese called Annibale to Rome, entrusting him with the execution of frescoes in his palace (Camerino, Gallery). This move to Rome was a turning-point in his career: confronted with Antiquity and the art of Raphael, Annibale Carracci became decisively oriented to the classical ideal of the High Renaissance. His style grew more severe, his compositions more structured, tectonic, more calculated and measured. Despite the opinion of some scholars (Longhi, Posner 1971), the Berlin *Landscape* is not a product of the Bolognese period but was done in Rome in about 1600, commissioned by Cardinal Farnese. It is evidently identical with a painting mentioned in a 1662 list of paintings in the Farnese palace that were to be sent from Rome to Parma, the residence of the Farnese Dukes. Presumably the *Landscape* belonged to the decoration planned as early as 1600 for a room in the so-called Palazzetto Farnese or Casino della Morte, a low annex to the Palazzo Farnese built in 1602–3 on the opposite side of Via Giulia (Whitfield, 1981). During his Bolognese period Annibale had been influenced by Titian's and Paolo Fiammingo's Venetian landscapes as well as those of the Bolognese artist Niccolò del' Abate, creating landscapes with hunters and fishermen, informal slices of nature in which the architectural element played very little part. In the Berlin *Landscape*, by contrast, a citadel rising at exactly the centre of the composition and underlined by a group of trees, gives the pictorial space a central emphasis with two lateral vistas and misty blue mountains on the horizon. These landscape views are in turn framed at the sides by groups of tall trees. The architecture of the citadel and the twin-arched bridge connecting it with the shore of the river on the right, were quite obviously inspired by the Tiber island (*isola tiberina*) with Ponte Fabricio in Rome (Whitfield, 1980, 1981). Groups of figures emphasize the three vertical aspects of the composition: a young, elegantly dressed couple playing music on the left; a heavy rowing boat with figures in the centre; and another boat with figures at the right. Further evidence that the picture was painted in Rome is the fact that another Bolognese artist of the Carracci school, G.F.Grimaldi, paraphrased Annibale's *Landscape* in about 1635–40, in a fresco in the Palazzo Peretti, Rome.

With the lunette-shaped landscape of *The Flight into Egypt*, in the Galleria Doria (from the chapel of the Palazzo Aldobrandini, *c.*1603–4), the Berlin *Landscape* is the most significant early example of classical landscape painting in Rome and one of the most monumental landscapes executed before Poussin. It strongly influenced not only Annibale's pupil and follower Domenichino, but also Poussin himself, not to mention Claude Lorrain. Despite the tectonic stringency of this 'structured' landscape, Annibale managed to retain the freshness of impression, translucency of surface, atmospheric vivacity, and the spontaneous rendering of details that characterize his early Bolognese landscapes.

G.F.Grimaldi
Landscape
Fresco
Rome, Palazzo Peretti-Fiano-Almagià

Michelangelo Merisi, called Il Caravaggio (1571–1610)
Amor Victorious
1602–3

Canvas, 156 × 113 cm ($61\frac{3}{8}$ × $44\frac{1}{2}$ in)
Acquired with the Giustiniani Collection, 1815
Cat. no. 369

Caravaggio came to Rome in about 1592–3 from Lombardy, where he had been deeply impressed by the art of Savoldo and Lotto, Romanino and Moretto. For a time he assisted in the workshop of the leading Late Mannerist, Giuseppe Cesari, but soon broke with the artificial rules of Roman-Florentine Mannerism to develop an absolutely new approach. His direct recourse to the reality of natural appearances, and his use of concentrated light and high-contrast chiaroscuro, revolutionized Roman art in about 1600 and made him, with Annibale Carracci, Elsheimer and Rubens, one of the pioneers of seventeenth-century painting. His first important public commission, the paintings for the Contarelli Chapel in S. Luigi del Francesi (lateral paintings 1599; two versions of central altarpiece 1602 and 1602–3), and his paintings for the side walls of the Cerasi Chapel in S. Maria del Popolo (1600–1), established his fame. Influential families of the Roman nobility bought and ordered pictures from him – the Mattei, Borghese and Barberini, but above all the Marchese Vincenzo Giustiniani (1564–1637), and his brother, Cardinal Benedetto Giustiniani (1544–1621), who were among his most important patrons and the most progressive art collectors in Rome. Of the five original Caravaggios which the King of Prussia purchased *en bloc* from the Giustiniani Collection in Paris in 1815, one, *Doubting Thomas*, came to Sanssouci in Potsdam. Of the four others which entered the Berlin Gallery collection, three were destroyed by fire in May 1945, in the Friedrichshain bunker. One remained – *Amor Victorious*, painted in 1602–3.

It shows the youthful god of love smiling in triumph, as Virgil wrote, over all – '*Omnia vincit amor*' (*Eclogae* 10:69) – over science, art, power and fame. Scattered at his feet like trophies (said the artist's biographer, Bellori, in 1672) are the instruments and symbols of the liberal arts, the laurels of immortal, particularly literary, fame, and armour representing the art of war and the glory for those skilled at it. At the left lie a musical score and two stringed instruments, a violin (invented in Cremona shortly before) and a lute; in front of them is a square and compass, tools of geometry. Behind Amor's right leg, half obscured by the laurel wreath, is an open manuscript closely filled with writing, and a reed pen; to his right at the edge of the painting, behind his extended left leg, are a crown and sceptre as symbols of terrestrial power. Amor seems to be seated on a blue globe studded with stars, that is, triumphing over the entire universe; but the celestial globe also symbolizes the art of astronomy. Incidentally, the artist seems to have added the globe as an afterthought, because the boy is not really sitting on its rounded surface but on the edge of a table or pedestal covered with drapery on which he props his left leg. As X-ray photographs and brushmarks showing through the final paint layer indicate, this edge once extended beyond the figure to the left, but then was painted over, and replaced by the globe. The boy's playfully coy, suggestively challenging pose – a travesty of Michelangelo's *Victor* (Florence, Palazzo Vecchio) – and his ambiguously scornful smile, together with the fact that Caravaggio's model was a boy of the streets, strengthens the interpretation suggested in the Giustiniani inventory (1638) and developed particularly by W.Friedlaender (*Caravaggio Studies*, 1955), that sensual love scorns human strivings towards moral and intellectual perfection. Besides this most widespread interpretation, recent commentators have pointed out the latent homo-erotic aspects in this and Caravaggio's other related early works (Posner, 1971). The conception of the image, whose extreme naturalism had no precedent, immediately caused literary reverberations and inspired numerous imitations on the part of Roman, Florentine, and Bolognese painters, whose figures of Amor were already thought by some contemporary commentators to represent the Genius of the Arts.

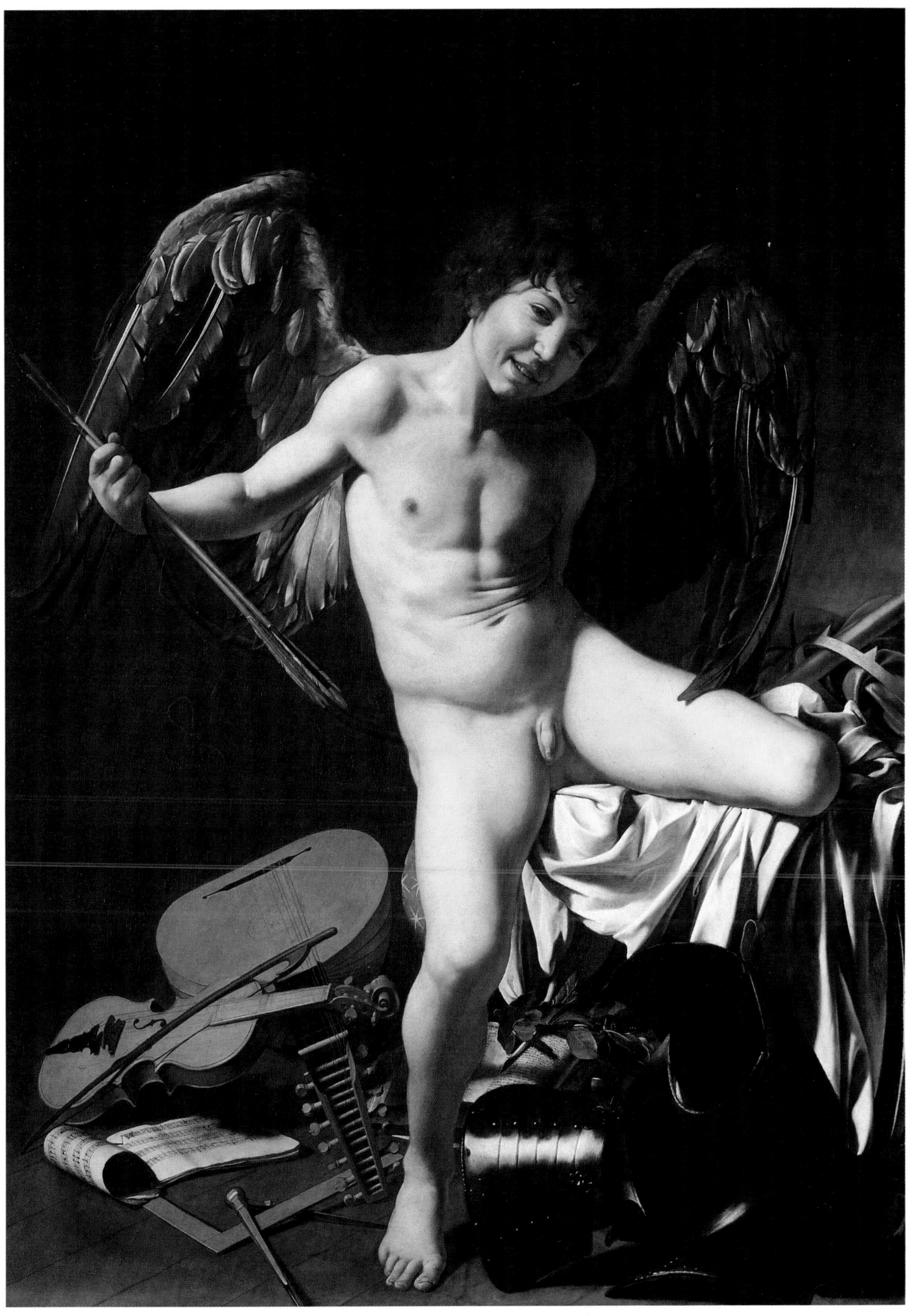

Orazio Gentileschi (1563–1639)

David with the Head of Goliath

*c.*1610

Copper, 36 × 28 cm (14$\frac{1}{8}$ × 11 in)
Acquired 1914
Property of the
Kaiser-Friedrich-Museums-Verein
Cat. no. 1723

Gentileschi was certainly the most important and independent of those artists in Rome who were influenced by Caravaggio. He knew Caravaggio personally and sometimes worked in competition with him during the first years of the century, until Caravaggio's flight from Rome in 1606. Yet he had not come into contact with his art until 1600–1, when Caravaggio's first publicly accessible works in Roman churches became known. While Gentileschi had been indebted to Roman Mannerism until 1600, in 1600–5 Gentileschi's style gradually began to take on Caravaggesque traits, a development that reached its peak in the years 1606–15, the period to which the present painting belongs.

Besides Caravaggio's influence and his own Tuscan heritage, during the first decade Gentileschi was impressed with the work of Adam Elsheimer, a German painter active in Rome – especially as regards the element of landscape and the use of small pictures on copper. *David with the Head of Goliath* is one of these.

It shows David bending over the giant's head, pondering his deed and its consequences. In comparison with previous interpretations of the theme, in which the action was represented at its brutal climax, Gentileschi's more introspective interpretation represented a new iconographical type, that is similar to Guido Reni's painting in the Louvre (*c.*1605) and goes back to Caravaggio's painting of the subject in the Galleria Borghese, Rome, which has David holding Goliath's just-severed and apparently not yet lifeless head up towards the spectator with a look of mixed disgust and pain. Yet instead of this direct look that follows the movement of his arm, Gentileschi, like Reni, gives David an attitude of pensiveness, turns his face out of the frontal plane to pure profile.

Unlike Caravaggio, whose genius would not allow him to repeat himself, Gentileschi frequently painted replicas or variants of his own compositions. The small copper panel in Berlin is just such a variant of his large painting with a life-size figure in the Galleria Spada, Rome. There, David's figure is cut off below the knee, and his right foot is not visible. The landscape background is completely different; the dark foil setting off the figure at the right does not consist of a grotto in a rugged cliff as here, but of a dark, tangled wood with two tree-trunks that catch the light, and dense foliage that fans out over the sky towards the left. Because of the full-length figure in the Berlin picture, some commentators have suggested that the Roman *David* may have been cropped along the bottom edge. However, this is apparently not the case. Gentileschi first conceived an even smaller format, as may be seen from the canvas, which consists of a central piece with strips of differently textured canvas added on all sides. Originally, the head of Goliath rested at the bottom edge of the canvas. In this seminal version, eye contact between David and the head of Goliath still existed, but it was weakened when the image was enlarged; in the Berlin version there is no eye-contact at all. Only now did the artist expand the figure to a full, standing figure, and alter David's stance by bringing his legs closer together, and making the figure more slender. Moreover, he altered the perspective by lowering the horizon line. The figure at this time was also given a completely different background, of that striated, slate-like, cool grey stone that Gentileschi was so fond of painting. He changed the position of Goliath's head, depicting it face down on the flat rock where David rests his foot. His sling lies in front of it, a detail absent from the Roman painting. David's right hand with the steel-grey sword is starkly silhouetted against the bright, partly overcast sky, and light from the right gleams on the tip of the blade.

Orazio Gentileschi
David with the Head of Goliath
Rome, Galleria Spada

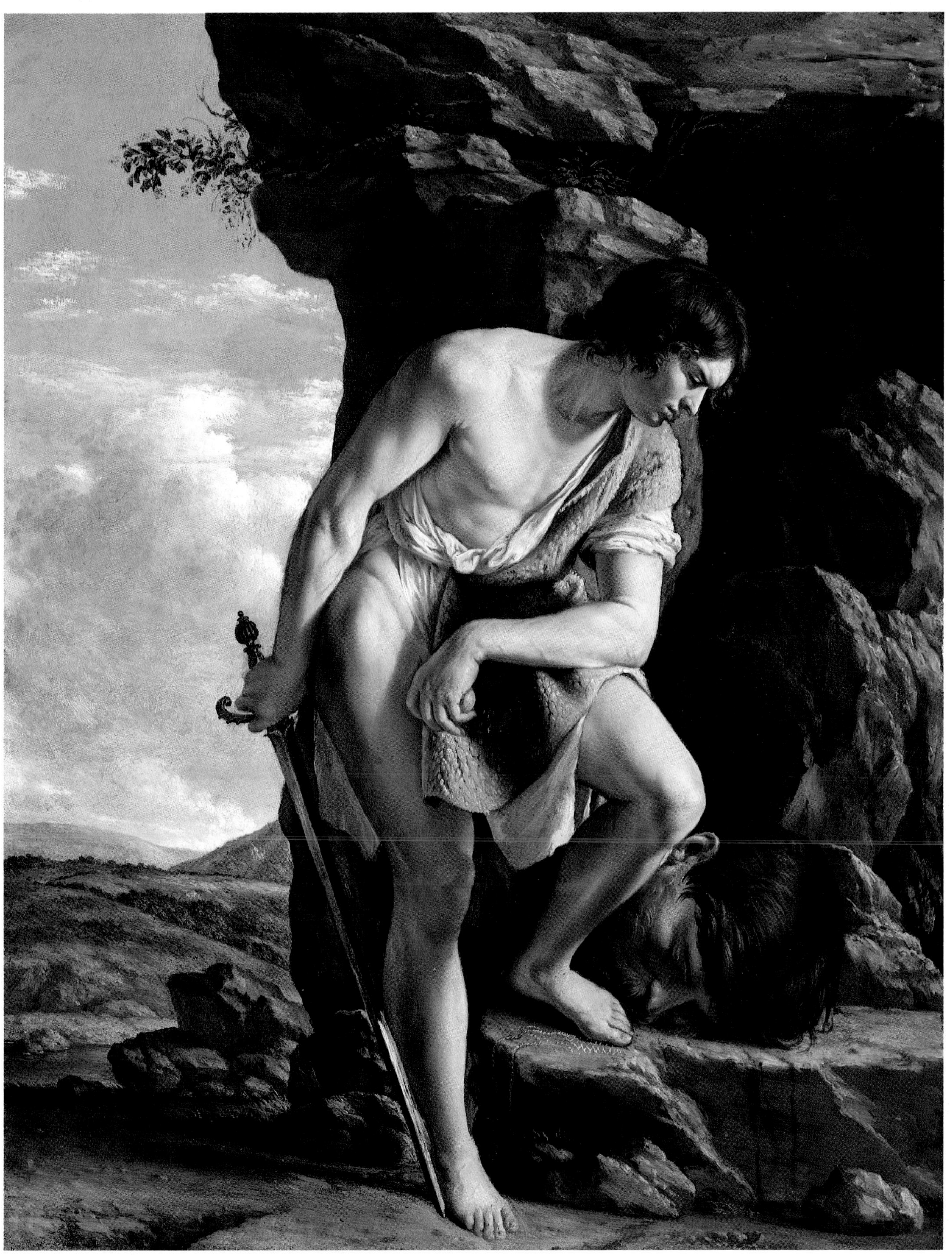

Georges de La Tour (1593–1652)
Old Peasant Couple Eating
*c.*1620

Canvas, 74 × 87 cm (29⅛ × 34¼ in)
Acquired 1976
Cat. no. 1/76

The work of Georges de La Tour, the great realist from Lorraine, named *peintre ordinaire du roi* in 1639 and extolled as a *peintre fameux* in 1644, fell into oblivion within decades after his death. Its rediscovery in the twentieth century was spurred by an essay written in 1915 by Hermann Voss, the outstanding connoisseur of Baroque painting who a few years later became a curator in the Berlin Gallery and whose efforts led to *The Finding of St Sebastian* being acquired in 1928 – one of those late *nocturnes* that once established La Tour's fame as the greatest *peintre de la réalité* alongside the Le Nain brothers. After the memorable 1972 La Tour exhibition in Paris, the Berlin painting proved to be a qualitatively inferior studio replica or copy of the original now in the Louvre, but the Berlin Gallery was able to compensate for the downgrading of this work in 1976 by buying *Old Peasant Couple Eating*. Unquestionably an authentic work of La Tour's earliest period, it was only discovered in 1974, after the Paris exhibition and the subsequent publication of monographs. This is one of the realistic 'daylight' scenes in which the artist depicted inhabitants of his home province of Lorraine: humble people, peasants, beggars, and itinerant musicians impoverished by war, plundering, and epidemics.

The old couple are almost life-size, in half-figure, on a tightly constricted format that brings them into extreme proximity to the spectator. Their simple meal consists of yellow split-peas eaten with short spoons from brown clay bowls. The old man on the right, bending forward, his shoulders hunched, looks down with a long-suffering, embittered gaze, holding his cane in a calloused, gouty hand. His wife, her spoon half-way to her mouth, pauses as if interrupted, the tendons in her neck protruding and her deep-set, dim eyes meeting ours. Bright, harsh and cool light falling obliquely from the left throws the couple's features into relief, revealing every wrinkle of their leathery skin, and glowing on the white cloak over the man's shoulder and on the greyed white of his wife's scarf.

The setting is indeterminate, in keeping with the tradition of Caravaggio's half-figure scenes, which may have been passed on to La Tour through the intermediary of Gerard Seghers of Antwerp, or by Hendrick Terbrugghen, who returned to Holland from Italy in 1614. The brushwork, incisive, nervous, clearly articulated and with very fine nuances in the faces and hands, grows much broader, more powerful and sweeping in the clothes, while the grey background has been applied lightly over a yellowish tone that shines around the contours of the heads.

The painting was executed at the start of La Tour's development in about 1620, when he had just moved from his birthplace, Vic-sur-Seille, to the burgeoning royal residence, Lunéville, where he enjoyed the status of master and spent the rest of his life. Yet despite its early date, *Old Peasant Couple Eating* became one of his more known works. Three seventeenth-century copies exist – one in the Musée Historique Lorain in Nancy, one in a German private collection and another in a French private collection. The subject of beggars and itinerant musicians performing or quarrelling originated in sixteenth-century Netherlandish art. In early seventeenth-century Lorraine it was particularly widespread: in the work of the court artist Jacques Bellange, and in that of Jacques Callot, who had returned from Florence in 1621. Callot's prints, especially his beggar sequence of 1622, were known to La Tour, though he definitely rejected their Mannerist, courtly tradition.

The allegorical significance of the image, its moral, is probably that poverty and need are human errors, self-inflicted sufferings that can be avoided. We are well informed about La Tour's prosperity and social behaviour. There is no reason to assume that the artist or his potential patron or buyer sympathized with the poor people he portrayed. The works most closely related to this one in artistic, thematic, and chronological terms are the two individual figures of peasants in San Francisco (probably inspired by popular street-theatre), and the *Beggars' Brawl* in the Getty Museum, Malibu (*c.*1625–30).

Jacques Callot
Two Beggar-women, 1622
Etching

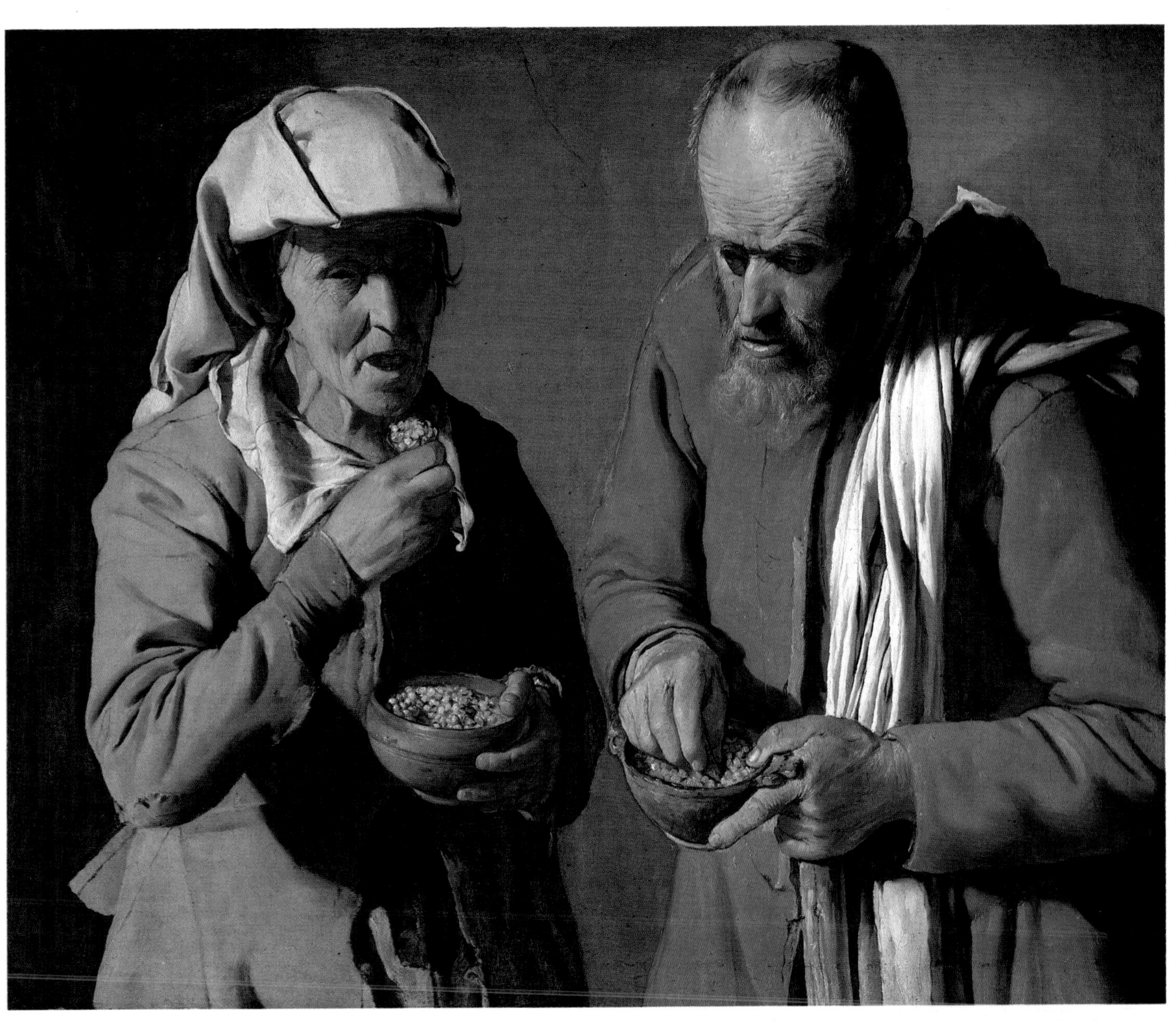

Claude Gellée, called Claude Lorrain (1600–82)
Landscape on the Italian Coast in Morning Light
1642

Canvas, 97 × 131 cm ($38\frac{1}{8} \times 51\frac{1}{2}$ in)
Inscribed: 'CLAUDE. IN. F/ROMAE 1642'
Acquired 1881
Cat. no. 448 B

With Poussin and his brother-in-law Gaspard Dughet, Claude Lorrain was the third great French painter of the seventeenth century to spend most of his life in Rome and to die there. Unlike Poussin but like Dughet he was exclusively a landscape painter. During a creative career of almost fifty years, he brought the classical approach to landscape developed by Paul Bril, Elsheimer, Annibale Carracci, Domenichino and Agostino Tassi to one of its highpoints. His landscape style, devoted above all to rendering the effects of sunlight emerging on the far horizon, suffusing great spaces, was an antipode to the more tectonically structured landscapes of Dughet and Poussin, although for a while his style shows certain affinities with the works of both of them.

Claude was born in 1600 in the still independent Dukedom of Lorraine. He was sent to Rome in 1613, where he was apparently apprenticed to Agostino Tassi; then after working as an assistant to Goffredo Wals in Naples (1618–22), he returned in 1625 for a year and a half to Nancy, Lorraine's capital. The first painting he dated after his return to Rome is inscribed 1629. After assisting on frescoes as an apprentice and journeyman, Claude turned exclusively to easel painting, doing works for the King of Spain, the Pope, cardinals, noblemen, and collectors in Italy and France. In about 1635 he began to record the compositions of his paintings in subsequent drawings, which he collected in an album called *Liber Veritatis* (London, British Museum) that contains practically all the works he did from 1637 to his death.

Before the Second World War the Berlin Gallery owned two important works by Claude Lorrain. One, a large, early landscape painted in about 1630–5 for the Marchese Vincenzo Giustiniani, was until recently believed to have been destroyed by fire in 1945, but it survives, somewhat damaged, in the Bode-Museum in East Berlin. The painting now in West Berlin, dated 1642, is included as no. 64 in Claude's *Liber Veritatis*.

The complicated genesis of this painting begins with a pen-and-wash drawing (New York, private collection), a composition sketch of the landscape without figures. Its design basically conforms to that of the painting, though some details have been radically altered. The flanking trees in the right foreground, for instance, are developed much further in the painting than in the drawing.

A woman dressed as a shepherdess sits on a rock in the foreground, listening to a shepherd play the flute. Behind them a man with a stick over his shoulder walks across a bridge; at the other end of the bridge two more people are visible. To the shepherd's right a staff or rod is stuck in the ground, apparently for no reason. Yet a glance at the X-ray photograph of the painting and Claude's drawing of it in the *Liber Veritatis* reveals its meaning. In the drawing, the shepherd is replaced by a young man clad in a short garment resembling a Greek *chiton* that leaves his left shoulder bare. His face is turned in profile to the young woman, to whom he presents something with his extended right hand. In his left-hand he holds a staff in exactly the same position as the disembodied staff in the painting. The X-ray photograph, by contrast, reveals his left hand in a gesture of pointing, while the female figure appears to be holding a stick in her right hand and resting it on her shoulder. Her legs are crossed differently in the drawing and in the X-ray, and her left arm is slightly extended. In the drawing she looks up at the man.

We have interpreted this scene as representing the meeting of Judah and Tamar, told in the Book of Genesis (38:14–20). On the way to Timnath, Judah meets Tamar, his widowed sister-in-law, sitting by the side of the road. Not recognizing her, he takes her for a harlot and desires her, promising to reward her with a kid from his flock. When she demands the further pledge of his signet ring, bracelets, and staff, he gives them to her and seduces her. The moral of the story is in the apparent sinfulness of its virtuous heroine, and the hero's shame when he discovers his mistake and its injustice.

Claude Lorrain
Composition Drawing
New York, Private Collection

Claude Lorrain
Drawing from the 'Liber Veritatis'
(detail)
London, British Museum

In an early phase of painting, as the X-ray shows, the artist represented Judah giving Tamar his bracelet, and Tamar already holding his staff. In a second, finished stage, similar to that recorded in the *Liber Veritatis* drawing, he is giving her the bracelet while holding his staff. The alteration of this group in the painting to a pastoral shepherd couple, was undoubtedly carried out in the seventeenth century. Though theoretically it could have been done by another hand, perhaps at the request of a patron, the change was probably made by Claude himself. When the painting was cleaned in 1952, the shepherd's staff, which had been deleted and painted over but which bled through the paint layer, reappeared. According to the *Liber Veritatis*, the painting was intended for a Parisian patron; from the early eighteenth century to 1818 it was in England, then came to Paris, where it was acquired by Wilhelm von Bode in 1881.

The Berlin painting (L.V. 64) was long assumed to be a companion piece to a painting recorded in drawing no. 65 of the *Liber*, which evidently originated in the same year and was also destined for Paris, but until recently it was thought to be lost (since 1784). Its subject, as in L.V. 65, was Tobias with the Angel, that is, another Old Testament scene. This painting was recently rediscovered in a private collection by Roethlisberger (*Master Drawings*, 1978); but though it was executed in the same year and is practically the same size as the Berlin landscape, Roethlisberger no longer believes that it is a companion piece.

Nicolas Poussin (1594–1665)
Landscape with the Evangelist St Matthew
1640

Canvas, 99 × 135 cm (39 × 53⅛ in)
Acquired 1873
Cat. no. 478 A

After a lyrical and romantic phase in his early years, Poussin turned more and more to a classical ideal in the tradition of Annibale Carracci and Raphael. Though he did not begin to paint autonomous landscape compositions until the late 1630s, just before his Paris stay (1640–2), landscape has always played a significant role as a background, heightening the poetic mood particularly of his early, neo-Venetian works.

In early seventeenth-century Rome, where Poussin worked from 1624 on, new departures in landscape painting were introduced by some of the most important and advanced artists of the age. There were the northerners, Elsheimer and Paul Bril, whose innovative approach led by way of Agostino Tassi to the atmospheric, romantic, light-suffused compositions of Claude Lorrain, Poussin's great French opposite. And there were the Bolognese figure painters Annibale Carracci and Domenichino, who conceived more stringently structured landscapes that led to the 'heroic' style of Poussin and his brother-in-law Gaspard Dughet, a style that largely determined the look of later Roman landscape painting.

Poussin's landscapes were painted primarily during the 1640s and early 1650s, at a time when his work exuded a great inner calm, clarity, and classical balance, a phase that lay between the large, classicizing, frequently multi-figured compositions of the 1630s and the compositions of his late period with their tragic mood. The Berlin *Landscape with the Evangelist St Matthew* is the earliest surviving example of this intermediate phase.

That the Berlin painting is related to Poussin's *Landscape with St John on Patmos* in Chicago has been known for a long time. Some art historians think they might both have belonged to an unfinished sequence of landscapes with the four Evangelists. Since the Berlin painting is recorded as being in the Barberini family since 1671, some had conjectured that both it and the Chicago painting were executed for Cardinal Francesco Barberini, one of the two powerful nephews of Pope Urban VIII. The most recent findings (Barroero, 1979; Corradini, 1979) indicate that both paintings were paid for on 28 October 1640 (the day Poussin left for Paris) by the Pope's private prelate, Monsignor Gian Maria Roscioli (Foligno 1609–Rome 1644). In all events, Roscioli entered payment of 40 scudi for the two paintings in his cash-book on that date. This would indicate that he, not Cardinal Barberini, commissioned the works. Roscioli owned a considerable art collection that included several works by Poussin. In his last will and testament, dictated the day before his untimely death on 25 September 1644, he bequeathed the Berlin painting to Cardinal Antonio Barberini Senior, the brother of Urban VIII. When Barberini died in 1646 the painting went to his nephew, Cardinal Antonio Barberini Junior, who was Cardinal Francesco's younger brother and lived in the Palazzo Barberini ai Giubbonari, also known as Casa Grande. The painting hung there until his death in 1671. From 1692 at the latest, it was in the Palazzo Barberini alle Quattro Fontane. The Chicago painting was evidently among those in Roscioli's collection sold by his brother after his death. It soon came to France, where Louis de Chatillon (1639–1734) engraved it. While the Berlin painting was still in the Palazzo Barberini, Gaspard Dughet made a chalk drawing after it, though he finished only the background landscape (Kunstmuseum Düsseldorf). From the Palazzo Barberini, the Berlin landscape passed in 1812 through inheritance to the Palazzo Sciarra, where it was acquired for the Berlin Gallery in 1873.

Unlike Claude Lorrain, but like Dughet in his later, Poussin-influenced landscapes and like Salvator Rosa in many of his, Poussin has employed a very high horizon line bounded by hills, from which the eye follows the dominant lines of the meandering river into the foreground. The two figures here, St Matthew and an angel holding his Gospel, are surrounded by fragments of antique columns and pedestals; their central position is accentuated by a temple ruin reaching above the horizon. In a landscape suffused with

Nicolas Poussin
Landscape with St John on Patmos
Chicago, The Art Institute of Chicago

Gaspard Dughet
Chalk Drawing after Poussin's Landscape with St Matthew the Evangelist
Düsseldorf, Kunstmuseum

great peace and clarity, Poussin has at once inimitably captured the appearance and mood of the Tiber Valley north of Rome (near Acqua Acetosa) and raised it to a timeless world.

Bernardo Strozzi (1582–1644)
Salome with the Head of John the Baptist
After 1630

Canvas, 124 × 94 cm ($48\frac{7}{8}$ × 37 in)
Acquired in Rome, 1914
Property of the
Kaiser-Friedrich-Museums-Verein
Cat. no. 1727

Though Strozzi's works have always been admired above all for their painterly qualities – sweeping, sumptuous brushwork, rich impasto, softly modelled volumes, and luminous colour – his style went through many changes. In Genoa, he began in a style on the threshold between Late Mannerism and Early Baroque, whose cool, glistening colour and polished modelling was influenced by Beccafumi's frescoes, by the paintings of Barocci and his Siennese followers Vanni and Salimbeni (then temporarily active in Genoa); later he was inspired by the Milanese artists Cerano and G.C.Procaccini. A naturalistic, sometimes even rustic phase followed, characterized by genre subjects with still-life objects, including kitchen scenes, that was influenced both by Flemish painting and by Fiasella (who had returned to Genoa from Rome in 1616). Strozzi's palette now became warmer, darker, and more harmoniously composed. During his later years in Genoa, he was influenced by the Genoese works of Rubens and van Dyck, then by those of Feti; but when he arrived in Venice, the great sixteenth-century tradition represented by Veronese and Titian became predominant.

Strozzi fled to Venice when his mother died in 1630. As he was a Capucine monk who had been granted lay status solely to care for his mother, he would have been forced to return to the monastery. *Salome with the Head of John the Baptist* was among the works of his early Venice years. While fourteenth- and fifteenth-century artists usually depicted Herod, Tetrarch of Galilee and Salome's stepfather, watching Salome dance at a feast, followed by John's execution and the presentation of his head to Salome or Herodias, Strozzi's image exemplifies a type developed from the early sixteenth century in Northern Italy. It emerged in Lombardy with Leonardo's followers, but particularly in Venice, with the Giorgione circle, the young Titian, Sebastiano del Piombo, and others. They reduced the scene to Salome in half-figure, holding John's head on a salver, either alone or accompanied by the executioner or a maid, and often with an expression of remorse or sorrow. Caravaggio in Rome began to employ this half-figure conception shortly after 1600, deepening the remorse in Salome's expression and painting the maid's features as if petrified in pain. Salome became a female counterpart to David, musing over Goliath's head. Strozzi's *Salome*, for a long time erroneously referred to as *Judith*, is indebted both to Caravaggio's conception and to the Venetian tradition of the early sixteenth century. In Strozzi's painting, too, the maid's expression of melancholy sorrow is stronger than that of Salome herself, who gingerly fondles a lock of the Baptist's hair.

A half-figure image of the same dimensions, *Hagar with the Angel* (Seattle, Museum of Art, Kress Collection), has frequently been called a companion piece to the Berlin *Salome*.

Johann Liss (*c.*1597–1631)
The Ecstasy of St Paul
*c.*1628–9

Canvas, 80 × 58.5 cm ($31\frac{1}{2}$ × 23 in)
Acquired 1919
Cat. no. 1858

J.Falck
The Ecstasy of St Peter,
*c.*1655
Engraving after D.Feti

Like the two other German artists, Elsheimer before him and, later, Schönfeld, Johann Liss of Oldenburg (Holstein) spent most of his productive life in Italy – primarily in Venice, but also in Rome. In 1616 he worked in Amsterdam and Haarlem, then presumably spent the years 1617–19 in Antwerp, where he was impressed by Jordaens's early painting. He then went by way of Paris to Venice, where his presence was recorded in 1621. During a stay in Rome (probably 1622–5), Liss was influenced by followers of Caravaggio such as Nicolas Regnier (who himself moved to Venice in 1626); Liss also became acquainted with the Baroque style of Guercino and Lanfranco, and with landscape painters of the Elsheimer circle such as Poelenburgh. His work in Venice was closely allied to that of the Mantuan, Feti (d. Venice 1623), whom he may already have met during his first years there; and it was influenced by the great sixteenth-century Venetian tradition, particularly as represented by Veronese.

The Ecstasy of St Paul stems from the final years of the artist's life. Towards the end of II Corinthians (12:2–4), St Paul says of himself, 'I knew a man in Christ above fourteen years ago . . . caught up to the third heaven. And I knew such a man . . . caught up into paradise, and [he] heard unspeakable words, which it is not lawful for a man to utter.' Liss depicts St Paul in the corner of his study, aroused by a vision of the Trinity in blinding light and glorious colour, with angels descending from on high. His hands are spread in a gesture partly of fright, partly of incredulous astonishment. A small book is open on a table, others are visible in the background, and pages are strewn on the floor in front of him. As one great angel pulls a curtain aside at the upper right, another, seen from the back and half in shade, has descended to Paul at the left, playing the lute. The descending diagonal of angels' figures crosses an ascending diagonal that connects the figure of St Paul with the Trinity group. In terms of colour, the deeper tones of the shadow at the bottom and right – a dark violet in Paul's mantle, the green of the curtain, and a dark blue in the angel to the left – culminate in lighter and more intense colours above – pinkish lilac in the violin-playing angel, white in the other angels, and a bright golden yellow in the representation of heaven. Fluent brushwork, the light, flocculent forms of the billowing, fluttering garments and swelling limbs of the angels, the gradual transitions from light to dark, and the luminous palette, merge into a whirling, sweeping, gloriously festive Baroque composition that anticipates the Venetian Settecento.

The composition is obviously related to Liss's almost contemporaneous *Vision of St Jerome*, his only known altar painting (S. Nicolò da Tolentino, Venice). Similarities between the angels in *The Ecstasy of St Paul* and those in Lanfranco's altarpiece in the Capucine church in Rome (1628–30) have led some critics to think that Liss may have made a second trip to Rome, in or after 1628 (Safarik, 1975). As a companion piece to Feti's *Ecstacy of St Peter*, Liss's painting was engraved in about 1655 by J.Falck for a volume devoted to the collection of Gerrit Reynst (1604–58), a wealthy merchant of Amsterdam. Reynst's brother, Jan, had lived in Venice for some time after 1625, and he may have acquired the painting there after Liss's death.

Diego Velázquez (1599–1660)
Portrait of a Lady
(Countess Monterrey ?)
*c.*1630–3

Canvas, 123 × 99 cm ($48\frac{1}{2}$ × 39 in)
Acquired 1887
Cat. no. 413 E

Standing beside a chair in front of a neutral, greyish-beige background, a distinguished middle-aged lady looks out at us with a slight turn of the head. She is portrayed at three-quarter's length, turned to the left; in keeping with the then conventional formula of courtly Spanish portraits, she rests her right hand on the back of the chair, and lets her left fall to her side, holding a closed fan that is just discernable. Her elaborate gown is of black, patterned velvet, with plastron and sleeves of bluish-black, and gold brocade embroidered with stars and trimmed with gold lace. She also wears a jet brooch on a long, heavy, golden chain formed of rosettes, a rose made of diamonds in her hair, and pearl earrings, a pearl necklace, and exquisite rings.

Velázquez, court painter to Philip IV in Madrid and the outstanding artist in Spain's golden age of painting, executed this portrait in the early 1630s, after returning from his first journey to Italy. It was the period of his great equestrian portraits of King Philip IV and the Duke of Olivares, and his hunting portraits of the King and his children. After Caravaggesque beginnings, his art had developed to full maturity. The strong chiaroscuro contrasts had given way to a diffuse daylight brightness, a silvery-grey tone that lay over local colours and unified them. The Berlin portrait belongs to this silver-grey phase, as can be seen from its predominant combination of black gown and light grey background, from which the brightly illuminated, softly modelled face framed by dark hair and the small, delicate hands emerge as the main accents. The face is modelled with that absolutely free, fluent brushwork so characteristic of Velázquez, while the drawing and modelling of the hands and extensive parts in the garment show a certain stolid dryness. This last trait has led some critics to believe that these passages were executed by Velázquez's workshop, probably by Juan Bautista del Mazo, Velázquez's principal assistant who in 1634 became the artist's son-in-law.

The identity of the model was long debated, and is still uncertain. While early commentators, relying on an inscription, thought she was the artist's wife, later opinion tended to identify her as Doña Inés de Zúniga, wife of Conde Duque de Olivares, Philip's powerful Minister of State. It is more probable, however, that the artist's model was Doña Leonora de Guzmán, Countess of Monterrey, sister of Conde Duque de Olivares and wife of the Count of Monterrey (who from 1628–31, during Velázquez's first Roman sojourn, was Spanish Ambassador in Rome and then, from 1631–7, Viceroy of Naples). The Count and Countess of Monterrey gave Velázquez their patronage while he was in Rome, and arranged for his care during an illness. This identification is corroborated by a similarity of features between the portrait and a marble statue of the Countess made in Naples in 1636, for her grave in Salamanca. Moreover, the Countess mentioned in a letter that Velázquez had painted her portrait at the request of her brother.

Francisco de Zurbaran (1598–1664)

Don Alonso Verdugo de Albornoz

*c.*1635

Canvas, 185 × 103 cm ($72\frac{7}{8} \times 40\frac{1}{2}$ in)
Inscribed lower right:
'fran. de zurbaran f./AETAS 12. A^S'
Acquired from the Alfred Morrison Collection, London, 1906
Cat. no. 404 C

Most of the Spanish paintings of the seventeenth century which once belonged to the Berlin gallery did not survive the last war; two important works by Murillo, a Ribera, and Zurbaran's *St Bonaventura and Thomas of Aquino* from the early 1627 series for the Franciscan Convent in Seville were destroyed by fire in 1945. Of the few paintings which were saved, Zurbaran's portrait of *Alonso Verdugo de Albornoz* is certainly the most important.

This is the artist's only signed portrait and one of only two known to have been painted from life. The commission, its occasion, and the resulting image are all unusual. The type of portrait, representing the sitter full-length in three-quarter view, standing with legs apart follows the tradition of official Spanish court portraits, but the sitter is a mere boy, a twelve-year-old decked out in an officer's uniform, a swagger stick in his left hand and his right resting on the hilt of a sword. An assumed seriousness of expression and his disdainful, manly gaze, belie his age. The portrait records the promotion of Alonso Verdugo (1623–95) to Captain of Horse Lancers in the bodyguard of his uncle, the influential Cardinal Gil de Albornoz, which had happened a year before in Carmona, a town near Seville. Since Alonso was born in 1623, and the inscription records that he was twelve at the time, the portrait must have been painted in 1635. The boy's rank is indicated by the red sash across his breastplate; his membership in the renowned Alcántara Military Order is shown by the green cross suspended beneath the family arms in the upper right corner of the picture.

Zurbaran painted this portrait soon after his return from Madrid, where in 1634 he had completed a Hercules cycle and two battle pictures for the Salón de Reinos, the throne chamber in the new royal palace, Buen Retiro, and where Philip IV had named him court painter. Though Velázquez had contributed his *Surrender at Breda* to the same sequence of battles, the style of his first maturity with its free and fluent brushwork left Zurbaran's rendering unaffected: for instance, the illumination in a hard light coming from the side, the pronounced chiaroscuro, and the modelling emphasize the shape of the figure and the density of every surface. The treatment of the highlights on the armour, the sharply delineated slashes in the breeches, and the hard contours of the white stockings, recall the Caravaggesque traits of Velázquez's early period, just as the overall conception recalls his portraits of the 1620s (*Don Carlos*, *c.*1626; Madrid, Prado).

Bartolomé Esteban Murillo (1618–82)
The Baptism of Christ
*c.*1655

Canvas, 233 × 160 cm (91¾ × 63 in)
Authentic signature, originally on lower cropped edge, reinserted at lower centre: 'MR.^{llo} f.'
Acquired 1968
Cat. no. 2/68

Murillo spent almost his entire life in his home town of Seville. Orphaned at ten, he was brought up by his brother-in-law, then apprenticed to Juan de Castillo. A trip to Madrid followed, in 1645 according to his biographer Palomino, but more likely some time between 1648 and 1650. While his early work with its strong, hard chiaroscuro modelling reveals the influence of Zurbaran, his mature style and especially his late *'estilo vaporoso'*, are characterized by rich impasto, the forms softly modelled in a warm light, and a light palette. His style was influenced by the works of Rubens and van Dyck, and to a lesser extent, by Velázquez and sixteenth-century Venetian painting, all of which Murillo may have seen in Madrid, not in Seville. Also, he frequently based his compositions on engravings after Italian, Flemish, and French works. His first large commission was a cycle of eleven paintings for the small cloister in the convent of S. Francisco in Seville (1645–6). These established his reputation, and soon Murillo had eclipsed Zurbaran to win official honours in 1655 as the city's leading artist. In 1660, he helped to found the Academy of Painting and later became its first president. Besides fulfilling this function, he devoted himself entirely to his work and his family. Among the major accomplishments of his mature period were series of paintings for the Capuchine monastery (1665–6 and 1668–70) and the Hospital de la Caridad (1670–4) in Seville.

The Berlin *Baptism of Christ* belongs to a group of four large, upright canvases representing scenes from the life of John the Baptist, which were originally in the refectory of S. Leandro, the convent of the Augustine nuns in Seville. All four works were seen and described there by F.Bruna as late as 1781; in 1812 the nuns sold them. Two of the series, *John the Baptist Pointing at Christ* (now in Chicago, Art Institute) and a lost painting whose subject is unknown, entered the famous collection of King Louis-Philippe of France in 1838. The Berlin painting and the fourth one, *John the Baptist with the Pharisees and Scribes* (now in Cambridge, Fitzwilliam Museum), were bought by Nathan Wetherell in 1812 and taken to England. The three surviving canvases were temporarily united at the Murillo exhibition recently held in Madrid (1982) and London (1983).

Very little is known about the circumstances of the commission or about its precise date of execution. According to A.Bravo (1837), the commission may have been related to the veneration of John the Baptist and John the Evangelist, in which the two Augustine convents Encarnación and S. Leandro competed with one another. The series is generally dated about 1655, to the beginning of Murillo's mature period, when he had overcome the hardness of modelling of his early style derived from Zurbaran, but still retained echoes of the strong chiaroscuro contrasts and dark palette. (A fifth painting, *St Augustine Washing Christ's Feet*, was earlier believed to be part of the group, forming the centre panel of a large retable, but this has since been disproved.)

In all three surviving paintings of the series the main figures are depicted standing, full-length, before a landscape background. The Berlin painting has been cropped on all sides, truncating the inscription with God's words in the sky. The composition was probably influenced by Rubens's *Baptism of Christ*, the altarpiece in St John's Church in Malines, which Murillo could have seen either in an engraving by W.Panneels dated 1630, or in one by A.Lommelin published by G.Hendricx.

In an attitude of humble submission, Christ's figure is subordinated to the looming figure of St John, whose features and gestures evoke great contained emotion. Both figures are subtly integrated into a harmonious composition based on a diagonal from lower left to upper right which is emphasized by the landscape.

Bartolomé Esteban Murillo
John the Baptist and the Pharisees
Cambridge, Fitzwilliam Museum

Bartolomé Esteban Murillo
John the Baptist Pointing at Christ
Chicago, The Art Institute of Chicago

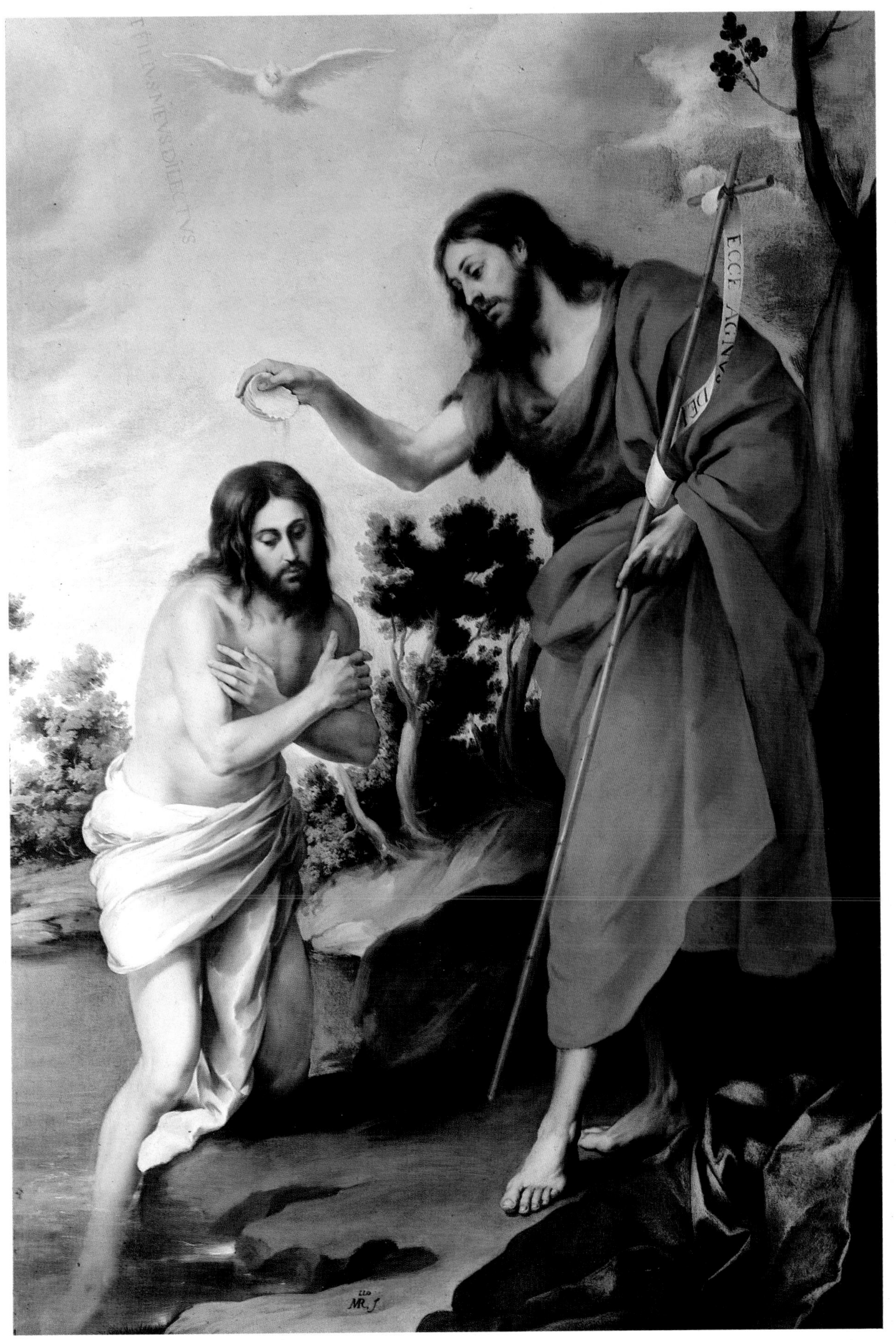
FILIVS MEVS DILECTVS
ECCE AGNVS DEI

Luca Giordano (1634–1705)
St Michael
*c.*1663

Canvas, 198 × 147 cm (78 × 57⅞ in)
Signed lower left: 'Giordano ./.F.'
Acquired 1971
Property of the
Kaiser-Friedrich-Museums-Verein
KFMV 261

St Michael Triumphing Over Satan and the Rebellious Angels is apparently an altarpiece that, judging by its dimensions, was intended for a side chapel rather than for a high altar – in what church we do not know. It was executed in about 1663, when Giordano had overcome the influence of Mattia Preti (active in Naples 1656–60) and the Venetian, Veronese-derived aspect of Preti's style, and began a short phase inspired by the great Bolognese painter, Guido Reni. Reni's influence made itself felt in brushwork of great fluency and lightness of touch, an airy translucence of surface particularly in passages of drapery, and a high-keyed, lucid palette. Reni's late masterpiece, *The Adoration of the Shepherds* in the choir of S. Martino, the church of the Carthusian convent in Naples, made a deep impact on Neapolitan painting. Its predominant colour triad of blue, white and red is found again in Giordano's *St Michael.* Still more direct inspiration came from Reni's famous altar painting, *St Michael*, executed shortly before 1636 for the Capuchine Church in Rome, the mother church of that order in Italy. Echoes of that painting merge here with those of still another renowned prototype: Raphael's *St Michael*, dated 1518, a painting presented to King Francis I of France by Lorenzo de' Medici. Giordano knew this composition from an engraving by Beatrizet. The motif of the lance which the angel grips with both hands, in the act of striking, and his almost dancing pose with his left leg extended behind him, were both inspired by Raphael. From Reni, on the other hand, came the diagonal composition, the inclination of the angel's head (though Giordano turns it from three-quarter into profile view), the facial type and wavy blond hair, and particularly the light, brilliant colours of the blue mail shirt and the pink, fluttering drapery. Finally, the influence of Giordano's presumed teacher, Ribera, is apparent in the figure of Satan – in the firm modelling of the body, the desperate gestures, and the grimacing face with its gaping mouth and bared teeth. These features are directly derived from an engraving by Ribera, dated 1622.

The influence of Ribera is even more evident (while that of Reni not yet detectable) in a much larger and darker altarpiece of *St Michael* in Vienna (Kunsthistorisches Museum), done about five or six years before the Berlin *St Michael.* Giordano devoted yet more altarpieces to the subject, which was widespread in sixteenth- and seventeenth-century art. St Michael, *miles christianus*, was a symbol of the triumph of the Catholic church over both Protestantism and the Turkish threat. Depictions of the saint were particularly numerous during the wars against the Turks: after Johann Sobieski's victory at Chozim in 1672, the liberation of Vienna in 1683 and of Budapest in 1686, the war against the Turks ended in an enthusiastically celebrated success. The triumphal character of Giordano's image, reflecting the optimism of the Roman church, is specially achieved by a festive, light palette. The elements derived from Raphael, Reni and Ribera have been transformed here into a High Baroque composition. The scene fairly bursts with the Baroque exuberance of the expansive movement with which St Michael quells Satan's final spasm.

Guido Reni
St Michael
Rome, Santa Maria della Concezione

Francesco Solimena (1657–1747)

The Virgin and Child Enthroned, with St Dominic and St Catherine of Sienna

(The Madonna of the Rosary)

*c.*1680–2

Canvas, 247 × 168 cm ($97\frac{1}{4}$ × $66\frac{1}{8}$ in)
Acquired 1971
Cat. no. 1/71

With Solimena's *Madonna of the Rosary*, acquired in 1971, the Berlin Gallery now also owns a work by the second great master of High and Late Baroque painting in Naples. The first was Giordano: during his ten-year absence from Naples, when Giordano lived in Madrid as court painter (1692–1702), Solimena's advance began, until by Giordano's death in 1705 he dominated the Neapolitan art scene. *The Madonna of the Rosary* is an early work, painted just two decades after Giordano's *St Michael*, when Solimena had yet to develop his cool, classicizing and academically oriented mature style characterized by strong chiaroscuro contrasts modelled in a cool palette. Here, as in other works of the early 1680s, his colour is still light and lucent with an emphasis on white and light red, the volumes burgeoning, the modelling loose, the impasto rich and the brushwork fluent – stylistic symptoms of the influence of Luca Giordano and Pietro da Cortona (the latter active in Rome and Florence). *The Madonna with the Rosary* – that is, the Virgin enthroned with the Christ Child who hands a rosary to St Dominic, founder of the Dominican order, while St Catherine of Sienna, the order's most important female saint, looks devoutly up at him – must have been intended as an altar painting for the Rosary Chapel of a Dominican church. It may be the work that Solimena's biographer, De Dominici (1743), mentions as being in the convent church at Sessa Aurunca in northern Campania, of which today only scant ruins remain. The theme appeared in visual art late in the fifteenth century, in connection with the spread of the brotherhood of the Rosary, but became frequent only in the course of the sixteenth century, particularly after Pope Gregory XIII established the Feast of the Rosary in 1573, to commemorate the Virgin's intercession in the Battle of Lepanto against the Turks (1571). While in most sixteenth-century depictions throughout Italy, and in seventeenth-century ones outside Rome, the Madonna is surrounded by many worshippers, Solimena paints only the two principal saints of the Dominican order, its founder and St Catherine of Sienna (1347–80; canonized 1461).

This compositional scheme with only these two saints rapidly came to dominate Roman painting. It was introduced into Naples by Giovanni Lanfranco, who had worked in Rome from 1602–33 and moved to Naples in 1634. His altarpiece of the Virgin Enthroned with two Carthusian Saints (based on his own *Madonna with the Rosary* in Perugia) for S. Martino in Naples (now Afragola, 1638), became the prototype for many altarpieces, including Solimena's in Berlin. Similarities are evident in the general conception, in the saint at the right with his foot on a pedestal and his face turned in profile to the Child, and in the column motif in the right background. Another similarity is the flowing red drapery, which in Lanfranco's painting is drawn up to the corner by a large angel at the upper left. Solimena, too, originally painted an angel in much the same position, holding a rose garland over the Virgin's head, and to his right, another flying putto holding up the drapery. The two figures are very clearly visible in the X-ray photograph. Though they were completely finished, the artist deleted them, perhaps to give the crowded composition more clarity and the diagonal orientation it now has. The golden green section of drapery was once part of the larger angel's garment, and in the space previously occupied by the angels there are now groups of cherubs' heads.

Francesco Solimena
Madonna of the Rosary
X-ray photograph
Berlin, Gemäldegalerie SMPK

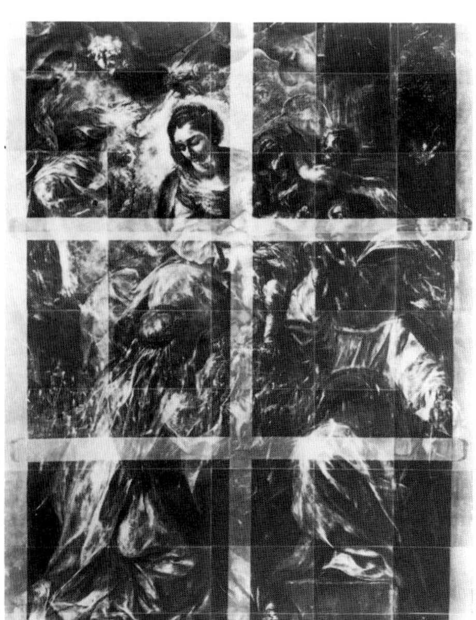

Sebastiano Ricci (1659–1734)
Bathsheba in her Bath
*c.*1725

Canvas, 109 × 142 cm (43 × 56 in)
Acquired by Frederick II before 1773
From the Royal Palaces, Berlin
Cat. no. 454

Sebastiano Ricci, a generation older than Tiepolo, was the first painter of the Venetian Settecento to liberate painting from the tenebrist tradition in Venetian painting of the later seventeenth century, inaugurating a new era that culminated in the work of Tiepolo. While in Rome from 1690–4, Ricci became acquainted with the High and Late Baroque style of Cortona and Gaulli, then saw the work of Magnasco in Milan and Giordano's frescoes in Florence. After returning to Venice in 1697, he created ceiling paintings in the Palazzo Mocenigo (*c.*1700; now Berlin, Gemäldegalerie SMPK) which reveal the influence of Giordano. A large ceiling fresco at Schönbrunn Castle in Vienna, followed in 1702. He spent 1706–8 in Florence, then returned to Venice, where in 1708 he executed a crucial work, the altarpiece in S. Giorgio Maggiore that marked an obvious recourse to the art of Veronese as well as to the composition of Titian's *Pesaro Madonna*. Passing through Paris in 1716 after four years in England, Ricci met Watteau and Lafosse, who celebrated him as a new Veronese.

The Berlin *Bathsheba* is a work of the artist's late Venetian period, probably painted in about 1724–5. It was acquired between 1764 and 1773 for the Picture Gallery at Sanssouci by Frederick the Great, who characteristically considered it to be a work of Veronese. Its true artist was not recognized until 1909, by Molmenti. Nor did the fact that its subject was the story of Bathsheba impress itself upon early commentators. In every Berlin catalogue from 1830 to 1921 the painting was listed as *After the Bath*, and in the 1931 edition as *The Toilette of Venus*. These misnamings are perhaps excusable because of the absence of David. The theme was finally identified solely by the figure of the girl messenger bringing a letter in the far left background.

The Bible story relates how David seduced Bathsheba, and when she became pregnant, sent her husband, Urias, into 'the forefront of the hottest battle', where he was soon killed. In Ricci's rendering, the moral of the story – David's punishment for the sin of leading Bathsheba into adultery – is entirely secondary to a celebration of feminine beauty. This treatment is typical of seventeenth- and eighteenth-century Italian painting, in which other female figures from the Old Testament and heroines of Roman history were assimilated in

Sebastiano Ricci
Bathsheba in her Bath
Budapest, Museum of Fine Arts

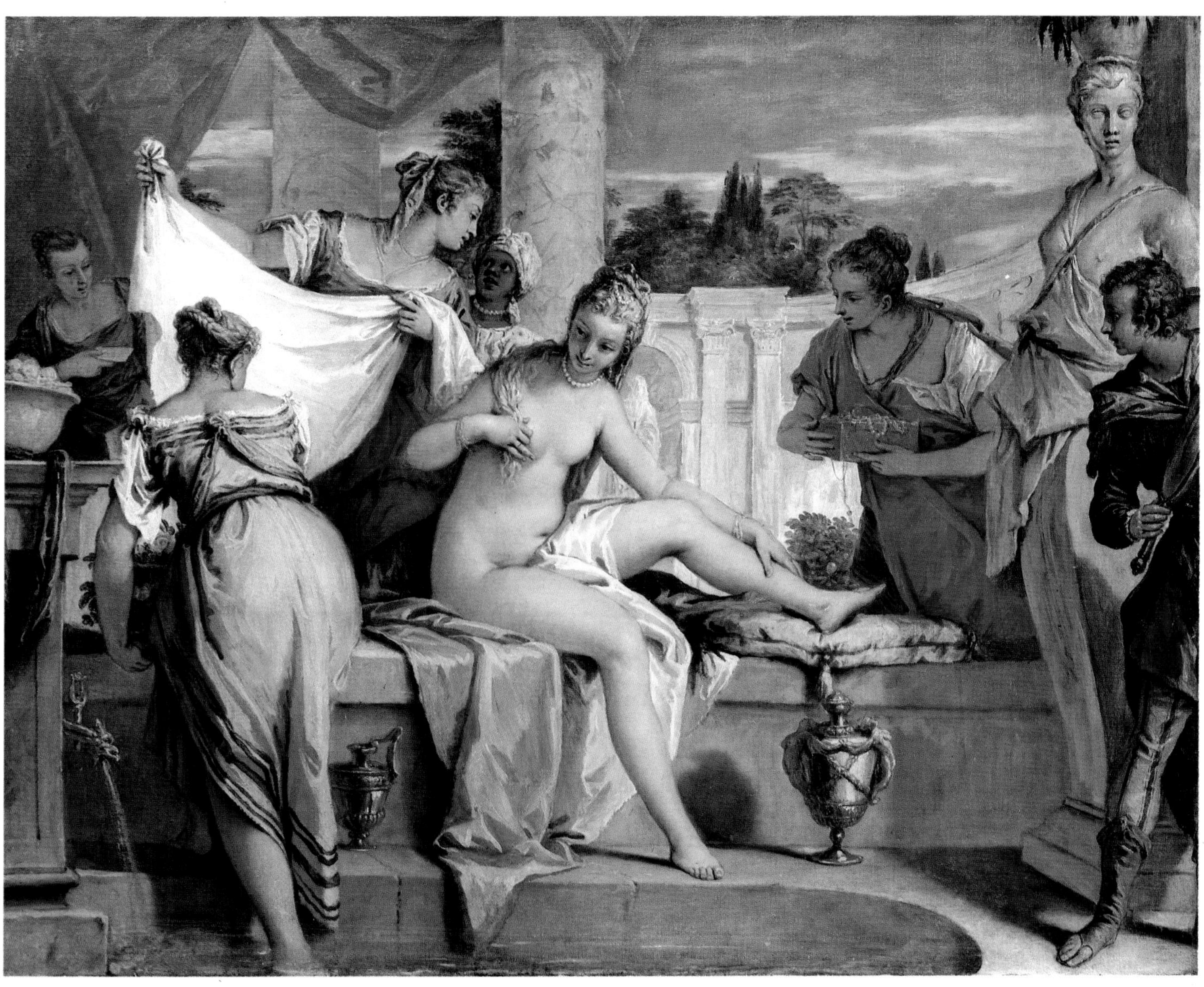

a similar way (Susanna, Lucretia, Cleopatra). The setting here, a Venetian Renaissance villa, is an architectural ambience often used especially by Veronese. Ricci also evokes the art of his great ancestor Veronese in the rendering of the figures and their luxurious garments, and in a festive colour scheme based on combinations of white, yellow, blue and red.

The same subject occurs in another Ricci painting of about the same date, a horizontal but somewhat larger format (Budapest, Museum of Fine Arts) of which two replicas exist, one and possibly both by his own hand. In this version, Bathsheba's head, instead of being shown frontally with a carefully arranged coiffure decked with pearls, and partly covered with a scarf, is seen in profile, her long, blonde hair loose and being combed by a maid. The scene is also set in a Palladian villa, though its background architecture is flat and parallel to the picture plane, while in the Berlin painting the bath has rounded ends and the background wall with its niches and pilasters describes an oval curve. This has a compositional counterbalance in the sweeping up of the white cloth by the maid at the left to protect Bathsheba from prying eyes.

Giovanni Battista Tiepolo (1696–1770)

The Martyrdom of St Agatha

*c.*1750

Canvas, 184 × 131 cm ($72\frac{1}{2}$ × $51\frac{1}{2}$ in)
Acquired 1878
Cat. no. 459 B

If Sebastiano Ricci and the somewhat younger Pellegrini and Amigoni rang in the Venetian Settecento, Tiepolo brought it to culmination. Particularly in his ceiling frescoes, he evoked heavenly realms of unprecedented vastness, and peopled them with mythological, historical, and allegorical figures in whose Baroque, declamatory, and yet ironically tinged pathos the declining Venetian aristocracy saw its former greatness.

One of Tiepolo's most classical images is the former high altarpiece of St Agatha, the church of the Benedictine Convent in Lendinara near Rovigo, painted in about 1750. It represents the death of the church's titular saint, who lived during the first half of the third century in Catania and suffered martyrdom in the year AD 251. Agatha came from a rich and noble family, and devoted her life to Christ from an early age. After being subjected to various temptations by the young Quintian, she was arrested and tortured. An executioner cut off her breasts. In the dungeon, St Peter appeared to her and healed her. When she was again being tortured, part of the building suddenly caved in, burying her tormentors beneath it, and an earthquake struck the town of Catania. After thanking the Lord for keeping her body inviolate, St Agatha died. During a later earthquake, the faithful took up the shroud covering her grave and quelled a flow of lava with it; her protection has been invoked against earthquakes ever since.

While Italian painters of the Early Baroque generally depicted St Agatha in the dungeon, being healed by St Peter, Tiepolo has represented her martyrdom. Collapsed on the steps of an ancient, ruined temple, she looks submissively towards heaven as a maid covers her wounds with a cloth and a servant holds a plate with her cut breasts. Intensely dramatic as the scene is, the artist none the less shied away from depicting the terrible moment itself. What dominates here is the impression of St Agatha's steadfast and tranquil faith in God. The composition centres around her figure, which is supported and, as it were, framed by the boy with the salver, and the maid bending tenderly towards her, in contrast to the violent and threatening figure of the executioner, his muscular arm angled to the right. The energy with which he twists his head to the left is met by a huge column opposite, whose vertical form symbolically repeats the vertical of St Agatha's pleading, trusting gaze.

As may be seen from an etching by Giambattista's son, Giandomenico, the painting originally had a semicircular upper edge, and the column extended higher, its top broken off, perhaps to evoke the collapse of the palace and the ensuing earthquake. Represented at the left was St Agatha's vision, Christ's heart in an aureole of flames, encompassed by a crown of thorns, and flanked by the heads of two angels. The painting was reported to be in poor condition as early as 1795. It was sold or otherwise removed from the church perhaps when the convent was secularized in 1810, but by 1832–5 at the latest. The church building was purchased in 1832 from the Austrian administration by a priest who presented it to the Capuchines; they refurnished it and dedicated the high altar to St Francis. St Agatha was venerated in a side altar, which in 1834 received a new altar painting. Tiepolo's canvas was apparently removed, and later a strip of about 15 cm wide was cut off the bottom edge.

Two preliminary drawings for the head of St Agatha are preserved in the Berlin Kupferstichkabinett, and a study for the hands of the boy holding a salver is in the Museo Correr, Venice.

Giandomenico Tiepolo
Engraving after Giovanni Battista Tiepolo's altar painting

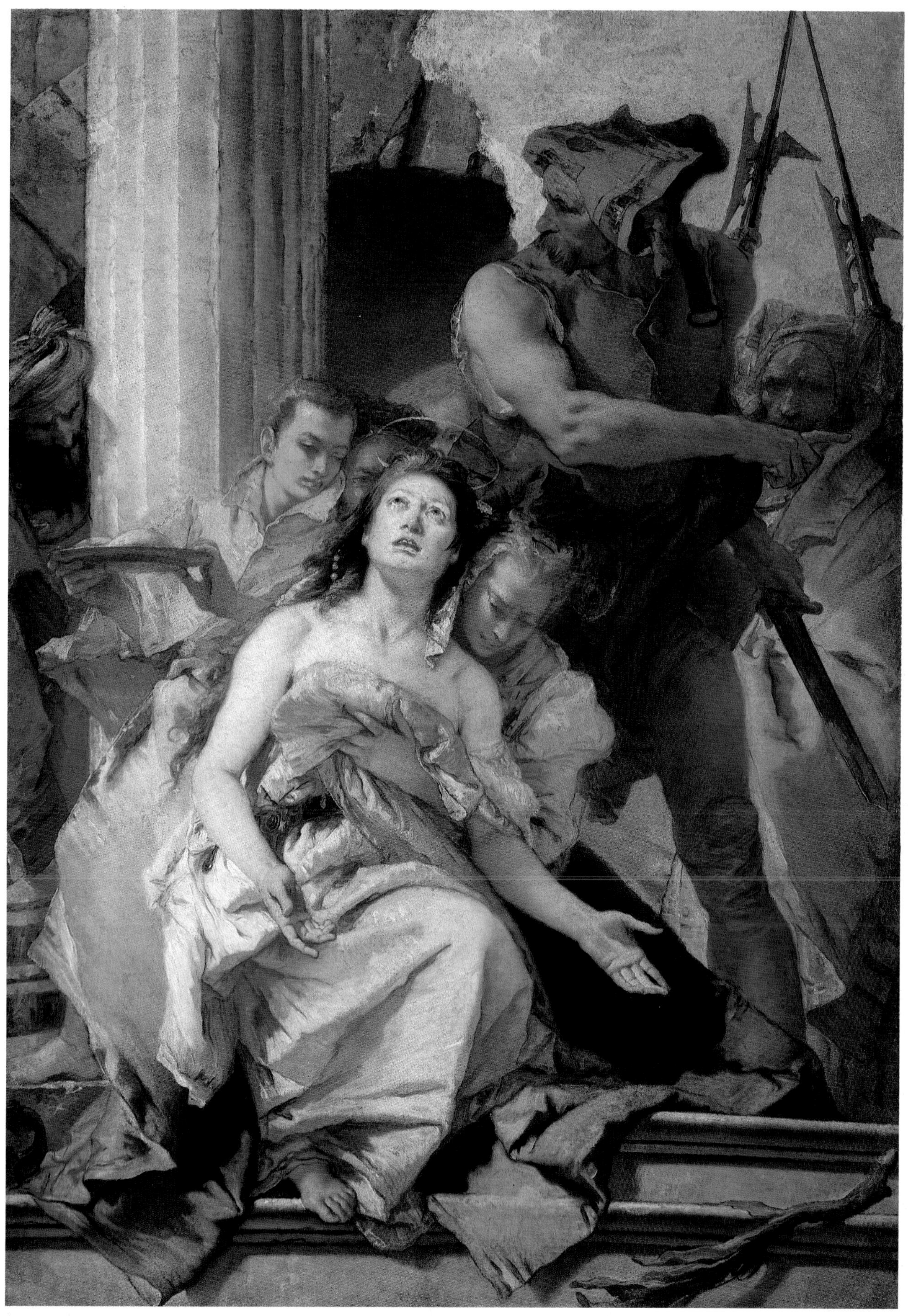

Giovanni Battista Tiepolo

Rinaldo and Armida in Armida's Magic Garden, Overheard by Carlo and Ubaldo – Rinaldo Bidding Armida Farewell

Canvas, 39 × 62 cm (15⅜ × 24⅜ in) (459 D)
and 39 × 61 cm (15⅜ × 24 in)
Acquired 1908 (459 D) and 1979
Cat. nos 459 D and 3/79

Tiepolo's agreement to execute works for the Würzburg Residence of Prince-Bishop Carl Philipp von Greiffenclau is first mentioned in an official letter of 29 May 1750. On 12 December of that year Tiepolo and his two sons, Domenico and Lorenzo, arrived in Würzburg, where the artist stayed for almost three years. With the ceiling fresco above the main stairwell, dated 1753, Tiepolo's art reached its greatest fulfilment. Besides frescoes in the *Kaisersaal* and paintings for the chapel (both 1752), his decorations of 1753 evidently included two medium-sized canvases (105 × 140 cm/41⅜ × 55 in) for other rooms of the Würzburg Residence. These were scenes from one of the best-known and most frequently illustrated love stories in Torquato Tasso's verse epic, *La Gerusalemme Liberata* (1581): *Rinaldo and Armida in Armida's Magic Garden* and *Rinaldo Bidding Armida Farewell*. For a long time the two paintings were shown in Munich (Alte Pinakothek), but they have again been on view in the Residence since 1974.

A small, *modello*-like sketch for the first of the two Tasso scenes was acquired for the Berlin Gallery in 1908, but it was not until 1979 that it also acquired a sketch for the other, from Cailleux in Paris. The two sketches for the Würzburg companion pieces are now reunited and their original context is restored, for they are related in composition and content. What is still debated is whether they represent preliminary, finished renderings (*modelli*) for the Würzburg canvases, as most scholars believe, or whether they are altered repetitions on a smaller format or *ricordi*, 'small variants' (*riduzioni in piccolo*) by the master's own hand, as suggested by Rizzi (1971), who dates them accordingly, to about 1755–60. As regards the first scene, the 'sketch' and finished painting are substantially similar in terms of composition, figures, and essential landscape details, though the placing of these does differ considerably. For the other scene, the compositions themselves diverge.

Tasso's verse epic and Ariosto's *Orlando Furioso* (1516) were the two main contemporary sources for imagery of this type in seventeenth- and eighteenth-century painting. The subject of these poems, the defence and victory of Christianity over the heathen Saracens, bore obvious analogies to such significant movements and events of the day as the Counter Reformation and the Turkish Wars. Nevertheless, instead of depicting scenes from the main plot involving Godfrey of Bouillon like the siege and fall of Jerusalem, most artists chose romantic and bucolic episodes. One of these was the encounter between Rinaldo, Christian crusader from the house of Este, and Armida, a sorceress sent from Damascus to spread confusion in the Christian camp. At first she succeeds. Infatuated by her charms, ten knights escort her out of camp, and others follow. When Rinaldo manages to free some of them from her magic spell, Armida calls a siren to lull him to sleep. Yet falling in love with him herself, she spirits him off to the Islands of Bliss far out in the sea. There, in her enchanted garden, Armida holds her magic mirror with her own image up to his eyes, and Rinaldo succumbs.

This scene from Canto XVI is represented in Tiepolo's first painting. Perched on the edge of the fountain is the parrot that in Tasso's poem sings praises of nature's beauty, of love, and of the transience of earthly things. Approaching from the right, the knights Carlo and Ubaldo come to reclaim Rinaldo for the Christian cause, armed with the Sage of Ascalon's overpowering diamond shield and wand.

In the second scene, Carlo and Ubaldo break the spell, tearing Rinaldo from Armida's arms. One of them supports the dazed Rinaldo, trying to restore him to reality as Armida, reclining at the left, points to the high garden wall as if to say there is no escape, though her pose and features bespeak resignation. Rinaldo's shield and helmet still lie beside her on the ground; her magic mirror, now powerless, lies forgotten in the shadow of the wall; Rinaldo still holds a garland of flowers. In the right background, a boat waits to take the crusaders back to their camp, where Godfrey of Bouillon will forgive Rinaldo and entrust

Giovanni Battista Tiepolo
Rinaldo and Armida in the Magic Garden
Würzburg, Residenz

Giovanni Battista Tiepolo
Rinaldo Bidding Armida Farewell
Würzburg, Residenz

him with new missions. This boat is absent from the Würzburg painting, whose format is not as long and narrow as the Berlin painting (which might be a fact against it being a preparatory sketch). The scene is reversed in the final painting. The only compositional element shared by both is the group of trees behind the garden wall. In the Würzburg painting Armida reclines in the right foreground, in the same direction as in the sketch, with her outstretched leg in an identical position, but looking to the left and holding a handkerchief to dry her tears. Rinaldo stands to the left, in front of the wall, in classical counterpoise, looking back over his shoulder at Armida as if to ask her forgiveness, his left hand to his breast in a gesture of pathos. The two knights turn towards Armida, holding up the diamond shield that makes her powerless. The figures' actions, so spontaneous in the Berlin painting, have here frozen into declamatory poses and theatrical gestures, and the relationship between the figures and landscape is altered to correspond. In the final version, the figures act out the scene on a foreground stage brought close by stronger chiaroscuro, while the landscape recedes further into the background.

Tiepolo had already treated the same theme ten years earlier, in about 1742, in Tasso scenes (now in Chicago and London) for the decoration of an entire room: Knox (1978) thinks these may have been in the Palazzo Dolfin-Manin in Venice. A pen drawing in Frankfurt for this early series contains a portico in the Palladian style which the artist employed in painting for the first time in the Berlin and Würzburg Rinaldo and Armida scenes. Tiepolo was again inspired by Tasso in 1757, with his frescoes for the Villa Valmarana, near Vicenza.

Giovanni Antonio Canal, called Canaletto (1697–1768)

The Campo di Rialto

1758–9

Canvas, 119 × 186 cm ($46\frac{7}{8} \times 73\frac{1}{4}$ in)
On loan from the Streitsche Stiftung, Berlin

This view of the Campo di Rialto, once the main marketplace and commercial centre of Venice, was painted in Canaletto's final years after his return from England, where he worked with short intervals from 1746 to 1755. It was commissioned by Sigismund Streit, a Berlin businessman and long-time resident of Venice. He also commissioned a companion piece with a view of the Canal Grande and Palazzo Foscari, where his home and office were located. The two paintings, together with other paintings, his library and fortune, were intended for Streit's former school, the Gymnasium Zum Grauen Kloster in Berlin. Streit also ordered two more paintings from Canaletto, depictions of Venetian festivities in *vedute* form: the *Festival on the Eve of St Martha's Name Day*, before the church of S. Marta on the Giudecca canal; and the *Festival of the Vigil of St Peter*, near S. Pietro di Castello. These paintings were the same size as the first two *vedute*, and they were perhaps meant to introduce a series on Venetian festivals. Streit indeed commissioned just such a series from the young Antonio Diziani, apparently because he was not satisfied with Canaletto's *Vigilia di S. Marta*. Both Canaletto's festival paintings are nocturnes; they form a pair and complement the two 'daylight' scenes, *Canal Grande* and *Campo di Rialto*.

Sigismund Streit (1687–1775) arrived in Venice in 1709, and by 1715 had established his own trading office. In 1739, at the age of fifty-two, he sat for his portrait to Amigoni, ten of whose Biblical and mythological paintings he later acquired, though probably not then intending to donate them to his former school or create a collection. Streit retired from business in 1750 and in 1754 moved permanently to Padua. Since he was a bachelor and had fallen out with his nephew who had been in his firm, Streit began to correspond with his old school about a donation from his estate. With this bequest in mind, he ordered four allegories with moral and educational allusions from Nogari in 1751–2, probably for the school library, and then the four Canaletto paintings, which were shipped to Berlin in 1763.

The Campo di S. Giacomo di Rialto, the city's main business and banking centre, was located across the Canal Grande from Streit's residence and office building, the Palazzo Foscari. Canaletto had depicted the square twice, looking in the opposite direction, with a view of the façade of S. Giacometto (Dresden and Ottawa), before this first attempt to paint the less interesting end of the square with its plain façades of the Fabbriche Vecchie di Rialto. These, built by Antonio Abbondi in 1520–2, were now the headquarters of the government Trade, Maritime and Food Agencies. The choice of this view evidently went back to Streit's wish to have a record of the graceful Porticato del Banco Giro, where the Venetian State Bank had its office.

We see clerks in black gowns and white ties working there at their desks; behind them in the passageway are notaries' windows; the offices of insurance agencies are not far away. Businessmen stroll through the square, conversing, negotiating. In his own description of the scene, Streit mentions the Jews with their compulsory red caps, and Armenians in long gowns and pointed hats. On the central column of the arcade is the *Gobbo di Rialto*, a sculpture by Pietro da Saló (1541) of a hunchbacked figure supporting a little staircase up the squat granite column, the *Colonna del bando*, where a *comandador* publicly announced new laws, proclamations, punishments, information about ships' arrivals and departures, and similar matters. Foreign businessmen were granted permission to convene at this column.

On the left is the *ruga degli orefici*, named after the goldsmiths who had their shops under the eaves and whose characteristic signs are clearly visible. High in the background is the campanile of S. Giovanni Elemosinario. Outside the shops, booths offer meat, fruit and vegetables, and pottery; awnings are spread over the perishable goods to protect them from the sun. In the foreground and along the right arcade, household goods, furniture (at

Canaletto
The Canal Grande, Venice, with Palazzo Foscari, Streit's Residence
Berlin, Gemäldegalerie SMPK, on loan from the Streitsche Stiftung

the far right, a *capoletto*), paintings, and other craft objects are on sale.

The wide-angle perspective makes the square appear much larger and more monumental than it actually is. The paving with meandering rectangular white stones still exists today. It was apparently carried out in 1758, which provides a *terminus post quem* for Canaletto's painting.

The monumentality of the space, the cool lucidity of its atmosphere, a great precision in the rendering of architectural detail, calligraphic brushwork, the palette with its dominating sandy beige, brown and red hues, and finally, a penchant for genre-like elaboration of detail – all these are characteristics of Canaletto's late style.

Francesco Guardi (1712–93)

The Balloon Ascent

1784

Canvas, 66 × 51 cm (26 × 20 in)
Acquired 1901
Property of the
Kaiser-Friedrich-Museums-Verein
Cat. no. 501 F

With Canaletto and Marieschi, Guardi was the third great eighteenth-century Venetian painter of views or *vedute*. In contrast to Canaletto, who focused on architecture and attempted a highly objective description of space, Guardi, in the painterly tradition of the Riccis and Magnasco, took figures and landscape as his point of departure. His approach was subjective, imaginative; his brushwork sketchy and nervous, giving his surfaces a vibrating effect that spread like a veil over the entire scene. In his late period he began to develop a reporter's eye for current events, as the present painting shows. It is devoted to the first balloon ascent in Venice, in 1784, a year after the Montgolfier brothers' pioneering flight. The balloon, or rather its gondola, was commissioned by the Procurator of S. Marco, Francesco Pesaro, and built by the Zanchi brothers. Though there is still some question as to who piloted the balloon, it cannot have been Count Francesco Zambeccari, as is frequently stated, because he was in London at the time. The balloon remained aloft for two hours and landed in a swampy area of the lagoon; and its flight was reported in newspapers, engravings, poems and commemorative medals. Though one of the engravings shows the ascent at the mouth of the Grand Canal, opposite the Piazzetta, above the Bacino di S. Marco, Guardi has it take place at the entrance to the Giudecca Canal. From a vantage point in the shade of the portico of the Customs House (*Dogana del Mar*) on the land between the Grand Canal and Giudecca Canal, a crowd of onlookers watches the balloon, which has just risen clear of a wooden platform surrounded by gondolas. In the background, on the far shore of the canal, is Palladio's Il Redentore church and the church of Le Zitelle. The charm of this unusual composition lies in the contrast between the repoussoir-like dark frame of the portico architecture in the foreground, and the expanse of blue, translucently clouded sky opening out behind it.

Giovanni Paolo Panini (1691–1765)

The Duc de Choiseul's Departure on St Peter's Square in Rome

1754

Canvas, 152 × 195 cm ($59\frac{7}{8} \times 76\frac{3}{4}$ in)
Signed lower left: 'I. P. PANINI/1754'
Collections of Hubert Robert, Paris; Mme V.e Robert, Paris, 1821
Donated by the Deutsche Klassenlotterie Berlin for the 150th anniversary of the Berlin Museums
Cat. no. 2/80

Panini, the leading painter of views, architecture, and ruins in eighteenth-century Rome, is represented in the Berlin Gallery with five works. The most outstanding among these is surely his *View of St Peter's Square with the Departure of the Duc de Choiseul*, which was acquired in 1980. Its large format, the number and unusual size of its figures, but particularly the importance of the scene depicted and the prominence of its patron and main protagonist, rank the painting high among Panini's works in Berlin and within his extensive œuvre as a whole.

Represented here is the ceremonial departure (from St Peter's) of the French Ambassador to the Holy See, Etienne-François de Choiseul, Comte de Stainville, later Duc de Choiseul, following his audience in St Peter's with Pope Benedict XIV in 1754, to inaugurate his three-year period in office. Choiseul had obtained this position, the first in his diplomatic career, thanks to the sponsorship of Madame de Pompadour. Choiseul's main objective was to negotiate with the Pope about dissension within the French church, which culminated in a conflict between the nationally oriented Gallicans and Jansenists, and the Roman oriented Jesuits. By the autumn of 1756, the deliberations were over. When on 16 October the Pope handed down to Choiseul his encyclica *Ex omnibus* – an event recorded by Batoni in a famous painting (Minneapolis Institute of Arts) – the Ambassador's mission had been accomplished, and he returned to Paris the following year.

Before the Berlin painting came to light in Paris in 1978, the only four works commissioned by Choiseul from Panini which were known were in a series to commemorate the Duke's diplomatic activities in Rome and his status as connoisseur and collector of classical and contemporary art: a *View of St Peter's Square with the Duke's Procession after a Papal Audience* (Scotland, Collection of the Duke of Sutherland); a *View of the Interior of St Peter's with Choiseul's Visit* (Boston, Atheneum); and two imaginary gallery interiors with *vedute* of ancient Rome (Stuttgart, Staatsgalerie) and modern Rome

G.P.Panini
Figure Study
London, British Museum

G.P.Panini
Figure Study
London, British Museum

G.P.Panini
Figure Study
Berlin, Kupferstichkabinett SMPK

(Boston, Museum of Fine Arts). These four paintings, rather larger than the one in Berlin, were executed in about 1756–7, towards the end of Choiseul's service in Rome; the *Gallery with Views of Modern Rome* is dated 1757. The Berlin painting is dated 1754, which places it at the beginning of Choiseul's ambassadorship. It probably represents the only surviving piece of the first series of views painted in 1754, which for unexplained reasons remained in the artist's possession until he passed them on to his pupil and friend, the painter Hubert Robert. Robert, who had come to Rome in Choiseul's retinue, owned over thirty paintings by Panini. Among these were the above-mentioned first series of four views of Rome commissioned by Choiseul, two of which – the imaginary galleries – were auctioned in Paris in 1809, a year after Robert's death, and whose whereabouts are still unknown. The other two were sold in 1821, after Robert's widow had died. The Berlin painting is apparently one of these, though the other is lost.

In terms of subject-matter and general conception, the Berlin painting corresponds to a similar view in the second series now in the Duke of Sutherland's collection. The long train of carriages sweeping in a wide curve across the square is arranged in much the same way in the two paintings, particularly in the foreground, though it does diverge in the background. Similarities are also evident in the strong lighting from the left, a swath of light glowing through the colonnade's narrow entrance across the square and picking out the Duke's carriage. By contrast, the large foreground figures of well-dressed ladies and gentlemen,

Louis Michel van Loo
Etienne François de Choiseul
Versailles, Musée National

clergy and humble onlookers, are in an area of shade and set off the scene behind. Vantage points and perspectives differ in the two paintings. In the Berlin view, the vantage point lies further to the right, and correspondingly, the obelisk appears to the left of the central axis of the church façade. The entire square appears to be rather nearer the spectator in the Berlin piece, and the architecture of the Vatican Palace is given with a different perspective foreshortening it. The figures represented in the Berlin work are quite different. Unlike those in pure or realistic views, where they play a subordinate role, here the figures play a much more important role. Their scale is larger than usual, and their careful rendering is based on preliminary drawings. Chalk drawings of individual figures and sections of buildings, and sketches of the square are preserved in an album in the British Museum, London; others are in the Berlin Kupferstichkabinett. In his Berlin painting, the artist has combined the *veduta reale* with an eye-witness account of a historical event.

FRENCH AND ENGLISH PAINTING OF THE EIGHTEENTH CENTURY

BY HENNING BOCK

Nicolas de Largillierre (1656–1746)
The Sculptor Nicolas Coustou in his Studio
*c.*1710–12

Canvas, 197 × 132 cm ($77\frac{1}{2}$ × 52 in)
Acquired 1980
Cat. no. 1/80

During the late seventeenth and early eighteenth centuries, Hyacinthe Rigaud (1659–1743) and Nicolas de Largillierre were the two leading portraitists in France – Rigaud more for the court society in Versailles, and Largillierre for the rich bourgoisie and nobility in Paris. Building on the Flemish tradition and the austere approach of English portraiture, and with the help of a well-organized workshop, Largillierre created an enormous œuvre of roughly two thousand portraits, still lifes, and history paintings. Pre-eminent among them are a small number of portraits of family members and friends, and of artists and writers on the Parisian scene. These are invariably works of unusual quality, and entirely by the artist's own hand. While some have the dignified distance of official portraits, others far transcend the conventions and compellingly capture the individuality of their sitters, making them the most personal and beautiful of Largillierre's works. This portrait of Nicolas Coustou is a particularly striking example of his ability to portray a man in all his individuality and strength of character while at the same time creating an image of an entire profession.

Nicolas Coustou, about the same age as Largillierre, was one of the most important sculptors of the period. Under Louis XIV and Louis XV he received extensive commissions to decorate great parks, churches in Paris, and above all the royal palaces in Trianon, Versailles, and Marly. A native of Lyons, he had come to Paris in 1676 and received his training from his uncle, the sculptor Antoine Coysevox. After spending the years 1683–6 in Rome on a scholarship he was accepted into the Académie in 1693. He became a professor in 1702, advanced to the position of rector in 1720, and finally, in 1733, to that of chancellor of the Académie.

The portrait shows Coustou in his studio. Though he is wearing a grand dress wig, his informal working clothes give the impression that he has just been interrupted at work. With a turn of the shoulders he faces us, frank and self-assured, extending his hand as if to invite perusal of the objects in his studio and the attributes of his profession. His right hand rests on a tripod before the clay model of a sculpture in progress. Though the colour scheme of the painting is dominated by a finely modulated range of brown, contrasting accents glow in the white of the shirt, in touches of complementary turquoise on the lining of the coat, and on the gold buttons.

Jean le Gros
Nicolas Coustou, 1725
Engraving after a painting by Dupuis, 1730

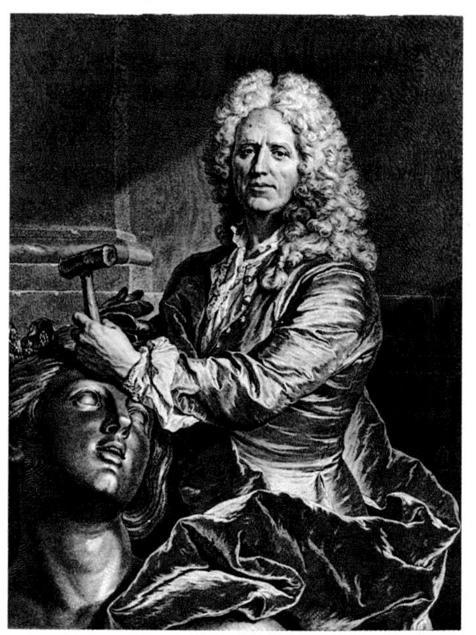

There has been some controversy about the model's identity, with some commentators arguing that he may possibly be the sculptor René Fremin (1672–1744). Yet this would seem unlikely since, first, the established portraits of Fremin bear little facial resemblance to the man depicted here; and secondly, the *bozzetti* or models given such prominence in the portrait are quite obvious clues to his identity. The *bozzetto* on the tripod is evidently a model for a large group called *Spring* that Coustou executed about 1712 for the garden façade of the Hôtel des Noailles on Rue St Honoré, Paris (the present site of the St James and Albany Hotel). The only surviving view of this side of the demolished building is found in an engraving by Blondel, while the sculpture itself has disappeared without a trace. An even more convincing argument for the sitter's identity is provided by the figures on the shelf at the upper right. The small armless *putto* occurs in several paintings by other artists of the eighteenth and nineteenth centuries. Chardin included it in his allegorical work *Le singe peintre* of 1743 (Chartres, Musée des Beaux-Arts); Cézanne had a plaster cast of this *putto* in his Aix-en-Provence house and employed it in a series of still lifes collectively titled *Amour en plâtre*. Still legible on the plinth of this cast is the fragmentary inscription, 'Fa... N. Cou...', quite concrete evidence that the sculptor portrayed here is indeed Nicolas Coustou.

The figurine of the standing youth on the right is apparently a small-scale replica of the famous Roman statue, *Antinous*, the original of which is in the Belvedere sculpture collection at the Vatican. From its discovery in the early sixteenth century, this piece

figured as one of the most perfect examples of classical art and as an ideal embodiment of the proportions of the human body. Largillierre himself had previously included it in his *Portrait of Charles Lebrun* (1686; Paris, Louvre) and a short time later in his *Portrait of Gerard Edelink* (*c.*1690; Norfolk, The Chrysler Museum), as an allusion to every artist's dependence on the doctrine of classical proportions and on the Greek and Roman ideal in art. Hence the *bozzetti* in this portrait of Coustou not only refer to a particular sculptor's work, but also convey a more general message about the artist's mission and his place within the history of his medium.

Still another feature of the portrait invites interpretation. Not by chance has Largillierre depicted his friend in working clothes, standing between a rough-hewn block of stone in the foreground and a lump of clay in the background. According to an academic theory then current, the artist was called upon to reveal the true idea in nature, which was veiled by imperfections and marred by accidental appearances. Only the work of art could reveal true perfection; only the creative imagination could infuse life into amorphous matter, give shape to a more beautiful, ideal world. The sculptor in the portrait accordingly, rather than presenting a finished piece, rests his working hand on a model, which like the crumpled drawing between the legs of the tripod evokes the intellectual process involved in the realization of a *prima idea*.

Beneath the surface of this apparently so realistic and informal portrait of a sculptor in his studio is a fundamental self-definition on the part of one of the major artists of the age.

Antoine Watteau (1684–1721)

The French Comedy
The Italian Comedy

After 1716

Canvas, each 37 × 48 cm ($14\frac{1}{2}$ × 19 in)
From the Royal Palaces, Berlin, 1830
Cat. nos 468 and 470

When Watteau died in 1721, barely thirty-seven years old, he left an œuvre whose most significant works had been created in the space of just over a decade. Born in Valenciennes in 1684, he had come to Paris in 1702 and been accepted into the Académie Royale in 1712, with the quite unusual distinction of being allowed to choose the subject of his reception picture himself. Though *Embarkation for Cythera* (now in the Louvre) was not finished until 1717, it immediately established Watteau as the painter of *fêtes galantes*, his own pictorial invention. Watteau travelled abroad only once, to England in 1719–20. Few of his works, including the two theatre paintings in Berlin, have come down to us in good condition, for Watteau's technique was often more than careless, and many of his paintings give only a faint idea of their original glory. His reputation as the greatest painter in early eighteenth-century France, however, stands undiminished.

The two Berlin theatre paintings were purchased by Frederick the Great for the small Picture Gallery at Sanssouci some time before 1766. They came to the Berlin Gallery in 1830, the only Watteaus from the Royal Collection and still, as P. Rosenberg noted in the catalogue to the great jubilee exhibition of 1984–5 (Washington, Paris, Berlin), among the artist's most famous works.

They figured as companion pieces from an early date, being already titled *L'amour au théâtre français* and *L'amour au théâtre italien* in the engravings made after them in 1734, when they were in the collection of Henri de Rosnel. In terms of subject-matter they are indeed related, though the dramatic principles followed by the two theatre groups could not be more different – improvisation with the *commedia dell'arte* and strict rules with the *comédie française*. Whether the two paintings were actually executed concurrently and intended as companion pieces, however, is impossible to say. They vary so widely in theme and composition that in the catalogue to the recent exhibition, one author suggested that the first version of *The French Comedy* was painted in about 1712, to which the artist added the central figures in about 1716. *The Italian Comedy*, according to the same essay, might not have been done until about 1718. This hypothesis is difficult to follow, let alone prove; a dating of both paintings to after 1716 would still seem justified by the concrete references they contain, to the return of the Italian actors to Paris in 1716 after their expulsion from France in 1697, and to the actor Poisson, whom Watteau portrays in the role of Crispin.

Antoine Watteau
Study for Amor
Basle, formerly Hirsch Collection

In *The French Comedy*, a mixed group of actors is depicted in a sunny clearing of a park. A few musicians and people clad as shepherds stand on the left, in the shadow of the trees, among them Pierrot and Gilles; in the centre, a couple is about to begin a courtly dance. Behind them, two actors touch glasses in a toast, one dressed as Amor with a quiver of arrows and elegant bow, the other as Bacchus with panther skin and vine wreath. Between them, in a dress of yellow and green and a shawl trimmed with bells, is Columbine as *La Folie*, a personification of the absurdity of sensual love. On the right, two couples look on: Harlequin turning to a young lady, and next to them, Crispin with a girl at his side. Crispin is the only figure in the painting who can still be identified with a known personage. His features are those of Paul Poisson (1658–1735), an actor brought to the Comédie Française in 1716 by the Duchesse de Berry, daughter of the regent.

None of the many attempts to explain the scene in terms of known contemporary plays has been quite convincing. Possibly Watteau's model was the 'Reconciliation of Amor and Bacchus', third intermezzo in the third act of the pastoral play *Les Fêtes de l'Amour et de Bacchus* by Molière, Benserade, Quinault, and Lully. Given its premiere performance in 1672, this play went on to become a great success, and was staged in Paris for the last time in 1716. Although it would explain the action in Watteau's painting, it falls short in terms of the figures involved. For instance, neither the prominent herm on the wall, nor the

presence of Columbine (*La Folie*), can be explained by reference to this play. Some commentators interpret the hooded herm as Momus, Son of the Night and symbol of foolish fault-finding. This would make Bacchus and Amor the embodiments of a reconciliation of spiritual and sensual love, as opposed to Momus and La Folie, who stand for blind passion. The young man and woman moving towards each other in a dance are involved in this conflict between spiritual and physical love.

The Italian Comedy, the only nocturne Watteau ever painted, shows twelve actors gathered out of doors, after a performance. Pierrot with his guitar stands in the centre; to his left are Columbine (with mask) and Isabella, who glances over at old Pantalone. To Pierrot's right are Harlequin throwing his arm up as if startled, then perhaps Pulcinella,

and Mezzetin with a torch, Doctor Marcisino leaning on his cane, and Scaramuccia. Attempts have been made to associate the image with a night scene in *L'heureuse surprise*, the first play performed by the troupe, at the Palais Royal, when they returned to Paris in 1716. Yet here, too, the correspondences are of only a very general nature. According to an advertisement for the 1734 engravings of the paintings that appeared in *Mercure de France* (1733), in this piece Watteau simply depicted his friends in costume. It should probably be understood as a kind of final scene, what Rosenberg has called a vaudeville of all the troupe's performances, in which the artist depicted characters from the *commedia dell'arte* in a nocturnal scene, combining theatrical illusion with reality.

Many preliminary drawings exist for both the Berlin theatre paintings.

Antoine Watteau

The Dance

(Iris)

*c.*1719

Canvas, 97 × 166 cm ($38\frac{1}{8} \times 65\frac{3}{8}$ in)
From the Royal Palaces, Berlin, 1830
On loan from the Federal Republic of Germany

Nothing is known about the genesis of this painting. It was first illustrated in the comprehensive volume of engravings *Recueil des dessins gravées*, published from 1721 to 1739 by Jean de Jullienne, after Watteau's death. In the facsimile engraving by Charles-Nicolas Cochin (before 1726?) the painting was titled *The Dance* and accompanied by this quatrain:

> *'Iris c'est de bonne heure avoir l'air à la danse,*
> *Vous exprimez déjà les tendres mouvemens,*
> *Qui nous font les jours conoitre à la Cadance,*
> *Le goust que vôtre Sexe a pour les intrumens.'*

The painting shows four children performing a pastoral play on a meadow at the edge of a wood. They have no audience apart from ourselves, who are invited to look on. Iris, the little dancer in her festive dress, seems to have just come on stage and to be waiting for her cue. She looks expectantly and, for all her childish innocence, rather self-consciously out at the spectator as she turns to face her imaginary audience. A few pastoral attributes lend deeper meaning to her dance – a heart, Cupid's arrow, and the basket of white and red roses. Symbols of the joys and sorrows of love, they allude to the fact that the little dancer will soon have grown out of her childish games.

Her three friends sit and watch from the shade of a tree. They are dressed as shepherds, one boy holding a long shepherd's crook while the other has just begun to play a tune on his flute; the girl between them leans back to watch, and beside them a brown and white dog has gone to sleep, oblivious of everything around him.

Yet the children's pastoral costumes are elegant and fashionable, and their play is an imitation of their elders' *fêtes galantes*. Nor is the stage really unsullied nature, but a wonderfully composed and artificial setting in which the shepherd and his flock and the old church in the background are included merely as evocative props.

This statement must be qualified, however, for as X-rays have shown, the round, central section of the painting is the only part that belongs to its original version, the corners having been added later. Yet Cochin's engraving, probably made before 1726, shows the painting in its present state. Who altered it and why, are questions no one has been able to answer. The painting itself must have been executed in 1719–20, when Watteau was in England for about a year.

Preliminary drawings of the heads of the three seated children have been preserved.

Antoine Watteau
The Dance
Without pieced-on sections

Jean François de Troy (1679–1752)
Bacchus and Ariadne
1717

Canvas, 140 × 165 cm ($55\frac{1}{8}$ × 65 in)
Signed: 'DE TROY 1717'
Acquired 1961
Property of the Kaiser-Friedrich-Museums-Verein
Cat. no. KFMV 241

Two episodes from Ovid's *Metamorphoses*, that inexhaustible source of subjects both dramatic and frivolous from the realm of Greek gods and goddesses, inspired two paintings by de Troy for the Regent of France, probably executed in 1717. The first recounted how Bacchus was reared by nymphs after the jealous Juno had driven his foster mother Ino mad, because she had adopted this son of Jupiter and his mistress, Semele (Ovid, *Metamorphoses* III, 310–17).

The second painting (colour plate) pictures the meeting of Bacchus and Ariadne on the island of Naxos (*Metamorphoses* VIII, 174–82). Ariadne, daughter of Minos, King of Crete, had assisted Theseus in his battle with the Minotaur and his escape from the labyrinth. On his return to Athens Theseus abducted the princess, but left her behind on Naxos. Bacchus, passing by with his revellers, discovered the abandoned girl and took her to be his wife. Four sons were born to them: Thaos, Staphylos, Oinopion and Peparethos. After Ariadne's death, Bacchus led her out of the underworld and up to Mount Olympus, where he threw her crown of light into the sky to shine forever in her memory among the stars (as the constellation *Corona Borealis*).

De Troy here represents the dramatic turning point of the story. Still visible in the far left distance is the ship on which fickle Theseus is sailing away. Bacchus has just arrived on the scene, climbed out of his panther-drawn chariot, and is listening with a gesture of commiseration to the desperate Ariadne's tale. Though she still points longingly to the ship, Cupid is already descending with the nuptial torch to enflame her with love for the god, as he is already enflamed by her charms. Yet Ariadne still seems not to notice Bacchus's advances, nor the bacchanalian revels in full swing around them. Maenads, nymphs and satyrs dance to their tambourines as Silenus, Bacchus's old mentor, approaches, fat and drunk on his donkey, supported by a satyr and led by a maenad. There is noise, frenzy, alcoholic and erotic transports on all sides. Yet the artist has depicted them without crass allusion: he has staged a riotous scene with the perfect taste and composure so typical of the Regency and Rococo.

The composition itself helps contain the turbulence, in a solidly constructed, almost classical arrangement. The main group acts as if on a stage bounded by the dark backdrop of trees in the centre and middle ground, while in the right and left foreground auxiliary groups of figures flank the main characters, leaving the centre free and yet remaining oriented towards it. An almost off-hand elegance characterizes both this image and its companion piece, *The Training of Bacchus*, and distinguishes both of them clearly from the great models for such bacchanalian themes in seventeenth-century Flemish painting, particularly the drastic revels of Jacob Jordaens.

Jean François de Troy belonged to a generation of French painters who were initially trained according to the strict observances of the Académie, but who then, under the impression of sixteenth- and seventeenth-century Italian and Flemish painting, translated the *grand goût* into a new idiom elegant in form and warm in palette. De Troy was a versatile talent, devoting himself as much to portraiture as to landscape, genre scenes, and mythological and historical subjects. The two Berlin paintings belong to his early period, having been executed after his return from Italy in 1708, when he was immediately accepted as a history painter into the Académie Royale.

Jean François de Troy
The Training of Bacchus
Berlin, Gemäldegalerie SMPK

Jean Restout (1692–1768)
The Magnanimity of Scipio
1728

Canvas, 132 × 197 cm (52 × 77½ in)
Signed: 'Restout 1728'
Rauceby Hall Collection, Lincs.
Acquired 1983
Cat. no. 3/83

In his history of Rome (*Ab urbe condita*, XXVI, 50) Titus Livius reports an event that took place during the Roman campaign against the Carthaginians in Spain. After the taking of New Carthage (Cartagena), a maiden of extraordinary beauty fell into the hands of the Roman commander, Publius Cornelius Scipio (*Africanus maior*, *c*.235–183 BC). Asked about her origins, Scipio's prisoner replied that she was the bride-to-be of Allucius, one of the noblest youths among the Celtiberians. Scipio sent for her parents and bridegroom, assured them that the girl's purity had been respected, and said that he was willing to set her free – on one condition, that Allucius become a friend of the Roman state. Declining the fine gifts offered to him by her parents, Scipio gave them instead to the young couple as a wedding present. Allucius, moved by Scipio's kindness and magnanimity, agreed to the deal and joined the Roman ranks.

Restout's painting follows its literary source very closely and represents the climax of the story. The Romans have erected their camp beneath the walls of the captured city. A low flight of steps under a baldachin provides a platform for their commander, who is distinguished by a red cloak even more brilliant than the many vivid colours around him. Allucius kneels down before him, grasping his hand in thanks, as Scipio indicates the young man's bride dressed in white, who approaches with her eyes demurely averted. At the right, her parents entreat the commander to accept their exquisite gifts, which are spread out before him on the ground like an opulent still-life. Auxiliary figures to left and right frame the composition and serve to focus our attention on the central event, as do the stage-like setting, the gestures of all the other figures, and the dramatic *mise en sène* of the whole.

This composition relies entirely on the classical canon of French history painting. As they advance from both sides, the actor's movements and gestures heighten the dramatic tension of the plot, which culminates in the figure of Scipio, its main character, at once reaching its climax and entering its dénouement. The local colours red, blue and white, are distributed in a manner that underlines the clear and logical placement of figures and accessories. Due to the low vantage point, only hints of the background landscape are visible, while the drama of virtue and magnanimity is played out large in the foreground as if just behind the footlights of a stage.

That the image has a moralizing tendency is undeniable. By relinquishing his prisoner, Scipio shows the true greatness of soul and noble selflessness which made him the finest embodiment of a virtuous man. And Restout, accordingly, concentrates less on the historical aspect of the event than on the example of humanitarian behaviour its represents. In this he may have drawn inspiration from several great seventeenth-century predecessors. As early as 1660–1, Charles Lebrun (1619–90) had already chosen a related subject from Roman history as a metaphor of a ruler's magnanimity, in his large painting *The Family of Darius Before Alexander* (Versailles, Musée National). Pierre Mignard (1612–95) and Jean Jouvenet (1644–1717) – the latter Restout's teacher – had developed the theme further, introducing important stylistic changes which allowed Restout, in his version, to take the decisive step from seventeenth-century Baroque pathos to the elegance in form and palette of the early Rococo. Actually, Restout was a religious painter who depicted few historical subjects. One of these was a large *Triumph of Bacchus*, commissioned in 1757 by Frederick the Great for the decoration of the Festival Hall in the Neues Palais, Potsdam.

The Magnanimity of Scipio once formed a companion piece to *Hector Taking Leave of Andromeda*, which was exhibited at the 1727 Salon. The two paintings were kept together in the Calonne Collection, Paris, until their sale in 1788. Though the companion piece is lost, its composition is recorded in a copy in the Halle Museum. By combining the two themes, Restout expanded on his fundamental message of the importance of virtue and selfless heroism. In this he conformed to one of the main purposes of history painting,

which was to inspire and educate by representing scenes of a timeless and ideal nature. It was to this high moral purpose that history painting owed its first rank among all the academic genres, a position it was able to maintain far into the nineteenth century.

Jean Baptiste Siméon Chardin (1699–1779)
The Young Draughtsman
1737

Canvas, 81 × 67 cm ($31\frac{7}{8} \times 26\frac{3}{8}$ in)
Signed: 'Chardin 1737'
From the Royal Palaces, Berlin
Acquired 1931
Cat. no. 2076

The subject of this painting is an allegorical one that was fairly common during the seventeenth and eighteenth centuries – a young artist at the beginning of his long and arduous training. This particular student, fine-featured and almost feminine, leans over a drawing table with his arm on a portfolio, sharpening the black crayon in a holder. He wears an apron to protect his fashionable coat, and his dark, three-cornered hat with a dangling ball for decoration serves not only elegance but also keeps his curly brown hair out of his eyes, the long back locks of which he has plaited in a loose braid. He has just finished a drawing on blue paper of the head of an old man or satyr, perhaps a copy after some Old Master, for that is what art students of the day were required to practice before going on to studies from life and, finally, free composition. Chardin is known to have been highly critical of this type of academic training.

The picture itself admittedly reveals little of this deeper, allegorical significance. What probably strikes the contemporary eye most about it is the superb feeling of calm it emanates. The boy's kindly, open gaze remains inward; the way he is poised over the table gives an impression of immobility, which lends the image more the appearance of a figurative still-life than an anecdote or scene. And though the motif might have something emblematic in its simplicity, this effect arises not so much from its symbolic meaning as from the solid structure of its composition and the lucidity of its colour scheme. The composition is built up of an interlocking scaffolding of planes and lines roughly parallel to the picture surface, beginning with the table edge and continuing through the offset diagonals of the portfolio and the boy's torso to run back and forth in a series of tense but balanced rhythms. These movements are finally brought back in upon themselves by the wide hat-brim and the direction of the boy's gaze. The background surrounds the figure like a protective cloak. Colour accents are few but emphatic – a blue in the drawing paper, and especially a small but forceful touch of red in the ribbons on the portfolio.

This high degree of abstraction with which the artist treated the theme was greatly admired during the nineteenth century, when an appreciation for this kind of noble simplicity of form finally developed. Painters ever since have admired the same qualities in Chardin – the painterly qualities which are so much in evidence here: a tranquillity and motionlessness that yet vibrate with the tension of a poised composition developed out of an interplay of pure forms, and a reserved mood resulting from a disciplined and rational employment of artistic means.

Two versions of *The Young Draughtsman* exist, both of them originals. One has been in the Louvre since 1944, and can be traced as far back as a sale in England in the year 1741. The other was acquired in 1931 by the Picture Gallery, after having been in the possession of the Prussian Royal House since its purchase for Frederick the Great in 1747, probably by Count Rothenburg – and after having been on the American art market for a short time following the partition of the royal estate in 1926. Both versions are signed and dated 1737, and hence are both authentic works by Chardin. They differ in details, but not at all in terms of their high quality.

Antoine Pesne (1683–1757)
Frederick the Great as Crown Prince
1739

Canvas, 78 × 63 cm ($30\frac{3}{4} \times 24\frac{3}{4}$ in)
Inscribed on the reverse: 'Original De S.A.R.Monseigneur le/Prince R. Peint a Reinsberg/par ant. Pesne en l'année 1739/et parvenue au Trone le 31 may 1740'
Acquired 1841
Cat. no. 489

Probably no other artist contributed more to our present picture of eighteenth-century Prussia than Antoine Pesne. Born in Paris in 1683, he became artist to the Prussian Court in 1711 and served under three monarchs: Frederick I, Frederick William I, and Frederick the Great. His portraits of the royal house, members of the court and nobility are both objective and effectively staged and, except perhaps for those turned out in series by his large workshop, of high artistic quality.

The true features of Frederick the Great remain shrouded in legend to this day. In monuments and portraits of the eighteenth and nineteenth centuries, he is invariably pictured as the great statesman or the military commander renowned for his victories in three Silesian Wars; or on the other hand, as the lonely old man and sage of Sanssouci. From Chodowiecki to Menzel, from Rauch's monument to Otto Gebühr's films of the 1930s, 'Old Fritz' has been the great king whom fate destined to lead Prussia to its belated place among the great powers of Europe.

Yet none of these images was truly authentic. Even as a young monarch, Frederick refused to sit to anyone for his portrait. The countless medals, commemorative coins, painted and modelled portraits, and the over 642 depictions of him in prints and drawings of the eighteenth century alone, may confirm his legendary fame, but they seldom give more than a stereotyped or idealized image of his features and bearing. Only while still Crown Prince did Frederick deign to have his likeness made – by Court Artist Pesne, and by the architect and artist Knobelsdorff. Of the few portraits antedating his accession to the throne on 31 May 1740, the present one, painted in 1739 at Rheinsberg, the Crown Prince's residence, is not only the last authentic portrait of Frederick but also the most human and characteristic.

'The King of Prussia is small, and quite well-fed without being fat. An intelligent physiognomy, attractive eyes, a round face, good-tempered and vivacious, quite lovely teeth, well-groomed brown hair, a noble appearance ... He interrogates one in a penetrating, witty way, and his questions require, even demand concise replies ... He is polite and goes out of his way to say obliging things,' wrote Duke Charles Philippe de Luynes in 1742. Pesne's portrait of Crown Prince Frederick, painted shortly before, captures many of these characteristics. Frederick appears here as Field Marshal in breastplate and orange riband of the Order of the Black Eagle over his shoulder, and a red velvet mantle embroidered with golden crowns. The large eyes in a regular, somewhat chubby face are directed straight at the observer. Frederick's contemporaries again and again emphasized the brilliance of his eyes in their attempts to describe his unusual personality and the vivacity of his presence.

Antoine Pesne
Frederick the Great
Holland, Huis Doorn

X-ray photographs of the painting have revealed that Pesne initially intended a partial reprise of his full-figure portrait of the Crown Prince of 1736 (Holland, Huis Doorn). In this very traditional portrait, Frederick stands to attention in commander's uniform with swagger stick, facing the observer frontally. A medal struck for Frederick's accession in 1740 shows exactly the same pose and half-length figure which the Gallery's portrait originally evinced.

In other words, the artist first literally repeated his earlier portrait, shortening it to half-length, but then decided to alter it considerably. After his reworking, all that remained of the original pose was the position of the head. The torso was turned from half-right to full-left, so that the Crown Prince now looks out at us over his left shoulder. With this change from the rather conventionally official and military posture of the earlier painting, Pesne transformed it into an image of a distinguished and self-assured prince on the threshold of sovereign power.

François Boucher (1703–70)
Venus and Cupid
*c.*1742

Canvas, 56 × 72 cm (22 × 28$\frac{3}{8}$ in)
Signed: 'F. Boucher'
Acquired 1978
Property of the
Kaiser-Friedrich-Museums-Verein
Cat. no. KFMV 272

The scene is set in a twilit clearing among the trees, near a mossy fountain, over the undulating edge of whose shell-shaped bowl water trickles into a brook. Venus reclines on an exquisite shawl of striped Indian silk shot through with gold threads. Her coyly innocent pose and coquettishly dislodged chemise reveal more of her charms than they were ever meant to conceal. Cupid, childishly engrossed, is playing with two white doves which he has tethered on a delicate blue ribbon. His red quiver is propped against Venus's seashell-chariot, which is decorated with white and red roses. Water, shell, and roses, together with the pearls in her blond hair, are the goddess's traditional attributes, evoking her mythical origin in the waves of the sea: Venus born of the foam.

Mythology, however, was for Boucher merely a welcome pretext to celebrate feminine beauty and, embodied in its goddess, the primal power of love. An engraving of the painting by Pierre Duclos (1742–1806) emphasized this more comprehensive significance by quoting a verse by Moraine:

'Déesse, qui donnés de si préssants desirs,
Qui remplissés nos cœurs d'ardeurs, d'inquiétude,
De sentimens jalous et de vifs déplaisirs,
Livrés-vous au sommeil dans cette solitude,
Césses de nous causer tant de tourmens divers;
Votre repos sera celui de l'Univers.'

Only when Venus sleeps is the world at peace; otherwise, everything is in constant restless motion, transient as the action on the stage of a theatre.

Boucher has masterfully translated a sensual theme into sensuous, delicately orchestrated colour. Between the muted browns of the background and the cool greens of the foreground foliage, light, glowing flesh tones, nuances of white, purple and opalescent violet luxuriously expand. It was with just such small-format paintings as this, probably intended for some expensively tasteful boudoir, that Boucher created his finest and most intimate works.

The picture in our collection originally had a companion piece, a *Diana at Rest* – the virginal goddess of the hunt contrasted with the goddess of love. The whereabouts of this painting has remained unknown since the pair was separated in 1783, at the auction of the Blondel d'Azaincourt collection in Paris.

With his scenes of pastoral dalliance, his landscapes and mythological subjects, designs for tapestries and decorations, and engraving sequences, Boucher shaped the taste of an entire epoch. He remained in royal favour for almost thirty years after having been admitted, as a history painter, into the Académie Royale in 1734 and commissioned by Louis XV only a year later to decorate the chambers of Queen Marie Leczinska at Versailles. His great benefactress, however, was Madame Pompadour, whom Louis XV raised to the rank of *Maîtresse en titre* in 1745 and who deluged Boucher with commissions. The artist later estimated his œuvre to comprise about a thousand paintings and ten thousand drawings. It certainly bears witness to a veritably inexhaustible flow of ideas, despite the routine touch of an overworked master which they sometimes reveal.

Joseph Vernet (1714–89)
View of Nogent-sur-Seine
1764

Canvas, 75 × 113 cm ($29\frac{1}{2} \times 44\frac{1}{2}$ in)
Signed: 'J. Vernet 1764'
Cailleux Collection, Paris
Acquired 1975
Cat. no. 2/75

Vernet was probably the most influential and highest regarded landscape painter in Europe during the eighteenth century. Connoisseurs and collectors deluged him with orders, which in his later years he was able to fulfil only with the assistance of a great workshop. An enormous life's work comprising almost two thousand paintings attests to his fame. His dramatic or idyllic landscapes and seascapes, cycles on the times of day or seasons, depictions of calm or stormy seas, and of ships returning home or wrecked and abandoned on treacherous rocks, met the sentimental tastes of his age to perfection.

After a long sojourn in Rome (1734–54) during which he established his reputation as a landscape artist, Vernet was honoured on his return to France by a commission to paint twenty-four views of the country's most important harbours – doubtless a significant political commission. Due to the years of travel its execution entailed, the artist was not able to settle finally in Paris until 1763.

That year brought a commission from the wealthy Jean de Boullongne, former Minister of Finance, to paint two views of Nogent-sur-Seine, a small village north of Paris at the point where the Paris–Troyes road crosses the Seine. Since the river was navigable up to the dam there, the village developed into a trading centre for goods of all kinds. Nearby, the local count had built a castle, La Chapelle-Godefroy, where he lived in retirement, devoting himself to the arts. He also established a stocking factory in a former convent there, which Vernet has portrayed in his painting. The companion piece showed the village itself, but only a fragment of it has survived, and is today in an English private collection.

The highroad crosses the Seine near Nogent over two bridges, one of which appears here – the Pont-Saint-Nicolas, built in 1728. To its right, before the machine building, lies the small harbour, and the stocking factory itself is located in the group of buildings in the background. The idyllic yet precisely rendered scene is suffused with the mild, warm light of morning, an illumination for which Vernet was renowned.

As in all of his pictures of this type, however, the landscape rendering goes beyond mere topographical exactness, and the figures serve the important function of making the landscape appear inhabited and busy, integrating nature in the human sphere. And accordingly, all social strata are represented. The gentleman accompanying two elegantly dressed ladies might well be the factory owner out on a tour of inspection. Of the other classes, there is a fisherman pulling in his nets; his wife with a basket of freshly caught fish on her arm; boatmen loading or unloading a barge; and a farmer with his wife riding on a mule. The landscape and its inhabitants merge into a well-ordered microcosm where everyone and everything has its proper place in the social system.

Vernet exhibited both views of Nogent-sur-Seine in the 1765 Salon, which definitely confirmed his triumph. It was this exhibition that inspired Diderot's famous review of Vernet's work, which begins with the dramatic cry, 'Twenty-five paintings, my friend! Twenty-five paintings? But what paintings!' He then goes on to describe them in detail, as though they were actual stretches of countryside, only at the end admitting that they were entirely invented by a great artist. But the highest praise he could give was to compare Vernet to the unchallenged old master of landscape, Claude Lorrain. 'Vernet is just as good as Claude Lorrain in the art of conjuring up mist on canvas; but he far surpasses him in the invention of scenes, the design of figures, the variety of his events, etc. The earlier man is only a great landscape painter; the latter, in my opinion, is truly a history painter. Claude chooses the rare moods in nature, and on that account is perhaps more exciting. The atmosphere in Vernet is more in the common run, and accordingly is more reassuringly familiar.'

Joseph Vernet
Nogent-sur-Seine
England, Private Collection

Elisabeth-Louise Vigée-Lebrun (1755–1842)
Prince Henry Lubomirski as the Genius of Fame
1789

Oak, 105 × 83 cm ($41\frac{3}{8}$ × $32\frac{5}{8}$ in)
Collection of Isabella Lubomirska, Paris, Warsaw, Lancut
Acquired 1974
Cat. no. 4/74

In autumn 1785, Princess Isabella Lubomirska, her opposition to King Stanislav August Poniatowski having become too apparent, left her Polish homeland to begin a six-year journey through Europe. She arrived in Paris in November 1786, where until the outbreak of revolution she resided in the Palais Royal and held a salon that became a favourite gathering place of Parisian society.

Among those accompanying her was the young Prince Henry Lubomirski (1777–1850) from a branch of her family in Kiev. The boy's extraordinary beauty and the childishly soulful cast of his features caused a great stir wherever he appeared. The rich princess, herself a collector and patron of the arts, not surprisingly had a series of portraits made of the boy, in Rome, Paris and London. The most significant of these was painted in Paris, in the early summer of 1789, when on the eve of revolution the princess offered Elisabeth Vigée-Lebrun, court artist to Queen Marie Antoinette, the unheard-of sum of twelve thousand francs to portray young Henry in the latest style, *à la grecque*.

The artist has placed her winged Cupid on a red drapery in the foreground of an expansive but mistily undefined landscape. He turns his head with its soft blond locks gently to the side, letting his large brown eyes stray into the distance. The expression on his regular features is perfectly described by Lavater's phrase, 'innocence and simplicity'. He holds a wreath of myrtle and laurel leaves, and a quiver with arrows lies forgotten before him on the ground. The delicate yet powerful-looking wings shimmer in subtle transitions from white to soft violet and a bluish-pink, echoing the light flesh tones, the strong red of the drapery, and the green wreath against a grey-blue sky. These colour nuances perfectly complement the idealized beauty and precociously knowing expression of the boy's face, to superbly exemplify the sentimental, Neo-Classical approach to portraiture.

The reference to Classical art is present in the attributes, but even more in the figure's pose, which refers directly back to a statue known as *Crouching Venus*, by Doidales. This Hellenistic sculpture of the third century BC was represented in many collections by Roman copies, cameos, and gems; but even more importantly, it was widely and popularly known through a figurine based on it. The *Portrait of Henry Lubomirski* relates quite directly to this sculpture. Despite all its refinement of colour and painterly surface, and despite the model's sentimental expression, the sculptural quality of the ancient Roman statue is its most striking characteristic. The emphasis on the principal view, the almost feminine softness of limb, the crouching pose, and the typical Roman movement of the body within a closed contour line, stylistically corroborate the artist's citation from antiquity. And nudity, in the eyes of a true Neo-Classicist, was inalienably part of the ideal style – even Napoleon had to succumb to Canova's apotheosis of him in a larger-than-life, nude statue of a Roman imperator.

Considering the Princess Lubomirska's admiration for Winckelmann, and also her enthusiasm for Lavater and Rousseau, it is no wonder that this portrait of a child should have had a special meaning. All the allegorical depictions of young Henry executed at the Princess's request during her European tour – as Amor, Bacchus, Amphion, Seraphim, or the Spirit of Fame – reflect not only her affection for him, but also her belief that his childish beauty contained the essence of a higher, ideal nature that only art could make visible.

Crouching Venus
third century BC
Rome, Museo Vaticano

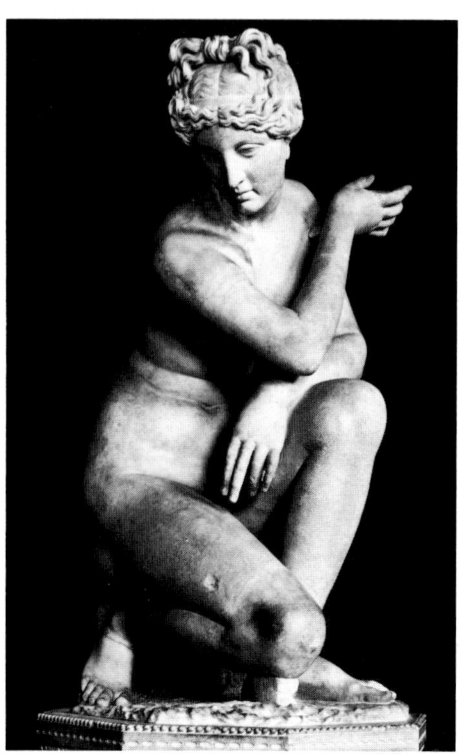

Joshua Reynolds (1723–92)

George Clive and his Family with an Indian Servant Girl

*c.*1765

Canvas, 140 × 171 cm ($55\frac{1}{8} \times 67\frac{3}{8}$ in)
Earl of Ellesmere, Bridgewater House, London
Acquired 1978
Cat. no. 1/78

Vying with the other European powers for political and economic supremacy during the eighteenth century, the British triumphed particularly in India. In 1757, Robert, Lord Clive of Plassey (1725–74) conquered and occupied the Bengal State, then during his service from 1764–7 as High Commander in East India, contributed decisively to British military successes. Among his personal aides was his cousin, George Clive (*c.*1720–79). Son of a clergyman, Clive joined the army and saw service in all the Indian campaigns. He returned to England a prosperous man and in 1763 was elected to Parliament as member for Bishop Castle. That same year he married Miss Sidney Bolton (1740–1814). In 1772, he commissioned the architect Robert Tayler to build him a fine estate, Mount Clare, in Roehampton outside London.

The Clives' eldest daughter was born in 1764, but she died in childhood. From her age in Reynolds's portrait of the family, we may conclude that it was executed about 1765–6.

As in so many of his large portraits, Reynolds relied here on the classical tradition of seventeenth-century Italian and Flemish portraiture, while enlivening it with a touch of the latest 'Indian' mode. For all its apparently relaxed atmosphere, the image is a masterpiece of formal representation, and its composition is arranged and balanced with extreme care. The family stands as if on an open veranda in the foreground, behind Clive lies a stretch of open hilly countryside with the golden glow of sunset still suffusing the horizon. Behind mother and child on the right, by contrast, a purple curtain obscures the view, closing out the world as if to evoke the family's domestic intimacy. The curtain is also a set-piece from centuries of official portraiture, the symbol of royal dignity and honour, used here to signify the social standing of the artist's sitters.

George Clive leans with easy self-assurance on the back of a red upholstered chair. Since the picture was not intended for official purposes, despite its open and veiled allusions, Clive wears the rather elaborate yet everyday clothes of a country gentleman. The group to his right is quite different, being separated from him not only physically. Mrs Clive and her Indian maid concentrate all their attention on the little girl, who, like her mother – and the maid – is superbly attired in the latest fashion.

Of special interest are the details here, which the artist has intentionally rendered with great precision. The exotic costumes worn by daughter and servant are intended to strike the eye, and to allude to the Clive family's close ties with the new British colony. The girl wears a light Indian cotton dress (an *anjarika* or *jama*) with pastel blue trim, of a kind worn by children of rich families at the courts of Indian princes. A scarf of fine silk with gold-embroidered border (*chaddar*) is fastened to her hair with a jewelled brooch, worn much as a contemporary Indian girl might wear a pretty flower. The charm bracelet (*bazuband*), worn Indian-style on her upper arm, has an arrangement of nine stones in the centre (*nauratna*) representing the nine planets, which play an important role in Indian astrology. The servant, judging by her ethnic type and her jewellery, may come from southern India, perhaps from the Madras region. Her hair, gathered in a topknot, and her necklace with three charms (*tali*) indicate that she is married. The medallion on her hairpin bears an ornament that is surely of magical significance, and on her wrist is a bracelet consisting of an ivory ring dyed with madder (*manjistha*) with gold ornaments and several black rings of a type still to be found today.

These numerous details are subtly integrated into the image and contribute to its opulent effect. A dominating, warm combination of brown (on the left), red and white (centre), and delicate grey (right) lends the painting that compelling colour which reveals Reynolds's debt to Flemish art. This consciousness of tradition, combined with an apparently unconstrained ease in conveying social status, lend Reynolds's portrait exactly the air of understated ceremony which his patrons expected of him.

X-rays of the painting show that his workshop contributed much to its execution, as was common practice with Reynolds. Evidently, only the three figures on the right were first blocked out on a smaller canvas. Then, to expand the composition, a piece of heavier canvas was spliced on to the left of the maid's figure, and certain passages were repainted – the landscape for instance, which was extended to Clive's right and behind the maid's head. As regards the figure of Mrs Clive, Reynolds obviously executed only the face, indicating the gown with a few cursory brushstrokes. The final and very careful rendering was probably undertaken by the foreman of Reynolds's workshop, who was responsible for drapery, or possibly by the well-known 'drapery man', Peter Toms. The child and servant, on the other hand, appear to have been painted entirely by Reynolds himself.

Joshua Reynolds

Lady Sunderlin

1786

Canvas, 236 × 145 cm (93 × 57 in)
Baron Ferdinand de Rothschild; Lord Burton
Acquired 1983
Cat. no. 4/83

The *Portrait of Lady Sunderlin*, among the most significant of the artist's late works, was executed almost contemporaneously with Gainsborough's fine late canvas in the Berlin Gallery, his group portrait of the Marsham children of 1787. Lady Sunderlin (1745–1831) was the eldest daughter of Godolphin Roopers of Great Berkamstead (Hertfordshire). In 1778 she married Richard Malone, a well-to-do London barrister who in 1785 was raised by George III to Baron Sunderlin of Lake Sunderlin. It was on this occasion that Reynolds received the commission for a full-length portrait of the Baron's wife, for which he was paid the sum of £157. 10*s* in November 1786.

For his life-size portrayal Reynolds chose the classical, Baroque scheme that van Dyck had introduced into England in the seventeenth century and that remained the prototype for official portraits far into the eighteenth century. In his annual lectures on the occasion of the Royal Academy awards, Reynolds, its President since 1768, repeatedly argued the importance of traditional pictorial formulas for the modern painter. Whenever his own work demanded an official portrait in the 'grand style', he did not hesitate to quote artists from Holbein and Michelangelo to van Dyck, frequently even giving his citations of the Classical masters an ironic twist. This is why a knowledge of Reynolds's borrowings and allusions and their translation into his own style is so crucial to an understanding of his portraits. If the composition, pose, and background landscape in the Berlin portrait rely on van Dyck, then the artist's reference to the courtly and official seventeenth century mode was surely meant to underline the social rank of his sitter.

The tall and slender Lady Sunderlin, forty-one years of age at the time, is portrayed in a light gown in front of a dark backdrop of trees. To her right, suffused in evening light, the landscape extends from bushes and hills in the foreground to a far horizon. Thanks to its warm hues and a free, vivid rendering, this landscape contributes much more to the superb effect of the portrait than is generally the case with such backdrops. Another touch of vivacity is the way Lady Sunderlin was apparently about to gather the folds of her long, white, sweeping silk gown when the artist caught the motion of her hand. While features such as these still go back to seventeenth-century tradition, contemporary details like the exquisite chiffon veil shot through with gold, the rich gold embroidery on the gathered sleeves, the nonchalantly looped golden girdle, and the blue turban *à bandeau* on the high-piled coiffure, reveal the influence of the latest Turkish mode. As early as 1777, the *Magazin à la Mode* had remarked about this oriental craze that 'with little or no operation, an English lady, taken from one of our polite assemblies and conducted to Constantinople, would be properly dressed to appear before the Grand Signior.'

The artist's combination of current fashion with a traditional portrait type, and of a subtle idealization of the model with a paint handling very modern in its fluency, make the image a particularly striking and lovely example of Reynolds's portrait art during the final years of his life.

Thomas Gainsborough (1727–88)

The Marsham Children

1787

Canvas, 243 × 182 cm ($95\frac{5}{8} \times 71\frac{5}{8}$ in)
Collection of Baron Elie de Rothschild, Paris
Acquired 1982
Cat. no. 4/82

In July 1787 the First Earl of Romney, Charles Marsham (1744–1811), commissioned the sixty-year-old Thomas Gainsborough to portray his four children, Charles (1777–1845), Frances (1778–1868), Harriot (1780–1825), and Amelia Charlotte (1782–1863). The Marsham family originated from Norfolk, had resided in Kent since the seventeenth century, and had been raised to the peerage in 1716. During the latter half of the eighteenth century, various members of the family had their likenesses painted by the best artists in London, among them Romney, Hoppner, Gardener, Zoffany, Reynolds, and of course Gainsborough.

The format of the painting is large and imposing. Yet between the life-size figures space has been left for an idyllic, late-summer landscape that contributes astonishingly to the effect of the image – the mild illumination and delicately tinted atmosphere create an outdoor mood verging on the romantic, a setting perfectly suited to complement the children's natural charm. Their everyday clothes reveal the artist's – or perhaps his patron's – intention to depict them not as miniature adults and future pillars of society, but simply as children at play. English painting of the eighteenth century is rich in such portraits of children who are as yet wonderfully free of the social airs of their elders.

The composition nonetheless subtly suggests the children's differences in age and status. The ten-year-old Charles, only son and heir of his father's title, is clearly distinguished from his sisters. He stands alone on the right, handing some hazelnuts to Frances, the next eldest at nine, who holds her skirt up to receive them. She in turn embraces the seven-year-old Harriot, while the youngest girl, red-headed Amelia Charlotte sits alone on the left with her arm around the family's favourite dog, Fidèle. She is the only one of the children to gaze out earnestly at the observer, while the others seem reserved and grouped statically.

As in many of Gainsborough's compositions, which were usually painted in dim studio light and sometimes even by candlelight in order better to gauge the overall effect, this one is entirely determined by alternating passages of light and dark. Numerous *pentimenti*, however, indicate that the artist altered certain details of the conception during the painting process. His short, nervous brushstrokes pull figures, landscape, and foliage together into a strangely vibrating, dense web of colour that recalls the early Rococo – Gainsborough had a high regard for Watteau – more than it anticipates the romantic style of Lawrence, not to mention Constable's realism. Reynolds greatly admired the evocative force of this open and in many passages even sketchy paint handling which during his final years Gainsborough developed into a unique stylistic technique, though it was certainly a far cry from Reynolds's own, very conscientious approach.

The development of English painting soon left Gainsborough's mature style behind. In the same year that he portrayed the Marsham children Thomas Lawrence arrived in London, and from then on, this young artist's romantic portraits set the standard. The extent to which taste changed may be seen from Lawrence's 1807 portrait of *The Angerstein Children* (colour plate p. 423). Though its composition is similar, it is nevertheless much more traditional than Gainsborough's, even employing the age-old symbol of sovereign dignity, the dark red curtain. And the warm, lucent palette brings a moodiness and sentimentality into the image that Gainsborough's cool and disciplined portraiture would never have countenanced.

Thomas Lawrence (1769–1830)
The Angerstein Children
1807

Canvas, 184 × 149 cm ($72\frac{1}{2} \times 58\frac{5}{8}$ in)
Acquired 1979
Cat. no. 2/79

In 1787 an eighteen-year-old pastel artist by the name of Thomas Lawrence arrived in London. Three years later this unknown young man was working on a life-size portrait of Queen Charlotte (London, National Gallery). His rapid success was enough to convince London that he, not the older Hoppner or Raeburn, was the true successor to the great Sir Joshua Reynolds. Lawrence was inundated with portrait commissions, but even more importantly, was accepted as a friend by many of the city's first families – the Lockes, the Boucheretts and the Angersteins. The rich banker John Julius Angerstein (1735–1823) in particular, co-founder of Lloyd's and advisor to Prime Minister Pitt, became Lawrence's paternal friend, advised him in his often terribly confused financial affairs, and supported him in his work. A welcome guest at Angerstein's Pall Mall residence and his country house, Woodlands, near Greenwich, the artist in turn advised the banker concerning his collection of Old Masters, and after his death in 1825, helped arrange its purchase by the English government to form the core of the National Gallery collections.

The Berlin portrait is one of the many Lawrence painted for the Angerstein family over the course of almost thirty years. It was begun on 17 August 1807, at Woodlands; but just two days later the artist was complaining in a letter that he was forced to do this most difficult of all subjects all at once. Everybody, the children included, ran back and forth, and nothing he could say would prevent them. Whether for this or other reasons, the painting was never finished, as so often with Lawrence; nevertheless, it was exhibited the following year at the Royal Academy.

The old John Julius Angerstein's four grandchildren, two boys and two girls, are shown at play in a garden based on the park at Woodlands. Grasping a broom on the right is the eldest, John Julius (1801–66), who is set off from the others by his pose and dark attire. In the centre the youngest Angerstein, Henry Frederick (1805–21), awkwardly attempts to dig with a spade much too big for him, and is prevented from falling by his sister, Carolina Amelia (1802[?]–79), as Elizabeth Julia (1803[?]–?) looks on. This carefully arranged and integrated composition of figures is still very much in the classical tradition of the eighteenth century.

The charm of the young faces, the children's chubby-cheeked engrossment in their play, and particularly the warm, luminous colours set among greyed whites, brilliant reds, and dark background hues, show Lawrence to be a true Romantic. It was above all in his renderings of children and mother and child groups that the notorious bachelor created the finest Romantic portraits in English art. Their moods range from natural insouciance to elegiac sentimentality; their apparent spontaneity and lightness of touch never reveal the slow and painstaking work that went into their composition and execution. The present work also shows signs of the afterthoughts so characteristic of Lawrence: a small bucket once lay in the left foreground, but was painted over as work progressed; and the red curtain at the top, a traditional symbol of nobility meant to suggest the portrait's official nature, was likewise a later addition. Moreover, whether at the request of his dissatisfied client or on his own account no one can say, Lawrence repeated the group in a completely new composition (Paris, Louvre). Here, a massive column, another traditional aristocratic attribute, heightens the more official, formal arrangement of the group, which lacks the relaxed charm of the somewhat earlier Berlin canvas.

Thomas Lawrence
The Angerstein Children
Paris, Musée du Louvre

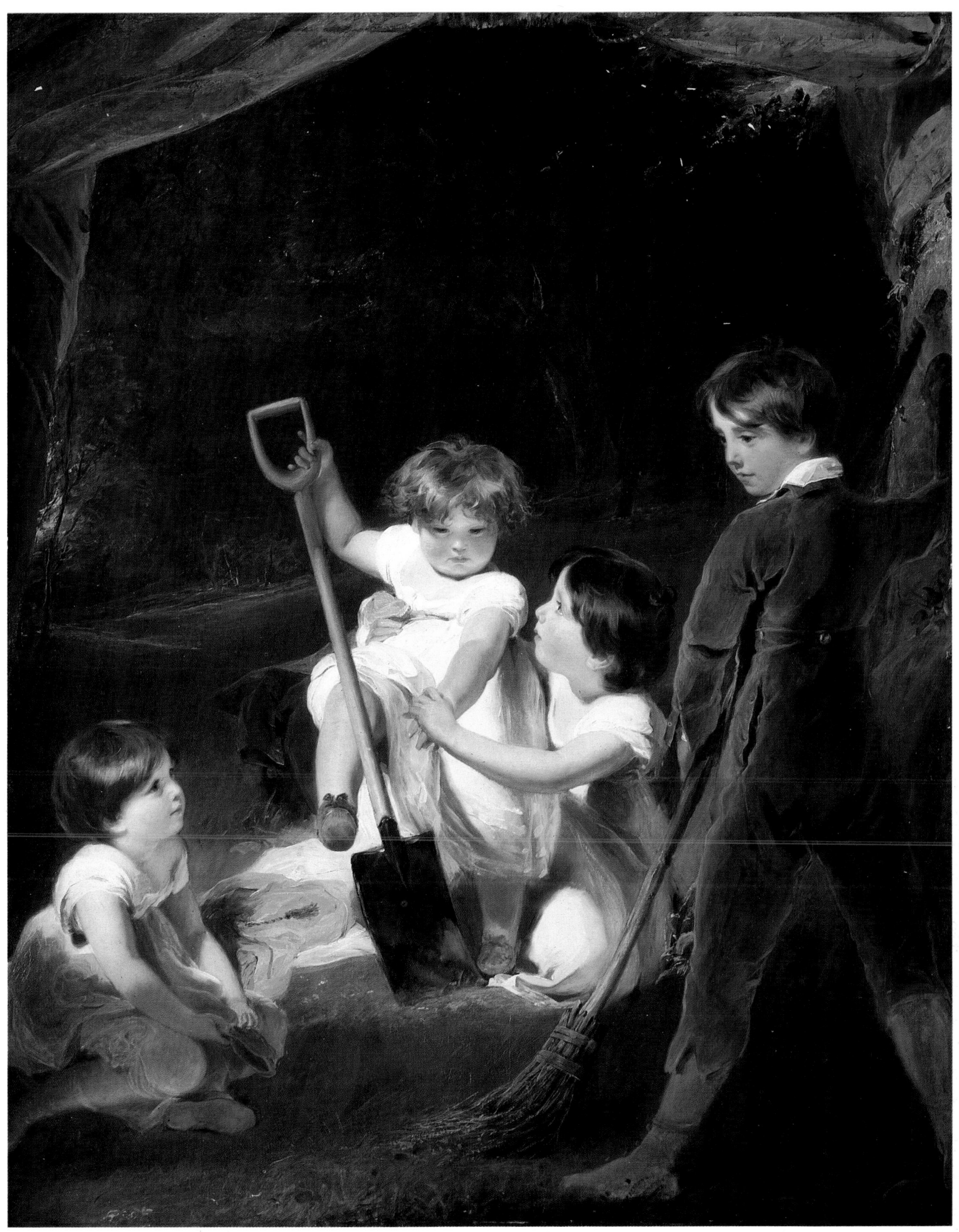

BIBLIOGRAPHY

A detailed history of the Berlin Museums has never before been written, although the subject would be interesting and important, including a look at the fourteen departments of the State Museums SMPK. However, in 1971 Rüdiger Klessmann produced an excellent outline of the history of the collection for the Gemäldegalerie. The following bibliography, therefore, lists only the more important works and the older relevant literature.

*

Waagen, G.F. *Verzeichnis der Gemälde-Sammlung des Königlichen Museums zu Berlin*, 1st edn, Berlin 1830; 14th edn, Berlin 1860.

Kugler, F. *Beschreibung der Gemälde-Galerie des Königlichen Museums zu Berlin*, Berlin 1838.

Meyer, J. and Bode, W. *Königliche Museen, Gemäldegalerie. Beschreibendes Verzeichnis . . . der Gemälde*, 1st edn, Berlin 1878; 9th edn, Berlin State Museum, Berlin 1931.

Staatliche Museen zu Berlin. *Die Gemäldegalerie*, 5 vols with illustrations, ed. by Irene Kunze, Berlin 1929–32.

Gemäldegalerie Berlin, Staatliche Museen Preussischer Kulturbesitz. *Verzeichnis der ausgestellten Werke des 13.–18. Jahrhunderts im Museum Dahlem*, 1st edn, Berlin 1956; 10th edn, Berlin 1966; English edn, Berlin 1968.

Redslob, E. *Gemäldegalerie Berlin-Dahlem, ehemals Kaiser-Friedrich-Museum*, Baden-Baden 1964.

Klessman, R. *Gemäldegalerie Berlin*, Essen 1971, English edn, London 1971.

Kaiser-Friedrich-Museums-Verein, Berlin. *Erwerbungen 1897–1972*, Berlin 1972.

Gemäldegalerie Berlin, Staatliche Museen Preussischer Kulturbesitz. *Katalog der ausgestellten Gemälde des 13.–18. Jahrhunderts*, Berlin 1975.

Gemäldegalerie Berlin, Staatliche Museen Preussischer Kulturbesitz. *Catalogue of Paintings 13th–18th Century*, translated by Linda B.Parshall, 2nd edn, Berlin 1978.

Gemäldegalerie, Berlin, Staatliche Museen Preussischer Kulturbesitz, from the series *Museum*, Braunschweig 1979.

Belser Kunstbibliothek *Die Meisterwerke aus der Gemäldegalerie Berlin, Staatliche Museen Preussischer Kulturbesitz*, Stuttgart and Zürich 1980.

Bock, H. and Köhler, W. H. *Gemäldegalerie; Staatlich Museen Preussischer Kulturbesitz, Berlin*, Touring Club Italiano, Milano 1982.

Gemäldegalerie, Berlin, Staatliche Museen Preussischer Kulturbesitz. *Gesamtverzeichnis der Gemälde*, Berlin/London 1986.

*

Illustrated booklets for the Staatliche Museen Preussischer Kulturbesitz:

Warnke, M. *Flämische Malerei des 17. Jahrhunderts*, Book 1, Berlin 1967.

Arndt, K. *Altniederländische Malerei*, Book 5, Berlin 1968.

Klessmann, R. *Holländische Malerei des 17. Jahrhunderts*, Books 11 & 12, Berlin 1969; 2nd revised edn 1983.

*

Bernhard, M. and Martin, K. *Verlorene Werke der Malerei. In Deutschland in der Zeit von 1939 bis 1945 zerstörte und verschollene Gemälde aus Museen und Galerien*, Munich 1965.

Bock, H., Gutbrod, R. and Riede, B. 'Die neue Gemäldegalerie. Einblicke – Einsichten – Aussichten', from the *Arbeit der Staatlichen Museen Preussischer Kulturbesitz*, special volume, 1983, pp. 133–51.

Bode, W. von 'Das Kaiser-Friedrich-Museum. Zur Eröffnung am 18.10.1904', *Museumskunde*, 1, 1905, pp. 1–16.

Bode, W. von 'Bruno Pauls Pläne zum Asiatischen Museum in Dahlem', *Jahrbuch der Preussischen Kunstsammlung*, 36, 1915, pp. 1–5.

Bode, W. von *Mein Leben*, 2 vols, Berlin 1930.

Börsch-Supan, H. 'Die Gemälde aus dem Vermächtnis der Amalie von Solms und aus der Oranischen Erbschaft in den brandenburgisch-preussischen Schlössern', *Zeitschrift für Kunstgeschichte*, 30, 1967, p. 143 ff.

Clemen, P. et al. 'Das Kaiser-Friedrich-Museum', *Zeitschrift für bildende Kunst NF.*, 16, 1905, p. 20 ff.

Eckhart, G. *Die Gemälde in der Bildergalerie von Sanssouci*, Potsdam 1980.

Geismeier, I. 'Gustav Friedrich Waagen – 45 Jahre Museumsarbeit', *Forschungen und Berichte/Staatliche Museen zu Berlin/DDR*, 20/21, 1980, pp. 130–7.

Geismeier, I. 'Fünfundsiebzig Jahre Bodemuseum 1904–1979', *Forschungen und Berichte/Staatliche Museen zu Berlin/DDR*, 23, 1983, pp. 130–7.

Girardet, C.-M. 'James Simon', *Jahrbuch Preussischer Kulturbesitz*, 19, 1982, pp. 77–98.

Hildebrand, J. and Theuerkauff, C. 'Die Brandenburgisch-Preussische Kunstkammer. Eine Auswahl aus den alten Beständen', exh. cat. *Staatliche Museen Preussischer Kulturbesitz*, Berlin 1981.

Kadatz, H.-J. and Murza, G. *Georg Wenzeslaus von Knobelsdorff, Baumeister Friedrichs II*, Leipzig 1983.

Kühn, M. 'Der Gemäldebesitz der brandenburgisch-preussischen Schlösser', *Gedenkschrift Ernst Gall*, Munich 1965, pp. 403–43.

Kühnel-Kunze, I. 'Bergung – Evakuierung – Rückführung, Die Berliner Museen in den Jahren 1939–59', *Jahrbuch Preussischer Kulturbesitz*, 1984, special volume 2.

Lowenthal-Hensel, C. 'Die Erwerbung der Sammlung Solly durch den preussischen Staat. Neue Forschungen zur Brandenburg-Preussischen Geschichte', 1, Cologne and Vienna, published from the archives of the *Preussischer Kulturbesitz*, 14, 1, pp. 109–59.

Lübbe, H. 'Wilhelm von Humboldt und die Berliner Museumsgründung 1830', *Jahrbuch Preussischer Kulturbesitz*, 17, 1980, pp. 87–110.

Lüdicke, R. *Die Preussischen Kulturminister und ihre Beamten im ersten Jahrhundert des Ministeriums 1817–1917*, Stuttgart and Berlin 1918.

Mielke, F. *Potsdamer Baukunst. Das klassische Potsdam*, Frankfurt, Berlin and Vienna 1981.

Plagemann, V. *Das deutsche Kunstmuseum* 1790–1870, Munich 1967.

Platz-Horster, G. 'Zur Geschichte der Berliner Gipssammlung', exh. cat. *Berlin und die Antike*, II, Berlin 1979, p. 273 ff.

Poensgen, G. 'Schinkel, Friedrich Wilhelm IV. und Ludwig Persius, in: Schinkel in der Mark', *Brandenburgische Jahrbücher*, 7, 1937, pp. 51–62.

Reuther, H. *Die Museumsinsel in Berlin*, Frankfurt, Berlin and Vienna 1977.

Staatliche Museen zu Berlin, (East), in cooperation with the Staatliche Schlösser und Gärten Potsdam-Sanssouci and with support from the Institut für Denkmalpflege der DDR, exh. cat. *Karl Friedrich Schinkel 1781–1841*, Berlin 1980–1.

Verwaltung der Staatlichen Schlösser und Gärten/Nationalgalerie, Staatliche Museen Preussischer Kulturbesitz, exh. cat. *Karl Friedrich Schinkel: Architektur, Malerei, Kunstgewerbe*, Berlin 1981.

Schöne, R. *Die Gründung und Organisation der Königlichen Museen in Berlin. Festschrift zur Feier ihres fünfzigjährigen Bestehens am 3. August 1880*, Berlin 1880, pp. 31–58.

Seidel, P. 'Zur Vorgeschichte der Berliner Museen', *Jahrbuch der Preussischen Kunstsammlungen*, 49, 1928, supplement pp. 55–174.

Spiero, S. 'Schinkels Altes Museum in Berlin. Seine Baugeschichte von den Anfängen bis zur Eröffnung', *Jahrbuch der Preussischen Kunstsammlungen*, 55, 1934, supplement pp. 41–86.

Stock, F. 'Urkunden zur Vorgeschichte des Berliner Museums', *Jahrbuch der Preussischen Kunstsammlungen*, 51, 1930, pp. 205–22.

Stock, F. 'Urkunden zur Einrichtung des Berliner Museums', *Jahrbuch der Preussischen Kunstsammlungen*, 58, 1937, supplement pp. 1–88.

Berliner Museen ed. Horst-Johs, catalogue and discussion, *Tümmers. Verzeichnis der Kataloge kunst- und kulturgeschichtlicher Museen in der Bundesrepublik Deutschland und Berlin (West)*, 1, Berlin 1975.

Waetzoldt, S. *Museumspolitik – Richard Schöne und Wilhelm von Bode. Kunstverwaltung, Bau- und Denkmal-Politik im Kaiserreich*, ed. E. Mai and S. Waetzoldt, Berlin 1981, pp. 481–90.

Waetzoldt, W. 'Die Staatlichen Museen zu Berlin 1830–1930', *Jahrbuch der Preussischen Kunstsammlungen*, 51, 1930, pp. 189–204.

Wescher, P. *Kunstraub unter Napoleon*, Berlin 1976.

INDEX OF COLOUR PLATES

W9-BQT-866

INTRODUCTION TO JAVA PROGRAMMING,
Seventh Edition

VideoNotes Access Card

Thank you for purchasing a new copy of *Introduction to Java Programming,* Seventh Edition, by Y. Daniel Liang. The information below provides instruction on how to access VideoNotes, Pearson's new visual tool for teaching and reinforcing key programming concepts and techniques.

VideoNotes are step-by-step videos that demonstrate how to solve problems from design through coding. VideoNotes allow for self-paced instruction with easy navigation including the ability to play, rewind, fast-forward, and stop within each VideoNote exercise.

– Margin icons in your textbook let you know that a VideoNotes tutorial is available for a particular concept or representative homework problem.

To access VideoNotes for Liang, 7e:

1. Go to www.prenhall.com/liang
2. Click on the title *Introduction to Java Programming*, Seventh Edition.
3. Click on the link to VideoNotes. There you can register as a First-Time User and Returning User.
4. Use a coin to scratch off the coating below and reveal your student access code.
   ***Do not use a knife or other sharp object as it may damage the code.*

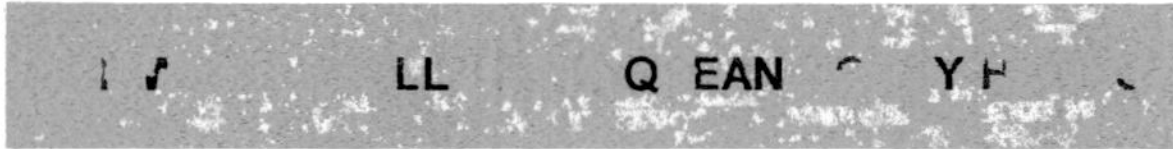

5. On the registration page, enter your student access code. Do not type the dashes. You can use lower or uppercase letters.
6. Follow the on-screen instructions. If you need help during the online registration process, simply click on Need Help?
7. Once your personal Login Name and Password are confirmed, you can begin viewing your VideoNotes.

To login to VideoNotes for the first time after you've registered:
Follow steps 1 and 2 to return to the VideoNotes link. Then, follow the prompts for "Returning Users" to enter your Login Name and Password.
Note to Instructors: For access to the Instructor Resource Center, contact your Pearson Representative.

IMPORTANT: The access code on this page can only be used once to establish a subscription to the Liang, *Introduction to Java Programming*, Seventh Edition VideoNotes. If this access code has already been scratched off, it may no longer be valid. If this is the case, you can purchase a subscription by going to the *www.prenhall.com/liang* website and selecting "Get Access."

Upper Saddle River, NJ 07458
www.prenhall.com

To get help with registration, visit *http://247.prenhall.com*

INTRODUCTION TO JAVA™ PROGRAMMING

INTRODUCTION TO JAVA™ PROGRAMMING

BRIEF VERSION

Seventh Edition

Y. Daniel Liang

Armstrong Atlantic State University

Upper Saddle River, New Jersey 07458

Library of Congress Cataloging-in Publication Data on File.

Editorial Director, Computer Science and Engineering: Marcia J. Horton
Executive Editor: Tracy Dunkelberger
Editorial Assistant: Melinda Haggerty
Director of Marketing: Margaret Waples
Marketing Manager: Christopher Kelly
Associate Editor: ReeAnne Davies
Senior Managing Editor: Scott Disanno
Production Editor: Irwin Zucker
Art Director: Kenny Beck
Media Editor: David Dulles
Media Editor: David Alick
Manufacturing Manager: Alan Fischer
Manufacturing Buyer: Lisa McDowell

© 2009 by Pearson Education, Inc. Upper Saddle River, New Jersey, 07458. All rights reserved. Printed in the United States of America. This publication is protected by Copyright and permission should be obtained from the publisher prior to any prohibited reproduction, storage in a retrieval system, or transmission in any form or by any means, electronic, mechanical, photocopying, recording, or likewise. For information regarding permission(s), write to: Rights and Permissions Department, Pearson Education, 1 Lake Street, Upper Saddle River, NJ 07458

The author and publisher of this book have used their best efforts in preparing this book. These efforts include the development, research, and testing of the theories and programs to determine their effectiveness. The author and publisher make no warranty of any kind, expressed or implied, with regard to these programs or the documentation contained in this book. The author and published shall not be liable in any event for incidental or consequential damages in connection with, or arising out of, the furnishing, performance, or use of these programs.

Pearson Education Ltd., London
Pearson Education Singapore, Pte, Ltd.
Pearson Education Canada, Inc.
Pearson Education-Japan
Pearson Education Australia PTY, Limited
Pearson Education North Asia, Ltd., Hong Kong
Pearson Education de Mexico, S. A. de C. V.
Pearson Education Malaysia, Pte. Ltd.
Pearson Education, Upper Saddle River, New Jersey

10 9 8 7 6 5 4 3 2 1

ISBN 10: 0-13-604258-9
ISBN 13: 978-0-13-604258-7

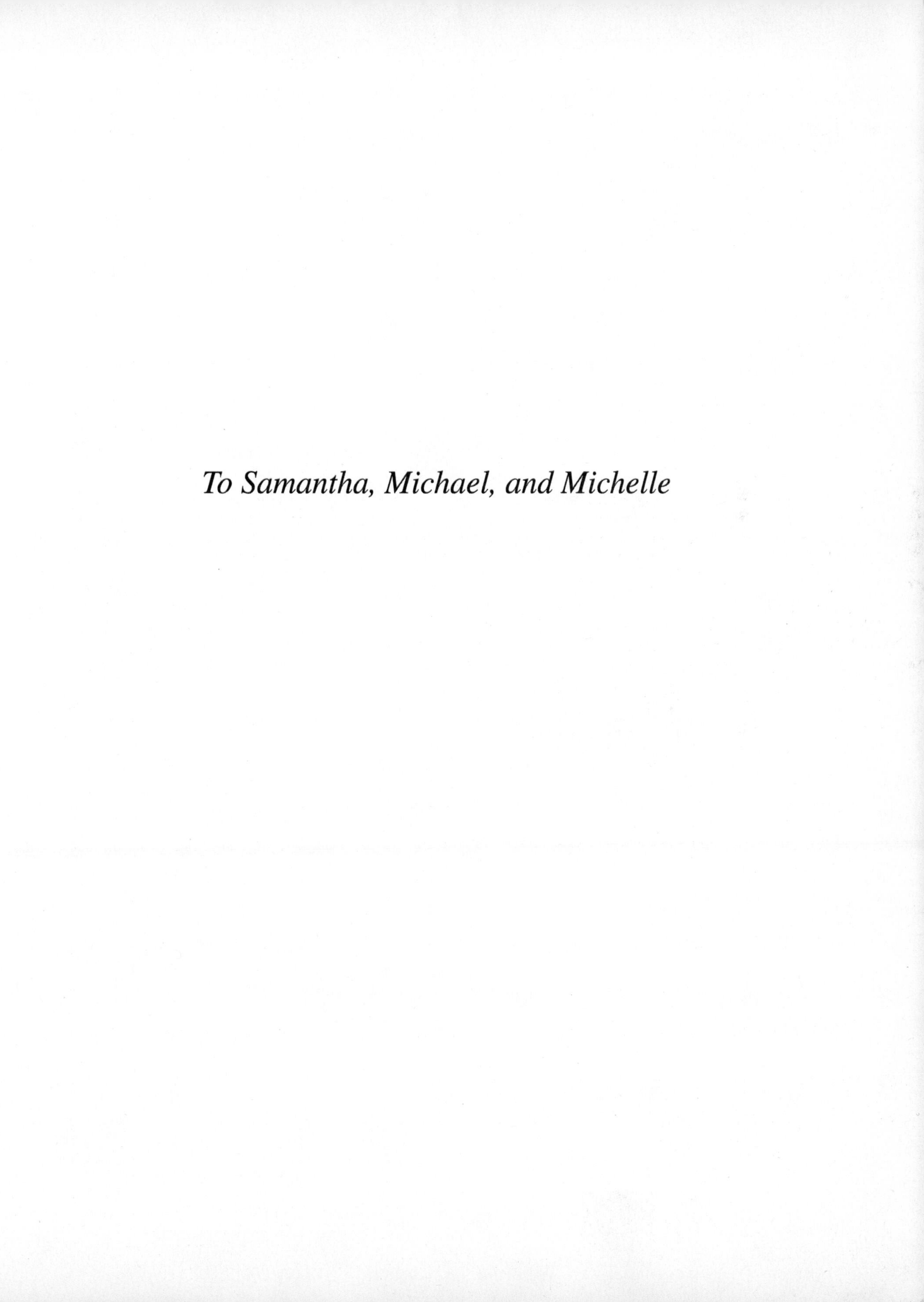

To Samantha, Michael, and Michelle

PREFACE

This book is a brief version of *Introduction to Java Programming, Comprehensive Version, 7E*. This version is designed for an introductory programming course, commonly known as *CS1*. This version contains the first twenty chapters in the comprehensive version.

Since 1997, six editions of *Introduction to Java Programming* have been published. Each new edition has substantially improved the previous one. This seventh edition is another great leap forward. We added the new Chapter 9, "Thinking in Objects," to bridge the differences between the procedural programming and object-oriented programming and show students when and how to apply OOP effectively. We expanded the coverage on data structures in Chapters 20–28 to serve a full course on data structures in the comprehensive version. We moved all advanced and nonessential language features to the Companion Web site, so that students can focus on problem solving and fundamental programming techniques in the early chapters. We refined the teaching method using the problem-driven approach. We enhanced the presentation to make the book more accessible to new programmers. We modified the contents to keep up with new Java technologies. We created a wide variety of new interesting examples and exercises to better motivate students. We renovated the Companion Web site to provide more useful supporting materials including a brand new *LiveLab*. We invite you to take a close look and be the judge.

The book uses the *fundamentals-first* and *problem-driven* pedagogy to teach problem solving and programming.

Fundamentals First

Both imperative and OOP are important programming paradigms with distinct advantages for certain applications. Some programs should be developed using the imperative approach, and others are better developed using the object-oriented approach. Today's students need to know both paradigms and use them effectively in harmony. This book introduces both imperative and OOP paradigms. Students will learn when and how to apply these two paradigms effectively.

imperative and OOP

The imperative paradigm is fundamental in programming. There are several strategies in teaching Java. This book adopts the fundamentals-first strategy. It begins with all the necessary and important basic concepts, then moves to object-oriented programming, and then to the use of the object-oriented approach to build interesting GUI applications and applets with exception handling and advanced features.

fundamentals-first

My own experience, confirmed by the experiences of many colleagues, demonstrates that new programmers in order to succeed must learn basic logic and fundamental programming techniques like loops and stepwise refinement. The fundamental concepts and techniques on loops, methods, and arrays are the foundation for programming. Building the foundation prepares students to learn object-oriented programming, GUI, and database and Web programming.

fundamental programming techniques

The fundamentals-first approach reinforces object-oriented programming by first presenting the procedural solutions and demonstrating how they can be improved using the object-oriented approach. Students can learn when and how to apply OOP effectively.

using OOP effectively

Problem-Driven

Programming isn't just syntax, classes, or objects. It is really *problem solving*. Variables, data types, operators and expressions, sequential statements, selection statements, loops, methods, and arrays are fundamental techniques for problem solving. From fundamental programming techniques to object-oriented programming, there are many layers of abstraction. Classes are simply a layer of abstraction. Applying the concept of abstraction in the design and implementation of software projects is the key to developing software. The overriding objective of

problem solving

the book, therefore, is to teach students to use many layers of abstraction in solving problems and to see problems in small and in large. The examples and exercises throughout the book center on problem solving and foster the concept of developing reusable components and using them to create practical projects.

problem-driven

This book uses the problem-driven approach to teach problem solving. Interesting and practical examples are used not only to illustrate syntax but also to teach problem solving and programming. Interesting and practical problems introduce each chapter and are solved within the chapter. The book uses a wide variety of problems with various levels of difficulty to motivate students. The problems cover many application areas in gaming, math, business, science, animation, and multimedia. Here are some representative problems in the book:

Example 1: We start Chapter 2 with a simple problem of computing a circle's area given its radius (§2.2, "Writing Simple Programs"). To solve this problem, we introduce variables for storing data and data types for declaring variables. We also introduce expressions for computing area. Initially, the input value for radius is coded in the program. This is not convenient. Later we introduce how to prompt the user to enter data at runtime using the `Scanner` class (§2.11) and the input dialog box (§2.16).

Example 2: The comparison operators and `boolean` type are introduced with the `AdditionQuiz` game (Listing 3.3) that automatically generates an addition question and grades the user's answers. Later we introduce the need for a selection statement in the `SubtractionQuiz` game (Listing 3.4) that automatically generates a subtraction question (i.e., `firstNumber - secondNumber`) and grades the user's answer. Since we require that the first number be greater than the second, a selection statement is introduced to write this program.

Example 3: The `SubtractionQuiz` game generates just one question. To repeatedly generate random questions, you have to use loops. In Chapter 4, we revise `SubtractionQuiz` to generate ten questions in `SubtractionQuizLoop` (Listing 4.3).

Example 4: The `GreatestCommonDivisor` program (Listing 4.8) computes the greatest common divisor (gcd) of two numbers. This program is not reusable because all the code is in the main method. To make the code modular and reusable, we revise the program to create a method for computing gcd in Listing 5.5.

Example 5: Listing 3.6, ComputeBMI.java, gives a program for computing Body Mass Index. Suppose you want to store the user's information. The program is difficult to expand in the procedural paradigm. We redesign the program using classes in §9.6, "Object-Oriented Thinking," and use this problem to demonstrate the advantages of using the object-oriented paradigm over the procedural paradigm.

Learning Strategies

learn from mistakes

A programming course is quite different from other courses. In a programming course, you learn from examples, from practice, and *from mistakes*. You need to devote a lot of time to writing programs, testing them, and fixing errors.

programmatic solution

For first-time programmers, learning Java is like learning any high-level programming language. The fundamental point in learning programming is to develop the critical skills of formulating programmatic solutions for real problems and translating them into programs using selection statements, loops, methods, and arrays.

object-oriented programming

Once you acquire the basic skills of writing programs using loops, methods, and arrays, you can begin to learn how to develop object-oriented software using class encapsulation and inheritance.

When you know how to program and understand the concept of object-oriented programming, learning Java becomes a matter of learning the Java API. The Java API establishes a framework for programmers to develop applications using Java. You have to use the classes and interfaces in the API and follow their conventions and rules to create applications. The best way to learn the Java API is to imitate examples and do exercises.

Java API

What's New in This Edition?

This edition substantially improves *Introduction to Java Programming, Sixth Edition*. The major improvements are as follows:

- The book is completely revised in every detail to enhance clarity, presentation, content, examples, and exercises. Every section has been reworked. — complete revision
- Nonessential language topics are moved to the Companion Web site so that students can focus on learning problem solving and programming techniques. These topics include the `&` and `|` operators, the discussion of how expressions are evaluated internally in Java, regular expressions, initialization blocks, how to package Java projects into archive files, etc. — focus on problem solving
- The book provides many new examples to stimulate student interest in programming in early chapters. For example, new guess number, body mass index, guess birth date, and Sudoku problems are provided in Chapters 3–6. — new examples
- A wide variety of new exercises in may application areas such as gaming, math, business, science, animation, and multimedia, are provided throughout the book. — new exercises
- The text introduces both console input using the `Scanner` class and GUI input using the `JOptionPane` class in Chapters 1–6. For consistency and ordering flexibility, the GUI examples are placed in separate sections and may be omitted. — separate GUI sections
- Design patterns are introduced throughout the book. — design patterns
- Chapter 7 in the preceding edition has been split into two chapters. The new Chapter 9 focuses on class design and explores the differences between the procedural paradigm and object-oriented paradigm. — new Chapter 9
- The code using `StringBuffer` is now replaced by `StringBuilder` to improve efficiency, starting from Chapter 8. — using **`StringBuilder`**
- Java 6 splash screen is introduced in §13.10, "Image Icons." — Java 6 splash screen

Pedagogical Features

The philosophy of the Liang Series is *teaching by example and learning by doing*. Basic features are explained by example so that you can learn by doing. The book uses the following elements to get the most from the material:

teaching by example
learning by doing

- **Objectives** list what students should have learned from the chapter. This will help them to determine whether they have met the objectives after completing the chapter.

- **Introduction** opens the discussion with the type of problems that will be solved in the chapter. The book is written using the problem-driven approach.
- **Examples,** carefully chosen and presented in an easy-to-follow style, teach programming concepts. The book uses many small, simple, and stimulating examples to demonstrate important ideas.
- **Chapter Summary** reviews the important subjects that students should understand and remember. It helps them to reinforce the key concepts they have learned in the chapter.
- **Review Questions** are grouped by sections to help students track their progress and evaluate their learning.
- **Programming Exercises** are grouped by sections to provide students with opportunities to apply on their own the new skills they have learned. The level of difficulty is rated as easy (no asterisk), moderate (*), hard (**), or challenging (***). The trick of learning programming is practice, practice, and practice. To that end, the book provides a great many exercises.
- **Notes, Tips,** and **Cautions** are inserted throughout the text to offer valuable advice and insight on important aspects of program development.

Note
Provides additional information on the subject and reinforces important concepts.

Tip
Teaches good programming style and practice.

Caution
Helps students steer away from the pitfalls of programming errors.

Design Guide
Provides the guidelines for designing programs.

Flexible Chapter Orderings

The book provides flexible chapter orderings to enable earlier coverage of GUI, exception handling, and recursion. Three common alternative orderings are shown as follows:

GUI Early Ordering	Exception and Binary I/O Early Ordering	Recursion Early Ordering
Chapter 10 Chapter 13 Chapter 14 Chapter 11 Chapter 15 Chapter 16 Chapter 17	Chapter 10 Chapter 18 Chapter 19	Chapter 6 Chapter 20

The accompanying diagram shows the chapter dependencies.

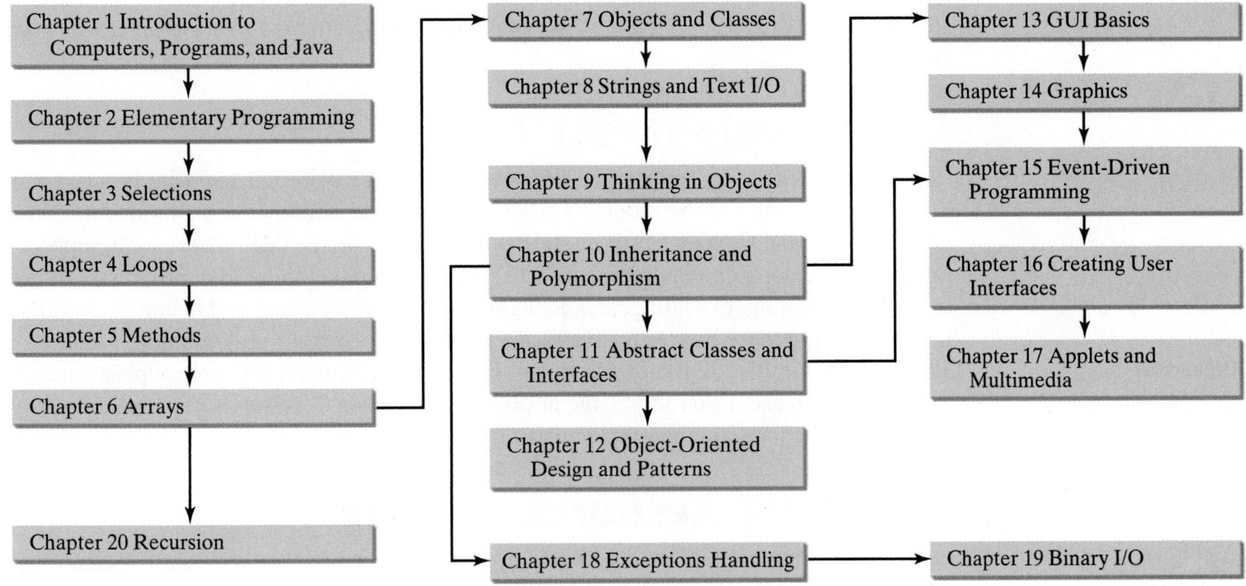

Organization of the Book

The chapters can be grouped into four parts that, taken together, form a solid introduction to problem solving and programming.

Part I: Fundamentals of Programming (Chapters 1–6)

The first part of the book is a stepping stone, preparing you to embark on the journey of learning Java. You will begin to know Java (Chapter 1), and will learn fundamental programming techniques with primitive data types (Chapter 2), control statements (Chapters 3–4), methods (Chapter 5), and arrays (Chapter 6).

Part II: Object-Oriented Programming (Chapters 7–12)

This part introduces object-oriented programming. Java is an object-oriented programming language that uses abstraction, encapsulation, inheritance, and polymorphism to provide great flexibility, modularity, and reusability in developing software. You will learn programming with objects and classes (Chapters 7-9), class inheritance (Chapter 10), polymorphism (Chapter 10), abstract classes (Chapter 11), interfaces (Chapter 11), and object-oriented design and patterns (Chapter 12). Processing strings will be introduced in Chapter 8.

Part III: GUI Programming (Chapters 13–17)

This part introduces Java GUI programming. Major topics include GUI basics (Chapter 13), drawing shapes (Chapter 14), event-driven programming (Chapter 15), creating graphical user interfaces (Chapter 16), and writing applets (Chapter 17). You will learn the architecture of Java GUI programming API and use the GUI components to develop applications and applets.

Part IV: Exception Handling, Binary IO, and Recursion (Chapters 18–20)

This part introduces the use of exception handling (Chapter 18) to make your programs robust and correct, the use of input and output to manage and process a large quantity of binary data stored in files (Chapter 19), and the use of recursive programming to solve inherently recursive problems.

Java Development Tools

You can use a text editor, such as the Windows Notepad or WordPad, to create Java programs, and to compile and run the programs from the command window. You can also use a Java development tool, such as TextPad, NetBeans, Eclipse, or JBuilder. These tools support an integrated development environment (IDE) for rapidly developing Java programs. Editing, compiling, building, executing, and debugging programs are integrated in one graphical user interface. Using these tools effectively can greatly increase your programming productivity. TextPad is a primitive IDE tool. NetBeans, Eclipse, and JBuilder are more sophisticated, but they are easy to use if you follow the tutorials. Tutorials on TextPad, NetBeans, Eclipse, and JBuilder can be found in the supplements on the Companion Web site.

IDE tutorials

Instructor Resource Materials

Instructor Resources associated with this book can be accessed via www.prenhall.com/liang or directly at www.cs.armstrong.edu/liang/intro7e . Access to some instructor material may require a password to the Pearson Instructor Resource Center (IRC). Contact your local Pearson Sales Representative for access to the IRC material.

The Instructor Resource site contains the following resources:

- **Interactive PowerPoint slides with interactive buttons** to view full-color, syntax-highlighted source code and to run programs without leaving the slides.
- **Solutions to all the review questions and exercises.** (Students will have access to the solutions of even-numbered programming exercises.)
- **Web-based quiz generator.** Instructors can choose chapters to generate quizzes from a large database of more than 2000 questions.
- **Sample Exams.** In general, each exam has four parts:
  - Multiple-choice questions or short-answer questions
  - Correct programming errors
  - Trace programs
  - Write programs
- **MyTest.** Testbank of exam questions

Web-Based Course Assessment and Management System (LiveLab)

This system provides three conveniences:

- **Automatic Grading System (AGS):** It can automatically grade programs
- **Quiz Creation/Submission/Grading System:** It enables instructors to create/modify quizzes and let students take them, and be graded automatically.

- **Tracking grades, attendance, etc.:** The system enables the students to track their own grades and instructors to view the grades of all students and track attendance.

The hallmark features of the **Automatic Grading System (AGS)** are as follows:

- Allows students to compile, run and submit exercises online (letting them know if their program runs correctly with student test casesóstudents can continue to run and submit the program before the due date)
- Allows instructors to review submissions; run programs with instructor test cases; correct them online; and provide feedback to students online.
- Allows instructors to create/modify their own exercises, create public and secret test cases, assign exercises, and set due dates.
- Provides more than 200 exercises that can be assigned to students.
- Allows instructors to sort and filter all exercises and check grades (by time frame, student, date, and/or exercise).
- Allows instructors to delete students from the system.
- Allows students and instructors to track grades on exercises.

Advantages and conveniences of **the Online Quiz System** are as follows:

- Allows instructors to create/modify quizzes from a test bank, from a text file, or create a completely new test online.
- Allows instructors to assign the quizzes to students, set a due date, and test time limit.
- Allows students and instructors to review submitted quizzes.
- Allows students and instructors to track grades on quizzes.

VideoNotes

VideoNotes are Pearson's new visual tool designed for teaching students key programming concepts and techniques and are available at www.prenhall.com/liang . These short step-by-step videos demonstrate how to solve problems from design through coding. VideoNotes allow for self-paced instruction with easy navigation including the ability to select, play, rewind, fast-forward, and stop within each VideoNote exercise.

VideoNote margin icons in your textbook let you know when a VideoNotes video is available for a particular concept or homework problem.

VideoNotes are free with the purchase of a new book. To *purchase* access to VideoNotes, go to www.prenhall.com/liang and click on VideoNotes under *Student Resources*.

GOAL

Gradiance Online Accelerated Learning (GOAL) is Pearson's premier online homework and assessment system and available at www.prenhall.com/liang. GOAL is designed to minimize student frustration while providing an interactive teaching experience outside the classroom.

With GOAL's immediate feedback and book-specific hints and pointers, students will have a more efficient and effective learning experience. GOAL delivers immediate assessment and feedback via two kinds of assignments: multiple choice homework exercises and interactive lab projects.

The homework consists of a set of multiple choice questions designed to test student knowledge of a solved problem. When answers are graded as incorrect, students are given a hint and directed back to a specific section in the course textbook for helpful information. The interactive Lab Projects, unlike syntax checkers and compilers, GOAL checks for both syntactic and semantic errors. GOAL determines if the student's program runs but more importantly, when checked against a hidden data set, verifies that it returns the correct result. By testing the code and providing immediate feedback, GOAL lets you know exactly which concepts the students have grasped and which ones need to be revisited.

Instructors should contact their local Pearson Sales Representative for sales and ordering information for the GOAL Student Access Code and Liang Introduction to Java Programming, 7eValue Pack.

Student Resources

Resources associated with this book can be accessed via www.prenhall.com/liang or directly at www.cs.armstrong.edu/liang/intro7e.

The Student Resource Web site contains the following resources:

- Answers to review questions
- Solutions to even-numbered programming exercises
- Source code for the examples in the book
- Interactive Self-Test (organized by sections for each chapter)
- LiveLabs
- Supplemental material
- Resource links
- Errata

Additional Supplemental Material

The text covers the essential subjects. The supplements extend the text to introduce additional topics that might be of interest to readers. The supplements listed in this table are available from the Companion Web site.

Supplements on the Companion Web Site

Part I General Supplements	Part II IDE Supplements
A Glossary	A TextPad Tutorial
B Installing and Configuring JDK	B JBuilder Tutorial
C Compiling and Running Java from the Command Window	C Learning Java Effectively with JBuilder
D Java Coding Style Guidelines	D NetBeans Tutorial
E Creating Desktop Shortcuts for Java Applications on Windows	E Learning Java Effectively with NetBeans
F Using Packages to Organize the Classes in the Text	F Eclipse Tutorial
	G Learning Java Effectively with Eclipse

H JBuilder 2007 Tutorial
I Visual GUI Development Using NetBeans

Part III Java Supplements
A Discussion on Operator and Operand Evaluations
B The & and | Operators
C Bitwise Operations
D Statement Labels with break and continue
E Enumerated Types
F Packages
G Regular Expressions
H Formatted Strings
I The Methods in the Object Class
J Hiding Data Fields and Static Methods
K Initialization Blocks
L Extended Discussions on Overriding Methods
M Design Patterns
N Text I/O Prior to JDK 1.5 (Reader and Writer Classes)
O Assertions
P Generics
Q Java Archiving
R Java 2D
S GridBagLayout | OverlayLayout | SpringLayout
T Networking Using Datagram Protocol
U Creating Internal Frames
V Pluggable Look and Feel
W UML Graphical Notations
X Testing Classes Using JUnit
Y JNI

Part IV Database Supplements
A SQL Statements for Creating and Initializing Tables Used in the Book
B MySQL Tutorial
C Oracle Tutorial
D Microsoft Access Tutorial
E Introduction to Database Systems
F Relational Database Concept
G Database Design
H SQL Basics
I Advanced SQL

Part V Web Programming Supplements
A HTML and XHTML Tutorial
B CSS Tutorial
C XML
D Java and XML
E Tomcat Tutorial
F More Examples on JSF and Visual Web Development

Part V Data Structures Supplements
A AVL Trees
B 2-3 Trees
C Red-Black Trees
D Hashing

Acknowledgments

I would like to thank Armstrong Atlantic State University for enabling me to teach what I write and for supporting me in writing what I teach. Teaching is the source of inspiration for continuing to improve the book. I am grateful to the instructors and students who have offered comments, suggestions, bug reports, and praise.

This book was greatly enhanced thanks to outstanding reviews for this and previous editions. The reviewers are: Elizabeth Adams (James Madison University), Yang Ang (University of Wollongong, Australia), Kevin Bierre (Rochester Institute of Technology), David Champion (DeVry Institute), James Chegwidden (Tarrant County College), Anup Dargar (University of North Dakota), Charles Dierbach (Towson University), Erica Eddy (University of Wisconsin at Parkside), Deena Engel (New York University), Henry A Etlinger (Rochester Institute of Technology), James Ten Eyck (Marist College), Olac Fuentes (University of Texas at El Paso), Harold Grossman (Clemson University), Ron Hofman (Red River College, Canada), Stephen Hughes (Roanoke College), Vladan Jovanovic (Georgia Southern University), Edwin Kay (Lehigh University), Larry King (University of Texas at Dallas), Nana Kofi (Langara College, Canada), Roger Kraft (Purdue University at Calumet), Hong Lin (DeVry Institute), Dan Lipsa (Armstrong Atlantic State University), James Madison (Rensselaer Polytechnic Institute), Frank Malinowski (Aelera Corporation), Tim Margush (University of Akron), Debbie Masada (Sun Microsystems), Blayne Mayfield (Oklahoma State University), John McGrath (J.P. McGrath Consulting), Shyamal Mitra (University of Texas at Austin), Michel Mitri (James Madison University), Kenrick Mock (University of Alaska Anchorage), Jun Ni (University of Iowa), Benjamin Nystuen (University of Colorado at Colorado Spring), Gavin Osborne (University of Saskatchewan), Kevin Parker (Idaho State University), Mark Pendergast (Florida Gulf Coast University), Richard Povinelli (Marquette University), Roger Priebe (University of Texas at Austin), Mary Ann Pumphrey (De Anza Junior College), Ronald F. Taylor (Wright State University), Carolyn Schauble (Colorado State University), David Scuse (University of Manitoba), Ashraf Shirani (San Jose State University), Daniel Spiegel (Kutztown University), Lixin Tao (Pace University), Russ Tront (Simon Fraser University), Deborah Trytten (University of Oklahoma), Kent Vidrine (George Washington University), and Bahram Zartoshty (California State University at Northridge).

It is a great pleasure, honor, and privilege to work with Prentice Hall. I would like to thank Marcia Horton, Tracy Dunkelberger, Margaret Waples, Chris Kelly, Erin Davis, Jake Warde, Melinda Haggerty, ReeAnne Davies, Vince O'Brien, Scott Disanno, Irwin Zucker, and their colleagues for organizing, producing, and promoting this project, and Robert Lentz for copy editing.

As always, I am indebted to my wife, Samantha, for her love, support, and encouragement.

Y. Daniel Liang
y.daniel.liang@gmail.com
www.cs.armstrong.edu/liang

BRIEF CONTENTS

CONTENTS

INTRODUCTION TO JAVA™ PROGRAMMING

CHAPTER 1

INTRODUCTION TO COMPUTERS, PROGRAMS, AND JAVA

Objectives

- To review computer basics, programs, and operating systems (§§1.2–1.4).
- To represent numbers in binary, decimal, and hexadecimal (§1.5).
- To explore the relationship between Java and the World Wide Web (§1.6).
- To distinguish the terms API, IDE, and JDK (§1.7).
- To write a simple Java program (§1.8).
- To display output on the console (§1.8).
- To create, compile, and run Java programs (§1.9).
- To explain the basic syntax of a Java program (§1.9).
- (GUI) To display output using the `JOptionPane` output dialog boxes (§1.10).

1.1 Introduction

why Java?

You use word processors to write documents, Web browsers to explore the Internet, and email programs to send email over the Internet. These are all examples of software that runs on computers. Software is developed using programming languages. There are many programming languages—so *why Java*? The answer is that Java enables users to develop and deploy applications on the Internet for servers, desktop computers, and small hand-held devices. The future of computing is being profoundly influenced by the Internet, and Java promises to remain a big part of that future. Java is *the* Internet programming language.

You are about to begin an exciting journey, learning a powerful programming language. At the outset, it is helpful to review computer basics, programs, and operating systems and to become familiar with number systems. If you are already familiar with such terms as CPU, memory, disks, operating systems, and programming languages, you may skip the review in §§1.2–1.4. You may also skip §1.5 and use it as reference when you have questions regarding binary and hexadecimal numbers.

1.2 What Is a Computer?

hardware
software

A computer is an electronic device that stores and processes data. It includes both *hardware* and *software*. In general, hardware comprises the visible, physical elements of the computer, and software provides the invisible instructions that control the hardware and make it perform specific tasks. Writing instructions for computers to perform is called computer programming. Knowing computer hardware isn't essential to your learning a programming language, but it does help you understand better the effect of the program instructions. This section introduces computer hardware components and their functions.

A computer consists of the following major hardware components (Figure 1.1):

- Central processing unit (CPU)
- Memory (main memory)
- Storage devices (disks, CDs, tapes)
- Input and output devices (monitors, keyboards, mice, printers)
- Communication devices [modems and network interface cards (NICs)]

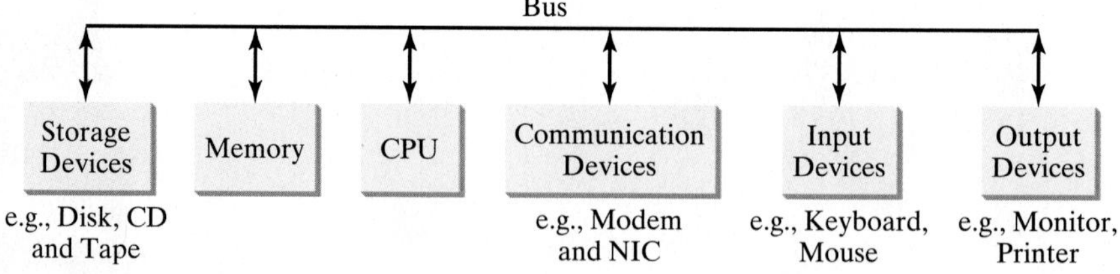

FIGURE 1.1 A computer consists of CPU, memory, storage devices, input devices, output devices, and communication devices.

The components are connected through a subsystem called a *bus* that transfers data or power between them.

1.2.1 Central Processing Unit

CPU

The *central processing unit* (CPU) is the computer's brain. It retrieves instructions from memory and executes them. The CPU usually has two components: a *control unit* and an *arithmetic/logic unit*. The control unit controls and coordinates the actions of the other components. The arithmetic and logic unit performs numeric operations (addition, subtraction, multiplication, division) and logical operations (comparisons).

Today's CPU is built on a small silicon semiconductor chip with millions of transistors. Every computer has an internal clock, which emits electronic pulses at a constant rate. These pulses are used to control and synchronize the pace of operations. The higher the clock speed, the more instructions are executed in a given period of time. The unit of measurement of clock speed is the *hertz* (Hz), with 1 hertz equaling 1 pulse per second. The clock speed of computers is usually stated in megahertz (MHz) (1 MHz is 1 million Hz). CPU speed has been improved continuously. Intel's Pentium 3 Processor runs at about 500 megahertz and its Intel Pentium 4 Processor at about 3 gigahertz (GHz) (1 GHz is 1000 MHz).

speed

hertz

megahertz

gigahertz

1.2.2 Memory

To store and process information, computers use *off* or *on* electrical states, referred to by convention as *0* and *1*. These 0s and 1s are interpreted as digits in the binary number system and called *bits* (*b*inary dig*its*). Data of various kinds, such as numbers, characters, and strings, are encoded as series of bits. Data and program instructions for the CPU to execute are stored as groups of bits, or bytes, each byte composed of eight bits, in a computer's *memory*. A memory unit is an ordered sequence of *bytes*, as shown in Figure 1.2.

bit

byte

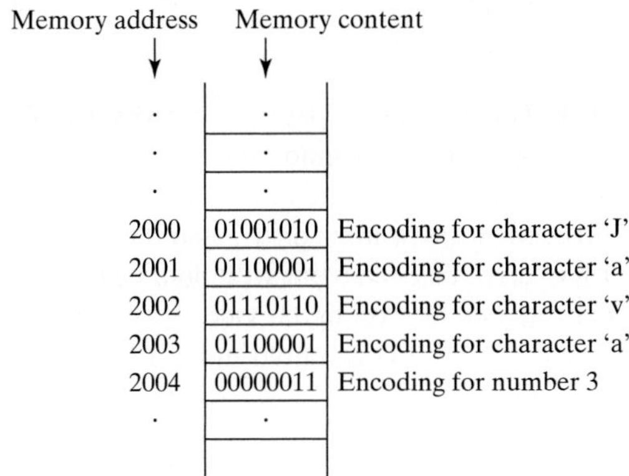

FIGURE 1.2 Memory stores data and program instructions.

The programmer need not be concerned about the encoding and decoding of data, which the system performs automatically, based on the encoding scheme. In the popular ASCII encoding scheme, for example, character `'J'` is represented by `01001010` in one byte.

A byte is the minimum storage unit. A small number such as `3` can be stored in a single byte. To store a number that cannot fit into a single byte, the computer uses several adjacent bytes. No two data items can share or split the same byte.

A memory byte is never empty, but its initial content may be meaningless to your program. The current content of a memory byte is lost whenever new information is placed in it.

A program and its data must be brought to memory before they can be executed.

Every byte has a unique address. The address is used to locate the byte for storing and retrieving data. Since the bytes can be accessed in any order, the memory is also referred to as *RAM* (random-access memory). Today's personal computers usually have at least 512 megabytes of RAM. A *megabyte* (abbreviated MB) is about 1 million bytes. For a precise definition of megabyte, please see http://en.wikipedia.org/wiki/Megabyte. Like the CPU, memory is built on silicon semiconductor chips containing thousands of transistors embedded on their surface. Compared to CPU chips, memory chips are less complicated, slower, and less expensive.

RAM

megabyte

megabyte URL

1.2.3 Storage Devices

Memory is volatile, because information is lost when the power is turned off. Programs and data are permanently stored on storage devices and, when the computer actually uses them are moved to memory, which is much faster than storage devices.

There are four main types of storage devices:

- Disk drives (hard disks and floppy disks)
- CD drives (CD-R, CD-RW, and DVD)
- Tape drives
- USB flash drives

drive

Drives are devices for operating a medium, such as disks, CDs, and tapes.

Disks

hard disk
floppy disk

There are two kinds of disks: *hard disks* and *floppy disks.* Personal computers have a hard drive with an optional 3.5-inch floppy disk drive. Hard disks provide much faster performance and larger capacity than floppy disks. A floppy disk has a fixed capacity of about 1.44 MB. The hard disks of the latest PCs store from 30 to 160 gigabytes. Often both disk drives are encased inside the computer, with the floppy disk being removable and the hard disk not. Removable hard disks are also available. Floppy disks are being replaced by CD-RW and flash drives.

CDs and DVDs

CD-R
CD-RW

CD stands for compact disk. There are two types of CD drives: *CD-R* and *CD-RW*. A CD-R is for read-only permanent storage; the user cannot modify its contents once they are recorded. A CD-RW can be used like a floppy disk, and thus can be both read and rewritten. A single CD can hold up to 700 MB. Most software is distributed through CD-ROMs. Most new PCs are equipped with a CD-RW drive that can work with both CD-R and CD-RW.

DVD stands for digital versatile disc or digital video disk. DVDs and CDs look alike, and you can use either to store data. A DVD can hold more information than a CD. A standard DVD storage capacity is 4.7 GB.

Tapes

Tapes are mainly used for backup of data and programs. Unlike disks and CDs, tapes store information sequentially. The computer must retrieve information in the order it was stored. Tapes are very slow. It would take one to two hours to back up a 1-gigabyte hard disk. The new trend is to back up data using flash drives or external hard disks.

USB Flash Drives

USB flash drives are devices for storing and transporting data. A flash drive is small—about the size of a pack of gum. It acts like a portable hard drive that can be plugged into the USB port of your computer. USB flash drives are currently available with up to 20 GB storage capacity.

1.2.4 Input and Output Devices

Input and output devices let the user communicate with the computer. The common input devices are *keyboards* and *mice*. The common output devices are *monitors* and *printers*.

The Keyboard

A computer *keyboard* resembles a typewriter keyboard except that it has extra keys for certain special functions.

function key

Function keys are located at the top of the keyboard and are numbered with prefix F. Their use depends on the software.

A *modifier key* is a special key (e.g., *Shift*, *Alt*, *Ctrl*) that modifies the normal action of another key when the two are pressed in combination. modifier key

The *numeric keypad,* located on the right-hand corner of the keyboard, is a separate set of keys for quick input of numbers. numeric keypad

Arrow keys, located between the main keypad and the numeric keypad, are used to move the cursor up, down, left, and right.

The *Insert, Delete, Page Up,* and *Page Dn keys*, located above the arrow keys, are used in word processing for performing insert, delete, page up, and page down.

The Mouse

A *mouse* is a pointing device. It is used to move an electronic pointer called a cursor around the screen or to click on an object on the screen to trigger it to respond.

The Monitor

The *monitor* displays information (text and graphics). The screen resolution and dot pitch determine the quality of the display.

The *screen resolution* specifies the number of pixels per square inch. Pixels (short for "picture elements") are tiny dots that form an image on the screen. A common resolution for a 17-inch screen, for example, is 1024 pixels wide and 768 pixels high. The resolution can be set manually. The higher the resolution, the sharper and clearer the image is. screen resolution

The *dot pitch* is the amount of space between pixels. Typically, it has ranges from 0.21 to 0.81 millimeters. The smaller the dot pitch, the better the display. dot pitch

1.2.5 Communication Devices

Computers can be networked through communication devices, such as the dialup modem (*mo*dulator/*dem*odulator), DSL, cable modem, and network interface card. A dialup modem uses a phone line and can transfer data at a speed up to 56,000 bps (bits per second). A DSL (digital subscriber line) also uses a phone line and can transfer data at a speed twenty times faster. A cable modem uses the TV cable line maintained by the cable company and is as fast as a DSL. A network interface card (NIC) is a device that connects a computer to a local area network (LAN). The LAN is commonly used in business, universities, and government organizations. A typical NIC called *10BaseT* can transfer data at 10 mbps (million bits per second).

modem
DSL
NIC
LAN
mbps

1.3 Programs

Computer *programs*, known as *software*, are instructions to the computer, telling it what to do. Computers do not understand human languages, so you need to use computer languages in computer programs. software

The computer's native language, which differs among different types of computers, is its *machine language*—a set of built-in primitive instructions. These instructions are in the form of binary code, so in telling the machine what to do, you have to enter binary code. Programming in machine language is a tedious process. Moreover, the programs are highly difficult to read and modify. For example, to add two numbers, you might have to write an instruction in binary like this: machine language

```
1101101010011010
```

Assembly language is a low-level programming language in which a mnemonic is used to represent each of the machine-language instructions. For example, to add two numbers, you might write an instruction in assembly code like this: assembly language

```
ADDF3 R1, R2, R3
```

assembler

Assembly languages were developed to make programming easy. However, since the computer cannot understand assembly language, a program called an *assembler* is used to convert assembly-language programs into machine code, as shown in Figure 1.3.

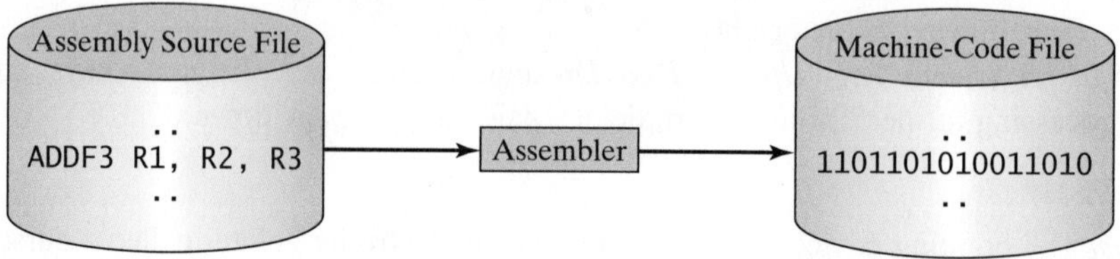

FIGURE 1.3 Assembler translates assembly-language instructions to machine code.

Assembly programs are written in terms of machine instructions with easy-to-remember mnemonic names. Since assembly language is machine dependent, an assembly program can be executed only on a particular kind of machine. The high-level languages were developed in order to overcome the platform-specific problem and make programming easier.

high-level language

The *high-level languages* are English-like and easy to learn and program. Here, for example, is a high-level language statement that computes the area of a circle with radius 5:

```
area = 5 * 5 * 3.1415;
```

There are over one hundred high-level languages. The well-known ones are:

- COBOL (COmmon Business Oriented Language)
- FORTRAN (FORmula TRANslation)
- BASIC (Beginner's All-purpose Symbolic Instruction Code)
- Pascal (named for Blaise Pascal)
- Ada (named for Ada Lovelace)
- C (whose developer designed B first)
- Visual Basic (Basic-like visual language developed by Microsoft)
- Delphi (Pascal-like visual language developed by Borland)
- C++ (an object-oriented language, based on C)
- C# (a Java-like language developed by Microsoft)
- Java

Each of these languages was designed for a specific purpose. COBOL was designed for business applications and now is used primarily for business data processing. FORTRAN was designed for mathematical computations and is used mainly for numeric computations. BASIC was designed to be learned and used easily. Ada was developed for the Department of Defense and is mainly used in defense projects. C combines the power of an assembly language with the ease of use and portability of a high-level language. Visual Basic and Delphi are used in developing graphical user interfaces and in rapid application development. C++ is popular for system software projects such as writing compilers and operating systems. The Microsoft Windows operating system was coded using C++.

source program
compiler

A program written in a high-level language is called a *source program or source code.* Since a computer cannot understand a source program, a program called a *compiler* is used to translate the source program into a machine-language program. The machine-language program is often then linked with other supporting library code to form an executable file. The executable file can be run on the machine, as shown in Figure 1.4. On Windows, executable files have extension .exe.

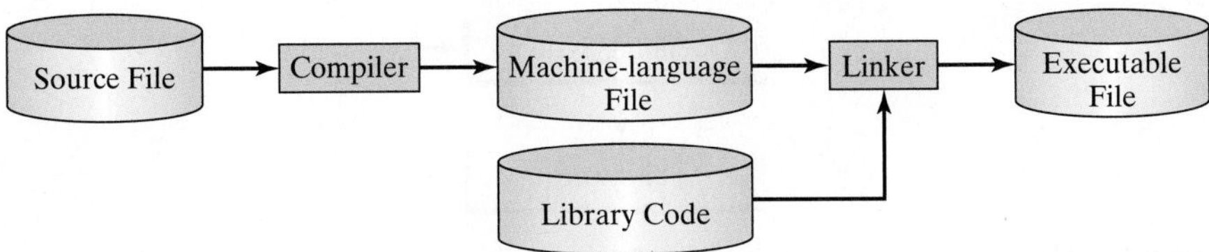

FIGURE 1.4 A source program is compiled into a machine-language file, which is then linked with the system library to form an executable file.

You can port (i.e., move) a source program to any machine with appropriate compilers. The source program must be recompiled, however, because the machine-language program can run only on a specific kind of machine. Nowadays computers are networked to work together. Java was designed to run on any platform. With Java, you write the program once and compile the source program into a special type of machine-language code known as *bytecode*. The bytecode can then run on any computer with a Java Virtual Machine (JVM), as shown in Figure 1.5. Java Virtual Machine is software that interprets Java bytecode.

bytecode

JVM

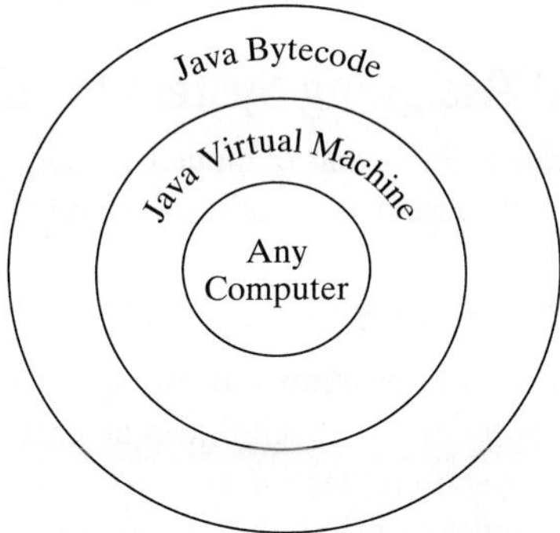

FIGURE 1.5 Java bytecode can be executed on any computer with a Java Virtual Machine.

Note

Java bytecode is interpreted. The difference between compiling and interpreting is as follows. Compiling translates the high-level code into a target-language code as a single unit. Interpreting translates the individual steps in a high-level program one at a time rather than the whole program as a single unit. Each step is executed immediately after it is translated.

compiling vs. interpreting

1.4 Operating Systems

The *operating system* (OS), the most important program that runs on a computer, enables it to manage and control its activities. Application programs, such as a Web browser or a word processor, cannot run without an operating system. You are probably using Microsoft Windows (currently the most popular PC operating system), Mac OS, or Linux. The interrelationship of hardware, operating system, application software, and the user is shown in Figure 1.6.

OS

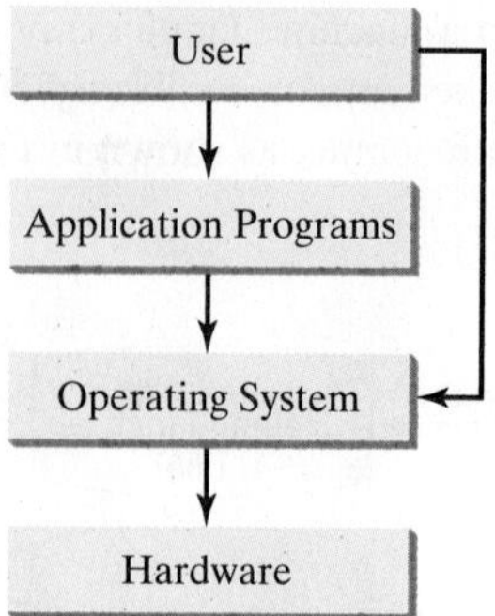

Figure 1.6 The operating system is the software that controls and manages the system.

The major tasks of the operating system are:

- Controlling and monitoring system activities
- Allocating and assigning system resources
- Scheduling operations

1.4.1 Controlling and Monitoring System Activities

Operating systems perform basic tasks, such as recognizing input from the keyboard, sending output to the monitor, keeping track of files and directories on the disk, and controlling peripheral devices, such as disk drives and printers. Operating systems also make sure that different programs and users running at the same time do not interfere with each other, and they are responsible for security, ensuring that unauthorized users do not access the system.

1.4.2 Allocating and Assigning System Resources

The OS is responsible for determining what computer resources a program needs (e.g., CPU, memory, disks, input and output devices) and for allocating and assigning them to run the program.

1.4.3 Scheduling Operations

The OS is responsible for scheduling programs to use the system resources efficiently. Many of today's operating systems support such techniques as *multiprogramming*, *multithreading*, or *multiprocessing* to increase system performance.

multiprogramming

Multiprogramming allows multiple programs to run simultaneously by sharing the CPU. The CPU is much faster than the other components. As a result, it is idle most of the time—for example, while waiting for data to be transferred from the disk or from other sources. A multiprogramming OS takes advantage of this by allowing multiple programs to use the CPU when it would otherwise be idle. For example, you may use a word processor to edit a file at the same time as the Web browser is downloading a file.

multithreading

Multithreading allows concurrency within a program, so that its subunits can run at the same time. For example, a word-processing program allows users to simultaneously edit text and save it to a file. In this example, editing and saving are two tasks within the same application. These two tasks may run on separate threads concurrently.

multiprocessing

Multiprocessing, or parallel processing, uses two or more processors together to perform a task. It is like a surgical operation where several doctors work together on one patient.

1.5 Number Systems

Pedagogical NOTE

You can skip this section and use it as reference when you have questions regarding binary and hexadecimal numbers.

Computers use binary numbers internally, because storage devices like memory and disks are made to store 0s and 1s. The binary number system has two digits, 0 and 1. A number or a character inside a computer is stored as a sequence of 0s and 1s. Each 0 or 1 is called a *bit*. binary number

Since we use decimal numbers in our daily life, binary numbers are not intuitive. When you write a number like 20 in a program, it is assumed to be a decimal number. Internally, computer software is used to convert decimal numbers into binary numbers, and vice versa. decimal number

You write programs using decimal number systems. However, if you write programs to deal with a system like an operating system, you need to use binary numbers to reach down to the "machine level." Binary numbers tend to be very long and cumbersome. Hexadecimal numbers are often used to abbreviate binary numbers, with each hexadecimal digit representing exactly four binary digits. The hexadecimal number system has sixteen digits: 0–9, A–F. The letters A, B, C, D, E, and F correspond to the decimal numbers 10, 11, 12, 13, 14, and 15. hexadecimal number

The digits in the decimal number system are 0, 1, 2, 3, 4, 5, 6, 7, 8, and 9. A decimal number is represented using a sequence of one or more of these digits. The value that each digit in the sequence represents depends on its position, which has a value that is an integral power of 10. For example, the digits 7, 4, 2, and 3 in decimal number 7423 represent 7000, 400, 20, and 3, respectively, as shown below:

$$\boxed{7\,|\,4\,|\,2\,|\,3} = 7 \times 10^3 + 4 \times 10^2 + 2 \times 10^1 + 3 \times 10^0$$

$$10^3\ 10^2\ 10^1\ 10^0 \quad = 7000 + 400 + 20 + 3 = 7423$$

The decimal number system has ten digits, and the position values are integral powers of 10. We say that 10 is the *base* or *radix* of the decimal number system. Similarly, the base of the binary number system is 2, since the binary number system has two digits, and the base of the hex number system is 16, since the hex number system has sixteen digits. base radix

If 1101 is a binary number, the digits 1, 1, 0, and 1 represent 1×2^3, 1×2^2, 0×2^1, and 1×2^0, respectively, as shown below:

$$\boxed{1\,|\,1\,|\,0\,|\,1} = 1 \times 2^3 + 1 \times 2^2 + 0 \times 2^1 + 1 \times 2^0$$

$$2^3\ 2^2\ 2^1\ 2^0 \quad = 8 + 4 + 0 + 1 = 13$$

If 7423 is a hex number, the digits 7, 4, 2, and 3 represent 7×16^3, 4×16^2, 2×16^1, and 3×16^0, respectively, as shown below:

$$\boxed{7\,|\,4\,|\,2\,|\,3} = 7 \times 16^3 + 4 \times 16^2 + 2 \times 16^1 + 3 \times 16^0$$

$$16^3\ 16^2\ 16^1\ 16^0 \quad = 28672 + 1024 + 32 + 3 = 29731$$

1.5.1 Conversions Between Binary Numbers and Decimal Numbers

Given a binary number $b_n b_{n-1} b_{n-2} \ldots b_2 b_1 b_0$, the equivalent decimal value is

$$b_n \times 2^n + b_{n-1} \times 2^{n-1} + b_{n-2} \times 2^{n-2} + \ \ldots \ + b_2 \times 2^2 + b_1 \times 2^1 + b_0 \times 2^0$$

The following are examples of converting binary numbers to decimals: binary to decimal

Binary	**Conversion Formula**	**Decimal**
10	$1 \times 2^1 + 0 \times 2^0$	2
1000	$1 \times 2^3 + 0 \times 2^2 + 0 \times 2^1 + 0 \times 2^0$	8
10101011	$1 \times 2^7 + 0 \times 2^6 + 1 \times 2^5 + 0 \times 2^4 + 1 \times 2^3 + 0 \times 2^2 +$ $1 \times 2^1 + 1 \times 2^0$	171

decimal to binary

To convert a decimal number d to a binary number is to find the bits $b_n, b_{n-1}, b_{n-2}, \ldots, b_2, b_1$, and b_0 such that

$$d = b_n \times 2^n + b_{n-1} \times 2^{n-1} + b_{n-2} \times 2^{n-2} + \ldots + b_2 \times 2^2 + b_1 \times 2^1 + b_0 \times 2^0$$

These bits can be found by successively dividing d by 2 until the quotient is 0. The remainders are $b_0, b_1, b_2, \ldots, b_{n-2}, b_{n-1}$, and b_n.

For example, the decimal number 123 is 1111011 in binary. The conversion is done as follows:

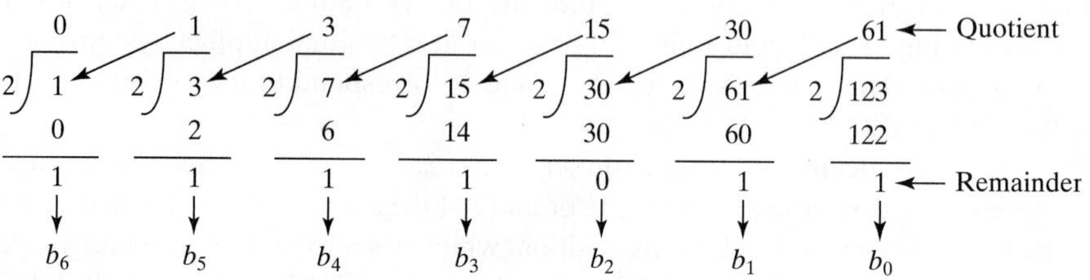

Tip

The Windows Calculator, as shown in Figure 1.7, is a useful tool for performing number conversions. To run it, choose *Programs*, *Accessories*, and *Calculator* from the Start button.

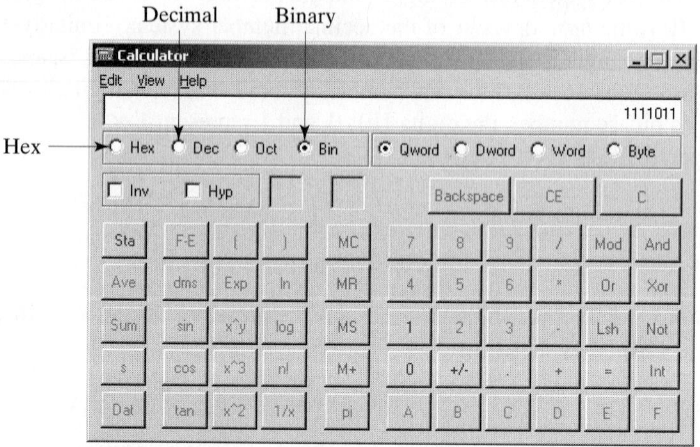

FIGURE 1.7 You can perform number conversions using the Windows Calculator.

1.5.2 Conversions Between Hexadecimal Numbers and Decimal Numbers

Given a hexadecimal number $h_n h_{n-1} h_{n-2} \ldots h_2 h_1 h_0$, the equivalent decimal value is

$$h_n \times 16^n + h_{n-1} \times 16^{n-1} + h_{n-2} \times 16^{n-2} + \ldots + h_2 \times 16^2 + h_1 \times 16^1 + h_0 \times 16^0$$

hex to decimal

The following are examples of converting hexadecimal numbers to decimals:

Hexadecimal	Conversion Formula	Decimal
7F	$7 \times 16^1 + 15 \times 16^0$	127
FFFF	$15 \times 16^3 + 15 \times 16^2 + 15 \times 16^1 + 15 \times 16^0$	65535
431	$4 \times 16^2 + 3 \times 16^1 + 1 \times 16^0$	1073

To convert a decimal number d to a hexadecimal number is to find the hexadecimal digits $h_n, h_{n-1}, h_{n-2}, \ldots, h_2, h_1$, and h_0 such that

decimal to hex

$$d = h_n \times 16^n + h_{n-1} \times 16^{n-1} + h_{n-2} \times 16^{n-2} + \ldots + h_2 \times 16^2 + h_1 \times 16^1 + h_0 \times 16^0$$

These numbers can be found by successively dividing d by 16 until the quotient is 0. The remainders are $h_0, h_1, h_2, \ldots, h_{n-2}, h_{n-1}$, and h_n.

For example, the decimal number 123 is 7B in hexadecimal. The conversion is done as follows:

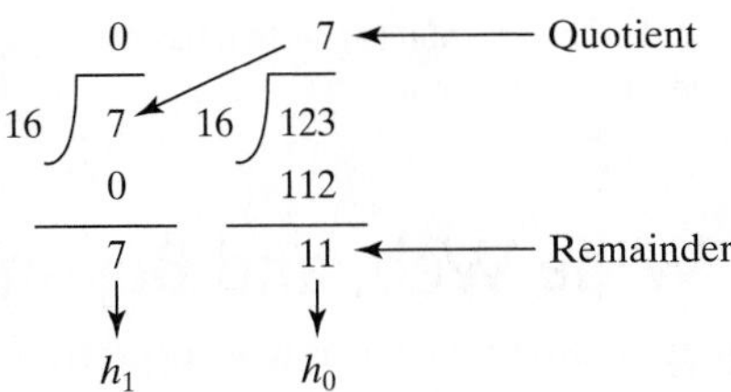

1.5.3 Conversions Between Binary Numbers and Hexadecimal Numbers

To convert a hexadecimal number to a binary number, simply convert each digit in the hexadecimal number into a four-digit binary number using Table 1.1.

hex to binary

TABLE 1.1 Converting Hexadecimal to Binary

Hexadecimal	*Binary*	*Decimal*
0	0000	0
1	0001	1
2	0010	2
3	0011	3
4	0100	4
5	0101	5
6	0110	6
7	0111	7
8	1000	8
9	1001	9
A	1010	10
B	1011	11
C	1100	12
D	1101	13
E	1110	14
F	1111	15

For example, the hexadecimal number 7B is 1111011, where 7 is 111 in binary, and B is 1011 in binary.

binary to hex

To convert a binary number to a hexadecimal, convert every four binary digits from right to left in the binary number into a hexadecimal number.

For example, the binary number 1110001101 is 38D, since 1101 is D, 1000 is 8, and 11 is 3, as shown below.

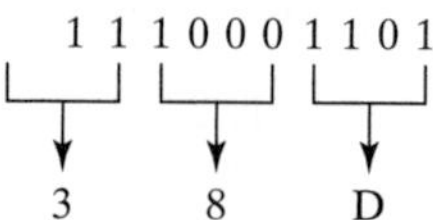

Note

Octal numbers are also useful. The octal number system has eight digits, 0 to 7. A decimal number 8 is represented as 10 in the octal system.

1.6 Java, World Wide Web, and Beyond

This book introduces Java programming. Java was developed by a team led by James Gosling at Sun Microsystems. Originally called *Oak*, it was designed in 1991 for use in embedded chips in consumer electronic appliances. In 1995, renamed *Java*, it was redesigned for developing Internet applications. For the history of Java, see java.sun.com/features/1998/05/birthday.html.

Java has become enormously popular. Its rapid rise and wide acceptance can be traced to its design characteristics, particularly its promise that you can write a program once and run it anywhere. As stated by Sun, Java is *simple*, *object-oriented*, *distributed*, *interpreted*, *robust*, *secure*, *architecture-neutral*, *portable*, *high-performance*, *multithreaded*, and *dynamic*. For the anatomy of Java characteristics, see www.cs.armstrong.edu/liang/intro7e/JavaCharacteristics.pdf.

Java is a full-featured, general-purpose programming language that is capable of developing robust mission-critical applications. Today, it is used not only for Web programming, but also for developing standalone applications across platforms on servers, desktops, and mobile devices. It was used to develop the code to communicate with and control the robotic rover that rolled on Mars. Many companies that once considered Java to be more hype than substance are now using it to create distributed applications accessed by customers and partners across the Internet. For every new project being developed today, companies are asking how they can use Java to make their work easier.

The World Wide Web is an electronic information repository that can be accessed on the Internet from anywhere in the world. The Internet is the infrastructure of the Web. The Internet has been around for more than thirty years. The colorful World Wide Web and sophisticated Web browsers are the major reason for its popularity.

The primary authoring language for the Web is the Hypertext Markup Language (HTML). HTML is a simple language for laying out documents, linking documents on the Internet, and bringing images, sound, and video alive on the Web. However, it cannot interact with the user except through simple forms. Web pages in HTML are essentially static and flat.

applet

Java initially became attractive because Java programs can be run from a Web browser. Such programs are called *applets*. Applets use a modern graphical user interface with buttons, text fields, text areas, radio buttons, and so on, to interact with users on the Web and process their requests. Applets make the Web responsive, interactive, and fun to use. Figure 1.8 shows an applet running from a Web browser.

Tip

For a demonstration of Java applets, visit java.sun.com/applets. This site provides a rich Java resource as well as links to other cool applet demo sites. java.sun.com is the official Sun Java Website.

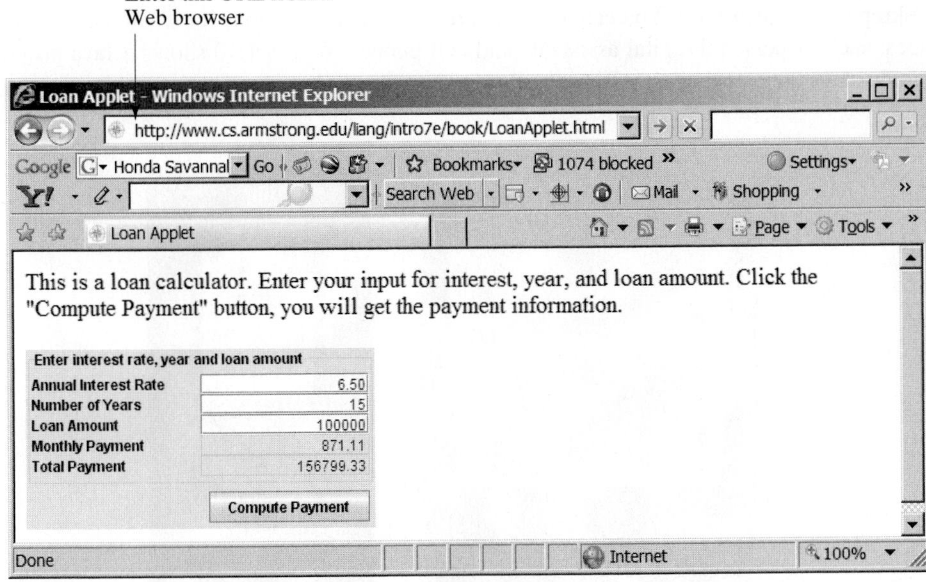

FIGURE 1.8 A Java applet for computing loan payments is embedded in an HTML page. The user can use the applet to compute the loan payments.

Java can also be used to develop applications on the server side. These applications can be run from a Web server to generate dynamic Web pages. The LiveLab accompanying this book, as shown in Figure 1.9, was developed using Java.

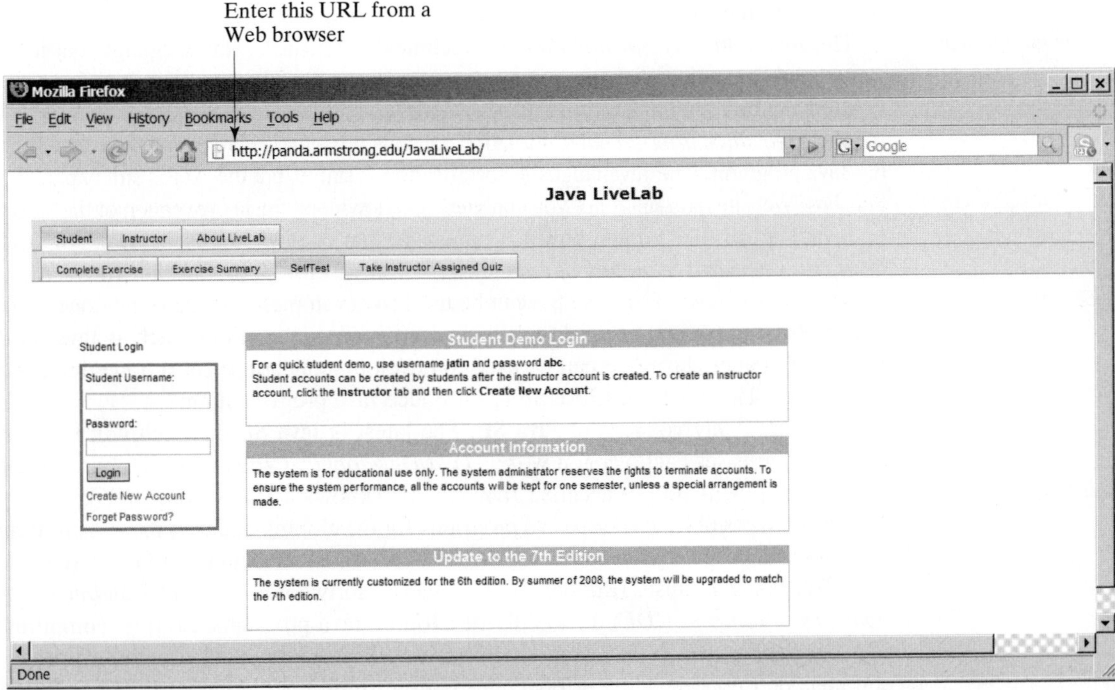

FIGURE 1.9 Java was used to develop the LiveLab for this book.

Java is a versatile programming language. You can use it to develop applications on your desktop and on the server. You can also use it to develop applications for small hand-held devices, such as personal digital assistants and cell phones. Figure 1.10 shows a Java program that displays the calendar on a BlackBerry© and on a cell phone.

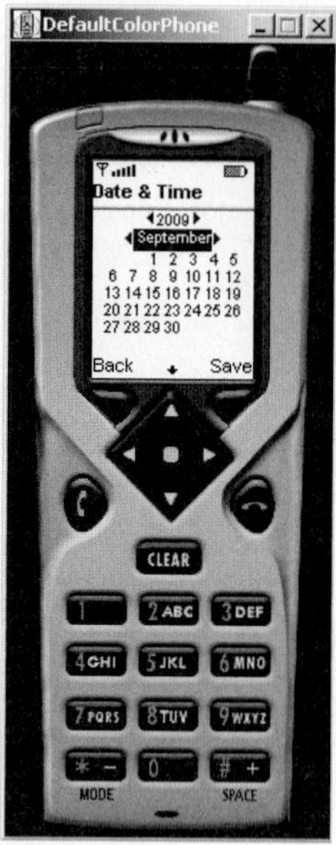

FIGURE 1.10 Java can be used to develop applications for hand-held and wireless devices, such as a BlackBerry© (left) and a cell phone (right).

1.7 The Java Language Specification, API, JDK, and IDE

Computer languages have strict rules of usage. If you do not follow the rules when writing a program, the computer will be unable to understand it. The Java language specification and Java API define the Java standard.

Java language specification

The *Java language specification* is a technical definition of the language that includes the syntax and semantics of the Java programming language. The complete Java language specification can be found at java.sun.com/docs/books/jls.

API

The *application program interface* (*API*) contains predefined classes and interfaces for developing Java programs. The Java language specification is stable, but the API is still expanding. At the Sun Java Website (java.sun.com), you can view and download the latest version of the Java API.

Java SE, EE, and ME

Java is a full-fledged and powerful language that can be used in many ways. It comes in three editions: *Java Standard Edition* (*Java SE*), *Java Enterprise Edition* (*Java EE*), and *Java Micro Edition* (*Java ME*). Java SE can be used to develop client-side standalone applications or applets. Java EE can be used to develop server-side applications, such as Java servlets and JavaServer Pages. Java ME can be used to develop applications for mobile devices, such as cell phones. This book uses Java SE to introduce Java programming.

JDK 1.6 = JDK 6

There are many versions of Java SE. The latest is Java SE 6, which will be used in this book. Sun releases each version with a *Java Development Toolkit* (JDK). For Java SE 6, the Java Development Toolkit is called *JDK 1.6* (also known as *Java 6* or *JDK 6*).

Java IDE

JDK consists of a set of separate programs for developing and testing Java programs, each of which is invoked from a command line. Besides JDK, you can use a Java development tool (e.g., NetBeans, Eclipse, JBuilder, and TextPad)—software that provides an *integrated development environment* (*IDE*) for rapidly developing Java programs. Editing, compiling, building, debugging, and online help are integrated in one graphical user interface. Just enter source code in one window or open an existing file in a window, then click a button, menu item, or function key to compile and run the program.

Pedagogical NOTE

If you wish to use NetBeans, Eclipse, JBuilder, or TextPad for developing Java programs, please see Supplement II for tutorials.

Supplement II

1.8 A Simple Java Program

application
applet

A Java program can be written in many ways. This book introduces Java applications, applets, and servlets. *Applications* are standalone programs that can be executed from any computer with a JVM. *Applets* are special kinds of Java programs that run from a Web browser. Servlets are special kinds of Java programs that run from a Web server to generate dynamic Web contents. Applets will be introduced in Chapter 17 and servlets in Chapter 39.

Let us begin with a simple Java program that displays the message "Welcome to Java!" on the console. The program is shown in Listing 1.1.

Video Note
Your first Java program

LISTING 1.1 Welcome.java

class
main method
comment
display message

```
1 public class Welcome {
2   public static void main(String[] args) {
3     // Display message Welcome to Java! to the console
4     System.out.println("Welcome to Java!");
5   }
6 }
```

```
Welcome to Java!
```

line numbers

The line numbers are not part of the program, but are displayed for reference purposes. So, don't type line numbers in your program.

class name

Line 1 defines a class. Every Java program must have at least one class. Each class has a name. By convention, class names start with an uppercase letter. In this example, the class name is `Welcome`.

main method

Line 2 defines the main method. In order to run a class, the class must contain a method named `main`. The JVM executes the program by invoking the `main` method.

A method is a construct that contains statements. The `main` method in this program contains the `System.out.println` statement. This statement prints a message "Welcome to Java!" to the console (line 4). Every statement in Java ends with a semicolon (`;`), known as the *statement terminator*.

statement terminator
reserved word

Reserved words, or *keywords,* have a specific meaning to the compiler and cannot be used for other purposes in the program. For example, when the compiler sees the word `class`, it understands that the word after `class` is the name for the class. Other reserved words in this program are `public`, `static`, and `void`.

comment

Line 3 is a *comment* that documents what the program is and how it is constructed. Comments help programmers to communicate and understand the program. They are not programming statements and thus are ignored by the compiler. In Java, comments are preceded by two slashes (`//`) on a line, called a *line comment*, or enclosed between `/*` and `*/` on one or several lines, called a *block comment*. When the compiler sees `//`, it ignores all text after `//` on the same line. When it sees `/*`, it scans for the next `*/` and ignores any text between `/*` and `*/`. Here are examples of comments:

```
// This application program prints Welcome to Java!
/* This application program prints Welcome to Java! */
/* This application program
   prints Welcome to Java! */
```

block

The braces in the program form a *block* that groups the components of the program. In Java, each block begins with an opening brace ({) and ends with a closing brace (}). Every class has a *class block* that groups the data and methods of the class. Every method has a *method block* that groups the statements in the method. Blocks can be *nested*, meaning that one block can be placed within another, as shown in the following code.

```
public class Welcome {
  public static void main(String[] args) {
    System.out.println("Welcome to Java!");
  }
}
```

Class block

Method block

matching braces

Tip

An opening brace must be matched by a closing brace. Whenever you type an opening brace, immediately type a closing brace to prevent the missing-brace error. Most Java IDEs automatically insert the closing brace for each opening brace.

Note

You are probably wondering why the `main` method is declared this way and why `System.out.println(...)` is used to display a message to the console. For the time being, simply accept that this is how things are done. Your questions will be fully answered in subsequent chapters.

syntax rules

Note

Like any programming language, Java has its own syntax, and you need to write code that obeys the syntax rules. If your program violates the rules—for example if the semicolon is missing, a brace is missing, a quotation mark is missing, or `String` is misspelled—the Java compiler will report syntax errors. Try to compile the program with these errors and see what the compiler reports.

The program in Listing 1.1 displays one message. Once you understand the program, it is easy to extend it to display more messages. For example, you can rewrite the program to display three messages, as shown in Listing 1.2.

LISTING 1.2 Welcome1.java

class
main method
display message

```
public class Welcome1 {
  public static void main(String[] args) {
    System.out.println("Programming is fun!");
    System.out.println("Fundamentals First");
    System.out.println("Problem Driven");
  }
}
```

```
Programming is fun!
Fundamentals First
Problem Driven
```

1.9 Creating, Compiling, and Executing a Java Program

You have to create your program and compile it before it can be executed. This process is repetitive, as shown in Figure 1.11. If your program has compilation errors, you have to fix them by modifying the program, then recompile it. If your program has runtime errors or does not produce the correct result, you have to modify the program, recompile it, and execute it again.

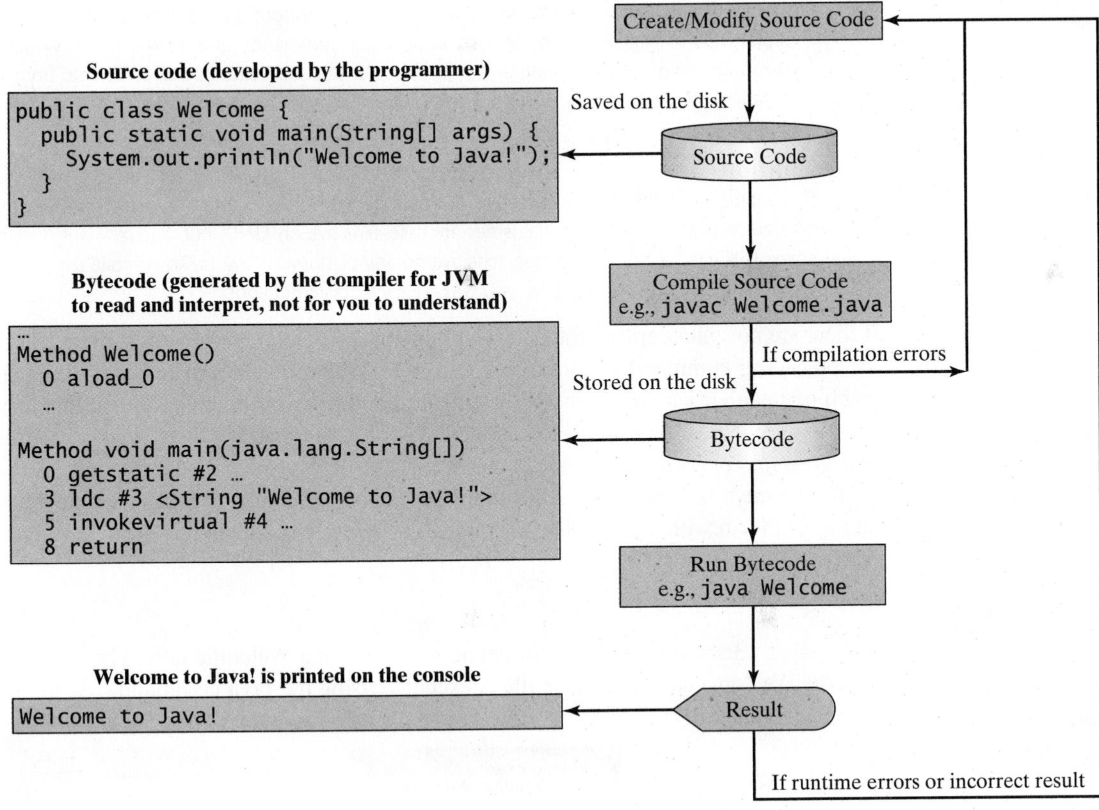

FIGURE 1.11 The Java program-development process consists of repeatedly creating/modifying source code, compiling, and executing programs.

You can use any text editor or IDE to create and edit a Java source-code file. Figure 1.12 shows how to use NotePad to create and edit the source-code file. editor

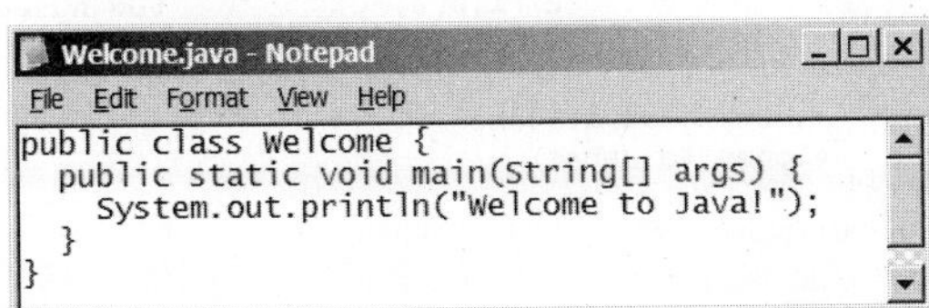

FIGURE 1.12 You can create the Java source file using Windows NotePad.

Note

The source file must end with the extension .java and must have the exact same name as the public class name. For example, the file for the source code in Listing 1.1 should be named Welcome.java, since the public class name is **Welcome**. .java file

A Java compiler translates a Java source file into a Java bytecode file. The following command compiles Welcome.java: compile

```
javac Welcome.java
```

Note

You must first install and configure JDK before compiling and running programs. See Supplement I.B, "Installing and Configuring JDK 6," on how to install JDK and set up the environment to compile and run Java programs. If you have trouble compiling and running programs, Supplement I.B

Supplement I.C

please see Supplement I.C, "Compiling and Running Java from the Command Window." This supplement also explains how to use basic DOS commands and how to use Windows NotePad and WordPad to create and edit files. All the supplements are accessible from the Companion Website.

Caution

case sensitive

Java source programs are case sensitive. It would be wrong, for example, to replace `main` in the program with `Main`. Program filenames are case sensitive on UNIX but generally not on Windows; JDK treats filenames as case sensitive on any platform. If you try to compile the program using **`javac welcome.java`**, you will get a file-not-found error.

.class bytecode file

If there are no syntax errors, the *compiler* generates a bytecode file with a .class extension. So the preceding command generates a file named **Welcome.class**. The bytecode is similar to machine instructions but is architecture neutral and can run on any platform that has a JVM. This is one of Java's primary advantages: *Java bytecode can run on a variety of hardware platforms and operating systems.*

run

To execute a Java program is to run the program's bytecode. You can execute the bytecode on any platform with a JVM. The following command runs the bytecode:

```
java Welcome
```

Video Note
Compile and run a Java program

Figure 1.13 shows the **javac** command for compiling Welcome.java. The compiler generated the Welcome.class file. This file is executed using the **java** command.

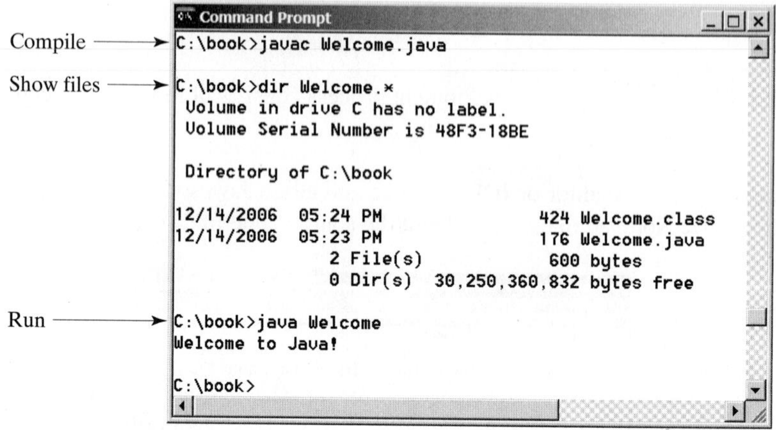

FIGURE 1.13 The output of Listing 1.1 displays the message Welcome to Java!

Note

c:\book

For simplicity and consistency, all source code and class files are placed under **c:\book** unless specified otherwise.

Caution

java ClassName

Do not use the extension .class in the command line when executing the program. Use **java ClassName** to run the program. If you use **java ClassName.class** in the command line, the system will attempt to fetch **ClassName.class.class**.

Tip

NoClassDefFoundError

NoSuchMethodError

If you execute a class file that does not exist, a `NoClassDefFoundError` will occur. If you execute a class file that does not have a `main` method or you mistype the `main` method (e.g., by typing `Main` instead of `main`), a `NoSuchMethodError` will occur.

Note

When executing a Java program, the JVM first loads the bytecode of the class to memory using a program called the *class loader*. If your program uses other classes, the class loader dynamically loads them just before they are needed. After a class is loaded, the JVM uses a program called *bytecode verifier* to check the validity of the bytecode and ensure that the bytecode does not violate Java's security restrictions. Java enforces strict security to make sure that Java programs arriving from the network do not harm your computer.

class loader

bytecode verifier

Pedagogical NOTE

Instructors may require students to use packages. For example, you may place all programs in this chapter in a package named *chapter1*. For instructions on how to use packages, please see Supplement I.F, "Using Packages to Organize the Classes in the Text."

using package

1.10 (GUI) Displaying Text in a Message Dialog Box

The program in Listing 1.1 displays the text on the console, as shown in Figure 1.13. You can rewrite the program to display the text in a message dialog box. To do so, you need to use the `showMessageDialog` method in the `JOptionPane` class. `JOptionPane` is one of the many predefined classes in the Java system that can be reused rather than "reinventing the wheel." You can use the `showMessageDialog` method to display any text in a message dialog box, as shown in Figure 1.14. The new program is given in Listing 1.3.

`JOptionPane`

`showMessageDialog`

Video Note
Display an output message dialog box

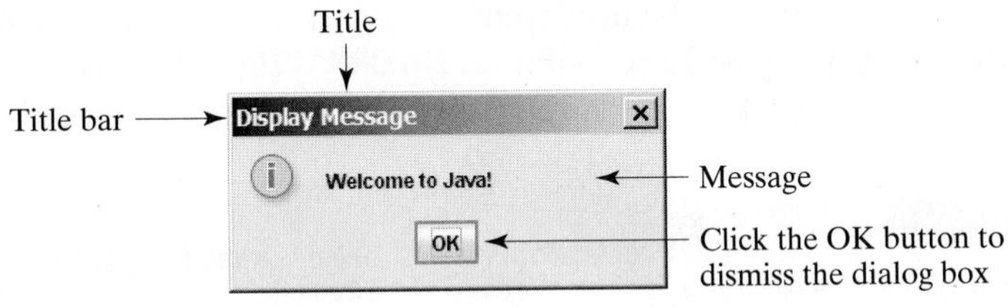

FIGURE 1.14 "Welcome to Java!" is displayed in a message box.

LISTING 1.3 `WelcomeInMessageDialogBox.java`

```
 1 /*  This application program displays Welcome to Java!
 2  *  in a message dialog box.
 3  */
 4 import javax.swing.JOptionPane;
 5
 6 public class WelcomeInMessageDialogBox {
 7   public static void main(String[] args) {
 8     // Display Welcome to Java! in a message dialog box
 9     JOptionPane.showMessageDialog(null, "Welcome to Java!");
10   }
11 }
```

block comment

import

main method

display message

This program uses a Java class `JOptionPane` (line 9). Java's predefined classes are grouped into packages. `JOptionPane` is in the `javax.swing` package. `JOptionPane` is imported to the program using the `import` statement in line 4 so that the compiler can locate the class without the full name `javax.swing.JOptionPane`.

package

Note

If you replace `JOptionPane` on line 9 with `javax.swing.JOptionPane`, you don't need to import it in line 4. `javax.swing.JOptionPane` is the full name for the `JOptionPane` class.

The `showMessageDialog` method is a *static* method. Such a method should be invoked by using the class name followed by a dot operator (`.`) and the method name with arguments. Methods will be introduced in Chapter 5, "Methods." The `showMessageDialog` method can be invoked with two arguments, as in line 9.

The first argument can always be `null`. `null` is a Java keyword that will be fully introduced in Chapter 7, "Objects and Classes." The second argument is a string for text to be displayed.

two versions of **`showMessageDialog`**

There are several ways to use the `showMessageDialog` method. For the time being, all you need to know are two ways to invoke it. One is to use a statement, as shown in the example:

```
JOptionPane.showMessageDialog(null, x);
```

where `x` is a string for the text to be displayed.

The other is to use a statement like this one:

```
JOptionPane.showMessageDialog(null, x,
  y, JOptionPane.INFORMATION_MESSAGE));
```

where `x` is a string for the text to be displayed, and `y` is a string for the title of the message box. The fourth argument can be `JOptionPane.INFORMATION_MESSAGE`, which causes the icon ( ) to be displayed in the message box, as shown in the following example.

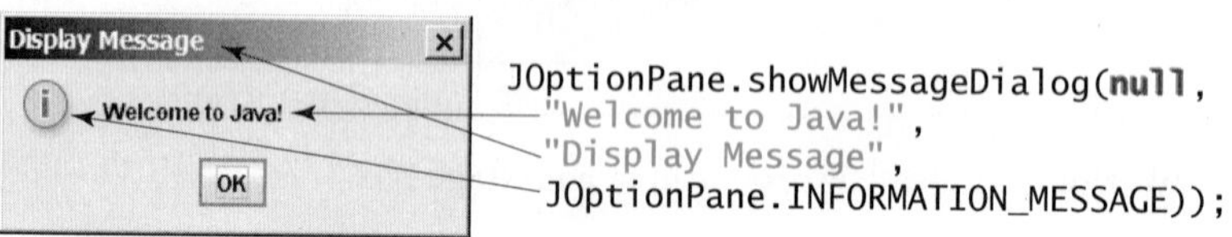

Note

specific import

There are two types of `import` statements: *specific import* and *wildcard import*. The *specific import* specifies a single class in the import statement. For example, the following statement imports `JOptionPane` from package `javax.swing`.

```
import javax.swing.JOptionPane;
```

wildcard import

The *wildcard import* imports all the classes in a package. For example, the following statement imports all classes from package `javax.swing`.

```
import javax.swing.*;
```

no performance difference

The information for the classes in an imported package is not read in at compile time or runtime unless the class is used in the program. The import statement simply tells the compiler where to locate the classes. There is no performance difference between a specific import and a wildcard import declaration.

Note

`java.lang`
implicitly imported

Recall that you have used the `System` class in the statement *`System.out.println("Welcome to Java");`* in Listing 1.1. The `System` class is not imported because it is in the `java.lang` package. All the classes in the `java.lang` package are *implicitly* imported in every Java program.

Key Terms

.class file 18
.java file 17
assembly language 6
binary numbers 3, 9
bit 3
block 16
block comment 15
byte 3
bytecode 7
bytecode verifier 19
cable modem 5
central processing unit (CPU) 2
class loader 19
comment 15
compiler 6
dot pitch 5
DSL (digital subscriber line) 5
hardware 2
hexadecimal numbers 9
high-level language 6
Integrated Development Environment (IDE) 14
java command 18
javac command 17
Java Development Toolkit (JDK) 14
Java Virtual Machine (JVM) 7
keyword (or reserved word) 15
line comment 15
machine language 5
main method 15
modem 5
memory 3
network interface card (NIC) 5
operating system (OS) 7
pixel 5
resolution 5
software 2
source code 6, 15
source file 6, 15
specific import 20
storage devices 4
statement 15
wildcard import 20

Note
The above terms are defined in the present chapter. Supplement I.A, "Glossary," on the Companion Web site lists all the key terms and descriptions in the book, organized by chapters.

Chapter Summary

- A computer is an electronic device that stores and processes data. A computer includes both *hardware* and *software*. In general, hardware is the visible, physical aspect of the computer, and software is the invisible instructions that control the hardware and make it perform tasks.

- Computer *programs*, known as *software*, are instructions to the computer. You tell a computer what to do through programs. Computer programming consists of writing instructions for computers to perform.

- The *machine language* is a set of primitive instructions built into every computer. *Assembly language* is a low-level programming language in which a mnemonic is used to represent each of the machine-language instructions.

- *High-level languages* are English-like and much easier to learn and program. There are over one hundred high-level languages. A program written in a high-level language is called a *source program*. Since a computer cannot understand a source program, a program called a *compiler* is used to translate it into a machine-language program, which is then linked with other supporting library code to form an executable file.

- The *operating system* (OS) is a program that manages and controls a computer's activities. Application programs, such as Web browsers and word processors, cannot run without an operating system.

- Java was developed by a team led by James Gosling at Sun Microsystems. It is an Internet programming language. Since its inception in 1995, it has quickly become a premier language for building software.

- Java is platform independent, meaning that you can write a program once and run it anywhere.

- Java programs can be embedded in HTML pages and downloaded by Web browsers to bring live animation and interaction to Web clients.

- Java source files end with the .java extension. Every class is compiled into a separate bytecode file that has the same name as the class and ends with the .class extension.

- To compile a Java source-code file from the command line, use the **javac** command. To run a Java class, use the **java** command.

- Every Java program is a set of class definitions. The keyword `class` introduces a class definition. The contents of the class are included in a block. A block begins with an opening brace (`{`) and ends with a closing brace (`}`). Methods are contained in a class.

- A Java application must have a `main` method. The `main` method is the entry point where the application program starts when it is executed.

Review Questions

Note

Answers to review questions are on the Companion Website.

Sections 1.2–1.4

1.1 Define hardware and software.

1.2 List the main components of the computer.

1.3 Define machine language, assembly language, and high-level programming language.

1.4 What is a source program? What is a compiler?

1.5 What is the JVM?

1.6 What is an operating system?

Section 1.5

1.7 Convert the following decimal numbers into hexadecimal and binary numbers.

```
100; 4340; 2000
```

1.8 Convert the following binary numbers into hexadecimal numbers and decimal numbers.

```
1000011001; 100000000; 100111
```

1.9 Convert the following hexadecimal numbers into binary and decimal numbers.

```
FEFA9; 93; 2000
```

Sections 1.6–1.7

1.10 Describe the history of Java. Can Java run on any machine? What is needed to run Java on a computer?

1.11 What are the input and output of a Java compiler?

1.12 List some Java development tools. Are tools like NetBeans, Eclipse, and JBuilder different languages from Java, or are they dialects or extensions of Java?

1.13 What is the relationship between Java and HTML?

Sections 1.8–1.10

1.14 Explain the Java keywords. List some Java keywords you learned in this chapter.

1.15 Is Java case sensitive? What is the case for Java keywords?

1.16 What is the Java source filename extension, and what is the Java bytecode filename extension?

1.17 What is a comment? Is the comment ignored by the compiler? How do you denote a comment line and a comment paragraph?

1.18 What is the statement to display a string on the console? What is the statement to display the message "Hello world" in a message dialog box?

1.19 The following program is wrong. Reorder the lines so that the program displays `morning` followed by `afternoon`.

```
  public static void main(String[] args) {
  }

public class Welcome {
    System.out.println("afternoon");
    System.out.println("morning");
}
```

1.20 Identify and fix the errors in the following code:

```
public class Welcome {
  public void Main(String[] args) {
    System.out.println('Welcome to Java!);
  }
}
```

1.21 What is the command to compile a Java program? What is the command to run a Java application?

1.22 If a `NoClassDefFoundError` occurs when you run a program, what is the cause of the error?

1.23 If a `NoSuchMethodError` occurs when you run a program, what is the cause of the error?

1.24 Why does the `System` class not need to be imported?

1.25 Are there any performance differences between the following two `import` statements?

```
import javax.swing.JOptionPane;
import javax.swing.*;
```

Programming Exercises

Note

level of difficulty

NOTE: Solutions to even-numbered exercises are on the Companion Website. Solutions to all exercises are on the Instructor Resource Website. The level of difficulty is rated easy (no star), moderate (*), hard (**), or challenging (***).

1.1 (*Creating, compiling, and running a Java program*) Create a source file containing a Java program. Perform the following steps to compile the program and run it (see §1.9, "Creating, Compiling, and Executing a Java Program" earlier in this chapter):

1. Create a file named **Welcome.java** for Listing 1.1. You can use any editor that will save your file in text format.
2. Compile the source file.
3. Run the bytecode.
4. Replace `"Welcome to Java"` with `"My first program"` in the program; save, compile, and run the program. You will see the message `"My first program"` displayed.
5. Replace `class` with `Class`, and recompile the source code. The compiler returns an error message because the Java program is case sensitive.
6. Change it back, and compile the program again.
7. Instead of using the command `java Welcome` to run the program, use `java Welcome.class`. What happens?

Video Note
Display five messages

1.2 (*Displaying five messages*) Write a Java program that displays `Welcome to Java` five times.

1.3* (*Displaying a pattern*) Write a Java program that displays the following pattern:

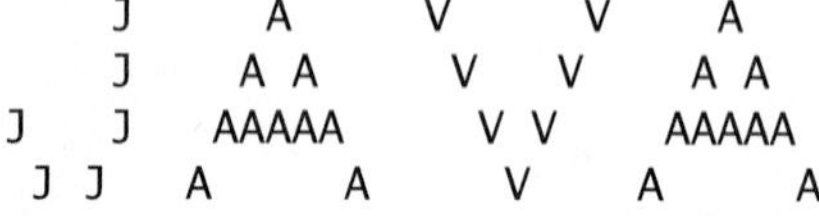

Chapter 2

Elementary Programming

Objectives

- To write Java programs to perform simple calculations (§2.2).
- To use identifiers to name variables, constants, methods, and classes (§2.3).
- To use variables to store data (§§2.4–2.5).
- To program with assignment statements and assignment expressions (§2.5).
- To use constants to store permanent data (§2.6).
- To declare Java primitive data types: `byte`, `short`, `int`, `long`, `float`, `double`, and `char` (§§2.7–2.9).
- To use Java operators to write numeric expressions (§§2.7–2.8).
- To represent characters using the `char` type (§2.9).
- To represent a string using the `String` type (§2.10).
- To obtain input from the console using the `Scanner` class (§§2.11–2.12).
- To become familiar with Java documentation, programming style, and naming conventions (§2.13).
- To distinguish syntax errors, runtime errors, and logic errors (§2.14).
- To debug logic errors (§2.15).
- (GUI) To obtain input using the `JOptionPane` input dialog boxes (§2.16).

2.1 Introduction

In Chapter 1 you learned how to create, compile, and run a Java program. Now you will learn how to solve practical problems programmatically. You will learn Java primitive data types and related subjects, such as variables, constants, data types, operators, expressions, and input and output.

2.2 Writing Simple Programs

problem

To begin, let's look at a simple problem for computing the area of a circle. How do we write a program for solving this problem?

algorithm

Writing a program involves designing algorithms and data structures, as well as translating algorithms into programming code. An *algorithm* describes how a problem is solved in terms of the actions to be executed and the order of their execution. Algorithms can help the programmer plan a program before writing it in a programming language. The algorithm for this program can be described as follows:

1. Read in the radius.
2. Compute the area using the following formula:

$$\text{area} = \text{radius} \times \text{radius} \times \pi$$

3. Display the area.

floating-point number
primitive data types

Data structures involve data representation and manipulation. Java provides data types for representing integers, floating-point numbers (i.e., numbers with a decimal point), characters, and Boolean types. These types are known as *primitive data types*. Java also supports array and string types as objects. Some advanced data structures, such as stacks, sets, and lists, have built-in implementation in Java.

To novice programmers, coding is a daunting task. When you *code*, you translate an algorithm into a programming language the computer understands. You already know that every Java program begins with a class declaration in which the keyword `class` is followed by the class name. Assume that you have chosen `ComputeArea` as the class name. The outline of the program would look like this:

```
public class ComputeArea {
  // Data and methods to be given later
}
```

As you know, every application must have a `main` method where program execution begins. So the program is expanded as follows:

```
public class ComputeArea {
  public static void main(String[] args) {
    // Step 1: Read in radius

    // Step 2: Compute area

    // Step 3: Display the area
  }
}
```

The program needs to read the radius entered by the user from the keyboard. This raises two important issues:

- Reading the radius.
- Storing the radius in the program.

Let's address the second issue first. In order to store the radius, the program needs to declare a symbol called a *variable* that will represent the radius. Variables are used to store data and computational results in the program.

variable

Rather than using x and y as variable names, choose descriptive names: in this case, radius for radius, and area for area. To let the compiler know what radius and area are, specify their data types—integer, float, or something else. Declare radius and area as double-precision floating-point numbers. The program can be expanded as follows:

descriptive names

```
public class ComputeArea {
  public static void main(String[] args) {
    double radius;
    double area;
    // Step 1: Read in radius

    // Step 2: Compute area

    // Step 3: Display the area
  }
}
```

The program declares radius and area as variables. The reserved word double indicates that radius and area are double-precision floating-point values stored in the computer.

The first step is to read in radius. Reading a number from the keyboard is not a simple matter. For the time being, let us assign a fixed number to radius in the program. In §2.11, "Console Input Using the Scanner Class," and §2.16, "Getting Input from Input Dialogs," you will learn how to obtain a numeric value from the console and from an input dialog.

The second step is to compute area by assigning the expression radius * radius * 3.14159 to area.

In the final step, print area on the console by using the System.out.println method.

The complete program is shown in Listing 2.1. A sample run of the program is shown in Figure 2.1.

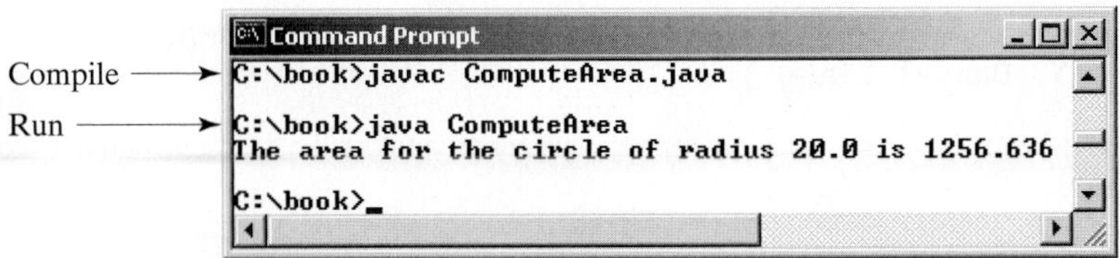

FIGURE 2.1 The program displays the area of a circle.

LISTING 2.1 ComputeArea.java

```
public class ComputeArea {
  /** Main method */
  public static void main(String[] args) {
    double radius; // Declare radius
    double area; // Declare area

    // Assign a radius
    radius = 20; // New value is radius

    // Compute area
    area = radius * radius * 3.14159;

    // Display results
```

Memory

radius: no value
area: no value
radius: 20
area: 1256.636

```
14      System.out.println("The area for the circle of radius " +
15        radius + " is " + area);
16    }
17 }
```

declaring variable

assign value

Variables such as **radius** and **area** correspond to memory locations. Every variable has a name, a type, a size, and a value. Line 4 declares that **radius** can store a **double** value. The value is not defined until you assign a value. Line 8 assigns **20** into **radius**. Similarly, line 5 declares variable **area**, and line 11 assigns a value into **area**. Figure 2.2 shows the value in the memory for **area** and **radius** as the program is executed.

line#	radius	area
4	no value	
5		no value
8	20	
11		1256.636

FIGURE 2.2 The variable values stored in the memory are changed during execution.

concatenating strings

concatenating strings with numbers

The plus sign (+) has two meanings: one for addition and the other for concatenating strings. The plus sign (+) in lines 14–15 is called a *string concatenation operator*. It combines two strings if two operands are strings. If one of the operands is a nonstring (e.g., a number), the nonstring value is converted into a string and concatenated with the other string. So the plus signs (+) in lines 14–15 concatenate strings into a longer string, which is then displayed in the output. Strings and string concatenation will be discussed further in §2.10, "The **String** Type."

Caution

breaking a long string

A string constant cannot cross lines in the source code. Thus the following statement would result in a compilation error:

```
System.out.println("Introduction to Java Programming,
  by Y. Daniel Liang");
```

To fix the error, break the string into separate substrings, and use the concatenation operator (+) to combine them:

```
System.out.println("Introduction to Java Programming, " +
  "by Y. Daniel Liang");
```

Tip

incremental development and testing

This example consists of three steps. It is a good approach to develop and test these steps incrementally by adding them one at a time.

2.3 Identifiers

naming identifiers

Just as every entity in the real world has a name, so you need to choose names for the things you will refer to in your programs. Programming languages use special names called *identifiers* for such programming entities as variables, constants, methods, classes, and packages. Here are the rules for naming identifiers:

- An identifier is a sequence of characters that consists of letters, digits, underscores (_), and dollar signs ($).
- An identifier must start with a letter, an underscore (_), or a dollar sign ($). It cannot start with a digit.

- An identifier cannot be a reserved word. (See Appendix A, "Java Keywords," for a list of reserved words.)
- An identifier cannot be **true**, **false**, or **null**.
- An identifier can be of any length.

For example, **$2**, **ComputeArea**, **area**, **radius**, and **showMessageDialog** are legal identifiers, whereas **2A** and **d+4** are not because they do not follow the rules. The Java compiler detects illegal identifiers and reports syntax errors.

Note

Since Java is case sensitive, **X** and **x** are different identifiers.

case-sensitive

Tip

Identifiers are used for naming variables, constants, methods, classes, and packages. Descriptive identifiers make programs easy to read. Besides choosing descriptive names for identifiers, you should follow naming conventions for different kinds of identifiers. Naming conventions are summarized in §2.15, "Programming Style and Documentation."

descriptive names

Tip

Do not name identifiers with the **$** character. By convention, the **$** character should be used only in mechanically generated source code.

the $ character

2.4 Variables

Variables are used to store data in a program. In the program in Listing 2.1, **radius** and **area** are variables of double-precision, floating-point type. You can assign any numerical value to **radius** and **area**, and the values of **radius** and **area** can be reassigned. For example, you can write the code shown below to compute the area for different radii:

```
// Compute the first area
radius = 1.0;
area = radius * radius * 3.14159;
System.out.println("The area is " + area + " for radius " + radius);

// Compute the second area
radius = 2.0;
area = radius * radius * 3.14159;
System.out.println("The area is " + area + " for radius " + radius);
```

2.4.1 Declaring Variables

Variables are for representing data of a certain type. To use a variable, you declare it by telling the compiler its name as well as what type of data it represents. This *variable declaration* tells the compiler to allocate appropriate memory space for the variable based on its data type. The syntax for declaring a variable is

```
datatype variableName;
```

Here are some examples of variable declarations:

declaring variable

```
int x;                 // Declare x to be an integer variable;
double radius;         // Declare radius to be a double variable;
double interestRate;   // Declare interestRate to be a double variable;
char a;                // Declare a to be a character variable;
```

The examples use the data types **int**, **double**, and **char**. Later you will be introduced to additional data types, such as **byte**, **short**, **long**, **float**, **char**, and **boolean**.

If variables are of the same type, they can be declared together, as follows:

```
datatype variable1, variable2, ..., variablen;
```

The variables are separated by commas. For example,

```
int i, j, k; // Declare i, j, and k as int variables
```

Note

naming variables

By convention, variable names are in lowercase. If a name consists of several words, concatenate all of them and capitalize the first letter of each word except the first. Examples of variables are radius and interestRate.

2.5 Assignment Statements and Assignment Expressions

assignment statement
assignment operator

After a variable is declared, you can assign a value to it by using an *assignment statement*. In Java, the equal sign (=) is used as the *assignment operator*. The syntax for assignment statements is as follows:

```
variable = expression;
```

expression

An *expression* represents a computation involving values, variables, and operators that, taking them together, evaluates to a value. For example, consider the following code:

```
int x = 1;                    // Assign 1 to variable x;
double radius = 1.0;          // Assign 1.0 to variable radius;
x = 5 * (3 / 2) + 3 * 2;      // Assign the value of the expression to x;
x = y + 1;                    // Assign the addition of y and 1 to x;
area = radius * radius * 3.14159; // Compute area
```

A variable can also be used in an expression. For example,

```
x = x + 1;
```

In this assignment statement, the result of x + 1 is assigned to x. If x is 1 before the statement is executed, then it becomes 2 after the statement is executed.

To assign a value to a variable, the variable name must be on the left of the assignment operator. Thus, 1 = x would be wrong.

Note:

In mathematics, x = x + 1 denotes an equation. However, in Java, x = x + 1 is an assignment statement that assigns a new value to x.

assignment expression

In Java, an assignment statement can also be treated as an expression that evaluates to the value being assigned to the variable on the left-hand side of the assignment operator. For this reason, an assignment statement is also known as an *assignment expression*. For example, the following statement is correct:

```
System.out.println(x = 1);
```

which is equivalent to

```
x = 1;
System.out.println(x);
```

The following statement is also correct:

```
i = j = k = 1;
```

which is equivalent to

```
k = 1;
j = k;
i = j;
```

Note

In an assignment statement, the data type of the variable on the left must be compatible with the data type of the value on the right. For example, `int x = 1.0` would be illegal because the data type of `x` is `int`. You cannot assign a `double` value (`1.0`) to an `int` variable without using type casting. Type casting is introduced in §2.8, "Numeric Type Conversions."

2.5.1 Declaring and Initializing Variables in One Step

Variables often have initial values. You can declare a variable and initialize it in one step. Consider, for instance, the following code:

```
int x = 1;
```

This is equivalent to the next two statements:

```
int x;
x = 1;
```

You can also use a shorthand form to declare and initialize variables of the same type together. For example,

```
int i = 1, j = 2;
```

Tip

A variable must be declared before it can be assigned a value. A variable declared in a method must be assigned a value before it can be used. Whenever possible, declare a variable and assign its initial value in one step. This will make the program easy to read and avoid programming errors.

2.6 Constants

The value of a variable may change during the execution of the program, but a *constant* represents permanent data that never changes. In our `ComputeArea` program, π is a constant. If you use it frequently, you don't want to keep typing `3.14159`; instead, you can define a constant for π. Here is the syntax for declaring a constant: constant

```
final datatype CONSTANTNAME = VALUE;
```

A constant must be declared and initialized in the same statement. The word `final` is a Java keyword which means that the constant cannot be changed. For example, in the `ComputeArea` program, you could define π as a constant and rewrite the program as follows:

```
// ComputeArea.java: Compute the area of a circle
public class ComputeArea {
  public static void main(String[] args) {
    final double PI = 3.14159; // Declare a constant

    // Assign a radius
    double radius = 20;

    // Compute area
    double area = radius * radius * PI ;
```

```
    // Display results
    System.out.println("The area for the circle of radius " +
      radius + " is " + area);
  }
}
```

Caution

naming constants

By convention, constants are named in uppercase: PI, not pi or Pi.

Note

benefits of constants

There are three benefits of using constants: (1) you don't have to repeatedly type the same value; (2) the value can be changed in a single location, if necessary; (3) a descriptive name for a constant makes the program easy to read.

2.7 Numeric Data Types and Operations

Every data type has a range of values. The compiler allocates memory space to store each variable or constant according to its data type. Java provides eight primitive data types for numeric values, characters, and Boolean values. This section introduces numeric data types.

Table 2.1 lists the six numeric data types, their ranges, and their storage sizes.

TABLE 2.1 Numeric Data Types

Name	*Range*	*Storage Size*
byte	-2^7 (−128) to $2^7 - 1$ (127)	8-bit signed
short	-2^{15} (−32768) to $2^{15} - 1$ (32767)	16-bit signed
int	-2^{31} (−2147483648) to $2^{31} - 1$ (2147483647)	32-bit signed
long	-2^{63} to $2^{63} - 1$ (i.e., −9223372036854775808 to 9223372036854775807)	64-bit signed
float	Negative range: −3.4028235E + 38 to −1.4E − 45 Positive range:1.4E–45 to 3.4028235E + 38	32-bit IEEE 754
double	Negative range:−1.7976931348623157E + 308 to−4.9E − 324 Positive range:4.9E − 324 to 1.7976931348623157E + 308	64-bit IEEE 754

Note

IEEE 754 is a standard approved by the Institute of Electrical and Electronics Engineers for representing floating-point numbers on computers. The standard has been widely adopted. Java has adopted the 32-bit **IEEE 754** for the float type and the 64-bit **IEEE 754** for the double type. The **IEEE 754** standard also defines special values in Appendix E, "Special Floating-Point Values."

integer types

Java uses four types for integers: byte, short, int, and long. Choose the type that is most appropriate for your variable. For example, if you know an integer stored in a variable is within a range of byte, declare the variable as a byte.

Java uses two types for floating-point numbers: `float` and `double`. The `double` type is twice as big as `float`. So, the `double` is known as *double precision*, while `float` is known as *single precision*. Normally, you should use the `double` type because it is more accurate than the `float` type. floating-point

Caution

When a variable is assigned a value that is too large to be stored, it causes *overflow*. For example, executing the following statement causes *overflow*, because the largest value that can be stored in a variable of the `int` type is `2147483647`. `2147483648` is too large. what is overflow?

```
int value = 2147483647 + 1;
```

When a variable is assigned a value that is too small to be stored, it causes *underflow*. For example, executing the following statement causes *underflow*, because the smallest value that can be stored in a variable of the `int` type is `-2147483648`. `-2147483649` is too small. what is underflow?

```
int value = -2147483648 - 1;
```

Java does not report warnings or errors on overflow and underflow. So be careful when working with numbers close to the maximum or minimum range of a given type.

2.7.1 Numeric Operators

The operators for numeric data types include the standard arithmetic operators: addition (+), subtraction (–), multiplication (*), division (/), and remainder (%), as shown in Table 2.2. operators +, –, *, /, %

TABLE 2.2 Numeric Operators

Name	*Meaning*	*Example*	*Result*
+	Addition	34 + 1	35
–	Subtraction	34.0 – 0.1	33.9
*	Multiplication	300 * 30	9000
/	Division	1.0 / 2.0	0.5
%	Remainder	20 % 3	2

The result of integer division is an integer. The fractional part is truncated. For example, `5 / 2` yields `2`, not `2.5`, and `-5 / 2` yields `-2`, not `-2.5`. integer division

The `%` operator yields the remainder after division. The left-hand operand is the dividend and the right-hand operand is the divisor. Therefore, `7 % 3` yields `1`, `12 % 4` yields `0`, `26 % 8` yields `2`, and `20 % 13` yields `7`.

```
  2        3        3                        1 ←— Quotient
3)7      4)12     8)26      Divisor ——→ 13)20 ←— Dividend
  6        12       24                       13
  1        0        2                        7 ←— Remainder
```

The % operator is often used for positive integers but can be used also with negative integers and floating-point values. The remainder is negative only if the dividend is negative. For example, -7 % 3 yields -1, -12 % 4 yields 0, -26 % -8 yields -2, and 20 % -13 yields 7.

Remainder is very useful in programming. For example, an even number % 2 is always 0 and an odd number % 2 is always 1. So you can use this property to determine whether a number is even or odd. Suppose today is Saturday, you and your friend are going to meet in 10 days. What day is in 10 days? You can find that the day is Tuesday using the following expression:

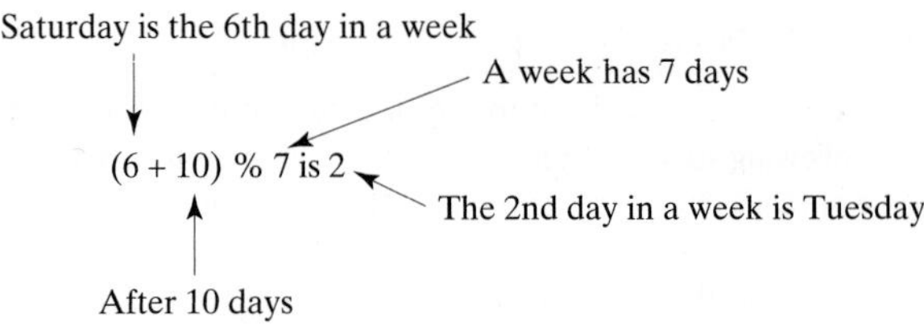

Listing 2.2 gives a program that obtains minutes and remaining seconds from an amount of time in seconds. For example, 500 seconds contains 8 minutes and 20 seconds.

LISTING 2.2 DisplayTime.java

divide

remainder

```
1 public class DisplayTime {
2   public static void main(String[] args) {
3     int seconds = 500;
4     int minutes = seconds / 60;
5     int remainingSeconds = seconds % 60;
6     System.out.println(seconds + " seconds is " + minutes +
7       " minutes and " + remainingSeconds + " seconds");
8   }
9 }
```

```
500 seconds is 8 minutes and 20 seconds
```

Line 4 obtains the minutes using seconds / 60. Line 5 (seconds % 60) obtains the remaining seconds after taking away the minutes.

unary operator

binary operator

The + and - operators can be both unary and binary. A *unary* operator has only one operand; a *binary* operator has two operands. For example, the - operator in -5 can be considered a unary operator to negate number 5, whereas the - operator in 4 - 5 is a binary operator for subtracting 5 from 4.

floating-point approximation

Note

Calculations involving floating-point numbers are approximated because these numbers are not stored with complete accuracy. For example,

```
System.out.println(1.0 - 0.1 - 0.1 - 0.1 - 0.1 - 0.1);
```

displays 0.5000000000000001, not 0.5, and

```
System.out.println(1.0 - 0.9);
```

displays 0.09999999999999998, not 0.1. Integers are stored precisely. Therefore, calculations with integers yield a precise integer result.

2.7.2 Numeric Literals

A *literal* is a constant value that appears directly in a program. For example, 34, 1000000, and 5.0 are literals in the following statements: literal

```
int i = 34;
long k = 1000000;
double d = 5.0;
```

Integer Literals

An integer literal can be assigned to an integer variable as long as it can fit into the variable. A compilation error would occur if the literal were too large for the variable to hold. The statement byte b = 128, for example, would cause a compilation error, because 128 cannot be stored in a variable of the byte type. (Note that the range for a byte value is from -128 to 127.)

An integer literal is assumed to be of the int type, whose value is between -2^{31} (−2147483648) and $2^{31} - 1$ (2147483647). To denote an integer literal of the long type, append the letter L or l to it (e.g., 2147483648L). L is preferred because l (lowercase L) can easily be confused with 1 (the digit one). To write integer 2147483648 in a Java program, you have to write it as denote 2147483648L, because 2147483648 exceeds the range for the int value.

long literal

Note

By default, an integer literal is a decimal number. To denote an octal integer literal, use a leading *0* (zero), and to denote a hexadecimal integer literal, use a leading *0x* or *0X* (zero x). For example, the following code displays the decimal value 65535 for hexadecimal number FFFF.

octal and hex literals

```
System.out.println( 0x FFFF);
```

Hexadecimal numbers, binary numbers, and octal numbers were introduced in §1.5, "Number Systems."

Floating-Point Literals

Floating-point literals are written with a decimal point. By default, a floating-point literal is treated as a double type value. For example, 5.0 is considered a double value, not a float value. You can make a number a float by appending the letter f or F, and you can make a number a double by appending the letter d or D. For example, you can use 100.2f or 100.2F for a float number, and 100.2d or 100.2D for a double number.

suffix f or F

suffix d or D

Note

The double type values are more accurate than the float type values. For example,

double vs. **float**

```
System.out.println("1.0 / 3.0 is " + 1.0 / 3.0);
```

displays 1.0 / 3.0 is 0.3333333333333333.

```
System.out.println("1.0F / 3.0F is " + 1.0F / 3.0F);
```

displays 1.0F / 3.0F is 0.33333334.

Scientific Notation

Floating-point literals can also be specified in scientific notation; for example, 1.23456e+2, the same as 1.23456e2, is equivalent to $1.23456 \times 10^2 = 123.456$, and 1.23456e-2 is equivalent to $1.23456 \times 10^{-2} = 0.0123456$. E (or e) represents an exponent and can be in either lowercase or uppercase.

> **Note**
>
> The `float` and `double` types are used to represent numbers with a decimal point. Why are they called *floating-point numbers*? These numbers are stored in scientific notation. When a number such as `50.534` is converted into scientific notation, such as `5.0534e+1`, its decimal point is moved (i.e., floated) to a new position.

why called floating-point?

2.7.3 Evaluating Java Expressions

Writing a numeric expression in Java involves a straightforward translation of an arithmetic expression using Java operators. For example, the arithmetic expression

$$\frac{3 + 4x}{5} - \frac{10(y - 5)(a + b + c)}{x} + 9\left(\frac{4}{x} + \frac{9 + x}{y}\right)$$

can be translated into a Java expression as:

```
(3 + 4 * x) / 5 – 10 * (y - 5) * (a + b + c) / x +
9 * (4 / x + (9 + x) / y)
```

evaluating an expression

Though Java has its own way to evaluate an expression behind the scene, the result of a Java expression and its corresponding arithmetic expression are the same. Therefore, you can safely apply the arithmetic rule for evaluating a Java expression. Operators contained within pairs of parentheses are evaluated first. Parentheses can be nested, in which case the expression in the inner parentheses is evaluated first. Multiplication, division, and remainder operators are applied next. If an expression contains several multiplication, division, and remainder operators, they are applied from left to right. Addition and subtraction operators are applied last. If an expression contains several addition and subtraction operators, they are applied from left to right. Here is an example of how an expression is evaluated:

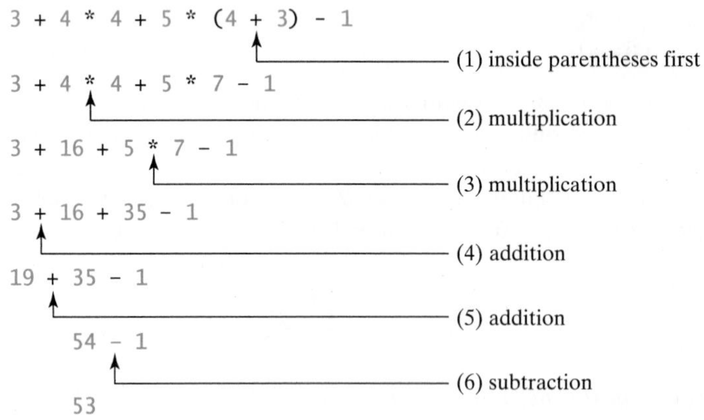

```
3 + 4 * 4 + 5 * (4 + 3) - 1
                    (1) inside parentheses first
3 + 4 * 4 + 5 * 7 - 1
                    (2) multiplication
3 + 16 + 5 * 7 - 1
                    (3) multiplication
3 + 16 + 35 - 1
                    (4) addition
19 + 35 - 1
                    (5) addition
  54 - 1
                    (6) subtraction
  53
```

Listing 2.3 gives a program that converts a Fahrenheit degree to Celsius using the formula $celsius = \left(\frac{5}{9}\right)(fahrenheit - 32)$.

LISTING 2.3 FahrenheitToCelsius.java

divide

```
public class FahrenheitToCelsius {
  public static void main(String[] args) {
    double fahrenheit = 100; // Say 100;
    double celsius = (5.0 / 9) * (fahrenheit - 32);
    System.out.println("Fahrenheit " + fahrenheit + " is " +
```

```
6         celsius + " in Celsius");
7   }
8 }
```

```
Fahrenheit 100.0 is 37.77777777777778 in Celsius
```

integer vs. decimal division

Be careful when applying division. Division of two integers yields an integer in Java. $\frac{5}{9}$ is translated to `5.0 / 9` instead of `5 / 9` in line 4, because `5 / 9` yields `0` in Java.

2.7.4 Shorthand Operators

Very often the current value of a variable is used, modified, and then reassigned back to the same variable. For example, the following statement adds the current value of `i` with `8` and assigns the result back to `i`:

```
i = i + 8;
```

shorthand operator

Java allows you to combine assignment and addition operators using a shorthand operator. For example, the preceding statement can be written as:

```
i += 8;
```

shorthand operator

The += is called the *addition assignment operator*. Other shorthand operators are shown in Table 2.3.

TABLE 2.3 Shorthand Operators

Operator	*Name*	*Example*	*Equivalent*
+=	Addition assignment	`i += 8`	`i = i + 8`
-=	Subtraction assignment	`f -= 8.0`	`f = f - 8.0`
*=	Multiplication assignment	`i *= 8`	`i = i * 8`
/=	Division assignment	`i /= 8`	`i = i / 8`
%=	Remainder assignment	`i %= 8`	`i = i % 8`

Caution

There are no spaces in the shorthand operators. For example, + = should be +=.

++ and --

There are two more shorthand operators for incrementing and decrementing a variable by `1`. This is handy because that's often how much the value needs to be changed. These two operators are ++ and --. They can be used in prefix or suffix notation, as shown in Table 2.4.

TABLE 2.4 Increment and Decrement Operators

Operator	*Name*	*Description*
`++var`	preincrement	The expression (`++var`) increments `var` by `1` and evaluates to the *new* value in `var` *after* the increment.
`var++`	postincrement	The expression (`var++`) evaluates to the *original* value in `var` and increments `var` by `1`.
`--var`	predecrement	The expression (`--var`) decrements `var` by `1` and evaluates to the *new* value in `var` *after* the decrement.
`var--`	postdecrement	The expression (`var--`) evaluates to the *original* value in `var` and decrements `var` by `1`.

If the operator is *before* (prefixed to) the variable, the variable is incremented or decremented by 1, then the *new* value of the variable is returned. If the operator is *after* (suffixed to) the variable, the original *old* value of the variable is returned, then the variable is incremented or decremented by 1. Therefore, the prefixes ++x and --x are referred to, respectively, as the *preincrement operator* and the *predecrement operator*; and the suffixes x++ and x-- are referred to, respectively, as the *postincrement operator* and the *postdecrement operator*. The prefix form of ++ (or --) and the suffix form of ++ (or --) are the same if they are used in isolation, but they cause different effects when used in an expression. The following code illustrates this:

preincrement, predecrement
postincrement, postdecrement

```
int i = 10;
int newNum = 10 * i++;
```

Same effect as

```
int newNum = 10 * i;
i = i + 1;
```

In this case, i is incremented by 1, then the *old* value of i is returned and used in the multiplication. So newNum becomes 100. If i++ is replaced by ++i as follows,

```
int i = 10;
int newNum = 10 * (++i);
```

Same effect as

```
i = i + 1;
int newNum = 10 * i;
```

i is incremented by 1, and the new value of i is returned and used in the multiplication. Thus newNum becomes 110.

Here is another example:

```
double x = 1.0;
double y = 5.0;
double z = x-- + (++y);
```

After all three lines are executed, y becomes 6.0, z becomes 7.0, and x becomes 0.0.

The increment operator ++ and the decrement operator -- can be applied to all integer and floating-point types. These operators are often used in loop statements. A *loop statement* is a structure that controls how many times an operation or a sequence of operations is performed in succession. This structure, and the subject of loop statements, are introduced in Chapter 4, "Loops."

Tip

Using increment and decrement operators makes expressions short, but it also makes them complex and difficult to read. Avoid using these operators in expressions that modify multiple variables or the same variable multiple times, such as this one: int k = ++i + i.

Note

Like the assignment operator (=), the operators (+=, -=, *=, /=, %=, ++, and --) can be used to form an assignment statement as well as an expression. For example, in the following code, x = 2 is a statement in the first line and an expression in the second line.

```
x = 2; // Statement
System.out.println(x = 2); // Expression
```

expression statement

If a statement is used as an expression, it is called an *expression statement*.

2.8 Numeric Type Conversions

Often it is necessary to mix numeric values of different types in a computation. Consider the following statements:

```
byte i = 100;
long k = i * 3 + 4;
double d = i * 3.1 + k / 2;
```

Are these statements correct? Java allows binary operations on values of different types. When performing a binary operation involving two operands of different types, Java automatically converts the operand based on the following rules:

converting operands

1. If one of the operands is **double**, the other is converted into **double**.
2. Otherwise, if one of the operands is **float**, the other is converted into **float**.
3. Otherwise, if one of the operands is **long**, the other is converted into **long**.
4. Otherwise, both operands are converted into **int**.

For example, the result of **1 / 2** is **0**, because both operands are **int** values. The result of **1.0 / 2** is **0.5**, since **1.0** is **double** and **2** is converted to **2.0**.

The range of numeric types increases in this order:

range increases →

byte, short, int, long, float, double

You can always assign a value to a numeric variable whose type supports a larger range of values; thus, for instance, you can assign a **long** value to a **float** variable. You cannot, however, assign a value to a variable of a type with smaller range unless you use *type casting*. Casting is an operation that converts a value of one data type into a value of another data type. Casting a variable of a type with a small range to a variable of a type with a larger range is known as *widening a type*. Casting a variable of a type with a large range to a variable of a type with a smaller range is known as *narrowing a type*. Widening a type can be performed automatically without explicit casting. Narrowing a type must be performed explicitly.

type casting

widening a type

narrowing a type

The syntax for casting gives the target type in parentheses, followed by the variable's name or the value to be cast. For example,

```
float f = (float)10.7;
int i = (int)f;
```

In the first line, the **double** value **10.7** is cast into **float**. In the second line, **i** has a value of **10**; the fractional part in **f** is *truncated*. Note that the fractional part is truncated, not rounded.

truncated

Caution

Casting is necessary if you are assigning a value to a variable of a smaller type range, such as assigning a **double** value to an **int** variable. A compilation error will occur if casting is not used in situations of this kind. Be careful when using casting. Lost information might lead to inaccurate results.

possible loss of precision

Note

Casting does not change the variable being cast. For example, **d** is not changed after casting in the following code:

```
double d = 4.5;
int i = (int)d;  // i becomes 4, but d is not changed
```

Note

To assign a variable of the **int** type to a variable of the **short** or **byte** type, explicit casting must be used. For example, the following statements have a compilation error:

```
int i = 1;
byte b = i; // Error because explicit casting is required
```

However, so long as the integer literal is within the permissible range of the target variable, explicit casting is not needed to assign an integer literal to a variable of the **short** or **byte** type. Please refer to §2.7.2, "Numeric Literals."

Listing 2.4 gives a program that displays the sales tax with two digits after the decimal point.

LISTING 2.4 SalesTax.java

```
1 public class SalesTax {
2   public static void main(String[] args) {
3     double purchaseAmount = 197.55;
4     double tax = purchaseAmount * 0.06;
5     System.out.println("Sales tax is " + (int)(tax * 100) / 100.0);
6   }
7 }
```

```
Sales tax is 11.85
```

formatting numbers

Variable **purchaseAmount** is **197.55** (line 3). The sales tax is **6%** of the purchase, so the **tax** is evaluated as **11.853** (line 4). The statement in line 5 displays the tax **11.85** with two digits after the decimal point. Note that **(int)(tax * 100)** is **1185**, so **(int)(tax * 100) / 100.0** is **11.85**.

2.9 Character Data Type and Operations

char type

The character data type, **char**, is used to represent a single character. A character literal is enclosed in single quotation marks. Consider the following code:

```
char letter = 'A';
char numChar = '4';
```

The first statement assigns character **A** to the **char** variable **letter**. The second statement assigns the digit character **4** to the **char** variable **numChar**.

Caution

char literal

A string literal must be enclosed in quotation marks. A character literal is a single character enclosed in single quotation marks. So **"A"** is a string, and **'A'** is a character.

2.9.1 Unicode and ASCII code

character encoding

Computers use binary numbers internally. A character is stored as a sequence of 0s and 1s in a computer. The process of converting a character to its binary representation is called *encoding*. There are different ways to encode a character. How characters are encoded is defined by an *encoding scheme*.

Unicode

original Unicode

Java supports *Unicode*, an encoding scheme established by the Unicode Consortium to support the interchange, processing, and display of written texts in the world's diverse languages. Unicode was originally designed as a 16-bit character encoding. The primitive data type **char** was intended to take advantage of this design by providing a simple data type that could hold any character. However, it turned out that the `65,536` characters possible in a 16-bit encoding are not sufficient to represent all the characters in the world. The Unicode standard therefore has been extended to allow up to `1,112,064` characters. Those characters that go beyond the original 16-bit limit are called *supplementary characters*. JDK 1.5 supports supplementary characters. The processing and representing of supplementary characters are beyond the scope of this book. For simplicity, this book considers only the original 16-bit Unicode characters. These characters can be stored in a `char` type variable.

supplementary Unicode

A 16-bit Unicode takes two bytes, preceded by `\u`, expressed in four hexadecimal digits that run from `'\u0000'` to `'\uFFFF'`. For example, the word "welcome" is translated into Chinese using two characters, 欢迎 . The Unicodes of these two characters are "`\u6B22\u8FCE`".

Listing 2.5 gives a program that displays two Chinese characters and three Greek letters.

LISTING 2.5 DisplayUnicode.java

```
import javax.swing.JOptionPane;

public class DisplayUnicode {
  public static void main(String[] args) {
    JOptionPane.showMessageDialog(null,
      "\u6B22\u8FCE \u03b1 \u03b2 \u03b3",
      "\u6B22\u8FCE Welcome",
      JOptionPane.INFORMATION_MESSAGE);
  }
}
```

If no Chinese font is installed on your system, you will not be able to see the Chinese characters. The Unicodes for the Greek letters α β γ are `\u03b1 \u03b2 \u03b3`.

Most computers use *ASCII* (*American Standard Code for Information Interchange*), a 7-bit encoding scheme for representing all uppercase and lowercase letters, digits, punctuation marks, and control characters. Unicode includes ASCII code, with `'\u0000'` to `'\u007F'` corresponding to the 128 ASCII characters. (See Appendix B, "The ASCII Character Set," for a list of ASCII characters and their decimal and hexadecimal codes.) You can use ASCII characters such as `'X'`, `'1'`, and `'$'` in a Java program as well as Unicodes. Thus, for example, the following statements are equivalent:

ASCII

```
char letter = 'A';
char letter = '\u0041'; // Character A's Unicode is 0041
```

Both statements assign character `A` to `char` variable `letter`.

Note

The increment and decrement operators can also be used on `char` variables to get the next or preceding Unicode character. For example, the following statements display character `b`.

char increment and decrement

```
char ch = 'a';
System.out.println(++ch);
```

2.9.2 Escape Sequences for Special Characters

Suppose you want to print a message with quotation marks in the output. Can you write a statement like this?

```
System.out.println("He said "Java is fun"");
```

No, this statement has a syntax error. The compiler thinks the second quotation character is the end of the string and does not know what to do with the rest of characters.

backslash

To overcome this problem, Java defines escape sequences to represent special characters, as shown in Table 2.5. An escape sequence begins with the backslash character (\) followed by a character that has a special meaning to the compiler.

TABLE 2.5 Java Escape Sequences

Character Escape Sequence	*Name*	*Unicode Code*
`\b`	Backspace	\u0008
`\t`	Tab	\u0009
`\n`	Linefeed	\u000A
`\f`	Formfeed	\u000C
`\r`	Carriage Return	\u000D
`\\`	Backslash	\u005C
`\'`	Single Quote	\u0027
`\"`	Double Quote	\u0022

So, now you can print the quoted message using the following statement:

```
System.out.println("He said \"Java is fun\"");
```

The output is

```
He said "Java is fun"
```

2.9.3 Casting between char and Numeric Types

A `char` value can be cast into any numeric type, and vice versa. When an integer is cast into a `char`, only its lower sixteen bits of data are used; the other part is ignored. For example, see the following code:

```
char ch = (char)0XAB0041; // The lower 16 bits hex code 0041 is
                          // assigned to ch
System.out.println(ch);   // ch is character A
```

When a floating-point value is cast into a `char`, the floating-point value is first cast into an `int`, which is then cast into a `char`.

```
char ch = (char)65.25;    // Decimal 65 is assigned to ch
System.out.println(ch);   // ch is character A
```

When a `char` is cast into a numeric type, the character's Unicode is cast into the specified numeric type.

```
int i = (int)'A'; // The Unicode of character A is assigned to i
System.out.println(i);  // i is 65
```

Implicit casting can be used if the result of a casting fits into the target variable. Otherwise, explicit casting must be used. For example, since the Unicode of `'a'` is `97`, which is within the range of a byte, these implicit castings are fine:

```
byte b = 'a';
int i = 'a';
```

But the following casting is incorrect, because the Unicode \uFFF4 cannot fit into a byte:

```
byte b = '\uFFF4';
```

To force assignment, use explicit casting, as follows:

```
byte b = (byte)'\uFFF4';
```

Any positive integer between 0 and FFFF in hexadecimal can be cast into a character implicitly. Any number not in this range must be cast into a char explicitly.

Note

numeric operators on characters

All numeric operators can be applied to char operands. A char operand is automatically cast into a number if the other operand is a number or a character. If the other operand is a string, the character is concatenated with the string. For example, the following statements

```
int i = '2' + '3'; // (int)'2' is 50 and (int)'3' is 51
System.out.println("i is " + i);

int j = 2 + 'a'; // (int)'a' is 97
System.out.println("j is " + j);
System.out.println(j + " is the Unicode for character " + (char)j);

System.out.println("Chapter " + '2');
```

display

```
i is 101
j is 99
99 is the Unicode for character c
Chapter 2
```

Note

The Unicodes for lowercase letters are consecutive integers starting from the Unicode for 'a', then for 'b', 'c', ..., and 'z'. The same is true for the uppercase letters. Furthermore, the Unicode for 'a' is greater than the Unicode for 'A'. So 'a' - 'A' is the same as 'b' - 'B'. For a lowercase letter *ch*, its corresponding uppercase letter is (char)('A' + (ch - 'a')).

2.10 The String Type

The char type represents only one character. To represent a string of characters, use the data type called String. For example, the following code declares the message to be a string with value "Welcome to Java".

```
String message = "Welcome to Java";
```

String is actually a predefined class in the Java library just like the System class and JOptionPane class. The String type is not a primitive type. It is known as a *reference type*. Any Java class can be used as a reference type for a variable. Reference data types will be thoroughly discussed in Chapter 7, "Classes and Objects." For the time being, you need to know only how to declare a String variable, how to assign a string to the variable, and how to concatenate strings.

concatenating strings and numbers

As first shown in Listing 2.1, two strings can be concatenated. The plus sign (+) is the concatenation operator if one of the operands is a string. If one of the operands is a nonstring (e.g., a number), the nonstring value is converted into a string and concatenated with the other string. Here are some examples:

```
// Three strings are concatenated
String message = "Welcome " + "to " + "Java";
```

```
// String Chapter is concatenated with number 2
String s = "Chapter" + 2; // s becomes Chapter2

// String Supplement is concatenated with character B
String s1 = "Supplement" + 'B'; // s becomes SupplementB
```

If neither of the operands is a string, the plus sign (+) is the addition operator that adds two numbers.

The shorthand += operator can also be used for string concatenation. For example, the following code appends the string " and Java is fun" with the string "Welcome to Java" in `message`.

```
message += " and Java is fun";
```

So the new `message` is "Welcome to Java and Java is fun".

Suppose that `i = 1` and `j = 2`, what is the output of the following statement?

```
System.out.println("i + j is " + i + j);
```

The output is "i + j is 12" because `"i + j is "` is concatenated with the value of `i` first. To force `i + j` to be executed first, enclose `i + j` in the parentheses, as follows:

```
System.out.println("i + j is " + (i + j));
```

2.11 Console Input Using the **Scanner** Class

In Listing 2.1, the radius is fixed in the source code. To use a different radius, you have to modify the source code and recompile it. Obviously, this is not convenient. You can use the `Scanner` class for console input.

Java uses `System.out` to refer to the standard output device and `System.in` to the standard input device. By default the output device is the console, and the input device is the keyboard. To perform console output, you simply use the `println` method to display a primitive value or a string to the console. Console input is not directly supported in Java, but you can use the `Scanner` class to create an object to read input from `System.in`, as follows:

```
Scanner input = new Scanner(System.in);
```

`Scanner` is a new class in JDK 1.5. The syntax *`new Scanner(System.in)`* creates an object of the `Scanner` type. The syntax *`Scanner input`* declares that `input` is a variable whose type is `Scanner`. The whole line *`Scanner input = new Scanner(System.in)`* creates a `Scanner` object and assigns its reference to the variable `input`. An object may contain methods. Invoking a method on an object is to ask the object to perform a task. A `Scanner` object contains the methods for reading input, as shown in Table 2.6:

TABLE 2.6 Methods for `Scanner` Objects

Method	*Description*
`nextByte()`	reads an integer of the `byte` type.
`nextShort()`	reads an integer of the `short` type.
`nextInt()`	reads an integer of the `int` type.
`nextLong()`	reads an integer of the `long` type.
`nextFloat()`	reads a number of the `float` type.
`nextDouble()`	reads a number of the `double` type.
`next()`	reads a string that ends before a whitespace.
`nextLine()`	reads a line of character (i.e., a string ending with a line separator).

A `Scanner` object reads an item separated by whitespaces. A whitespace character is `' '`, `'\t'`, `'\f'`, `'\r'`, or `'\n'`. For example, the following statements prompt the user to enter a `double` value from the console.

whitespace

```
System.out. print("Enter a double value: ");
Scanner input = new Scanner(System.in);
double d = input.nextDouble();
```

The `print` method is identical to the `println` method except that `println` moves the cursor to the next line after displaying the string, but `print` does not advance the cursor to the next line when completed.

`print` vs. `println`

More details on objects will be introduced in Chapter 7, "Objects and Classes." For the time being, simply accept that this is how to obtain input from the console.

Listing 2.6 gives an example that reads various types of data from the console using the `Scanner` class.

Video Note
Obtain console input

LISTING 2.6 TestScanner.java

```
1 import java.util.Scanner; // Scanner is in java.util
2
3 public class TestScanner {
4   public static void main(String args[]) {
5     // Create a Scanner
6     Scanner input = new Scanner(System.in);
7
8     // Prompt the user to enter an integer
9     System.out.print("Enter an integer: ");
10    int intValue = input.nextInt();
11    System.out.println("You entered the integer " + intValue);
12
13    // Prompt the user to enter a double value
14    System.out.print("Enter a double value: ");
15    double doubleValue = input.nextDouble();
16    System.out.println("You entered the double value "
17      + doubleValue);
18
19    // Prompt the user to enter a string
20    System.out.print("Enter a string without space: ");
21    String string = input.next();
22    System.out.println("You entered the string " + string);
23  }
24 }
```

import class

create a `Scanner`

read an `int`

read a `double`

read a `string`

```
Enter an integer: 4 ↵Enter
You entered the integer 4

Enter a double value: 23.55 ↵Enter
You entered the double value 23.55

Enter a string without space: Java ↵Enter
You entered the string Java
```

The `Scanner` class is in the `java.util` package. It is imported in line 1. Line 6 creates a `Scanner` object. Line 10 reads an `int` value. Line 15 reads a `double` value. Line 21 reads a string.

avoiding input errors

Important Caution

To *avoid input errors*, do not use **nextLine()** after **nextByte()**, **nextShort()**, **nextInt()**, **nextLong()**, **nextFloat()**, **nextDouble()**, and **next()**. The reasons will be explained in §8.7.3, "How Does **Scanner** Work?"

2.12 Case Studies

In the preceding sections, you learned about variables, constants, primitive data types, operators, expressions, and console input. You are now ready to use them to write interesting programs. This section presents three problems: computing loan payments, breaking a sum of money down into smaller units, and displaying the current time.

2.12.1 Problem: Computing Loan Payments

The problem is to write a program that computes loan payments. The loan can be a car loan, a student loan, or a home mortgage loan. The program lets the user enter the interest rate, number of years, and loan amount, and displays the monthly and total payments.

The formula to compute the monthly payment is as follows:

$$\frac{loanAmount \times monthlyInterestRate}{1 - \dfrac{1}{(1 + monthlyInterestRate)^{numberOfYears \times 12}}}$$

You don't have to know how this formula is derived. Nonetheless, given the monthly interest rate, number of years, and loan amount, you can use it to compute the monthly payment.

pow(a, b) method

In the formula, you have to compute $(1 + monthlyInterestRate)^{numberOfYears \times 12}$. The **pow(a, b)** method in the **Math** class can be used to compute a^b. The **Math** class, which comes with the Java API, is available to all Java programs. The **Math** class is introduced in Chapter 5, "Methods."

Here are the steps in developing the program:

1. Prompt the user to enter the annual interest rate, number of years, and loan amount.
2. Obtain the monthly interest rate from the annual interest rate.
3. Compute the monthly payment using the preceding formula.
4. Compute the total payment, which is the monthly payment multiplied by 12 and multiplied by the number of years.
5. Display the monthly payment and total payment.

Video Note
Program Mathematical computations

Listing 2.7 gives the complete program.

LISTING 2.7 ComputeLoan.java

import class

create a **Scanner**

```
import java.util.Scanner;

public class ComputeLoan {
  public static void main(String[] args) {
    // Create a Scanner
    Scanner input = new Scanner(System.in);

```

```
8      // Enter yearly interest rate
9      System.out.print("Enter yearly interest rate, for example 8.25: ");
10     double annualInterestRate = input.nextDouble();
11
12     // Obtain monthly interest rate
13     double monthlyInterestRate = annualInterestRate / 1200;
14
15     // Enter number of years
16     System.out.print(
17       "Enter number of years as an integer, for example 5: ");
18     int numberOfYears = input.nextInt();
19
20     // Enter loan amount
21     System.out.print("Enter loan amount, for example 120000.95: ");
22     double loanAmount = input.nextDouble();
23
24     // Calculate payment
25     double monthlyPayment = loanAmount * monthlyInterestRate / (1
26       - 1 / Math.pow(1 + monthlyInterestRate, numberOfYears * 12));
27     double totalPayment = monthlyPayment * numberOfYears * 12;
28
29     // Format to keep two digits after the decimal point
30     monthlyPayment = (int)(monthlyPayment * 100) / 100.0;
31     totalPayment = (int)(totalPayment * 100) / 100.0;
32
33     // Display results
34     System.out.println("The monthly payment is " + monthlyPayment);
35     System.out.println("The total payment is " + totalPayment);
36   }
37 }
```

enter interest rate

enter years

enter loan amount

monthlyPayment

totalPayment

display result

```
Enter yearly interest rate, for example 8.25: 5.75 ↵Enter
Enter number of years as an integer, for example 5: 15 ↵Enter
Enter loan amount, for example 120000.95: 250000 ↵Enter
The monthly payment is 2076.02
The total payment is 373684.53
```

Line 10 reads the yearly interest rate, which is converted into monthly interest rate in line 13. If you entered an input other than a numeric value, a runtime error would occur. In Chapter 18, "Exception Handling," you will learn how to handle the exception so that the program can continue to run.

Each variable in a method such as `main` must be declared once and only once. Choose the most appropriate data type for the variable. For example, `numberOfYears` is best declared as an `int` (line 18), although it could be declared as a `long`, `float`, or `double`. Note that `byte` might be the most appropriate for `numberOfYears`. For simplicity, however, the examples in this book will use `int` for integer and `double` for floating-point values.

The formula for computing the monthly payment is translated into Java code in lines 25–27.

The statements in lines 30–31 are for formatting the number to keep two digits after the decimal point. For example, if `monthlyPayment` is `2076.0252175`, `(int)(monthlyPayment * 100)` is `207602`. Therefore, `(int)(monthlyPayment * 100) / 100.0` yields `2076.02`.

formatting numbers

java.lang package

The program uses the Scanner class, imported in line 1. The program also uses the Math class; why isn't it imported? The Math class is in the java.lang package. All classes in the java.lang package are implicitly imported. So, there is no need to explicitly import the Math class.

2.12.2 Problem: Counting Monetary Units

Suppose you want to develop a program that classifies a given amount of money into smaller monetary units. The program lets the user enter an amount as a double value representing a total in dollars and cents, and outputs a report listing the monetary equivalent in dollars, quarters, dimes, nickels, and pennies, as shown in the sample output.

Your program should report the maximum number of dollars, then the maximum number of quarters, and so on, in this order.

Here are the steps in developing the program:

1. Prompt the user to enter the amount as a decimal number, such as 11.56.
2. Convert the amount (e.g., 11.56) into cents (1156).
3. Divide the cents by 100 to find the number of dollars. Obtain the remaining cents using the cents remainder 100.
4. Divide the remaining cents by 25 to find the number of quarters. Obtain the remaining cents using the remaining cents remainder 25.
5. Divide the remaining cents by 10 to find the number of dimes. Obtain the remaining cents using the remaining cents remainder 10.
6. Divide the remaining cents by 5 to find the number of nickels. Obtain the remaining cents using the remaining cents remainder 5.
7. The remaining cents are the pennies.
8. Display the result.

The complete program is given in Listing 2.8.

LISTING 2.8 ComputeChange.java

import class
enter input
dollars

```
import java.util.Scanner;

public class ComputeChange {
  public static void main(String[] args) {
    // Create a Scanner
    Scanner input = new Scanner(System.in);

    // Receive the amount
    System.out.print(
      "Enter an amount in double, for example 11.56: ");
    double amount = input.nextDouble();

    int remainingAmount = (int)(amount * 100);

    // Find the number of one dollars
    int numberOfOneDollars = remainingAmount / 100;
    remainingAmount = remainingAmount % 100;

```

quarters

dimes

nickels

pennies

prepare output

```
19      // Find the number of quarters in the remaining amount
20      int numberOfQuarters = remainingAmount / 25;
21      remainingAmount = remainingAmount % 25;
22
23      // Find the number of dimes in the remaining amount
24      int numberOfDimes = remainingAmount / 10;
25      remainingAmount = remainingAmount % 10;
26
27      // Find the number of nickels in the remaining amount
28      int numberOfNickels = remainingAmount / 5;
29      remainingAmount = remainingAmount % 5;
30
31      // Find the number of pennies in the remaining amount
32      int numberOfPennies = remainingAmount;
33
34      // Display results
35      String output = "Your amount " + amount + " consists of \n" +
36        "\t" + numberOfOneDollars + " dollars\n" +
37        "\t" + numberOfQuarters + " quarters\n" +
38        "\t" + numberOfDimes + " dimes\n" +
39        "\t" + numberOfNickels + " nickels\n" +
40        "\t" + numberOfPennies + " pennies";
41      System.out.println(output);
42    }
43 }
```

```
Enter an amount in double, for example 11.56: 11.56 ↵Enter
Your amount 11.56 consists of
11 dollars
2 quarters
0 dimes
1 nickels
1 pennies
```

The variable **amount** stores the amount entered from the console (line 11). This variable is not changed because the amount has to be used at the end of the program to display the results. The program introduces the variable **remainingAmount** (line 13) to store the changing **remainingAmount**.

The variable **amount** is a **double** decimal representing dollars and cents. It is converted to an **int** variable **remainingAmount**, which represents all the cents. For instance, if **amount** is **11.56**, then the initial **remainingAmount** is **1156**. The division operator yields the integer part of the division. So **1156 / 100** is **11**. The remainder operator obtains the remainder of the division. So **1156 % 100** is **56**.

The program extracts the maximum number of singles from the total amount and obtains the remaining amount in the variable **remainingAmount** (lines 16–17). It then extracts the maximum number of quarters from **remainingAmount** and obtains a new **remainingAmount** (lines 20–21). Continuing the same process, the program finds the maximum number of dimes, nickels, and pennies in the remaining amount.

loss of precision

One serious problem with this example is the possible loss of precision when casting a **double** amount to an **int remainingAmount**. This could lead to an inaccurate result. If you try to enter the amount **10.03**, **10.03 * 100** becomes **1002.9999999999999**. You will find that the program displays **10** dollars and **2** pennies. To fix the problem, enter the amount as an integer value representing cents (see Exercise 2.9).

As shown in the sample output, 0 dimes, 1 nickels, and 1 pennies are displayed in the result. It would be better not to display 0 dimes, and to display 1 nickel and 1 penny using the singular forms of the words. You will learn how to use selection statements to modify this program in the next chapter (see Exercise 3.7).

2.12.3 Problem: Displaying the Current Time

The problem is to develop a program that displays the current time in GMT (Greenwich Mean Time) in the format hour:minute:second, such as 13:19:8.

currentTimeMillis

The **currentTimeMillis** method in the **System** class returns the current time in milliseconds elapsed since the time **00:00:00** on January 1, 1970 GMT, as shown in Figure 2.3. This time is known as the *Unix epoch,* because **1970** was the year when the Unix operating system was formally introduced.

Unix epoch

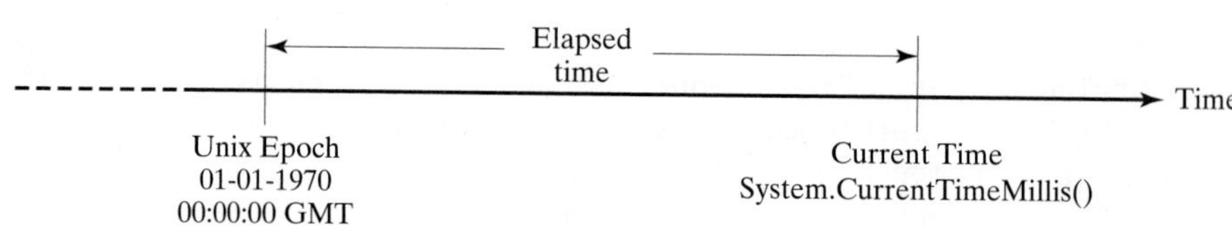

FIGURE 2.3 The **System.currentTimeMillis()** returns the number of milliseconds since the Unix epoch.

You can use this method to obtain the current time, and then compute the current second, minute, and hour as follows.

1. Obtain the total milliseconds since midnight, Jan 1, 1970, in **totalMilliseconds** by invoking **System.currentTimeMillis()** (e.g., 1103203148368 milliseconds).
2. Obtain the total seconds **totalSeconds** by dividing **totalMilliseconds** by 1000 (e.g., 1103203148368 milliseconds / 1000 = 1103203148 seconds).
3. Compute the current second from **totalSeconds % 60** (e.g., 1103203148 seconds % 60 = 8,which is the current second).
4. Obtain the total minutes **totalMinutes** by dividing **totalSeconds** by 60 (e.g., 1103203148 seconds / 60 = 18386719 minutes).
5. Compute the current minute from **totalMinutes % 60** (e.g., 18386719 minutes % 60 = 19, which is the current minute).
6. Obtain the total hours **totalHours** by dividing **totalMinutes** by 60 (e.g.,18386719 minutes / 60 = 306445 hours).
7. Compute the current hour from **totalHours % 24** (e.g., 306445 hours % 24 = 19, which is the current hour).

Listing 2.9 gives the complete program.

Video Note
Use operators / and %

LISTING 2.9 ShowCurrentTime.java

totalMilliseconds

```
public class ShowCurrentTime {
  public static void main(String[] args) {
    // Obtain the total milliseconds since the midnight, Jan 1, 1970
    long totalMilliseconds = System.currentTimeMillis();

    // Obtain the total seconds since the midnight, Jan 1, 1970
```

```
 7     long totalSeconds = totalMilliseconds / 1000;
 8
 9     // Compute the current second in the minute in the hour
10     int currentSecond = (int)(totalSeconds % 60);
11
12     // Obtain the total minutes
13     long totalMinutes = totalSeconds / 60;
14
15     // Compute the current minute in the hour
16     int currentMinute = (int)(totalMinutes % 60);
17
18     // Obtain the total hours
19     long totalHours = totalMinutes / 60;
20
21     // Compute the current hour
22     int currentHour = (int)(totalHours % 24);
23
24     // Display results
25     System.out.println("Current time is " + currentHour + ":"
26       + currentMinute + ":" + currentSecond + " GMT");
27   }
28 }
```

totalSeconds

currentSecond

totalMinutes

currentMinute

totalHours

currentHour

preparing output

```
Current time is 13:19:8 GMT
```

When `System.currentTimeMillis()` (line 4) is invoked, it returns the difference, measured in milliseconds, between the current GMT and midnight, January 1, 1970 GMT. This method returns the milliseconds as a `long` value.

2.13 Programming Style and Documentation

programming style

documentation

Programming style deals with what programs look like. A program can compile and run properly even if written on only one line, but writing it all on one line would be bad programming style because it would be hard to read. *Documentation* is the body of explanatory remarks and comments pertaining to a program. Programming style and documentation are as important as coding. Good programming style and appropriate documentation reduce the chance of errors and make programs easy to read. So far you have learned some good programming styles. This section summarizes them and gives several guidelines. More detailed guidelines can be found in Supplement I.D, "Java Coding Style Guidelines," on the Companion Website.

2.13.1 Appropriate Comments and Comment Styles

Include a summary at the beginning of the program to explain what the program does, its key features, its supporting data structures, and any unique techniques it uses. In a long program, you should also include comments that introduce each major step and explain anything that is difficult to read. It is important to make comments concise so that they do not crowd the program or make it difficult to read.

javadoc comment

In addition to line comment `//` and block comment `/*`, Java supports comments of a special type, referred to as *javadoc comments*. javadoc comments begin with `/**` and end with `*/`. They can be extracted into an HTML file using JDK's `javadoc` command. For more information, see java.sun.com/j2se/javadoc.

Use javadoc comments (`/** ... */`) for commenting on an entire class or an entire method. These comments must precede the class or the method header in order to be extracted in a javadoc HTML file. For commenting on steps inside a method, use line comments (`//`).

2.13.2 Naming Conventions

Make sure that you choose descriptive names with straightforward meanings for the variables, constants, classes, and methods in your program. Names are case sensitive. Listed below are the conventions for naming variables, methods, and classes.

naming variables and methods

- Use lowercase for variables and methods. If a name consists of several words, concatenate them into one, making the first word lowercase and capitalizing the first letter of each subsequent word—for example, the variables `radius` and `area` and the method `showInputDialog`.

naming classes

- Capitalize the first letter of each word in a class name—for example, the class names `ComputeArea`, `Math`, and `JOptionPane`.

naming constants

- Capitalize every letter in a constant, and use underscores between words—for example, the constants `PI` and `MAX_VALUE`.

It is important to become familiar with the naming conventions. Understanding them will help you to understand Java programs. If you stick with the naming conventions, other programmers will better understand your program.

naming classes

Caution

Do not choose class names that are already used in the Java library. For example, since the `Math` class is defined in Java, you should not name your class `Math`.

using full descriptive names

Tip

Avoid using abbreviations for identifiers. Using complete words is more descriptive. For example, `numberOfStudents` is better than `numStuds`, `numOfStuds`, or `numOfStudents`.

2.13.3 Proper Indentation and Spacing

indent code

A consistent indentation style makes programs clear and easy to read. *Indentation* is used to illustrate the structural relationships between a program's components or statements. Java can read the program even if all of the statements are in a straight line, but it is easier to read and maintain code that is aligned properly. Indent each subcomponent or statement at least *two* spaces more than the structure within which it is nested.

A single space should be added on both sides of a binary operator, as shown in the following statement:

```
int i= 3+4 * 4;
```
← Bad style

```
int i = 3 + 4 * 4;
```
← Good style

A single space line should be used to separate segments of the code to make the program easier to read.

2.13.4 Block Styles

A block is a group of statements surrounded by braces. There are two popular styles, *next-line* style and *end-of-line* style, as shown below.

The next-line style aligns braces vertically and makes programs easy to read, whereas the end-of-line style saves space and may help avoid some subtle programming errors. Both are acceptable block styles. The choice depends on personal or organizational preference. You should use a style consistently. Mixing styles is not recommended. This book uses the *end-of-line* style to be consistent with the Java API source code.

```
public class Test
{
  public static void main(String[] args)
  {
    System.out.println("Block Styles");
  }
}
```

Next-line style

```
public class Test {
  public static void main(String[] args) {
    System.out.println("Block Styles");
  }
}
```

End-of-line style

2.14 Programming Errors

Programming errors are unavoidable, even for experienced programmers. Errors can be categorized into three types: syntax errors, runtime errors, and logic errors.

2.14.1 Syntax Errors

syntax errors

Errors that occur during compilation are called *syntax errors* or *compilation errors*. Syntax errors result from errors in code construction, such as mistyping a keyword, omitting some necessary punctuation, or using an opening brace without a corresponding closing brace. These errors are usually easy to detect, because the compiler tells you where they are and what caused them. For example, compiling the following program results in a syntax error, as shown in Figure 2.4.

syntax error

```
// ShowSyntaxErrors.java: The program contains syntax errors
public class ShowSyntaxErrors {
  public static void main(String[] args) {
    i = 30;
    System.out.println(i + 4);
  }
}
```

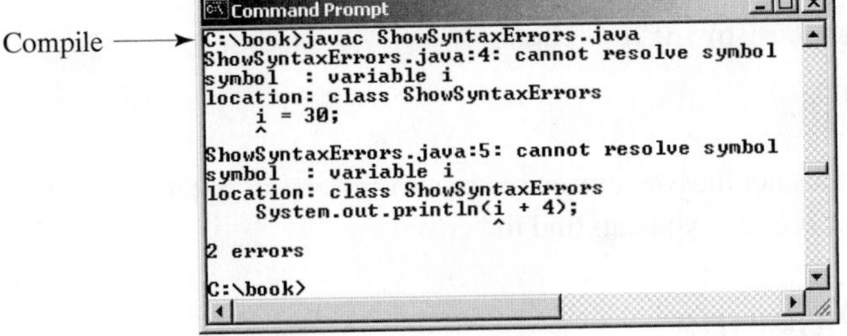

FIGURE 2.4 The compiler reports syntax errors.

Two errors are detected. Both are the result of not declaring variable `i`. Since a single error will often display many lines of compilation errors, it is a good practice to start debugging from the top line and work downward. Fixing errors that occur earlier in the program may also fix additional errors that occur later.

2.14.2 Runtime Errors

runtime errors

Runtime errors are errors that cause a program to terminate abnormally. Runtime errors occur while an application is running if the environment detects an operation that is impossible to carry out. Input errors typically cause runtime errors.

An *input error* occurs when the user enters an unexpected input value that the program cannot handle. For instance, if the program expects to read in a number, but instead the user enters a string, this causes data-type errors to occur in the program. To prevent input errors, the program should prompt the user to enter the correct type of values. It may display a message like "Please enter an integer" before reading an integer from the keyboard.

Another common source of runtime errors is division by zero. This happens when the divisor is zero for integer divisions. For instance, the following program would cause a runtime error, as shown in Figure 2.5.

```
// ShowRuntimeErrors.java: Program contains runtime errors
public class ShowRuntimeErrors {
  public static void main(String[] args) {
    int i = 1 / 0;
  }
}
```

Run

FIGURE 2.5 The runtime error causes the program to terminate abnormally.

2.14.3 Logic Errors

logic errors

Logic errors occur when a program does not perform the way it was intended to. Errors of this kind occur for many different reasons. For example, suppose you wrote the following program to add `number1` to `number2`.

```
// ShowLogicErrors.java: The program contains a logic error
public class ShowLogicErrors {
  public static void main(String[] args) {
    // Add number1 to number2
    int number1 = 3;
    int number2 = 3;
    number2 += number1 + number2;
    System.out.println("number2 is " + number2);
  }
}
```

The program does not have syntax errors or runtime errors, but it does not print the correct result for `number2`. See if you can find the error.

2.15 Debugging

In general, syntax errors are easy to find and easy to correct because the compiler gives indications as to where the errors came from and why they are there. Runtime errors are not difficult to find either, since the Java interpreter displays them on the console when the program aborts. Finding logic errors, on the other hand, can be very challenging.

Logic errors are called *bugs*. The process of finding and correcting errors is called *debugging*. A common approach to debugging is to use a combination of methods to narrow down to the part of the program where the bug is located. You can *hand-trace* the program (i.e., catch errors by reading the program), or you can insert print statements in order to show the values of the variables or the execution flow of the program. This approach might work for a short, simple program. But for a large, complex program, the most effective approach for debugging is to use a debugger utility.

bugs
debugging
hand-traces

JDK includes a command-line debugger (jdb), which is invoked with a class name. jdb is itself a Java program, running its own copy of Java interpreter. All the Java IDE tools, such as NetBeans, Eclipse, and JBuilder, include integrated debuggers. The debugger utilities let you follow the execution of a program. They vary from one system to another, but they all support most of the following helpful features:

debugging in IDE

- **`Executing a single statement at a time:`** The debugger allows you to execute one statement at a time so that you can see the effect of each.
- **`Tracing into or stepping over a method:`** If a method is being executed, you can ask the debugger to enter the method and execute one statement at a time in the method, or you can ask it to step over the entire method. You should step over the entire method if you know that the method works. For example, always step over system-supplied methods, such as `System.out.println`.
- **`Setting breakpoints:`** You can also set a breakpoint at a specific statement. Your program pauses when it reaches a breakpoint and displays the line with the breakpoint. You can set as many breakpoints as you want. Breakpoints are particularly useful when you know where your programming error starts. You can set a breakpoint at that line and have the program execute until it reaches the breakpoint.
- **`Displaying variables:`** The debugger lets you select several variables and display their values. As you trace through a program, the content of a variable is continuously updated.
- **`Displaying call stacks:`** The debugger lets you trace all of the method calls and lists all pending methods. This feature is helpful when you need to see a large picture of the program-execution flow.
- **`Modifying variables:`** Some debuggers enable you to modify the value of a variable when debugging. This is convenient when you want to test a program with different samples but do not want to leave the debugger.

Pedagogical Note

An IDE not only helps debug errors but also is an effective pedagogical tool. Supplement II shows you how to use a debugger to trace programs and how debugging can help in learning Java effectively.

learning tool

2.16 (GUI) Getting Input from Input Dialogs

You can obtain input from the console. Alternatively, you may obtain input from an input dialog box by invoking the `JOptionPane.showInputDialog` method, as shown in Figure 2.6.

`JOptionPane` class

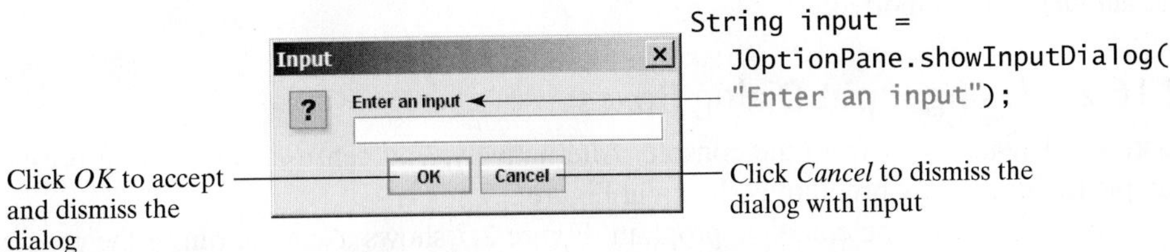
Input
Enter an input
OK
Cancel
String input =
JOptionPane.showInputDialog(
"Enter an input");
Click *OK* to accept and dismiss the dialog
Click *Cancel* to dismiss the dialog with input

FIGURE 2.6 The input dialog box enables the user to enter a string.

When this method is executed, a dialog is displayed to enable you to enter an input value. After entering a string, click OK to accept the input and dismiss the dialog box. The input is returned from the method as a string.

Note

showInputDialog method

There are several ways to use the **showInputDialog** method. For the time being, you need to know only two ways to invoke it.

One is to use a statement like this one:

```
JOptionPane.showInputDialog(x);
```

where **x** is a string for the prompting message.

The other is to use a statement as shown in the example:

```
String string = JOptionPane.showInputDialog(null, x,
   y, JOptionPane.QUESTION_MESSAGE);
```

where **x** is a string for the prompting message, and **y** is a string for the title of the input dialog box, as shown in the following example.

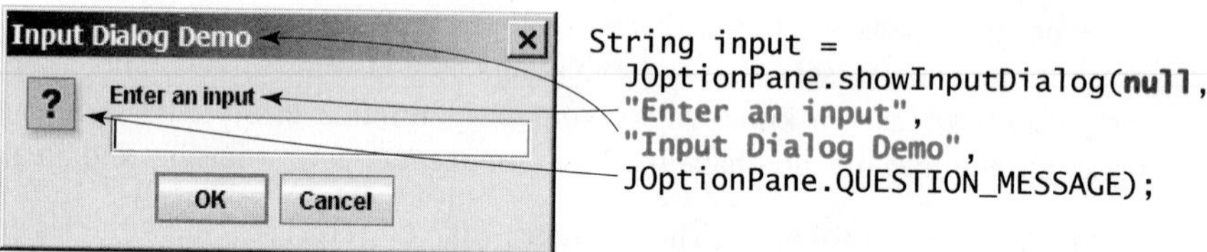
Input Dialog Demo
?
Enter an input
OK
Cancel
String input =
JOptionPane.showInputDialog(null,
"Enter an input",
"Input Dialog Demo",
JOptionPane.QUESTION_MESSAGE);

2.16.1 Converting Strings to Numbers

The input returned from the input dialog box is a string. If you enter a numeric value such as **123**, it returns **"123"**. You have to convert a string into a number to obtain the input as a number.

Integer.parseInt method

To convert a string into an **int** value, use the **parseInt** method in the **Integer** class, as follows:

```
int intValue = Integer.parseInt(intString);
```

where **intString** is a numeric string such as **"123"**.

Double.parseDouble method

To convert a string into a **double** value, use the **parseDouble** method in the **Double** class, as follows:

```
double doubleValue = Double.parseDouble(doubleString);
```

where **doubleString** is a numeric string such as **"123.45"**.

The **Integer** and **Double** classes are both included in the **java.lang** package, and thus are automatically imported.

2.16.2 Using Input Dialog Boxes

Listing 2.7 reads input from the console. Alternatively, you can use input dialog boxes. A sample run of the new program is shown in Figure 2.7.

Listing 2.10 gives the complete program. Figure 2.7 shows a sample run of the program.

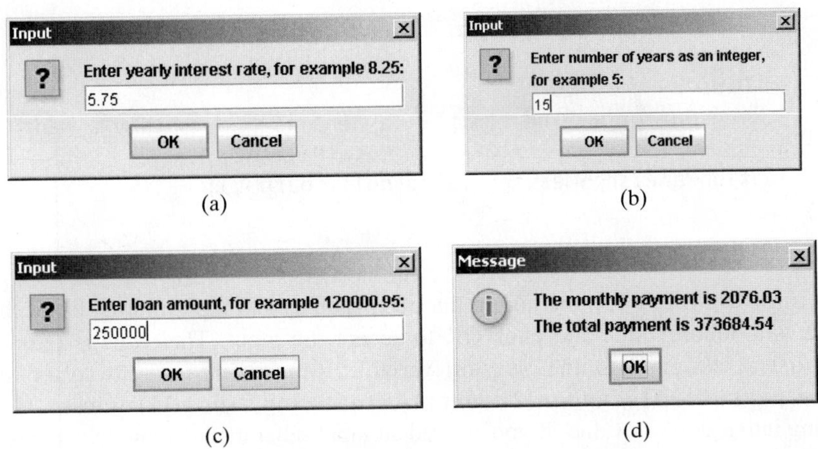

FIGURE 2.7 The program accepts the annual interest rate (a), number of years (b), and loan amount (c), then displays the monthly payment and total payment (d).

LISTING 2.10 ComputeLoanUsingInputDialog.java

```java
import javax.swing.JOptionPane;

public class ComputeLoanUsingInputDialog {
  public static void main(String[] args) {
    // Enter yearly interest rate
    String annualInterestRateString = JOptionPane.showInputDialog(
      "Enter yearly interest rate, for example 8.25:");

    // Convert string to double
    double annualInterestRate =
      Double.parseDouble(annualInterestRateString);

    // Obtain monthly interest rate
    double monthlyInterestRate = annualInterestRate / 1200;

    // Enter number of years
    String numberOfYearsString = JOptionPane.showInputDialog(
      "Enter number of years as an integer, \nfor example 5:");

    // Convert string to int
    int numberOfYears = Integer.parseInt(numberOfYearsString);

    // Enter loan amount
    String loanString = JOptionPane.showInputDialog(
      "Enter loan amount, for example 120000.95:");

    // Convert string to double
    double loanAmount = Double.parseDouble(loanString);

    // Calculate payment
    double monthlyPayment = loanAmount * monthlyInterestRate / (1
      - 1 / Math.pow(1 + monthlyInterestRate, numberOfYears * 12));
    double totalPayment = monthlyPayment * numberOfYears * 12;

    // Format to keep two digits after the decimal point
    monthlyPayment = (int)(monthlyPayment * 100) / 100.0;
```

enter interest rate

convert string to double

monthlyPayment

totalPayment

preparing output

```
37       totalPayment = (int)(totalPayment * 100) / 100.0;
38
39       // Display results
40       String output = "The monthly payment is " + monthlyPayment +
41         "\nThe total payment is " + totalPayment;
42       JOptionPane.showMessageDialog(null, output);
43     }
44 }
```

The **showInputDialog** method in lines 6–7 displays an input dialog. Enter the interest rate as a double value and click OK to accept the input. The value is returned as a string that is assigned to the **String** variable **annualInterestRateString**. The **Double.parseDouble(annualInterestRateString)** (line 11) is used to convert the string into a **double** value. If you entered an input other than a numeric value or clicked *Cancel* in the input dialog box, a runtime error would occur. In Chapter 18, "Exception Handling," you will learn how to handle the exception so that the program can continue to run.

JOptionPane or **Scanner**?

Pedagogical Note

For obtaining input you can use **JOptionPane** or **Scanner**, whichever is convenient. For consistency most examples in the book use **Scanner** for getting input. You can easily revise the examples using **JOptionPane** for getting input.

Key Terms

algorithm 26
assignment operator (=) 30
assignment statement 30
backslash (\) 42
byte type 33
casting 39
char type 40
constant 31
data type 32
debugger 55
debugging 55
declaration 29
decrement operator (−−) 37
double type 32
encoding 40
final 31
float type 32
floating-point number 26
expression 30
expression statement 38
identifier 28
increment operator (++) 37
incremental development and testing 28
indentation 52
int type 32
literal 35
logic error 54
long type 32
narrowing (of types) 39
operator 33
primitive data type 26
runtime error 54
short type 32
syntax error 53
supplementary Unicode 41
Unicode 40
Unix epoch 50
variable 27
widening (of types) 39
whitespace 45

Chapter Summary

- Java provides four integer types (**byte**, **short**, **int**, **long**) that represent integers of four different sizes, and two floating-point types (**float**, **double**) that represent floating-point numbers of two different precisions. Character type (**char**) represents a single character. These are called primitive data types. Java's primitive types are portable across all computer platforms. They have exactly the same values on all platforms. When they are declared, the variables of these types are created and assigned memory space.

- Java provides operators that perform numeric operations: + (addition), – (subtraction), * (multiplication), / (division), and % (remainder). Integer division (/) yields an integer result. The remainder operator (%) yields the remainder of the division.

- The increment operator (++) and the decrement operator (––) increment or decrement a variable by 1. If the operator is prefixed to the variable, the variable is first incremented or decremented by 1, then used in the expression. If the operator is a suffix to the variable, the variable is incremented or decremented by 1, but then the original old value is used in the expression.

- All the numeric operators can be applied to characters. When an operand is a character, the character's Unicode value is used in the operation.

- You can use casting to convert a value of one type into another type. Casting a variable of a type with a small range to a variable of a type with a larger range is known as *widening a type*. Casting a variable of a type with a large range to a variable of a type with a smaller range is known as *narrowing a type*. Widening a type can be performed automatically without explicit casting. Narrowing a type must be performed explicitly.

- Programming errors can be categorized into three types: syntax errors, runtime errors, and logic errors. Errors that occur during compilation are called *syntax errors* or *compilation errors. Runtime errors* are errors that cause a program to terminate abnormally. *Logic errors* occur when a program does not perform the way it was intended to.

REVIEW QUESTIONS

Sections 2.2–2.6

2.1 Which of the following identifiers are valid?

```
applet, Applet, a++, --a, 4#R, $4, #44, apps
```

2.2 Which of the following are Java keywords?

```
class, public, int, x, y, radius
```

2.3 Translate the following algorithm into Java code:

- Step 1: Declare a `double` variable named `miles` with initial value `100`;
- Step 2: Declare a `double` constant named `MILE_TO_KILOMETER` with value `1.609`;
- Step 3: Declare a `double` variable named `kilometer`, multiply miles and `MILE_TO_KILOMETER`, and assign the result to `kilometer`.
- Step 4: Display `kilometer` to the console.

What is `kilometer` after Step 4?

2.4 What are the benefits of using constants? Declare an `int` constant `SIZE` with value `20`.

Section 2.7 Numeric Data Types and Operations

2.5 Assume that `int a = 1` and `double d = 1.0`, and that each expression is independent. What are the results of the following expressions?

```
a = 46 / 9;
a = 46 % 9 + 4 * 4 - 2;
a = 45 + 43 % 5 * (23 * 3 % 2);
a %= 3 / a + 3;
d = 4 + d * d + 4;
d += 1.5 * 3 + (++a);
d -= 1.5 * 3 + a++;
```

2.6 Show the result of the following remainders.

```
56 % 6
78 % -4
-34 % 5
-34 % -5
5 % 1
1 % 5
```

2.7 Find the largest and smallest `byte`, `short`, `int`, `long`, `float`, and `double`. Which of these data types requires the least amount of memory?

2.8 What is the result of `25 / 4`? How would you rewrite the expression if you wished the result to be a floating-point number?

2.9 Are the following statements correct? If so, show the output.

```
System.out.println("the output for 25 / 4 is " + 25 / 4);
System.out.println("the output for 25 / 4.0 is " + 25 / 4.0);
```

2.10 How would you write the following arithmetic expression in Java?

$$\frac{4}{3(r + 34)} - 9(a + bc) + \frac{3 + d(2 + a)}{(a + bd)}$$

2.11 Suppose `m` and `r` are integers. Write a Java expression for mr^2 to obtain a floating-point result?

2.12 Which of these statements are true?

(a) Any expression can be used as a statement.
(b) The expression `x++` can be used as a statement.
(c) The statement `x = x + 5` is also an expression.
(d) The statement `x = y = x = 0` is illegal.

2.13 Which of the following are correct literals for floating-point numbers?

`12.3, 12.3e+2, 23.4e-2, -334.4, 20, 39F, 40D`

2.14 Identify and fix the errors in the following code:

```
public class Test {
  public void main(string[] args) {
    int i;
    int k = 100.0;
    int j = i + 1;

    System.out.println("j is " + j + " and
      k is " + k);
  }
}
```

Section 2.8 Numeric Type Conversions

2.15 Can different types of numeric values be used together in a computation?

2.16 What does an explicit conversion from a `double` to an `int` do with the fractional part of the *double* value? Does casting change the variable being cast?

2.17 Show the following output.

```
float f = 12.5F;
int i = (int)f;
System.out.println("f is " + f);
System.out.println("i is " + i);
```

Section 2.9 Character Data Type and Operations

2.18 Use print statements to find out the ASCII code for `'1'`, `'A'`, `'B'`, `'a'`, `'b'`. Use print statements to find out the character for the decimal code 40, 59, 79, 85, 90. Use print statements to find out the character for the hexadecimal code 40, 5A, 71, 72, 7A.

2.19 Which of the following are correct literals for characters?

```
'1', '\u345dE', '\u3fFa','\b', \t
```

2.20 How do you display characters \ and "?

2.21 Evaluate the following:

```
int i = '1';
int j = '1' + '2';
int k = 'a';
char c = 90;
```

2.22 Can the following conversions involving casting be allowed? If so, find the converted result.

```
char c = 'A';
i = (int)c;

float f = 1000.34f;
int i = (int)f;

double d = 1000.34;
int i = (int)d;

int i = 97;
char c = (char)i;
```

Section 2.10 The `String` Type

2.23 Show the output of the following statements (write a program to verify your result):

```
System.out.println("1" + 1);
System.out.println('1' + 1);
System.out.println("1" + 1 + 1);
System.out.println("1" + (1 + 1));
System.out.println('1' + 1 + 1);
```

2.24 Evaluate the following expressions (write a program to verify your result):

```
1 + "Welcome " + 1 + 1
1 + "Welcome " + (1 + 1)
```

```
1 + "Welcome " + ('\u0001' + 1)
1 + "Welcome " + 'a' + 1
```

Sections 2.11–2.12

2.25 How do you convert a decimal string into a `double` value? How do you convert an integer string into an `int` value?

2.26 How do you obtain the current minute using the `System.currentTimeMillis()` method?

Sections 2.14–2.15

2.27 What are the naming conventions for class names, method names, constants, and variables? Which of the following items can be a constant, a method, a variable, or a class according to the Java naming conventions?

`MAX_VALUE, Test, read, readInt`

2.28 Reformat the following program according to the programming style and documentation guidelines. Use the next-line brace style.

```
public class Test
{
  // Main method
  public static void main(String[] args) {
  /** Print a line */
  System.out.println("2 % 3 = "+2%3);
  }
}
```

2.29 Describe syntax errors, runtime errors, and logic errors.

Section 2.16 (GUI) Getting Input from Input Dialogs

2.30 Why do you have to import `JOptionPane` but not the `Math` class?

2.31 How do you prompt the user to enter an input using a dialog box?

2.32 How do you convert a string to an integer? How do you convert a string to a double?

Programming Exercises

fixed input

Pedagogical Note

Students may first write a program with a fixed input value and later modify it using the console input or an input dialog box. The solutions are provided for both console and dialog boxes.

learn from examples

Debugging Tip

The compiler usually gives a reason for a syntax error. If you don't know how to correct it, compare your program closely with similar examples in the text character by character.

Sections 2.2–2.8

2.1 (*Converting Celsius to Fahrenheit*) Write a program that reads a Celsius degree in double from the console, then converts it to Fahrenheit and displays the result. The formula for the conversion is as follows:

```
fahrenheit = (9 / 5) * celsius + 32
```

Hint: In Java, 9 / 5 is 1, so you need to write 9.0 / 5 in the program to obtain the correct result.

2.2 (*Computing the volume of a cylinder*) Write a program that reads in the radius and length of a cylinder and computes volume using the following formulas:

```
area = radius * radius * π
volume = area * length
```

2.3 (*Converting feet into meters*) Write a program that reads a number in feet, converts it to meters, and displays the result. One foot is 0.305 meters.

2.4 (*Converting pounds into kilograms*) Write a program that converts pounds into kilograms. The program prompts the user to enter a number in pounds, converts it to kilograms, and displays the result. One pound is 0.454 kilograms.

2.5* (*Financial application: calculating tips*) Write a program that reads the subtotal and the gratuity rate, and computes the gratuity and total. For example, if the user enters 10 for subtotal and 15% for gratuity rate, the program displays $1.5 as gratuity and $11.5 as total.

2.6** (*Summing the digits in an integer*) Write a program that reads an integer between 0 and 1000 and adds all the digits in the integer. For example, if an integer is 932, the sum of all its digits is 14.

Hint: Use the % operator to extract digits, and use the / operator to remove the extracted digit. For instance, 932 % 10 = 2 and 932 / 10 = 93.

Section 2.9 Character Data Type and Operations

2.7* (*Converting an uppercase letter to lowercase*) Write a program that converts an uppercase letter to a lowercase letter. The character is typed in the source code as a literal value. In Chapter 9, "Strings and Text I/O," you will learn how to enter a character input.

Hint: In the ASCII table (see Appendix B), uppercase letters appear before lowercase letters. The offset between any uppercase letter and its corresponding lowercase letter is the same. So you can find a lowercase letter from its corresponding uppercase letter, as follows:

```
int offset = (int)'a' - (int)'A';
int unicodeForUppercase = (int)uppercase;
int unicodeForLowercase = unicodeForUppercase + offset;
char lowercase = (char)unicodeForLowercase;
```

2.8* (*Finding the character of an ASCII code*) Write a program that receives an ASCII code (an integer between 0 and 128) and displays its character. For example, if the user enters 97, the program displays character a.

Sections 2.10–2.12

2.9* (*Financial application: monetary units*) Rewrite Listing 2.8, ComputeChange.java, to fix the possible loss of accuracy when converting a double value to an int value. Enter the input as an integer whose last two digits represent the cents. For example, the input 1156 represents 11 dollars and 56 cents.

Section 2.16 (GUI) Getting Input from Input Dialogs

2.10* (*Using the GUI input*) Rewrite Listing 2.8, ComputeChange.java, using the GUI input and output.

Comprehensive

2.11* (*Financial application: payroll*) Write a program that reads the following information and prints a payroll statement:

Employee's name (e.g., Smith)

Number of hours worked in a week (e.g., 10)

Hourly pay rate (e.g., 6.75)

Federal tax withholding rate (e.g., 20%)

State tax withholding rate (e.g., 9%)

Write this program in two versions: (a) Use dialog boxes to obtain input and display output; (b) Use console input and output. A sample run of the console input and output is shown below:

```
Enter employee's name: Smith ↵Enter
Enter number of hours worked in a week: 10 ↵Enter
Enter hourly pay rate: 6.75 ↵Enter
Enter federal tax withholding rate: 0.20 ↵Enter
Enter state tax withholding rate: 0.09 ↵Enter
Employee Name: Smith
Hours Worked:  10.0
Pay Rate:  $6.75
Gross Pay:  $67.5
Deductions:
  Federal Withholding (20.0%):  $13.5
  State Withholding (9.0%):  $6.07
  Total Deduction:  $19.57
Net Pay:  $47.92
```

2.12* (*Financial application: calculating interest*) If you know the balance and the annual percentage interest rate, you can compute the interest on the next monthly payment using the following formula:

$$\text{interest} = \text{balance} \times (\text{annualInterestRate} \,/\, 1200)$$

Write a program that reads the balance and the annual percentage interest rate and displays the interest for the next month in two versions: (a) Use dialog boxes to obtain input and display output; (b) Use console input and output. A sample run of the console input and output is shown below:

```
Enter balance: 100000 ↵Enter
Enter annual interest rate: 4.625 ↵Enter
The interest is 385.41
```

2.13* (*Financial application: calculating the future investment value*) Write a program that reads in investment amount, annual interest rate, and number of years, and displays the future investment value using the following formula:

$$\text{futureInvestmentValue} = \text{investmentAmount} \times (1 + \text{monthlyInterestRate})^{\text{numberOfYears}*12}$$

For example, if you enter amount **1000**, annual interest rate **3.25%**, and number of years **1**, the future investment value is **1032.98**.

Hint: Use the **Math.pow(a, b)** method to compute **a** raised to the power of **b**.

2.14 (*Health application: computing BMI*) Body Mass Index (BMI) is a measure of health on weight. It can be calculated by taking your weight in kilograms and dividing by the square of your height in meters. Write a program that prompts the user to enter a weight in pounds and height in inches and display the BMI. Note that one pound is **0.45359237** kilograms and one inch is **0.0254** meters.

Video Note
Compute BMI

2.15**(*Financial application: compound value*) Suppose you save **$100** *each* month into a savings account with the annual interest rate 5%. So, the monthly interest rate is 0.05 / 12 = 0.00417. After the first month, the value in the account becomes

```
100 * (1 + 0.00417) = 100.417
```

After the second month, the value in the account becomes,

```
(100 + 100.417) * (1 + 0.00417) = 201.252
```

After the third month, the value in the account becomes,

```
(100 + 201.252) * (1 + 0.00417) = 302.507
```

and so on.

Write a program to display the account value after the sixth month. (In Exercise 4.30, you will use a loop to simplify the code and display the account value for any month.)

2.16 (*Science: calculating energy*) Write a program that calculates the energy needed to heat water from an initial temperature to a final temperature. Your program should prompt the user to enter the amount of water in kilograms and the initial and final temperatures of the water. The formula to compute the energy is

```
Q = M * (final temperature - initial temperature) * 4184
```

where **M** is the weight of water in kilograms, temperatures are in degrees Celsius, and energy **Q** is measured in joules.

2.17* (*Science: wind-chill temperature*) How cold is it outside? The temperature alone is not enough to provide the answer. Other factors including wind speed, relative humidity, and sunshine play important roles in determining coldness outside. In 2001, the National Weather Service (NWS) implemented the new wind-chill temperature to measure the coldness using temperature and wind speed. The formula is given as follows:

$$t_{wc} = 35.74 + 0.6215t_a - 35.75v^{0.16} + 0.4275t_a v^{0.16}$$

where t_a is the outside temperature measured in degrees Fahrenheit and v is the speed measured in miles per hour. t_{wc} is the wind-chill temperature. The formula cannot be used for wind speeds below 2 mph or temperatures below -58°F or above 41°F.

Write a program that prompts the user to enter a temperature between −58°F and 41°F and a wind speed greater than or equal to **2** and displays the wind-chill temperature. Use **Math.pow(a, b)** to compute $v^{0.16}$ (see §2.12.1).

2.18 (*Printing a table*) Write a program that displays the following table:

```
a     b     pow(a, b)
1     2     1
2     3     8
3     4     81
4     5     1024
5     6     15625
```

CHAPTER 3

SELECTIONS

Objectives

- To declare `boolean` type and use Boolean values `true` and `false` (§3.2).
- To apply relational operators (<, <=, ==, !=, >, >=) and logic operators (!, &&, ||, ^) to write Boolean expressions (§3.2).
- To use Boolean expressions to control selection statements (§§3.3–3.5).
- To implement selection control using `if` and nested `if` statements (3.3).
- To implement selection control using `switch` statements (§3.4).
- To write expressions using the conditional operator (§3.5).
- To display formatted output using the `System.out.printf` method and to format strings using the `String.format` method (§3.6).
- To examine the rules governing operator precedence and associativity (§3.7).
- (GUI) To get user confirmation using confirmation dialogs (§3.8).

3.1 Introduction

problem

If you assign a negative value for **radius** in Listing 2.1, ComputeArea.java, the program prints an invalid result. If the radius is negative, you don't want the program to compute the area. How can you deal with this situation?

pseudocode

Like all high-level programming languages, Java provides selection statements that let you choose actions with two or more alternative courses. You can use selection statements in the following *pseudocode* (i.e., natural language mixed with programming code) to rewrite Listing 2.1:

```
if the radius is negative
  the program displays a message indicating a wrong input;
else
  the program computes the area and displays the result;
```

Selection statements use conditions. Conditions are Boolean expressions. This chapter first introduces Boolean types, values, operators, and expressions.

3.2 boolean Data Type and Operations

comparison operators

How do you compare two values, such as whether a radius is greater than **0**, equal to **0**, or less than **0**? Java provides six *comparison operators* (also known as *relational operators*), shown in Table 3.1, which can be used to compare two values. The result of the comparison is a Boolean value: **true** or **false**. For example, the following statement displays **true**:

```
double radius = 1;
System.out.println(radius > 0);
```

TABLE 3.1 Comparison Operators

Operator	*Name*	*Example*	*Result*
<	less than	1 < 2	true
<=	less than or equal to	1 <= 2	true
>	greater than	1 > 2	false
>=	greater than or equal to	1 >= 2	false
==	equal to	1 == 2	false
!=	not equal to	1 != 2	true

compare characters

Note

You can also compare characters. Comparing characters is the same as comparing their Unicodes. For example, **'a'** is larger than **'A'** because the Unicode of **'a'** is larger than the Unicode of **'A'**.

== vs. =

Caution

The equality comparison operator is two equal signs (==), not a single equal sign (=). The latter symbol is for assignment.

Boolean variable

A variable that holds a Boolean value is known as a *Boolean variable*. The **boolean** data type is used to declare Boolean variables. A **boolean** variable can hold one of the two values: **true** and **false**. For example, the following statement assigns **true** to the variable **lightsOn**:

```
boolean lightsOn = true;
```

`true` and `false` are literals, just like a number such as `10`. They are reserved words and cannot be used as identifiers in your program.

Boolean literals

Boolean operators

Boolean operators, also known as logical operators, operate on Boolean values to create a new Boolean value. Table 3.2 gives a list of Boolean operators. Table 3.3 defines the not (`!`) operator. The not (`!`) operator negates `true` to `false` and `false` to `true`. Table 3.4 defines the and (`&&`) operator. The and (`&&`) of two Boolean operands is `true` if and only if both operands are `true`. Table 3.5 defines the or (`||`) operator. The or (`||`) of two Boolean operands is `true` if at least one of the operands is `true`. Table 3.6 defines the exclusive or (`^`) operator. The exclusive or (`^`) of two Boolean operands is `true` if and only if the two operands have different Boolean values.

TABLE 3.2 Boolean Operators

Operator	*Name*	*Description*
`!`	not	logical negation
`&&`	and	logical conjunction
`||`	or	logical disjunction
`^`	exclusive or	logical exclusion

TABLE 3.3 Truth Table for Operator `!`

p	*!p*	*Example*
`true`	`false`	`!(1 > 2)` is `true`, because `(1 > 2)` is `false`.
`false`	`true`	`!(1 > 0)` is `false`, because `(1 > 0)` is `true`.

TABLE 3.4 Truth Table for Operator `&&`

p1	*p2*	*p1 && p2*	*Example*
`false`	`false`	`false`	`(2 > 3) && (5 > 5)` is `false`, because
`false`	`true`	`false`	either `(2 > 3)` or `(5 > 5)` is `false`.
`true`	`false`	`false`	`(3 > 2) && (5 > 5)` is `false`, because `(5 > 5)` is `false`.
`true`	`true`	`true`	`(3 > 2) && (5 >= 5)` is `true`, because `(3 > 2)` and `(5 >= 5)` are both `true`.

TABLE 3.5 Truth Table for Operator `||`

p1	*p2*	*p1 || p2*	*Example*
`false`	`false`	`false`	`(2 > 3) || (5 > 5)` is `false`, because `(2 > 3)` and `(5 > 5)` are both `false`.
`false`	`true`	`true`	
`true`	`false`	`true`	`(3 > 2) || (5 > 5)` is `true`, because `(3 > 2)` is `true`.
`true`	`true`	`true`	

TABLE 3.6 Truth Table for Operator `^`

p1	*p2*	*p1 ^ p2*	*Example*
`false`	`false`	`false`	`(2 > 3) ^ (5 > 1)` is `true`, because `(2 > 3)` is false and `(5 > 1)` is `true`.
`false`	`true`	`true`	
`true`	`false`	`true`	`(3 > 2) ^ (5 > 1)` is `false`, because both `(3 > 2)` and `(5 > 1)` are `true`.
`true`	`true`	`false`	

Listing 3.1 gives a program that checks whether a number is divisible by 2 and 3, whether a number is divisible by 2 or 3, and whether a number is divisible by 2 or 3 but not both:

LISTING 3.1 TestBoolean.java

import class

input

and

or

exclusive or

```
1 import java.util.Scanner;
2
3 public class TestBoolean {
4   public static void main(String[] args) {
5     // Create a Scanner
6     Scanner input = new Scanner(System.in);
7
8     // Receive an input
9     System.out.print("Enter an integer: ");
10    int number = input.nextInt();
11
12    System.out.println("Is " + number +
13      "\n\tdivisible by 2 and 3? " +
14      (number % 2 == 0 && number % 3 == 0)
15      + "\n\tdivisible by 2 or 3? " +
16      (number % 2 == 0 || number % 3 == 0) +
17      "\n\tdivisible by 2 or 3, but not both? "
18      + (number % 2 == 0 ^ number % 3 == 0));
19  }
20 }
```

```
Enter an integer: 18 ↵Enter
Is 18
  divisible by 2 and 3? true
  divisible by 2 or 3? true
  divisible by 2 or 3, but not both? false
```

A long string is formed by concatenating the substrings in lines 12–18. The three \n characters display the string in four lines. `(number % 2 == 0 && number % 3 == 0)` (line 14) checks whether the number is divisible by 2 and 3. `(number % 2 == 0 || number % 3 == 0)` (line 16) checks whether the number is divisible by 2 or 3. `(number % 2 == 0 ^ number % 3 == 0)` (line 18) checks whether the number is divisible by 2 or 3, but not both.

Caution

In mathematics, the expression

```
1 <= numberOfDaysInAMonth <= 31
```

incompatible operands

is correct. However, it does not make sense in Java, because `1 <= numberOfDaysInAMonth` is evaluated to a `boolean` value, which cannot be compared with `31`. Here, two operands (a `boolean` value and a numeric value) are *incompatible*. The correct expression in Java is

```
(1 <= numberOfDaysInAMonth) && (numberOfDaysInAMonth <= 31)
```

Note

cannot cast **boolean**

As shown in the preceding chapter, a `char` value can be cast into an `int` value, and vice versa. A `boolean` value, however, cannot be cast into a value of other types, nor can a value of other types be cast into a `boolean` value.

Note

De Morgan's law

De Morgan's law, named after Indian-born British mathematician and logician Augustus De Morgan (1806-1871), can be used to simplify Boolean expressions. The law states

`!(condition1 && condition2)` is same as `!condition1 || !condition2`
`!(condition1 || condition2)` is same as `!condition1 && !condition2`

For example,

`!(n == 2 || n == 3)` is same as `n != 2 && n != 3`
`!(n % 2 == 0 && n % 3 == 0)` is same as `n % 2 != 0 || n % 3 != 0`

Note

When evaluating `p1 && p2`, Java first evaluates `p1` and then, if `p1` is `true`, evaluates `p2`; if `p1` is `false`, it does not evaluate `p2`. When evaluating `p1 || p2`, Java first evaluates `p1` and then, if `p1` is `false`, evaluates `p2`; if `p1` is `true`, it does not evaluate `p2`. Therefore, `&&` is referred to as the *conditional* or *short-circuit AND* operator, and `||` is referred to as the *conditional* or *short-circuit OR* operator.

conditional operator
short-circuit operator

3.2.1 Problem: Determining Leap Year

A year is a *leap year* if it is divisible by 4 but not by 100 or if it is divisible by 400. So you can use the following Boolean expression to check whether a year is a leap year:

leap year

(year % 4 == 0 && year % 100 != 0) || (year % 400 == 0)

Listing 3.2 gives the program that lets the user enter a year and checks whether it is a leap year.

LISTING 3.2 LeapYear.java

```
import java.util.Scanner;

public class LeapYear {
  public static void main(String args[]) {
    // Create a Scanner
    Scanner input = new Scanner(System.in);
    System.out.print("Enter a year: ");
    int year = input.nextInt();

    // Check if the year is a leap year
    boolean isLeapYear =
      (year % 4 == 0 && year % 100 != 0) || (year % 400 == 0);

    // Display the result
    System.out.println(year + " is a leap year? " + isLeapYear);
  }
}
```

input
leap year?
display result

```
Enter a year: 2008 ↵Enter
2008 is a leap year? true
```

```
Enter a year: 2002 ↵Enter
2002 is a leap year? false
```

3.2.2 Problem: A Simple Math Learning Tool

Suppose you want to develop a program to let a first-grader practice addition. The program randomly generates two single-digit integers, `number1` and `number2`, and displays to the student a question such as "What is 7 + 9?", as shown in the sample output. After the student types the answer, the program displays a message to indicate whether the answer is true or false.

There are several ways to generate random numbers. For now, generate the first integer using `System.currentTimeMillis() % 10` and the second using `System.currentTimeMillis() * 7 % 10`. Listing 3.3 gives the program. Lines 5–6 generate two numbers, `number1` and `number2`. Line 14 obtains an answer from the user. The answer is graded in line 18 using a Boolean expression `number1 + number2 == answer`.

Video Note
Program addition quiz

LISTING 3.3 AdditionQuiz.java

generate number1 (line 5); generate number2 (line 6); show question (line 11); display result (line 16)

```
 1 import java.util.Scanner;
 2
 3 public class AdditionQuiz {
 4   public static void main(String[] args) {
 5     int number1 = (int)(System.currentTimeMillis() % 10);
 6     int number2 = (int)(System.currentTimeMillis() * 7 % 10);
 7
 8     // Create a Scanner
 9     Scanner input = new Scanner(System.in);
10
11     System.out.print(
12       "What is " + number1 + " + " + number2 + "? ");
13
14     int answer = input.nextInt();
15
16     System.out.println(
17       number1 + " + " + number2 + " = " + answer + " is " +
18       (number1 + number2 == answer));
19   }
20 }
```

```
What is 1 + 7? 8 [Enter]
1 + 7 = 8 is true
```

```
What is 4 + 8? 9 [Enter]
4 + 8 = 9 is false
```

3.3 `if` Statements

why `if` statement?

The preceding program displays a message such as "6 + 2 = 7 is false." If you wish the message to be "6 + 2 = 7 is incorrect," you have to use a selection statement to carry out this minor change.

This section introduces selection statements. Java has several types of selection statements: simple `if` statements, `if . . . else` statements, nested `if` statements, `switch` statements, and conditional expressions.

3.3.1 Simple if Statements

A simple `if` statement executes an action if and only if the condition is `true`. The syntax for a simple `if` statement is shown below:

`if` statement

```
if (booleanExpression) {
  statement(s);
}
```

The execution flow chart is shown in Figure 3.1(a).

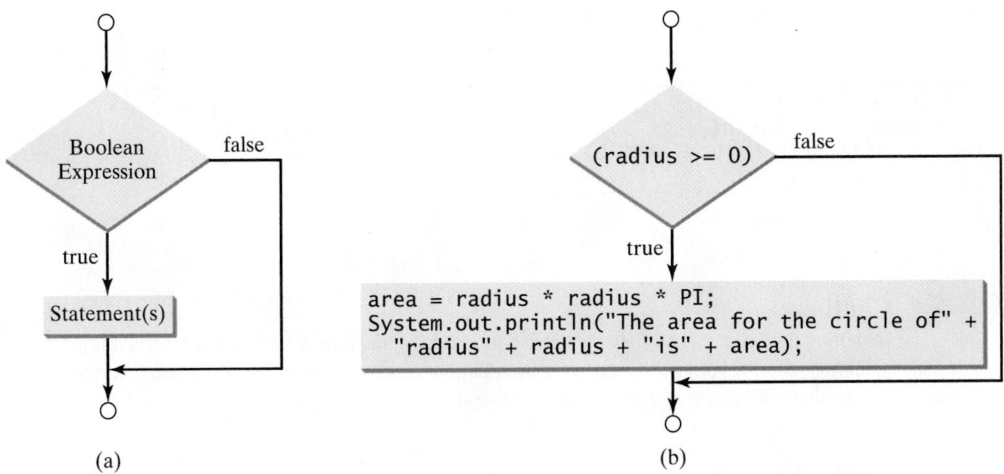

FIGURE 3.1 An `if` statement executes statements if the `booleanExpression` evaluates to `true`.

If the `booleanExpression` evaluates to `true`, the statements in the block are executed. As an example, see the following code:

```
if (radius >= 0) {
  area = radius * radius * PI;
  System.out.println("The area for the circle of radius " +
    radius + " is " + area);
}
```

The flow chart of the preceding statement is shown in Figure 3.1(b). If the value of `radius` is greater than or equal to `0`, then the `area` is computed and the result is displayed; otherwise, the two statements in the block will not be executed.

As another example, the following statement determines whether a number is even or odd:

```
if (number % 2 == 0)
  System.out.println(number + " is even.");

if (number % 2 != 0)
  System.out.println(number + " is odd.");
```

The booleanExpression is enclosed in parentheses. For example, the code in (a) below is wrong. It should be corrected, as shown in (b).

```
if (i > 0) && (i < 10) {
  System.out.println("i is an " +
    + "integer between 0 and 10");
}
```

(a) Wrong

```
if ((i > 0) && (i < 10))
  System.out.println("i is an " +
    + "integer between 0 and 10");
```

(b) Correct

The braces can be omitted if they enclose a single statement. For example, the following statements are equivalent.

```
if ((i > 0) && (i < 10)) {
  System.out.println("i is an " +
    + "integer between 0 and 10");
}
```

(a)

Equivalent

```
if ((i > 0) && (i < 10))
  System.out.println("i is an " +
    + "integer between 0 and 10");
```

(b)

Caution

Forgetting the braces when they are needed for grouping multiple statements is a common programming error. If you modify the code by adding new statements in an if statement without braces, you will have to insert the braces if they are not already in place.

Caution

Adding a semicolon at the end of an if clause, as shown in (a) below, is a common mistake.

Logic Error

```
if (radius >= 0);
{
  area = radius * radius * PI;
  System.out.println("The area "
    + " is " + area);
}
```

(a)

Equivalent

Empty Body

```
if (radius >= 0) { };
{
  area = radius * radius * PI;
  System.out.println("The area "
    + " is " + area);
}
```

(b)

This mistake is hard to find, because it is neither a compilation error nor a runtime error; it is a logic error. The code in (a) is equivalent to that in (b) with an empty block.

This error often occurs when you use the next-line block style. Using the end-of-line block style will prevent this error.

3.3.2 if . . . else Statements

A simple if statement takes an action if the specified condition is true. If the condition is false, nothing is done. But what if you want to take alternative actions when the condition is false? You can use an if . . . else statement. The actions that an if . . . else statement specifies differ based on whether the condition is true or false.

Here is the syntax for this type of statement:

if-else statement

```
if (booleanExpression) {
  statement(s)-for-the-true-case;
}
```

```
else {
  statement(s)-for-the-false-case;
}
```

The flow chart of the statement is shown in Figure 3.2.

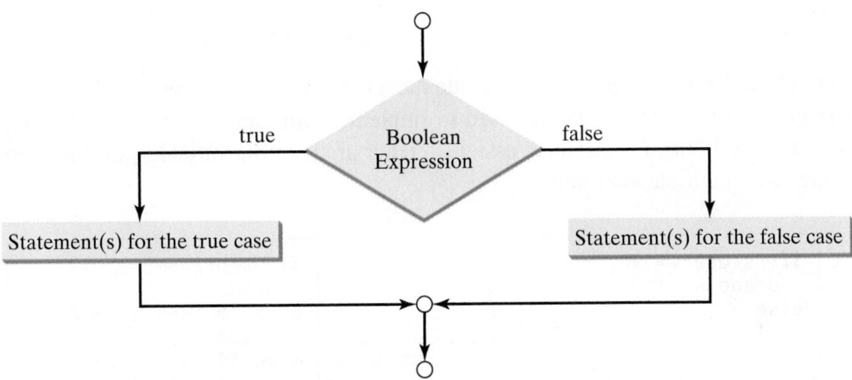

FIGURE 3.2 An `if . . . else` statement executes statements for the `true` case if the `boolean` expression evaluates to `true`; otherwise, statements for the `false` case are executed.

If the `booleanExpression` evaluates to `true`, the `statement(s)` for the true case are executed; otherwise, the `statement(s)` for the false case are executed. For example, consider the following code:

```
if (radius >= 0) {
  area = radius * radius * PI;
  System.out.println("The area for the circle of radius " +
    radius + " is " + area);
}
else {
  System.out.println("Negative input");
}
```

If `radius >= 0` is `true`, `area` is computed and displayed; if it is `false`, the message `"Negative input"` is printed.

As usual, the braces can be omitted if there is only one statement within them. The braces enclosing the `System.out.println("Negative input")` statement can therefore be omitted in the preceding example.

Using the `if ... else` statement, you can rewrite the code for determining whether a number is even or odd in the preceding section, as follows:

```
if (number % 2 == 0)
  System.out.println(number + " is even.");
else
  System.out.println(number + " is odd.");
```

This is more efficient because whether `number % 2` is `0` is tested only once.

3.3.3 Nested `if` Statements

The statement in an `if` or `if . . . else` statement can be any legal Java statement, including another `if` or `if . . . else` statement. The inner `if` statement is said to be *nested* inside the outer `if` statement. The inner `if` statement can contain another `if` statement; in fact, there is no limit to the depth of the nesting. For example, the following is a nested `if` statement:

nested `if` statement

```
if (i > k) {
  if (j > k)
    System.out.println("i and j are greater than k");
}
else
  System.out.println("i is less than or equal to k");
```

The `if (j > k)` statement is nested inside the `if (i > k)` statement.

The nested `if` statement can be used to implement multiple alternatives. The statement given in Figure 3.3(a), for instance, assigns a letter grade to the variable `grade` according to the score, with multiple alternatives.

```
if (score >= 90.0)
  grade = 'A';
else
  if (score >= 80.0)
    grade = 'B';
  else
    if (score >= 70.0)
      grade = 'C';
    else
      if (score >= 60.0)
        grade = 'D';
      else
        grade = 'F';
```

(a)

Equivalent

This is better

```
if (score >= 90.0)
  grade = 'A';
else if (score >= 80.0)
  grade = 'B';
else if (score >= 70.0)
  grade = 'C';
else if (score >= 60.0)
  grade = 'D';
else
  grade = 'F';
```

(b)

FIGURE 3.3 A preferred format for multiple alternative `if` statements is shown in (b).

The execution of this `if` statement proceeds as follows. The first condition `(score >= 90.0)` is tested. If it is `true`, the grade becomes `'A'`. If it is `false`, the second condition `(score >= 80.0)` is tested. If the second condition is `true`, the grade becomes `'B'`. If that condition is `false`, the third condition and the rest of the conditions (if necessary) continue to be tested until a condition is met or all of the conditions prove to be `false`. If all of the conditions are `false`, the grade becomes `'F'`. Note that a condition is tested only when all of the conditions that come before it are `false`.

The `if` statement in Figure 3.3(a) is equivalent to the `if` statement in Figure 3.3(b). In fact, Figure 3.3(b) is the preferred writing style for multiple alternative `if` statements. This style avoids deep indentation and makes the program easy to read.

matching `else` with `if`

Note

The `else` clause matches the most recent unmatched `if` clause in the same block. For example, the statement in (a) below is equivalent to the statement in (b).

```
int i = 1;
int j = 2;
int k = 3;

if (i > j)
  if (i > k)
    System.out.println("A");
else
    System.out.println("B");
```

(a)

Equivalent

This is better with correct indentation

```
int i = 1;
int j = 2;
int k = 3;

if (i > j)
  if (i > k)
    System.out.println("A");
  else
    System.out.println("B");
```

(b)

The compiler ignores indentation. Nothing is printed from the statement in (a) and (b). To force the else clause to match the first if clause, you must add a pair of braces:

```
int i = 1; int j = 2; int k = 3;

if(i > j) {
  if (i > k)
    System.out.println("A");
}
else
  System.out.println("B");
```

This statement prints B.

Tip

assign boolean variable

Often new programmers write the code that assigns a test condition to a boolean variable like the code in (a):

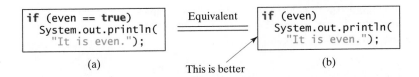

```
if (number % 2 == 0)
  even = true;
else
  even = false;
```

(a)

Equivalent

This is shorter

```
boolean even
  = number % 2 == 0;
```

(b)

The code can be simplified by assigning the test value directly to the variable, as shown in (b).

Caution

test boolean value

To test whether a boolean variable is true or false in a test condition, it is redundant to use the equality comparison operator like the code in (a):

```
if (even == true)
  System.out.println(
    "It is even.");
```

(a)

Equivalent

This is better

```
if (even)
  System.out.println(
    "It is even.");
```

(b)

Instead, it is better to use the boolean variable directly, as shown in (b). Another good reason to use the boolean variable directly is to avoid errors that are difficult to detect. Using the = operator instead of the == operator to compare equality of two items in a test condition is a common error. It could lead to the following erroneous statement:

```
if (even = true)
  System.out.println("It is even.");
```

This statement does not have syntax errors. It assigns true to even so that even is always true.

3.3.4 Problem: An Improved Math Learning Tool

Suppose you want to develop a program for a first-grader to practice subtraction. The program randomly generates two single-digit integers, number1 and number2, with number1 > number2 and displays to the student a question such as "What is 9 − 2?" After the student enters the answer, the program displays a message to indicate whether the answer is correct.

The previous programs generate random numbers using System.currentTimeMillis(). A better way to generate a random number is to use the random() method in the Math class.

random() method

Invoking this method returns a random double value **d** such that $0.0 \leq d < 1.0$. So, **(int)(Math.random() * 10)** returns a random single-digit integer (i.e., a number between 0 and 9).

The program may work as follows:

- Generate two single-digit integers into **number1** and **number2**.
- If **number1 < number2**, swap **number1** with **number2**.
- Prompt the student to answer "What is number1 – number2?"
- Check the student's answer and display whether the answer is correct.

The complete program is shown in Listing 3.4.

Video Note
Program subtraction quiz

Listing 3.4 SubtractionQuiz.java

random numbers

get answer

check the answer

```
 1 import java.util.Scanner;
 2
 3 public class SubtractionQuiz {
 4   public static void main(String[] args) {
 5     // 1. Generate two random single-digit integers
 6     int number1 = (int)(Math.random() * 10);
 7     int number2 = (int)(Math.random() * 10);
 8
 9     // 2. If number1 < number2, swap number1 with number2
10     if (number1 < number2) {
11       int temp = number1;
12       number1 = number2;
13       number2 = temp;
14     }
15
16     // 3. Prompt the student to answer "What is number1 - number2?"
17     System.out.print
18       ("What is " + number1 + " - " + number2 + "? ");
19     Scanner input = new Scanner(System.in);
20     int answer = input.nextInt();
21
22     // 4. Grade the answer and display the result
23     if (number1 - number2 == answer)
24       System.out.println("You are correct!");
25     else
26       System.out.println("Your answer is wrong.\n" + number1 + " - "
27         + number2 + " should be " + (number1 - number2));
28   }
29 }
```

```
What is 6 - 6? 0 ↵Enter
You are correct!
```

```
What is 9 - 2? 5 ↵Enter
Your answer is wrong.
9 - 2 should be 7
```

To swap two variables **number1** and **number2**, a temporary variable **temp** (line 11) is used to first hold the value in **number1**. The value in **number2** is assigned to **number1** (line 12), and the value in **temp** is assigned to **number2**.

3.3.5 Problem: Lottery

Suppose you want to develop a program to play lottery. The program randomly generates a lottery of a two-digit number, prompts the user to enter a two-digit number, and determines whether the user wins according to the following rule:

1. If the user input matches the lottery in exact order, the award is $10,000.
2. If the user input matches the lottery, the award is $3,000.
3. If one digit in the user input matches a digit in the lottery, the award is $1,000.

The complete program is shown in Listing 3.5.

LISTING 3.5 Lottery.java

```
1 import java.util.Scanner;
2
3 public class Lottery {
4   public static void main(String[] args) {
5     // Generate a lottery
6     int lottery = (int)(Math.random() * 100);
7
8     // Prompt the user to enter a guess
9     Scanner input = new Scanner(System.in);
10    System.out.print("Enter your lottery pick (two digits): ");
11    int guess = input.nextInt();
12
13    // Check the guess
14    if (guess == lottery)
15      System.out.println("Exact match: you win $10,000");
16    else if (guess % 10 == lottery / 10
17        && guess / 10 == lottery % 10)
18      System.out.println("Match all digits: you win $3,000");
19    else if (guess % 10 == lottery / 10 || guess % 10 == lottery % 10
20        || guess / 10 == lottery / 10 || guess / 10 == lottery % 10)
21      System.out.println("Match one digit: you win $1,000");
22    else
23      System.out.println("Sorry, no match");
24  }
25 }
```

generate a lottery

enter a guess

exact match?

match all digits?

match one digit?

```
Enter your lottery pick (two digits): 45 ↵Enter
Sorry, no match
```

```
Enter your lottery pick: 23 ↵Enter
Exact match: you win $10,000
```

The program generates a lottery using the `Math.random()` method (line 6) and prompts the user to enter a guess (line 11). The program then checks the guess against the lottery number in this order:

1. First check whether the guess matches the lottery exactly (line 14).
2. If not, check whether the reversal of the guess matches the lottery (lines 16–17).

3. If not, check whether one digit is in the lottery (lines 19-20).
4. If not, nothing matches.

Note that `guess % 10` obtains the last digit from `guess` and `guess / 10` obtains the first digit from `guess`, since `guess` is a two-digit number.

3.3.6 Problem: Computing Body Mass Index

Body Mass Index (BMI) is a measure of health on weight. It can be calculated by taking your weight in kilograms and dividing by the square of your height in meters. The interpretation of BMI for people 16 years or older is as follows:

BMI	Interpretation
below 16	serious underweight
16-18	underweight
18-24	normal weight
24-29	overweight
29-35	seriously overweight
above 35	gravely overweight

Write a program that prompts the user to enter a weight in pounds and height in inches and display the BMI. Note that one pound is `0.45359237` kilograms and one inch is `0.0254` meters. Listing 3.6 gives the program.

Video Note
Use multiple alternative if statements

LISTING 3.6 ComputeBMI.java

```
import java.util.Scanner;

public class ComputeBMI {
  public static void main(String[] args) {
    Scanner input = new Scanner(System.in);

    // Prompt the user to enter weight in pounds
    System.out.print("Enter weight in pounds: ");
    double weight = input.nextDouble();

    // Prompt the user to enter height in inches
    System.out.print("Enter height in inches: ");
    double height = input.nextDouble();

    final double KILOGRAMS_PER_POUND = 0.45359237; // Constant
    final double METERS_PER_INCH = 0.0254; // Constant

    // Compute BMI
    double bmi = weight * KILOGRAMS_PER_POUND /
      ((height * METERS_PER_INCH) * (height * METERS_PER_INCH));

    // Display result
    System.out.println("Your BMI is " + bmi);
    if (bmi < 16)
      System.out.println("You are seriously underweight");
    else if (bmi < 18)
      System.out.println("You are underweight");
    else if (bmi < 24)
      System.out.println("You are normal weight");
    else if (bmi < 29)
      System.out.println("You are overweight");
    else if (bmi < 35)
      System.out.println("You are seriously overweight");
```

input weight

input height

compute bmi

display output

```
34      else
35        System.out.println("You are gravely overweight");
36    }
37 }
```

```
Enter weight in pounds: 146 ↵Enter
Enter height in inches: 70 ↵Enter
Your BMI is 20.948603801493316
You are normal weight
```

Two constants `KILOGRAMS_PER_POUND` and `METERS_PER_INCH` are defined in lines 15–16. Using constants here makes programs easy to read.

3.3.7 Problem: Computing Taxes

The United States federal personal income tax is calculated based on filing status and taxable income. There are four filing statuses: single filers, married filing jointly, married filing separately, and head of household. The tax rates vary every year. Table 3.7 shows the rates for 2002. If you are, say, single with a taxable income of $10,000, the first $6,000 is taxed at 10% and the other $4,000 is taxed at 15%. So your tax is $1,200.

TABLE 3.7 2002 U.S. Federal Personal Tax Rates

Tax rate	*Single filers*	*Married filing jointly or qualifying widow/widower*	*Married filing separately*	*Head of household*
10%	Up to $6,000	Up to $12,000	Up to $6,000	Up to $10,000
15%	$6,001 – $27,950	$12,001 – $46,700	$6,001 – $23,350	$10,001 – $37,450
27%	$27,951 – $67,700	$46,701 – $112,850	$23,351 – $56,425	$37,451 – $96,700
30%	$67,701 – $141,250	$112,851 – $171,950	$56,426 – $85,975	$96,701 – $156,600
35%	$141,251 – $307,050	$171,951 – $307,050	$85,976 – $153,525	$156,601 – $307,050
38.6%	$307,051 or more	$307,051 or more	$153,526 or more	$307,051 or more

You are to write a program to compute personal income tax. Your program should prompt the user to enter the filing status and taxable income and compute the tax. Enter `0` for single filers, `1` for married filing jointly, `2` for married filing separately, and `3` for head of household.

Your program computes the tax for the taxable income based on the filing status. The filing status can be determined using `if` statements outlined as follows:

```
if (status == 0) {
  // Compute tax for single filers
}
else if (status == 1) {
  // Compute tax for married filing jointly
}
else if (status == 2) {
  // Compute tax for married filing separately
}
else if (status == 3) {
  // Compute tax for head of household
}
else {
  // Display wrong status
}
```

For each filing status there are six tax rates. Each rate is applied to a certain amount of taxable income. For example, of a taxable income of $400,000 for single filers, $6,000 is taxed at 10%, (27,950 − 6,000) at 15%, (67,700 − 27,950) at 27%, (141,250 − 67,700) at 35%, and (400,000 − 307,050) at 38.6%.

Listing 3.7 gives the solution to compute taxes for single filers. The complete solution is left as an exercise.

LISTING 3.7 ComputeTax.java

input status

input income

compute tax

```
import java.util.Scanner;

public class ComputeTax {
  public static void main(String[] args) {
    // Create a Scanner
    Scanner input = new Scanner(System.in);

    // Prompt the user to enter filing status
    System.out.print(
      "(0-single filer, 1-married jointly,\n" +
      "2-married separately, 3-head of household)\n" +
      "Enter the filing status: ");
    int status = input.nextInt();

    // Prompt the user to enter taxable income
    System.out.print("Enter the taxable income: ");
    double income = input.nextDouble();

    // Compute tax
    double tax = 0;

    if (status == 0) { // Compute tax for single filers
      if (income <= 6000)
        tax = income * 0.10;
      else if (income <= 27950)
        tax = 6000 * 0.10 + (income - 6000) * 0.15;
      else if (income <= 67700)
        tax = 6000 * 0.10 + (27950 - 6000) * 0.15 +
          (income - 27950) * 0.27;
      else if (income <= 141250)
        tax = 6000 * 0.10 + (27950 - 6000) * 0.15 +
          (67700 - 27950) * 0.27 + (income - 67700) * 0.30;
      else if (income <= 307050)
        tax = 6000 * 0.10 + (27950 - 6000) * 0.15 +
          (67700 - 27950) * 0.27 + (141250 - 67700) * 0.30 +
          (income - 141250) * 0.35;
      else
        tax = 6000 * 0.10 + (27950 - 6000) * 0.15 +
          (67700 - 27950) * 0.27 + (141250 - 67700) * 0.30 +
          (307050 - 141250) * 0.35 + (income - 307050) * 0.386;
    }
    else if (status == 1) { // Compute tax for married filing jointly
      // Left as exercise
    }
    else if (status == 2) { // Compute tax for married filing separately
      // Left as exercise
    }
    else if (status == 3) { // Compute tax for head of household
      // Left as exercise
    }
```

```
51      else {
52        System.out.println("Error: invalid status");
53        System.exit(0);
54      }
55
56      // Display the result
57      System.out.println("Tax is " + (int)(tax * 100) / 100.0);
58    }
59  }
```

exit program

display output

```
(0-single filer, 1-married jointly,
2-married separately, 3-head of household)
Enter the filing status: 0 ↵Enter
Enter the taxable income: 400000 ↵Enter
Tax is 130598.7
```

The program receives the filing status and taxable income. The multiple alternative `if` statements (lines 22, 42, 45, 48, 51) check the filing status and compute the tax based on the filing status.

System.exit(0)

`System.exit(0)` (line 53) is defined in the `System` class. Invoking this method terminates the program. The argument `0` indicates that the program is terminated normally.

An initial value of `0` is assigned to `tax` (line 20). A syntax error would occur if it had no initial value, because all of the other statements that assign values to `tax` are within the `if` statement. The compiler thinks that these statements may not be executed and therefore reports a syntax error.

test all cases

To test a program, you should provide the input that covers all cases. For this program, your input should cover all statuses (`0`, `1`, `2`, `3`). For each status, test the tax for each of the six brackets. So, there are a total of 24 cases.

Tip

For all programs, you should write a small amount of code and test it before moving on to add more code. This is called *incremental development and testing*. This approach makes debugging easier, because the errors are likely in the new code you just added.

incremental development and testing

3.3.8 Problem: Guessing Birth Dates

You can find out your friend's birth date by asking five questions. Each question asks whether the date is in one of five sets of numbers, as shown in Figure 3.4:

The birth date is the sum of the first numbers in the sets where the date appears. For example, if the birth date is `19`, it appears in Set1, Set3, and Set5. The first numbers in these three sets are `1`, `2`, and `16`. Their sum is `19`.

The way the numbers are placed in the five sets is intrigue. The numbers are not put together by accident. The starting numbers in each set are 1, 2, 4, 8, and 16, which correspond to 1, 10, 100, 1000, and 10000 in binary. If a date's binary number has a digit 1 in position k, the number should appear in Setk. For example, number 19 is 10011, so it appears in Set1, Set2, and Set5. It is binary 1 + 10 + 10000 = 10011 or decimal 1 + 2 + 16 = 19. Number 31 is 11111, so it appears in Set1, Set2, Set3, Set4, and Set5. It is binary 1 + 10 + 100 + 1000 + 10000 = 11111 and it is decimal 1 + 2 + 4 + 8 + 16 = 31.

Listing 3.8 gives a program that prompts the user to answer whether the date is in Set1 (lines 41–47), in Set2 (lines 50–56), in Set3 (lines 59–65), in Set4 (lines 68–74), and in Set5 (lines 77–83). If the number is in the set, the program adds the first number in the set to `date` (lines 47, 56, 65, 74, 83).

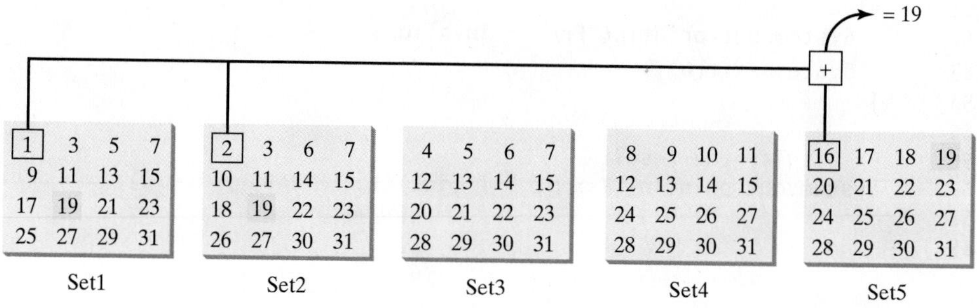

= 19

Set1			
1	3	5	7
9	11	13	15
17	19	21	23
25	27	29	31

Set2			
2	3	6	7
10	11	14	15
18	19	22	23
26	27	30	31

Set3			
4	5	6	7
12	13	14	15
20	21	22	23
28	29	30	31

Set4			
8	9	10	11
12	13	14	15
24	25	26	27
28	29	30	31

Set5			
16	17	18	19
20	21	22	23
24	25	26	27
28	29	30	31

FIGURE 3.4 The birth date is the sum of the first numbers in the sets where the date appears.

LISTING 3.8 GuessBirthDate.java

date to be determined

```
import java.util.Scanner;

public class GuessBirthDate {
  public static void main(String[] args) {
    String set1 =
      " 1  3  5  7\n" +
      " 9 11 13 15\n" +
      "17 19 21 23\n" +
      "25 27 29 31";

    String set2 =
      " 2  3  6  7\n" +
      "10 11 14 15\n" +
      "18 19 22 23\n" +
      "26 27 30 31";

    String set3 =
      " 4  5  6  7\n" +
      "12 13 14 15\n" +
      "20 21 22 23\n" +
      "28 29 30 31";

    String set4 =
      " 8  9 10 11\n" +
      "12 13 14 15\n" +
      "24 25 26 27\n" +
      "28 29 30 31";

    String set5 =
      "16 17 18 19\n" +
      "20 21 22 23\n" +
      "24 25 26 27\n" +
      "28 29 30 31";

    int date = 0;

    // Create a Scanner
    Scanner input = new Scanner(System.in);

    // Prompt the user to answer questions
    System.out.print("Is your birthdate in Set1?\n");
    System.out.print(set1);
    System.out.print("\nEnter 0 for No and 1 for Yes: ");
    int answer = input.nextInt();
```

```

    if (answer == 1)
      date += 1;

    // Prompt the user to answer questions
    System.out.print("\nIs your birthdate in Set2?\n");
    System.out.print(set2);
    System.out.print("\nEnter 0 for No and 1 for Yes: ");
    answer = input.nextInt();

    if (answer == 1)
      date += 2;

    // Prompt the user to answer questions
    System.out.print("Is your birthdate in Set3?\n");
    System.out.print(set3);
    System.out.print("\nEnter 0 for No and 1 for Yes: ");
    answer = input.nextInt();

    if (answer == 1)
      date += 4;

    // Prompt the user to answer questions
    System.out.print("\nIs your birthdate in Set4?\n");
    System.out.print(set4);
    System.out.print("\nEnter 0 for No and 1 for Yes: ");
    answer = input.nextInt();

    if (answer == 1)
      date += 8;

    // Prompt the user to answer questions
    System.out.print("\nIs your birthdate in Set5?\n");
    System.out.print(set5);
    System.out.print("\nEnter 0 for No and 1 for Yes: ");
    answer = input.nextInt();

    if (answer == 1)
      date += 16;

    System.out.println("\nYour birthdate is " + date + "!");
  }
}
```

in Set1?

in Set2?

in Set3?

in Set4?

in Set5?

```
Is your birth date in Set1?
 1  3  5  7
 9 11 13 15
17 19 21 23
25 27 29 31
Enter 0 for No and 1 for Yes: 1 ↵Enter

Is your birth date in Set2?
 2  3  6  7
10 11 14 15
18 19 22 23
26 27 30 31
Enter 0 for No and 1 for Yes: 1 ↵Enter
```

```
Is your birth date in Set3?
 4  5  6  7
12 13 14 15
20 21 22 23
28 29 30 31
Enter 0 for No and 1 for Yes: 0 ↵Enter

Is your birth date in Set4?
 8  9 10 11
12 13 14 15
24 25 26 27
28 29 30 31
Enter 0 for No and 1 for Yes: 0 ↵Enter

Is your birth date in Set5?
16 17 18 19
20 21 22 23
24 25 26 27
28 29 30 31
Enter 0 for No and 1 for Yes: 1 ↵Enter
Your birth date is 19
```

3.4 **switch** Statements

The `if` statement in Listing 3.5 makes selections based on a single `true` or `false` condition. There are four cases for computing taxes, which depend on the value of `status`. To fully account for all the cases, nested `if` statements were used. Overuse of nested `if` statements makes a program difficult to read. Java provides a `switch` statement to handle multiple conditions efficiently. You could write the following `switch` statement to replace the nested `if` statement in Listing 3.5:

```
switch (status) {
  case 0:  compute taxes for single filers;
           break;
  case 1:  compute taxes for married filing jointly;
           break;
  case 2:  compute taxes for married filing separately;
           break;
  case 3:  compute taxes for head of household;
           break;
  default: System.out.println("Errors: invalid status");
           System.exit(0);
}
```

The flow chart of the preceding `switch` statement is shown in Figure 3.5.

This statement checks to see whether the status matches the value `0`, `1`, `2`, or `3`, in that order. If matched, the corresponding tax is computed; if not matched, a message is displayed. Here is the full syntax for the `switch` statement:

switch statement

```
switch (switch-expression) {
  case value1: statement(s)1;
               break;
  case value2: statement(s)2;
               break;
```

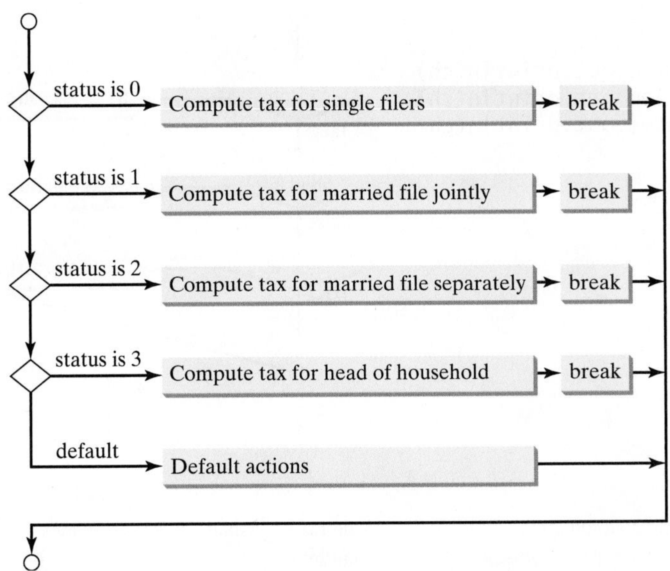

FIGURE 3.5 The `switch` statement checks all cases and executes the statements in the matched case.

```
   ...
   case valueN: statement(s)N;
                break;
   default:     statement(s)-for-default;
}
```

The `switch` statement observes the following rules:

- The `switch-expression` must yield a value of `char`, `byte`, `short`, or `int` type and must always be enclosed in parentheses.
- The `value1`, ..., and `valueN` must have the same data type as the value of the `switch-expression`. Note that `value1`, ..., and `valueN` are constant expressions, meaning that they cannot contain variables, such as `1 + x`.
- When the value in a `case` statement matches the value of the `switch-expression`, the statements *starting from this case* are executed until either a `break` statement or the end of the switch statement is reached.
- The keyword `break` is optional. The `break` statement immediately ends the `switch` statement.
- The `default` case, which is optional, can be used to perform actions when none of the specified cases matches the `switch-expression`.
- The `case` statements are checked in sequential order, but the order of the cases (including the default case) does not matter. However, it is good programming style to follow the logical sequence of the cases and place the default case at the end.

Caution

Do not forget to use a `break` statement when one is needed. Once a case is matched, the statements starting from the matched case are executed until a `break` statement or the end of the `switch` statement is reached. This is referred to as *fall-through behavior*. For example, the following code prints character a three times if `ch` is 'a':

without **break**

fall-through behavior

```
switch (ch) {
  case 'a': System.out.println(ch);
  case 'b': System.out.println(ch);
  case 'c': System.out.println(ch);
}
```

Tip

To avoid programming errors and improve code maintainability, it is a good idea to put a comment in a case clause if **break** is purposely omitted.

3.5 Conditional Expressions

You might want to assign a value to a variable that is restricted by certain conditions. For example, the following statement assigns 1 to y if x is greater than 0, and -1 to y if x is less than or equal to 0.

```
if (x > 0)
  y = 1;
else
  y = -1;
```

Alternatively, as in this example, you can use a conditional expression to achieve the same result.

```
y = (x > 0) ? 1 : -1;
```

Conditional expressions are in a completely different style, with no explicit if in the statement. The syntax is shown below:

conditional expression

```
booleanExpression ? expression1 : expression2;
```

The result of this conditional expression is **expression1** if **booleanExpression** is true; otherwise the result is **expression2**.

Suppose you want to assign the larger number between variable **num1** and **num2** to **max**. You can simply write a statement using the conditional expression:

```
max = (num1 > num2) ? num1 : num2;
```

For another example, the following statement displays the message "num is even" if **num** is even, and otherwise displays "num is odd."

```
System.out.println((num % 2 == 0) ? "num is even" : "num is odd");
```

Note

The symbols ? and : appear together in a conditional expression. They form a conditional operator. It is called a *ternary operator* because it uses three operands. It is the only ternary operator in Java.

3.6 Formatting Console Output

If you wish to display only two digits after the decimal point in a floating-point value, you may write the code like this:

```
double x = 2.0 / 3;
System.out.println("x is " + (int)(x * 100) / 100.0);
```

```
x is 0.66
```

However, a better way to accomplish this task is to format the output using the `printf` method. The syntax to invoke this method is

printf

```
System.out.printf(format, item1, item2, ..., itemk)
```

where `format` is a string that may consist of substrings and format specifiers.

A format specifier specifies how an item should be displayed. An item may be a numeric value, a character, a Boolean value, or a string. A simple specifier consists of a percent sign (%) and a conversion code. Table 3.8 lists some frequently used simple specifiers:

specifier

TABLE 3.8 Frequently Used Specifiers

Specifier	*Output*	*Example*
%b	a Boolean value	true or false
%c	a character	'a'
%d	a decimal integer	200
%f	a floating-point number	45.460000
%e	a number in standard scientific notation	4.556000e+01
%s	a string	"Java is cool"

Here is an example:

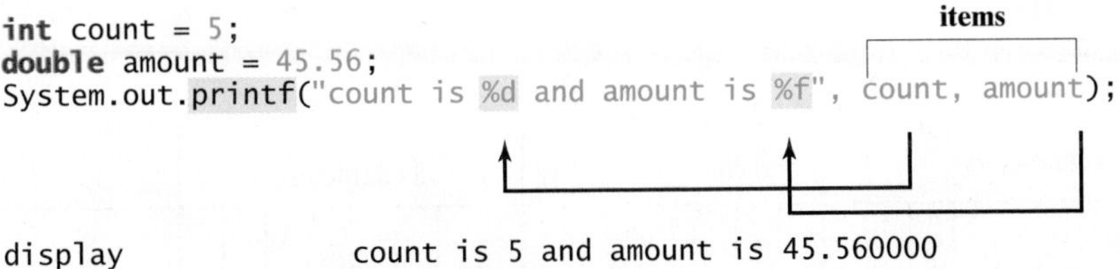

Items must match the specifiers in order, in number, and in exact type. For example, the specifier for `count` is `%d` and for `amount` is `%f`. By default, a floating-point value is displayed with six digits after the decimal point. You can specify the width and precision in a specifier, as shown in the examples in Table 3.9.

The code presented in the beginning of this section for displaying only two digits after the decimal point in a floating-point value can be revised using the `printf` method as follows:

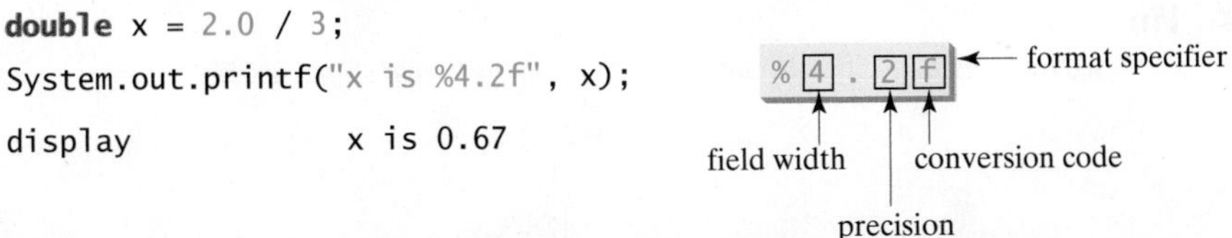

TABLE 3.9 Examples of Specifying Width and Precision

Example	*Output*
`%5c`	Output the character and add four spaces before the character item.
`%6b`	Output the Boolean value and add one space before the false value and two spaces before the true value.
`%5d`	Output the integer item with width at least 5. If the number of digits in the item is $<$ 5, add spaces before the number. If the number of digits in the item is $>$ 5, the width is automatically increased.
`%10.2f`	Output the floating-point item with width at least 10 including a decimal point and two digits after the point. Thus there are 7 digits allocated before the decimal point. If the number of digits before the decimal point in the item is $<$ 7, add spaces before the number. If the number of digits before the decimal point in the item is $>$ 7, the width is automatically increased.
`%10.2e`	Output the floating-point item with width at least 10 including a decimal point, two digits after the point and the exponent part. If the displayed number in scientific notation has width less than 10, add spaces before the number.
`%12s`	Output the string with width at least 12 characters. If the string item has less than 12 characters, add spaces before the string. If the string item has more than 12 characters, the width is automatically increased.

left justify

By default, the output is right justified. You can put the minus sign (-) in the specifier to specify that the item is left justified in the output within the specified field. For example, the following statements

```
System.out.printf("%8d%8s%8.1f\n", 1234, "Java", 5.6);
System.out.printf("%-8d%-8s%-8.1f \n", 1234, "Java", 5.6);
```

display

```
|  8 characters  |  8 characters  |  8 characters  |
    1234    Java     5.6
1234    Java    5.6
```

Caution

The items must match the specifiers in exact type. The item for the specifier `%f` or `%e` must be a floating-point type value such as 40.0, not 40. Thus an `int` variable cannot match `%f` or `%e`.

Tip

The `%` sign denotes a specifier. To output a literal `%` in the format string, use `%%`.

3.7 Operator Precedence and Associativity

Operator precedence and associativity determine the order in which operators are evaluated. Suppose that you have this expression:

```
3 + 4 * 4 > 5 * (4 + 3) - 1
```

What is its value? What is the execution order of the operators?

Arithmetically, the expression in the parentheses is evaluated first. (Parentheses can be nested, in which case the expression in the inner parentheses is executed first.) When evaluating an expression without parentheses, the operators are applied according to the precedence rule and the associativity rule.

precedence

The precedence rule defines precedence for operators, as shown in Table 3.10, which contains the operators you have learned so far. Operators are listed in decreasing order of precedence from top to bottom. Operators with the same precedence appear in the same group. (See Appendix C, "Operator Precedence Chart," for a complete list of Java operators and their precedence.)

TABLE 3.10 Operator Precedence Chart

Precedence	*Operator*
↓	var++ and var-- (Postfix)
	+, - (Unary plus and minus), ++var and --var (Prefix)
	(type) (Casting)
	! (Not)
	*, /, % (Multiplication, division, and remainder)
	+, - (Binary addition and subtraction)
	<, <=, >, >= (Comparison)
	==, != (Equality)
	^ (Exclusive OR)
	&& (AND)
	|| (OR)
	=, +=, -=, *=, /=, %= (Assignment operator)

associativity

If operators with the same precedence are next to each other, their *associativity* determines the order of evaluation. All binary operators except assignment operators are *left associative.* For example, since + and - are of the same precedence and are left associative, the expression

```
a - b + c - d   ===equivalent===   ((a - b) + c) - d
```

Assignment operators are *right associative*. Therefore, the expression

```
a = b += c = 5   ===equivalent===   a = (b += (c = 5))
```

Suppose a, b, and c are 1 before the assignment; after the whole expression is evaluated, a becomes 6, b becomes 6, and c becomes 5. Note that left associativity for the assignment operator would not make sense.

Note

behind scenes

Java has its own way to evaluate an expression internally. The result of a Java evaluation is the same as its corresponding arithmetic evaluation. Interested readers may refer to Supplement IV.M for more discussions on how an expression is evaluated in Java *behind the scenes*.

3.8 (GUI) Confirmation Dialogs

You have used `showMessageDialog` to display a message dialog box and `showInputDialog` to display an input dialog box. Occasionally it is useful to answer a question with a confirmation dialog box. A confirmation dialog can be created using the following statement:

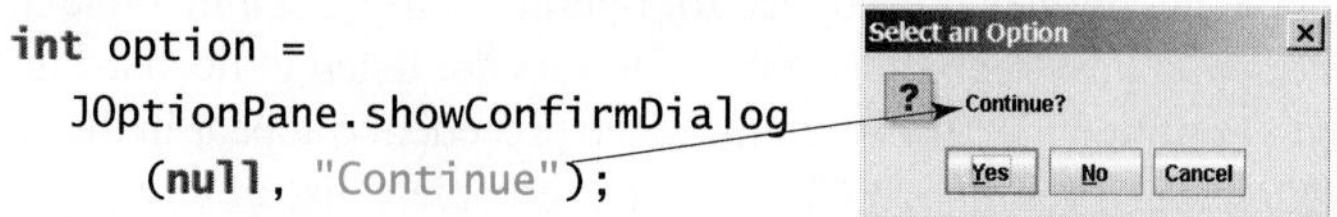


```
int option =
  JOptionPane.showConfirmDialog
    (null, "Continue");
```

When a button is clicked, the method returns an option value. The value is `JOptionPane.YES_OPTION` (`0`) for the *Yes* button, `JOptionPane.NO_OPTION` (`1`) for the *No* button, and `JOptionPane.CANCEL_OPTION` (`2`) for the *Cancel* button.

You may rewrite the guess-birth-date program in Listing 3.8 using confirmation dialog boxes, as shown in Listing 3.9. Figure 3.6 shows a sample run of the program for the date 19.

LISTING 3.9 `GuessBirthDateUsingConfirmationDialog.java`

import class

```
import javax.swing.JOptionPane;

public class GuessBirthDateUsingConfirmationDialog {
  public static void main(String[] args) {
```

set1

```
    String set1 =
      " 1  3  5  7\n" +
      " 9 11 13 15\n" +
      "17 19 21 23\n" +
      "25 27 29 31";
```

set2

```
    String set2 =
      " 2  3  6  7\n" +
      "10 11 14 15\n" +
      "18 19 22 23\n" +
      "26 27 30 31";
```

set3

```
    String set3 =
      " 4  5  6  7\n" +
      "12 13 14 15\n" +
      "20 21 22 23\n" +
      "28 29 30 31";
```

set4

```
    String set4 =
      " 8  9 10 11\n" +
      "12 13 14 15\n" +
      "24 25 26 27\n" +
      "28 29 30 31";
```

set5

```
    String set5 =
      "16 17 18 19\n" +
      "20 21 22 23\n" +
      "24 25 26 27\n" +
      "28 29 30 31";

```

```
    int date = 0;

    // Prompt the user to answer questions
    int answer = JOptionPane.showConfirmDialog(null,
      "Is your birthdate in these numbers?\n" + set1);

    if (answer == JOptionPane.YES_OPTION)
      date += 1;

    answer = JOptionPane.showConfirmDialog(null,
      "Is your birthdate in these numbers?\n" + set2);

    if (answer == JOptionPane.YES_OPTION)
      date += 2;

    answer = JOptionPane.showConfirmDialog(null,
      "Is your birthdate in these numbers?\n" + set3);

    if (answer == JOptionPane.YES_OPTION)
      date += 4;

    answer = JOptionPane.showConfirmDialog(null,
      "Is your birthdate in these numbers?\n" + set4);

    if (answer == JOptionPane.YES_OPTION)
      date += 8;

    answer = JOptionPane.showConfirmDialog(null,
      "Is your birthdate in these numbers?\n" + set5);

    if (answer == JOptionPane.YES_OPTION)
      date += 16;

    JOptionPane.showMessageDialog(null, "Your birthdate is " +
      date + "!");
  }
}
```

confirmation dialog

in set1?

in set2?

in set3?

in set4?

in set5?

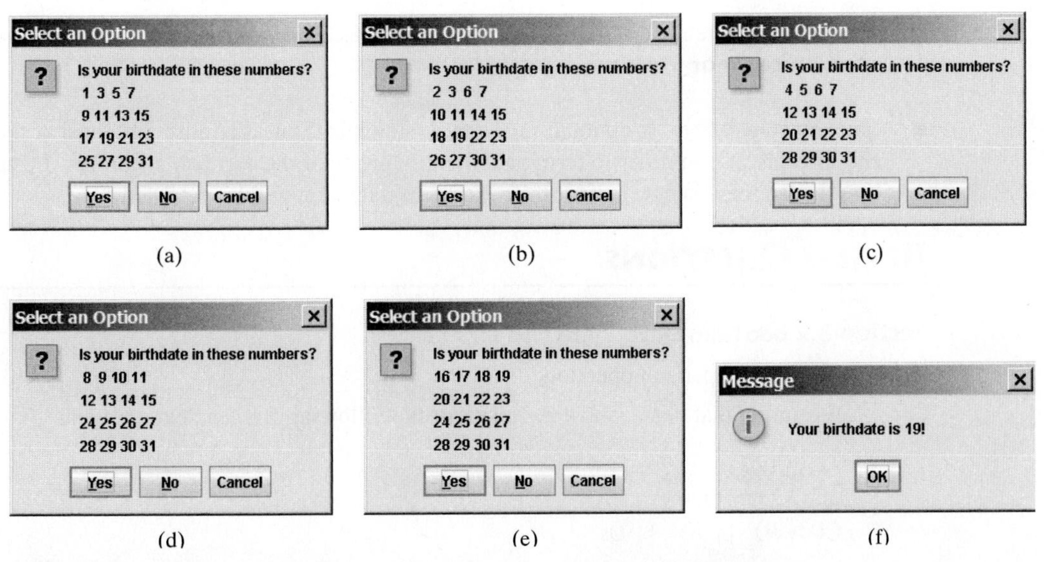

FIGURE 3.6 Click Yes in (a), No in (b), Yes in (c), Yes in (d), and No in (e).

The program displays confirmation boxes to prompt the user to answer whether a number is in Set1 (line 38), Set2 (line 44), Set3 (line 50), Set4 (line 56), and Set5 (line 62). If the answer is Yes, the first number in the set is added to `date` (lines 42, 48, 54, 60, and 66).

KEY TERMS

boolean expression 68
boolean value 68
`boolean` type 68
`break` statement 86
conditional operator 88
fall-through behavior 87
operator associativity 91
operator precedence 91
selection statement 72
short-circuit evaluation 71

CHAPTER SUMMARY

- The `boolean` type represents a `true` or `false` value.
- The relational operators (<, <=, ==, !=, >, >=) work with numbers and characters, and yield a Boolean value.
- The Boolean operators &&, ||, !, and ^ operate with Boolean values and variables.
- When evaluating `p1 && p2`, Java first evaluates `p1` and then evaluates `p2` if `p1` is `true`; if `p1` is `false`, it does not evaluate `p2`. When evaluating `p1 || p2`, Java first evaluates `p1` and then evaluates `p2` if `p1` is `false`; if `p1` is `true`, it does not evaluate `p2`. Therefore, && is referred to as the *conditional* or *short-circuit AND* operator, and || is referred to as the *conditional* or *short-circuit OR* operator.
- Selection statements are used for programming with alternative courses. There are several types of selection statements: `if` statements, `if . . . else` statements, nested `if` statements, `switch` statements, and conditional expressions.
- The various `if` statements all make control decisions based on a Boolean expression. Based on the `true` or `false` evaluation of the expression, these statements take one of two possible courses.
- The `switch` statement makes control decisions based on a switch expression of type `char`, `byte`, `short`, or `int`.
- The keyword `break` is optional in a switch statement, but it is normally used at the end of each case in order to terminate the remainder of the `switch` statement. If the `break` statement is not present, the next `case` statement will be executed.

REVIEW QUESTIONS

Section 3.2 `boolean` Data Type and Operations

3.1 List six comparison operators.

3.2 Assuming that `x` is `1`, show the result of the following Boolean expressions.

```
(true) && (3 > 4)
!(x > 0) && (x > 0)
(x > 0) || (x < 0)
```

```
(x != 0) || (x == 0)
(x >= 0) || (x < 0)
(x != 1) == !(x == 1)
```

3.3 Write a Boolean expression that evaluates to true if a number stored in variable num is between 1 and 100.

3.4 Write a Boolean expression that evaluates to true if a number stored in variable num is between 1 and 100 or the number is negative.

3.5 Assume that x and y are int type. Which of the following are legal Java expressions?

```
x > y > 0
x = y && y
x /= y
x or y
x and y
(x != 0) || (x = 0)
```

3.6 Can the following conversions involving casting be allowed? If so, find the converted result.

```
boolean b = true;
i = (int)b;

int i = 1;
boolean b = (boolean)i;
```

3.7 Suppose that x is 1. What is x after the evaluation of the following expression?

```
(x >= 1) && (x++ > 1)
```

3.8 Suppose that x is 1. What is x after the evaluation of the following expression?

```
(x > 1) && (x++ > 1)
```

3.9 Show the output of the following program:

```
public class Test {
  public static void main(String[] args) {
    char x = 'a';
    char y = 'c';

    System.out.println(++y);
    System.out.println(y++);
    System.out.println(x > y);
    System.out.println(x - y);
  }
}
```

3.10 Write a Boolean expression that evaluates true if age is greater than 13 and less than 18.

3.11 Write a Boolean expression that evaluates true if weight is greater than 50 or height is greater than 160.

3.12 Write a Boolean expression that evaluates true if weight is greater than 50 and height is greater than 160.

3.13 Write a Boolean expression that evaluates true if either weight is greater than 50 or height is greater than 160, but not both.

Section 3.3 if Statements

3.14 Suppose x = 3 and y = 2; show the output, if any, of the following code. What is the output if x = 3 and y = 4? What is the output if x = 2 and y = 2? Draw a flow chart of the following code:

```
if (x > 2) {
  if (y > 2) {
    z = x + y;
    System.out.println("z is " + z);
  }
}
else
  System.out.println("x is " + x);
```

3.15 Which of the following statements are equivalent? Which ones are correctly indented?

```
if (i > 0) if
(j > 0)
x = 0; else
if (k > 0) y = 0;
else z = 0;
```

(a)

```
if (i > 0) {
  if (j > 0)
    x = 0;
  else if (k > 0)
    y = 0;
}
else
  z = 0;
```

(b)

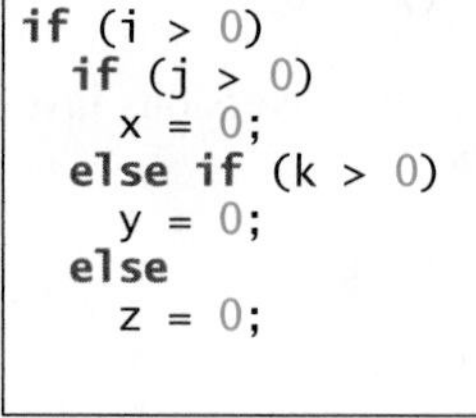

```
if (i > 0)
  if (j > 0)
    x = 0;
  else if (k > 0)
    y = 0;
  else
    z = 0;
```

(c)

```
if (i > 0)
  if (j > 0)
    x = 0;
  else if (k > 0)
    y = 0;
else
  z = 0;
```

(d)

3.16 Suppose x = 2 and y = 3. Show the output, if any, of the following code. What is the output if x = 3 and y = 2? What is the output if x = 3 and y = 3? (*Hint*: Indent the statement correctly first.)

```
if (x > 2)
  if (y > 2) {
    int z = x + y;
    System.out.println("z is " + z);
  }
else
  System.out.println("x is " + x);
```

3.17 Are the following two statements equivalent?

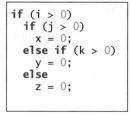

```
if (income <= 10000)
  tax = income * 0.1;
else if (income <= 20000)
  tax = 1000 +
    (income - 10000) * 0.15;
```

```
if (income <= 10000)
  tax = income * 0.1;
else if (income > 10000 &&
         income <= 20000)
  tax = 1000 +
    (income - 10000) * 0.15;
```

3.18 Which of the following is a possible output from invoking `Math.random()`?

`323.4, 0.5, 34, 1.0, 0.0, 0.234`

3.19 How do you generate a random integer i such that $0 \leq i < 20$? How do you generate a random integer i such that $10 \leq i < 20$? How do you generate a random integer i such that $10 \leq i \geq 50$?

3.20 Write an if statement that assigns 1 to x if y is greater than 0.

3.21 Write an if statement that increases pay by 3% if score is greater than 90.

3.22 Write an if statement that increases pay by 3% if score is greater than 90, otherwise increases pay by 1%.

3.23 Rewrite the following statement using a Boolean expression:

```
if (count % 10 == 0)
  newLine = true;
else
  newLine = false;
```

Section 3.4 switch Statements

3.24 What data types are required for a switch variable? If the keyword break is not used after a case is processed, what is the next statement to be executed? Can you convert a switch statement to an equivalent if statement, or vice versa? What are the advantages of using a switch statement?

3.25 What is y after the following switch statement is executed?

```
x = 3; y = 3;
switch (x + 3) {
  case 6:  y = 1;
  default: y += 1;
}
```

3.26 Use a switch statement to rewrite the following if statement and draw the flow chart for the switch statement:

```
if (a == 1)
  x += 5;
else if (a == 2)
  x += 10;
else if (a == 3)
  x += 16;
else if (a == 4)
  x += 34;
```

3.27 Write a switch statement that assigns a String variable dayName with Sunday, Monday, Tuesday, Wednesday, Thursday, Friday, Saturday, if day is 0, 1, 2, 3, 4, 5, 6, accordingly.

Section 3.5 Conditional Expressions

3.28 Rewrite the following if statement using the conditional operator:

```
if (count % 10 == 0)
  System.out.print(count + "\n");
else
  System.out.print(count + " ");
```

3.29 Rewrite the following statement using a conditional expression:

```
if (temperature > 90)
  pay = pay * 1.5;
else
  pay = pay * 1.1;
```

Section 3.6 Formatting Console Output

3.30 What are the specifiers for outputting a Boolean value, a character, a decimal integer, a floating-point number, and a string?

3.31 What is wrong in the following statements?

```
(a) System.out.printf("%5d %d", 1, 2, 3);
(b) System.out.printf("%5d %f", 1);
(c) System.out.printf("%5d %f", 1, 2);
```

3.32 Show the output of the following statements.

```
(a) System.out.printf("amount is %f %e\n", 32.32, 32.32);
(b) System.out.printf("amount is %5.4f %5.4e\n", 32.32, 32.32);
(c) System.out.printf("%6b\n", (1 > 2));
(d) System.out.printf("%6s\n", "Java");
(e) System.out.printf("%-6b%s\n", (1 > 2), "Java");
(f) System.out.printf("%6b%-s\n", (1 > 2), "Java");
```

3.33 How do you create a formatted string?

Section 3.7 Operator Precedence and Associativity

3.34 List the precedence order of the Boolean operators. Evaluate the following expressions:

```
true || true && false
true && true || false
```

3.35 True or false? All the binary operators except = are left associative.

3.36 Evaluate the following expressions:

```
2 * 2 - 3 > 2 && 4 - 2 > 5
2 * 2 - 3 > 2 || 4 - 2 > 5
```

Section 3.8 (GUI) Confirmation Dialogs

3.37 How do you display a confirmation dialog? What value is returned when invoking `JOptionPane.showConfirmDialog`?

Programming Exercises

Pedagogical Note

think before coding

For each exercise, students should carefully analyze the problem requirements and design strategies for solving the problem before coding.

Pedagogical Note

document analysis and design

Instructors may ask students to document analysis and design for selected exercises. Students should use their own words to analyze the problem, including the input, output, and what needs to be computed, and describe how to solve the problem using English or pseudocode.

Debugging Tip

learn from mistakes

Before you ask for help, read and explain the program to yourself, and trace it using several representative inputs by hand or using an IDE debugger. You learn how to program by debugging your own mistakes.

Note

Do not use selection statements for Exercises 3.1–3.6.

Section 3.2 `boolean` Data Type and Operations

3.1* (*Validating triangles*) Write a program that reads three edges for a triangle and determines whether the input is valid. The input is valid if the sum of any two edges is greater than the third edge. Here are the sample runs of this program:

```
Enter three edges: 1 2 1 ↵Enter
Can edges 1, 2, and 1 form a triangle? false
```

```
Enter three edges: 2 2 1 ↵Enter
Can edges 2, 2, and 1 form a triangle? true
```

3.2 (*Checking whether a number is even*) Write a program that reads an integer and checks whether it is even. Here are the sample runs of this program:

```
Enter an integer: 25 ↵Enter
Is 25 an even number? false
```

```
Enter an integer: 2000 ↵Enter
Is 2000 an even number? true
```

3.3* (Using the &&, || and ^ operators) Write a program that prompts the user to enter an integer and determines whether it is divisible by 5 and 6, whether it is divisible by 5 or 6, and whether it is divisible by 5 or 6, but not both. Here is a sample run of this program:

```
Enter an integer: 10 ↵Enter
Is 10 divisible by 5 and 6? false
Is 10 divisible by 5 or 6? true
Is 10 divisible by 5 or 6, but not both? true
```

3.4** (*Game: learning addition*) Write a program that generates two integers under 100 and prompts the user to enter the addition of these two integers. The program then reports true if the answer is correct, false otherwise. The program is similar to Listing 3.3.

3.5** (*Game: addition for three numbers*) The program in Listing 3.3 generates two integers and prompts the user to enter the addition of these two integers. Revise the program to generate three single-digit integers and prompt the user to enter the addition of these three integers.

3.6* (*Using the input dialog box*) Rewrite Listing 3.2, LeapYear.java, using the input dialog box.

Section 3.3 `if` Statements

3.7 (*Financial application: monetary units*) Modify Listing 2.8, ComputeChange.java, to display the nonzero denominations only, using singular words for single units like 1 dollar and 1 penny, and plural words for more than one unit like 2 dollars and 3 pennies. (Use input 23.67 to test your program.)

3.8* (*Sorting three integers*) Write a program that sorts three integers. The integers are entered from the input dialogs and stored in variables num1, num2, and num3, respectively. The program sorts the numbers so that $num1 \leq num2 \leq num3$.

Video Note
Sort three integers

3.9 (*Computing the perimeter of a triangle*) Write a program that reads three edges for a triangle and computes the perimeter if the input is valid. Otherwise, display that the input is invalid. The input is valid if the sum of any two edges is greater than the third edge. (Also see Exercise 3.1.)

3.10 (*Financial application: computing taxes*) Listing 3.7 gives the source code to compute taxes for single filers. Complete Listing 3.7 to give the complete source code.

3.11* (*Finding the number of days in a month*) Write a program that prompts the user to enter the month and year, and displays the number of days in the month. For example, if the user entered month 2 and year 2000, the program should display that February 2000 has 29 days. If the user entered month 3 and year 2005, the program should display that March 2005 has 31 days.

3.12 (*Checking a number*) Write a program that prompts the user to enter an integer and checks whether the number is divisible by both 5 and 6, or neither of them, or just one of them. Here are some sample outputs for inputs 10, 30, and 23.

```
10 is divisible by 5 or 6, but not both
30 is divisible by both 5 and 6
23 is not divisible by either 5 or 6
```

3.13* (*Game: addition quiz*) Listing 3.4, SubtractionQuiz.java, randomly generates a subtraction question. Revise the program to randomly generate an addition question with two integers less than 100.

3.14 (*Game: head or tail*) Write a program that lets the user guess the head or tail of a coin. The program randomly generates an integer 0 or 1, which represents the head or tail of a coin. The program prompts the user to enter a guess and reports whether the guess is correct or incorrect.

3.15* (*Game: lottery*) Revise Listing 3.5, Lottery.java, to generate a lottery of a three-digit number. The program prompts the user to enter a three-digit number and determines whether the user wins according to the following rule:

1. If the user input matches the lottery in exact order, the award is $10,000.
2. If the user input matches the lottery, the award is $3,000.
3. If one digit in the user input matches a digit in the lottery, the award is $1,000.

3.16 (*Random character*) Write a program that displays a random uppercase letter.

3.17* (*Game: scissor, rock, paper*) Write a program that plays the popular scissor-rock-paper game. The program randomly generates a number 0, 1, or 2 representing scissor, rock, and paper. The program prompts the user to enter a number 0, 1, or 2 and displays a message indicating whether the user or the computer wins or draws. Note that a scissor can cut a paper, a rock can knock a scissor, and a paper can wrap a rock.

3.18* (*Health application: BMI*) Revise Listing 3.6, ComputeBMI.java, to let the user enter weight, feet, and inches. For example, if a person is 5 feet and 10 inches, you will enter 5 for feet and 10 for inches.

3.19** (*Checking ISBN*) An **ISBN** (International Standard Book Number) consists of 10 digits $d_1d_2d_3d_4d_5d_6d_7d_8d_9d_{10}$. The last digit d_{10} is a checksum, which is calculated from the other nine digits using the following formula:

$$(d_1 \times 1 + d_2 \times 2 + d_3 \times 3 + d_4 \times 4 + d_5 \times 5 +$$

$$d_6 \times 6 + d_7 \times 7 + d_8 \times 8 + d_9 \times 9) \% 11$$

If the checksum is 10, the last digit is denoted X according to the ISBN convention. Write a program that prompts the user to enter the first 9 digits and displays the 10-digit ISBN (including leading zeros). Your program should read the input as an integer.

3.20* (*Science: wind chill temperature*) Exercise 2.17 gives a formula to compute the wind chill temperature. The formula is valid for the temperature in the range between −58°F and above 41°F and wind speed greater than or equal to 2. Write a program that prompts the user to enter a temperature and a wind speed. The program displays the wind chill temperature if the input is valid, otherwise, displays a message that indicates whether the temperature and/or wind speed is invalid.

CHAPTER 4

LOOPS

Objectives

- To use `while`, `do-while`, and `for` loop statements to control the repetition of statements (§§4.2–4.4).
- To understand the flow of control in loop statements (§§4.2–4.4).
- To use Boolean expressions to control loop statements (§§4.2–4.4).
- To discover the similarities and differences between three types of loops (§4.5).
- To write nested loops (§4.6).
- To learn the techniques for minimizing numerical errors (§4.7).
- To learn loops from a variety of examples (§4.8).
- To implement program control with `break` and `continue` (§4.9).
- (GUI) To control a loop with a confirmation dialog (§4.10).

4.1 Introduction

Suppose that you need to print a string (e.g., "Welcome to Java!") a hundred times. It would be tedious to have to write the following statement a hundred times:

```
System.out.println("Welcome to Java!");
```

problem

why loop?

So, how do you solve this problem?

Java provides a powerful control structure called a *loop* that controls how many times an operation or a sequence of operations is performed in succession. Using a loop statement, you simply tell the computer to print a string a hundred times without having to code the print statement a hundred times.

Loops are structures that control repeated executions of a block of statements. The concept of looping is fundamental to programming. Java provides three types of loop statements: while loops, do-while loops, and for loops.

4.2 The **while** Loop

The syntax for the while loop is as follows:

while loop

```
while (loop-continuation-condition) {
  // Loop body
  Statement(s);
}
```

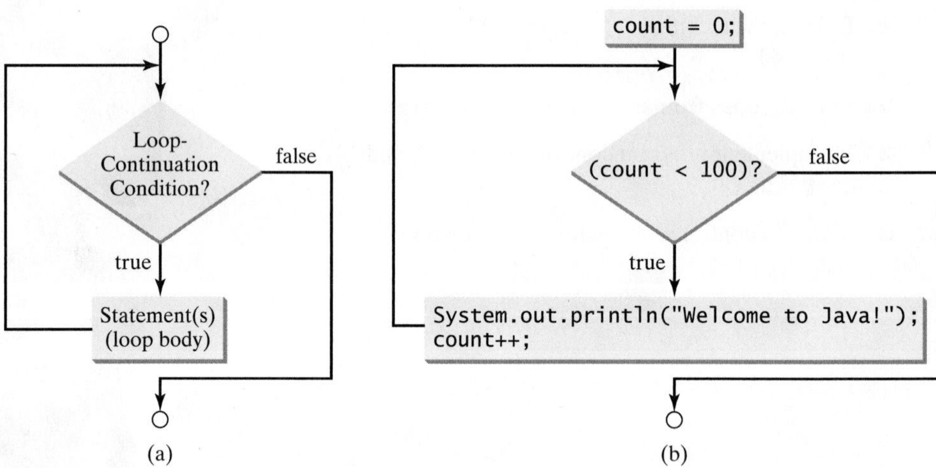

FIGURE 4.1 The while loop repeatedly executes the statements in the loop body when the loop-continuation condition evaluates to true.

loop body

iteration

The while loop flow chart is shown in Figure 4.1(a). The part of the loop that contains the statements to be repeated is called the *loop body*. A one-time execution of a loop body is referred to as an *iteration of the loop*. Each loop contains a loop-continuation condition, a Boolean expression that controls the execution of the body. It is evaluated each time to determine if the loop body is executed. If its evaluation is true, the loop body is executed; if its evaluation is false, the entire loop terminates and the program control turns to the statement that follows the while loop. For example, the following while loop prints "Welcome to Java!" a hundred times.

```
int count = 0;
while (count < 100) {
```

```
    System.out.println("Welcome to Java!");
    count++;
  }
```

The flow chart of the preceding statement is shown in Figure 4.1(b). The variable `count` is initially `0`. The loop checks whether (`count < 100`) is true. If so, it executes the loop body to print the message `"Welcome to Java!"` and increments count by `1`. It repeatedly executes the loop body until (`count < 100`) becomes false. When (`count < 100`) is `false` (i.e., when `count` reaches `100`), the loop terminates and the next statement after the loop statement is executed.

Note

The `loop-continuation-condition` must always appear inside the parentheses. The braces enclosing the loop body can be omitted only if the loop body contains one or no statement.

Caution

Make sure that the `loop-continuation-condition` eventually becomes `false` so that the program will terminate. A common programming error involves *infinite loops*. That is, the program cannot terminate because of a mistake in the `loop-continuation-condition`. For instance, if you forgot to increase `count` (`count++`) in the code, the program would not stop.

infinite loop

4.2.1 Problem: Guessing Numbers

The problem is to guess what a number a computer has in mind. You will write a program that randomly generates an integer between `0` and `100`, inclusive. The program prompts the user to enter a number continuously until the number matches the randomly generated number. For each user input, the program tells the user whether the input is too low or too high, so the user can choose the next input intelligently. Here is a sample run:

```
Guess a magic number between 0 and 100

Enter your guess: 50 ↵Enter
Your guess is too high

Enter your guess: 25 ↵Enter
Your guess is too high

Enter your guess: 12 ↵Enter
Your guess is too high

Enter your guess: 6 ↵Enter
Your guess is too low

Enter your guess: 9 ↵Enter
Your guess is too high

Enter your guess: 7 ↵Enter
Your guess is too low

Enter your guess: 8 ↵Enter
Yes, the number is 8
```

intelligent guess

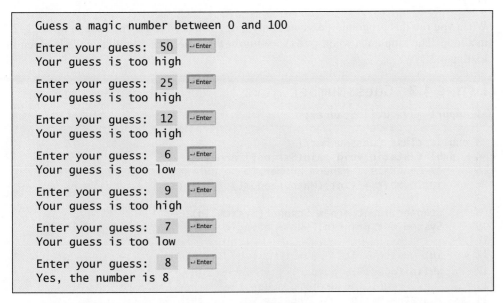

The magic number is between `0` and `100`. To minimize the number of guesses, enter `50` first. If your guess is too high, the magic number is between `0` and `49`. If your guess is too low, the magic number is between `51` and `100`. So, you can eliminate half of the numbers from further consideration after one guess.

think before coding

code incrementally

How do you write this program? Do you immediately begin coding? No. It is important to *think before coding*. Think how you would solve the problem without writing a program. You need first to generate a random number between 0 and 100, inclusively, then to prompt the user to enter a guess, and then to compare the guess with the random number.

It is a good practice to *code incrementally* one step at a time. For programs involving loops, if you don't know how to write a loop right away, you may first write the code for executing the loop one time, and then figure out how to repeatedly execute the code in a loop. For this program, you may create an initial draft, as shown in Listing 4.1:

Video Note
Guess a number

Listing 4.1 GuessNumberOneTime.java

generate a number · enter a guess · correct guess? · too high? · too low?

```
 1 import java.util.Scanner;
 2 
 3 public class GuessNumberOneTime {
 4   public static void main(String[] args) {
 5     // Generate a random number to be guessed
 6     int number = (int)(Math.random() * 101);
 7 
 8     Scanner input = new Scanner(System.in);
 9     System.out.println("Guess a magic number between 0 and 100");
10 
11     // Prompt the user to guess the number
12     System.out.print("\nEnter your guess: ");
13     int guess = input.nextInt();
14 
15     if (guess == number)
16       System.out.println("Yes, the number is " + number);
17     else if (guess > number)
18       System.out.println("Your guess is too high");
19     else
20       System.out.println("Your guess is too low");
21   }
22 }
```

When you run this program, it executes only once. You need to put the code in lines 11–20 in a loop. The loop ends when `guess == number` is true. The complete code is given in Listing 4.2.

Listing 4.2 GuessNumber.java

generate a number · enter a guess

```
import java.util.Scanner;

public class GuessNumber {
  public static void main(String[] args) {
    // Generate a random number to be guessed
    int number = (int)(Math.random() * 101);

    Scanner input = new Scanner(System.in);
    System.out.println("Guess a magic number between 0 and 100");

    int guess = -1;
    while (guess != number) {
      // Prompt the user to guess the number
      System.out.print("\nEnter your guess: ");
      guess = input.nextInt();

      if (guess == number)
        System.out.println("Yes, the number is " + number);
```

```
19       else if (guess > number)
20         System.out.println("Your guess is too high");
21       else
22         System.out.println("Your guess is too low");
23     }
24   } // End of loop
25 }
```

too high?

too low?

The program generates the magic number in line 6 and prompts the user to enter a guess continuously in a loop (lines 12–23). For each guess, the program checks whether the guess is correct, too high, or too low (lines 17–22). When the guess is correct, the program exits the loop (line 12). Note that `guess` is initialized to `-1`. Initializing it to a value between `0` and `100` would be wrong, because that could be the number to be guessed.

4.2.2 Problem: An Advanced Math Learning Tool

The Math subtraction learning tool program in Listing 3.4, SubtractionQuiz.java, generates just one question for each run. You can use a loop to generate questions repeatedly. Listing 4.3 gives a program that generates five questions and, after a student answers all five, reports the number of correct answers. The program also displays the time spent on the test and lists all the questions.

Listing 4.3 SubtractionQuizLoop.java

Video Note
Multiple subtraction quiz

```
import java.util.Scanner;

public class SubtractionQuizLoop {
  public static void main(String[] args) {
    final int NUMBER_OF_QUESTIONS = 5; // Number of questions
    int correctCount = 0; // Count the number of correct answers
    int count = 0; // Count the number of questions
    long startTime = System.currentTimeMillis();
    String output = ""; // output string is initially empty
    Scanner input = new Scanner(System.in);

    while (count < NUMBER_OF_QUESTIONS) {
      // 1. Generate two random single-digit integers
      int number1 = (int)(Math.random() * 10);
      int number2 = (int)(Math.random() * 10);

      // 2. If number1 < number2, swap number1 with number2
      if (number1 < number2) {
        int temp = number1;
        number1 = number2;
        number2 = temp;
      }

      // 3. Prompt the student to answer "What is number1 – number2?"
      System.out.print(
        "What is " + number1 + " - " + number2 + "? ");
      int answer = input.nextInt();

      // 4. Grade the answer and display the result
      if (number1 - number2 == answer) {
        System.out.println("You are correct!");
        correctCount++;
      }
      else
```

get start time

loop

display a question

grade an answer

increase correct count

increase control variable; prepare output; end loop; get end time; test time; display result

```
35         System.out.println("Your answer is wrong.\n" + number1
36           + " - " + number2 + " should be " + (number1 - number2));
37
38       // Increase the count
39       count++;
40
41       output += "\n" + number1 + "-" + number2 + "=" + answer +
42         ((number1 - number2 == answer) ? " correct" : " wrong");
43     }
44
45     long endTime = System.currentTimeMillis();
46     long testTime = endTime - startTime;
47
48     System.out.println("Correct count is " + correctCount +
49       "\nTest time is " + testTime / 1000 + " seconds\n" + output);
50   }
51 }
```

```
What is 9 – 2? 7 [Enter]
You are correct!

What is 3 – 0? 3 [Enter]
You are correct!

What is 3 – 2? 1 [Enter]
You are correct!

What is 7 – 4? 4 [Enter]
Your answer is wrong.
7 – 4 should be 3

What is 7 – 5? 4 [Enter]
Your answer is wrong.
7 – 5 should be 2

Correct count is 3
Test time is 1021 seconds

9–2=7 correct
3–0=3 correct
3–2=1 correct
7–4=4 wrong
7–5=4 wrong
```

The program uses the control variable **count** to control the execution of the loop. **count** is initially **0** (line 7) and is increased by **1** in each iteration (line 39). A subtraction question is displayed and processed in each iteration. The program obtains the time before the test starts in line 8 and the time after the test ends in line 45, and computes the test time in line 46. The test time is in milliseconds and is converted to seconds in line 49.

4.2.3 Controlling a Loop with a Sentinel Value

sentinel value

Another common technique for controlling a loop is to designate a special value when reading and processing a set of values. This special input value, known as a *sentinel value*, signifies the end of the loop.

Listing 4.4 writes a program that reads and calculates the sum of an unspecified number of integers. The input **0** signifies the end of the input. Do you need to declare a new variable for each input value? No. Just use one variable named **data** (line 12) to store the input value and use a variable named `sum` (line 15) to store the total. Whenever a value is read, assign it to `data` and, if it is not zero, add it to `sum` (line 17).

LISTING 4.4 SentinelValue.java

```
1 import java.util.Scanner;
2
3 public class SentinelValue {
4   /** Main method */
5   public static void main(String[] args) {
6     // Create a Scanner
7     Scanner input = new Scanner(System.in);
8
9     // Read an initial data
10    System.out.print(
11      "Enter an int value (the program exits if the input is 0): ");
12    int data = input.nextInt();
13
14    // Keep reading data until the input is 0
15    int sum = 0;
16    while (data != 0) {
17      sum += data;
18
19      // Read the next data
20      System.out.print(
21        "Enter an int value (the program exits if the input is 0): ");
22      data = input.nextInt();
23    }
24
25    System.out.println("The sum is " + sum);
26  }
27 }
```

input

loop

end of loop

display result

```
Enter an int value (the program exits if the input is 0): 2 ↵Enter
Enter an int value (the program exits if the input is 0): 3 ↵Enter
Enter an int value (the program exits if the input is 0): 4 ↵Enter
Enter an int value (the program exits if the input is 0): 0 ↵Enter
The sum is 9
```

If `data` is not `0`, it is added to `sum` (line 17) and the next item of input data is read (lines 20–22). If `data` is `0`, the loop body is no longer executed and the `while` loop terminates. The input value `0` is the sentinel value for this loop. Note that if the first input read is `0`, the loop body never executes, and the resulting sum is `0`.

Caution

Don't use floating-point values for equality checking in a loop control. Since floating-point values are approximations for some values, using them could result in imprecise counter values and inaccurate results. This example uses `int` value for `data`. If a floating-point type value is used for `data`, `(data != 0)` may be `true` even though `data` is exactly `0`.

Here is a good example provided by a reviewer of this book:

```
// data should be zero
double data = Math.pow(Math.sqrt(2), 2) - 2;

if (data == 0)
  System.out.println("data is zero");
```

```
else
  System.out.println("data is not zero");
```

numeric error

Like **pow**, **sqrt** is a method in the **Math** class for computing the square root of a number. The variable **data** in the above code should be zero, but it is not, because of rounding-off errors.

4.3 The do-while Loop

The **do-while** loop is a variation of the **while** loop. Its syntax is given below:

do-while loop

```
do {
  // Loop body;
  Statement(s);
} while (loop-continuation-condition);
```

Its execution flow chart is shown in Figure 4.2.

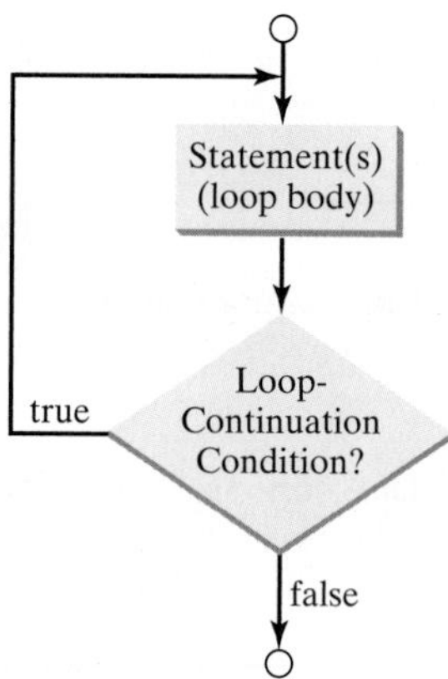

FIGURE 4.2 The **do-while** loop executes the loop body first, then checks the **loop-continuation-condition** to determine whether to continue or terminate the loop.

The loop body is executed first. Then the **loop-continuation-condition** is evaluated. If the evaluation is true, the loop body is executed again; if it is false, the **do-while** loop terminates. The difference between a **while** loop and a **do-while** loop is the order in which the **loop-continuation-condition** is evaluated and the loop body executed. The **while** loop and the **do-while** loop have equal expressive power. Sometimes one is a more convenient choice than the other. For example, you can rewrite the **while** loop in Listing 4.4 using a **do-while** loop, as shown in Listing 4.5:

LISTING 4.5 TestDoWhile.java

```
import java.util.Scanner;

public class TestDoWhile {
  /** Main method */
  public static void main(String[] args) {
    int data;
    int sum = 0;

    // Create a Scanner
    Scanner input = new Scanner(System.in);

```

```
    // Keep reading data until the input is 0
    do {
      // Read the next data
      System.out.print(
        "Enter an int value (the program exits if the input is 0): ");
      data = input.nextInt();

      sum += data;
    } while (data != 0);

    System.out.println("The sum is " + sum);
  }
}
```

loop

end loop

```
Enter an int value (the program exits if the input is 0): 3 ↵Enter
Enter an int value (the program exits if the input is 0): 5 ↵Enter
Enter an int value (the program exits if the input is 0): 6 ↵Enter
Enter an int value (the program exits if the input is 0): 0 ↵Enter
The sum is 14
```

Tip

Use the **do-while** loop if you have statements inside the loop that must be executed *at least once*, as in the case of the **do-while** loop in the preceding **TestDoWhile** program. These statements must appear before the loop as well as inside the loop if you use a **while** loop.

4.4 The **for** Loop

Often you write a loop in the following common form:

```
i = initialValue;  // Initialize loop control variable
while (i < endValue) {
  // Loop body
  ...
  i++; // Adjust loop control variable
}
```

A **for** loop can be used to simplify the proceding loop:

```
for (i = initialValue; i < endValue; i++) {
  // Loop body
  ...
}
```

In general, the syntax of a **for** loop is as shown below:

for loop

```
for (initial-action; loop-continuation-condition;
     action-after-each-iteration) {
  // Loop body;
  Statement(s);
}
```

The flow chart of the **for** loop is shown in Figure 4.3(a).

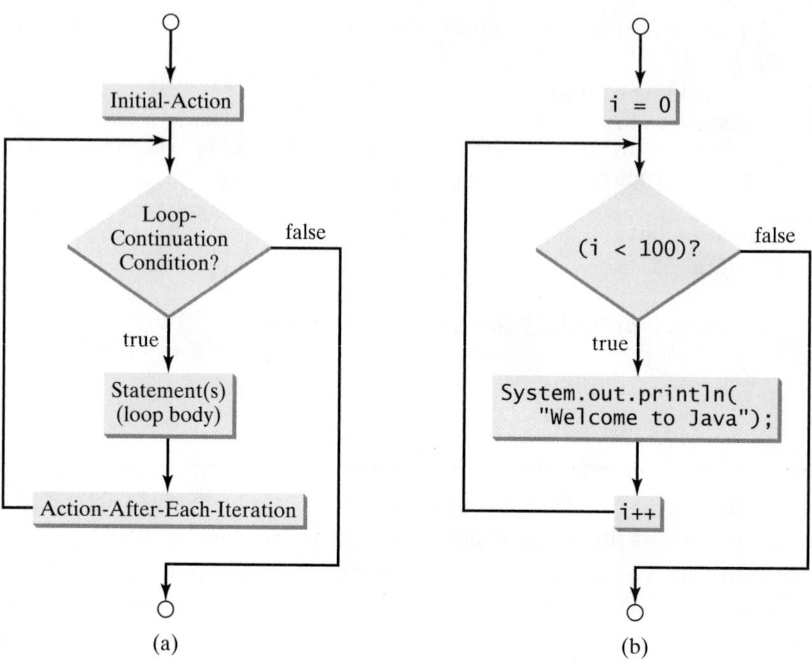

FIGURE 4.3 A `for` loop performs an initial action once, then repeatedly executes the statements in the loop body, and performs an action after an iteration when the `loop-continuation-condition` evaluates to `true`.

The `for` loop statement starts with the keyword `for`, followed by a pair of parentheses enclosing the control structure of the loop. This structure consists of `initial-action`, `loop-continuation-condition`, and `action-after-each-iteration`. The control structure is followed by the loop body enclosed inside braces. The `initial-action`, `loop-continuation-condition`, and `action-after-each-iteration` are separated by semicolons.

control variable

A `for` loop generally uses a variable to control how many times the loop body is executed and when the loop terminates. This variable is referred to as a *control variable*. The `initial-action` often initializes a control variable, the `action-after-each-iteration` usually increments or decrements the control variable, and the `loop-continuation-condition` tests whether the control variable has reached a termination value. For example, the following `for` loop prints `Welcome to Java!` a hundred times:

```
int i;
for (i = 0; i < 100; i++) {
  System.out.println("Welcome to Java!");
}
```

The flow chart of the statement is shown in Figure 4.3(b). The `for` loop initializes `i` to `0`, then repeatedly executes the `println` statement and evaluates `i++` while `i` is less than `100`.

`initial-action`

The `initial-action`, `i = 0`, initializes the control variable, `i`. The `loop-continuation-condition`, `i < 100`, is a Boolean expression. The expression is evaluated at the beginning of each iteration. If this condition is true, execute the loop body. If it is false, the loop terminates and the program control turns to the line following the loop.

`action-after-each-iteration`

The `action-after-each-iteration`, `i++`, is a statement that adjusts the control variable. This statement is executed after each iteration. It increments the control variable. Eventually, the value of the control variable should force the `loop-continuation-condition` to become false. Otherwise the loop is infinite.

The loop control variable can be declared and initialized in the for loop. Here is an example:

```
for (int i = 0; i < 100; i++) {
  System.out.println("Welcome to Java!");
}
```

If there is only one statement in the loop body, as in this example, the braces can be omitted. omitting braces

Tip

The control variable must be declared inside the control structure of the loop or before the loop. If the loop control variable is used only in the loop, and not elsewhere, it is good programming practice to declare it in the `initial-action` of the `for` loop. If the variable is declared inside the loop control structure, it cannot be referenced outside the loop. In the preceding code, for example, you cannot reference `i` outside the `for` loop, because it is declared inside the `for` loop. declare control variable

Note

The `initial-action` in a `for` loop can be a list of zero or more comma-separated variable declaration statements or assignment expressions. For example, for loop variations

```
for (int i = 0, j = 0; (i + j < 10); i++, j++) {
  // Do something
}
```

The `action-after-each-iteration` in a `for` loop can be a list of zero or more comma-separated statements. For example,

```
for (int i = 1; i < 100; System.out.println(i), i++);
```

This example is correct, but it is not a good example, because it makes the code difficult to read. Normally, you declare and initialize a control variable as an initial action, and increment or decrement the control variable as an action after each iteration.

Note

If the `loop-continuation-condition` in a `for` loop is omitted, it is implicitly true. Thus the statement given below in (a), which is an infinite loop, is correct. Nevertheless, it is better to use the equivalent loop in (c) to avoid confusion:

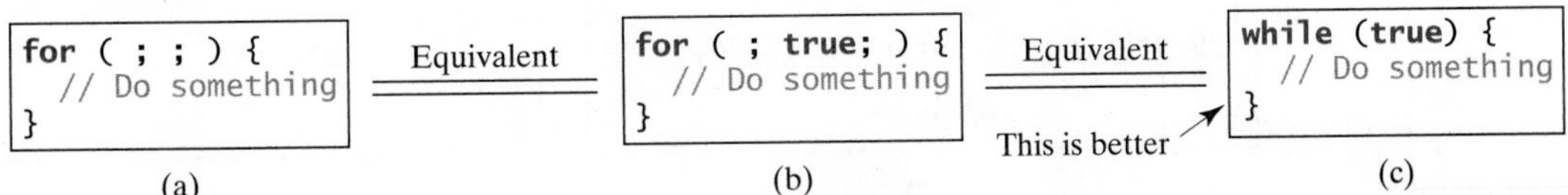

```
for ( ; ; ) {
  // Do something
}
```

(a)

Equivalent

```
for ( ; true; ) {
  // Do something
}
```

(b)

Equivalent

This is better

```
while (true) {
  // Do something
}
```

(c)

4.5 Which Loop to Use?

The `while` loop and `for` loop are called *pre-test loops* because the continuation condition is checked before the loop body is executed. The `do-while` loop is called a *post-test loop* because the condition is checked after the loop body is executed. The three forms of loop statements, `while`, `do-while`, and `for`, are expressively equivalent; that is, you can write a loop in any of these three forms. For example, a `while` loop in (a) in the following figure can always be converted into the `for` loop in (b): pre-test loop post-test loop

```
while (loop-continuation-condition) {
  // Loop body
}
```

(a)

Equivalent

```
for ( ; loop-continuation-condition; ) {
  // Loop body
}
```

(b)

A **for** loop in (a) in the next figure can generally be converted into the **while** loop in (b) except in certain special cases (see Review Question 4.13 for such a case):

```
for (initial-action;
     loop-continuation-condition;
     action-after-each-iteration) {
  // Loop body;
}
```

(a)

Equivalent

```
initial-action;
while (loop-continuation-condition) {
  // Loop body;
  action-after-each-iteration;
}
```

(b)

Use the loop statement that is most intuitive and comfortable for you. In general, a **for** loop may be used if the number of repetitions is known, as, for example, when you need to print a message a hundred times. A **while** loop may be used if the number of repetitions is not known, as in the case of reading the numbers until the input is 0. A **do-while** loop can be used to replace a **while** loop if the loop body has to be executed before the continuation condition is tested.

Caution

Adding a semicolon at the end of the **for** clause before the loop body is a common mistake, as shown below in (a). In (a), the semicolon signifies the end of the loop prematurely. The loop body is actually empty, as shown in (b). (a) and (b) are equivalent.

Error

```
for (int i = 0; i < 10; i++);
{
  System.out.println("i is " + i);
}
```

(a)

Empty Body

```
for (int i = 0; i < 10; i++)  { };
{
  System.out.println("i is " + i);
}
```

(b)

Similarly, the loop in (c) is also wrong. (c) is equivalent to (d).

Error

```
int i = 0;
while (i < 10);
{
  System.out.println("i is " + i);
  i++;
}
```

(c)

Empty Body

```
int i = 0;
while (i < 10) { };
{
  System.out.println("i is " + i);
  i++;
}
```

(d)

These errors often occur when you use the next-line block style. Using the end-of-line block style can avoid errors of this type.

In the case of the **do-while** loop, the semicolon is needed to end the loop.

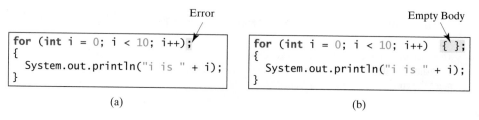

```
int i = 0;
do {
  System.out.println("i is " + i);
  i++;
} while (i < 10);
```

Correct

4.6 Nested Loops

Nested loops consist of an outer loop and one or more inner loops. Each time the outer loop is repeated, the inner loops are reentered, and started anew.

Listing 4.6 presents a program that uses nested **for** loops to print a multiplication table.

LISTING 4.6 `MultiplicationTable.java`

```
1 public class MultiplicationTable {
2   /** Main method */
3   public static void main(String[] args) {
4     // Display the table heading
5     System.out.println("           Multiplication Table");
6
7     // Display the number title
8     System.out.print("    ");
9     for (int j = 1; j <= 9; j++)
10      System.out.print("   " + j);
11
12    System.out.println("\n-----------------------------------------");
13    String output = "";
14
15    // Print table body
16    for (int i = 1; i <= 9; i++) {
17      output += i + " | ";
18      for (int j = 1; j <= 9; j++) {
19        // Display the product and align properly
20        if (i * j < 10)
21          output += "   " + i * j;
22        else
23          output += "  " + i * j;
24      }
25      output += "\n";
26    }
27
28    // Display result
29    System.out.println(output);
30  }
31 }
```

table title (line 5)

table body (line 16)

nested loop (line 18)

```
           Multiplication Table
         1   2   3   4   5   6   7   8   9
-----------------------------------------
1 |      1   2   3   4   5   6   7   8   9
2 |      2   4   6   8  10  12  14  16  18
3 |      3   6   9  12  15  18  21  24  27
4 |      4   8  12  16  20  24  28  32  36
5 |      5  10  15  20  25  30  35  40  45
6 |      6  12  18  24  30  36  42  48  54
7 |      7  14  21  28  35  42  49  56  63
8 |      8  16  24  32  40  48  56  64  72
9 |      9  18  27  36  45  54  63  72  81
```

The program displays a title (line 5) on the first line in the output. The first **for** loop (lines 9-10) displays the numbers **1** through **9** on the second line. A dash (**-**) line is displayed on the third line (line 12).

The next loop (lines 16–26) is a nested **for** loop with the control variable **i** in the outer loop and **j** in the inner loop. For each **i**, the product **i * j** is displayed on a line in the inner loop, with j being 1, 2, 3, ..., 9. The if statement in the inner loop (lines 20–23) is used so that the product will be aligned properly. If the product is a single digit, it is displayed with an extra space before it.

Video Note
Minimize numeric errors

4.7 Minimizing Numeric Errors

Numeric errors involving floating-point numbers are inevitable. This section discusses how to minimize such errors through an example.

Listing 4.7 presents an example summing a series that starts with 0.01 and ends with 1.0. The numbers in the series will increment by 0.01, as follows: 0.01 + 0.02 + 0.03 and so on.

LISTING 4.7 TestSum.java

loop

```
 1 public class TestSum {
 2   public static void main(String[] args) {
 3     // Initialize sum
 4     float sum = 0;
 5
 6     // Add 0.01, 0.02, ..., 0.99, 1 to sum
 7     for (float i = 0.01f; i <= 1.0f; i = i + 0.01f)
 8       sum += i;
 9
10     // Display result
11     System.out.println("The sum is " + sum);
12   }
13 }
```

```
The sum is 50.499985
```

The for loop (lines 7-8) repeatedly adds the control variable i to sum. This variable, which begins with 0.01, is incremented by 0.01 after each iteration. The loop terminates when i exceeds 1.0.

The for loop initial action can be any statement, but it is often used to initialize a control variable. From this example, you can see that a control variable can be a float type. In fact, it can be any data type.

double precision

The exact sum should be 50.50, but the answer is 50.499985. The result is imprecise because computers use a fixed number of bits to represent floating-point numbers, and thus cannot represent some floating-point numbers exactly. If you change float in the program to double, as follows, you should see a slight improvement in precision, because a double variable takes 64 bits, whereas a float variable takes 32 bits.

```
// Initialize sum
double sum = 0;

// Add 0.01, 0.02, ..., 0.99, 1 to sum
for (double i = 0.01; i <= 1.0; i = i + 0.01)
  sum += i;
```

numeric error

However, you will be stunned to see that the result is actually 49.50000000000003. What went wrong? If you print out i for each iteration in the loop, you will see that the last i is slightly larger than 1 (not exactly 1). This causes the last i not to be added into sum. The fundamental problem is that the floating-point numbers are represented by approximation. To fix the problem, use an integer count to ensure that all the numbers are added to sum. Here is the new loop:

```
double currentValue = 0.01;

for (int count = 0; count < 100; count++) {
  sum += currentValue;
  currentValue += 0.01;
}
```

After this loop, sum is 50.50000000000003. This loop adds the numbers from small to big. What happens if you add numbers from big to small (i.e., 1.0, 0.99, 0.98, ..., 0.02, 0.01 in this order) as follows:

```
double currentValue = 1.0;

for (int count = 0; count < 100; count++) {
  sum += currentValue;
  currentValue -= 0.01;
}
```

After this loop, sum is 50.49999999999995. Adding from big to small is less accurate than adding from small to big. This phenomenon is an artifact of the finite-precision arithmetic. Adding a very small number to a very big number can have no effect if the true result requires more precision than the variable can store. For example, the inaccurate result of 100000000.0 + 0.000000001 is 100000000.0. To obtain more accurate results, carefully select the order of computation. Adding the smaller numbers before the big numbers is one way to minimize error.

avoiding numeric error

4.8 Case Studies

Loop are fundamental in programming. The ability to write loops is essential in learning Java programming. *If you can write programs using loops, you know how to program!* For this reason, this section presents three additional examples of solving problems using loops.

4.8.1 Problem: Finding the Greatest Common Divisor

The greatest common divisor of two integers 4 and 2 is 2. The greatest common divisor of two integers 16 and 24 is 8. How do you find the greatest common divisor? Let the two input integers be n1 and n2. You know that number 1 is a common divisor, but it may not be the greatest common divisor. So you can check whether k (for k = 2, 3, 4, and so on) is a common divisor for n1 and n2, until k is greater than n1 or n2. Store the common divisor in a variable named gcd. Initially, gcd is 1. Whenever a new common divisor is found, it becomes the new gcd. When you have checked all the possible common divisors from 2 up to n1 or n2, the value in variable gcd is the greatest common divisor. The idea can be translated into the following loop:

GCD

```
int gcd = 1;
int k = 2;

while (k <= n1 && k <= n2) {
  if (n1 % k == 0 && n2 % k == 0)
    gcd = k;
  k++;
}

// After the loop, gcd is the greatest common divisor for n1 and n2
```

Listing 4.8 presents the program that prompts the user to enter two positive integers and finds their greatest common divisor.

LISTING 4.8 GreatestCommonDivisor.java

```
import java.util.Scanner;

public class GreatestCommonDivisor {
  /** Main method */
  public static void main(String[] args) {
    // Create a Scanner
    Scanner input = new Scanner(System.in);

    // Prompt the user to enter two integers
    System.out.print("Enter first integer: ");
    int n1 = input.nextInt();
    System.out.print("Enter second integer: ");
    int n2 = input.nextInt();

    int gcd = 1;
    int k = 2;
    while (k <= n1 && k <= n2) {
      if (n1 % k == 0 && n2 % k == 0)
        gcd = k;
      k++;
    }

    System.out.println("The greatest common divisor for " + n1 +
      " and " + n2 + " is " + gcd);
  }
}
```

input

input

gcd

check divisor

output

```
Enter first integer: 125 ↵Enter
Enter second integer: 2525 ↵Enter
The greatest common divisor for 125 and 2525 is 25
```

think before you type

How did you write this program? Did you immediately begin to write the code? No. It is important to *think before you type*. Thinking enables you to generate a logical solution for the problem without concern about how to write the code. Once you have a logical solution, type the code to translate the solution into a Java program. The translation is not unique. For example, you could use a `for` loop to rewrite the code as follows:

```
for (int k = 2; k <= n1 && k <= n2; k++) {
  if (n1 % k == 0 && n2 % k == 0)
    gcd = k;
}
```

multiple solutions

A problem often has multiple solutions. The GCD problem can be solved in many ways. Exercise 4.15 suggests another solution. A more efficient solution is to use the classic Euclidean algorithm. See http://www.cut-the-knot.org/blue/Euclid.shtml for more information.

erroneous solutions

You might think that a divisor for a number `n1` cannot be greater than `n1 / 2`. So you would attempt to improve the program using the following loop:

```
for (int k = 2; k <= n1 / 2 && k <= n2 / 2; k++) {
  if (n1 % k == 0 && n2 % k == 0)
    gcd = k;
}
```

This revision is wrong. Can you find the reason? See Review Question 4.10 for the answer.

4.8.2 Problem: Finding the Sales Amount

You have just started a sales job in a department store. Your pay consists of a base salary and a commission. The base salary is $5,000. The scheme shown below is used to determine the commission rate.

Sales Amount	Commission Rate
$0.01–$5,000	8 percent
$5,000.01–$10,000	10 percent
$10,000.01 and above	12 percent

Your goal is to earn $30,000 a year. This section writes a program that finds the minimum amount of sales you have to generate in order to make $30,000.

Since your base salary is $5,000, you have to make $25,000 in commissions to earn $30,000 a year. What is the sales amount for a $25,000 commission? If you know the sales amount, the commission can be computed as follows:

```
if (salesAmount >= 10000.01)
  commission =
    5000 * 0.08 + 5000 * 0.1 + (salesAmount - 10000) * 0.12;
else if (salesAmount >= 5000.01)
  commission = 5000 * 0.08 + (salesAmount - 5000) * 0.10;
else
  commission = salesAmount * 0.08;
```

This suggests that you can try to find the `salesAmount` to match a given commission through incremental approximation. For `salesAmount` of $0.01 (1 cent), find `commission`. If `commission` is less than $25,000, increment `salesAmount` by 0.01 and find commission again. If `commission` is still less than $25,000, repeat the process until it is greater than or equal to $25,000. This is a tedious job for humans, but it is exactly what a computer is good for. You can write a loop and let a computer execute it painlessly. The idea can be translated into the following loop:

```
Set COMMISSION_SOUGHT as a constant;
Set an initial salesAmount;

do {
  Increase salesAmount by 1 cent;
  Compute the commission from the current salesAmount;
} while (commission < COMMISSION_SOUGHT);
```

The complete program is given in Listing 4.9.

LISTING 4.9 `FindSalesAmount.java`

constants

loop

```
public class FindSalesAmount {
  /** Main method */
  public static void main(String[] args) {
    // The commission sought
    final double COMMISSION_SOUGHT = 25000;
    final double INITIAL_SALES_AMOUNT = 0.01;
    double commission = 0;
    double salesAmount = INITIAL_SALES_AMOUNT;

    do {
```

compute commission

end loop

output

```
11        // Increase salesAmount by 1 cent
12        salesAmount += 0.01;
13
14        // Compute the commission from the current salesAmount;
15        if (salesAmount >= 10000.01)
16          commission =
17            5000 * 0.08 + 5000 * 0.1 + (salesAmount - 10000) * 0.12;
18        else if (salesAmount >= 5000.01)
19          commission = 5000 * 0.08 + (salesAmount - 5000) * 0.10;
20        else
21          commission = salesAmount * 0.08;
22      } while (commission < COMMISSION_SOUGHT);
23
24      // Display the sales amount
25      System.out.println(
26        "The sales amount $" + (int)(salesAmount * 100) / 100.0 +
27        "\nis needed to make a commission of $" + COMMISSION_SOUGHT);
28    }
29  }
```

```
The sales amount $210833.34
is needed to make a commission of $25000.0
```

The do-while loop (lines 10–22) is used to repeatedly compute commission for an incremental salesAmount. The loop terminates when commission is greater than or equal to a constant COMMISSION_SOUGHT.

In Exercise 4.17, you will rewrite this program to let the user enter COMMISSION_SOUGHT dynamically from an input dialog.

You can improve the performance of this program by estimating a higher INITIAL_SALES_AMOUNT (e.g., 25000).

What is wrong if salesAmount is incremented after the commission is computed, as follows?

```
do {
  // Compute the commission from the current salesAmount;
  if (salesAmount >= 10000.01)
    commission =
      5000 * 0.08 + 5000 * 0.1 + (salesAmount - 10000) * 0.12;
  else if (salesAmount >= 5000.01)
    commission = 5000 * 0.08 + (salesAmount - 5000) * 0.10;
  else
    commission = salesAmount * 0.08;

  // Increase salesAmount by 1 cent
  salesAmount += 0.01;
} while (commission < COMMISSION_SOUGHT);
```

off-by-one error

The change is erroneous because, when the loop ends, salesAmount is 1 cent more than is needed for the commission. This is a common error in loops, known as the *off-by-one* error.

Tip

constants

This example uses constants COMMISSION_SOUGHT and INITIAL_SALES_AMOUNT. Using constants makes programs easy to read and maintain.

4.8.3 Problem: Displaying a Pyramid of Numbers

The problem is to write a program that prompts the user to enter an integer from `1` to `15` and displays a pyramid, as shown in the following sample output:

```
Enter the number of lines: 11 ↵Enter
                                1
                             2  1  2
                          3  2  1  2  3
                       4  3  2  1  2  3  4
                    5  4  3  2  1  2  3  4  5
                 6  5  4  3  2  1  2  3  4  5  6
              7  6  5  4  3  2  1  2  3  4  5  6  7
           8  7  6  5  4  3  2  1  2  3  4  5  6  7  8
        9  8  7  6  5  4  3  2  1  2  3  4  5  6  7  8  9
    10  9  8  7  6  5  4  3  2  1  2  3  4  5  6  7  8  9 10
 11 10  9  8  7  6  5  4  3  2  1  2  3  4  5  6  7  8  9 10 11
```

Your program receives the input for an integer (`numberOfLines`) that represents the total number of lines. It displays all the lines one by one. Each line has three parts. The first part comprises the spaces before the numbers; the second part, the leading numbers, such as `3 2 1` in line 3; and the last part, the ending numbers, such as `2 3` in line 3.

Each number occupies three spaces. Display an empty space before a double-digit number, and display two empty spaces before a single-digit number.

You can use an outer loop to control the lines. At the nth row, there are `(numberOfLines – n) * 3` leading spaces, the leading numbers are `n`, `n-1`, . . . , `1`, and the ending numbers are `2`, . . . , `n`. You can use three separate inner loops to print each part.

Here is the algorithm for the problem:

```
Input numberOfLines;

for (int row = 1; row <= numberOfLines; row++) {
  Print (numberOfLines - row) * 3 leading spaces;
  Print leading numbers row, row - 1, ..., 1;
  Print ending numbers 2, 3, ..., row - 1, row;
  Start a new line;
}
```

The complete program is given in Listing 4.10.

LISTING 4.10 PrintPyramid.java

```java
import java.util.Scanner;

public class PrintPyramid {
  public static void main(String[] args) {
    // Create a Scanner
    Scanner input = new Scanner(System.in);

    // Prompt the user to enter the number of lines
    System.out.print("Enter the number of lines: ");
    int numberOfLines = input.nextInt();

    if (numberOfLines < 1 || numberOfLines > 15) {
      System.out.println("You must enter a number from 1 to 15");
      System.exit(0);
    }
```

print lines
print spaces
print leading numbers
print ending numbers
a new line

```
16
17      // Print lines
18      for (int row = 1; row <= numberOfLines; row++) {
19        // Print NUMBER_OF_LINES - row) leading spaces
20        for (int column = 1; column <= numberOfLines - row; column++)
21          System.out.print("   ");
22
23        // Print leading numbers row, row - 1, ..., 1
24        for (int num = row; num >= 1; num--)
25          System.out.print((num >= 10) ? " " + num : "  " + num);
26
27        // Print ending numbers 2, 3, ..., row - 1, row
28        for (int num = 2; num <= row; num++)
29          System.out.print((num >= 10) ? " " + num : "  " + num);
30
31        // Start a new line
32        System.out.println();
33      }
34    }
35 }
```

The program uses the **print** method (lines 21, 25, and 29) to display a string to the console. The conditional expression **(num >= 10) ? " "+ num : " " + num** in lines 25 and 29 returns a string with a single empty space before the number if the number is greater than or equal to **10**, and otherwise returns a string with two empty spaces before the number.

Printing patterns like this one and the ones in Exercises 4.18 and 4.19 are good exercise for practicing loop control statements. The key is to understand the pattern and to describe it using loop control variables.

The last line in the outer loop (line 32), **System.out.println()**, does not have any argument in the method. This call moves the cursor to the next line.

4.9 Keywords **break** and **continue**

Two keywords, **break** and **continue**, can be used in loop statements to provide additional control.

break

- **break** immediately ends the innermost loop that contains it. In other words, **break** breaks out of a loop.

continue

- **continue** ends only the current iteration. Program control goes to the end of the loop body. In other words, **continue** breaks out of an iteration.

You have already used the keyword **break** in a **switch** statement. You can also use **break** and **continue** in a loop. Normally, these two keywords are used with an **if** statement. Listings 4.11 and 4.12 present two programs to demonstrate the effect of the **break** and **continue** keywords in a loop.

The program in Listing 4.11 adds the integers from **1** to **20** in this order to **sum** until **sum** is greater than or equal to **100**. Without the **if** statement (line 9), the program calculates the sum of the numbers from **1** to **20**. But with the **if** statement, the loop terminates when **sum** becomes greater than or equal to **100**.

LISTING 4.11 TestBreak.java

```
1 public class TestBreak {
2   public static void main(String[] args) {
3     int sum = 0;
4     int number = 0;
5
```

```
    while (number < 20) {
      number++;
      sum += number;
      if (sum >= 100) break;
    }

    System.out.println("The number is " + number);
    System.out.println("The sum is " + sum);
  }
}
```

break

```
The number is 14
The sum is 105
```

If you changed the `if` statement as shown below,

```
if (sum == 100) break;
```

the output would be as follows:

```
The number is 20
The sum is 210
```

In this case, the `if` condition will never be true. Therefore, the `break` statement will never be executed.

The program in Listing 4.12 adds all the integers from `1` to `20` except `10` and `11` to `sum`. With the `if` statement in the program (line 8), the `continue` statement is executed when number becomes `10` or `11`. The `continue` statement ends the current iteration so that the rest of the statement in the loop body is not executed; therefore, number is not added to `sum` when it is `10` or `11`.

LISTING 4.12 TestContinue.java

```
1 public class TestContinue {
2   public static void main(String[] args) {
3     int sum = 0;
4     int number = 0;
5
6     while (number < 20) {
7       number++;
8       if (number == 10 || number == 11) continue;
9       sum += number;
10    }
11
12    System.out.println("The sum is " + sum);
13  }
14 }
```

continue

```
The sum is 189
```

Without the `if` statement in the program, the output would be as follows:

```
The sum is 210
```

In this case, all of the numbers are added to **sum**, even when **number** is 10 or 11. Therefore, the result is **210**, which is **21** more than it was with the **if** statement.

Note

The **continue** statement is always inside a loop. In the **while** and **do-while** loops, the **loop-continuation-condition** is evaluated immediately after the **continue** statement. In the **for** loop, the **action-after-each-iteration** is performed, then the **loop-continuation-condition** is evaluated immediately after the **continue** statement.

You can always write a program without using **break** or **continue** in a loop. See Review Question 4.14. In general, it is appropriate to use **break** and **continue** if their use simplifies coding and makes programs easier to read.

Listing 4.2 gives a program for guessing a number. You can rewrite it using a **break** statement, as shown in Listing 4.13.

LISTING 4.13 GuessNumberUsingBreak.java

generate a number

loop continuously

enter a guess

break

```
import java.util.Scanner;

public class GuessNumberUsingBreak {
  public static void main(String[] args) {
    // Generate a random number to be guessed
    int number = (int)(Math.random() * 101);

    Scanner input = new Scanner(System.in);
    System.out.println("Guess a magic number between 0 and 100");

    while (true) {
      // Prompt the user to guess the number
      System.out.print("\nEnter your guess: ");
      int guess = input.nextInt();

      if (guess == number) {
        System.out.println("Yes, the number is " + number);
        break;
      }
      else if (guess > number)
        System.out.println("Your guess is too high");
      else
        System.out.println("Your guess is too low");
    } // End of loop
  }
}
```

Using the **break** statement makes the program simpler and easier to read.

Note

goto

Some programming languages have a **goto** statement. The **goto** statement would indiscriminately transfer the control to any statement in the program and execute it. Using it will make your program vulnerable to errors. The **break** and **continue** statements in Java are different from **goto** statements. They operate only in a loop or a switch statement. The **break** statement breaks out of the loop, and the **continue** statement breaks out of the current iteration in the loop.

4.9.1 Problem: Displaying Prime Numbers

An integer greater than 1 is *prime* if its only positive divisor is 1 or itself. For example, 2, 3, 5, and 7 are prime numbers, but 4, 6, 8, and 9 are not.

The problem is to display the first 50 prime numbers in five lines, each of which contains ten numbers. The problem can be broken into the following tasks:

- Determine whether a given number is prime.
- For number = 2, 3, 4, 5, 6, ..., test whether it is prime.
- Count the prime numbers.
- Print each prime number, and print ten numbers per line.

Obviously, you need to write a loop and repeatedly test whether a new **number** is prime. If the **number** is prime, increase the count by 1. The **count** is 0 initially. When it reaches 50, the loop terminates.

Here is the algorithm for the problem:

```
Set the number of prime numbers to be printed as
  a constant NUMBER_OF_PRIMES;
Use count to track the number of prime numbers and
  set an initial count to 0;
Set an initial number to 2;

while (count < NUMBER_OF_PRIMES) {
  Test if number is prime;

  if number is prime {
    Print the prime number and increase the count;
  }

  Increment number by 1;
}
```

To test whether a number is prime, check whether it is divisible by 2, 3, 4, up to **number/2**. If a divisor is found, the number is not a prime. The algorithm can be described as follows:

```
Use a boolean variable isPrime to denote whether
  the number is prime; Set isPrime to true initially;

for (int divisor = 2; divisor <= number / 2; divisor++) {
  if (number % divisor == 0) {
    Set isPrime to false
    Exit the loop;
  }
}
```

The complete program is given in Listing 4.14.

LISTING 4.14 PrimeNumber.java

```
public class PrimeNumber {
  public static void main(String[] args) {
    final int NUMBER_OF_PRIMES = 50; // Number of primes to display
    final int NUMBER_OF_PRIMES_PER_LINE = 10; // Display 10 per line
    int count = 0; // Count the number of prime numbers
    int number = 2; // A number to be tested for primeness

```

count prime numbers

check primeness

exit loop

print if prime

```
8       System.out.println("The first 50 prime numbers are \n");
9
10      // Repeatedly find prime numbers
11      while (count < NUMBER_OF_PRIMES) {
12        // Assume the number is prime
13        boolean isPrime = true; // Is the current number prime?
14
15        // Test if number is prime
16        for (int divisor = 2; divisor <= number / 2; divisor++) {
17          if (number % divisor == 0) { // If true, number is not prime
18            isPrime = false; // Set isPrime to false
19            break; // Exit the for loop
20          }
21        }
22
23        // Print the prime number and increase the count
24        if (isPrime) {
25          count++; // Increase the count
26
27          if (count % NUMBER_OF_PRIMES_PER_LINE == 0) {
28            // Print the number and advance to the new line
29            System.out.println(number);
30          }
31          else
32            System.out.print(number + " ");
33        }
34
35        // Check if the next number is prime
36        number++;
37      }
38    }
39  }
```

```
The first 50 prime numbers are

2 3 5 7 11 13 17 19 23 29
31 37 41 43 47 53 59 61 67 71
73 79 83 89 97 101 103 107 109 113
127 131 137 139 149 151 157 163 167 173
179 181 191 193 197 199 211 223 227 229
```

subproblem

This is a complex program for novice programmers. The key to developing a programmatic solution to this problem, and to many other problems, is to break it into subproblems and develop solutions for each of them in turn. Do not attempt to develop a complete solution in the first trial. Instead, begin by writing the code to determine whether a given number is prime, then expand the program to test whether other numbers are prime in a loop.

To determine whether a number is prime, check whether it is divisible by a number between 2 and number/2 inclusive. If so, it is not a prime number; otherwise, it is a prime number. For a prime number, display it. If the count is divisible by 10, advance to a new line. The program ends when the count reaches 50.

The program uses the break statement in line 19 to exit the for loop as soon as the number is found to be a nonprime. You can rewrite the loop (lines 16-21) without using the break statement, as follows:

```
for (int divisor = 2; divisor <= number / 2 && isPrime;
     divisor++) {
```

```
    // If true, the number is not prime
    if (number % divisor == 0) {
      // Set isPrime to false, if the number is not prime
      isPrime = false;
    }
  }
```

However, using the **break** statement makes the program simpler and easier to read in this case.

4.10 (GUI) Controlling a Loop with a Confirmation Dialog

confirmation dialog

A sentinel-controlled loop can be implemented using a confirmation dialog. The answers *Yes* or *No* continue or terminate the loop. The template of the loop may look as follows:

```
int option = 0;
while (option == JOptionPane.YES_OPTION) {
  System.out.println("continue loop");
  option = JOptionPane.showConfirmDialog(null, "Continue?");
}
```

Listing 4.15 rewrites Listing 4.4, SentinelValue.java, using a confirmation dialog box. A sample run is shown in Figure 4.4.

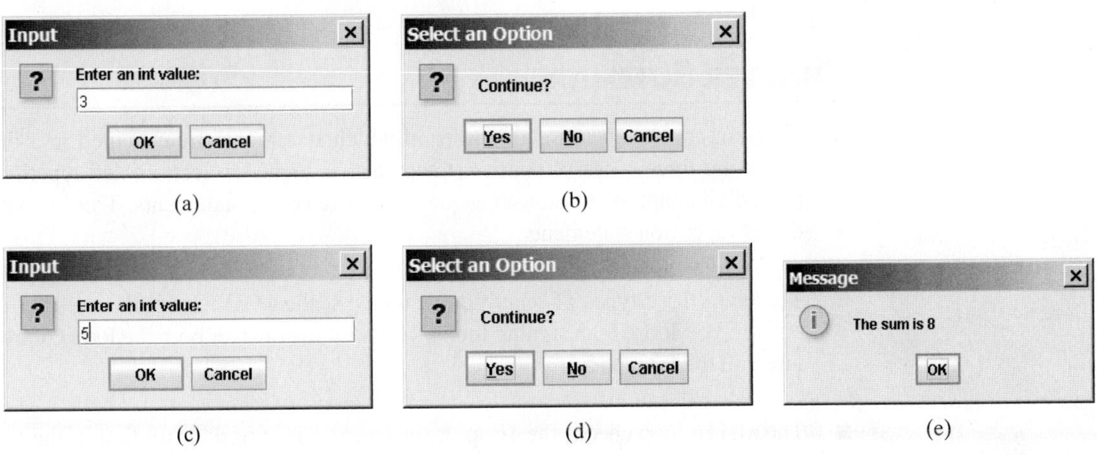

FIGURE 4.4 The user enters 3 in (a), clicks Yes in (b), enters 5 in (c), clicks No in (d), and the result is shown in (e).

LISTING 4.15 SentinelValueUsingConfirmationDialog.java

```
import javax.swing.JOptionPane;

public class SentinelValueUsingConfirmationDialog {
  public static void main(String[] args) {
    int sum = 0;

    // Keep reading data until the user answers No
    int option = 0;
    while (option == JOptionPane.YES_OPTION) {
      // Read the next data
      String dataString = JOptionPane.showInputDialog(
        "Enter an int value: ");
      int data = Integer.parseInt(dataString);

```

confirmation option

check option

input dialog

confirmation dialog

message dialog

```
15         sum += data;
16
17         option = JOptionPane.showConfirmDialog(null, "Continue?");
18       }
19
20       JOptionPane.showMessageDialog(null, "The sum is " + sum);
21     }
22 }
```

A program displays an input dialog to prompt the user to enter an integer (line 11) and adds it to `sum` (line 15). Line 17 displays a confirmation dialog to let the user decide whether to continue the input. If the user clicks *Yes*, the loop continues; otherwise the loop exits. Finally the program displays the result in a message dialog box (line 20).

Key Terms

`break` statement 122
`continue` statement 122
loop control structure 113
infinite loop 105
iteration 104
labeled continue statement 123
loop 104
`loop-continuation-condition` 104
loop body 104
nested loop 115
off-by-one error 120
sentinel value 108

Chapter Summary

- Program control specifies the order in which statements are executed in a program. There are three types of control statements: sequence, selection, and repetition. The preceding chapters introduced sequence and selection statements. This chapter introduced repetition statements.

- There are three types of repetition statements: the `while` loop, the `do-while` loop, and the `for` loop. In designing loops, you need to consider both the loop control structure and the loop body.

- The `while` loop checks the `loop-continuation-condition` first. If the condition is `true`, the loop body is executed; if it is `false`, the loop terminates. The `do-while` loop is similar to the `while` loop, except that the `do-while` loop executes the loop body first and then checks the `loop-continuation-condition` to decide whether to continue or to terminate.

- Since the `while` loop and the `do-while` loop contain the `loop-continuation-condition`, which is dependent on the loop body, the number of repetitions is determined by the loop body. The `while` loop and the `do-while` loop are often used when the number of repetitions is unspecified.

- The `for` loop is generally used to execute a loop body a predictable number of times; this number is not determined by the loop body. The loop control has three parts. The first part is an initial action that often initializes a control variable. The second part, the `loop-continuation-condition`, determines whether the loop body is to be executed. The third part is executed after each iteration and is often used to adjust the control variable. Usually, the loop control variables are initialized and changed in the control structure.

- Two keywords, break and continue, can be used in a loop. The keyword break breaks out of a loop. The keyword continue breaks out of an iteration.

Review Questions

Sections 4.2–4.4

4.1 What is wrong if guess is initialized to 0 in line 11 in Listing 4.1?

4.2 How many times is the following loop body repeated? What is the printout of the loop?

```
int i = 1;
while (i > 10)
  if ((i++) % 2 == 0)
    System.out.println(i);
```

(a)

```
int i = 1;
while (i < 10)
  if ((i++) % 2 == 0)
    System.out.println(i);
```

(b)

4.3 What are the differences between a while loop and a do-while loop?

4.4 Do the following two loops result in the same value in sum?

```
for (int i = 0; i < 10; ++i) {
  sum += i;
}
```

(a)

```
for (int i = 0; i < 10; i++) {
  sum += i;
}
```

(b)

4.5 What are the three parts of a for loop control? Write a for loop that prints the numbers from 1 to 100.

4.6 What does the following statement do?

```
for ( ; ; ) {
  do something;
}
```

4.7 If a variable is declared in the for loop control, can it be used after the loop exits?

4.8 Can you convert a for loop to a while loop? List the advantages of using for loops.

4.9 Convert the following for loop statement to a while loop and to a do-while loop:

```
long sum = 0;
for (int i = 0; i <= 1000; i++)
  sum = sum + i;
```

4.10 Will the program work if n1 and n2 are replaced by n1 / 2 and n2 / 2 in line 15 in Listing 4.8?

Section 4.9 Keywords break and continue

4.11 What is the keyword break for? What is the keyword continue for? Will the following program terminate? If so, give the output.

```
int balance = 1000;
while (true) {
  if (balance < 9)
    break;
  balance = balance - 9;
}

System.out.println("Balance is "
  + balance);
```

(a)

```
int balance = 1000;
while (true) {
  if (balance < 9)
    continue;
  balance = balance - 9;
}

System.out.println("Balance is "
  + balance);
```

(b)

4.12 Can you always convert a `while` loop into a `for` loop? Convert the following `while` loop into a `for` loop.

```
int i = 1;
int sum = 0;
while (sum < 10000) {
  sum = sum + i;
  i++;
}
```

4.13 The `for` loop on the left is converted into the `while` loop on the right. What is wrong? Correct it.

```
for (int i = 0; i < 4; i++) {
  if (i % 3 == 0) continue;
  sum += i;
}
```

Converted
Wrong conversion

```
int i = 0;
while (i < 4) {
  if(i % 3 == 0) continue;
  sum += i;
  i++;
}
```

4.14 Rewrite the programs `TestBreak` and `TestContinue` in Listings 4.9 and 4.10 without using `break` and `continue`.

4.15 After the `break` statement is executed in the following loop, which statement is executed? Show the output.

```
for (int i = 1; i < 4; i++) {
  for (int j = 1; j < 4; j++) {
    if (i * j > 2)
      break;

    System.out.println(i * j);
  }

  System.out.println(i);
}
```

4.16 After the `continue` statement is executed in the following loop, which statement is executed? Show the output.

```
for (int i = 1; i < 4; i++) {
  for (int j = 1; j < 4; j++) {
    if (i * j > 2)
      continue;

    System.out.println(i * j);
  }
```

```
    System.out.println(i);
  }
```

Comprehensive

4.17 Identify and fix the errors in the following code:

```
public class Test {
  public void main(String[] args) {
    for (int i = 0; i < 10; i++);
      sum += i;

    if (i < j);
      System.out.println(i)
    else
      System.out.println(j);

    while (j < 10);
    {
      j++;
    };

    do {
      j++;
    } while (j < 10)
  }
}
```

4.18 What is wrong with the following programs?

```
public class ShowErrors {
  public static void main(String[] args) {
    int i;
    int j = 5;

    if (j > 3)
      System.out.println(i + 4);
  }
}
```

(a)

```
public class ShowErrors {
  public static void main(String[] args) {
    for (int i = 0; i < 10; i++);
      System.out.println(i + 4);
  }
}
```

(b)

4.19 Show the output of the following programs:

```
public class Test {
  /** Main method */
  public static void main(String[] args) {
    for (int i = 1; i < 5; i++) {
      int j = 0;
      while (j < i) {
        System.out.print(j + " ");
        j++;
      }
    }
  }
}
```

(a)

```
public class Test {
  /** Main method */
  public static void main(String[] args) {
    int i = 0;
    while (i < 5) {
      for (int j = i; j > 1; j--)
        System.out.print(j + " ");
      System.out.println("****");
      i++;
    }
  }
}
```

(b)

```
public class Test {
  public static void main(String[] args) {
    int i = 5;
    while (i >= 1) {
      int num = 1;
      for (int j = 1; j <= i; j++) {
        System.out.print(num + "xxx");
        num *= 2;
      }

      System.out.println();
      i--;
    }
  }
}
```

(c)

```
public class Test {
  public static void main(String[] args) {
    int i = 1;
    do {
      int num = 1;
      for (int j = 1; j <= i; j++) {
        System.out.print(num + "G");
        num += 2;
      }

      System.out.println();
      i++;
    } while (i <= 5);
  }
}
```

(d)

4.20 Reformat the following programs according to the programming style and documentation guidelines proposed in §2.13. Use the next-line brace style.

```
public class Test {
  public static void main(String[] args) {
    int i = 0;
    if (i>0)
    i++;
    else
    i--;
    char grade;

    if (i >= 90)
     grade = 'A';
    else
      if (i >= 80)
       grade = 'B';

  }
}
```

(a)

```
public class Test {
  public static void main(String[] args) {
  for (int i = 0; i<10; i++)
    if (i>0)
      i++;
    else
      i--;
  }
}
```

(b)

4.21 Count the number of iterations in the following loops.

```
int count = 0;
while (count < n) {
  count++;
}
```

(a)

```
for (int count = 0;
   count <= n; count++) {
}
```

(b)

```
int count = 5;
while (count < n) {
  count++;
}
```

(c)

```
int count = 5;
while (count < n) {
  count = count + 3;
}
```

(d)

PROGRAMMING EXERCISES

Pedagogical Note

A problem often can be solved in many different ways. Students are encouraged to explore various solutions.

explore solutions

Sections 4.2-4.7

4.1* (*Repeating additions*) Listing 4.1, SubtractionQuizLoop.java, generates ten random subtraction questions. Revise the program to generate ten random addition questions for two integers between 1 and 15. Display the correct count and test time.

4.2* (*Counting positive and negative numbers and computing the average of numbers*) Write a program that reads an unspecified number of integers, determines how many positive and negative values have been read, and computes the total and average of the input values, not counting zeros. Your program ends with the input 0. Display the average as a floating-point number. (For example, if you entered 1, 2, and 0, the average should be 1.5.)

4.3 (*Conversion from kilograms to pounds*) Write a program that displays the following table (note that 1 kilogram is 2.2 pounds):

```
Kilograms     Pounds

1             2.2
3             6.6
...
197           433.4
199           437.8
```

4.4 (*Conversion from miles to kilometers*) Write a program that displays the following table (note that 1 mile is 1.609 kilometers):

```
Miles      Kilometers

1          1.609
2          3.218
...
9          14.481
10         16.09
```

4.5 (*Conversion from kilograms to pounds*) Write a program that displays the following two tables side by side (note that 1 kilogram is 2.2 pounds):

```
Kilograms     Pounds     Pounds    Kilograms

1             2.2        20        9.09
3             6.6        25        11.36
...
197           433.4      510       231.82
199           437.8      515       234.09
```

4.6 (*Conversion from miles to kilometers*) Write a program that displays the following two tables side by side (note that 1 mile is 1.609 kilometers):

```
Miles     Kilometers     Kilometers     Miles

1         1.609          20             12.430
2         3.218          25             15.538
...
9         14.481         60             37.290
10        16.09          65             40.398
```

4.7** (*Financial application: computing future tuition*) Suppose that the tuition for a university is $10,000 this year and increases 5% every year. Write a program that uses a loop to compute the tuition in ten years. Write another program that computes the total cost of four years' worth of tuition starting ten years from now.

4.8 (*Finding the highest score*) Write a program that prompts the user to enter the number of students and each student's name and score, and finally displays the student with the highest score.

4.9* (*Finding the two highest scores*) Write a program that prompts the user to enter the number of students and each student's name and score, and finally displays the student with the highest score and the student with the second-highest score.

4.10 (*Finding numbers divisible by* `5` *and* `6`) Write a program that displays all the numbers from `100` to `1000`, ten per line, that are divisible by `5` and `6`.

4.11 (*Finding numbers divisible by* `5` *or* `6`*, but not both*) Write a program that displays all the numbers from `100` to `200`, ten per line, that are divisible by `5` or `6`, but not both.

4.12 (*Finding the smallest* `n` *such that* $n^2 > 12{,}000$) *Use a* `while` loop to find the smallest integer `n` such that n^2 is greater than 12,000.

4.13 (*Finding the largest* `n` *such that* $n^3 < 12{,}000$) *Use a* `while` loop to find the largest integer `n` such that n^3 is less than 12,000.

4.14* (*Displaying the ACSII character table*) Write a program that prints the characters in the ASCII character table from '`!`' to '`~`'. Print ten characters per line. The ASCII table is printed in Appendix B.

Section 4.8 Case Studies

4.15* (*Computing the greatest common divisor*) Another solution for Listing 4.8 to find the greatest common divisor of two integers `n1` and `n2` is as follows: First find `d` to be the minimum of `n1` and `n2`, then check whether `d`, `d-1`, `d-2`, ..., `2`, or `1` is a divisor for both `n1` and `n2` in this order. The first such common divisor is the greatest common divisor for `n1` and `n2`. Write a program that prompts the user to enter two positive integers and displays the gcd.

4.16** (*Finding the factors of an integer*) Write a program that reads an integer and displays all its smallest factors in increasing order. For example, if the input integer is `120`, the output should be as follows: `2, 2, 2, 3, 5`.

4.17* (*Financial application: finding the sales amount*) Rewrite Listing 4.9, FindSalesAmount.java, as follows:

- Use a `for` loop instead of a `do-while` loop.
- Let the user enter `COMMISSION_SOUGHT` instead of fixing it as a constant.

4.18* (*Printing four patterns using loops*) Use nested loops that print the following patterns in four separate programs:

```
Pattern I      Pattern II     Pattern III    Pattern IV
1              1 2 3 4 5 6              1    1 2 3 4 5 6
1 2            1 2 3 4 5              2 1      1 2 3 4 5
1 2 3          1 2 3 4              3 2 1        1 2 3 4
1 2 3 4        1 2 3              4 3 2 1          1 2 3
1 2 3 4 5      1 2              5 4 3 2 1            1 2
1 2 3 4 5 6    1              6 5 4 3 2 1              1
```

4.19** (*Printing numbers in a pyramid pattern*) Write a nested **for** loop that prints the following output:

```
                              1
                          1   2   1
                      1   2   4   2   1
                  1   2   4   8   4   2   1
              1   2   4   8  16   8   4   2   1
          1   2   4   8  16  32  16   8   4   2   1
      1   2   4   8  16  32  64  32  16   8   4   2   1
  1   2   4   8  16  32  64 128  64  32  16   8   4   2   1
```

Hint: Here is the pseudocode solution:

```
for the row from 0 to 7 {
  Pad leading blanks in a row using a loop like this:
  for the column from 1 to 7-row
    System.out.print("    ");

  Print left half of the row for numbers 1, 2, 4, up to
    2^row using a look like this:
  for the column from 0 to row
    System.out.print("    " + (int)Math.pow(2, column));

  Print the right half of the row for numbers
    2^(row-1), 2^(row-2), ..., 1 using a loop like this:
  for (int column = row - 1; column >= 0; col--)
    System.out.print("    " + (int)Math.pow(2, column));

  Start a new line
  System.out.println();
}
```

You need to figure out how many spaces to print before the number. This depends on the number. If a number is a single digit, print four spaces. If a number has two digits, print three spaces. If a number has three digits, print two spaces.

The **Math.pow()** method was introduced in §2.12.1, "Problem: Computing Loan Payments." Can you write this program without using it?

4.20* (*Printing prime numbers between* 2 *and* 1000) Modify Listing 4.14 to print all the prime numbers between 2 and 1000, inclusively. Display eight prime numbers per line.

Comprehensive

4.21** (*Financial application: comparing loans with various interest rates*) Write a program that lets the user enter the loan amount and loan period in number of years and displays the monthly and total payments for each interest rate starting from 5% to 8%, with an increment of 1/8. Suppose you enter the loan amount 10,000 for five years; display a table as follows:

```
Loan Amount: 10000
Number of Years: 5
Interest Rate          Monthly Payment    Total Payment

5%                     188.71             11322.74
5.125%                 189.28             11357.13
```

```
5.25%          189.85          11391.59
...
7.85%          202.16          12129.97
8.0%           202.76          12165.83
```

Video Note
Display loan schedule

4.22** (*Financial application: loan amortization schedule*) The monthly payment for a given loan pays the principal and the interest. The monthly interest is computed by multiplying the monthly interest rate and the balance (the remaining principal). The principal paid for the month is therefore the monthly payment minus the monthly interest. Write a program that lets the user enter the loan amount, number of years, and interest rate, and displays the amortization schedule for the loan. Suppose you enter the loan amount 10,000 for one year with an interest rate of 7%, display a table as follows:

```
Loan Amount: 10000
Number of Years: 1
Annual Interest Rate: 7%

Monthly Payment: 865.26
Total Payment: 10383.21

Payment#      Interest      Principal      Balance
1             58.33         806.93         9193.07
2             53.62         811.64         8381.43
...
11            10.0          855.26         860.27
12            5.01          860.25         0.01
```

Note

The balance after the last payment may not be zero. If so, the last payment should be the normal monthly payment plus the final balance.

Hint: Write a loop to print the table. Since monthly payment is the same for each month, it should be computed before the loop. The balance is initially the loan amount. For each iteration in the loop, compute the interest and principal, and update the balance. The loop may look like this:

```
for (i = 1; i <= numberOfYears * 12; i++) {
  interest = monthlyInterestRate * balance;
  principal = monthlyPayment - interest;
  balance = balance - principal;
  System.out.println(i + "\t\t" + interest
    + "\t\t" + principal + "\t\t" + balance);
}
```

4.23* (*Obtaining more accurate results*) In computing the following series, you will obtain more accurate results by computing from right to left rather than from left to right:

$$1 + \frac{1}{2} + \frac{1}{3} + \ldots + \frac{1}{n}$$

Write a program that compares the results of the summation of the preceding series, computing from left to right and from right to left with n = 50000.

4.24* (*Summing a series*) Write a program to sum the following series:

$$\frac{1}{3} + \frac{3}{5} + \frac{5}{7} + \frac{7}{9} + \frac{9}{11} + \frac{11}{13} + \ldots + \frac{95}{97} + \frac{97}{99}$$

4.25**(*Computing* π) You can approximate π by using the following series:

$$\pi = 4\left(1 - \frac{1}{3} + \frac{1}{5} - \frac{1}{7} + \frac{1}{9} - \frac{1}{11} + \frac{1}{13} - \ldots - \frac{1}{2i-1} + \frac{1}{2i+1}\right)$$

Write two separate programs. The first program displays the π value for `i` = `10000`, `20000`, ..., and `100000`. The second program finds out how many terms of this series you need to use before you first get `3.14159`.

4.26**(*Computing e*) You can approximate `e` by using the following series:

$$e = 1 + \frac{1}{1!} + \frac{1}{2!} + \frac{1}{3!} + \frac{1}{4!} + \ldots + \frac{1}{i!}$$

Write a program that displays the `e` value for `i` = `10000`, `20000`, ..., and `100000`. (*Hint*: Since $i! = i \times (i-1) \times \ldots \times 2 \times 1$, $\frac{1}{i!}$ is $\frac{1}{i(i-1)!}$. Initialize `e` and `item` to be 1 and keep adding a new `item` to `e`. The new item is the previous item divided by `i` for i = `2, 3, 4, ...`)

4.27**(*Displaying leap years*) Write a program that displays all the leap years, ten per line, in the twenty-first century (from `2001` to `2100`).

4.28**(*Displaying the first days of each month*) Write a program that prompts the user to enter the year and first day of the year, and displays the first day of each month in the year on the console. For example, if the user entered the year `2005`, and `6` for Saturday, January 1, 2005, your program should display the following output (Note that Sunday is `0`):

```
January 1, 2005 is Saturday
...
December 1, 2005 is Thursday
```

4.29**(*Displaying calendars*) Write a program that prompts the user to enter the year and first day of the year, and displays the calendar table for the year on the console. For example, if the user entered the year `2005`, and `6` for Saturday, January 1, 2005, your program should display the calendar for each month in the year, as follows:

January 2005

Sun	Mon	Tue	Wed	Thu	Fri	Sat
						1
2	3	4	5	6	7	8
9	10	11	12	13	14	15
16	17	18	19	20	21	22
23	24	25	26	27	28	29
30	31					

...

December 2005

Sun	Mon	Tue	Wed	Thu	Fri	Sat
				1	2	3
4	5	6	7	8	9	10
11	12	13	14	15	16	17
18	19	20	21	22	23	24
25	26	27	28	29	30	31

4.30* (*Financial application: compound value*) Suppose you save **$100** *each* month into a savings account with the annual interest rate **5%**. So, the monthly interest rate is **0.05 / 12 = 0.00417**. After the first month, the value in the account becomes

```
100 * (1 + 0.00417) = 100.417
```

After the second month, the value in the account becomes

```
(100 + 100.417) * (1 + 0.00417) = 201.252
```

After the third month, the value in the account becomes

```
(100 + 201.252) * (1 + 0.00417) = 302.507
```

and so on.

Write a program that prompts the user to enter an amount (e.g., **100**), the annual interest rate (e.g., **5**), and the number of months (e.g., **6**), and displays the amount in the savings account after the given month.

4.31* (*Financial application: computing CD value*) Suppose you put $10,000 into a CD with an annual percentage yield of 5.75%. After one month, the CD is worth

```
10000 + 10000 * 5.75 / 1200 = 10047.91
```

After two months, the CD is worth

```
10047.91 + 10047.91 * 5.75 / 1200 = 10096.06
```

After three months, the CD is worth

```
10096.06 + 10096.06 * 5.75 / 1200 = 10144.43
```

and so on.

Write a program that prompts the user to enter an amount (e.g., **10000**), the annual percentage yield (e.g., **5.75**), and the number of months (e.g., **18**), and displays a table as shown in the sample output.

```
Enter the initial deposit amount: 10000 ↵Enter
Enter annual percentage yield: 5.75 ↵Enter
Enter maturity period (number of months): 18 ↵Enter

Month        CD Value
1            10047.91
2            10096.06
...
17           10846.56
18           10898.54
```

4.32** (*Perfect number*) A positive integer is called a *perfect number* if it is equal to the sum of all of its positive divisors, excluding itself. For example, `6` is the first perfect number because `6 = 3 + 2 + 1`. The next is `28 = 14 + 7 + 4 + 2 + 1`. There are four perfect numbers less than `10000`. Write a program to find all these four numbers.

4.33** (*Game: lottery*) Revise Listing 3.5, Lottery.java, to generate a lottery of a two-digit number. The two digits in the number are distinct. (*Hint*: Generate the first digit. Use a loop to continuously generate the second digit until it is different from the first digit.)

4.34*** (*Game: scissor, rock, paper*) Exercise 3.17 gives a program that plays the scissor-rock-paper game. Revise the program to let the user continuously play until either the user or the computer wins more than two times.

4.35* (*Summation*) You can prove that the following summation is `24`.

$$\frac{1}{1+\sqrt{2}} + \frac{1}{\sqrt{2}+\sqrt{3}} + \frac{1}{\sqrt{3}+\sqrt{4}} + \ldots + \frac{1}{\sqrt{624}+\sqrt{625}}$$

Write a program to verify your result.

4.36** (*Business application: checking ISBN*) Use loops to simplify Exercise 3.19.

4.37** (*Decimal to binary*) Write a program that prompts the user to enter a decimal integer and displays its corresponding binary value. Don't use Java's `Integer.toBinaryString(int)` in this program.

4.38** (*Decimal to hex*) Write a program that prompts the user to enter a decimal integer and displays its corresponding hexadecimal value. Don't use Java's `Integer.toHexString(int)` in this program.

CHAPTER 5

METHODS

Objectives

- To define methods, invoke methods, and pass arguments to a method (§5.2–5.5).
- To develop reusable code that is modular, easy to read, easy to debug, and easy to maintain (§5.6).
- To use method overloading and understand ambiguous overloading (§5.7).
- To determine the scope of variables (§5.8).
- To solve mathematics problems using the methods in the `Math` class (§§5.9–5.10).
- To apply the concept of method abstraction in software development (§5.11).
- To design and implement methods using stepwise refinement (§5.11).

5.1 Introduction

why method?

A method is a construct for grouping statements together to perform a function. Using a method, you can write the code once for performing the function in a program and reuse it in many other programs. For example, often you need to find the maximum between two numbers. Whenever you need this function, you have to write the following code:

```
int result;

if (num1 > num2)
  result = num1;
else
  result = num2;
```

If you define this function for finding a maximum number between any two numbers in a method, you don't have to repeatedly write the same code. You need to define it just once and reuse it in other programs.

In the preceding chapters, you have already used such methods as System.out.println, JOptionPane.showMessageDialog, JOptionPane.showInputDialog, Integer.parseInt, Double.parseDouble, System.exit, Math.pow, and Math.random. These methods are defined in the Java library. In this chapter, you will learn how to create your own methods and apply method abstraction to solve complex problems.

5.2 Defining a Method

The syntax for defining a method is as follows:

```
modifier returnValueType methodName(list of parameters) {
  // Method body;
}
```

Let's take a look at a method created to find which of two integers is bigger. This method, named max, has two int parameters, num1 and num2, the larger of which is returned by the method. Figure 5.1 illustrates the components of this method.

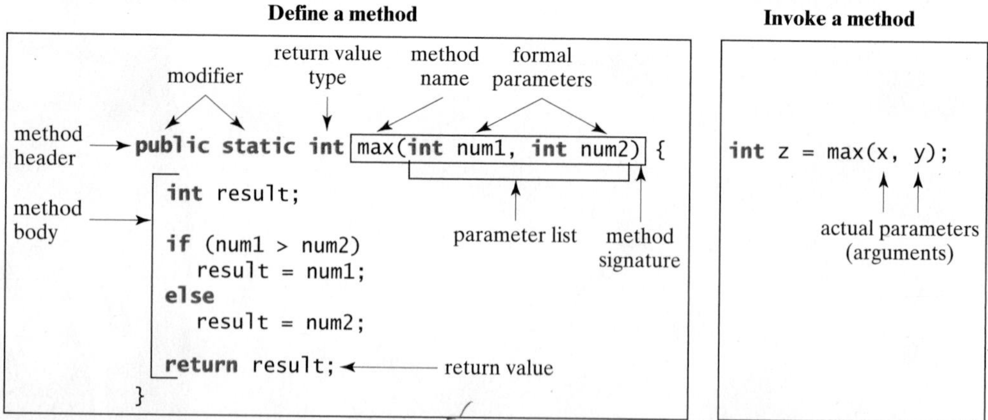

FIGURE 5.1 A method declaration consists of a method header and a method body.

method header

The *method header* specifies the *modifiers*, *return value type*, *method name*, and *parameters* of the method. The static modifier is used for all the methods in this chapter. The reason for using it will be discussed in Chapter 7, "Objects and Classes."

A method may return a value. The `returnValueType` is the data type of the value the method returns. Some methods perform desired operations without returning a value. In this case, the `returnValueType` is the keyword `void`. For example, the `returnValueType` is `void` in the `main` method, as well as in `System.exit`, `System.out.println`, and `JOptionPane.showMessageDialog`. The method that returns a value is called a *value-returning method*, and the method that does not return a value is called a *void method.*

value-returning method

void method

The variables defined in the method header are known as *formal parameters* or simply *parameters*. A parameter is like a placeholder. When a method is invoked, you pass a value to the parameter. This value is referred to as an *actual parameter* or *argument*. The *parameter list* refers to the type, order, and number of the parameters of a method. The method name and the parameter list together constitute the *method signature*. Parameters are optional; that is, a method may contain no parameters. For example, the `Math.random()` method has no parameters.

parameter

argument

parameter list

method signature

The method body contains a collection of statements that define what the method does. The method body of the `max` method uses an `if` statement to determine which number is larger and return the value of that number. A return statement using the keyword `return` is *required* for a value-returning method to return a result. The method terminates when a return statement is executed.

Note

In certain other languages, methods are referred to as *procedures* and *functions*. A value-returning method is called a *function*; a void method is called a *procedure*.

Caution

You need to declare a separate data type for each parameter. For instance, `int num1, num2` should be replaced by `int num1, int num2`.

5.3 Calling a Method

In creating a method, you give a definition of what the method is to do. To use a method, you have to *call* or *invoke* it. There are two ways to call a method; the choice is based on whether the method returns a value or not.

If the method returns a value, a call to the method is usually treated as a value. For example,

```
int larger = max(3, 4);
```

calls `max(3, 4)` and assigns the result of the method to the variable `larger`. Another example of a call that is treated as a value is

```
System.out.println(max(3, 4));
```

which prints the return value of the method call `max(3, 4)`.

If the method returns `void`, a call to the method must be a statement. For example, the method `println` returns `void`. The following call is a statement:

```
System.out.println("Welcome to Java!");
```

Note

A value-returning method can also be invoked as a statement in Java. In this case, the caller simply ignores the return value. This is rare but is permissible if the caller is not interested in the return value.

When a program calls a method, program control is transferred to the called method. A called method returns control to the caller when its return statement is executed or when its method-ending closing brace is reached.

Listing 5.1 shows a complete program that is used to test the `max` method.

Video Note
Declare/use max method

LISTING 5.1 TestMax.java

main method
invoke max
declare method

```
1 public class TestMax {
2   /** Main method */
3   public static void main(String[] args) {
4     int i = 5;
5     int j = 2;
6     int k = max(i, j);
7     System.out.println("The maximum between " + i +
8       " and " + j + " is " + k);
9   }
10
11  /** Return the max between two numbers */
12  public static int max(int num1, int num2) {
13    int result;
14
15    if (num1 > num2)
16      result = num1;
17    else
18      result = num2;
19
20    return result;
21  }
22 }
```

```
The maximum between 5 and 2 is 5
```

main method

This program contains the main method and the max method. The main method is just like any other method except that it is invoked by the JVM.

The main method's header is always the same, like the one in this example, with the modifiers public and static, return value type void, method name main, and a parameter of the String[] type. String[] indicates that the parameter is an array of String, a subject addressed in Chapter 6, "Arrays."

The statements in main may invoke other methods that are defined in the class that contains the main method or in other classes. In this example, the main method invokes max(i, j), which is defined in the same class with the main method.

max method

When the max method is invoked (line 6), variable i's value 5 is passed to num1, and variable j's value 2 is passed to num2 in the max method. The flow of control transfers to the max method. The max method is executed. When the return statement in the max method is executed, the max method returns the control to its caller (in this case the caller is the main method). This process is illustrated in Figure 5.2.

pass the value i

pass the value j

```
public static void main(String[] args) {
  int i = 5;
  int j = 2;
  int k = max(i, j);

  System.out.println(
    "The maximum between " + i +
    " and " + j + " is " + k);
}
```

```
public static int max(int num1, int num2) {
  int result;

  if (num1 > num2)
    result = num1;
  else
    result = num2;

  return result;
}
```

FIGURE 5.2 When the max method is invoked, the flow of control transfers to the max method. Once the max method is finished, it returns control back to the caller.

Caution

A `return` statement is required for a value-returning method. The method shown below in (a) is logically correct, but it has a compilation error because the Java compiler thinks it possible that this method does not return any value.

```
public static int sign(int n) {
  if (n > 0)
    return 1;
  else if (n == 0)
    return 0;
  else if (n < 0)
    return -1;
}
```

(a)

Should be

```
public static int sign(int n) {
  if (n > 0)
    return 1;
  else if (n == 0)
    return 0;
  else
    return -1;
}
```

(b)

To fix this problem, delete `if (n < 0)` in (a), so that the compiler will see a `return` statement to be reached regardless of how the `if` statement is evaluated.

Note

Methods enable code sharing and reuse. The `max` method can be invoked from any class besides `TestMax`. If you create a new class, you can invoke the `max` method using `ClassName.methodName` (i.e., `TestMax.max`).

reusing method

5.3.1 Call Stacks

Each time a method is invoked, the system stores parameters and variables in an area of memory known as a *stack*, which stores elements in last-in, first-out fashion. When a method calls another method, the caller's stack space is kept intact, and new space is created to handle the new method call. When a method finishes its work and returns to its caller, its associated space is released.

stack

Understanding call stacks helps you to comprehend how methods are invoked. The variables defined in the `main` method are `i`, `j`, and `k`. The variables defined in the `max` method are `num1`, `num2`, and `result`. The variables `num1` and `num2` are defined in the method signature and are parameters of the method. Their values are passed through method invocation. Figure 5.3 illustrates the variables in the stack.

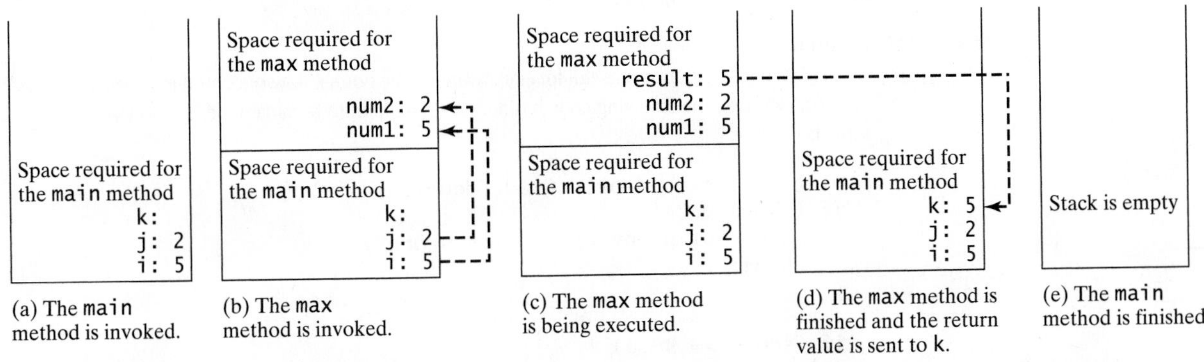

FIGURE 5.3 When the `max` method is invoked, the flow of control transfers to the `max` method. Once the `max` method is finished, it returns control back to the caller.

5.4 void Method Example

The preceding section gives an example of a value-returning method. This section shows how to declare and invoke a `void` method. Listing 5.2 gives a program that declares a method named `printGrade` and invokes it to print the grade for a given score.

Video Note
Use void method

LISTING 5.2 TestVoidMethod.java

`main` method
invoke `printGrade`
`printGrade` method

```
1 public class TestVoidMethod {
2   public static void main(String[] args) {
3     System.out.print("The grade is ");
4     printGrade(78.5);
5   }
6
7   public static void printGrade(double score) {
8     if (score >= 90.0) {
9       System.out.println('A');
10    }
11    else if (score >= 80.0) {
12      System.out.println('B');
13    }
14    else if (score >= 70.0) {
15      System.out.println('C');
16    }
17    else if (score >= 60.0) {
18      System.out.println('D');
19    }
20    else {
21      System.out.println('F');
22    }
23  }
24 }
```

```
The grade is C
```

invoke void method

The `printGrade` method is a `void` method. It does not return any value. A call to a `void` method must be a statement. So, it is invoked as a statement in line 3 in the `main` method. This statement, like any Java statement, is terminated with a semicolon.

return in void method

Note

A `return` statement is not needed for a `void` method, but it can be used for terminating the method and returning to the method's caller. The syntax is simply

```
return;
```

This is rare but sometimes is useful for circumventing the normal flow of control in a `void` function. For example, the following code has a return statement to terminate the function when the score is invalid.

```
public static void printGrade(double score) {
  if (score < 0 || score > 100) {
    System.out.println("Invalid score");
    return;
  }

  if (score >= 90.0) {
    System.out.println('A');
  }
  else if (score >= 80.0) {
    System.out.println('B');
  }
  else if (score >= 70.0) {
    System.out.println('C');
  }
```

```
    else if (score >= 60.0) {
      System.out.println('D');
    }
    else {
      System.out.println('F');
    }
  }
```

5.5 Passing Parameters by Values

parameter order association

The power of a method is its ability to work with parameters. You can use **println** to print any string and **max** to find the maximum between any two **int** values. When calling a method, you need to provide arguments, which must be given in the same order as their respective parameters in the method specification. This is known as *parameter order association*. For example, the following method prints a message **n** times:

```
public static void nPrintln(String message, int n) {
  for (int i = 0; i < n; i++)
    System.out.println(message);
}
```

You can use **nPrintln("Hello", 3)** to print **"Hello"** three times. The **nPrintln("Hello", 3)** statement passes the actual string parameter, **"Hello"**, to the parameter, **message**; passes **3** to **n**; and prints **"Hello"** three times. However, the statement **nPrintln(3, "Hello")** would be wrong. The data type of **3** does not match the data type for the first parameter, **message**, nor does the second parameter, **"Hello"**, match the second parameter, **n**.

Caution

The arguments must match the parameters in *order*, *number*, and *compatible type*, as defined in the method signature. Compatible type means that you can pass an argument to a parameter without explicit casting, such as passing an **int** value argument to a **double** value parameter.

pass-by-value

When you invoke a method with a parameter, the value of the argument is passed to the parameter. This is referred to as *pass-by-value*. If the argument is a variable rather than a literal value, the value of the variable is passed to the parameter. The variable is not affected, regardless of the changes made to the parameter inside the method. As shown in Listing 5.3, the value of **x** (**1**) is passed to the parameter **n** to invoke the **increment** function (line 5). **n** is incremented by **1** in the function (line 10), but **x** is not changed no matter what the function does.

LISTING 5.3 Increment.java

```
 1 public class Increment {
 2   public static void main(String[] args) {
 3     int x = 1;
 4     System.out.println("Before the call, x is " + x);
 5     increment(x);
 6     System.out.println("after the call, x is " + x);
 7   }
 8
 9   public static void increment(int n) {
10     n++;
11     System.out.println("n inside the function is " + n);
12   }
13 }
```

invoke increment

increment **n**

```
Before the call, x is 1
n inside the function is 2
after the call, x is 1
```

Listing 5.4 gives another program that demonstrates the effect of passing by value. The program creates a method for swapping two variables. The swap method is invoked by passing two arguments. Interestingly, the values of the arguments are not changed after the method is invoked.

LISTING 5.4 TestPassByValue.java

false swap

```
1 public class TestPassByValue {
2   /** Main method */
3   public static void main(String[] args) {
4     // Declare and initialize variables
5     int num1 = 1;
6     int num2 = 2;
7
8     System.out.println("Before invoking the swap method, num1 is " +
9       num1 + " and num2 is " + num2);
10
11    // Invoke the swap method to attempt to swap two variables
12    swap(num1, num2);
13
14    System.out.println("After invoking the swap method, num1 is " +
15      num1 + " and num2 is " + num2);
16  }
17
18  /** Swap two variables */
19  public static void swap(int n1, int n2) {
20    System.out.println("\tInside the swap method");
21    System.out.println("\t\tBefore swapping n1 is " + n1
22      + " n2 is " + n2);
23
24    // Swap n1 with n2
25    int temp = n1;
26    n1 = n2;
27    n2 = temp;
28
29    System.out.println("\t\tAfter swapping n1 is " + n1
30      + " n2 is " + n2);
31  }
32 }
```

```
Before invoking the swap method, num1 is 1 and num2 is 2
  Inside the swap method
    Before swapping n1 is 1 n2 is 2
    After swapping n1 is 2 n2 is 1
After invoking the swap method, num1 is 1 and num2 is 2
```

Before the swap method is invoked (line 12), num1 is 1 and num2 is 2. After the swap method is invoked, num1 is still 1 and num2 is still 2. Their values are not swapped after the swap method is invoked. As shown in Figure 5.4, the values of the arguments num1 and num2 are passed to n1 and n2, but n1 and n2 have their own memory locations independent of num1 and num2. Therefore, changes in n1 and n2 do not affect the contents of num1 and num2.

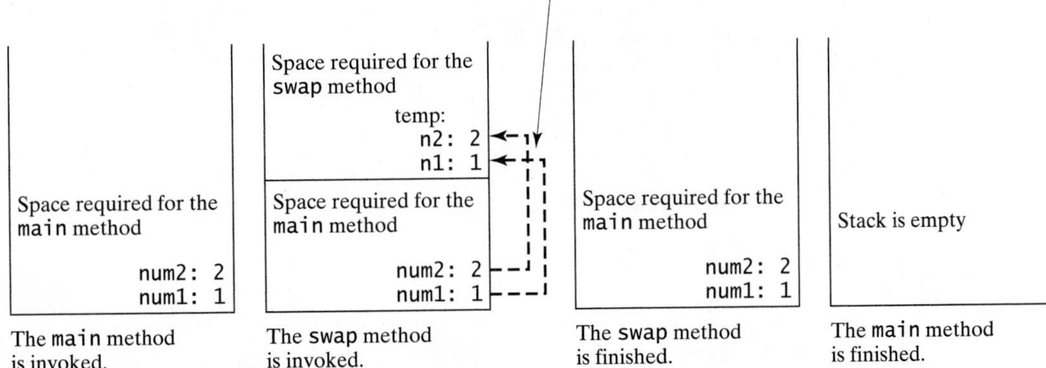

FIGURE 5.4 The values of the variables are passed to the parameters of the method.

Another twist is to change the parameter name `n1` in `swap` to `num1`. What effect does this have? No change occurs, because it makes no difference whether the parameter and the argument have the same name. The parameter is a variable in the method with its own memory space. The variable is allocated when the method is invoked, and it disappears when the method is returned to its caller.

Note

For simplicity, Java programmers often say *passing an argument* `x` *to a parameter* `y`, which actually means *passing the value of* `x` *to* `y`.

5.6 Modularizing Code

Methods can be used to reduce redundant code and enable code reuse. Methods can also be used to modularize code and improve the quality of the program.

Listing 4.8 gives a program that prompts the user to enter two integers and displays their greatest common divisor. You can rewrite the program using a method, as shown in Listing 5.5.

LISTING 5.5 GreatestCommonDivisorMethod.java

Video Note
Modularize code

```
import java.util.Scanner;

public class GreatestCommonDivisorMethod {
  /** Main method */
  public static void main(String[] args) {
    // Create a Scanner
    Scanner input = new Scanner(System.in);

    // Prompt the user to enter two integers
    System.out.print("Enter first integer: ");
    int n1 = input.nextInt();
    System.out.print("Enter second integer: ");
    int n2 = input.nextInt();

    System.out.println("The greatest common divisor for " + n1 +
      " and " + n2 + " is " + gcd(n1, n2));
  }

  /** Return the gcd of two integers */
```

invoke **gcd**

compute gcd

return gcd

```
  public static int gcd(int n1, int n2) {
    int gcd = 1; // Initial gcd is 1
    int k = 2;   // Possible gcd

    while (k <= n1 && k <= n2) {
      if (n1 % k == 0 && n2 % k == 0)
        gcd = k; // Update gcd
      k++;
    }

    return gcd; // Return gcd
  }
}
```

```
Enter first integer: 45 ↵Enter
Enter second integer: 75 ↵Enter
The greatest common divisor for 45 and 75 is 15
```

By enclosing the code for obtaining the gcd in a method, this program has several advantages:

1. It isolates the problem for computing the gcd from the rest of the code in the main method. Thus, the logic becomes clear and the program is easier to read.
2. The errors on computing gcd are confined in the `gcd` method, which narrows the scope of debugging.
3. The `gcd` method now can be reused by other programs.

Listing 5.6 applies the concept of code modularization to improve Listing 4.14, PrimeNumber.java.

Listing 5.6 PrimeNumberMethod.java

invoke **printPrimeNumbers**

printPrimeNumbers method

invoke **isPrime**

```
public class PrimeNumberMethod {
  public static void main(String[] args) {
    System.out.println("The first 50 prime numbers are \n");
    printPrimeNumbers(50);
  }

  public static void printPrimeNumbers(int numberOfPrimes) {
    final int NUMBER_OF_PRIMES = 50; // Number of primes to display
    final int NUMBER_OF_PRIMES_PER_LINE = 10; // Display 10 per line
    int count = 0; // Count the number of prime numbers
    int number = 2; // A number to be tested for primeness

    // Repeatedly find prime numbers
    while (count < numberOfPrimes) {
      // Print the prime number and increase the count
      if (isPrime(number)) {
        count++; // Increase the count

        if (count % NUMBER_OF_PRIMES_PER_LINE == 0) {
          // Print the number and advance to the new line
          System.out.printf("%-5s\n", number);
        }
        else
          System.out.printf("%-5s", number);
      }
```

```

        // Check if the next number is prime
        number++;
      }
    }

    /** Check whether number is prime */
    public static boolean isPrime(int number) {
      for (int divisor = 2; divisor <= number / 2; divisor++) {
        if (number % divisor == 0) { // If true, number is not prime
          return false; // number is not a prime
        }
      }

      return true; // number is prime
    }
}
```

isPrime method

```
The first 50 prime numbers are

2    3    5    7    11   13   17   19   23   29
31   37   41   43   47   53   59   61   67   71
73   79   83   89   97   101  103  107  109  113
127  131  137  139  149  151  157  163  167  173
179  181  191  193  197  199  211  223  227  229
```

We divided a large problem into two subproblems. As a result, the new program is easier to read and easier to debug. Moreover, the methods `printPrimeNumbers` and `isPrime` can be reused by other programs.

5.7 Overloading Methods

The `max` method that was used earlier works only with the `int` data type. But what if you need to determine which of two floating-point numbers has the maximum value? The solution is to create another method with the same name but different parameters, as shown in the following code:

```
public static double max(double num1, double num2) {
  if (num1 > num2)
    return num1;
  else
    return num2;
}
```

If you call `max` with `int` parameters, the `max` method that expects `int` parameters will be invoked; if you call `max` with `double` parameters, the `max` method that expects `double` parameters will be invoked. This is referred to as *method overloading*; that is, two methods have the same name but different parameter lists within one class. The Java compiler determines which method is used based on the method signature.

method overloading

Listing 5.7 is a program that creates three methods. The first finds the maximum integer, the second finds the maximum double, and the third finds the maximum among three double values. All three methods are named `max`.

LISTING 5.7 TestMethodOverloading.java

```
public class TestMethodOverloading {
  /** Main method */
  public static void main(String[] args) {
```

```
4     // Invoke the max method with int parameters
5     System.out.println("The maximum between 3 and 4 is "
6       + max(3, 4));
7
8     // Invoke the max method with the double parameters
9     System.out.println("The maximum between 3.0 and 5.4 is "
10      + max(3.0, 5.4));
11
12    // Invoke the max method with three double parameters
13    System.out.println("The maximum between 3.0, 5.4, and 10.14 is "
14      + max(3.0, 5.4, 10.14));
15  }
16
17  /** Return the max between two int values */
18  public static int max(int num1, int num2) {
19    if (num1 > num2)
20      return num1;
21    else
22      return num2;
23  }
24
25  /** Find the max between two double values */
26  public static double max(double num1, double num2) {
27    if (num1 > num2)
28      return num1;
29    else
30      return num2;
31  }
32
33  /** Return the max among three double values */
34  public static double max(double num1, double num2, double num3) {
35    return max(max(num1, num2), num3);
36  }
37 }
```

overloaded **max** (line 18)

overloaded **max** (line 26)

overloaded **max** (line 34)

```
The maximum between 3 and 4 is 4
The maximum between 3.0 and 5.4 is 5.4
The maximum between 3.0, 5.4, and 10.14 is 10.14
```

When calling `max(3, 4)` (line 6), the `max` method for finding the maximum of two integers is invoked. When calling `max(3.0, 5.4)` (line 10), the `max` method for finding the maximum of two doubles is invoked. When calling `max(3.0, 5.4, 10.14)` (line 14), the `max` method for finding the maximum of three double values is invoked.

Can you invoke the `max` method with an `int` value and a `double` value, such as `max(2, 2.5)`? If so, which of the `max` methods is invoked? The answer to the first question is yes. The answer to the second is that the `max` method for finding the maximum of two `double` values is invoked. The argument value 2 is automatically converted into a `double` value and passed to this method.

You may be wondering why the method `max(double, double)` is not invoked for the call `max(3, 4)`. Both `max(double, double)` and `max(int, int)` are possible matches for `max(3, 4)`. The Java compiler finds the most specific method for a method invocation. Since the method `max(int, int)` is more specific than `max(double, double)`, `max(int, int)` is used to invoke `max(3, 4)`.

Tip

Overloading methods can make programs clearer and more readable. Methods that perform closely related tasks should be given the same name.

Note

Overloaded methods must have different parameter lists. You cannot overload methods based on different modifiers or return types.

Note

ambiguous invocation

Sometimes there are two or more possible matches for an invocation of a method, but the compiler cannot determine the most specific match. This is referred to as *ambiguous invocation*. Ambiguous invocation causes a compilation error. Consider the following code:

```
public class AmbiguousOverloading {
  public static void main(String[] args) {
    System.out.println(max(1, 2));
  }

  public static double max(int num1, double num2) {
    if (num1 > num2)
      return num1;
    else
      return num2;
  }

  public static double max(double num1, int num2) {
    if (num1 > num2)
      return num1;
    else
      return num2;
  }
}
```

Both `max(int, double)` and `max(double, int)` are possible candidates to match `max(1, 2)`. Since neither is more specific than the other, the invocation is ambiguous, resulting in a compilation error.

5.8 The Scope of Variables

local variable

The *scope of a variable* is the part of the program where the variable can be referenced. A variable defined inside a method is referred to as a *local variable*.

The scope of a local variable starts from its declaration and continues to the end of the block that contains the variable. A local variable must be declared and assigned a value before it can be used.

A parameter is actually a local variable. The scope of a method parameter covers the entire method.

A variable declared in the initial action part of a `for` loop header has its scope in the entire loop. But a variable declared inside a `for` loop body has its scope limited in the loop body from its declaration to the end of the block that contains the variable, as shown in Figure 5.5.

You can declare a local variable with the same name multiple times in different nonnested blocks in a method, but you cannot declare a local variable twice in nested blocks, as shown in Figure 5.6.

Caution

Do not declare a variable inside a block and then attempt to use it outside the block. Here is an example of a common mistake:

```
for (int i = 0; i < 10; i++) {
}

System.out.println(i);
```

The last statement would cause a syntax error because variable `i` is not defined outside of the `for` loop.

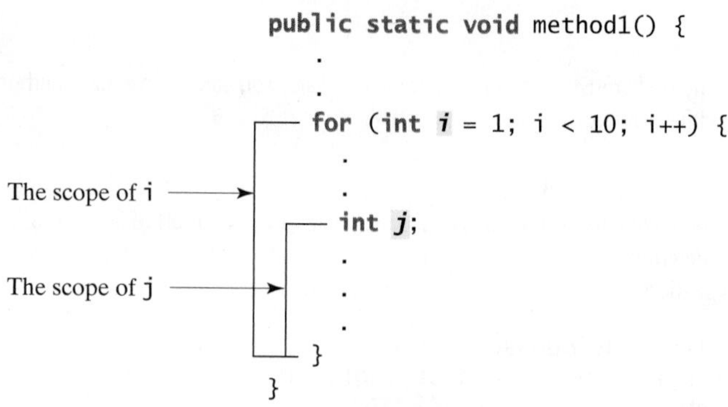

FIGURE 5.5 A variable declared in the initial action part of a `for` loop header has its scope in the entire loop.

It is fine to declare `i` in two nonnested blocks

```
public static void method1() {
  int x = 1;
  int y = 1;

  for (int i = 1; i < 10; i++) {
    x += i;
  }

  for (int i = 1; i < 10; i++) {
    y += i;
  }
}
```

It is wrong to declare `i` in two nested blocks

```
public static void method2() {

  int i = 1;
  int sum = 0;

  for (int i = 1; i < 10; i++)
    sum += i;
  }

}
```

FIGURE 5.6 A variable can be declared multiple times in nonnested blocks, but can be declared only once in nested blocks.

5.9 The `Math` Class

The `Math` class contains the methods needed to perform basic mathematical functions. You have already used the `pow(a, b)` method to compute a^b in Listing 2.7, ComputeLoan.java, and the `Math.random()` method in Listing 3.3, AdditionQuiz.java. This section introduces other useful methods in the `Math` class. They can be categorized as *trigonometric methods*, *exponent methods*, and *service methods*. Besides methods, the `Math` class provides two useful `double` constants, `PI` and `E` (the base of natural logarithms). You can use these constants as `Math.PI` and `Math.E` in any program.

5.9.1 Trigonometric Methods

The `Math` class contains the following trigonometric methods:

```
public static double sin(double radians)
public static double cos(double radians)
public static double tan(double radians)
public static double asin(double radians)
public static double acos(double radians)
```

```
public static double atan(double radians)
public static double toRadians(double degree)
public static double toDegrees(double radians)
```

Each method has a single `double` parameter, and its return type is `double`. The parameter represents an angle in radians. One degree is equal to $\pi/180$ in radians. For example, `Math.sin(Math.PI)` returns the trigonometric sine of π. Since JDK 1.2, the `Math` class has also provided the method `toRadians(double angdeg)` for converting an angle in degrees to radians, and the method `toDegrees(double angrad)` for converting an angle in radians to degrees.

For example,

```
Math.sin(0) returns 0.0
Math.sin(Math.toRadians(270)) returns -1.0
Math.sin(Math.PI / 6) returns 0.5
Math.sin(Math.PI / 2) returns 1.0
Math.cos(0) returns 1.0
Math.cos(Math.PI / 6) returns 0.866
Math.cos(Math.PI / 2) returns 0
```

5.9.2 Exponent Methods

There are five methods related to exponents in the `Math` class:

```
/** Return e raised to the power of x (e^x) */
public static double exp(double x)

/** Return the natural logarithm of x (ln(x) = log_e(x)) */
public static double log(double x)

/** Return the base 10 logarithm of x (log_10(x)) */
public static double log10(double x)

/** Return a raised to the power of b (a^b) */
public static double pow(double a, double b)

/** Return the square root of x (√x) */
public static double sqrt(double x)
```

Note that the parameter in the `sqrt` method must not be negative.

For example,

```
Math.exp(1) returns 2.71828
Math.log(Math.E) returns 1.0
Math.log10(10) returns 1.0
Math.pow(2, 3) returns 8.0
Math.pow(3, 2) returns 9.0
Math.pow(3.5, 2.5) returns 22.91765
Math.sqrt(4) returns 2.0
Math.sqrt(10.5) returns 3.24
```

5.9.3 The Rounding Methods

The `Math` class contains five rounding methods:

```
/** x is rounded up to its nearest integer. This integer is
  * returned as a double value. */
public static double ceil(double x)
```

```
/** x is rounded down to its nearest integer. This integer is
  * returned as a double value. */
public static double floor(double x)

/** x is rounded to its nearest integer. If x is equally close
  * to two integers, the even one is returned as a double. */
public static double rint(double x)

/** Return (int)Math.floor(x + 0.5). */
public static int round(float x)

/** Return (long)Math.floor(x + 0.5). */
public static long round(double x)
```

For example,

```
Math.ceil(2.1) returns 3.0
Math.ceil(2.0) returns 2.0
Math.ceil(-2.0) returns -2.0
Math.ceil(-2.1) returns -2.0
Math.floor(2.1) returns 2.0
Math.floor(2.0) returns 2.0
Math.floor(-2.0) returns -2.0
Math.floor(-2.1) returns -3.0
Math.rint(2.1) returns 2.0
Math.rint(2.0) returns 2.0
Math.rint(-2.0) returns -2.0
Math.rint(-2.1) returns -2.0
Math.rint(2.5) returns 2.0
Math.rint(-2.5) returns -2.0
Math.round(2.6f) returns 3 // Returns int
Math.round(2.0) returns 2  // Returns long
Math.round(-2.0f) returns -2
Math.round(-2.6) returns -3
```

5.9.4 The min, max, and abs Methods

The min and max methods are overloaded to return the minimum and maximum numbers between two numbers (int, long, float, or double). For example, max(3.4, 5.0) returns 5.0, and min(3, 2) returns 2.

The abs method is overloaded to return the absolute value of the number (int, long, float, and double). For example,

```
Math.max(2, 3) returns 3
Math.max(2.5, 3) returns 3.0
Math.min(2.5, 3.6) returns 2.5
Math.abs(-2) returns 2
Math.abs(-2.1) returns 2.1
```

5.9.5 The random Method

The Math class also has a powerful method, random, which generates a random double value greater than or equal to 0.0 and less than 1.0 (0 <= Math.random() < 1.0). This method is very useful. Listing 3.4, SubtractQuiz.java, uses this method to generate a single-digit integer. You can use it to write a simple expression to generate random numbers in any range. For example,

`(int) (Math.random( ) * 10)` ⟶ Returns a random integer between 0 and 9

`50 + (int) (Math.random( ) * 50)` ⟶ Returns a random integer between 50 and 99

In general,

`a + Math.random( ) * b` ⟶ Returns a random number between a and a + b excluding a + b

Tip

You can view the complete documentation for the Math class online from http://java.sun.com/javase/6/docs/api/index.html, as shown in Figure 5.7.

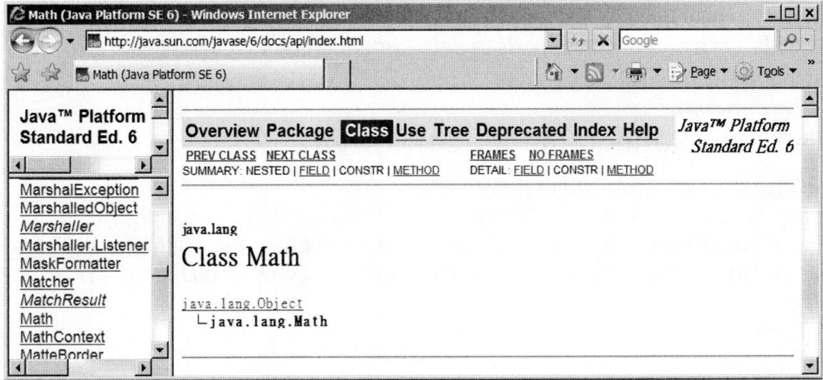

FIGURE 5.7 You can view the documentation for Java API online.

Note

Not all classes need a main method. The Math class and JOptionPane class do not have main methods. These classes contain methods for other classes to use.

5.10 Case Study: Generating Random Characters

Computer programs process numerical data and characters. You have seen many examples that involve numerical data. It is also important to understand characters and how to process them. This section presents an example for generating random characters.

As introduced in §2.9, every character has a unique Unicode between 0 and FFFF in hexadecimal (65535 in decimal). To generate a random character is to generate a random integer between 0 and 65535 using the following expression (note that since 0 <= Math.random() < 1.0, you have to add 1 to 65535):

```
(int)(Math.random() * (65535 + 1))
```

Now let us consider how to generate a random lowercase letter. The Unicodes for lowercase letters are consecutive integers starting from the Unicode for 'a', then that for 'b', 'c', ..., and 'z'. The Unicode for 'a' is

```
(int)'a'
```

So a random integer between `(int)'a'` and `(int)'z'` is

```
(int)((int)'a' + Math.random() * ((int)'z' - (int)'a' + 1)
```

As discussed in §2.9.4, all numeric operators can be applied to the **char** operands. The **char** operand is cast into a number if the other operand is a number or a character. Thus the preceding expression can be simplified as follows:

```
'a' + Math.random() * ('z' - 'a' + 1)
```

and a random lowercase letter is

```
(char)('a' + Math.random() * ('z' - 'a' + 1))
```

To generalize the foregoing discussion, a random character between any two characters **ch1** and **ch2** with **ch1 < ch2** can be generated as follows:

```
(char)(ch1 + Math.random() * (ch2 - ch1 + 1))
```

This is a simple but useful discovery. Let us create a class named **RandomCharacter** in Listing 5.8 with five overloaded methods to get a certain type of character randomly. You can use these methods in your future projects.

LISTING 5.8 RandomCharacter.java

getRandomCharacter

getRandomLowerCaseLetter()

getRandomUpperCaseLetter()

getRandomDigitCharacter()

getRandomCharacter()

```
public class RandomCharacter {
  /** Generate a random character between ch1 and ch2 */
  public static char getRandomCharacter(char ch1, char ch2) {
    return (char)(ch1 + Math.random() * (ch2 - ch1 + 1));
  }

  /** Generate a random lowercase letter */
  public static char getRandomLowerCaseLetter() {
    return getRandomCharacter('a', 'z');
  }

  /** Generate a random uppercase letter */
  public static char getRandomUpperCaseLetter() {
    return getRandomCharacter('A', 'Z');
  }

  /** Generate a random digit character */
  public static char getRandomDigitCharacter() {
    return getRandomCharacter('0', '9');
  }

  /** Generate a random character */
  public static char getRandomCharacter() {
    return getRandomCharacter('\u0000', '\uFFFF');
  }
}
```

Listing 5.9 gives a test program that displays 175 random lowercase letters.

LISTING 5.9 TestRandomCharacter.java

```
public class TestRandomCharacter {
  /** Main method */
```

```
  public static void main(String[] args) {
    final int NUMBER_OF_CHARS = 175;
    final int CHARS_PER_LINE = 25;

    // Print random characters between 'a' and 'z', 25 chars per line
    for (int i = 0; i < NUMBER_OF_CHARS; i++) {
      char ch = RandomCharacter.getRandomLowerCaseLetter() ;
      if ((i + 1) % CHARS_PER_LINE == 0)
        System.out.println(ch);
      else
        System.out.print(ch);
    }
  }
}
```

constants

lower-case letter

5.11 Method Abstraction and Stepwise Refinement

The key to developing software is to apply the concept of abstraction. You will learn many levels of abstraction from this book. *Method abstraction* is achieved by separating the use of a method from its implementation. The client can use a method without knowing how it is implemented. The details of the implementation are encapsulated in the method and hidden from the client who invokes the method. This is known as *information hiding* or *encapsulation*. If you decide to change the implementation, the client program will not be affected, provided that you do not change the method signature. The implementation of the method is hidden from the client in a "black box," as shown in Figure 5.8.

method abstraction

information hiding

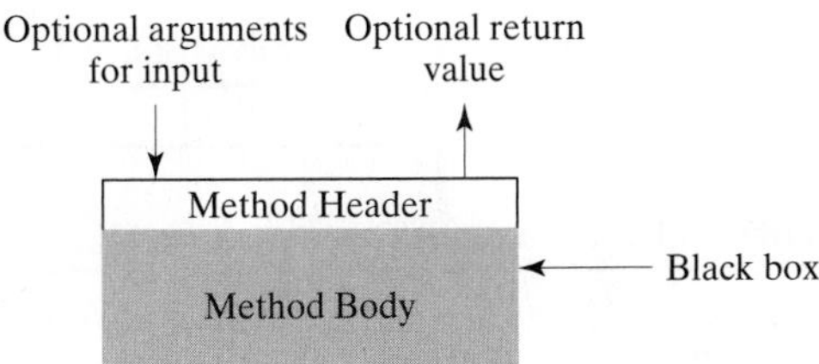

FIGURE 5.8 The method body can be thought of as a black box that contains the detailed implementation for the method.

You have already used the `System.out.print` method to display a string, the `JOptionPane.showInputDialog` method to read a string from a dialog box, and the `max` method to find the maximum number. You know how to write the code to invoke these methods in your program, but as a user of these methods, you are not required to know how they are implemented.

The concept of method abstraction can be applied to the process of developing programs. When writing a large program, you can use the *divide-and-conquer* strategy, also known as *stepwise refinement*, to decompose it into subproblems. The subproblems can be further decomposed into smaller, more manageable problems.

divide and conquer

stepwise refinement

Suppose you write a program that displays the calendar for a given month of the year. The program prompts the user to enter the year and the month, and then displays the entire calendar for the month, as shown in the following sample output:

```
Enter full year (e.g., 2001): 2006 ↵Enter
Enter month in number between 1 and 12: 6 ↵Enter
          June 2006
-----------------------------
 Sun Mon Tue Wed Thu Fri Sat
                   1   2   3
   4   5   6   7   8   9  10
  11  12  13  14  15  16  17
  18  19  20  21  22  23  24
  25  26  27  28  29  30
```

Let us use this example to demonstrate the divide-and-conquer approach.

5.11.1 Top-Down Design

How would you get started on such a program? Would you immediately start coding? Beginning programmers often start by trying to work out the solution to every detail. Although details are important in the final program, concern for detail in the early stages may block the problem-solving process. To make problem solving flow as smoothly as possible, this example begins by using method abstraction to isolate details from design and only later implements the details.

For this example, the problem is first broken into two subproblems: get input from the user, and print the calendar for the month. At this stage, the creator of the program should be concerned with what the subproblems will achieve, not with how to get input and print the calendar for the month. You can draw a structure chart to help visualize the decomposition of the problem (see Figure 5.9(a)).

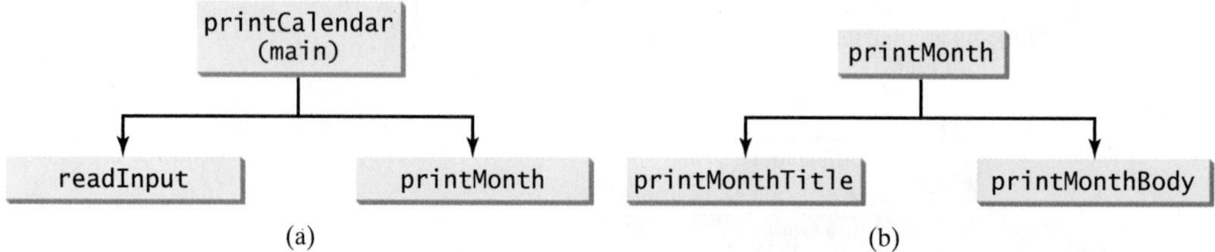

FIGURE 5.9 The structure chart shows that the printCalendar problem is divided into two subproblems, readInput and printMonth, and that printMonth is divided into two smaller subproblems, printMonthTitle and printMonthBody.

Use the JOptionPane.showInputDialog method to display input dialog boxes that prompt the user to enter the year and the month.

The problem of printing the calendar for a given month can be broken into two subproblems: print the month title, and print the month body, as shown in Figure 5.9(b). The month title consists of three lines: month and year, a dash line, and the names of the seven days of the week. You need to get the month name (e.g., January) from the numeric month (e.g., 1). This is accomplished in getMonthName (see Figure 5.10(a)).

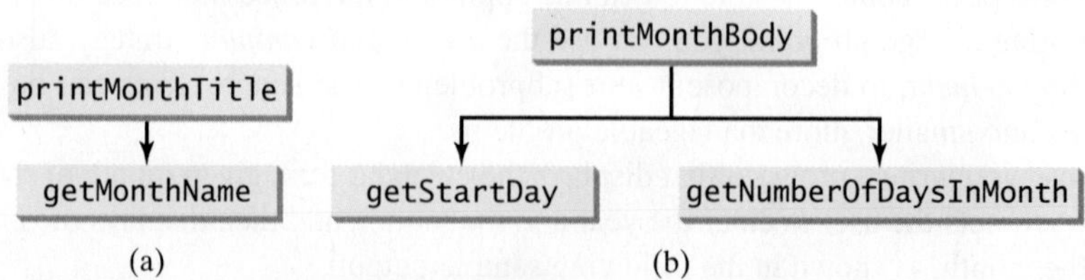

FIGURE 5.10 (a) To printMonthTitle, you need getMonthName. (b) The printMonthBody problem is refined into several smaller problems.

In order to print the month body, you need to know which day of the week is the first day of the month (getStartDay) and how many days the month has (getNumberOfDaysInMonth), as shown in Figure 5.10(b). For example, December 2005 has 31 days, and the first of the month is Thursday.

How would you get the start day for the first date in a month? There are several ways to do so. The simplest approach is to use the Calendar class in §11.3, "Example: Calendar and GregorianCalendar." For now, an alternative approach is used. Assume you know that the start day (startDay1800 = 3) for Jan 1, 1800, was Wednesday. You could compute the total number of days (totalNumberOfDays) between Jan 1, 1800, and the first date of the calendar month. The start day for the calendar month is (totalNumberOfDays + startDay1800) % 7, since every week has seven days. So the getStartDay problem can be further refined as getTotalNumberOfDays, as shown in Figure 5.11(a).

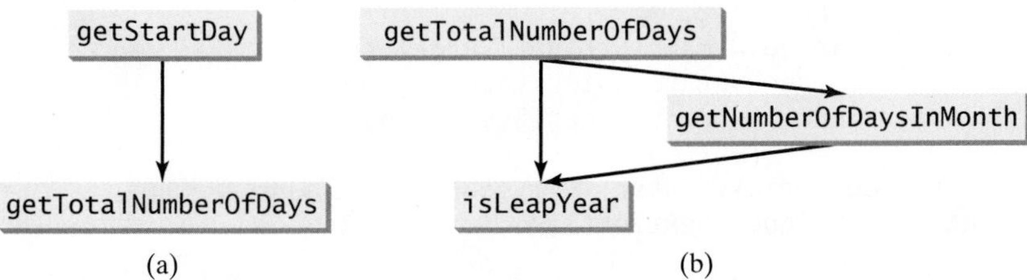

FIGURE 5.11 (a) To getStartDay, you need getTotalNumberOfDays. (b) The getTotalNumberOfDays problem is refined into two smaller problems.

To get the total number of days, you need to know whether the year is a leap year and the number of days in each month. So getTotalNumberOfDays is further refined into two subproblems: isLeapYear and getNumberOfDaysInMonth, as shown in Figure 5.11(b). The complete structure chart is shown in Figure 5.12.

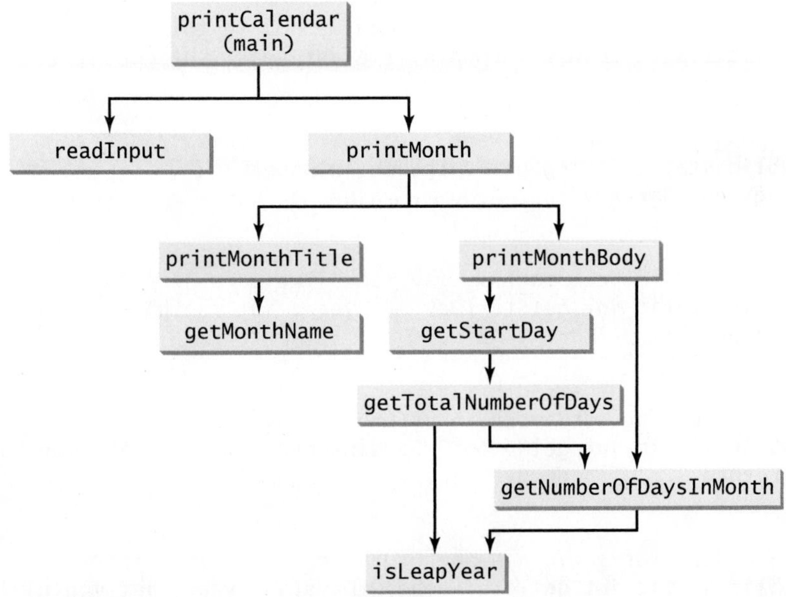

FIGURE 5.12 The structure chart shows the hierarchical relationship of the subproblems in the program.

5.11.2 Top-Down or Bottom-Up Implementation

Now we turn our attention to implementation. In general, a subproblem corresponds to a method in the implementation, although some are so simple that this is unnecessary. You would need to decide which modules to implement as methods and which to combine in other methods. Decisions of this kind should be based on whether the overall program will be easier to read as a result of your choice. In this example, the subproblem `readInput` can be simply implemented in the `main` method.

top-down approach

stub

You can use either a "top-down" approach or a "bottom-up" approach. The top-down approach implements one method in the structure chart at a time from the top to the bottom. Stubs can be used for the methods waiting to be implemented. A *stub* is a simple but incomplete version of a method. The use of stubs enables you to quickly build the framework of the program. Implement the `main` method first, and then use a stub for the `printMonth` method. For example, let `printMonth` display the year and the month in the stub. Thus, your program may begin like this:

```
public class PrintCalendar {
  /** Main method */
  public static void main(String[] args) {
    // Prompt the user to enter year
    Scanner input = new Scanner(System.in);

    System.out.print("Enter full year (e.g., 2001): ");
    int year = input.nextInt();

    // Prompt the user to enter month
    System.out.print("Enter month as number between 1 and 12: ");
    int month = input.nextInt();

    // Print calendar for the month of the year
    printMonth(year, month);
  }

  /** A stub for printMonth may look like this */
  public static void printMonth(int year, int month) {
    System.out.print(month + " " + year);
  }

  /** A stub for printMonthTitle may look like this */
  public static void printMonthTitle(int year, int month) {
  }

  /** A stub for getMonthName may look like this */
  public static String getMonthName(int month) {
    return "January"; // A dummy value
  }

  /** A stub for getStartDay may look like this */
  public static int getStartDay(int year, int month) {
    return 1; // A dummy value
  }

  /** A stub for getNumberOfDaysInMonth may look like this */
  public static int getNumberOfDaysInMonth(int year, int month) {
    return 31; // A dummy value
  }

  /** A stub for getTotalNumberOfDays may look like this */
  public static int getTotalNumberOfDays(int year, int month) {
    return 10000; // A dummy value
  }
```

```
  /** A stub for getTotalNumberOfDays may look like this */
  public static boolean isLeapYear(int year) {
    return true; // A dummy value
  }
}
```

Compile and test the program, and fix any errors. You can now implement the printMonth method. For methods invoked from the printMonth method, you can again use stubs.

bottom-up approach

The bottom-up approach implements one method in the structure chart at a time from the bottom to the top. For each method implemented, write a test program to test it. The top-down and bottom-up approaches are both fine. Both approaches implement methods incrementally, help to isolate programming errors, and make debugging easy. Sometimes they can be used together.

5.11.3 Implementation Details

The isLeapYear(int year) method can be implemented using the following code:

```
return (year % 400 == 0 || (year % 4 == 0 && year % 100 != 0));
```

Use the following facts to implement getTotalNumberOfDaysInMonth(int year, int month):

- January, March, May, July, August, October, and December have 31 days.
- April, June, September, and November have 30 days.
- February has 28 days during a regular year and 29 days during a leap year. A regular year, therefore, has 365 days, a leap year 366 days.

To implement getTotalNumberOfDays(int year, int month), you need to compute the total number of days (totalNumberOfDays) between January 1, 1800, and the first day of the calendar month. You could find the total number of days between the year 1800 and the calendar year and then figure out the total number of days prior to the calendar month in the calendar year. The sum of these two totals is totalNumberOfDays.

To print a body, first pad some space before the start day and then print the lines for every week.

The complete program is given in Listing 5.10.

LISTING 5.10 PrintCalendar.java

```
import java.util.Scanner;

public class PrintCalendar {
  /** Main method */
  public static void main(String[] args) {
    // Prompt the user to enter year
    Scanner input = new Scanner(System.in);

    // Prompt the user to enter year
    System.out.print("Enter full year (e.g., 2001): ");
    int year = input.nextInt();

    // Prompt the user to enter month
    System.out.print("Enter month in number between 1 and 12: ");
    int month = input.nextInt();

```

```
    // Print calendar for the month of the year
    printMonth(year, month);
  }

  /** Print the calendar for a month in a year */
```

printMonth

```
  static void printMonth(int year, int month) {
    // Print the headings of the calendar
    printMonthTitle(year, month);

    // Print the body of the calendar
    printMonthBody(year, month);
  }

  /** Print the month title, e.g., May, 1999 */
```

printMonthTitle

```
  static void printMonthTitle(int year, int month) {
    System.out.println("         " + getMonthName(month)
      + " " + year);
    System.out.println("-----------------------------");
    System.out.println(" Sun Mon Tue Wed Thu Fri Sat");
  }

  /** Get the English name for the month */
```

getMonthName

```
  static String getMonthName(int month) {
    String monthName = null;
    switch (month) {
      case 1: monthName = "January"; break;
      case 2: monthName = "February"; break;
      case 3: monthName = "March"; break;
      case 4: monthName = "April"; break;
      case 5: monthName = "May"; break;
      case 6: monthName = "June"; break;
      case 7: monthName = "July"; break;
      case 8: monthName = "August"; break;
      case 9: monthName = "September"; break;
      case 10: monthName = "October"; break;
      case 11: monthName = "November"; break;
      case 12: monthName = "December";
    }

    return monthName;
  }

  /** Print month body */
```

getMonthBody

```
  static void printMonthBody(int year, int month) {
    // Get start day of the week for the first date in the month
    int startDay = getStartDay(year, month);

    // Get number of days in the month
    int numberOfDaysInMonth = getNumberOfDaysInMonth(year, month);

    // Pad space before the first day of the month
    int i = 0;
    for (i = 0; i < startDay; i++)
      System.out.print("    ");

    for (i = 1; i <= numberOfDaysInMonth; i++) {
      if (i < 10)
        System.out.print("   " + i);
      else
        System.out.print("  " + i);
```

```
      if ((i + startDay) % 7 == 0)
        System.out.println();
    }

    System.out.println();
  }

  /** Get the start day of month/1/year */
  static int getStartDay(int year, int month) {
    final int START_DAY_FOR_JAN_1_1800 = 3;
    // Get total number of days from 1/1/1800 to month/1/year
    int totalNumberOfDays = getTotalNumberOfDays(year, month);

    // Return the start day for month/1/year
    return (totalNumberOfDays + START_DAY_FOR_JAN_1_1800) % 7;
  }

  /** Get the total number of days since January 1, 1800 */
  static int getTotalNumberOfDays(int year, int month) {
    int total = 0;

    // Get the total days from 1800 to 1/1/year
    for (int i = 1800; i < year; i++)
      if (isLeapYear(i))
        total = total + 366;
      else
        total = total + 365;

    // Add days from Jan to the month prior to the calendar month
    for (int i = 1; i < month; i++)
      total = total + getNumberOfDaysInMonth(year, i);

    return total;
  }

  /** Get the number of days in a month */
  static int getNumberOfDaysInMonth(int year, int month) {
    if (month == 1 || month == 3 || month == 5 || month == 7 ||
      month == 8 || month == 10 || month == 12)
      return 31;

    if (month == 4 || month == 6 || month == 9 || month == 11)
      return 30;

    if (month == 2) return isLeapYear(year) ? 29 : 28;

    return 0; // If month is incorrect
  }

  /** Determine if it is a leap year */
  static boolean isLeapYear(int year) {
    return year % 400 == 0 || (year % 4 == 0 && year % 100 != 0);
  }
}
```

getStartDay

getTotalNumberOfDays

getNumberOfDaysInMonth

isLeapYear

The program does not validate user input. For instance, if the user enters either a month not in the range between `1` and `12` or a year before `1800`, the program displays an erroneous calendar. To avoid this error, add an `if` statement to check the input before printing the calendar.

This program prints calendars for a month but could easily be modified to print calendars for a whole year. Although it can print months only after January `1800`, it could be modified to trace the day of a month before `1800`.

Note

Method abstraction modularizes programs in a neat, hierarchical manner. Programs written as collections of concise methods are easier to write, debug, maintain, and modify. This writing style also promotes method reusability.

Tip

incremental development and testing

When implementing a large program, use the top-down or bottom-up approach. Do not write the entire program at once. Using these approaches seems to take more development time (because you repeatedly compile and run the program), but it actually saves time and makes debugging easier.

Key Terms

actual parameter 143
argument 143
ambiguous invocation 153
divide and conquer 159
formal parameter (i.e., parameter) 143
information hiding 159
method 142
method abstraction 159
method overloading 151
method signature 143
modifier 142
pass-by-value 147
parameter 142
return type 142
return value 142
scope of variable 153
stepwise refinement 159
stub 162

Chapter Summary

- Making programs modular and reusable is one of the central goals in software engineering. Java provides many powerful constructs that help to achieve this goal. Methods are one such construct.

- The method header specifies the *modifiers*, *return value type*, *method name*, and *parameters* of the method. The static modifier is used for all the methods in this chapter.

- A method may return a value. The `returnValueType` is the data type of the value the method returns. If the method does not return a value, the `returnValueType` is the keyword `void`.

- The *parameter list* refers to the type, order, and number of the parameters of a method. The method name and the parameter list together constitute the *method signature*. Parameters are optional; that is, a method may contain no parameters.

- A return statement can also be used in a `void` method for terminating the method and returning to the method's caller. This is useful occasionally for circumventing the normal flow of control in a method.

- The arguments that are passed to a method should have the same number, type, and order as the parameters in the method definition.

- When a program calls a method, program control is transferred to the called method. A called method returns control to the caller when its return statement is executed or when its method-ending closing brace is reached.

- A value-returning method can also be invoked as a statement in Java. In this case, the caller simply ignores the return value. In the majority of cases, a call to a method with return value is treated as a value. In some cases, however, the caller is not interested in the return value.

- Each time a method is invoked, the system stores parameters and local variables in a space known as a *stack*. When a method calls another method, the caller's stack space is kept intact, and new space is created to handle the new method call. When a method finishes its work and returns to its caller, its associated space is released.

- A method can be overloaded. This means that two methods can have the same name, as long as their method parameter lists differ.

- The scope of a local variable is limited locally to a method. The scope of a local variable starts from its declaration and continues to the end of the block that contains the variable. A local variable must be declared before it can be used, and it must be initialized before it is referenced.

- *Method abstraction* is achieved by separating the use of a method from its implementation. The client can use a method without knowing how it is implemented. The details of the implementation are encapsulated in the method and hidden from the client who invokes the method. This is known as *information hiding* or *encapsulation*.

- Method abstraction modularizes programs in a neat, hierarchical manner. Programs written as collections of concise methods are easier to write, debug, maintain, and modify than would otherwise be the case. This writing style also promotes method reusability.

- When implementing a large program, use the top-down or bottom-up coding approach. Do not write the entire program at once. These approaches seem to take more time for coding (because you are repeatedly compiling and running the program), but they actually save time and makes debugging easier.

Review Questions

Sections 5.2–5.3

5.1 What are the benefits of using a method? How do you declare a method? How do you invoke a method?

5.2 What is the `return` type of a `main` method?

5.3 Can you simplify the `max` method in Listing 5.1 using the conditional operator?

5.4 True or false? A call to a method with a `void` return type is always a statement itself, but a call to a value-returning method is always a component of an expression.

5.5 What would be wrong with not writing a `return` statement in a value-returning method? Can you have a `return` statement in a `void` method, such as the following?

```
public static void main(String[] args) {
  int i;
  while (true) {
    // Prompt the user to enter an integer
    String intString = JOptionPane.showInputDialog(
      "Enter an integer:");

    // Convert a string into int
    int i = Integer.parseInt(intString);
    if (i == 0)
      return;
    System.out.println("i = " + i);
  }
}
```

Does the **return** statement in the following method cause syntax errors?

```
public static void xMethod(double x, double y) {
  System.out.println(x + y);
  return x + y;
}
```

5.6 Define the terms parameter, argument, and method signature.

5.7 Write method headers for the following methods:

- Computing a sales commission, given the sales amount and the commission rate.
- Printing the calendar for a month, given the month and year.
- Computing a square root.
- Testing whether a number is even, and returning `true` if it is.
- Printing a message a specified number of times.
- Computing the monthly payment, given the loan amount, number of years, and annual interest rate.
- Finding the corresponding uppercase letter, given a lowercase letter.

5.8 Identify and correct the errors in the following program:

```
public class Test {
  public static method1(int n, m) {
    n += m;
    xMethod(3.4);
  }

  public static int xMethod(int n) {
    if (n > 0) return 1;
    else if (n == 0) return 0;
    else if (n < 0) return -1;
  }
}
```

5.9 Reformat the following program according to the programming style and documentation guidelines proposed in §2.13, "Programming Style and Documentation." Use the next-line brace style.

```
public class Test {
  public static double xMethod(double i,double j)
  {
  while (i<j) {
    j--;
  }
```

```
        return j;
      }
    }
```

Section 5.4 Passing Parameters

5.10 How is an argument passed to a method? Can the argument have the same name as its parameter?

5.11 What is pass-by-value? Show the result of the following programs:

```
public class Test {
  public static void main(String[] args) {
    int max = 0;
    max(1, 2, max);
    System.out.println(max);
  }

  public static void max(
      int value1, int value2, int max) {
    if (value1 > value2)
      max = value1;
    else
      max = value2;
  }
}
```

(a)

```
public class Test {
  public static void main(String[] args) {
    // Initialize times
    int times = 3;
    System.out.println("Before the call,"
      + " variable times is " + times);

    // Invoke nPrintln and display times
    nPrintln("Welcome to Java!", times);
    System.out.println("After the call,"
      + "variable times is " + times);
  }

  // Print the message n times
  public static void nPrintln(
      String message, int n) {
    while (n > 0) {
      System.out.println("n = " + n);
      System.out.println(message);
      n--;
    }
  }
}
```

(b)

```
public class Test {
  public static void main(String[] args) {
    int i = 1;
    while (i <= 6) {
      xMethod(i, 2);
      i++;
    }
  }

  public static void xMethod(
      int i, int num) {
    for (int j = 1; j <= i; j++) {
      System.out.print(num + " ");
      num *= 2;
    }

    System.out.println();
  }
}
```

(c)

```
public class Test {
  public static void main(String[] args) {
    int i = 0;
    while (i <= 4) {
      xMethod(i);
      i++;
    }

    System.out.println("i is " + i);
  }

  public static void xMethod(int i) {
    do {
      if (i % 3 != 0)
        System.out.print(i + " ");
      i--;
    }
    while (i >= 1);

    System.out.println();
  }
}
```

(d)

5.12 For (a) in the preceding question, show the contents of the stack just before the method max is invoked, just entering max, just before max is returned, and right after max is returned.

Section 5.7 Overloading Methods

5.13 What is method overloading? Is it permissible to define two methods that have the same name but different parameter types? Is it permissible to define two methods in a class that have identical method names and parameter lists but different return value types or different modifiers?

5.14 What is wrong in the following program?

```
public class Test {
  public static void method(int x) {
  }

  public static int method(int y) {
    return y;
  }
}
```

Section 5.8 The Scope of Local Variables

5.15 Identify and correct the errors in the following program:

```
public class Test {
  public static void main(String[] args) {
    nPrintln("Welcome to Java!", 5);
  }

  public static void nPrintln(String message, int n) {
    int n = 1;
    for (int i = 0; i < n; i++)
      System.out.println(message);
  }
}
```

Section 5.9 The Math Class

5.16 True or false? The argument for trigonometric methods represents an angle in radians.

5.17 Write an expression that returns a random integer between 34 and 55. Write an expression that returns a random integer between 0 and 999. Write an expression that returns a random number between 5.5 and 55.5. Write an expression that returns a random lowercase letter.

5.18 Evaluate the following method calls:

(a) Math.sqrt(4)
(b) Math.sin(2 * Math.PI)
(c) Math.cos(2 * Math.PI)
(d) Math.pow(2, 2)
(e) Math.log(Math.E)
(f) Math.exp(1)
(g) Math.max(2, Math.min(3, 4))
(h) Math.rint(−2.5)
(i) Math.ceil(−2.5)
(j) Math.floor(−2.5)
(k) Math.round(−2.5f)

(l) Math.round(−2.5)
(m) Math.rint(2.5)
(n) Math.ceil(2.5)
(o) Math.floor(2.5)
(p) Math.round(2.5f)
(q) Math.round(2.5)
(r) Math.round(Math.abs(−2.5))

Programming Exercises

Sections 5.2–5.7

5.1 (*Converting an uppercase letter to lowercase*) Write a method that converts an uppercase letter to a lowercase letter. Use the following method header:

```
public static char upperCaseToLowerCase(char ch)
```

If the character is not an uppercase letter, the method simply returns the character itself. For example, `upperCaseToLowerCase('B')` returns `b` and `upperCaseToLowerCase('5')` returns `5`. See Exercise 2.7 on how to convert an uppercase letter to lowercase.

5.2* (*Summing the digits in an integer*) Write a method that computes the sum of the digits in an integer. Use the following method header:

```
public static int sumDigits(long n)
```

For example, `sumDigits(234)` returns `9` (2 + 3 + 4).

Hint: Use the `%` operator to extract digits, and the `/` operator to remove the extracted digit. For instance, to extract `4` from `234`, use `234 % 10` (=4). To remove `4` from `234`, use `234 / 10` (=23). Use a loop to repeatedly extract and remove the digit until all the digits are extracted.

5.3* (*Displaying an integer reversed*) Write the following method to display an integer in reverse order:

```
public static void reverse(int number)
```

For example, `reverse(3456)` displays `6543`.

5.4** (*Returning an integer reversed*) Write the following method to return an integer reversed:

```
public static int reverse(int number)
```

For example, `reverse(3456)` returns `6543`.

5.5* (*Sorting three numbers*) Write the following method to display three numbers in increasing order:

```
public static void sort(double num1, double num2, double num3)
```

5.6* (*Displaying patterns*) Write a method to display a pattern as follows:

```
              1
            2 1
          3 2 1
...
n n-1 ... 3 2 1
```

The method header is

```
public static void displayPattern(int n)
```

5.7* (*Financial application: computing the future investment value*) Write a method that computes future investment value at a given interest rate for a specified number of years. The future investment is determined using the formula in Exercise 2.9.

Use the following method header:

```
public static double futureInvestmentValue(
  double investmentAmount, double monthlyInterestRate, int
  years)
```

For example, `futureInvestmentValue(10000, 0.05/12, 5)` returns `12833.59`.

Write a test program that prompts the user to enter the investment amount (e.g., 1000) and the interest rate (e.g., 9%), and prints a table that displays future value for the years from 1 to 30, as shown below:

```
The amount invested: 1000
Annual interest rate: 9%
Years          Future Value
  1               1093.8
  2               1196.41
...
 29             13467.25
 30             14730.57
```

5.8 (*Conversions between Celsius and Fahrenheit*) Write a class that contains the following two methods:

```
/** Converts from Celsius to Fahrenheit */
public static double celsiusToFahrenheit(double celsius)


/** Converts from Fahrenheit to Celsius */
public static double fahrenheitToCelsius(double fahrenheit)
```

The formula for the conversion is:

```
fahrenheit = (9.0 / 5) * celsius + 32
```

Write a test program that invokes these methods to display the following tables:

```
Celsius        Fahrenheit          Fahrenheit        Celsius

 40.0          104.0               120.0             48.89
 39.0          102.2               110.0             43.33
...
 32.0           89.6                40.0              4.44
 31.0           87.8                30.0             -1.11
```

5.9 (*Conversions between feet and meters*) Write a class that contains the following two methods:

```
/** Converts from feet to meters */
public static double footToMeter(double foot)

/** Converts from meters to feet */
public static double meterToFoot(double meter)
```

The formula for the conversion is:

```
meter = 0.305 * foot
```

Write a test program that invokes these methods to display the following tables:

```
Feet       Meters    |   Meters     Feet
 1.0       0.305     |   20.0        65.574
 2.0       0.61      |   25.0        81.967
...
 9.0       2.745     |   60.0       196.721
10.0       3.05      |   65.0       213.115
```

5.10 (*Using the* `isPrime` *Method*) Listing 5.6, PrimeNumberMethod.java, provides the `isPrime(int number)` method for testing whether a number is prime. Use this method to find the number of prime numbers less than `10000`.

5.11 (*Financial application: computing commissions*) Write a method that computes the commission, using the scheme in §4.8.2, "Problem: Finding the Sales Amount." The header of the method is as follows:

```
public static double computeCommission(double salesAmount)
```

Write a test program that displays the following table:

```
SalesAmount        Commission
 10000                900.0
 15000               1500.0
   ...
 95000              11100.0
100000              11700.0
```

5.12** (*Displaying characters*) Write a method that prints characters using the following header:

```
public static void printChars(char ch1, char ch2,
  int numberPerLine)
```

This method prints the characters between `ch1` and `ch2` with the specified numbers per line. Write a test program that prints ten characters per line from `'1'` to `'Z'`.

5.13* (*Summing series*) Write a method to compute the following series:

$$m(i) = \frac{1}{2} + \frac{2}{3} + \ldots + \frac{i}{i+1}$$

Write a test program that displays the following table:

```
i                m(i)
1                0.5
2                1.1667
...
19               16.4023
20               17.3546
```

5.14* (*Computing series*) Write a method to compute the following series:

$$m(i) = 4\left(1 - \frac{1}{3} + \frac{1}{5} - \frac{1}{7} + \frac{1}{9} - \frac{1}{11} + \frac{1}{13} - \ldots + \frac{1}{2i-1} - \frac{1}{2i+1}\right)$$

5.15* (*Financial application: printing a tax table*) Listing 3.7 gives a program to compute tax. Write a method for computing tax using the following header:

```
public static double computetax(int status, double taxableIncome)
```

Use this method to write a program that prints a tax table for taxable income from $50,000 to $60,000 with intervals of $50 for all four statuses, as follows:

```
Taxable      Single      Married      Married      Head of
Income                   Joint        Separate     a House
 50000        9846        7296        10398         8506
 50050        9859        7309        10411         8519
 ...
 59950       12532        9982        13190        11192
 60000       12546        9996        13205        11206
```

5.16* (*Number of days in a year*) Write a method that returns the number of days in a year using the following header:

```
public static int numberOfDaysInAYear(int year)
```

Write a test program that displays the number of days in year `2000`, . . . , and `2010`.

Section 5.9 The `Math` Class

5.17* (*Displaying matrix of 0s and 1s*) Write a method that displays an `n`-by-`n` matrix using the following header:

```
public static void printMatrix(int n)
```

Each element is 0 or 1, which is generated randomly. Write a test program that prints a 3-by-3 matrix that may look like this:

0 1 0
0 0 0
1 1 1

5.18 (*Using the `Math.sqrt` method*) Write a program that prints the following table using the `sqrt` method in the `Math` class.

```
Number      SquareRoot
0              0.0000
2              1.4142
...
18             4.2426
20             4.4721
```

5.19* (*The `MyTriangle` class*) Create a class named `MyTriangle` that contains the following two methods:

```
/** Returns true if the sum of any two sides is
 *  greater than the third side. */
public static boolean isValid(
  double side1, double side2, double side3)

/** Returns the area of the triangle. */
public static double area(
  double side1, double side2, double side3)
```

The formula for computing the area is

$$s = (side1 + side2 + side3)/2;$$

$$area = \sqrt{s(s - side1)(s - side2)(s - side3)}$$

Write a test program that reads three sides for a triangle and computes the area if the input is valid. Otherwise, it displays that the input is invalid.

5.20 (*Using trigonometric methods*) Print the following table to display the `sin` value and `cos` value of degrees from 0 to 360 with increments of 10 degrees. Round the value to keep four digits after the decimal point.

```
Degree      Sin         Cos
0           0.0         1.0
10          0.1736      0.9848
...
350         -0.1736     0.9848
360         0.0         1.0
```

5.21** (*Computing mean and standard deviation*) In business applications, you are often asked to compute the mean and standard deviation of data. The mean is simply the average of the numbers. The standard deviation is a statistic that tells you how tightly all the various data are clustered around the mean in a set of data. For example, what is the average age of the students in a class? How close are the ages? If all the students are the same age, the deviation is 0. Write a program that prompts the user to enter ten numbers, and displays the mean and standard deviations of these numbers using the following formula:

$$mean = \frac{\sum_{i=1}^{n} x_i}{n} = \frac{x_1 + x_2 + \ldots + x_n}{n} \qquad deviation = \sqrt{\frac{\sum_{i=1}^{n} x_i^2 - \frac{\left(\sum_{i=1}^{n} x_i\right)^2}{n}}{n-1}}$$

5.22** (*Approximating the square root*) Implement the `sqrt` method. The square root of a number, `num`, can be approximated by repeatedly performing a calculation using the following formula:

```
nextGuess = (lastGuess + (num / lastGuess)) / 2
```

When `nextGuess` and `lastGuess` are almost identical, `nextGuess` is the approximated square root.

The initial guess can be any positive value (e.g., `1`). This value will be the starting value for `lastGuess`. If the difference between `nextGuess` and `lastGuess` is less than a very small number, such as `0.0001`, you can claim that `nextGuess` is the approximated square root of `num`. If not, `nextGuess` becomes the `lastGuess` and continue the approximation process.

Sections 5.10–5.11

5.23* (*Generating random characters*) Use the methods in `RandomCharacter` in Listing 5.8 to print 100 uppercase letters and then 100 single digits, and print ten per line.

5.24** (*Displaying current date and time*) Listing 2.9, ShowCurrentTime.java, displays the current time. Improve this example to display the current date and time. The calendar example in Listing 5.10, PrintCalendar.java, should give you some ideas on how to find year, month, and day.

5.25** (*Converting milliseconds to hours, minutes, and seconds*) Write a method that converts milliseconds to hours, minutes, and seconds using the following header:

```
public static String convertMillis(long millis)
```

The method returns a string as hours:minutes:seconds. For example, `convertMillis(5500)` returns a string 0:0:5, `convertMillis(100000)` returns a string 0:1:40, and `convertMillis(555550000)` returns a string 154:19:10.

Comprehensive

Video Note
Find emirp prime

5.26** (*Emirp*) An *emirp* (prime spelled backward) is a prime number whose reversal is also a prime. For example, 17 is a prime and 71 is a prime. So 17 and 71 are emirps. Write a program that displays the first 100 emirps. Display 10 numbers per line and align the numbers properly, as follows:

```
  2    3    5    7   11   13   17   31   37   71
 73   79   97  101  107  113  131  149  151  157
...
```

5.27** (*Palindromic prime*) A *palindromic prime* is a prime number and also palindromic. For example, 131 is a prime and also a palindromic prime. So are 17 and 71. Write a program that displays the first 100 palindromic prime numbers. Display 10 numbers per line and align the numbers properly, as follows:

```
  2    3    5    7   11  101  131  151  181  191
313  353  373  383  727  757  787  797  919  929
...
```

5.28** (*Mersenne prime*) A prime number is called a *Mersenne prime* if it can be written in the form $2^p - 1$ for some positive integer p. Write a program that finds all Mersenne primes with $p \leq 31$ and displays the output as follows:

```
p        2^p - 1
2           3
3           7
5          31
...
```

5.29** (*Game: craps*) Craps is a popular dice game played in casinos. Write a program to play a variation of the game, as follows:

Roll two dice. Each die has six faces representing values 1, 2, …, and 6, respectively. Check the sum of the two dice. If the sum is 2, 3, or 12 (called *craps*), you lose; if the sum is 7 or 11 (called *natural*), you win; if the sum is another value (i.e., 4, 5, 6, 8, 9, or 10), a *point* is established. Continue to roll the dice until either a 7 or the same point value is rolled. If 7 is rolled, you lose. Otherwise, you win.

Your program acts as a single player. Here are some sample runs.

```
You rolled 5 + 6 = 11
You win
```

```
You rolled 1 + 2 = 3
You lose
```

```
You rolled 4 + 4 = 8
point is 8
You rolled 6 + 2 = 8
You win
```

```
You rolled 3 + 2 = 5
point is 5
You rolled 2 + 5 = 7
You lose
```

5.30** (*Twin primes*) Twin primes are a pair of prime numbers that differ by 2. For example, 3 and 5 are twin primes, 5 and 7 are twin primes, and 11 and 13 are twin primes. Write a program to find all twin primes less than 1000. Display the output as follows:

```
(3, 5)
(5, 7)
...
```

5.31**(*Financial: credit card number validation)* Credit card numbers follow certain patterns. A credit card number must have between 13 and 16 digits. It must start with:

- 4 for Visa cards
- 5 for Master cards
- 37 for American Express cards
- 6 for Discover cards

In 1954, Hans Luhn of IBM proposed an algorithm for validating credit card numbers. The algorithm is useful to determine if a card number is entered correctly or if a credit card is scanned correctly by a scanner. Almost all credit card numbers are generated following this validity check, commonly known as the *Luhn check* or the *Mod 10 check*, which can be described as follows (for illustration, consider the card number 4388576018402625):

1. Double every second digit from right to left. If doubling of a digit results in a two-digit number, add up the two digits to get a single-digit number.
   2 * 2 = 4
   2 * 2 = 4
   4 * 2 = 8
   1 * 2 = 2
   6 * 2 = 12 (1 + 2 = 3)
   5 * 2 = 10 (1 + 0 = 1)
   8 * 2 = 16 (1 + 6 = 7)
   4 * 2 = 8
2. Now add all single-digit numbers from Step 1.
   4 + 4 + 8 + 2 + 3 + 1 + 7 + 8 = 37
3. Add all digits in the odd places from right to left in the card number.
   5 + 6 + 0 + 8 + 0 + 7 + 8 + 3 = 37
4. Sum the results from Step 2 and Step 3.
   37 + 37 = 74

5. If the result from Step 4 is divisible by 10, the card number is valid; otherwise, it is invalid. For example, the number 4388576018402625 is invalid, but the number 4388576018410707 is valid.

Write a program that prompts the user to enter a credit card number as a `long` integer. Display whether the number is valid. Design your program to use the following methods:

```
/** Return true if the card number is valid */
public boolean isValid(long number)

/** Get the result from Step 2 */
public static int sumOfEvenPlace(long number)

/** Return this number if it is a single digit, otherwise, return
 * the sum of the two digits */
public static int getDigit(int number)

/** Return sum of odd place digits in number */
public static int sumOfOddPlace(long number)
```

5.32** (*Game: chance of winning at craps*) Revise Exercise 5.29 to run it 10000 times and display the number of winning games.

CHAPTER 6

ARRAYS

Objectives

- To describe why arrays are necessary in programming (§6.1).
- To learn the steps involved in using arrays: declaring array reference variables and creating arrays (§§6.2.1–6.2.2).
- To initialize the values in an array (§6.2.3).
- To access array elements using indexed variables (§6.2.4).
- To simplify programming using the for-each loops (§6.2.5).
- To declare, create, and initialize an array using an array initializer (§6.2.6).
- To copy contents from one array to another (§6.3).
- To develop and invoke methods with array arguments and return value (§6.4–6.5).
- To declare a method with variable-length argument list (§6.6).
- To search elements using the linear (§6.7.1) or binary (§6.7.2) search algorithm.
- To sort an array using the selection sort (§6.8.1)
- To sort an array using the insertion sort algorithm (§6.8.2).
- To use the methods in the `Arrays` class (§6.9).
- To declare and create two-dimensional arrays to solve interesting problems such as Sudoku (§6.10).
- To declare and create multidimensional arrays (§6.11).

6.1 Introduction

why array?

Often you will have to store a large number of values during the execution of a program. Suppose, for instance, that you need to read 100 numbers, compute their average, and find out how many numbers are above the average. Your program first reads the numbers and computes their average, and then compares each number with the average to determine whether it is above the average. The numbers must all be stored in variables in order to accomplish this task. You have to declare 100 variables and repeatedly write almost identical code one hundred times. From the standpoint of practicality, it is impossible to write a program this way. So, how do you solve this problem?

what is array?

An efficient, organized approach is needed. Java and most other high-level languages provide a data structure, the *array*, which stores a fixed-size sequential collection of elements of the same type. In this case, you can store all 100 numbers into an array and access the numbers through a single array variable.

6.2 Array Basics

An array is used to store a collection of data, but it is often more useful to think of an array as a collection of variables of the same type. Instead of declaring individual variables, such as `number0`, `number1`, ..., and `number99`, you declare one array variable such as `numbers` and use `numbers[0]`, `numbers[1]`, ..., and `numbers[99]` to represent individual variables. This section introduces how to declare array variables, create arrays, and process arrays using indexed variables.

6.2.1 Declaring Array Variables

To use an array in a program, you must declare a variable to reference the array and specify the type of array the variable can reference. Here is the syntax for declaring an array variable:

preferred syntax

```
dataType[] arrayRefVar;
```

For example, the following code snippets are examples of this syntax:

```
double[] myList;
```

Note

preferred syntax

You can also use `dataType arrayRefVar[]` to declare an array variable. This style comes from the C language and was adopted in Java to accommodate C programmers. The style `dataType[] arrayRefVar` is preferred

6.2.2 Creating Arrays

Unlike declarations for primitive data type variables, the declaration of an array variable does not allocate any space in memory for the array. It creates only a storage location for the reference to an array. If a variable does not contain a reference to an array, the value of the variable is `null`. You cannot assign elements to an array unless it has already been created. After an array variable is declared, you can create an array by using the `new` operator with the following syntax:

```
arrayRefVar = new dataType[arraySize];
```

This statement does two things: (1) it creates an array using `new dataType[arraySize];` (2) it assigns the reference of the newly created array to the variable `arrayRefVar`.

new operator

Declaring an array variable, creating an array, and assigning the reference of the array to the variable can be combined in one statement, as shown below:

```
dataType[] arrayRefVar = new dataType[arraySize];
```

or

```
dataType arrayRefVar[] = new dataType[arraySize];
```

Here is an example of such a statement:

```
double[] myList = newdouble[10];
```

This statement declares an array variable, `myList`, creates an array of ten elements of `double` type, and assigns its reference to `myList`. To assign values to the elements, use the syntax:

```
arrayRefVar[index] = value;
```

For example, the following code initializes the array.

```
myList[0] = 5.6;
myList[1] = 4.5;
myList[2] = 3.3;
myList[3] = 13.2;
myList[4] = 4.0;
myList[5] = 34.33;
myList[6] = 34.0;
myList[7] = 45.45;
myList[8] = 99.993;
myList[9] = 11123;
```

The array is pictured in Figure 6.1.

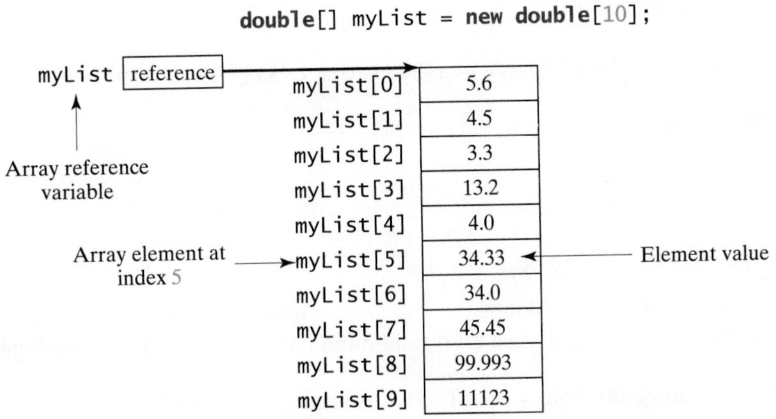

```
double[] myList = new double[10];
```

myList reference

Array reference variable

myList[0]	5.6
myList[1]	4.5
myList[2]	3.3
myList[3]	13.2
myList[4]	4.0
myList[5]	34.33
myList[6]	34.0
myList[7]	45.45
myList[8]	99.993
myList[9]	11123

Array element at index 5

Element value

FIGURE 6.1 The array `myList` has ten elements of `double` type and `int` indices from `0` to `9`.

array vs. array variable

Note

An array variable that appears to hold an array actually contains a reference to that array. Strictly speaking, an array variable and an array are different, but most of the time the distinction can be ignored. Thus it is all right to say, for simplicity, that `myList` is an array, instead of stating, at greater length, that `myList` is a variable that contains a reference to an array of ten double elements.

6.2.3 Array Size and Default Values

array length

When space for an array is allocated, the array size must be given, to specify the number of elements that can be stored in it. The size of an array cannot be changed after the array is created. Size can be obtained using `arrayRefVar.length`. For example, `myList.length` is `10`.

default values

When an array is created, its elements are assigned the default value of `0` for the numeric primitive data types, `'\u0000'` for `char` types, and `false` for `boolean` types.

6.2.4 Array Indexed Variables

0 based

The array elements are accessed through the index. Array indices are `0` based; that is, they start from `0` to `arrayRefVar.length-1`. In the example in Figure 6.1, `myList` holds ten `double` values, and the indices are from `0` to `9`.

indexed variables

Each element in the array is represented using the following syntax, known as an *indexed variable:*

```
arrayRefVar[index];
```

For example, `myList[9]` represents the last element in the array `myList`.

Caution

Some languages use parentheses to reference an array element, as in `myList(9)`. But Java uses brackets, as in `myList[9]`.

After an array is created, an indexed variable can be used in the same way as a regular variable. For example, the following code adds the values in `myList[0]` and `myList[1]` to `myList[2]`.

```
myList[2] = myList[0] + myList[1];
```

The following loop assigns `0` to `myList[0]`, `1` to `myList[1]`, . . . , and `9` to `myList[9]`:

```
for (int i = 0; i < myList.length; i++) {
  myList[i] = i;
}
```

6.2.5 Array Initializers

Java has a shorthand notation, known as the *array initializer*, which combines in one statement declaring an array, creating an array, and initializing, using the following syntax:

```
dataType[] arrayRefVar = {value0, value1, ..., valuek};
```

For example,

```
double[] myList = {1.9, 2.9, 3.4, 3.5};
```

This statement declares, creates, and initializes the array myList with four elements, which is equivalent to the statements shown below:

```
double[] myList = new double[4];
myList[0] = 1.9;
myList[1] = 2.9;
myList[2] = 3.4;
myList[3] = 3.5;
```

Caution

The new operator is not used in the array initializer syntax. Using an array initializer, you have to declare, create, and initialize the array all in one statement. Splitting it would cause a syntax error. Thus the next statement is wrong:

```
double[] myList;
myList = {1.9, 2.9, 3.4, 3.5};
```

6.2.6 Processing Arrays

When processing array elements, you will often use a for loop—for two reasons:

- All of the elements in an array are of the same type. They are evenly processed in the same fashion by repeatedly using a loop.
- Since the size of the array is known, it is natural to use a for loop.

Here are some examples of processing arrays:

1. (*Initializing arrays with random values*) The following loop initializes the array myList with random values between 0.0 and 100.0, but less than 100.0.

```
for (int i = 0; i < myList.length; i++) {
  myList[i] = Math.random() * 100;
}
```

2. (*Printing arrays*) To print an array, you have to print each element in the array using a loop like the following:

```
for (int i = 0; i < myList.length; i++) {
  System.out.print(myList[i] + " ");
}
```

Tip

For an array of the char[] type, it can be printed using one print statement. For example, the following code displays Dallas:

print character array

```
char[] city = {'D', 'a', 'l', 'l', 'a', 's'};
System.out.println(city);
```

3. (*Summing all elements*) Use a variable named total to store the sum. Initially total is 0. Add each element in the array to total using a loop like this:

```
double total = 0;
for (int i = 0; i < myList.length; i++) {
  total += myList[i];
}
```

4. (*Finding the largest element*) Use a variable named max to store the largest element. Initially max is myList[0]. To find the largest element in the array myList,

compare each element in myList with max, and update max if the element is greater than max.

```
double max = myList[0];
for (int i = 1; i < myList.length; i++) {
  if (myList[i] > max) max = myList[i];
}
```

5. (*Finding the smallest index of the largest element*) Often you need to locate the largest element in an array. If an array has more than one largest element, find the smallest index of such an element. Suppose the array myList is {1, 5, 3, 4, 5, 5}. The largest element is 5 and the smallest index for 5 is 1. Use a variable named max to store the largest element and a variable named indexOfMax to denote the index of the largest element. Initially max is myList[0], and indexOfMax is 0. Compare each element in myList with max, and update max and indexOfMax if the element is greater than max.

```
double max = myList[0];
int indexOfMax = 0;
for (int i = 1; i < myList.length; i++) {
  if (myList[i] > max) {
    max = myList[i];
    indexOfMax = i;
  }
}
```

What is the consequence if **(myList[i] > max)** is replaced by **(myList[i] >= max)**?

6. (*Shifting elements*) Sometimes you need to shift the elements left or right. Here is an example to shift the elements one position to the left and fill the last element with the first element:

```
double temp = myList[0]; // Retain the first element

// Shift elements left
for (int i = 1; i < myList.length; i++) {
  myList[i - 1] = myList[i];
}

// Move the first element to fill in the last position
myList[myList.length - 1] = temp;
```


6.2.7 For-each Loops

JDK 1.5 introduced a new for loop, known as a *for-each loop* or *enhanced for loop*, which enables you to traverse the complete array sequentially without using an index variable. For example, the following code displays all the elements in the array myList:

```
for (double element: myList) {
  System.out.println(element);
}
```

You can read the code as "for each element in myList do the following." Note that the variable, element, must be declared the same type as the elements in myList.

In general, the syntax for a for-each loop is

```
for (elementType element: arrayRefVar) {
  // Process the element
}
```

You still have to use an index variable if you wish to traverse the array in a different order or change the elements in the array.

6.2.8 Problem: Analyzing Array Elements

The problem is to write a program that reads six integers, finds the largest of them, and counts its occurrences. Suppose that you entered 3, 5, 2, 5, 5, 5; the program finds that the largest is 5 and the occurrence count for 5 is 4.

An intuitive solution is to first read the numbers and store them in an array, then find the largest number in the array, and finally count the occurrences of the largest number in the array. The program is given in Listing 6.1.

LISTING 6.1 TestArray.java

```
import java.util.Scanner;

public class TestArray {
  /** Main method */
  public static void main(String[] args) {
    final int TOTAL_NUMBERS = 6;
    int[] numbers = new int[TOTAL_NUMBERS];

    // Create a Scanner
    Scanner input = new Scanner(System.in);

    // Read all numbers
    for (int i = 0; i < numbers.length; i++) {
      System.out.print("Enter a number: ");

      // Convert string into integer
      numbers[i] = input.nextInt();
    }

    // Find the largest
    int max = numbers[0];
    for (int i = 1; i < numbers.length; i++) {
      if (max < numbers[i])
        max = numbers[i];
    }

    // Find the occurrence of the largest number
    int count = 0;
    for (int i = 0; i < numbers.length; i++) {
      if (numbers[i] == max) count++;
    }

    // Prepare the result
    String output = "The array is ";
    for (int i = 0; i < numbers.length; i++) {
      output += numbers[i] + " ";
    }

    output += "\nThe largest number is " + max;
    output += "\nThe occurrence count of the largest number "
      + "is " + count;

    // Display the result
    System.out.println(output);
  }
}
```

create array

store numbers

update max

count occurrence

prepare output

output

```
Enter a number: 3 ↵Enter
Enter a number: 5 ↵Enter
Enter a number: 2 ↵Enter
Enter a number: 5 ↵Enter
Enter a number: 5 ↵Enter
Enter a number: 5 ↵Enter
The array is 3 5 2 5 5 5
The largest number is 5
The occurrence count of the largest number is 4
```

The program declares and creates an array of six integers (line 7). It finds the largest number in the array (lines 21–25), counts its occurrences (lines 28–31), and displays the result (lines 34–44). To display the array, you need to display each element in the array using a loop.

Without using the `numbers` array, you would have to declare a variable for each number entered, because all the numbers are compared to the largest number to count its occurrences after it is found.

Caution

ArrayIndexOutOfBounds Exception

Accessing an array out of bounds is a common programming error that throws a runtime `ArrayIndexOutOfBoundsException`. To avoid it, make sure that you do not use an index beyond `arrayRefVar.length - 1`.

off-by-one error

Programmers often mistakenly reference the first element in an array with index `1`, but it should be `0`. This is called the *off-by-one error*.

6.2.9 Problem: Assigning Grades

The problem is to write a program that reads student scores, gets the best score, and then assigns grades based on the following scheme:

Grade is A if score is >= best − 10;

Grade is B if score is >= best − 20;

Grade is C if score is >= best − 30;

Grade is D if score is >= best − 40;

Grade is F otherwise.

The program prompts the user to enter the total number of students, then prompts the user to enter all of the scores, and concludes by displaying the grades.

The program reads the scores, then finds the best score, and finally assigns grades to the students based on the preceding scheme. Listing 6.2 gives the solution to the problem.

Video Note
Assign grades

Listing 6.2 AssignGrade.java

```java
import java.util.Scanner;

public class AssignGrade {
  /** Main method */
  public static void main(String[] args) {
    // Create a Scanner
    Scanner input = new Scanner(System.in);

    // Get number of students
    System.out.print("Please enter number of students: ");
```

```
11      int numberOfStudents = input.nextInt();
12
13      int[] scores = new int[numberOfStudents]; // Array scores
14      int best = 0; // The best score
15      char grade; // The grade
16
17      // Read scores and find the best score
18      for (int i = 0; i < scores.length; i++) {
19        System.out.print("Please enter a score: ");
20        scores[i] = input.nextInt();
21
22        if (scores[i] > best)
23          best = scores[i];
24      }
25
26      // Declare and initialize output string
27      String output = " ";
28
29      // Assign and display grades
30      for (int i = 0; i < scores.length; i++) {
31        if (scores[i] >= best - 10)
32          grade = 'A';
33        else if (scores[i] >= best - 20)
34          grade = 'B';
35        else if (scores[i] >= best - 30)
36          grade = 'C';
37        else if (scores[i] >= best - 40)
38          grade = 'D';
39        else
40          grade = 'F';
41
42        output += "Student " + i + " score is " +
43          scores[i] + " and grade is " + grade + "\n";
44      }
45
46      // Display the result
47      System.out.println(output);
48    }
49  }
```

number of students

create array

get a score

update best

assign grade

display grade

```
Please enter number of students: 4 ↵Enter
Please enter a score: 40 ↵Enter
Please enter a score: 50 ↵Enter
Please enter a score: 60 ↵Enter
Please enter a score: 70 ↵Enter
Student 0 score is 40 and grade is C
Student 1 score is 50 and grade is B
Student 2 score is 60 and grade is A
Student 3 score is 70 and grade is A
```

The program declares and creates **scores** as an array of **int** type in order to store the students' scores (line 13), after the user enters the number of students into **numberOfStudents** in line 11. The size of the array is set at runtime; it cannot be changed once the array is created.

The array is not needed to find the best score, but it is needed to keep all of the scores so that grades can be assigned later on, and it is needed when scores are printed along with the students' grades.

6.3 Copying Arrays

Often, in a program, you need to duplicate an array or a part of an array. In such cases you could attempt to use the assignment statement (=), as follows:

```
list2 = list1;
```

copy reference

garbage collection

This statement does not copy the contents of the array referenced by list1 to list2, but merely copies the reference value from list1 to list2. After this statement, list1 and list2 reference to the same array, as shown in Figure 6.2. The array previously referenced by list2 is no longer referenced; it becomes garbage, which will be automatically collected by the Java Virtual Machine.

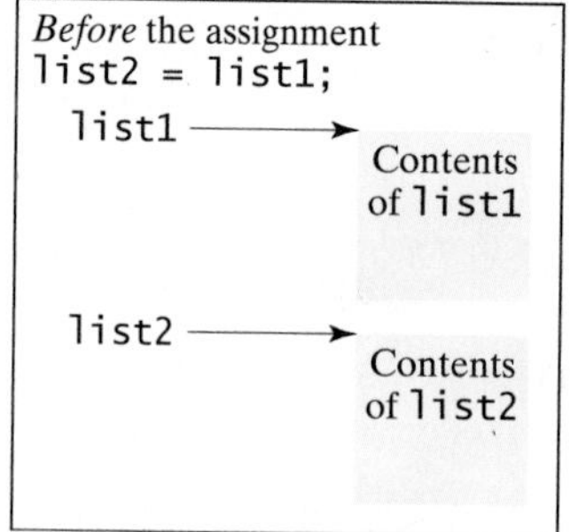

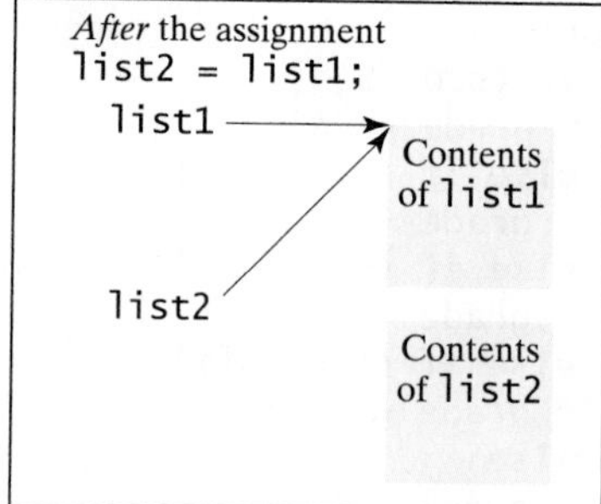

Figure 6.2 Before the assignment statement, list1 and list2 point to separate memory locations. After the assignment, the reference of the list1 array is passed to list2.

In Java, you can use assignment statements to copy primitive data type variables, but not arrays. Assigning one array variable to another array variable actually copies one reference to another and makes both variables point to the same memory location.

There are three ways to copy arrays:

- Use a loop to copy individual elements one by one.
- Use the static arraycopy method in the System class.
- Use the clone method to copy arrays; this will be introduced in Chapter 10, "Inheritance and Polymorphism."

You can write a loop to copy every element from the source array to the corresponding element in the target array. The following code, for instance, copies sourceArray to targetArray using a for loop.

```
int[] sourceArray = {2, 3, 1, 5, 10};
int[] targetArray = new int[sourceArray.length];
for (int i = 0; i < sourceArray.length; i++) {
  targetArray[i] = sourceArray[i];
}
```

arraycopy method

Another approach is to use the arraycopy method in the java.lang.System class to copy arrays instead of using a loop. The syntax for arraycopy is shown below:

```
arraycopy(sourceArray, src_pos, targetArray, tar_pos, length);
```

The parameters src_pos and tar_pos indicate the starting positions in sourceArray and targetArray, respectively. The number of elements copied from sourceArray to targetArray is indicated by length. For example, you can rewrite the loop using the following statement:

```
System.arraycopy(sourceArray, 0, targetArray, 0, sourceArray.length);
```

The arraycopy method does not allocate memory space for the target array. The target array must have already been created with its memory space allocated. After the copying takes place, targetArray and sourceArray have the same content but independent memory locations.

Note

The arraycopy method violates the Java naming convention. By convention, this method should be named arrayCopy (i.e., with an uppercase C).

6.4 Passing Arrays to Methods

Just as you can pass primitive type values to methods, you can also pass arrays to methods. For example, the following method displays the elements in an int array.

```
public static void printArray(int[] array) {
  for (int i = 0; i < array.length; i++) {
    System.out.print(array[i] + " ");
  }
}
```

You can invoke it by passing an array. For example, the following statement invokes the printArray method to display 3, 1, 2, 6, 4, and 2.

```
printArray(newint[]{3, 1, 2, 6, 4, 2});
```

Note

The preceding statement creates an array using the following syntax:

```
new dataType[]{value0, value1, ..., valuek};
```

There is no explicit reference variable for the array. Such array is called an *anonymous array*. anonymous arrays

Java uses *pass-by-value* to pass arguments to a method. There are important differences between passing the values of variables of primitive data types and passing arrays. pass-by-value

- For an argument of a primitive type, the argument's value is passed.
- For an argument of an array type, the value of the argument is a reference to an array; this reference value is passed to the method. Semantically, it can be best described as *pass-by-sharing*, i.e., the array in the method is the same as the array being passed. So if you change the array in the method, you will see the change outside the method. pass-by-sharing

Take the following code, for example:

```
public class Test {
  public static void main(String[] args) {
    int x = 1; // x represents an int value
    int[] y = new int[10]; // y represents an array of int values

    m(x, y); // Invoke m with arguments x and y
```

```
    System.out.println("x is " + x);
    System.out.println("y[0] is " + y[0]);
  }

  public static void m(int number, int[] numbers) {
    number = 1001; // Assign a new value to number
    numbers[0] = 5555; // Assign a new value to numbers[0]
  }
}
```

You will see that after m is invoked, x remains 1, but y[0] is 5555. This is because y and numbers reference to the same array, although y and numbers are independent variables, as illustrated in Figure 6.3. When invoking m(x, y), the values of x and y are passed to number and numbers. Since y contains the reference value to the array, numbers now contains the same reference value to the same array.

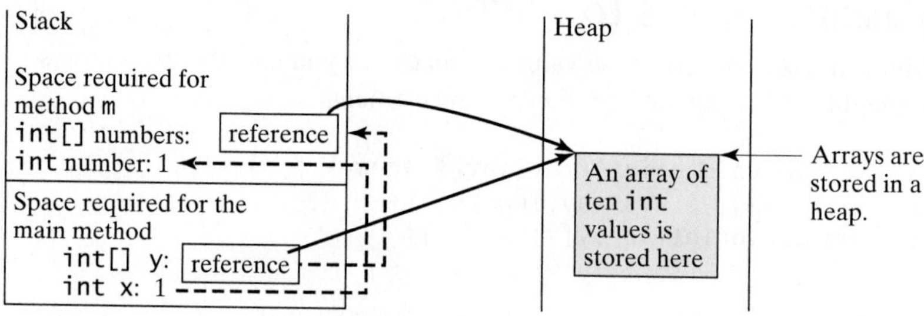

FIGURE 6.3 The primitive type value in x is passed to number, and the reference value in y is passed to numbers.

heap

Note

The JVM stores the array in an area of memory called the *heap*, which is used for dynamic memory allocation where blocks of memory are allocated and freed in an arbitrary order.

6.4.1 Passing Array Arguments

Listing 6.3 gives another program that shows the difference between passing a primitive data type value and an array reference variable to a method.

The program contains two methods for swapping elements in an array. The first method, named swap, fails to swap two int arguments. The second method, named swapFirstTwoInArray, successfully swaps the first two elements in the array argument.

LISTING 6.3 TestPassArray.java

false swap

```
public class TestPassArray {
  /** Main method */
  public static void main(String[] args) {
    int[] a = {1, 2};

    // Swap elements using the swap method
    System.out.println("Before invoking swap");
    System.out.println("array is {" + a[0] + ", " + a[1] + "}");
    swap(a[0], a[1]);
    System.out.println("After invoking swap");
    System.out.println("array is {" + a[0] + ", " + a[1] + "}");

```

```
    // Swap elements using the swapFirstTwoInArray method
    System.out.println("Before invoking swapFirstTwoInArray");
    System.out.println("array is {" + a[0] + ", " + a[1] + "}");
    swapFirstTwoInArray(a);
    System.out.println("After invoking swapFirstTwoInArray");
    System.out.println("array is {" + a[0] + ", " + a[1] + "}");
  }

  /** Swap two variables */
  public static void swap(int n1, int n2) {
    int temp = n1;
    n1 = n2;
    n2 = temp;
  }

  /** Swap the first two elements in the array */
  public static void swapFirstTwoInArray(int[] array) {
    int temp = array[0];
    array[0] = array[1];
    array[1] = temp;
  }
}
```

swap array elements

```
Before invoking swap
array is {1, 2}
After invoking swap
array is {1, 2}
Before invoking swapFirstTwoInArray
array is {1, 2}
After invoking swapFirstTwoInArray
array is {2, 1}
```

As shown in Figure 6.4, the two elements are not swapped using the **swap** method. However, they are swapped using the **swapFirstTwoInArray** method. Since the parameters in the **swap** method are primitive type, the values of **a[0]** and **a[1]** are passed to **n1** and **n2** inside the method when invoking **swap(a[0], a[1])**. The memory locations for **n1** and **n2** are

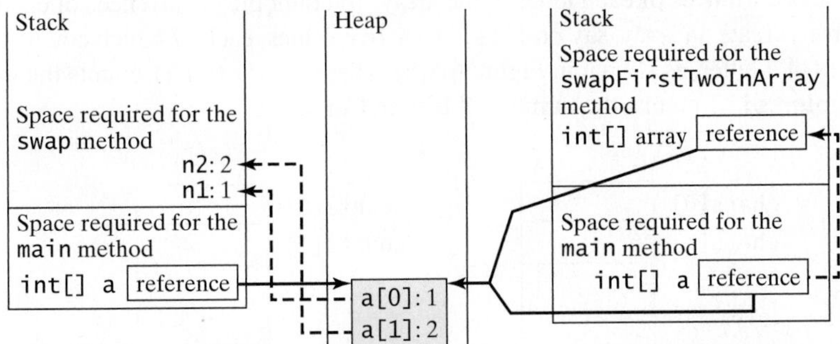

Invoke swap(int n1, int n2). The primitive type values in a[0] and a[1] are passed to the swap method.

The arrays are stored in a heap.

Invoke swapFirstTwoInArray(int[] array). The reference value in a is passed to the swapFirstTwoInArray method.

FIGURE 6.4 When passing an array to a method, the reference of the array is passed to the method.

independent of the ones for `a[0]` and `a[1]`. The contents of the array are not affected by this call.

The parameter in the `swapFirstTwoInArray` method is an array. As shown in Figure 6.4, the reference of the array is passed to the method. Thus the variables `a` (outside the method) and `array` (inside the method) both refer to the same array in the same memory location. Therefore, swapping `array[0]` with `array[1]` inside the method `swapFirstTwoInArray` is the same as swapping `a[0]` with `a[1]` outside of the method.

6.5 Returning an Array from a Method

You can pass arrays when invoking a method. A method may also return an array. For example, the method shown below returns an array that is the reversal of another array:

create array

return array

```
1 public static int[] reverse(int[] list) {
2   int[] result = new int[list.length];
3
4   for (int i = 0, j = result.length - 1;
5        i < list.length; i++, j--) {
6     result[j] = list[i];
7   }
8
9   return result;
10 }
```

list

result

Line 2 creates a new array `result`. Lines 4–7 copy elements from array `list` to array `result`. Line 9 returns the array. For example, the following statement returns a new array `list2` with elements `6, 5, 4, 3, 2, 1`.

```
int[] list1 = {1, 2, 3, 4, 5, 6};
int[] list2 = reverse(list1);
```

6.5.1 Case Study: Counting the Occurrences of Each Letter

Listing 6.4 presents a program to count the occurrences of each letter in an array of characters. The program does the following:

1. Generate `100` lowercase letters randomly and assign them to an array of characters, as shown in Figure 6.5(a). You can obtain a random letter by using the `getRandomLowerCaseLetter()` method in the `RandomCharacter` class in Listing 5.8.

2. Count the occurrences of each letter in the array. To count the occurrences of each letter in the array, create an array, say `counts`, of `26 int` values, each of which counts the occurrences of a letter, as shown in Figure 6.5(b). That is, `counts[0]` counts the number of `a`'s, `counts[1]` counts the number of `b`'s, and so on.

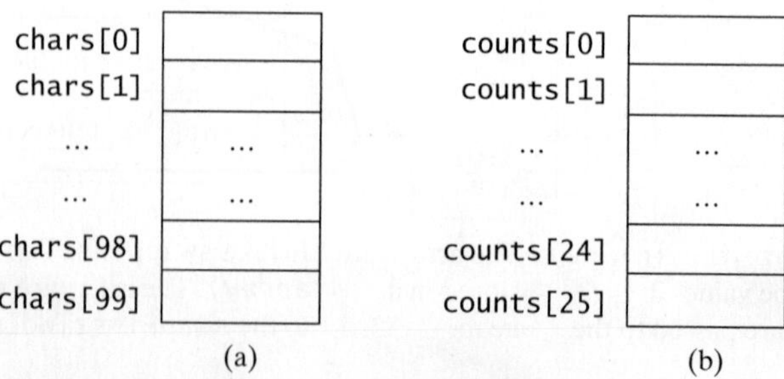

FIGURE 6.5 The `chars` array stores `100` characters, and the `counts` array stores `26` counts, each of which counts the occurrences of a letter.

LISTING 6.4 CountLettersInArray.java

```
public class CountLettersInArray {
  /** Main method */
  public static void main(String[] args) {
    // Declare and create an array
    char[] chars = createArray();

    // Display the array
    System.out.println("The lowercase letters are:");
    displayArray(chars);

    // Count the occurrences of each letter
    int[] counts = countLetters(chars);

    // Display counts
    System.out.println();
    System.out.println("The occurrences of each letter are:");
    displayCounts(counts);
  }

  /** Create an array of characters */
  public static char[] createArray() {
    // Declare an array of characters and create it
    char[] chars = new char[100];

    // Create lowercase letters randomly and assign
    // them to the array
    for (int i = 0; i < chars.length; i++)
      chars[i] = RandomCharacter.getRandomLowerCaseLetter();

    // Return the array
    return chars;
  }

  /** Display the array of characters */
  public static void displayArray(char[] chars) {
    // Display the characters in the array 20 on each line
    for (int i = 0; i < chars.length; i++) {
      if ((i + 1) % 20 == 0)
        System.out.println(chars[i] + " ");
      else
        System.out.print(chars[i] + " ");
    }
  }

  /** Count the occurrences of each letter */
  public static int[] countLetters(char[] chars) {
    // Declare and create an array of 26 int
    int[] counts = new int[26];

    // For each lowercase letter in the array, count it
    for (int i = 0; i < chars.length; i++)
      counts[chars[i] - 'a']++;

    return counts;
  }

  /** Display counts */
  public static void displayCounts(int[] counts) {
```

create array

pass array

return array

pass array

count

```
59      for (int i = 0; i < counts.length; i++) {
60        if ((i + 1) % 10 == 0)
61          System.out.println(counts[i] + " " + (char)(i + 'a'));
62        else
63          System.out.print(counts[i] + " " + (char)(i + 'a') + " ");
64      }
65    }
66 }
```

```
The lowercase letters are:
e y l s r i b k j v j h a b z n w b t v
s c c k r d w a m p w v u n q a m p l o
a z g d e g f i n d x m z o u l o z j v
h w i w n t g x w c d o t x h y v z y z
q e a m f w p g u q t r e n n w f c r f

The occurrences of each letter are:
5 a 3 b 4 c 4 d 4 e 4 f 4 g 3 h 3 i 3 j
2 k 3 l 4 m 6 n 4 o 3 p 3 q 4 r 2 s 4 t
3 u 5 v 8 w 3 x 3 y 6 z
```

The `createArray` method (lines 21–32) generates an array of `100` random lowercase letters. Line 5 invokes the method and assigns the array to `chars`. What would be wrong if you rewrote the code as follows?

```
char[] chars = new char[100];
chars = createArray();
```

You would be creating two arrays. The first line would create an array by using `new char[100]`. The second line would create an array by invoking `createArray()` and assign the reference of the array to `chars`. The array created in the first line would be garbage because it is no longer referenced. Java automatically collects garbage behind the scenes. Your program would compile and run correctly, but it would create an array unnecessarily.

Invoking `getRandomLowerCaseLetter()` (line 28) returns a random lowercase letter. This method is defined in the `RandomCharacter` class in Listing 5.8.

The `countLetters` method (lines 46–55) returns an array of `26` `int` values, each of which stores the number of occurrences of a letter. The method processes each letter in the array and increases its count by one. A brute-force approach to count the occurrences of each letter might be as follows:

```
for (int i = 0; i < chars.length; i++)
  if (chars[i] == 'a')
    counts[0]++;
  else if (chars[i] == 'b')
    counts[1]++;
  ...
```

But a better solution is given in lines 51–52.

```
for (int i = 0; i < chars.length; i++)
  counts[chars[i] - 'a']++;
```

If the letter (`chars[i]`) is `'a'`, the corresponding count is `counts['a' - 'a']` (i.e., `counts[0]`). If the letter is `'b'`, the corresponding count is `counts['b' - 'a']` (i.e., `counts[1]`) since the Unicode of `'b'` is one more than that of `'a'`. If the letter is `'z'`, the corresponding count is `counts['z' - 'a']` (i.e., `counts[25]`), since the Unicode of `'z'` is `25` more than that of `'a'`.

Figure 6.6 shows the call stack and heap *during* and *after* executing `createArray`. See Review Question 6.14 to show the call stack and heap for other methods in the program.

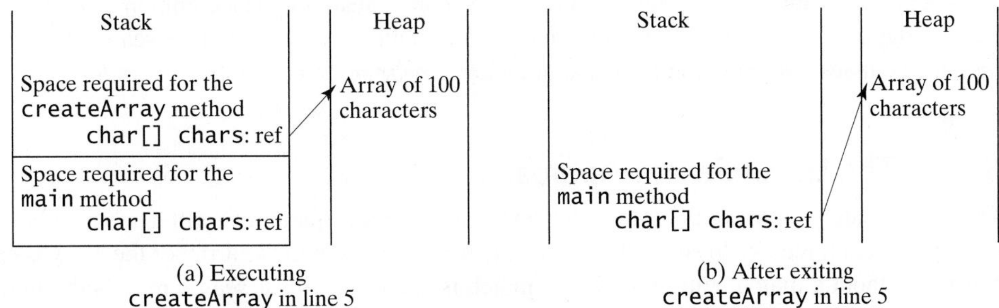

FIGURE 6.6 (a) An array of 100 characters is created when executing `createArray`. (b) This array is returned and assigned to the variable `chars` in the `main` method.

6.6 Variable-Length Argument Lists

You can pass a variable number of arguments of the same type to a method. The parameter in the method is declared as follows:

```
typeName... parameterName
```

In the method declaration, you specify the type followed by an ellipsis (...). Only one variable-length parameter may be specified in a method, and this parameter must be the last parameter. Any regular parameters must precede it.

Java treats a variable-length parameter as an array. You can pass an array or a variable number of arguments to a variable-length parameter. When invoking a method with a variable number of arguments, Java creates an array and passes the arguments to it. Listing 6.5 contains a method that prints the maximum value in a list of an unspecified number of values.

LISTING 6.5 `VarArgsDemo.java`

```
1 public class VarArgsDemo {
2   public static void main(String[] args) {
3     printMax(34, 3, 3, 2, 56.5);
4     printMax(new double[]{1, 2, 3});
5   }
6
7   public static void printMax(double... numbers) {
8     if (numbers.length == 0) {
9       System.out.println("No argument passed");
10      return;
11    }
12
13    double result = numbers[0];
14
15    for (int i = 1; i < numbers.length; i++)
16      if (numbers[i] > result)
17        result = numbers[i];
18
19    System.out.println("The max value is " + result);
20  }
21 }
```

pass variable-length arg list

pass an array arg

a variable-length arg parameter

Line 3 invokes the `printMax` method with a variable-length argument list passed to the array `numbers`. If no arguments are passed, the length of the array is `0` (line 8).

Line 4 invokes the `printMax` method with an array.

6.7 Searching Arrays

linear search
binary search

Searching is the process of looking for a specific element in an array—for example, discovering whether a certain score is included in a list of scores. Searching is a common task in computer programming. Many algorithms and data structures are devoted to searching. This section discusses two commonly used approaches, *linear search* and *binary search*.

6.7.1 The Linear Search Approach

The linear search approach compares the key element `key` sequentially with each element in the array. It continues to do so until the key matches an element in the array or the array is exhausted without a match being found. If a match is made, the linear search returns the index of the element in the array that matches the key. If no match is found, the search returns `-1`. The `linearSearch` method in Listing 6.6 gives the solution:

LISTING 6.6 `LinearSearch.java`

```
public class LinearSearch {
  /** The method for finding a key in the list */
  public static int linearSearch(int[] list, int key) {
    for (int i = 0; i < list.length; i++) {
      if (key == list[i])
        return i;
    }
    return -1;
  }
}
```

[0] [1] [2] ...
list
key Compare key with `list[i]` for i = 0, 1, ...

To better understand this method, trace it with the following statements:

```
int[] list = {1, 4, 4, 2, 5, -3, 6, 2};
int i = linearSearch(list, 4);  // Returns 1
int j = linearSearch(list, -4); // Returns -1
int k = linearSearch(list, -3); // Returns 5
```

The linear search method compares the key with each element in the array. The elements in the array can be in any order. On average, the algorithm will have to compare half of the elements in an array before finding the key, if it exists. Since the execution time of a linear search increases linearly as the number of array elements increases, linear search is inefficient for a large array.

6.7.2 The Binary Search Approach

Binary search is the other common search approach for a list of values. For binary search to work, the elements in the array must already be ordered. Without loss of generality, assume that the array is in ascending order. The binary search first compares the key with the element in the middle of the array. Consider the following three cases:

- If the key is less than the middle element, you need to continue to search for the key only in the first half of the array.

- If the key is equal to the middle element, the search ends with a match.
- If the key is greater than the middle element, you need to continue to search for the key only in the second half of the array.

Clearly, the binary search method eliminates half of the array after each comparison. Suppose that the array has *n* elements. For convenience, let n be a power of 2. After the first comparison, there are n/2 elements left for further search; after the second comparison, (n/2)/2 elements are left. After the kth comparison, $n/2^k$ elements are left for further search. When $k = \log_2 n$, only one element is left in the array, and you need only one more comparison. Therefore, in the worst case when using the binary search approach, you need $\log_2 n+1$ comparisons to find an element in the sorted array. In the worst case for a list of 1024 (2^{10}) elements, binary search requires only 11 comparisons, whereas a linear search requires 1023 comparisons in the worst case.

The portion of the array being searched shrinks by half after each comparison. Let low and high denote, respectively, the first index and last index of the array that is currently being searched. Initially, low is 0 and high is list.length-1. Let mid denote the index of the middle element. So mid is (low + high)/2. Figure 6.7 shows how to find key 11 in the list {2, 4, 7, 10, 11, 45, 50, 59, 60, 66, 69, 70, 79} using binary search.

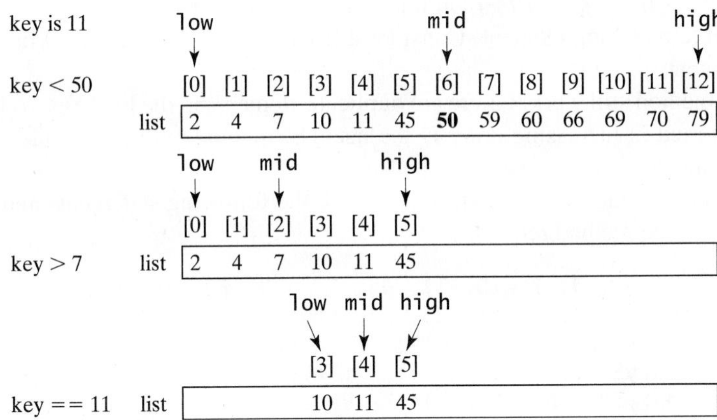

FIGURE 6.7 Binary search eliminates half of the list from further consideration after each comparison.

The binary search returns the index of the search key if it is contained in the list. Otherwise, it returns −(insertion point + 1) The insertion point is the point at which the key would be inserted into the list. For example, the insertion point for key 5 is 2, so the binary search returns − 3; the insertion point for key 51 is 7, so the binary search returns − 8.

You now know how the binary search works. The next task is to implement it in Java, as shown in Listing 6.7.

LISTING 6.7 BinarySearch.java

```
public class BinarySearch {
  /** Use binary search to find the key in the list */
  public static int binarySearch(int[] list, int key) {
    int low = 0;
```

first half

second half

```
5      int high = list.length - 1;
6
7      while (high >= low) {
8        int mid = (low + high) / 2;
9        if (key < list[mid])
10         high = mid - 1;
11       else if (key == list[mid])
12         return mid;
13       else
14         low = mid + 1;
15     }
16
17     return -low - 1; // Now high < low
18   }
19 }
```

You start by comparing the key with the middle element in the list whose `low` index is `0` and `high` index is `list.length-1`. If `key < list[mid]`, set the `high` index to `mid-1`; if `key == list[mid]`, a match is found and return `mid`; if `key > list[mid]`, set the `low` index to `mid+1`. Continue the search until `low > high` or a match is found. If `low > high`, return `-low - 1`, where `low` is the insertion point.

What happens if `(high >= low)` in line 7 is replaced by `(high > low)`? The search would miss a possible matching element. Consider a list with just one element. The search would miss the element.

Does the method still work if there are duplicate elements in the list? Yes, as long as the elements are sorted in increasing order in the list. The method returns the index of one of the matching elements if the element is in the list.

To better understand this method, trace it with the following statements and identify `low` and `high` when the method returns.

```
int[] list = {2, 4, 7, 10, 11, 45, 50, 59, 60, 66, 69, 70, 79};
int i = binarySearch(list, 2); // Returns 0
int j = binarySearch(list, 11); // Returns 4
int k = binarySearch(list, 12); // Returns -6
int l = binarySearch(list, 1); // Returns -1
int m = binarySearch(list, 3); // Returns -2
```

Here is the table that lists the `low` and `high` values when the method exits and the value returned from invoking the method.

Method	Low	High	Value Returned
binarySearch(list, 2)	0	1	0
binarySearch(list, 11)	3	5	4
binarySearch(list, 12)	5	4	−6
binarySearch(list, 1)	0	−1	−1
binarySearch(list, 3)	1	0	−2

why `-low - 1`?

If the key matches an element in the list, the method returns the index of the element. This index is a nonnegative integer (*including* `0`). If the key is not in the list, `low` is the index where the element would be inserted. In this case, the method returns `-low - 1`. It would be more intuitive to return just `-low`. But this would be wrong. Suppose the key is smaller than `list[0]` (e.g., `binarySearch(list, 1)`). When the method exits, `low` is `0`. Returning

`-low` would be `-0`. There is no difference between `-0` and `0`. `-0` would indicate that the element is not in the list, while `0` would indicate that the key matches the first element in the list (e.g., `binarySearch(list, 2)`). So, returning `-low` for a nonmatching case could conflict with returning `0` for the matching case on `list[0]`. For this reason, the method is designed to return `-low - 1` for a nonmatching case.

Note

Linear search is useful for finding an element in a small array or an unsorted array, but it is inefficient for large arrays. Binary search is more efficient, but requires that the array be presorted.

binary search benefits

6.8 Sorting Arrays

Sorting, like searching, is a common task in computer programming. It would be used, for instance, if you wanted to display the grades from Listing 6.2, "Assigning Grades," in alphabetical order. Many different algorithms have been developed for sorting. This section introduces two simple, intuitive sorting algorithms: *selection sort* and *insertion sort.*

6.8.1 Selection Sort

Suppose that you want to sort a list in ascending order. Selection sort finds the largest number in the list and places it last. It then finds the largest number remaining and places it next to last, and so on until the list contains only a single number. Figure 6.8 shows how to sort a list {`2`, `9`, `5`, `4`, `8`, `1`, `6`} using selection sort.

Select 9 (the largest) and swap it with 6 (the last) in the list	swap 2 9 5 4 8 1 6	
Select 8 (the largest) and swap it with 1 (the last) in the remaining list	swap 2 6 5 4 8 1 9	The number 9 is now in the correct position and thus no longer needs to be considered.
Select 6 (the largest) and swap it with 1 (the last) in the remaining list	swap 2 6 5 4 1 8 9	The number 8 is now in the correct position and thus no longer needs to be considered.
Select 5 (the largest) and swap it with 4 (the last) in the remaining list	swap 2 1 5 4 6 8 9	The number 6 is now in the correct position and thus no longer needs to be considered.
4 is the largest and last in the list. No swap is necessary	2 1 4 5 6 8 9	The number 5 is now in the correct position and thus no longer needs to be considered.
Select 2 (the largest) and swap it with 1 (the last) in the remaining list	swap 2 1 4 5 6 8 9	The number 4 is now in the correct position and thus no longer needs to be considered.
Since there is only one number remaining in the list, sort is completed	1 2 4 5 6 8 9	The number 2 is now in the correct position and thus no longer needs to be considered.

FIGURE 6.8 Selection sort repeatedly selects the largest number and swaps it with the last number in the list.

You know how the selection-sort approach works. The task now is to implement it in Java. Beginners find it difficult to develop a complete solution on the first attempt. Start by writing the code for the first iteration to find the largest element in the list and swap it with the last element, and then observe what would be different for the second iteration, the third, and so on. The insight this gives will enable you to write a loop that generalizes all the iterations.

The solution can be described as follows:

```
for (int i = list.length - 1; i >= 1; i-) {
  select the largest element in list[0..i];
  swap the largest with list[i], if necessary;
  // list[i] is in its correct position.
  // The next iteration apply on list[0..i-1]
}
```

Listing 6.8 implements the solution.

Video Note
Selection sort

LISTING 6.8 SelectionSort.java

select

swap

```
1 public class SelectionSort {
2   /** The method for sorting the numbers */
3   public static void selectionSort(double[] list) {
4     for (int i = list.length - 1; i >= 1; i--) {
5       // Find the maximum in the list[0..i]
6       double currentMax = list[0];
7       int currentMaxIndex = 0;
8
9       for (int j = 1; j <= i; j++) {
10        if (currentMax < list[j]) {
11          currentMax = list[j];
12          currentMaxIndex = j;
13        }
14      }
15
16      // Swap list[i] with list[currentMaxIndex] if necessary;
17      if (currentMaxIndex != i) {
18        list[currentMaxIndex] = list[i];
19        list[i] = currentMax;
20      }
21    }
22  }
23 }
```

The `selectionSort(double[] list)` method sorts any array of double elements. The method is implemented with a nested `for` loop. The outer loop (with the loop control variable `i`) (line 4) is iterated in order to find the largest element in the list, which ranges from `list[0]` to `list[i]`, and exchange it with the current last element, `list[i]`.

The variable `i` is initially `list.length-1`. After each iteration of the outer loop, `list[i]` is in the right place. Eventually, all the elements are put in the right place; therefore, the whole list is sorted.

To better understand this method, trace it with the following statements:

```
selectionSort(new double[]{2, 1});
selectionSort(new double[]{2, 3, 1});
selectionSort(new double[]{1, 2, 1});
```

6.8.2 Insertion Sort

Suppose that you want to sort a list in ascending order. The insertion-sort algorithm sorts a list of values by repeatedly inserting a new element into a sorted sublist until the whole list is sorted. Figure 6.9 shows how to sort the list {2, 9, 5, 4, 8, 1, 6} using insertion sort.

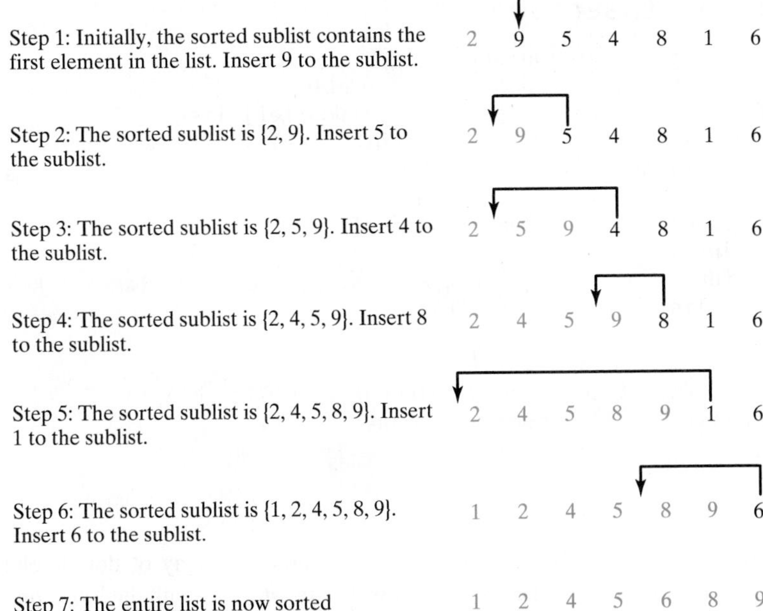

Step 1: Initially, the sorted sublist contains the first element in the list. Insert 9 to the sublist.
2 9 5 4 8 1 6
Step 2: The sorted sublist is {2, 9}. Insert 5 to the sublist.
2 9 5 4 8 1 6
Step 3: The sorted sublist is {2, 5, 9}. Insert 4 to the sublist.
2 5 9 4 8 1 6
Step 4: The sorted sublist is {2, 4, 5, 9}. Insert 8 to the sublist.
2 4 5 9 8 1 6
Step 5: The sorted sublist is {2, 4, 5, 8, 9}. Insert 1 to the sublist.
2 4 5 8 9 1 6
Step 6: The sorted sublist is {1, 2, 4, 5, 8, 9}. Insert 6 to the sublist.
1 2 4 5 8 9 6
Step 7: The entire list is now sorted
1 2 4 5 6 8 9

FIGURE 6.9 Insertion sort repeatedly inserts a new element into a sorted sublist.

The algorithm can be described as follows:

```
for (int i = 1; i < list.length; i++) {
  insert list[i] into a sorted sublist list[0..i-1] so that
  list[0..i] is sorted.
}
```

To insert `list[i]` into `list[0..i-1]`, save `list[i]` into a temporary variable, say `currentElement`. Move `list[i-1]` to `list[i]` if `list[i-1]` > `currentElement`, move `list[i-2]` to `list[i-1]` if `list[i-2]` > `currentElement`, and so on, until `list[i-k]` <= `currentElement` or `k` > `i` (we pass the first element of the sorted list). Assign `currentElement` to `list[i-k+1]`. For example, to insert 4 into {2, 5, 9} in Step 3 in Figure 6.10, move `list[2]` (9) to `list[3]` since 9 > 4, move `list[1]` (5) to `list[2]` since 5 > 4, Finally, move `currentElement` (4) to `list[1]`.

The algorithm can be expanded and implemented as in Listing 6.9.

	[0]	[1]	[2]	[3]	[4]	[5]	[6]	
list	2	5	9	4				Step 1: Save 4 to a temporary variable `currentElement`
list	2	5		9				Step 2: Move `list[2]` to `list[3]`
list	2		5	9				Step 3: Move `list[1]` to `list[2]`
list	2	4	5	9				Step 4: Assign `currentElement` to `list[1]`

FIGURE 6.10 A new element is inserted into a sorted sublist.

LISTING 6.9 InsertionSort.java

shift

insert

```
1 public class InsertionSort {
2   /** The method for sorting the numbers */
3   public static void insertionSort(double[] list) {
4     for (int i = 1; i < list.length; i++) {
5       /** insert list[i] into a sorted sublist list[0..i-1] so that
6            list[0..i] is sorted. */
7       double currentElement = list[i];
8       int k;
9       for (k = i - 1; k >= 0 && list[k] > currentElement; k–) {
10        list[k + 1] = list[k];
11      }
12
13      // Insert the current element into list[k + 1]
14      list[k + 1] = currentElement;
15    }
16  }
17 }
```

The `insertionSort(double[] list)` method sorts any array of double elements. The method is implemented with a nested `for` loop. The outer loop (with the loop control variable `i`) (line 4) is iterated in order to obtain a sorted sublist, which ranges from `list[0]` to `list[i]`. The inner loop (with the loop control variable `k`) inserts `list[i]` into the sublist from `list[0]` to `list[i-1]`.

To better understand this method, trace it with the following statements:

```
insertionSort(new double[]{2, 1});
insertionSort(new double[]{2, 3, 1});
insertionSort(new double[]{1, 2, 1});
```

6.9 The **Arrays** Class

The `java.util.Arrays` class contains various static methods for sorting and searching arrays, comparing arrays, and filling array elements. These methods are overloaded for all primitive types.

sort

You can use the `sort` method to sort a whole array or a partial array. For example, the following code sorts an array of numbers and an array of characters.

```
double[] numbers = {6.0, 4.4, 1.9, 2.9, 3.4, 3.5};
java.util.Arrays.sort(numbers); // Sort the whole array

char[] chars = {'a', 'A', '4', 'F', 'D', 'P'};
java.util.Arrays.sort(chars, 1, 3); // Sort part of the array
```

Invoking `sort(numbers)` sorts the whole array `numbers`. Invoking `sort(chars, 1, 3)` sorts a partial array from `chars[1]` to `chars[3-1 ]`.

binarySearch

You can use the `binarySearch` method to search for a key in an array. The array must be presorted in increasing order. If the key is not in the array, the method returns `–(insertion point + 1)`. For example, the following code searches the keys in an array of integers and an array of characters.

```
int[] list = {2, 4, 7, 10, 11, 45, 50, 59, 60, 66, 69, 70, 79};
System.out.println("(1) Index is " +
  java.util.Arrays.binarySearch(list, 11));
System.out.println("(2) Index is " +
  java.util.Arrays.binarySearch(list, 12));
```

```
char[] chars = {'a', 'c', 'g', 'x', 'y', 'z'};
System.out.println("(3) Index is " +
  java.util.Arrays.binarySearch(chars, 'a'));
System.out.println("(4) Index is " +
  java.util.Arrays.binarySearch(chars, 't'));
```

The output of the preceding code is

(1) Index is 4
(2) Index is −6
(3) Index is 0
(4) Index is −4

You can use the `equals` method to check whether two arrays are equal. Two arrays are equal if they have the same contents. In the following code, `list1` and `list2` are equal, but `list2` and `list3` are not. `equals`

```
int[] list1 = {2, 4, 7, 10};
int[] list2 = {2, 4, 7, 10};
int[] list3 = {4, 2, 7, 10};
System.out.println(java.util.Arrays.equals(list1, list2)); // true
System.out.println(java.util.Arrays.equals(list2, list3)); // false
```

You can use the `fill` method to fill in all or part of the array. For example, the following code fills `list1` with `5` and fills `8` into elements `list2[1]` and `list2[3-1]`. `fill`

```
int[] list1 = {2, 4, 7, 10};
int[] list2 = {2, 4, 7, 10};
java.util.Arrays.fill(list1, 5); // Fill 5 to the whole array
java.util.Arrays.fill(list2, 1, 3, 8); // Fill 8 to a partial array
```

6.10 Two-Dimensional Arrays

Thus far, you have used one-dimensional arrays to model linear collections of elements. You can use a two-dimensional array to represent a matrix or a table. For example, the following table that describes the distances between the cities can be represented using a two-dimensional array.

Distance Table (in miles)

	Chicago	Boston	New York	Atlanta	Miami	Dallas	Houston
Chicago	0	983	787	714	1375	967	1087
Boston	983	0	214	1102	1763	1723	1842
New York	787	214	0	888	1549	1548	1627
Atlanta	714	1102	888	0	661	781	810
Miami	1375	1763	1549	661	0	1426	1187
Dallas	967	1723	1548	781	1426	0	239
Houston	1087	1842	1627	810	1187	239	0

6.10.1 Declaring Variables of Two-Dimensional Arrays and Creating Two-Dimensional Arrays

Here is the syntax for declaring a two-dimensional array:

```
dataType[][] arrayRefVar;
```

or

```
dataType arrayRefVar[][]; // This style is allowed, but not preferred
```

As an example, here is how you would declare a two-dimensional array variable `matrix` of `int` values:

```
int[][] matrix;
```

or

```
int matrix[][]; // This style is allowed, but not preferred
```

You can create a two-dimensional array of `5` by `5` `int` values and assign it to `matrix` using this syntax:

```
matrix = new int[5][5];
```

Two subscripts are used in a two-dimensional array, one for the row, and the other for the column. As in a one-dimensional array, the index for each subscript is of the `int` type and starts from `0`, as shown in Figure 6.11(a).

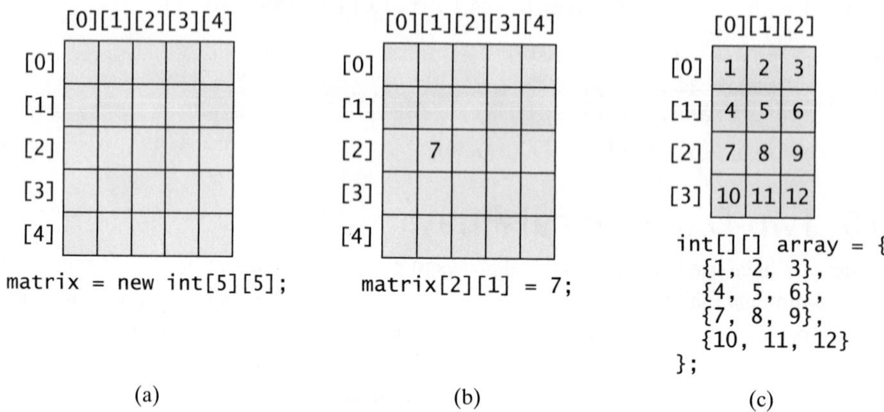

FIGURE 6.11 The index of each subscript of a two-dimensional array is an `int` value, starting from `0`.

To assign the value 7 to a specific element at row `2` and column `1`, as shown in Figure 6.11(b), you can use the following:

```
matrix[2][1] = 7;
```

Caution

It is a common mistake to use `matrix[2, 1]` to access the element at row 2 and column 1. In Java, each subscript must be enclosed in a pair of square brackets.

You can also use an array initializer to declare, create, and initialize a two-dimensional array. For example, the following code in (a) creates an array with the specified initial values, as shown in Figure 6.11(c). This is equivalent to the code in (b).

```
int[][] array = {
  {1, 2, 3},
  {4, 5, 6},
  {7, 8, 9},
  {10, 11, 12}
};
```

(a)

Equivalent

```
int[][] array = new int[4][3];
array[0][0] = 1; array[0][1] = 2; array[0][2] = 3;
array[1][0] = 4; array[1][1] = 5; array[1][2] = 6;
array[2][0] = 7; array[2][1]  8; array[2][2] = 9;
array[3][0] = 10; array[3][1] = 11; array[3][2] = 12;
```

(b)

6.10.2 Obtaining the Lengths of Two-Dimensional Arrays

A two-dimensional array is actually an array in which each element is a one-dimensional array. The length of an array `x` is the number of elements in the array, which can be obtained using `x.length`. `x[0]`, `x[1]`, . . . , and `x[x.length-1]` are arrays. Their lengths can be obtained using `x[0].length`, `x[1].length`, . . . , and `x[x.length-1].length`.

For example, suppose `x = new int[3][4]`, `x[0]`, `x[1]`, and `x[2]` are one-dimensional arrays and each contains four elements, as shown in Figure 6.12. `x.length` is `3`, and `x[0].length`, `x[1].length`, and `x[2].length` are `4`.

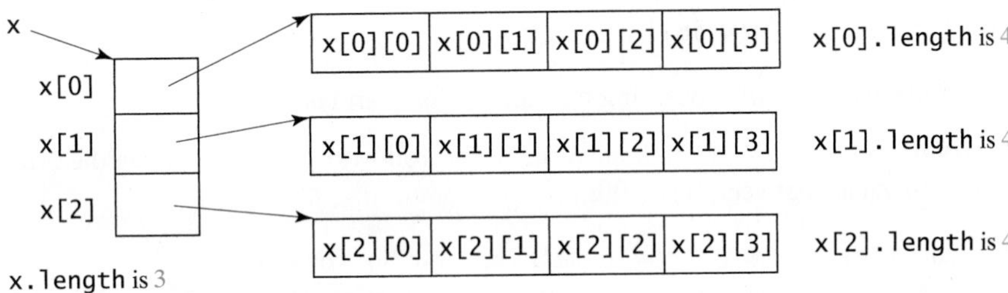

FIGURE 6.12 A two-dimensional array is a one-dimensional array in which each element is another one-dimensional array.

6.10.3 Ragged Arrays

Each row in a two-dimensional array is itself an array. Thus the rows can have different lengths. An array of this kind is known as a *ragged array*. Here is an example of creating a ragged array:

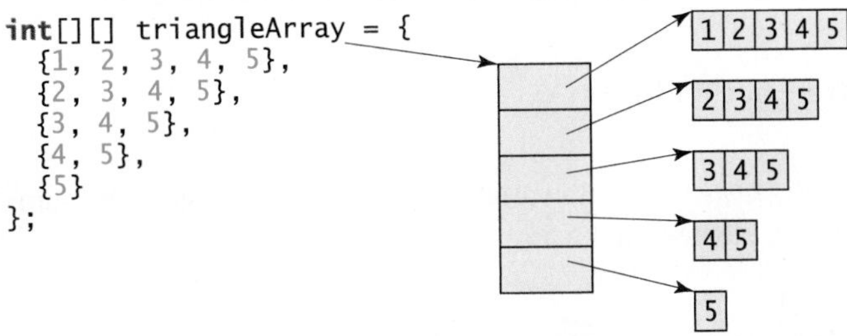

As can be seen, `triangleArray[0].length` is 5, `triangleArray[1].length` is 4, `triangleArray[2].length` is 3, `triangleArray[3].length` is 2, and `triangleArray[4].length` is 1.

If you don't know the values in a ragged array in advance, but know the sizes, say the same as before, you can create a ragged array using the syntax that follows:

```
int[][] triangleArray = new int[5][];
triangleArray[0] = new int[5];
```

```
triangleArray[1] = new int[4];
triangleArray[2] = new int[3];
triangleArray[3] = new int[2];
triangleArray[4] = new int[1];
```

You can now assign values to the array. For example,

```
triangleArray[0][3] = 50;
triangleArray[4][0] = 45;
```

Note

The syntax `new int[5][]` for creating an array requires the first index to be specified. The syntax `new int[][]` would be wrong.

6.10.4 Processing Two-Dimensional Arrays

Suppose an array `matrix` is declared as follows:

```
int[][] matrix = new int[10][10];
```

Here are some examples of processing two-dimensional arrays:

1. (*Initializing arrays with random values*) The following loop initializes the array with random values between 0 and 99:

```
for (int row = 0; row < matrix.length; row++) {
  for (int column = 0; column < matrix[row].length ; column++) {
    matrix[row][column] = (int)(Math.random() * 100);
  }
}
```

2. (*Printing arrays*) To print a two-dimensional array, you have to print each element in the array using a loop like the following:

```
for (int row = 0; row < matrix.length ; row++) {
  for (int column = 0; column < matrix[row].length ; column++) {
    System.out.print(matrix[row][column] + " ");
  }

  System.out.println();
}
```

3. (*Summing all elements*) Use a variable named `total` to store the sum. Initially `total` is `0`. Add each element in the array to `total` using a loop like this:

```
int total = 0;
for (int row = 0; row < matrix.length; row++) {
  for (int column = 0; column < matrix[row].length; column++) {
    total += matrix[row][column];
  }
}
```

4. (*Summing elements by column*) For each column, use a variable named `total` to store its sum. Add each element in the column to `total` using a loop like this:

```
for (int column = 0; column < matrix[0].length; column++) {
  int total = 0;
```

```
    for (int row = 0; row < matrix.length; row++)
      total += matrix[row][column];
    System.out.println("Sum for column " + column + " is " + total);
  }
```

5. (*Which row has the largest sum?*) Use variables maxRow and indexOfMaxRow to track the largest sum and index of the row. For each row, compute its sum and update maxRow and indexOfMaxRow if the new sum is greater.

```
int maxRow = 0;
int indexOfMaxRow = 0;

// Get sum of the first row in maxRow
for (int column = 0; column < matrix[0].length; column++) {
  maxRow += matrix[0][column];
}

for (int row = 1; row < matrix.length; row++) {
  int totalOfThisRow = 0;
  for (int column = 0; column < matrix[row].length; column++) {
    totalOfThisRow += matrix[row][column];
    if (totalOfThisRow > maxRow) {
      maxRow = totalOfThisRow;
      indexOfMaxRow = row;
    }
  }
}

System.out.println("Row " + indexOfMaxRow
  + " has the maximum sum" + " of " + maxRow);
```

6.10.5 Problem: Grading a Multiple-Choice Test

The problem is to write a program that grades multiple-choice tests. Suppose there are eight students and ten questions, and the answers are stored in a two-dimensional array. Each row records a student's answers to the questions. For example, the following array stores the test.

Students' Answers to the Questions:

	0	1	2	3	4	5	6	7	8	9
Student 0	A	B	A	C	C	D	E	E	A	D
Student 1	D	B	A	B	C	A	E	E	A	D
Student 2	E	D	D	A	C	B	E	E	A	D
Student 3	C	B	A	E	D	C	E	E	A	D
Student 4	A	B	D	C	C	D	E	E	A	D
Student 5	B	B	E	C	C	D	E	E	A	D
Student 6	B	B	A	C	C	D	E	E	A	D
Student 7	E	B	E	C	C	D	E	E	A	D

The key is stored in a one-dimensional array:

Key to the Questions:

	0	1	2	3	4	5	6	7	8	9
Key	D	B	D	C	C	D	A	E	A	D

Your program grades the test and displays the result. It compares each student's answers with the key, counts the number of correct answers, and displays it. Listing 6.10 gives the program.

LISTING 6.10 GradeExam.java

2-D array

1-D array

compare with key

```
1 public class GradeExam {
2   /** Main method */
3   public static void main(String[] args) {
4     // Students' answers to the questions
5     char[][] answers = {
6       {'A', 'B', 'A', 'C', 'C', 'D', 'E', 'E', 'A', 'D'},
7       {'D', 'B', 'A', 'B', 'C', 'A', 'E', 'E', 'A', 'D'},
8       {'E', 'D', 'D', 'A', 'C', 'B', 'E', 'E', 'A', 'D'},
9       {'C', 'B', 'A', 'E', 'D', 'C', 'E', 'E', 'A', 'D'},
10      {'A', 'B', 'D', 'C', 'C', 'D', 'E', 'E', 'A', 'D'},
11      {'B', 'B', 'E', 'C', 'C', 'D', 'E', 'E', 'A', 'D'},
12      {'B', 'B', 'A', 'C', 'C', 'D', 'E', 'E', 'A', 'D'},
13      {'E', 'B', 'E', 'C', 'C', 'D', 'E', 'E', 'A', 'D'}};
14
15    // Key to the questions
16    char[] keys = {'D', 'B', 'D', 'C', 'C', 'D', 'A', 'E', 'A', 'D'};
17
18    // Grade all answers
19    for (int i = 0; i < answers.length; i++) {
20      // Grade one student
21      int correctCount = 0;
22      for (int j = 0; j < answers[i].length; j++) {
23        if (answers[i][j] == keys[j])
24          correctCount++;
25      }
26
27      System.out.println("Student " + i + "'s correct count is " +
28        correctCount);
29    }
30  }
31 }
```

```
Student 0's correct count is 7
Student 1's correct count is 6
Student 2's correct count is 5
Student 3's correct count is 4
Student 4's correct count is 8
Student 5's correct count is 7
Student 6's correct count is 7
Student 7's correct count is 7
```

The statement in lines 5–13 declares, creates, and initializes a two-dimensional array of characters and assigns the reference to **answers** of the **char[][]** type.

The statement in line 16 declares, creates, and initializes an array of **char** values and assigns the reference to **keys** of the **char[]** type.

Each row in the array **answers** stores a student's answer, which is graded by comparing it with the key in the array **keys**. The result is displayed immediately after a student's answer is graded.

6.10.6 Problem: Finding a Closest Pair

The GPS navigation system is becoming increasingly popular. The system uses the graph and geometric algorithms to calculate distances and map a route. This section presents a geometric problem for finding a closest pair of points.

Given a set of points, the closest-pair problem is to find the two points that are nearest to each other. In Figure 6.13, for example, points `(1, 1)` and `(2, 0.5)` are closest to each other. There are several ways to solve this problem. An intuitive approach is to compute the distances between all pairs of points and find the one with the minimum distance, as implemented in Listing 6.11.

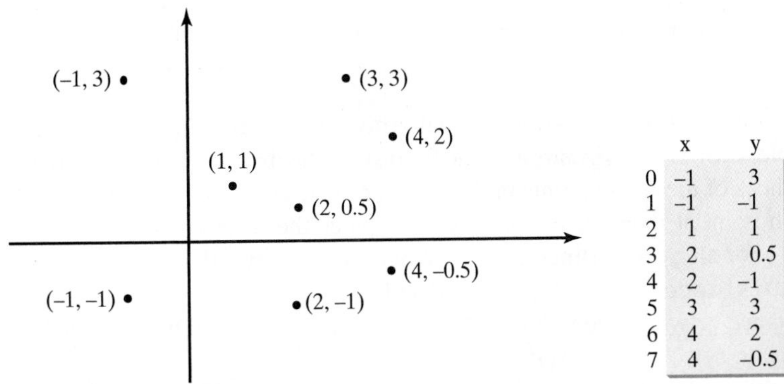

	x	y
0	–1	3
1	–1	–1
2	1	1
3	2	0.5
4	2	–1
5	3	3
6	4	2
7	4	–0.5

FIGURE 6.13 Points can be represented in a two-dimensional array.

LISTING 6.11 FindNearestPoints.java

```
public class FindNearestPoints {
  public static void main(String[] args) {
    // Each row in points represents a point
    double[][] points = {{-1, 3}, {-1, -1}, {1, 1},
      {2, 0.5}, {2, -1}, {3, 3}, {4, 2}, {4, -0.5}};

    // p1 and p2 are the indices in the points array
    int p1 = 0, p2 = 1; // Initial two points
    double shortestDistances = distance(points[p1][0], points[p1][1],
      points[p2][0], points[p2][1]); // Initialize shortestDistances

    // Compute distance for every two points
    for (int i = 0; i < points.length; i++) {
      for (int j = i + 1; j < points.length; j++) {
        double distance = distance(points[i][0], points[i][1],
          points[j][0], points[j][1]); // Find distance

        if (shortestDistances > distance) {
          p1 = i; // Update p1
          p2 = j; // Update p2
          shortestDistances = distance; // Update shortestDistances
        }
      }
    }

    // Display result
```

2-D array

track two points

track **shortestDistance**

for each point **i**

for each point **j**

distance between **i** and **j**

update **shortestDistance**

distance between two points

```
27     System.out.println("The closest two points are " +
28       "(" + points[p1][0] + ", " + points[p1][1] + ") and (" +
29       points[p2][0] + ", " + points[p2][1] + ")");
30   }
31
32   /** Compute the distance between two points (x1, y1) and (x2, y2)*/
33   public static double distance(
34       double x1, double y1, double x2, double y2) {
35     return Math.sqrt((x2 - x1) * (x2 - x1) + (y2 - y1) * (y2 - y1));
36   }
37 }
```

```
The closest two points are (1.0, 1.0) and (2.0, 0.5)
```

The points are stored in a two-dimensional array named `points` (lines 4–5). The program uses variable `shortestDistances` (line 9) to store the distance between two nearest points, and the indices of these two points in the `points` array are stored in `p1` and `p2` (line 8).

For each point at index `i`, the program computes the distance between `points[i]` and `points[j]` for all `j > i` (lines 13–24). Whenever a shorter distance is found, the variable `shortestDistances`, `p1`, and `p2` are updated (lines 18–22).

The distance between two points `(x1, y1)` and `(x2, y2)` can be computed using the formula $\sqrt{(x_2 - x_1)^2 + (y_2 - y_1)^2}$ (lines 33–36).

The program assumes that the plain has at least two points. You can easily modify the program to handle the case if the plain has zero or one point.

Note that there might be more than one closest pair of points with the same minimum distance. The program finds one such pair.

6.10.7 Problem: Sudoku

Video Note
Solve Sudoku

This book teaches you how to program using a wide variety of problems with various levels of difficulty. This section presents an interesting problem of a sort that appears in the newspaper every day. It is a number-placement puzzle, commonly known as *Sudoku*. This is a challenge problem. Feel free to skip it if you wish.

The objective is to fill the grid (see Figure 6.14(a)) so that every row, every column, and every 3 × 3 box contains the numbers 1 to 9, as shown in Figure 6.14(b).

How do you write a program to solve this problem? Your program searches a solution for an input of a 9-by-9 grid Sudoku puzzle. Note that there may be multiple solutions for an input. The program will find one such solution if exists. The grid can be represented using a

5	3			7				
6			1	9	5			
	9	8					6	
8				6				3
4			8		3			1
7				2				6
	6							
			4	1	9			5
				8			7	9

(a) Input

5	3	4	6	7	8	9	1	2
6	7	2	1	9	5	3	4	8
1	9	8	3	4	2	5	6	7
8	5	9	7	6	1	4	2	3
4	2	6	8	5	3	7	9	1
7	1	3	9	2	4	8	5	6
9	6	1	5	3	7	2	8	4
2	8	7	4	1	9	6	3	5
3	4	5	2	8	6	1	7	9

(b) Output

FIGURE 6.14 (b) is the solution to the Sudoku puzzle in (a).

two-dimensional array. For example, the grid in Figure 6.14(a) can be represented as shown in Figure 6.15(a). The value 0 indicates a free cell whose value will be filled by the program.

```
int[][] grid =
  {{5, 3, 0, 0, 7, 0, 0, 0, 0},
   {6, 0, 0, 1, 9, 5, 0, 0, 0},
   {0, 9, 8, 0, 0, 0, 0, 6, 0},
   {8, 0, 0, 0, 6, 0, 0, 0, 3},
   {4, 0, 0, 8, 0, 3, 0, 0, 1},
   {7, 0, 0, 0, 2, 0, 0, 0, 6},
   {0, 6, 0, 0, 0, 0, 2, 8, 0},
   {0, 0, 0, 4, 1, 9, 0, 0, 5},
   {0, 0, 0, 0, 8, 0, 0, 7, 9}
  };
```

(a)

```
int[][] freeCellList =
  {{0, 2}, {0, 3}, {0, 5}, {0, 6}, {0, 7}, {0, 8},
   {1, 1}, {1, 2}, {1, 6}, {1, 7}, {1, 8},
   {2, 0}, {2, 3}, {2, 4}, {2, 5}, {2, 6}, {2, 8},
   {3, 1}, {3, 2}, {3, 3}, {3, 5}, {3, 6}, {3, 7},
   {4, 1}, {4, 2}, {4, 4}, {4, 6}, {4, 7},
   {5, 1}, {5, 2}, {5, 3}, {5, 5}, {5, 6}, {5, 7},
   {6, 0}, {6, 2}, {6, 3}, {6, 4}, {6, 5}, {6, 8},
   {7, 0}, {7, 1}, {7, 2}, {7, 6}, {7, 7},
   {8, 0}, {8, 1}, {8, 2}, {8, 3}, {8, 5}, {8, 6}
  };
```

(b)

FIGURE 6.15 (a) is a two-dimensional array representation for the grid; (b) is a two-dimensional array representation for the free cells.

To better facilitate search on free cells, the program stores free cells in a two-dimensional array, as shown 6.15(b). Each row in the array has two columns, which indicate the subscripts of the free cell in the grid. For example, {`freeCellList[0][0]`, `freeCellList[0][1]`} (i.e., {0, 2}) is the subscript for the first free cell in the grid and {`freeCellList[1][0]`, `freeCellList[1][1]`} (i.e., {0, 3}) is the subscript for the second free cell in the grid.

An intuitive approach to solve this problem is to start from the first free cell, then the second, and so on. Fill each free cell with the smallest value possible. For example, you can fill 1 into `grid[0][2]`, 2 into `grid[0][3]`, 4 into `grid[0][5]`, 8 into `grid[0][6]`, and 9 into `grid[0][7]`, as shown in Figure 6.16(a).

5	3	*1*	*2*	7	*4*	*8*	*9*	
6			1	9	5			
	9	8					6	
8				6				3
4			8		3			1
7				2				6
	6							
			4	1	9			5
				8			7	9

(a)

5	3	*1*	*2*	7	*4*	*9*	*8*	
6			1	9	5			
	9	8					6	
8				6				3
4			8		3			1
7				2				6
	6							
			4	1	9			5
				8			7	9

(b)

FIGURE 6.16 The program attempts to fill in free cells.

Now look at `grid[0][8]`. There is no possible value to fill in this cell. You need to backtrack to the previous free cell at `grid[0][7]` and reset its value. Since `grid[0][7]` is already 9, no new value is possible. So you have to backtrack to its previous free cell at `grid[0][6]` and change its value to 9. Continue to move forward to set `grid[0][7]` to 8, as shown in Figure 6.16(b). Now there is still no possible value for `grid[0][8]`. Backtrack to `grid[0][7]`, no possible new value for this cell. Backtrack to `grid[0][6]`, no possible new value for this cell. Backtrack to `grid[0][5]` and change it to 6. Now continue to move forward.

backtrack

The search moves forward and backward continuously until one of the following two cases arises:

- All free cells are filled. A solution is found.
- The search is backtracked to the first free cell with no new possible value. The puzzle has no solution.

Listing 6.12 gives the solution to the program.

LISTING 6.12 Sudoku.java

read input
input valid?
search
print result
read input
return grid
get free-cell list
count free cells
create free-cell list

```java
import java.util.Scanner;

public class Sudoku {
  public static void main(String[] args) {
    // Read a Sudoku puzzle
    int[][] grid = readAPuzzle();

    if (!isValid(grid))
      System.out.println("Invalid input");
    else if (search(grid)) {
      System.out.println("The solution is found:");
      printGrid(grid);
    }
    else
      System.out.println("No solution");
  }

  /** Read a Sudoku puzzle from the keyboard */
  public static int[][] readAPuzzle() {
    // Create a Scanner
    Scanner input = new Scanner(System.in);

    System.out.println("Enter a Sudoku puzzle:");
    int[][] grid = new int[9][9];
    for (int i = 0; i < 9; i++)
      for (int j = 0; j < 9; j++)
        grid[i][j] = input.nextInt();

    return grid;
  }

  /** Obtain a list of free cells from the puzzle */
  public static int[][] getFreeCellList(int[][] grid) {
    // Determine the number of free cells
    int numberOfFreeCells = 0;
    for (int i = 0; i < 9; i++)
      for (int j = 0; j < 9; j++)
        if (grid[i][j] == 0)
          numberOfFreeCells++;

    // Store free cell positions into freeCellList
    int[][] freeCellList = new int[numberOfFreeCells][2];
    int count = 0;
    for (int i = 0; i < 9; i++)
      for (int j = 0; j < 9; j++)
        if (grid[i][j] == 0) {
          freeCellList[count][0] = i;
          freeCellList[count++][1] = j;
        }
```

```

    return freeCellList;
  }

  /** Print the values in the grid */
  public static void printGrid(int[][] grid) {
    for (int i = 0; i < 9; i++) {
      for (int j = 0; j < 9; j++)
        System.out.print(grid[i][j] + " ");
      System.out.println();
    }
  }

  /** Search for a solution */
  public static boolean search(int[][] grid) {
    int[][] freeCellList = getFreeCellList(grid); // Free cells
    int k = 0; // Start from the first free cell
    boolean found = false; // Solution found?

    while (!found) {
      int i = freeCellList[k][0];
      int j = freeCellList[k][1];
      if (grid[i][j] == 0)
        grid[i][j] = 1; // Start with 1

      if (isValid(i, j, grid)) {
        if (k + 1 == freeCellList.length) { // No more free cells
          found = true; // A solution is found
        }
        else { // Move to the next free cell
          k++;
        }
      }
      else if (grid[i][j] < 9) {
        grid[i][j] = grid[i][j] + 1; // Check the next possible value
      }
      else { // grid[i][j] is 9, backtrack
        while (grid[i][j] == 9) {
          grid[i][j] = 0; // Reset to free cell
          if (k == 0) {
            return false; // No possible value
          }
          k--; // Backtrack
          i = freeCellList[k][0];
          j = freeCellList[k][1];
        }

        grid[i][j] = grid[i][j] + 1; // Check the next possible value
      }
    }

    return true; // A solution is found
  }

  /** Check whether grid[i][j] is valid in the grid */
  public static boolean isValid(int i, int j, int[][] grid) {
    // Check whether grid[i][j] is valid at the i's row
    for (int column = 0; column < 9; column++)
      if (column != j && grid[i][column] == grid[i][j])
```

print grid

search a solution

continuous search

start with 1

is valid?

found

to next free cell

increase cell value

reset cell value

no solution

backtrack

check valid

check row

check column

check box

valid grid?

```
109          return false;
110
111      // Check whether grid[i][j] is valid at the j's column
112      for (int row = 0; row < 9; row++)
113        if (row != i && grid[row][j] == grid[i][j])
114          return false;
115
116      // Check whether grid[i][j] is valid in the 3 by 3 box
117      for (int row = (i / 3) * 3; row < (i / 3) * 3 + 3; row++)
118        for (int col = (j / 3) * 3; col < (j / 3) * 3 + 3; col++)
119          if (row != i && col != j && grid[row][col] == grid[i][j])
120            return false;
121
122      return true; // The current value at grid[i][j] is valid
123    }
124
125    /** Check whether the fixed cells are valid in the grid */
126    public static boolean isValid(int[][] grid) {
127      for (int i = 0; i < 9; i++)
128        for (int j = 0; j < 9; j++)
129          if (grid[i][j] != 0 && !isValid(i, j, grid)) return false;
130
131      return true; // The fixed cells are valid
132    }
133  }
```

```
Enter a puzzle:
0 6 0 1 0 4 0 5 0 ↵Enter
0 0 8 3 0 5 6 0 0 ↵Enter
2 0 0 0 0 0 0 0 1 ↵Enter
8 0 0 4 0 7 0 0 6 ↵Enter
0 0 6 0 0 0 3 0 0 ↵Enter
7 0 0 9 0 1 0 0 4 ↵Enter
5 0 0 0 0 0 0 0 2 ↵Enter
0 0 7 2 0 6 9 0 0 ↵Enter
0 4 0 5 0 8 0 7 0 ↵Enter

The solution is found:
9 6 3 1 7 4 2 5 8
1 7 8 3 2 5 6 4 9
2 5 4 6 8 9 7 3 1
8 2 1 4 3 7 5 9 6
4 9 6 8 5 2 3 1 7
7 3 5 9 6 1 8 2 4
5 8 9 7 1 3 4 6 2
3 1 7 2 4 6 9 8 5
6 4 2 5 9 8 1 7 3
```

The program invokes the **readAPuzzle()** method (line 6) to read a Sudoku puzzle and return a two-dimensional array representing a Sudoku grid. There are three possible outputs from the program:

- The input is invalid (line 9)

- A solution is found (line 11).
- No solution is found (line 15).

The `getFreeCellList(int[][] grid)` method returns a two-dimensional array storing the free cell positions. `freeCellList[i][j]` indicates a free cell at row index `i` and column index `j`. The method first counts the number of free cells (lines 35-39), then creates the array for storing free cell positions (lines 42-49).

The `search(int[][] grid)` method starts search from the first free cell with `k = 0` (line 66), where `k` points to the current free cell being considered, as shown below:

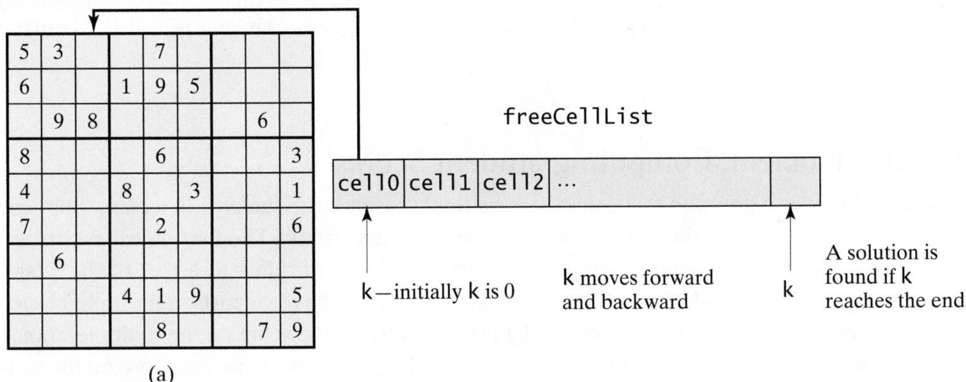

(a)

The value in a free cell starts with `1` (line 73). If the value is valid, the next cell is considered (line 80). If the value is not valid, its next value is considered (line 84). If the value is aready `9`, the search is backtracked (lines 87–95). All the backtracked cells become free again and their values are reset to `0` (line 88).

The `search` method returns `true` when no more free cells are left (lines 76–78) and returns `false` when the first cell has to be backtracked (lines 89–91).

The `isValid(i, j, grid)` method checks whether the current value at `grid[i][j]` is valid. It checks whether `grid[i][j]` appears more than once at row `i` (lines 107-109), at column `j` (lines 112–114), and in the 3 × 3 box (lines 117–120). Note that the starting row subscript and column subscript of the 3 × 3 box for `grid[i][j]` are `i / 3` and `j / 3`. This observation results in the short code in lines 117–120.

Tip

It is cumbersome to enter 81 numbers from the console. When you test the program, you may store the input in a file, say sudoku.txt, and run the program using the following command: input file

```
java Sudoku < sudoku.txt
```

Note

This program is not user friendly. You can improve it by providing a GUI interface. See Exercise 17.25.

6.11 Multidimensional Arrays

In the preceding section, you used a two-dimensional array to represent a matrix or a table. Occasionally, you will need to represent *n*-dimensional data structures. In Java, you can create *n*-dimensional arrays for any integer *n*.

The way to declare two-dimensional array variables and create two-dimensional arrays can be generalized to declare *n*-dimensional array variables and create *n*-dimensional arrays for

$n >= 3$. For example, the following syntax declares a three-dimensional array variable scores, creates an array, and assigns its reference to scores.

```
double[][][] scores = new double[10][5][2];
```

A multidimensional array is actually an array in which each element is another array. A three-dimensional array consists of an array of two-dimensional arrays, each of which is an array of one-dimensional arrays. For example, suppose `x = new int[2][2][5]`, `x[0]` and `x[1]` are two-dimensional arrays. `X[0][0]`, `x[0][1]`, `x[1][0]`, and `x[1][1]` are one-dimensional arrays and each contains five elements. `x.length` is `2`, `x[0].length` and `x[1].length` are `2`, and `X[0][0].length`, `x[0][1].length`, `x[1][0].length`, and `x[1][1].length` are `5`.

6.11.1 Problem: Computing Student Scores

Listing 6.13 gives a program that calculates the total score for the students in a class. Suppose the scores are stored in a three-dimensional array named `scores`. The first index in `scores` refers to a student, the second refers to an exam, and the third refers to a part of the exam. Suppose there are seven students, five exams, and each exam has two parts: a multiple-choice part and a programming part. `scores[i][j][0]` represents the score on the multiple-choice part for the `i`'s student on the `j`'s exam. `scores[i][j][1]` represents the score on the programming part for the `i`'s student on the `j`'s exam. The program processes the `scores` array for all the students. For each student, it adds the two scores from all exams to `totalScore` and displays `totalScore`. Your program displays the total score for each student, as shown in the sample output.

LISTING 6.13 TotalScore.java

3-D array

```
public class TotalScore {
  /** Main method */
  public static void main(String[] args) {
    double[][][] scores = {
      {{7.5, 20.5}, {9.0, 22.5}, {15, 33.5}, {13, 21.5}, {15, 2.5}},
      {{4.5, 21.5}, {9.0, 22.5}, {15, 34.5}, {12, 20.5}, {14, 9.5}},
      {{6.5, 30.5}, {9.4, 10.5}, {11, 33.5}, {11, 23.5}, {10, 2.5}},
      {{6.5, 23.5}, {9.4, 32.5}, {13, 34.5}, {11, 20.5}, {16, 7.5}},
      {{8.5, 26.5}, {9.4, 52.5}, {13, 36.5}, {13, 24.5}, {16, 2.5}},
      {{9.5, 20.5}, {9.4, 42.5}, {13, 31.5}, {12, 20.5}, {16, 6.5}},
      {{1.5, 29.5}, {6.4, 22.5}, {14, 30.5}, {10, 30.5}, {16, 6.0}}};

    // Calculate and display total score for each student
    for (int i = 0; i < scores.length; i++) {
      double totalScore = 0;
      for (int j = 0; j < scores[i].length ; j++)
        for (int k = 0; k < scores[i][j].length; k++)
          totalScore += scores[i][j][k];

      System.out.println("Student " + i + "'s score is " +
        totalScore);
    }
  }
}
```

```
Student 0's score is 160.0
Student 1's score is 163.0
Student 2's score is 147.4
Student 3's score is 174.4
Student 4's score is 201.4
Student 5's score is 181.4
Student 6's score is 165.9
```

To understand this program, it is essential to know how data in the three-dimensional array are interpreted. `scores[0]` is a two-dimensional array that stores all the exam scores for the first student. `scores[0][0]` is `{7.5, 20.5}`, a one-dimensional array, which stores two scores for the two parts of the first student's first exam. `scores[0][0][0]` is `7.5`, which is the score for the first part of the first student's first exam. `scores[5]` is a two-dimensional array that stores all the exam scores for the sixth student. `scores[5][4]` is `{16, 6.5}`, a one-dimensional array, which stores two scores for the two parts of the sixth student's fifth exam. `scores[5][4][1]` is `6.5`, which is the score for the second part of the sixth student's fifth exam.

The statement in lines 4–11 declares, creates, and initializes a three-dimensional array of `double` values and assigns the reference to `scores` of the `double[][][]` type.

The scores for each student are added in lines 16–18, and the result is displayed in lines 20–21. The `for` loop in line 14 process the scores for all the students.

6.11.2 Problem: Guessing Birth Dates

Listing 3.8, GuessBirthDate.java, gives a program that guesses a birth date. The program can be simplified by storing the numbers in five sets in a three-dimensional array, and it prompts the user for the answers using a loop, as shown in Listing 6.14. The sample run of the program can be the same as shown in Listing 3.8.

LISTING 6.14 `GuessBirthDateUsingArray.java`

three-dimensional array

```
import java.util.Scanner;

public class GuessBirthDateUsingArray {
  public static void main(String[] args) {
    int date = 0; // Date to be determined
    int answer;

    int[][][] dates = {
      {{ 1,  3,  5,  7},
       { 9, 11, 13, 15},
       {17, 19, 21, 23},
       {25, 27, 29, 31}},
      {{ 2,  3,  6,  7},
       {10, 11, 14, 15},
       {18, 19, 22, 23},
       {26, 27, 30, 31}},
      {{ 4,  5,  6,  7},
       {12, 13, 14, 15},
       {20, 21, 22, 23},
       {28, 29, 30, 31}},
      {{ 8,  9, 10, 11},
       {12, 13, 14, 15},
       {24, 25, 26, 27},
       {28, 29, 30, 31}},
      {{16, 17, 18, 19},
       {20, 21, 22, 23},
```

```
27          {24, 25, 26, 27},
28          {28, 29, 30, 31}}};
29
30      // Create a Scanner
31      Scanner input = new Scanner(System.in);
32
33      for (int i = 0; i < 5; i++) {
```

Set i

```
34        System.out.println("Is your birth date in Set" + (i + 1) + "?");
35        for (int j = 0; j < 4; j++) {
36          for (int k = 0; k < 4; k++)
37            System.out.print(dates[i][j][k] + "  ");
38          System.out.println();
39        }
40
41        System.out.print("\nEnter 0 for No and 1 for Yes: ");
42        answer = input.nextInt();
43
44        if (answer == 1)
```

add to Set i

```
45          date += dates[i][0][0] ;
46      }
47
48      System.out.println("Your birth date is " + date);
49    }
50 }
```

A three-dimensional array `dates` is created in Lines 8–28. This array stores five sets of numbers. Each set is a 4-by-4 two-dimensional array.

The loop starting from line 33 displays the numbers in each set and prompts the user to answer whether the date is in the set (lines 41–42). If the date is in the set, the first number (`dates[i][0][0]`) in the set is added to variable `date` (line 45).

Key Terms

anonymous array 189
array 180
array initializer 182
binary search 196
garbage collection 188
index 182
indexed variable 182
insertion sort 200
linear search 196
multidimensional array 215
ragged array 205
selection sort 199

Chapter Summary

- A variable is declared as an array type using the syntax `dataType[] arrayRefVar` or `dataType arrayRefVar[]`. The style `dataType[] arrayRefVar` is preferred, although `dataType arrayRefVar[]` is legal.

- Unlike declarations for primitive data type variables, the declaration of an array variable does not allocate any space in memory for the array. An array variable is not a primitive data type variable. An array variable contains a reference to an array.

- You cannot assign elements to an array unless it has already been created. You can create an array by using the `new` operator with the following syntax: `new dataType[arraySize]`.

- Each element in the array is represented using the syntax `arrayRefVar[index]`. An index must be an integer or an integer expression.

- After an array is created, its size becomes permanent and can be obtained using `arrayRefVar.length`. Since the index of an array always begins with `0`, the last index is always `arrayRefVar.length - 1`. An out-of-bounds error will occur if you attempt to reference elements beyond the bounds of an array.
- Programmers often mistakenly reference the first element in an array with index `1`, but it should be `0`. This is called the *index off-by-one error.*
- When an array is created, its elements are assigned the default value of `0` for the numeric primitive data types, `'\u0000'` for char types, and `false` for `boolean` types.
- Java has a shorthand notation, known as the *array initializer*, which combines in one statement declaring an array, creating an array, and initializing, using the syntax: `dataType[] arrayRefVar = {value0, value1, ..., valuek}`.
- When you pass an array argument to a method, you are actually passing the reference of the array; that is, the called method can modify the elements in the caller's original array.
- You can use arrays of arrays to form multidimensional arrays. For example, a two-dimensional array is declared as an array of arrays using the syntax `dataType[][] arrayRefVar` or `dataType arrayRefVar[][]`.

Review Questions

Section 6.2 Array Basics

6.1 How do you declare and create an array?

6.2 How do you access elements of an array?

6.3 Is memory allocated for an array when it is declared? When is the memory allocated for an array? What is the printout of the following code?

```
int x = 30;
int[] numbers = new int[x];
x = 60;
System.out.println("x is " + x);
System.out.println("The size of numbers is " + numbers.length);
```

6.4 Indicate true or false for the following statements:

- Every element in an array has the same type.
- The array size is fixed after it is declared.
- The array size is fixed after it is created.
- The elements in an array must be of primitive data type.

6.5 Which of the following statements are valid array declarations?

```
int i = new int(30);
double d[] = new double[30];
char[] r = new char(1..30);
int i[] = (3, 4, 3, 2);
float f[] = {2.3, 4.5, 6.6};
char[] c = new char();
```

6.6 What is the array index type? What is the lowest index?

6.7 What is the representation of the third element in an array named a?

6.8 What happens when your program attempts to access an array element with an invalid index?

6.9 Identify and fix the errors in the following code:

```
public class Test {
  public static void main(String[] args) {
    double[100] r;

    for (int i = 0; i < r.length(); i++);
      r(i) = Math.random * 100;
  }
}
```

Section 6.3 Copying Arrays

6.10 Use the arraycopy() method to copy the following array to a target array t:

```
int[] source = {3, 4, 5};
```

6.11 Once an array is created, its size cannot be changed. Does the following code resize the array?

```
int[] myList;
myList = new int[10];
// Some time later you want to assign a new array to myList
myList = new int[20];
```

Sections 6.4–6.5

6.12 When an array is passed to a method, a new array is created and passed to the method. Is this true?

6.13 Show the output of the following two programs:

```
public class Test {
  public static void main(String[] args) {
    int number = 0;
    int[] numbers = new int[1];

    m(number, numbers);

    System.out.println("number is " + number
      + " and numbers[0] is " + numbers[0]);
  }

  public static void m(int x, int[] y) {
    x = 3;
    y[0] = 3;
  }
}
```

(a)

```
public class Test {
  public static void main(String[] args) {
    int[] list = {1, 2, 3, 4, 5};
    reverse(list);
    for (int i = 0; i < list.length; i++)
      System.out.print(list[i] + " ");
  }

  public static void reverse(int[] list) {
    int[] newList = new int[list.length];

    for (int i = 0; i < list.length; i++)
      newList[i] = list[list.length - 1 - i];

    list = newList;
  }
}
```

(b)

6.14 Where are the arrays stored during execution? Show the contents of the stack and heap during and after executing createArray, displayArray, countLetters, displayCounts in Listing 6.4,

Section 6.6 Variable-Length Argument Lists

6.15 What is wrong in the following method declaration?

```
public static void print(String... strings, double... numbers)
public static void print(double... numbers, String name)
public static double... print(double d1, double d2)
```

6.16 Can you invoke the `printMax` method in Listing 6.5 using the following statements?

```
printMax(1, 2, 2, 1, 4);
printMax(new double[]{1, 2, 3});
printMax(new int[]{1, 2, 3});
```

Sections 6.7–6.8

6.17 Use Figure 6.7 as an example to show how to apply the binary search approach to a search for key `10` and key `12` in list {`2, 4, 7, 10, 11, 45, 50, 59, 60, 66, 69, 70, 79`}.

6.18 Use Figure 6.8 as an example to show how to apply the selection-sort approach to sort {`3.4, 5, 3, 3.5, 2.2, 1.9, 2`}.

6.19 Use Figure 6.9 as an example to show how to apply the insertion-sort approach to sort {`3.4, 5, 3, 3.5, 2.2, 1.9, 2`}.

6.20 How do you modify the `selectionSort` method in Listing 6.8 to sort numbers in decreasing order?

6.21 How do you modify the `insertionSort` method in Listing 6.9 to sort numbers in decreasing order?

Section 6.9 The Arrays Class

6.22 What types of array can be sorted using the `java.util.Arrays.sort` method? Does this `sort` method create a new array?

6.23 To apply `java.util.Arrays.binarySearch(array, key)`, should the array be sorted in increasing order, in decreasing order, or neither?

6.24 Show the contents of the array after the execution of each line.

```
int[] list = {2, 4, 7, 10};
java.util.Arrays.fill(list, 7);
java.util.Arrays.fill(list, 1, 3, 8);
System.out.print(java.util.Arrays.equals(list, list));
```

Section 6.10 Two-Dimensional Arrays

6.25 Declare and create a `4`-by-`5` `int` matrix.

6.26 Can the rows in a two-dimensional array have different lengths?

6.27 What is the output of the following code?

```
int[][] array = new int[5][6];
int[] x = {1, 2};
array[0] = x;
System.out.println("array[0][1] is " + array[0][1]);
```

6.28 Which of the following statements are valid array declarations?

```
int[][] r = new int[2];

int[] x = new int[];

int[][] y = new int[3][];
```

6.29 True or false? Every valid Sudoku input has a solution. If false, give an example.

Programming Exercises

Section 6.2 Array Basics

6.1 (*Analyzing input*) Write a program that reads ten numbers, computes their average, and finds out how many numbers are above the average.

6.2 (*Alternative solution to Listing 6.1, "Testing Arrays"*) The solution of Listing 6.1 counts the occurrences of the largest number by comparing *each number* with the largest. So you have to use an array to store all the numbers. Another way to solve the problem is to maintain two variables, `max` and `count`. `max` stores the current max number, and `count` stores its occurrences. Initially, assign the first number to `max` and `1` to `count`. Compare each subsequent number with `max`. If the number is greater than `max`, assign it to `max` and reset `count` to `1`. If the number is equal to `max`, increment `count` by `1`. Use this approach to rewrite Listing 6.1.

6.3 (*Reversing the numbers entered*) Write a program that reads ten integers and displays them in the reverse of the order in which they were read.

6.4 (*Analyzing scores*) Write a program that reads an unspecified number of scores and determines how many scores are above or equal to the average and how many scores are below the average. Enter a negative number to signify the end of the input. Assume that the maximum number of scores is `10`.

6.5** (*Printing distinct numbers*) Write a program that reads in ten numbers and displays distinct numbers (i.e., if a number appears multiple times, it is displayed only once). (*Hint*: Read a number and store it to an array if it is new. If the number is already in the array, discard it. After the input, the array contains the distinct numbers.)

6.6* (*Revising Listing 4.14, PrimeNumber.java*) Listing 4.14 determines whether a number `n` is prime by checking whether `2`, `3`, `4`, `5`, `6`, ..., `n/2` is a divisor. If a divisor is found, `n` is not prime. A more efficient approach to determine whether `n` is prime is to check whether any of the prime numbers less than or equal to $\sqrt{n}$ can divide `n` evenly. If not, `n` is prime. Rewrite Listing 4.14 to display the first 50 prime numbers using this approach. You need to use an array to store the prime numbers and later use them to check whether they are possible divisors for `n`.

6.7* (*Counting single digits*) Write a program that generates `100` random integers between `0` and `9` and displays the count for each number. (*Hint*: Use `(int)(Math.random() * 10)` to generate a random integer between `0` and `9`. Use an array of ten integers, say `counts`, to store the counts for the number of `0`'s, `1`'s, ..., `9`'s.)

Sections 6.4–6.5

6.8 (*Averaging an array*) Write two overloaded methods that return the average of an array with the following headers:

```
public static int average(int[] array);
public static double average(double[] array);
```

Use {`1, 2, 3, 4, 5, 6`} and {`6.0, 4.4, 1.9, 2.9, 3.4, 3.5`} to test the methods.

6.9 (*Finding the smallest element*) Write a method that finds the smallest element in an array of integers. Use {`1, 2, 4, 5, 10, 100, 2, -22`} to test the method.

6.10 (*Finding the index of the smallest element*) Write a method that returns the index of the smallest element in an array of integers. If there are more than one such elements, return the smallest index. Use {`1, 2, 4, 5, 10, 100, 2, -22`} to test the method.

6.11* (*Computing deviation*) Exercise 5.21 computes the standard deviation of numbers. This exercise uses a different but equivalent formula to compute the standard deviation of n numbers.

$$mean = \frac{\sum_{i=1}^{n} x_i}{n} = \frac{x_1 + x_2 + \cdots + x_n}{n} \qquad deviation = \sqrt{\frac{\sum_{i=1}^{n}(x_i - mean)^2}{n - 1}}$$

To compute deviation with this formula, you have to store the individual numbers using an array, so that they can be used after the mean is obtained. Use $\{1, 2, 3, 4, 5, 6, 7, 8, 9, 10\}$ to test the method.

Your program should contain the following methods:

```
/** Method for computing deviation of double values*/
public static double deviation(double[] x)

/** Method for computing deviation of int values*/
public static double deviation(int[] x)

/** Method for computing mean of an array of double values*/
public static double mean(double[] x)

/** Method for computing mean of an array of int values*/
public static double mean(int[] x)
```

6.12* (*Reversing an array*) The `reverse` method in §6.5 reverses an array by copying it to a new array. Rewrite the method without creating new arrays.

Section 6.6 Variable-Length Argument Lists

6.13* (*Random number chooser*) Write a method that returns a random number between `1` and `54`, excluding the numbers passed in the argument. The method header is specified as follows:

```
public static int getRandom(int... numbers)
```

6.14 (*Computing gcd*) Write a method that returns the gcd of an unspecified number of integers. The method header is specified as follows:

```
public static int gcd(int... numbers)
```

Sections 6.7–6.9

6.15 (*Financial application: finding the sales amount*) Rewrite Listing 4.9, FindSalesAmount.cpp, using the binary search approach. Since the sales amount is between `1` and `COMMISSION_SOUGHT/0.08`, you can use a binary search to improve it.

6.16 (*Execution time*) Write a program that randomly generates an array of `100000` integers and a key. Estimate the execution time of invoking the `linearSearch` method in Listing 6.6. Sort the array and estimate the execution time of invoking the `binarySearch` method in Listing 6.7. You can use the following code template to obtain the execution time:

```
long startTime = System.currentTimeMillis();
perform the task;
long endTime = System.currentTimeMillis();
long executionTime = endTime - startTime;
```

6.17* (*Revising selection sort*) In §6.8.1, you used selection sort to sort an array. The selection sort method repeatedly finds the largest number in the current array and swaps it with the last number in the array. Rewrite this program by finding the smallest number and swapping it with the first number in the array.

6.18** (*Bubble sort*) Write a sort method that uses the bubble-sort algorithm. The bubble-sort algorithm makes several passes through the array. On each pass, successive neighboring pairs are compared. If a pair is in decreasing order, its values are swapped; otherwise, the values remain unchanged. The technique is called a *bubble sort* or *sinking sort* because the smaller values gradually "bubble" their way to the top and the larger values "sink" to the bottom. Use {`6.0`, `4.4`, `1.9`, `2.9`, `3.4`, `2.9`, `3.5`} to test the method.

6.19** (*Sorting students*) Write a program that prompts the user to enter the number of students, and student names and their scores, and prints student names in decreasing order of their scores.

Section 6.10 Two-dimensional Arrays

6.20* (*Summing all the numbers in a matrix*) Write a method that sums all the integers in a matrix of integers. Use {{`1`, `2`, `4`, `5`}, {`6`, `7`, `8`, `9`}, {`10`, `11`, `12`, `13`}, {`14`, `15`, `16`, `17`}} to test the method.

6.21* (*Summing the major diagonal in a matrix*) Write a method that sums all the integers in the major diagonal in an $n \times n$ matrix of integers. Use {{`1`, `2`, `4`, `5`}, {`6`, `7`, `8`, `9`}, {`10`, `11`, `12`, `13`}, {`14`, `15`, `16`, `17`}} to test the method.

6.22* (*Sorting students on grades*) Rewrite Listing 6.10, GradeExam.java, to display the students in increasing order of the number of correct answers.

6.23** (*Computing the weekly hours for each employee*) Suppose the weekly hours for all employees are stored in a two-dimensional array. Each row records an employee's seven-day work hours with seven columns. For example, the following array stores the work hours for eight employees. Write a program that displays employees and their total hours in decreasing order of the total hours.

	Su	M	T	W	H	F	Sa
Employee 0	2	4	3	4	5	8	8
Employee 1	7	3	4	3	3	4	4
Employee 2	3	3	4	3	3	2	2
Employee 3	9	3	4	7	3	4	1
Employee 4	3	5	4	3	6	3	8
Employee 5	3	4	4	6	3	4	4
Employee 6	3	7	4	8	3	8	4
Employee 7	6	3	5	9	2	7	9

6.24 (*Adding two matrices*) Write a method to add two matrices. The header of the method is as follows:

```
public static int[][] addMatrix(int[][] a, int[][] b)
```

In order to be added, the two matrices must have the same dimensions and the same or compatible types of elements. As shown below, two matrices are added by adding the two elements of the arrays with the same index:

$$\begin{pmatrix} a_{11} & a_{12} & a_{13} \\ a_{21} & a_{22} & a_{23} \\ a_{31} & a_{32} & a_{33} \end{pmatrix} + \begin{pmatrix} b_{11} & b_{12} & b_{13} \\ b_{21} & b_{22} & b_{23} \\ b_{31} & b_{32} & b_{33} \end{pmatrix} = \begin{pmatrix} a_{11}+b_{11} & a_{12}+b_{12} & a_{13}+b_{13} \\ a_{21}+b_{21} & a_{22}+b_{22} & a_{23}+b_{23} \\ a_{31}+b_{31} & a_{32}+b_{32} & a_{33}+b_{33} \end{pmatrix}$$

6.25** (*Multiplying two matrices*) Write a method to multiply two matrices. The header of the method is as follows:

```
public static int[][] multiplyMatrix(int[][] a, int[][] b)
```

To multiply matrix a by matrix b, the number of columns in a must be the same as the number of rows in b, and the two matrices must have elements of the same or compatible types. Let c be the result of the multiplication, and a, b, and c are denoted as follows:

$$\begin{pmatrix} a_{11} & a_{12} & a_{13} \\ a_{21} & a_{22} & a_{23} \\ a_{31} & a_{32} & a_{33} \end{pmatrix} \times \begin{pmatrix} b_{11} & b_{12} & b_{13} \\ b_{21} & b_{22} & b_{23} \\ b_{31} & b_{32} & b_{33} \end{pmatrix} = \begin{pmatrix} c_{11} & c_{12} & c_{13} \\ c_{21} & c_{22} & c_{23} \\ c_{31} & c_{32} & c_{33} \end{pmatrix}$$

where $c_{ij} = a_{i1} \times b_{1j} + a_{i2} \times b_{2j} + a_{i3} \times b_{3j}$.

6.26* (*Points nearest to each other*) Listing 6.11 gives a program that finds two points in a two-dimensional space nearest to other. Revise the program that finds two points in a three-dimensional space nearest to each other. Use a two-dimensional array to represent the points. Test the program using the following points:

Video Note
Find points nearest to each other

```
double[][] points = {{-1, 0, 3}, {-1, -1, -1}, {4, 1, 1},
  {2, 0.5, 9}, {3.5, 2, -1}, {3, 1.5, 3}, {-1.5, 4, 2},
  {5.5, 4, -0.5}};
```

The formula for computing the distance between two points (x1, y1, z1) and (x2, y2, z2) is $\sqrt{(x_2 - x_1)^2 + (y_2 - y_1)^2 + (z_2 - z_1)^2}$.

6.27** (*All closest pairs of points*) Revise Listing 6.11, FindNearestPoints.java, to find all closest pairs of points with same minimum distance.

Comprehensive

6.28* (*Game: TicTacToe board*) Write a program that randomly fills in 0s and 1s into a TicTacToe board, prints the board, and finds the rows, columns, or diagonals with all 0s or 1s. Use a two-dimensional array to represent a TicTacToe board. Here is a sample run of the program:

```
001
001
111
All 1's on row 2
All 1's on column 2
```

6.29*** (*Game: bean machine*) The bean machine, also known as a quincunx or the Galton box, is a device for statistic experiments named after English scientist Sir Francis Galton. It consists of an upright board with evenly spaced nails (or pegs) in a triangular form, as shown in Figure 6.17.

Balls are dropped from the opening of the board. Every time a ball hits a nail, it has a 50% of chance to fall to the left and a 50% of chance to fall to the right. The piles of balls are accumulated in the slots at the bottom of the board.

Write a program that simulates the bean machine. Your program should prompt the user to enter the number of the balls and the number of the slots in the machine. Simulate the falling of each ball by printing its path. For example, the path for the ball in Figure 6.17(b) is LLRRLLR and the path for the ball in Figure 6.17(c) is RLRRLRR. Display the final buildup of the balls in the slots in a histogram. Here is a sample run of the program:

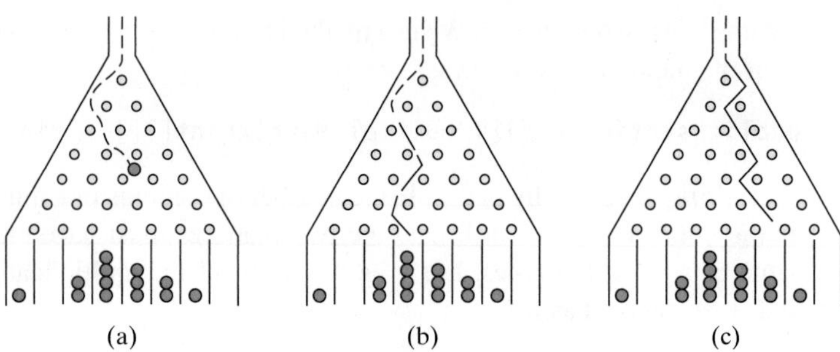

FIGURE 6.17 Each ball takes a random path and falls into a slot.

```
Enter the number of balls to drop: 5 ↵Enter
Enter the number of slots in the bean machine: 7 ↵Enter

LRLRLRR
RRLLLRR
LLRLLRR
RRLLLLL
LRLRRLR

    0
    0
   000
```

Hint: Create an array named `slots`. Each element in `slots` stores the number of balls in a slot. Each ball falls into a slot via a path. The number of R's in a path is the position of the slot where the ball falls. For example, for the path LRLRLRR, the ball falls into `slots[4]`, and for the path is RRLLLLL, the ball falls into `slots[2]`.

6.30*** (*Game: playing a TicTacToe game*) In a game of TicTacToe, two players take turns marking an available cell in a 3 × 3 grid with their respective tokens (either X or O). When one player has placed three tokens in a horizontal, vertical, or diagonal row on the grid, the game is over and that player has won. A draw (no winner) occurs when all the cells on the grid have been filled with tokens and neither player has achieved a win. Create a program for playing TicTacToe, as follows:

1. The program prompts the first player to enter an X token, and then prompts the second player to enter an O token. Whenever a token is entered, the program refreshes the board and determines the status of the game (win, draw, or unfinished).
2. To place a token, display two dialog boxes to prompt the user to enter the row and the column for the token.

6.31** (*Game: nine heads and tails*) Nine coins are placed in a 3-by-3 matrix with some face up and some face down. You can represent the state of the coins using a 3-by-3 matrix with values 0 (head) and 1 (tail). Here are some examples:

```
0 0 0   1 0 1   1 1 0   1 0 1   1 0 0
0 1 0   0 0 1   1 0 0   1 1 0   1 1 1
0 0 0   1 0 0   0 0 1   1 0 0   1 1 0
```

Each state can also be represented using a binary number. For example, the preceding matrices correspond to the numbers

```
000010000 101001100 110100001 101110100 100111110
```

There are a total of 512 possibilities. So, you can use decimal numbers 0, 1, 2, 3, . . . , and 511 to represent all states of the matrix. Write a program that prompts the user to enter a number between 0 and 511 and displays the corresponding matrix with characters H and T. Here is a sample output:

```
Enter a number between 0 and 511: 7 ↵Enter
H H H
H H H
T T T
```

The user entered 7, which corresponds to 000000111. Since 0 stands for H and 1 for T, the output is correct.

6.32** (*Financial application: computing tax*) Rewrite Listing 3.7, ComputeTax.java, using arrays. For each filing status, there are six tax rates. Each rate is applied to a certain amount of taxable income. For example, from the taxable income of $400,000 for a single filer, $6,000 is taxed at 10%, (27,950 – 6,000) at 15%, (67,700 – 27,950) at 27%, (141,250 – 67,700) at 30%, (307,050 – 141,250) at 35%, and (400,000 – 307,050) at 38.6%. The six rates are the same for all filing statuses, which can be represented in the following array:

```
double[] rates = {0.10, 0.15, 0.27, 0.30, 0.35, 0.386};
```

The brackets for each rate for all the filing statuses can be represented in a two-dimensional array as follows:

```
int[][] brackets = {
  {6000, 27950, 67700, 141250, 307050},    // Single filer
  {12000, 46700, 112850, 171950, 307050}, // Married jointly
  {6000, 23350, 56425, 85975, 153525},   // Married separately
  {10000, 37450, 96700, 156600, 307050}  // Head of household
};
```

Suppose the taxable income is $400,000 for single filers. The tax can be computed as follows:

```
tax = brackets[0][0] * rates[0] +
  (brackets[0][1] - brackets[0][0]) * rates[1] +
  (brackets[0][2] - brackets[0][1]) * rates[2] +
  (brackets[0][3] - brackets[0][2]) * rates[3] +
  (brackets[0][4] - brackets[0][3]) * rates[4] +
  (400000 - brackets[0][4]) * rates[5]
```

6.33** (*Game: locker puzzle*) A school has 100 lockers and 100 students. All lockers are closed on the first day of school. As the students enter, the first student, denoted S1, opens every locker. Then the second student, S2, begins with the second locker, denoted L2, and closes every other locker. Student S3 begins with the third locker and changes every third locker (closes it if it was open, and opens it if it was closed). Student S4 begins with locker L4 and changes every fourth locker. Student S5 starts with L5 and changes every fifth locker, and so on, until student S100 changes L100.

After all the students have passed through the building and changed the lockers, which lockers are open? Write a program to find your answer.

(*Hint*: Use an array of 100 elements, each of which stores the number of the times a locker has changed. If a locker changes an even number of times, it is closed; otherwise, it is open.)

6.34** (*Game: checker board*) Write a program that randomly fills in 0s and 1s into an 8×8 checker board, prints the board, and finds the rows, columns, or diagonals with all 0s or 1s. Use a two-dimensional array to represent a checker board. Here is a sample run of the program:

```
10101000
10100001
11100011
10100001
11100111
10000001
10100111
00100001
All 0's on subdiagonal
```

6.35*** (*Game: Eight Queens*) The classic Eight Queens puzzle is to place eight queens on a chessboard such that no two queens can attack each other (i.e., no two queens are on the same row, same column, or same diagonal). There are many possible solutions. Write a program that displays one such solution. A sample output is shown below:

```
|Q| | | | | | | |
| | | | |Q| | | |
| | | | | | | |Q|
| | | | | |Q| | |
| | |Q| | | | | |
| | | | | | |Q| |
| |Q| | | | | | |
| | | |Q| | | | |
```

6.36*** (*Game: multiple Sudoku solutions*) A Sudoku problem may have multiple solutions. Modify Listing 6.12, Sudoku.java, to display the total number of the solutions. Display two solutions if multiple solutions exist.

6.37*** (*Game: multiple Eight Queens solutions*) Exercise 6.35 finds one solution for the eight queens problem. Write a program to count all possible solutions for the eight queens problem and displays all solutions.

CHAPTER 7

OBJECTS AND CLASSES

Objectives

- To describe objects and classes, and use classes to model objects (§7.2).
- To use UML graphical notations to describe classes and objects (§7.2).
- To construct objects using constructors (§7.3).
- To access objects via object reference variables (§7.4).
- To define a reference variable using a reference type (§7.4.1).
- To access an object's data and methods (§7.4.2).
- To declare a class and create an object from a class (§7.4.3).
- To assign default values for an object's data fields (§7.4.4).
- To distinguish between object reference variables and primitive data type variables (§7.4.5).
- To use classes `Date`, `Random`, and `JFrame` in the Java library (§7.5).
- To distinguish between instance and static variables and methods (§7.6).
- To declare private data fields with appropriate `get` and `set` methods (§7.7).
- To encapsulate data fields to make classes easy to maintain (§7.8).
- To differentiate between primitive-type arguments and object-type arguments (§7.9).
- To develop methods with object arguments (§7.9).
- To store and process objects in arrays (§7.10).

7.1 Introduction

After learning the material in earlier chapters, you are able to solve many programming problems using selections, loops, methods, and arrays. However, these Java features are not sufficient for developing graphical user interfaces and large-scale software systems. Suppose you want to develop a GUI (graphical user interface, pronounced *goo-ee*) as shown in Figure 7.1. How do you program it?

why OOP?

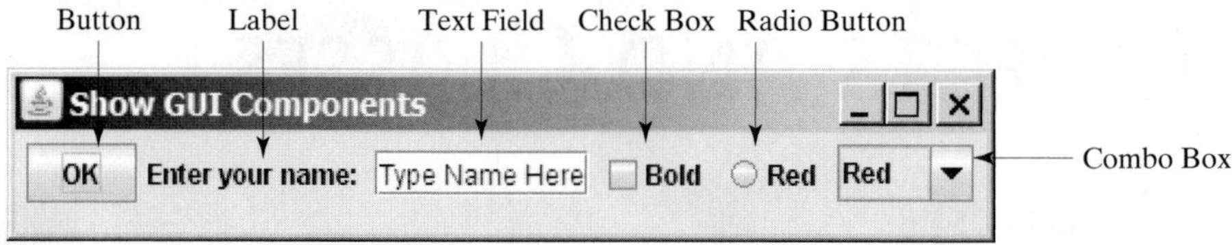

FIGURE 7.1 The GUI component objects can be displayed.

This chapter begins the introduction of object-oriented programming, which will enable you to develop GUI and large-scale software systems effectively.

7.2 Defining Classes for Objects

object

Object-oriented programming (OOP) involves programming using objects. An *object* represents an entity in the real world that can be distinctly identified. For example, a student, a desk, a circle, a button, and even a loan can all be viewed as objects. An object has a unique identity, state, and behaviors.

state

- The *state* of an object is represented by *data fields* (also known as *properties*) with their current values.

behavior

- The *behavior* of an object is defined by a set of methods. To invoke a method on an object is to ask the object to perform a task.

A circle object, for example, has a data field, `radius`, which is the property that characterizes a circle. One behavior of a circle is that its area can be computed using the method `getArea()`.

Objects of the same type are defined using a common class. A class is a template or blueprint that defines what an object's data and methods will be. An object is an instance of a class. You can create many instances of a class. Creating an instance is referred to as *instantiation*. The terms *object* and *instance* are often interchangeable. The relationship between classes and objects is analogous to the-relationship between apple pie recipes and apple pies. You can make as many apple pies as you want from a single recipe. Figure 7.2 shows a class named `Circle` and its three objects.

instantiation
object
instance

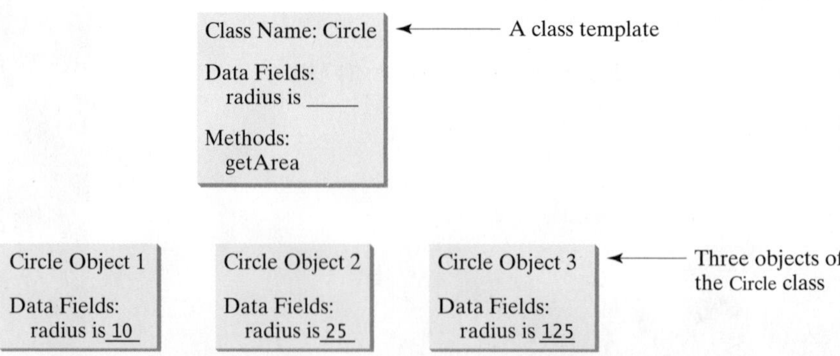

FIGURE 7.2 A class is a template for creating objects.

A Java class uses variables to define data fields and methods to define behaviors. Additionally, a class provides methods of a special type, known as *constructors*, which are invoked when a new object is created. A constructor is a special kind of method. A constructor can perform any action, but constructors are designed to perform initializing actions, such as initializing the data fields of objects. Figure 7.3 shows an example of the class for `Circle` objects.

class
data field
method
constructor

```
class Circle {
  /** The radius of this circle */
  double radius = 1.0;                          <-- Data field

  /** Construct a circle object */
  Circle() {
  }
                                                <-- Constructors
  /** Construct a circle object */
  Circle(double newRadius) {
    radius = newRadius;
  }

  /** Return the area of this circle */
  double getArea() {                            <-- Method
    return radius * radius * Math.PI;
  }
}
```

FIGURE 7.3 A class is a construct that defines objects of the same type.

The `Circle` class is different from all of the other classes you have seen thus far. It does not have a `main` method and therefore cannot be run; it is merely a definition used to declare and create `Circle` objects. For convenience, the class that contains the `main` method will be referred to as the *main class* in this book.

main class

The illustration of class templates and objects in Figure 7.3 can be standardized using UML (Unified Modeling Language) notations. This notation, as shown in Figure 7.4, is called a *UML class diagram*, or simply a *class diagram*. In the class diagram, the data field is denoted as

class diagram

```
dataFieldName: dataFieldType
```

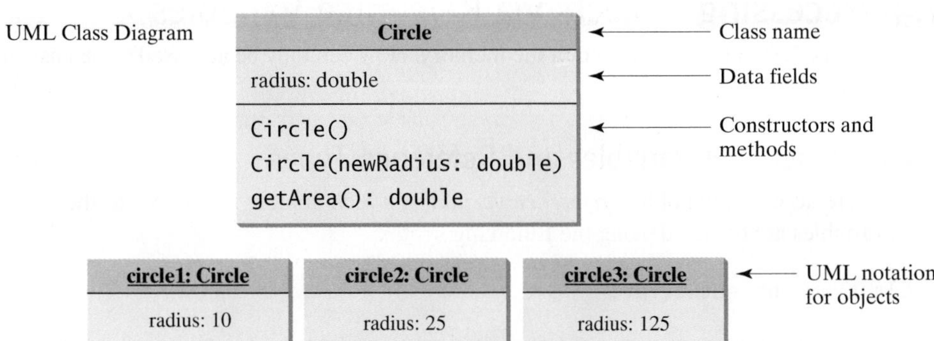

FIGURE 7.4 Classes and objects can be represented using UML notations.

The constructor is denoted as

```
ClassName(parameterName: parameterType)
```

The method is denoted as

```
methodName(parameterName: parameterType): returnType
```

7.3 Constructing Objects Using Constructors

overloaded constructors

Constructors are used to construct objects. The constructor has exactly the same name as the defining class. Like regular methods, constructors can be overloaded (i.e., multiple constructors with the same name but different signatures), making it easy to construct objects with different initial data values.

To construct an object from a class, invoke a constructor of the class using the `new` operator, as follows:

```
new ClassName(arguments);
```

For example, `new Circle()` creates an object of the `Circle` class using the first constructor defined in the `Circle` class, and `new Circle(5)` creates an object using the second constructor defined in the `Circle` class.

no-arg constructor

A class normally provides a constructor without arguments (e.g., `Circle()`). Such a constructor is referred to as a *no-arg* or *no-argument constructor.*

default constructor

A class may be declared without constructors. In this case, a no-arg constructor with an empty body is implicitly declared in the class. This constructor, called *a default constructor*, is provided automatically *only if no constructors are explicitly declared in the class.*

Constructors are a special kind of method, with three differences:

constructor's name

- Constructors must have the same name as the class itself.

no return type

- Constructors do not have a return type—not even `void`.

new operator

- Constructors are invoked using the `new` operator when an object is created. Constructors play the role of initializing objects.

Caution

It is a common mistake to put the `void` keyword in front of a constructor. For example,

```
public void Circle() {
}
```

In this case, `Circle()` is a method, not a constructor.

7.4 Accessing Objects via Reference Variables

Newly created objects are allocated in the memory. How can they be accessed? The answer is given in this section.

7.4.1 Reference Variables and Reference Types

reference variable

Objects are accessed via object *reference variables*, which contain references to the objects. Such variables are declared using the following syntax:

```
ClassName objectRefVar;
```

reference type

A class defines a type, known as a *reference type*. Any variable of the class type can reference an instance of the class. The following statement declares the variable `myCircle` to be of the `Circle` type:

```
Circle myCircle;
```

The variable `myCircle` can reference a `Circle` object. The next statement creates an object and assigns its reference to `myCircle`.

```
myCircle = new Circle();
```

Using the syntax shown below, you can write one statement that combines the declaration of an object reference variable, the creation of an object, and the assigning of an object reference to the variable.

```
ClassName objectRefVar = new ClassName();
```

Here is an example:

```
Circle myCircle = new Circle();
```

The variable `myCircle` holds a reference to a `Circle` object.

Note

An object reference variable that appears to hold an object actually contains a reference to that object. Strictly speaking, an object reference variable and an object are different, but most of the time the distinction can be ignored. So it is fine, for simplicity, to say that `myCircle` is a `Circle` object rather than use a more long-winded description that `myCircle` is a variable that contains a reference to a `Circle` object.

object vs. object reference variable

Note

Arrays are treated as objects in Java. Arrays are created using the `new` operator. An array variable is actually a variable that contains a reference to an array.

array object

7.4.2 Accessing an Object's Data and Methods

After an object is created, its data can be accessed and its methods invoked using the *dot operator* (`.`), also known as the *object member access operator*:

dot operator

- `objectRefVar.dataField` references a data field in the object.
- `objectRefVar.method(arguments)` invokes a method on the object.

For example, `myCircle.radius` references the radius in `myCircle`, and `myCircle.getArea()` invokes the `getArea` method on `myCircle`. Methods are invoked as operations on objects.

The data field `radius` is referred to as an *instance variable* because it is dependent on a specific instance. For the same reason, the method `getArea` is referred to as an *instance method*, because you can invoke it only on a specific instance. The object on which an instance method is invoked is called a *calling object*.

instance variable

instance method

calling object

Note

Most of the time, you create an object and assign it to a variable. Later you can use the variable to reference the object. Occasionally, an object does not need to be referenced later. In this case, you can create an object without explicitly assigning it to a variable, as shown below:

```
new Circle();
```

or

```
System.out.println("Area is " + new Circle(5).getArea());
```

The former statement creates a `Circle` object. The latter creates a `Circle` object and invokes its `getArea` method to return its area. An object created in this way is known as an *anonymous object*.

anonymous object

7.4.3 Example: Declaring Classes and Creating Objects

Listing 7.1 is a program that declares a circle class. To avoid a naming conflict with several improved versions of the `Circle` class introduced later in this book, the `Circle` class in this example is named `Circle1`.

The program constructs a circle object with radius 5 and an object with radius 1 and displays the radius and area of each of the two circles. Change the radius of the second object to 100 and display its new radius and area.

LISTING 7.1 TestCircle1.java

main class
main method
create object
create object
class **Circle1**
data field
no-arg constructor
second constructor
method

```
public class TestCircle1 {
  /** Main method */
  public static void main(String[] args) {
    // Create a circle with radius 5.0
    Circle1 myCircle = new Circle1(5.0);
    System.out.println("The area of the circle of radius "
      + myCircle.radius + " is " + myCircle.getArea());

    // Create a circle with radius 1
    Circle1 yourCircle = new Circle1();
    System.out.println("The area of the circle of radius "
      + yourCircle.radius + " is " + yourCircle.getArea());

    // Modify circle radius
    yourCircle.radius = 100;
    System.out.println("The area of the circle of radius "
      + yourCircle.radius + " is " + yourCircle.getArea() );
  }
}

// Define the circle class with two constructors
class Circle1 {
  double radius;

  /** Construct a circle with radius 1 */
  Circle1() {
    radius = 1.0;
  }

  /** Construct a circle with a specified radius */
  Circle1(double newRadius) {
    radius = newRadius;
  }

  /** Return the area of this circle */
  double getArea() {
    return radius * radius * Math.PI;
  }
}
```

```
The area of the circle of radius 5.0 is 78.53981633974483
The area of the circle of radius 1.0 is 3.141592653589793
The area of the circle of radius 100.0 is 31415.926535897932
```

The program contains two classes. The first class, `TestCircle1`, is the main class. Its sole purpose is to test the second class, `Circle1`. When you run the program, the Java runtime system invokes the `main` method in the main class.

You can put the two classes into one file, but only one class in the file can be a public class. Furthermore, the public class must have the same name as the file name. Therefore, the file name is TestCircle1.java since `TestCircle1` is public.

The main class contains the `main` method (line 3) that creates two objects. The constructor `Circle1(5.0)` was used to create `myCircle` with a radius of `5.0` (line 5), and the constructor `Circle1()` was used to create `yourCircle` with a radius of `1.0` (line 10).

These two objects (referenced by `myCircle` and `yourCircle`) have different data but have the same methods. Therefore, you can compute their respective areas by using the `getArea()` method.

To write the `getArea` method in a procedural programming language like Pascal, you would pass radius as an argument to the method. But in object-oriented programming, `radius` and `getArea` are defined for the object. The `radius` is a data member in the object, which is accessible by the `getArea` method. In procedural programming languages, data and methods are separated, but in an object-oriented programming language, data and methods are coupled together.

The `getArea` method is an instance method that is always invoked by an instance in which the `radius` is specified.

There are many ways to write Java programs. For instance, you can combine the two classes in the example into one, as shown in Listing 7.2:

Listing 7.2 Circle1.java

```
public class Circle1 {
  /** Main method */
  public static void main(String[] args) {
    // Create a circle with radius 5.0
    Circle1 myCircle = new Circle1(5.0);
    System.out.println("The area of the circle of radius "
      + myCircle.radius + " is " + myCircle.getArea());

    // Create a circle with radius 1
    Circle1 yourCircle = new Circle1();
    System.out.println("The area of the circle of radius "
      + yourCircle.radius + " is " + yourCircle.getArea());

    // Modify circle radius
    yourCircle.radius = 100;
    System.out.println("The area of the circle of radius "
      + yourCircle.radius + " is " + yourCircle.getArea());
  }

  double radius;

  /** Construct a circle with radius 1 */
  Circle1() {
    radius = 1.0;
  }

  /** Construct a circle with a specified radius */
  Circle1(double newRadius) {
    radius = newRadius;
  }

  /** Return the area of this circle */
  double getArea() {
    return radius * radius * Math.PI;
  }
}
```

main method

no-arg constructor

second constructor

method

Since the combined class has a main method, it can be executed by the Java interpreter. The main method creates myCircle as a Circle1 object and then displays radius and finds area in myCircle. This demonstrates that you can test a class by simply adding a main method in the same class.

Caution

invoking methods

Recall that you use Math.methodName(arguments) (e.g., Math.pow(3, 2.5)) to invoke a method in the Math class. Can you invoke getArea() using Circle1.getArea()? The answer is no. All the methods in the Math class are static methods, which are defined using the static keyword. However, getArea() is an instance method, and thus nonstatic. It must be invoked from an object using objectRefVar.methodName(arguments) (e.g., myCircle.getArea()). More explanations will follow in §7.6, "Static Variables, Constants, and Methods."

7.4.4 Reference Data Fields and the null Value

reference data fields

The data fields can be of reference types. For example, the following Student class contains a data field name of the String type. String is a predefined Java class.

```
class Student {
  String name; // name has default value null
  int age; // age has default value 0
  boolean isScienceMajor; // isScienceMajor has default value false
  char gender; // c has default value '\u0000'
}
```

null value

If a data field of a reference type does not reference any object, the data field holds a special Java value, null. null is a literal just like true and false. While true and false are Boolean literals, null is a literal for a reference type.

default field values

The default value of a data field is null for a reference type, 0 for a numeric type, false for a boolean type, and '\u0000' for a char type. However, Java assigns no default value to a local variable inside a method. The following code displays the default values of data fields name, age, isScienceMajor, and gender for a Student object:

```
class Test {
  public static void main(String[] args) {
    Student student = new Student();
    System.out.println("name? " + student.name );
    System.out.println("age? " + student.age);
    System.out.println("isScienceMajor? " + student.isScienceMajor);
    System.out.println("gender? " + student.gender);
  }
}
```

The following code has a compilation error because local variables x and y are not initialized:

```
class Test {
  public static void main(String[] args) {
    int x; // x has no default value
    String y; // y has no default value
    System.out.println("x is " + x);
    System.out.println("y is " + y);
  }
}
```

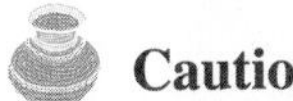

Caution

`NullPointerException` is a common runtime error. It happens when you invoke a method on a reference variable with `null` value. Make sure you assign an object reference to the variable before invoking the method through the reference variable.

`NullPointerException`

7.4.5 Differences Between Variables of Primitive Types and Reference Types

Every variable represents a memory location that holds a value. When you declare a variable, you are telling the compiler what type of value the variable can hold. For a variable of a primitive type, the value is of the primitive type. For a variable of a reference type, the value is a reference to where an object is located. For example, as shown in Figure 7.5, the value of `int` variable `i` is `int` value `1`, and the value of `Circle` object `c` holds a reference to where the contents of the `Circle` object are stored in the memory.

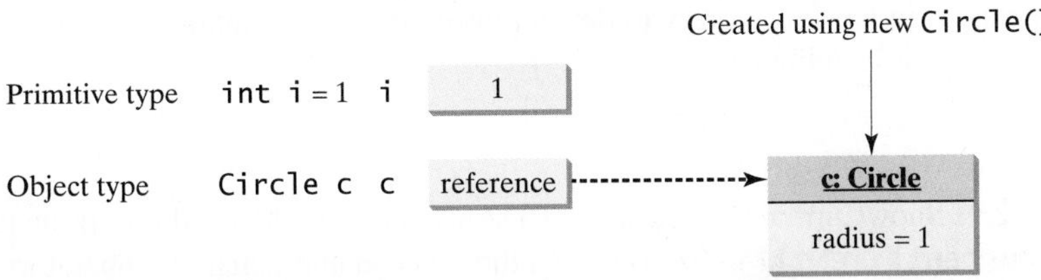

FIGURE 7.5 A variable of a primitive type holds a value of the primitive type, and a variable of a reference type holds a reference to where an object is stored in memory.

When you assign one variable to another, the other variable is set to the same value. For a variable of a primitive type, the real value of one variable is assigned to the other variable. For a variable of a reference type, the reference of one variable is assigned to the other variable. As shown in Figure 7.6, the assignment statement `i = j` copies the contents of `j` into `i` for primitive variables. As shown in Figure 7.7, the assignment statement `c1 = c2` copies the reference of `c2` into `c1` for reference variables. After the assignment, variables `c1` and `c2` refer to the same object.

Primitive type assignment `i = j`

Before:		After:	
i	1	i	2
j	2	j	2

FIGURE 7.6 Primitive variable `j` is copied to variable `i`.

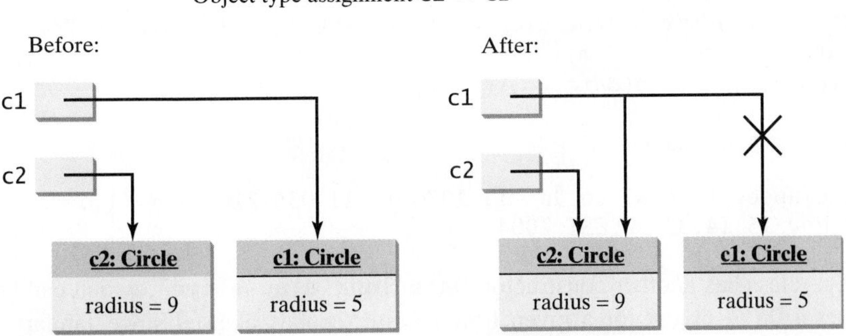

FIGURE 7.7 Reference variable `c2` is copied to variable `c1`.

Note

garbage
garbage collection

As shown in Figure 7.7, after the assignment statement `c1 = c2`, `c1` points to the same object referenced by `c2`. The object previously referenced by `c1` is no longer useful and therefore is now known as *garbage*. Garbage occupies memory space. The Java runtime system detects garbage and automatically reclaims the space it occupies. This process is called *garbage collection*.

Tip

If you know that an object is no longer needed, you can explicitly assign `null` to a reference variable for the object. The JVM will automatically collect the space if the object is not referenced by any reference variable.

7.5 Using Classes from the Java Library

Listing 7.1 declared the `Circle1` class and created objects from the class. You will frequently use the classes in the Java library to develop programs. This section gives some examples of the classes in the Java library.

7.5.1 The `Date` Class

`java.util.Date` class

In Listing 2.9, ShowCurrentTime.java, you learned how to obtain the current time using `System.currentTimeMillis()`. You used the division and remainder operators to extract current second, minute, and hour. Java provides a system-independent encapsulation of date and time in the `java.util.Date` class, as shown in Figure 7.8.

java.util.Date	
+Date()	Constructs a Date object for the current time.
+Date(elapseTime: long)	Constructs a Date object for a given time in milliseconds elapsed since January 1, 1970, GMT.
+toString(): String	Returns a string representing the date and time.
+getTime(): long	Returns the number of milliseconds since January 1, 1970, GMT.
+setTime(elapseTime: long): void	Sets a new elapse time in the object.

The + sign indicates public modifier

FIGURE 7.8 A `Date` object represents a specific date and time.

You can use the no-arg constructor in the `Date` class to create an instance for the current date and time, its `getTime()` method to return the elapsed time since January 1, 1970, GMT, and its `toString` method to return the date and time as a string. For example, the following code

create object
get elapsed time
invoke `toString`

```
java.util.Date date = new java.util.Date();
System.out.println("The elapsed time since Jan 1, 1970 is " +
  date.getTime() + " milliseconds");
System.out.println(date.toString());
```

displays the output like this:

```
The elapsed time since Jan 1, 1970 is 1100547210284 milliseconds
Mon Nov 15 14:33:30 EST 2004
```

The `Date` class has another constructor, `Date(long elapseTime)`, which can be used to construct a `Date` object for a given time in milliseconds elapsed since January 1, 1970, GMT.

7.5.2 The Random Class

You have used `Math.random()` to obtain a random double value between `0.0` and `1.0` (excluding `1.0`). Another way to generate random numbers is to use the `java.util.Random` class, as shown in Figure 7.9, which can generate a random `int`, `long`, `double`, `float`, and `boolean` value.

java.util.Random	
`+Random()`	Constructs a Random object with the current time as its seed.
`+Random(seed: long)`	Constructs a Random object with a specified seed.
`+nextInt(): int`	Returns a random int value.
`+nextInt(n: int): int`	Returns a random int value between 0 and n (exclusive).
`+nextLong(): long`	Returns a random long value.
`+nextDouble(): double`	Returns a random double value between 0.0 and 1.0 (exclusive).
`+nextFloat(): float`	Returns a random float value between 0.0F and 1.0F (exclusive).
`+nextBoolean(): boolean`	Returns a random boolean value.

FIGURE 7.9 A Random object can be used to generate random values.

When you create a Random object, you have to specify a seed or use the default seed. The no-arg constructor creates a Random object using the current elapsed time as its seed. If two Random objects have the same seed, they will generate identical sequences of numbers. For example, the following code creates two Random objects with the same seed, 3.

```
Random random1 = new Random(3);
System.out.print("From random1: ");
for (int i = 0; i < 10; i++)
  System.out.print(random1.nextInt(1000) + " ");

Random random2 = new Random(3);
System.out.print("\nFrom random2: ");
for (int i = 0; i < 10; i++)
  System.out.print(random2.nextInt(1000) + " ");
```

The code generates the same sequence of random `int` values:

```
From random1: 734 660 210 581 128 202 549 564 459 961
From random2: 734 660 210 581 128 202 549 564 459 961
```

Note

The capability of generating the same sequence of random values is useful in software testing and many other applications. In software testing, you can test your program using a fixed sequence of numbers before using different sequences of random numbers. same sequence

7.5.3 Displaying GUI Components

Pedagogical Note

Graphical user interface (GUI) components are good examples for teaching OOP. Simple GUI examples are introduced for this purpose. The complete introduction on GUI programming is covered starting from Chapter 13, "GUI Basics."

When you develop programs to create graphical user interfaces, you will use Java classes such as `JFrame`, `JButton`, `JRadioButton`, `JComboBox`, and `JList` to create frames, buttons, radio buttons, combo boxes, lists, and so on. Listing 7.3 is an example that creates two windows using the `JFrame` class. The output of the program is shown in Figure 7.10.

Window 1
Window 2

FIGURE 7.10 The program creates two windows using the `JFrame` class.

LISTING 7.3 TestFrame.java

create an object
invoke a method
create an object
invoke a method

```
1 import javax.swing.JFrame;
2
3 public class TestFrame {
4   public static void main(String[] args) {
5     JFrame frame1 = new JFrame();
6     frame1.setTitle("Window 1");
7     frame1.setSize(200, 150);
8     frame1.setLocation(200, 100);
9     frame1.setDefaultCloseOperation(JFrame.EXIT_ON_CLOSE);
10    frame1.setVisible(true);
11
12    JFrame frame2 = new JFrame();
13    frame2.setTitle("Window 2");
14    frame2.setSize(200, 150);
15    frame2.setLocation(410, 100);
16    frame2.setDefaultCloseOperation(JFrame.EXIT_ON_CLOSE);
17    frame2.setVisible(true);
18  }
19 }
```

This program creates two objects of the `JFrame` class (lines 5, 12) and then uses the methods `setTitle`, `setSize`, `setLocation`, `setDefaultCloseOperation`, and `setVisible` to set the properties of the objects. The `setTitle` method sets a title for the window (lines 6, 13). The `setSize` method sets the window's width and height (lines 7, 14). The `setLocation` method specifies the location of the window's upper-left corner (lines 8, 15). The `setDefaultCloseOperation` method terminates the program when the frame is closed (lines 8, 16). The `setVisible` method displays the window.

You can add graphical user interface components, such as buttons, labels, text fields, check boxes, and combo boxes to the window. The components are defined using classes. Listing 7.4 gives an example of creating a graphical user interface, as shown in Figure 7.1.

LISTING 7.4 GUIComponents.java

Video Note
Use classes

create a button
create a label
create a text field
create a check box

```
import javax.swing.*;

public class GUIComponents {
  public static void main(String[] args) {
    // Create a button with text OK
    JButton jbtOK = new JButton("OK");

    // Create a label with text "Enter your name: "
    JLabel jlblName = new JLabel("Enter your name: ");

    // Create a text field with text "Type Name Here"
    JTextField jtfName = new JTextField("Type Name Here");

    // Create a check box with text bold
    JCheckBox jchkBold = new JCheckBox("Bold");
```

```
16
17     // Create a radio button with text red
18     JRadioButton jrbRed = new JRadioButton("Red");
19
20     // Create a combo box with choices red, green, and blue
21     JComboBox jcboColor = new JComboBox(new String[]{"Red",
22       "Green", "Blue"});
23
24     // Create a panel to group components
25     JPanel panel = new JPanel();
26     panel.add(jbtOK); // Add the button to the panel
27     panel.add(jlblName); // Add the label to the panel
28     panel.add(jtfName); // Add the text field to the panel
29     panel.add(jchkBold); // Add the check box to the panel
30     panel.add(jrbRed); // Add the radio button to the panel
31     panel.add(jcboColor); // Add the combo box to the panel
32
33     JFrame frame = new JFrame(); // Create a frame
34     frame.add(panel); // Add the panel to the frame
35     frame.setTitle("Show GUI Components");
36     frame.setSize(450, 100);
37     frame.setLocation(200, 100);
38     frame.setDefaultCloseOperation(JFrame.EXIT_ON_CLOSE);
39     frame.setVisible(true);
40   }
41 }
```

create a radio button
create a combo box
create a panel
add to panel
create a frame
add panel to frame
display frame

This program creates GUI objects using the classes `JButton`, `JLabel`, `JTextField`, `JCheckBox`, `JRadioButton`, and `JComboBox` (lines 6–22). It then creates a panel object using the `JPanel` class (line 25) and adds the button, label, text field, check box, radio button, and combo box to the panel (lines 26–31). The program then creates a frame and adds a panel to the frame (line 34). The frame is displayed in line 39.

7.6 Static Variables, Constants, and Methods

instance variable

The data field `radius` in the circle class in Listing 7.1 is known as an *instance variable*. An instance variable is tied to a specific instance of the class; it is not shared among objects of the same class. For example, suppose that you create the following objects:

```
Circle circle1 = new Circle();
Circle circle2 = new Circle(5);
```

The `radius` in `circle1` is independent of the `radius` in `circle2` and is stored in a different memory location. Changes made to `circle1`'s `radius` do not affect `circle2`'s `radius`, and vice versa.

static variable

If you want all the instances of a class to share data, use *static variables*, also known as *class variables*. Static variables store values for the variables in a common memory location. Because of this common location, all objects of the same class are affected if one object changes the value of a static variable. Java supports static methods as well as static variables. *Static methods* can be called without creating an instance of the class.

static method

Let us modify the `Circle` class by adding a static variable `numberOfObjects` to count the number of circle objects created. When the first object of this class is created, `numberOfObjects` is `1`. When the second object is created, `numberOfObjects` becomes `2`. The UML of the new circle class is shown in Figure 7.11. The `Circle` class defines the instance variable `radius` and the static variable `numberOfObjects`, the instance methods `getRadius`, `setRadius`, and `getArea`, and the static method `getNumberOfObjects`. (Note that static variables and functions are underlined in the UML class diagram.)

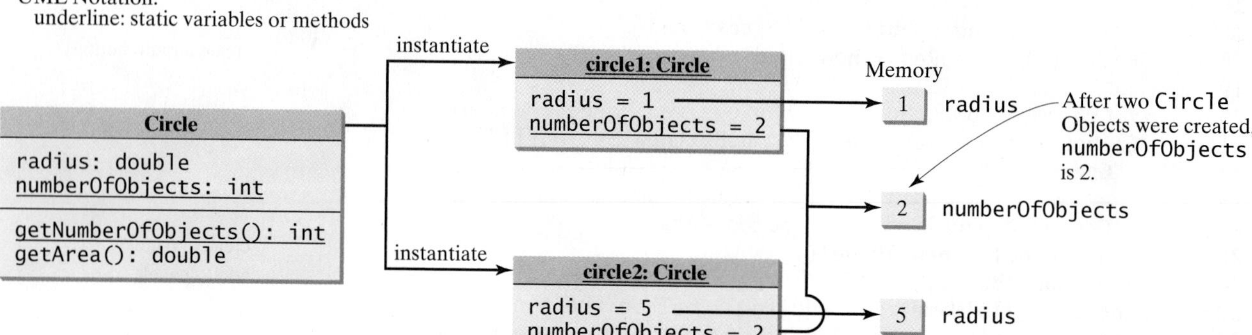

FIGURE 7.11 Instance variables belong to the instances and have memory storage independent of one another. Static variables are shared by all the instances of the same class.

To declare a static variable or a static method, put the modifier `static` in the variable or method declaration. The static variable `numberOfObjects` and the static method `getNumberOfObjects()` can be declared as follows:

declare static variable

```
static int numberOfObjects;
```

declare static method

```
static int getNumberObjects() {
  return numberOfObjects;
}
```

Constants in a class are shared by all objects of the class. Thus, constants should be declared `final static`. For example, the constant `PI` in the `Math` class is defined as:

declare constant

```
final static double PI = 3.14159265358979323846;
```

The new circle class, named `Circle2`, is declared in Listing 7.5:

Video Note
static vs. instance

LISTING 7.5 Circle2.java

static variable; increase by 1; increase by 1; static method

```
public class Circle2 {
  /** The radius of the circle */
  double radius;

  /** The number of objects created */
  static int numberOfObjects = 0;

  /** Construct a circle with radius 1 */
  Circle2() {
    radius = 1.0;
    numberOfObjects++;
  }

  /** Construct a circle with a specified radius */
  Circle2(double newRadius) {
    radius = newRadius;
    numberOfObjects++;
  }

  /** Return numberOfObjects */
  static int getNumberOfObjects() {
    return numberOfObjects;
  }
```

```

  /** Return the area of this circle */
  double getArea() {
    return radius * radius * Math.PI;
  }
}
```

Method `getNumberOfObjects()` in `Circle2` is a static method. Other examples of static methods are `showMessageDialog` and `showInputDialog` in the `JOptionPane` class, and all the methods in the `Math` class. The `main` method is static, too.

Instance methods (e.g., `getArea()`) and instance data (e.g., `radius`) belong to instances and can be used only after the instances are created. They are accessed via a reference variable. Static methods (e.g., `getNumberOfObjects()`) and static data (e.g., `numberOfObjects`) can be accessed from a reference variable or from their class name.

The program in Listing 7.6 demonstrates how to use instance and static variables and methods, and illustrates the effects of using them.

LISTING 7.6 `TestCircle2.java`

```
public class TestCircle2 {
  /** Main method */
  public static void main(String[] args) {
    // Create c1
    Circle2 c1 = new Circle2();

    // Display c1 BEFORE c2 is created
    System.out.println("Before creating c2");
    System.out.println("c1 is : radius (" + c1.radius +
      ") and number of Circle objects (" +
      c1.numberOfObjects + ")");

    // Create c2
    Circle2 c2 = new Circle2(5);

    // Change the radius in c1
    c1.radius = 9;

    // Display c1 and c2 AFTER c2 was created
    System.out.println("\nAfter creating c2 and modifying " +
      "c1's radius to 9");
    System.out.println("c1 is : radius (" + c1.radius +
      ") and number of Circle objects (" +
      c1.numberOfObjects + ")");
    System.out.println("c2 is : radius (" + c2.radius +
      ") and number of Circle objects (" +
      c2.numberOfObjects + ")");
  }
}
```

static variable

instance variable

static variable

static variable

```
Before creating c2
c1 is : radius (1.0) and number of Circle objects (1)

After creating c2 and modifying c1's radius to 9
c1 is : radius (9.0) and number of Circle objects (2)
c2 is : radius (5.0) and number of Circle objects (2)
```

The main method creates two circles, c1 and c2 (lines 5, 14). The instance variable radius in c1 is modified to become 9 (line 17). This change does not affect the instance variable radius in c2, since these two instance variables are independent. The static variable numberOfObjects becomes 1 after c1 is created (line 5), and it becomes 2 after c2 is created (line 14).

Note that PI is a constant defined in Math, and Math.PI references the constant. c.numberOfObjects could be replaced by Circle2.numberOfObjects. This improves readability, because the reader can easily recognize the static variable. You can also replace Circle2.numberOfObjects by Circle2.getNumberOfObjects().

use class name

Tip

Use ClassName.methodName(arguments) to invoke a static method and ClassName.staticVariable. This improves readability, because the user can easily recognize the static method and data in the class.

static import

Note

You can use a new JDK 1.5 feature to directly import static variables and methods from a class. The imported data and methods can be referenced or called without specifying a class. For example, you can use PI (instead of Math.PI), and random() (instead of Math.random()), if you have the following import statement in the class:

```
import static java.lang.Math.*;
```

Static variables and methods can be used from instance or static methods in the class. However, instance variables and methods can be used only from instance methods, not from static methods, since static variables and methods don't belong to a particular object. Thus the code given below is wrong.

```
public class Foo {
  int i = 5;
  static int k = 2;

  public static void main(String[] args) {
    int j = i; // Wrong because i is an instance variable
    m1(); // Wrong because m1() is an instance method
  }

  public void m1() {
    // Correct since instance and static variables and methods
    // can be used in an instance method
    i = i + k + m2(i, k);
  }

  public static int m2(int i, int j) {
    return (int)(Math.pow(i, j));
  }
}
```

instance or static?

Design Guide

How do you decide whether a variable or method should be an instance one or a static one? A variable or method that is dependent on a specific instance of the class should be an instance variable or method. A variable or method that is not dependent on a specific instance of the class should be a static variable or method. For example, every circle has its own radius. Radius is dependent on a specific circle. Therefore, radius is an instance variable of the Circle class. Since the getArea method is dependent on a specific circle, it is an instance method. None of the methods in the Math class, such as random, pow, sin, and cos, is dependent on a specific instance. Therefore, these methods are static methods. The main method is static and can be invoked directly from a class.

Caution

It is a common design error to declare an instance method that should have been declared static. For example, the following method `factorial(int n)` should be declared static, because it is independent of any specific instance.

common design error

```
public class Test {
  public int factorial(int n) {
    int result = 1;
    for (int i = 1; i <= n; i++)
      result *= i;

    return result;
  }
}
```

(a) Wrong design

```
public class Test {
  public static int factorial(int n) {
    int result = 1;
    for (int i = 1; i <= n; i++)
      result *= i;

    return result;
  }
}
```

(b) Correct design

7.7 Visibility Modifiers

Java provides several modifiers that control access to data fields, methods, and classes. This section introduces the `public`, `private`, and default modifiers.

- `public` makes classes, methods, and data fields accessible from any class. public
- `private` makes methods and data fields accessible only from within its own class. private
- If `public` or `private` is not used, then by default the classes, methods, and data fields are accessible by any class in the same package. This is known as *package-private* or *package-access*. package-private

Note

Packages can be used to organize classes. To do so, you need to add the following line as the first noncomment and nonblank statement in the program:

using packages

```
package packageName;
```

If a class is declared without the package statement, the class is said to be placed in the *default package*.

Java recommends that you place classes into packages rather using a default package. For simplicity, however, this book uses default packages. For more information on packages, see Supplement III.F, "Packages."

Figure 7.12 illustrates how a public, default, and private data field or method in class `C1` can be accessed from a class `C2` in the same package, and from a class `C3` in a different package.

```
package p1;

public class C1 {
  public int x;
  int y;
  private int z;

  public void m1() {
  }
  void m2() {
  }
  private void m3() {
  }
}

public class C2 {
  void aMethod() {
    C1 o = new C1();
    can access o.x;
    can access o.y;
    cannot access o.z;

    can invoke o.m1();
    can invoke o.m2();
    cannot invoke o.m3();
  }
}
```

```
package p2;

public class C3 {
  void aMethod() {
    C1 o = new C1();
    can access o.x;
    cannot access o.y;
    cannot access o.z;

    can invoke o.m1();
    cannot invoke o.m2();
    cannot invoke o.m3();
  }
}
```

FIGURE 7.12 The private modifier restricts access to its defining class, the default modifier restricts access to a package, and the public modifier enables unrestricted access.

If a class is not declared public, it can be accessed only within the same package, as shown in Figure 7.13.

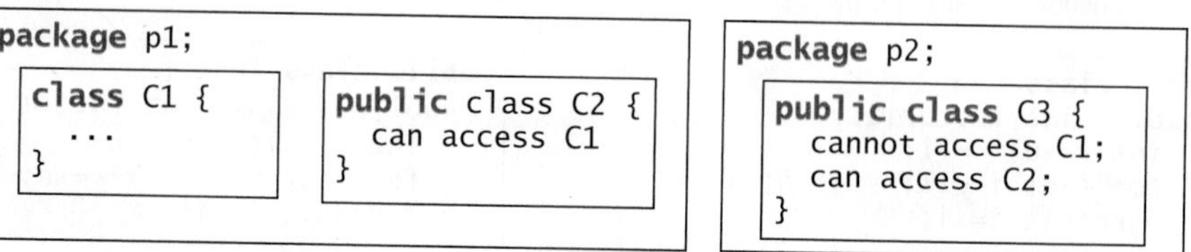

FIGURE 7.13
A nonpublic class has package-access.

inside access

A visibility modifier specifies how data fields and methods in a class can be accessed from the outside of the class. There is no restriction on accessing data fields and methods from inside the class. As shown in Figure 7.14(b), an object foo of the Foo class cannot access its private members, because foo is in the Test class. As shown in Figure 7.14(a), an object foo of the Foo class can access its private members, because foo is declared inside its own class.

```
public class Foo {
  private boolean x;

  public static void main(String[] args) {
    Foo foo = new Foo();
    System.out.println(foo.x);
    System.out.println(foo.convert());
  }

  private int convert() {
    return x ? 1 : -1;
  }
}
```

(a) This is OK because object foo is used inside the Foo class

```
public class Test {
  public static void main(String[] args) {
    Foo foo = new Foo();
    System.out.println(foo.x);
    System.out.println(foo.convert());
  }
}
```

(b) This is wrong because x and convert are private in Foo.

FIGURE 7.14
An object can access its private members if it is declared in its own class.

Caution

The private modifier applies only to the members of a class. The public modifier can apply to a class or members of a class. Using modifiers public and private on local variables would cause a compile error.

Note

private constructor

In most cases, the constructor should be public. However, if you want to prohibit the user from creating an instance of a class, use a private constructor. For example, there is no reason to create an instance from the Math class, because all of its data fields and methods are static. To prevent the user from creating objects from the Math class, the constructor in java.lang.Math is defined as follows:

```
private Math() {
}
```

7.8 Data Field Encapsulation

The data fields `radius` and `numberOfObjects` in the `Circle2` class in Listing 7.5 can be modified directly (e.g., `myCircle.radius = 5` or `Circle2.numberOfObjects = 10`). This is not a good practice—for two reasons:

- First, data may be tampered with. For example, `numberOfObjects` is to count the number of objects created, but it may be set to an arbitrary value (e.g., `Circle2.numberOfObjects = 10`).
- Second, it makes the class difficult to maintain and vulnerable to bugs. Suppose you want to modify the `Circle2` class to ensure that the radius is nonnegative after other programs have already used the class. You have to change not only the `Circle2` class, but also the programs that use the `Circle2` class. Such programs are often referred to as *clients*. This is because the clients may have modified the radius directly (e.g., `myCircle.radius = -5`).

client

To prevent direct modifications of data fields, you should declare the fields private, using the `private` modifier. This is known as *data field encapsulation*.

data field encapsulation

A private data field cannot be accessed by an object through a direct reference outside the class that defines the private field. But often a client needs to retrieve and modify a data field. To make a private data field accessible, provide a *get* method to return the value of the data field. To enable a private data field to be updated, provide a *set* method to set a new value.

Note

Colloquially, a `get` method is referred to as a *getter* (or *accessor*), and a `set` method is referred to as a *setter* (or *mutator*).

accessor
mutator

A `get` method has the following signature:

```
public returnType getPropertyName()
```

If the `returnType` is `boolean`, the `get` method should be defined as follows by convention:

boolean accessor

```
public boolean isPropertyName()
```

A `set` method has the following signature:

```
public void setPropertyName(dataType propertyValue)
```

Let us create a new circle class with a private data field radius and its associated accessor and mutator methods. The class diagram is shown in Figure 7.15. The new circle class, named `Circle3`, is declared in Listing 7.7:

Video Note
Data field encapsulation

LISTING 7.7 `Circle3.java`

```
public class Circle3 {
  /** The radius of the circle */
  private double radius = 1;

  /** The number of the objects created */
  private static int numberOfObjects = 0;

  /** Construct a circle with radius 1 */
  public Circle3() {
    numberOfObjects++;
  }

```

encapsulate **radius**

encapsulate **numberOfObjects**

access method (line 20) · mutator method (line 25) · access method (line 30)

```
13   /** Construct a circle with a specified radius */
14   public Circle3(double newRadius) {
15     radius = newRadius;
16     numberOfObjects++;
17   }
18
19   /** Return radius */
20   public double getRadius() {
21     return radius;
22   }
23
24   /** Set a new radius */
25   public void setRadius(double newRadius) {
26     radius = (newRadius >= 0) ? newRadius : 0;
27   }
28
29   /** Return numberOfObjects */
30   public static int getNumberOfObjects() {
31     return numberOfObjects;
32   }
33
34   /** Return the area of this circle */
35   public double getArea() {
36     return radius * radius * Math.PI;
37   }
38 }
```

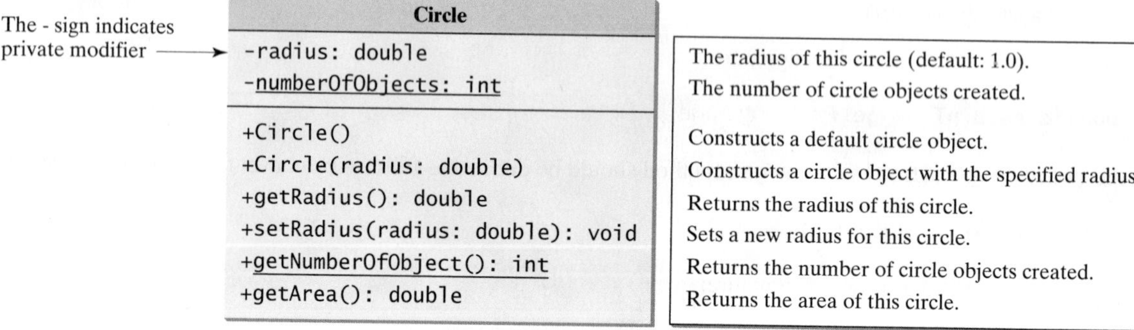

FIGURE 7.15 The `Circle` class encapsulates circle properties and provides get/set and other methods.

The `getRadius()` method (lines 20–22) returns the radius, and the `setRadius(newRadius)` method (line 25–27) sets a new radius into the object. If the new radius is negative, `0` is set to the radius in the object. Since these methods are the only ways to read and modify radius, you have total control over how the `radius` property is accessed. If you have to change the implementation of these methods, you need not change the client programs. This makes the class easy to maintain.

Listing 7.8 gives a client program that uses the `Circle` class to create a `Circle` object and modifies the radius using the `setRadius` method.

LISTING 7.8 TestCircle3.java

```
public class TestCircle3 {
  /** Main method */
  public static void main(String[] args) {
    // Create a Circle with radius 5.0
    Circle3 myCircle = new Circle3(5.0);
```

```
    System.out.println("The area of the circle of radius "
      + myCircle.getRadius() + " is " + myCircle.getArea());

    // Increase myCircle's radius by 10%
    myCircle.setRadius(myCircle.getRadius() * 1.1);
    System.out.println("The area of the circle of radius "
      + myCircle.getRadius() + " is " + myCircle.getArea());
  }
}
```

invoke instance method

invoke instance method

The data field radius is declared private. Private data can be accessed only within their defining class. You cannot use myCircle.radius in the client program. A compilation error would occur if you attempted to access private data from a client.

Since numberOfObjects is private, it cannot be modified. This prevents tampering. For example, the user cannot set numberOfObjects to 100. The only way to make it 100 is to create 100 objects of the Circle class.

Suppose you combined TestCircle and Circle into one class by moving the main method in TestCircle into Circle. Could you use myCircle.radius in the main method? See Review Question 7.12 for the answer.

Note

When you compile TestCircle3.java, the Java compiler automatically compiles Circle3.java if it has not been compiled since the last change.

Design Guide

To prevent data from being tampered with and to make the class easy to maintain, declare data fields private.

7.9 Passing Objects to Methods

You can pass objects to methods. Like passing an array, passing an object is actually passing the reference of the object. The following code passes the myCircle object as an argument to the printCircle method:

```
public class TestPassObject {
  public static void main(String[] args) {
    // Circle3 is defined in Listing 7.7
    Circle3 myCircle = new Circle3(5.0);
    printCircle(myCircle);
  }

  public static void printCircle(Circle3 c) {
    System.out.println("The area of the circle of radius "
      + c.getRadius() + " is " + c.getArea());
  }
}
```

pass an object

pass-by-value

Java uses exactly one mode of passing arguments: pass-by-value. In the preceding code, the value of myCircle is passed to the printCircle method. This value is a reference to a Circle object.

Let us demonstrate the difference between passing a primitive type value and passing a reference value with the program in Listing 7.9:

LISTING 7.9 TestPassObject.java

```
public class TestPassObject {
  /** Main method */
  public static void main(String[] args) {
```

pass object

object parameter

```
 4     // Create a Circle object with radius 1
 5     Circle3 myCircle = new Circle3(1);
 6
 7     // Print areas for radius 1, 2, 3, 4, and 5.
 8     int n = 5;
 9     printAreas(myCircle, n);
10
11     // See myCircle.radius and times
12     System.out.println("\n" + "Radius is " + myCircle.getRadius());
13     System.out.println("n is " + n);
14   }
15
16   /** Print a table of areas for radius */
17   public static void printAreas(Circle3 c, int times) {
18     System.out.println("Radius \t\tArea");
19     while (times >= 1) {
20       System.out.println(c.getRadius() + "\t\t" + c.getArea());
21       c.setRadius(c.getRadius() + 1);
22       times--;
23     }
24   }
25 }
```

```
Radius                Area
  1.0            3.141592653589793
  2.0           12.566370614359172
  3.0           29.274333882308138
  4.0           50.26548245743669
  5.0           79.53981633974483

Radius is 6.0
n is 5
```

The `Circle3` class is defined in Listing 7.7. The program passes a `Circle3` object `myCircle` and an integer value from `n` to invoke `printAreas(myCircle, n)` (line 9), which prints a table of areas for radii `1`, `2`, `3`, `4`, as shown in the sample output.

Figure 7.16 shows the call stack for executing the methods in the program. Note that the objects are stored in a heap.

When passing an argument of a primitive data type, the value of the argument is passed. In this case, the value of `n` (`5`) is passed to `times`. Inside the `printAreas` method, the content of `times` is changed; this does not affect the content of `n`.

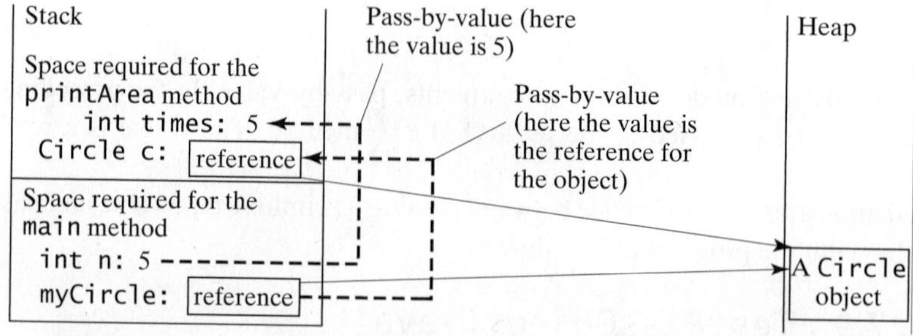

FIGURE 7.16 The value of `n` is passed to `times`, and the reference of `myCircle` is passed to `c` in the `printAreas` method.

When passing an argument of a reference type, the reference of the object is passed. In this case, `c` contains a reference for the object that is also referenced via `myCircle`. Therefore, changing the properties of the object through `c` inside the `printAreas` method has the same effect as doing so outside the method through the variable `myCircle`. Pass-by-value on references can be best described as *pass-by-sharing* semantically; i.e., the object referenced in the method is the same as the object being passed.

pass-by-sharing

7.10 Array of Objects

In Chapter 6, "Arrays," arrays of primitive type elements were created. You can also create arrays of objects. For example, the following statement declares and creates an array of ten `Circle` objects:

```
Circle[] circleArray = new Circle[10];
```

To initialize the `circleArray`, you can use a `for` loop like this one:

```
for (int i = 0; i < circleArray.length; i++) {
  circleArray[i] = new Circle();
}
```

An array of objects is actually an *array of reference variables*. So, invoking `circleArray[1].getArea()` involves two levels of referencing, as shown in Figure 7.17. `circleArray` references the entire array. `circleArray[1]` references a `Circle` object.

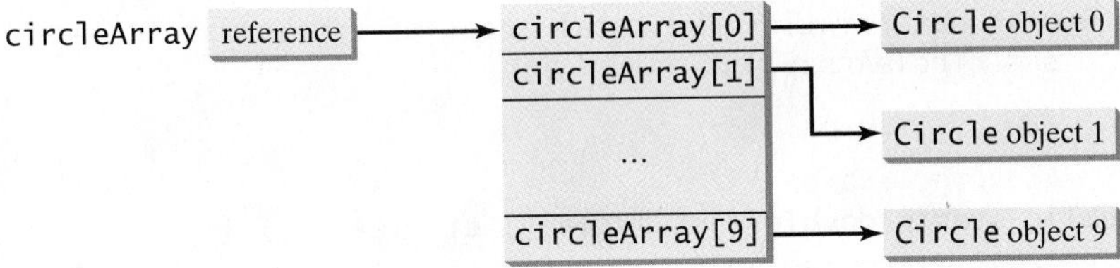

FIGURE 7.17 In an array of objects, an element of the array contains a reference to an object.

Note

When an array of objects is created using the `new` operator, each element in the array is a reference variable with a default value of `null`.

Listing 7.10 gives an example that demonstrates how to use an array of objects. The program summarizes the areas of an array of circles. The program creates `circleArray`, an array composed of five `Circle` objects; it then initializes circle radii with random values, and displays the total area of the circles in the array.

LISTING 7.10 TotalArea.java

```
public class TotalArea {
  /** Main method */
  public static void main(String[] args) {
    // Declare circleArray
    Circle3[] circleArray;

    // Create circleArray
    circleArray = createCircleArray() ;
```

array of objects

return array of objects

pass array of objects

pass array of objects

```
 9
10     // Print circleArray and total areas of the circles
11     printCircleArray(circleArray);
12   }
13
14   /** Create an array of Circle objects */
15   public static Circle3[] createCircleArray() {
16     Circle3[] circleArray = new Circle3[5];
17
18     for (int i = 0; i < circleArray.length; i++) {
19       circleArray[i] = new Circle3(Math.random() * 100);
20     }
21
22     // Return Circle array
23     return circleArray;
24   }
25
26   /** Print an array of circles and their total area */
27   public static void printCircleArray(Circle3[] circleArray) {
28     System.out.println("Radius\t\t\t\t" + "Area");
29     for (int i = 0; i < circleArray.length; i++) {
30       System.out.print(circleArray[i].getRadius() + "\t\t" +
31         circleArray[i].getArea() + '\n');
32     }
33
34     System.out.println("----------------------------------------------");
35
36     // Compute and display the result
37     System.out.println("The total areas of circles is \t" +
38       sum(circleArray));
39   }
40
41   /** Add circle areas */
42   public static double sum(Circle3[] circleArray) {
43     // Initialize sum
44     double sum = 0;
45
46     // Add areas to sum
47     for (int i = 0; i < circleArray.length; i++)
48       sum += circleArray[i].getArea();
49
50     return sum;
51   }
52 }
```

```
Radius                              Area
46.74450345121816                   6864.532638610253
69.07475859903327                   14989.551008666382
 7.406606050399822                    172.34090289657104
34.837951903312394                  3812.8972598630908
69.54563440024302                   15194.612150185108
-----------------------------------------------------------
The total areas of circles is       41033.9339602214
```

The program invokes **createCircleArray()** (line 8) to create an array of five **Circle** objects. Several **Circle** classes were introduced in this chapter. This example uses the **Circle** class introduced in §7.8, "Data Field Encapsulation."

The circle radii are randomly generated using the `Math.random()` method (line 19). The `createCircleArray` method returns an array of `Circle` objects (line 23). The array is passed to the `printCircleArray` method, which displays the radius and area of each circle and the total area of the circles.

The sum of the areas of the circle is computed using the `sum` method (line 38), which takes the array of `Circle` objects as the argument and returns a `double` value for the total area.

Key Terms

accessor method (getter) 247
class 231
constructor 231
data field encapsulation 247
default constructor 232
dot operator (.) 233
instance 230
instance method 233
instance variable 233
instantiation 230
mutator method (setter) 247
`null` 236
no-arg constructor 237
object-oriented programming (OOP) 230
Unified Modeling Language (UML) 230
package-private (or package-access) 245
private 245
public 245
reference variable 232
reference type 232
static method 241
static variable 241

Chapter Summary

- A class is a template for objects. It defines the properties of objects, and provides constructors for creating objects and methods for manipulating them.

- A class is also a data type. You can use it to declare object reference variables. An object reference variable that appears to hold an object actually contains a reference to that object. Strictly speaking, an object reference variable and an object are different, but most of the time the distinction can be ignored.

- An object is an instance of a class. You use the `new` operator to create an object, and the dot (`.`) operator to access members of that object through its reference variable.

- An instance variable or method belongs to an instance of a class. Its use is associated with individual instances. A static variable is a variable shared by all instances of the same class. A static method is a method that can be invoked without using instances.

- Every instance of a class can access the class's static variables and methods. However, it is better to invoke static variables and methods using `ClassName.variable` and `ClassName.method` for clarity.

- Modifiers specify how the class, method, and data are accessed. A `public` class, method, or data is accessible to all clients. A `private` method or data is only accessible inside the class.

- You can provide a `get` method or a `set` method to enable clients to see or modify the data. Colloquially, a `get` method is referred to as a *getter* (or *accessor*), and a `set` method is referred to as a *setter* (or *mutator*).
- A get method has the signature `public returnType getPropertyName()`. If the `returnType` is `boolean`, the get method should be defined as `public boolean isPropertyName()`. A set method has the signature `public void setPropertyName(dataType propertyValue)`.
- All parameters are passed to methods using pass-by-value. For a parameter of a primitive type, the actual value is passed; for a parameter of a reference type, the reference for the object is passed.
- A Java array is an object that can contain primitive type values or object type values. When an array of objects is created, its elements are assigned the default value of `null`.

Review Questions

Sections 7.2–7.4

7.1 Describe the relationship between an object and its defining class. How do you declare a class? How do you declare an object reference variable? How do you create an object? How do you declare and create an object in one statement?

7.2 What are the differences between constructors and methods?

7.3 Is an array an object or a primitive type value? Can an array contain elements of an object type as well as a primitive type? Describe the default value for the elements of an array.

7.4 What is wrong with the following program?

```
public class ShowErrors {
  public static void main(String[] args) {
    ShowErrors t = new ShowErrors(5);
  }
}
```

(a)

```
public class ShowErrors {
  public static void main(String[] args) {
    ShowErrors t = new ShowErrors();
    t.x();
  }
}
```

(b)

```
public class ShowErrors {
  public void method1() {
    Circle c;
    System.out.println("What is radius "
      + c.getRadius());
    c = new Circle();
  }
}
```

(c)

```
public class ShowErrors {
  public static void main(String[] args) {
    C c = new C(5.0);
    System.out.println(c.value);
  }
}

class C {
  int value = 2;
}
```

(d)

7.5 What is wrong in the following code?

```
class Test {
  public static void main(String[] args) {
    A a = new A();
    a.print();
  }
}

class A {
  String s;

  A(String s) {
    this.s = s;
  }

  public void print() {
    System.out.print(s);
  }
}
```

7.6 What is the printout of the following code?

```
public class Foo {
  private boolean x;

  public static void main(String[] args) {
    Foo foo = new Foo();
    System.out.println(foo.x);
  }
}
```

Section 7.5 Using Classes from the Java Library

7.7 How do you create a `Date` for the current time? How do you display the current time?

7.8 How do you create a `JFrame`, set a title in a frame, and display a frame?

7.9 Which packages contain the classes `Date`, `JFrame`, `JOptionPane`, `System`, and `Math`?

Section 7.6 Static Variables, Constants, and Methods

7.10 Suppose that the class `Foo` is defined in (a). Let `f` be an instance of `Foo`. Which of the statements in (b) are correct?

```
public class Foo {
  int i;
  static String s;

  void imethod() {
  }

  static void smethod() {
  }
}
```

(a)

```
System.out.println(f.i);
System.out.println(f.s);
f.imethod();
f.smethod();
System.out.println(Foo.i);
System.out.println(Foo.s);
Foo.imethod();
Foo.smethod();
```

(b)

7.11 Add the `static` keyword in the place of `?` if appropriate.

```
public class Test {
  private int count;

  public ? void main(String[] args) {
```

```
    ...
  }

  public ? int getCount() {
    return count;
  }

  public ? int factorial(int n) {
    int result = 1;
    for (int i = 1; i <= n; i++)
      result *= i;

    return result;
  }
}
```

7.12 Can you invoke an instance method or reference an instance variable from a static method? Can you invoke a static method or reference a static variable from an instance method? What is wrong in the following code?

```
public class Foo {
  public static void main(String[] args) {
    method1();
  }

  public void method1() {
    method2();
  }

  public static void method2() {
    System.out.println("What is radius " + c.getRadius());
  }

  Circle c = new Circle();
}
```

Sections 7.7-7.8

7.13 What is an accessor method? What is a mutator method? What are the naming conventions for accessor methods and mutator methods?

7.14 What are the benefits of data field encapsulation?

7.15 In the following code, `radius` is private in the `Circle` class, and `myCircle` is an object of the `Circle` class. Does the following highlighted code cause any problems? Explain why.

```
public class Circle {
  private double radius = 1.0;

  /** Find the area of this circle */
  double getArea() {
    return radius * radius * Math.PI;
  }

  public static void main(String[] args) {
    Circle myCircle = new Circle();
    System.out.println("Radius is " + myCircle.radius);
  }
}
```

Section 7.9 Passing Objects to Methods

7.16 Describe the difference between passing a parameter of a primitive type and passing a parameter of a reference type. Show the output of the following program:

```
public class Test {
  public static void main(String[] args) {
    Count myCount = new Count();
    int times = 0;

    for (int i = 0; i < 100; i++)
      increment(myCount, times);

    System.out.println("count is " + myCount.count);
    System.out.println("times is " + times);
  }

  public static void increment(Count c, int times) {
    c.count++;
    times++;
  }
}
```

```
public class Count {
  public int count;

  Count(int c) {
    count = c;
  }

  Count() {
    count = 1;
  }
}
```

7.17 Show the output of the following program:

```
public class Test {
  public static void main(String[] args) {
    Circle circle1 = new Circle(1);
    Circle circle2 = new Circle(2);

    swap1(circle1, circle2);
    System.out.println("After swap1: circle1 = " +
      circle1.radius + " circle2 = " + circle2.radius);

    swap2(circle1, circle2);
    System.out.println("After swap2: circle1 = " +
      circle1.radius + " circle2 = " + circle2.radius);
  }

  public static void swap1(Circle x, Circle y) {
    Circle temp = x;
    x = y;
    y = temp;
  }

  public static void swap2(Circle x, Circle y) {
    double temp = x.radius;
    x.radius = y.radius;
    y.radius = temp;
  }
}

class Circle {
  double radius;
  Circle(double newRadius) {
    radius = newRadius;
  }
}
```

7.18 Show the printout of the following code:

```
public class Test {
  public static void main(String[] args) {
    int[] a = {1, 2};
    swap(a[0], a[1]);
    System.out.println("a[0] = " + a[0]
      + " a[1] = " + a[1]);
  }

  public static void swap(int n1, int n2) {
    int temp = n1;
    n1 = n2;
    n2 = temp;
  }
}
```

(a)

```
public class Test {
  public static void main(String[] args) {
    int[] a = {1, 2};
    swap(a);
    System.out.println("a[0] = " + a[0]
      + " a[1] = " + a[1]);
  }

  public static void swap(int[] a) {
    int temp = a[0];
    a[0] = a[1];
    a[1] = temp;
  }
}
```

(b)

```
public class Test {
  public static void main(String[] args) {
    T t = new T();
    swap(t);
    System.out.println("e1 = " + t.e1
      + " e2 = " + t.e2);
  }

  public static void swap(T t) {
    int temp = t.e1;
    t.e1 = t.e2;
    t.e2 = temp;
  }
}

class T {
  int e1 = 1;
  int e2 = 2;
}
```

(c)

```
public class Test {
  public static void main(String[] args) {
    T t1 = new T();
    T t2 = new T();
    System.out.println("t1's i = " +
      t1.i + " and j = " + t1.j);
    System.out.println("t2's i = " +
      t2.i + " and j = " + t2.j);
  }
}

class T {
  static int i = 0;
  int j = 0;

  T() {
    i++;
    j = 1;
  }
}
```

(d)

7.19 What is the output of the following program?

```
import java.util.Date;

public class Test {
  public static void main(String[] args) {
    Date date = null;
    m1(date);
    System.out.println(date);
  }

  public static void m1(Date date) {
    date = new java.util.Date();
  }
}
```

(a)

```
import java.util.Date;

public class Test {
  public static void main(String[] args) {
    Date date = new Date(1234567);
    m1(date);
    System.out.println(date.getTime());
  }

  public static void m1(Date date) {
    date = new java.util.Date(7654321);
  }
}
```

(b)

```
import java.util.Date;

public class Test {
  public static void main(String[] args) {
    Date date = new Date(1234567);
    m1(date);
    System.out.println(date.getTime());
  }

  public static void m1(Date date) {
    date.setTime(7654321);
  }
}
```

(c)

```
import java.util.Date;

public class Test {
  public static void main(String[] args) {
    Date date = new Date(1234567);
    m1(date);
    System.out.println(date.getTime());
  }

  public static void m1(Date date) {
    date = null;
  }
}
```

(d)

Section 7.10 Array of Objects

7.20 What is wrong in the following code?

```
public class Test {
  public static void main(String[] args) {
    java.util.Date[] dates = new java.util.Date[10];
    System.out.println(dates[0]);
    System.out.println(dates[0].toString());
  }
}
```

PROGRAMMING EXERCISES

Pedagogical Note

The exercises in Chapters 7–12 achieve three objectives:

three objectives

- Design classes and draw UML class diagrams;
- Implement classes from the UML;
- Use classes to develop applications.

Solutions for the UML diagrams for the even-numbered exercises can be downloaded from the Student Web site and all others can be downloaded from the Instructor Web site.

7.1 (*The `Rectangle` class*) Design a class named `Rectangle` to represent a rectangle. The class contains:

- Two `double` data fields named `width` and `height` that specify the width and height of the rectangle. The default values are `1` for both `width` and `height`.
- A string data field named `color` that specifies the color of a rectangle. Hypothetically, assume that all rectangles have the same color. The default color is `white`.
- A no-arg constructor that creates a default rectangle.
- A constructor that creates a rectangle with the specified `width` and `height`.
- The accessor and mutator methods for all three data fields.
- A method named `getArea()` that returns the area of this rectangle.
- A method named `getPerimeter()` that returns the perimeter.

Draw the UML diagram for the class. Implement the class. Write a test program that creates two `Rectangle` objects. Assign width `4` and height `40` to the first object and width 3.5 and height 35.9 to the second object. Assign color red to all Rectangle objects. Display the properties of both objects and find their areas and perimeters.

Video Note
Fan class

7.2 (*The* Fan *class*) Design a class named Fan to represent a fan. The class contains:

- Three constants named SLOW, MEDIUM, and FAST with values 1, 2, and 3 to denote the fan speed.
- An int data field named speed that specifies the speed of the fan (default SLOW).
- A boolean data field named on that specifies whether the fan is on (default false).
- A double data field named radius that specifies the radius of the fan (default 5).
- A string data field named color that specifies the color of the fan (default blue).
- A no-arg constructor that creates a default fan.
- The accessor and mutator methods for all four data fields.
- A method named toString() that returns a string description for the fan. If the fan is on, the method returns the fan speed, color, and radius in one combined string. If the fan is not on, the method returns fan color and radius along with the string "fan is off" in one combined string.

Draw the UML diagram for the class. Implement the class. Write a test program that creates two Fan objects. Assign maximum speed, radius 10, color yellow, and turn it on to the first object. Assign medium speed, radius 5, color blue, and turn it off to the second object. Display the objects by invoking their toString method.

7.3 (*The* Account *class*) Design a class named Account that contains:

- An int data field named id for the account (default 0).
- A double data field named balance for the account (default 0).
- A double data field named annualInterestRate that stores the current interest rate (default 0).
- A Date data field named dateCreated that stores the date when the account was created.
- A no-arg constructor that creates a default account.
- The accessor and mutator methods for id, balance, and annualInterestRate.
- The accessor method for dateCreated.
- A method named getMonthlyInterestRate() that returns the monthly interest rate.
- A method named withdraw that withdraws a specified amount from the account.
- A method named deposit that deposits a specified amount to the account.

Draw the UML diagram for the class. Implement the class. Write a test program that creates an Account object with an account ID of 1122, a balance of $20,000, and an annual interest rate of 4.5%. Use the withdraw method to withdraw $2,500, use the deposit method to deposit $3,000, and print the balance, the monthly interest, and the date when this account was created.

7.4 (*The* Stock *class*) Design a class named Stock that contains:

- A string data field named symbol for the stock's symbol.
- A string data field named name for the stock's name.
- A double data field named previousClosingPrice that stores the stock price for the previous day.
- A double data field named currentPrice that stores the stock price for the current time.

- A constructor that creates a stock with specified symbol and name.
- The accessor methods for all data fields.
- The mutator methods for `previousClosingPrice` and `currentPrice`.
- A method named `getChangePercent()` that returns the percentage changed from `previousClosingPrice` to `currentPrice`.

Draw the UML diagram for the class. Implement the class. Write a test program that creates a `Stock` object with the stock symbol SUNW, the name Sun Microsystems Inc, and the previous closing price of `100`. Set a new current price to `90` and display the price-change percentage.

7.5* (*Using the `GregorianCalendar` class*) Java API has the `GregorianCalendar` class in the `java.util` package that can be used to obtain the year, month, and day of a date. The no-arg constructor constructs an instance for the current date, and the methods `get(GregorianCalendar.YEAR)`, `get(GregorianCalendar.MONTH)`, and `get(GregorianCalendar.DAY_OF_MONTH)` return the year, month, and day. Write a program to perform two tasks:

- Display the current year, month, and day.
- The `GregorianCalendar` class has the `setTimeInMillis(long)`, which can be used to set a specified elapsed time since January 1, 1970. Set the value to `1234567898765L` and display the year, month, and day.

7.6** (*Displaying calendars*) Rewrite the `PrintCalendar` class in §5.11, "Method Abstraction and Stepwise Refinement," to display calendars in a message dialog box. Since the output is generated from several static methods in the class, you may define a static `String` variable `output` for storing the output and display it in a message dialog box.

CHAPTER 8

STRINGS AND TEXT I/O

Objectives

- To use the `String` class to process fixed strings (§8.2).
- To use the `Character` class to process a single character (§8.3).
- To use the `StringBuilder`/`StringBuffer` class to process flexible strings (§8.4).
- To distinguish among the `String`, `StringBuilder`, and `StringBuffer` classes (§8.2–8.4).
- To learn how to pass arguments to the `main` method from the command line (§8.5).
- To discover file properties and to delete and rename files using the `File` class (§8.6).
- To write data to a file using the `PrintWriter` class (§8.7.1).
- To read data from a file using the `Scanner` class (§8.7.2).
- (GUI) To open files using a dialog box (§8.8).

8.1 Introduction

problem

Often you encounter problems that involve string processing and file input and output. Suppose you need to write a program that replaces all occurrences of a word in a file with a new word. How do you solve this problem? This chapter introduces strings and text files, which will enable you to solve this type of problem. Another purpose of this chapter is to show how to program using the classes in the Java library.

8.2 The String Class

A *string* is a sequence of characters. In many languages, strings are treated as arrays of characters, but in Java a string is an object. The String class has 11 constructors and more than 40 methods for manipulating strings. The String class not only is very useful in programming but also is a good example for learning classes and objects.

8.2.1 Constructing a String

You can create a string object from a string value or from an array of characters. To create a string from a string literal, use a syntax like this one:

```
String newString = new String(stringLiteral);
```

The argument stringLiteral is a sequence of characters enclosed inside double quotes. The following statement creates a String object message for the string literal "Welcome to Java":

```
String message = new String("Welcome to Java");
```

string literal object

Java treats a string literal as a String object. So the following statement is valid:

```
String message = "Welcome to Java";
```

You can also create a string from an array of characters. For example, the following statements create the string "Good Day".

```
char[] charArray = {'G', 'o', 'o', 'd', ' ', 'D', 'a', 'y'};
String message = new String(charArray);
```

Note

string variable, string object, string value

A String variable holds a reference to a String object that stores a string value. Strictly speaking, the terms *String variable*, *String object*, and *string value* are different, but most of the time the distinctions between them can be ignored. For simplicity, the term *string* will often be used to refer to String variable, String object, and string value.

8.2.2 Immutable Strings and Interned Strings

immutable

A String object is immutable; its contents cannot be changed. Does the following code change the contents of the string?

```
String s = "Java";
s = "HTML";
```

The answer is no. The first statement creates a String object with the content "Java" and assigns its reference to s. The second statement creates a new String object with the content "HTML" and assigns its reference to s. The first String object still exists after the assignment, but it can no longer be accessed, because variable s now points to the new object, as shown in Figure 8.1.

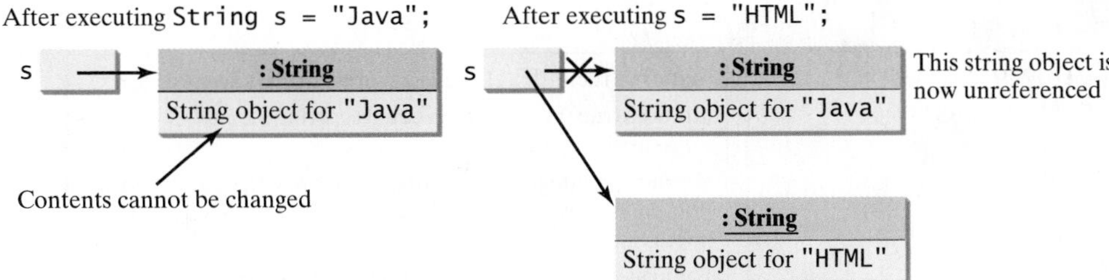

FIGURE 8.1 Strings are immutable; once created, their contents cannot be changed.

Since strings are immutable and are ubiquitous in programming, to improve efficiency and save memory, the JVM uses a unique instance for string literals with the same character sequence. Such an instance is called *interned*. For example, the following statements: interned string

```
String s1 = "Welcome to Java";

String s2 = new String("Welcome to Java");

String s3 = "Welcome to Java";

System.out.println("s1 == s2 is " + (s1 == s2));
System.out.println("s1 == s3 is " + (s1 == s3));
```

s1
s3
: String
Interned string object for "Welcome to Java"

s2
: String
A string object for "Welcome to Java"

display

```
s1 == s2 is false
s1 == s3 is true
```

In the preceding statements, `s1` and `s3` refer to the same interned string "Welcome to Java", therefore `s1 == s3` is true. However, `s1 == s2` is false, because `s1` and `s2` are two different string objects, even though they have the same contents.

8.2.3 String Comparisons

The `String` class provides the methods for comparing strings, as shown in Figure 8.2.

How do you compare the contents of two strings? You might attempt to use the == operator, as follows: ==

```
if (string1 == string2)
  System.out.println("string1 and string2 are the same object");
else
  System.out.println("string1 and string2 are different objects");
```

However, the == operator only checks whether `string1` and `string2` refer to the same object; it does not tell you whether `string1` and `string2` contain the same contents. Therefore, you cannot use the == operator to find out whether two string variables have the same contents. Instead, you should use the `equals` method for an equality comparison of the contents of objects. The code given below, for instance, can be used to compare two strings.

`string1.equals(string2)`

```
if (string1.equals(string2))
  System.out.println("string1 and string2 have the same contents");
else
  System.out.println("string1 and string2 are not equal");
```

java.lang.String	
+equals(s1: String): boolean	Returns true if this string is equal to string s1.
+equalsIgnoreCase(s1: String): boolean	Returns true if this string is equal to string s1 case insensitive.
+compareTo(s1: String): int	Returns an integer greater than 0, equal to 0, or less than 0 to indicate whether this string is greater than, equal to, or less than s1.
+compareToIgnoreCase(s1: String): int	Same as compareTo except that the comparison is case insensitive.
+regionMatches(toffset: int, s1: String, offset: int, len: int): boolean	Returns true if the specified subregion of this string exactly matches the specified subregion in string s1.
+regionMatches(ignoreCase: boolean, toffset: int, s1: String, offset: int, len: int): boolean	Same as the preceding method except that you can specify whether the match is case sensitive.
+startsWith(prefix: String): boolean	Returns true if this string starts with the specified prefix.
+endsWith(suffix: String): boolean	Returns true if this string ends with the specified suffix.

FIGURE 8.2 The String class contains the methods for comparing strings.

For example, the following statements display true and then false.

```
String s1 = new String("Welcome to Java");
String s2 = "Welcome to Java";
String s3 = "Welcome to C++";
System.out.println(s1.equals(s2)); // true
System.out.println(s1.equals(s3)); // false
```

The compareTo method can also be used to compare two strings. For example, consider the following code:

s1.compareTo(s2)

```
s1.compareTo(s2)
```

The method returns the value 0 if s1 is equal to s2, a value less than 0 if s1 is lexicographically (i.e., Unicode ordering) less than s2, and a value greater than 0 if s1 is lexicographically greater than s2.

The actual value returned from the compareTo method depends on the offset of the first two distinct characters in s1 and s2 from left to right. For example, suppose s1 is "abc" and s2 is "abg", and s1.compareTo(s2) returns -4. The first two characters (a vs. a) from s1 and s2 are compared. Because they are equal, the second two characters (b vs. b) are compared. Because they are also equal, the third two characters (c vs. g) are compared. Since the character c is 4 less than g, the comparison returns -4.

Caution

Syntax errors will occur if you compare strings by using comparison operators, such as >, >=, <, or <=. Instead, you have to use s1.compareTo(s2).

Note

The equals method returns true if two strings are equal, and false if they are not equal. The compareTo method returns 0, a positive integer, or a negative integer, depending on whether one string is equal to, greater than, or less than the other string.

The String class also provides equalsIgnoreCase, compareToIgnoreCase, and regionMatches methods for comparing strings. The equalsIgnoreCase and compareToIgnoreCase methods ignore the case of the letters when comparing two strings. The regionMatches method compares portions of two strings for equality. You can also use str.startsWith(prefix) to check whether string str starts with a specified prefix, and str.endsWith(suffix) to check whether string str ends with a specified suffix.

8.2.4 String Length, Characters, and Combining Strings

The String class provides the methods for obtaining length, retrieving individual characters, and concatenating strings, as shown in Figure 8.3.

java.lang.String	
+length(): int	Returns the number of characters in this string.
+charAt(index: int): char	Returns the character at the specified index from this string.
+concat(s1: String): String	Returns a new string that concatenates this string with string s1.

FIGURE 8.3 The String class contains the methods for getting string length, individual characters, and combining strings.

You can get the length of a string by invoking its length() method. For example, message.length() returns the length of the string message.

length()

Caution

length is a method in the String class but is a property of an array object. So you have to use s.length() to get the number of characters in string s, and a.length to get the number of elements in array a.

length()

The s.charAt(index) method can be used to retrieve a specific character in a string s, where the index is between 0 and s.length()-1. For example, message.charAt(0) returns the character W, as shown in Figure 8.4.

charAt(index)

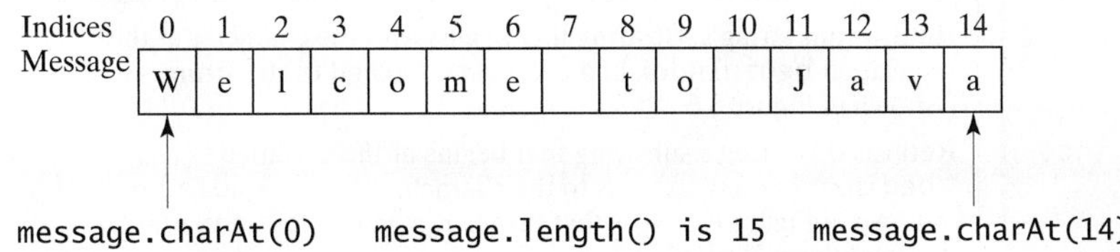

FIGURE 8.4 A String object is represented using an array internally.

Note

When you use a string, you often know its literal value. For convenience, Java allows you to use the string literal to refer directly to strings without creating new variables. Thus, "Welcome to Java".charAt(0) is correct and returns W.

string literal

Note

A string value is represented using a private array variable internally. The array cannot be accessed outside of the String class. The String class provides many public methods, such as length() and charAt(index), to retrieve the array information. This is a good example of encapsulation: the detailed data structure of the class is hidden from the user through the private modifier, and thus the user cannot directly manipulate the internal data structure. If the array were not private, the user would be able to change the string content by modifying the array. This would violate the tenet that the String class is immutable.

encapsulating string

Caution

Attempting to access characters in a string `s` out of bounds is a common programming error. To avoid it, make sure that you do not use an index beyond `s.length() - 1`. For example, `s.charAt(s.length())` would cause a `StringIndexOutOfBoundsException`.

string index range

You can use the `concat` method to concatenate two strings. The statement shown below, for example, concatenates strings `s1` and `s2` into `s3`:

`s1.concat(s2)`

```
String s3 = s1.concat(s2);
```

Since string concatenation is heavily used in programming, Java provides a convenient way to accomplish it. You can use the plus (+) sign to concatenate two or more strings. So the above statement is equivalent to

`s1 + s2`

```
String s3 = s1 + s2;
```

The following code combines the strings `message`, `" and "`, and `"HTML"` into one string:

```
String myString = message + " and " + "HTML";
```

Recall that the + sign can also concatenate a number with a string. In this case, the number is converted into a string and then concatenated. Note that at least one of the operands must be a string in order for concatenation to take place.

8.2.5 Obtaining Substrings

You can obtain a single character from a string using the `charAt` method. You can also obtain a substring from a string using the `substring` method in the `String` class, as shown in Figure 8.5.

java.lang.String	
`+substring(beginIndex: int): String`	Returns this string's substring that begins with the character at the specified `beginIndex` and extends to the end of the string, as shown in Figure 8.6.
`+substring(beginIndex: int, endIndex: int): String`	Returns this string's substring that begins at the specified `beginIndex` and extends to the character at index `endIndex - 1`, as shown in Figure 8.6. Note that the character at `endIndex` is not part of the substring.

FIGURE 8.5 The `String` class contains the methods for obtaining substrings.

For example,

```
String message = "Welcome to Java".substring(0, 11) + "HTML";
```

The string `message` now becomes `"Welcome to HTML"`.

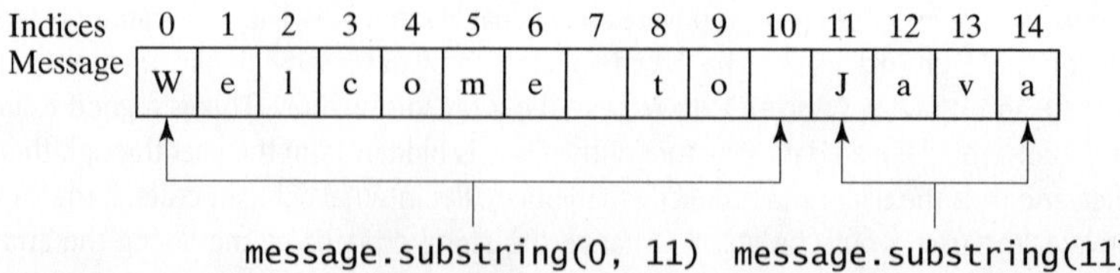

FIGURE 8.6 The `substring` method obtains a substring from a string.

Note

If beginIndex is endIndex, substring(beginIndex, endIndex) returns an empty string with length 0. If beginIndex > endIndex, it would be a runtime error.

beginIndex <= endIndex

8.2.6 Converting, Replacing, and Splitting Strings

The String class provides the methods for converting, replacing, and splitting strings, as shown in Figure 8.7.

java.lang.String	
+toLowerCase(): String	Returns a new string with all characters converted to lowercase.
+toUpperCase(): String	Returns a new string with all characters converted to uppercase.
+trim(): String	Returns a new string with blank characters trimmed on both sides.
+replace(oldChar: char, newChar: char): String	Returns a new string that replaces all matching characters in this string with the new character.
+replaceFirst(oldString: String, newString: String): String	Returns a new string that replaces the first matching substring in this string with the new substring.
+replaceAll(oldString: String, newString: String): String	Returns a new string that replaces all matching substrings in this string with the new substring.
+split(delimiter: String): String[]	Returns an array of strings consisting of the substrings split by the delimiter.

FIGURE 8.7 The String class contains the methods for converting, replacing, and splitting strings.

Once a string is created, its contents cannot be changed. The methods toLowerCase, toUpperCase, trim, replace, replaceFirst, and replaceAll return a new string derived from the original string (without changing the original string!). The toLowerCase and toUpperCase methods return a new string by converting all the characters in the string to lowercase or uppercase. The trim method returns a new string by eliminating blank characters from both ends of the string. Several versions of the replace methods are provided to replace a character or a substring in the string with a new character or a new substring.

For example,

```
"Welcome".toLowerCase() returns a new string, welcome.
"Welcome".toUpperCase() returns a new string, WELCOME.
"  Welcome  ".trim() returns a new string, Welcome.
"Welcome".replace('e', 'A') returns a new string, WAlcomA.
"Welcome".replaceFirst("e", "AB") returns a new string, WABlcome.
"Welcome".replace("e", "AB") returns a new string, WABlcomAB.
"Welcome".replace("el", "AB") returns a new string, WABlcome.
```

toLowerCase()
toUpperCase()
trim()
replace
replaceFirst
replace
replace

The split method can be used to extract tokens from a string with the specified delimiters. For example, the following code

split

```
String[] tokens = "Java#HTML#Perl".split("#", 0);
for (int i = 0; i < tokens.length; i++)
  System.out.print(tokens[i] + " ");
```

displays

Java HTML Perl

8.2.7 Matching, Replacing and Splitting by Patterns

You can match, replace, or split a string by specifying a pattern. This is an extremely useful and powerful feature, commonly known as *regular expression*. Regular expressions seem complex to beginning students. For this reason, two simple patterns are used in this section. Please refer to Supplement III.F, "Regular Expressions," for further studies.

regular expression

matches(regex)

Let us begin with the `matches` method in the `String` class. At first glance, the `matches` method is very similar to the `equals` method. For example, the following two statements both evaluate to `true`.

```
"Java".matches("Java");
"Java".equals("Java");
```

However, the `matches` method is more powerful. It can match not only a fixed string, but also a set of strings that follow a pattern. For example, the following statements all evaluate to `true`.

```
"Java is fun".matches("Java.*" )
"Java is cool".matches("Java.*" )
"Java is powerful".matches("Java.*")
```

`"Java.*"` in the preceding statements is a regular expression. It describes a string pattern that begins with Java followed by *any* zero or more characters. Here, the substring `.*` matches any zero or more characters.

The `replaceAll`, `replaceFirst`, and `split` methods can be used with a regular expression. For example, the following statement returns a new string that replaces $, +, or # in `"a+b$#c"` with the string NNN.

replaceAll(regex)

```
String s = "a+b$#c".replaceAll("[$+#]", "NNN");
System.out.println(s);
```

Here the regular expression `[$+#]` specifies a pattern that matches $, +, or #. So, the output is aNNNbNNNNNNc.

The following statement splits the string into an array of strings delimited by some punctuation marks.

split(regex)

```
String[] tokens = "Java,C?C#,C++".split("[.,:;?]");

for (int i = 0; i < tokens.length; i++)
  System.out.println(tokens[i]);
```

Here the regular expression `[.,:;?]` specifies a pattern that matches ., ,, :, ;, ?. Each of these characters is a delimiter for splitting the string. So, the string is split into `Java`, C, C#, and C++, which are stored into array `tokens`.

8.2.8 Finding a Character or a Substring in a String

The `String` class provides several overloaded `indexOf` and `lastIndexOf` methods to find a character or a substring in a string, as shown in Figure 8.8.

For example,

indexOf

```
"Welcome to Java".indexOf('W') returns 0.
"Welcome to Java".indexOf('o') returns 4.
"Welcome to Java".indexOf('o', 5) returns 8.
"Welcome to Java".indexOf("come") returns 3.
"Welcome to Java".indexOf("Java", 5) returns 11.
"Welcome to Java".indexOf("java", 5) returns -1.
```

java.lang.String	
+indexOf(ch: char): int	Returns the index of the first occurrence of ch in the string. Returns -1 if not matched.
+indexOf(ch: char, fromIndex: int): int	Returns the index of the first occurrence of ch after fromIndex in the string. Returns -1 if not matched.
+indexOf(s: String): int	Returns the index of the first occurrence of string s in this string. Returns -1 if not matched.
+indexOf(s: String, fromIndex: int): int	Returns the index of the first occurrence of string s in this string after fromIndex. Returns -1 if not matched.
+lastIndexOf(ch: int): int	Returns the index of the last occurrence of ch in the string. Returns -1 if not matched.
+lastIndexOf(ch: int, fromIndex: int): int	Returns the index of the last occurrence of ch before fromIndex in this string. Returns -1 if not matched.
+lastIndexOf(s: String): int	Returns the index of the last occurrence of string s. Returns -1 if not matched.
+lastIndexOf(s: String, fromIndex: int): int	Returns the index of the last occurrence of string s before fromIndex. Returns -1 if not matched.

FIGURE 8.8 The String class contains the methods for matching substrings.

lastIndexOf

```
"Welcome to Java".lastIndexOf('W') returns 0.
"Welcome to Java".lastIndexOf('o') returns 8.
"Welcome to Java".lastIndexOf('o', 5) returns 4.
"Welcome to Java".lastIndexOf("come") returns 3.
"Welcome to Java".lastIndexOf("Java", 5) returns -1.
"Welcome to Java".lastIndexOf("java", 5) returns -1.
```

8.2.9 Conversion between Strings and Arrays

Strings are not arrays, but a string can be converted into an array, and vice versa. To convert a string to an array of characters, use the toCharArray method. For example, the following statement converts the string "Java" to an array.

toCharArray

```
char[] chars = "Java".toCharArray();
```

So chars[0] is 'J', chars[1] is 'a', chars[2] is 'v', and chars[3] is 'a'.

You can also use the getChars(int srcBegin, int srcEnd, char[] dst, int dstBegin) method to copy a substring of the string from index srcBegin to index srcEnd-1 into a character array dst starting from index dstBegin. For example, the following code copies a substring "3720" in "CS3720" from index 2 to index 6-1 into the character array dst starting from index 4.

getChars

```
char[] dst = {'J', 'A', 'V', 'A', '1', '3', '0', '1'};
"CS3720".getChars(2, 6, dst, 4);
```

Thus dst becomes {'J', 'A', 'V', 'A', '3', '7', '2', '0'}.

To convert an array of characters into a string, use the String(char[]) constructor or the valueOf(char[]) method. For example, the following statement constructs a string from an array using the String constructor.

```
String str = new String(new char[]{'J', 'a', 'v', 'a'});
```

The next statement constructs a string from an array using the valueOf method.

valueOf

```
String str = String.valueOf(new char[]{'J', 'a', 'v', 'a'});
```

8.2.10 Converting Characters and Numeric Values to Strings

overloaded **valueOf**

The static `valueOf` method can be used to convert an array of characters into a string. There are several overloaded versions of the `valueOf` method that can be used to convert a character and numeric values to strings with different parameter types, `char`, `double`, `long`, `int`, and `float`, as shown in Figure 8.9.

java.lang.String	
+valueOf(c: char): String	Returns a string consisting of the character c.
+valueOf(data: char[]): String	Returns a string consisting of the characters in the array.
+valueOf(d: double): String	Returns a string representing the double value.
+valueOf(f: float): String	Returns a string representing the float value.
+valueOf(i: int): String	Returns a string representing the int value.
+valueOf(l: long): String	Returns a string representing the long value.

FIGURE 8.9 The `String` class contains the static methods for creating strings from primitive type values.

For example, to convert a double value `5.44` to a string, use `String.valueOf(5.44)`. The return value is a string consisting of the characters `'5'`, `'.'`, `'4'`, and `'4'`.

Note

Use `Double.parseDouble(str)` or `Integer.parseInt(str)` to convert a string to a `double` value or an `int` value.

8.2.11 Problem: Checking Palindromes

A string is a palindrome if it reads the same forward and backward. The words "mom," "dad," and "noon," for instance, are all palindromes.

The problem is to write a program that prompts the user to enter a string and reports whether the string is a palindrome. One solution is to check whether the first character in the string is the same as the last character. If so, check whether the second character is the same as the second-to-last character. This process continues until a mismatch is found or all the characters in the string are checked, except for the middle character if the string has an odd number of characters.

To implement this idea, use two variables, say `low` and `high`, to denote the position of two characters at the beginning and the end in a string `s`, as shown in Listing 8.1 (lines 22, 25). Initially, `low` is `0` and `high` is `s.length() - 1`. If the two characters at these positions match, increment `low` by `1` and decrement `high` by `1` (lines 31-32). This process continues until (`low >= high`) or a mismatch is found.

Video Note
Check palindrome

LISTING 8.1 CheckPalindrome.java

```
1 import java.util.Scanner;
2
3 public class CheckPalindrome {
4   /** Main method */
5   public static void main(String[] args) {
6     // Create a Scanner
7     Scanner input = new Scanner(System.in);
8
9     // Prompt the user to enter a string
```

```
10     System.out.print("Enter a string: ");
11     String s = input.nextLine();
12
13     if (isPalindrome(s))
14       System.out.println(s + " is a palindrome");
15     else
16       System.out.println(s + " is not a palindrome");
17   }
18
19   /** Check if a string is a palindrome */
20   public static boolean isPalindrome(String s) {
21     // The index of the first character in the string
22     int low = 0;
23
24     // The index of the last character in the string
25     int high = s.length() - 1;
26
27     while (low < high) {
28       if (s.charAt(low) != s.charAt(high))
29         return false; // Not a palindrome
30
31       low++;
32       high--;
33     }
34
35     return true; // The string is a palindrome
36   }
37 }
```

input string

low index

high index

update indices

```
Enter a string: noon ↵Enter
noon is a palindrome

Enter a string: moon ↵Enter
moon is not a palindrome
```

The `nextLine()` method in the `Scanner` class (line 11) reads a line into `s`. `isPalindrome(s)` checks whether `s` is a palindrome (line 13).

8.3 The **Character** Class

Java provides a wrapper class for every primitive data type. These classes are `Character`, `Boolean`, `Byte`, `Short`, `Integer`, `Long`, `Float`, and `Double` for `char`, `boolean`, `byte`, `short`, `int`, `long`, `float`, and `double`. All these classes are in the `java.lang` package. They enable the primitive data values to be treated as objects. They also contain useful methods for processing primitive values. This section introduces the `Character` class. The other wrapper classes will be introduced in Chapter 11, "Abstract Classes and Interfaces."

The `Character` class has a constructor and several methods for determining a character's category (uppercase, lowercase, digit, etc.) and for converting characters from uppercase to lowercase, and vice versa, as shown in Figure 8.10.

You can create a `Character` object from a `char` value. For example, the following statement creates a `Character` object for the character `'a'`.

```
Character character = new Character('a');
```

java.lang.Character	
+Character(value: char)	Constructs a character object with char value.
+charValue(): char	Returns the char value from this object.
+compareTo(anotherCharacter: Character): int	Compares this character with another.
+equals(anotherCharacter: Character): boolean	Returns true if this character is equal to another.
+isDigit(ch: char): boolean	Returns true if the specified character is a digit.
+isLetter(ch: char): boolean	Returns true if the specified character is a letter.
+isLetterOrDigit(ch: char): boolean	Returns true if the character is a letter or a digit.
+isLowerCase(ch: char): boolean	Returns true if the character is a lowercase letter.
+isUpperCase(ch: char): boolean	Returns true if the character is an uppercase letter.
+toLowerCase(ch: char): char	Returns the lowercase of the specified character.
+toUpperCase(ch: char): char	Returns the uppercase of the specified character.

FIGURE 8.10 The Character class provides the methods for manipulating a character.

The charValue method returns the character value wrapped in the Character object. The compareTo method compares this character with another character and returns an integer that is the difference between the Unicodes of this character and the other character. The equals method returns true if and only if the two characters are the same. For example, suppose charObject is new Character('b'):

```
charObject.compareTo(new Character('a')) returns 1
charObject.compareTo(new Character('b')) returns 0
charObject.compareTo(new Character('c')) returns  – 1
charObject.compareTo(new Character('d') returns  – 2
charObject.equals(new Character('b')) returns true
charObject.equals(new Character('d')) returns false
```

Most of the methods in the Character class are static methods. The isDigit(char ch) method returns true if the character is a digit. The isLetter(char ch) method returns true if the character is a letter. The isLetterOrDigit(char ch) method returns true if the character is a letter or a digit. The isLowerCase(char ch) method returns true if the character is a lowercase letter. The isUpperCase(char ch) method returns true if the character is an uppercase letter. The toLowerCase(char ch) method returns the lowercase letter for the character, and the toUpperCase(char ch) method returns the uppercase letter for the character.

8.3.1 Problem: Counting Each Letter in a String

The problem is to write a program that prompts the user to enter a string and counts the number of occurrences of each letter in the string regardless of case.

Here are the steps to solve this problem:

1. Convert all the uppercase letters in the string to lowercase using the toLowerCase method in the String class.
2. Create an array, say counts of 26 int values, each of which counts the occurrences of a letter. That is, counts[0] counts the number of a's, counts[1] counts the number of b's, and so on.
3. For each character in the string, check whether it is a (lowercase) letter. If so, increment the corresponding count in the array.

LISTING 8.2 CountEachLetter.java

```
1 import java.util.Scanner;
2
3 public class CountEachLetter {
4   /** Main method */
5   public static void main(String[] args) {
6     // Create a Scanner
7     Scanner input = new Scanner(System.in);
8
9     // Prompt the user to enter a string
10    System.out.print("Enter a string: ");
11    String s = input.nextLine();
12
13    // Invoke the countLetters method to count each letter
14    int[] counts = countLetters(s.toLowerCase()) ;
15
16    // Display results
17    for (int i = 0; i < counts.length; i++) {
18      if (counts[i] != 0)
19        System.out.println((char)('a' + i) + " appears  " +
20          counts[i] + ((counts[i] == 1) ? " time" : " times"));
21    }
22  }
23
24  /** Count each letter in the string */
25  public static int[] countLetters(String s) {
26    int[] counts = new int[26];
27
28    for (int i = 0; i < s.length(); i++) {
29      if (Character.isLetter(s.charAt(i)))
30        counts[s.charAt(i) - 'a']++;
31    }
32
33    return counts;
34  }
35 }
```

input string

count letters

count a letter

```
Enter a string: abababx ↵Enter
a appears  3 times
b appears  3 times
x appears  1 time
```

The main method reads a line (line 11) and counts the number of occurrences of each letter in the string by invoking the `countLetters` method (line 14). Since the case of the letters is ignored, the program uses the `toLowerCase` method to convert the string into all lowercase and pass the new string to the `countLetters` method.

The `countLetters` method (lines 25–34) returns an array of `26` elements. Each element counts the number of occurrences of a letter in the string `s`. The method processes each character in the string. If the character is a letter, its corresponding count is increased by 1. For example, if the character (`s.charAr(i)`) is `'a'`, the corresponding count is `counts['a' - 'a']` (i.e., `counts[0]`). If the character is `'b'`, the corresponding count is `counts['b' - 'a']` (i.e., `counts[1]`), since the Unicode of `'b'` is `1` more than that of `'a'`. If the character is 'z', the corresponding count is counts['z' - 'a'] (i.e., counts[25]), since the Unicode of 'z' is 25 more than that of 'a'.

8.4 The StringBuilder/StringBuffer Class

The StringBuilder/StringBuffer class is an alternative to the String class. In general, a StringBuilder/StringBuffer can be used wherever a string is used. StringBuilder/StringBuffer is more flexible than String. You can add, insert, or append new contents into a string builder or a string buffer, whereas the value of a String object is fixed, once the string is created.

StringBuilder

The StringBuilder class is similar to StringBuffer except that the methods for modifying buffer in StringBuffer are synchronized. Use StringBuffer if it may be accessed by multiple tasks concurrently. Using StringBuilder is more efficient if it is accessed by a single task. The constructors and methods in StringBuffer and StringBuilder are almost the same. This section covers StringBuilder. You may replace StringBuilder by StringBuffer. The program can compile and run without any other changes.

StringBuilder constructors

The StringBuilder class has three constructors and more than 30 methods for managing the builder and modifying strings in the builder. You can create an empty string builder or a string builder from a string using the constructors, as shown in Figure 8.11.

java.lang.StringBuilder	
+StringBuilder()	Constructs an empty string builder with capacity 16.
+StringBuilder(capacity: int)	Constructs a string builder with the specified capacity.
+StringBuilder(s: String)	Constructs a string builder with the specified string.

FIGURE 8.11 The StringBuilder class contains the constructors for creating instances of StringBuilder.

8.4.1 Modifying Strings in the StringBuilder

You can append new contents at the end of a string builder, insert new contents at a specified position in a string builder, and delete or replace characters in a string builder, using the methods listed in Figure 8.12:

The StringBuilder class provides several overloaded methods to append boolean, char, char array, double, float, int, long, and String into a string builder. For example, the following code appends strings and characters into stringBuilder to form a new string, "Welcome to Java".

append

```
StringBuilder stringBuilder = new StringBuilder();

stringBuilder.append("Welcome");
stringBuilder.append(' ');
stringBuilder.append("to");
stringBuilder.append(' ');
stringBuilder.append("Java");
```

The StringBuilder class also contains overloaded methods to insert boolean, char, char array, double, float, int, long, and String into a string builder. Consider the following code:

insert

```
stringBuilder.insert(11, "HTML and ");
```

Suppose stringBuilder contains "Welcome to Java" before the insert() method is applied. This code inserts "HTML and " at position 11 in stringBuilder (just before J). The new stringBuilder is "Welcome to HTML and Java".

java.lang.StringBuilder	
`+append(data: char[]): StringBuilder`	Appends a `char` array into this string builder.
`+append(data: char[], offset: int, len: int): StringBuilder`	Appends a subarray in `data` into this string builder.
`+append(v: aPrimitiveType): StringBuilder`	Appends a primitive type value as a string to this builder.
`+append(s: String): StringBuilder`	Appends a string to this string builder.
`+delete(startIndex: int, endIndex: int): StringBuilder`	Deletes characters from `startIndex` to `endIndex`.
`+deleteCharAt(index: int): StringBuilder`	Deletes a character at the specified index.
`+insert(index: int, data: char[], offset: int, len: int): StringBuilder`	Inserts a subarray of the data in the array to the builder at the specified index.
`+insert(offset: int, data: char[]): StringBuilder`	Inserts data into this builder at the position offset.
`+insert(offset: int, b: aPrimitiveType): StringBuilder`	Inserts a value converted to a string into this builder.
`+insert(offset: int, s: String): StringBuilder`	Inserts a string into this builder at the position offset.
`+replace(startIndex: int, endIndex: int, s: String): StringBuilder`	Replaces the characters in this builder from `startIndex` to `endIndex` with the specified string.
`+reverse(): StringBuilder`	Reverses the characters in the builder.
`+setCharAt(index: int, ch: char): void`	Sets a new character at the specified index in this builder.

FIGURE 8.12 The `StringBuilder` class contains the methods for modifying string builders.

You can also delete characters from a string in the builder using the two `delete` methods, reverse the string using the `reverse` method, replace characters using the `replace` method, or set a new character in a string using the `setCharAt` method.

For example, suppose `stringBuilder` contains `"Welcome to Java"` before each of the following methods is applied.

`stringBuilder.delete(8, 11)` changes the builder to `Welcome Java`. **delete**
`stringBuilder.deleteCharAt(8)` changes the builder to `Welcome o Java`. **deleteCharAt**
`stringBuilder.reverse()` changes the builder to `avaJ ot emocleW`. **reverse**
`stringBuilder.replace(11, 15, "HTML")` changes the builder to `Welcome to HTML`. **replace**
`stringBuilder.setCharAt(0, 'w')` sets the builder to `welcome to Java`. **setCharAt**

All these modification methods except `setCharAt` do two things:

1. Change the contents of the string builder
2. Return the reference of the string builder

For example, the following statement

```
StringBuilder stringBuilder1 = stringBuilder.reverse();
```

reverses the string in the builder and assigns the reference of the builder to `stringBuilder1`. Thus, `stringBuilder` and `stringBuilder1` both point to the same `StringBuilder` object. Recall that a value-returning method may be invoked as a statement, if you are not interested in the return value of the method. In this case, the return value is simply ignored. For example, in the following statement

ignore return value

```
stringBuilder.reverse();
```

the return value is ignored.

String or StringBuilder?

Tip

If a string does not require any change, use String rather than StringBuilder. Java can perform some optimizations for String, such as sharing interned strings.

8.4.2 The toString, capacity, length, setLength, and charAt Methods

The StringBuilder class provides the additional methods for manipulating a string builder and obtaining its properties, as shown in Figure 8.13.

java.lang.StringBuilder	
+toString(): String	Returns a string object from the string builder.
+capacity(): int	Returns the capacity of this string builder.
+charAt(index: int): char	Returns the character at the specified index.
+length(): int	Returns the number of characters in this builder.
+setLength(newLength: int): void	Sets a new length in this builder.
+substring(startIndex: int): String	Returns a substring starting at startIndex.
+substring(startIndex: int, endIndex: int): String	Returns a substring from startIndex to endIndex-1.
+trimToSize(): void	Reduces the storage size used for the string builder.

FIGURE 8.13 The StringBuilder class contains the methods for modifying string builders.

capacity()

The capacity() method returns the current capacity of the string builder. The capacity is the number of characters it is able to store without having to increase its size.

length()
setLength(int)

The length() method returns the number of characters actually stored in the string builder. The setLength(newLength) method sets the length of the string builder. If the newLength argument is less than the current length of the string builder, the string builder is truncated to contain exactly the number of characters given by the newLength argument. If the newLength argument is greater than or equal to the current length, sufficient null characters ('\u0000') are appended to the string builder so that length becomes the newLength argument. The newLength argument must be greater than or equal to 0.

charAt(int)

The charAt(index) method returns the character at a specific index in the string builder. The index is 0 based. The first character of a string builder is at index 0, the next at index 1, and so on. The index argument must be greater than or equal to 0, and less than the length of the string builder.

length and capacity

Note

The length of the string is always less than or equal to the capacity of the builder. The length is the actual size of the string stored in the builder, and the capacity is the current size of the builder. The builder's capacity is automatically increased if more characters are added to exceed its capacity. Internally, a string builder is an array of characters, so the builder's capacity is the size of the array. If the builder's capacity is exceeded, the array is replaced by a new array. The new array size is 2 * (the previous array size + 1).

initial capacity

Tip

You can use new StringBuilder(initialCapacity) to create a StringBuilder with a specified initial capacity. By carefully choosing the initial capacity, you can make your program more efficient. If the capacity is always larger than the actual length of the builder, the JVM will never need to reallocate memory for the builder. On the other hand, if the capacity is too large, you will waste memory space. You can use the `trimToSize()` method to reduce the capacity to the actual size.

trimToSize()

8.4.3 Problem: Ignoring Nonalphanumeric Characters When Checking Palindromes

Listing 8.1, "Checking Palindromes," considered all the characters in a string to check whether it was a palindrome. Write a new program that ignores nonalphanumeric characters in checking whether a string is a palindrome.

Here are the steps to solve the problem:

1. Filter the string by removing the nonalphanumeric characters. This can be done by creating an empty string builder, adding each alphanumeric character in the string to a string builder, and returning the string from the string builder. You can use the `isLetterOrDigit(ch)` method in the `Character` class to check whether character `ch` is a letter or a digit.

2. Obtain a new string that is the reversal of the filtered string. Compare the reversed string with the filtered string using the `equals` method.

The complete program is shown in Listing 8.3.

LISTING 8.3 PalindromeIgnoreNonAlphanumeric.java

```
import java.util.Scanner;

public class PalindromeIgnoreNonAlphanumeric {
  /** Main method */
  public static void main(String[] args) {
    // Create a Scanner
    Scanner input = new Scanner(System.in);

    // Prompt the user to enter a string
    System.out.print("Enter a string: ");
    String s = input.nextLine();

    // Display result
    System.out.println("Ignoring nonalphanumeric characters, \nis "
      + s + " a palindrome? " + isPalindrome(s));
  }

  /** Return true if a string is a palindrome */
  public static boolean isPalindrome(String s) {
    // Create a new string by eliminating nonalphanumeric chars
    String s1 = filter(s);

    // Create a new string that is the reversal of s1
    String s2 = reverse(s1);

    // Compare if the reversal is the same as the original string
    return s2.equals(s1);
  }

  /** Create a new string by eliminating nonalphanumeric chars */
  public static String filter(String s) {
    // Create a string builder
    StringBuilder stringBuilder = new StringBuilder();
```

check palindrome

add letter or digit

```
34
35       // Examine each char in the string to skip alphanumeric char
36       for (int i = 0; i < s.length(); i++) {
37         if (Character.isLetterOrDigit(s.charAt(i))) {
38           stringBuilder.append(s.charAt(i));
39         }
40       }
41
42       // Return a new filtered string
43       return stringBuilder.toString();
44     }
45
46     /** Create a new string by reversing a specified string */
47     public static String reverse(String s) {
48       StringBuilder stringBuilder = new StringBuilder(s);
49       stringBuilder.reverse(); // Use the reverse method
50       return stringBuilder.toString();
51     }
52   }
```

```
Enter a string: ab<c>cb?a ↵Enter
Ignoring nonalphanumeric characters,
is ab<c>cb?a a palindrome? true

Enter a string: abcc><?cab ↵Enter
Ignoring nonalphanumeric characters,
is abcc><?cab a palindrome? false
```

The `filter(String s)` method (lines 31–44) examines each character in string `s` and copies it to a string builder if the character is a letter or a numeric character. The `filter` method returns the string in the builder. The `reverse(String s)` method (lines 47–51) creates a new string that reverses the specified string `s`. The `filter` and `reverse` methods both return a new string. The original string is not changed.

The program in Listing 8.1 checks whether a string is a palindrome by comparing pairs of characters from both ends of the string. Listing 8.3 uses the `reverse` method in the `StringBuilder` class to reverse the string, then compares whether the two strings are equal to determine whether the original string is a palindrome.

8.5 Command-Line Arguments

Perhaps you have already noticed the unusual declarations for the `main` method, which has parameter `args` of `String[]` type. It is clear that `args` is an array of strings. The `main` method is just like a regular method with a parameter. You can call a regular method by passing actual parameters. Can you pass arguments to `main`? Yes, of course you can. For example, the `main` method in class `B` is invoked by a method in `A`, as shown below:

```
public class A {
  public static void main(String[] args) {
    String[] strings = {"New York",
      "Boston", "Atlanta"};
    B.main(strings);
  }
}
```

```
public class B {
  public static void main(String[] args) {
    for (int i = 0; i < args.length; i++)
      System.out.println(args[i]);
  }
}
```

A main method is just a regular method. Furthermore, you can pass arguments from the command line.

8.5.1 Passing Strings to the main Method

You can pass strings to a main method from the command line when you run the program. The following command line, for example, starts the program TestMain with three strings: arg0, arg1, and arg2:

```
java TestMain arg0 arg1 arg2
```

arg0, arg1, and arg2 are strings, but they don't have to appear in double quotes on the command line. The strings are separated by a space. A string that contains a space must be enclosed in double quotes. Consider the following command line:

```
java TestMain "First num" alpha 53
```

It starts the program with three strings: "First num", alpha, and 53, a numeric string. Since "First num" is a string, it is enclosed in double quotes. Note that 53 is actually treated as a string. You can use "53" instead of 53 in the command line.

When the main method is invoked, the Java interpreter creates an array to hold the command-line arguments and pass the array reference to args. For example, if you invoke a program with n arguments, the Java interpreter creates an array like this one:

```
args = new String[n];
```

The Java interpreter then passes args to invoke the main method.

Note

If you run the program with no strings passed, the array is created with new String[0]. In this case, the array is empty with length 0. args references to this empty array. Therefore, args is not null, but args.length is 0.

8.5.2 Problem: Calculator

Suppose you are to develop a program that performs arithmetic operations on integers. The program receives three arguments: an integer followed by an operator and another integer. For example, to add two integers, use this command:

```
java Calculator 2 + 3
```

The program will display the following output:

```
2 + 3 = 5
```

Figure 8.14 shows sample runs of the program.

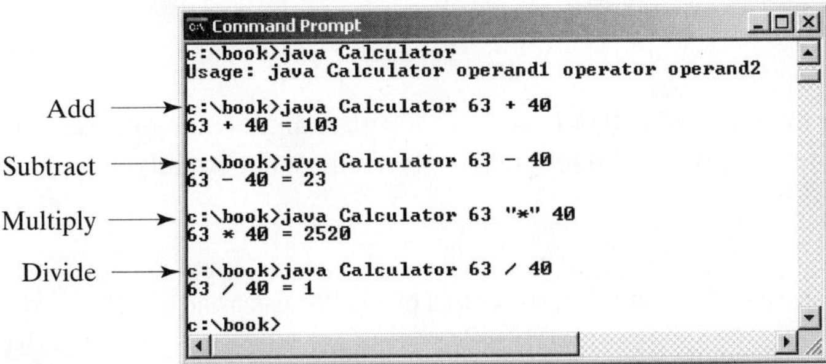

FIGURE 8.14 The program takes three arguments (operand1 operator operand2) from the command line and displays the expression and the result of the arithmetic operation.

The strings passed to the main program are stored in **args**, which is an array of strings. The first string is stored in **args[0]**, and **args.length** is the number of strings passed.

Here are the steps in the program:

1. Use **args.length** to determine whether three arguments have been provided in the command line. If not, terminate the program using **System.exit(0)**.
2. Perform a binary arithmetic operation on the operands **args[0]** and **args[2]** using the operator specified in **args[1]**.

The program is shown in Listing 8.4.

Video Note
Command-line argument

LISTING 8.4 Calculator.java

check operator

```
1 public class Calculator {
2   /** Main method */
3   public static void main(String[] args) {
4     // Check number of strings passed
5     if (args.length != 3) {
6       System.out.println(
7         "Usage: java Calculator operand1 operator operand2");
8       System.exit(0);
9     }
10
11     // The result of the operation
12     int result = 0;
13
14     // Determine the operator
15     switch (args[1].charAt(0)) {
16       case '+': result = Integer.parseInt(args[0]) +
17                          Integer.parseInt(args[2]);
18                 break;
19       case '-': result = Integer.parseInt(args[0]) -
20                          Integer.parseInt(args[2]);
21                 break;
22       case '*': result = Integer.parseInt(args[0]) *
23                          Integer.parseInt(args[2]);
24                 break;
25       case '/': result = Integer.parseInt(args[0]) /
26                          Integer.parseInt(args[2]);
27     }
28
29     // Display result
30     System.out.println(args[0] + ' ' + args[1] + ' ' + args[2]
31       + " = " + result);
32   }
33 }
```

Integer.parseInt(args[0]) (line 15) converts a digital string into an integer. The string must consist of digits. If not, the program will terminate abnormally.

special * character

Note

In the sample run, "*" had to be used instead of * for the command

```
java Calculator 63 "*" 40
```

In JDK 1.1 and above, the * symbol refers to all the files in the current directory when it is used on a command line. Therefore, in order to specify the multiplication operator, the * must be enclosed in quote marks in the command line. The following program displays all the files in the current directory when issuing the command `java Test *`:

```
public class Test {
  public static void main(String[] args) {
    for (int i = 0; i < args.length; i++)
      System.out.println(args[i]);
  }
}
```

8.6 The **File** Class

Data stored in variables, arrays, and objects are temporary; they are lost when the program terminates. To permanently store the data created in a program, you need to save them in a file on a disk or a CD. The file can be transported and can be read later by other programs. Since data are stored in files, this section introduces how to use the `File` class to obtain file properties and to delete and rename files. The next section introduces how to read/write data from/to text files. why file?

Every file is placed in a directory in the file system. An *absolute file name* contains a file name with its complete path and drive letter. For example, **c:\book\Welcome.java** is the absolute file name for the file **Welcome.java** on the Windows operating system. Here **c:\book** is referred to as the *directory path* for the file. Absolute file names are machine dependent. On the Unix platform, the absolute file name may be **/home/liang/book/Welcome.java**, where **/home/liang/book** is the directory path for the file **Welcome.java**. absolute file name directory path

The `File` class is intended to provide an abstraction that deals with most of the machine-dependent complexities of files and path names in a machine-independent fashion. The `File` class contains the methods for obtaining file properties and for renaming and deleting files, as shown in Figure 8.15. However, *the* `File` *class does not contain the methods for reading and writing file contents.*

The file name is a string. The `File` class is a wrapper class for the file name and its directory path. For example, `new File("c:\\book")` creates a `File` object for the directory **c:\book**, and `new File("c:\\book\\test.dat")` creates a `File` object for the file **c:\\book\\test.dat**, both on Windows. You can use the `File` class's `isDirectory()` method to check whether the object represents a directory, and the `isFile()` method to check whether the object represents a file.

Caution

The directory separator for Windows is a backslash (`\`). The backslash is a special character in Java and should be written as `\\` in a string literal (see Table 2.5). \ in file names

Note

Constructing a `File` *instance does not create a file on the machine.* You can create a `File` instance for any filename regardless whether it exists or not. You can invoke the `exists()` method on a `File` instance to check whether the file exists.

Do not use absolute file names in your program. If you use a file name such as `"c:\\book\\Welcome.java"`, it will work on Windows but not on other platforms. You should use a file name relative to the current directory. For example, you may create a `File` object using `new File("Welcome.java")` for the file **Welcome.java** in the current directory. You may create a `File` object using `new File("image/us.gif")` for the file **us.gif** under the **image** directory in the current directory. The forward slash (`/`) is the Java directory separator, which is the same as on Unix. The statement `new File("image/us.gif")` works on Windows, Unix, or any other platform. relative file name Java directory separator (/)

java.io.File	
+File(pathname: String)	Creates a File object for the specified path name. The path name may be a directory or a file.
+File(parent: String, child: String)	Creates a File object for the child under the directory parent. The child may be a file name or a subdirectory.
+File(parent: File, child: String)	Creates a File object for the child under the directory parent. The parent is a File object. In the preceding constructor, the parent is a string.
+exists(): boolean	Returns true if the file or the directory represented by the File object exists.
+canRead(): boolean	Returns true if the file represented by the File object exists and can be read.
+canWrite(): boolean	Returns true if the file represented by the File object exists and can be written.
+isDirectory(): boolean	Returns true if the File object represents a directory.
+isFile(): boolean	Returns true if the File object represents a file.
+isAbsolute(): boolean	Returns true if the File object is created using an absolute path name.
+isHidden(): boolean	Returns true if the file represented in the File object is hidden. The exact definition of *hidden* is system dependent. On Windows, you can mark a file hidden in the File Properties dialog box. On Unix systems, a file is hidden if its name begins with a period character '.'.
+getAbsolutePath(): String	Returns the complete absolute file or directory name represented by the File object.
+getCanonicalPath(): String	Returns the same as getAbsolutePath() except that it removes redundant names, such as "." and "..", from the path name, resolves symbolic links (on Unix platforms), and converts drive letters to standard uppercase (on Win32 platforms).
+getName(): String	Returns the last name of the complete directory and file name represented by the File object. For example, new File("c:\\book\\test.dat").getName() returns test.dat.
+getPath(): String	Returns the complete directory and file name represented by the File object. For example, new File("c:\\book\\test.dat").getPath() returns c:\book\test.dat.
+getParent(): String	Returns the complete parent directory of the current directory or the file represented by the File object. For example, new File("c:\\book\\test.dat").getParent() returns c:\book.
+lastModified(): long	Returns the time that the file was last modified.
+length(): long	Returns the size of the file, or 0 if it does not exist or if it is a directory.
+listFile(): File[]	Returns the files under the directory for a directory File object.
+delete(): boolean	Deletes this file. The method returns true if the deletion succeeds.
+renameTo(dest: File): boolean	Renames this file. The method returns true if the operation succeeds.

FIGURE 8.15 The File class can be used to obtain file and directory properties and to delete and rename files.

Listing 8.5 demonstrates how to create a File object and use the methods in the File class to obtain its properties. The program creates a File object for the file **us.gif**. This file is stored under the **image** directory in the current directory.

LISTING 8.5 TestFileClass.java

create a File
exists()
length()
canRead()
canWrite()
isDirectory()
isFile()
isAbsolute()
isHidden()
getAbsolutePath()

```
public class TestFileClass {
  public static void main(String[] args) {
    java.io.File file = new java.io.File("image/us.gif");
    System.out.println("Does it exist? " + file.exists() );
    System.out.println("The file has " + file.length() + " bytes");
    System.out.println("Can it be read? " + file.canRead());
    System.out.println("Can it be written? " + file.canWrite());
    System.out.println("Is it a directory? " + file.isDirectory());
    System.out.println("Is it a file? " + file.isFile());
    System.out.println("Is it absolute? " + file.isAbsolute());
    System.out.println("Is it hidden? " + file.isHidden());
    System.out.println("Absolute path is " +
      file.getAbsolutePath());
```

```
14     System.out.println("Last modified on " +
15       new java.util.Date(file.lastModified()));
16   }
17 }
```

`lastModified()`

The `lastModified()` method returns the date and time when the file was last modified, measured in milliseconds since the beginning of Unix time (00:00:00 GMT, January 1, 1970). The `Date` class is used to display it in a readable format in lines 14–15.

Figure 8.16(a) shows a sample run of the program on Windows, and Figure 8.16(b), a sample run on Unix. As shown in the figures, the path-naming conventions on Windows are different from those on Unix.

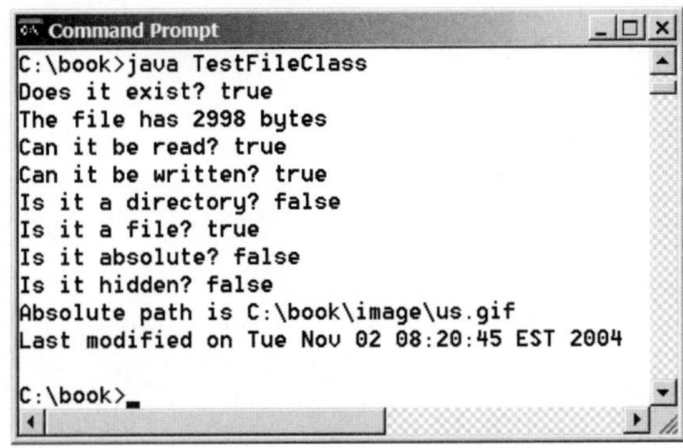

(a) On Windows

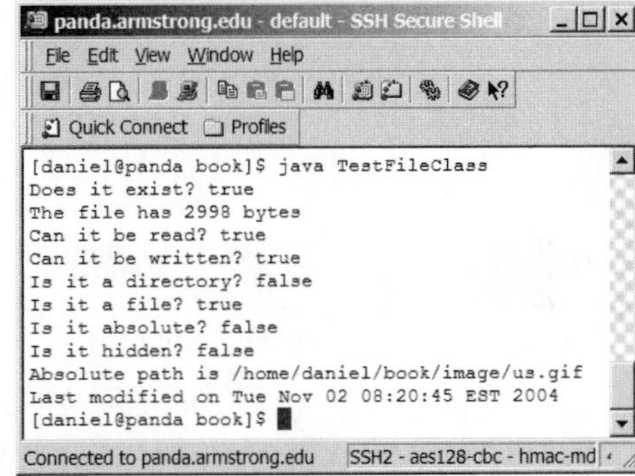

(b) On Unix

FIGURE 8.16 The program creates a `File` object and displays file properties.

8.7 File Input and Output

A `File` object encapsulates the properties of a file or a path, but does not contain the methods for reading/writing data from/to a file. In order to perform I/O, you need to create objects using appropriate Java I/O classes. The objects contain the methods for reading/writing data from/to a file. This section introduces how to read/write strings and numeric values from/to a text file using the `Scanner` and `PrintWriter` classes.

8.7.1 Writing Data Using `PrintWriter`

The `java.io.PrintWriter` class can be used to write data to a text file. First, you have to create a `PrintWriter` object for a text file as follows:

```
PrintWriter output = new PrintWriter(filename);
```

Then, you can invoke the `print`, `println`, and `printf` methods on the `PrintWriter` object to write data to a file. Figure 8.17 summarizes frequently used methods in `PrintWriter`.

Listing 8.6 gives an example that creates an instance of `PrintWriter` and writes two lines to the file "scores.txt". Each line consists of first name (a string), middle name initial (a character), last name (a string), and score (an integer).

Video Note
Write/read data to/from files

LISTING 8.6 `WriteData.java`

```
public class WriteData {
  public static void main(String[] args) throws Exception {
    java.io.File file = new java.io.File("scores.txt");
```

throws an exception

create `File` object

file exist? · create **PrintWriter** · print data · close file

```
4      if (file.exists()) {
5        System.out.println("File already exists");
6        System.exit(0);
7      }
8
9      // Create a file
10     java.io.PrintWriter output = new java.io.PrintWriter(file);
11
12     // Write formatted output to the file
13     output.print("John T Smith ");
14     output.println(90);
15     output.print("Eric K Jones ");
16     output.println(85);
17
18     // Close the file
19     output.close();
20   }
21 }
```


java.io.PrintWriter	
+PrintWriter(filename: String)	Creates a PrintWriter object for the specified file.
+print(s: String): void	Writes a string.
+print(c: char): void	Writes a character.
+print(cArray: char[]): void	Writes an array of characters.
+print(i: int): void	Writes an int value.
+print(l: long): void	Writes a long value.
+print(f: float): void	Writes a float value.
+print(d: double): void	Writes a double value.
+print(b: boolean): void	Writes a boolean value.
Also contains the overloaded println methods.	A println method acts like a print method; additionally it prints a line separator. The line separator string is defined by the system. It is \r\n on Windows and \n on Unix.
Also contains the overloaded printf methods.	The printf method was introduced in §3.6, "Formatting Console Output."

FIGURE 8.17 The `PrintWriter` class contains the methods for writing data to a text file.

Lines 3–7 check whether the file scores.txt exists. If so, exit the program (line 6).

create a file

Invoking the constructor `new PrintWriter(String filename)` will create a new file if the file does not exist. If the file already exists, the current content in the file will be discarded.

throws Exception

Invoking the constructor `new PrintWriter(String filename)` may throw an I/O exception. Java forces you to write the code to deal with this type of exception. You will learn how to handle it in Chapter 19, "Exception Handling." For now, simply declare `throws Exception` in the method declaration (line 2).

print method

You have used the `System.out.print` and `System.out.println` methods to write text to the console. `System.out` is a standard Java object for the console. You can create objects for writing text to any file using `print`, `println`, and `printf` (lines 13–16).

close file

The `close()` method must be used to close the file. If this method is not invoked, the data may not be saved properly in the file.

8.7.2 Reading Data Using Scanner

The `java.util.Scanner` class was used to read strings and primitive values from the console in §2.11, "Console Input Using the Scanner Class." A `Scanner` breaks its input into tokens delimited by whitespace characters. To read from the keyboard, you create a Scanner for System.in, as follows:

```
Scanner input = new Scanner(System.in);
```

To read from a file, create a Scanner for a file, as follows:

```
Scanner input = new Scanner(new File(filename));
```

Figure 8.18 summarizes frequently used methods in Scanner.

java.util.Scanner	
+Scanner(source: File)	Creates a scanner that produces values scanned from the specified file.
+Scanner(source: String)	Creates a scanner that produces values scanned from the specified string.
+close()	Closes this scanner.
+hasNext(): boolean	Returns true if this scanner has more data to be read.
+next(): String	Returns next token as a string delimited by a white space.
+nextLine(): String	Returns a line ending with the line separator.
+nextByte(): byte	Returns next token as a byte.
+nextShort(): short	Returns next token as a short.
+nextInt(): int	Returns next token as an int.
+nextLong(): long	Returns next token as a long.
+nextFloat(): float	Returns next token as a float.
+nextDouble(): double	Returns next token as a double.
+useDelimiter(pattern: String): Scanner	Sets this scanner's delimiting pattern.

FIGURE 8.18 The Scanner class contains the methods for scanning data.

Listing 8.7 gives an example that creates an instance of Scanner and reads data from the file "scores.txt".

LISTING 8.7 ReadData.java

```
import java.util.Scanner;

public class ReadData {
  public static void main(String[] args) throws Exception {
    // Create a File instance
    java.io.File file = new java.io.File("scores.txt");

    // Create a Scanner for the file
    Scanner input = new Scanner(file);

    // Read data from a file
    while (input.hasNext()) {
      String firstName = input.next();
      String mi = input.next();
      String lastName = input.next();
      int score = input.nextInt();
      System.out.println(
        firstName + " " + mi + " " + lastName + " " + score);
    }

    // Close the file
    input.close();
  }
}
```


create a File

create a Scanner

has next?
read items

close file

File class

Note that new Scanner(String) creates a Scanner for a given string. To create a Scanner to read data from a file, you have to use the java.io.File class to create an instance of the File using the constructor *new File(filename)* (line 6), and use new Scanner(File) to create a Scanner for the file (line 9).

throws Exception

Invoking the constructor *new Scanner(File)* may throw an I/O exception. So the main method declares *throws Exception* in line 6.

Each iteration in the while loop reads first name, mi, last name, and score from the text file (lines 12–19). The file is closed in line 22.

close file

It is not necessary to close the input file (line 22), but it is a good practice to do so to release the resources occupied by the file.

8.7.3 How Does Scanner Work?

token-reading method

change delimiter

The nextByte(), nextShort(), nextInt(), nextLong(), nextFloat(), nextDouble(), and next() methods are known as *token-reading methods*, because they read tokens separated by delimiters. By default, the delimiters are whitespace. You can use the useDelimiter(String regex) method to set a new pattern for delimiters.

How does an input method work? A token-reading method first skips any delimiters (whitespace by default), then reads a token ending at a delimiter. The token is then automatically converted into a value of the byte, short, int, long, float, or double type for nextByte(), nextShort(), nextInt(), nextLong(), nextFloat(), and nextDouble(), respectively. For the next() method, no conversion is performed. If the token does not match the expected type, a runtime exception java.util.InputMismatchException will be thrown.

InputMismatchException

next() vs. **nextLine()**

Both methods next() and nextLine() read a string. The next() method reads a string delimited by delimiters, but nextLine() reads a line ending with a line separator. Recall that the line separator is platform dependent. It is \r\n on Windows and \n on Unix.

Note

line separator

The line separator string is defined by the system. It is \r\n on Windows and \n on Unix. To get the line separator on a particular platform, use

```
String lineSeparator = System.getProperty("line.separator");
```

If you enter input from a keyboard, a line ends with the ENTER key, which corresponds to the \n character.

behavior of **nextLine()**

The token-reading method does not read the delimiter after the token. If the nextLine() is invoked after a token-reading method, the method reads characters that start from this delimiter and end with the line separator. The line separator is read, but is not part of the string returned by nextLine().

input from file

Suppose a text file named test.txt contains a line

```
34 567
```

After the following code is executed,

```
Scanner input = new Scanner(new File("test.txt"));
int intValue = input.nextInt();
String line = input.nextLine();
```

intValue contains 34 and line contains characters ' ', '5', '6', '7'.

What happens if the input is *entered from the keyboard*? Suppose you enter 34, the ENTER key, 567, and the ENTER key for the following code:

```
Scanner input = new Scanner(System.in);
int intValue = input.nextInt();
String line = input.nextLine();
```

You will get 34 in intValue, and an empty string in line. Why? Here is the reason. The token-reading method nextInt() reads in 34 and stops at the delimiter, which is a line separator (the ENTER key) in this case. The nextLine() method ends after reading the line separator and returns the string read before the line separator. Since there are no characters before the line separator, line is empty.

input from keyboard

8.7.4 Problem: Replacing Text

Suppose you are to write a program named ReplaceText that replaces all occurrence of a string in a text file with a new string. The file name and strings are passed as command-line arguments as follows:

```
java ReplaceText sourceFile targetFile oldString newString
```

For example, invoking

```
java ReplaceText FormatString.java t.txt StringBuilder StringBuffer
```

replaces all the occurrences of StringBuilder by StringBuffer in FormatString.java and saves the new file in t.txt.

Listing 8.8 gives the solution to the problem. The program checks the number of arguments passed to the main method (lines 7–11), checks whether the source and target files exist (lines 14–25), creates a Scanner for the source file (line 28), creates a PrintWriter for the target file, and repeatedly reads a line from the source file (line 33), replaces the text (line 33), and writes a new line to the target file (line 34). You must close the output file (line 38) to ensure that data is saved to the file properly.

LISTING 8.8 ReplaceText.java

```
 1 import java.io.*;
 2 import java.util.*;
 3
 4 public class ReplaceText {
 5   public static void main(String[] args) throws Exception {
 6     // Check command line-parameter usage
 7     if (args.length != 4) {
 8       System.out.println(
 9         "Usage: java ReplaceText sourceFile targetFile oldStr newStr");
10       System.exit(0);
11     }
12
13     // Check if source file exists
14     File sourceFile = new File(args[0]);
15     if (!sourceFile.exists()) {
16        System.out.println("Source file " + args[0] + " does not exist");
17        System.exit(0);
18     }
19
20     // Check if target file exists
21     File targetFile = new File(args[1]);
22     if (targetFile.exists()) {
23       System.out.println("Target file " + args[1] + " already exists");
24       System.exit(0);
25     }
26
27     // Create input and output files
28     Scanner input = new Scanner(sourceFile);
29     PrintWriter output = new PrintWriter(targetFile);
```

check command usage

source file exists?

target file exists?

create a **Scanner**

create a **PrintWriter**

has next?
read a line
close file

```
    while (input.hasNext() ) {
      String s1 = input.nextLine();
      String s2 = s1.replaceAll(args[2], args[3]);
      output.println(s2);
    }

    input.close();
    output.close();
  }
}
```

8.8 (GUI) File Dialogs

Java provides the `javax.swing.JFileChooser` class for displaying a file dialog, as shown in Figure 8.19. From this dialog box, the user can choose a file.

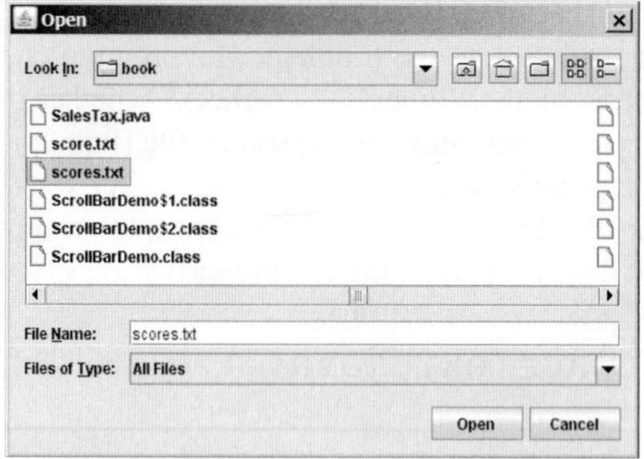

FIGURE 8.19 `JFileChooser` can be used to display a file dialog for opening a file.

Listing 8.9 gives a program that prompts the user to choose a file and displays the contents of the file on the console.

LISTING 8.9 ReadFileUsingJFileChooser.java

create a **JFileChooser**
display file chooser
check status
getSelectedFile

```
import java.util.Scanner;
import javax.swing.JFileChooser;

public class ReadFileUsingJFileChooser {
  public static void main(String[] args) throws Exception {
    JFileChooser fileChooser = new JFileChooser();
    if (fileChooser.showOpenDialog(null)
        == JFileChooser.APPROVE_OPTION ) {
      // Get the selected file
      java.io.File file = fileChooser.getSelectedFile();

      // Create a Scanner for the file
      Scanner input = new Scanner(file);

      // Read text from the file
      while (input.hasNext()) {
        System.out.println(input.nextLine());
      }

```

```
20       // Close the file
21       input.close();
22     }
23     else {
24       System.out.println("No file selected");
25     }
26   }
27 }
```

The program creates a `JFileChooser` in line 6. The `showOpenDialog(null)` method displays a dialog box, as shown in Figure 8.19. The method returns an `int` value, either `APPROVE_OPTION` or `CANCEL_OPTION`, which indicates whether the *Open* button or the *Cancel* button was clicked.

showOpenDialog

APPROVE_OPTION

The `getSelectedFile()` method (line 10) returns the selected file from the file dialog box. Line 13 creates a scanner for the file. The program continuously reads the lines from the file and displays them to the console (lines 16-18).

getSelectedFile

Chapter Summary

- Strings are objects encapsulated in the `String` class. A string can be constructed using one of the 11 constructors or using a string literal shorthand initializer.
- A `String` object is immutable; its contents cannot be changed. To improve efficiency and save memory, the JVM stores string literals in a unique object if two literal strings have the same character sequence. This unique object is called an interned string object.
- You can get the length of a string by invoking its `length()` method, retrieve a character at the specified `index` in the string using the `charAt(index)` method, and use the `indexOf` and `lastIndexOf` methods to find a character or a substring in a string.
- You can use the `concat` method to concatenate two strings, or the plus (+) sign to concatenate two or more strings.
- You can use the `substring` method to obtain a substring from the string.
- You can use the `equals` and `compareTo` methods to compare strings. The `equals` method returns `true` if two strings are equal, and `false` if they are not equal. The `compareTo` method returns `0`, a positive integer, or a negative integer, depending on whether one string is equal to, greater than, or less than the other string.
- The `Character` class is a wrapper class for a single character. The `Character` class provides useful static methods to determine whether a character is a letter (`isLetter(char)`), a digit (`isDigit(char)`), uppercase (`isUpperCase(char)`), or lowercase (`isLowerCase(char)`).
- The `StringBuilder`/`StringBuffer` class can be used to replace the `String` class. The `String` object is immutable, but you can add, insert, or append new contents into a `StringBuilder`/`StringBuffer` object. Use `String` if the string contents do not require any change, and use `StringBuilder`/`StringBuffer` if they change.
- You can pass strings to the `main` method from the command line. Strings passed to the `main` program are stored in `args`, which is an array of strings. The first string is represented by `args[0]`, and `args.length` is the number of strings passed.

- The File class is used to obtain file properties and manipulate files. It does not contain the methods for reading/writing data from/to a file.
- You can use Scanner to read string and primitive data values from a text file and use PrintWriter to write data to a text file.
- The JFileChooser class can be used to display files graphically.

REVIEW QUESTIONS

Section 8.2 The String Class

8.1 Suppose that s1, s2, s3, and s4 are four strings, given as follows:

```
String s1 = "Welcome to Java";
String s2 = s1;
String s3 = new String("Welcome to Java");
String s4 = s3.intern();
```

What are the results of the following expressions?

```
(1) s1 == s2                       (13) s1.length()
(2) s2 == s3                       (14) s1.substring(5)
(3) s1.equals(s2)                  (15) s1.substring(5, 11)
(4) s2.equals(s3)                  (16) s1.startsWith("Wel")
(5) s1.compareTo(s2)               (17) s1.endsWith("Java")
(6) s2.compareTo(s3)               (18) s1.toLowerCase()
(7) s1 == s4                       (19) s1.toUpperCase()
(8) s1.charAt(0)                   (20) "  Welcome ".trim()
(9) s1.indexOf('j')                (21) s1.replace('o', 'T')
(10) s1.indexOf("to")              (22) s1.replaceAll("o", "T")
(11) s1.lastIndexOf('a')           (23) s1.replaceFirst("o", "T")
(12) s1.lastIndexOf("o", 15)       (24) s1.toCharArray()
```

To create a string "Welcome to Java", you may use a statement like this:

```
String s = "Welcome to Java";
```

Or

```
String s = new String("Welcome to Java);
```

Which one is better? Why?

8.2 Suppose that s1 and s2 are two strings. Which of the following statements or expressions are incorrect?

```
String s = new String("new string");
String s3 = s1 + s2;
String s3 = s1 - s2;
s1 == s2;
s1 >= s2;
s1.compareTo(s2);
int i = s1.length();
char c = s1(0);
char c = s1.charAt(s1.length());
```

8.3 What is the printout of the following code?

```
String s1 = "Welcome to Java";
String s2 = s1.replace("o", "abc");
System.out.println(s1);
System.out.println(s2);
```

8.4 Let s1 be " Welcome " and s2 be " welcome ". Write the code for the following statements:

- Check whether s1 is equal to s2 and assign the result to a Boolean variable isEqual.
- Check whether s1 is equal to s2 ignoring case and assign the result to a Boolean variable isEqual.
- Compare s1 with s2 and assign the result to an int variable x.
- Compare s1 with s2 ignoring case and assign the result to an int variable x.
- Check whether s1 has prefix "AAA" and assign the result to a Boolean variable b.
- Check whether s1 has suffix "AAA" and assign the result to a Boolean variable b.
- Assign the length of s1 to an int variable x.
- Assign the first character of s1 to a char variable x.
- Create a new string s3 that combines s1 with s2.
- Create a substring of s1 starting from index 1.
- Create a substring of s1 from index 1 to index 4.
- Create a new string s3 that converts s1 to lowercase.
- Create a new string s3 that converts s1 to uppercase.
- Create a new string s3 that trims blank spaces on both ends of s1.
- Replace all occurrences of character e with E in s1 and assign the new string to s3.
- Split "Welcome to Java and HTML" into an array tokens delimited by a space.
- Assign the index of the first occurrence of character e in s1 to an int variable x.
- Assign the index of the last occurrence of string abc in s1 to an int variable x.

8.5 Does any method in the String class change the contents of the string?

8.6 Suppose string s is created using new String(); what is s.length()?

8.7 How do you convert a char, an array of characters, or a number to a string?

8.8 Why does the following code cause a NullPointerException?

```
public class Test {
  private String text;

  public Test(String s) {
    String text  = s;
  }

  public static void main(String[] args) {
    Test test = new Test("ABC");
    System.out.println(test.text.toLowerCase());
  }
}
```

8.9 What is wrong in the following program?

```
public class Test  {
  String text;

  public void Test(String s) {
    this.text  = s;
  }

  public static void main(String[] args) {
    Test test = new Test("ABC");
    System.out.println(test);
  }
}
```

Section 8.3 The Character Class

8.10 How do you determine whether a character is in lowercase or uppercase?

8.11 How do you determine whether a character is alphanumeric?

Section 8.4 The StringBuilder/StringBuffer Class

8.12 What is the difference between `StringBuilder` and `StringBuffer`?

8.13 How do you create a string builder for a string? How do you get the string from a string builder?

8.14 Write three statements to reverse a string `s` using the `reverse` method in the `StringBuilder` class.

8.15 Write a statement to delete a substring from a string `s` of `20` characters, starting at index `4` and ending with index `10`. Use the `delete` method in the `StringBuilder` class.

8.16 What is the internal structure of a string and a string builder?

8.17 Suppose that `s1` and `s2` are given as follows:

```
StringBuilder s1 = new StringBuilder("Java");
StringBuilder s2 = new StringBuilder("HTML");
```

Show the value of `s2` after each of the following statement. Assume that the statements are independent.

```
(1) s1.append(" is fun");       (7) s1.deleteCharAt(3);
(2) s1.append(s2);              (8) s1.delete(1, 3);
(3) s1.insert(2, "is fun");     (9) s1.reverse();
(4) s1.insert(1, s2);           (10) s1.replace(1, 3, "Computer");
(5) s1.charAt(2);               (11) s1.substring(1, 3);
(6) s1.length();                (12) s1.substring(2);
```

8.18 Show the output of the following program:

```
public class Test {
  public static void main(String[] args) {
    String s = "Java";
    StringBuilder builder = new StringBuilder(s);
    change(s, builder);

    System.out.println(s);
```

```
    System.out.println(builder);
  }

  private static void change(String s, StringBuilder builder) {
    s = s + " and HTML";
    builder.append(" and HTML");
  }
}
```

Section 8.5 Command-Line Arguments

8.19 This book declares the `main` method as

```
public static void main(String[] args)
```

Can it be replaced by one of the following lines?

```
public static void main(String args[])
public static void main(String[] x)
public static void main(String x[])
static void main(String x[])
```

8.20 Show the output of the following program when invoked using

1. **java Test I have a dream**
2. **java Test "1 2 3"**
3. **java Test**
4. **java Test** "*"
5. **java Test** *

```
public class Test {
  public static void main(String[] args) {
    System.out.println("Number of strings is " + args.length);
    for (int i = 0; i < args.length; i++)
      System.out.println(args[i]);
  }
}
```

Section 8.6 The `File` Class

8.21 What is wrong about creating a `File` object using the following statement?

```
new File("c:\book\test.dat");
```

8.22 How do you check whether a file already exists? How do you delete a file? How do you rename a file? Can you find the file size (the number of bytes) using the `File` class?

8.23 Can you use the `File` class for I/O? Does creating a `File` object create a file on the disk?

Section 8.7 File Input and Output

8.24 How do you create a `PrintWriter` to write data to a file? What is the reason to declare `throws Exception` in the main method in Listing 8.6, WriteData.java. What would happen if the `close()` method were not invoked in Listing 8.6.

8.25 Show the contents of the file temp.txt after the following program is executed.

```
public class Test {
  public static void main(String[] args) throws Exception {
```

```
      java.io.PrintWriter output = new
        java.io.PrintWriter("temp.txt");
      output.printf("amount is %f %e\r\n", 32.32, 32.32);
      output.printf("amount is %5.4f %5.4e\r\n", 32.32, 32.32);
      output.printf("%6b\r\n", (1 > 2));
      output.printf("%6s\r\n", "Java");
      output.close();
    }
  }
```

8.26 How do you create a Scanner to read data from a file? What is the reason to declare throws Exception in the main method in Listing 8.7, ReadData.java? What would happen if the close() method were not invoked in Listing 8.7.

8.27 What will happen if you attempt to create a Scanner for a nonexistent file? What will happen if you attempt to create a PrintWriter for an existing file?

8.28 Is the line separator the same on all platforms? What is the line separator on Windows?

8.29 Suppose you enter 45 57.8 789, then press the ENTER key. Show the contents of the variables after the following code is executed.

```
Scanner input = new Scanner(System.in);
int intValue = input.nextInt();
double doubleValue = input.nextDouble();
String line = input.nextLine();
```

8.30 Suppose you enter 45, the ENTER key, 57.8, the ENTER key, 789, the ENTER key. Show the contents of the variables after the following code is executed.

```
Scanner input = new Scanner(System.in);
int intValue = input.nextInt();
double doubleValue = input.nextDouble();
String line = input.nextLine();
```

Programming Exercises

Sections 8.2-8.3

8.1* (*Checking SSN*) Write a program that prompts the user to enter a social security number in the format DDD-DD-DDDD, where D is a digit. The program displays "valid SSN" for a correct social security number and "invalid SSN" otherwise.

8.2** (*Checking substrings*) You can check whether a string is a substring of another string by using the indexOf method in the String class. Write your own method for this function. Write a program that prompts the user to enter two strings, and check whether the first string is a substring of the second.

8.3** (*Checking password*) Some Web sites impose certain rules for passwords. Write a method that checks whether a string is a valid password. Suppose the password rule is as follows:

- A password must have at least eight characters.
- A password consists of only letters and digits.
- A password must contain at least two digits.

Write a test program that prompts the user to enter a password and displays "Valid Password" if the rule is followed or "Invalid Password" otherwise.

8.4 (*Occurrences of a specified character*) Write a method that finds the number of occurrences of a specified character in the string using the following header:

```
public static int count(String str, char a)
```

For example, `count("Welcome", 'e')` returns `2`.

8.5** (*Occurrences of each digit in a string*) Write a method that counts the occurrences of each digit in a string using the following header:

```
public static int[] count(String s)
```

The method counts how many times a digit appears in the string. The return value is an array of ten elements, each of which holds the count for a digit. For example, after executing `int[] counts = count("12203AB3")`, `counts[0]` is `1`, `counts[1]` is `1`, `counts[2]` is `2`, `counts[3]` is `2`.

Write a `main` method to display the count for `"SSN is 343 32 4545 and ID is 434 34 4323"`.

8.6* (*Counting the letters in a string*) Write a method that counts the number of letters in the string using the following header:

```
public static int countLetters(String s)
```

Write a `main` method to invoke `countLetters("Java in 2008")` and display its return value.

8.7* (*Hex to decimal*) Write a method that parses a hex number as a string into a decimal integer. The method header is as follows:

```
public static int parseHex(String hexString)
```

For example, `hexString` A5 is 165 ($10 \times 16 + 5 = 165$) and FAA is 4010 ($15 \times 16^2 + 10 \times 16 + 10 = 4010$). So `parseHex("A5")` returns `165`, and `parseHex("FAA")` returns `4010`. Use hex strings ABC and 10A to test the method. Note that `Integer.parseInt("FAA", 16)` parses a hex string to a decimal value. Do not use this method in this exercise.

8.8* (*Binary to decimal*) Write a method that parses a binary number as a string into a decimal integer. The method header is as follows:

```
public static int parseBinary(String binaryString)
```

For example, `binaryString` 10001 is 17 ($1 \times 2^4 + 0 \times 2^3 + 0 \times 2^2 + 0 \times 2 + 1 = 17$). So, `parseBinary("10001")` returns `17`. Use binary string 11111111 to test the method. Note that `Integer.parseInt("10001", 2)` parses a binary string to a decimal value. Do not use this method in this exercise.

Section 8.4 The StringBuilder/StringBuffer Class

8.9** (*Decimal to hex*) Write a method that parses a decimal number into a hex number as a string. The method header is as follows:

```
public static String convertDecimalToHex(int value)
```

See §1.5, "Number Systems," for converting a decimal into a hex. Use decimal `298` and `9123` to test the method.

8.10** (*Decimal to binary*) Write a method that parses a decimal number into a binary number as a string. The method header is as follows:

Video Note
Convert a decimal number into a binary number

```
public static String convertDecimalToBinary(int value)
```

See §1.5, "Number Systems," for converting a decimal into a binary. Use decimal 298 and 9123 to test the method.

8.11** (*Sorting characters in a string*) Write a method that returns a sorted string using the following header:

```
public static String sort(String s)
```

For example, sort("acb") returns abc.

8.12** (*Anagrams*) Write a method that checks whether two words are anagrams. Two words are anagrams if they contain the same letters in any order. For example, "silent" and "listen" are anagrams. The header of the method is as follows:

```
public static boolean isAnagram(String s1, String s2)
```

Write a main method to invoke isAnagram("silent", "listen"), isAnagram("garden", "ranged"), and isAnagram("split", "lisp").

Section 8.5 Command-Line Arguments

8.13* (*Passing a string to check palindromes*) Rewrite Listing 8.1 by passing the string as a command-line argument.

8.14* (*Summing integers*) Write two programs. The first program passes an unspecified number of integers as separate strings to the main method and displays their total. The second program passes an unspecified number of integers delimited by one space in a string to the main method and displays their total. Name the two programs Exercise8_14a and Exercise8_14b, as shown in Figure 8.20.

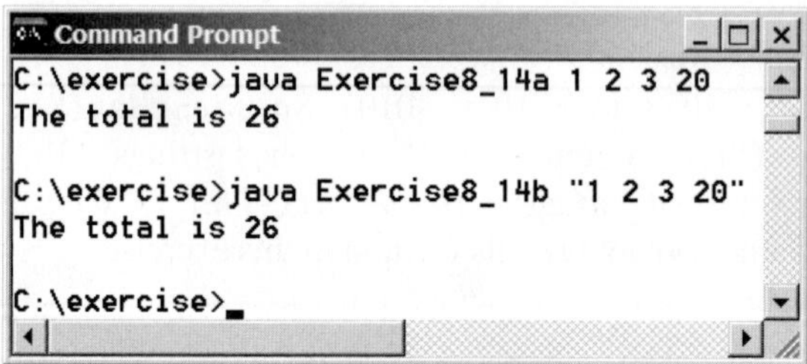

FIGURE 8.20 The program adds all the numbers passed from the command line.

8.15* (*Finding the number of uppercase letters in a string*) Write a program that passes a string to the main method and displays the number of uppercase letters in a string.

Sections 8.7-8.8

8.16** (*Reformatting Java source code*) Write a program that converts the Java source code from the next-line brace style to the end-of-line brace style. For example, the following Java source in (a) uses the next-line brace style. Your program converts it to the end-of-line brace style in (b).

```
public class Test
{
  public static void main(String[] args)
  {
    // Some statements
  }
}
```

(a) Next-line brace style

```
public class Test {
  public static void main(String[] args) {
    // Some statements
  }
}
```

(b) End-of-line brace style

Your program can be invoked from the command line with the Java source-code file as the argument. It converts the Java source code to a new format. For example, the following command converts the Java source code file **Test.java** to the end-of-line brace style.

```
java Exercise8_16 Test.java
```

8.17* (*Counting characters, words, and lines in a file*) Write a program that will count the number of characters (excluding control characters `'\r'` and `'\n'`), words, and lines, in a file. Words are separated by spaces, tabs, carriage return, or line-feed characters. The file name should be passed as a command-line argument, as shown in Figure 8.21.

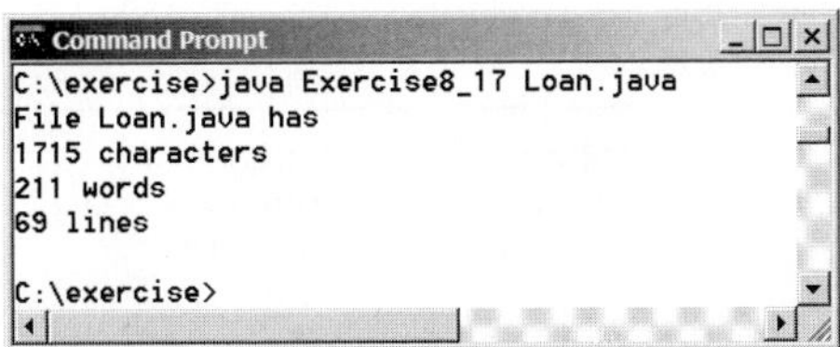

FIGURE 8.21 The program displays the number of characters, words, and lines in the given file.

8.18* (*Processing scores in a text file*) Suppose that a text file **Exercise8_18.txt** contains an unspecified number of scores. Write a program that reads the scores from the file and displays their total and average. Scores are separated by blanks.

8.19* (*Writing/Reading data*) Write a program to create a file named **Exercise8_19.txt** if it does not exist. Write `100` integers created randomly into the file using text I/O. Integers are separated by spaces in the file. Read the data back from the file and display the sorted data.

8.20** (*Replacing text*) Listing 8.8, ReplaceText.java, gives a program that replaces text in a source file and saves the change into a new file. Revise the program to save the change into the original file. For example, invoking

```
java Exercise8_20 file oldString newString
```

replaces `oldString` in the source file with `newString`.

8.21** (*Removing text*) Write a program that removes all the occurrences of a specified string from a text file. For example, invoking

```
java Exercise8_21 John filename
```

removes string `John` from the specified file.

Comprehensive

8.22** (*Guessing the capitals*) Write a program that repeatedly prompts the user to enter a capital for a state, as shown in Figure 8.22(a). Upon receiving the user input, the program reports whether the answer is correct, as shown in Figure 8.22(b). Assume that `50` states and their capitals are stored in a two-dimensional array, as

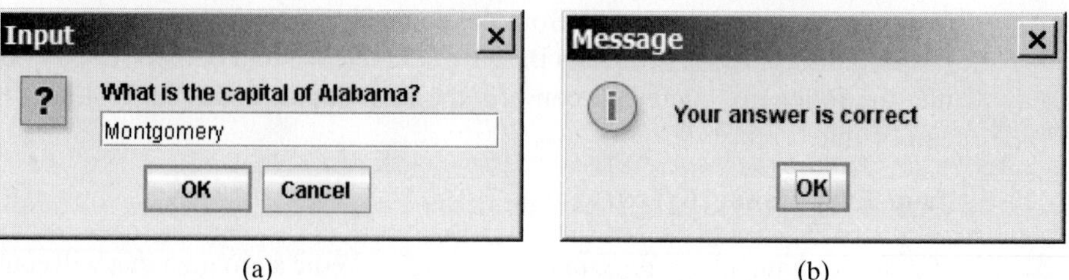

(a) (b)

FIGURE 8.22 The program prompts the user to enter the capital in (a) and reports the correctness of the answer.

shown in Figure 8.23. The program prompts the user to answer all ten states' capitals and displays the total correct count.

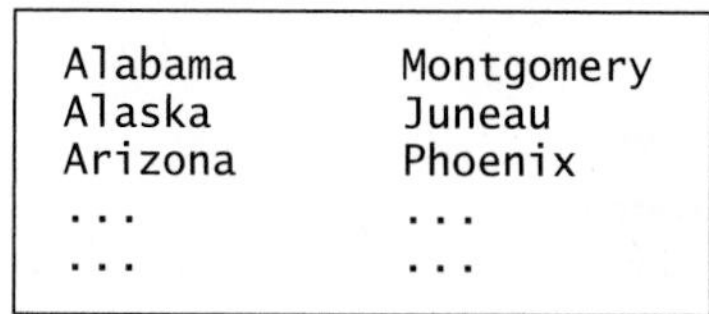

FIGURE 8.23 A two-dimensional array stores states and their capitals.

8.23** (*Implementing the* `String` *class*) The `String` class is provided in the Java library. Provide your own implementation for the following methods (name the new class `MyString1`):

```
public MyString1(char[] chars);
public char charAt(int index);
public int length();
public MyString1 substring(int begin, int end);
public char[] toChars();
public MyString1 toLowerCase();
public boolean equals(MyString1 s);
public static MyString1 valueOf(int i);
```

8.24** (*Implementing the* `String` *class*) The `String` class is provided in the Java library. Provide your own implementation for the following methods (name the new class `MyString2`):

```
public MyString2(char[] chars);
public int compare(String s);
public MyString2 substring(int begin);
public MyString2 toUpperCase();
public char[] toChars();
public static MyString2 valueOf(boolean b);
```

8.25 (*Implementing the* `Character` *class*) The `Character` class is provided in the Java library. Provide your own implementation for this class. Name the new class `MyCharacter`.

8.26** (*Implementing the* `StringBuilder` *class*) The `StringBuilder` class is provided in the Java library. Provide your own implementation for the following methods (name the new class `MyStringBuilder1`):

```
public MyStringBuilder1();
public MyStringBuilder1(char[] chars);
public MyStringBuilder1(String s);
public MyStringBuilder1 append(MyStringBuilder1 s);
public MyStringBuilder1 append(int i);
public int length();
public char charAt(int index);
public MyStringBuilder1 toLowerCase();
public MyStringBuilder1 substring(int begin, int end);
public String toString();
```

8.27** (*Implementing the* `StringBuilder` *class*) The `StringBuilder` class is provided in the Java library. Provide your own implementation for the following methods (name the new class `MyStringBuilder2`):

```
public MyStringBuilder2();
public MyStringBuilder2(char[] chars);
public MyStringBuilder2(String s);
public MyStringBuilder2 insert(int offset, MyStringBuilder2 s);
public MyStringBuilder2 reverse();
public MyStringBuilder2 substring(int begin);
public MyStringBuilder2 toUpperCase();
```

8.28* (*Common prefix*) Write a method that returns the common prefix of two strings. For example, the common prefix of `"distance"` and `"disinfection"` is `"dis"`. The header of the method is as follows:

```
public static String prefix(String s1, String s2)
```

If the two strings have no common prefix, the method returns an empty string.

Write a `main` method that prompts the user to enter two strings and display their common prefix.

8.29** (*New string* `split` *method*) The `split` method in the `String` class returns an array of strings consisting of the substrings split by the delimiters. However, the delimiters are not returned. Implement the following new method that returns an array of strings consisting of the substrings split by the matches, including the matches.

```
public static String[] split(String s, String regex)
```

For example, `split("ab#12#453", "#")` returns `ab`, `#`, `12`, `#`, `453` in an array of `String`, and `split("a?b?gf#e", "[?#]")` returns `a`, `b`, `?`, `b`, `gf`, `#`, and `e` in an array of `String`.

8.30** (*Financial: credit card number validation*) Rewrite Exercise 5.31 using a string input for credit card number. Redesign the program using the following method:

```
/** Get the result from Step 2 */
public static int sumOfEvenPlace(String cardNumber)
```

```
/** Return this number if it is a single digit, otherwise,
    return the sum of the two digits */
public static int getDigit(int number)

/** Return sum of odd place digits in number */
public static int sumOfOddPlace(String cardNumber)
```

8.31**(*Checking ISBN*) Use string operations to simplify Exercise 3.19. Enter the first 9-digit of an ISBN number as a string.

CHAPTER 9

THINKING IN OBJECTS

Objectives

- To create immutable objects from immutable classes to protect the contents of objects (§9.2).
- To determine the scope of variables in the context of a class (§9.3).
- To use the keyword `this` to refer to the calling object itself (§9.4).
- To apply class abstraction to develop software (§9.5).
- To explore the differences between the procedural paradigm and object-oriented paradigm (§9.6).
- To design programs using the object-oriented paradigm (§§9.7–9.9).

9.1 Introduction

The preceding two chapters introduced the concept of objects and classes. You learned how to program using objects from several classes in the Java API (e.g., `Date`, `Random`, `JFrame`, `String`, `StringBuilder`, `File`, `Scanner`, `PrintWriter`). This chapter focuses on class design. Several examples will illustrate the advantages of object-oriented programming. To begin, we will introduce some language features supporting these examples.

9.2 Immutable Objects and Classes

immutable object
immutable class

Normally, you create an object and allow its contents to be changed later. Occasionally, it is desirable to create an object whose contents cannot be changed once the object is created. We call such an object an *immutable object* and its class an *immutable class*. The `String` class, for example, is immutable. If you deleted the `set` method in the `Circle` class in Listing 7.7, the class would be immutable because radius is private and cannot be changed without a `set` method.

A class with all private data fields and no mutators is not necessarily immutable. An example is the class `Student`.

Student class

```
public class Student {
  private int id;
  private String name;
  private java.util.Date dateCreated;

  public Student(int ssn, String newName) {
    id = ssn;
    name = newName;
    dateCreated = new java.util.Date();
  }

  public int getId() {
    return id;
  }

  public String getName() {
    return name;
  }

  public java.util.Date getDateCreated() {
    return dateCreated;
  }
}
```

As shown in the following code, the data field `dateCreated` is returned using the `getDateCreated()` method. This is a reference to a `Date` object. Through this reference, the content for `dateCreated` can be changed.

```
public class Test {
  public static void main(String[] args) {
    Student student = new Student(111223333, "John");
    java.util.Date dateCreated = student.getDateCreated();
    dateCreated.setTime(200000); // Now dateCreated field is changed!
  }
}
```

For a class to be immutable, it must meet the following requirements:

- Declare all data fields private;
- Provide no mutator methods;
- Provide no accessor method that returns a reference to a data field that is mutable.

9.3 The Scope of Variables

Chapter 5, "Methods," discussed local variables and their scope rules. Local variables are declared and used inside a method locally. This section discusses the scope rules of all the variables in the context of a class.

Instance and static variables in a class are referred to as the *class's variables* or *data fields*. A variable defined inside a method is referred to as a local variable. The scope of a class's variables is the entire class, regardless of where the variables are declared. A class's variables and methods can be declared in any order in the class, as shown in Figure 9.1(a). The exception is when a data field is initialized based on a reference to another data field. In such cases, the other data field must be declared first, as shown in Figure 9.1(b). For consistency, this book declares data fields at the beginning of the class.

```
public class Circle {
  public double findArea() {
    return radius * radius * Math.PI;
  }
  private double radius = 1;
}
```

(a) Variable radius and method findArea() can be declared in any order.

```
public class Foo {
  private int i;
  private int j = i + 1;
}
```

(b) i has to be declared before j because j's initial value is dependent on i.

FIGURE 9.1 Members of a class can be declared in any order, with one exception.

You can declare a class's variable only once, but you can declare the same variable name in a method many times in different nonnesting blocks.

If a local variable has the same name as a class's variable, the local variable takes precedence and the class's variable with the same name is *hidden*. For example, in the following program, x is defined as an instance variable and as a local variable in the method.

```
class Foo {
  int x = 0; // Instance variable
  int y = 0;

  Foo() {
  }

  void p() {
    int x = 1; // Local variable
    System.out.println("x = " + x);
    System.out.println("y = " + y);
  }
}
```

What is the printout for f.p(), where f is an instance of Foo? The printout for f.p() is 1 for x and 0 for y. Here is why:

- x is declared as a data field with the initial value of 0 in the class, but is also defined in the method p() with an initial value of 1. The latter x is referenced in the System.out.println statement.
- y is declared outside the method p(), but is accessible inside it.

Tip

To avoid confusion and mistakes, do not use the names of instance or static variables as local variable names, except for method parameters.

9.4 The this Reference

hidden data fields

The this keyword is the name of a reference that refers to a calling object itself. One common use of the this keyword is to reference a class's *hidden data fields*. For example, a property name is often used as the parameter name in a set method for the property. In this case, you need to reference the hidden property name in the method in order to set a new value to it. A hidden static variable can be accessed simply by using the ClassName.StaticVariable reference. A hidden instance variable can be accessed by using the keyword this, as shown in Figure 9.2(a).

```
public class Foo {
  int i = 5;
  static double k = 0;

  void setI(int i) {
    this.i = i;
  }

  static void setK(double k) {
    Foo.k = k;
  }
}
```

(a)

```
Suppose that f1 and f2 are two objects of Foo.

Invoking f1.setI(10) is to execute
   this.i = 10, where this refers f1

Invoking f2.setI(45) is to execute
   this.i = 45, where this refers f2
```

(b)

FIGURE 9.2 The keyword this refers to the calling object that invokes the method.

The line this.i = i means "assign the value of parameter i to the data field i of the calling object." The keyword this refers to the object that invokes the instance method setI, as shown in Figure 9.2(b). The line Foo.k = k means that the value in parameter k is assigned to the static data field k of the class, which is shared by all the objects of the class.

call another constructor

Another common use of the this keyword is to enable a constructor to invoke another constructor of the same class. For example, you can redefine the Circle class as follows:

```
public class Circle {
  private double radius;

  public Circle(double radius) {
    this.radius = radius;
  }

  public Circle() {
    this(1.0);
  }

  public double getArea() {
    return this.radius * this.radius * Math.PI;
  }
}
```

this must be explicitly used to reference the data field radius of the object being constructed

this is used to invoke another constructor

Every instance variable belongs to an instance represented by this, which is normally omitted

The line this(1.0) in the second constructor invokes the first constructor with a double value argument.

Tip

If a class has multiple constructors, it is better to implement them using `this(arg-list)` as much as possible. In general, a constructor with no or fewer arguments can invoke the constructor with more arguments using `this(arg-list)`. This often simplifies coding and makes the class easier to read and to maintain.

Note

Java requires that the `this(arg-list)` statement appear first in the constructor before any other statements.

9.5 Class Abstraction and Encapsulation

In Chapter 5, "Methods," you learned about method abstraction and used it in program development. Java provides many levels of abstraction. *Class abstraction* is the separation of class implementation from the use of a class. The creator of a class describes it and lets the user know how it can be used. The collection of methods and fields that are accessible from outside the class, together with the description of how these members are expected to behave, serves as the *class's contract*. As shown in Figure 9.3, the user of the class does not need to know how the class is implemented. The details of implementation are encapsulated and hidden from the user. This is known as *class encapsulation*. For example, you can create a `Circle` object and find the area of the circle without knowing how the area is computed.

class abstraction

class encapsulation

FIGURE 9.3 Class abstraction separates class implementation from the use of the class.

Class abstraction and encapsulation are two sides of the same coin. There are many real-life examples that illustrate the concept of class abstraction. Consider building a computer system, for instance. Your personal computer is made up of many components, such as a CPU, CD-ROM, floppy disk, motherboard, fan, and so on. Each component can be viewed as an object that has properties and methods. To get the components to work together, all you need to know is how each component is used and how it interacts with the others. You don't need to know how they work internally. The internal implementation is encapsulated and hidden from you. You can build a computer without knowing how a component is implemented.

The computer-system analogy precisely mirrors the object-oriented approach. Each component can be viewed as an object of the class for the component. For example, you might have a class that models all kinds of fans for use in a computer, with properties like fan size and speed, and methods like start, stop, and so on. A specific fan is an instance of this class with specific property values.

As another example, consider getting a loan. A specific loan can be viewed as an object of a `Loan` class. Interest rate, loan amount, and loan period are its data properties, and computing monthly payment and total payment are its methods. When you buy a car, a loan object is created by instantiating the class with your loan interest rate, loan amount, and loan period. You can then use the methods to find the monthly payment and total payment of your loan. As a user of the `Loan` class, you don't need to know how these methods are implemented.

Video Note
Loan class

Listing 2.7, ComputeLoan.java, presented a program for computing loan payments. The program cannot be reused in other programs. One way to fix this problem is to define static methods for computing monthly payment and total payment. However, this solution has limitations. Suppose you wish to associate a date with the loan. The ideal way is to create an object that ties the properties for loan information and date together. Figure 9.4 shows the UML class diagram for the Loan class.

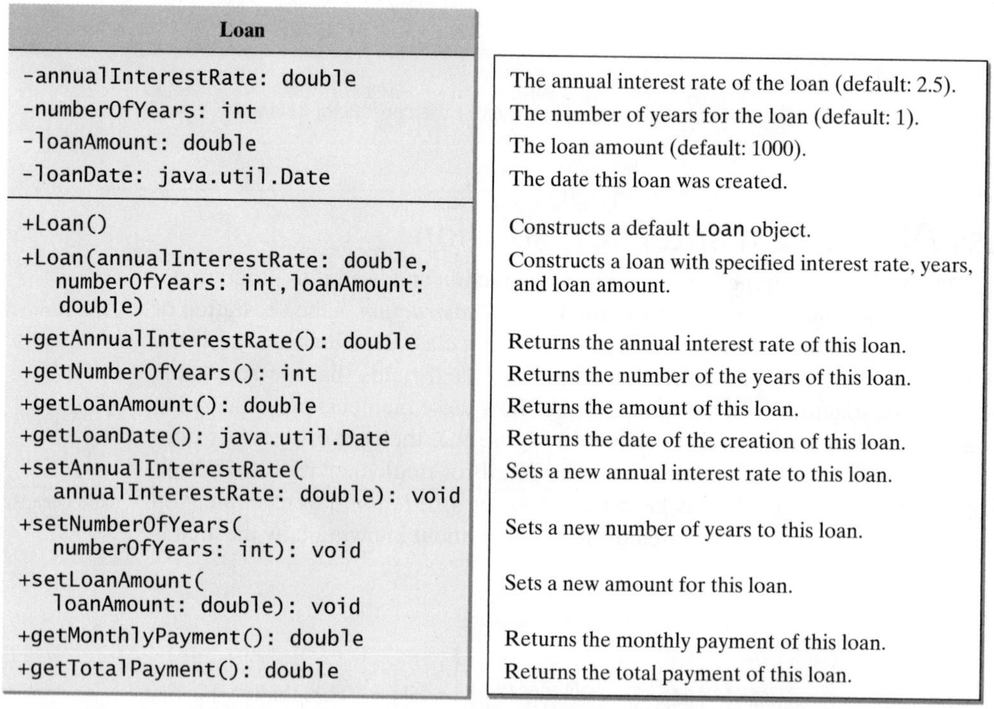

Loan	
-annualInterestRate: double	The annual interest rate of the loan (default: 2.5).
-numberOfYears: int	The number of years for the loan (default: 1).
-loanAmount: double	The loan amount (default: 1000).
-loanDate: java.util.Date	The date this loan was created.
+Loan()	Constructs a default Loan object.
+Loan(annualInterestRate: double, numberOfYears: int,loanAmount: double)	Constructs a loan with specified interest rate, years, and loan amount.
+getAnnualInterestRate(): double	Returns the annual interest rate of this loan.
+getNumberOfYears(): int	Returns the number of the years of this loan.
+getLoanAmount(): double	Returns the amount of this loan.
+getLoanDate(): java.util.Date	Returns the date of the creation of this loan.
+setAnnualInterestRate(annualInterestRate: double): void	Sets a new annual interest rate to this loan.
+setNumberOfYears(numberOfYears: int): void	Sets a new number of years to this loan.
+setLoanAmount(loanAmount: double): void	Sets a new amount for this loan.
+getMonthlyPayment(): double	Returns the monthly payment of this loan.
+getTotalPayment(): double	Returns the total payment of this loan.

FIGURE 9.4 The Loan class models the properties and behaviors of loans.

The UML diagram in Figure 9.4 serves as the contract for the Loan class. Throughout the book, you will play the role of both class user and class writer. The user can use the class without knowing how the class is implemented. Assume that the Loan class is available. Let us begin by writing a test program that uses the Loan class in Listing 9.1.

LISTING 9.1 TestLoanClass.java

```
import java.util.Scanner;

public class TestLoanClass {
  /** Main method */
  public static void main(String[] args) {
    // Create a Scanner
    Scanner input = new Scanner(System.in);

    // Enter yearly interest rate
    System.out.print(
      "Enter yearly interest rate, for example, 8.25: ");
    double annualInterestRate = input.nextDouble();

    // Enter number of years
    System.out.print("Enter number of years as an integer: ");
    int numberOfYears = input.nextInt();

    // Enter loan amount
    System.out.print("Enter loan amount, for example, 120000.95: ");
```

```
20       double loanAmount =  input.nextDouble();
21
22       // Create Loan object
23       Loan loan =
24         new Loan(annualInterestRate, numberOfYears, loanAmount);
25
26       // Format to keep two digits after the decimal point
27       double monthlyPayment =
28         (int)(loan.getMonthlyPayment () * 100) / 100.0;
29       double totalPayment =
30         (int)(loan.getTotalPayment () * 100) / 100.0;
31
32       // Display results
33       System.out.println("The loan was created on " +
34         loan.getLoanDate().toString() + "\nThe monthly payment is " +
35         monthlyPayment + "\nThe total payment is " + totalPayment);
36     }
37   }
```

create Loan object

invoke instance method

invoke instance method

```
Enter yearly interest rate, for example, 8.25: 2.5 ↵Enter
Enter number of years as an integer: 5 ↵Enter
Enter loan amount, for example, 120000.95: 1000 ↵Enter
The loan was created on Sat Jun 10 21:12:50 EDT 2006
The monthly payment is 17.74
The total payment is 1064.84
```

The **main** method reads interest rate, payment period (in years), and loan amount; creates a **Loan** object; and then obtains the monthly payment (lines 27–28) and total payment (lines 29–30) using the instance methods in the **Loan** class.

The **Loan** class can be implemented as in Listing 9.2.

LISTING 9.2 Loan.java

```
public class Loan {
  private double annualInterestRate;
  private int numberOfYears;
  private double loanAmount;
  private java.util.Date loanDate;

  /** Default constructor */
  public Loan() {
    this(2.5, 1, 1000);
  }

  /** Construct a loan with specified annual interest rate,
      number of years and loan amount */
  public Loan(double annualInterestRate, int numberOfYears,
      double loanAmount) {
    this.annualInterestRate = annualInterestRate;
    this.numberOfYears = numberOfYears;
    this.loanAmount = loanAmount;
    loanDate = new java.util.Date();
  }

  /** Return annualInterestRate */
  public double getAnnualInterestRate() {
```

no-arg constructor

constructor

```
    return annualInterestRate;
  }

  /** Set a new annualInterestRate */
  public void setAnnualInterestRate(double annualInterestRate) {
    this.annualInterestRate = annualInterestRate;
  }

  /** Return numberOfYears */
  public int getNumberOfYears() {
    return numberOfYears;
  }

  /** Set a new numberOfYears */
  public void setNumberOfYears(int numberOfYears) {
    this.numberOfYears = numberOfYears;
  }

  /** Return loanAmount */
  public double getLoanAmount() {
    return loanAmount;
  }

  /** Set a newloanAmount */
  public void setLoanAmount(double loanAmount) {
    this.loanAmount = loanAmount;
  }

  /** Find monthly payment */
  public double getMonthlyPayment() {
    double monthlyInterestRate = annualInterestRate / 1200;
    double monthlyPayment = loanAmount * monthlyInterestRate / (1 -
      (Math.pow(1 / (1 + monthlyInterestRate), numberOfYears * 12)));
    return monthlyPayment;
  }

  /** Find total payment */
  public double getTotalPayment() {
    double totalPayment = getMonthlyPayment() * numberOfYears * 12;
    return totalPayment;
  }

  /** Return loan date */
  public java.util.Date getLoanDate() {
    return loanDate;
  }
}
```

From a class developer's perspective, a class is designed for use by many different customers. In order to be useful in a wide range of applications, a class should provide a variety of ways for customization through constructors, properties, and methods.

The Loan class contains two constructors, four get methods, three set methods, and the methods for finding monthly payment and total payment. You can construct a Loan object by using the no-arg constructor or the one with three parameters: annual interest rate, number of years, and loan amount. When a loan object is created, its date is stored in the loanDate field. The getLoanDate method returns the date. The three get methods, getAnnualInterest, getNumberOfYears, and getLoanAmount, return annual interest rate, payment years, and loan amount, respectively. All the data properties and methods in this class are tied to a specific instance of the Loan class. Therefore, they are instance variables or methods.

Important Pedagogical TIP

The UML diagram for the Loan class is shown in Figure 9.4. Students should begin by writing a test program that uses the Loan class even though they don't know how the Loan class is implemented. This has three benefits:

- It demonstrates that developing a class and using a class are two separate tasks.
- It enables you to skip the complex implementation of certain classes without interrupting the sequence of the book.
- It is easier to learn how to implement a class if you are familiar with the class through using it.

For all the examples from now on, you may first create an object from the class and try to use its methods and then turn your attention to its implementation.

9.6 Object-Oriented Thinking

Chapters 1–6 introduced fundamental programming techniques for problem solving using loops, methods, and arrays. The study of these techniques lays a solid foundation for object-oriented programming. Classes provide more flexibility and modularity for building reusable software. This section improves the solution for a problem introduced in Chapter 3 using the object-oriented approach. From the improvements, you will gain insight on the differences between the procedural programming and object-oriented programming and see the benefits of developing reusable code using objects and classes.

Listing 3.6, ComputeBMI.java, presented a program for computing body mass index. The program cannot be reused in other programs. To make the code reusable, define a static method to compute body mass index as follows:

```
public static double getBMI(double weight, double height)
```

This method is useful for computing body mass index for a specified weight and height. However, it has limitations. Suppose you need to associate the weight and height with a person's name and birth date. You may declare separate variables to store these values. But these values are not tightly coupled. The ideal way to couple them is to create an object that contains them. Since these values are tied to individual objects, they should be stored in instance data fields. You can declare a class named BMI, as shown in Figure 9.5.

Video Note
BMI class

The get methods for these data fields are provided in the class, but omitted in the UML diagram for brevity.

BMI	
-name: String	The name of the person.
-age: int	The age of the person.
-weight: double	The weight of the person in pounds.
-height: double	The height of the person in inches.
+BMI(name: String, age: int, weight: double, height: double)	Creates a BMI object with the specified name, age, weight, and height.
+BMI(name: String, weight: double, height: double)	Creates a BMI object with the specified name, weight, height, and a default age 20.
+getBMI(): double	Returns the BMI
+getStatus(): String	Returns the BMI status (e.g., normal, overweight, etc.)

Figure 9.5 The BMI class encapsulates BMI information.

Assume that the BMI class is available. Listing 9.3 gives a test program that uses this class.

Listing 9.3 UseBMIClass.java

create object
invoke instance method
create object
invoke instance method

```
1 public class UseBMIClass {
2   public static void main(String[] args) {
3     BMI bmi1 = new BMI("John Doe", 18, 145, 70);
4     System.out.println("The BMI for " + bmi1.getName() + " is "
5       + bmi1.getBMI() + " " + bmi1.getStatus());
6
7     BMI bmi2 = new BMI("Peter King", 215, 70);
8     System.out.println("The BMI for " + bmi2.getName() + " is "
9       + bmi2.getBMI() + " " + bmi2.getStatus());
10  }
11 }
```

```
The BMI for John Doe is 20.81 normal weight
The BMI for Peter King is 30.85 seriously overweight
```

Line 3 creates an object bmi1 for John Doe and line 7 creates an object bmi2 for Peter King. You can use the instance methods getName(), getBMI(), and getStatus() to return the BMI information in a BMI object.

The BMI class can be implemented as in Listing 9.4.

Listing 9.4 BMI.java

constructor
constructor
getBMI
getStatus

```
public class BMI {
  private String name;
  private int age;
  private double weight; // in pounds
  private double height; // in inches
  public final double KILOGRAMS_PER_POUND = 0.45359237;
  public final double METERS_PER_INCH = 0.0254;

  public BMI(String name, int age, double weight, double height) {
    this.name = name;
    this.age = age;
    this.weight = weight;
    this.height = height;
  }

  public BMI(String name, double weight, double height) {
    this(name, 20, weight, height);
  }

  public double getBMI() {
    double bmi = weight * KILOGRAMS_PER_POUND /
      ((height * METERS_PER_INCH) * (height * METERS_PER_INCH));
    return Math.round(bmi * 100) / 100.0;
  }

  public String getStatus() {
    double bmi = getBMI();
    if (bmi < 16)
```

```
      return "seriously underweight";
    else if (bmi < 18)
      return "underweight";
    else if (bmi < 24)
      return "normal weight";
    else if (bmi < 29)
      return "overweight";
    else if (bmi < 35)
      return "seriously overweight";
    else
      return "gravely overweight";
  }

  public String getName() {
    return name;
  }

  public int getAge() {
    return age;
  }

  public double getWeight() {
    return weight;
  }

  public double getHeight() {
    return height;
  }
}
```

The mathematic formula for computing the BMI using weight and height is given in §3.3.6. The instance method `getBMI()` returns the BMI. Since the weight and height are instance data fields in the object, the `getBMI()` method can use these properties to compute the BMI for the object.

The instance method `getStatus()` returns a string that interprets the BMI. The interpretation is also given in §3.3.6.

Procedural vs. Object-Oriented Paradigms

This example demonstrates the advantages of using the object-oriented paradigm over the procedural paradigm. The procedural paradigm focuses on designing methods. The object-oriented paradigm couples data and methods together into objects. Software design using the object-oriented paradigm focuses on objects and operations on objects. The object-oriented approach combines the power of the procedural paradigm with an added dimension that integrates data with operations into objects.

In procedural programming, data and operations on the data are separate, and this methodology requires sending data to methods. Object-oriented programming places data and the operations that pertain to them within a single entity called an *object*; this approach solves many of the problems inherent in procedural programming. The object-oriented programming approach organizes programs in a way that mirrors the real world, in which all objects are associated with both attributes and activities. Using objects improves software reusability and makes programs easier to develop and easier to maintain. Programming in Java involves thinking in terms of objects; a Java program can be viewed as a collection of cooperating objects.

9.7 Designing the **Course** Class

The philosophy of this book is *teaching by example and learning by doing*. To this extent, the book provides a wide variety of examples to demonstrate object-oriented programming. The following three sections offer additional examples on designing classes.

Suppose you need to process course information. Each course has a name and students who take the course. You should be able to add/drop a student to/from the course. You can use a class to model the courses, as shown in Figure 9.6.

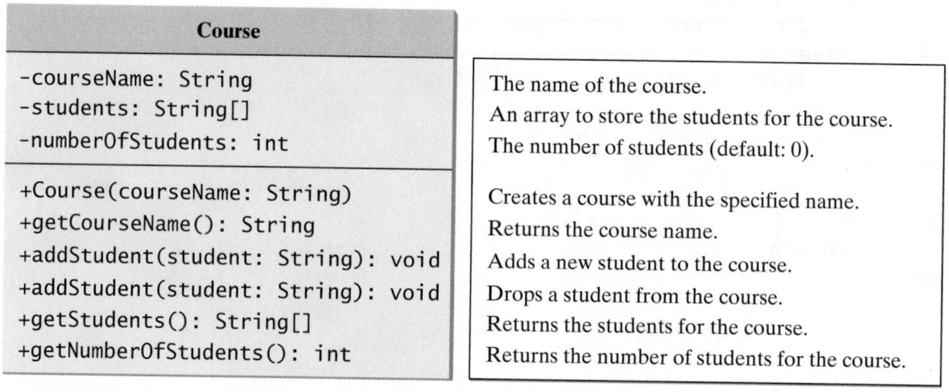

Course	
-courseName: String	The name of the course.
-students: String[]	An array to store the students for the course.
-numberOfStudents: int	The number of students (default: 0).
+Course(courseName: String)	Creates a course with the specified name.
+getCourseName(): String	Returns the course name.
+addStudent(student: String): void	Adds a new student to the course.
+addStudent(student: String): void	Drops a student from the course.
+getStudents(): String[]	Returns the students for the course.
+getNumberOfStudents(): int	Returns the number of students for the course.

FIGURE 9.6 The `Course` class models the courses.

A `Course` object can be created using the constructor `Course(String name)` by passing a course name. You can add students to the course using the `addStudent(String student)` method, drop a student from the course using the `dropStudent (String student)` method, and return all the students for the course using the `getStudents()` method. Suppose the class is available; Listing 9.5 gives a test class that creates two courses and adds students to them.

LISTING 9.5 TestCourse.java

create a course

add a student

number of students

return students

```
public class TestCourse {
  public static void main(String[] args) {
    Course course1 = new Course("Data Structures");
    Course course2 = new Course("Database Systems");

    course1.addStudent("Peter Jones");
    course1.addStudent("Brian Smith");
    course1.addStudent("Anne Kennedy");

    course2.addStudent("Peter Jones");
    course2.addStudent("Steve Smith");

    System.out.println("Number of students in course1: "
      + course1.getNumberOfStudents());
    String[] students = course1.getStudents();
    for (int i = 0; i < course1.getNumberOfStudents() ; i++)
      System.out.print(students[i] + ", ");

    System.out.println();
    System.out.print("Number of students in course2: "
      + course2.getNumberOfStudents());
  }
}
```

```
Number of students in course1: 3
Peter Jones, Brian Smith, Anne Kennedy,
Number of students in course2: 2
```

The Course class is implemented in Listing 9.6. It uses an array to store the students for the course. For simplicity, assume that the maximum course enrollment is 100. The array is created using new String[100] in line 3. The addStudent method (line 10) adds a student to the array. Whenever a new student is added to the course, numberOfStudents is increased (line 11). The getStudents method returns the array. The dropStudent method (line 27) is left as an exercise.

LISTING 9.6 Course.java

```
1 public class Course {
2   private String courseName;
3   private String[] students = new String[100];
4   private int numberOfStudents;
5
6   public Course(String courseName) {
7     this.courseName = courseName;
8   }
9
10  public void addStudent(String student) {
11    students[numberOfStudents] = student;
12    numberOfStudents++;
13  }
14
15  public String[] getStudents() {
16    return students;
17  }
18
19  public int getNumberOfStudents() {
20    return numberOfStudents;
21  }
22
23  public String getCourseName() {
24    return courseName;
25  }
26
27  public void dropStudent(String student) {
28    // Left as an exercise in Exercise 9.9
29  }
30 }
```

create students

add a course

return students

number of students

The array size is fixed to be 100 (line 3) in Listing 9.6. You can improve it to automatically increase the array size in Exercise 9.9.

When you create a Course object, an array object is created. A Course object contains a reference to the array. For simplicity, you can say that the Course object contains the array.

The user can create a Course and manipulate it through the public methods addStudent, dropStudent, getNumberOfStudents, and getStudents. However, the user doesn't need to know how these methods are implemented. The Course class encapsulates the internal implementation. This example uses an array to store students. You may use a different data structure to store students. The program that uses Course does not need to change as long as the contract of the public methods remains unchanged.

9.8 Designing a Class for Stacks

Recall that a stack is a data structure that holds objects in a last-in, first-out fashion, as shown in Figure 9.7.

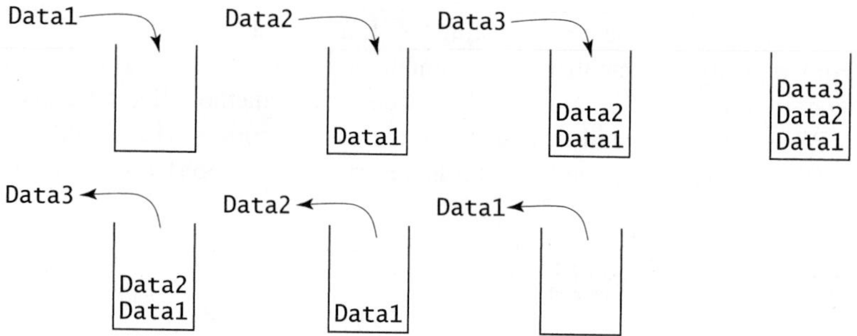

FIGURE 9.7 A stack holds objects in a last-in, first-out fashion.

stack

Stacks have many applications. For example, the compiler uses a stack to process method invocations. When a method is invoked, its parameters and local variables are pushed into a stack. When a method calls another method, the new method's parameters and local variables are pushed into the stack. When a method finishes its work and returns to its caller, its associated space is released from the stack.

You can define a class to model stacks. For simplicity, assume the stack holds the `int` values. So, name the stack class `StackOfIntegers`. The UML diagram for the class is shown in Figure 9.8.

StackOfIntegers	
-elements: int[]	An array to store integers in the stack.
-size: int	The number of integers in the stack.
+StackOfIntegers()	Constructs an empty stack with a default capacity of 16.
+StackOfIntegers(capacity: int)	Constructs an empty stack with a specified capacity.
+empty(): boolean	Returns true if the stack is empty.
+peek(): int	Returns the integer at the top of the stack without removing it from the stack.
+push(value: int): int	Stores an integer into the top of the stack.
+pop(): int	Removes the integer at the top of the stack and returns it.
+getSize(): int	Returns the number of elements in the stack.

FIGURE 9.8 The `StackOfIntegers` class encapsulates the stack storage and provides the operations for manipulating the stack.

Suppose that the class is available. Let us write a test program in Listing 9.7 that uses the class to create a stack (line 3), stores ten integers 0, 1, 2, . . . , and 9 (line 6), and displays them in reverse order (line 9).

LISTING 9.7 TestStackOfIntegers.java

create a stack

```
1 public class TestStackOfIntegers {
2   public static void main(String[] args) {
3     StackOfIntegers stack = new StackOfIntegers();
```

```

    for (int i = 0; i < 10; i++)
      stack.push(i);

    while (!stack.empty())
      System.out.print(stack.pop() + " ");
  }
}
```

push to stack

pop from stack

```
9 8 7 6 5 4 3 2 1 0
```

Video Note
StackOfInteger class

How do you implement the `StackOfIntegers` class? The elements in the stack are stored in an array named `elements`. When you create a stack, the array is also created. The no-arg constructor creates an array with the default capacity of `16`. The variable `size` counts the number of elements in the stack, and `size - 1` is the index of the element at the top of the stack, as shown in Figure 9.9. For an empty stack, `size` is `0`.

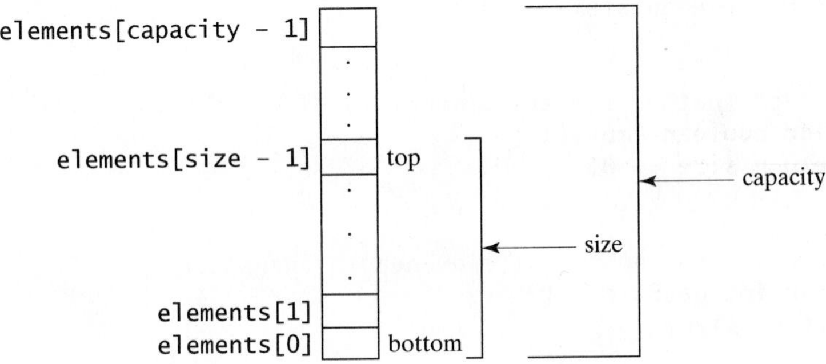

FIGURE 9.9 The `StackOfIntegers` class encapsulates the stack storage and provides the operations for manipulating the stack.

The `StackOfIntegers` class is implemented in Listing 9.8. The methods `empty()`, `peek()`, `pop()`, and `getSize()` are easy to implement. To implement `push(int value)`, assign `value` to `elements[size]` if `size < capacity` (line 24). If the stack is full (i.e., `size >= capacity`), create a new array of twice the current capacity (line 19), copy the contents of the current array to the new array (line 20), and assign the reference of the new array to the current array in the stack (line 21). Now you can add the new value to the array (line 24).

LISTING 9.8 StackOfIntegers.java

```
 1 public class StackOfIntegers {
 2   private int[] elements;
 3   private int size;
 4   public static final int DEFAULT_CAPACITY = 16;
 5
 6   /** Construct a stack with the default capacity 16 */
 7   public StackOfIntegers() {
 8     this(DEFAULT_CAPACITY);
 9   }
10
11   /** Construct a stack with the specified maximum capacity */
12   public StackOfIntegers(int capacity) {
```

max capacity 16

double the capacity

add to stack

```
    elements = new int[capacity];
  }

  /** Push a new integer into the top of the stack */
  public int push(int value) {
    if (size >= elements.length) {
      int[] temp = new int[elements.length * 2];
      System.arraycopy(elements, 0, temp, 0, elements.length);
      elements = temp;
    }

    return elements[size++] = value;
  }

  /** Return and remove the top element from the stack */
  public int pop() {
    return elements[-size];
  }

  /** Return the top element from the stack */
  public int peek() {
    return elements[size - 1];
  }

  /** Test whether the stack is empty */
  public boolean empty() {
    return size == 0;
  }

  /** Return the number of elements in the stack */
  public int getSize() {
    return size;
  }
}
```

9.9 Designing the **GuessDate** Class

Listing 3.8, GuessBirthDate.java, and Listing 6.14, GuessBirthDateUsingArray.java, presented two programs for guessing birth dates. Both programs use the same data developed with the procedural paradigm. The majority of code in these two programs is to define the five sets of data. You cannot reuse the code in these two programs. To make the code reusable, design a class to encapsulate the data, as defined in Figure 9.10.

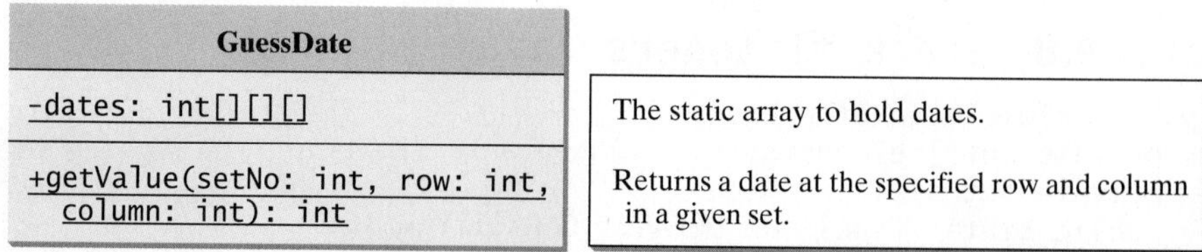

FIGURE 9.10 The `GuessDate` class defines data for guessing birth dates.

Note that `getValue` is defined as a static method because it is not dependent on a specific object of the `GuessDate` class. The `GuessDate` class encapsulates `dates` as a private member. The user of this class does not need to know how `dates` is implemented and does not even need to know the existence of the `dates` field in the class. All that the user needs to know is how to use this method to access dates. Suppose this class is available. As shown in Figure 3.4, there are five sets of dates. Invoking `getValue(setNo, row, column)` returns the date at the specified row and column in the given set. For example, `getValue(1, 0, 0)` returns `16`.

Assume that the `GuessDate` class is available. Listing 9.9 gives a test program that uses this class.

Listing 9.9 UseGuessDateClass.java

```
import java.util.Scanner;

public class UseGuessDateClass {
  public static void main(String[] args) {
    int date = 0; // Date to be determined
    int answer;

    // Create a Scanner
    Scanner input = new Scanner(System.in);

    for (int i = 0; i < 5; i++) {
      System.out.println("Is your birth date in Set" + (i + 1) + "?");
      for (int j = 0; j < 4; j++) {
        for (int k = 0; k < 4; k++)
          System.out.print(GuessDate.getValue(i, j, k) + "  ");
        System.out.println();
      }

      System.out.print("\nEnter 0 for No and 1 for Yes: ");
      answer = input.nextInt();

      if (answer == 1)
        date + = GuessDate.getValue(i, 0, 0);
    }

    System.out.println("Your birth date is " + date);
  }
}
```

invoke static method

invoke static method

```
Is your birth date in Set1?
1  3  5  7
9  11  13  15
17  19  21  23
25  27  29  31
Enter 0 for No and 1 for Yes: 0 ↵Enter

Is your birth date in Set2?
2  3  6  7
10  11  14  15
18  19  22  23
26  27  30  31
Enter 0 for No and 1 for Yes: 1 ↵Enter

Is your birth date in Set3?
4  5  6  7
12  13  14  15
20  21  22  23
28  29  30  31
Enter 0 for No and 1 for Yes: 0 ↵Enter
```

```
Is your birth date in Set4?
8  9  10  11
12  13  14  15
24  25  26  27
28  29  30  31
Enter 0 for No and 1 for Yes: 1 ↵Enter

Is your birth date in Set5?
16  17  18  19
20  21  22  23
24  25  26  27
28  29  30  31
Enter 0 for No and 1 for Yes: 1 ↵Enter

Your birth date is 26
```

Since `getValue` is a static method, you don't need to create an object in order to invoke it. `GuessDate.getValue(i, j, k)` (line 15) returns the date at row `i` and column `k` in Set `i`.

The `GuessDate` class can be implemented in Listing 9.10.

LISTING 9.10 GuessDate.java

static field

private constructor

static method

```
 1 public class GuessDate {
 2   private final static int[][][] dates = {
 3     {{ 1,  3,  5,  7},
 4      { 9, 11, 13, 15},
 5      {17, 19, 21, 23},
 6      {25, 27, 29, 31}},
 7     {{ 2,  3,  6,  7},
 8      {10, 11, 14, 15},
 9      {18, 19, 22, 23},
10      {26, 27, 30, 31}},
11     {{ 4,  5,  6,  7},
12      {12, 13, 14, 15},
13      {20, 21, 22, 23},
14      {28, 29, 30, 31}},
15     {{ 8,  9, 10, 11},
16      {12, 13, 14, 15},
17      {24, 25, 26, 27},
18      {28, 29, 30, 31}},
19     {{16, 17, 18, 19},
20      {20, 21, 22, 23},
21      {24, 25, 26, 27},
22      {28, 29, 30, 31}}};
23
24   /** Prevent the user from creating objects from GuessDate */
25   private GuessDate() {
26   }
27
28   /** Return a date at the specified row and column in a given set */
29   public static int getValue(int setNo, int k, int j) {
30     return dates[setNo][k][j];
31   }
32 }
```

This class uses a three-dimensional array to store dates (lines 2–22). You may use a different data structure (i.e., five two-dimensional arrays for representing five sets of numbers). The implementation of the `getValue` method will change, but the program that uses `GuessDate` does not need to change as long as the contract of the public method `getValue` remains unchanged. This shows the benefit of data encapsulation.

benefit of data encapsulation

The class defines a private no-arg constructor (line 25) to prevent the user from creating objects for this class. Since all methods are static in this class, there is no need to create objects from this class.

private constructor

Key Terms

immutable class 307
immutable object 307
stack 307
`this` keyword 305

Chapter Summary

- An immutable object cannot be modified once it is created. To prevent users from modifying an object, you may declare immutable classes.

- The scope of instance and static variables is the entire class, regardless of where the variables are declared. Instance and static variables can be declared anywhere in the class. For consistency, they are declared at the beginning of the class.

- The keyword `this` can be used to refer to the calling object. It can also be used inside a constructor to invoke another constructor of the same class.

- The procedural paradigm focuses on designing methods. The object-oriented paradigm couples data and methods together into objects. Software design using the object-oriented paradigm focuses on objects and operations on objects. The object-oriented approach combines the power of the procedural paradigm with an added dimension that integrates data with operations into objects.

Review Questions

Section 9.2 Immutable Objects and Classes

9.1 If a class contains only private data fields and no set methods, is the class immutable?

9.2 If all the data fields in a class are private and primitive type, and the class contains no `set` methods, is the class immutable?

9.3 Is the following class immutable?

```
class A {
  private int[] values;
  public int[] getValues() {
    return values;
  }
}
```

9.4 If you redefine the `Loan` class in the preceding chapter without `set` methods, is the class immutable?

Section 9.3 The Scope of Variables

9.5 What is the output of the following program?

```
public class Foo {
  static int i = 0;
  static int j = 0;

  public static void main(String[] args) {
    int i = 2;
    int k = 3;

    {
      int j = 3;
      System.out.println("i + j is " + i + j);
    }

    k = i + j;
    System.out.println("k is " + k);
    System.out.println("j is " + j);
  }
}
```

Section 9.4 The `this` Reference

9.6 Describe the role of the `this` keyword. What is wrong in the following code?

```
public class C {
  int p;

  public C() {
    System.out.println("C's no-arg constructor invoked");
    this(0);
  }

  public C(int p) {
    p = p;
  }

  public void setP(int p) {
    p = p;
  }
}
```

Programming Exercises

9.1* *(The `Time` class)* Design a class named `Time`. The class contains:

- Data fields `hour`, `minute`, and `second` that represent a time.
- A no-arg constructor that creates a `Time` object for the current time. (The data fields value will represent the current time.)
- A constructor that constructs a `Time` object with a specified elapsed time since midnight, Jan 1, 1970, in milliseconds. (The data fields value will represent this time.)
- Three `get` methods for the data fields `hour`, `minute`, and `second`, respectively.

Draw the UML diagram for the class. Implement the class. Write a test program that creates two `Time` objects (using `new Time()` and `new Time(555550000)`) and display their hour, minute, and second.

(*Hint*: The current time can be obtained using `System.currentTime()`, as shown in Listing 2.9, ShowCurrentTime.java. The other constructor sets the hour, minute, and second for the specified elapsed time. For example, if the elapsed time is `555550000` milliseconds, the hour is `10`, the minute is `19`, and the second is `10`.)

9.2 (*The* `BMI` *class*) Add the following new constructor in the `BMI` class:

```
/** Construct a BMI with the specified name, age, weight,
 * feet and inches
 */
public BMI(String name, int age, double weight, int feet,
  int inches)
```

9.3 (*The* `MyInteger` *class*) Design a class named `MyInteger`. The class contains:

- An `int` data field named `value` that stores the `int` value represented by this object.
- A constructor that creates a `MyInteger` object for the specified `int` value.
- A `get` method that return the `int` value.
- Methods `isEven()`, `isOdd()`, and `isPrime()` that return `true` if the value is even, odd, or prime, respectively.
- Static methods `isEven(int)`, `isOdd(int)`, and `isPrime(int)` that return `true` if the specified value is even, odd, or prime, respectively.
- Static methods `isEven(MyInteger)`, `isOdd(MyInteger)`, and `isPrime(MyInteger)` that return `true` if the specified value is even, odd, or prime, respectively.
- Methods `equals(int)` and `equals(MyInteger)` that return `true` if the value in the object is equal to the specified value.
- A static method `parseInt(char[])` that converts an array of numeric characters to an `int` value.

Draw the UML diagram for the class. Implement the class. Write a client program that tests all methods in the class.

9.4 (*The* `MyPoint` *class*) Design a class named `MyPoint` to represent a point with `x`- and `y`-coordinates. The class contains:

Video Note
Design and implement `MyPoint` class

- Two data fields `x` and `y` that represent the coordinates with get methods.
- A no-arg constructor that creates a point (`0`, `0`).
- A constructor that constructs a point with specified coordinates.
- Two `get` methods for data fields `x` and `y`, respectively.
- A method named `distance` that returns the distance from this point to another point of the `MyPoint` type.
- A method named `distance` that returns the distance from this point to another point with specified -`x` and `y`-coordinates.

Draw the UML diagram for the class. Implement the class. Write a test program that creates two points (`0`, `0`) and (`10`, `30.5`) and displays the distance between them.

9.5* (*Displaying the prime factors*) Write a program that receives a positive integer and displays all its smallest factors in decreasing order. For example, if the integer is `120`, the smallest factors are displayed as `5, 3, 2, 2, 2`. Use the `StackOfIntegers` class to store the factors (e.g., `2`, `2`, `2`, `3`, `5`) and retrieve and display them in reverse order.

9.6* (*Displaying the prime numbers*) Write a program that displays all the prime numbers less than `120` in decreasing order. Use the `StackOfIntegers` class to store the prime numbers (e.g., `2`, `3`, `5`, ...) and retrieve and display them in reverse order.

9.7** (*Game: ATM machine*) Use the `Account` class created in Exercise 7.3 to simulate an ATM machine. Create ten accounts in an array with id `0`, `1`, ..., `9`, and initial balance $100. The system prompts the user to enter an id. If the id is entered incorrectly, ask the user to enter a correct id. Once an id is accepted, the main menu is displayed as shown in the sample output. You can enter a choice 1 for viewing the current balance, 2 for withdrawing money, 3 for depositing money, and 4 for exiting the main menu. Once you exit, the system will prompt for an id again. So, once the system starts, it will not stop.

```
Enter an id: 4 ↵Enter

Main menu
1: check balance
2: withdraw
3: deposit
4: exit
Enter a choice: 1 ↵Enter
The balance is 100.0

Main menu
1: check balance
2: withdraw
3: deposit
4: exit
Enter a choice: 2 ↵Enter
Enter an amount to withdraw: 3 ↵Enter

Main menu
1: check balance
2: withdraw
3: deposit
4: exit
Enter a choice: 1 ↵Enter
The balance is 97.0

Main menu
1: check balance
2: withdraw
3: deposit
4: exit
Enter a choice: 3 ↵Enter
Enter an amount to deposit: 10 ↵Enter

Main menu
1: check balance
2: withdraw
3: deposit
4: exit
Enter a choice: 1 ↵Enter
The balance is 107.0

Main menu
1: check balance
2: withdraw
3: deposit
4: exit
Enter a choice: 4 ↵Enter

Enter an id:
```

9.8*** (*Financial: the* Tax *class*) Exercise 6.32 writes a program for computing taxes using arrays. Design a class named Tax to contain the following instance data fields:

- int filingStatus: One of the four tax filing statuses: 0—single filer, 1—married filing jointly, 2—married filing separately, and 3—head of household. Use the public static constants SINGLE_FILER (0), MARRIED_JOINTLY (1), MARRIED_SEPARATELY (2), HEAD_OF_HOUSEHOLD (3) to represent the status.
- int[][] brackets: Stores the tax brackets for each filing status.
- double[] rates: Stores tax rates for each bracket.
- double taxableIncome: Stores the taxable income.

Provide the get and set methods for each data field and the getTax() method that returns the tax. Also provide a no-arg constructor and the constructor Tax(filingStatus, brackets, rates, taxableIncome).

Draw the UML diagram for the class. Implement the class. Write a test program that uses the Tax class to print the 2001 and 2002 tax tables for taxable income from $50,000 to $60,000 with intervals of $1,000 for all four statuses. The tax rates for the year 2002 were given in Table 3.7. The tax rates for 2001 are shown in Table 9.1.

TABLE 9.1 2001 United States Federal Personal Tax Rates

Tax rate	*Single filers*	*Married filing jointly or qualifying widow(er)*	*Married filing separately*	*Head of household*
15%	Up to $27,050	Up to $45,200	Up to $22,600	Up to $36,250
27.5%	$27,051–$65,550	$45,201–$109,250	$22,601–$54,625	$36,251–$93,650
30.5%	$65,551–$136,750	$109,251–$166,500	$54,626–$83,250	$93,651–$151,650
35.5%	$136,751–$297,350	$166,501–$297,350	$83,251–$148,675	$151,651–$297,350
39.1%	$297,351 or more	$297,351 or more	$148,676 or more	$297,351 or more

9.9** (*The* Course *class*) Revise the Course class as follows:

- The array size is fixed in Listing 9.6. Improve it to automatically increase the array size by creating a new larger array and copying the contents of the current array to it.
- Implement the dropStudent method.
- Add a new method named clear() that removes all students from the course.

Write a test program that creates a course, adds three students, removes one, and displays the students in the course.

9.10* (*Game: The* GuessDate *class*) Modify the GuessDate class in Listing 9.10. Instead of representing dates in a three-dimensional array, use five two-dimensional arrays to represent the five sets of numbers. So you need to declare:

```
private static int[][] set1 = {{ 1,  3,  5,  7}, ... };
private static int[][] set2 = {{ 2,  3,  6,  7}, ... };
private static int[][] set3 = {{ 4,  5,  6,  7}, ... };
private static int[][] set4 = {{ 8,  9, 10, 11}, ... };
private static int[][] set5 = {{16, 17, 18, 19}, ... };
```

9.11* (*Geometry: The `Circle2D` class*) Define the `Circle2D` class that contains:

- Two `double` data fields named `x` and `y` that specify the center of the circle with `get` methods.
- A data field `radius` with a `get` method.
- A no-arg constructor that creates a default circle with (`0`, `0`) for (`x`, `y`) and `1` for `radius`.
- A constructor that creates a circle with the specified `x`, `y`, and `radius`.
- A method `getArea()` that returns the area of the circle.
- A method `getPerimeter()` that returns the perimeter of the circle.
- A method `contains(double x, double y)` that returns `true` if the specified point (`x`, `y`) is inside this circle. See Figure 9.11(a).
- A method `contains(Circle2D circle)` that returns `true` if the specified circle is inside this circle. See Figure 9.11(b).
- A method `overlaps(Circle2D circle)` that returns `true` if the specified circle overlaps with this circle. See Figure 9.11(c).

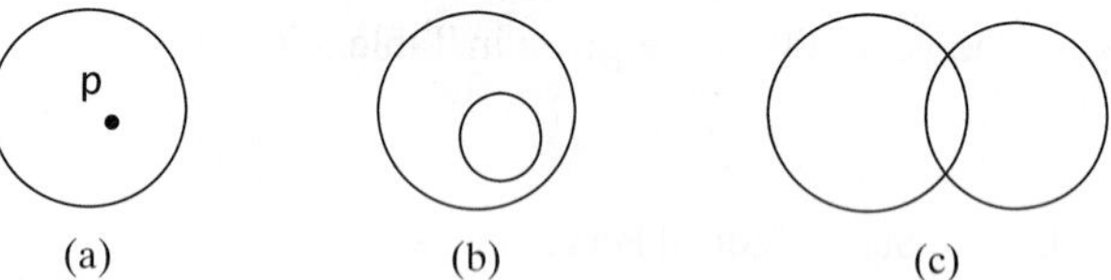

FIGURE 9.11 (a) A point is inside the circle. (b) A circle is inside another circle. (c) A circle overlaps another circle.

Draw the UML diagram for the class. Implement the class. Write a test program that creates a `Circle2D` object `c1` (`new Circle2D(2, 2, 5.5)`), displays its area and perimeter, and displays the result of `c1.contains(3, 3)`, `c1.contains(new Circle2D(4, 5, 10.5))`, and `c1.overlaps(new Circle2D(3, 5, 2.3))`.

9.12* (*Geometry: The `Rectangle2D` class*) Define the `Rectangle2D` class that contains:

- Two `double` data fields named `x` and `y` that specify the center of the rectangle with `get` and `set` methods. (Assume that the rectangle sides are parallel to `x`- or `y`- axes.)
- The data fields `width` and `height` with `get` and `set` methods.
- A no-arg constructor that creates a default rectangle with (`0`, `0`) for (`x`, `y`) and `1` for both `width` and `height`.
- A constructor that creates a rectangle with the specified `x`, `y`, and `radius`.
- A method `getArea()` that returns the area of the rectangle.
- A method `getPerimeter()` that returns the perimeter of the rectangle.
- A method `contains(double x, double y)` that returns `true` if the specified point (`x`, `y`) is inside this rectangle. See Figure 9.12(a).
- A method `contains(Rectangle2D r)` that returns `true` if the specified rectangle is inside this rectangle. See Figure 9.12(b).
- A method `overlaps(Rectangle2D r)` that returns `true` if the specified rectangle overlaps with this rectangle. See Figure 9.12(c).

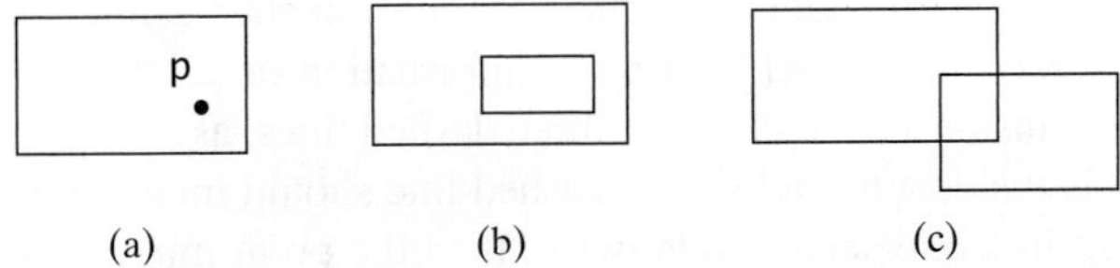

FIGURE 9.12 (a) A point is inside the rectangle. (b) A rectangle is inside another rectangle. (c) A rectangle overlaps another rectangle.

Draw the UML diagram for the class. Implement the class. Write a test program that creates a `Rectangle2D` objects `r1` (`new Rectangle2D(2, 2, 5.5, 4.9)`), displays its area and perimeter, and displays the result of `r1.contains(3, 3)`, `r1.contains(new Rectangle2D(4, 5, 10.5, 3.2))`, and `r1.overlaps(new Rectangle2D(3, 5, 2.3, 5.4))`.

9.13*** (*Geometry: The `Triangle2D` class*) Define the `Triangle2D` *class that contains:*

- Three points named `p1`, `p2`, and `p3` with the type `MyPoint` with `get` and `set` methods. `MyPoint` is defined in Exercise 9.4.
- A no-arg constructor that creates a default triangle with points (`0`, `0`), (`1`, `1`), and (`2`, `5`).
- A constructor that creates a triangle with the specified points.
- A method `getArea()` that returns the area of the triangle.
- A method `getPerimeter()` that returns the perimeter of the triangle.
- A method `contains(MyPoint p)` that returns `true` if the specified point `p` is inside this triangle. See Figure 9.13(a).
- A method `contains(Triangle2D t)` that returns `true` if the specified triangle is inside this triangle. See Figure 9.13(b).
- A method `overlaps(Triangle2D t)` that returns `true` if the specified triangle overlaps with this triangle. See Figure 9.13(c).

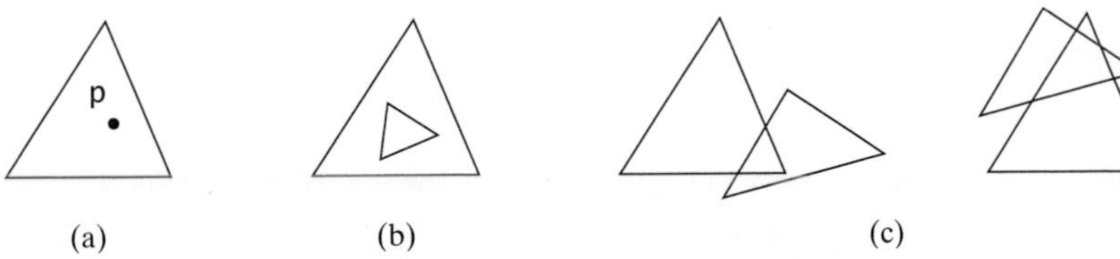

FIGURE 9.13 (a) A point is inside the triangle. (b) A triangle is inside another triangle. (c) A triangle overlaps another triangle.

Draw the UML diagram for the class. Implement the class. Write a test program that creates a `Triangle2D` objects `t1` (`new Triangle2D(new MyPoint(2.5, 2), new MyPoint(4.2, 3), MyPoint(5, 3.5))`), displays its area and perimeter, and displays the result of `t1.contains(3, 3)`, `r1.contains(new Triangle2D(new MyPoint(2.9, 2), new MyPoint(4, 1), MyPoint(1, 3.4)))`, and `t1.overlaps(new Triangle2D(new MyPoint(2, 5.5), new MyPoint(4, -3), MyPoint(2, 6.5)))`.

(*Hint*: For the formula to compute the area of a triangle, see Exercise 5.19. Use the `java.awt.geo.Line2D` class in the Java API to implement the `contains` and `overlaps` methods. The `Line2D` class contains the methods for checking whether two line segments intersect and whether a line contains a point, etc. Please see the Java API for more information on `Line2D`. To detect whether a point is inside a triangle, draw three dashed lines, as shown in Figure 9.14. If the point is inside a triangle, each dashed line should intersect a side only once. If a dashed line intersects a side twice, then the point must be outside the triangle.)

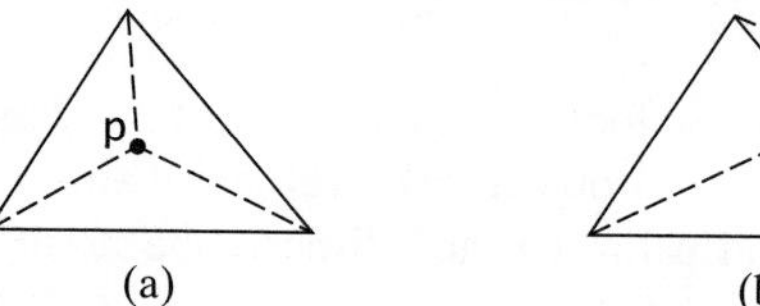

FIGURE 9.14 (a) A point is inside the triangle. (b) A point is outside the triangle.

CHAPTER 10

INHERITANCE AND POLYMORPHISM

Objectives

- To develop a subclass from a superclass through inheritance (§10.2).
- To illustrate inheritance by creating a custom frame that extends `JFrame` (§10.3).
- To invoke the superclass's constructors and methods using the `super` keyword (§10.4).
- To override instance methods in the subclass (§10.5).
- To distinguish differences between overriding and overloading (§10.6).
- To explore the methods `toString()` and `equals(Object)` in the `Object` class (§10.7).
- To discover polymorphism, dynamic binding, and generic programming (§10.8).
- To describe casting and explain why explicit downcasting is necessary (§10.9).
- To store, retrieve, and manipulate objects in an `ArrayList` (§10.10).
- To implement a `Stack` class using `ArrayList` (§10.11).
- To restrict access to data and methods to subclasses using the `protected` visibility modifier (§10.12).
- To prevent class extending and method overriding using the `final` modifier (§10.13).

10.1 Introduction

inheritance

Object-oriented programming allows you to derive new classes from existing classes. This is called *inheritance*. Inheritance is an important and powerful feature in Java for reusing software. In fact, every class you define in Java is inherited from an existing class, either explicitly or implicitly. The classes you created in the preceding chapters were all extended implicitly from the `java.lang.Object` class.

why inheritance?

Suppose you are to define classes to model circles, rectangles, and triangles. These classes have many common features. What is the best way to design these classes so to avoid redundancy? The answer is to use inheritance.

Recall that you create an instance of `JFrame` and add components into the frame in Listing 7.4 GUIComponents.java. Suppose you wish to display two identical frames with the same components in each, as shown in Figure 10.1. Do you have to write the same code repeatedly for creating two frames and adding the same type of components to each frame? There are several ways to solve this problem. An effective way is to use inheritance.

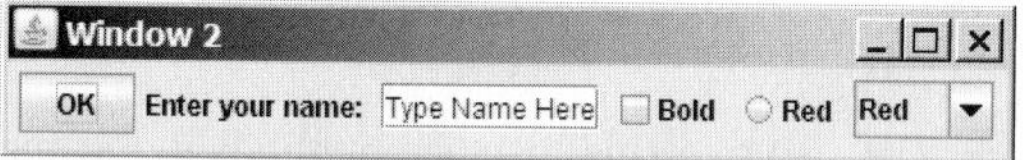

FIGURE 10.1 The program displays two windows with the same components.

This chapter introduces inheritance, which will enable you to solve these problems effectively.

10.2 Superclasses and Subclasses

subclass
superclass

In Java terminology, a class `C1` extended from another class `C2` is called a *subclass*, and `C2` is called a *superclass*. A superclass is also referred to as a *parent class*, or a *base class*, and a subclass as a *child class*, an *extended class*, or a *derived class*. A subclass inherits accessible data fields and methods from its superclass, and may also add new data fields and methods.

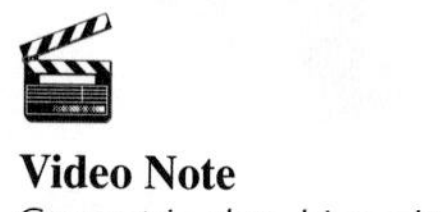

Video Note
Geometric class hierarchy

Consider geometric objects. Suppose you want to design the classes to model geometric objects such as circles and rectangles. Geometric objects have many common properties and behaviors. They can be drawn in a certain color, filled or unfilled. Thus a general class `GeometricObject` can be used to model all geometric objects. This class contains the properties `color` and `filled` and their appropriate get and set methods. Assume that this class also contains the `dateCreated` property and the `getDateCreated()` and `toString()` methods. The `toString()` method returns a string representation for the object. Since a circle is a special type of geometric object, it shares common properties and methods with other geometric objects. Thus it makes sense to define the `Circle` class that extends the `GeometricObject` class. Likewise, `Rectangle` can also be declared as a subclass of `GeometricObject`. Figure 10.2 shows the relationship among these classes. An arrow pointing to the superclass is used to denote the inheritance relationship between the two classes involved.

The `Circle` class inherits all accessible data fields and methods from the `GeometricObject` class. In addition, it has a new data field, `radius`, and its associated `get` and `set` methods. It also contains the `getArea()`, `getPerimeter()`, and `getDiameter()` methods for returning the area, perimeter, and diameter of the circle.

The `Rectangle` class inherits all accessible data fields and methods from the `GeometricObject` class. In addition, it has the data fields `width` and `height`, and the associated `get` and `set` methods. It also contains the `getArea()` and `getPerimeter()` methods for returning the area and perimeter of the rectangle.

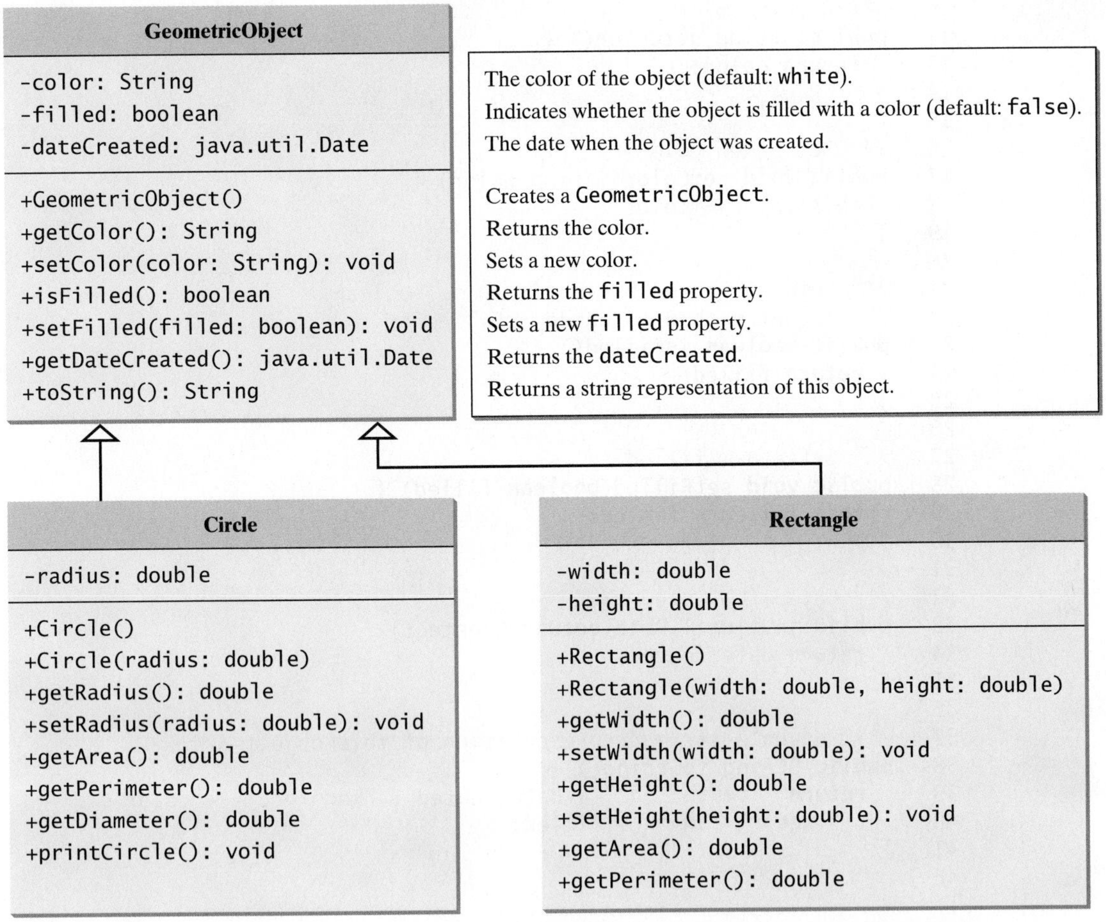

GeometricObject	
-color: String	The color of the object (default: white).
-filled: boolean	Indicates whether the object is filled with a color (default: false).
-dateCreated: java.util.Date	The date when the object was created.
+GeometricObject()	Creates a GeometricObject.
+getColor(): String	Returns the color.
+setColor(color: String): void	Sets a new color.
+isFilled(): boolean	Returns the filled property.
+setFilled(filled: boolean): void	Sets a new filled property.
+getDateCreated(): java.util.Date	Returns the dateCreated.
+toString(): String	Returns a string representation of this object.

Circle
-radius: double
+Circle()
+Circle(radius: double)
+getRadius(): double
+setRadius(radius: double): void
+getArea(): double
+getPerimeter(): double
+getDiameter(): double
+printCircle(): void

Rectangle
-width: double
-height: double
+Rectangle()
+Rectangle(width: double, height: double)
+getWidth(): double
+setWidth(width: double): void
+getHeight(): double
+setHeight(height: double): void
+getArea(): double
+getPerimeter(): double

FIGURE 10.2 The GeometricObject class is the superclass for Circle and Rectangle.

The GeometricObject, Circle, and Rectangle classes are shown in Listings 10.1, 10.2, and 10.3.

Note

avoid naming conflict

To avoid naming conflict with the improved GeometricObject, Circle, and Rectangle classes introduced in the next chapter, name these classes GeometricObject1, Circle4, and Rectangle1 in this chapter. For convenience, we will still refer to them in the text as GeometricObject, Circle, and Rectangle classes. The best way to avoid naming conflict would be to place these classes in a different package. However, for simplicity and consistency, all classes in this book are placed in the default package.

LISTING 10.1 GeometricObject1.java

data fields

constructor

date constructed

```
public class GeometricObject1 {
  private String color = "white";
  private boolean filled;
  private java.util.Date dateCreated;

  /** Construct a default geometric object */
  public GeometricObject1() {
    dateCreated = new java.util.Date();
  }

```

methods

```
  /** Return color */
  public String getColor() {
    return color;
  }

  /** Set a new color */
  public void setColor(String color) {
    this.color = color;
  }

  /** Return filled. Since filled is boolean,
     its get method is named isFilled */
  public boolean isFilled() {
    return filled;
  }

  /** Set a new filled */
  public void setFilled(boolean filled) {
    this.filled = filled;
  }

  /** Get dateCreated */
  public java.util.Date getDateCreated() {
    return dateCreated;
  }

  /** Return a string representation of this object */
  public String toString() {
    return "created on " + dateCreated + "\ncolor: " + color +
      " and filled: " + filled;
  }
}
```

LISTING 10.2 `Circle4.java`

data fields

```
public class Circle4 extends GeometricObject1 {
  private double radius;
```

constructor

```
  public Circle4() {
  }

  public Circle4(double radius) {
    this.radius = radius;
  }
```

methods

```
  /** Return radius */
  public double getRadius() {
    return radius;
  }

  /** Set a new radius */
  public void setRadius(double radius) {
    this.radius = radius;
  }

  /** Return area */
  public double getArea() {
    return radius * radius * Math.PI;
  }

```

```
  /** Return diameter */
  public double getDiameter() {
    return 2 * radius;
  }

  /** Return perimeter */
  public double getPerimeter() {
    return 2 * radius * Math.PI;
  }

  /* Print the circle info */
  public void printCircle() {
    System.out.println("The circle is created " + getDateCreated() +
      " and the radius is " + radius);
  }
}
```

LISTING 10.3 Rectangle1.java

```
public class Rectangle1 extends GeometricObject1 {
  private double width;
  private double height;

  public Rectangle1() {
  }

  public Rectangle1(double width, double height) {
    this.width = width;
    this.height = height;
  }

  /** Return width */
  public double getWidth() {
    return width;
  }

  /** Set a new width */
  public void setWidth(double width) {
    this.width = width;
  }

  /** Return height */
  public double getHeight() {
    return height;
  }

  /** Set a new height */
  public void setHeight(double height) {
    this.height = height;
  }

  /** Return area */
  public double getArea() {
    return width * height;
  }

  /** Return perimeter */
  public double getPerimeter() {
    return 2 * (width + height);
  }
}
```

data fields

constructor

methods

The `Circle` class extends the `GeometricObject` class. The reserved word `extends` (line 1) tells the compiler that the `Circle` class extends the `GeometricObject` class, thus inheriting the methods `getColor`, `setColor`, `isFilled`, `setFilled`, and `toString`.

The following code in Listing 10.4 creates objects of `Circle` and `Rectangle` and invokes the methods on these objects.

LISTING 10.4 TestCircleRectangle.java

Circle object
invoke **toString**

Rectangle object
invoke **toString**

```
public class TestCircleRectangle {
  public static void main(String[] args) {
    Circle4 circle = new Circle4(1);
    System.out.println("A circle " + circle.toString());
    System.out.println("The radius is " + circle.getRadius());
    System.out.println("The area is " + circle.getArea());
    System.out.println("The diameter is " + circle.getDiameter());

    Rectangle1 rectangle = new Rectangle1(2, 4);
    System.out.println("\nA rectangle " + rectangle.toString());
    System.out.println("The area is " + rectangle.getArea() );
    System.out.println("The perimeter is " +
      rectangle.getPerimeter());
  }
}
```

```
A circle created on Fri Dec 22 10:07:02 CST 2006
color: white and filled: false
The radius is 1.0
The area is 3.141592653589793
The diameter is 2.0

A rectangle created on Fri Dec 22 10:07:02 CST 2006
color: white and filled: false
The area is 8.0
The perimeter is 12.0
```

The following points regarding inheritance are worthwhile to note:

more in subclass

- Contrary to the conventional interpretation, a subclass is not a subset of its superclass. In fact, a subclass usually contains more information and functions than its superclass.

nonextensible is-a

- Not all is-a relationships should be modeled using inheritance. For example, a square is a rectangle, but you should not declare a `Square` class to extend a `Rectangle` class, because there is nothing to extend (or supplement) from a rectangle to a square. Rather you should declare a `Square` class to extend the `GeometricObject` class. For class `A` to extend class `B`, `A` should contain more detailed information than `B`.

no blind extension

- Inheritance is used to model the *is-a* relationship. Do not blindly extend a class just for the sake of reusing methods. For example, it makes no sense for a `Tree` class to extend a `Person` class, even though they share common properties such as height and weight, etc. A subclass and its superclass must have the is-a relationship.

multiple inheritance

- Some programming languages allow you to derive a subclass from several classes. This capability is known as *multiple inheritance*. Java, however, does not allow multiple inheritance. A Java class may inherit directly from only one superclass.

This restriction is known as *single inheritance*. If you use the **extends** keyword to define a subclass, it allows only one parent class. Nevertheless, multiple inheritance can be achieved through interfaces, which will be introduced in §11.4, "Interfaces."

single inheritance

10.3 Extending the **JFrame** Class

Video Note
Extend **JFrame**

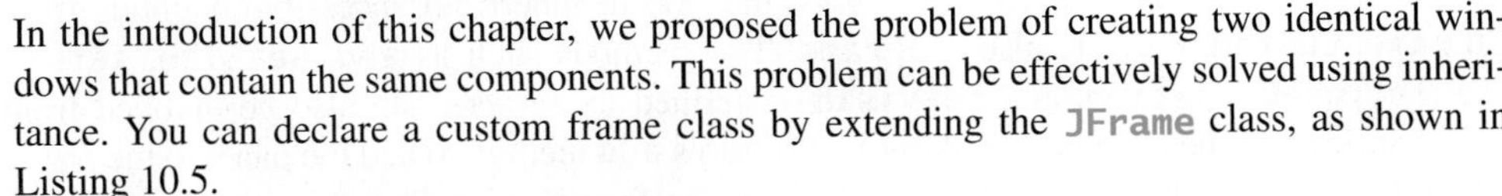

In the introduction of this chapter, we proposed the problem of creating two identical windows that contain the same components. This problem can be effectively solved using inheritance. You can declare a custom frame class by extending the JFrame class, as shown in Listing 10.5.

LISTING 10.5 UseCustomFrame.java

```
import javax.swing.*;

public class UseCustomFrame {
  public static void main(String[] args) {
    JFrame frame1 = new CustomFrame(); // Create a frame
    frame1.setTitle("Window 1"); // Set frame title
    frame1.setLocation(200, 100); // Set frame location
    frame1.setVisible(true); // Display frame

    JFrame frame2 = new CustomFrame(); // Create another frame
    frame2.setTitle("Window 2"); // Set frame title
    frame2.setLocation(200, 300); // Set frame location
    frame2.setVisible(true); // Display frame
  }
}

class CustomFrame extends JFrame {
  public CustomFrame() {
    // Create a button with text OK
    JButton jbtOK = new JButton("OK");

    // Create a label with text "Enter your name: "
    JLabel jlblName = new JLabel("Enter your name: ");

    // Create a text field with text "Type Name Here"
    JTextField jtfName = new JTextField("Type Name Here");

    // Create a check box with text bold
    JCheckBox jchkBold = new JCheckBox("Bold");

    // Create a radio button with text red
    JRadioButton jrbRed = new JRadioButton("Red");

    // Create a combo box with choices red, green, and blue
    JComboBox jcboColor = new JComboBox(new String[]{"Red",
      "Green", "Blue"});

    // Create a panel to group components
    JPanel panel = new JPanel();
    panel.add(jbtOK); // Add the button to the panel
    panel.add(jlblName); // Add the label to the panel
    panel.add(jtfName); // Add the text field to the panel
    panel.add(jchkBold); // Add the check box to the panel
    panel.add(jrbRed); // Add the radio button to the panel
    panel.add(jcboColor); // Add the combo box to the panel

```

create frame

create frame

custom frame class

frame constructor

```
47       add(panel); // Add the panel to the frame
48       setSize(450, 70); // Set frame's size
49       setDefaultCloseOperation(JFrame.EXIT_ON_CLOSE);
50     }
51 }
```

The CustomFrame class extends JFrame (line 17) to inherit all accessible methods from JFrame. CustomFrame is also a JFrame. The methods such as add, setSize, setDefaultCloseOperation, and setVisible defined in JFrame can also be invoked from CustomFrame. The program invokes the JFrame's add method to add the panel to the frame (line 47), invokes the setSize method to set the frame's size (line 48), and invokes the setDefaultCloseOperation method to terminate the program when the frame is closed (line 49).

In the main method, two instances frame1 and frame2 of CustomFrame are created by invoking new CustomFrame() (lines 5, 10). frame1 and frame2 are instances of CustomFrame and also instances of JFrame. frame1 can invoke all the accessible methods defined in JFrame. So frame1 can invoke setLocation(200, 100) to set the location for frame1 (line 7) and invoke setVisible(true) to display the frame (line 8).

10.4 Using the **super** Keyword

A subclass inherits accessible data fields and methods from its superclass. Does it inherit constructors? Can superclass constructors be invoked from subclasses? This section addresses these questions and their ramification.

§9.4, "The this Reference," introduced the use of the keyword this to reference the calling object. The keyword super refers to the superclass of the class in which super appears. It can be used in two ways:

- To call a superclass constructor.
- To call a superclass method.

10.4.1 Calling Superclass Constructors

The syntax to call a superclass constructor is:

```
super(), or super(parameters);
```

The statement super() invokes the no-arg constructor of its superclass, and the statement super(arguments) invokes the superclass constructor that matches the arguments. The statement super() or super(arguments) must appear in the first line of the subclass constructor; this is the only way to invoke a superclass constructor.

Caution

You must use the keyword super to call the superclass constructor, and the call must be the first statement in the constructor. Invoking a superclass constructor's name in a subclass causes a syntax error.

Note

A constructor is used to construct an instance of a class. Unlike properties and methods, the constructors of a superclass are not inherited in the subclass. They can only be invoked from the constructors of the subclasses, using the keyword super.

10.4.2 Constructor Chaining

A constructor may invoke an overloaded constructor or its superclass's constructor. If neither of them is invoked explicitly, the compiler puts `super()` as the first statement in the constructor. For example,

```
public A() {
}
```

Equivalent

```
public A() {
  super();
}
```

```
public A(double d) {
  // some statements
}
```

Equivalent

```
public A(double d) {
  super();
  // some statements
}
```

In any case, constructing an instance of a class invokes the constructors of all the superclasses along the inheritance chain. A superclass's constructor is called before the subclass's constructor. This is called *constructor chaining*. Consider the following code:

constructor chaining

```
1 public class Faculty extends Employee {
2   public static void main(String[] args) {
3     new Faculty();
4   }
5
6   public Faculty() {
7     System.out.println("(4) Invoke Faculty's no-arg constructor");
8   }
9 }
10
11 class Employee extends Person {
12   public Employee() {
13     this("(2) Invoke Employee's overloaded constructor");
14     System.out.println("(3) Invoke Employee's no-arg constructor");
15   }
16
17   public Employee(String s) {
18     System.out.println(s);
19   }
20 }
21
22 class Person {
23   public Person() {
24     System.out.println("(1) Invoke Person's no-arg constructor");
25   }
26 }
```

invoke overloaded constructor

```
(1) Invoke Person's no-arg constructor
(2) Invoke Employee's overloaded constructor
(3) Invoke Employee's no-arg constructor
(4) Invoke Faculty's no-arg constructor
```

The program produces the preceding output. Why? Let us discuss the reason. In line 3, `new Faculty()` invokes `Faculty`'s no-arg constructor. Since `Faculty` is a subclass of `Employee`, `Employee`'s no-arg constructor is invoked before any statements in `Faculty`'s constructor are executed. `Employee`'s no-arg constructor invokes `Employee`'s second constructor (line 12). Since `Employee` is a subclass of `Person`, `Person`'s no-arg constructor is invoked before any statements in `Employee`'s second constructor are executed.

Caution

no-arg constructor

If a class is designed to be extended, it is better to provide a no-arg constructor to avoid programming errors. Consider the following code:

```
public class Apple extends Fruit {
}

class Fruit {
  public Fruit(String name) {
    System.out.println("Fruit's constructor is invoked");
  }
}
```

Since no constructor is explicitly defined in `Apple`, `Apple`'s default no-arg constructor is declared implicitly. Since `Apple` is a subclass of `Fruit`, `Apple`'s default constructor automatically invokes `Fruit`'s no-arg constructor. However, `Fruit` does not have a no-arg constructor because `Fruit` has an explicit constructor defined. Therefore, the program cannot be compiled.

Design Guide

no-arg constructor

It is better to provide a no-arg constructor (if desirable) for every class to make the class easy to extend and to avoid errors.

10.4.3 Calling Superclass Methods

The keyword `super` can also be used to reference a method other than the constructor in the superclass. The syntax is like this:

```
super.method(parameters);
```

You could rewrite the `printCircle()` method in the `Circle` class as follows:

```
public void printCircle() {
  System.out.println("The circle is created " +
    super.getDateCreated() + " and the radius is " + radius);
}
```

It is not necessary to put `super` before `getDateCreated()` in this case, however, because `getDateCreated` is a method in the `GeometricObject` class and is inherited by the `Circle` class. Nevertheless, in some cases, as shown in the next section, the keyword `super` is needed.

Caution

no multiple **supers**

You can use `super.p()` to invoke the method `p()` defined in the superclass. Suppose `A` extends `B`, and `B` extends `C`, and a method `p()` is defined in `C`. Can you invoke `super.super.p()` from `A`? The answer is no. It is illegal to have such a chain of `supers` in Java.

10.5 Overriding Methods

method overriding

A subclass inherits methods from a superclass. Sometimes it is necessary for the subclass to modify the implementation of a method defined in the superclass. This is referred to as *method overriding*.

The `toString` method in the `GeometricObject` class returns the string representation for a geometric object. This method can be overridden to return the string representation for a circle. To override it, add the following new method in Listing 10.2, Circle4.java:

```
public class Circle4 extends GeometricObject1 {
  // Other methods are omitted

```

```
4   /** Override the toString method defined in GeometricObject */
5   public String toString() {
6     return super.toString() + "\nradius is " + radius;
7   }
8 }
```

toString in superclass

The toString() method is defined in the GeometricObject class and modified in the Circle class. Both methods can be used in the Circle class. To invoke the toString method defined in the GeometricObject class from the Circle class, use super.toString() (line 6).

Can a subclass of Circle access the toString method defined in the GeometricObject class using a syntax such as super.super.toString()? No. This is a syntax error.

no super.super.methodName()

Several points are worth noting:

- Private data fields in a superclass are not accessible outside the class. Therefore, they cannot be used directly in a subclass. They can, however, be accessed/mutated through public accessor/mutator if defined in the superclass.

private data fields

- An instance method can be overridden only if it is accessible. Thus a private method cannot be overridden, because it is not accessible outside its own class. If a method defined in a subclass is private in its superclass, the two methods are completely unrelated.

override accessible instance method

- Like an instance method, a static method can be inherited. However, a static method cannot be overridden. If a static method defined in the superclass is redefined in a subclass, the method defined in the superclass is hidden. The hidden static methods can be invoked using the syntax SuperClassName.staticMethodName.

cannot override static method

10.6 Overriding vs. Overloading

You have learned about overloading methods in §5.7, "Overloading Methods." Overloading a method is a way to provide more than one method with the same name but with different signatures to distinguish them. To override a method, the method must be defined in the subclass using the same signature and same return type as in its superclass.

same signature
same return type

Let us use an example to show the differences between overriding and overloading. In (a), the method p(int i) in class A overrides the same method defined in class B. However, in (b), the method p(double i) in class A and the method p(int i) in class B are two overloaded methods. The method p(int i) in class B is inherited in A.

```
public class Test {
  public static void main(String[] args) {
    A a = new A();
    a.p(10);
  }
}

class B {
  public void p(int i) {
  }
}

class A extends B {
  // This method overrides the method in B
  public void p(int i) {
    System.out.println(i);
  }
}
```

(a)

```
public class Test {
  public static void main(String[] args) {
    A a = new A();
    a.p(10);
  }
}

class B {
  public void p(int i) {
  }
}

class A extends B {
  // This method overloads the method in B
  public void p(double i) {
    System.out.println(i);
  }
}
```

(b)

When you run the Test class in (a), a.p(10) invokes the p(int i) method defined in class A, so the program displays 10. When you run the Test class in (b), a.p(10) invokes the p(int i) method defined in class B, so nothing is printed.

10.7 The Object Class and Its Methods

Every class in Java is descended from the java.lang.Object class. If no inheritance is specified when a class is defined, the superclass of the class is Object by default. For example, the following two class declarations are the same:

```
public class Circle {
  ...
}
```

Equivalent

```
public class Circle extends Object {
  ...
}
```

Classes like String, StringBuffer, Loan, and GeometricObject are implicitly subclasses of Object (as are all the main classes you have seen in this book so far). It is important to be familiar with the methods provided by the Object class so that you can use them in your classes. Two methods in the Object class to be discussed here are toString and equals.

toString()

The signature of the toString() method is

```
public String toString()
```

string representation

Invoking toString() on an object returns a string that describes the object. By default, it returns a string consisting of a class name of which the object is an instance, an at sign (@), and the object's memory address in hexadecimal. For example, consider the following code for the Loan class defined in Listing 9.2:

```
Loan loan = new Loan();
System.out.println(loan.toString());
```

The code displays something like Loan@15037e5. This message is not very helpful or informative. Usually you should override the toString method so that it returns a descriptive string representation of the object. For example, the toString method in the GeometricObject class in Listing 10.1 was overridden as follows:

```
public String toString() {
  return "color: " + color + "and is filled: " + filled;
}
```

print object

Note

You can also pass an object to invoke System.out.println(object) or System.out.print(object). This is equivalent to invoking System.out.println(object.toString()) or System.out.print(object.toString()). So you could replace System.out.println(loan.toString()) with System.out.println(loan).

equals(Object)

The signature of the equals method is

```
public boolean equals(Object o)
```

This method tests whether two objects are equal. The syntax for invoking it is:

```
object1.equals(object2);
```

The default implementation of the `equals` method in the `Object` class is:

```
public boolean equals(Object obj) {
  return (this == obj);
}
```

This implementation checks whether two reference variables point to the same object using the == operator. You should override this method in your custom class to test whether two distinct objects have the same content.

You have already used the `equals` method to compare two strings in §9.2, "The `String` Class." The `equals` method in the `String` class is inherited from the `Object` class and is modified in the `String` class to test whether two strings are identical in content. You can override the `equals` method in the `Circle` class to compare whether two circles are equal based on their radius as follows:

```
public boolean equals(Object o) {
  if (o instanceof Circle) {
    return radius == ((Circle)o).radius;
  }
  else
    return false;
}
```

Note

== vs. equals

The == comparison operator is used for comparing two primitive data type values or for determining whether two objects have the same references. The `equals` method is intended to test whether two objects have the same contents, provided that the method is modified in the defining class of the objects. The == operator is stronger than the `equals` method, in that the == operator checks whether the two reference variables refer to the same object.

Caution

equals(Object)

Using the signature `equals(SomeClassName obj)` (e.g., `equals(Circle c)` to override the `equals` method in a subclass is a common mistake. You should use `equals(Object obj)`. See Review Question 10.12.

10.8 Polymorphism, Dynamic Binding, and Generic Programming

The three pillars of object-oriented programming are encapsulation, inheritance, and polymorphism. You have already learned the first two. This section introduces polymorphism.

subtype
supertype
declared type

Before getting into the detail, let us define two useful terms: subtype and supertype. A class defines a type. A type defined by a subclass is called a *subtype* and a type defined by its superclass is called a *supertype*. A variable must be declared a type. The type of a variable is called its *declared type*. A variable of a reference type can hold a `null` value or a reference to an object. An object is an instance of a class.

The inheritance relationship enables a subclass to inherit features from its superclass with additional new features. A subclass is a specialization of its superclass; every instance of a subclass is an instance of its superclass, but not vice versa. For example, every circle is an object, but not every object is a circle. Therefore, you can always pass an instance of a subclass to a parameter of its superclass type. Consider the code in Listing 10.6:

LISTING 10.6 `PolymorphismDemo.java`

```
public class PolymorphismDemo {
  public static void main(String[] args) {
```

polymorphic call

dynamic binding

override **toString()**

override **toString()**

```
 3     m(new GraduateStudent());
 4     m(new Student());
 5     m(new Person());
 6     m(new Object());
 7   }
 8
 9   public static void m(Object x) {
10     System.out.println(x.toString());
11   }
12 }
13
14 class GraduateStudent extends Student {
15 }
16
17 class Student extends Person {
18   public String toString() {
19     return "Student";
20   }
21 }
22
23 class Person extends Object {
24   public String toString() {
25     return "Person";
26   }
27 }
```

```
Student
Student
Person
java.lang.Object@130c19b
```

The program produces the preceding output. Why? Let us discuss the reason. Method **m** (line 9) takes a parameter of the **Object** type. You can invoke **m** with any object (e.g., **new GraduateStudent()**, **new Student()**, **new Person()**, and **new Object()**)in lines 3-6). An object of a subclass can be used wherever its superclass object is required. This is commonly known as *polymorphism* (from a Greek word meaning "many forms"). In simple terms, polymorphism means that a variable of supertype can refer to a subtype object.

polymorphism

When the method **m(Object x)** is executed, the argument **x**'s **toString** method is invoked. **x** may be an instance of **GraduateStudent**, **Student**, **Person**, or **Object**. Classes **GraduateStudent**, **Student**, **Person**, and **Object** have their own implementations of the **toString** method. Which implementation is used will be determined dynamically by the Java Virtual Machine at runtime. This capability is known as *dynamic binding*.

dynamic binding

Dynamic binding works as follows: Suppose an object **o** is an instance of classes C_1, C_2, ..., C_{n-1}, and C_n, where C_1 is a subclass of C_2, C_2 is a subclass of C_3, ..., and C_{n-1} is a subclass of C_n, as shown in Figure 10.3. That is, C_n is the most general class, and C_1 is the most specific class. In Java, C_n is the **Object** class. If **o** invokes a method **p**, the JVM searches the implementation for the method **p** in C_1, C_2, ..., C_{n-1}, and C_n, in this order, until it is found. Once

C_n ◁— C_{n-1} ◁— ..... ◁— C_2 ◁— C_1

java.lang.Object

If o is an instance of C_1, o is also an instance of C_2, C_3, ..., C_{n-1}, and C_n

FIGURE 10.3 The method to be invoked is dynamically bound at runtime.

an implementation is found, the search stops and the first-found implementation is invoked. For example, when m(new GraduateStudent()) is invoked in line 3, the toString method defined in the Student class is used.

Matching a method signature and binding a method implementation are two separate issues. The *declared type* of the reference variable decides which method to match at compile time. The compiler finds a matching method according to parameter type, number of parameters, and order of the parameters at compile time. A method may be implemented in several subclasses. The JVM dynamically binds the implementation of the method at runtime, decided by the *actual class* of the object referenced by the variable. matching vs. binding

Dynamic binding enables new classes to be loaded on the fly without recompilation. There is no need for developers to create, and for users to install, major new software versions. New features can be incorporated transparently as needed. For example, suppose you have placed the classes Test, GraduateStudent, Student, Person in four separate files. If you change GraduateStudent as follows: benefits of dynamic binding

```
class GraduateStudent extends Student {
  public String toString() {
    return "Graduate Student";
  }
}
```

you have a new version of GraduateStudent with a new toString method, but you don't have to recompile the classes Test, Student, and Person. When you run Test, the JVM dynamically binds the new toString method for the object of GraduateStudent when executing m(new GraduateStudent()).

Polymorphism allows methods to be used generically for a wide range of object arguments. This is known as *generic programming*. If a method's parameter type is a superclass (e.g., Object), you may pass to this method an object of any of the parameter's subclasses (e.g., Student or String). When an object (e.g., a Student object or a String object) is used in the method, the particular implementation of the method of the object invoked (e.g., toString) is determined dynamically. generic programming

10.9 Casting Objects and the instanceof Operator

You have already used the casting operator to convert variables of one primitive type to another. Casting can also be used to convert an object of one class type to another within an inheritance hierarchy. In the preceding section, the statement

```
m(new Student());
```

assigns the object new Student() to a parameter of the Object type. This statement is equivalent to

```
Object o = new Student(); // Implicit casting
m(o);
```

The statement Object o = new Student(), known as *implicit casting*, is legal because an instance of Student is automatically an instance of Object. implicit casting

Suppose you want to assign the object reference o to a variable of the Student type using the following statement:

```
Student b = o;
```

In this case a compilation error would occur. Why does the statement Object o = new Student() work when Student b = o doesn't? The reason is that a Student object is

explicit casting

always an instance of Object, but an Object is not necessarily an instance of Student. Even though you can see that o is really a Student object, the compiler is not clever enough to know it. To tell the compiler that o is a Student object, use an *explicit casting*. The syntax is similar to the one used for casting among primitive data types. Enclose the target object type in parentheses and place it before the object to be cast, as follows:

```
Student b = (Student)o; // Explicit casting
```

upcasting

downcasting

ClassCastException

instanceof

It is always possible to cast an instance of a subclass to a variable of a superclass (known as *upcasting*), because an instance of a subclass is *always* an instance of its superclass. When casting an instance of a superclass to a variable of its subclass (known as *downcasting*), explicit casting must be used to confirm your intention to the compiler with the (SubclassName) cast notation. For the casting to be successful, you must make sure that the object to be cast is an instance of the subclass. If the superclass object is not an instance of the subclass, a runtime *ClassCastException* occurs. For example, if an object is not an instance of Student, it cannot be cast into a variable of Student. It is a good practice, therefore, to ensure that the object is an instance of another object before attempting a casting. This can be accomplished by using the instanceof operator. Consider the following code:

```
Object myObject = new Circle();
... // Some lines of code
/** Perform casting if myObject is an instance of Circle */
if (myObject instanceof Circle) {
  System.out.println("The circle diameter is " +
    ((Circle)myObject).getDiameter());
  ...
}
```

You may be wondering why casting is necessary. Variable myObject is declared Object. The *declared type* decides which method to match at compile time. Using myObject.-getDiameter() would cause a compilation error, because the Object class does not have the getDiameter method. The compiler cannot find a match for myObject.getDiameter(). It is necessary to cast myObject into the Circle type to tell the compiler that myObject is also an instance of Circle.

Why not declare myObject as a Circle type in the first place? To enable generic programming, it is a good practice to declare a variable with a supertype, which can accept a value of any subtype.

Note

lowercase keywords

instanceof is a Java keyword. Every letter in a Java keyword is in lowercase.

Tip

casting analogy

To help understand casting, you may also consider the analogy of fruit, apple, and orange with the Fruit class as the superclass for Apple and Orange. An apple is a fruit, so you can always safely assign an instance of Apple to a variable for Fruit. However, a fruit is not necessarily an apple, so you have to use explicit casting to assign an instance of Fruit to a variable of Apple.

Listing 10.7 demonstrates polymorphism and casting. The program creates two objects (lines 5-6), a circle and a rectangle, and invokes the displayObject method to display them (lines 9-10). The displayObject method displays the area and diameter if the object is a circle (line 15), and the area if the object is a rectangle (line 21).

LISTING 10.7 TestPolymorphismCasting.java

```
1 public class TestPolymorphismCasting {
2   /** Main method */
```

```
3    public static void main(String[] args) {
4      // Declare and initialize two objects
5      Object object1 = new Circle4(1);
6      Object object2 = new Rectangle1(1, 1);
7
8      // Display circle and rectangle
9      displayObject(object1);
10     displayObject(object2);
11   }
12
13   /** A method for displaying an object */
14   public static void displayObject(Object object) {
15     if (object instanceof Circle4) {
16       System.out.println("The circle area is " +
17         ((Circle4)object).getArea());
18       System.out.println("The circle diameter is " +
19         ((Circle4)object).getDiameter());
20     }
21     else if (object instanceof Rectangle1) {
22       System.out.println("The rectangle area is " +
23         ((Rectangle1)object).getArea());
24     }
25   }
26 }
```

polymorphic call

polymorphic call

```
The circle area is 3.141592653589793
The circle diameter is 2.0
The rectangle area is 1.0
```

The `displayObject(Object object)` method is an example of generic programming. It can be invoked by passing any instance of `Object`.

The program uses implicit casting to assign a `Circle` object to `object1` and a `Rectangle` object to `object2` (lines 5–6), and then invokes the `displayObject` method to display the information on these objects (lines 9–10).

In the `displayObject` method (lines 14–25), explicit casting is used to cast the object to `Circle` if the object is an instance of `Circle`, and the methods `getArea` and `getDiameter` are used to display the area and diameter of the circle.

Casting can be done only when the source object is an instance of the target class. The program uses the `instanceof` operator to ensure that the source object is an instance of the target class before performing a casting (line 15).

Explicit casting to `Circle` (lines 17, 19) and to `Rectangle` (line 23) is necessary because the `getArea` and `getDiameter` methods are not available in the `Object` class.

Caution

The object member access operator (`.`) precedes the casting operator. Use parentheses to ensure that casting is done before the `.` operator, as in

```
((Circle)object).getArea());
```

. precedes casting

10.10 The `ArrayList` Class

Video Note
`ArrayList` class

You can create an array to store objects. But, once the array is created, the array's size is fixed. Java provides the `ArrayList` class that can be used to store an unlimited number of objects. Figure 10.4 shows some methods in `ArrayList`.

java.util.ArrayList	
+ArrayList()	Creates an empty list.
+add(o: Object): void	Appends a new element o at the end of this list.
+add(index: int, o: Object): void	Adds a new element o at the specified index in this list.
+clear(): void	Removes all the elements from this list.
+contains(o: Object): boolean	Returns true if this list contains the element o.
+get(index: int): Object	Returns the element from this list at the specified index.
+indexOf(o: Object): int	Returns the index of the first matching element in this list.
+isEmpty(): boolean	Returns true if this list contains no elements.
+lastIndexOf(o: Object): int	Returns the index of the last matching element in this list.
+remove(o: Object): boolean	Removes the element o from this list.
+size(): int	Returns the number of elements in this list.
+remove(index: int): boolean	Removes the element at the specified index.
+set(index: int, o: Object): Object	Sets the element at the specified index.

FIGURE 10.4 An `ArrayList` stores an unlimited number of objects.

Listing 10.8 is an example of using `ArrayList`. The program creates an `ArrayList` using its no-arg constructor (line 4). The `add` method adds any instance of `Object` into the list. Since `String` is a subclass of `Object`, strings can be added to the list. The `add` method (lines 7-17) adds an object to the end of list. So, after `cityList.add("London")` (line 7), the list contains

```
[London]
```

add(Object)

After `cityList.add("New York")` (line 9), the list contains

```
[London, New York]
```

After adding Paris, Toronto, Hong Kong, and Singapore (lines 11-17), the list would contain

```
[London, New York, Paris, Toronto, Hong Kong, Singapore]
```

size()

Invoking `size()` (line 21) returns the size of the list, which is currently `6`. Invoking `contains("Toronto")` (line 23) checks whether the object is in the list. In this case, it returns `true`, since Toronto is in the list. Invoking `indexOf("New York")` (line 25) returns the index of the object in the list, which is `1`. If the object is not in the list, it returns `-1`. The `isEmpty()` method (line 27) checks whether the list is empty. It returns `false`, since the list is not empty.

add(index, Object)

The statement `cityList.add(2, "Beijing")` (line 30) inserts an object to the list at the specified index. After this statement, the list becomes

```
[London, New York, Beijing, Paris, Toronto, Hong Kong, Singapore]
```

remove(Object)

The statement `cityList.remove("Toronto")` (line 35) removes the object from the list. After this statement, the list becomes

```
[London, New York, Beijing, Paris, Hong Kong, Singapore]
```

remove(index)

The statement `cityList.remove(1)` (line 40) removes the object at the specified index from the list. After this statement, the list becomes

```
[London, Beijing, Paris, Hong Kong, Singapore]
```

The statement in line 44 is same as

```
System.out.println(cityList);
```

The `toString()` method returns a string representation for the list in the form of `[e0.toString(), e1.toString(), ..., ek.toString()]`, where `e0`, `e1`, ..., and `ek` are the elements in the list.

toString()

The `get(index)` method (line 48) returns the object at the specified index.

getIndex()

Listing 10.8 TestArrayList.java

```
1 public class TestArrayList {
2   public static void main(String[] args) {
3     // Create a list to store cities
4     java.util.ArrayList cityList = new java.util.ArrayList();
5
6     // Add some cities in the list
7     cityList.add("London");
8     // cityList now contains [London]
9     cityList.add("New York");
10    // cityList now contains [London, New York]
11    cityList.add("Paris");
12    // cityList now contains [London, New York, Paris]
13    cityList.add("Toronto");
14    // cityList now contains [London, New York, Paris, Toronto]
15    cityList.add("Hong Kong");
16    // contains [London, New York, Paris, Toronto, Hong Kong]
17    cityList.add("Singapore");
18    // contains [London, New York, Paris, Toronto,
19    //           Hong Kong, Singapore]
20
21    System.out.println("List size? " + cityList.size());
22    System.out.println("Is Toronto in the list? " +
23      cityList.contains("Toronto"));
24    System.out.println("The location of New York in the list? "
25      + cityList.indexOf("New York"));
26    System.out.println("Is the list empty? " +
27      cityList.isEmpty()); // Print false
28
29    // Insert a new city at index 2
30    cityList.add(2, "Beijing");
31    // contains [London, New York, Beijing, Paris, Toronto,
32    //           Hong Kong, Singapore]
33
34    // Remove a city from the list
35    cityList.remove("Toronto");
36    // contains [London, New York, Beijing, Paris,
37    //           Hong Kong, Singapore]
38
39    // Remove a city at index 1
40    cityList.remove(1);
41    // contains [London, Beijing, Paris, Hong Kong, Singapore]
42
43    // Display the contents in the list
44    System.out.println(cityList.toString());
45
46    // Display the contents in the list in reverse order
47    for (int i = cityList.size() - 1; i> = 0; i--)
48      System.out.print(cityList.get(i) + " ");
49    System.out.println();
```

create **ArrayList** (line 4)
add element (line 7)
list size (line 21)
contains element? (line 23)
element index (line 25)
is empty? (line 27)
remove element (line 35)
remove element (line 40)
toString() (line 44)
get element (line 48)

create **ArrayList**

```
    // Create a list to store two circles
    java.util.ArrayList list = new java.util.ArrayList();

    // Add two circles
    list.add(new Circle4(2));
    list.add(new Circle4(3));

    // Display the area of the first circle in the list
    System.out.println("The area of the circle? " +
      ((Circle4)list.get(0)).getArea());
  }
}
```

```
List size? 6
Is Toronto in the list? True
The location of New York in the list? 1
Is the list empty? false
[London, Beijing, Paris, Hong Kong, Singapore]
Singapore Hong Kong Paris Beijing London
The area of the circle? 12.566370614359172
```

compiler warning

Note

You will get the following warning when compiling this program from the command prompt:

```
Note: TestArrayList.java uses unchecked or unsafe operations.
Note: Recompile with -Xlint:unchecked for details.
```

This warning can be eliminated using generic types discussed in Chapter 21, "Generics." For now, ignore it. Despite the warning, the program will be compiled just fine to produce a .class file.

array vs. **ArrayList**

`ArrayList` objects can be used like arrays, but there are many differences. Table 10.1 lists their similarities and differences.

TABLE 10.1 Differences and Similarities between Arrays and `ArrayList`

Operation	*Array*	*ArrayList*
Creating an array/ArrayList	`Object[] a = new Object[10]`	`ArrayList list = new ArrayList();`
Accessing an element	`a[index]`	`list.get(index);`
Updating an element	`a[index] = "London";`	`list.set(index, "London");`
Returning size	`a.length`	`list.size();`
Adding a new element		`list.add("London");`
Inserting a new element		`list.add(index, "London");`
Removing an element		`list.remove(index);`
Removing an element		`list.remove(Object);`
Removing all elements		`list.clear();`

Once an array is created, its size is fixed. You can access an array element using the square bracket notation (e.g., `a[index]`). When an `ArrayList` is created, its size is `0`. You cannot use the `get` and `set` methods if the element is not in the list. It is easy to add, insert, and remove elements in a list, but it is rather complex to add, insert, and remove elements in an array. You have to write the code to manipulate the array in order to perform these operations.

Note

Vector class

`java.util.Vector` is also a class for storing objects, which is very similar to the `ArrayList` class. All the methods in `ArrayList` are also available in `Vector`. The `Vector` class was introduced in JDK 1.1. The `ArrayList` class introduced in JDK 1.2 was intended to replace the `Vector` class.

10.11 A Custom Stack Class

"Designing a Class for Stacks" in §9.8 presented a stack class for storing `int` values. This section introduces a stack class to store objects. You can use an `ArrayList` to implement `Stack`, as shown in Listing 10.9. The UML diagram for the class is shown in Figure 10.5.

MyStack	
-list: ArrayList	A list to store elements.
+isEmpty(): boolean	Returns true if this stack is empty.
+getSize(): int	Returns the number of elements in this stack.
+peek(): Object	Returns the top element in this stack.
+pop(): Object	Returns and removes the top element in this stack.
+push(o: Object): Object	Adds a new element to the top of this stack.
+search(o: Object): int	Returns the position of the first element in the stack from the top that matches the specified element.

FIGURE 10.5 The `MyStack` class encapsulates the stack storage and provides the operations for manipulating the stack.

LISTING 10.9 MyStack.java

```
public class MyStack {
  private java.util.ArrayList list = new java.util.ArrayList();

  public boolean isEmpty() {
    return list.isEmpty();
  }

  public int getSize() {
    return list.size();
  }

  public Object peek() {
    return list.get(getSize() - 1);
  }

  public Object pop() {
    Object o = list.get(getSize() - 1);
    list.remove(getSize() - 1);
    return o;
  }

  public Object push(Object o) {
    list.add(o);
    return o;
  }

```

array list

stack empty?

get stack size

peek stack

remove

add

search

```
27   public int search(Object o) {
28     return list.lastIndexOf(o);
29   }
30
31   /** Override the toString in the Object class */
32   public String toString() {
33     return "stack: " + list.toString();
34   }
35 }
```

An array list is created to store the elements in the stack (line 2). The `isEmpty()` method (lines 4-6) is the same as `list.isEmpty()`. The `getSize()` method (lines 8-10) is the same as `list.size()`. The `peek()` method (lines 12-14) looks at the element at the top of the stack without removing it. The end of the list is the top of the stack. The `pop()` method (lines 16-20) removes the top element from the stack and returns it. The `push(Object element)` method (lines 22-25) adds the specified element to the stack. The `search(Object element)` method checks whether the specified element is in the stack, and returns the index of first-matching element in the stack from the top by invoking `list.lastIndexOf(o)`. The `toString()` method (lines 32-34) defined in the `Object` class is overridden to display the contents of the stack by invoking `list.toString()`. The `toString()` method implemented in `ArrayList` returns a string representation of all the elements in an array list.

Design Guide

composition
has-a
is-a

In Listing 10.9, `MyStack` contains `ArrayList`. The relationship between `MyStack` and `ArrayList` is called *composition*. While inheritance models an is-a relationship, composition models a has-a relationship. You may also implement `MyStack` as a subclass of `ArrayList` (see Exercise 10.4). Using composition is better, however, because it enables you to declare a completely new stack class without inheriting the unnecessary and inappropriate methods from `ArrayList`.

10.12 The **protected** Data and Methods

The modifier `protected` can be applied to data and methods in a class. A protected datum or a protected method in a public class can be accessed *by any class in the same package or its subclasses*, even if the subclasses are in different packages.

The modifiers `private`, `protected`, and `public` are known as *visibility* or *accessibility modifiers* because they specify how class and class members are accessed. The visibility of these modifiers increases in this order:

Visibility increases →
private, none (if no modifier is used), protected, public

Table 10.2 summarizes the accessibility of the members in a class. Figure 10.6 illustrates how a public, protected, default, and private datum or method in class `C1` can be accessed from a class `C2` in the same package, from a subclass `C3` in the same package, from a subclass `C4` in a different package, and from a class `C5` in a different package.

TABLE 10.2 Data and Methods Visibility

Modifier on members in a class	*Accessed from the same class*	*Accessed from the same package*	*Accessed from a subclass*	*Accessed from a different package*
Public	✓	✓	✓	✓
Protected	✓	✓	✓	–
(default)	✓	✓	–	–
private	✓	–	–	–

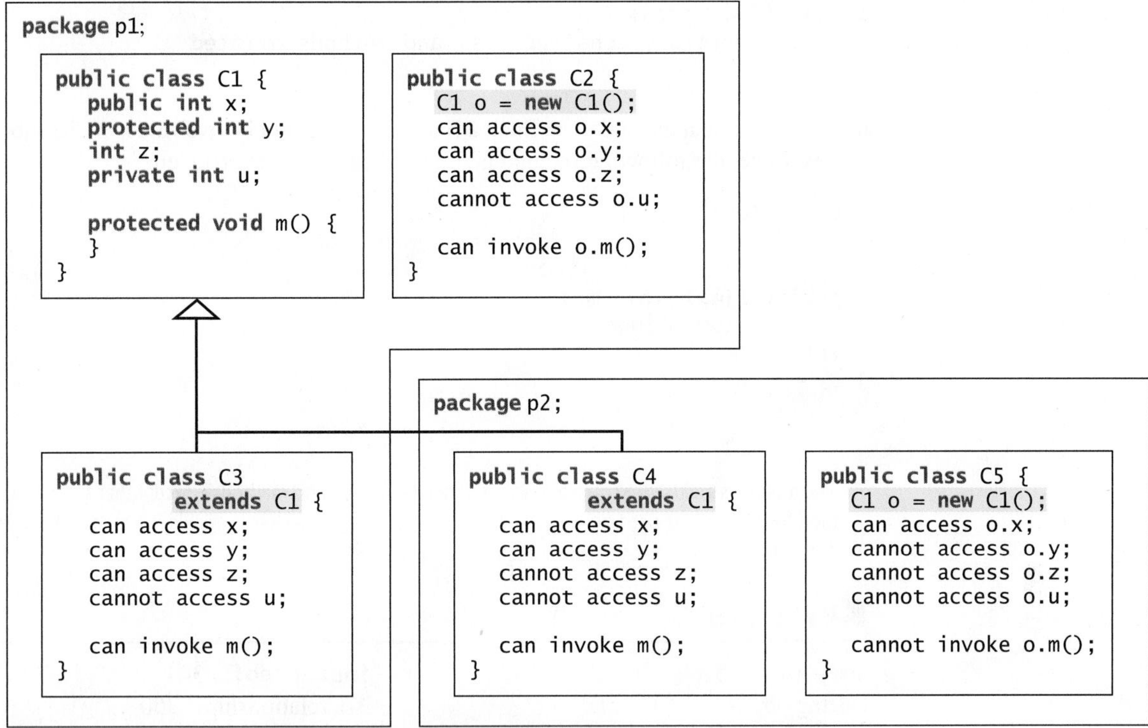

FIGURE 10.6 Visibility modifiers are used to control how data and methods are accessed.

Use the `private` modifier to hide the members of the class completely so that they cannot be accessed directly from outside the class. Use no modifiers in order to allow the members of the class to be accessed directly from any class within the same package but not from other packages. Use the `protected` modifier to enable the members of the class to be accessed by the subclasses in any package or classes in the same package. Use the `public` modifier to enable the members of the class to be accessed by any class.

Your class can be used in two ways: for creating instances of the class, and for creating subclasses by extending the class. Make the members `private` if they are not intended for use from outside the class. Make the members `public` if they are intended for the users of the class. Make the fields or methods `protected` if they are intended for the extenders of the class but not the users of the class.

The `private` and `protected` modifiers can be used only for members of the class. The `public` modifier and the default modifier (i.e., no modifier) can be used on members of the class as well on the class. A class with no modifier (i.e., not a public class) is not accessible by classes from other packages.

Note

A subclass may override a protected method in its superclass and change its visibility to public. However, a subclass cannot weaken the accessibility of a method defined in the superclass. For example, if a method is defined as public in the superclass, it must be defined as public in the subclass.

change visibility

10.13 Preventing Extending and Overriding

You may occasionally want to prevent classes from being extended. In such cases, use the `final` modifier to indicate that a class is final and cannot be a parent class. The `Math` class, introduced in Chapter 5, "Methods," is a final class. The `String`, `StringBuilder`, and `StringBuffer` classes, introduced in Chapter 8, "Strings and Text I/O," are also final classes. For example, the following class is final and cannot be extended.

```
public final class C {
  // Data fields, constructors, and methods omitted
}
```

You also can define a method to be final; a final method cannot be overridden by its subclasses. For example, the following method is final and cannot be overridden.

```
public class Test {
  // Data fields, constructors, and methods omitted

  public final void m() {
    // Do something
  }
}
```

Note

The modifiers are used on classes and class members (data and methods), except that the `final` modifier can also be used on local variables in a method. A final local variable is a constant inside a method.

Key Terms

array list 345
casting objects 343
composition 350
constructor chaining 337
dynamic binding 342
`final` 351
generic programming 343
has-a relationship 350
inheritance 330
`instanceof` 344
is-a relationship 350
override 339
polymorphism 342
`protected` 350
subclass 330
subtype 341
superclass 330
supertype 341

Chapter Summary

- You can derive a new class from an existing class. This is known as *class inheritance*. The new class is called a *subclass*, *child class*, or *extended class*. The existing class is called a *superclass*, *parent class*, or *base class*.
- A constructor is used to construct an instance of a class. Unlike properties and methods, the constructors of a superclass are not inherited in the subclass. They can be invoked only from the constructors of the subclasses, using the keyword `super`.
- A constructor may invoke an overloaded constructor or its superclass's constructor. The call must be the first statement in the constructor. If none of them is invoked explicitly, the compiler puts `super()` as the first statement in the constructor.
- To override a method, the method must be defined in the subclass using the same signature as in its superclass.
- An instance method can be overridden only if it is accessible. Thus a private method cannot be overridden, because it is not accessible outside its own class. If a method defined in a subclass is private in its superclass, the two methods are completely unrelated.
- Like an instance method, a static method can be inherited. However, a static method cannot be overridden. If a static method defined in the superclass is redefined in a subclass, the method defined in the superclass is hidden.

- Every class in Java is descended from the `java.lang.Object` class. If no inheritance is specified when a class is defined, its superclass is `Object`.
- If a method's parameter type is a superclass (e.g., `Object`), you may pass an object to this method of any of the parameter's subclasses (e.g., `Circle` or `String`). When an object (e.g., a `Circle` object or a `String` object) is used in the method, the particular implementation of the method of the object that is invoked (e.g., `toString`) is determined dynamically.
- It is always possible to cast an instance of a subclass to a variable of a superclass, because an instance of a subclass is *always* an instance of its superclass. When casting an instance of a superclass to a variable of its subclass, explicit casting must be used to confirm your intention to the compiler with the (`SubclassName`) cast notation.
- You can override an instance method, but you cannot override a field (instance or static) or a static method. If you declare a field or a static method in a subclass with the same name as one in the superclass, the one in the superclass is hidden, but it still exists. You can reference the hidden field or static method using the `super` keyword in the subclass. The hidden field or method can also be accessed via a reference variable of the superclass's type.
- When invoking an instance method from a reference variable, the *actual class of the object* referenced by the variable decides which implementation of the method is used *at runtime*. When accessing a field or a static method, the *declared type* of the reference variable decides which method is used *at compile time*.
- You can use `obj instanceof AClass` to check whether an object is an instance of a class.
- You can use the `protected` modifier to prevent the data and methods from being accessed by nonsubclasses from a different package.
- You can use the `final` modifier to indicate that a class is final and cannot be a parent class.

REVIEW QUESTIONS

Sections 10.2–10.6

10.1 What is the printout of running the class `C` in (a)? What problem arises in compiling the program in (b)?

```
class A {
  public A() {
    System.out.println(
      "A's no-arg constructor is invoked");
  }
}

class B extends A {
}

public class C {
  public static void main(String[] args) {
    B b = new B();
  }
}
```

(a)

```
class A {
  public A(int x) {
  }
}

class B extends A {
  public B() {
  }
}

public class C {
  public static void main(String[] args) {
    B b = new B();
  }
}
```

(b)

10.2 True or false?

1. A subclass is a subset of a superclass.
2. When invoking a constructor from a subclass, its superclass's no-arg constructor is always invoked.
3. You can override a private method defined in a superclass.
4. You can override a static method defined in a superclass.

10.3 Identify the problems in the following classes:

```
public class Circle {
  private double radius;

  public Circle(double radius) {
    radius = radius;
  }

  public double getRadius() {
    return radius;
  }

  public double getArea() {
    return radius * radius * Math.PI;
  }
}

class B extends Circle {
  private double length;

  B(double radius, double length) {
    Circle(radius);
    length = length;
  }

  /** Override getArea() */
  public double getArea() {
    return getArea() * length;
  }
}
```

10.4 How do you explicitly invoke a superclass's constructor from the subclass?

10.5 How do you invoke an overridden superclass method from the subclass?

10.6 Explain the difference between method overloading and method overriding.

10.7 If a method in a subclass has the same signature as a method in its superclass with the same return type, is the method overridden or overloaded?

10.8 If a method in a subclass has the same signature as a method in its superclass with a different return type, will this be a problem?

10.9 If a method in a subclass has the same name as a method in its superclass with different parameter types, is the method overridden or overloaded?

Section 10.7 The `Object` Class and Its Methods

10.10 Does every class have a `toString` method and an `equals` method? Where do they come from? How are they used? Is it appropriate to override these methods?

10.11 Show the output of following program:

```
public class Test {
  public static void main(String[] args) {
```

```
    A a = new A(3);
  }
}

class A extends B {
  public A(int t) {
    System.out.println("A's constructor is invoked");
  }
}

class B {
  public B() {
    System.out.println("B's constructor is invoked");
  }
}
```

Is the no-arg constructor of `Object` invoked when `new A(3)` is invoked?

10.12 When overriding the `equals` method, a common mistake is mistyping its signature in the subclass. For example, the `equals` method is incorrectly written as `equals(Circle circle)`, as shown in (a) in the following code; instead, it should be `equals(Object circle)`, as shown in (b). Show the output of running class `Test` with the `Circle` class in (a) and in (b), respectively.

```
public class Test {
  public static void main(String[] args) {
    Object circle1 = new Circle();
    Object circle2 = new Circle();
    System.out.println(circle1.equals(circle2));
  }
}
```

```
class Circle {
  double radius;

  public boolean equals(Circle circle) {
    return this.radius == circle.radius;

  }
}
```

(a)

```
class Circle {
  double radius;

  public boolean equals(Object circle) {
    return this.radius ==
      ((Circle)circle).radius;
  }
}
```

(b)

Sections 10.8–10.9

10.13 For the `GeometricObject` and `Circle` classes in Listings 10.1 and 10.2, answer the following questions:

(a) Are the following Boolean expressions true or false?

```
Circle circle = new Circle(1);
GeometricObject object1 = new GeometricObject();
(circle instanceof GeometricObject)
(object1 instanceof GeometricObject)
(circle instanceof Circle)
(object1 instanceof Circle)
```

(b) Can the following statements be compiled?

```
Circle circle = new Circle(5);
GeometricObject object = circle;
```

(c) Can the following statements be compiled?

```
GeometricObject object = new GeometricObject();
Circle circle = (Circle)object;
```

10.14 Suppose that `Fruit`, `Apple`, `Orange`, `Golden Delicious Apple`, and `Macintosh Apple` are declared, as shown in Figure 10.7.

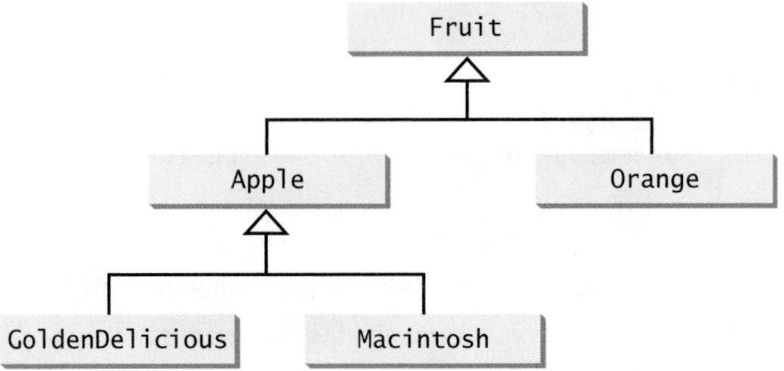

FIGURE 10.7 `GoldenDelicious` and `Macintosh` are subclasses of `Apple`, `Apple` and `Orange` are subclasses of `Fruit`.

Assume that the following declaration is given:

```
Fruit fruit = new GoldenDelicious();
Orange orange = new Orange();
```

Answer the following questions:

(1) Is `fruit instanceof Fruit`?
(2) Is `fruit instanceof Orange`?
(3) Is `fruit instanceof Apple`?
(4) Is `fruit instanceof GoldenDelicious`?
(5) Is `fruit instanceof Macintosh`?
(6) Is `orange instanceof Orange`?
(7) Is `orange instanceof Fruit`?
(8) Is `orange instanceof Apple`?
(9) Suppose the method `makeApple` is defined in the `Apple` class. Can `fruit` invoke this method? Can `orange` invoke this method?
(10) Suppose the method `makeOrangeJuice` is defined in the `Orange` class. Can `orange` invoke this method? Can `fruit` invoke this method?
(11) Is the statement `Orange p = new Apple()` legal?
(12) Is the statement `Macintosh p = new Apple()` legal?
(13) Is the statement `Apple p = new Macintosh()` legal?

10.15 What is wrong in the following code?

```
public class Test {
  public static void main(String[] args) {
    Object fruit = new Fruit();
    Object apple = (Apple)fruit;
  }
}

class Apple extends Fruit {
}

class Fruit {
}
```

Section 10.10 The ArrayList Class

10.16 How do you create an ArrayList? How do you append an object to a list? How do you insert an object at the beginning of a list? How do you find the number of objects in a list? How do you remove a given object from a list? How do you remove the last object from the list? How do you check whether a given object is in a list? How do you retrieve an object at a specified index from a list?

10.17 There are three errors in the following code. Identify them.

```
ArrayList list = new ArrayList();
list.add("New York");
list.add("Austin");
list.add(new java.util.Date());
String city = list.get(0);
list.set(3, "Dallas");
System.out.println(list.get(3));
```

Sections 10.12-10.13

10.18 What modifier should you use on a class so that a class in the same package can access it, but a class in a different package cannot access it?

10.19 What modifier should you use so that a class in a different package cannot access the class, but its subclasses in any package can access it?

10.20 In the following code, classes A and B are in the same package. If the question marks are replaced by blanks, can class B be compiled? If the question marks are replaced by private, can class B be compiled? If the question marks are replaced by protected, can class B be compiled?

```
package p1;

public class A {
  ?   int i;

  ?   void m() {
    ...
  }
}
```

(a)

```
package p1;

public class B extends A {
  public void m1(String[] args) {
    System.out.println(i);
    m();
  }
}
```

(b)

10.21 In the following code, classes A and B are in different packages. If the question marks are replaced by blanks, can class B be compiled? If the question marks are replaced by private, can class B be compiled? If the question marks are replaced by protected, can class B be compiled?

```
package p1;

public class A {
  ?   int i;

  ?   void m() {
    ...
  }
}
```

(a)

```
package p2;

public class B extends A {
  public void m1(String[] args) {
    System.out.println(i);
    m();
  }
}
```

(b)

10.22 How do you prevent a class from being extended? How do you prevent a method from being overridden?

Comprehensive

10.23 Define the following terms: inheritance, superclass, subclass, the keywords `super` and `this`, casting objects, the modifiers `protected` and `final`.

10.24 Indicate true or false for the following statements:

- A protected datum or method can be accessed by any class in the same package.
- A protected datum or method can be accessed by any class in different packages.
- A protected datum or method can be accessed by its subclasses in any package.
- A final class can have instances.
- A final class can be extended.
- A final method can be overridden.
- You can always successfully cast an instance of a subclass to a superclass.
- You can always successfully cast an instance of a superclass to a subclass.

10.25 Describe the difference between method matching and method binding.

10.26 What is polymorphism? What is dynamic binding? What is generic programming? What are the advantages of dynamic binding?

PROGRAMMING EXERCISES

Sections 10.2–10.5

10.1 (*The `Triangle` class*) Design a class named `Triangle` that extends `GeometricObject`. The class contains:

- Three `double` data fields named `side1`, `side2`, and `side3` with default values `1.0` to denote three sides of the triangle.
- A no-arg constructor that creates a default triangle.
- A constructor that creates a triangle with the specified `side1`, `side2`, and `side3`.
- The accessor methods for all three data fields.
- A method named `getArea()` that returns the area of this triangle.
- A method named `getPerimeter()` that returns the perimeter of this triangle.
- A method named `toString()` that returns a string description for the triangle.

For the formula to compute the area of a triangle, see Exercise 5.19. The `toString()` method is implemented as follows:

```
return "Triangle: side1 = " + side1 + " side2 = " + side2 +
  " side3 = " + side3;
```

Draw the UML diagram that involves the classes `Triangle` and `GeometricObject`. Implement the class. Write a test program that creates a `Triangle` object with sides `1`, `1.5`, `1`, setting color `yellow` and filled `true`, and displaying the area, perimeter, color, and whether filled or not.

Sections 10.6–10.9

10.2 (*The `Person`, `Student`, `Employee`, `Faculty`, and `Staff` classes*) Design a class named `Person` and its two subclasses named `Student` and `Employee`. Make `Faculty` and `Staff` subclasses of `Employee`. A person has a name, address, phone number, and email address. A student has a class status (freshman, sophomore, junior, or senior). Define the status as a constant. An employee has an office, salary, and date-hired. Define a class named `MyDate` that contains the fields `year`, `month`, and `day`. A faculty member has office hours and a rank. A staff member has a title. Override the `toString` method in each class to display the class name and the person's name.

Draw the UML diagram for the classes. Implement the classes. Write a test program that creates a `Person`, `Student`, `Employee`, `Faculty`, and `Staff`, and invokes their `toString()` methods.

10.3 (*Subclasses of `Account`*) In Exercise 7.3, the `Account` class was created to model a bank account. An account has the properties account number, balance, annual interest rate, and date created, and methods to deposit and withdraw. Create two subclasses for checking and saving accounts. A checking account has an overdraft limit, but a savings account cannot be overdrawn.

Draw the UML diagram for the classes. Implement the classes. Write a test program that creates objects of `Account`, `SavingsAccount`, and `CheckingAccount` and invokes their `toString()` methods.

10.4 (*Implementing `MyStack` using inheritance*) In Listing 10.9, `MyStack` is implemented using composition. Create a new stack class that extends `ArrayList`.

Video Note
Implement **MyStack** using inheritance

Draw the UML diagram for the classes. Implement `MyStack`. Write a test program that prompts the user to enter five strings and displays them in reverse order.

10.5 (*The `Course` class*) Rewrite the `Course` class in Listing 9.8. Use an `ArrayList` to replace an array to store students.

10.6 (*Using `ArrayList`*) *Write a program that creates an* `ArrayList` and adds a `Loan` object, a `Date` object, a string, a `JFrame` object, and a `Circle` object to the list, and use a loop to display all the elements in the list by invoking the object's `toString()` method.

10.7*** (*Implementing `ArrayList`*) `ArrayList` is implemented in the Java API. Implement `ArrayList` and the methods defined in Figure 10.4. (*Hint*: Use an array to store the elements in `ArrayList`. If the size of the `ArrayList` exceeds the capacity of the current array, create a new array that doubles the size of the current array and copy the contents of the current to the new array.)

CHAPTER 11

ABSTRACT CLASSES AND INTERFACES

Objectives

- To design and use abstract classes (§11.2).
- To process a calendar using the `Calendar` and `GregorianCalendar` classes (§11.3).
- To specify common behavior for objects using interfaces (§11.4).
- To define interfaces and declare classes that implement interfaces (§11.4).
- To define a natural order using the `Comparable` interface (§11.5).
- To enable objects to listen for action events using the `ActionListener` interface (§11.6).
- To make objects cloneable using the `Cloneable` interface (§11.7).
- To explore the similarities and differences between an abstract class and an interface (§11.8).
- To create objects for primitive values using the wrapper classes (`Byte`, `Short`, `Integer`, `Long`, `Float`, `Double`, `Character`, and `Boolean`) (§11.9).
- To create a generic sort method (§11.10).
- To simplify programming using automatic conversion between primitive types and wrapper class types (§11.11).
- To use the `BigInteger` and `BigDecimal` classes for computing very large numbers with arbitrary precisions (§11.12).

11.1 Introduction

problem

You have learned how to write simple programs to create and display GUI components. Can you write the code to respond to user actions, such as clicking a button? As shown in Figure 11.1, when a button is clicked, a message is displayed on the console.

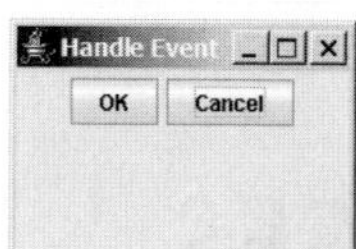

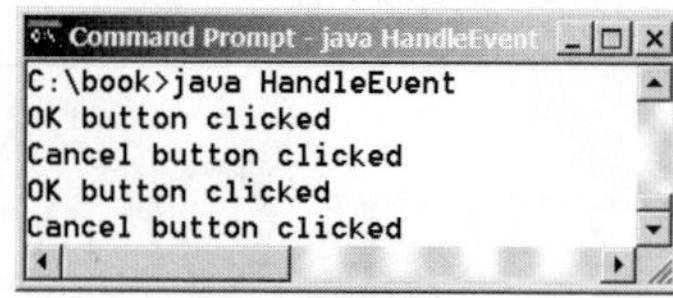

FIGURE 11.1 The program responds to button-clicking action events.

In order to write such code, you have to know interfaces. An interface is for defining common behavior for classes. Before discussing interfaces, we introduce a closely related subject: abstract classes.

11.2 Abstract Classes

abstract class

In the inheritance hierarchy, classes become more specific and concrete *with each new subclass*. If you move from a subclass back up to a superclass, the classes become more general and less specific. Class design should ensure that a superclass contains common features of its subclasses. Sometimes a superclass is so abstract that it cannot have any specific instances. Such a class is referred to as an *abstract class*.

abstract method

abstract modifier

In Chapter 10, `GeometricObject` was declared as the superclass for `Circle` and `Rectangle`. `GeometricObject` models common features of geometric objects. Both `Circle` and `Rectangle` contain the `getArea()` and `getPerimeter()` methods for computing the area and perimeter of a circle and a rectangle. Since you can compute areas and perimeters for all geometric objects, it is better to declare the `getArea()` and `getPerimeter()` methods in the `GeometricObject` class. However, these methods cannot be implemented in the `GeometricObject` class, because their implementation depends on the specific type of geometric object. Such methods are referred to as *abstract methods* and are denoted using the *`abstract` modifier* in the method header. After you declare the methods in `GeometricObject`, it becomes an abstract class. Abstract classes are denoted using the `abstract` modifier in the class header. In UML graphic notation, the names of abstract classes and their abstract methods are italicized, as shown in Figure 11.2. Listing 11.1 gives the source code for the new `GeometricObject` class.

LISTING 11.1 GeometricObject.java

abstract class

Video Note
Abstract
GeometricObject class

```java
public abstract class GeometricObject {
  private String color = "white";
  private boolean filled;
  private java.util.Date dateCreated;

  /** Construct a default geometric object */
  protected GeometricObject() {
    dateCreated = new java.util.Date();
  }

  /** Return color */
  public String getColor() {
    return color;
  }

```

```
  /** Set a new color */
  public void setColor(String color) {
    this.color = color;
  }

  /** Return filled. Since filled is boolean,
   *  the get method is named isFilled */
  public boolean isFilled() {
    return filled;
  }

  /** Set a new filled */
  public void setFilled(boolean filled) {
    this.filled = filled;
  }

  /** Get dateCreated */
  public java.util.Date getDateCreated() {
    return dateCreated;
  }

  /** Return a string representation of this object */
  public String toString() {
    return "created on " + dateCreated + "\ncolor: " + color +
      " and filled: " + filled;
  }

  /** Abstract method getArea */
  public abstract double getArea();

  /** Abstract method getPerimeter */
  public abstract double getPerimeter();
}
```

abstract method

abstract method

Abstract classes are like regular classes with data fields and methods, but you cannot create instances of abstract classes using the new operator. An abstract method is a method signature without implementation. Its implementation is provided by the subclasses. A class that contains abstract methods must be declared abstract.

why protected constructor?

The constructor in the abstract class is declared protected, because it is used only by subclasses. When you create an instance of a concrete subclass, the subclass's parent class constructor is invoked to initialize data fields defined in the parent class.

implementing **Circle**
implementing **Rectangle**

The GeometricObject abstract class provides the common features (data and methods) for geometric objects. Because you don't know how to compute areas and perimeters of geometric objects, getArea and getPerimeter are defined as abstract methods. These methods are implemented in the subclasses. The implementation of Circle and Rectangle is the same as in Listings 10.2 and 10.3, except that they extend the GeometricObject class defined in this chapter, as follows:

LISTING 11.2 Circle.java

extends **GeometricObject**

```
public class Circle extends GeometricObject {
  // Same as lines 2-40 in Listing 10.2, so omitted
}
```

LISTING 11.3 Rectangle.java

extends **GeometricObject**

```
public class Rectangle extends GeometricObject {
  // Same as lines 2-41 in Listing 10.3, so omitted
}
```

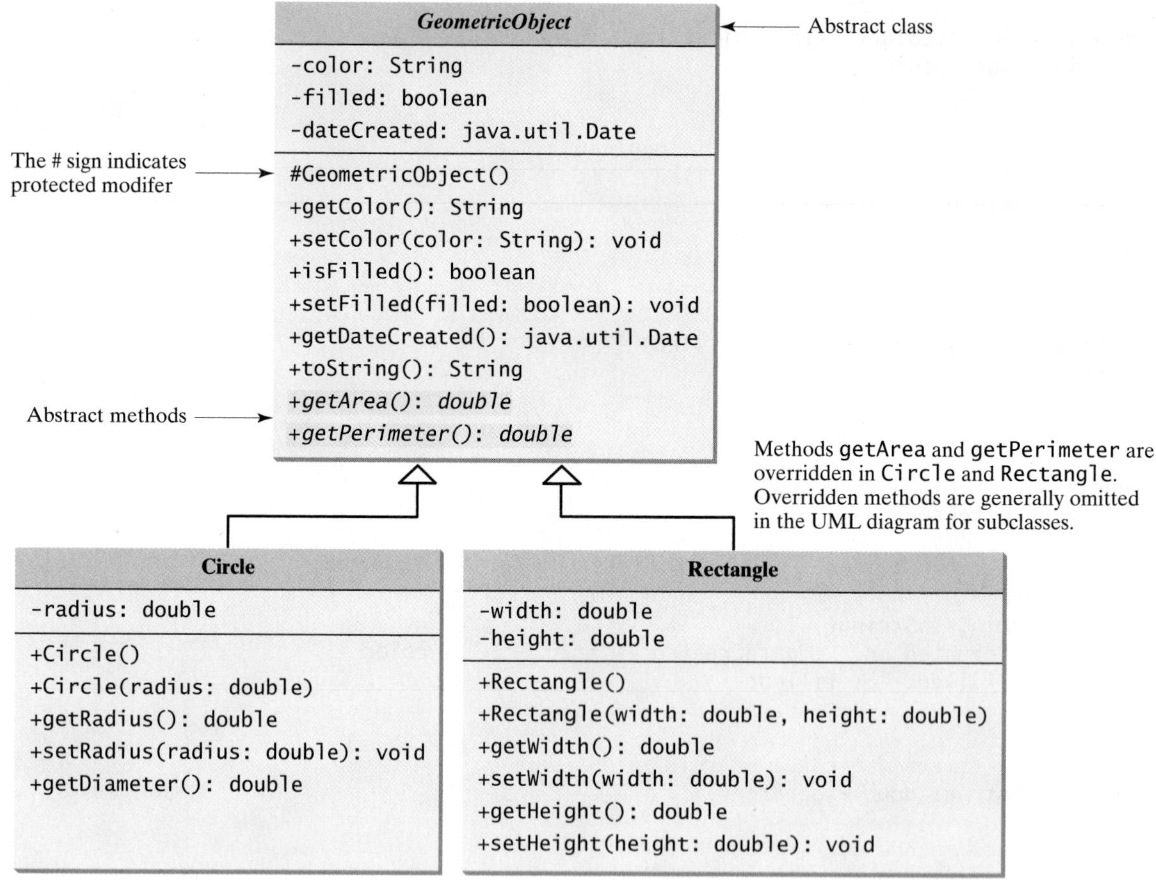

FIGURE 11.2 The new `GeometricObject` class contains abstract methods.

11.2.1 Why Abstract Methods?

You may be wondering what advantage is gained by defining the methods `getArea` and `getPerimeter` as abstract in the `GeometricObject` class instead of defining them only in each subclass. The following example shows the benefits of retaining them in the `GeometricObject` class.

The example in Listing 11.4 creates two geometric objects, a circle and a rectangle, invokes the `equalArea` method to check whether the two objects have equal areas, and invokes the `displayGeometricObject` method to display the objects.

LISTING 11.4 TestGeometricObject.java

create a circle
create a rectangle

```java
public class TestGeometricObject {
  /** Main method */
  public static void main(String[] args) {
    // Declare and initialize two geometric objects
    GeometricObject geoObject1 = new Circle(5);
    GeometricObject geoObject2 = new Rectangle(5, 3);

    System.out.println("The two objects have the same area? " +
      equalArea(geoObject1, geoObject2));

    // Display circle
    displayGeometricObject(geoObject1);

```

```
14     // Display rectangle
15     displayGeometricObject(geoObject2);
16   }
17
18   /** A method for comparing the areas of two geometric objects */
19   public static boolean equalArea(GeometricObject object1,
20       GeometricObject object2) {
21     return object1.getArea() == object2.getArea();
22   }
23
24   /** A method for displaying a geometric object */
25   public static void displayGeometricObject(GeometricObject object) {
26     System.out.println();
27     System.out.println("The area is " + object.getArea());
28     System.out.println("The perimeter is " + object.getPerimeter());
29   }
30 }
```

equalArea

displayGeometricObject

```
The two objects have the same area? false

The area is 78.53981633974483
The perimeter is 31.41592653589793

The area is 15.0
The perimeter is 16.0
```

The methods `getArea()` and `getPerimeter()` defined in the `GeometricObject` class are overridden in the `Circle` class and the `Rectangle` class. The statements (lines 5–6)

```
GeometricObject geoObject1 = new Circle(5);
GeometricObject geoObject2 = new Rectangle(5, 3);
```

create a new circle and rectangle and assign them to the variables `geoObject1` and `geoObject2`. These two variables are of the `GeometricObject` type.

When invoking `equalArea(geoObject1, geoObject2)` (line 9), the `getArea` method defined in the `Circle` class is used for `object1.getArea()`, since `geoObject1` is a circle, and the `getArea` method defined in the `Rectangle` class is used for `object2.getArea()`, since `geoObject2` is a rectangle.

Similarly, when invoking `displayGeometricObject(geoObject1)` (line 12), the methods `getArea` and `getPerimeter` defined in the `Circle` class are used, and when invoking `displayGeometricObject(geoObject2)` (line 15), the methods `getArea` and `getPerimeter` defined in the `Rectangle` class are used. The JVM dynamically determines which of these methods to invoke at runtime, depending on the type of object.

Note that if the `getArea` and `getPerimeter` methods were not defined in `GeometricObject`, you cannot define the `equalArea` and `displayObject` methods in this program. So, you now see the benefits of defining the abstract methods in `GeometricObject`.

why abstract methods?

11.2.2 Interesting Points on Abstract Classes

The following points on abstract classes are worth noting:

abstract method in abstract class

- An abstract method cannot be contained in a nonabstract class. If a subclass of an abstract superclass does not implement all the abstract methods, the subclass must be declared abstract. In other words, in a nonabstract subclass extended from an abstract class, all the abstract methods must be implemented, even if they are not used in the subclass. Also note that abstract methods are nonstatic.

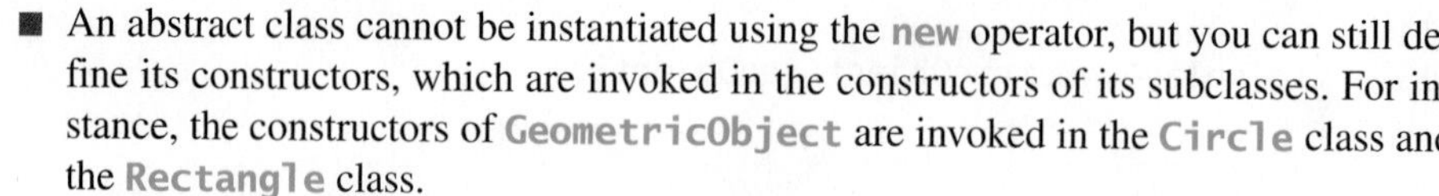

object cannot be created from abstract class

- An abstract class cannot be instantiated using the `new` operator, but you can still define its constructors, which are invoked in the constructors of its subclasses. For instance, the constructors of `GeometricObject` are invoked in the `Circle` class and the `Rectangle` class.

abstract class without abstract method

- A class that contains abstract methods must be abstract. However, it is possible to declare an abstract class that contains no abstract methods. In this case, you cannot create instances of the class using the `new` operator. This class is used as a base class for defining a new subclass.

superclass of abstract class may be concrete

- A subclass can be abstract even if its superclass is concrete. For example, the `Object` class is concrete, but its subclasses, such as `GeometricObject`, may be abstract.

concrete method overridden to be abstract

- A subclass can override a method from its superclass to declare it `abstract`. This is *very unusual*, but is useful when the implementation of the method in the superclass becomes invalid in the subclass. In this case, the subclass must be declared abstract.

abstract class as type

- You cannot create an instance from an abstract class using the `new` operator, but an abstract class can be used as a data type. Therefore, the following statement, which creates an array whose elements are of the `GeometricObject` type, is correct.

```
GeometricObject[] objects = new GeometricObject[10];
```

Video Note
Calendar and **GregorianCalendar** classes

11.3 Example: Calendar and GregorianCalendar

abstract **add** method

An instance of `java.util.Date` represents a specific instant in time with millisecond precision. `java.util.Calendar` is an abstract base class for extracting detailed calendar information, such as year, month, date, hour, minute, and second. Subclasses of `Calendar` can implement specific calendar systems, such as the Gregorian calendar, the lunar calendar, and the Jewish calendar. Currently, `java.util.GregorianCalendar` for the Gregorian calendar is supported in Java, as shown in Figure 11.3. The `add` method is abstract in the `Calendar` class, because its implementation is dependent on a concrete calendar system.

java.util.Calendar	
#Calendar()	Constructs a default calendar.
+get(field: int): int	Returns the value of the given calendar field.
+set(field: int, value: int): void	Sets the given calendar to the specified value.
+set(year: int, month: int, dayOfMonth: int): void	Sets the calendar with the specified year, month, and date. The month parameter is 0 based; that is, 0 is for January.
+getActualMaximum(field: int): int	Returns the maximum value that the specified calendar field could have.
+add(field: int, amount: int): void	Adds or subtracts the specified amount of time to the given calendar field.
+getTime(): java.util.Date	Returns a `Date` object representing this calendar's time value (million second offset from the Unix epoch).
+setTime(date: java.util.Date): void	Sets this calendar's time with the given `Date` object.

java.util.GregorianCalendar	
+GregorianCalendar()	Constructs a `GregorianCalendar` for the current time.
+GregorianCalendar(year: int, month: int, dayOfMonth: int)	Constructs a `GregorianCalendar` for the specified year, month, and day of month.
+GregorianCalendar(year: int, month: int, dayOfMonth: int, hour:int, minute: int, second: int)	Constructs a `GregorianCalendar` for the specified year, month, day of month, hour, minute, and second. The month parameter is 0 based; that is, 0 is for January.

FIGURE 11.3 The abstract `Calendar` class defines common features of various calendars.

You can use `new GregorianCalendar()` to construct a default `GregorianCalendar` with the current time and `new GregorianCalendar(year, month, date)` to construct a `GregorianCalendar` with the specified `year`, `month`, and `date`. The `month` parameter is `0` based—that is, `0` is for January.

constructing calendar

The `get(int field)` method defined in the `Calendar` class is useful for extracting the date and time information from a `Calendar` object. The fields are defined as constants, as shown in Table 11.1.

`get(field)`

TABLE 11.1 Field constants in the `Calendar` class

Constant	*Description*
YEAR	The year of the calendar.
MONTH	The month of the calendar with 0 for January.
DATE	The day of the calendar.
HOUR	The hour of the calendar (12-hour notation).
HOUR_OF_DAY	The hour of the calendar (24-hour notation).
MINUTE	The minute of the calendar.
SECOND	The second of the calendar.
DAY_OF_WEEK	The day number within the week with 1 for Sunday.
DAY_OF_MONTH	Same as DATE.
DAY_OF_YEAR	The day number in the year with 1 for the first day of the year.
WEEK_OF_MONTH	The week number within the month.
WEEK_OF_YEAR	The week number within the year.
AM_PM	Indicator for AM or PM (0 for AM and 1 for PM).

Listing 11.5 gives an example that displays the date and time information for the current time.

LISTING 11.5 `TestCalendar.java`

```
import java.util.*;

public class TestCalendar {
  public static void main(String[] args) {
    // Construct a Gregorian calendar for the current date and time
    Calendar calendar = new GregorianCalendar();
    System.out.println("Current time is " + new Date());
    System.out.println("YEAR:\t" + calendar.get(Calendar.YEAR));
    System.out.println("MONTH:\t" + calendar.get(Calendar.MONTH));
    System.out.println("DATE:\t" + calendar.get(Calendar.DATE));
    System.out.println("HOUR:\t" + calendar.get(Calendar.HOUR));
    System.out.println("HOUR_OF_DAY:\t" +
      calendar.get(Calendar.HOUR_OF_DAY));
    System.out.println("MINUTE:\t" + calendar.get(Calendar.MINUTE));
    System.out.println("SECOND:\t" + calendar.get(Calendar.SECOND));
    System.out.println("DAY_OF_WEEK:\t" +
      calendar.get(Calendar.DAY_OF_WEEK));
    System.out.println("DAY_OF_MONTH:\t" +
      calendar.get(Calendar.DAY_OF_MONTH));
    System.out.println("DAY_OF_YEAR: " +
```

calendar for current time

extract fields in calendar

```
      calendar.get(Calendar.DAY_OF_YEAR));
    System.out.println("WEEK_OF_MONTH: " +
      calendar.get(Calendar.WEEK_OF_MONTH));
    System.out.println("WEEK_OF_YEAR: " +
      calendar.get(Calendar.WEEK_OF_YEAR));
    System.out.println("AM_PM: " + calendar.get(Calendar.AM_PM));

    // Construct a calendar for September 11, 2001
    Calendar calendar1 = new GregorianCalendar(2001, 8, 11);
    System.out.println("September 11, 2001 is a " +
      dayNameOfWeek(calendar1.get(Calendar.DAY_OF_WEEK)));
  }

  public static String dayNameOfWeek(int dayOfWeek) {
    switch (dayOfWeek) {
      case 1: return "Sunday";
      case 2: return "Monday";
      case 3: return "Tuesday";
      case 4: return "Wednesday";
      case 5: return "Thursday";
      case 6: return "Friday";
      case 7: return "Saturday";
      default: return null;
    }
  }
}
```

create a calendar

```
Current time is Sun Sep 09 21:23:59 EDT 2007
YEAR:           2007
MONTH:          8
DATE:           9
HOUR:           9
HOUR_OF_DAY:    21
MINUTE:         23
SECOND:         59
DAY_OF_WEEK:    1
DAY_OF_MONTH:   9
DAY_OF_YEAR:    252
WEEK_OF_MONTH:  3
WEEK_OF_YEAR:   37
AM_PM:          1
September 11, 2001 is a Tuesday
```

set(field, value)

The `set(int field, value)` method defined in the `Calendar` class can be used to set a field. For example, you can use `calendar.set(Calendar.DAY_OF_MONTH, 1)` to set the `calendar` to the first day of the month.

add(field, amount)

The `add(field, value)` method adds or subtracts the specified amount to a given field. For example, to subtract five days from the current time of the calendar, you must call `add(Calendar.DAY_OF_MONTH, -5)`.

getActualMaximum(field)

To obtain the number of days in a month, use `calendar.getActualMaximum(Calendar.DAY_OF_MONTH)`. For example, if the `calendar` were for March, this method would return `31`.

setTime(Date)
getTime()

You can set a time represented in a `Date` object for the `calendar` by invoking `calendar.setTime(date)` and retrieve the time by invoking `calendar.getTime()`.

11.4 Interfaces

Video Note
The concept of interface

An interface is a classlike construct that contains only constants and abstract methods. In many ways an interface is similar to an abstract class, but the intent of an interface is to specify common behavior for objects. For example, using appropriate interfaces, you can specify that the objects are comparable, edible, and cloneable.

To distinguish an interface from a class, Java uses the following syntax to declare an interface:

```
modifier interface  InterfaceName {
  /** Constant declarations */
  /** Method signatures */
}
```

Here is an example of an interface:

```
public interface Edible {
  /** Describe how to eat */
  public abstract String howToEat();
}
```

An interface is treated like a special class in Java. Each interface is compiled into a separate bytecode file, just like a regular class. As with an abstract class, you cannot create an instance from an interface using the `new` operator, but in most cases you can use an interface more or less the same way you use an abstract class. For example, you can use an interface as a data type for a variable, as the result of casting, and so on.

You can now use the `Edible` interface to specify whether an object is edible. This is accomplished by letting the class for the object implement this interface using the `implements` keyword. For example, the classes `Chicken` and `Fruit` in Listing 11.6 (lines 14, 23) implement the `Edible` interface. The relationship between the class and the interface is known as *interface inheritance*. Since interface inheritance and class inheritance are essentially the same, we will simply refer to both as inheritance.

interface inheritance

Listing 11.6 TestEdible.java

```
1 public class TestEdible {
2   public static void main(String[] args) {
3     Object[] objects = {new Tiger(), new Chicken(), new Apple()};
4     for (int i = 0; i < objects.length; i++)
5       if (objects[i] instanceof Edible)
6         System.out.println(((Edible)objects[i]).howToEat());
7   }
8 }
9
10 class Animal {
11   // Data fields, constructors, and methods omitted here
12 }
13
14 class Chicken extends Animal implements Edible {
15   public String howToEat() {
16     return "Chicken: Fry it";
17   }
18 }
19
20 class Tiger extends Animal {
21 }
22
23 abstract class Fruit implements Edible {
```

`Animal` class

`implements Edible`
`howToEat()`

`Tiger` class

`implements Edible`

Apple class

Orange class

```
24   // Data fields, constructors, and methods omitted here
25 }
26
27 class Apple extends Fruit {
28   public String howToEat() {
29     return "Apple: Make apple cider";
30   }
31 }
32
33 class Orange extends Fruit {
34   public String howToEat() {
35     return "Orange: Make orange juice";
36   }
37 }
```

```
Chicken: Fry it
Apple: Make apple cider
```

The `Chicken` class extends `Animal` and implements `Edible` to specify that chickens are edible. When a class implements an interface, it implements all the methods defined in the interface with the exact signature and return type. The `Chicken` class provides the implementation for the `howToEat` method (lines 15–17).

The `Fruit` class implements `Edible`. Since it does not implement the `howToEat` method, `Fruit` must be denoted `abstract` (line 23). The concrete subclasses of `Fruit` must provide implementation for the `howToEach` method. The `Apple` and `Orange` classes implement the `howToEat` method (lines 28, 34).

The main method creates an array with three objects for `Tiger`, `Chicken`, and `Apple` (line 3) and invokes the `howToEat` method if the element is edible.

omitting modifiers

Note

Since all data fields are ***public final static*** and all methods are ***public abstract*** in an interface, Java allows these modifiers to be omitted. Therefore the following declarations are equivalent:

```
public interface T {
  public static  final int K = 1;

  public abstract  void p();
}
```

Equivalent

```
public interface T {
  int K = 1;

  void p();
}
```

accessing constants

Tip

A constant defined in an interface can be accessed using the syntax `InterfaceName.CONSTANT_NAME` (e.g., `T.K`).

11.5 Example: The **Comparable** Interface

Suppose you want to design a generic method to find the larger of two objects. The objects can be students, circles, rectangles, or squares. Since compare methods are different for different types of objects, you need to define a generic compare method to determine the order of the two objects. Then you can tailor the method to compare students, circles, or rectangles. For example, you can use student ID as the key for comparing students, radius as the key for comparing circles, and area as the key for comparing rectangles. You can use an interface to define a generic compareTo method, as follows:

java.lang.Comparable

```
// Interface for comparing objects, defined in java.lang
package java.lang;

public interface Comparable {
  public int compareTo(Object o);
}
```

The compareTo method determines the order of this object with the specified object o, and returns a negative integer, zero, or a positive integer if this object is less than, equal to, or greater than the specified object o.

Many classes in the Java library (e.g., String and Date) implement Comparable to define a natural order for the objects. If you examine the source code of these classes, you will see the keyword implements used in the classes, as shown below:

```
public class String extends Object
    implements Comparable  {
  // class body omitted
}
```

```
public class Date extends Object
    implements Comparable  {
  // class body omitted
}
```

Thus, strings are comparable, and so are dates. Let s be a String object and d be a Date object. All the following expressions are true.

```
s instanceof String
s instanceof Object
s instanceof Comparable
```

```
d instanceof java.util.Date
d instanceof Object
d instanceof Comparable
```

A generic max method for finding the larger of two objects can be declared, as shown in (a) or (b):

```
// Max.java: Find a maximum object
public class Max {
  /** Return the maximum of two objects */
  public static Comparable max
      (Comparable o1, Comparable o2) {
    if (o1.compareTo(o2) > 0)
      return o1;
    else
      return o2;
  }
}
```

(a)

```
// Max.java: Find a maximum object
public class Max {
  /** Return the maximum of two objects */
  public static Object max
      (Object o1, Object o2) {
    if (((Comparable)o1 ).compareTo(o2) > 0)
      return o1;
    else
      return o2;
  }
}
```

(b)

The max method in (a) is simpler than the one in (b). In the Max class in (b), o1 is declared as Object, and (Comparable)o1 tells the compiler to cast o1 into Comparable so that the compareTo method can be invoked from o1. However, no casting is needed in the Max class in (a), since o1 is declared as Comparable. (a) is simpler

The max method in (a) is more robust than the one in (b). You must invoke the max method with two comparable objects. Suppose you invoke max with two noncomparable objects: (a) is more robust

```
Max.max(anyObject1, anyObject2);
```

The compiler will detect the error using the max method in (a), because anyObject1 is not an instance of Comparable. Using the max method in (b), this line of code will compile fine but will have a runtime ClassCastException, because anyObject1 is not an instance of Comparable and cannot be cast into Comparable.

From now on, assume that the max method in (a) is in the text. Since strings are comparable and dates are comparable, you can use the max method to find the larger of two instances of String or Date. Here is an example:

```
String s1 = "abcdef";
String s2 = "abcdee";
String s3 = (String)Max.max(s1, s2);
```

```
Date d1 = new Date();
Date d2 = new Date();
Date d3 = (Date)Max.max(d1, d2);
```

The return value from the max method is of the Comparable type. So you need to cast it to String or Date explicitly.

You cannot use the max method to find the larger of two instances of Rectangle, because Rectangle does not implement Comparable. However, you can declare a new rectangle class that implements Comparable. The instances of this new class are comparable. Let this new class be named ComparableRectangle, as shown in Listing 11.7.

LISTING 11.7 ComparableRectangle.java

implements **Comparable**

implement **compareTo**

```
public class ComparableRectangle extends Rectangle
    implements Comparable {
  /** Construct a ComparableRectangle with specified properties */
  public ComparableRectangle(double width, double height) {
    super(width, height);
  }

  /** Implement the compareTo method defined in Comparable */
  public int compareTo(Object o) {
    if (getArea() > ((ComparableRectangle)o).getArea())
      return 1;
    else if (getArea() < ((ComparableRectangle)o).getArea())
      return -1;
    else
      return 0;
  }
}
```

ComparableRectangle extends Rectangle and implements Comparable, as shown in Figure 11.4. The keyword implements indicates that ComparableRectangle inherits all the constants from the Comparable interface and implements the methods in the interface. The compareTo method compares the areas of two rectangles. An instance of ComparableRectangle is also an instance of Rectangle, GeometricObject, Object, and Comparable.

Notation:
The interface name and the method names are italicized. The dashed lines and hollow triangles are used to point to the interface.

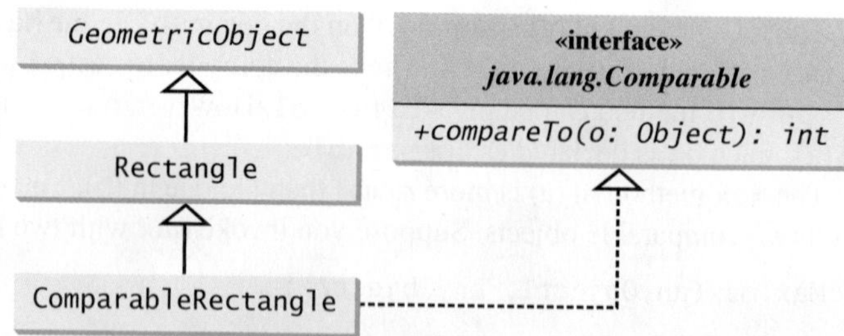

FIGURE 11.4 ComparableRectangle extends Rectangle and implements Comparable.

You can now use the max method to find the larger of two objects of ComparableRectangle. Here is an example:

```
ComparableRectangle rectangle1 = new ComparableRectangle(4, 5);
ComparableRectangle rectangle2 = new ComparableRectangle(3, 6);
System.out.println(Max.max(rectangle1, rectangle2));
```

An interface provides another form of generic programming. It would be difficult to use a generic max method to find the maximum of the objects without using an interface in this example, because multiple inheritance would be necessary to inherit Comparable and another class, such as Rectangle, at the same time.

The Object class contains the equals method, which is intended for the subclasses of the Object class to override in order to compare whether the contents of the objects are the same. Suppose that the Object class contains the compareTo method, as defined in the Comparable interface; the new max method can be used to compare a list of *any* objects. Whether a compareTo method should be included in the Object class is debatable. Since the compareTo method is not defined in the Object class, the Comparable interface is created in Java to enable objects to be compared if they are instances of the Comparable interface. It is strongly recommended (though not required) that compareTo should be consistent with equals. That is, for two objects o1 and o2, o1.compareTo(o2) == 0 if and only if o1.equals(o2) is true.

11.6 Example: The **ActionListener** Interface

Now you are ready to write a simple program to address the problem proposed in the introduction of this chapter. The program displays two buttons in the frame, as shown in Figure 11.1. To respond to a button click, you need to write the code to process the clicking button action. The button is a *source object* where the action originates. You need to create an object capable of handling the action event on a button. This object is called a *listener*. Not all objects can be listeners for an action event. To be a listener, two requirements must be met:

ActionListener interface

1. The object must be an instance of the ActionListener interface. The ActionListener interface contains the actionPerformed method for processing the event.

addActionListener (listener)

2. The ActionListener object listener must be registered with the source using the method source.addActionListener(listener).

Listing 11.8 gives the code that processes the ActionEvent on the two buttons. When you click the *OK* button, the message "OK button clicked" is displayed. When you click the *Cancel* button, the message "Cancel button clicked" is displayed, as shown in Figure 11.1.

Listing 11.8 HandleEvent.java

```
import javax.swing.*;
import java.awt.event.*;

public class HandleEvent extends JFrame {
  public HandleEvent() {
    // Create two buttons
    JButton jbtOK = new JButton("OK");
    JButton jbtCancel = new JButton("Cancel");

    // Create a panel to hold buttons
    JPanel panel = new JPanel();
    panel.add(jbtOK);
```

```
13       panel.add(jbtCancel);
14
15       add(panel); // Add panel to the frame
16
17       // Register listeners
```

create listener

register listener

```
18       OKListenerClass listener1 = new OKListenerClass();
19       CancelListenerClass listener2 = new CancelListenerClass();
20       jbtOK.addActionListener(listener1);
21       jbtCancel.addActionListener(listener2);
22     }
23
24     public static void main(String[] args) {
25       JFrame frame = new HandleEvent();
26       frame.setTitle("Handle Event");
27       frame.setSize(200, 150);
28       frame.setLocation(200, 100);
29       frame.setDefaultCloseOperation(JFrame.EXIT_ON_CLOSE);
30       frame.setVisible(true);
31     }
32   }
33
```

listener class

process event

```
34   class OKListenerClass implements ActionListener {
35     public void actionPerformed(ActionEvent e) {
36       System.out.println("OK button clicked");
37     }
38   }
39
```

listener class

process event

```
40   class CancelListenerClass implements ActionListener {
41     public void actionPerformed(ActionEvent e) {
42       System.out.println("Cancel button clicked");
43     }
44   }
```

Two listener classes are declared in lines 34–44. Each listener class implements `ActionListener` to process `ActionEvent`. The object `listener1` is an instance of `OKListenerClass` (line 18), which is registered with the button `jbtOK` (line 20). When the OK button is clicked, the `actionPerformed(ActionEvent)` method (line 36) in `OKListenerClass` is invoked to process the event. The object `listener2` is an instance of `CancelListenerClass` (line 19), which is registered with the button `jbtCancel` in line 21. When the OK button is clicked, the `actionPerformed(ActionEvent)` method (line 42) in `CancelListenerClass` is invoked to process the event. More discussions on how to process events will be covered in Chapter 15, "Event-driven Programming."

11.7 Example: The `Cloneable` Interface

Often it is desirable to create a copy of an object. You need to use the `clone` method and understand the `Cloneable` interface, which is the subject of this section.

An interface contains constants and abstract methods, but the `Cloneable` interface is a special case. The `Cloneable` interface in the `java.lang` package is defined as follows:

`java.lang.Cloneable`

```
package java.lang;

public interface Cloneable {
}
```

marker interface

This interface is empty. An interface with an empty body is referred to as a *marker interface*. A marker interface does not contain constants or methods. It is used to denote that a class possesses certain desirable properties. A class that implements the `Cloneable` interface is marked cloneable, and its objects can be cloned using the `clone()` method defined in the `Object` class.

Many classes in the Java library (e.g., `Date`, `Calendar`, and `ArrayList`) implement `Cloneable`. Thus, the instances of these classes can be cloned. For example, the following code

```
Calendar calendar = new GregorianCalendar(2003, 2, 1);
Calendar calendarCopy = (Calendar)calendar.clone();
System.out.println("calendar == calendarCopy is " +
  (calendar == calendarCopy));
System.out.println("calendar.equals(calendarCopy) is " +
  calendar.equals(calendarCopy));
```

displays

```
calendar == calendarCopy is false
calendar.equals(calendarCopy) is true
```

how to implement **Cloneable**

To declare a custom class that implements the `Cloneable` interface, the class must override the `clone()` method in the `Object` class. Listing 11.9 declares a class named `House` that implements `Cloneable` and `Comparable`.

LISTING 11.9 House.java

```
public class House implements Cloneable, Comparable {
  private int id;
  private double area;
  private java.util.Date whenBuilt;

  public House(int id, double area) {
    this.id = id;
    this.area = area;
    whenBuilt = new java.util.Date();
  }

  public double getId() {
    return id;
  }

  public double getArea() {
    return area;
  }

  public java.util.Date getWhenBuilt() {
    return whenBuilt;
  }

  /** Override the protected clone method defined in the Object
    class, and strengthen its accessibility */
  public Object clone() throws CloneNotSupportedException {
    return super.clone();
  }

  /** Implement the compareTo method defined in Comparable */
  public int compareTo(Object o) {
    if (area > ((House)o).area)
      return 1;
    else if (area < ((House)o).area)
      return -1;
```

This exception is thrown if **House** does not implement **Cloneable**

```
36       else
37         return 0;
38     }
39 }
```

The House class implements the clone method (lines 26-28) defined in the Object class. The definition is:

```
protected native Object clone() throws CloneNotSupportedException;
```

The keyword native indicates that this method is not written in Java, but is implemented in the JVM for the native platform. The keyword protected restricts the method to be accessed in the same package or in a subclass. For this reason, the House class must override the method and change the visibility modifier to public so that the method can be used in any package. Since the clone method implemented for the native platform in the Object class performs the task of cloning objects, the clone method in the House class simply invokes super.clone(). The clone method defined in the Object class may throw CloneNotSupportedException.

CloneNotSupported-Exception

The House class implements the compareTo method (lines 31-38) defined in the Comparable interface. The method compares the areas of two houses.

You can now create an object of the House class and create an identical copy from it, as follows:

```
House house1 = new House(1, 1750.50);
House house2 = (House)house1.clone();
```

house1 and house2 are two different objects with identical contents. The clone method in the Object class copies each field from the original object to the target object. If the field is of a primitive type, its value is copied. For example, the value of area (double type) is copied from house1 to house2. If the field is of an object, the reference of the field is copied. For example, the field whenBuilt is of the Date class, so its reference is copied into house2, as shown in Figure 11.5. Therefore, house1.whenBuilt == house2.whenBuilt is true, although house1 == house2 is false. This is referred to as a *shallow copy* rather than a *deep copy*, meaning that if the field is of an object, the reference of the field is copied rather than its contents.

shallow copy

deep copy

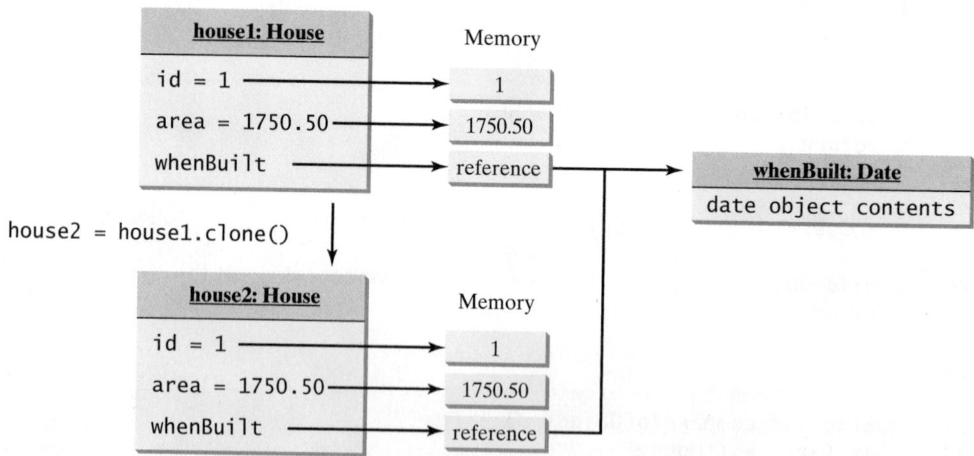

FIGURE 11.5 The clone method copies the values of primitive type fields and the references of object type fields.

If you want to perform a deep copy, you can override the `clone` method with custom cloning operations after invoking `super.clone()`. See Exercise 11.4.

Note

You learned how to use the `arraycopy` method to copy arrays in Chapter 6, "Arrays." This method provides shallow copies. It works fine for arrays of primitive data type elements, but not for arrays of object type elements. To support a deep copy, you have to deal with how to copy individual object elements in the array.

Caution

If the `House` class does not override the `clone()` method, the program will receive a syntax error, because `clone()` is protected in `java.lang.Object`. If `House` does not implement `java.lang.Cloneable`, invoking `super.clone()` (line 28) in House.java would cause a `CloneNotSupportedException`. Thus, to enable cloning an object, the class for the object must override the `clone()` method and implement `Cloneable`.

11.8 Interfaces vs. Abstract Classes

An interface can be used the same way as an abstract class, but declaring an interface is different from declaring an abstract class. Table 11.2 summarizes the differences.

TABLE 11.2 Interfaces vs. Abstract Classes

	Variables	*Constructors*	*Methods*
Abstract class	No restrictions	Constructors are invoked by subclasses through constructor chaining. An abstract class cannot be instantiated using the new operator.	No restrictions.
Interface	All variables must be `public static final`.	No constructors. An interface cannot be instantiated using the new operator.	All methods must be public abstract instance methods

Java allows only *single inheritance* for class extension, but multiple extensions for interfaces. For example,

```
public class NewClass extends BaseClass
    implements Interface1, ..., InterfaceN {
  ...
}
```

An interface can inherit other interfaces using the `extends` keyword. Such an interface is called a *subinterface*. For example, `NewInterface` in the following code is a subinterface of `Interface1`, ..., and `InterfaceN`. subinterface

```
public interface NewInterface extends Interface1, ..., InterfaceN {
  // constants and abstract methods
}
```

A class implementing `NewInterface` must implement the abstract methods defined in `NewInterface`, `Interface1`, ..., and `InterfaceN`. An interface can extend other interfaces, but not classes. A class can extend its superclass and implement *multiple interfaces*.

All classes share a single root, the `Object` class, but there is no single root for interfaces. Like a class, an interface also defines a type. A variable of an interface type can reference any instance of the class that implements the interface. If a class implements an interface, the interface is like a superclass for the class. You can use an interface as a data type and cast a variable of an interface type to its subclass, and vice versa. For example, suppose that `c` is an instance of `Class2` in Figure 11.6. `c` is also an instance of `Object`, `Class1`, `Interface1`, `Interface1_1`, `Interface1_2`, `Interface2_1`, and `Interface2_2`.

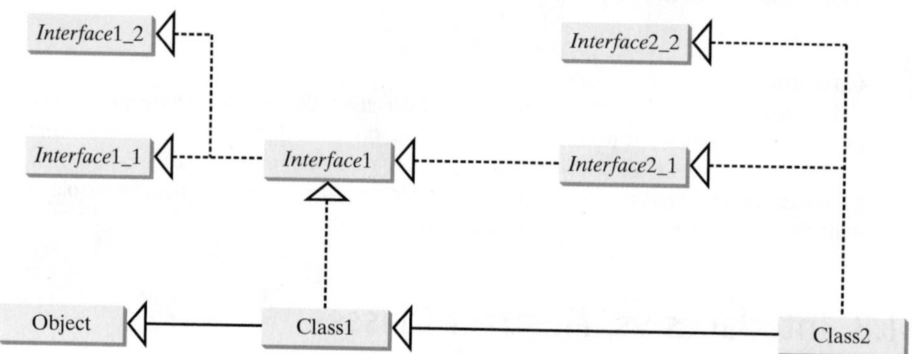

FIGURE 11.6 `Class1` implements `Interface1`; `Interface1` extends `Interface1_1` and `Interface1_2`. `Class2` extends `Class1` and implements `Interface2_1` and `Interface2_2`.

naming convention

Note

Class names are nouns. Interface names may be adjectives or nouns. For example, both `java.lang.Comparable` and `java.awt.event.ActionListener` are interfaces. `Comparable` is an adjective, and `ActionListener` is a noun.

Design Guide

is-a relationship

is-kind-of relationship

Abstract classes and interfaces can both be used to specify common behaviour of objects. How do you decide whether to use an interface or a class? In general, a *strong is-a relationship* that clearly describes a parent-child relationship should be modeled using classes. For example, Gregorian calendar is a calendar, so the relationship between the class `java.util.GregorianCalendar` and `java.util.Calendar` is modeled using class inheritance. A *weak is-a relationship*, also known as an *is-kind-of relationship*, indicates that an object possesses a certain property. A weak is-a relationship can be modeled using interfaces. For example, all strings are comparable, so the `String` class implements the `Comparable` interface.

interface preferred

In general, interfaces are preferred over classes because an interface can represent a common supertype for unrelated classes. Interfaces are more flexible than classes. Consider the `Animal` class. Suppose the `howToEat` method is defined in the `Animal` class, as follows:

`Animal` class

```
abstract class Animal {
  public String howToEat();
}
```

Two subclasses of `Animal` are defined as follows:

`Chicken` class

```
class Chicken extends Animal {
  public String howToEat() {
    return "Fry it";
  }
}
```

Duck class

```
class Duck extends Animal {
  public String howToEat() {
    return "Roast it";
  }
}
```

Given this inheritance hierarchy, polymorphism enables you to hold a reference to a Chicken object or a Duck object in a variable of type Animal, as in the following code:

```
public static void main(String[] args) {
  Animal animal = new Chicken();
  eat(animal);

  animal = new Duck();
  eat(animal);
}

public static void eat(Animal animal) {
  animal.howToEat();
}
```

The JVM dynamically decides which howToEat method to invoke based on the actual object that invokes the method.

You can add another subclass (e.g., Turkey) to the animal family. However, there is a restriction. The subclass must be for another animal.

Interfaces don't have this restriction. Interfaces give you more flexibility than classes, because you don't have make everything fit into one type of class. You may define the howToEat() method in an interface and let it serve as a common supertype for other classes. For example,

```
public static void main(String[] args) {
  Edible stuff = new Chicken();
  eat(stuff);

  stuff = new Duck();
  eat(stuff);

  stuff = new Broccoli();
  eat(stuff);
}

public static void eat(Edible stuff) {
  stuff.howToEat();
}
```

Edible interface

```
interface Edible {
  public String howToEat() ;
}
```

Chicken class

```
class Chicken implements Edible {
  public String howToEat() {
    return "Fry it";
  }
}
```

Duck class

```
class Duck implements Edible {
  public String howToEat() {
    return "Roast it";
  }
}
```

Broccoli class

```
class Broccoli implements Edible {
  public String howToEat() {
    return "Stir-fry it";
  }
}
```

To define a class that represents edible objects, simply let the class implement the `Edible` interface. The class is now a subtype of the `Edible` type. Any `Edible` object can be passed to invoke the `eat` method.

11.9 Processing Primitive Data Type Values as Objects

Owing to performance considerations, primitive data types are not used as objects in Java. Because of the overhead of processing objects, the language's performance would be adversely affected if primitive data types were treated as objects. However, many Java methods require the use of objects as arguments. For example, the `add(object)` method in the `ArrayList` class adds an object to an `ArrayList`. Java offers a convenient way to incorporate, or wrap, a primitive data type into an object (e.g., wrapping `int` into the `Integer` class, and wrapping `double` into the `Double` class). The corresponding class is called a *wrapper class*. By using a wrapper object instead of a primitive data type variable, you can take advantage of generic programming.

wrapper class
why wrapper class?

Java provides `Boolean`, `Character`, `Double`, `Float`, `Byte`, `Short`, `Integer`, and `Long` wrapper classes for primitive data types. These classes are grouped in the `java.lang` package. Their inheritance hierarchy is shown in Figure 11.7.

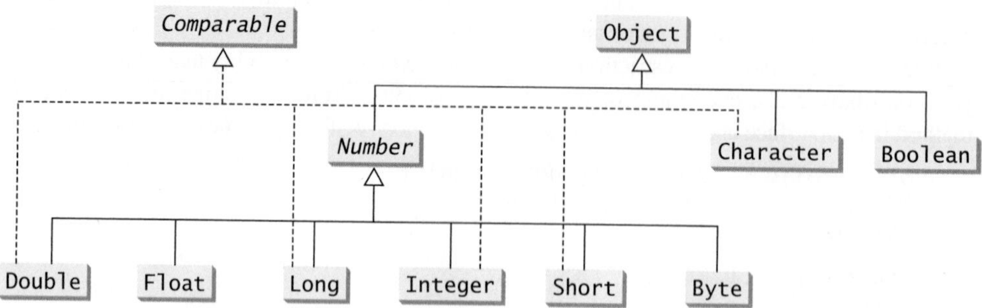

FIGURE 11.7 The `Number` class is an abstract superclass for `Double`, `Float`, `Long`, `Integer`, `Short`, and `Byte`.

naming convention

Note

Most wrapper class names for a primitive type are the same as the primitive data type name with the first letter capitalized. The exceptions are `Integer` and `Character`.

Each numeric wrapper class extends the abstract `Number` class, which contains the methods `doubleValue()`, `floatValue()`, `intValue()`, `longValue()`, `shortValue()`, and `byteValue()`. These methods "convert" objects into primitive type values. Each wrapper class overrides the `toString`, and `equals`, methods defined in the `Object` class. Since all the numeric wrapper classes and the `Character` class implement the `Comparable` interface, the `compareTo` method is implemented in these classes.

Wrapper classes are very similar to each other. The `Character` class was introduced in Chapter 8, "Strings and Text I/O." The `Boolean` class wraps a Boolean value `true` or `false`. This section uses `Integer` and `Double` as examples to introduce the numeric wrapper classes. The key features of `Integer` and `Double` are shown in Figure 11.8.

constructors

You can construct a wrapper object either from a primitive data type value or from a string representing the numeric value—for example, `new Double(5.0)`, `new Double("5.0")`, `new Integer(5)`, and `new Integer("5")`.

no no-arg constructor
immutable

The wrapper classes do not have no-arg constructors. The instances of all wrapper classes are immutable; this means that, once the objects are created, their internal values cannot be changed.

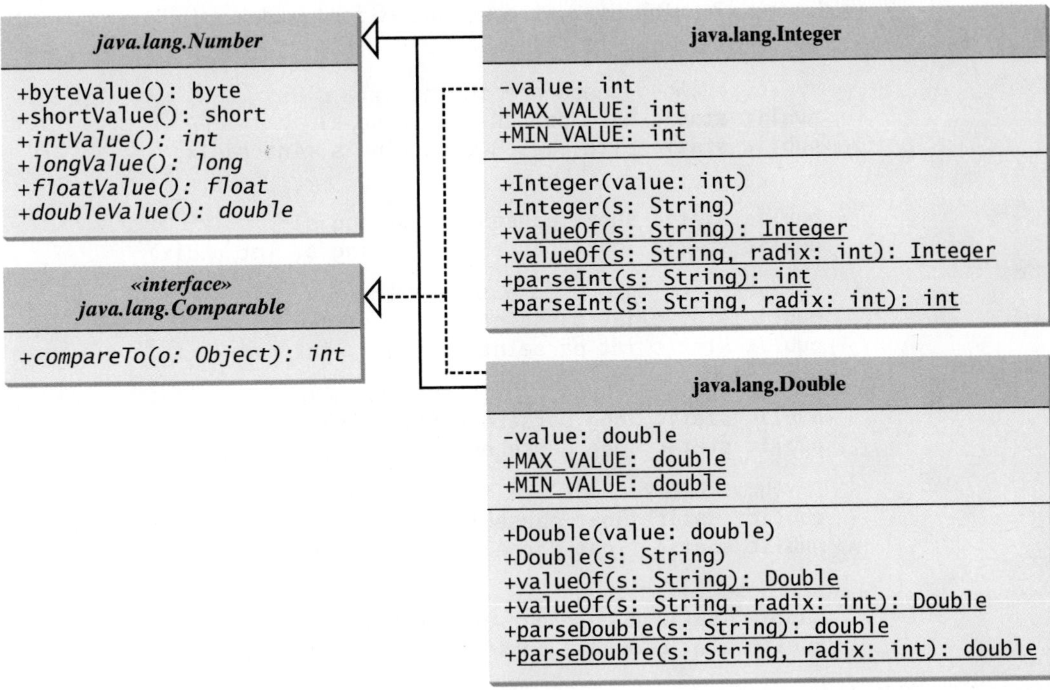

FIGURE 11.8 The wrapper classes provide constructors, constants, and conversion methods for manipulating various data types.

Each numeric wrapper class has the constants `MAX_VALUE` and `MIN_VALUE`. `MAX_VALUE` represents the maximum value of the corresponding primitive data type. For `Byte`, `Short`, `Integer`, and `Long`, `MIN_VALUE` represents the minimum `byte`, `short`, `int`, and `long` values. For `Float` and `Double`, `MIN_VALUE` represents the minimum *positive* `float` and `double` values. The following statements display the maximum integer (2,147,483,647), the minimum positive float (1.4E-45), and the maximum double floating-point number (1.79769313486231570e+308d).

constants

```
System.out.println("The maximum integer is " + Integer.MAX_VALUE);
System.out.println("The minimum positive float is " +
  Float.MIN_VALUE);
System.out.println(
  "The maximum double precision floating-point number is " +
  Double.MAX_VALUE);
```

Each numeric wrapper class implements the abstract methods `doubleValue()`, `floatValue()`, `intValue()`, `longValue()`, and `shortValue()`, which are defined in the `Number` class. These methods return a `double`, `float`, `int`, `long`, or `short` value for the wrapper object.

conversion methods

The numeric wrapper classes have a useful static method, `valueOf(String s)`. This method creates a new object initialized to the value represented by the specified string. For example,

static **valueOf** methods

```
Double doubleObject = Double.valueOf("12.4");
Integer integerObject = Integer.valueOf("12");
```

You have used the `parseInt` method in the `Integer` class to parse a numeric string into an `int` value and the `parseDouble` method in the `Double` class to parse a numeric string into a `double` value. Each numeric wrapper class has two overloaded parsing methods to parse a numeric string into an appropriate numeric value based on `10` (decimal) or any specified

static parsing methods

radix (e.g., 2 for binary, 8 for octal, and 16 for hexadecimal). These methods are shown below:

```
// These two methods are in the Byte class
public static byte parseByte(String s)
public static byte parseByte(String s, int radix)

// These two methods are in the Short class
public static short parseShort(String s)
public static short parseShort(String s, int radix)

// These two methods are in the Integer class
public static int parseInt(String s)
public static int parseInt(String s, int radix)

// These two methods are in the Long class
public static long parseLong(String s)
public static long parseLong(String s, int radix)

// These two methods are in the Float class
public static float parseFloat(String s)
public static float parseFloat(String s, int radix)

// These two methods are in the Double class
public static double parseDouble(String s)
public static double parseDouble(String s, int radix)
```

For example,

```
Integer.parseInt("11", 2) returns 3;
Integer.parseInt("12", 8) returns 10;
Integer.parseInt("13", 10) returns 13;
Integer.parseInt("1A", 16) returns 26;
```

`Integer.parseInt("12", 2)` would raise a runtime exception because `12` is not a binary number.

11.10 Sorting an Array of Objects

This example presents a static generic method for sorting an array of comparable objects. The objects are instances of the `Comparable` interface, and they are compared using the `compareTo` method. The method can be used to sort an array of any objects as long as their classes implement the `Comparable` interface.

To test the method, the program sorts an array of integers, an array of double numbers, an array of characters, and an array of strings. The program is shown in Listing 11.10.

LISTING 11.10 GenericSort.java

```
public class GenericSort {
  public static void main(String[] args) {
    // Create an Integer array
    Integer[] intArray = {new Integer(2), new Integer(4),
      new Integer(3)};

    // Create a Double array
    Double[] doubleArray = {new Double(3.4), new Double(1.3),
      new Double(-22.1)};

    // Create a Character array
    Character[] charArray = {new Character('a'),
      new Character('J'), new Character('r')};

```

```
    // Create a String array
    String[] stringArray = {"Tom", "John", "Fred"};

    // Sort the arrays
    sort(intArray);
    sort(doubleArray);
    sort(charArray);
    sort(stringArray);

    // Display the sorted arrays
    System.out.print("Sorted Integer objects: ");
    printList(intArray);
    System.out.print("Sorted Double objects: ");
    printList(doubleArray);
    System.out.print("Sorted Character objects: ");
    printList(charArray);
    System.out.print("Sorted String objects: ");
    printList(stringArray);
  }

  /** Sort an array of comparable objects */
  public static void sort(Comparable[] list) {
    Comparable currentMax;
    int currentMaxIndex;

    for (int i = list.length - 1; i >= 1; i--) {
      // Find the maximum in the list[0..i]
      currentMax = list[i];
      currentMaxIndex = i;

      for (int j = i - 1; j >= 0; j--) {
        if (currentMax.compareTo(list[j]) < 0) {
          currentMax = list[j];
          currentMaxIndex = j;
        }
      }

      // Swap list[i] with list[currentMaxIndex] if necessary;
      if (currentMaxIndex != i) {
        list[currentMaxIndex] = list[i];
        list[i] = currentMax;
      }
    }
  }

  /** Print an array of objects */
  public static void printList(Object[] list) {
    for (int i = 0; i < list.length; i++)
      System.out.print(list[i] + " ");
    System.out.println();
  }
}
```

sort **Integer** objects
sort **Double** objects
sort **Character** objects
sort **String** objects

generic sort method

compareTo

```
Sorted Integer objects: 2 3 4
Sorted Double objects: -22.1 1.3 3.4
Sorted Character objects: J a r
Sorted String objects: Fred John Tom
```

The algorithm for the `sort` method is the same as in §6.8.1, "Selection Sort." The `sort` method in §6.8.1 sorts an array of double values. The `sort` method in this example can sort an array of any object type, provided that the objects are also instances of the `Comparable` interface. This is another example of *generic programming*, a subject discussed in §10.8, "Polymorphism, Dynamic Binding, and Generic Programming." Generic programming enables a method to operate on arguments of generic types, making it reusable with multiple types.

`Integer`, `Double`, `Character`, and `String` implement `Comparable`, so the objects of these classes can be compared using the `compareTo` method. The sort method uses the `compareTo` method to determine the order of the objects in the array.

Tip

`Arrays.sort` method

Java provides a static `sort` method for sorting an array of any object type in the `java.util.Arrays` class, provided that the elements in the array are comparable. Thus you can use the following code to sort arrays in this example:

```
java.util.Arrays.sort(intArray);
java.util.Arrays.sort(doubleArray);
java.util.Arrays.sort(charArray);
java.util.Arrays.sort(stringArray);
```

Note

Arrays are objects. An array is an instance of the `Object` class. Furthermore, if `A` is a subtype of `B`, every instance of `A[]` is an instance of `B[]`. Therefore, the following statements are all true:

```
new int[10] instanceof Object
new Integer[10] instanceof Object
new Integer[10] instanceof Comparable[]
new Integer[10] instanceof Number[]
new Number[10] instanceof Object[]
```

Caution

Although an `int` value can be assigned to a `double` type variable, `int[]` and `double[]` are two incompatible types. Therefore, you cannot assign an `int[]` array to a variable of `double[]` or `Object[]` type.

11.11 Automatic Conversion between Primitive Types and Wrapper Class Types

Java allows primitive types and wrapper classes to be converted automatically. For example, the following statement in (a) can be simplified as in (b) due to autoboxing:

```
Integer intObject = new Integer(2);
```

(a)

Equivalent

```
Integer intObject = 2;
```

autoboxing (b)

boxing

unboxing

Converting a primitive value to a wrapper object is called *boxing*. The reverse conversion is called *unboxing*. The compiler will automatically box a primitive value that appears in a context requiring an object, and will unbox an object that appears in a context requiring a primitive value. Consider the following example:

```
Integer[] intArray = {1, 2, 3};
System.out.println(intArray[0] + intArray[1] + intArray[2]);
```

In line 1, primitive values 1, 2, and 3 are automatically boxed into objects new Integer(1), new Integer(2), and new Integer(3). In line 2, objects intArray[0], intArray[1], and intArray[2] are automatically converted into int values that are added together.

11.12 The **BigInteger** and **BigDecimal** Classes

If you need to compute with very large integers or high-precision floating-point values, you can use the BigInteger and BigDecimal classes in the java.math package. Both are *immutable*. Both extend the Number class and implement the Comparable interface. The largest integer of the long type is Long.MAX_VALUE (i.e., 9223372036854775807). An instance of BigInteger can represent an integer of any size. You can use new BigInteger(String) and new BigDecimal(String) to create an instance of BigInteger and BigDecimal, use the add, subtract, multiple, divide, and remainder methods to perform arithmetic operations, and use the compareTo method to compare two big numbers. For example, the following code creates two BigInteger objects and multiplies them.

immutable

```
BigInteger a = new BigInteger("9223372036854775807");
BigInteger b = new BigInteger("2");
BigInteger c = a.multiply(b); // 9223372036854775807 * 2
System.out.println(c);
```

The output is 18446744073709551614.

There is no limit to the precision of a BigDecimal object. The divide method may throw an ArithmeticException if the result cannot be terminated. However, you can use the overloaded divide(BigDecimal d, int scale, int roundingMode) method to specify a scale and a rounding mode to avoid this exception, where scale is the minimum number of digits after the decimal point. For example, the following code creates two BigDecimal objects and performs division with scale 20 and rounding mode BigDecimal.ROUND_UP.

```
BigDecimal a = new BigDecimal(1.0);
BigDecimal b = new BigDecimal(3);
BigDecimal c = a.divide(b, 20, BigDecimal.ROUND_UP);
System.out.println(c);
```

The output is 0.33333333333333333334.

Note that the factorial of an integer can be very large. Listing 11.11 gives a method that can return the factorial of any integer.

LISTING 11.11 LargeFactorial.java

```
import java.math.*;

public class LargeFactorial {
  public static void main(String[] args) {
    System.out.println("50! is \n" + factorial(50));
  }

  public static BigInteger factorial(long n) {
    BigInteger result = BigInteger.ONE;
    for (int i = 1; i <= n; i++)
      result = result.multiply(new BigInteger(i + ""));

    return result;
  }
}
```

constant

multiply

```
50! is
30414093201713378043612608166064768844377641568960512000000000000
```

`BigInteger.ONE` (line 9) is a constant defined in the `BigInteger` class. `BigInteger.ONE` is same as `new BigInteger("1")`.

A new result is obtained by invoking the `multiply` method (line 11).

Key Terms

abstract class 362
abstract method 362
deep copy 376
interface 369
marker interface 374
multiple inheritance 373
subinterface 377
shallow copy 376
single inheritance 377
wrapper class 380

Chapter Summary

- Abstract classes are like regular classes with data and methods, but you cannot create instances of abstract classes using the `new` operator.
- An abstract method cannot be contained in a nonabstract class. If a subclass of an abstract superclass does not implement all the inherited abstract methods of the superclass, the subclass must be declared abstract.
- A class that contains abstract methods must be abstract. However, it is possible to declare an abstract class that contains no abstract methods.
- A subclass can be abstract even if its superclass is concrete.
- An interface is a classlike construct that contains only constants and abstract methods. In many ways, an interface is similar to an abstract class, but an abstract class can contain constants and abstract methods as well as variables and concrete methods.
- An interface is treated like a special class in Java. Each interface is compiled into a separate bytecode file, just like a regular class.
- The `java.lang.Comparable` interface defines the `compareTo` method. Many classes in the Java library implement `Comparable`.
- The `java.lang.Cloneable` interface is a marker interface. An object of the class that implements the `Cloneable` interface is cloneable.
- A class can extend only one superclass but can implement one or more interfaces.
- An interface can extend one or more interfaces.
- Many Java methods require the use of objects as arguments. Java offers a convenient way to incorporate, or wrap, a primitive data type into an object (e.g., wrapping `int` into the `Integer` class, and wrapping `double` into the `Double` class).

The corresponding class is called a *wrapper class*. By using a wrapper object instead of a primitive data type variable, you can take advantage of generic programming.

- Java can automatically convert a primitive type value to its corresponding wrapper object in the context and vice versa.

- The `BigInteger` class is useful to compute and process integers of any size. The `BigDecimal` class can be used to compute and process floating-point numbers with any arbitrary precision.

Review Questions

Section 11.2 Abstract Classes

11.1 Which of the following class definitions defines a legal abstract class?

```
class A {
  abstract void unfinished() {
  }
}
```

(a)

```
public class abstract A {
  abstract void unfinished();
}
```

(d)

```
class A {
  abstract void unfinished();
}
```

(b)

```
abstract class A {
  protected void unfinished();
}
```

(e)

```
abstract class A {
  abstract void unfinished();
}
```

(c)

```
abstract class A {
  abstract int unfinished();
}
```

(f)

11.2 The `getArea` and `getPerimeter` methods may be removed from the `GeometricObject` class. What are the benefits of defining `getArea` and `getPerimeter` as abstract methods in the `GeometricObject` class?

11.3 True or false? An abstract class can be used just like a nonabstract class except that you cannot use the `new` operator to create an instance from the abstract class.

Sections 11.4–11.8

11.4 Which of the following is a correct interface?

```
interface A {
  void print() { };
}
```

(a)

```
abstract interface A extends I1, I2 {
  abstract void print() { };
}
```

(c)

```
abstract interface A {
  print();
}
```

(b)

```
interface A {
  void print();
}
```

(d)

11.5 True or false? If a class implements Comparable, the object of the class can invoke the compareTo method.

11.6 Two max methods are defined in §11.5. Explain why the max with the signature max(Comparable, Comparable) is better than the one with the signature max(Object, Object).

11.7 You can define the compareTo method in a class without implementing the Comparable interface. What are the benefits of implementing the Comparable interface?

11.8 True or false? If a class implements java.awt.event.ActionListener, the object of the class can invoke the actionPerformed method.

11.9 Can you invoke the clone() method to clone an object if the class for the object does not implement the java.lang.Cloneable? Does the Date class implement Cloneable?

11.10 What would happen if the House class (defined in Listing 11.9) did not override the clone() method or if House did not implement java.lang.Cloneable?

11.11 Show the printout of the following code:

```
java.util.Date date = new java.util.Date();
java.util.Date date1 = (java.util.Date)(date.clone());
System.out.println(date == date1);
System.out.println(date.equals(date1));
```

11.12 Show the printout of the following code:

```
java.util.ArrayList list = new java.util.ArrayList();
list.add("New York"); list.add(new java.util.Date());
  java.util.ArrayList list1 =
(java.util.ArrayList)(list.clone());
System.out.println(list == list1);
System.out.println(list.get(0) == list1.get(0));
System.out.println(list.get(1) == list1.get(1));
```

11.13 What is wrong in the following code?

```
public class Test {
  public static void main(String[] args) {
    GeometricObject x = new Circle(3);
    GeometricObject y = x.clone();
    System.out.println(x == y);
  }
}
```

Section 11.9 Processing Primitive Data Type Values as Objects

11.14 Describe primitive-type wrapper classes. Why do you need these wrapper classes?

11.15 Can each of the following statement be compiled?

```
Integer i = new Integer("23");
Integer i = new Integer(23);
Integer i = Integer.valueOf("23");
Integer i = Integer.parseInt("23", 8);
Double d = new Double();
Double d = Double.valueOf("23.45");
int i = (Integer.valueOf("23")).intValue();
double d = (Double.valueOf("23.4")).doubleValue();
```

```
int i = (Double.valueOf("23.4")).intValue();
String s = (Double.valueOf("23.4")).toString();
```

11.16 How do you convert an integer into a string? How do you convert a numeric string into an integer? How do you convert a double number into a string? How do you convert a numeric string into a double value?

11.17 Why do the following two lines of code compile but cause a runtime error?

```
Number numberRef = new Integer(0);
Double doubleRef = (Double)numberRef;
```

11.18 Why do the following two lines of code compile but cause a runtime error?

```
Number[] numberArray = new Integer[2];
numberArray[0] = new Double(1.5);
```

11.19 What is wrong in the following code?

```
public class Test {
  public static void main(String[] args) {
    Number x = new Integer(3);
    System.out.println(x.intValue());
    System.out.println(x.compareTo(new Integer(4)));
  }
}
```

11.20 What is wrong in the following code?

```
public class Test {
  public static void main(String[] args) {
    Number x = new Integer(3);
    System.out.println(x.intValue());
    System.out.println((Integer)x.compareTo(new Integer(4)));
  }
}
```

11.21 What is output of the following code?

```
public class Test {
  public static void main(String[] args) {
    System.out.println(Integer.parseInt("10"));
    System.out.println(Integer.parseInt("10", 10));
    System.out.println(Integer.parseInt("10", 16));
  }
}
```

Sections 11.10–11.12

11.22 What are the autoboxing and autounboxing features? Are the following statements correct?

```
Number x = 3;
Integer x = 3;
Double x = 3;
Double x = 3.0;
int x = new Integer(3);
int x = new Integer(3) + new Integer(4);
double y = 3.4;
```

```
y.intValue();
JOptionPane.showMessageDialog(null, 45.5);
```

11.23 Can you assign `new int[10]`, `new String[100]`, `new Object[50]`, or `new Calendar[20]` into a variable of `Object[]` type?

11.24 What is the output of the following code?

```
public class Test {
  public static void main(String[] args) {
    java.math.BigInteger x = new java.math.BigInteger("3");
    java.math.BigInteger y = new java.math.BigInteger("7");
    x.add(y);
    System.out.println(x);
  }
}
```

Comprehensive

11.25 Define the following terms: abstract classes, interfaces. What are the similarities and differences between abstract classes and interfaces?

11.26 Indicate true or false for the following statements:

- An abstract class can have instances created using the constructor of the abstract class.
- An abstract class can be extended.
- An interface is compiled into a separate bytecode file.
- A subclass of a nonabstract superclass cannot be abstract.
- A subclass cannot override a concrete method in a superclass to declare it abstract.
- An abstract method must be nonstatic.
- An interface can have static methods.
- An interface can extend one or more interfaces.
- An interface can extend an abstract class.
- An abstract class can extend an interface.

Programming Exercises

Sections 11.1–11.7

11.1* (*Enabling `GeometricObject` comparable*) Modify the `GeometricObject` class to implement the `Comparable` interface, and define a static `max` method in the `GeometricObject` class for finding the larger of two `GeometricObject` objects. Draw the UML diagram and implement the new `GeometricObject` class. Write a test program that uses the `max` method to find the larger of two circles and the larger of two rectangles.

11.2* (*The `ComparableCircle` class*) Create a class named `ComparableCircle` that extends `Circle` and implements `Comparable`. Draw the UML diagram and implement the `compareTo` method to compare the circles on the basis of area. Write a test class to find the larger of two instances of `ComparableCircle` objects.

11.3* (*The `Colorable` interface*) Design an interface named `Colorable` with a void method named `howToColor()`. Every class of a colorable object must implement the `Colorable` interface. Design a class named `Square` that extends `GeometricObject` and implements `Colorable`. Implement `howToColor` to display a message on how to color the square.

Draw a UML diagram that involves Colorable, Square, and GeometricObject. Write a test program that creates an array of five GeometricObject. For each object in the array, invoke its howToColor method if it is colorable.

11.4* (*Revising the House class*) Rewrite the House class in Listing 11.9 to perform a deep copy on the whenBuilt field.

11.5* (*Enabling Circle comparable*) Rewrite the Circle class in Listing 10.2 to extend GeometricObject and implement the Comparable interface. Override the equals method in the Object class. Two Circle objects are equal if their radii are the same. Draw the UML diagram that involves Circle, GeometricObject, and Comparable.

11.6* (*Enabling Rectangle comparable*) Rewrite the Rectangle class in Listing 10.3 to extend GeometricObject and implement the Comparable interface. Override the equals method in the Object class. Two Rectangle objects are equal if their areas are the same. Draw the UML diagram that involves Rectangle, GeometricObject, and Comparable.

Video Note
Redesign the **Rectangle** class

11.7* (*The Octagon class*) Write a class named Octagon that extends GeometricObject and implements the Comparable and Cloneable interfaces. Assume that all eight sides of the octagon are of equal size. The area can be computed using the following formula:

$$area = \left(2 + 4/\sqrt{2}\right)side*side$$

Draw the UML diagram that involves Octagon, GeometricObject, Comparable, and Cloneable. Write a test program that creates an Octagon object with side value 5 and displays its area and perimeter. Create a new object using the clone method and compare the two objects using the compareTo method.

11.8* (*Summing the areas of geometric objects*) Write a method that sums the areas of all the geometric objects in an array. The method signature is:

```
public static double sumArea(GeometricObject[] a)
```

Write a test program that creates an array of four objects (two circles and two rectangles) and computes their total area using the sumArea method.

11.9* (*Finding the largest object*) Write a method that returns the largest object in an array of objects. The method signature is:

```
public static Object max(Comparable[] a)
```

All the objects are instances of the Comparable interface. The order of the objects in the array is determined using the compareTo method.

Write a test program that creates an array of ten strings, an array of ten integers, and an array of ten dates, and finds the largest string, integer, and date in the arrays.

11.10** (*Displaying calendars*) Rewrite the PrintCalendar class in Listing 5.10 to display a calendar for a specified month using the Calendar and GregorianCalendar classes. Your program receives the month and year from the command line. For example:

```
java Exercise11_10 1 2007
```

This displays the calendar shown in Figure 11.9.

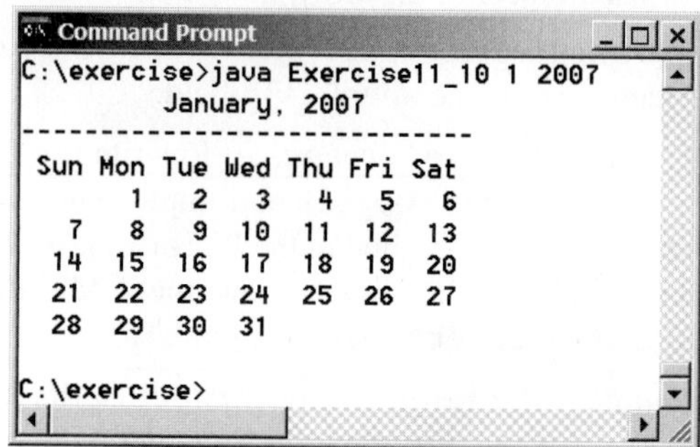

FIGURE 11.9 The program displays a calendar for *January 2007*.

You also can run the program without the year. In this case, the year is the current year. If you run the program without specifying a month and a year, the month is the current month.

Section 11.12 The BigInteger and BigDecimal Classes

11.11** (*Divisible by 5 or 6*) Find the first ten numbers (greater than Long.MAX_VALUE) that are divisible by 5 or 6.

11.12** (*Divisible by 2 or 3*) Find the first ten numbers with 50 decimal digits that are divisible by 2 or 3.

11.13** (*Square numbers*) Find the first ten square numbers that are greater than Long.MAX_VALUE. A square number is a number in the form of n^2.

11.14** (*Large prime numbers*) Write a program that finds five prime numbers larger than long.MAX_VALUE.

11.15** (*Mersenne prime*) A prime number is called a *Mersenne prime* if it can be written in the form $2^p - 1$ for some positive integer p. Write a program that finds all Mersenne primes with $p \leq 100$ and displays the output as shown below. (You have to use BigInteger to store the number, because it is too big to be stored in long. Your program may take several hours to complete.)

```
p        2^p - 1

2           3
3           7
5          31
...
```

CHAPTER 12

OBJECT-ORIENTED DESIGN AND PATTERNS

Objectives

- To describe the software life cycle (§12.2).
- To discover classes and determine responsibilities of each class (§12.3).
- To describe relationship types: association, aggregation, composition, dependency, strong inheritance, and weak inheritance (§12.4).
- To declare classes to represent the relationships (§12.4).
- To design systems by identifying the classes and discovering the relationships among these classes (§12.5).
- To implement the `Rational` class and process rational numbers using this class (§12.6).
- To design classes that follow the class-design guidelines (§12.7).
- To explain the concept of framework-based programming using the Java API (§12.8).
- To apply design patterns for developing sound software systems (§12.9).

12.1 Introduction

The preceding chapters introduced objects, classes, class inheritance, and interfaces. You learned the concepts of object-oriented programming. This chapter focuses on the analysis and design of software systems using the object-oriented approach. You will learn class-design guidelines and the techniques and patterns for designing reusable classes.

12.2 Software Life Cycle

Developing a software project is an engineering process. Software products, no matter how large or how small, have the same life cycle: requirements specification, analysis, design, implementation, testing, deployment, and maintenance, as shown in Figure 12.1.

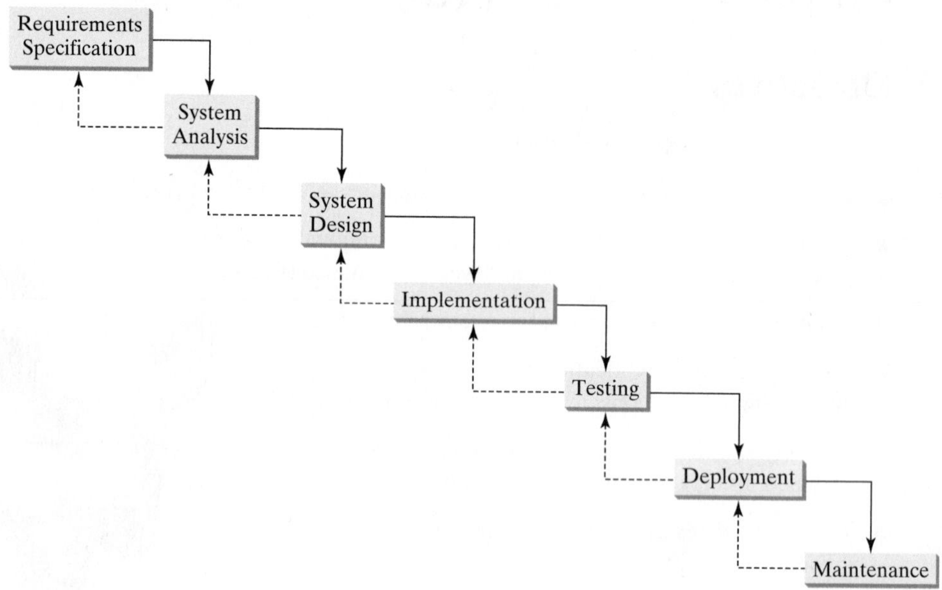

FIGURE 12.1 Developing a project involves requirements specification, system analysis, system design, implementation, testing, deployment, and maintenance.

requirements specification

Requirements specification is a formal process that seeks to understand the problem and to document in detail what the software system needs to do. This phase involves close interaction between users and developers. Most of the examples in this book are simple, and their requirements are clearly stated. In the real world, however, problems are not well defined. You need to work closely with your customer and study a problem carefully to identify its requirements.

system analysis

System analysis seeks to analyze the business process in terms of data flow, and to identify the system's input and output. Part of the analysis entails modeling the system's behavior. The model is intended to capture the essential elements of the system and to define services to the system.

system design

System design is the process of designing the system's components. This phase involves the use of many levels of abstraction to decompose the problem into manageable components, identify classes and interfaces, and establish relationships among the classes and interfaces.

implementation

Implementation is translating the system design into programs. Separate programs are written for each component and put to work together. This phase requires the use of a programming language like Java. The implementation involves coding, testing, and debugging.

testing

Testing ensures that the code meets the requirements specification and weeds out bugs. An independent team of software engineers not involved in the design and implementation of the project usually conducts such testing.

Deployment makes the project available for use. For a Java applet, this means installing it on a Web server; for a Java application, installing it on the client's computer. A project usually consists of many classes. An effective approach for deployment is to package all the classes into a Java archive file, as described in Supplement III.Q, "Packaging and Deploying Java Projects." deployment

Maintenance is concerned with changing and improving the product. A software product must continue to perform and improve in a changing environment. This requires periodic upgrades of the product to fix newly discovered bugs and incorporate changes. maintenance

This chapter is concerned mainly with object-oriented design. While there are many object-oriented methodologies, UML has become the industry-standard notation for object-oriented modeling, and itself leads to a methodology. The process of designing classes calls for identifying the classes and discovering the relationships among them.

12.3 Discovering Classes

The key to object-oriented programming is to model the application in terms of cooperative objects. Careful design of classes is critical when a project is being developed.

There are many levels of abstraction in system design. You have learned method abstraction and have applied it to the development of large programs. Methods are means to group statements. Classes extend abstraction to a higher level and provide a means of grouping methods. Classes do more than just group methods, however; they also contain data fields. Methods and data fields together describe the properties and behaviors of classes.

The power of classes is further extended by inheritance. Inheritance enables a class to extend the contract and the implementation of an existing class without knowing the details of the existing class. In the development of a Java program, class abstraction is applied to decompose the problem into a set of related classes, and method abstraction is applied to design individual classes.

Your first task is to identify classes and determine the responsibilities of each class. There are many strategies for identifying classes in a system, one of which is to study how the system works and select a number of use cases, or scenarios. A simple rule is to look for nouns in the problem description. For example, to design an information system for a university, obviously you will identify student, faculty, and courses as classes.

Once the classes are identified, you will determine the responsibilities of each class, i.e., the methods carried out by the objects of the class. A simple rule is to look for verbs in the problem description and match the verbs to appropriate objects. For example, in the information system for a university, a student registers for a course. Obviously, registering for courses is the responsibility of the `Student` class. The `Course` class is involved in this operation, which is known as a *collaborator* for the operation.

One popular way of facilitating the discovery process is by creating CRC cards. CRC stands for *classes*, *responsibilities*, and *collaborators*. Use an index card for each class, as shown in Figure 12.2. CRC cards

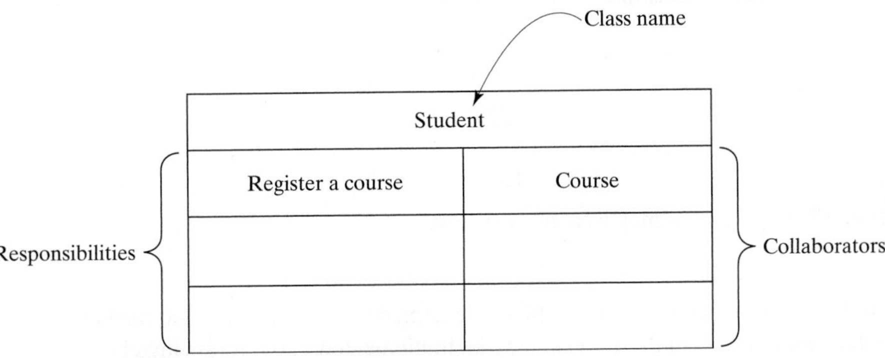

FIGURE 12.2 A CRC card for the `Student` class.

At the top of the card, write the class name. Each row has two columns. Write a responsibility in the left column. If the responsibility involves a collaborator class, write it in the corresponding right column.

12.4 Discovering Class Relationships

The common relationships among classes are: *association*, *aggregation*, *composition*, *dependency*, and *inheritance*.

12.4.1 Association

association

Association is a general binary relationship that describes an activity between two classes. For example, a student taking a course is an association between the `Student` class and the `Course` class, and a faculty member teaching a course is an association between the `Faculty` class and the `Course` class. These associations can be represented in UML graphical notation, as shown in Figure 12.3.

FIGURE 12.3 A student may take any number of courses, and a faculty member teaches at most three courses. A course may have from five to 60 students and is taught by only one faculty member.

An association is illustrated by a solid line between two classes with an optional label that describes the relationship. In Figure 12.3, the labels are *Take* and *Teach*. Each relationship may have an optional small black triangle that indicates the direction of the relationship. In Figure 12.3, the direction indicates that a student takes a course, as opposed to a course taking a student.

Each class involved in the relationship may have a role name that describes the role it plays in the relationship. In Figure 12.3, *teacher* is the role name for `Faculty`.

Each class involved in an association may specify a *multiplicity*. A multiplicity could be a number or an interval that specifies how many objects of the class are involved in the relationship. The character * means an unlimited number of objects, and the interval `m..n` means that the number of objects should be between `m` and `n`, inclusive. In Figure 12.3, each student may take any number of courses, and each course must have at least five students and at most 60 students. Each course is taught by only one faculty member, and a faculty member may teach from zero to three courses per semester.

Association may exist between objects of the same class. For example, a person may have a supervisor. This is illustrated in Figure 12.4.

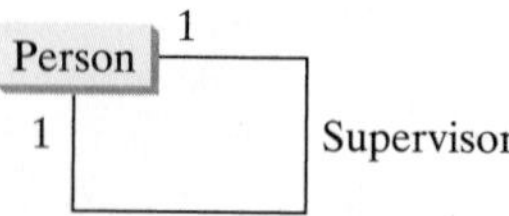

FIGURE 12.4 A person may have a supervisor.

In Java code, an association can be implemented using data fields and methods. For example, the relationships in Figure 12.3 may be implemented in the following classes:

```
public class Student {
  private Course[]
    courseList;

  public void addCourse(
    Course s)
}
```

```
public class Course {
  private Student[]
    classList;
  private Faculty faculty;

  public void addStudent(
    Student s)

  public void setFaculty(
    Faculty faculty)
}
```

```
public class Faculty {
  private Course[]
    courseList;

  public void addCourse(
    Course c)
}
```

Note

There are many possible ways to implement relationships. For example, the student and faculty information in the Course class can be omitted, since they are already in the Student and Faculty class. Likewise, if you don't need to know the courses a student takes or a faculty member teaches, the data field courseList and the addCourse method in Student or Faculty can be omitted.

many possible implementations

12.4.2 Aggregation and Composition

aggregation
aggregating object
aggregated object

Aggregation is a special form of association that represents an ownership relationship between two objects. Aggregation models *has-a* relationships. The owner object is called an *aggregating object*, and its class an *aggregating class*. The subject object is called an *aggregated object*, and its class an *aggregated class*. The association "a person has a supervisor" in Figure 12.4 is actually an aggregation.

composition

An object may be owned by several other aggregating objects. If an object is exclusively owned by an aggregating object, the relationship between the object and its aggregating object is referred to as *composition*. For example, "a student has a name" is a composition relationship between the Student class and the Name class, whereas "a student has an address" is an aggregation relationship between the Student class and the Address class, since an address may be shared by several students. In UML, a filled diamond is attached to an aggregating class (e.g., Student) to denote the composition relationship with an aggregated class (e.g., Name), and an empty diamond is attached to an aggregating class (e.g., Student) to denote the aggregation relationship with an aggregated class (e.g., Address), as shown in Figure 12.5.

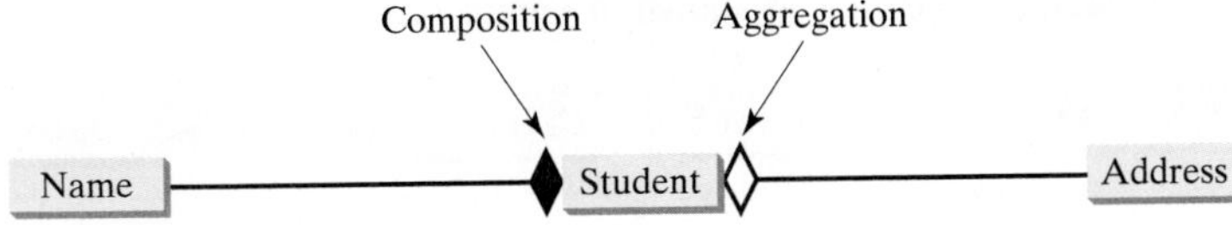

FIGURE 12.5 A student has a name and an address.

An aggregation relationship is usually represented as a data field in the aggregating class. For example, the relationship in Figure 12.5 can be represented as follows:

```
public class Name {
  ...
}
```

Aggregated class

```
public class Person {
  private Name name;
  private Address address;

  ...
}
```

Aggregating class

```
public class Address {
  ...
}
```

Aggregated class

In the relationship "a person has a supervisor," as shown in Figure 12.4, a supervisor can be represented as a data field in the `Person` class, as follows:

```
public class Person {
  // The type for the data is the class itself
  private Person supervisor;

  ...
}
```

If a person has several supervisors, as shown in Figure 12.6, you may use an array or an `ArrayList` to store the supervisors.

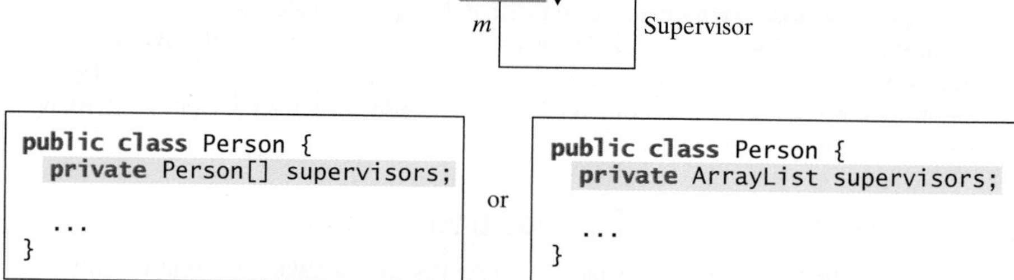

FIGURE 12.6 A person may have several supervisors.

aggregation or composition

Note

For simplicity, since aggregation and composition relationships are translated into the same class template, both are called composition.

12.4.3 Dependency

client

supplier

A *dependency* describes a relationship between two classes where one (called *client*) uses the other (called *supplier*). In UML, draw a dashed line with an arrow from the client class to the supplier class. For example, the `ArrayList` class uses `Object` because you can add objects to an `ArrayList`. The relationship between `ArrayList` and `Object` can be described using dependency, as shown in Figure 12.7(a). The `Calendar` class uses `Date` because you can set a calendar with a specified `Date` object. The relationship between `Calendar` and `Date` can be described using dependency, as shown in Figure 12.7(b).

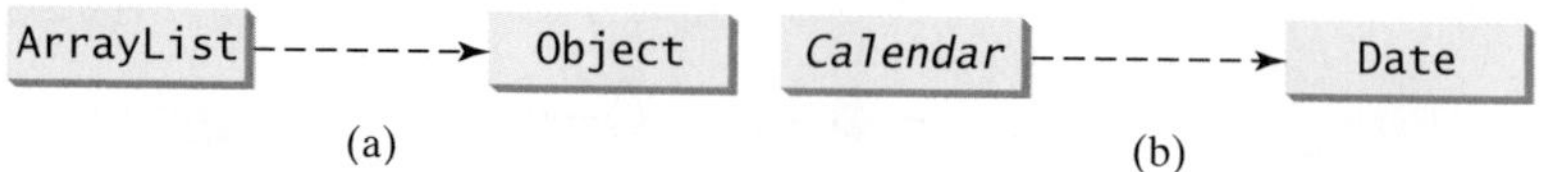

FIGURE 12.7 (a) `ArrayList` uses `Object`. (b) `Calendar` uses `Date`.

In Java code, a dependency can be implemented using a method in the client class. The method contains a parameter of the supplier class type. For example, the `ArrayList` class has the `add(Object)` method that adds an object to the `ArrayList`. The `Calendar` class has the `setTime(Date)` method that sets a new time in the calendar.

```
public class ArrayList {
  public void add(Object o)

  ...
}
```

```
public abstract class Calendar {
  public void setTime(Date d)

  ...
}
```

12.4.4 Comparing Dependency, Association, Aggregation, and Composition

Dependency, association, aggregation, and composition all describe dependent relationships between two classes. The difference is the degree of *coupling* with composition being the strongest, followed by aggregation, association, and dependency in this order.

coupling increases
→
dependency, association, aggregation, composition

If class **A** contains a method with a parameter whose type is class **B**, as shown in Figure 12.8(a), **A** is said to be dependent on **B**. If class **A** contains a data field whose type is class **B**, as shown in Figure 12.8(b), the relationship between the classes is association.

```
public class A {
  public void aMethod(B b)
    ...
}
```

(a) Dependency

```
public class A {
  private B b;
    ...
}
```

(b) Association

FIGURE 12.8 Association is stronger than dependency.

Association can be viewed as a special case of dependency. Aggregation is a special case of association where it describes a has-a relationship. Composition is a special case of aggregation where it describes an exclusive has-a relationship.

12.4.5 Inheritance

strong is-a

weak is-a

Inheritance models the *is-a* relationship between two classes. A strong is-a relationship describes a direct inheritance relationship between two classes. A weak is-a relationship conveys that a class has certain properties. A strong is-a relationship can be represented using class inheritance. For example, the relationship "a faculty member is a person" (shown in Figure 12.9(a)) is a strong is-a relationship and can be represented using the class in Figure 12.9(b).

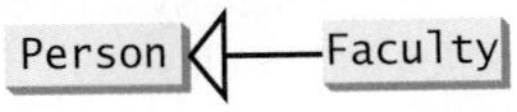

Person ◁— Faculty

(a)

```
public class Faculty extends Person {
  ...
}
```

(b)

FIGURE 12.9 `Faculty` extends `Person`.

A weak is-a relationship is better represented using interfaces. For example, the weak is-a relationship "students are comparable based on their grades" (shown in Figure 12.10(a)) can be represented by implementing the `Comparable` interface, as shown in Figure 12.10(b).

```
public class Student extends Person
    implements Comparable {
  ...

  /** Implement the compareTo method */
  public int compareTo(Object object) {
    ...
  }
}
```

(a) (b)

FIGURE 12.10 Student extends Person and implements Comparable.

Video Note
Object-oriented design

12.5 Case Study: Object-Oriented Design

This case study models borrowing loans to demonstrate how to identify classes, discover the relationships between classes, and apply class abstraction in object-oriented program development.

For simplicity, the example does not attempt to build a complete system for storing, processing, and manipulating loans for borrowers; instead it focuses on modeling borrowers and the loans for the borrowers. The following steps are usually involved in building an object-oriented system:

1. Identify classes for the system.
2. Establish relationships among classes.
3. Describe the attributes and methods in each class.
4. Implement the classes.

identify classes

The first step is to identify classes for the system. Since a borrower is a person who obtains a loan, and a person has a name and an address, you can identify the following classes: `Person`, `Name`, `Address`, `Borrower`, and `Loan`.

Identifying objects is not easy for novice programmers. How do you find the right objects? There is no unique solution, even for simple problems. Software development is more an art than a science. The quality of a program ultimately depends on the programmer's intuition, experience, and knowledge. This example identifies five classes: `Name`, `Address`, `Person`, `Borrower`, and `Loan`. There are several alternatives. One would combine `Name`, `Address`, `Person`, and `Borrower` into one class. This design is not good because it would put unrelated entities into one class. Is there a good justification for combining name with person into the `Person` class? Yes, but separating them makes `Name` reusable. The many ways to design classes have different advantages. You need to consider trade-offs to choose one.

establish relationships

The second step is to establish relationships among the classes. The relationship is derived from the system analysis. The first two steps are intertwined. When you identify classes, you also think about the relationships among them. Establishing relationships among objects helps you understand the interactions among them. An object-oriented system consists of a collection of interrelated cooperative objects. The relationships for the classes in this example are illustrated in Figure 12.11.

FIGURE 12.11 A borrower is a person who has a loan.

describe attributes

The third step is to describe the attributes and methods in each of the classes you have identified. The `Name` class has the properties `firstName`, `mi`, and `lastName`, their associated `get` and `set` methods, and the `getFullName` method for returning the full name. You can compare names in alphabetical order of last name, first name, and mi. The `Address` class has the properties `street`, `city`, `state`, and `zip`, their associated `get` and `set` methods, and the `getAddress` method for returning the full address. The `Loan` class, presented in Listing 9.2, has the properties `annualInterestRate`, `numberOfYears`, and `loanAmount`, their associated `get` and `set` methods, and `getMonthlyPayment` and `getTotalPayment` methods. The `Person` class has the properties `name` and `address`, their associated `get` and `set` methods, and the `toString` method for displaying complete information about the person. `Borrower` is a subclass of `Person`. Additionally, `Borrower` has the `loan` property and its associated `get` and `set` methods, and the `toString` method for displaying the person and the loan payments. You can compare persons according to their names. Figure 12.11 is expanded to Figure 12.12.

```
«interface»
java.lang.Comparable
```

```
Name
-firstName: String
-mi: char
-lastName: String
+Name(firstName: String,
  mi: char, lastName:
  String)
+getFirstName(): String
+getMi(): char
+getLastName(): String
+getFullName(): String
```

```
Person
-name: Name
-address: Address
+Person()
+Person(name: Name, address:
 Address)
+getName(): Name
+setName(name: Name): void
+getAddress(): Address
+setAddress(address: Address):
 void
+toString(): String
```

```
Address
-street: String
-city: String
-state: String
-zip: String
+Address(street: String,
 city: String,state:
 String, zip: String)
+getStreet(): String
+getCity(): String
+getState(): String
+getZip(): String
+getFullAddress(): String
```

```
Loan
```

Defined in Listing 9.2

```
Borrower
-loan: Loan
+Borrower()
+Borrower(name: Name, address:
 Address)
+getLoan(): Loan
+setLoan(loan: Loan): void
+toString(): String
```

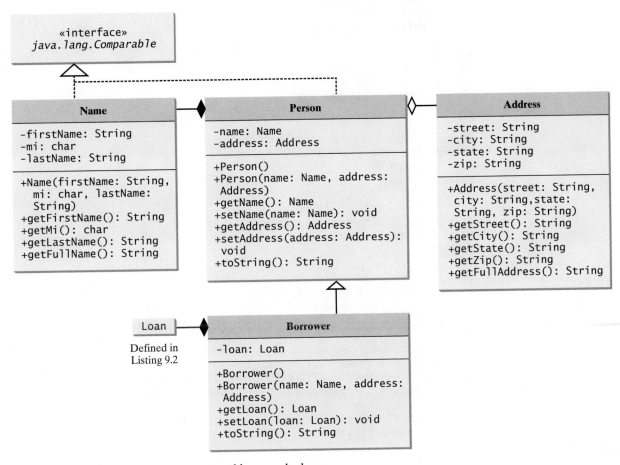

FIGURE 12.12 A borrower has a name, an address, and a loan.

Note

steps intertwined

The first three steps are often *intertwined*. For example, when you discover a class, you think of its responsibilities. You may identify new classes as collaborators. You will discover the relationships among these classes.

coding

The fourth step is to write the code for the classes. The program is long, but most of the coding is for the `get` and `set` methods. Once an object is identified, its properties and methods can be defined by analyzing the requirements and scenarios of the system. It is a good practice to provide complete **get** and **set** methods. These may not be needed for your current project, but they will be useful in other projects, because your classes are designed for reuse in future projects. Listings 12.1, 12.2, 12.3, and 12.4 give the **Name**, **Address**, **Person**, and **Borrower** classes.

LISTING 12.1 Name.java

Name class

constructor

```
public final class Name implements Comparable {
  private String firstName;
  private char mi;
  private String lastName;

  /** Construct a name with firstName, mi, and lastName */
  public Name(String firstName, char mi, String lastName) {
    this.firstName = firstName;
    this.mi = mi;
    this.lastName = lastName;
  }

  /** Return firstName */
  public String getFirstName() {
    return firstName;
  }

  /** Return middle name initial */
  public char getMi() {
    return mi;
  }

  /** Return lastName */
  public String getLastname() {
    return lastName;
  }

  /** Obtain full name */
  public String getFullName() {
    return firstName + ' ' + mi + ' ' + lastName;
  }

  /** Implement compareTo in the Comparable interface */
  public int compareTo(Object o) {
    if (!lastName.equals(((Name)o).lastName)) {
      return lastName.compareTo(((Name)o).lastName);
    }
    else if (!firstName.equals(((Name)o).firstName)) {
      return firstName.compareTo(((Name)o).firstName);
    }
    else {
      return mi - ((Name)o).mi;
    }
  }
}
```

LISTING 12.2 Address.java

Address class

```
public final class Address {
  private String street;
  private String city;
  private String state;
```

```
  private String zip;

  /** Create an address with street, city, state, and zip */
  public Address(String street, String city,
    String state, String zip) {
    this.street = street;
    this.city = city;
    this.state = state;
    this.zip = zip;
  }

  /** Return street */
  public String getStreet() {
    return street;
  }

  /** Return city */
  public String getCity() {
    return city;
  }

  /** Return state */
  public String getState() {
    return state;
  }

  /** Return zip */
  public String getZip() {
    return zip;
  }

  /** Get full address */
  public String getFullAddress() {
    return street + '\n' + city + ", " + state + ' ' + zip + '\n';
  }
}
```

constructor

Note

To avoid naming conflict with the **Person** class defined in Chapter 10, name the class **Person1** here.

LISTING 12.3 Person1.java

```
public class Person1 implements Comparable {
  private Name name;
  private Address address;

  /** Construct a person with default properties */
  public Person1() {
    this(new Name("Jill", 'S', "Barr"),
      new Address("100 Main", "Savannah", "GA", "31411"));
  }

  /** Construct a person with specified name and address */
  public Person1(Name name, Address address) {
    this.name = name;
    this.address = address;
  }

  /** Return name */
```

Person class

constructor

constructor

```
  public Name getName() {
    return name;
  }

  /** Set a new name */
  public void setName(Name name) {
    this.name = name;
  }

  /** Return address */
  public Address getAddress() {
    return address;
  }

  /** Set a new address */
  public void setAddress(Address address) {
    this.address = address;
  }

  /** Override the toString method */
  public String toString() {
    return '\n' + name.getFullName() + '\n' +
      address.getFullAddress() + '\n';
  }

  /** Implement compareTo in the Comparable interface */
  public int compareTo(Object o) {
    return name.compareTo(((Person1)o).name);
  }
}
```

LISTING 12.4 Borrower.java

Borrower class

```
public class Borrower extends Person1 {
  private Loan loan;

  /** Construct a borrower with default properties */
  public Borrower() {
    super();
  }

  /** Create a borrower with specified name and address */
  public Borrower(Name name, Address address) {
    super(name, address);
  }

  /** Return loan */
  public Loan getLoan() {
    return loan;
  }

  /** Set a new loan */
  public void setLoan(Loan loan) {
    this.loan = loan;
  }

  /** String representation for borrower */
  public String toString() {
    return super.toString() +
```

```
      "Monthly payment is " + loan.getMonthlyPayment() + '\n' +
      "Total payment is " + loan.getTotalPayment();
  }
}
```

Listing 12.5 is a test program that uses the classes Name, Address, Borrower, and Loan.

LISTING 12.5 BorrowLoan.java

BorrowLoan class

```
public class BorrowLoan {
  /** Main method */
  public static void main(String[] args) {
    // Create a name
    Name name = new Name("John", 'D', "Smith");

    // Create an address
    Address address = new Address("100 Main Street", "Savannah",
      "GA", "31419");

    // Create a loan
    Loan loan = new Loan(5.5, 15, 250000);

    // Create a borrower
    Borrower borrower = new Borrower(name, address);

    borrower.setLoan(loan);

    // Display loan information
    System.out.println(borrower);
  }
}
```

```
John D Smith
100 Main Street
Savannah, GA 31419

Monthly payment is 2042.7086365528232
Total payment is 367687.5545795082
```

12.6 Case Study: The **Rational** Class

Video Note
Rational class

A rational number has a numerator and a denominator in the form a/b, where a is the numerator and b is the denominator. For example, 1/3, 3/4, and 10/4 are rational numbers.

A rational number cannot have a denominator of 0, but a numerator of 0 is fine. Every integer a is equivalent to a rational number a/1. Rational numbers are used in exact computations involving fractions—for example, 1/3 = 0.33333.... This number cannot be precisely represented in floating-point format using data type double or float. To obtain the exact result, we must use rational numbers.

Java provides data types for integers and floating-point numbers, but not for rational numbers. This section shows how to design a class to represent rational numbers.

Since rational numbers share many common features with integers and floating-point numbers, and Number is the root class for numeric wrapper classes, it is appropriate to define Rational as a subclass of Number. Since rational numbers are comparable, the Rational class should also implement the Comparable interface. Figure 12.13 illustrates the Rational class and its relationship to the Number class and the Comparable interface.

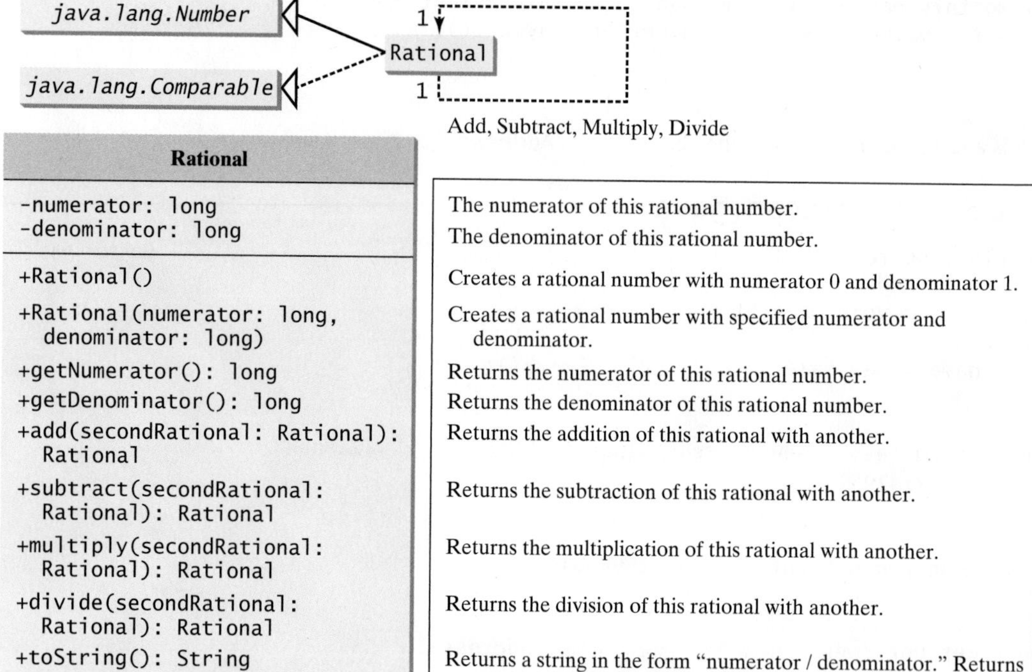

FIGURE 12.13 The properties, constructors, and methods of the `Rational` class are illustrated in UML.

A rational number consists of a numerator and a denominator. There are many equivalent rational numbers—for example, $1/3 = 2/6 = 3/9 = 4/12$. The numerator and the denominator of 1/3 have no common divisor except 1, so 1/3 is said to be in lowest terms.

To reduce a rational number to its lowest terms, you need to find the greatest common divisor (GCD) of the absolute values of its numerator and denominator, and then divide both numerator and denominator by this value. You can use the method for computing the GCD of two integers `n` and `d`, as suggested in Listing 4.8, GreatestCommonDivisor.java. The numerator and denominator in a `Rational` object are reduced to their lowest terms.

As usual, let us first write a test program to create two `Rational` objects and test its methods. Listing 12.6 is a test program.

LISTING 12.6 TestRationalClass.java

create a Rational
create a Rational
add

```
public class TestRationalClass {
  /** Main method */
  public static void main(String[] args) {
    // Create and initialize two rational numbers r1 and r2.
    Rational r1 = new Rational(4, 2);
    Rational r2 = new Rational(2, 3);

    // Display results
    System.out.println(r1 + " + " + r2 + " = " + r1.add(r2));
    System.out.println(r1 + " - " + r2 + " = " + r1.subtract(r2));
    System.out.println(r1 + " * " + r2 + " = " + r1.multiply(r2));
    System.out.println(r1 + " / " + r2 + " = " + r1.divide(r2));
    System.out.println(r2 + " is " + r2.doubleValue());
  }
}
```

```
2 + 2/3 = 8/3
2 - 2/3 = 4/3
2 * 2/3 = 4/3
2 / 2/3 = 3
2/3 is 0.6666666666666666
```

The `main` method creates two rational numbers, `r1` and `r2` (lines 5–6), and displays the results of `r1` + `r2`, `r1` - `r2`, `r1` x `r2`, and `r1` / `r2` (lines 9–12). To perform `r1` + `r2`, invoke `r1.add(r2)` to return a new `Rational` object. Similarly, `r1.subtract(r2)` is for `r1` - `r2`, `r1.multiply(r2)` for `r1` x `r2`, and `r1.divide(r2)` for `r1` / `r2`.

The `doubleValue()` method displays the double value of `r2` (line 13). The `doubleValue()` method is defined in `java.lang.Number` and overridden in `Rational`.

Note that when a string is concatenated with an object using the plus sign (+), the object's string representation from the `toString()` method is used to concatenate with the string. So `r1` + " + " + `r2` + " = " + `r1.add(r2)` is equivalent to `r1.toString()` + " + " + `r2.toString()` + " = " + `r1.add(r2).toString()`.

The `Rational` class is implemented in Listing 12.7.

LISTING 12.7 Rational.java

```
public class Rational extends Number implements Comparable {
  // Data fields for numerator and denominator
  private long numerator = 0;
  private long denominator = 1;

  /** Construct a rational with default properties */
  public Rational() {
    this(0, 1);
  }

  /** Construct a rational with specified numerator and denominator */
  public Rational(long numerator, long denominator) {
    long gcd = gcd(numerator, denominator);
    this.numerator = ((denominator > 0) ? 1 : -1) * numerator / gcd;
    this.denominator = Math.abs(denominator) / gcd;
  }

  /** Find GCD of two numbers */
  private static long gcd(long n, long d) {
    long n1 = Math.abs(n);
    long n2 = Math.abs(d);
    int gcd = 1;

    for (int k = 1; k <= n1 && k <= n2; k++) {
      if (n1 % k == 0 && n2 % k == 0)
        gcd = k;
    }

    return gcd;
  }

  /** Return numerator */
  public long getNumerator() {
    return numerator;
  }

  /** Return denominator */
```

```
  public long getDenominator() {
    return denominator;
  }

```

$\frac{a}{b} + \frac{c}{d} = \frac{ad + bc}{bd}$

```
  /** Add a rational number to this rational */
  public Rational add(Rational secondRational) {
    long n = numerator * secondRational.getDenominator() +
      denominator * secondRational.getNumerator();
    long d = denominator * secondRational.getDenominator();
    return new Rational(n, d);
  }

```

$\frac{a}{b} - \frac{c}{d} = \frac{ad - bc}{bd}$

```
  /** Subtract a rational number from this rational */
  public Rational subtract(Rational secondRational) {
    long n = numerator * secondRational.getDenominator()
      - denominator * secondRational.getNumerator();
    long d = denominator * secondRational.getDenominator();
    return new Rational(n, d);
  }

```

$\frac{a}{b} \times \frac{c}{d} = \frac{ac}{bd}$

```
  /** Multiply a rational number to this rational */
  public Rational multiply(Rational secondRational) {
    long n = numerator * secondRational.getNumerator();
    long d = denominator * secondRational.getDenominator();
    return new Rational(n, d);
  }

```

$\frac{a}{b} \div \frac{c}{d} = \frac{ad}{bc}$

```
  /** Divide a rational number from this rational */
  public Rational divide(Rational secondRational) {
    long n = numerator * secondRational.getDenominator();
    long d = denominator * secondRational.numerator;
    return new Rational(n, d);
  }

  /** Override the toString() method */
  public String toString() {
    if (denominator == 1)
      return numerator + "";
    else
      return numerator + "/" + denominator;
  }

  /** Override the equals method in the Object class */
  public boolean equals(Object parm1) {
    if ((this.subtract((Rational)(parm1))).getNumerator() == 0)
      return true;
    else
      return false;
  }

  /** Implement the abstract intValue method in java.lang.Number */
  public int intValue() {
    return (int)doubleValue();
  }

  /** Implement the abstract floatValue method in java.lang.Number */
  public float floatValue() {
```

```
95      return (float)doubleValue();
96    }
97
98    /** Implement the doubleValue method in java.lang.Number */
99    public double doubleValue() {
100     return numerator * 1.0 / denominator;
101   }
102
103   /** Implement the abstract longValue method in java.lang.Number */
104   public long longValue() {
105     return (long)doubleValue();
106   }
107
108   /** Implement the compareTo method in java.lang.Comparable */
109   public int compareTo(Object o) {
110     if ((this.subtract((Rational)o)).getNumerator() > 0)
111       return 1;
112     else if ((this.subtract((Rational)o)).getNumerator() < 0)
113       return -1;
114     else
115       return 0;
116   }
117 }
```

The rational number is encapsulated in a `Rational` object. Internally, a rational number is represented in its lowest terms (line 13), and the numerator determines its sign (line 14). The denominator is always positive (line 15).

The `gcd()` method (lines 19–30 in the `Rational` class) is private; it is not intended for use by clients. The `gcd()` method is only for internal use by the `Rational` class. The `gcd()` method is also static, since it is not dependent on any particular `Rational` object.

The `abs(x)` method (lines 20–21 in the `Rational` class) is defined in the `Math` class that returns the absolute value of `x`.

Two `Rational` objects can interact with each other to perform add, subtract, multiply, and divide operations. These methods return a new `Rational` object (lines 43–70).

The methods `toString` and `equals` in the `Object` class are overridden in the `Rational` class (lines 73–91). The `toString()` method returns a string representation of a `Rational` object in the form `numerator/denominator`, or simply `numerator` if `denominator` is `1`. The `equals(Object other)` method returns true if this rational number is equal to the other rational number.

The abstract methods `intValue`, `longValue`, `floatValue`, and `doubleValue` in the `Number` class are implemented in the `Rational` class (lines 88–106). These methods return `int`, `long`, `float`, and `double` value for this rational number.

The `compareTo(Object other)` method in the `Comparable` interface is implemented in the `Rational` class (lines 109–117) to compare this rational number to the other rational number.

Tip

The `get` methods for the properties `numerator` and `denominator` are provided in the `Rational` class, but the `set` methods are not provided, so, once a `Rational` object is created, its contents cannot be changed. The `Rational` class is immutable. A well-known example of an immutable class is the `String` class. The wrapper classes introduced in §11.9, "Processing Primitive Data Type Values as Objects," are also immutable.

immutable

Tip

encapsulation

The numerator and denominator are represented using two variables. It is possible to use an array of two integers to represent the numerator and denominator. See Exercise 12.4. The signatures of the public methods in the `Rational` class are not changed, although the internal representation of a rational number is changed. This is a good example to illustrate the idea that the data fields of a class should be kept private so as to encapsulate the implementation of the class from the use of the class.

overflow

The `Rational` class has serious limitations. It can easily overflow. For example, the following code will display an incorrect result, because the denominator is too large.

```
public class Test {
  public static void main(String[] args) {
    Rational r1 = new Rational(1, 123456789);
    Rational r2 = new Rational(1, 123456789);
    Rational r3 = new Rational(1, 123456789);
    System.out.println("r1 * r2 * r3 is " +
      r1.multiply(r2.multiply(r3)));
  }
}
```

```
r1 * r2 * r3 is -1/2204193661661244627
```

To fix it, you may implement the `Rational` class using the `BigInteger` for numerator and denominator (see Exercises 12.3 and 12.5).

12.7 Class Design Guidelines

You have learned how to design classes from the preceding two examples and from many other examples in the preceding chapters. Here are some guidelines.

12.7.1 Cohesion

coherent purpose

A class should describe a single entity, and all the class operations should logically fit together to support a coherent purpose. You can use a class for students, for example, but you should not combine students and staff in the same class, because students and staff have different entities.

separating responsibilities

A single entity with too many responsibilities can be broken into several classes to separate responsibilities. The classes `String`, `StringBuilder`, and `StringBuffer` all deal with strings, for example, but have different responsibilities. The `String` class deals with immutable strings, the `StringBuilder` class is for creating mutable strings, and the `StringBuffer` class is similar to `StringBuilder` except that `StringBuffer` contains synchronized methods for updating strings.

The `Date`, `Calendar`, and `GregorianCalendar` classes all deal with date and time, but have different responsibilities. The `Date` class represents a specific time. `Calendar` is an abstract class for extracting detailed calendar information from a specific time. `GregorianCalendar` implements a concrete calendar system.

12.7.2 Consistency

naming conventions

Follow standard Java programming style and naming conventions. Choose informative names for classes, data fields, and methods. A popular style is to place the data declaration before the constructor, and place constructors before methods.

Choose names consistently. It is not a good practice to choose different names for similar operations. For example, the `length()` method returns the size of a `String`, a `StringBuilder`, and a `StringBuffer`. But the `size()` method is used to return the size of an `ArrayList`. For consistency it would be better to use the same name. naming consistency

In general, you should consistently provide a public no-arg constructor for constructing a default instance. If a class does not support a no-arg constructor, document the reason. If no constructors are defined explicitly, a public default no-arg constructor with an empty body is assumed. If a constructor does not invoke an overloaded constructor or its superclass's constructor, it invokes its superclass no-arg constructor by default. no-arg constructor

If you want to prevent users from creating an object for a class, you may declare a private constructor in the class, as is the case for the `Math` class. The constructors in abstract classes should always be declared `protected`.

12.7.3 Encapsulation

A class should use the `private` modifier to hide its data from direct access by clients. This makes the class easy to maintain. encapsulating data fields

Provide a `get` method only if you want the field to be readable, and provide a `set` method only if you want the field to be updateable. For example, the `Rational` class provides `get` methods for numerator and denominator, but no `set` methods, because `Rational` is an immutable class.

A class should also hide methods not intended for client use. The `gcd` method in the `Rational` class in the preceding section is private, for example, because it is only for internal use within the class.

A class can present two contracts: one for the users of the class, and one for the extenders of the class. Make the fields `private` and the accessor and mutator methods `public` if they are intended for the users of the class. Make the fields or methods `protected` if they are intended for extenders of the class. The contract for extenders encompasses the contract for users. The extended class may increase the visibility of an instance method from `protected` to `public`, or may change its implementation, but you should never change the implementation in a way that violates the contract. private vs. protected

12.7.4 Clarity

Cohesion, consistency, and encapsulation are good guidelines for achieving design clarity. Additionally, a class should have a clear contract that is easy to explain and easy to understand. easy to explain

Users can incorporate classes in many different combinations, orders, and environments. Therefore, you should design a class that imposes no restrictions on what or when the user can do with it, design the properties in a way that lets the user set them in any order and with any combination of values, and design methods that function independently of their order of occurrence. For example, the `Loan` class contains the properties `loanAmount`, `numberOfYears`, and `annualInterestRate`. The values of these properties can be set in any order. independent methods

Methods should be defined intuitively without generating confusion. For example, the `substring(int beginIndex, int endIndex)` method in the `String` class is somehow confusing. The method returns a substring from `beginIndex` to `endIndex - 1`, rather than `endIndex`. intuitive meaning

You should not declare a data field that can be derived from other data fields. For example, the following `Person` class has two data fields: `birthDate` and `age`. Since `age` can be derived from `birthDate`, age should not be declared as a data field. independent properties

```
public class Person {
  private java.util.Date birthDate;
  int age;

  ...
}
```

12.7.5 Completeness

Classes are designed for use by many different customers. In order to be useful in a wide range of applications, a class should provide a variety of ways for customization through properties and methods. For example, the String class contains more than 50 methods that are useful for a variety of applications. The Calendar class defines many time fields as constants, such as YEAR, MONTH, DATE, HOUR, HOUR_OF_DAY, MINUTE, SECOND, and DAY_OF_WEEK, and provides many methods for extracting date and time and for setting a new date and time in the calendar.

12.7.6 Instance vs. Static

A variable or method that is dependent on a specific instance of the class should be an instance variable or method. A variable that is shared by all the instances of a class should be declared static. For example, the variable numberOfObjects in Circle3 in Listing 7.7, is shared by all the objects of the SimpleCircle1 class, and therefore is declared static. A method that is not dependent on a specific instance should be declared as a static method. For instance, the getNumberOfObjects method in Circle3 and the gcd method in Rational are not tied to any specific instance, and therefore are declared as static methods.

Always reference static variables and methods from a class name (rather than a reference variable) to improve readability and avoid errors.

Do not pass a parameter from a constructor to initialize a static data field. It is better to use a set method to change the static data field. The class in (a) below is better replaced by (b).

```
public class SomeThing {
  int t1;
  static int t2;

  public SomeThing(int t1, int t2) {
    ...
  }
}
```

(a)

```
public class SomeThing {
  int t1;
  static int t2;

  public SomeThing(int t1) {
    ...
  }

  public static void setT2(int t2) {
    SomeThing.t2 = t2;
  }
}
```

(b)

common design error

Instance and static are integral parts of object-oriented programming. A data field or method is either instance or static. Do not mistakenly overlook static data fields or methods. It is a common design error to declare an instance method that should have been declared static. For example, the factorial(int n) method for computing the factorial of n should be declared static, because it is independent of any specific instance.

A constructor is always instance, because it is used to create a specific instance. A static variable or method can be invoked from an instance method, but an instance variable or method cannot be invoked from a static method.

12.7.7 Inheritance vs. Aggregation

The difference between inheritance and aggregation is the difference between an is-a and a has-a relationship. For example, an apple is a fruit; thus, you would use inheritance to model the relationship between the classes Apple and Fruit. A person has a name; thus, you would use aggregation to model the relationship between the classes Person and Name.

12.7.8 Interfaces vs. Abstract Classes

Both interfaces and abstract classes can be used to specify common behaviour for objects. How do you decide whether to use an interface or a class? In general, a *strong is-a relationship* that clearly describes a parent-child relationship should be modeled using classes. For example, since an orange is a fruit, their relationship should be modeled using class inheritance. A *weak is-a relationship*, also known as an *is-kind-of relationship*, indicates that an object possesses a certain property. A weak is-a relationship can be modeled using interfaces. For example, all strings are comparable, so the `String` class implements the `Comparable` interface. A circle or a rectangle is a geometric object, so `Circle` can be designed as a subclass of `GeometricObject`. Circles are different and comparable based on their radii, so `Circle` can implement the `Comparable` interface.

Interfaces are more flexible than abstract classes, because a subclass can extend only one superclass but can implement any number of interfaces. However, interfaces cannot contain concrete methods. The virtues of interfaces and abstract classes can be combined by creating an interface with an abstract class that implements it. Then you can use the interface or the abstract class, whichever is convenient. For this reason, such classes are known as *convenience classes*. For example, in the Java Collections Framework, introduced in Chapter 22, the `AbstractCollection` class is a convenience class for the `Collection` interface, and the `AbstractSet` class is a convenience class for the `Set` interface.

12.8 Framework-Based Programming Using Java API

The Java *API* (*Application Program Interface*) consists of numerous classes and interfaces grouped into more than a dozen packages, as shown in Table 12.1. API

TABLE 12.1 Some Java API packages

Package	*Description*
`java.lang`	contains core Java classes and interfaces (e.g., `System`, `Math`, `Object`, `String`, `StringBuffer`, `Number`, `Character`, `Boolean`, `Byte`, `Short`, `Integer`, `Long`, `Float`, `Double`, `Comparable`, and `Cloneable`). This package is implicitly imported to every Java program.
`javax.swing`	contains the lightweight graphical user interface components (e.g., `JOptionPane`, `JFrame`, `JButton`) for developing Swing GUI programs.
`java.util`	contains utility classes and interfaces, such as `Scanner`, `Arrays`, `ArrayList`, `Date`, `Calendar`, and `GregorianCalendar`.
`java.io`	contains classes and interfaces for IO, such as `File` and `PrintWriter`.
`java.math`	contains classes `BigInteger` for performing arbitrary-precision integer arithmetic and `BigDecimal` for performing arbitrary-precision decimal arithmetic.
`java.net`	contains classes for network programming.
`java.applet`	contains classes for supporting applets.
`java.awt`	contains classes for supporting GUI programming.

You have used several classes and interfaces in the `java.lang`, `javax.swing`, `java.util`, and `java.io` packages. These are just a few of the classes and interfaces you have learned. To create comprehensive projects, you have to use more classes and interfaces in the Java API. The classes and interfaces in the Java API establish a framework for programmers to develop applications using Java. For example, the classes and interfaces in the Java GUI API establish a framework for developing GUI programs. You have to use these classes and interfaces and follow their conventions and rules to create applications. This is referred to as *framework-based programming*.

framework-based programming

Once you understand the concept of Java and object-oriented programming, the most important lesson from now on is learning how to use the API to develop useful programs. The most effective way to achieve this is to imitate good examples. The book provides many carefully designed examples to demonstrate the concept of framework-based programming using the Java API. You will learn the Java GUI programming framework in Chapters 13–17, the Java exception–handling framework in Chapter 18, and the Java I/O framework in Chapter 19.

12.9 Design Patterns

reuse code

One important benefit of object-oriented programming is to *reuse code*. For example, to create a button, you simply use the `JButton` class to create an instance of `JButton`. The `JButton` class is already defined in the Java API, so you can use it without having to reinvent the wheel. Design patterns are proven sound software strategies for designing classes. Applying design patterns is like *reusing experience*. You can apply successful patterns to develop new software without reinventing new solution strategies.

reuse experience

The formal recognition of design patterns was presented in a groundbreaking book, *Design Patterns: Elements of Reusable Object-Oriented Software*, by Erich Gamma, Richard Helm, Ralph Johnson, and John Vlissides. The book profoundly influenced object-oriented software development. The authors are respectfully nicknamed the "*Gang of Four*" and their book is commonly known as the *gang-of-four book*.

the gang-of-four book

The gang-of-four book argues that expert designers do not solve every problem from scratch. Rather, they reuse solutions that have worked for them in the past. When they find a good solution, they use it over and over again. Design patterns can speed up the development process by providing almost ready-made solutions that have been used earlier and proved to be effective and efficient. The gang-of-four book records experiences in designing object-oriented software as design patterns, documenting 23 of them.

23 design patterns

To apply design patterns effectively, you need to familiarize yourself with the most popular and effective ones. The best way to learn these patterns is by examples. We will illustrate design patterns throughout the book with concrete examples.

learn design patterns

As an example, this section introduces the *Singleton pattern*. This pattern declares a class that can be used to instantiate a unique instance. Occasionally, it is desirable to restrict instantiation of a class to exactly one object. For example, there may be many printers in a system, but there should be only one printer spooler. So, your system should ensure that only one printer spooler object is created.

Singleton pattern

The Singleton pattern can be implemented by creating a class with a private constructor and a static constant that references an instance of the class. Listing 12.8 shows an example of such class.

Listing 12.8 Singleton.java

create object

private constructor

```
public final class Singleton {
  private static final Singleton uniqueInstance = new Singleton();

  private Singleton() {
  }

```

```
7   public static Singleton getInstance() {
8     return uniqueInstance;
9   }
10 }
```

access point

An object of the `Singleton` class is created in line 2. Since the constructor is private (line 4), it prevents the client from creating objects using `new Singleton()`. The only way to access the object is through the `getInstance()` method (line 7), which returns the reference of the object (line 8). For example, the following code displays `true`, since `object1` and `object2` refer to the same object.

```
Singleton object1 = Singleton.getInstance();
Singleton object2 = Singleton.getInstance();
System.out.println(object1 == object2);
```

Key Terms

aggregated object 397
aggregation 397
aggregating object 397
Application Program Interface (API) 413
association 396
composition 397
CRC cards 395
dependency 398
design pattern 414
framework-based programming 414

Chapter Summary

- Software life cycle involves *requirements specification, system analysis, system design, implementation, testing, deployment,* and *maintenance.*

- The process of designing classes calls for identifying the classes and discovering the relationships among them.

- The common relationships among classes are *association*, *aggregation*, *composition*, *dependency*, and *inheritance*.

- Some guidelines for class design are *cohesion*, *consistency*, *encapsulation*, *clarity*, and *completeness*.

- A property shared by all the instances of a class should be declared as a static property. Don't mistakenly overlook static data fields or methods. A method not tied to a specific instance should be declared static.

- The difference between inheritance and aggregation is the difference between an is-a and a has-a relationship.

- Both interfaces and abstract classes can be used to specify common behavior of objects. How do you decide whether to use an interface or a class? In general, a *strong is-a relationship* that clearly describes a parent-child relationship should be modeled using classes. A weak is-a relationship can be modeled using interfaces.

- Interfaces are more flexible than abstract classes, because a subclass can extend only one superclass but can implement any number of interfaces. However, interfaces cannot contain concrete methods.

- Design patterns are proven sound software strategies for designing classes. Applying design patterns is like *reusing experience*. You can apply successful patterns to develop new software without reinventing new solution strategies.

Review Questions

Section 12.3 Discovering Relationships among Objects

12.1 What are the common types of relationships among classes? Describe the graphical notations for modeling the relationships among classes.

12.2 What relationship is appropriate for the following classes? Draw the relationships using UML diagrams.

- Company and Employee
- Course and Faculty
- Student and Person
- House and Window
- Account and Savings Account
- The `JOptionPane` class and the `String` class
- The `Loan` class and the `Date` class

Section 12.6 The `Rational` Class

12.3 Show the output of the following code:

```
public class Test {
  public static void main(String[] args) {
    Rational r1 = new Rational(1, 3);
    Rational r2 = new Rational(2, 4);
    System.out.println(r1 + " + " + r2 + " = " + r1.add(r2));
    System.out.println(r2 + " + " + r1 + " = " + r2.add(r1));
    System.out.println(r1 + " - " + r2 + " = " +
      r1.subtract(r2));
    System.out.println(r2 + " - " + r1 + " = " +
      r2.subtract(r1));
    System.out.println(r1 + " * " + r2 + " = " +
      r1.multiply(r2));
    System.out.println(r2 + " * " + r1 + " = " +
      r2.multiply(r1));
    System.out.println(r1 + " / " + r2 + " = " +
      r1.divide(r2));
    System.out.println(r2 + " / " + r1 + " = " +
      r2.divide(r1));
    System.out.println(r1 + " = " + r1.doubleValue());
    System.out.println(r2 + " = " + r2.doubleValue());
  }
}
```

12.4 What is wrong in the following code?

```
Number r = new Rational();
System.out.println(r);
System.out.println(r.doubleValue());
System.out.println(r.add(new Rational()));
System.out.println((Rational)r.add(new Rational()));
System.out.println(((Rational)r).add(new Rational()));
```

12.5 What is wrong in the following code?

```
Number r = new Number();
System.out.println(r);
```

12.6 Is the following code correct?

```
Comparable r = new Rational();
System.out.println(r);
```

(a)

```
Comparable r = new Rational();
System.out.println(
  r.compareTo(new Rational()));
```

(b)

Section 12.7 Class Design Guidelines

12.7 What is cohesion? Give examples of cohesive class design.

12.8 What is consistency? Give examples of inconsistent class design.

12.9 What is encapsulation? What are the benefits of data field encapsulation?

12.10 When is it appropriate to use the `protected` modifier?

12.11 Which of the following is poor design?

- A data field is derived from other data fields in the same class.
- A method must be invoked after/before invoking another method in the same class.
- A method is an instance method, but it does not reference any instance data fields or invoke instance methods.
- A parameter is passed from a constructor to initialize a static data field.

12.12 Which of the following is incorrect?

- A static method may reference instance data fields or invoke instance methods.
- An instance method may reference static data fields or invoke static methods.
- A constructor may be static.
- A constructor may be private.
- A constructor may invoke a static method.
- A constructor may invoke an overloaded constructor.
- A constructor invokes its superclass no-arg constructor by default if it does not invoke an overloaded constructor or its superclass's constructor.
- An abstract class contains constructors.
- The constructors in an abstract class are public.
- The constructors in an abstract class are private.
- You may declare a final abstract class.
- An interface may contain constructors.
- An interface may contain instance data fields.
- An interface may contain static methods.

PROGRAMMING EXERCISES

12.1* (*Multiple loans*) For the case study in §12.5, suppose that a borrower may have multiple loans. Redesign the system and redraw the UML diagrams to reflect the change. Use an array list to store multiple loans. You need a method that adds a new loan, a method that removes an existing loan, and a method that returns all loans in a list. Implement the new design and write a test program that creates a borrower with three loans, and display borrower and loan information.

Video Note
Design/implement classes for **Person** and **Student**

12.2** (*The* `Person` *and* `Student` *classes*) Design the `Student` class that extends `Person`. Implement the `compareTo` method in the `Person` class to compare persons in alphabetical order of their last name. Implement the `compareTo` method to compare students in alphabetical order of their major and last name. Draw a UML diagram that involves `Person`, `Student`, `Comparable`, and `Name`.

Write a program with the following four methods:

```
/** Sort an array of comparable objects  */
public static void sort(Comparable[] list)

/** Pirnt an array of objects */
public static void printList(Object[] object)

/** Return the max object in an array of comparable objects */
public static Comparable max(Comparable[] list)
```

`main` method: Test the `sort`, `printList`, and `max` methods using an array of four students, an array of four strings, an array of 100 random rationals, and an array of 100 random integers.

12.3 (*Using the* `Rational` class) Write a program that will compute the following summation series using the `Rational` class:

$$\frac{1}{2} + \frac{2}{3} + \frac{3}{4} + \ldots + \frac{98}{99} + \frac{99}{100}$$

You will discover that output is incorrect because of integer overflow (too large). To fix this problem, see Exercise 12.5.

12.4* (*Demonstrating the benefits of encapsulation*) Rewrite the `Rational` class in §12.6 using a new internal representation for numerator and denominator. Declare an array of two integers as follows:

```
private long[] r = new long[2];
```

Use `r[0]` to represent the numerator and `r[1]` to represent the denominator. The signatures of the methods in the `Rational` class are not changed, so a client application that uses the previous `Rational` class can continue to use this new `Rational` class without being recompiled.

12.5** (*Using* `BigInteger` for the `Rational` class) Redesign and implement the `Rational` class in §12.6 using `BigInteger` for numerator and denominator.

12.6* (*Creating a rational number calculator*) Write a program similar to Listing 8.4, Calculator.java. Instead of using integers, use rationals, as shown in Figure 12.14. You will need to use the `split` method in the `String` class, introduced in §8.2.6, "Converting, Replacing, and Splitting Strings," to retrieve the numerator string and denominator string, and convert strings into integers using the `Integer.parseInt` method.

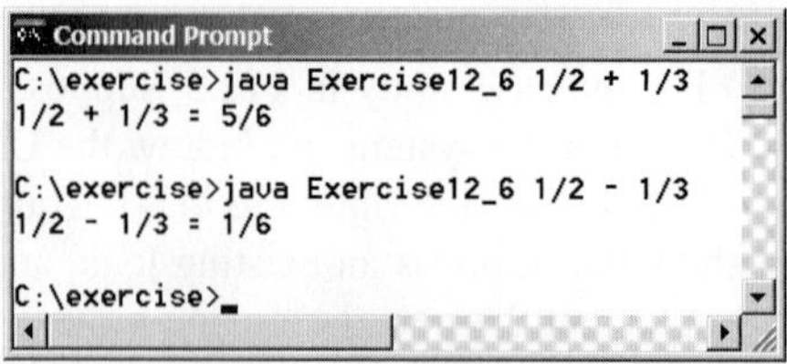

FIGURE 12.14 The program takes three arguments (operand1, operator, and operand2) from the command line and displays the expression and the result of the arithmetic operation.

CHAPTER 13

GUI BASICS

Objectives

- To distinguish between Swing and AWT (§13.2).
- To describe the Java GUI API hierarchy (§13.3).
- To create user interfaces using frames, panels, and simple GUI components (§13.4).
- To understand the role of layout managers (§13.5).
- To use the `FlowLayout`, `GridLayout`, and `BorderLayout` managers to layout components in a container (§13.5).
- To specify colors and fonts using the `Color` and `Font` classes (§§13.6–13.7).
- To use `JPanel` as subcontainers (§13.8).
- To apply common features such as borders, tool tips, fonts, and colors on Swing components (§13.9).
- To use borders to visually group user-interface components (§13.9).
- To create image icons using the `ImageIcon` class (§13.10).

13.1 Introduction

The design of the API for Java GUI programming is an excellent example of how the object-oriented principle is applied. In the preceding chapters, we used simple GUI examples to demonstrate OOP. In the chapters that follow, you will learn the framework of Java GUI API and use the GUI components to develop user-friendly interfaces for applications and applets.

This chapter introduces the basics of Java GUI programming. Specifically, it discusses GUI components and their relationships, containers and layout managers, colors, fonts, borders, image icons, and tool tips.

13.2 Swing vs. AWT

Why do the GUI component classes have the prefix *J*? Instead of `JButton`, why not name it simply `Button`? In fact, there is a class already named `Button` in the `java.awt` package.

When Java was introduced, the GUI classes were bundled in a library known as the Abstract Windows Toolkit (AWT). For every platform on which Java runs, the AWT components are automatically mapped to the platform-specific components through their respective agents, known as *peers*. AWT is fine for developing simple graphical user interfaces, but not for developing comprehensive GUI projects. Besides, AWT is prone to platform-specific bugs, because its peer-based approach relies heavily on the underlying platform. With the release of Java 2, the AWT user-interface components were replaced by a more robust, versatile, and flexible library known as *Swing components*. Swing components are painted directly on canvases using Java code, except for components that are subclasses of `java.awt.Window` or `java.awt.Panel`, which must be drawn using native GUI on a specific platform. Swing components are less dependent on the target platform and use less of the native GUI resource. For this reason, Swing components that don't rely on native GUI are referred to as *lightweight components,* and AWT components are referred to as *heavyweight components*.

Swing components

lightweight

heavyweight

To distinguish new Swing component classes from their AWT counterparts, the names of Swing GUI component classes begin with a prefixed *J*. Although AWT components are still supported in Java 2, it is better to learn to how program using Swing components, because the AWT user-interface components will eventually fade away. This book uses Swing GUI components exclusively.

why prefix J?

13.3 The Java GUI API

The GUI API contains the essential classes listed below. Their hierarchical relationships are shown in Figures 13.1 and 13.2.

The GUI classes can be classified into three groups: *container classes*, *component classes,* and *helper classes*. The container classes, such as `JFrame`, `JPanel`, and `JApplet`, are used to contain other components. The GUI component classes, such as `JButton`, `JTextField`, `JTextArea`, `JComboBox`, `JList`, `JRadioButton`, and `JMenu`, are subclasses of `JComponent`. The helper classes, such as `Graphics`, `Color`, `Font`, `FontMetrics`, and `Dimension`, are used to support GUI components.

Note

The `JFrame`, `JApplet`, `JDialog`, and `JComponent` classes and their subclasses are grouped in the `javax.swing` package. All the other classes in Figure 13.1 are grouped in the `java.awt` package.

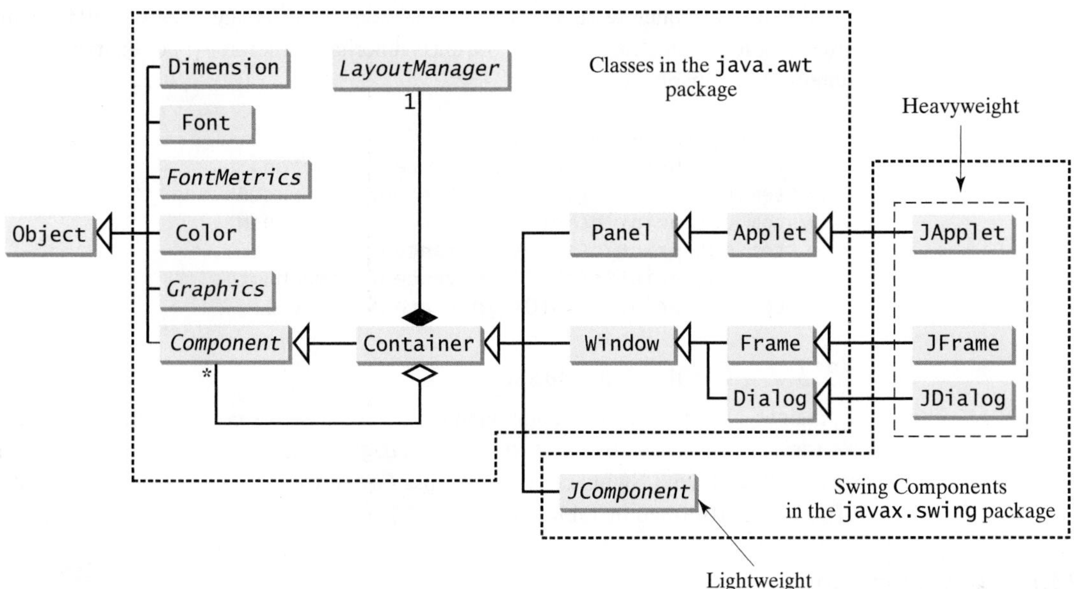

FIGURE 13.1 Java GUI programming utilizes the classes shown in this hierarchical diagram.

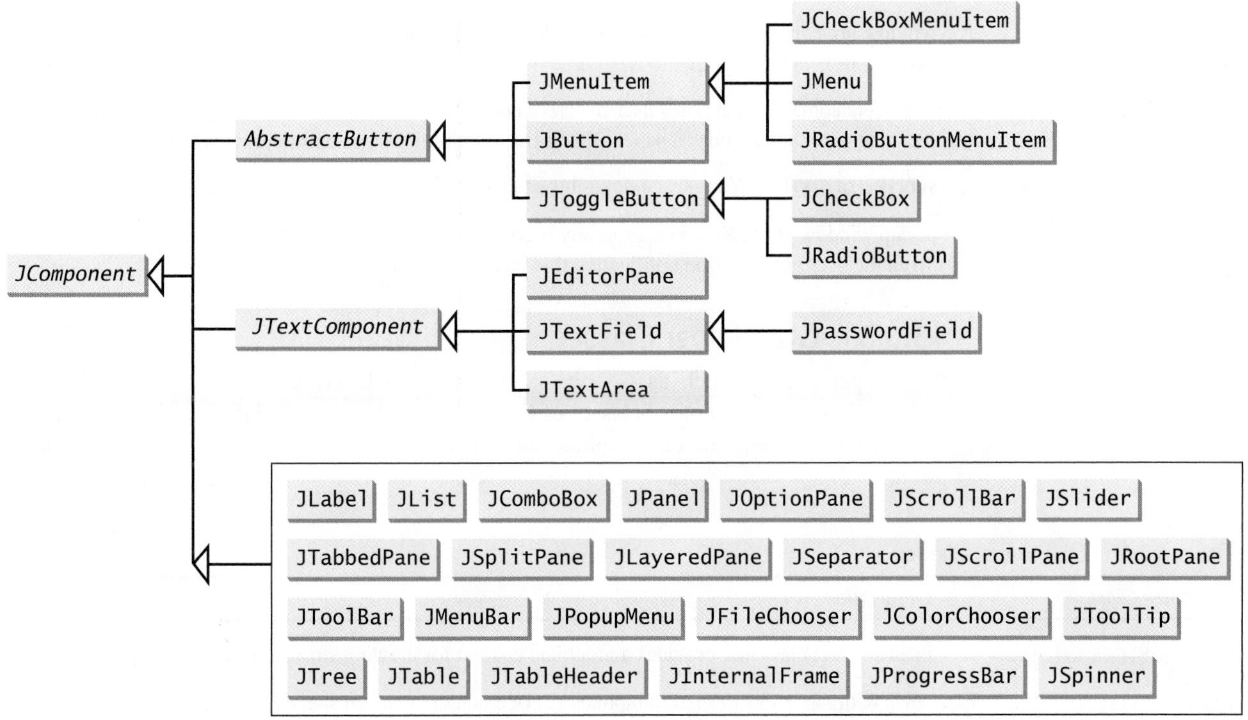

FIGURE 13.2 `JComponent` and its subclasses are the basic elements for building graphical user interfaces.

13.3.1 Swing GUI Components

`Component` is a superclass of all the user-interface classes, and `JComponent` is a superclass of all the lightweight Swing components, Since `JComponent` is an abstract class, you cannot use `new JComponent()` to create an instance of `JComponent`. However, you can use the constructors of concrete subclasses of JComponent to create JComponent instances. It is important to become familiar with the class inheritance hierarchy. For example, the following statements all display true.

```
JButton jbtOK = new JButton("OK");
System.out.println(jbtOK instanceof JButton);
System.out.println(jbtOK instanceof AbstractButton);
System.out.println(jbtOK instanceof JComponent);
System.out.println(jbtOK instanceof Container);
System.out.println(jbtOK instanceof Component);
System.out.println(jbtOK instanceof Object);
```

13.3.2 Container Classes

Container classes are GUI components that are used to contain other GUI components. Window, Panel, Applet, Frame, and Dialog are the container classes for AWT components. To work with Swing components, use Container, JFrame, JDialog, JApplet, and JPanel, as described in Table 13.1.

TABLE 13.1 GUI Container Classes

Container Class	*Description*
java.awt.Container	is used to group components. Frames, panels, and applets are its subclasses.
javax.swing.JFrame	is a window not contained inside another window. It is the container that holds other Swing user-interface components in Java GUI applications.
javax.swing.JPanel	is an invisible container that holds user-interface components. Panels can be nested. You can place panels inside a container that includes a panel. JPanel is often used as a canvas to draw graphics.
javax.swing.JApplet	is a subclass of Applet. You must extend JApplet to create a Swing-based Java applet.
javax.swing.JDialog	is a popup window or message box generally used as a temporary window to receive additional information from the user or to provide notification that an event has occurred.

13.3.3 GUI Helper Classes

The helper classes, such as Graphics, Color, Font, FontMetrics, Dimension, and LayoutManager, are not subclasses of Component. They are used to describe the properties of GUI components, such as graphics context, colors, fonts, and dimension, as described in Table 13.2.

TABLE 13.2 GUI Helper Classes

Container Class	*Description*
java.awt.Graphics	is an abstract class that provides a graphical context for drawing strings, lines, and simple shapes.
java.awt.Color	deals with the colors of GUI components. For example, you can specify background or foreground colors in components like JFrame and JPanel, or you can specify colors of lines, shapes, and strings in drawings.
java.awt.Font	specifies fonts for the text and drawings on GUI components. For example, you can specify the font type (e.g., SansSerif), style (e.g., bold), and size (e.g., 24 points) for the text on a button.
java.awt.FontMetrics	is an abstract class used to get the properties of the fonts.
java.awt.Dimension	encapsulates the width and height of a component (in integer precision) in a single object.
java.awt.LayoutManager	is an interface, whose instances specify how components are arranged in a container.

Note

The helper classes are in the **java.awt** package. The Swing components do not replace all the classes in AWT, only the AWT GUI component classes (e.g., **Button**, **TextField**, **TextArea**). The AWT helper classes remain unchanged.

13.4 Frames

To create a user interface, you need to create either a frame or an applet to hold the user-interface components. Creating Java applets will be introduced in Chapter 17, "Applets and Multimedia." This section introduces frames.

13.4.1 Creating a Frame

To create a frame, use the **JFrame** class, as shown in Figure 13.3.

javax.swing.JFrame	
+JFrame()	Creates a default frame with no title.
+JFrame(title: String)	Creates a frame with the specified title.
+setSize(width: int, height: int): void	Specifies the size of the frame.
+setLocation(x: int, y: int): void	Specifies the upper-left-corner location of the frame.
+setVisible(visible: boolean): void	Sets true to display the frame.
+setDefaultCloseOperation(mode: int): void	Specifies the operation when the frame is closed.
+setLocationRelativeTo(c: Component): void	Sets the location of the frame relative to the specified component. If the component is null, the frame is centered on the screen.
+pack(): void	Automatically sets the frame size to hold the components in the frame.

FIGURE 13.3 **Frame** is a top-level container to hold GUI components.

The program in Listing 13.1 creates a frame:

LISTING 13.1 MyFrame.java

```
import javax.swing.*;                                              // import package

public class MyFrame {
  public static void main(String[] args) {
    JFrame frame = new JFrame("MyFrame"); // Create a frame         // create frame
    frame.setSize(400, 300); // Set the frame size                  // set size
    frame.setLocationRelativeTo(null); // New since JDK 1.4         // center frame
    frame.setDefaultCloseOperation(JFrame.EXIT_ON_CLOSE);           // close upon exit
    frame.setVisible(true); // Display the frame                    // display the frame
  }
}
```

The frame is not displayed *until* the **frame.setVisible(true)** method is invoked. **frame.setSize(400, 300)** specifies that the frame is **400** pixels wide and **300** pixels high. If the **setSize** method is not used, the frame will be sized to display just the title bar. Since the **setSize** and **setVisible** methods are both defined in the **Component** class, they are inherited by the **JFrame** class. Later you will see that these methods are also useful in many other subclasses of **Component**.

When you run the **MyFrame** program, a window will be displayed on-screen (see Figure 13.4(a)).

FIGURE 13.4 (a) The program creates and displays a frame with the title `MyFrame`. (b) An OK button is added to the frame.

Invoking `setLocationRelativeTo(null)` (line 7) centers the frame on the screen. Invoking `setDefaultCloseOperation(JFrame.EXIT_ON_CLOSE)` (line 8) tells the program to terminate when the frame is closed. If this statement is not used, the program does not terminate when the frame is closed. In that case, you have to stop the program by pressing Ctrl+C at the DOS prompt window in Windows or stop the process by using the kill command in Unix.

Note

pixel and resolution

Recall that a pixel is the smallest unit of space available for drawing on the screen. You can think of a pixel as a small rectangle and think of the screen as paved with pixels. The *resolution* specifies the number of pixels per square inch. The more pixels the screen has, the higher the screen's resolution. The higher the resolution, the finer the detail you can see.

Note

`setSize` before centering

You should invoke `setSize(w, h)` method before invoking `setLocationRelativeTo(null)` to center the frame.

13.4.2 Adding Components to a Frame

The frame shown in Figure 13.4(a) is empty. Using the `add` method, you can add components into the frame, as in Listing 13.2.

LISTING 13.2 MyFrameWithComponents.java

create a button · add to frame · set size · exit upon closing window · center the frame · set visible

```
import javax.swing.*;

public class MyFrameWithComponents {
  public static void main(String[] args) {
    JFrame frame = new JFrame("MyFrameWithComponents");

    // Add a button into the frame
    JButton jbtOK = new JButton("OK");
    frame.add(jbtOK);

    frame.setSize(400, 300);
    frame.setDefaultCloseOperation(JFrame.EXIT_ON_CLOSE);
    frame.setLocationRelativeTo(null); // Center the frame
    frame.setVisible(true);
  }
}
```

Each `JFrame` contains a content pane. A content pane is an instance of `java.awt.Container`. The GUI components such as buttons are placed in the content pane in a frame. Prior to JDK 1.5, you had to use the `getContentPane` method in the `JFrame` class to return the content pane of the frame, and then invoke the content pane's add method to place a component into the content pane, as follows:

```
java.awt.Container container = frame.getContentPane();
container.add(jbtOK);
```

This was cumbersome. JDK 1.5 allows you to place components to the content pane by invoking a frame's add method, as follows:

```
frame.add(jbtOK);
```

This new feature is called *content pane delegation*. Strictly speaking, a component is added into the content pane of a frame. For simplicity we say that a component is added to a frame.

content pane delegation

An object of JButton was created using new JButton("OK"), and this object was added to the content pane of the frame (line 9).

The add(Component comp) method defined in the Container class adds an instance of Component to the container. Since JButton is a subclass of Component, an instance of JButton is also an instance of Component. To remove a component from a container, use the remove method. The following statement removes the button from the container:

```
container.remove(jbtOK);
```

When you run the program MyFrameWithComponents, the window will be displayed as in Figure 13.4(b). The button is always centered in the frame and occupies the entire frame no matter how you resize it. This is because components are put in the frame by the content pane's layout manager, and the default layout manager for the content pane places the button in the center. In the next section, you will use several different layout managers to place components in other locations as desired.

13.5 Layout Managers

In many other window systems, the user-interface components are arranged by using hard-coded pixel measurements. For example, put a button at location (10, 10) in the window. Using hard-coded pixel measurements, the user interface might look fine on one system but be unusable on another. Java's layout managers provide a level of abstraction that automatically maps your user interface on all window systems.

The Java GUI components are placed in containers, where they are arranged by the container's layout manager. In the preceding program, you did not specify where to place the OK button in the frame, but Java knows where to place it because the layout manager works behind the scenes to place components in the correct locations. A layout manager is created using a layout manager class. Every layout manager class implements the LayoutManager interface.

Layout managers are set in containers using the setLayout(LayoutManager) method. For example, you can use the following statements to create an instance of *X*Layout and set it in a container:

```
LayoutManager layoutManager = new XLayout();
container.setLayout(layoutManager);
```

This section introduces three basic layout managers: FlowLayout, GridLayout, and BorderLayout.

13.5.1 FlowLayout

FlowLayout is the simplest layout manager. The components are arranged in the container from left to right in the order in which they were added. When one row is filled, a new row is started. You can specify the way the components are aligned by using one of three constants:

FlowLayout.RIGHT, FlowLayout.CENTER, or FlowLayout.LEFT. You can also specify the gap between components in pixels. The constructors and methods in FlowLayout are shown in Figure 13.5.

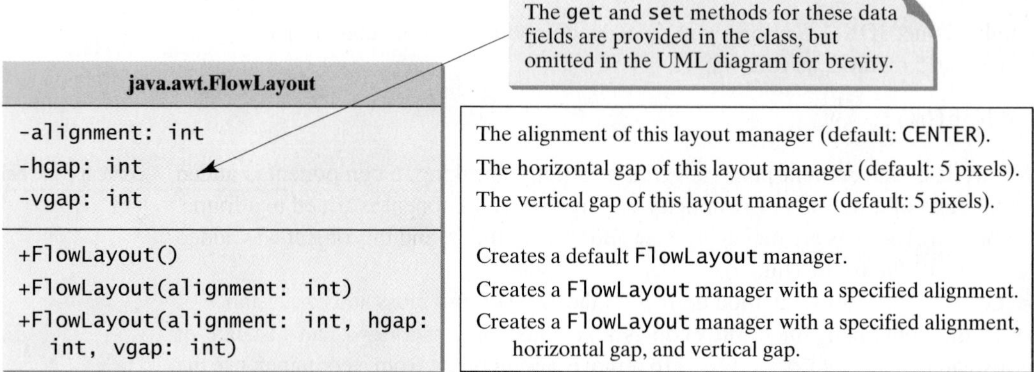

FIGURE 13.5 FlowLayout lays out components row by row.

Listing 13.3 gives a program that demonstrates flow layout. The program adds three labels and text fields into the frame with a FlowLayout manager, as shown in Figure 13.6.

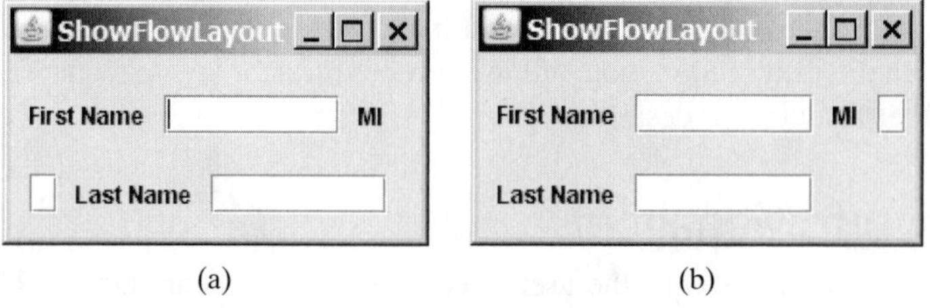

FIGURE 13.6 The components are added by the FlowLayout manager to fill in the rows in the container one after another.

Video Note
Test layout managers

LISTING 13.3 ShowFlowLayout.java

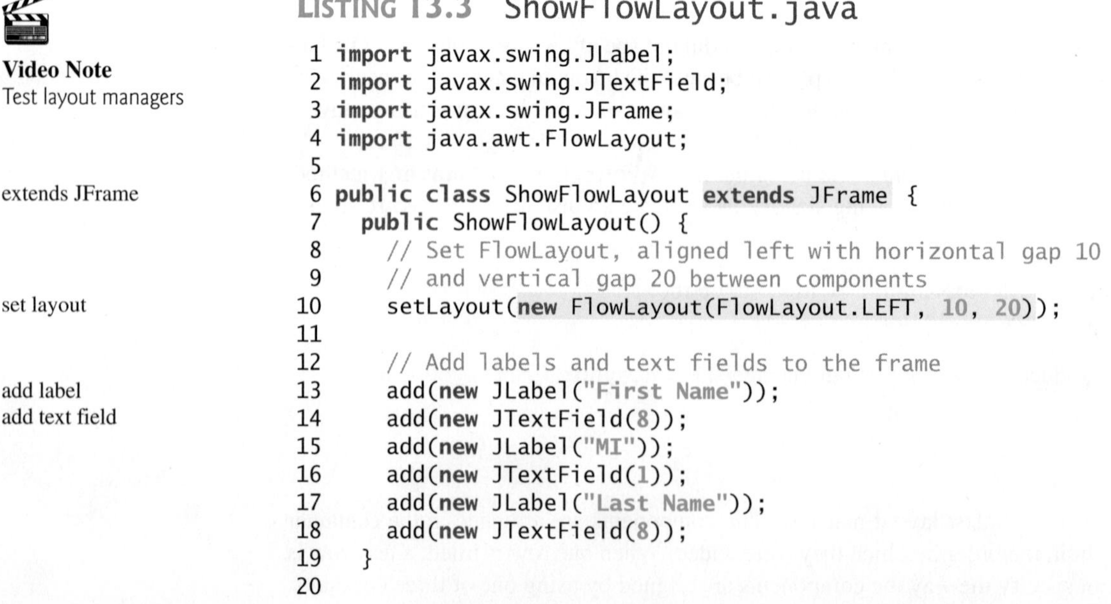

extends JFrame

set layout

add label

add text field

```
import javax.swing.JLabel;
import javax.swing.JTextField;
import javax.swing.JFrame;
import java.awt.FlowLayout;

public class ShowFlowLayout extends JFrame {
  public ShowFlowLayout() {
    // Set FlowLayout, aligned left with horizontal gap 10
    // and vertical gap 20 between components
    setLayout(new FlowLayout(FlowLayout.LEFT, 10, 20));

    // Add labels and text fields to the frame
    add(new JLabel("First Name"));
    add(new JTextField(8));
    add(new JLabel("MI"));
    add(new JTextField(1));
    add(new JLabel("Last Name"));
    add(new JTextField(8));
  }

```

```
21   /** Main method */
22   public static void main(String[] args) {
23     ShowFlowLayout frame = new ShowFlowLayout();
24     frame.setTitle("ShowFlowLayout");
25     frame.setSize(200, 200);
26     frame.setLocationRelativeTo(null); // Center the frame
27     frame.setDefaultCloseOperation(JFrame.EXIT_ON_CLOSE);
28     frame.setVisible(true);
29   }
30 }
```

create frame

set visible

This example creates a program using a style different from the programs in the preceding section, where frames were created using the JFrame class. This example creates a class named ShowFlowLayout that extends the JFrame class (line 6). The main method in this program creates an instance of ShowFlowLayout (line 23). The constructor of ShowFlowLayout constructs and places the components in the frame. This is the preferred style of creating GUI applications—for three reasons:

- Creating a GUI application means creating a frame, so it is natural to define a frame to extend JFrame.
- The frame may be further extended to add new components or functions.
- The class can be easily reused. For example, you can create multiple frames by creating multiple instances of the class.

Using one style consistently makes programs easy to read. From now on, most of the GUI main classes will extend the JFrame class. The constructor of the main class constructs the user interface. The main method creates an instance of the main class and then displays the frame.

In this example, the FlowLayout manager is used to place components in a frame. If you resize the frame, the components are automatically rearranged to fit in it. In Figure 13.6(a), the first row has three components, but in Figure 13.6(b), the first row has four components, because the width has been increased.

If you replace the setLayout statement (line 10) with setLayout(new FlowLayout(FlowLayout.RIGHT, 0, 0)), all the rows of buttons will be right-aligned with no gaps.

An anonymous FlowLayout object was created in the statement (line 10):

```
setLayout(new FlowLayout(FlowLayout.LEFT, 10, 20));
```

which is equivalent to:

```
FlowLayout layout = new FlowLayout(FlowLayout.LEFT, 10, 20);
setLayout(layout);
```

This code creates an explicit reference to the object layout of the FlowLayout class. The explicit reference is not necessary, because the object is not directly referenced in the ShowFlowLayout class.

The setTitle method (line 24) is defined in the java.awt.Frame class. Since JFrame is a subclass of Frame, you can use it to set a title for an object of JFrame.

Suppose you add the same button into the container ten times, will ten buttons appear in the container? No, only the last one will be displayed.

Caution

Do not forget to put the new operator before a layout manager class when setting a layout style—for example, setLayout(new FlowLayout()).

Note

The constructor `ShowFlowLayout()` does not explicitly invoke the constructor `JFrame()`, but the constructor `JFrame()` is invoked implicitly. See §10.4.2, "Constructor Chaining."

13.5.2 `GridLayout`

The `GridLayout` manager arranges components in a grid (matrix) formation with the number of rows and columns defined by the constructor. The components are placed in the grid from left to right, starting with the first row, then the second, and so on, in the order in which they are added. The constructors and methods in `GridLayout` are shown in Figure 13.7.

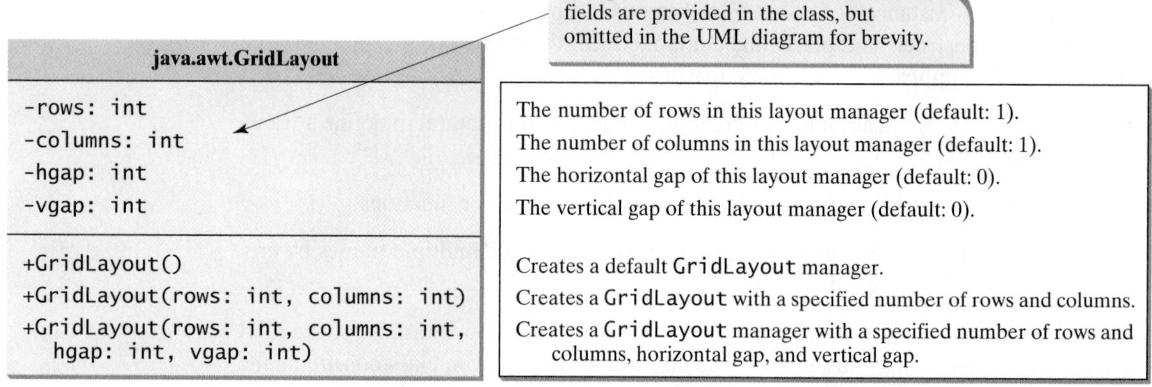

The get and set methods for these data fields are provided in the class, but omitted in the UML diagram for brevity.
java.awt.GridLayout
-rows: int
-columns: int
-hgap: int
-vgap: int
+GridLayout()
+GridLayout(rows: int, columns: int)
+GridLayout(rows: int, columns: int, hgap: int, vgap: int)
The number of rows in this layout manager (default: 1).
The number of columns in this layout manager (default: 1).
The horizontal gap of this layout manager (default: 0).
The vertical gap of this layout manager (default: 0).
Creates a default GridLayout manager.
Creates a GridLayout with a specified number of rows and columns.
Creates a GridLayout manager with a specified number of rows and columns, horizontal gap, and vertical gap.

FIGURE 13.7 `GridLayout` lays out components in equal-sized cells on a grid.

You can specify the number of rows and columns in the grid. The basic rule is as follows:

- The number of rows or the number of columns can be zero, but not both. If one is zero and the other is nonzero, the nonzero dimension is fixed, while the zero dimension is determined dynamically by the layout manager. For example, if you specify zero rows and three columns for a grid that has ten components, `GridLayout` creates three fixed columns of four rows, with the last row containing one component. If you specify three rows and zero columns for a grid that has ten components, `GridLayout` creates three fixed rows of four columns, with the last row containing two components.
- If both the number of rows and the number of columns are nonzero, the number of rows is the dominating parameter; that is, the number of rows is fixed, and the layout manager dynamically calculates the number of columns. For example, if you specify three rows and three columns for a grid that has ten components, `GridLayout` creates three fixed rows of four columns, with the last row containing two components.

Listing 13.4 gives a program that demonstrates grid layout. The program is similar to the one in Listing 13.3. It adds three labels and three text fields to the frame of `GridLayout` instead of `FlowLayout`, as shown in Figure 13.8.

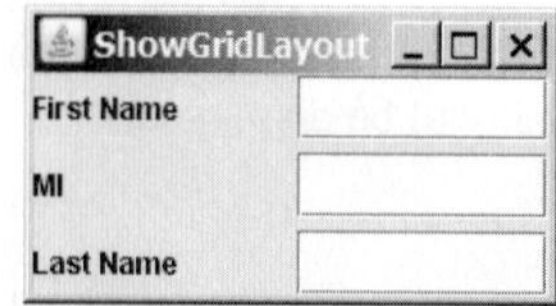

FIGURE 13.8 The `GridLayout` manager divides the container into grids; then the components are added to fill in the cells row by row.

LISTING 13.4 ShowGridLayout.java

```
 1 import javax.swing.JLabel;
 2 import javax.swing.JTextField;
 3 import javax.swing.JFrame;
 4 import java.awt.GridLayout;
 5
 6 public class ShowGridLayout extends JFrame {
 7   public ShowGridLayout() {
 8     // Set GridLayout, 3 rows, 2 columns, and gaps 5 between
 9     // components horizontally and vertically
10     setLayout(new GridLayout(3, 2, 5, 5));
11
12     // Add labels and text fields to the frame
13     add(new JLabel("First Name"));
14     add(new JTextField(8));
15     add(new JLabel("MI"));
16     add(new JTextField(1));
17     add(new JLabel("Last Name"));
18     add(new JTextField(8));
19   }
20
21   /** Main method */
22   public static void main(String[] args) {
23     ShowGridLayout frame = new ShowGridLayout();
24     frame.setTitle("ShowGridLayout");
25     frame.setSize(200, 125);
26     frame.setLocationRelativeTo(null); // Center the frame
27     frame.setDefaultCloseOperation(JFrame.EXIT_ON_CLOSE);
28     frame.setVisible(true);
29   }
30 }
```

set layout

add label

add text field

create a frame

set visible

If you resize the frame, the layout of the buttons remains unchanged (i.e., the number of rows and columns does not change, and the gaps don't change either).

All components are given equal size in the container of `GridLayout`.

Replacing the `setLayout` statement (line 8) with `setLayout(new GridLayout(3, 10))` would still yield three rows and *two* columns. The columns parameter is ignored because the rows parameter is nonzero. The actual number of columns is calculated by the layout manager.

What would happen if the `setLayout` statement (line 10) were replaced with `setLayout(new GridLayout(4, 2))` or with `setLayout(new GridLayout(2, 2))`? Please try it yourself.

Note

In `FlowLayout` and `GridLayout`, the order in which the components are added to the container is important. It determines the location of the components in the container.

13.5.3 `BorderLayout`

The `BorderLayout` manager divides the window into five areas: East, South, West, North, and Center. Components are added to a `BorderLayout` by using `add(Component, index)`, where `index` is a constant `BorderLayout.EAST`, `BorderLayout.SOUTH`, `BorderLayout.WEST`, `BorderLayout.NORTH`, or `BorderLayout.CENTER`. The constructors and methods in `BorderLayout` are shown in Figure 13.9.

The components are laid out according to their preferred sizes and where they are placed in the container. The North and South components can stretch horizontally; the East and West

The get and set methods for these data fields are provided in the class, but omitted in the UML diagram for brevity.

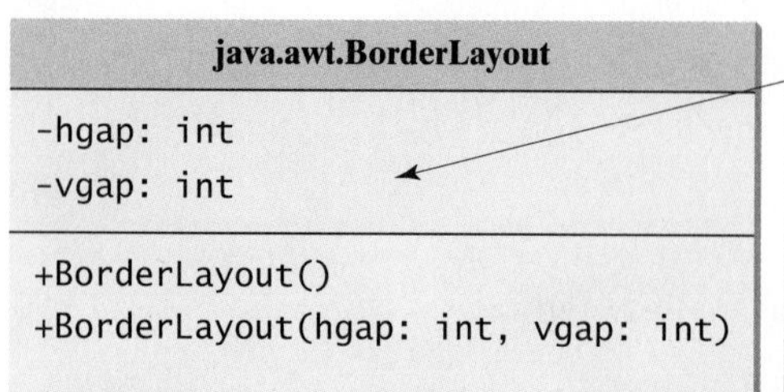

The horizontal gap of this layout manager (default: 0).

The vertical gap of this layout manager (default: 0).

Creates a default BorderLayout manager.

Creates a BorderLayout manager with a specified number of horizontal gap, and vertical gap.

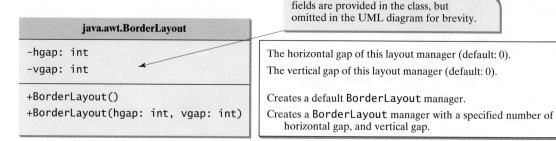

FIGURE 13.9 BorderLayout lays out components in five areas.

components can stretch vertically; the Center component can stretch both horizontally and vertically to fill any empty space.

Listing 13.5 gives a program that demonstrates border layout. The program adds five buttons labeled East, South, West, North, and Center into the frame with a BorderLayout manager, as shown in Figure 13.10.

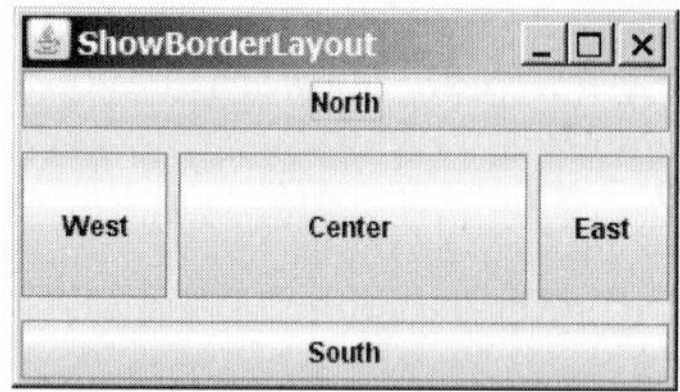

FIGURE 13.10 BorderLayout divides the container into five areas, each of which can hold a component.

LISTING 13.5 ShowBorderLayout.java

set layout

add buttons

create a frame

```
import javax.swing.JButton;
import javax.swing.JFrame;
import java.awt.BorderLayout;

public class ShowBorderLayout extends JFrame {
  public ShowBorderLayout() {
    // Set BorderLayout with horizontal gap 5 and vertical gap 10
    setLayout(new BorderLayout(5, 10));

    // Add buttons to the frame
    add(new JButton("East"), BorderLayout.EAST);
    add(new JButton("South"), BorderLayout.SOUTH);
    add(new JButton("West"), BorderLayout.WEST);
    add(new JButton("North"), BorderLayout.NORTH);
    add(new JButton("Center"), BorderLayout.CENTER);
  }

  /** Main method */
  public static void main(String[] args) {
    ShowBorderLayout frame = new ShowBorderLayout();
    frame.setTitle("ShowBorderLayout");
    frame.setSize(300, 200);
    frame.setLocationRelativeTo(null); // Center the frame
```

```
24     frame.setDefaultCloseOperation(JFrame.EXIT_ON_CLOSE);
25     frame.setVisible(true);
26   }
27 }
```

set visible

The buttons are added to the frame (lines 11–15). Note that the add method for BorderLayout is different from the one for FlowLayout and GridLayout. With BorderLayout you specify where to put the components.

It is unnecessary to place components to occupy all the areas. If you remove the East button from the program and rerun it, you will see that the center stretches rightward to occupy the East area.

Note

BorderLayout interprets the absence of an index specification as BorderLayout.CENTER. For example, add(component) is the same as add(Component, BorderLayout.CENTER). If you add two components into a container of BorderLayout, as follows,

```
container.add(component1);
container.add(component2);
```

only the last component is displayed.

13.5.4 Properties of Layout Managers

Layout managers have properties that can be changed dynamically. FlowLayout has alignment, hgap, and vgap properties. You can use the setAlignment, setHgap, and setVgap methods to specify the alignment and the horizontal and vertical gaps. GridLayout has the rows, columns, hgap, and vgap properties. You can use the setRows, setColumns, setHgap, and setVgap methods to specify the number of rows, the number of columns, and the horizontal and vertical gaps. BorderLayout has the hgap and vgap properties. You can use the setHgap and setVgap methods to specify the horizontal and vertical gaps.

In the preceding sections, an anonymous layout manager is used because the properties of a layout manager do not change, once it is created. If you have to change the properties of a layout manager dynamically, the layout manager must be explicitly referenced by a variable. You can then change the properties of the layout manager through the variable. For example, the following code creates a layout manager and sets its properties:

```
// Create a layout manager
FlowLayout flowLayout = new FlowLayout();

// Set layout properties
flowLayout.setAlignment(FlowLayout.RIGHT);
flowLayout.setHgap(10);
flowLayout.setVgap(20);
```

13.5.5 The validate and doLayout Methods

A container can have only one layout manager at a time. You can change its layout manager by using the setLayout(aNewLayout) method and then use the validate() method to force the container to again lay out the components in the container using the new layout manager. **validate()**

If you use the same layout manager but change its properties, you need to use the doLayout() method to force the container to re-lay out the components using the new properties of the layout manager. **doLayout()**

13.6 The **Color** Class

You can set colors for GUI components by using the java.awt.Color class. Colors are made of red, green, and blue components, each represented by an unsigned byte value that describes its intensity, ranging from 0 (darkest shade) to 255 (lightest shade). This is known as the *RGB model*.

You can create a color using the following constructor:

```
public Color(int r, int g, int b);
```

in which r, g, and b specify a color by its red, green, and blue components. For example,

```
Color color = new Color(128, 100, 100);
```

Note

IllegalArgumentException

The arguments r, g, b are between 0 and 255. If a value beyond this range is passed to the argument, an IllegalArgumentException will occur.

You can use the setBackground(Color c) and setForeground(Color c) methods defined in the java.awt.Component class to set a component's background and foreground colors. Here is an example of setting the background and foreground of a button:

```
JButton jbtOK = new JButton();
jbtOK.setBackground(color);
jbtOK.setForeground(new Color(100, 1, 1));
```

Alternatively, you can use one of the 13 standard colors (black, blue, cyan, darkGray, gray, green, lightGray, magenta, orange, pink, red, white, yellow) defined as constants in java.awt.Color. The following code, for instance, sets the foreground color of a button to red:

```
jbtOK.setForeground(Color.red);
```

Note

color constants

The standard color names are constants, but they are named as variables with lowercase for the first word and uppercase for the first letters of subsequent words. Thus the color names violate the Java naming convention. Since JDK 1.4, you can also use the new constants BLACK, BLUE, CYAN, DARK_GRAY, GRAY, GREEN, LIGHT_GRAY, MAGENTA, ORANGE, PINK, RED, WHITE, and YELLOW.

13.7 The **Font** Class

You can create a font using the java.awt.Font class and set fonts for the components using the setFont method in the Component class.

The constructor for Font is:

```
public Font(String name, int style, int size);
```

You can choose a font name from SansSerif, Serif, Monospaced, Dialog, or DialogInput, choose a style from Font.PLAIN (0), Font.BOLD (1), Font.ITALIC (2), and Font.BOLD + Font.ITALIC (3), and specify a font size of any positive integer. For example, the following statements create two fonts and set one font to a button.

```
Font font1 = new Font("SansSerif", Font.BOLD, 16);
Font font2 = new Font("Serif", Font.BOLD + Font.ITALIC, 12);
```

```
JButton jbtOK = new JButton("OK");
jbtOK.setFont(font1);
```

Tip

If your system supports other fonts, such as "Times New Roman," you can use it to create a Font object. To find the fonts available on your system, you need to create an instance of java.awt.GraphicsEnvironment using its static method getLocalGraphicsEnvironment(). GraphicsEnvironment is an abstract class that describes the graphics environment on a particular system. You can use its getAllFonts() method to obtain all the available fonts on the system, and its getAvailableFontFamilyNames() method to obtain the names of all the available fonts. For example, the following statements print all the available font names in the system:

find available fonts

```
GraphicsEnvironment e =
  GraphicsEnvironment.getLocalGraphicsEnvironment();
String[] fontnames = e.getAvailableFontFamilyNames();

for (int i = 0; i < fontnames.length; i++)
  System.out.println(fontnames[i]);
```

13.8 Using Panels as Subcontainers

Video Note
Organize components using panels

Suppose that you want to place ten buttons and a text field in a frame. The buttons are placed in grid formation, but the text field is placed on a separate row. It is difficult to achieve the desired look by placing all the components in a single container. With Java GUI programming, you can divide a window into panels. Panels act as subcontainers to group user-interface components. You add the buttons in one panel, and then add the panel into the frame.

The Swing version of panel is JPanel. You can use new JPanel() to create a panel with a default FlowLayout manager or new JPanel(LayoutManager) to create a panel with the specified layout manager. Use the add(Component) method to add a component to the panel. For example, the following code creates a panel and adds a button to it:

```
JPanel p = new JPanel();
p.add(new JButton("OK"));
```

Panels can be placed inside a frame or inside another panel. The following statement places panel p into frame f:

```
f.add(p);
```

Listing 13.6 gives an example that demonstrates using panels as subcontainers. The program creates a user interface for a microwave oven, as shown in Figure 13.11.

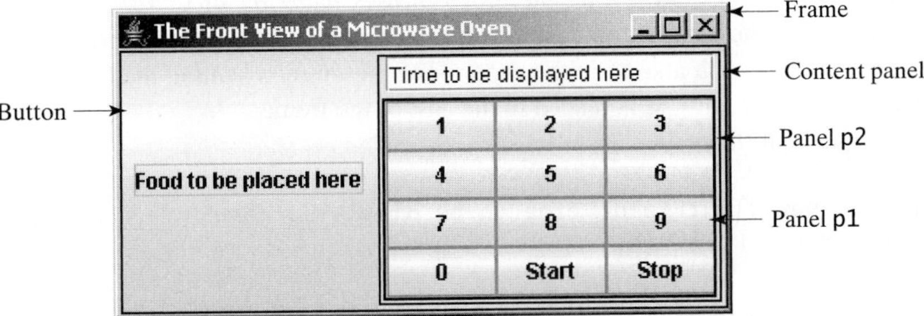

FIGURE 13.11 The program uses panels to organize components.

LISTING 13.6 TestPanels.java

panel p1

panel p2

add p2 to frame

```
1 import java.awt.*;
2 import javax.swing.*;
3
4 public class TestPanels extends JFrame {
5   public TestPanels() {
6     // Create panel p1 for the buttons and set GridLayout
7     JPanel p1 = new JPanel();
8     p1.setLayout(new GridLayout(4, 3));
9
10    // Add buttons to the panel
11    for (int i = 1; i <= 9; i++) {
12      p1.add(new JButton("" + i));
13    }
14
15    p1.add(new JButton("" + 0));
16    p1.add(new JButton("Start"));
17    p1.add(new JButton("Stop"));
18
19    // Create panel p2 to hold a text field and p1
20    JPanel p2 = new JPanel(new BorderLayout());
21    p2.add(new JTextField("Time to be displayed here"),
22      BorderLayout.NORTH);
23    p2.add(p1, BorderLayout.CENTER);
24
25    // add contents into the frame
26    add(p2, BorderLayout.EAST);
27    add(new JButton("Food to be placed here"),
28      BorderLayout.CENTER);
29  }
30
31  /** Main method */
32  public static void main(String[] args) {
33    TestPanels frame = new TestPanels();
34    frame.setTitle("The Front View of a Microwave Oven");
35    frame.setSize(400, 250);
36    frame.setLocationRelativeTo(null); // Center the frame
37    frame.setDefaultCloseOperation(JFrame.EXIT_ON_CLOSE);
38    frame.setVisible(true);
39  }
40 }
```

The **setLayout** method is defined in **java.awt.Container**. Since **JPanel** is a subclass of **Container**, you can use **setLayout** to set a new layout manager in the panel (line 8). Lines 7–8 can be replaced by **JPanel p1 = new JPanel(new GridLayout(4, 3))**.

To achieve the desired layout, the program uses panel **p1** of **GridLayout** to group the number buttons, the *Stop* button, and the *Start* button, and panel **p2** of **BorderLayout** to hold a text field in the north and **p1** in the center. The button representing the food is placed in the center of the frame, and **p2** is placed in the east of the frame.

The statement (lines 21–23)

```
p2.add(new JTextField("Time to be displayed here"),
  BorderLayout.NORTH);
```

creates an instance of **JTextField** and adds it to **p2**. **JTextField** is a GUI component that can be used for user input as well as to display values.

Note

It is worthwhile to note that the `Container` class is the superclass for GUI component classes, such as `JButton`. Every GUI component is a container. In theory, you could use the `setLayout` method to set the layout in a button and add components into a button, because all the public methods in the `Container` class are inherited into `JButton`, but for practical reasons you should not use buttons as containers.

superclass **`Container`**

13.9 Common Features of Swing GUI Components

Video Note
Swing common properties

You have used several GUI components (e.g., `JFrame`, `Container`, `JPanel`, `JButton`, `JLabel`, `JTextField`) in this chapter. Many more GUI components will be introduced in this book. It is important to understand the common features of Swing GUI components. The `Component` class is the root for all GUI components and containers. All Swing GUI components (except `JFrame`, `JApplet`, and `JDialog`) are subclasses of `JComponent`, as shown in Figures 13.1 and 13.2. Figure 13.12 lists some frequently used methods in `Component`, `Container`, and `JComponent` for manipulating properties like font, color, size, tool tip text, and border.

`Component`
`Container`
`JComponent`

The `get` and `set` methods for these data fields are provided in the class, but omitted in the UML diagram for brevity.

java.awt.Component	
`-font: java.awt.Font`	The font of this component.
`-background: java.awt.Color`	The background color of this component.
`-foreground: java.awt.Color`	The foreground color of this component.
`-preferredSize: java.awt.Dimension`	The preferred size of this component.
`-visible: boolean`	Indicates whether this component is visible.
`+getWidth(): int`	Returns the width of this component.
`+getHeight(): int`	Returns the height of this component.
`+getX(): int`	`getX()` and `getY()` return the coordinate of the component's upper-left corner within its parent component.
`+getY(): int`	

java.awt.Container	
`+add(comp: Component): Component`	Adds a component to the container.
`+add(comp: Component, index: int): Component`	Adds a component to the container with the specified index.
`+remove(comp: Component): void`	Removes the component from the container.
`+getLayout(): LayoutManager`	Returns the layout manager for this container.
`+setLayout(l: LayoutManager): void`	Sets the layout manager for this container.
`+paintComponents(g: Graphics): void`	Paints each of the components in this container.

The `get` and `set` methods for these data fields are provided in the class, but omitted in the UML diagram for brevity.

javax.swing.JComponent	
`-toolTipText: String`	The tool tip text for this component. Tool tip text is displayed when the mouse points on the component without clicking.
`-border: javax.swing.border.Border`	The border for this component.

FIGURE 13.12 All the Swing GUI components inherit the public methods from `Component`, `Container`, and `JComponent`.

A *tool tip* is text displayed on a component when you move the mouse on the component. It is often used to describe the function of a component.

You can set a border on any object of the `JComponent` class. Swing has several types of borders. To create a titled border, use `new TitledBorder(String title)`. To create a line border, use `new LineBorder(Color color, int width)`, where `width` specifies the thickness of the line.

Listing 13.7 is an example to demonstrate Swing common features. The example creates a panel `p1` to hold three buttons (line 8) and a panel `p2` to hold two labels (line 25) as shown in Figure 13.13. The background of the button `jbtLeft` is set to white (line 12) and the foreground of the button `jbtCenter` is set to green (line 13). The tool tip of the button `jbtRight` is set in line 14. Titled borders are set on panels `p1` and `p2` (lines 18, 36) and line borders are set on the labels (lines 32-33).

LISTING 13.7 TestSwingCommonFeatures.java

set background (line 12)
set foreground (line 13)
set tool tip text (line 14)
set titled border (line 18)
create a font (line 21)
create a border (line 22)
set foreground (line 28)
set font (line 30)
set line border (line 32)
set titled border (line 36)

```
 1 import java.awt.*;
 2 import javax.swing.*;
 3 import javax.swing.border.*;
 4
 5 public class TestSwingCommonFeatures extends JFrame {
 6   public TestSwingCommonFeatures() {
 7     // Create a panel to group three buttons
 8     JPanel p1 = new JPanel(new FlowLayout(FlowLayout.LEFT, 2, 2));
 9     JButton jbtLeft = new JButton("Left");
10     JButton jbtCenter = new JButton("Center");
11     JButton jbtRight = new JButton("Right");
12     jbtLeft.setBackground(Color.WHITE);
13     jbtCenter.setForeground(Color.GREEN);
14     jbtRight.setToolTipText("This is the Right button");
15     p1.add(jbtLeft);
16     p1.add(jbtCenter);
17     p1.add(jbtRight);
18     p1.setBorder(new TitledBorder("Three Buttons"));
19
20     // Create a font and a line border
21     Font largeFont = new Font("TimesRoman", Font.BOLD, 20);
22     Border lineBorder = new LineBorder(Color.BLACK, 2);
23
24     // Create a panel to group two labels
25     JPanel p2 = new JPanel(new GridLayout(1, 2, 5, 5));
26     JLabel jlblRed = new JLabel("Red");
27     JLabel jlblOrange = new JLabel("Orange");
28     jlblRed.setForeground(Color.RED);
29     jlblOrange.setForeground(Color.ORANGE);
30     jlblRed.setFont(largeFont);
31     jlblOrange.setFont(largeFont);
32     jlblRed.setBorder(lineBorder);
33     jlblOrange.setBorder(lineBorder);
34     p2.add(jlblRed);
35     p2.add(jlblOrange);
36     p2.setBorder(new TitledBorder("Two Labels"));
37
38     // Add two panels to the frame
39     setLayout(new GridLayout(2, 1, 5, 5));
40     add(p1);
41     add(p2);
42   }
43
```

```
44   public static void main(String[] args) {
45     // Create a frame and set its properties
46     JFrame frame = new TestSwingCommonFeatures();
47     frame.setTitle("TestSwingCommonFeatures");
48     frame.setSize(300, 150);
49     frame.setLocationRelativeTo(null); // Center the frame
50     frame.setDefaultCloseOperation(JFrame.EXIT_ON_CLOSE);
51     frame.setVisible(true);
52   }
53 }
```

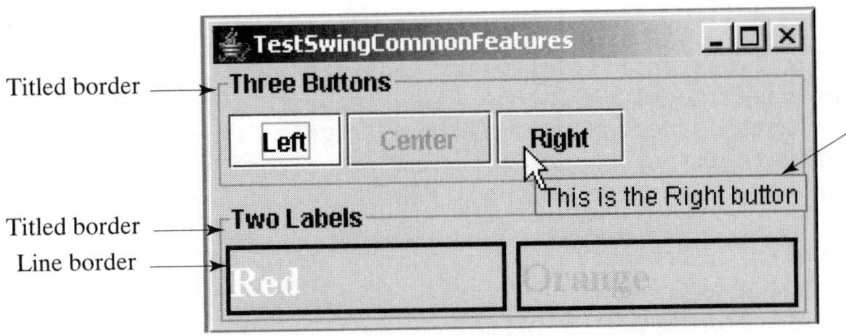

FIGURE 13.13 The font, color, border, and tool tip text are set in the message panel.

Note

property default values

The same property may have different default values in different components. For example, the `visible` property in `JFrame` is `false` by default, but it is `true` in every instance of `JComponent` (e.g., `JButton` and `JLabel`) by default. To display a `JFrame`, you have to invoke `setVisible(true)` to set the `visible` property `true`, but you don't have to set this property for a `JButton` or a `JLabel`, because it is already `true`. To make a `JButton` or a `JLabel` invisible, you may invoke `setVisible(false)` on. Please run the program and see the effect after inserting the following two statements in line 37.

```
jbtLeft.setVisible(false);
jlblRed.setVisible(false);
```

13.10 Image Icons

image file format

An icon is a fixed-size picture; typically it is small and used to decorate components. Images are normally stored in image files. Java currently supports three image formats: GIF (Graphics Interchange Format), JPEG (Joint Photographic Experts Group), and PNG (Portable Network Graphics). The image filenames for these types end with .gif, .jpg, and .png, respectively. If you have a bitmap file or image files in other formats, you can use image-processing utilities to convert them into GIF, JPEG, or PNG format for use in Java.

To display an image icon, first create an `ImageIcon` object using `new javax.swing.ImageIcon(filename)`. For example, the following statement creates an icon from an image file `us.gif` in the `image` directory under the current class path:

create **ImageIcon**

```
ImageIcon icon = new ImageIcon("image/us.gif");
```

file path character

"`image/us.gif`" is located in "`c:\book\image\us.gif`." The back slash (\) is the Windows file path notation. In Unix, the forward slash (/) should be used. In Java, the forward slash (/) is used to denote a relative file path under the Java classpath (e.g., `image/left.gif`, as in this example).

Tip

naming files consistently

File names are not case sensitive in Windows but are case sensitive in Unix. To enable your programs to run on all platforms, name all the image files consistently, using lowercase.

An image icon can be displayed in a label or a button using `new JLabel(imageIcon)` or `new JButton(imageIcon)`. Listing 13.8 demonstrates displaying icons in labels and buttons. The example creates two labels and two buttons with icons, as shown in Figure 13.14.

LISTING 13.8 TestImageIcon.java

create image icons

a label with image

a button with image

```
import javax.swing.*;
import java.awt.*;

public class TestImageIcon extends JFrame {
  private ImageIcon usIcon = new ImageIcon("image/us.gif");
  private ImageIcon myIcon = new ImageIcon("image/my.jpg");
  private ImageIcon frIcon = new ImageIcon("image/fr.gif");
  private ImageIcon ukIcon = new ImageIcon("image/uk.gif");

  public TestImageIcon() {
    setLayout(new GridLayout(1, 4, 5, 5));
    add(new JLabel(usIcon));
    add(new JLabel(myIcon));
    add(new JButton(frIcon));
    add(new JButton(ukIcon));
  }

  /** Main method */
  public static void main(String[] args) {
    TestImageIcon frame = new TestImageIcon();
    frame.setTitle("TestImageIcon");
    frame.setSize(200, 200);
    frame.setLocationRelativeTo(null); // Center the frame
    frame.setDefaultCloseOperation(JFrame.EXIT_ON_CLOSE);
    frame.setVisible(true);
  }
}
```

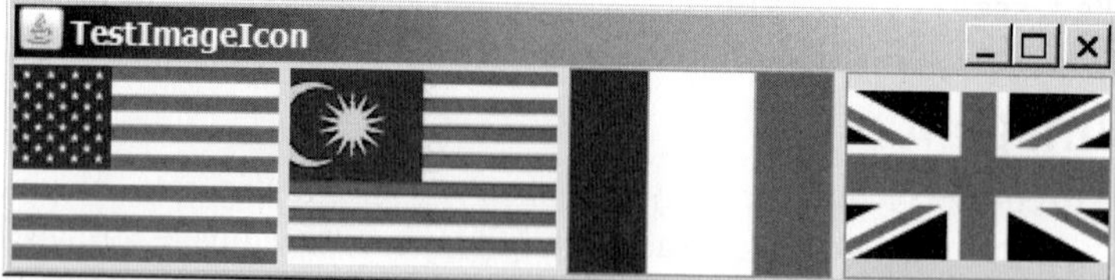

FIGURE 13.14 The image icons are displayed in labels and buttons.

Note

GUI components cannot be shared by containers, because one GUI component can appear in only one container at a time. Therefore, the relationship between a component and a container is the composition denoted by a solid diamond, as shown in Figure 13.1.

Note

sharing borders and icons

Borders and icons can be shared. Thus you can create a border or icon and use it to set the `border` or `icon` property for any GUI component. For example, the following statements set a border `b` for two panels `p1` and `p2`:

```
p1.setBorder(b);
p2.setBorder(b);
```

The following statements set an icon in two buttons `jbt1` and `jbt2`:

```
jbt1.setIcon(icon);
jbt2.setIcon(icon);
```

Tip

A splash screen is an image that is displayed while the application is starting up. If your program takes a long time to load, you may display a splash screen to alert the user. For example, the following command:

splash screen

```
java -splash:image/us.gif TestImageIcon
```

displays an image while the program `TestImageIcon` is being loaded.

Key Terms

AWT 420
heavyweight component 420
lightweight component 420
Swing 420
splash screen 439

Chapter Summary

- Every container has a layout manager that is used to position and place components in the container in the desired locations. Three simple and frequently-used layout managers are `FlowLayout`, `GridLayout`, and `BorderLayout`.

- You can use a `JPanel` as a subcontainer to group components to achieve a desired layout.

- Use the `add` method to place components to a `JFrame` or a `JPanel`. By default, the frame's layout is `BorderLayout`, and the `JPanel`'s layout is `FlowLayout`.

- You can set colors for GUI components by using the `java.awt.Color` class. Colors are made of red, green, and blue components, each of which is represented by an unsigned byte value that describes its intensity, ranging from `0` (darkest shade) to `255` (lightest shade). This is known as the *RGB model.*

- The syntax to create a `Color` object is `Color color = new Color(r, g, b)`, in which `r`, `g`, and `b` specify a color by its red, green, and blue components. Alternatively, you can use one of the 13 standard colors (`BLACK`, `BLUE`, `CYAN`, `DARK_GRAY`, `GRAY`, `GREEN`, `LIGHT_GRAY`, `MAGENTA`, `ORANGE`, `PINK`, `RED`, `WHITE`, `YELLOW`) defined as constants in `java.awt.Color`.

- Every Swing GUI component is a subclass of `javax.swing.JComponent`, and `JComponent` is a subclass of `java.awt.Component`. The properties `font`, `background`, `foreground`, `height`, `width`, and `preferredSize` in `Component` are inherited in these subclasses, as are `toolTipText` and `border` in `JComponent`.

- You can use borders on any Swing components. You can create an image icon using the `ImageIcon` class and display it in a label and a button. Icons and borders can be shared.

Review Questions

Sections 13.3–13.4

13.1 Which class is the root of the Java GUI component classes? Is a container class a subclass of Component? Which class is the root of the Swing GUI component classes?

13.2 Explain the difference between AWT GUI components, such as java.awt.Button, and Swing components, such as javax.swing.JButton.

13.3 How do you create a frame? How do you set the size for a frame? How do you get the size of a frame? How do you add components to a frame? What would happen if the statements frame.setSize(400, 300) and frame.setVisible(true) were swapped in the MyFrameWithComponents class in §13.4.2, "Adding Components to a Frame"?

13.4 Determine whether the following statements are true or false:

- You can add a button to a frame.
- You can add a frame to a panel.
- You can add a panel to a frame.
- You can add any number of components to a panel or a frame.
- You can derive a class from JButton, JPanel, JFrame, or JApplet.

13.5 The following program is supposed to display a button in a frame, but nothing is displayed. What is the problem?

```
public class Test extends javax.swing.JFrame {
  public Test() {
    add(new javax.swing.JButton("OK"));
  }

  public static void main(String[] args) {
    javax.swing.JFrame frame = new javax.swing.JFrame();
    frame.setSize(100, 200);
    frame.setVisible(true);
  }
}
```

13.6 Which of the following statements have syntax errors?

```
Component c1 = new Component();
JComponent c2 = new JComponent();
Component c3 = new JButton();
JComponent c4 = new JButton();
Container c5 = new JButton();
c5.add(c4);
Object c6 = new JButton();
c5.add(c6);
```

Section 13.5 Layout Managers

13.7 Why do you need to use layout managers? What is the default layout manager for a frame? How do you add a component to a frame?

13.8 Describe FlowLayout. How do you create a FlowLayout manager? How do you add a component to a FlowLayout container? Is there a limit to the number of components that can be added to a FlowLayout container?

13.9 Describe GridLayout. How do you create a GridLayout manager? How do you add a component to a GridLayout container? Is there a limit to the number of components that can be added to a GridLayout container?

13.10 Describe `BorderLayout`. How do you create a `BorderLayout` manager? How do you add a component to a `BorderLayout` container?

Sections 13.6–13.7

13.11 How do you create a color? What is wrong about creating a `Color` using `new Color(400, 200, 300)`? Which of two colors is darker, `new Color(10, 0, 0)` or `new Color(200, 0, 0)`?

13.12 How do you create a font? How do you find all available fonts on your system?

Section 13.8 Using Panels as Subcontainers

13.13 How do you create a panel with a specified layout manager?

13.14 What is the default layout manager for a `JPanel`? How do you add a component to a `JPanel`?

13.15 Can you use the `setTitle` method in a panel? What is the purpose of using a panel?

13.16 Since a GUI component class such as `JButton` is a subclass of `Container`, can you add components into a button?

Sections 13.9–13.10

13.17 How do you set background color, foreground color, font, and tool tip text on a Swing GUI component? Why is the tool tip text not displayed in the following code?

```
import javax.swing.*;

public class Test extends JFrame {
  private JButton jbtOK = new JButton("OK");

  public static void main(String[] args) {
    // Create a frame and set its properties
    JFrame frame = new Test();
    frame.setTitle("Logic Error");
    frame.setSize(200, 100);
    frame.setDefaultCloseOperation(JFrame.EXIT_ON_CLOSE);
    frame.setVisible(true);
  }

  public Test() {
    jbtOK.setToolTipText("This is a button");
    add(new JButton("OK"));
  }
}
```

13.18 Show the output of the following code:

```
import javax.swing.*;

public class Test {
  public static void main(String[] args) {
    JButton jbtOK = new JButton("OK");
    System.out.println(jbtOK.isVisible());
    JFrame frame = new JFrame();
    System.out.println(frame.isVisible());
  }
}
```

13.19 How do you create an `ImageIcon` from the file image/us.gif in the class directory?

13.20 What happens if you add a button to a container several times, as shown below? Does it cause syntax errors? Does it cause runtime errors?

```
JButton jbt = new JButton();
JPanel panel = new JPanel();
panel.add(jbt);
panel.add(jbt);
panel.add(jbt);
```

13.21 Will the following code display three buttons? Will the buttons display the same icon?

```
import javax.swing.*;
import java.awt.*;

public class Test extends JFrame  {
  public static void main(String[] args) {
    // Create a frame and set its properties
    JFrame frame = new Test();
    frame.setTitle("ButtonIcons");
    frame.setSize(200, 100);
    frame.setDefaultCloseOperation(JFrame.EXIT_ON_CLOSE);
    frame.setVisible(true);
  }

  public Test() {
    ImageIcon usIcon = new ImageIcon("image/usIcon.gif");
    JButton jbt1 = new JButton(usIcon);
    JButton jbt2 = new JButton(usIcon);

    JPanel p1 = new JPanel();
    p1.add(jbt1);

    JPanel p2 = new JPanel();
    p2.add(jbt2);

    JPanel p3 = new JPanel();
    p2.add(jbt1);

    add(p1, BorderLayout.NORTH);
    add(p2, BorderLayout.SOUTH);
    add(p3, BorderLayout.CENTER);
  }
}
```

13.22 Can a border or an icon be shared by GUI components?

Programming Exercises

Section 13.5 Layout Managers

13.1 (*Using the `FlowLayout` manager*) Write a program that meets the following requirements (see Figure 13.15):

- Create a frame and set its layout to `FlowLayout`.
- Create two panels and add them to the frame.
- Each panel contains three buttons. The panel uses `FlowLayout`.

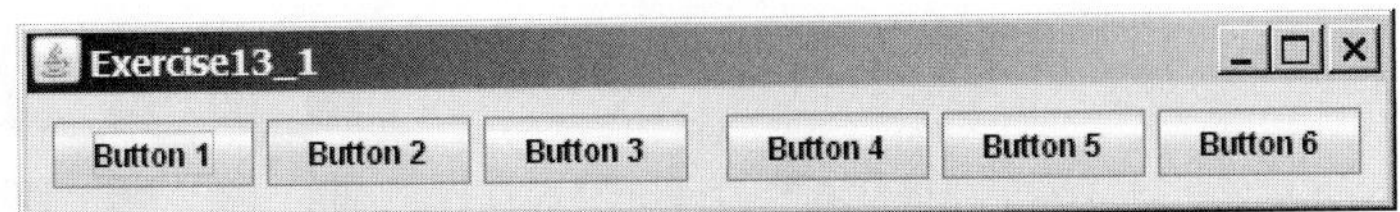

FIGURE 13.15 Exercise 13.1 places the first three buttons in one panel and the other three buttons in another panel.

13.2 (*Using the* `BorderLayout` *manager*) Rewrite the preceding program to create the same user interface, but instead of using `FlowLayout` for the frame, use `BorderLayout`. Place one panel in the south of the frame, and the other panel in the center.

13.3 (*Using the* `GridLayout` *manager*) Rewrite the preceding program to create the same user interface. Instead of using `FlowLayout` for the panels, use a `GridLayout` of two rows and three columns.

13.4 (*Using* `JPanel` *to group buttons*) Rewrite the preceding program to create the same user interface. Instead of creating buttons and panels separately, define a class that extends the `JPanel` class. Place three buttons in your panel class, and create two panels from the user-defined panel class.

13.5 (*Displaying labels*) Write a program that displays four lines of text in four labels, as shown in Figure 13.16(a). Add a line border on each label.

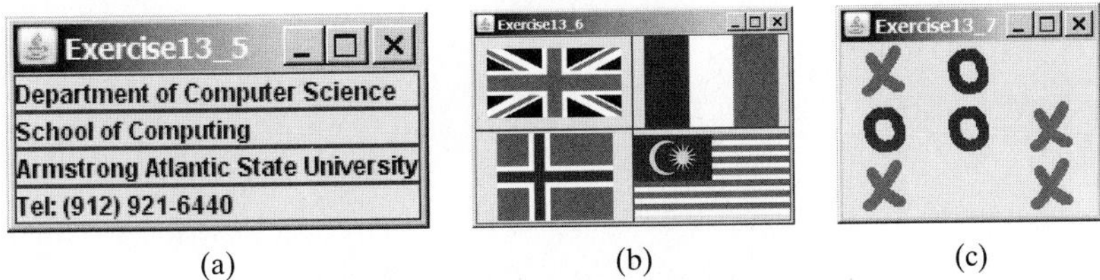

FIGURE 13.16 (a) Exercise 13.5 displays four labels. (b) Exercise 13.6 displays four icons. (c) A TicTacToe board is displayed with image icons in labels.

13.6 (*Displaying icons*) Write a program that displays four icons in four labels, as shown in Figure 13.16(b). Add a line border on each label. (Use any images of your choice or the ones in the book, which can be obtained along with the book's source code.)

13.7** (*Game: displaying a TicTacToe board*) Display a frame that contains nine labels. A label may display an image icon for X, an image icon for O, or nothing, as shown in Figure 13.16(c). What to display is randomly decided. Use the `Math.random()` method to generate an integer `0`, `1`, or `2`, which corresponds to displaying a cross image icon, a not image icon, or nothing. The cross and not images are in the files `x.gif` and `o.gif`, which are under the `image` directory in www.cs.armstrong.edu/liang/intro7e/evennumberedexercise.zip).

13.8* (*Swing common features*) Display a frame that contains six labels. Set the background of the labels to white. Set the foreground of the labels to black, blue, cyan, green, magenta, and orange, respectively, as shown in Figure 13.17(a). Set the border of each label to a line border with the yellow color. Set the font of each label to TimesRoman, bold, and 20 pixels. Set the text and tool tip text of each label to the name of its foreground color.

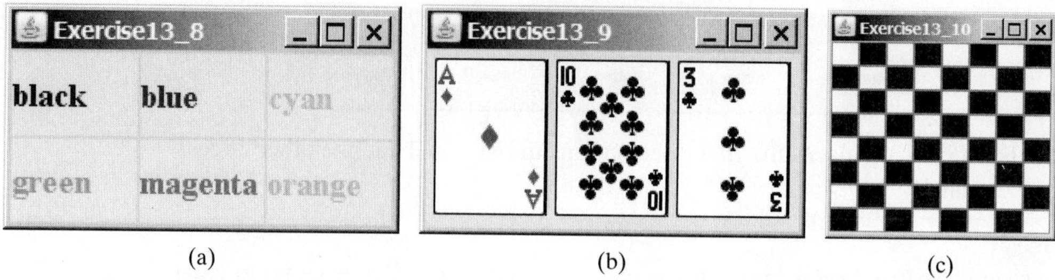

(a) (b) (c)

FIGURE 13.17 (a) Six labels are placed in the frame. (b) Three cards are randomly selected (c) A checkerboard is displayed using buttons.

13.9* (*Game: displaying four cards*) Display a frame that contains three labels. Each label displays a card, as shown in Figure 13.17(b). The card image files are named 1.png, 2.png, ..., 54.png, and stored in the `image/card` directory. All three cards are distinct and selected randomly. The image files can be obtained from www.cs.armstrong.edu/liang/intro7e/evennumberedexercise.zip.

Video Note
Display a checker board

13.10* (*Game: displaying a checkerboard*) Write a program that displays a checkerboard in which each white and black cell is a `JButton` with a background black or white, as shown in Figure 13.17(c).

CHAPTER 14

GRAPHICS

Objectives

- To describe Java coordinate systems in a GUI component (§14.2).
- To draw things using the methods in the `Graphics` class (§14.3).
- To explain how and when a `Graphics` object is created (§14.3).
- To override the `paintComponent` method to draw things on a GUI component (§14.4).
- To use a panel as a canvas to draw things (§14.5).
- To draw strings, lines, rectangles, ovals, arcs, and polygons (§§14.6, 14.8–14.9).
- To obtain font properties using `FontMetrics` and know how to center a message (§14.10).
- To display an image in a GUI component (§14.13).
- To develop reusable GUI components `FigurePanel`, `MessagePanel`, `StillClock`, and `ImageViewer` (§§14.7, 14.11, 14.12, 14.14).

14.1 Introduction

If you want to draw shapes such as a bar chart, a clock, or a stop sign, as shown in Figure 14.1, how can you do so?

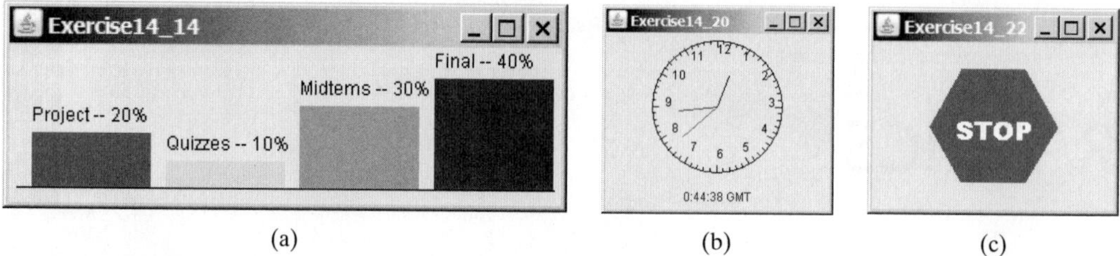

FIGURE 14.1 You can draw shapes using the drawing methods in the `Graphics` class.

You can accomplish the task using the `Graphics` class. This chapter describes how to draw strings, lines, rectangles, ovals, arcs, polygons, and images, and how to develop reusable GUI components.

14.2 Graphical Coordinate Systems

To paint, you need to specify where to paint. Each component has its own coordinate system with the origin (`0`, `0`) at the upper-left corner of the component. The *x* coordinate increases to the right, and the *y* coordinate increases downward. Note that the Java coordinate system differs from the conventional coordinate system, as shown in Figure 14.2.

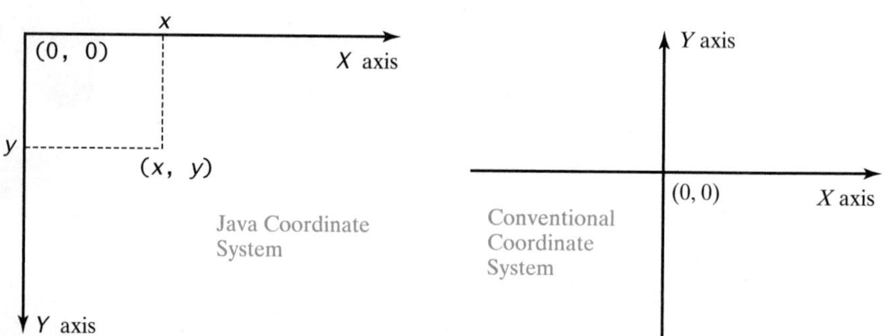

FIGURE 14.2 The Java coordinate system is measured in pixels, with `(0, 0)` at its upper-left corner.

The location of the upper-left corner of a component `c1` (e.g., a button) inside its parent component `c2` (e.g., a panel) can be located using `c1.getX()` and `c1.getY()`. As shown in Figure 14.3, `(x1, y1) = (c1.getX(), c1.getY())`, `(x2, y2) = (c2.getX(), c2.getY())`, and `(x3, y3) = (c3.getX(), c3.getY())`.

14.3 The `Graphics` Class

You can draw strings, lines, rectangles, ovals, arcs, polygons, and polylines, using the methods in the `Graphics` class, as shown in Figure 14.4.

The `Graphics` class is an abstract class that provides a device-independent graphics interface for displaying figures and images on the screen on different platforms. Whenever a component (e.g., a button, a label, a panel) is displayed, the JVM automatically creates a `Graphics`

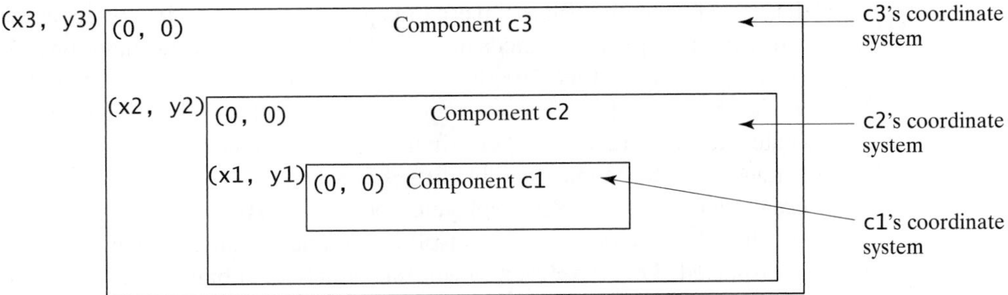

FIGURE 14.3 Each GUI component has its own coordinate system.

java.awt.Graphics	
`+setColor(color: Color): void`	Sets a new color for subsequent drawings.
`+setFont(font: Font): void`	Sets a new font for subsequent drawings.
`+drawString(s: String, x: int, y: int): void`	Draws a string starting at point `(x, y)`.
`+drawLine(x1: int, y1: int, x2: int, y2: int): void`	Draws a line from `(x1, y1)` to `(x2, y2)`.
`+drawRect(x:int, y: int, w: int, h: int): void`	Draws a rectangle with specified upper-left corner point at `(x,y)` and width `w` and height `h`.
`+fillRect(x: int, y: int, w: int, h: int): void`	Draws a filled rectangle with specified upper-left corner point at `(x, y)` and width `w` and height `h`.
`+drawRoundRect(x: int, y: int, w: int, h: int, aw: int, ah: int): void`	Draws a round-cornered rectangle with specified arc width `aw` and arc height `ah`.
`+fillRoundRect(x: int, y: int, w: int, h: int, aw: int, ah: int): void`	Draws a filled round-cornered rectangle with specified arc width `aw` and arc height `ah`.
`+draw3DRect(x: int, y: int, w: int, h: int, raised: boolean): void`	Draws a 3-D rectangle raised above the surface or sunk into the surface.
`+fill3DRect(x: int, y: int, w: int, h: int, raised: boolean): void`	Draws a filled 3-D rectangle raised above the surface or sunk into the surface.
`+drawOval(x: int, y: int, w: int, h: int): void`	Draws an oval bounded by the rectangle specified by the parameters `x`, `y`, `w`, and `h`.
`+fillOval(x: int, y: int, w: int, h: int): void`	Draws a filled oval bounded by the rectangle specified by the parameters `x`, `y`, `w`, and `h`.
`+drawArc(x: int, y: int, w: int, h: int, startAngle: int, arcAngle: int): void`	Draws an arc conceived as part of an oval bounded by the rectangle specified by the parameters `x`, `y`, `w`, and `h`.
`+fillArc(x: int, y: int, w: int, h: int, startAngle: int, arcAngle: int): void`	Draws a filled arc conceived as part of an oval bounded by the rectangle specified by the parameters `x`, `y`, `w`, and `h`.
`+drawPolygon(xPoints: int[], yPoints: int[], nPoints: int): void`	Draws a closed polygon defined by arrays of `x`- and `y`-coordinates. Each pair of `(x[i], y[i])` coordinates is a point.
`+fillPolygon(xPoints: int[], yPoints: int[], nPoints: int): void`	Draws a filled polygon defined by arrays of `x`- and `y`-coordinates. Each pair of `(x[i], y[i])`-coordinates is a point.
`+drawPolygon(g: Polygon): void`	Draws a closed polygon defined by a `Polygon` object.
`+fillPolygon(g: Polygon): void`	Draws a filled polygon defined by a `Polygon` object.
`+drawPolyline(xPoints: int[], yPoints: int[], nPoints: int): void`	Draws a polyline defined by arrays of `x`- and `y`-coordinates. Each pair of `(x[i], y[i])`-coordinates is a point.

FIGURE 14.4 The `Graphics` class contains the methods for drawing strings and shapes.

object for the component on the native platform. This object can be obtained using the `getGraphics()` method. For example, the `Graphics` object for a label `jlblBanner` can be obtained using

```
Graphics graphics = jlblBanner.getGraphics();
```

Think of a GUI component as a piece of paper and the Graphics object as a pencil or paintbrush. You can apply the methods in the Graphics class to draw things on a GUI component.

To help understand the Graphics class, we first present an intuitive, but not practical, example in Listing 14.1. The program creates a label in line 5. When the main method is executed, the constructor TestGetGraphics is executed (line 13) and the label is added to the frame (line 8). At this time, the Graphics object for the label has not been created because the label has not been displayed. Therefore, jlblBanner.getGraphics() returns null (line 9). After the frame is displayed in line 18, all the components in the frame are also displayed. The Graphics object for the label is obtained in line 21. A line is drawn from (0, 0) to (50, 50) on the label, as shown in Figure 14.5.

LISTING 14.1 TestGetGraphics.java

```
 1 import javax.swing.*;
 2 import java.awt.Graphics;
 3
 4 public class TestGetGraphics extends JFrame {
 5   private JLabel jlblBanner = new JLabel("Banner");
 6
 7   public TestGetGraphics() {
 8     add(jlblBanner);
 9     System.out.println(jlblBanner.getGraphics());
10   }
11
12   public static void main(String[] args) {
13     TestGetGraphics frame = new TestGetGraphics();
14     frame.setTitle("TestGetGraphics");
15     frame.setSize(200, 100);
16     frame.setLocationRelativeTo(null); // Center the frame
17     frame.setDefaultCloseOperation(JFrame.EXIT_ON_CLOSE);
18     frame.setVisible(true);
19     JOptionPane.showMessageDialog(null,
20       "Delay on purpose\nClick OK to dismiss the dialog");
21     Graphics graphics = frame.jlblBanner.getGraphics();
22     graphics.drawLine(0, 0, 50, 50);
23   }
24 }
```

create a label (line 5)
add a label (line 8)
create a frame (line 13)
display frame (line 18)
for delay purpose (line 19)
get graphics (line 21)
draw line (line 22)

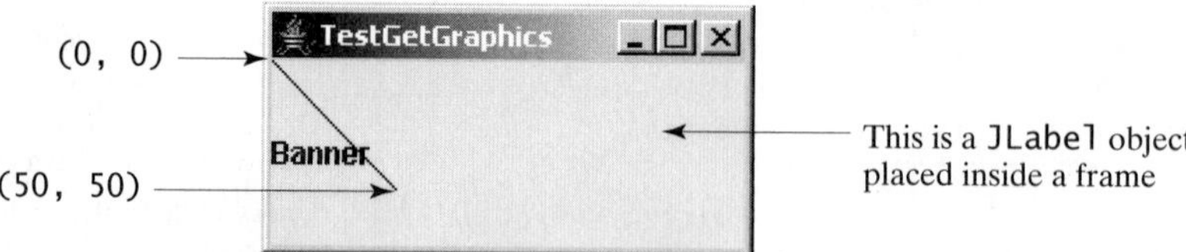

FIGURE 14.5 A line is drawn on a label, and the label is placed inside the frame.

When you run this program, the frame is displayed (line 18), then a message dialog box is displayed (line 19). What is the purpose of having a message dialog box in this program? It is to delay the execution of lines 21 and 22. Without the delay, you might not see the line (line 22). The reason will be discussed in the next section.

When you create a label with a text such as new JLabel("Banner"), you see the text on the label when the label is displayed. The text is actually painted on the label using the drawString method in the Graphics class internally.

Every GUI component has a Graphics object that can be obtained using getGraphics() after the component is displayed. You may rewrite this example using a button, a text field, or a text area rather a label. Note that jlblBanner.getGraphics() returns null in line 9, because `jlblBanner` has not been displayed yet. It is displayed when the frame is set visible in line 18.

In line 11, `jlblBanner.getGraphics()` is used to return a `Graphics` object. In line 21, why do you have to use `frame.jlblBanner.getGraphics()` in the `main` method? This is because `jlblBanner` is an instance variable, and it cannot be referenced directly in a static method.

14.4 The **paintComponent** Method

The program in Listing 14.1 has two problems:

1. If you resize the frame, the line disappears.
2. It is awkward to program because you have to make sure that the component is displayed before obtaining its `Graphics` object using the `getGraphics()` method. For this reason, lines 21 and 22 are placed after the frame is displayed in line 18.

Because of these two problems, you should avoid programming using the `getGraphics()` method. To fix the first problem, you need to know its cause. When you resize the frame, the JVM automatically invokes the `paintComponent` method of a Swing component (e.g., a `JLabel`) to redisplay the graphics on the component. Since you did not draw a line in the `paintComponent` method, the line is gone when the frame is resized. To permanently display the line, you need to draw the line in the `paintComponent` method. The signature of the `paintComponent` method is as follows:

```
protected void paintComponent(Graphics g)
```

This method, defined in the `JComponent` class, is invoked whenever a component is first displayed or redisplayed. The `Graphics` object `g` is created automatically by the JVM for every visible GUI component. The JVM obtains the `Graphics` object and passes it to invoke `paintComponent`.

In order to draw things on a component (e.g., a `JLabel`) consistently, you need to declare a class that extends a Swing GUI component class and overrides its `paintComponent` method to specify what to draw. The program in Listing 14.1 can be rewritten as shown in Listing 14.2. The output is the same as shown in Figure 14.5. When you resize the frame, the JVM invokes the `paintComponent` method to repaint the line and the text.

LISTING 14.2 TestPaintComponent.java

```
import javax.swing.*;
import java.awt.Graphics;

public class TestPaintComponent extends JFrame {
  public TestPaintComponent() {
    add(new NewLabel("Banner"));
  }

  public static void main(String[] args) {
    TestPaintComponent frame = new TestPaintComponent();
    frame.setTitle("TestPaintComponent");
    frame.setSize(200, 100);
    frame.setLocationRelativeTo(null); // Center the frame
    frame.setDefaultCloseOperation(JFrame.EXIT_ON_CLOSE);
    frame.setVisible(true);
  }
}

```

create a label

new label class
override **paintComponent**
draw things in the superclass
draw line

```
19 class NewLabel extends JLabel {
20   public NewLabel(String text) {
21     super(text);
22   }
23
24   protected void paintComponent(Graphics g) {
25     super.paintComponent(g);
26     g.drawLine(0, 0, 50, 50);
27   }
28 }
```

The `paintComponent` method is automatically invoked to paint graphics when the component is first displayed or whenever the component needs to be redisplayed. The text "banner" is drawn in the `paintComponent` method defined in the `JLabel` class. Invoking `super.paintComponent(g)` (line 25) displays the text in the label, and invoking the `drawLine` method (line 26) draws a line.

The JVM invokes `paintComponent` to draw things on a component. The user should never invoke `paintComponent` directly. For this reason, the protected visibility is sufficient for `paintComponent`.

14.5 Drawing Graphics on Panels

Panels are invisible and are used as small containers that group components to achieve a desired layout. Another important use of `JPanel` is for drawing. You can draw things on any Swing GUI component, but normally you should use a `JPanel` as a canvas upon which to draw things.

To draw in a `JPanel`, you create a new class that extends `JPanel` and overrides the `paintComponent` method to tell the panel how to draw things. Listing 14.3 is an example to demonstrate drawings on a panel. The example declares the `NewPanel` class, which extends `JPanel` and overrides the `paintComponent` method to draw a line (line 22) and a string (line 23), as shown in Figure 14.6.

LISTING 14.3 TestPanelDrawing.java

create a label
new panel class
override **paintComponent**
draw things in the superclass
draw line

```
 1 import javax.swing.*;
 2 import java.awt.Graphics;
 3
 4 public class TestPanelDrawing extends JFrame {
 5   public TestPanelDrawing() {
 6     add(new NewPanel());
 7   }
 8
 9   public static void main(String[] args) {
10     TestPanelDrawing frame = new TestPanelDrawing();
11     frame.setTitle("TestPanelDrawing");
12     frame.setSize(200, 100);
13     frame.setLocationRelativeTo(null); // Center the frame
14     frame.setDefaultCloseOperation(JFrame.EXIT_ON_CLOSE);
15     frame.setVisible(true);
16   }
17 }
18
19 class NewPanel extends JPanel {
20   protected void paintComponent(Graphics g) {
21     super.paintComponent(g);
22     g.drawLine(0, 0, 50, 50);
```

```
23      g.drawString("Banner", 0, 40);
24    }
25 }
```

FIGURE 14.6 A line and a string are drawn on a panel.

All the drawing methods have parameters that specify the locations of the subjects to be drawn. All measurements in Java are made in pixels. The string "Banner" is drawn at location (0, 40).

Note

Invoking `super.paintComponent(g)` (line 23) is necessary to ensure that the viewing area is cleared before a new drawing is displayed.

super.paint-Component(g)

Tip

Some textbooks declare a canvas class by subclassing `JComponent`. The problem is that you have to write the code to paint the background color if you wish to set a background in the canvas. A simple `setBackground(Color color)` method will not set a background color in a `JComponent`.

extends JComponent?

14.6 Drawing Strings, Lines, Rectangles, and Ovals

The `drawString(String s, int x, int y)` method draws a string starting at the point `(x, y)`, as shown in Figure 14.7(a).

drawString

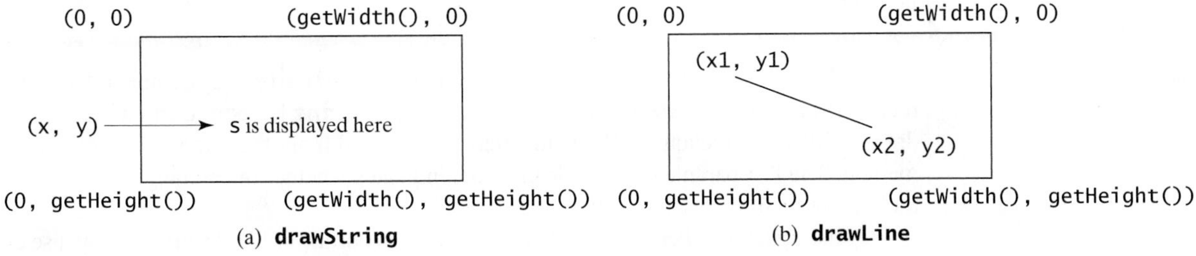

FIGURE 14.7 (a) The `drawString(s, x, y)` method draws a string starting at `(x, y)`. (b) The `drawLine(x1, y1, x2, y2)` method draws a line between two specified points.

The `drawLine(int x1, int y1, int x2, int y2)` method draws a straight line from point `(x1, y1)` to point `(x2, y2)`, as shown in Figure 14.7(b).

drawLine

Java provides six methods for drawing rectangles in outline or filled with color. You can draw or fill plain rectangles, round-cornered rectangles, or three-dimensional rectangles.

The `drawRect(int x, int y, int w, int h)` method draws a plain rectangle and the `fillRect(int x, int y, int w, int h)` method draws a filled rectangle. The parameters `x` and `y` represent the upper-left corner of the rectangle, and `w` and `h` are its width and height (see Figure 14.8).

drawRect
fillRect

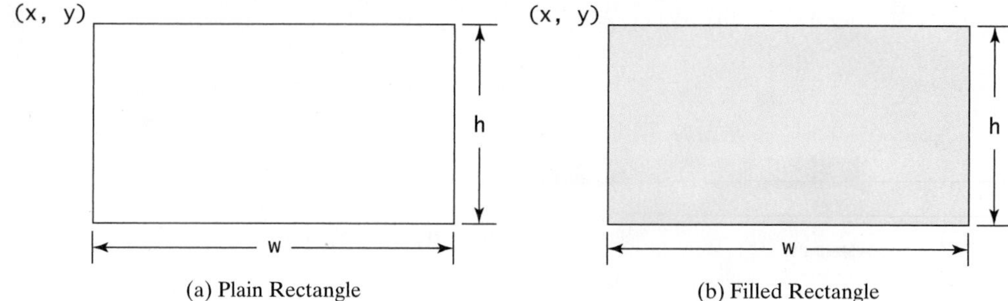

(a) Plain Rectangle (b) Filled Rectangle

FIGURE 14.8 (a) The `drawRect(x, y, w, h)` method draws a rectangle. (b) The `fillRect(x, y, w, h)` method draws a filled rectangle.

drawRoundRect
fillRoundRect

The `drawRoundRect(int x, int y, int w, int h, int aw, int ah)` method draws a round-cornered rectangle, and the `fillRoundRect(int x, int y, int w, int h, int aw, int ah)` method draws a filled round-cornered rectangle. Parameters `x`, `y`, `w`, and `h` are the same as in the `drawRect` method, parameter `aw` is the horizontal diameter of the arcs at the corner, and `ah` is the vertical diameter of the arcs at the corner (see Figure 14.9(a)). In other words, `aw` and `ah` are the width and the height of the oval that produces a quarter-circle at each corner.

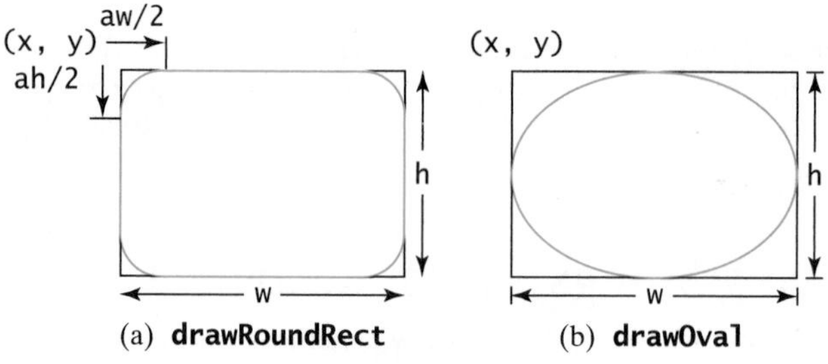

(a) **drawRoundRect** (b) **drawOval**

FIGURE 14.9 (a) The `drawRoundRect(x, y, w, h, aw, ah)` method draws a round-cornered rectangle. (b) The `drawOval(x, y, w, h)` method draws an oval based on its bounding rectangle.

draw3DRect
fill3DRect

The `draw3DRect(int x, int y, int w, int h, boolean raised)` method draws a 3D rectangle and the `fill3DRect(int x, int y, int w, int h, boolean raised)` method draws a filled 3D rectangle. The parameters `x`, `y`, `w`, and `h` are the same as in the `drawRect` method. The last parameter, a Boolean value, indicates whether the rectangle is raised above the surface or sunk into the surface.

drawOval
fillOval

Depending on whether you wish to draw an oval in outline or filled solid, you can use either the `drawOval(int x, int y, int w, int h)` method or the `fillOval(int x, int y, int w, int h)` method. An oval is drawn based on its bounding rectangle. Parameters `x` and `y` indicate the top-left corner of the bounding rectangle, and `w` and `h` indicate the width and height, respectively, of the bounding rectangle, as shown in Figure 14.9(b).

Video Note
`FigurePanel` class

14.7 Case Study: The `FigurePanel` Class

This example develops a useful class for displaying various figures. The class enables the user to set the figure type and specify whether the figure is filled, and displays the figure on a panel. The UML diagram for the class is shown in Figure 14.10. The panel can display lines,

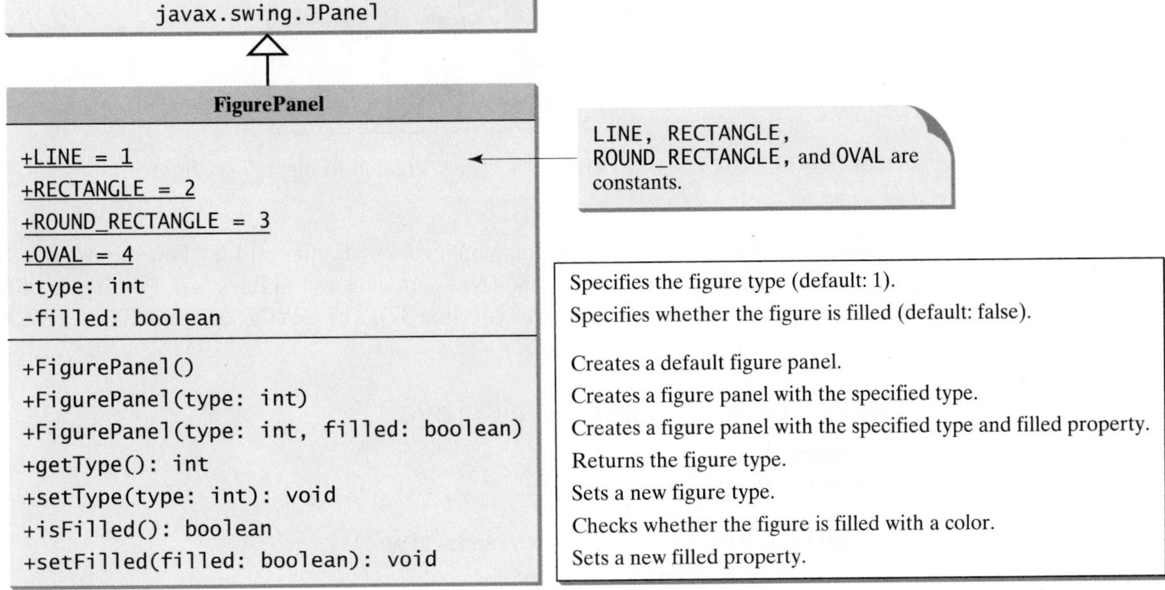

FIGURE 14.10 FigurePanel displays various types of figures on the panel.

rectangles, round-cornered rectangles, and ovals. Which figure to display is decided by the `type` property. If the `filled` property is `true`, the rectangle, round-cornered rectangle, and oval are filled in the panel.

The UML diagram serves as the contract for the `FigurePanel` class. The user can use the class without knowing how the class is implemented. Let us begin by writing a program in Listing 14.4 that uses the class to display six figure panels, as shown in Figure 14.11.

LISTING 14.4 TestFigurePanel.java

create figures

```
import java.awt.*;
import javax.swing.*;

public class TestFigurePanel extends JFrame {
  public TestFigurePanel() {
    setLayout(new GridLayout(2, 3, 5, 5));
    add(new FigurePanel(FigurePanel.LINE));
    add(new FigurePanel(FigurePanel.RECTANGLE));
    add(new FigurePanel(FigurePanel.ROUND_RECTANGLE));
    add(new FigurePanel(FigurePanel.OVAL));
    add(new FigurePanel(FigurePanel.RECTANGLE, true));
    add(new FigurePanel(FigurePanel.ROUND_RECTANGLE, true));
  }

  public static void main(String[] args) {
    TestFigurePanel frame = new TestFigurePanel();
    frame.setSize(400, 200);
    frame.setTitle("TestFigurePanel");
    frame.setLocationRelativeTo(null); // Center the frame
    frame.setDefaultCloseOperation(JFrame.EXIT_ON_CLOSE);
    frame.setVisible(true);
  }
}
```

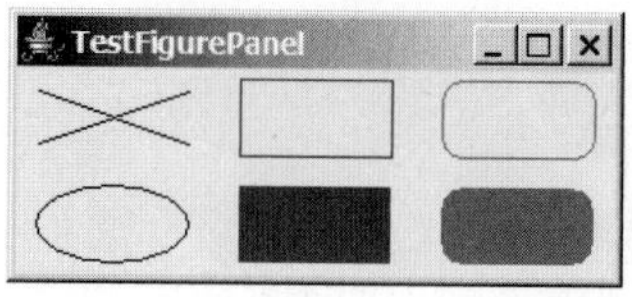

FIGURE 14.11 Six FigurePanel objects are created to display six figures.

The FigurePanel class is implemented in Listing 14.5. Four constants, LINE, RECTANGLE, ROUND_RECTANGLE, and OVAL, are declared in lines 6–9. Four types of figures are drawn according to the type property (line 37). The setColor method (lines 39, 44, 53, 62) sets a new color for the drawing.

LISTING 14.5 FigurePanel.java

```
1 import java.awt.*;
2 import javax.swing.JPanel;
3
4 public class FigurePanel extends JPanel {
5   // Define constants
6   public static final int LINE = 1;
7   public static final int RECTANGLE = 2;
8   public static final int ROUND_RECTANGLE = 3;
9   public static final int OVAL = 4;
10
11  private int type = 1;
12  private boolean filled = false;
13
14  /** Construct a default FigurePanel */
15  public FigurePanel() {
16  }
17
18  /** Construct a FigurePanel with the specified type */
19  public FigurePanel(int type) {
20    this.type = type;
21  }
22
23  /** Construct a FigurePanel with the specified type and filled */
24  public FigurePanel(int type, boolean filled) {
25    this.type = type;
26    this.filled = filled;
27  }
28
29  /** Draw a figure on the panel */
30  protected void paintComponent(Graphics g) {
31    super.paintComponent(g);
32
33    // Get the appropriate size for the figure
34    int width = getSize().width;
35    int height = getSize().height;
36
37    switch (type) {
38      case LINE: // Display two cross lines
39        g.setColor(Color.BLACK);
40        g.drawLine(10, 10, width - 10, height - 10);
41        g.drawLine(width - 10, 10, 10, height - 10);
42        break;
43      case RECTANGLE: // Display a rectangle
44        g.setColor(Color.BLUE);
```

constants

override paintComponent(g)

check type

draw lines

```
45          if (filled)
46            g.fillRect((int)(0.1 * width), (int)(0.1 * height),
47              (int)(0.8 * width), (int)(0.8 * height));
48          else
49            g.drawRect((int)(0.1 * width), (int)(0.1 * height),
50              (int)(0.8 * width), (int)(0.8 * height));
51          break;
52        case ROUND_RECTANGLE: // Display a round-cornered rectangle
53          g.setColor(Color.RED);
54          if (filled)
55            g.fillRoundRect((int)(0.1 * width), (int)(0.1 * height),
56              (int)(0.8 * width), (int)(0.8 * height), 20, 20);
57          else
58            g.drawRoundRect((int)(0.1 * width), (int)(0.1 * height),
59              (int)(0.8 * width), (int)(0.8 * height), 20, 20);
60          break;
61        case OVAL: // Display an oval
62          g.setColor(Color.BLACK);
63          if (filled)
64            g.fillOval((int)(0.1 * width), (int)(0.1 * height),
65              (int)(0.8 * width), (int)(0.8 * height));
66          else
67            g.drawOval((int)(0.1 * width), (int)(0.1 * height),
68              (int)(0.8 * width), (int)(0.8 * height));
69      }
70    }
71
72    /** Set a new figure type */
73    public void setType(int type) {
74      this.type = type;
75      repaint();
76    }
77
78    /** Return figure type */
79    public int getType() {
80      return type;
81    }
82
83    /** Set a new filled property */
84    public void setFilled(boolean filled) {
85      this.filled = filled;
86      repaint();
87    }
88
89    /** Check if the figure is filled */
90    public boolean isFilled() {
91      return filled;
92    }
93
94    /** Specify preferred size */
95    public Dimension getPreferredSize() {
96      return new Dimension(80, 80);
97    }
98  }
```

fill a rectangle

draw a rectangle

fill round-cornered rect

draw round-cornered rect

fill an oval

draw an oval

repaint panel

repaint panel

override **getPreferredSize()**

The **repaint** method (lines 75, 86) is defined in the **Component** class. Invoking **repaint** causes the **paintComponent** method to be called. The **repaint** method is invoked to refresh the viewing area. Typically, you call it if you have new things to display.

don't invoke **paintComponent**

Caution

The paintComponent method should never be invoked directly. It is invoked either by the JVM whenever the viewing area changes or by the repaint method. You should override the paintComponent method to tell the system how to paint the viewing area, but never override the repaint method.

request repaint using **repaint()**

Note

The repaint method lodges a request to update the viewing area and returns immediately. Its effect is asynchronous, meaning that it is up to the JVM to execute the paintComponent method.

getPreferedSize()

The getPreferredSize() method (lines 95–97), defined in Component, is overridden in FigurePanel to specify the preferred size for the layout manager to consider when laying out a FigurePanel object. This property may or may not be considered by the layout manager, depending on its rules. For example, a component uses its preferred size in a container with a FlowLayout manager, but its preferred size may be ignored if it is placed in a container with a GridLayout manager. It is a good practice to override getPreferredSize() in a subclass of JPanel to specify a preferred size, because the default preferred size for a JPanel is 0 by 0.

14.8 Drawing Arcs

An arc is conceived as part of an oval bounded by a rectangle. The methods to draw or fill an arc are as follows:

```
drawArc(int x, int y, int w, int h, int startAngle, int arcAngle);
fillArc(int x, int y, int w, int h, int startAngle, int arcAngle);
```

Parameters x, y, w, and h are the same as in the drawOval method; parameter startAngle is the starting angle; arcAngle is the spanning angle (i.e., the angle covered by the arc). Angles are measured in degrees and follow the usual mathematical conventions (i.e., 0 degrees is in the easterly direction, and positive angles indicate counterclockwise rotation from the easterly direction); see Figure 14.12.

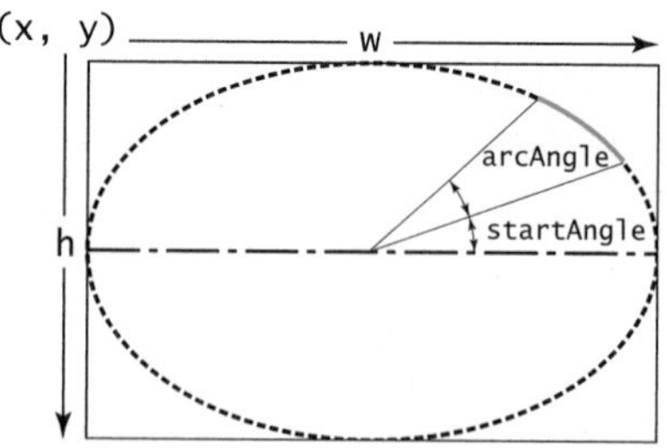

FIGURE 14.12 The drawArc method draws an arc based on an oval with specified angles.

Listing 14.6 is an example of how to draw arcs; the output is shown in Figure 14.13.

LISTING 14.6 DrawArcs.java

```
import javax.swing.JFrame;
import javax.swing.JPanel;
import java.awt.Graphics;

public class DrawArcs extends JFrame {
  public DrawArcs() {
```

```
    setTitle("DrawArcs");
    add(new ArcsPanel());
  }

  /** Main method */
  public static void main(String[] args) {
    DrawArcs frame = new DrawArcs();
    frame.setSize(250, 300);
    frame.setLocationRelativeTo(null); // Center the frame
    frame.setDefaultCloseOperation(JFrame.EXIT_ON_CLOSE);
    frame.setVisible(true);
  }
}

// The class for drawing arcs on a panel
class ArcsPanel extends JPanel {
  // Draw four blades of a fan
  protected void paintComponent(Graphics g) {
    super.paintComponent(g);

    int xCenter = getWidth() / 2;
    int yCenter = getHeight() / 2;
    int radius = (int)(Math.min(getWidth(), getHeight()) * 0.4);

    int x = xCenter - radius;
    int y = yCenter - radius;

    g.fillArc(x, y, 2 * radius, 2 * radius, 0, 30);
    g.fillArc(x, y, 2 * radius, 2 * radius, 90, 30);
    g.fillArc(x, y, 2 * radius, 2 * radius, 180, 30);
    g.fillArc(x, y, 2 * radius, 2 * radius, 270, 30);
  }
}
```

add a panel

override **paintComponent**

30° arc from 0°

30° arc from 90°

30° arc from 180°

30° arc from 270°

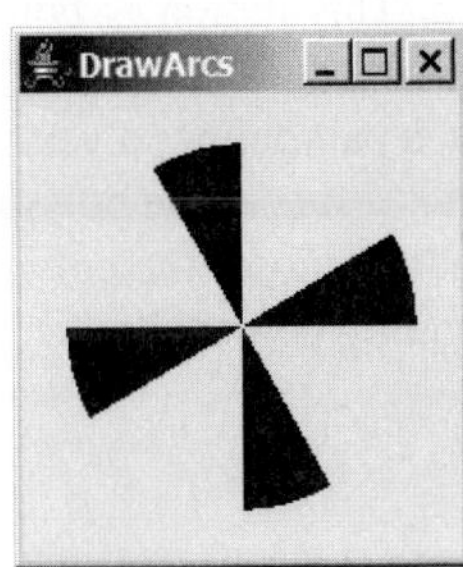

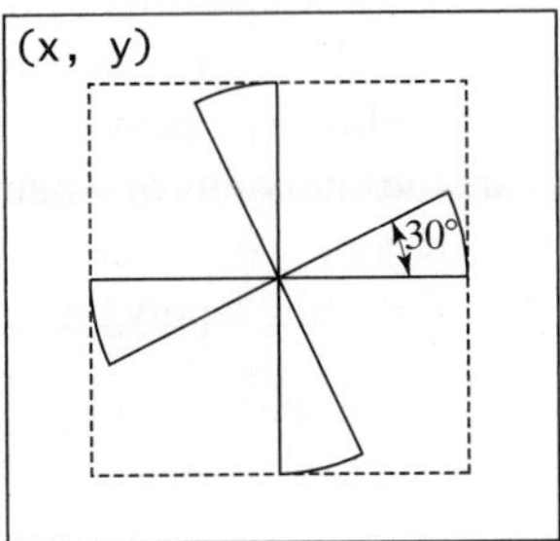

FIGURE 14.13 The program draws four filled arcs.

negative degrees

Angles may be negative. A negative starting angle sweeps clockwise from the easterly direction, as shown in Figure 14.14. A negative spanning angle sweeps clockwise from the starting angle. The following two statements draw the same arc:

```
g.fillArc(x, y, 2 * radius, 2 * radius, -30, -20);
g.fillArc(x, y, 2 * radius, 2 * radius, -50, 20);
```

The first statement uses negative starting angle -30 and negative spanning angle -20, as shown in Figure 14.14(a). The second statement uses negative starting angle -50 and positive spanning angle 20, as shown in Figure 14.14(b).

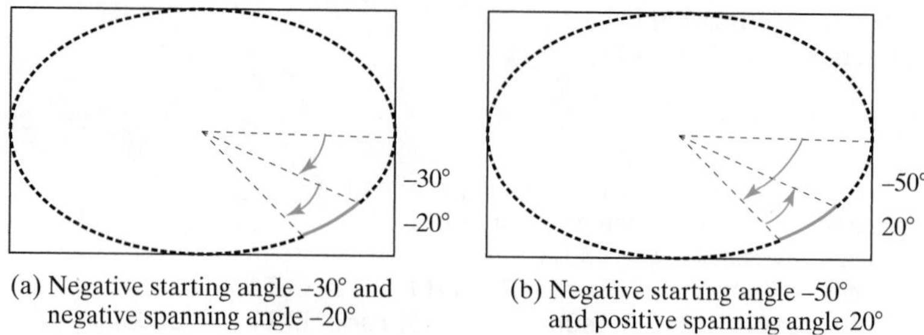

(a) Negative starting angle -30° and negative spanning angle -20°

(b) Negative starting angle -50° and positive spanning angle 20°

FIGURE 14.14 Angles may be negative.

14.9 Drawing Polygons and Polylines

To draw a polygon, first create a Polygon object using the Polygon class, as shown in Figure 14.15.

java.awt.Polygon	
+xpoints: int[]	x-coordinates of all points in the polygon.
+ypoints: int[]	y-coordinates of all points in the polygon.
+npoints: int	The number of points in the polygon.
+Polygon()	Creates an empty polygon.
+Polygon(xpoints: int[], ypoints: int[], npoints: int)	Creates a polygon with the specified points.
+addPoint(x: int, y: int)	Appends a point to the polygon.

FIGURE 14.15 The Polygon class models a polygon.

A polygon is a closed two-dimensional region. This region is bounded by an arbitrary number of line segments, each of which is one side (or edge) of the polygon. A polygon comprises a list of (x, y)-coordinate pairs in which each pair defines a vertex of the polygon, and two successive pairs are the endpoints of a line that is a side of the polygon. The first and final pairs of (x, y) points are joined by a line segment that closes the polygon.

Here is an example of creating a polygon and adding points into it:

```
Polygon polygon = new Polygon();
polygon.addPoint(40, 20);
polygon.addPoint(70, 40);
polygon.addPoint(60, 80);
polygon.addPoint(45, 45);
polygon.addPoint(20, 60);
```

After these points are added, xpoints is {40, 70, 60, 45, 20}, ypoints is {20, 40, 80, 45, 60}, and npoints is 5. xpoints, ypoints, and npoints are public data fields in Polygon, which is a bad design. In principle, all data fields should be kept private.

To draw or fill a polygon, use one of the following methods in the Graphics class:

```
drawPolygon(Polygon polygon);

fillPolygon(Polygon polygon);

drawPolygon(int[] xpoints, int[] ypoints, int npoints);

fillPolygon(int[] xpoints, int[] ypoints, int npoints);
```

For example:

```
int x[] = {40, 70, 60, 45, 20};
int y[] = {20, 40, 80, 45, 60};
g.drawPolygon(x, y, x.length);
```

The drawing method opens the polygon by drawing lines between point `(x[i], y[i])` and point `(x[i+1], y[i+1])` for `i = 0, ... , x.length-1`; it closes the polygon by drawing a line between the first and last points (see Figure 14.16(a)).

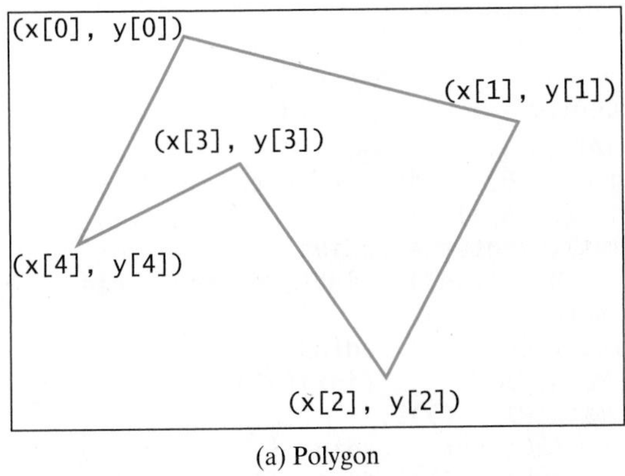

(a) Polygon

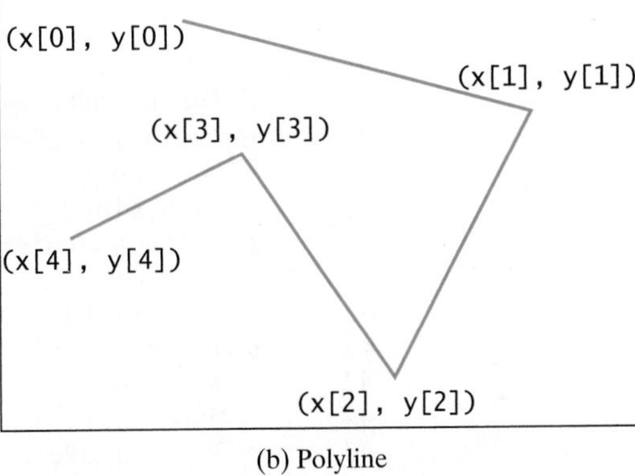

(b) Polyline

FIGURE 14.16 The `drawPolygon` method draws a polygon, and the `polyLine` method draws a polyline.

To draw a polyline, use the `drawPolyline(int[] x, int[] y, int nPoints)` method, which draws a sequence of connected lines defined by arrays of `x`- and `y`-coordinates. For example, the following code draws the polyline, as shown in Figure 14.16(b).

```
int x[] = {40, 70, 60, 45, 20};
int y[] = {20, 40, 80, 45, 60};
g.drawPolygon(x, y, x.length);
```

Listing 14.7 is an example of how to draw a hexagon, with the output shown in Figure 14.17.

LISTING 14.7 DrawPolygon.java

```
import javax.swing.JFrame;
import javax.swing.JPanel;
import java.awt.Graphics;
import java.awt.Polygon;

public class DrawPolygon extends JFrame {
  public DrawPolygon() {
    setTitle("DrawPolygon");
    add(new PolygonsPanel());
  }

  /** Main method */
  public static void main(String[] args) {
    DrawPolygon frame = new DrawPolygon();
    frame.setSize(200, 250);
    frame.setLocationRelativeTo(null); // Center the frame
    frame.setDefaultCloseOperation(JFrame.EXIT_ON_CLOSE);
    frame.setVisible(true);
  }
}

```

add a panel

paintComponent

add a point

draw polygon

```
// Draw a polygon in the panel
class PolygonsPanel extends JPanel {
  protected void paintComponent(Graphics g) {
    super.paintComponent(g);

    int xCenter = getWidth() / 2;
    int yCenter = getHeight() / 2;
    int radius = (int)(Math.min(getWidth(), getHeight()) * 0.4);

    // Create a Polygon object
    Polygon polygon = new Polygon();

    // Add points to the polygon in this order
    polygon.addPoint(xCenter + radius, yCenter);
    polygon.addPoint((int)(xCenter + radius *
      Math.cos(2 * Math.PI / 6)), (int)(yCenter - radius *
      Math.sin(2 * Math.PI / 6)));
    polygon.addPoint((int)(xCenter + radius *
      Math.cos(2 * 2 * Math.PI / 6)), (int)(yCenter - radius *
      Math.sin(2 * 2 * Math.PI / 6)));
    polygon.addPoint((int)(xCenter + radius *
      Math.cos(3 * 2 * Math.PI / 6)), (int)(yCenter - radius *
      Math.sin(3 * 2 * Math.PI / 6)));
    polygon.addPoint((int)(xCenter + radius *
      Math.cos(4 * 2 * Math.PI / 6)), (int)(yCenter - radius *
      Math.sin(4 * 2 * Math.PI / 6)));
    polygon.addPoint((int)(xCenter + radius *
      Math.cos(5 * 2 * Math.PI / 6)), (int)(yCenter - radius *
      Math.sin(5 * 2 * Math.PI / 6)));

    // Draw the polygon
    g.drawPolygon(polygon);
  }
}
```

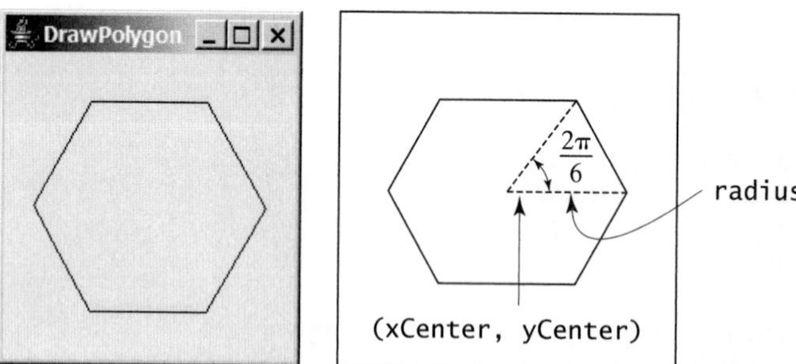

FIGURE 14.17 The program uses the drawPolygon method to draw a polygon.

14.10 Centering a String Using the FontMetrics Class

You can display a string at any location in a panel. Can you display it centered? To do so, you need to use the FontMetrics class to measure the exact width and height of the string for a particular font. FontMetrics can measure the following attributes for a given font (see Figure 14.18):

- **Leading,** pronounced *ledding*, is the amount of space between lines of text.
- **Ascent** is the distance from the baseline to the ascent line. The top of most characters in the font will be under the ascent line, but some may extend above the ascent line.

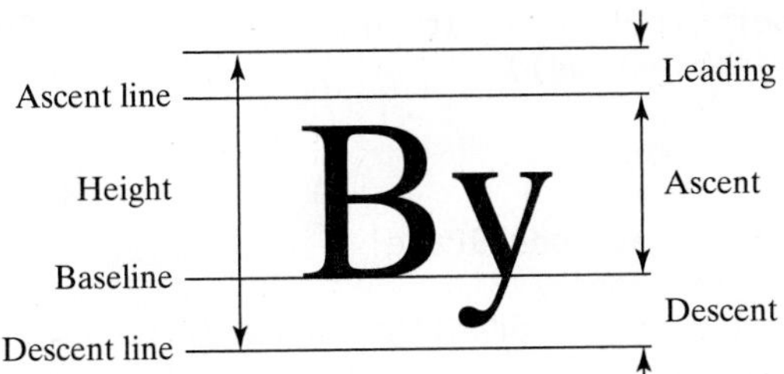

FIGURE 14.18 The `FontMetrics` class can be used to determine the font properties of characters for a given font.

- **Descent** is the distance from the baseline to the descent line. The bottom of most descending characters (e.g., *j*, *y*, and *g*) in the font will be above the descending line, but some may extend below the descending line.
- **Height** is the sum of leading, ascent, and descent.

`FontMetrics` is an abstract class. To get a `FontMetrics` object for a specific font, use the following `getFontMetrics` methods defined in the `Graphics` class:

- `public FontMetrics getFontMetrics(Font font)`
  Returns the font metrics of the specified font.

- `public FontMetrics getFontMetrics()`
  Returns the font metrics of the current font.

You can use the following instance methods in the `FontMetrics` class to obtain the attributes of a font and the width of a string when it is drawn using the font:

```
public int getAscent() // Return the ascent
public int getDescent() // Return the descent
public int getLeading() // Return the leading
public int getHeight() // Return the height
public int stringWidth(String str) // Return the width of the string
```

Listing 14.8 gives an example that displays a message in the center of the panel, as shown in Figure 14.19.

LISTING 14.8 `TestCenterMessage.java`

```
import javax.swing.*;
import java.awt.*;

public class TestCenterMessage extends JFrame {
  public TestCenterMessage() {
    CenterMessage messagePanel = new CenterMessage();
    add(messagePanel);
    messagePanel.setBackground(Color.WHITE);
    messagePanel.setFont(new Font("Californian FB", Font.BOLD, 30));
  }

  /** Main method */
  public static void main(String[] args) {
    TestCenterMessage frame = new TestCenterMessage();
    frame.setSize(300, 150);
    frame.setLocationRelativeTo(null); // Center the frame
```

create a message panel
add a message panel
set background
set font

override **paintComponent**

get **FontMetrics**

```
17     frame.setDefaultCloseOperation(JFrame.EXIT_ON_CLOSE);
18     frame.setVisible(true);
19   }
20 }
21
22 class CenterMessage extends JPanel {
23   /** Paint the message */
24   protected void paintComponent(Graphics g) {
25     super.paintComponent(g);
26
27     // Get font metrics for the current font
28     FontMetrics fm = g.getFontMetrics();
29
30     // Find the center location to display
31     int stringWidth = fm.stringWidth("Welcome to Java");
32     int stringAscent = fm.getAscent();
33
34     // Get the position of the leftmost character in the baseline
35     int xCoordinate = getWidth() / 2 - stringWidth / 2;
36     int yCoordinate = getHeight() / 2 + stringAscent / 2;
37
38     g.drawString("Welcome to Java", xCoordinate, yCoordinate);
39   }
40 }
```

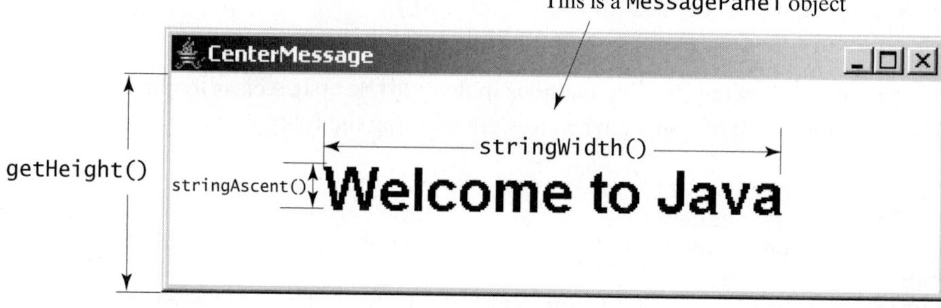

Figure 14.19 The program uses the **FontMetrics** class to measure the string width and height, and displays it at the center of the panel.

The methods **getWidth()** and **getHeight()** (lines 35–36) defined in the **Component** class, return the component's width and height, respectively.

yCoordinate is the height of the baseline for the first character of the string to be displayed. Since the message is **centered**, **yCoordinate** should be **getHeight() / 2 + h / 2**, where **h** is the ascent of the string.

xCoordinate is the width of the baseline for the first character of the string to be displayed. Since the message is **centered**, **xCoordinate** should be **getWidth() / 2 - stringWidth / 2**.

14.11 Case Study: The MessagePanel Class

Video Note
MessagePanel class

This case study develops a useful class that displays a message in a panel. The class enables the user to set the location of the message, center the message, and move the message with the specified interval. The contract of the class is shown in Figure 14.20.

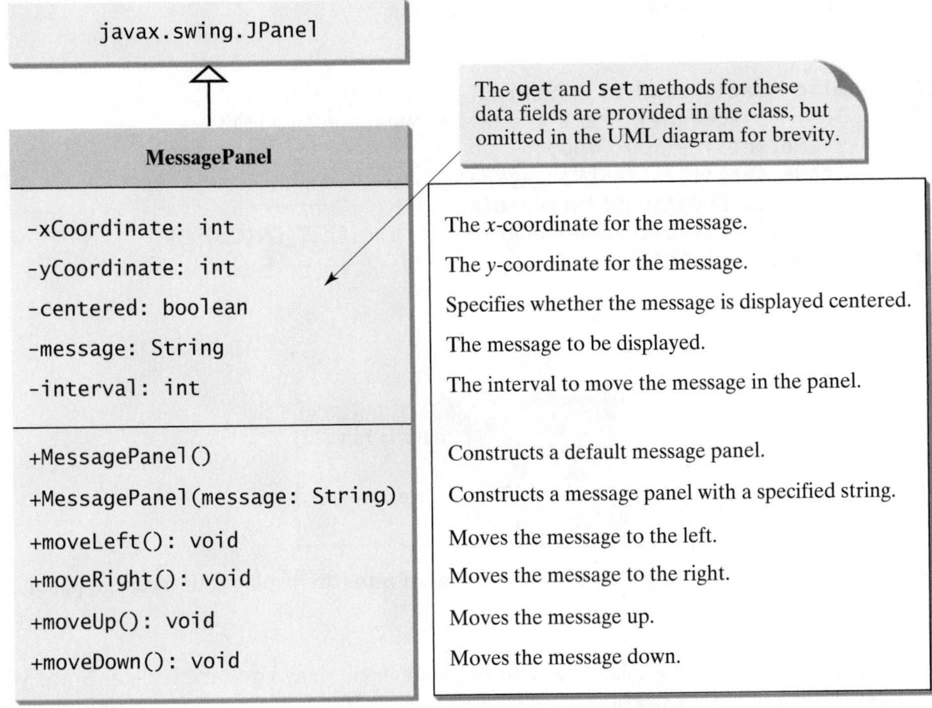

FIGURE 14.20 `MessagePanel` displays a message on the panel.

Let us first write a test program in Listing 14.9 that uses the `MessagePanel` class to display four message panels, as shown in Figure 14.21.

LISTING 14.9 TestMessagePanel.java

```
import java.awt.*;
import javax.swing.*;

public class TestMessagePanel extends JFrame {
  public TestMessagePanel() {
    MessagePanel messagePanel1 = new MessagePanel("Wecome to Java");
    MessagePanel messagePanel2 = new MessagePanel("Java is fun");
    MessagePanel messagePanel3 = new MessagePanel("Java is cool");
    MessagePanel messagePanel4 = new MessagePanel("I love Java");
    messagePanel1.setFont(new Font("SansSerif", Font.ITALIC, 20));
    messagePanel2.setFont(new Font("Courie", Font.BOLD, 20));
    messagePanel3.setFont(new Font("Times", Font.ITALIC, 20));
    messagePanel4.setFont(new Font("Californian FB", Font.PLAIN, 20));
    messagePanel1.setBackground(Color.red);
    messagePanel2.setBackground(Color.cyan);
    messagePanel3.setBackground(Color.green);
    messagePanel4.setBackground(Color.white);
    messagePanel1.setCentered(true);

    setLayout(new GridLayout(2, 2));
    add(messagePanel1);
    add(messagePanel2);
    add(messagePanel3);
```

create message panel

set font

set background

add message panel

```java
    add(messagePanel4);
  }

  public static void main(String[] args) {
    TestMessagePanel frame = new TestMessagePanel();
    frame.setSize(300, 200);
    frame.setTitle("TestMessagePanel");
    frame.setLocationRelativeTo(null); // Center the frame
    frame.setDefaultCloseOperation(JFrame.EXIT_ON_CLOSE);
    frame.setVisible(true);
  }
}
```

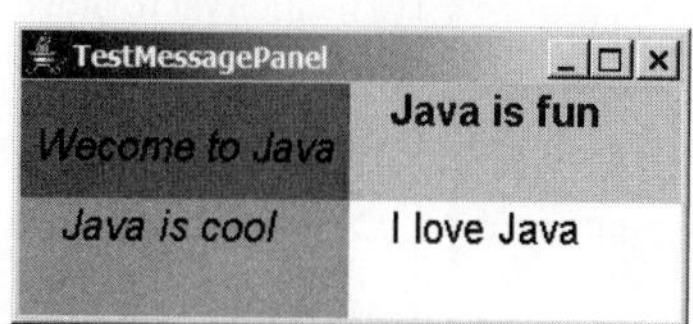

FIGURE 14.21 `TestMessagePanel` uses `MessagePanel` to display four message panels.

skip implementation?

The rest of this section explains how to implement the `MessagePanel` class. Since you can use the class without knowing how it is implemented, you may skip the implementation if you wish.

The `MessagePanel` class is implemented in Listing 14.10. The program seems long but is actually simple, because most of the methods are `get` and `set` methods, and each method is relatively short and easy to read.

LISTING 14.10 MessagePanel.java

```java
import java.awt.FontMetrics;
import java.awt.Dimension;
import java.awt.Graphics;
import javax.swing.JPanel;

public class MessagePanel extends JPanel {
  /** The message to be displayed */
  private String message = "Welcome to Java";

  /** The x-coordinate where the message is displayed */
  private int xCoordinate = 20;

  /** The y-coordinate where the message is displayed */
  private int yCoordinate = 20;

  /** Indicate whether the message is displayed in the center */
  private boolean centered;

  /** The interval for moving the message horizontally and vertically */
  private int interval = 10;

  /** Construct with default properties */
  public MessagePanel() {
  }

```

```
  /** Construct a message panel with a specified message */
  public MessagePanel(String message) {
    this.message = message;
  }

  /** Return message */
  public String getMessage() {
    return message;
  }

  /** Set a new message */
  public void setMessage(String message) {
    this.message = message;
    repaint();
  }
```

repaint panel

```
  /** Return xCoordinator */
  public int getXCoordinate() {
    return xCoordinate;
  }

  /** Set a new xCoordinator */
  public void setXCoordinate(int x) {
    this.xCoordinate = x;
    repaint();
  }
```

repaint panel

```
  /** Return yCoordinator */
  public int getYCoordinate() {
    return yCoordinate;
  }

  /** Set a new yCoordinator */
  public void setYCoordinate(int y) {
    this.yCoordinate = y;
    repaint();
  }
```

repaint panel

```
  /** Return centered */
  public boolean isCentered() {
    return centered;
  }

  /** Set a new centered */
  public void setCentered(boolean centered) {
    this.centered = centered;
    repaint();
  }
```

repaint panel

```
  /** Return interval */
  public int getInterval() {
    return interval;
  }

  /** Set a new interval */
  public void setInterval(int interval) {
    this.interval = interval;
    repaint();
  }

```

repaint panel

override **paintComponent**

check centered

override **getPreferredSize**

```
86   /** Paint the message */
87   protected void paintComponent(Graphics g) {
88     super.paintComponent(g);
89
90     if (centered) {
91       // Get font metrics for the current font
92       FontMetrics fm = g.getFontMetrics();
93
94       // Find the center location to display
95       int stringWidth = fm.stringWidth(message);
96       int stringAscent = fm.getAscent();
97       // Get the position of the leftmost character in the baseline
98       xCoordinate = getWidth() / 2 - stringWidth / 2;
99       yCoordinate = getHeight() / 2 + stringAscent / 2;
100    }
101
102    g.drawString(message, xCoordinate, yCoordinate);
103  }
104
105  /** Move the message left */
106  public void moveLeft() {
107    xCoordinate -= interval;
108    repaint();
109  }
110
111  /** Move the message right */
112  public void moveRight() {
113    xCoordinate += interval;
114    repaint();
115  }
116
117  /** Move the message up */
118  public void moveUp() {
119    yCoordinate -= interval;
120    repaint();
121  }
122
123  /** Move the message down */
124  public void moveDown() {
125    yCoordinate += interval;
126    repaint();
127  }
128
129  /** Override get method for preferredSize */
130  public Dimension getPreferredSize() {
131    return new Dimension(200, 30);
132  }
133 }
```

The `paintComponent` method displays the message centered, if the `centered` property is true (line 90). `message` is initialized to "Welcome to Java" in line 8. If it is not initialized, a `NullPointerException` runtime error would occur when you create a `MessagePanel` using the no-arg constructor, because `message` would be `null` in line 102.

Caution

The `MessagePanel` class uses the properties `xCoordinate` and `yCoordinate` to specify the position of the message displayed on the panel. Do not use the property names `x` and `y`, because they are already defined in the `Component` class to return the position of the component in the parent's coordinate system using `getX()` and `getY()`.

Note

The `Component` class has the `setBackground`, `setForeground`, and `setFont` methods. These methods are for setting colors and fonts for the entire component. Suppose you want to draw several messages in a panel with different colors and fonts; you have to use the `setColor` and `setFont` methods in the `Graphics` class to set the color and font for the current drawing.

Note

design classes for reuse

One of the key features of Java programming is the reuse of classes. Throughout the book, reusable classes are developed and later reused. `MessagePanel` is an example of this, as are `Loan` in §9.5 and `FigurePanel` in §14.7. It can be reused whenever you need to display a message on a panel. To make your class reusable in a wide range of applications, you should provide a variety of ways to use it. `MessagePanel` provides many properties and methods that will be used in several examples in the book. §14.12 presents another useful and reusable class for displaying a clock on a panel graphically.

14.12 Case Study: The `StillClock` Class

Video Note
`StillClock` class

This case study develops a class that displays a clock on a panel. The contract of the class is shown in Figure 14.22.

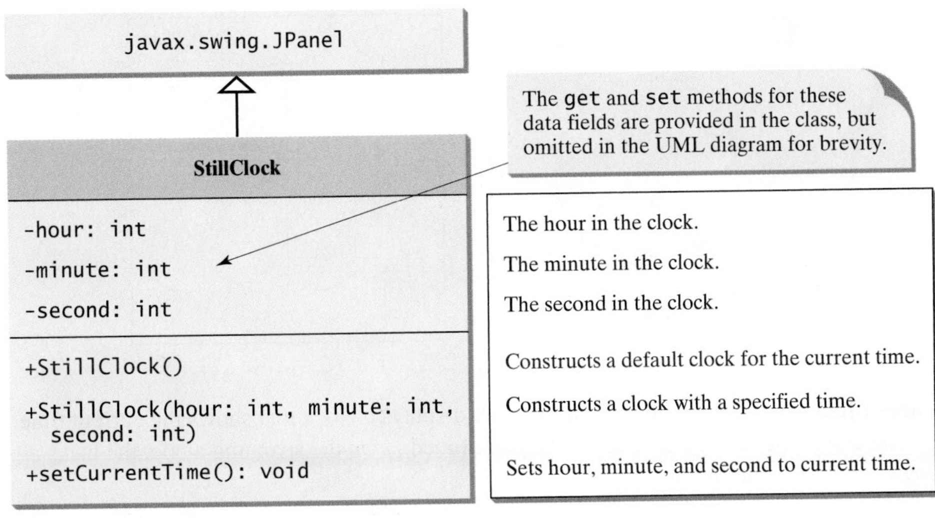

FIGURE 14.22 `StillClock` displays an analog clock.

Let us first write a test program in Listing 14.11 that uses the `StillClock` class to display an analog clock and uses the `MessagePanel` class to display the hour, minute, and second in a panel, as shown in Figure 14.23(a).

LISTING 14.11 `DisplayClock.java`

create a clock

```
import java.awt.*;
import javax.swing.*;

public class DisplayClock extends JFrame {
  public DisplayClock() {
    // Create an analog clock for the current time
    StillClock clock = new StillClock();

    // Display hour, minute, and seconds in the message panel
```

create a message panel

add a clock

add a message panel

```
    MessagePanel messagePanel = new MessagePanel(clock.getHour() +
      ":" + clock.getMinute() + ":" + clock.getSecond());
    messagePanel.setCentered(true);
    messagePanel.setForeground(Color.blue);
    messagePanel.setFont(new Font("Courie", Font.BOLD, 16));

    // Add the clock and message panel to the frame
    add(clock);
    add(messagePanel, BorderLayout.SOUTH);
  }

  public static void main(String[] args) {
    DisplayClock frame = new DisplayClock();
    frame.setTitle("DisplayClock");
    frame.setSize(300, 350);
    frame.setLocationRelativeTo(null); // Center the frame
    frame.setDefaultCloseOperation(JFrame.EXIT_ON_CLOSE);
    frame.setVisible(true);
  }
}
```

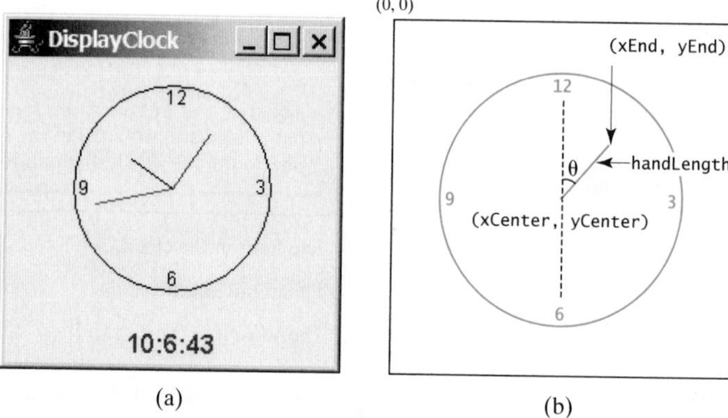

FIGURE 14.23 (a) The DisplayClock program displays a clock that shows the current time. (b) The end point of a clock hand can be determined given the spanning angle, the hand length, and the center point.

skip implementation?

The rest of this section explains how to implement the `StillClock` class. Since you can use the class without knowing how it is implemented, you may skip the implementation if you wish.

implementation

To draw a clock, you need to draw a circle and three hands for second, minute, and hour. To draw a hand, you need to specify the two ends of the line. As shown in Figure 14.23(b), one end is the center of the clock at `(xCenter, yCenter)`; the other end, at `(xEnd, yEnd)`, is determined by the following formula:

```
xEnd = xCenter + handLength × sin(θ)
yEnd = yCenter - handLength × cos(θ)
```

Since there are sixty seconds in one minute, the angle for the second hand is

```
second × (2π/60)
```

The position of the minute hand is determined by the minute and second. The exact minute value combined with seconds is `minute + second/60`. For example, if the time is 3 minutes and 30 seconds, the total minutes are 3.5. Since there are sixty minutes in one hour, the angle for the minute hand is

```
(minute + second/60) × (2π/60)
```

Since one circle is divided into twelve hours, the angle for the hour hand is

```
(hour + minute/60 + second/(60 × 60)) × (2π/12)
```

For simplicity, you can omit the seconds in computing the angles of the minute hand and the hour hand, because they are very small and can be neglected. Therefore, the end points for the second hand, minute hand, and hour hand can be computed as:

```
xSecond = xCenter + secondHandLength × sin(second × (2π/60))
ySecond = yCenter - secondHandLength × cos(second × (2π/60))
xMinute = xCenter + minuteHandLength × sin(minute × (2π/60))
yMinute = yCenter - minuteHandLength × cos(minute × (2π/60))
xHour = xCenter + hourHandLength × sin((hour + minute/60) × (2π/60))
yHour = yCenter - hourHandLength × cos((hour + minute/60) × (2π/60))
```

The StillClock class is implemented in Listing 14.12.

LISTING 14.12 StillClock.java

```
import java.awt.*;
import javax.swing.*;
import java.util.*;

public class StillClock extends JPanel {
  private int hour;
  private int minute;
  private int second;

  /** Construct a default clock with the current time*/
  public StillClock() {
    setCurrentTime();
  }

  /** Construct a clock with specified hour, minute, and second */
  public StillClock(int hour, int minute, int second) {
    this.hour = hour;
    this.minute = minute;
    this.second = second;
  }

  /** Return hour */
  public int getHour() {
    return hour;
  }

  /** Set a new hour */
  public void setHour(int hour) {
    this.hour = hour;
    repaint();
  }

  /** Return minute */
  public int getMinute() {
    return minute;
  }

```

repaint panel

repaint panel

repaint panel

override **paintComponent**

```
  /** Set a new minute */
  public void setMinute(int minute) {
    this.minute = minute;
    repaint();
  }

  /** Return second */
  public int getSecond() {
    return second;
  }

  /** Set a new second */
  public void setSecond(int second) {
    this.second = second;
    repaint();
  }

  /** Draw the clock */
  protected void paintComponent(Graphics g) {
    super.paintComponent(g);

    // Initialize clock parameters
    int clockRadius =
      (int)(Math.min(getWidth(), getHeight()) * 0.8 * 0.5);
    int xCenter = getWidth() / 2;
    int yCenter = getHeight() / 2;

    // Draw circle
    g.setColor(Color.black);
    g.drawOval(xCenter - clockRadius, yCenter - clockRadius,
      2 * clockRadius, 2 * clockRadius);
    g.drawString("12", xCenter - 5, yCenter - clockRadius + 12);
    g.drawString("9", xCenter - clockRadius + 3, yCenter + 5);
    g.drawString("3", xCenter + clockRadius - 10, yCenter + 3);
    g.drawString("6", xCenter - 3, yCenter + clockRadius - 3);

    // Draw second hand
    int sLength = (int)(clockRadius * 0.8);
    int xSecond = (int)(xCenter + sLength *
      Math.sin(second * (2 * Math.PI / 60)));
    int ySecond = (int)(yCenter - sLength *
      Math.cos(second * (2 * Math.PI / 60)));
    g.setColor(Color.red);
    g.drawLine(xCenter, yCenter, xSecond, ySecond);

    // Draw minute hand
    int mLength = (int)(clockRadius * 0.65);
    int xMinute = (int)(xCenter + mLength *
      Math.sin(minute * (2 * Math.PI / 60)));
    int yMinute = (int)(yCenter - mLength *
      Math.cos(minute * (2 * Math.PI / 60)));
    g.setColor(Color.blue);
    g.drawLine(xCenter, yCenter, xMinute, yMinute);

    // Draw hour hand
    int hLength = (int)(clockRadius * 0.5);
    int xHour = (int)(xCenter + hLength *
      Math.sin((hour % 12 + minute / 60.0) * (2 * Math.PI / 12)));
    int yHour = (int)(yCenter - hLength *
      Math.cos((hour % 12 + minute / 60.0) * (2 * Math.PI / 12)));
```

```
98      g.setColor(Color.green);
99      g.drawLine(xCenter, yCenter, xHour, yHour);
100   }
101
102   public void setCurrentTime() {
103     // Construct a calendar for the current date and time
104     Calendar calendar = new GregorianCalendar();
105
106     // Set current hour, minute and second
107     this.hour = calendar.get(Calendar.HOUR_OF_DAY);
108     this.minute = calendar.get(Calendar.MINUTE);
109     this.second = calendar.get(Calendar.SECOND);
110   }
111
112   public Dimension getPreferredSize() {
113     return new Dimension(200, 200);
114   }
115 }
```

get current time

override `getPreferredSize`

The program enables the clock size to adjust as the frame resizes. Every time you resize the frame, the `paintComponent` method is automatically invoked to paint the new frame. The `paintComponent` method displays the clock in proportion to the panel width (`getWidth()`) and height (`getHeight()`) (lines 60–63 in `StillClock`).

14.13 Displaying Images

You learned how to create image icons and display them in labels and buttons in §13.10, "Image Icons." For example, the following statements create an image icon and display it in a label:

```
ImageIcon icon = new ImageIcon("image/us.gif");
JLabel jlblImage = new JLabel(imageIcon);
```

An image icon displays a fixed-size image. To display an image in a flexible size, you need to use the `java.awt.Image` class. An image can be created from an image icon using the `getImage()` method as follows:

```
Image image = imageIcon.getImage();
```

Using a label as an area for displaying images is simple and convenient, but you don't have much control over how the image is displayed. A more flexible way to display images is to use the `drawImage` method of the `Graphics` class on a panel. Four versions of the `drawImage` method are shown in Figure 14.24.

`ImageObserver` is an asynchronous update interface that receives notifications of image information as the image is constructed. The `Component` class implements `ImageObserver`. Therefore, every GUI component is an instance of `ImageObserver`. To draw images using the `drawImage` method in a Swing component, such as `JPanel`, override the `paintComponent` method to tell the component how to display the image in the panel.

Listing 14.13 gives the code that displays an image from `image/us.gif`. The file `image/us.gif` (line 20) is under the class directory. An `Image` object is obtained in line 21. The `drawImage` method displays the image to fill in the whole panel, as shown in Figure 14.25.

java.awt.Graphics	
+drawImage(image: Image, x: int, y: int, bgcolor: Color, observer: ImageObserver): void	Draws the image in a specified location. The image's top-left corner is at (*x*, *y*) in the graphics context's coordinate space. Transparent pixels in the image are drawn in the specified color bgcolor. The observer is the object on which the image is displayed. The image is cut off if it is larger than the area it is being drawn on.
+drawImage(image: Image, x: int, y: int, observer: ImageObserver): void	Same as the preceding method except that it does not specify a background color.
+drawImage(image: Image, x: int, y: int, width: int, height: int, observer: ImageObserver): void	Draws a scaled version of the image that can fill all of the available space in the specified rectangle.
+drawImage(image: Image, x: int, y: int, width: int, height: int, bgcolor: Color, observer: ImageObserver): void	Same as the preceding method except that it provides a solid background color behind the image being drawn.

FIGURE 14.24 You can apply the drawImage method on a Graphics object to display an image in a GUI component.

LISTING 14.13 DisplayImage.java

```
import java.awt.*;
import javax.swing.*;

public class DisplayImage extends JFrame {
  public DisplayImage() {
    add(new ImagePanel());
  }

  public static void main(String[] args) {
    JFrame frame = new DisplayImage();
    frame.setTitle("DisplayImage");
    frame.setSize(300, 300);
    frame.setLocationRelativeTo(null); // Center the frame
    frame.setDefaultCloseOperation(JFrame.EXIT_ON_CLOSE);
    frame.setVisible(true);
  }

  // Inner class: Define the panel for showing an image
  static class ImagePanel extends JPanel {
    ImageIcon imageIcon = new ImageIcon("image/us.gif");
    Image image = imageIcon.getImage();

    /** Draw image on the panel */
    public void paintComponent(Graphics g) {
      super.paintComponent(g);

      if (image != null)
        g.drawImage(image, 0, 0, getWidth(), getHeight(), this);
    }
  }
}
```

add panel

inner class

create image icon

get image

override **paintComponent**

draw image

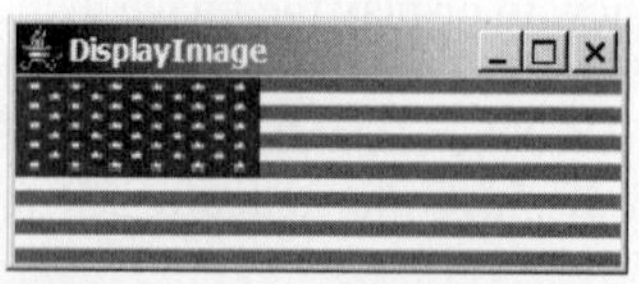

FIGURE 14.25 An image is displayed in a panel.

14.14 Case Study: The **ImageViewer** Class

Displaying an image is a common task in Java programming. This case study develops a reusable component named `ImageViewer` that displays an image on a panel. The class contains the properties `image`, `stretched`, `xCoordinate`, and `yCoordinate`, with associated accessor and mutator methods, as shown in Figure 14.26.

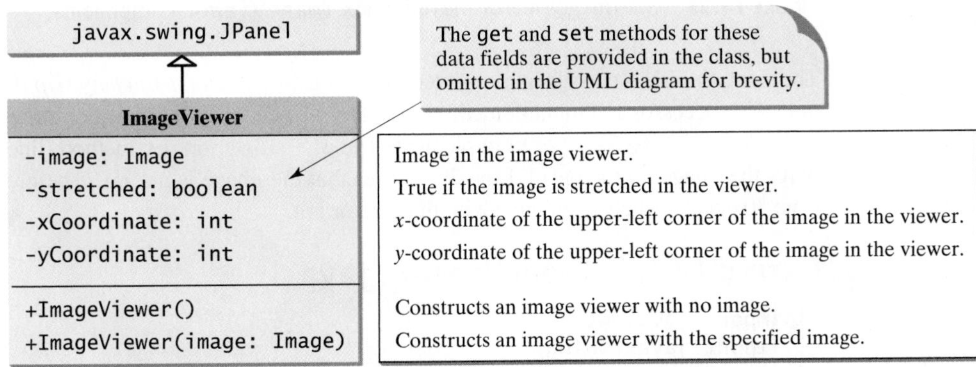

FIGURE 14.26 The `ImageViewer` class displays an image on a panel.

You can use images in Swing components like `JLabel` and `JButton`, but these images are not stretchable. The image in an `ImageViewer` can be stretched.

stretchable image

Let us write a test program in Listing 14.14 that displays six images using the `ImageViewer` class. Figure 14.27 shows a sample run of the program.

LISTING 14.14 `SixFlags.java`

create image

create image viewer

```
import javax.swing.*;
import java.awt.*;

public class SixFlags extends JFrame {
  public SixFlags() {
    Image image1 = new ImageIcon("image/us.gif").getImage();
    Image image2 = new ImageIcon("image/ca.gif").getImage();
    Image image3 = new ImageIcon("image/india.gif").getImage();
    Image image4 = new ImageIcon("image/uk.gif").getImage();
    Image image5 = new ImageIcon("image/china.gif").getImage();
    Image image6 = new ImageIcon("image/norway.gif").getImage();

    setLayout(new GridLayout(2, 0, 5, 5));
    add(new ImageViewer(image1));
    add(new ImageViewer(image2));
    add(new ImageViewer(image3));
    add(new ImageViewer(image4));
    add(new ImageViewer(image5));
    add(new ImageViewer(image6));
  }

  public static void main(String[] args) {
    SixFlags frame = new SixFlags();
    frame.setTitle("SixFlags");
    frame.setSize(400, 320);
    frame.setLocationRelativeTo(null); // Center the frame
    frame.setDefaultCloseOperation(JFrame.EXIT_ON_CLOSE);
    frame.setVisible(true);
  }
}
```

FIGURE 14.27 Six images are displayed in six `ImageViewer` components.

implementation

skip implementation?

The `ImageViewer` class is implemented in Listing 14.15. (*Note: You may skip the implementation.*) The accessor and mutator methods for the properties `image`, `stretched`, `xCoordinate`, and `yCoordinate` are easy to implement. The `paintComponent` method (lines 26–35) displays the image on the panel. Line 29 ensures that the image is not `null` before displaying it. Line 30 checks whether the image is stretched or not.

LISTING 14.15 ImageViewer.java

properties

constructor

constructor

image null?

stretched

non-stretched

```
1 import java.awt.*;
2 import javax.swing.*;
3
4 public class ImageViewer extends JPanel {
5   /** Hold value of property image. */
6   private java.awt.Image image;
7
8   /** Hold value of property stretched. */
9   private boolean stretched = true;
10
11   /** Hold value of property xCoordinate. */
12   private int xCoordinate;
13
14   /** Hold value of property yCoordinate. */
15   private int yCoordinate;
16
17   /** Construct an empty image viewer */
18   public ImageViewer() {
19   }
20
21   /** Construct an image viewer for a specified Image object */
22   public ImageViewer(Image image) {
23     this.image = image;
24   }
25
26   protected void paintComponent(Graphics g) {
27     super.paintComponent(g);
28
29     if (image != null)
30       if (isStretched())
31         g.drawImage(image, xCoordinate, yCoordinate,
32           getSize().width, getSize().height, this);
33       else
34         g.drawImage(image, xCoordinate, yCoordinate, this);
35   }
36
37   /** Return value of property image */
38   public java.awt.Image getImage() {
39     return image;
40   }
41
```

```
  /** Set a new value for property image */
  public void setImage(java.awt.Image image) {
    this.image = image;
    repaint();
  }

  /** Return value of property stretched */
  public boolean isStretched() {
    return stretched;
  }

  /** Set a new value for property stretched */
  public void setStretched(boolean stretched) {
    this.stretched = stretched;
    repaint();
  }

  /** Return value of property xCoordinate */
  public int getXCoordinate() {
    return xCoordinate;
  }

  /** Set a new value for property xCoordinate */
  public void setXCoordinate(int xCoordinate) {
    this.xCoordinate = xCoordinate;
    repaint();
  }

  /** Return value of property yCoordinate */
  public int getYCoordinate() {
    return yCoordinate;
  }

  /** Set a new value for property yCoordinate */
  public void setYCoordinate(int yCoordinate) {
    this.yCoordinate = yCoordinate;
    repaint();
  }
}
```

CHAPTER SUMMARY

- Each component has its own coordinate system with the origin (`0, 0`) at the upper-left corner of the window. The *x*-coordinate increases to the right, and the *y*-coordinate increases downward.

- The `Graphics` class is an abstract class for displaying figures and images on the screen on different platforms. The `Graphics` class is implemented on the native platform in the JVM. When you use the `paintComponent(g)` method to paint on a GUI component, this `g` is an instance of a concrete subclass of the abstract `Graphics` class for the specific platform. The `Graphics` class encapsulates the platform details and enables you to draw things uniformly without concern for the specific platform.

- Invoking `super.paintComponent(g)` is necessary to ensure that the viewing area is cleared before a new drawing is displayed. The user can request the component to be redisplayed by invoking the `repaint()` method defined in the `Component` class. Invoking `repaint()` causes `paintComponent` to be invoked by the JVM. The user should never invoke paintComponent directly. For this reason, the protected visibility is sufficient for paintComponent.

- Normally you use JPanel as a canvas. To draw on a JPanel, you create a new class that extends JPanel and overrides the paintComponent method to tell the panel how to draw things.

- You can set fonts for the components or subjects you draw, and use font metrics to measure font size. Fonts and font metrics are encapsulated in the classes Font and FontMetrics. FontMetrics can be used to compute the exact length and width of a string, which is helpful for measuring the size of a string in order to display it in the right position.

- The Component class has the setBackground, setForeground, and setFont methods. These methods are used to set colors and fonts for the entire component. Suppose you want to draw several messages in a panel with different colors and fonts; you have to use the setColor and setFont methods in the Graphics class to set the color and font for the current drawing.

- To display an image, first create an image icon. You can then use ImageIcon's getImage() method to get an Image object for the image and draw the image using the drawImage method in the java.awt.Graphics class.

REVIEW QUESTIONS

Sections 14.2–14.3

14.1 Suppose that you want to draw a new message below an existing message. Should the x-coordinate, y-coordinate, or both increase or decrease?

14.2 Why does jlblBanner.getGraphics() in line 9 in Listing 14.1 return null? What is the reason for showing the message dialog box in line 19 in Listing 14.1? In line 9, jlblBanner.getGraphics() is used to return a Graphics object. In line 21, why do you have to use frame.jlblBanner.getGraphics() in the main method?

Sections 14.4–14.5

14.3 Describe the paintComponent method. Where is it defined? How is it invoked? Can it be directly invoked? How can the program cause this method be invoked?

14.4 Why is the paintComponent method protected? What happens if you change it to public or private in a subclass? Why is super.paintComponent(g) invoked in line 25 in Listing 14.2 and in line 21 in Listing 14.3?

14.5 Can you draw things on any Swing GUI component? Why should you use a panel as a canvas for drawings rather than a label or a button?

Sections 14.6–14.9

14.6 Describe the methods for drawing strings, lines, rectangles, round-cornered rectangles, 3D rectangles, ovals, arcs, polygons, and polylines.

14.7 Describe the methods for filling rectangles, round-cornered rectangle, ovals, arcs, and polygons.

14.8 How do you get and set colors and fonts in a Graphics object?

14.9 Write a statement to draw the following shapes:

- Draw a thick line from (10, 10) to (70, 30). You can draw several lines next to each other to create the effect of one thick line.
- Draw/fill a rectangle of width 100 and height 50 with the upper-left corner at (10, 10).
- Draw/fill a round-cornered rectangle with width 100, height 200, corner horizontal diameter 40, and corner vertical diameter 20.
- Draw/fill a circle with radius 30.
- Draw/fill an oval with width 50 and height 100.
- Draw the upper half of a circle with radius 50.
- Draw/fill a polygon connecting the following points: (20, 40), (30, 50), (40, 90), (90, 10), (10, 30).

Sections 14.10–14.12

14.10 How do you find the leading, ascent, descent, and height of a font? How do you find the exact length in pixels of a string in a `Graphics` object?

14.11 If `message` is not initialized in line 8 in Listing 14.10, MessagePanel.java, what will happen when you create a `MessagePanel` using its no-arg constructor?

14.12 The following program is supposed to display a message on the panel, but nothing is displayed. There are problems in lines 2 and 14. Correct them.

```
 1 public class TestDrawMessage extends javax.swing.JFrame {
 2   public void TestDrawMessage() {
 3     add(new DrawMessage());
 4   }
 5
 6   public static void main(String[] args) {
 7     javax.swing.JFrame frame = new TestDrawMessage();
 8     frame.setSize(100, 200);
 9     frame.setVisible(true);
10   }
11 }
12
13 class DrawMessage extends javax.swing.JPanel {
14   protected void PaintComponent(java.awt.Graphics g) {
15     super.paintComponent(g);
16     g.drawString("Welcome to Java", 20, 20);
17   }
18 }
```

Sections 14.13–14.14

14.13 How do you create an `Image` object from the `ImageIcon` object?

14.14 How do you create an `ImageIcon` object from an `Image` object?

14.15 Describe the `drawImage` method in the `Graphics` class.

14.16 Explain the differences between displaying images in a `JLabel` and in a `JPanel`.

14.17 Which package contains `ImageIcon`, and which contains `Image`?

PROGRAMMING EXERCISES

Sections 14.2–14.9

14.1* (*Displaying a* 3×3 *grid*) Write a program that displays a 3×3 grid, as shown in Figure 14.28(a). Use red color for vertical lines and blue color for horizontal lines.

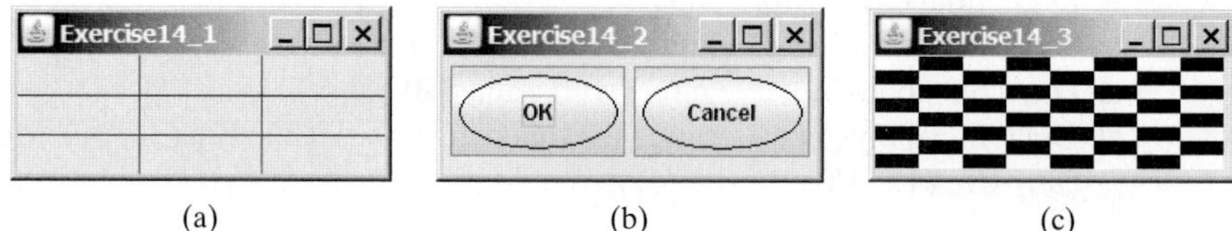

(a) (b) (c)

FIGURE 14.28 (a) Exercise 14.1 displays a grid. (b) Exercise 14.2 displays two objects of `OvalButton`. (c) Exercise 14.3 displays a checkerboard.

14.2** (*Creating a custom button class*) Develop a custom button class named `OvalButton` that extends `JButton` and displays the button text inside an oval. Figure 14.28(b) shows two buttons created using the `OvalButton` class.

14.3* (*Displaying a checkerboard*) Exercise 13.10 displays a checkerboard in which each white and black cell is a `JButton`. Rewrite a program that draws a checkerboard on a `JPanel` using the drawing methods in the `Graphics` class, as shown in Figure 14.28(c).

14.4* (*Displaying a multiplication table*) Write a program that displays a multiplication table in a panel using the drawing methods, as shown in Figure 14.29(a).

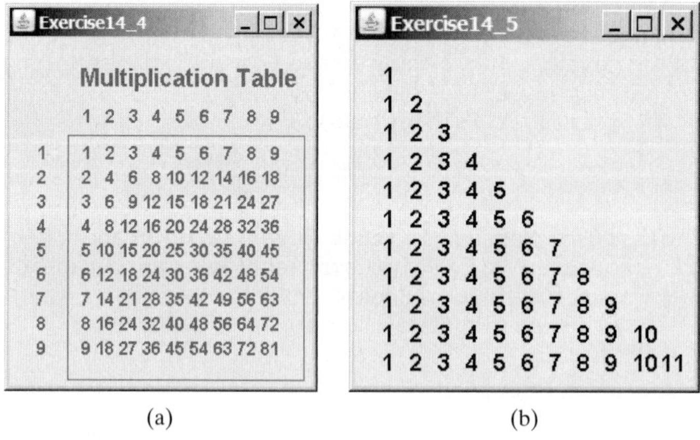

(a) (b)

FIGURE 14.29 (a) Exercise 14.4 displays a multiplication table. (b) Exercise 14.5 displays numbers in a triangle formation.

14.5** (*Displaying numbers in a triangular pattern*) Write a program that displays numbers in a triangular pattern, as shown in Figure 14.29(b). The number of lines in the display changes to fit the window as the window resizes.

14.6** (*Improving* `FigurePanel`) The `FigurePanel` class in Listing 14.5 can display lines, rectangles, round-cornered rectangles, and ovals. Add appropriate new code in the class to display arcs and polygons. Write a test program to display the shapes as shown in Figure 14.30(a) using the new `FigurePanel` class.

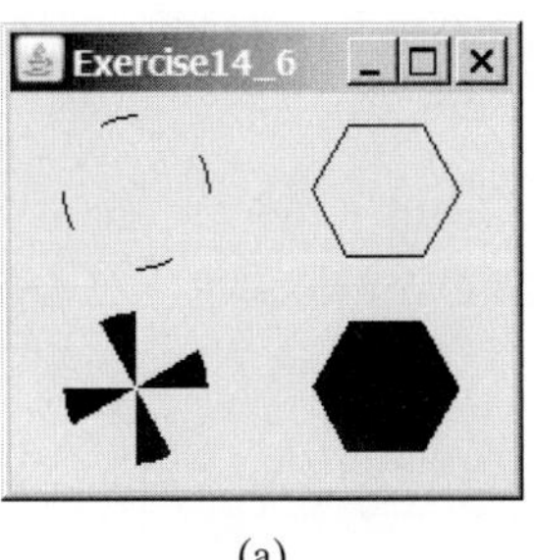

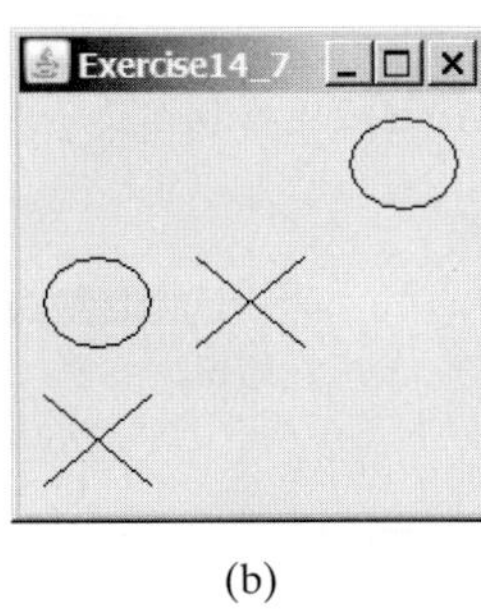

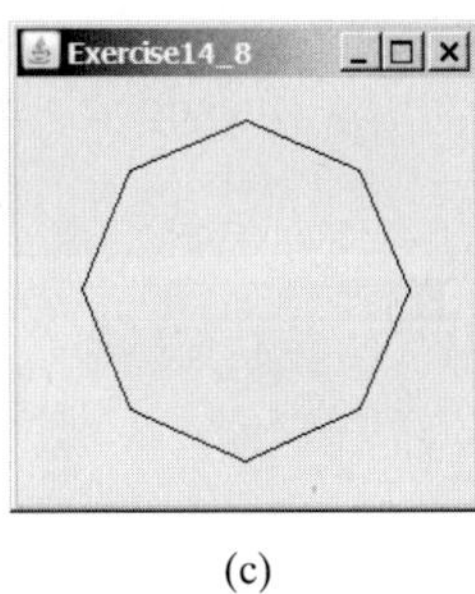

(a) (b) (c)

FIGURE 14.30 (a) Four panels of geometric figures are displayed in a frame of `GridLayout`. (b) `TicTacToe` cells display X, O, or nothing randomly. (c) Exercise 14.8 draws an octagon.

14.7** (*Displaying a TicTacToe board*) Create a custom panel that displays `X`, `O`, or nothing. What to display is randomly decided whenever a panel is repainted. Use the `Math.random()` method to generate an integer `0`, `1`, or `2`, which corresponds to displaying `X`, `O`, or nothing. Create a frame that contains nine custom panels, as shown in Figure 14.30(b).

14.8** (*Drawing an octagon*) Write a program that draws an octagon, as shown in Figure 14.30(c).

14.9* (*Creating four fans*) Write a program that places four fans in a frame of `GridLayout` with two rows and two columns, as shown in Figure 14.31(a).

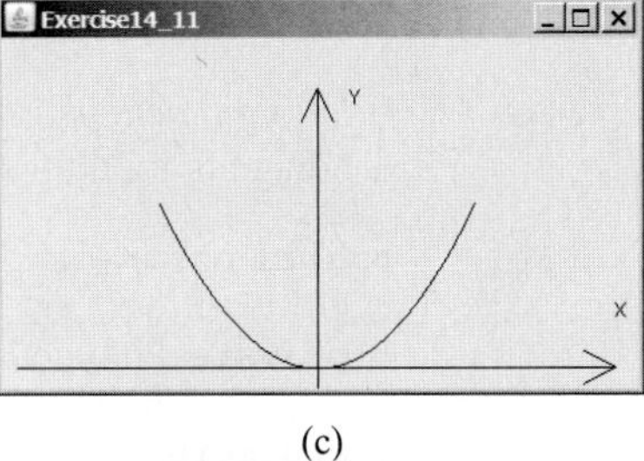

(a) (b) (c)

FIGURE 14.31 (a) Exercise 14.9 draws four fans. (b) Exercise 14.10 draws a cylinder. (c) Exercise 14.11 draws a diagram for function $f(x) = x^2$.

14.10* (*Creating a cylinder*) Write a program that draws a cylinder, as shown in Figure 14.31(b).

14.11** (*Plotting the square function*) Write a program that draws a diagram for the function $f(x) = x^2$ (see Figure 14.31(c)).

Hint: Add points to a polygon `p` using the following loop:

```
double scaleFactor = 0.1;

for (int x = -100; x <= 100; x++) {
  p.addPoint(x + 200, 200 - (int)(scaleFactor * x * x));
}
```

Connect the points using `g.drawPolyline(p.xpoints, p.ypoints, p.npoints)` for a `Graphics` object `g`. `p.xpoints` returns an array of `x`-coordinates, `p.ypoints` returns an array of `y`-coordinates, and `p.npoints` returns the number of points in `Polygon` object `p`.

Video Note
Plot a sine function

14.12** (*Plotting the sine function*) Write a program that draws a diagram for the sine function, as shown in Figure 14.32(a).

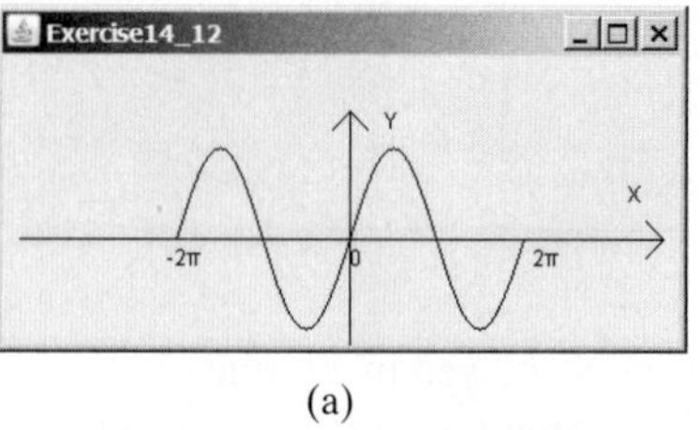

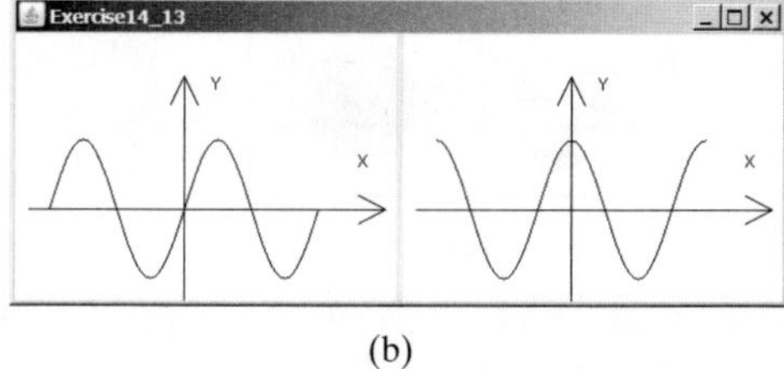

(a) (b)

FIGURE 14.32 (a) Exercise 14.12 draws a diagram for function $f(x) = sin(x)$. (b) Exercise 14.13 draws the sine and cosine functions.

Hint: The Unicode for π is `\u03c0`. To display -2π, use `g.drawString("-2\u03c0", x, y)`. For a trigonometric function like `sin(x)`, `x` is in radians. Use the following loop to add the points to a polygon `p`:

```
for (intx = -100; x <= 100; x++) {
  p.addPoint(x + 200,
    100 - (int)(50 * Math.sin((x / 100.0) * 2 * Math.PI)));
}
```

-2π is at (100, 100), the center of the axis is at (200, 100), and 2π is at (300, 100). Use the `drawPolyline` method in the `Graphics` class to connect the points.

14.13** (*Plotting functions using abstract methods*) Write an abstract class that draws the diagram for a function. The class is defined as follows:

```
public abstract class AbstractDrawFunction extends JPanel {
  /** Polygon to hold the points */
  private Polygon p = new Polygon();

  protected AbstractDrawFunction () {
    drawFunction();
  }

  /** Return the y-coordinate */
  abstract double f(double x);

  /** Obtain points for x-coordinates 100, 101, ..., 300 */
  public void drawFunction() {
    for (int x = -100; x <= 100; x++) {
      p.addPoint(x + 200, 200 - (int)f(x));
    }
  }

  /** Implement paintComponent to draw axes, labels, and
   *  connecting points
   */
  protected void paintComponent(Graphics g) {
    // To be completed by you
  }
}
```

Test the class with the following functions:

```
f(x) = x²;
f(x) = sin(x);
f(x) = cos(x);
f(x) = tan(x);
f(x) = cos(x) + 5sin(x);
f(x) = 5cos(x) + sin(x);
f(x) = log(x) + x²;
```

For each function, create a class that extends the `AbstractDrawFunction` class and implements the `f` method. Figure 14.32(b) displays the drawings for the sine function and the cosine function.

14.14** (*Displaying a bar chart*) Write a program that uses a bar chart to display the percentages of the overall grade represented by projects, quizzes, midterm exams, and the final exam, as shown in Figure 14.1(a). Suppose that projects take `20` percent and are displayed in red, quizzes take `10` percent and are displayed in blue, midterm exams take `30` percent and are displayed in green, and the final exam takes `40` percent and is displayed in orange.

14.15** (*Displaying a pie chart*) Write a program that uses a pie chart to display the percentages of the overall grade represented by projects, quizzes, midterm exams, and the final exam, as shown in Figure 14.33(a). Suppose that projects take `20` percent and are displayed in red, quizzes take `10` percent and are displayed in blue, midterm exams take `30` percent and are displayed in green, and the final exam takes `40` percent and is displayed in orange.

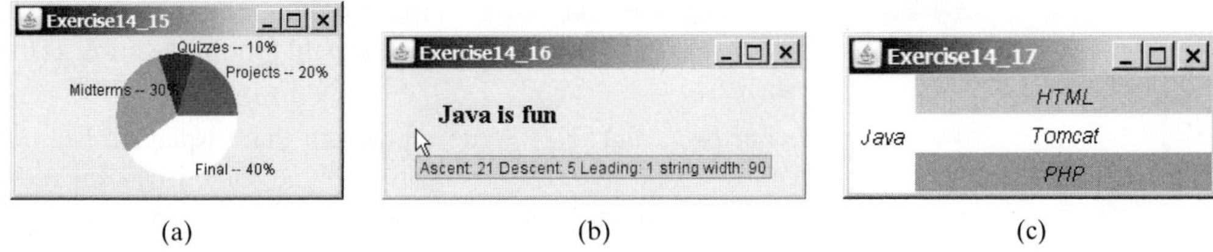

(a) (b) (c)

FIGURE 14.33 (a) Exercise 14.15 uses a pie chart to show the percentages of projects, quizzes, midterm exams, and final exam in the overall grade. (b) Exercise 14.16 displays font properties in a tool tip text. (c) Exercise 14.17 uses `MessagePanel` to display four strings.

14.16 (*Obtaining font information*) Write a program that displays the message "Java is fun" in a panel. Set the panel's font to `TimesRoman`, `bold`, and `20` pixel. Display the font's leading, ascent, descent, height, and the string width as a tool tip text for the panel, as shown in Figure 14.33(b).

14.17 (*Using the `MessagePanel` class*) Write a program that displays four messages, as shown in Figure 14.33(c).

14.18 (*Using the `StillClock` class*) Write a program that displays two clocks. The hour, minute, and second values are `4`, `20`, `45` for the first clock, and `22`, `46`, `15` for the second clock, as shown in Figure 14.34(a).

14.19* (*Random time*) Modify the `StillClock` class with three new Boolean properties: `hourHandVisible`, `minuteHandVisible`, and `secondHandVisible`, and their associated accessor and mutator methods. You can use the `set` methods to make a hand visible or invisible. Write a test program that displays only the hour

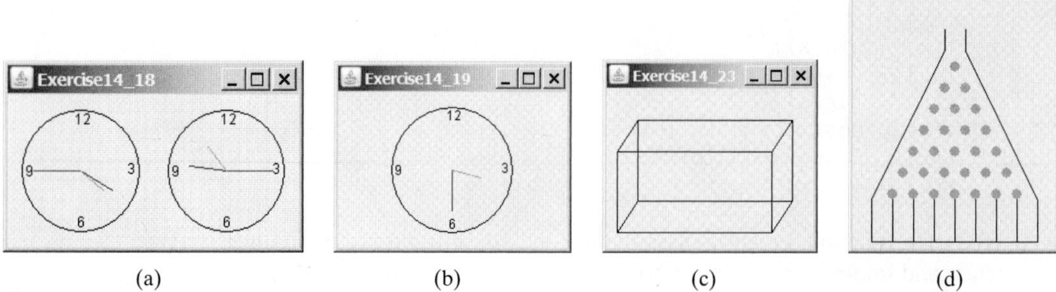

(a) (b) (c) (d)

FIGURE 14.34 (a) Exercise 14.18 displays two clocks. (b) Exercise 14.19 displays a clock with random hour and minute values. (c) Exercise 14.23 displays a rectanguloid. (d) Exercise 14.24 simulates a bean machine.

and minute hands. The hour and minute values are randomly generated. The hour is between `0` and `11`, and the minute is either `0` or `30`, as shown in Figure 14.34(b).

14.20** (*Drawing a detailed clock*) Modify the `StillClock` class in §14.12, "Case Study: The `StillClock` Class," to draw the clock with more details on the hours and minutes, as shown in Figure 14.1(b).

14.21** (*Displaying a TicTacToe board with images*) Rewrite Exercise 13.7 to display an image in a `JPanel` instead of displaying an image icon in a `JLabel`.

14.22* (*Displaying a STOP sign*) Write a program that displays a STOP sign, as shown in Figure 14.1(c). The hexagon is in red and the sign is in white. (*Hint*: See Listing 14.7, DrawPolygon.java, and Listing 14.8, TestCenterMessage.java.)

14.23 (*Displaying a rectanguloid*) Write a program that displays a rectanguloid, as shown in Figure 14.34(c). The cube should grow and shrink as the frame grows or shrinks.

14.24 (*Game: bean machine*) Write a program that displays a bean machine introduced in Exercise 6.29. The bean machine should be centered in a resizable panel, as shown in Figure 14.34(d).

CHAPTER 15

EVENT-DRIVEN PROGRAMMING

Objectives

- To describe events, event sources, and event classes (§15.2).
- To declare listener classes, register listener objects with the source object, and write the code to handle events (§15.3).
- To declare listener classes using inner classes (§15.3.1).
- To declare listener classes using anonymous inner classes (§15.3.2).
- To write programs to deal with `ActionEvent` (§15.3.3).
- To write programs to deal with `WindowEvent` (§15.3.4).
- To simplify coding for listener classes using listener interface adapters (§15.3.5).
- To write programs to deal with `MouseEvent` (§15.4).
- To write programs to deal with `KeyEvent` (§15.5).
- To use the `javax.swing.Timer` class to control animations (§15.6).

15.1 Introduction

problem

Suppose you wish to write a program that animates a rising flag, as shown in Figure 15.1. How do you accomplish the task? There are several solutions to this problem. An effective way to solve it is to use event-driven programming, which is the subject of this chapter.

FIGURE 15.1 A flag is rising upward.

event-driven programming

All the programs so far execute in a procedural order. This chapter introduces *event-driven programming*, in which code is executed when an event occurs (e.g., a button click, or a mouse movement).

§11.6, "Example: The `ActionListener` Interface," gave you a taste of event-driven programming. You probably have many questions, such as why a listener class is declared to implement the `ActionListener` interface. This chapter will give you all the answers.

15.2 Event and Event Source

event

When you run Java GUI programs, the program interacts with the user, and the events drive its execution. An *event* can be defined as a signal to the program that something has happened. Events are triggered either by external user actions, such as mouse movements, button clicks, and keystrokes, or by internal program activities, such as a timer. The program can choose to respond to or ignore an event.

fire event
source object

The component on which an event is *fired* or *generated* is called the *source object* or *source component*. For example, a button is the source object for a button-clicking action event. An event is an instance of an event class. The root class of the event classes is `java.util.EventObject`. The hierarchical relationships of some event classes are shown in Figure 15.2.

getSource()

An event object contains whatever properties are pertinent to the event. You can identify the source object of an event using the `getSource()` instance method in the `EventObject` class. The subclasses of `EventObject` deal with special types of events, such as action events, window events, component events, mouse events, and key events. Table 15.1 lists external user actions, source objects, and event types fired.

EventObject
AWTEvent
ListSelectionEvent
ActionEvent
AdjustmentEvent
ComponentEvent
ItemEvent
TextEvent
ContainerEvent
FocusEvent
InputEvent
PaintEvent
WindowEvent
MouseEvent
KeyEvent

FIGURE 15.2 An event is an object of the `EventObject` class.

TABLE 15.1 User Action, Source Object, and Event Type

User Action	*Source Object*	*Event Type Fired*
Click a button	`JButton`	`ActionEvent`
Press return on a text field	`JTextField`	`ActionEvent`
Select a new item	`JComboBox`	`ItemEvent`, `ActionEvent`
Select item(s)	`JList`	`ListSelectionEvent`
Click a check box	`JCheckBox`	`ItemEvent`, `ActionEvent`
Click a radio button	`JRadioButton`	`ItemEvent`, `ActionEvent`
Select a menu item	`JMenuItem`	`ActionEvent`
Move the scroll bar	`JScrollBar`	`AdjustmentEvent`
Window opened, closed, iconified, deiconified, or closing	`Window`	`WindowEvent`
Mouse pressed, released, clicked, entered, or exited	`Component`	`MouseEvent`
Mouse moved or dragged	`Component`	`MouseEvent`
Key released or pressed	`Component`	`KeyEvent`
Component added or removed from the container	`Container`	`ContainerEvent`
Component moved, resized, hidden, or shown	`Component`	`ComponentEvent`
Component gained or lost focus	`Component`	`FocusEvent`

Note

If a component can fire an event, any subclass of the component can fire the same type of event. For example, every GUI component can fire `MouseEvent`, `KeyEvent`, `FocusEvent`, and `ComponentEvent`, since `Component` is the superclass of all GUI components.

Note

All the event classes in Figure 15.2 are included in the `java.awt.event` package except `ListSelectionEvent`, which is in the `javax.swing.event` package. AWT events were originally designed for AWT components, but many Swing components fire them.

15.3 Listeners, Registrations, and Handling Events

Java uses a delegation-based model for event handling: a source object fires an event, and an object interested in the event handles the event. The latter object is called a *listener*. For an object to be a listener for an event on a source object, two things are needed, as shown in Figure 15.3.

listener

1. The listener object must be an instance of the corresponding event-listener interface to ensure that the listener has the correct method for processing the event. Java provides a listener interface for every type of GUI event. The listener interface is usually named `XListener` for `XEvent`, with the exception of `MouseMotionListener`. For example,

listener interface

*X*Listener/*X*Event

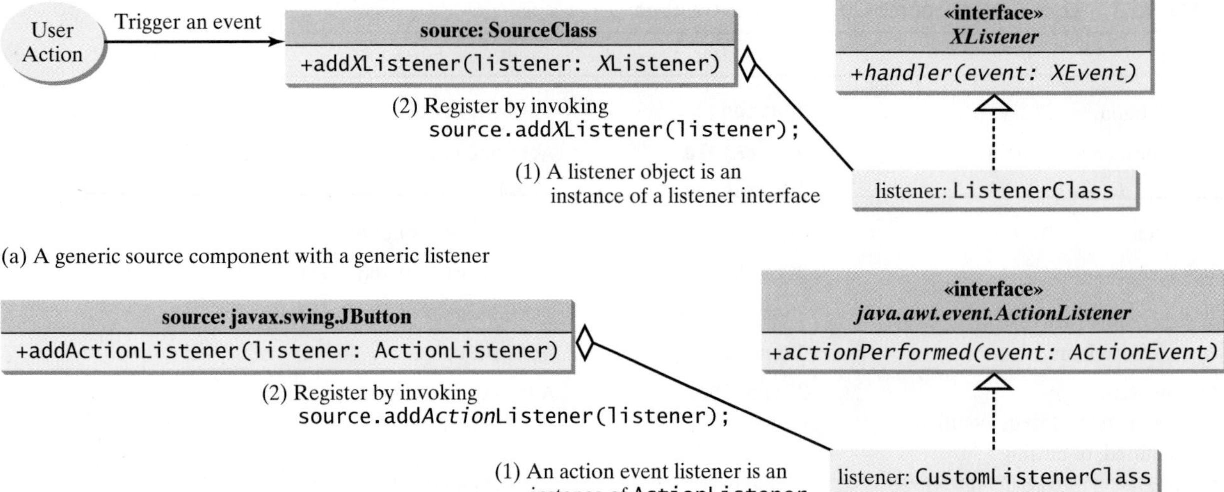

(a) A generic source component with a generic listener

(b) A `JButton` source component with an `ActionListener`

FIGURE 15.3 A listener must be an instance of a listener interface and must be registered with a source component.

ActionEvent/ActionListener

handler

the corresponding listener interface for `ActionEvent` is `ActionListener`; each listener for `ActionEvent` should implement the `ActionListener` interface. Table 15.2 lists event types, the corresponding listener interfaces, and the methods defined in the listener interfaces. The listener interface contains the method(s), known as the *handler(s)*, invoked by the source object to process the event.

register listener

2. The listener object must be registered by the source object. Registration methods are dependent on the event type. For `ActionEvent`, the method is `addActionListener`. In general, the method is named `addXListener` for `XEvent`. A source object may fire several types of events. For each event, the source object maintains a list of listeners and notifies all the registered listeners by invoking the *handler* on the listener object to respond to the event, as shown in Figure 15.4. (Figure 15.4 shows the internal implementation of a source class. You don't have to know how a source class like `JButton` is implemented in order to use it. Nevertheless, knowing this will help you to understand the Java event-driven programming framework and is the first step in being able to develop custom source components in the future).

Let's revisit Listing 11.8, HandleEvent.java. Since a `JButton` object fires `ActionEvent`, a listener object for `ActionEvent` must be an instance of `ActionListener`, so the listener class implements `ActionListener` in line 34. The source object invokes `addActionListener(listener)` to register a listener, as follows:

create source object
create listener object
register listener

```
JButton jbtOK = new JButton("OK"); // Line 7 in Listing 11.8
ActionListener listener1 = new OKListener(); // Line 18 in Listing 11.8
jbtOK.addActionListener(listener1); // Line 20 in Listing 11.8
```

TABLE 15.2 Events, Event Listeners, and Listener Methods

Event Class (Handlers)	*Listener Interface*	*Listener Methods*
ActionEvent	ActionListener	actionPerformed(ActionEvent)
ItemEvent	ItemListener	itemStateChanged(ItemEvent)
MouseEvent	MouseListener	mousePressed(MouseEvent)
		mouseReleased(MouseEvent)
		mouseEntered(MouseEvent)
		mouseExited(MouseEvent)
		mouseClicked(MouseEvent)
	MouseMotionListener	mouseDragged(MouseEvent)
		mouseMoved(MouseEvent)
KeyEvent	KeyListener	keyPressed(KeyEvent)
		keyReleased(KeyEvent)
		keyTyped(KeyEvent)
WindowEvent	WindowListener	windowClosing(WindowEvent)
		windowOpened(WindowEvent)
		windowIconified(WindowEvent)
		windowDeiconified (WindowEvent)
		windowClosed(WindowEvent)
		windowActivated(WindowEvent)
		windowDeactivated(WindowEvent)
ContainerEvent	ContainerListener	componentAdded(ContainerEvent)
		componentRemoved(ContainerEvent)
ComponentEvent	ComponentListener	componentMoved(ComponentEvent)
		componentHidden(ComponentEvent)
		componentResized(ComponentEvent)
		componentShown(ComponentEvent)
FocusEvent	FocusListener	focusGained(FocusEvent)
		focusLost(FocusEvent)
AdjustmentEvent	AdjustmentListener	adjustmentValueChanged(AdjustmentEvent)

When you click the button, the `JButton` object fires an `ActionEvent` and passes it to invoke the listener's `actionPerformed` method to handle the event.

The event object contains information pertinent to the event, which can be obtained using the methods, as shown in Figure 15.5. For example, you can use `e.getSource()` to obtain the source object in order to determine whether it is a button, a check box, or a radio button. For an action event, you can use `e.getWhen()` to obtain the time when the event occurs.

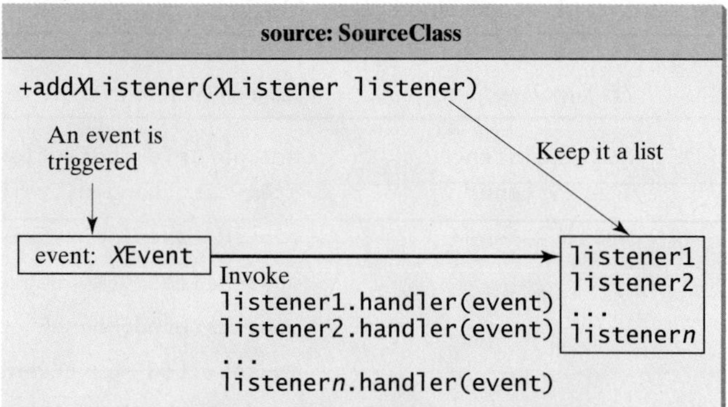

(a) Internal function of a generic source object

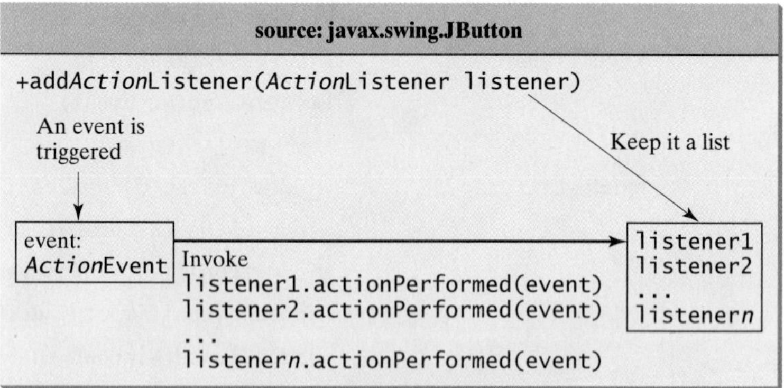

(b) Internal function of a `JButton` object

FIGURE 15.4 The source object notifies the listeners of the event by invoking the handler of the listener object.

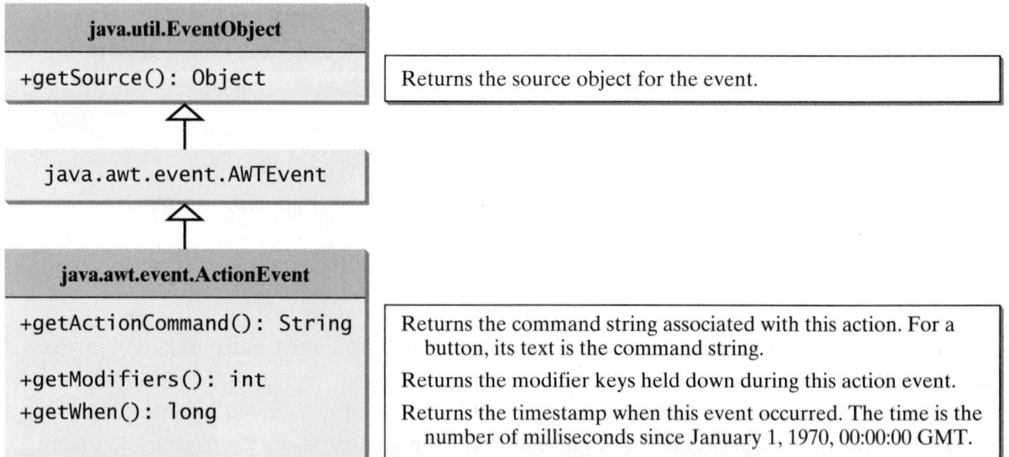

FIGURE 15.5 You can obtain useful information from an event object.

Listing 15.1 gives an example that uses the event object in the handler. This example displays two buttons, *OK* and *Cancel*, in a frame. A message is displayed on the console to indicate which button is clicked and when, as shown in Figure 15.6.

LISTING 15.1 SimpleEventDemo.java

Video Note
Create source and listener

```
 1 import javax.swing.*;
 2 import java.awt.event.*;
 3 
 4 public class SimpleEventDemo extends JFrame {
 5   public SimpleEventDemo() {
 6     // Create two buttons
 7     JButton jbtOK = new JButton("OK");
 8     JButton jbtCancel = new JButton("Cancel");
 9 
10     // Create a panel to hold buttons
11     JPanel panel = new JPanel();
12     panel.add(jbtOK);
13     panel.add(jbtCancel);
14 
15     add(panel); // Add panel to the frame
16 
17     // Register listeners
18     ListenerClass listener = new ListenerClass();
19     jbtOK.addActionListener(listener);
20     jbtCancel.addActionListener(listener);
21   }
22 
23   public static void main(String[] args) {
24     JFrame frame = new SimpleEventDemo();
25     frame.setTitle("Handle Event");
26     frame.setSize(200, 150);
27     frame.setLocation(200, 100);
28     frame.setDefaultCloseOperation(JFrame.EXIT_ON_CLOSE);
29     frame.setVisible(true);
30   }
31 }
32 
33 class ListenerClass implements ActionListener {
34   public void actionPerformed(ActionEvent e) {
35     System.out.println("The " + e.getActionCommand() + " button "
36       + "is clicked at\n  " + new java.util.Date(e.getWhen()));
37   }
38 }
```

create listener
register listener

listener class
handle event

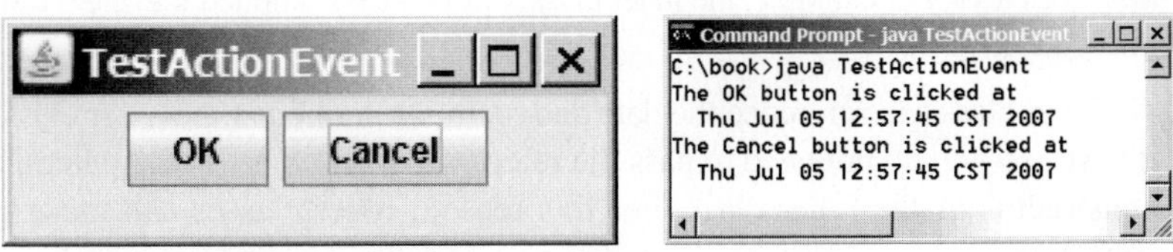

FIGURE 15.6 The program responds to the button action events.

The program creates a listener from `ListenerClass` (line 18). The listener is registered with both the *OK* button and the *Cancel* button (lines 19–20).

The button objects `jbtOK` and `jbtCancel` are the source of `ActionEvent`. Clicking a button causes the `actionPerformed` method in the listener to be invoked. The `e.getActionCommand()` method returns the action command from the button (line 35). By default, a button's action command is the label of the button.

The `e.getWhen()` method returns the time of the action in milliseconds since January 1, 1970, 00:00:00 GMT. The `Date` class converts the time to year, month, date, hours, minutes, and seconds (line 36).

15.3.1 Inner Class Listeners

A listener class is designed specifically to create a listener object for a GUI component (e.g., a button). The listener class will not be shared by other applications and therefore is appropriately defined inside the frame class as an inner class.

inner class

An *inner class*, or *nested class,* is a class defined within the scope of another class. The code in Figure 15.7(a) declares two separate classes, `Test` and `A`. The code in Figure 15.7(b) declares `A` as an inner class in `Test`.

```
public class Test {
  ...
}

public class A {
  ...
}
```

(a)

```
public class Test {
  ...

  // Inner class
  public class A {
    ...
  }
}
```

(b)

```
// OuterClass.java: inner class demo
public class OuterClass {
  private int data;

  /** A method in the outer class */
  public void m() {
    // Do something
  }

  // An inner class
  class InnerClass {
    /** A method in the inner class */
    public void mi() {
      // Directly reference data and method
      // defined in its outer class
      data++;
      m();
    }
  }
}
```

(c)

FIGURE 15.7 Inner classes combine dependent classes into the primary class.

The class `InnerClass` defined inside `OuterClass` in Figure 15.6(c) is another example of an inner class. An inner class may be used just like a regular class. Normally, you declare a class an inner class if it is used only by its outer class. An inner class has the following features:

- An inner class is compiled into a class named `OuterClassName$InnerClassName.class`. For example, the inner class `A` in `Test` is compiled into `Test$A.class` in Figure 15.6(b).
- An inner class can reference the data and methods defined in the outer class in which it nests, so you do not need to pass the reference of an object of the outer class to the constructor of the inner class. For this reason, inner classes can make programs simple and concise.
- An inner class can be declared with a visibility modifier subject to the same visibility rules applied to a member of the class.
- An inner class can be declared `static`. A `static` inner class can be accessed using the outer class name. A `static` inner class cannot access nonstatic members of the outer class.
- Objects of an inner class are often created in the outer class. But you can also create an object of an inner class from another class. If the inner class is nonstatic, you must

first create an instance of the outer class, then use the following syntax to create an object for the inner class:

```
OuterClass.InnerClass innerObject = outerObject.new InnerClass();
```

- If the inner class is static, use the following syntax to create an object for it:

```
OuterClass.InnerClass innerObject = new OuterClass.InnerClass();
```

Tip

A simple use of inner classes is to combine dependent classes into a primary class. This reduces the number of source files. It also makes class files easy to organize, since all the class files are named with the primary class as the prefix. For example, rather than creating two source files, Test.java and A.java, in Figure 15.6(a), you can combine class **A** into class **Test** and create just one source file Test.java in Figure 15.6(b). The resulting class files are Test.class and Test$A.class.

Listing 15.2 modifies Listing 15.1 using an inner class.

LISTING 15.2 SimpleEventDemoInnerClass.java

```
import javax.swing.*;
import java.awt.event.*;

public class SimpleEventDemoInnerClass extends JFrame {
  public SimpleEventDemoInnerClass() {
    // Create two buttons
    JButton jbtOK = new JButton("OK");
    JButton jbtCancel = new JButton("Cancel");

    // Create a panel to hold buttons
    JPanel panel = new JPanel();
    panel.add(jbtOK);
    panel.add(jbtCancel);

    add(panel); // Add panel to the frame

    // Register listeners
    ListenerClass listener = new ListenerClass();
    jbtOK.addActionListener(listener);
    jbtCancel.addActionListener(listener);
  }

  /** Main method */
  public static void main(String[] args) {
    JFrame frame = new SimpleEventDemoInnerClass();
    frame.setTitle("SimpleEventDemoInnerClass");
    frame.setLocationRelativeTo(null); // Center the frame
    frame.setDefaultCloseOperation(JFrame.EXIT_ON_CLOSE);
    frame.setSize(220, 80);
    frame.setVisible(true);
  }

  private static class ListenerClass implements ActionListener {
    public void actionPerformed(ActionEvent e) {
      System.out.println("The " + e.getActionCommand() + " button "
        + "is clicked at\n  " + new java.util.Date(e.getWhen()));
    }
  }
}
```

create listener
register listener

listener class
handle event

Listing 15.2 is the same as Listing 15.1 except that `ListenerClass` is now an inner class. Since the listener class will not be used by applications outside the frame class, it is declared `private`. Since `ListenerClass` does not refer to any instance members of the outer class, it is declared as a static inner class (line 33).

15.3.2 Anonymous Class Listeners

anonymous inner class

Inner classes can be shortened using anonymous inner classes. An *anonymous inner class* is an inner class without a name. It combines declaring an inner class and creating an instance of the class in one step. An anonymous inner class is declared as follows:

```
new SuperClassName/InterfaceName() {
  // Implement or override methods in superclass or interface

  // Other methods if necessary
}
```

Since an anonymous inner class is a special kind of inner class, it is treated like an inner class with the following features:

- An anonymous inner class must always extend a superclass or implement an interface, but it cannot have an explicit `extends` or `implements` clause.
- An anonymous inner class must implement all the abstract methods in the superclass or in the interface.
- An anonymous inner class always uses the no-arg constructor from its superclass to create an instance. If an anonymous inner class implements an interface, the constructor is `Object()`.
- An anonymous inner class is compiled into a class named `OuterClassName$n.class`. For example, if the outer class `Test` has two anonymous inner classes, they are compiled into `Test$1.class` and `Test$2.class`.

Listing 15.3 gives an example that handles the events from four buttons, as shown in Figure 15.8.

LISTING 15.3 AnonymousListenerDemo.java

```
import javax.swing.*;
import java.awt.event.*;

public class AnonymousListenerDemo extends JFrame {
  public AnonymousListenerDemo() {
    // Create four buttons
    JButton jbtNew = new JButton("New");
    JButton jbtOpen = new JButton("Open");
    JButton jbtSave = new JButton("Save");
    JButton jbtPrint = new JButton("Print");

    // Create a panel to hold buttons
    JPanel panel = new JPanel();
    panel.add(jbtNew);
    panel.add(jbtOpen);
    panel.add(jbtSave);
    panel.add(jbtPrint);

    add(panel);

    // Create and register anonymous inner class listener
    jbtNew.addActionListener(new ActionListener() {
```

anonymous listener

handle event

```
23        public void actionPerformed(ActionEvent e) {
24          System.out.println("Process New");
25        }
26      });
27
28      jbtOpen.addActionListener(new ActionListener() {
29        public void actionPerformed(ActionEvent e) {
30          System.out.println("Process Open");
31        }
32      });
33
34      jbtSave.addActionListener(new ActionListener() {
35        public void actionPerformed(ActionEvent e) {
36          System.out.println("Process Save");
37        }
38      });
39
40      jbtPrint.addActionListener(new ActionListener() {
41        public void actionPerformed(ActionEvent e) {
42          System.out.println("Process Print");
43        }
44      });
45    }
46
47    /** Main method */
48    public static void main(String[] args) {
49      JFrame frame = new AnonymousListenerDemo();
50      frame.setTitle("AnonymousListenerDemo");
51      frame.setLocationRelativeTo(null); // Center the frame
52      frame.setDefaultCloseOperation(JFrame.EXIT_ON_CLOSE);
53      frame.pack();
54      frame.setVisible(true);
55    }
56  }
```

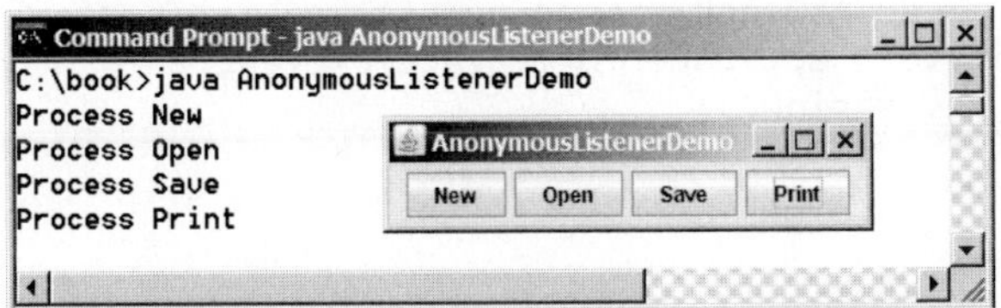

FIGURE 15.8 The program handles the events from four buttons.

The program creates four listeners using anonymous inner classes (lines 22–44). Without using anonymous inner classes, you would have to create four separate classes. An anonymous listener works the same way as an inner class listener. The program is condensed using an anonymous inner class.

Anonymous inner classes are compiled into `OuterClassName$#.class`, where `#` starts at `1` and is incremented for each anonymous class encountered by the compiler. In this example, the anonymous inner class is compiled into `AnonymousListenerDemo$1.class`, `AnonymousListenerDemo$2.class`, `AnonymousListenerDemo$3.class`, and `AnonymousListenerDemo$4.class`.

Instead of using the `setSize` method to set the size for the frame, the program uses the `pack()` method (line 53), which automatically sizes up the frame according to the size of the components placed in it.

pack()

Pedagogical Note

Handing events using anonymous inner classes has become a standard in Java. From here on, this book will use anonymous inner classes to implement listeners.

Video Note
Enlarge and shrink a ball

15.3.3 Example: Enlarging or Shrinking a Circle

This example presents a program in Listing 15.4 that uses two buttons to control the size of a circle, as shown in Figure 15.9.

LISTING 15.4 ControlBall.java

buttons; ball canvas; button listener; button listener; **BallCanvas** inner class; enlarge radius

```
import javax.swing.*;
import java.awt.*;
import java.awt.event.*;

public class ControlBall extends JFrame {
  private JButton jbtEnlarge = new JButton("Enlarge");
  private JButton jbtShrink = new JButton("Shrink");
  private BallCanvas canvas = new BallCanvas();

  public ControlBall() {
    JPanel panel = new JPanel(); // Use the panel to group buttons
    panel.add(jbtEnlarge);
    panel.add(jbtShrink);

    this.add(canvas, BorderLayout.CENTER); // Add canvas to center
    this.add(panel, BorderLayout.SOUTH); // Add buttons to the frame

    jbtEnlarge.addActionListener(new ActionListener() {
      public void actionPerformed(ActionEvent e) {
        canvas.enlarge();
      }
    });

    jbtShrink.addActionListener(new ActionListener() {
      public void actionPerformed(ActionEvent e) {
        canvas.shrink();
      }
    });
  }

  /** Main method */
  public static void main(String[] args) {
    JFrame frame = new ControlBall();
    frame.setTitle("ControlBall");
    frame.setLocationRelativeTo(null); // Center the frame
    frame.setDefaultCloseOperation(JFrame.EXIT_ON_CLOSE);
    frame.setSize(200, 200);
    frame.setVisible(true);
  }

  public static class BallCanvas extends JPanel {
    private int radius = 5; // Default ball radius

    /** Enlarge the ball */
    public void enlarge() {
      radius += 1;
      repaint();
```

```
48     }
49
50     /** Shrink the ball */
51     public void shrink() {
52       radius -= 1;
53       repaint();
54     }
55
56     /** Repaint the ball */
57     protected void paintComponent(Graphics g) {
58       super.paintComponent(g);
59       g.drawOval(getWidth() / 2 - radius, getHeight() / 2 - radius,
60         2 * radius, 2 * radius);
61     }
62   }
63 }
```

shrink radius

paint the ball

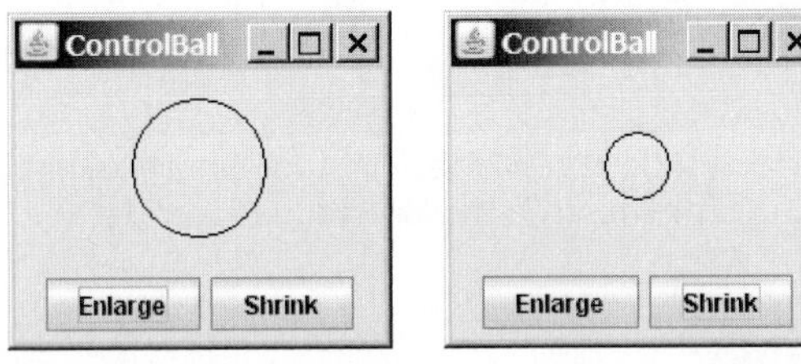

FIGURE 15.9 The user clicks the *Enlarge* and *Shrink* buttons to enlarge and shrink the size of the circle.

The BallCanvas class extends JPanel to display a ball centered in the panel (lines 59–60). Since BallCanvas does not refer to any instance members of BallControl, it is declared as a static inner class in ControlBall (line 41).

When the *Enlarge* button is clicked, it invokes the BallCanvas's enlarge method (line 20), which enlarges the radius of the ball by 1 (line 46).

When the *Shrink* button is clicked, it invokes the BallCanvas's shrink method (line 26), which shrinks the radius of the ball by 1 (line 52).

15.3.4 Example: Handling Window Events

This example writes a program that demonstrates handling window events. Any subclass of the Window class can fire the following window events: window opened, closing, closed, activated, deactivated, iconified, and deiconified. The program in Listing 15.5 creates a frame, listens to the window events, and displays a message to indicate the occurring event. Figure 15.10 shows a sample run of the program.

LISTING 15.5 TestWindowEvent.java

```
import java.awt.event.*;
import javax.swing.JFrame;

public class TestWindowEvent extends JFrame {
  public static void main(String[] args) {
    TestWindowEvent frame = new TestWindowEvent();
    frame.setSize(220, 80);
    frame.setLocationRelativeTo(null); // Center the frame
    frame.setDefaultCloseOperation(JFrame.EXIT_ON_CLOSE);
    frame.setTitle("TestWindowEvent");
```

```
    frame.setVisible(true);
  }

  public TestWindowEvent() {
    addWindowListener(new WindowListener() {
      /**
       * Handler for window deiconified event
       * Invoked when a window is changed from a minimized
       * to a normal state.
       */
```

implement handler

```
      public void windowDeiconified(WindowEvent event) {
        System.out.println("Window deiconified");
      }

      /**
       * Handler for window iconified event
       * Invoked when a window is changed from a normal to a
       * minimized state. For many platforms, a minimized window
       * is displayed as the icon specified in the window's
       * iconImage property.
       */
```

implement handler

```
      public void windowIconified(WindowEvent event) {
        System.out.println("Window iconified");
      }

      /**
       * Handler for window activated event
       * Invoked when the window is set to be the user's
       * active window, which means the window (or one of its
       * subcomponents) will receive keyboard events.
       */
```

implement handler

```
      public void windowActivated(WindowEvent event) {
        System.out.println("Window activated");
      }

      /**
       * Handler for window deactivated event
       * Invoked when a window is no longer the user's active
       * window, which means that keyboard events will no longer
       * be delivered to the window or its subcomponents.
       */
```

implement handler

```
      public void windowDeactivated(WindowEvent event) {
        System.out.println("Window deactivated");
      }

      /**
       * Handler for window opened event
       * Invoked the first time a window is made visible.
       */
      public void windowOpened(WindowEvent event) {
        System.out.println("Window opened");
      }

      /**
       * Handler for window closing event
       * Invoked when the user attempts to close the window
       * from the window's system menu.  If the program does not
       * explicitly hide or dispose the window while processing
```

```
       * this event, the window close operation will be cancelled.
       */
      public void windowClosing(WindowEvent event) {
        System.out.println("Window closing");
      }

      /**
       * Handler for window closed event
       * Invoked when a window has been closed as the result
       * of calling dispose on the window.
       */
      public void windowClosed(WindowEvent event) {
        System.out.println("Window closed");
      }
    });
  }
}
```

implement handler

implement handler

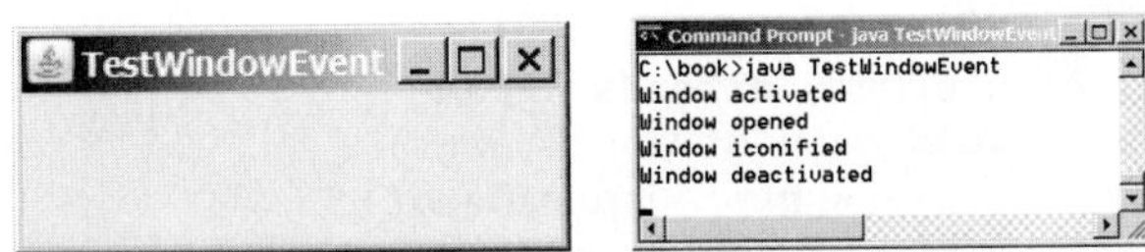

FIGURE 15.10 The window events are displayed on the console when you run the program from the command prompt.

The WindowEvent can be fired by the Window class or by any subclass of Window. Since JFrame is a subclass of Window, it can fire WindowEvent.

TestWindowEvent extends JFrame and implements WindowListener. The WindowListener interface defines several abstract methods (windowActivated, windowClosed, windowClosing, windowDeactivated, windowDeiconified, windowIconified, windowOpened) for handling window events when the window is activated, closed, closing, deactivated, deiconified, iconified, or opened.

When a window event, such as activation, occurs, the windowActivated method is triggered. Implement the windowActivated method with a concrete response if you want the event to be processed.

15.3.5 Listener Interface Adapters

Because the methods in the WindowListener interface are abstract, you must implement all of them even if your program does not care about some of the events. For convenience, Java provides support classes, called *convenience adapters*, which provide default implementations for all the methods in the listener interface. The default implementation is simply an empty body. Java provides convenience listener adapters for every AWT listener interface with multiple handlers. A *convenience listener adapter* is named *X*Adapter for *X*Listener. For example, WindowAdapter is a convenience listener adapter for WindowListener. Table 15.3 lists the convenience adapters.

convenience adapter

Using WindowAdapter, the preceding example can be simplified as shown in Listing 15.6, if you are interested only in the window activated event. The WindowAdapter class is used to create an anonymous listener instead of WindowListener (line 15). The windowActivated handler is implemented in line 16.

TABLE 15.3 Convenience Adapters

Adapter	*Interface*
`WindowAdapter`	`WindowListener`
`MouseAdapter`	`MouseListener`
`MouseMotionAdapter`	`MouseMotionListener`
`KeyAdapter`	`KeyListener`
`ContainerAdapter`	`ContainerListener`
`ComponentAdapter`	`ComponentListener`
`FocusAdapter`	`FocusListener`

LISTING 15.6 AdapterDemo.java

register listener
implement handler

```
import java.awt.event.*;
import javax.swing.JFrame;

public class AdapterDemo extends JFrame {
  public static void main(String[] args) {
    AdapterDemo frame = new AdapterDemo();
    frame.setSize(220, 80);
    frame.setLocationRelativeTo(null); // Center the frame
    frame.setDefaultCloseOperation(JFrame.EXIT_ON_CLOSE);
    frame.setTitle("AdapterDemo");
    frame.setVisible(true);
  }

  public AdapterDemo() {
    addWindowListener(new WindowAdapter() {
      public void windowActivated(WindowEvent event) {
        System.out.println("Window activated");
      }
    });
  }
}
```

15.4 Mouse Events

A mouse event is fired whenever a mouse is pressed, released, clicked, moved, or dragged on a component. The mouse-event object captures the event, such as the number of clicks associated with it or the location (x- and y-coordinates) of the mouse, as shown in Figure 15.11.

Since the `MouseEvent` class inherits `InputEvent`, you can use the methods defined in the `InputEvent` class on a `MouseEvent` object.

`Point` class

The `java.awt.Point` class represents a point on a component. The class contains two public variables, `x` and `y`, for coordinates. To create a `Point`, use the following constructor:

```
Point(int x, int y)
```

This constructs a `Point` object with the specified `x`- and `y`-coordinates. Normally, the data fields in a class should be private. This class has two public data fields, which is not a good practice.

Java provides two listener interfaces, `MouseListener` and `MouseMotionListener`, to handle mouse events, as shown in Figure 15.12. Implement the `MouseListener` interface to listen for such actions as pressing, releasing, entering, exiting, or clicking the mouse, and

java.awt.event.InputEvent	
`+getWhen(): long`	Returns the timestamp when this event occurred.
`+isAltDown(): boolean`	Returns true if the `Alt` key is pressed on this event.
`+isControlDown(): boolean`	Returns true if the `Control` key is pressed on this event.
`+isMetaDown(): boolean`	Returns true if the `Meta` mouse button is pressed on this event.
`+isShiftDown(): boolean`	Returns true if the `Shift` key is pressed on this event.

java.awt.event.MouseEvent	
`+getButton(): int`	Indicates which mouse button has been clicked.
`+getClickCount(): int`	Returns the number of mouse clicks associated with this event.
`+getPoint():java.awt.Point`	Returns a `Point` object containing the *x*- and *y*-coordinates.
`+getX(): int`	Returns the *x*-coordinate of the mouse point.
`+getY(): int`	Returns the *y*-coordinate of the mouse point.

FIGURE 15.11 The `MouseEvent` class encapsulates information for mouse events.

«interface» *java.awt.event.MouseListener*	
`+mousePressed(e: MouseEvent): void`	Invoked after the mouse button has been pressed on the source component.
`+mouseReleased(e: MouseEvent): void`	Invoked after the mouse button has been released on the source component.
`+mouseClicked(e: MouseEvent): void`	Invoked after the mouse button has been clicked (pressed and released) on the source component.
`+mouseEntered(e: MouseEvent): void`	Invoked after the mouse enters the source component.
`+mouseExited(e: MouseEvent): void`	Invoked after the mouse exits the source component.

«interface» *java.awt.event.MouseMotionListener*	
`+mouseDragged(e: MouseEvent): void`	Invoked after a mouse button is moved with a button pressed.
`+mouseMoved(e: MouseEvent): void`	Invoked after a mouse button is moved without a button pressed.

FIGURE 15.12 The `MouseListener` interface handles mouse pressed, released, clicked, entered, and exited events. The `MouseMotionListener` interface handles mouse dragged and moved events.

implement the `MouseMotionListener` interface to listen for such actions as dragging or moving the mouse.

15.4.1 Example: Moving a Message on a Panel Using a Mouse

This example writes a program that displays a message in a panel, as shown in Listing 15.7. You can use the mouse to move the message. The message moves as the mouse drags and is always displayed at the mouse point. A sample run of the program is shown in Figure 15.13.

Video Note
Move message using the mouse

LISTING 15.7 MoveMessageDemo.java

create a panel

inner class

set a new message

anonymous listener

override handler

new location

repaint

```
import java.awt.*;
import java.awt.event.*;
import javax.swing.*;

public class MoveMessageDemo extends JFrame {
  public MoveMessageDemo() {
    // Create a MovableMessagePanel instance for moving a message
   MovableMessagePanel p = new MovableMessagePanel("Welcome to Java");

    // Place the message panel in the frame
    setLayout(new BorderLayout());
    add(p);
  }

  /** Main method */
  public static void main(String[] args) {
    MoveMessageDemo frame = new MoveMessageDemo();
    frame.setTitle("MoveMessageDemo");
    frame.setSize(200, 100);
    frame.setLocationRelativeTo(null); // Center the frame
    frame.setDefaultCloseOperation(JFrame.EXIT_ON_CLOSE);
    frame.setVisible(true);
  }

  // Inner class: MovableMessagePanel draws a message
  static class MovableMessagePanel extends JPanel {
    private String message = "Welcome to Java";
    private int x = 20;
    private int y = 20;

    /** Construct a panel to draw string s */
    public MovableMessagePanel(String s) {
      message = s;
      addMouseMotionListener(new MouseMotionAdapter() {
        /** Handle mouse dragged event */
        public void mouseDragged(MouseEvent e) {
          // Get the new location and repaint the screen
          x = e.getX();
          y = e.getY();
          repaint();
        }
      });
    }

    /** Paint the component */
    protected void paintComponent(Graphics g) {
      super.paintComponent(g);
      g.drawString(message, x, y);
    }
  }
}
```

FIGURE 15.13 You can move the message by dragging the mouse.

The `MovableMessagePanel` class extends `JPanel` to draw a message (line 26). Additionally, it handles redisplaying the message when the mouse is dragged. This class is declared as an inner class inside the main class because it is used only in this class. Furthermore, the inner class is declared static because it does not reference any instance members of the main class.

The `MouseMotionListener` interface contains two handlers, `mouseMoved` and `mouseDragged`, for handling mouse-motion events. When you move the mouse with the button pressed, the `mouseDragged` method is invoked to repaint the viewing area and display the message at the mouse point. When you move the mouse without pressing the button, the `mouseMoved` method is invoked.

Because the listener is interested only in the mouse dragged event, the anonymous inner class listener extends `MouseMotionAdapter` to override the `mouseDragged` method. If the inner class implemented the `MouseMotionListener` interface, you would have to implement all of the handlers, even if your listener did not care about some of the events.

The `mouseDragged` method is invoked when you move the mouse with a button pressed. This method obtains the mouse location using `getX` and `getY` methods (lines 38–39) in the `MouseEvent` class. This becomes the new location for the message. Invoking the `repaint()` method (line 40) causes `paintComponent` to be invoked (line 46), which displays the message in a new location.

15.5 Key Events

Key events enable the use of the keys to control and perform actions or get input from the keyboard. A key event is fired whenever a key is pressed, released, or typed on a component. The `KeyEvent` object describes the nature of the event (namely, that a key has been pressed, released, or typed) and the value of the key, as shown in Figure 15.14. Java provides the `KeyListener` to handle key events, as shown in Figure 15.15.

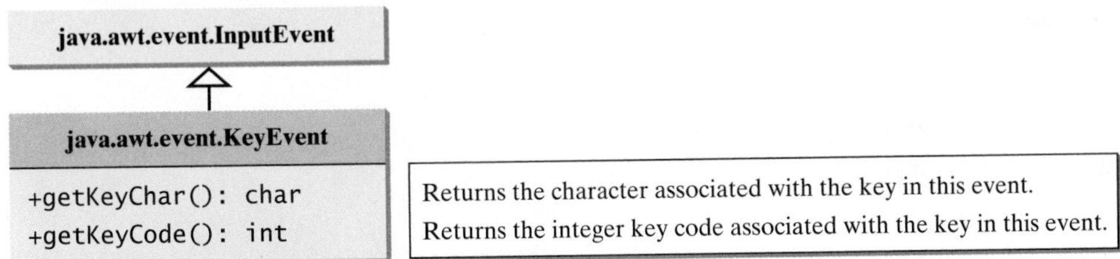

FIGURE 15.14 The `KeyEvent` class encapsulates information about key events.

«interface»
java.awt.event.KeyListener

+keyPressed(e: KeyEvent): void	Invoked after a key is pressed on the source component.
+keyReleased(e: KeyEvent): void	Invoked after a key is released on the source component.
+keyTyped(e: KeyEvent): void	Invoked after a key is pressed and then released on the source component.

FIGURE 15.15 The `KeyListener` interface handles key pressed, released, and typed events.

The `keyPressed` handler is invoked when a key is pressed, the `keyReleased` handler is invoked when a key is released, and the `keyTyped` handler is invoked when a Unicode character is entered. If a key does not have a Unicode (e.g., function keys, modifier keys, action keys, and control keys), the `keyTyped` handler will be not be invoked.

Every key event has an associated key character or key code that is returned by the `getKeyChar()` or `getKeyCode()` method in `KeyEvent`. The key codes are constants defined in Table 15.4. For a key of the Unicode character, the key code is the same as the

TABLE 15.4 Key Constants

Constant	*Description*	*Constant*	*Description*
VK_HOME	The Home key	VK_SHIFT	The Shift key
VK_END	The End key	VK_BACK_SPACE	The Backspace key
VK_PGUP	The Page Up key	VK_CAPS_LOCK	The Caps Lock key
VK_PGDN	The Page Down key	VK_NUM_LOCK	The Num Lock key
VK_UP	The up-arrow key	VK_ENTER	The Enter key
VK_DOWN	The down-arrow key	VK_UNDEFINED	The keyCode unknown
VK_LEFT	The left-arrow key	VK_F1 to VK_F12	The function keys from F1 to F12
VK_RIGHT	The right-arrow key		
VK_ESCAPE	The Esc key	VK_0 to VK_9	The number keys from 0 to 9
VK_TAB	The Tab key	VK_A to VK_Z	The letter keys from A to Z
VK_CONTROL	The Control key		

Unicode value. For the key pressed and key released events, `getKeyCode()` returns the value as defined in the table. For the key typed event, `getKeyCode()` returns `VK_UNDEFINED`.

The program in Listing 15.8 displays a user-input character. The user can move the character up, down, left, and right, using the arrow keys `VK_UP`, `VK_DOWN`, `VK_LEFT`, and `VK_RIGHT`. Figure 15.16 contains a sample run of the program.

FIGURE 15.16 The program responds to key events by displaying a character and moving it up, down, left, or right.

LISTING 15.8 KeyEventDemo.java

create a panel

focusable

```
import java.awt.*;
import java.awt.event.*;
import javax.swing.*;

public class KeyEventDemo extends JFrame {
  private KeyboardPanel keyboardPanel = new KeyboardPanel();

  /** Initialize UI */
  public KeyEventDemo() {
    // Add the keyboard panel to accept and display user input
    add(keyboardPanel);

    // Set focus
    keyboardPanel.setFocusable(true);
  }

  /** Main method */
  public static void main(String[] args) {
    KeyEventDemo frame = new KeyEventDemo();
```

```
20      frame.setTitle("KeyEventDemo");
21      frame.setSize(300, 300);
22      frame.setLocationRelativeTo(null); // Center the frame
23      frame.setDefaultCloseOperation(JFrame.EXIT_ON_CLOSE);
24      frame.setVisible(true);
25    }
26
27    // Inner class: KeyboardPanel for receiving key input
28    static class KeyboardPanel extends JPanel {
29      private int x = 100;
30      private int y = 100;
31      private char keyChar = 'A'; // Default key
32
33      public KeyboardPanel() {
34        addKeyListener(new KeyAdapter() {
35          public void keyPressed(KeyEvent e) {
36            switch (e.getKeyCode()) {
37              case KeyEvent.VK_DOWN: y += 10; break;
38              case KeyEvent.VK_UP: y -= 10; break;
39              case KeyEvent.VK_LEFT: x -= 10; break;
40              case KeyEvent.VK_RIGHT: x += 10; break;
41              default: keyChar = e.getKeyChar();
42            }
43
44            repaint();
45          }
46        });
47      }
48
49      /** Draw the character */
50      protected void paintComponent(Graphics g) {
51        super.paintComponent(g);
52
53        g.setFont(new Font("TimesRoman", Font.PLAIN, 24));
54        g.drawString(String.valueOf(keyChar), x, y);
55      }
56    }
57  }
```

inner class

register listener

override handler

get the key pressed

repaint

redraw character

The `KeyboardPanel` class extends `JPanel` to display a character (line 28). This class is declared as an inner class inside the main class, because it is used only in this class. Furthermore, the inner class is declared static, because it does not reference any instance members of the main class.

Because the program gets input from the keyboard, it listens for `KeyEvent` and extends `KeyAdapter` to handle key input (line 34).

When a key is pressed, the `keyPressed` handler is invoked. The program uses `e.getKeyCode()` to obtain the key code and `e.getKeyChar()` to get the character for the key. When a nonarrow key is pressed, the key is displayed (line 41). When an arrow key is pressed, the character moves in the direction indicated by the arrow key (lines 37–40).

focusable

Only a focused component can receive `KeyEvent`. To make a component focusable, set its `isFocusable` property to `true` (line 14).

efficient?

Every time the component is repainted, a new font is created for the `Graphics` object in line 53. This is not efficient. It is better to create the font once as a data field.

15.6 Animation Using the **Timer** Class

Video Note
Animate a clock

Not all source objects are GUI components. The `javax.swing.Timer` class is a source component that fires an `ActionEvent` at a predefined rate. Figure 15.17 lists some of the methods in the class.

javax.swing.Timer	
+Timer(delay: int, listener: ActionListener)	Creates a Timer object with a specified delay in milliseconds and an ActionListener.
+addActionListener(listener: ActionListener): void	Adds an ActionListener to the timer.
+start(): void	Starts this timer.
+stop(): void	Stops this timer.
+setDelay(delay: int): void	Sets a new delay value for this timer.

FIGURE 15.17 A `Timer` object fires an `ActionEvent` at a fixed rate.

A `Timer` object serves as the source of an `ActionEvent`. The listeners must be instances of `ActionListener` and registered with a `Timer` object. You create a `Timer` object using its sole constructor with a delay and a listener, where `delay` specifies the number of milliseconds between two action events. You can add additional listeners using the `addActionListener` method, and adjust the `delay` using the `setDelay` method. To start the timer, invoke the `start()` method. To stop the timer, invoke the `stop()` method.

The `Timer` class can be used to control animations. For example, you can use it to display a moving message, as shown in Figure 15.18, with the code in Listing 15.9.

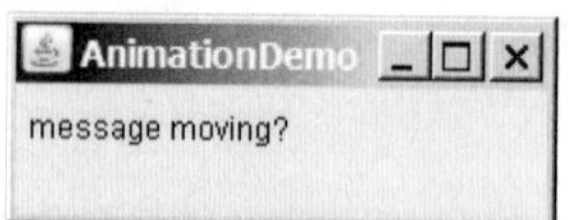

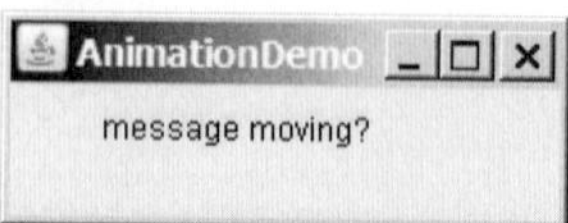

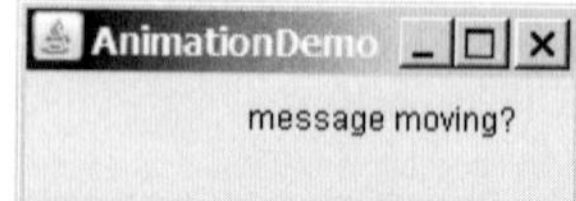

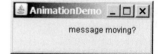

FIGURE 15.18 A message moves in the panel.

LISTING 15.9 AnimationDemo.java

create panel

```
import java.awt.*;
import java.awt.event.*;
import javax.swing.*;

public class AnimationDemo extends JFrame {
  public AnimationDemo() {
    // Create a MovingMessagePanel for displaying a moving message
    add(new MovingMessagePanel("message moving?"));
  }

  /** Main method */
  public static void main(String[] args) {
    AnimationDemo frame = new AnimationDemo();
    frame.setTitle("AnimationDemo");
    frame.setSize(280, 100);
    frame.setLocationRelativeTo(null); // Center the frame
    frame.setDefaultCloseOperation(JFrame.EXIT_ON_CLOSE);
    frame.setVisible(true);
  }

  // Inner class: Displaying a moving message
  static class MovingMessagePanel extends JPanel {
    private String message = "Welcome to Java";
    private int xCoordinate = 0;
    private int yCoordinate = 20;

```

```
27     public MovingMessagePanel(String message) {
28       this.message = message;
29
30       // Create a timer
31       Timer timer = new Timer(1000, new TimerListener());
32       timer.start();
33     }
34
35     /** Paint message */
36     protected void paintComponent(Graphics g) {
37       super.paintComponent(g);
38
39       if (xCoordinate > getWidth()) {
40         xCoordinate = -20;
41       }
42       xCoordinate += 5;
43       g.drawString(message, xCoordinate, yCoordinate);
44     }
45
46     class TimerListener implements ActionListener {
47       /** Handle ActionEvent */
48       public void actionPerformed(ActionEvent e) {
49         repaint();
50       }
51     }
52   }
53 }
```

set message
create timer
start timer
reset x-coordinate
move message
listener class
event handler
repaint

The MovingMessagePanel class extends JPanel to display a message (line 22). This class is declared as an inner class inside the main class, because it is used only in this class. Furthermore, the inner class is declared static, because it does not reference any instance members of the main class.

An inner class listener is declared in line 46 to listen for ActionEvent. Line 31 creates a Timer for the listener. The timer is started in line 32. The timer fires an ActionEvent every second, and the listener responds in line 49 to repaint the panel. When a panel is painted, its x-coordinate is increased (line 42), so the message is displayed to the right. When the x-coordinate exceeds the bound of the panel, it is reset to -20 (line 40), so the message continues moving from left to right.

In §14.12, "Case Study: The StillClock Class," you drew a StillClock to show the current time. The clock does not tick after it is displayed. What can you do to make the clock display a new current time every second? The key to making the clock tick is to repaint it every second with a new current time. You can use a timer to control the repainting of the clock with the code in Listing 15.10.

LISTING 15.10 ClockAnimation.java

```
import java.awt.event.*;
import javax.swing.*;

public class ClockAnimation extends StillClock {
  public ClockAnimation() {
    // Create a timer with delay 1000 ms
    Timer timer = new Timer(1000, new TimerListener());
    timer.start();
  }

  private class TimerListener implements ActionListener {
    /** Handle the action event */
```

create timer
start timer
listener class

implement handler

set new time

repaint

```
13     public void actionPerformed(ActionEvent e) {
14       // Set new time and repaint the clock to display current time
15       setCurrentTime();
16       repaint();
17     }
18   }
19
20   /** Main method */
21   public static void main(String[] args) {
22     JFrame frame = new JFrame("ClockAnimation");
23     ClockAnimation clock = new ClockAnimation();
24     frame.add(clock);
25     frame.setSize(200, 200);
26     frame.setLocationRelativeTo(null); // Center the frame
27     frame.setDefaultCloseOperation(JFrame.EXIT_ON_CLOSE);
28     frame.setVisible(true);
29   }
30 }
```

The program displays a running clock, as shown in Figure 15.19. `ClockAnimation` extends `StillClock` and repaints the clock every `1` second triggered by a timer. Line 7 creates a `Timer` for a `ClockAnimation`. The timer is started in line 8 when a `ClockAnimation` is constructed. The timer fires an `ActionEvent` every second, and the listener responds in line 15 to set a new time and repaint the clock. The `setCurrentTime()` method defined in `StillClock` sets the current time in the clock.

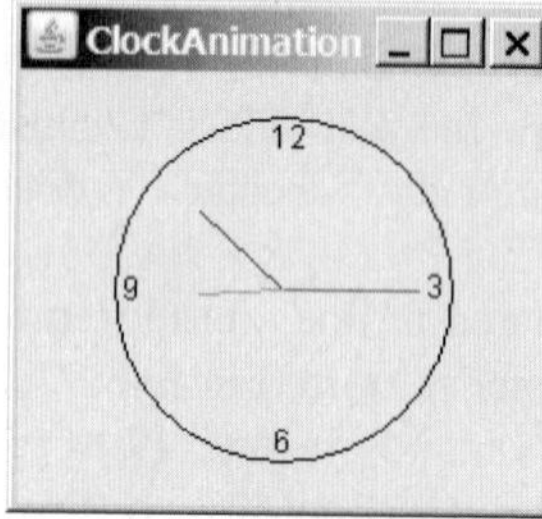

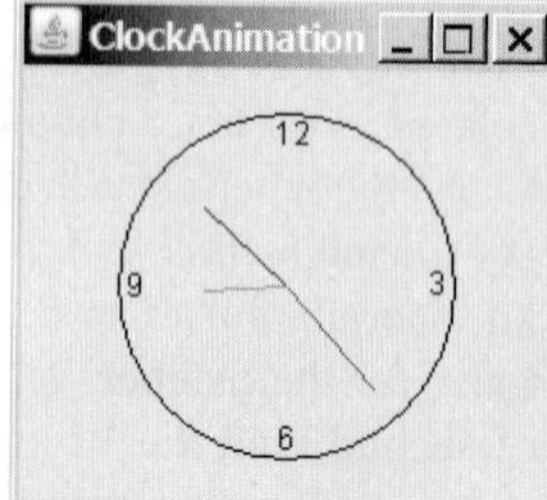

FIGURE 15.19 A live clock is displayed in the panel.

KEY TERMS

CHAPTER SUMMARY

- The root class of the event classes is `java.util.EventObject`. The subclasses of `EventObject` deal with special types of events, such as action events, window events, component events, mouse events, and key events. You can identify the source object of an event using the `getSource()` instance method in the `EventObject` class. If a component can fire an event, any subclass of the component can fire the same type of event.

- The listener object's class must implement the corresponding event-listener interface. Java provides a listener interface for every event class. The listener interface is usually named `XListener` for `XEvent`, with the exception of `MouseMotionListener`. For example, the corresponding listener interface for `ActionEvent` is `ActionListener`; each listener for `ActionEvent` should implement the `ActionListener` interface. The listener interface contains the method(s), known as the *handler(s)*, which process the events.

- The listener object must be registered by the source object. Registration methods are dependent on the event type. For `ActionEvent`, the method is `addActionListener`. In general, the method is named `addXListener` for `XEvent`.

- An *inner class*, or *nested class*, is a class defined within the scope of another class. An inner class can reference the data and methods defined in the outer class in which it nests, so you need not pass the reference of the outer class to the constructor of the inner class.

- Convenience adapters are support classes that provide default implementations for all the methods in the listener interface. Java provides convenience listener adapters for every AWT listener interface with multiple handlers. A convenience listener adapter is named *X*Adapter for *X*Listener.

- A source object may fire several types of events. For each event, the source object maintains a list of listeners and notifies all the registered listeners by invoking the *handler* on the listener object to process the event.

- A mouse event is fired whenever a mouse is clicked, released, moved, or dragged on a component. The mouse event object captures the event, such as the number of clicks associated with it or the location (`x`- and `y`-coordinates) of the mouse point.

- Java provides two listener interfaces, `MouseListener` and `MouseMotionListener`, to handle mouse events, implement the `MouseListener` interface to listen for such actions as mouse pressed, released, clicked, entered, or exited, and implement the `MouseMotionListener` interface to listen for such actions as mouse dragged or moved.

- A `KeyEvent` object describes the nature of the event (namely, that a key has been pressed, released, or typed) and the value of the key.

- The `keyPressed` handler is invoked when a key is pressed, the `keyReleased` handler is invoked when a key is released, and the `keyTyped` handler is invoked when a Unicode character key is entered. If a key does not have a Unicode (e.g., function keys, modifier keys, action keys, and control keys), the `keyTyped` handler will be not be invoked.

- You can use the `Timer` class to control Java animations. A timer fires an `ActionEvent` at a fixed rate. The listener updates the painting to simulate an animation.

Review Questions

Sections 15.2–15.3

15.1 Can a button fire a `WindowEvent`? Can a button fire a `MouseEvent`? Can a button fire an `ActionEvent`?

15.2 Why must a listener be an instance of an appropriate listener interface? Explain how to register a listener object and how to implement a listener interface.

15.3 Can a source have multiple listeners? Can a listener listen on multiple sources? Can a source be a listener for itself?

15.4 How do you implement a method defined in the listener interface? Do you need to implement all the methods defined in the listener interface?

15.5 Can an inner class be used in a class other than the class in which it nests?

15.6 Can the modifiers `public`, `private`, and `static` be used on inner classes?

15.7 If class `A` is an inner class in class `B`, what is the .class file for `A`? If class B contains two anonymous inner classes, what are the .class file names for these two classes?

15.8 What is wrong in the following code?

```
import java.swing.*;
import java.awt.*;

public class Test extends JFrame {
  public Test() {
    JButton jbtOK = new JButton("OK");
    add(jbtOK);
  }

  private class Listener
      implements ActionListener {
    public void actionPerform
        (ActionEvent e) {
      System.out.println
        (jbtOK.getActionCommand());
    }
  }

  /** Main method omitted */
}
```

(a)

```
import java.awt.event.*;
import javax.swing.*;

public class Test extends JFrame {
  public Test() {
    JButton jbtOK = new JButton("OK");
    add(jbtOK);
    jbtOK.addActionListener(
      new ActionListener() {
        public void actionPerformed
            (ActionEvent e) {
          System.out.println
            (jbtOK.getActionCommand());
        }
    } // Something missing here
  }

  /** Main method omitted */
}
```

(b)

15.9 What is the difference between the `setSize(width, height)` method and the `pack()` method in `JFrame`?

Sections 15.4–15.5

15.10 What method do you use to get the source of an event? What method do you use to get the timestamp for an action event, a mouse event, or a key event? What method do you use to get the mouse point position for a mouse event? What method do you use to get the key character for a key event?

15.11 What is the listener interface for mouse pressed, released, clicked, entered, and exited? What is the listener interface for mouse moved and dragged?

15.12 Does every key in the keyboard have a Unicode? Is a key code in the `KeyEvent` class equivalent to a Unicode?

15.13 Is the `keyPressed` handler invoked after a key is pressed? Is the `keyReleased` handler invoked after a key is released? Is the `keyTyped` handler invoked after *any* key is typed?

Section 15.6 Animation Using the `Timer` Class

15.14 How do you create a timer? How do you start a timer? How do you stop a timer?

15.15 Does the `Timer` class have a no-arg constructor? Can you add multiple listeners to a timer?

Programming Exercises

Sections 15.2–15.3

15.1 (*Finding which button has been clicked on the console*) Add the code to Exercise 13.1 that will display a message on the console indicating which button has been clicked.

15.2 (*Using* `ComponentEvent`) Any GUI component can fire a `ComponentEvent`. The `ComponentListener` defines the `componentMoved`, `componentResized`, `componentShown`, and `componentHidden` methods for processing component events. Write a test program to demonstrate `ComponentEvent`.

15.3* (*Moving the ball*) Write a program that moves the ball in a panel. You should define a panel class for displaying the ball and provide the methods for moving the button left, right, up, and down, as shown in Figure 15.20(a).

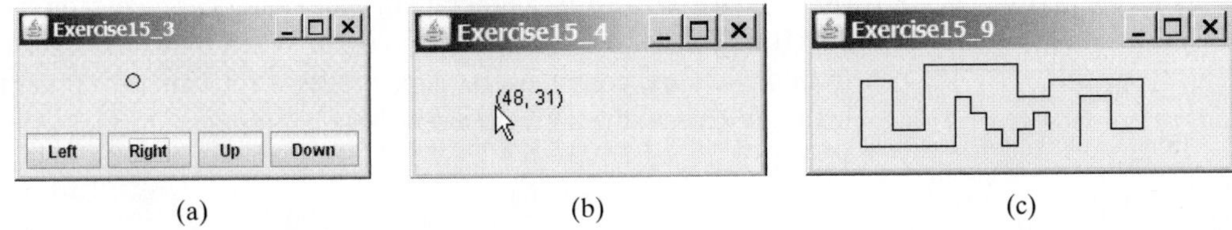

(a) (b) (c)

FIGURE 15.20 (a) Exercise 15.3 displays which button is clicked on a message panel. (b) Exercise 15.4 displays the mouse position. (c) Exercise 15.9 uses the arrow keys to draw the lines.

Section 15.4 Mouse Events

15.4* (*Displaying the mouse position*) Write two programs, such that one displays the mouse position when the mouse is clicked (see Figure 15.20(b)) and the other displays the mouse position when the mouse is pressed and ceases to display it when the mouse is released.

15.5* (*Setting background color using a mouse*) Write a program that displays the background color of a panel as black when the mouse is pressed and as white when the mouse is released.

15.6** (*Alternating two messages*) Write a program to rotate two messages "Java is fun" and "Java is powerful" displayed on a panel with a mouse click.

Section 15.5 Key Events

15.7** (*Entering and displaying a string*) Write a program that receives a string from the keyboard and displays it on a panel. The *Enter* key signals the end of a string. Whenever a new string is entered, it is displayed on the panel.

15.8* (*Displaying a character*) Write a program to get a character input from the keyboard and display the character where the mouse points.

15.9* (*Drawing lines using the arrow keys*) Write a program that draws line segments using the arrow keys. The line starts from the center of the frame and draws toward east, north, west, or south when the right-arrow key, up-arrow key, left-arrow key, or down-arrow key is clicked, as shown in Figure 15.20(c).

Section 15.6 Animation Using the `Timer` Class

15.10* (*Displaying a flashing label*) Write a program that displays a flashing label.

(*Hint*: To make the label flash, you need to repaint the panel alternately with the label and without it (blank screen) at a fixed rate. Use a `boolean` variable to control the alternation.)

15.11* (*Controlling a moving label*) Modify Listing 15.9, AnimationDemo.java, to control a moving label using the mouse. The label freezes when the mouse is pressed, and moves again when the button is released.

15.12** (*Displaying a running fan*) Listing 14.6, DrawArcs.java, displays a motionless fan. Write a program that displays a running fan.

15.13** (*Slide show*) Twenty-five slides are stored as image files (slide0.jpg, slide1.jpg, ..., slide24.jpg) in the image directory downloadable along with the source code in the book. The size of each image is 800 × 600. Write a Java application that automatically displays the slides repeatedly. Each slide is shown for a second. The slides are displayed in order. When the last slide finishes, the first slide is redisplayed, and so on. (*Hint*: Place a label in the frame and set a slide as an image icon in the label.)

Video Note
Animate a rising flag

15.14** (*Raising flag*) Write a Java program that animates raising a flag, as shown in Figure 15.1. (See §14.13, "Displaying Images," on how to display images.)

15.15** (*Racing car*) Write a Java program that simulates car racing, as shown in Figure 15.21(a). The car moves from left to right. When it hits the right end, it restarts from the left and continues the same process. You can use a timer to control animation. Redraw the car with a new base coordinates (x, y), as shown in Figure 15.21(b).

FIGURE 15.21 (a) Exercise 15.15 displays a moving car. (b) You can redraw a car with a new base point.

15.16* (*Moving a circle using keys*) Write a program that moves a circle up, down, left, or right using the arrow keys.

15.17** (*Moving a circle using mouse*) Write a program that displays a circle with radius **10** pixels. You can point the mouse inside the circle and drag (i.e., move with mouse pressed) the circle wherever the mouse goes, as shown in Figure 15.22(b).

FIGURE 15.22 (a)–(b) You can point, drag, and move the circle. (c) When you click a circle, a new circle is displayed at a random location. (d) After 20 circles are clicked, the time spent in the panel is displayed.

15.18*** (*Game: eye-hand coordination*) Write a program that displays a circle of radius `10` pixels filled with a random color at a random location on a panel, as shown in Figure 15.22(c). When you click the circle, it is gone and a new random-colored circle is displayed at another random location. After twenty circles are clicked, display the time spent in the panel, as shown in Figure 15.22(d).

15.19** (*Geometry: inside a circle?*) Write a program that draws a fixed circle centered at (`100`, `60`) with radius `50`. Whenever a mouse is moved, display the message indicating whether the mouse point is inside the circle, as shown in Figure 15.23(a).

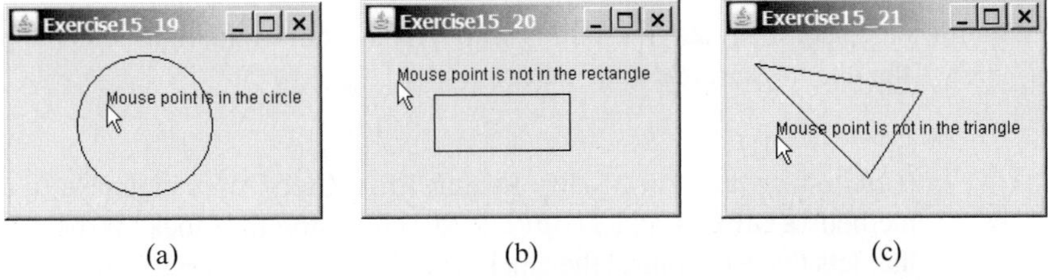

FIGURE 15.23 Detect whether a point is inside a circle, a rectangle, or a triangle.

15.20** (*Geometry: inside a rectangle?*) Write a program that draws a fixed rectangle centered at (`100`, `60`) with width `100` and height `40`. Whenever a mouse is moved, display the message indicating whether the mouse point is inside the rectangle, as shown in Figure 15.23(b). To detect whether a point is inside a rectangle, use the `Rectangle2D` class defined in Exercise 9.12.

15.21** (*Geometry: inside a triangle?*) Write a program that draws a fixed triangle with three vertices at (`20`, `20`), (`100`, `100`), and (`140`, `40`). Whenever a mouse is moved, display the message indicating whether the mouse point is inside the triangle, as shown in Figure 15.23(c). To detect whether a point is inside a triangle, use the `Triangle2D` class defined in Exercise 9.13.

15.22*** (*Game: bean machine animation*) Write a program that animates a bean machine introduced in Exercise 14.24. The animation terminates after ten balls are dropped, as shown in Figure 15.24.

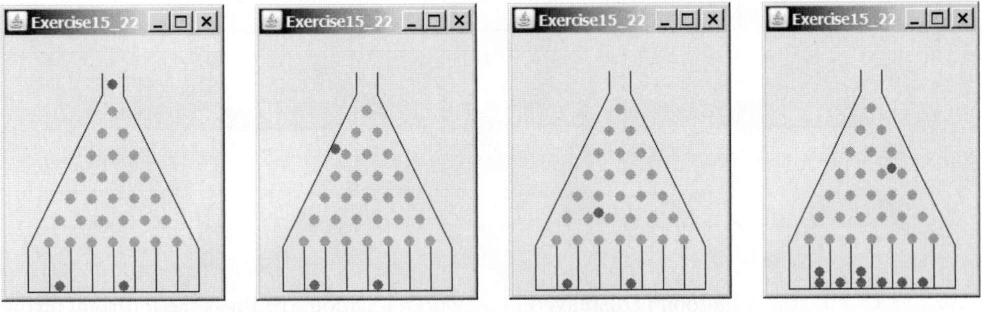

FIGURE 15.24 The balls are dropped to the bean machine.

15.23*** (*Geometry: closest pair of points*) Write a program that lets the user click on the panel to dynamically create points. Initially, the panel is empty. When a panel has two or more points, highlight the pair of closest points. Whenever a new point is created, a new pair of closest points is highlighted. Display the points using small circles and highlight the points using filled circles, as shown in Figure 15.25(a–c). (*Hint:* store the points in an `ArrayList`.)

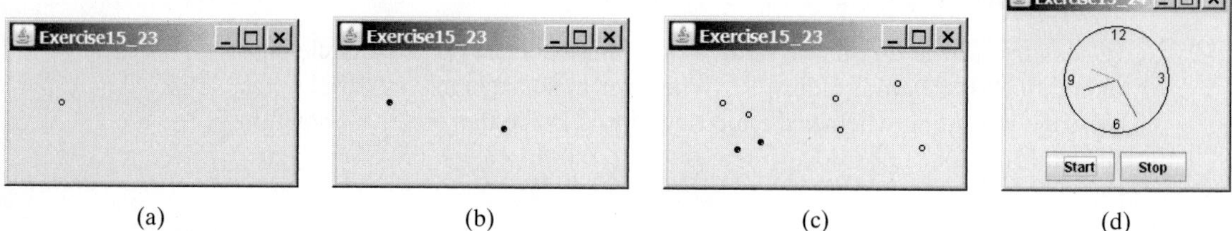

FIGURE 15.25 (a)–(c) Exercise15.23 allows the user to create new points with a mouse click and highlights the pair of the closest points. (d) Exercise15.24 allows the user to start and stop a clock.

15.24* (*Controlling a clock*) Modify Listing 15.10 ClockAnimation.java to add two methods `start()` and `stop()` to start and stop the clock. Write a program that lets the user control the clock with the *Start* and *Stop* buttons, as shown in Figure 15.25(d).

15.25*** (*Game: hitting balloons*) Write a program that displays a balloon in a random position in a panel (Figure 15.26(a)). Use the left and right arrow keys to point the gun left or right to aim at the balloon (Figure 15.26(b)). Press the up arrow key to fire a small ball from the gun (Figure 15.26(c)). Once the ball hits the balloon, the debris is displayed (Figure 15.26(e)) and a new balloon is displayed in a random location (Figure 15.26(f)). If the ball misses the balloon, the ball disappears once it hits the boundary of the panel. You can then press the up arrow key to fire another ball. Whenever you press the left or the right arrow key, the gun turns 5 degrees left or right. (Instructors may modify the game as follows: 1. display the number of the balloons destroyed; 2. display a countdown timer (e.g., 60 seconds) and terminate the game once the time expires; 3. allow the balloon to rise dynamically.)

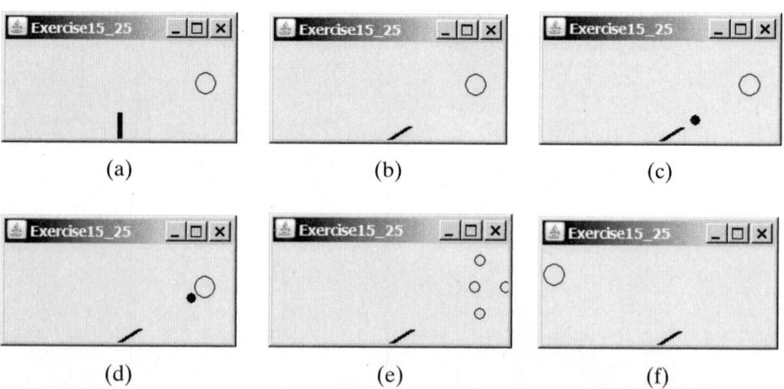

FIGURE 15.26 (a) A balloon is displayed in a random location; (b) Press the left/right arrow keys to aim the balloon; (c) Press the up arrow key to fire a ball; (d) The ball moves straight toward the balloon; (e) The ball hits the balloon; (f) A new balloon is displayed in a random position.

CHAPTER 16

CREATING USER INTERFACES

Objectives

- To create graphical user interfaces with various user-interface components: `JButton`, `JCheckBox`, `JRadioButton`, `JLabel`, `JTextField`, `JTextArea`, `JComboBox`, `JList`, `JScrollBar`, and `JSlider` (§§16.2–16.11).
- To create listeners for various types of events (§§16.2–16.11).
- To explore `JButton` (§16.2)
- To explore `JCheckBox` (§16.3)
- To explore `JRadioButton` (§16.4)
- To explore `JLabel` (§16.5)
- To explore `JTextField` (§16.6)
- To explore `JTextArea` (§16.7)
- To explore `JComboBox` (§16.8)
- To explore `JList` (§16.9)
- To explore `JScrollBar` (§16.10)
- To explore `JSlider` (§16.11)
- To display multiple windows in an application (§16.12).

16.1 Introduction

GUI

A graphical user interface (GUI) makes a system user-friendly and easy to use. Creating a GUI requires creativity and knowledge of how GUI components work. Since the GUI components in Java are very flexible and versatile, you can create a wide assortment of useful user interfaces.

Many Java IDEs provide tools for visually designing and developing GUI interfaces. This enables you to rapidly assemble the elements of a user interface (UI) for a Java application or applet with minimum coding. Tools, however, cannot do everything. You have to modify the programs they produce. Consequently, before you begin to use the visual tools, you must understand the basic concepts of Java GUI programming.

Previous chapters briefly introduced several GUI components. This chapter introduces the frequently used GUI components in detail (see Figure 16.1). Since there are no new concepts introduced in this chapter, instructors may assign this chapter for students to study on their own.

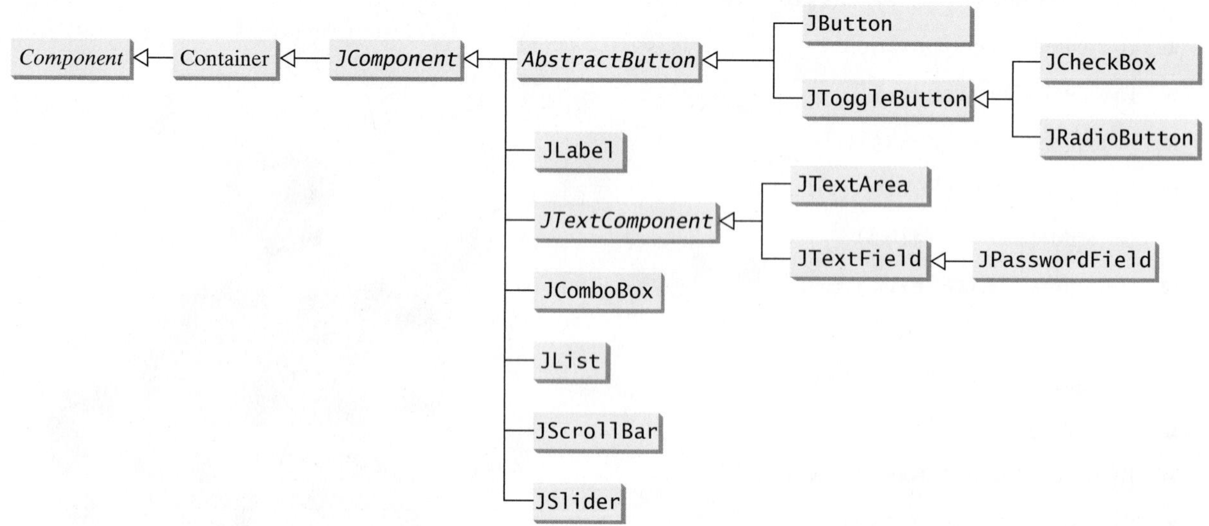

FIGURE 16.1 These Swing GUI components are frequently used to create user interfaces.

naming convention for components

Note

Throughout this book, the prefixes `jbt`, `jchk`, `jrb`, `jlbl`, `jtf`, `jpf`, `jta`, `jcbo`, `jlst`, `jscb`, and `jsld` are used to name reference variables for `JButton`, `JCheckBox`, `JRadioButton`, `JLabel`, `JTextField`, `JPasswordField`, `JTextArea`, `JComboBox`, `JList`, `JScrollBar`, and `JSlider`.

16.2 Buttons

`AbstractButton`

A *button* is a component that triggers an action event when clicked. Swing provides regular buttons, toggle buttons, check box buttons, and radio buttons. The common features of these buttons are represented in `javax.swing.AbstractButton`, as shown in Figure 16.2.

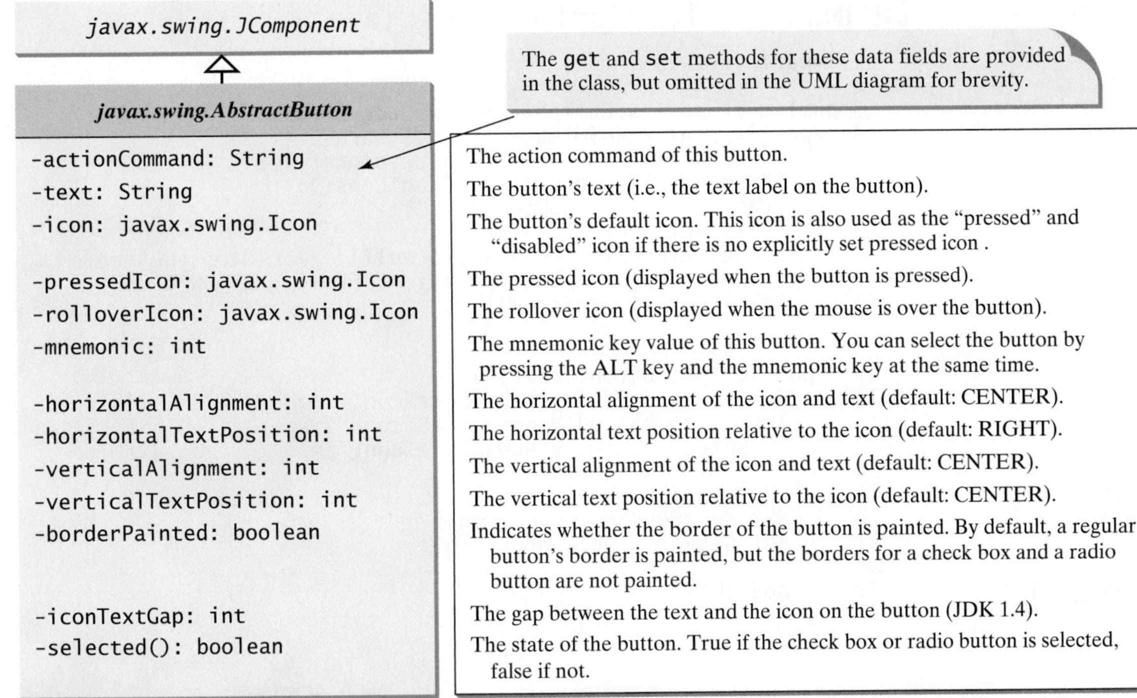

FIGURE 16.2 `AbstractButton` defines common features of different types of buttons.

This section introduces the regular buttons defined in the `JButton` class. `JButton` inherits `AbstractButton` and provides several constructors to create buttons, as shown in Figure 16.3. **JButton**

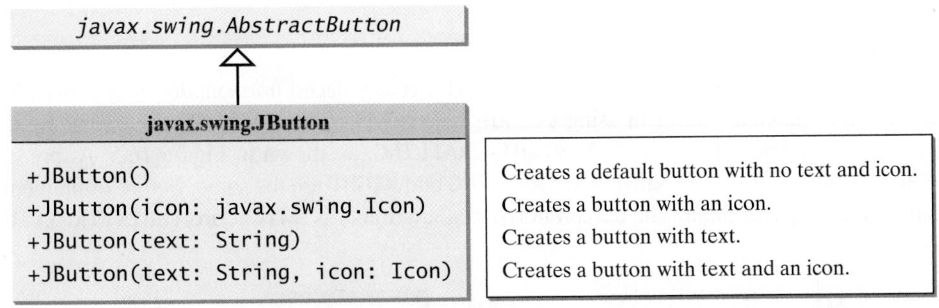

FIGURE 16.3 `JButton` defines a regular push button.

16.2.1 Icons, Pressed Icons, and Rollover Icons

A regular button has a default icon, a pressed icon, and a rollover icon. Normally, you use the default icon. The other icons are for special effects. A pressed icon is displayed when a button is pressed, and a rollover icon is displayed when the mouse is over the button but not pressed. For example, Listing 16.1 displays the American flag as a regular icon, the Canadian flag as a pressed icon, and the British flag as a rollover icon, as shown in Figure 16.4.

LISTING 16.1 TestButtonIcons.java

create icons
regular icon
pressed icon
rollover icon
add a button

```
import javax.swing.*;

public class TestButtonIcons extends JFrame  {
  public static void main(String[] args) {
    // Create a frame and set its properties
    JFrame frame = new TestButtonIcons();
    frame.setTitle("ButtonIcons");
    frame.setSize(200, 100);
    frame.setLocationRelativeTo(null); // Center the frame
    frame.setDefaultCloseOperation(JFrame.EXIT_ON_CLOSE);
    frame.setVisible(true);
  }

  public TestButtonIcons() {
    ImageIcon usIcon = new ImageIcon("image/usIcon.gif");
    ImageIcon caIcon = new ImageIcon("image/caIcon.gif");
    ImageIcon ukIcon = new ImageIcon("image/ukIcon.gif");

    JButton jbt = new JButton("Click it", usIcon);
    jbt.setPressedIcon(caIcon);
    jbt.setRolloverIcon(ukIcon);

    add(jbt);
  }
}
```

(a) Default icon (b) Pressed icon (c) Rollover icon

FIGURE 16.4 A button can have several types of icons.

16.2.2 Alignments

horizontal alignment

Horizontal alignment specifies how the icon and text are placed horizontally on a button. You can set the horizontal alignment using `setHorizontalAlignment(int)` with one of the five constants `LEADING`, `LEFT`, `CENTER`, `RIGHT`, `TRAILING`, as shown in Figure 16.5. At present, `LEADING` and `LEFT` are the same, and `TRAILING` and `RIGHT` are the same. Future implementation may distinguish them. The default horizontal alignment is `SwingConstants.TRAILING`.

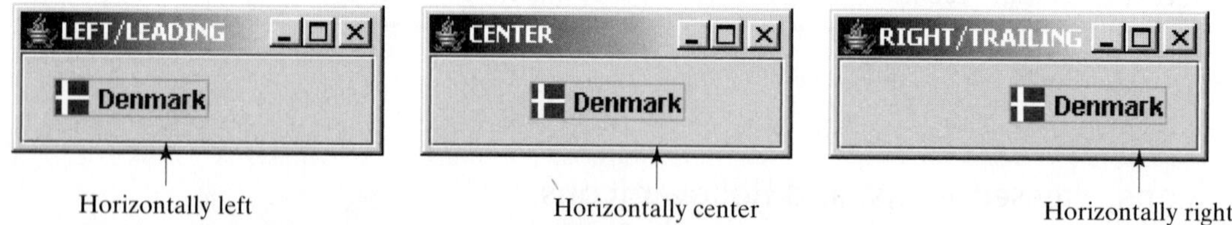

FIGURE 16.5 You can specify how the icon and text are placed on a button horizontally.

vertical alignment

Vertical alignment specifies how the icon and text are placed vertically on a button. You can set the vertical alignment using `setVerticalAlignment(int)` with one of the three constants `TOP`, `CENTER`, `BOTTOM`, as shown in Figure 16.6. The default vertical alignment is `SwingConstants.CENTER`.

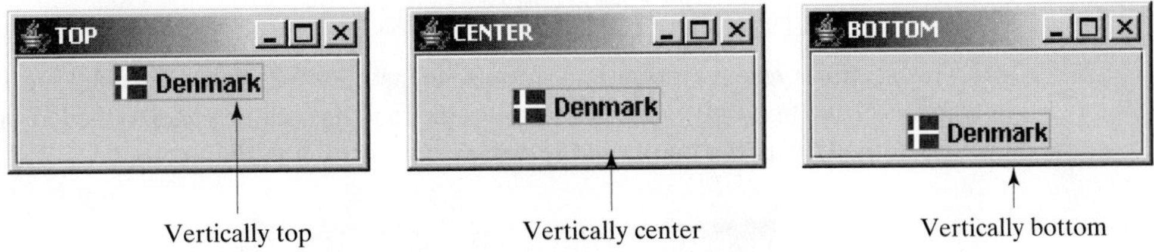

FIGURE 16.6 You can specify how the icon and text are placed on a button vertically.

16.2.3 Text Positions

Horizontal text position specifies the horizontal position of the text relative to the icon. You can set the horizontal text position using `setHorizontalTextPosition(int)` with one of the five constants `LEADING`, `LEFT`, `CENTER`, `RIGHT`, `TRAILING`, as shown in Figure 16.7. At present, `LEADING` and `LEFT` are the same, and `TRAILING` and `RIGHT` are the same. Future implementation may distinguish them. The default horizontal text position is `SwingConstants.RIGHT`.

horizontal text position

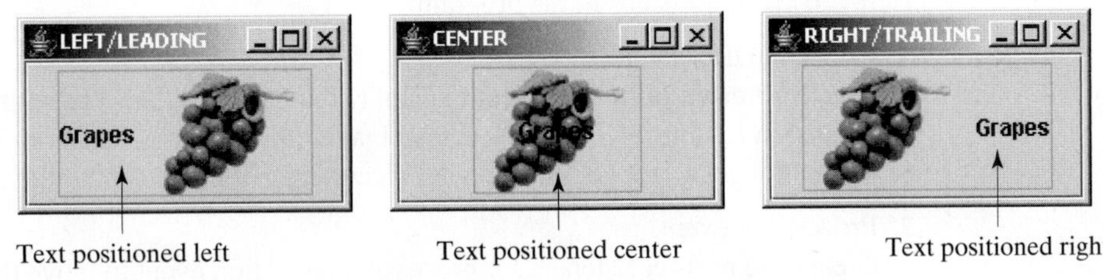

FIGURE 16.7 You can specify the horizontal position of the text relative to the icon.

Vertical text position specifies the vertical position of the text relative to the icon. You can set the vertical text position using `setVerticalTextPosition(int)` with one of the three constants `TOP`, `CENTER`, `BOTTOM`, as shown in Figure 16.8. The default vertical text position is `SwingConstants.CENTER`.

vertical text position

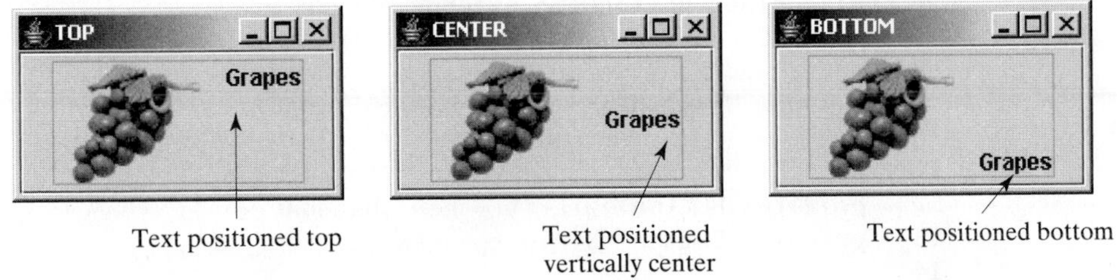

FIGURE 16.8 You can specify the vertical position of the text relative to the icon.

Note

The constants `LEFT`, `CENTER`, `RIGHT`, `LEADING`, `TRAILING`, `TOP`, and `BOTTOM` used in `AbstractButton` are also used in many other Swing components. These constants are centrally defined in the `javax.swing.SwingConstants` interface. Since all Swing GUI components implement `SwingConstants`, you can reference the constants through `SwingConstants` or a GUI component. For example, `SwingConstants.CENTER` is the same as `JButton.CENTER`.

`SwingConstants`

`JButton` can generate many types of events, but often you need to respond to an `ActionEvent`. When a button is pressed, it generates an `ActionEvent`.

Video Note
Use buttons

16.2.4 Using Buttons

This section presents a program, shown in Listing 16.2, that displays a message on a panel and uses two buttons, <= and => to move the message on the panel to the left or right. The layout of the UI and the output of the program are shown in Figure 16.9.

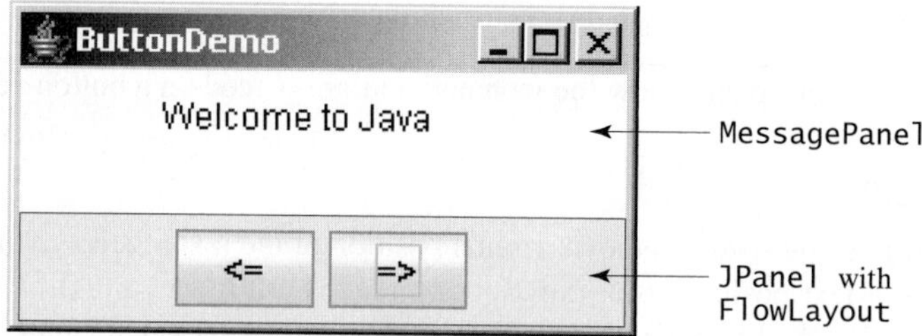

FIGURE 16.9 Clicking the <= and => buttons causes the message on the panel to move to the left and right, respectively.

Here are the major steps in the program:

1. Create the user interface.
   Create a `MessagePanel` object to display the message. The `MessagePanel` class was created in Listing 14.10, MessagePanel.java. Place it in the center of the frame. Create two buttons, <= and =>, on a panel. Place the panel in the south of the frame.
2. Process the event.
   Create and register listeners for processing the action event to move the message left or right according to whether the left or right button was clicked.

LISTING 16.2 ButtonDemo.java

JFrame ← CheckBoxDemo

```java
import java.awt.*;
import java.awt.event.ActionListener;
import java.awt.event.ActionEvent;
import javax.swing.*;

public class ButtonDemo extends JFrame {
  // Create a panel for displaying message
  protected MessagePanel messagePanel
    = new MessagePanel("Welcome to Java");

  // Declare two buttons to move the message left and right
  private JButton jbtLeft = new JButton("<=");
  private JButton jbtRight = new JButton("=>");

  public static void main(String[] args) {
    ButtonDemo frame = new ButtonDemo();
    frame.setTitle("ButtonDemo");
    frame.setSize(250, 100);
    frame.setLocationRelativeTo(null); // Center the frame
    frame.setDefaultCloseOperation(JFrame.EXIT_ON_CLOSE);
    frame.setVisible(true);
  }

  public ButtonDemo() {
    // Set the background color of messagePanel
    messagePanel.setBackground(Color.white);

    // Create Panel jpButtons to hold two Buttons "<=" and “right =>"
    JPanel jpButtons = new JPanel();
```

create frame

create UI

```
30      jpButtons.setLayout(new FlowLayout());
31      jpButtons.add(jbtLeft);
32      jpButtons.add(jbtRight);
33
34      // Set keyboard mnemonics
35      jbtLeft.setMnemonic('L');
36      jbtRight.setMnemonic('R');
37
38      // Set icons and remove text
39      // jbtLeft.setIcon(new ImageIcon("image/left.gif"));
40      // jbtRight.setIcon(new ImageIcon("image/right.gif"));
41      // jbtLeft.setText(null);
42      // jbtRight.setText(null);
43
44      // Set tool tip text on the buttons
45      jbtLeft.setToolTipText("Move message to left");
46      jbtRight.setToolTipText("Move message to right");
47
48      // Place panels in the frame
49      setLayout(new BorderLayout());
50      add(messagePanel, BorderLayout.CENTER);
51      add(jpButtons, BorderLayout.SOUTH);
52
53      // Register listeners with the buttons
54      jbtLeft.addActionListener(new ActionListener() {
55        public void actionPerformed(ActionEvent e) {
56          messagePanel.moveLeft();
57        }
58      });
59      jbtRight.addActionListener(new ActionListener() {
60        public void actionPerformed(ActionEvent e) {
61          messagePanel.moveRight();
62        }
63      });
64    }
65 }
```

mnemonic

tool tip

register listener

register listener

`messagePanel` (line 10) is deliberately declared `protected` so that it can be referenced by a subclass in future examples.

You can set an icon image on the button by using the `setIcon` method. If you uncomment the following code in lines 39–42:

```
// jbtLeft.setIcon(new ImageIcon("image/left.gif"));
// jbtRight.setIcon(new ImageIcon("image/right.gif"));
// jbtLeft.setText(null);
// jbtRight.setText(null);
```

the texts are replaced by the icons, as shown in Figure 16.10(a). `"image/left.gif"` is located in `"c:\book\image\left.gif"`. Note that the back slash is the Windows file path notation. In Java, the forward slash should be used.

You can set text and an icon on a button at the same time, if you wish, as shown in Figure 16.10(b). By default, the text and icon are centered horizontally and vertically.

The button can also be accessed by using the keyboard mnemonics. Pressing ALT+L is equivalent to clicking the <= button, since you set the mnemonic property to `'L'` in the left button (line 35). If you change the left button text to `"Left"` and the right button to `"Right"`, the `L` and `R` in the captions of these buttons will be underlined, as shown in Figure 16.10(b).

Each button has a tool-tip text (lines 45–46), which appears when the mouse is set on the button without clicking, as shown in Figure 16.10(c).

(a)

(b)

(c)

FIGURE 16.10 You can set an icon on a `JButton` and access a button using mnemonic keys.

locating **MessagePanel**

Note

Since `MessagePanel` is not in the Java API, you should place MessagePanel.java in the same directory with ButtonDemo.java.

16.3 Check Boxes

toggle button

A *toggle button* is a two-state button like a light switch. `JToggleButton` inherits `AbstractButton` and implements a toggle button. Often `JToggleButton`'s subclasses `JCheckBox` and `JRadioButton` are used to enable the user to toggle a choice on or off. This section introduces `JCheckBox`. `JRadioButton` will be introduced in the next section.

`JCheckBox` inherits all the properties from `AbstractButton`, such as `text`, `icon`, `mnemonic`, `verticalAlignment`, `horizontalAlignment`, `horizontalTextPosition`, `verticalTextPosition`, and `selected`, and provides several constructors to create check boxes, as shown in Figure 16.11.

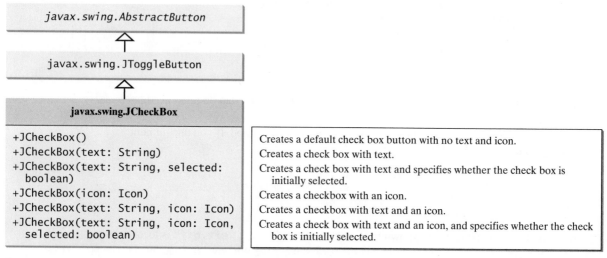

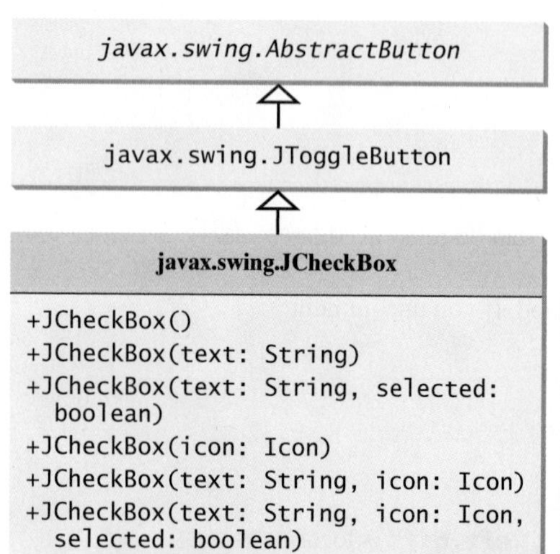

Creates a default check box button with no text and icon.
Creates a check box with text.
Creates a check box with text and specifies whether the check box is initially selected.
Creates a checkbox with an icon.
Creates a checkbox with text and an icon.
Creates a check box with text and an icon, and specifies whether the check box is initially selected.

FIGURE 16.11 `JCheckBox` defines a check box button.

Here is an example of a check box with text Student, red foreground, white background, mnemonic key `'S'`, and initially selected.

```
JCheckBox jchk = new JCheckBox("Student", true);
jchk.setForeground(Color.RED);
jchk.setBackground(Color.WHITE);
jchk.setMnemonic('S');
```

When a check box is clicked (checked or unchecked), it fires an `ItemEvent` and then an `ActionEvent`. To see if a check box is selected, use the `isSelected()` method.

Listing 16.3 gives a program that adds three check boxes named *Centered*, *Bold*, and *Italic* to the preceding example to let the user specify whether the message is centered, bold, or italic, as shown in Figure 16.12.

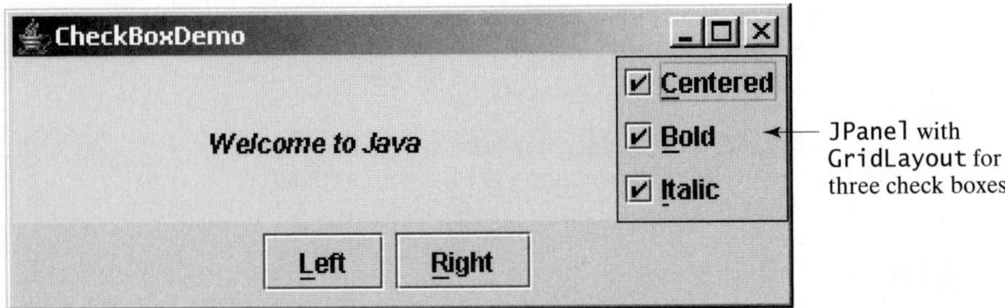

FIGURE 16.12 Three check boxes are added to specify how the message is displayed.

There are at least two approaches to writing this program. The first is to revise the preceding `ButtonDemo` class to insert the code for adding the check boxes and processing their events. The second is to create a subclass that extends `ButtonDemo`. Please implement the first approach as an exercise. Listing 16.3 gives the code to implement the second approach.

Video Note
Use check boxes

LISTING 16.3 CheckBoxDemo.java

JFrame ← ButtonDemo ← CheckBoxDemo

```
import java.awt.*;
import java.awt.event.*;
import javax.swing.*;

public class CheckBoxDemo extends ButtonDemo {
  // Create three check boxes to control the display of message
  private JCheckBox jchkCentered = new JCheckBox("Centered");
  private JCheckBox jchkBold = new JCheckBox("Bold");
  private JCheckBox jchkItalic = new JCheckBox("Italic");

  public static void main(String[] args) {
    CheckBoxDemo frame = new CheckBoxDemo();
    frame.setTitle("CheckBoxDemo");
    frame.setSize(500, 200);
    frame.setLocationRelativeTo(null); // Center the frame
    frame.setDefaultCloseOperation(JFrame.EXIT_ON_CLOSE);
    frame.setVisible(true);
  }

  public CheckBoxDemo() {
    // Set mnemonic keys
    jchkCentered.setMnemonic('C');
    jchkBold.setMnemonic('B');
    jchkItalic.setMnemonic('I');

    // Create a new panel to hold check boxes
    JPanel jpCheckBoxes = new JPanel();
    jpCheckBoxes.setLayout(new GridLayout(3, 1));
    jpCheckBoxes.add(jchkCentered);
    jpCheckBoxes.add(jchkBold);
    jpCheckBoxes.add(jchkItalic);
    add(jpCheckBoxes, BorderLayout.EAST);

    // Register listeners with the check boxes
    jchkCentered.addActionListener(new ActionListener() {
```

create frame

create UI

register listener

register listener

set a new font

```
36       public void actionPerformed(ActionEvent e) {
37         messagePanel.setCentered(jchkCentered.isSelected());
38       }
39     });
40     jchkBold.addActionListener(new ActionListener() {
41       public void actionPerformed(ActionEvent e) {
42         setNewFont();
43       }
44     });
45     jchkItalic.addActionListener(new ActionListener() {
46       public void actionPerformed(ActionEvent e) {
47         setNewFont();
48       }
49     });
50   }
51
52   private void setNewFont() {
53     // Determine a font style
54     int fontStyle = Font.PLAIN;
55     fontStyle += (jchkBold.isSelected() ? Font.BOLD : Font.PLAIN);
56     fontStyle += (jchkItalic.isSelected() ? Font.ITALIC : Font.PLAIN);
57
58     // Set font for the message
59     Font font = messagePanel.getFont();
60     messagePanel.setFont(
61       new Font(font.getName(), fontStyle, font.getSize()));
62   }
63 }
```

CheckBoxDemo extends ButtonDemo and adds three check boxes to control how the message is displayed. When a CheckBoxDemo is constructed (line 12), its superclass's no-arg constructor is invoked, so you don't have to rewrite the code that is already in the constructor of ButtonDemo.

When a check box is checked or unchecked, the listener's actionPerformed method is invoked to process the event. When the *Centered* check box is checked or unchecked, the centered property of the MessagePanel class is set to true or false.

The current font name and size used in MessagePanel are obtained from messagePanel.getFont() using the getName() and getSize() methods. The font styles (Font.BOLD and Font.ITALIC) are specified in the check boxes. If no font style is selected, the font style is Font.PLAIN. Font styles are combined by adding together the selected integers representing the fonts.

The keyboard mnemonics *C*, *B*, and *I* are set on the check boxes *Centered*, *Bold*, and *Italic*, respectively (lines 22–24). You can use a mouse gesture or a shortcut key to select a check box.

The setFont method (line 60) defined in the Component class is inherited in the MessagePanel class. This method automatically invokes the repaint method. Invoking setFont in messagePanel automatically repaints the message.

A check box fires an ActionEvent and an ItemEvent when it is clicked. You could process either the ActionEvent or the ItemEvent to redisplay the message. The example processes the ActionEvent. If you wished to process the ItemEvent, you could create a listener for ItemEvent and register it with a check box, as shown below:

```
public class CheckBoxDemoUsingItemEvent extends ButtonDemo {
  ... // Same as in CheckBoxDemo.java, so omitted

  public CheckBoxDemoUsingItemEvent() {
    ... // Same as in CheckBoxDemo.java, so omitted
```

```
      // TO listen for ItemEvent
      jchkCentered.addItemListener(new ItemListener() {
        /** Handle ItemEvent */
        public void itemStateChanged(ItemEvent e) {
          messagePanel.setCentered(jchkCentered.isSelected());
        }
      });
    }
  }
```

16.4 Radio Buttons

Radio buttons, also known as *option buttons*, enable you to choose a single item from a group of choices. In appearance radio buttons resemble check boxes, but check boxes display a square that is either checked or blank, whereas radio buttons display a circle that is either filled (if selected) or blank (if not selected).

`JRadioButton` inherits `AbstractButton` and provides several constructors to create radio buttons, as shown in Figure 16.13. These constructors are similar to the constructors for `JCheckBox`.

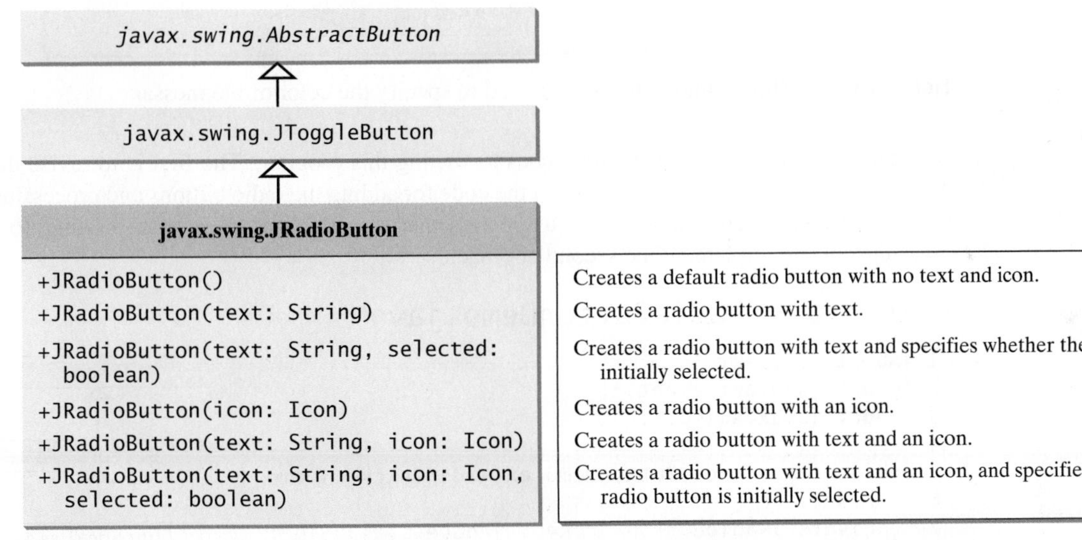

FIGURE 16.13 `JRadioButton` defines a radio button.

Here is an example of a radio button with text `Student`, `RED` foreground, `WHITE` background, mnemonic key `'S'`, and initially selected.

```
JRadioButton jrb = new JRadioButton("Student", true);
jrb.setForeground(Color.RED);
jrb.setBackground(Color.WHITE);
jrb.setMnemonic('S');
```

To group radio buttons, you need to create an instance of `java.swing.ButtonGroup` and use the `add` method to add them to it, as follows:

```
ButtonGroup group = new ButtonGroup();
group.add(jrb1);
group.add(jrb2);
```

This code creates a radio button group for radio buttons `jrb1` and `jrb2` so that `jrb1` and `jrb2` are selected mutually exclusively. Without grouping, `jrb1` and `jrb2` would be independent.

Note

`ButtonGroup` is not a subclass of `java.awt.Component`, so a `ButtonGroup` object cannot be added to a container.

When a radio button is changed (selected or deselected), it fires an `ItemEvent` and then an `ActionEvent`. To see if a radio button is selected, use the `isSelected()` method.

Listing 16.4 gives a program that adds three radio buttons named *Red*, *Green*, and *Blue* to the preceding example to let the user choose the color of the message, as shown in Figure 16.14.

FIGURE 16.14 Three radio buttons are added to specify the color of the message.

Again there are at least two approaches to writing this program. The first is to revise the preceding `CheckBoxDemo` class to insert the code for adding the radio buttons and processing their events. The second is to create a subclass that extends `CheckBoxDemo`. Listing 16.4 gives the code to implement the second approach.

Video Note
Use radio buttons

LISTING 16.4 RadioButtonDemo.java

create frame

create UI

```
import java.awt.*;
import java.awt.event.*;
import javax.swing.*;

public class RadioButtonDemo extends CheckBoxDemo {
  // Declare radio buttons
  private JRadioButton jrbRed, jrbGreen, jrbBlue;

  public static void main(String[] args) {
    RadioButtonDemo frame = new RadioButtonDemo();
    frame.setSize(500, 200);
    frame.setLocationRelativeTo(null); // Center the frame
    frame.setDefaultCloseOperation(JFrame.EXIT_ON_CLOSE);
    frame.setTitle("RadioButtonDemo");
    frame.setVisible(true);
  }

  public RadioButtonDemo() {
    // Create a new panel to hold check boxes
    JPanel jpRadioButtons = new JPanel();
    jpRadioButtons.setLayout(new GridLayout(3, 1));
    jpRadioButtons.add(jrbRed = new JRadioButton("Red"));
    jpRadioButtons.add(jrbGreen = new JRadioButton("Green"));
```

JFrame
ButtonDemo
CheckBoxDemo
RadioButtonDemo

```
24      jpRadioButtons.add(jrbBlue = new JRadioButton("Blue"));
25      add(jpRadioButtons, BorderLayout.WEST);
26
27      // Create a radio button group to group three buttons
28      ButtonGroup group = new ButtonGroup();
29      group.add(jrbRed);
30      group.add(jrbGreen);
31      group.add(jrbBlue);
32
33      // Set keyboard mnemonics
34      jrbRed.setMnemonic('E');
35      jrbGreen.setMnemonic('G');
36      jrbBlue.setMnemonic('U');
37
38      // Register listeners for check boxes
39      jrbRed.addActionListener(new ActionListener() {
40        public void actionPerformed(ActionEvent e) {
41          messagePanel.setForeground(Color.red);
42        }
43      });
44      jrbGreen.addActionListener(new ActionListener() {
45        public void actionPerformed(ActionEvent e) {
46          messagePanel.setForeground(Color.green);
47        }
48      });
49      jrbBlue.addActionListener(new ActionListener() {
50        public void actionPerformed(ActionEvent e) {
51          messagePanel.setForeground(Color.blue);
52        }
53      });
54
55      // Set initial message color to blue
56      jrbBlue.setSelected(true);
57      messagePanel.setForeground(Color.blue);
58    }
59  }
```

group buttons

register listener

register listener

register listener

RadioButtonDemo extends CheckBoxDemo and adds three radio buttons to specify the message color. When a radio button is clicked, the radio button's action event listener sets the corresponding foreground color in messagePanel.

The keyboard mnemonics 'R' and 'B' are already set for the Right button and Bold check box. To avoid conflict, the keyboard mnemonics 'E', 'G', and 'U' are set on the radio buttons *Red*, *Green*, and *Blue*, respectively (lines 34–36).

The program creates a ButtonGroup and puts three JRadioButton instances (jrbRed, jrbGreen, and jrbBlue) in the group (lines 28–31).

A radio button fires an ActionEvent and an ItemEvent when it is selected or deselected. You could process either the ActionEvent or the ItemEvent to choose a color. The example processes the ActionEvent. Please rewrite the code using the ItemEvent as an exercise.

16.5 Labels

A *label* is a display area for a short text, an image, or both. It is often used to label other components (usually text fields). Figure 16.15 lists the constructors and methods in JLabel.

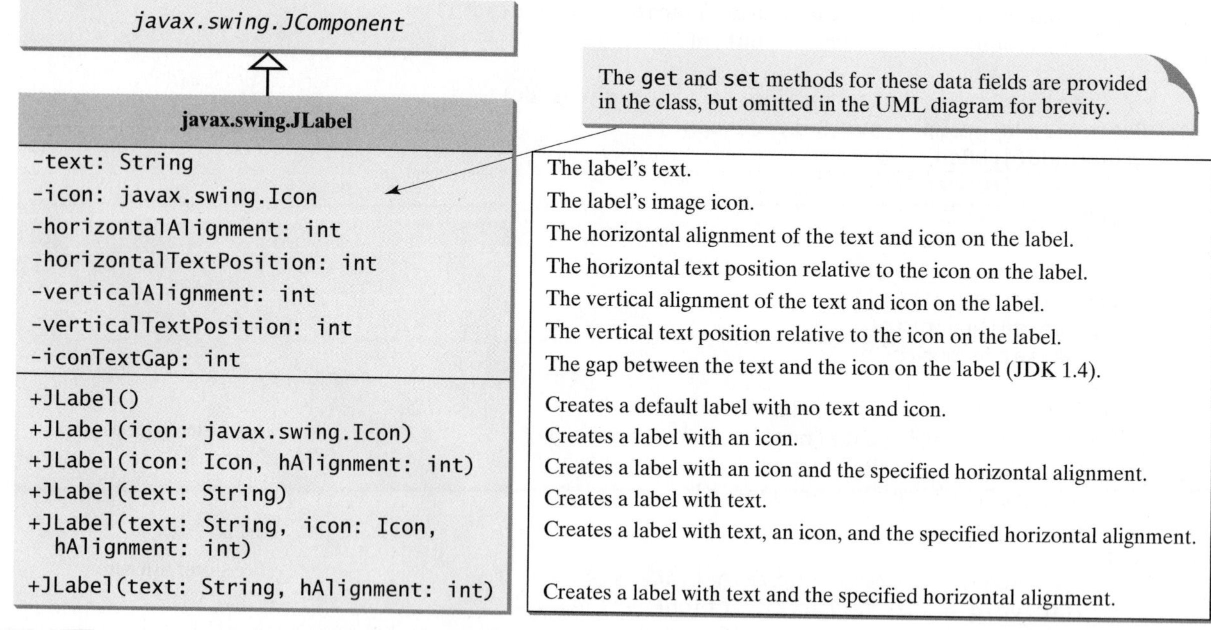

FIGURE 16.15 `JLabel` displays text or an icon, or both.

`JLabel` inherits all the properties from `JComponent` and has many properties similar to the ones in `JButton`, such as `text`, `icon`, `horizontalAlignment`, `verticalAlignment`, `horizontalTextPosition`, `verticalTextPosition`, and `iconTextGap`. For example, the following code displays a label with text and an icon:

```
// Create an image icon from an image file
ImageIcon icon = new ImageIcon("image/grapes.gif");

// Create a label with a text, an icon,
// with centered horizontal alignment
JLabeljlbl = new JLabel("Grapes", icon, SwingConstants.CENTER);

//Set label's text alignment and gap between text and icon
jlbl.setHorizontalTextPosition(SwingConstants.CENTER);
jlbl.setVerticalTextPosition(SwingConstants.BOTTOM);
jlbl.setIconTextGap(5);
```

Text and Icon Label

Grapes

16.6 Text Fields

A *text field* can be used to enter or display a string. `JTextField` is a subclass of `JTextComponent`. Figure 16.16 lists the constructors and methods in `JTextField`.

`JTextField` inherits `JTextComponent`, which inherits `JComponent`. Here is an example of creating a non-editable text field with red foreground color and right horizontal alignment:

```
JTextField jtfMessage = new JTextField("T-Strom");
jtfMessage.setEditable(false);
jtfMessage.setForeground(Color.RED);
jtfMessage.setHorizontalAlignment(SwingConstants.RIGHT);
```

When you move the cursor in the text field and press the *Enter* key, it fires an `ActionEvent`.

Listing 16.5 gives a program that adds a text field to the preceding example to let the user set a new message, as shown in Figure 16.17.

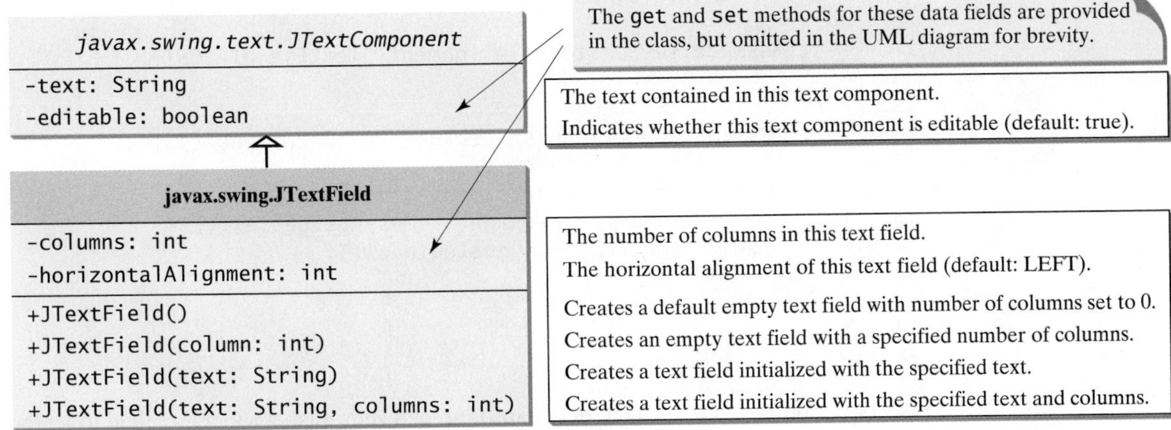

FIGURE 16.16 `JTextField` enables you to enter or display a string.

FIGURE 16.17 A label and a text field are added to set a new message.

Listing 16.5 creates a subclass that extends `RadioButtonDemo`.

Video Note
Use labels and text fields

LISTING 16.5 TextFieldDemo.java

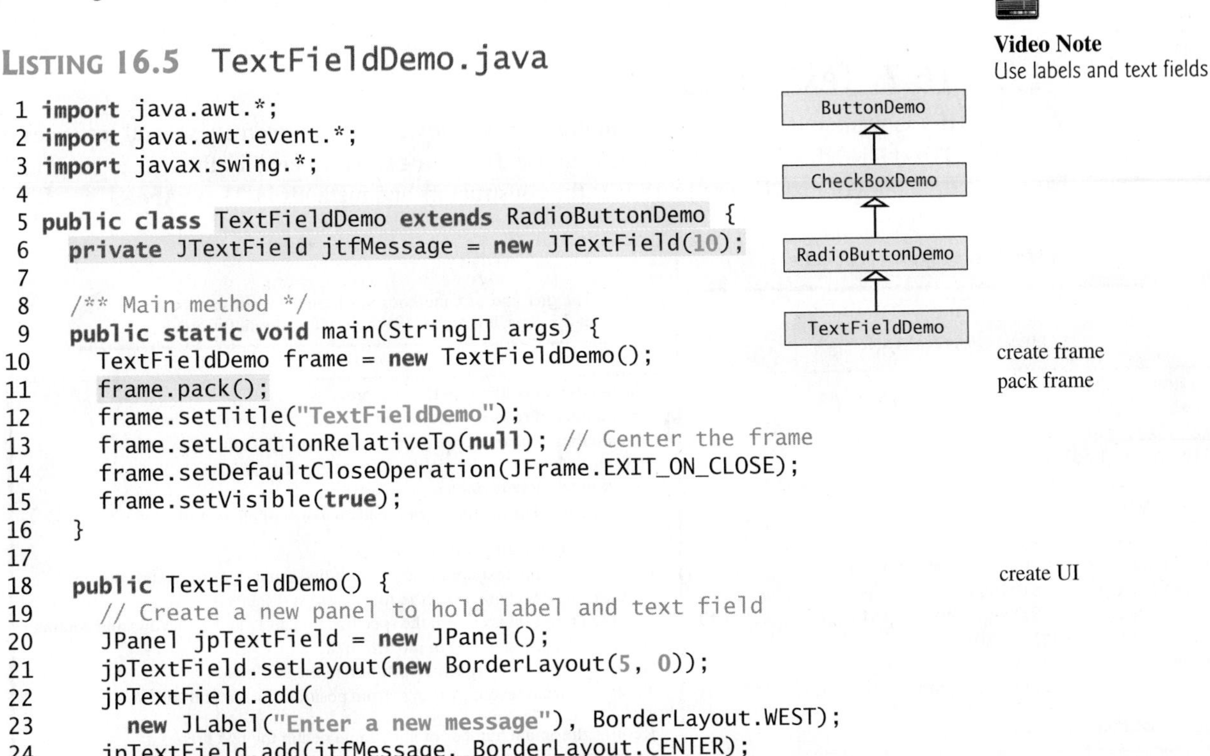


```java
import java.awt.*;
import java.awt.event.*;
import javax.swing.*;

public class TextFieldDemo extends RadioButtonDemo {
  private JTextField jtfMessage = new JTextField(10);

  /** Main method */
  public static void main(String[] args) {
    TextFieldDemo frame = new TextFieldDemo();              // create frame
    frame.pack();                                           // pack frame
    frame.setTitle("TextFieldDemo");
    frame.setLocationRelativeTo(null); // Center the frame
    frame.setDefaultCloseOperation(JFrame.EXIT_ON_CLOSE);
    frame.setVisible(true);
  }

  public TextFieldDemo() {                                  // create UI
    // Create a new panel to hold label and text field
    JPanel jpTextField = new JPanel();
    jpTextField.setLayout(new BorderLayout(5, 0));
    jpTextField.add(
      new JLabel("Enter a new message"), BorderLayout.WEST);
    jpTextField.add(jtfMessage, BorderLayout.CENTER);
```

listener

```
25      add(jpTextField, BorderLayout.NORTH);
26
27      jtfMessage.setHorizontalAlignment(JTextField.RIGHT);
28
29      // Register listener
30      jtfMessage.addActionListener(new ActionListener() {
31        /** Handle ActionEvent */
32        public void actionPerformed(ActionEvent e) {
33          messagePanel.setMessage(jtfMessage.getText());
34          jtfMessage.requestFocusInWindow();
35        }
36      });
37    }
38 }
```

`TextFieldDemo` extends `RadioButtonDemo` and adds a label and a text field to let the user enter a new message. After you set a new message in the text field and press the *Enter* key, a new message is displayed. Pressing the *Enter* key on the text field triggers an action event. The listener sets a new message in `messagePanel` (line 33).

pack()

The `pack()` method (line 11) automatically sizes up the frame according to the size of the components placed in it.

requestFocusInWindow()

The `requestFocusInWindow()` method (line 34) defined in the `Component` class requests the component to receive input focus. Thus, `jtfMessage.requestFocusInWindow()` requests the input focus on `jtfMessage`. You will see the cursor on `jtfMessage` after the `actionPerformed` method is invoked.

JPasswordField

Note

If a text field is used for entering a password, use `JPasswordField` to replace `JTextField`. `JPasswordField` extends `JTextField` and hides the input text with echo charaters (e.g., ******). By default, the echo character is *. You can specify a new echo character using the `setEchoChar(char)` method.

16.7 Text Areas

If you want to let the user enter multiple lines of text, you have to create several instances of `JTextField`. A better alternative is to use `JTextArea`, which enables the user to enter multiple lines of text. Figure 16.18 lists the constructors and methods in `JTextArea`.

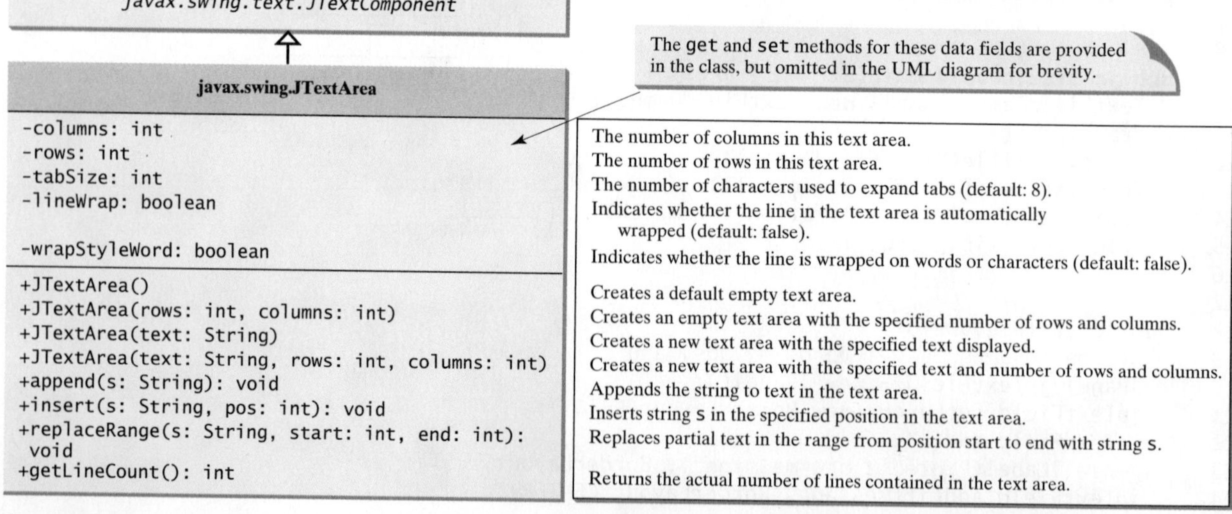

FIGURE 16.18 `JTextArea` enables you to enter or display multiple lines of characters.

Like JTextField, JTextArea inherits JTextComponent, which contains the methods getText, setText, isEditable, and setEditable. Here is an example of creating a text area with five rows and 20 columns, line-wrapped on words, red foreground color, and Courier font, bold, 20 pixels.

```
JTextArea jtaNote = new JTextArea("This is a text area", 5, 20);
jtaNote.setLineWrap(true);          // wrap line
jtaNote.setWrapStyleWord(true);     // wrap word
jtaNote.setForeground(Color.RED);
jtaNote.setFont(new Font("Courier", Font.BOLD, 20));
```

JTextArea does not handle scrolling, but you can create a JScrollPane object to hold an instance of JTextArea and let JScrollPane handle scrolling for JTextArea, as follows:

```
// Create a scroll pane to hold text area
JScrollPane scrollPane = new JScrollPane(jta = new JTextArea());
add(scrollPane, BorderLayout.CENTER);
```

Listing 16.7 gives a program that displays an image and a text in a label, and a text in a text area, as shown in Figure 16.19.

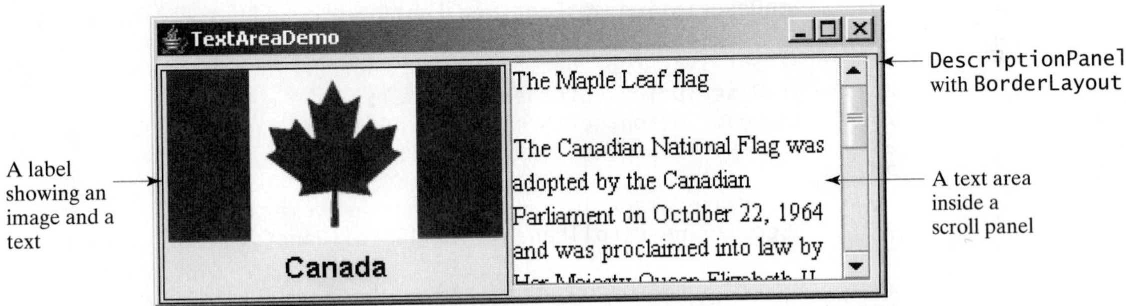

FIGURE 16.19 The program displays an image in a label, a title in a label, and a text in the text area.

Here are the major steps in the program:

1. Create a class named DescriptionPanel that extends JPanel, as shown in Listing 16.6. This class contains a text area inside a scroll pane, and a label for displaying an image icon and a title. This class is used in the present example and will be reused in later examples.
2. Create a class named TextAreaDemo that extends JFrame, as shown in Listing 16.7. Create an instance of DescriptionPanel and add it to the center of the frame. The relationship between DescriptionPanel and TextAreaDemo is shown in Figure 16.20.

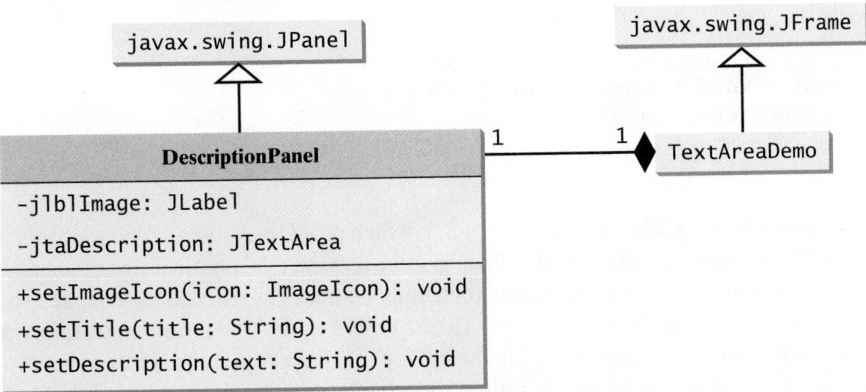

FIGURE 16.20 TextAreaDemo uses DescriptionPanel to display an image, title, and text description of a national flag.

LISTING 16.6 DescriptionPanel.java

label · text area · label properties · wrap line · wrap word · read only · scroll pane

```
 1 import javax.swing.*;
 2 import java.awt.*;
 3
 4 public class DescriptionPanel extends JPanel {
 5   /** Label for displaying an image icon and a text */
 6   private JLabel jlblImageTitle = new JLabel();
 7
 8   /** Text area for displaying text */
 9   private JTextArea jtaDescription = new JTextArea();
10
11   public DescriptionPanel() {
12     // Center the icon and text and place the text under the icon
13     jlblImageTitle.setHorizontalAlignment(JLabel.CENTER);
14     jlblImageTitle.setHorizontalTextPosition(JLabel.CENTER);
15     jlblImageTitle.setVerticalTextPosition(JLabel.BOTTOM);
16
17     // Set the font in the label and the text field
18     jlblImageTitle.setFont(new Font("SansSerif", Font.BOLD, 16));
19     jtaDescription.setFont(new Font("Serif", Font.PLAIN, 14));
20
21     // Set lineWrap and wrapStyleWord true for the text area
22     jtaDescription.setLineWrap(true);
23     jtaDescription.setWrapStyleWord(true);
24     jtaDescription.setEditable(false);
25
26     // Create a scroll pane to hold the text area
27     JScrollPane scrollPane = new JScrollPane(jtaDescription);
28
29     // Set BorderLayout for the panel, add label and scrollpane
30     setLayout(new BorderLayout(5, 5));
31     add(scrollPane, BorderLayout.CENTER);
32     add(jlblImageTitle, BorderLayout.WEST);
33   }
34
35   /** Set the title */
36   public void setTitle(String title) {
37     jlblImageTitle.setText(title);
38   }
39
40   /** Set the image icon */
41   public void setImageIcon(ImageIcon icon) {
42     jlblImageTitle.setIcon(icon);
43   }
44
45   /** Set the text description */
46   public void setDescription(String text) {
47     jtaDescription.setText(text);
48   }
49 }
```

The text area is inside a `JScrollPane` (line 27), which provides scrolling functions for the text area. Scroll bars automatically appear if there is more text than the physical size of the text area, and disappear if the text is deleted and the remaining text does not exceed the text area size.

The `lineWrap` property is set to `true` (line 21) so that the line is automatically wrapped when the text cannot fit in one line. The `wrapStyleWord` property is set to `true` (line 23) so that the line is wrapped on words rather than characters. The text area is set non-editable (line 24), so you cannot edit the description in the text area.

It is not necessary to create a separate class for `DescriptionPanel` in this example. Nevertheless, this class was created for reuse in the next example, where you will use it to display a description panel for various images.

LISTING 16.7 `TextAreaDemo.java`

```
1 import java.awt.*;
2 import javax.swing.*;
3
4 public class TextAreaDemo extends JFrame {
5   // Declare and create a description panel
6   private DescriptionPanel descriptionPanel = new DescriptionPanel();
7
8   public static void main(String[] args) {
9     TextAreaDemo frame = new TextAreaDemo();
10    frame.pack();
11    frame.setLocationRelativeTo(null); // Center the frame
12    frame.setDefaultCloseOperation(JFrame.EXIT_ON_CLOSE);
13    frame.setTitle("TextAreaDemo");
14    frame.setVisible(true);
15  }
16
17  public TextAreaDemo() {
18    // Set title, text and image in the description panel
19    descriptionPanel.setTitle("Canada");
20    String description = "The Maple Leaf flag \n\n" +
21      "The Canadian National Flag was adopted by the Canadian " +
22      "Parliament on October 22, 1964 and was proclaimed into law " +
23      "by Her Majesty Queen Elizabeth II (the Queen of Canada) on " +
24      "February 15, 1965. The Canadian Flag (colloquially known " +
25      "as The Maple Leaf Flag) is a red flag of the proportions " +
26      "two by length and one by width, containing in its center a " +
27      "white square, with a single red stylized eleven-point " +
28      "mapleleaf centered in the white square.";
29    descriptionPanel.setDescription(description);
30    descriptionPanel.setImageIcon(new ImageIcon("image/ca.gif"));
31
32    // Add the description panel to the frame
33    setLayout(new BorderLayout());
34    add(descriptionPanel, BorderLayout.CENTER);
35  }
36 }
```

create **decriptionPanel**

create frame

create UI

add **decriptionPanel**

`TextAreaDemo` simply creates an instance of `DescriptionPanel` (line 6), and sets the title (line 19), image (line 30), and text in the description panel (line 29). `DescriptionPanel` is a subclass of `JPanel`. `DescriptionPanel` contains a label for displaying an image icon and a text title, and a text area for displaying a description of the image.

16.8 Combo Boxes

A *combo box*, also known as a *choice list* or *drop-down list*, contains a list of items from which the user can choose. It is useful in limiting a user's range of choices and avoids the cumbersome validation of data input. Figure 16.21 lists several frequently used constructors and methods in `JComboBox`.

The following statements create a combo box with four items, red foreground, white background, and the second item selected.

```
JComboBox jcb = new JComboBox(new Object[]
  {"Item 1", "Item 2", "Item 3", "Item 4"});
jcb.setForeground(Color.RED);
jcb.setBackground(Color.WHITE);
jcb.setSelectedItem("Item 2");
```

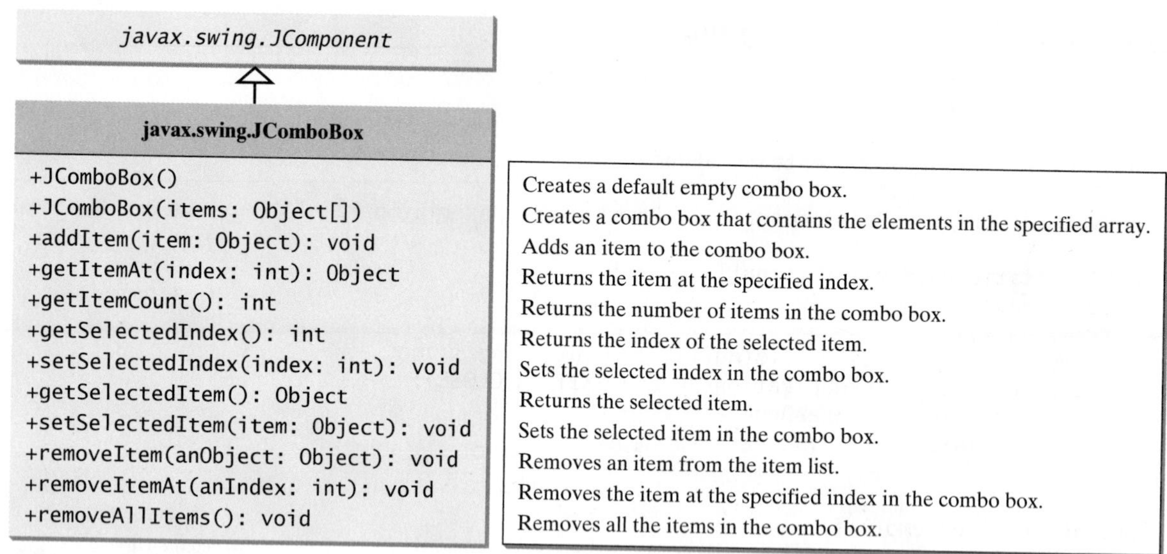
javax.swing.JComponent
javax.swing.JComboBox
+JComboBox()
+JComboBox(items: Object[])
+addItem(item: Object): void
+getItemAt(index: int): Object
+getItemCount(): int
+getSelectedIndex(): int
+setSelectedIndex(index: int): void
+getSelectedItem(): Object
+setSelectedItem(item: Object): void
+removeItem(anObject: Object): void
+removeItemAt(anIndex: int): void
+removeAllItems(): void
Creates a default empty combo box.
Creates a combo box that contains the elements in the specified array.
Adds an item to the combo box.
Returns the item at the specified index.
Returns the number of items in the combo box.
Returns the index of the selected item.
Sets the selected index in the combo box.
Returns the selected item.
Sets the selected item in the combo box.
Removes an item from the item list.
Removes the item at the specified index in the combo box.
Removes all the items in the combo box.

FIGURE 16.21 `JComboBox` enables you to select an item from a set of items.

`JComboBox` can generate `ActionEvent` and `ItemEvent`, among many other events. Whenever an item is selected, an `ActionEvent` is fired. Whenever a new item is selected, `JComboBox` generates `ItemEvent` twice, once for deselecting the previously selected item, and the other for selecting the currently selected item. Note that no `ItemEvent` is fired if the current item is reselected. To respond to an `ItemEvent`, you need to implement the `itemStateChanged(ItemEvent e)` handler for processing a choice. To get data from a `JComboBox` menu, you can use `getSelectedItem()` to return the currently selected item, or `e.getItem()` method to get the item from the `itemStateChanged(ItemEvent e)` handler.

Listing 16.8 gives a program that lets users view an image and a description of a country's flag by selecting the country from a combo box, as shown in Figure 16.22.

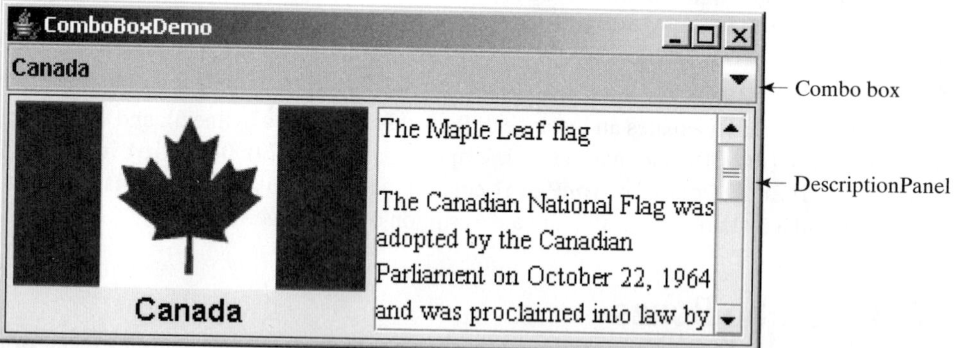
ComboBoxDemo
Canada
Combo box
Canada
The Maple Leaf flag
The Canadian National Flag was adopted by the Canadian Parliament on October 22, 1964 and was proclaimed into law by
DescriptionPanel

FIGURE 16.22 A country's info, including a flag image and a description of the flag, is displayed when the country is selected in the combo box.

Here are the major steps in the program:

1. Create the user interface.

   Create a combo box with country names as its selection values. Create a `DescriptionPanel` object. The `DescriptionPanel` class was introduced in the preceding example. Place the combo box in the north of the frame and the description panel in the center of the frame.

2. Process the event.
   Create a listener to implement the `itemStateChanged` handler to set the flag title, image, and text in the description panel for the selected country name.

LISTING 16.8 ComboBoxDemo.java

```
import java.awt.*;
import java.awt.event.*;
import javax.swing.*;

public class ComboBoxDemo extends JFrame {
  // Declare an array of Strings for flag titles
  private String[] flagTitles = {"Canada", "China", "Denmark",
    "France", "Germany", "India", "Norway", "United Kingdom",
    "United States of America"};

  // Declare an ImageIcon array for the national flags of 9 countries
  private ImageIcon[] flagImage = {
    new ImageIcon("image/ca.gif"),
    new ImageIcon("image/china.gif"),
    new ImageIcon("image/denmark.gif"),
    new ImageIcon("image/fr.gif"),
    new ImageIcon("image/germany.gif"),
    new ImageIcon("image/india.gif"),
    new ImageIcon("image/norway.gif"),
    new ImageIcon("image/uk.gif"),
    new ImageIcon("image/us.gif")
  };

  // Declare an array of strings for flag descriptions
  private String[] flagDescription = new String[9];

  // Declare and create a description panel
  private DescriptionPanel descriptionPanel = new DescriptionPanel();

  // Create a combo box for selecting countries
  private JComboBox jcbo = new JComboBox(flagTitles);

  public static void main(String[] args) {
    ComboBoxDemo frame = new ComboBoxDemo();
    frame.pack();
    frame.setTitle("ComboBoxDemo");
    frame.setLocationRelativeTo(null); // Center the frame
    frame.setDefaultCloseOperation(JFrame.EXIT_ON_CLOSE);
    frame.setVisible(true);
  }

  public ComboBoxDemo() {
    // Set text description
    flagDescription[0] = "The Maple Leaf flag \n\n" +
      "The Canadian National Flag was adopted by the Canadian " +
      "Parliament on October 22, 1964 and was proclaimed into law " +
      "by Her Majesty Queen Elizabeth II (the Queen of Canada) on " +
      "February 15, 1965. The Canadian Flag (colloquially known " +
      "as The Maple Leaf Flag) is a red flag of the proportions " +
      "two by length and one by width, containing in its center a " +
      "white square, with a single red stylized eleven-point " +
      "mapleleaf centered in the white square.";
    flagDescription[1] = "Description for China ... ";
```

country

image icon

description

combo box

create UI

listener

```
54     flagDescription[2] = "Description for Denmark ... ";
55     flagDescription[3] = "Description for France ... ";
56     flagDescription[4] = "Description for Germany ... ";
57     flagDescription[5] = "Description for India ... ";
58     flagDescription[6] = "Description for Norway ... ";
59     flagDescription[7] = "Description for UK ... ";
60     flagDescription[8] = "Description for US ... ";
61
62     // Set the first country (Canada) for display
63     setDisplay(0);
64
65     // Add combo box and description panel to the list
66     add(jcbo, BorderLayout.NORTH);
67     add(descriptionPanel, BorderLayout.CENTER);
68
69     // Register listener
70     jcbo.addItemListener(new ItemListener() {
71       /** Handle item selection */
72       public void itemStateChanged(ItemEvent e) {
73         setDisplay(jcbo.getSelectedIndex());
74       }
75     });
76   }
77
78   /** Set display information on the description panel */
79   public void setDisplay(int index) {
80     descriptionPanel.setTitle(flagTitles[index]);
81     descriptionPanel.setImageIcon(flagImage[index]);
82     descriptionPanel.setDescription(flagDescription[index]);
83   }
84 }
```

The listener listens to ItemEvent from the combo box and implements ItemListener (lines 70–75). Instead of using ItemEvent, you may rewrite the program to use ActionEvent for handling combo box item selection.

The program stores the flag information in three arrays: flagTitles, flagImage, and flagDescription (lines 7–25). The array flagTitles contains the names of nine countries, the array flagImage contains images of the nine countries' flags, and the array flagDescription contains descriptions of the flags.

The program creates an instance of DescriptionPanel (line 28), which was presented in Listing 16.6, TextAreasDemo.java. The program creates a combo box with initial values from flagTitles (line 31). When the user selects an item in the combo box, the ItemStateChanged handler is executed, finds the selected index, and sets its corresponding flag title, flag image, and flag description on the panel.

16.9 Lists

A *list* is a component that basically performs the same function as a combo box but enables the user to choose a single value or multiple values. The Swing JList is very versatile. Figure 16.23 lists several frequently used constructors and methods in JList.

selectionMode is one of the three values (SINGLE_SELECTION, SINGLE_INTERVAL_SELECTION, MULTIPLE_INTERVAL_SELECTION) defined in javax.swing.ListSelectionModel that indicate whether a single item, single-interval item, or multiple-interval item can be selected. Single selection allows only one item to be selected. Single-interval selection allows multiple selections, but the selected items must be contiguous. Multiple-interval selection allows selections of multiple contiguous items without restrictions, as shown in Figure 16.24. The default value is MULTIPLE_INTERVAL_SELECTION.

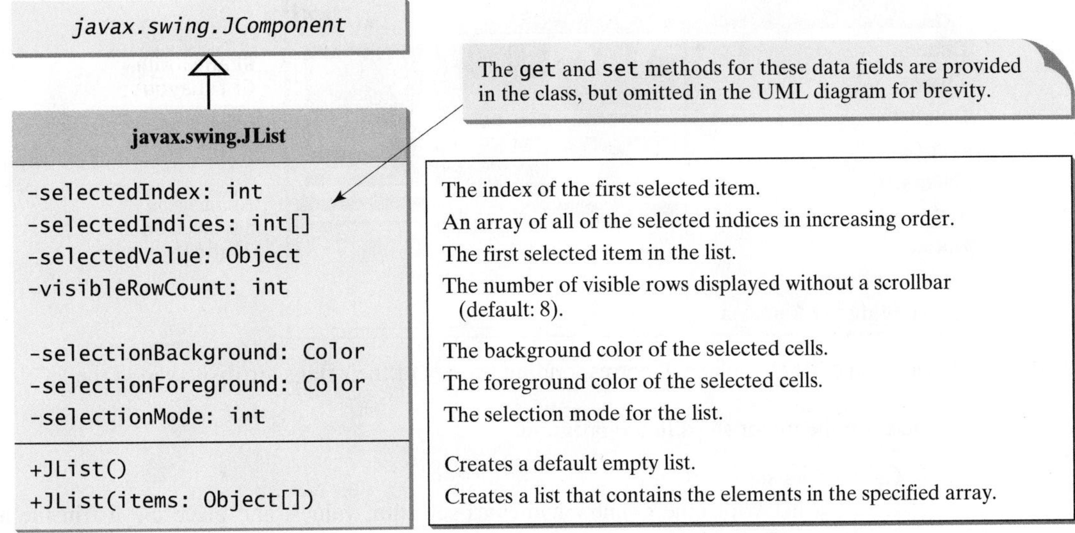

FIGURE 16.23 `JList` enables you to select multiple items from a set of items.

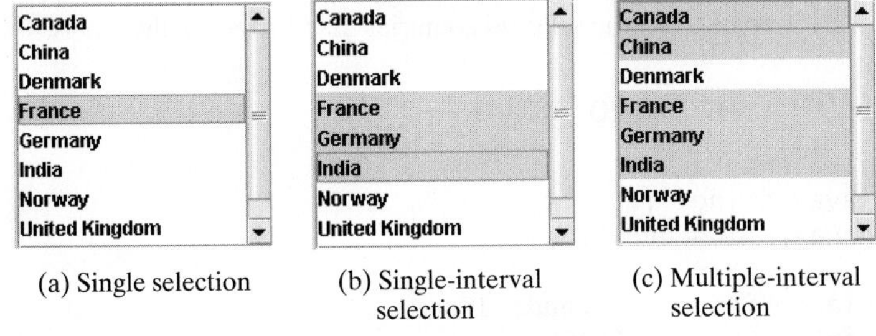

(a) Single selection (b) Single-interval selection (c) Multiple-interval selection

FIGURE 16.24 `JList` has three selection modes: single selection, single-interval selection, and multiple-interval selection.

The following statements create a list with six items, `red` foreground, `white` background, `pink` selection foreground, `black` selection background, and visible row count `4`.

```
JList jlst = new JList(new Object[]
  {"Item 1", "Item 2", "Item 3", "Item 4", "Item 5", "Item 6"});
jlst.setForeground(Color.RED);
jlst.setBackground(Color.WHITE);
jlst.setSelectionForeground(Color.PINK);
jlst.setSelectionBackground(Color.BLACK);
jlst.setVisibleRowCount(4);
```

Lists do not scroll automatically. To make a list scrollable, create a scroll pane and add the list to it. Text areas are made scrollable in the same way.

`JList` generates `javax.swing.event.ListSelectionEvent` to notify the listeners of the selections. The listener must implement the `valueChanged` handler in the `javax.swing.event.ListSelectionListener` interface to process the event.

Listing 16.9 gives a program that lets users select countries in a list and display the flags of the selected countries in the labels. Figure 16.25 shows a sample run of the program.

FIGURE 16.25 When the countries in the list are selected, corresponding images of their flags are displayed in the labels.

Here are the major steps in the program:

1. Create the user interface.
   Create a list with nine country names as selection values, and place the list inside a scroll pane. Place the scroll pane in the west of the frame. Create nine labels to be used to display the countries' flag images. Place the labels in the panel, and place the panel in the center of the frame.

2. Process the event.
   Create a listener to implement the `valueChanged` method in the `ListSelection-Listener` interface to set the selected countries' flag images in the labels.

LISTING 16.9 ListDemo.java

```
import java.awt.*;
import javax.swing.*;
import javax.swing.event.*;

public class ListDemo extends JFrame {
  final int NUMBER_OF_FLAGS = 9;

  // Declare an array of Strings for flag titles
  private String[] flagTitles = {"Canada", "China", "Denmark",
    "France", "Germany", "India", "Norway", "United Kingdom",
    "United States of America"};

  // The list for selecting countries
  private JList jlst = new JList(flagTitles);

  // Declare an ImageIcon array for the national flags of 9 countries
  private ImageIcon[] imageIcons = {
    new ImageIcon("image/ca.gif"),
    new ImageIcon("image/china.gif"),
    new ImageIcon("image/denmark.gif"),
    new ImageIcon("image/fr.gif"),
    new ImageIcon("image/germany.gif"),
    new ImageIcon("image/india.gif"),
    new ImageIcon("image/norway.gif"),
    new ImageIcon("image/uk.gif"),
    new ImageIcon("image/us.gif")
  };

  // Arrays of labels for displaying images
  private JLabel[] jlblImageViewer = new JLabel[NUMBER_OF_FLAGS];

```

```
32   public static void main(String[] args) {
33     ListDemo frame = new ListDemo();
34     frame.setSize(650, 500);
35     frame.setTitle("ListDemo");
36     frame.setLocationRelativeTo(null); // Center the frame
37     frame.setDefaultCloseOperation(JFrame.EXIT_ON_CLOSE);
38     frame.setVisible(true);
39   }
40
41   public ListDemo() {
42     // Create a panel to hold nine labels
43     JPanel p = new JPanel(new GridLayout(3, 3, 5, 5));
44
45     for (int i = 0; i < NUMBER_OF_FLAGS; i++) {
46       p.add(jlblImageViewer[i] = new JLabel());
47       jlblImageViewer[i].setHorizontalAlignment
48         (SwingConstants.CENTER);
49     }
50
51     // Add p and the list to the frame
52     add(p, BorderLayout.CENTER);
53     add(new JScrollPane(jlst), BorderLayout.WEST);
54
55     // Register listeners
56     jlst.addListSelectionListener(new ListSelectionListener() {
57       /** Handle list selection */
58       public void valueChanged(ListSelectionEvent e) {
59         // Get selected indices
60         int[] indices = jlst.getSelectedIndices();
61
62         int i;
63         // Set icons in the labels
64         for (i = 0; i < indices.length; i++) {
65           jlblImageViewer[i].setIcon(imageIcons[indices[i]]);
66         }
67
68         // Remove icons from the rest of the labels
69         for (; i < NUMBER_OF_FLAGS; i++) {
70           jlblImageViewer[i].setIcon(null);
71         }
72       }
73     });
74   }
75 }
```

create frame

create UI

event handler

The anonymous inner class listener listens to `ListSelectionEvent` for handling the selection of country names in the list (lines 56–73). `ListSelectionEvent` and `ListSelectionListener` are defined in the `javax.swing.event` package, so this package is imported in the program (line 3).

The program creates an array of nine labels for displaying flag images for nine countries. The program loads the images of the nine countries into an image array (lines 17–27) and creates a list of the nine countries in the same order as in the image array (lines 9–11). Thus the index `0` of the image array corresponds to the first country in the list.

The list is placed in a scroll pane (line 53) so that it can be scrolled when the number of items in the list extends beyond the viewing area.

By default, the selection mode of the list is multiple-interval, which allows the user to select multiple items from different blocks in the list. When the user selects countries in the list, the `valueChanged` handler (lines 58–72) is executed, which gets the indices of the selected item and sets their corresponding image icons in the label to display the flags.

16.10 Scroll Bars

`JScrollBar` is a component that enables the user to select from a range of values, as shown in Figure 11.26.

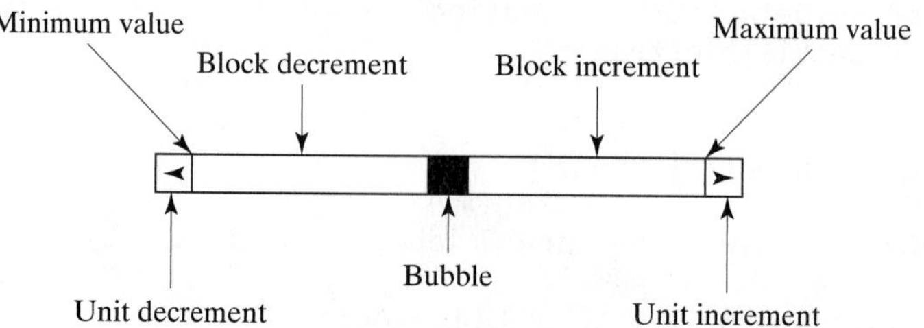

FIGURE 16.26 A scroll bar represents a range of values graphically.

Normally, the user changes the value of the scroll bar by making a gesture with the mouse. For example, the user can drag the scroll bar's bubble up and down, or click in the scroll bar's unit-increment or block-increment areas. Keyboard gestures can also be mapped to the scroll bar. By convention, the Page Up and Page Down keys are equivalent to clicking in the scroll bar's block-increment and block-decrement areas.

Note

The width of the scroll bar's track corresponds to `maximum + visibleAmount`. When a scroll bar is set to its maximum value, the left side of the bubble is at `maximum`, and the right side is at `maximum + visibleAmount`.

`JScrollBar` has the following properties, as shown in Figure 16.27.

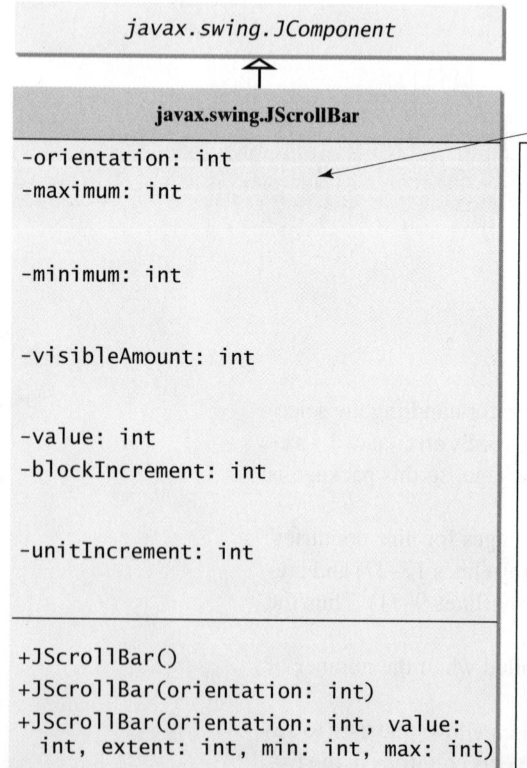

The get and set methods for these data fields are provided in the class, but omitted in the UML diagram for brevity.

Specifies horizontal or vertical style, default is horizontal.

Specifies the maximum value the scroll bar represents when the bubble reaches the right end of the scroll bar for horizontal style or the bottom of the scroll bar for vertical style.

Specifies the minimum value the scroll bar represents when the bubble reaches the left end of the scroll bar for horizontal style or the top of the scroll bar for vertical style.

Specifies the relative width of the scroll bar's bubble. The actual width appearing on the screen is determined by the maximum value and the value of `visibleAmount`.

Represents the current value of the scroll bar.

Specifies value added (subtracted) when the user activates the block-increment (decrement) area of the scroll bar, as shown in Figure 16.26.

Specifies the value added (subtracted) when the user activates the unit-increment (decrement) area of the scroll bar, as shown in Figure 16.26.

Creates a default vertical scroll bar.

Creates a scroll bar with the specified orientation.

Creates a scroll bar with the specified orientation, value, extent, minimum, and maximum.

FIGURE 16.27 `JScrollBar` enables you to select from a range of values.

When the user changes the value of the scroll bar, the scroll bar generates an instance of `AdjustmentEvent`, which is passed to every registered listener. An object that wishes to be notified of changes to the scroll bar's value must implement the `adjustmentValueChanged` method in the `AdjustmentListener` interface defined in the package `java.awt.event`.

Listing 16.10 gives a program that uses horizontal and vertical scroll bars to control a message displayed on a panel. The horizontal scroll bar is used to move the message to the left or the right, and the vertical scroll bar to move it up and down. A sample run of the program is shown in Figure 16.28.

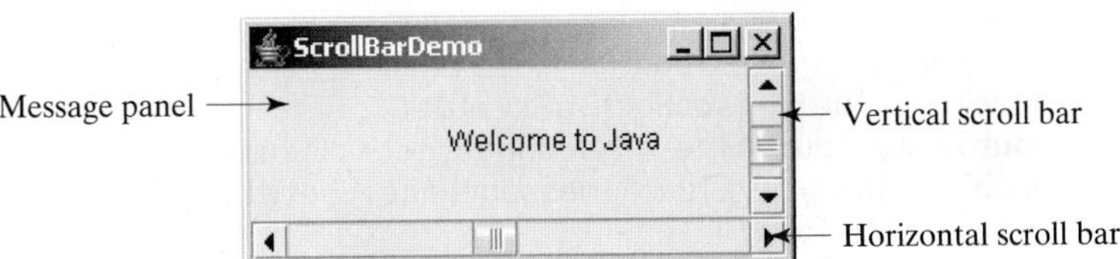

FIGURE 16.28 The scroll bars move the message on a panel horizontally and vertically.

Here are the major steps in the program:

1. Create the user interface.
   Create a `MessagePanel` object and place it in the center of the frame. Create a vertical scroll bar and place it in the east of the frame. Create a horizontal scroll bar and place it in the south of the frame.

2. Process the event.
   Create a listener to implement the `adjustmentValueChanged` handler to move the message according to the bar movement in the scroll bars.

LISTING 16.10 ScrollBarDemo.java

```
import java.awt.*;
import java.awt.event.*;
import javax.swing.*;

public class ScrollBarDemo extends JFrame {
  // Create horizontal and vertical scroll bars
  private JScrollBar jscbHort =
    new JScrollBar(JScrollBar.HORIZONTAL);
  private JScrollBar jscbVert =
    new JScrollBar(JScrollBar.VERTICAL);

  // Create a MessagePanel
  private MessagePanel messagePanel =
    new MessagePanel("Welcome to Java");

  public static void main(String[] args) {
    ScrollBarDemo frame = new ScrollBarDemo();
    frame.setTitle("ScrollBarDemo");
    frame.setLocationRelativeTo(null); // Center the frame
    frame.setDefaultCloseOperation(JFrame.EXIT_ON_CLOSE);
    frame.pack();
```

horizontal scroll bar

vertical scroll bar

create frame

create UI

add scroll bar

adjustment listener

adjustment listener

```
22     frame.setVisible(true);
23   }
24
25   public ScrollBarDemo() {
26     // Add scroll bars and message panel to the frame
27     setLayout(new BorderLayout());
28     add(messagePanel, BorderLayout.CENTER);
29     add(jscbVert, BorderLayout.EAST);
30     add(jscbHort, BorderLayout.SOUTH);
31
32     // Register listener for the scroll bars
33     jscbHort.addAdjustmentListener(new AdjustmentListener() {
34       public void adjustmentValueChanged(AdjustmentEvent e) {
35         // getValue() and getMaximumValue() return int, but for better
36         // precision, use double
37         double value = jscbHort.getValue();
38         double maximumValue = jscbHort.getMaximum();
39         double newX = (value * messagePanel.getWidth() /
40           maximumValue);
41         messagePanel.setXCoordinate((int)newX);
42       }
43     });
44     jscbVert.addAdjustmentListener(new AdjustmentListener() {
45       public void adjustmentValueChanged(AdjustmentEvent e) {
46         // getValue() and getMaximumValue() return int, but for better
47         // precision, use double
48         double value = jscbVert.getValue();
49         double maximumValue = jscbVert.getMaximum();
50         double newY = (value * messagePanel.getHeight() /
51           maximumValue);
52         messagePanel.setYCoordinate((int)newY);
53       }
54     });
55   }
56 }
```

The program creates two scroll bars (`jscbVert` and `jscbHort`) (lines 7–10) and an instance of `MessagePanel` (`messagePanel`) (lines 13–14). `messagePanel` is placed in the center of the frame; `jscbVert` and `jscbHort` are placed in the east and south sections of the frame (lines 29–30), respectively.

You can specify the orientation of the scroll bar in the constructor or use the `setOrientation` method. By default, the property value is `100` for `maximum`, `0` for `minimum`, `10` for `blockIncrement`, and `10` for `visibleAmount`.

When the user drags the bubble, or clicks the increment or decrement unit, the value of the scroll bar changes. An instance of `AdjustmentEvent` is generated and passed to the listener by invoking the `adjustmentValueChanged` handler. The listener for the vertical scroll bar moves the message up and down (lines 33–43), and the listener for the horizontal bar moves the message to right and left (lines 44–54).

The maximum value of the vertical scroll bar corresponds to the height of the panel, and the maximum value of the horizontal scroll bar corresponds to the width of the panel. The ratio between the current and maximum values of the horizontal scroll bar is the same as the ratio between the `x` value and the width of the message panel. Similarly, the ratio between the current and maximum values of the vertical scroll bar is the same as the ratio between the `y` value and the height of the message panel. The `x`-coordinate and `y`-coordinate are set in response to the scroll bar adjustments (lines 39, 49).

16.11 Sliders

`JSlider` is similar to `JScrollBar`, but `JSlider` has more properties and can appear in many forms. Figure 16.29 shows two sliders.

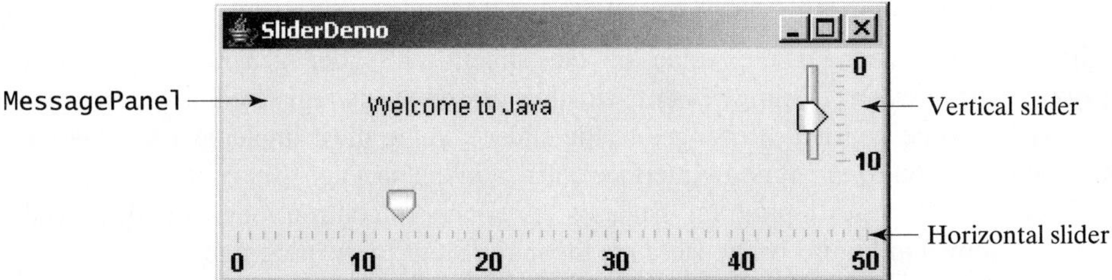

FIGURE 16.29 The sliders move the message on a panel horizontally and vertically.

`JSlider` lets the user graphically select a value by sliding a knob within a bounded interval. The slider can show both major tick marks and minor tick marks between them. The number of pixels between the tick marks is controlled by the `majorTickSpacing` and `minorTickSpacing` properties. Sliders can be displayed horizontally or vertically, with or without ticks, and with or without labels. The frequently used constructors and properties in `JSlider` are shown in Figure 16.30.

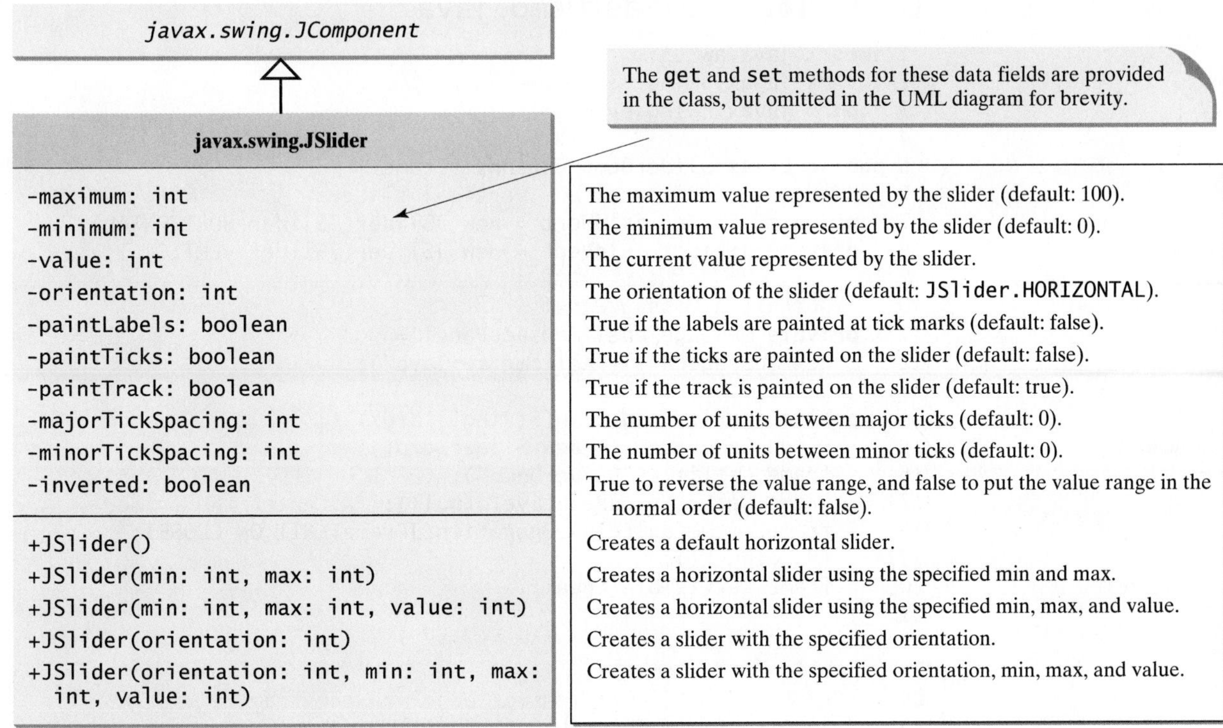

FIGURE 16.30 `JSlider` enables you to select from a range of values.

Note

The values of a vertical scroll bar increase from top to bottom, but the values of a vertical slider decrease from top to bottom.

Note

By convention, the **get** method for a Boolean property is named *is<PropertyName>()*. In the **JSlider** class, the **get** methods for **paintLabels**, **paintTicks**, **paintTrack**, and **inverted** are **getPaintLabels()**, **getPaintTicks()**, **getPaintTrack()**, and **getInverted()**, which violate the naming convention.

When the user changes the value of the slider, the slider generates an instance of **javax.swing.event.ChangeEvent**, which is passed to any registered listeners. Any object that wishes to be notified of changes to the slider's value must implement **stateChanged** method in the **ChangeListener** interface defined in the package **javax.swing.event**.

Listing 16.11 writes a program that uses the sliders to control a message displayed on a panel, as shown in Figure 16.29. Here are the major steps in the program:

1. Create the user interface.
   Create a **MessagePanel** object and place it in the center of the frame. Create a vertical slider and place it in the east of the frame. Create a horizontal slider and place it in the south of the frame.

2. Process the event.
   Create a listener to implement the **stateChanged** handler in the **ChangeListener** interface to move the message according to the knot movement in the slider.

LISTING 16.11 SliderDemo.java

horizontal slider
vertical slider
create frame
create UI
slider properties

```
import java.awt.*;
import javax.swing.*;
import javax.swing.event.*;

public class SliderDemo extends JFrame {
  // Create horizontal and vertical sliders
  private JSlider jsldHort = new JSlider(JSlider.HORIZONTAL);
  private JSlider jsldVert = new JSlider(JSlider.VERTICAL);

  // Create a MessagePanel
  private MessagePanel messagePanel =
    new MessagePanel("Welcome to Java");

  public static void main(String[] args) {
    SliderDemo frame = new SliderDemo();
    frame.setTitle("SliderDemo");
    frame.setLocationRelativeTo(null); // Center the frame
    frame.setDefaultCloseOperation(JFrame.EXIT_ON_CLOSE);
    frame.pack();
    frame.setVisible(true);
  }

  public SliderDemo() {
    // Add sliders and message panel to the frame
    setLayout(new BorderLayout(5, 5));
    add(messagePanel, BorderLayout.CENTER);
    add(jsldVert, BorderLayout.EAST);
    add(jsldHort, BorderLayout.SOUTH);

    // Set properties for sliders
    jsldHort.setMaximum(50);
    jsldHort.setPaintLabels(true);
    jsldHort.setPaintTicks(true);
```

```
34      jsldHort.setMajorTickSpacing(10);
35      jsldHort.setMinorTickSpacing(1);
36      jsldHort.setPaintTrack(false);
37      jsldVert.setInverted(true);
38      jsldVert.setMaximum(10);
39      jsldVert.setPaintLabels(true);
40      jsldVert.setPaintTicks(true);
41      jsldVert.setMajorTickSpacing(10);
42      jsldVert.setMinorTickSpacing(1);
43
44      // Register listener for the sliders
45      jsldHort.addChangeListener(new ChangeListener() {
46        /** Handle scroll bar adjustment actions */
47        public void stateChanged(ChangeEvent e) {
48          // getValue() and getMaximumValue() return int, but for better
49          // precision, use double
50          double value = jsldHort.getValue();
51          double maximumValue = jsldHort.getMaximum();
52          double newX = (value * messagePanel.getWidth() /
53            maximumValue);
54          messagePanel.setXCoordinate((int)newX);
55        }
56      });
57      jsldVert.addChangeListener(new ChangeListener() {
58        /** Handle scroll bar adjustment actions */
59        public void stateChanged(ChangeEvent e) {
60          // getValue() and getMaximumValue() return int, but for better
61          // precision, use double
62          double value = jsldVert.getValue();
63          double maximumValue = jsldVert.getMaximum();
64          double newY = (value * messagePanel.getHeight() /
65            maximumValue);
66          messagePanel.setYCoordinate((int) newY);
67        }
68      });
69    }
70  }
```

listener

listener

`JSlider` is similar to `JScrollBar` but has more features. As shown in this example, you can specify maximum, labels, major ticks, and minor ticks on a `JSlider` (lines 31–35). You can also choose to hide the track (line 36). Since the values of a vertical slider decrease from top to bottom, the `setInverted` method reverses the order (line 37).

`JSlider` fires `ChangeEvent` when the slider is changed. The listener needs to implement the `stateChanged` handler in `ChangeListener` (lines 45–68). Note that `JScrollBar` fires `AdjustmentEvent` when the scroll bar is adjusted.

16.12 Creating Multiple Windows

Occasionally, you may want to create multiple windows in an application. The application opens a new window to perform a specified task. The new windows are called *subwindows,* and the main frame is called the *main window.*

To create a subwindow from an application, you need to create a subclass of `JFrame` that defines the task and tells the new window what to do. You can then create an instance of this subclass in the application and launch the new window by setting the frame instance to be visible.

Listing 16.12 gives a program that creates a main window with a text area in the scroll pane and a button named *Show Histogram.* When the user clicks the button, a new window appears that displays a histogram to show the occurrences of the letters in the text area. Figure 16.31 contains a sample run of the program.

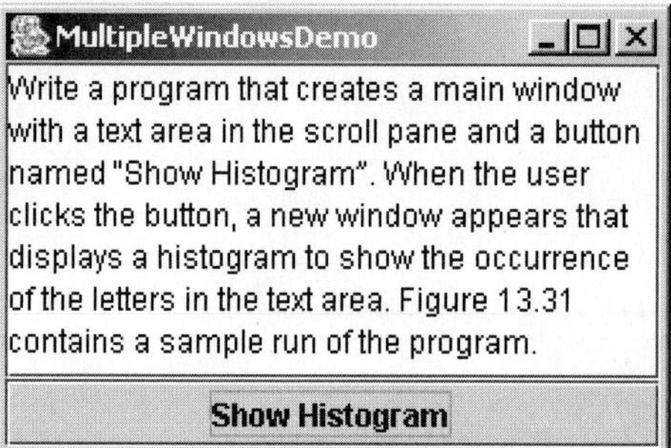

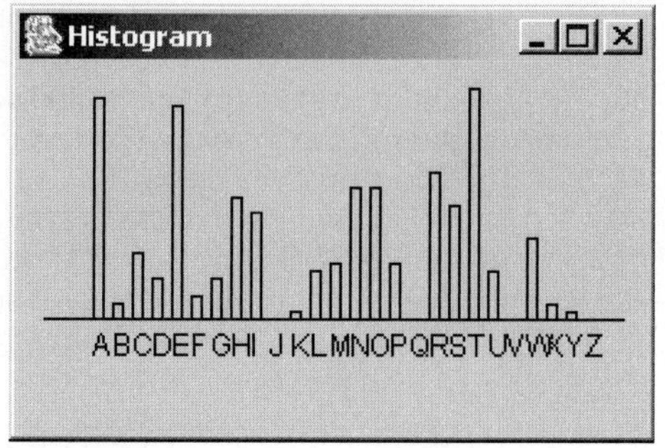

FIGURE 16.31 The histogram is displayed in a separate frame.

Here are the major steps in the program:

1. Create a main class for the frame named `MultipleWindowsDemo` in Listing 16.12. Add a text area inside a scroll pane, and place the scroll pane in the center of the frame. Create a button "Show Histogram" and place it in the south of the frame.
2. Create a subclass of `JPanel` named `Histogram` in Listing 16.13. The class contains a data field named `count` of the `int[]` type, which counts the occurrences of `26` letters. The values in `count` are displayed in the histogram.
3. Implement the `actionPerformed` handler in `MultipleWindowsDemo`, as follows:
   a. Create an instance of `Histogram`. Count the letters in the text area and pass the count to the `Histogram` object.
   b. Create a new frame and place the `Histogram` object in the center of frame. Display the frame.

LISTING 16.12 MultipleWindowsDemo.java

create subframe
create subframe
create UI

```
import java.awt.*;
import java.awt.event.*;
import javax.swing.*;

public class MultipleWindowsDemo extends JFrame {
  private JTextArea jta;
  private JButton jbtShowHistogram = new JButton("Show Histogram");
  private Histogram histogram = new Histogram();

  // Create a new frame to hold the histogram panel
  private JFrame histogramFrame = new JFrame();

  public MultipleWindowsDemo() {
    // Store text area in a scroll pane
    JScrollPane scrollPane = new JScrollPane(jta = new JTextArea());
    scrollPane.setPreferredSize(new Dimension(300, 200));
    jta.setWrapStyleWord(true);
    jta.setLineWrap(true);

    // Place scroll pane and button in the frame
    add(scrollPane, BorderLayout.CENTER);
    add(jbtShowHistogram, BorderLayout.SOUTH);

    // Register listener
    jbtShowHistogram.addActionListener(new ActionListener() {
      /** Handle the button action */
      public void actionPerformed(ActionEvent e) {
        // Count the letters in the text area
```

```
        int[] count = countLetters();

        // Set the letter count to histogram for display
        histogram.showHistogram(count);

        // Show the frame
        histogramFrame.setVisible(true);
      }
    });

    // Create a new frame to hold the histogram panel
    histogramFrame.add(histogram);
    histogramFrame.pack();
    histogramFrame.setTitle("Histogram");
  }

  /** Count the letters in the text area */
  private int[] countLetters() {
    // Count for 26 letters
    int[] count = new int[26];

    // Get contents from the text area
    String text = jta.getText();

    // Count occurrence of each letter (case insensitive)
    for (int i = 0; i < text.length(); i++) {
      char character = text.charAt(i);

      if ((character >= 'A') && (character <= 'Z')) {
        count[character - 'A']++;
      }
      else if ((character >= 'a') && (character <= 'z')) {
        count[character - 'a']++;
      }
    }

    return count; // Return the count array
  }

  public static void main(String[] args) {
    MultipleWindowsDemo frame = new MultipleWindowsDemo();
    frame.setLocationRelativeTo(null); // Center the frame
    frame.setDefaultCloseOperation(JFrame.EXIT_ON_CLOSE);
    frame.setTitle("MultipleWindowsDemo");
    frame.pack();
    frame.setVisible(true);
  }
}
```

display subframe

create main frame

LISTING 16.13 Histogram.java

```
import javax.swing.*;
import java.awt.*;

public class Histogram extends JPanel {
  // Count the occurrence of 26 letters
  private int[] count;

  /** Set the count and display histogram */
  public void showHistogram(int[] count) {
    this.count = count;
```

```
    repaint();
  }

  /** Paint the histogram */
```

paint histogram

```
  protected void paintComponent(Graphics g) {
    if (count == null) return; // No display if count is null

    super.paintComponent(g);

    // Find the panel size and bar width and interval dynamically
    int width = getWidth();
    int height = getHeight();
    int interval = (width - 40) / count.length;
    int individualWidth = (int)(((width - 40) / 24) * 0.60);

    // Find the maximum count. The maximum count has the highest bar
    int maxCount = 0;
    for (int i = 0; i < count.length; i++) {
      if (maxCount < count[i])
        maxCount = count[i];
    }

    // x is the start position for the first bar in the histogram
    int x = 30;

    // Draw a horizontal base line
    g.drawLine(10, height - 45, width - 10, height - 45);
    for (int i = 0; i < count.length; i++) {
      // Find the bar height
      int barHeight =
        (int)(((double)count[i] / (double)maxCount) * (height - 55));

      // Display a bar (i.e. rectangle)
      g.drawRect(x, height - 45 - barHeight, individualWidth,
        barHeight);

      // Display a letter under the base line
      g.drawString((char)(65 + i) + "", x, height - 30);

      // Move x for displaying the next character
      x += interval;
    }
  }

  /** Override getPreferredSize */
```

preferredSize

```
  public Dimension getPreferredSize() {
    return new Dimension(300, 300);
  }
}
```

The program contains two classes: `MultipleWindowsDemo` and `Histogram`. Their relationship is shown in Figure 16.32.

`MultipleWindowsDemo` is a frame that holds a text area in a scroll pane and a button. `Histogram` is a subclass of `JPanel` that displays a histogram for the occurrences of letters in the text area.

When the user clicks the *Show Histogram* button, the handler counts the occurrences of letters in the text area. Letters are counted regardless of their case. Nonletter characters are not counted. The count is stored in an `int` array of twenty-six elements. The first element stores the count for letter '*a*' or '*A*', and the last element in the array stores the count for letter '*z*' or

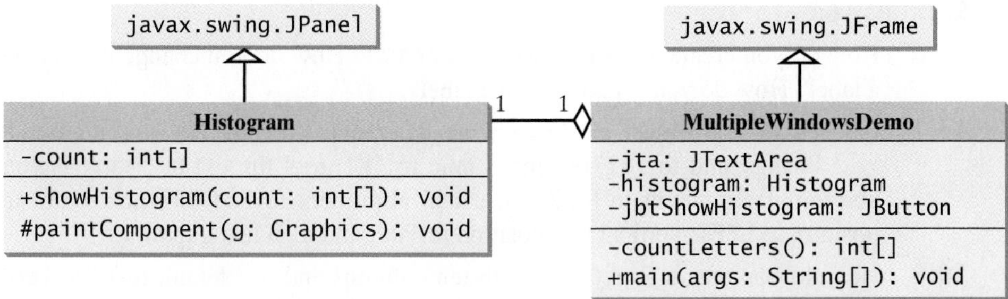

FIGURE 16.32 `MultipleWindowsDemo` uses `Histogram` to display a histogram of the occurrences of the letters in a text area in the frame.

'Z'. The `count` array is passed to the histogram for display. The `MultipleWindowsDemo` class contains a `main` method. The `main` method creates an instance of `MultipleWindowsDemo` and displays the frame. The `MultipleWindowsDemo` class also contains an instance of `JFrame`, named `histogramFrame`, which holds an instance of `Histogram`. When the user clicks the *Show Histogram* button, `histogramFrame` is set visible to display the histogram.

The height and width of the bars in the histogram are determined dynamically according to the window size of the histogram.

You cannot add an instance of `JFrame` to a container. For example, adding `histogramFrame` to the main frame would cause a runtime exception. However, you can create a frame instance and set it visible to launch a new window.

CHAPTER SUMMARY

- You learned how to create graphical user interfaces using Swing GUI components `JButton`, `JCheckBox`, `JRadioButton`, `JLabel`, `JTextField`, `JTextArea`, `JComboBox`, `JList`, `JScrollBar`, and `JSlider`. You also learned how to handle events on these components.

- You can display a text and icon on buttons (`JButton`, `JCheckBox`, `JRadioButton`) and labels `Jlabel`).

REVIEW QUESTIONS

Sections 16.2–16.4

16.1 How do you create a button labeled OK? How do you change text on a button? How do you set an icon, pressed icon, and rollover icon in a button?

16.2 Given a `JButton` object `jbtOK`, write statements to set the button's foreground to `red`, background to `yellow`, mnemonic to `'K'`, tool tip text to `"Click OK to proceed"`, horizontal alignment to `RIGHT`, vertical alignment to `BOTTOM`, horizontal text position to `LEFT`, vertical text position to `TOP`, and icon text gap to 5.

16.3 How do you create a check box? How do you create a check box with the box checked initially? How do you determine whether a check box is selected?

16.4 What is wrong if the statement `super.actionPerformed(e)` in Listing 16.3, `CheckBoxDemo.java`, is omitted?

16.5 How do you create a radio button? How do you create a radio button with the button selected initially? How do you group the radio buttons together? How do you determine whether a radio button is selected?

Sections 16.5–16.9

16.6 How do you create a label named `"Address"`? How do you change the name on a label? How do you set an icon in a label?

16.7 Given a `JLabel` object `jlblMap`, write statements to set the label's foreground to `red`, background to `yellow`, mnemonic to `'K'`, tool tip text to `"Map image"`, horizontal alignment to `RIGHT`, vertical alignment to `BOTTOM`, horizontal text position to `LEFT`, vertical text position to `TOP`, and icon text gap to `5`.

16.8 How do you create a text field with ten columns and the default text `"Welcome to Java"`? How do you write the code to check whether a text field is empty?

16.9 How do you create a text area with 10 rows and `20` columns? How do you insert three lines into the text area? How do you create a scrollable text area?

16.10 How do you create a combo box, add three items to it, and retrieve a selected item?

16.11 How do you create a list with an array of strings?

Sections 16.10–16.12

16.12 How do you create a horizontal scroll bar? What event can a scroll bar generate?

16.13 How do you create a vertical slider? What event can a slider generate?

16.14 Explain how to create and show multiple frames in an application.

Programming Exercises

Pedagogical Note

additional exercises

Instructors may assign txercises 17.5–17.27 from the next chapter as exercises for this chapter. Instead of writing Java applets, ask students to write Java applications.

Sections 16.2–16.5

16.1* (*Revising Listing 16.2,* `ButtonDemo.java`) Rewrite Listing 16.2 to add a group of radio buttons to select background colors. The available colors are red, yellow, white, gray, and green (see Figure 16.33).

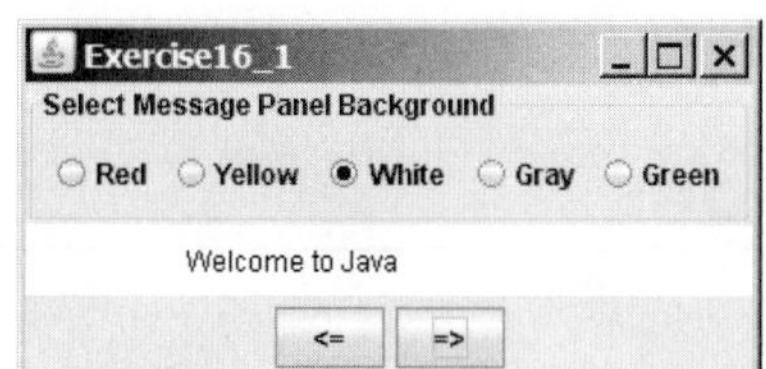

Figure 16.33 The <= and => buttons move the message on the panel, and you can also set the background color for the message.

16.2* (*Selecting geometric figures*) Write a program that draws various figures, as shown in Figure 16.34. The user selects a figure from a radio button and specifies

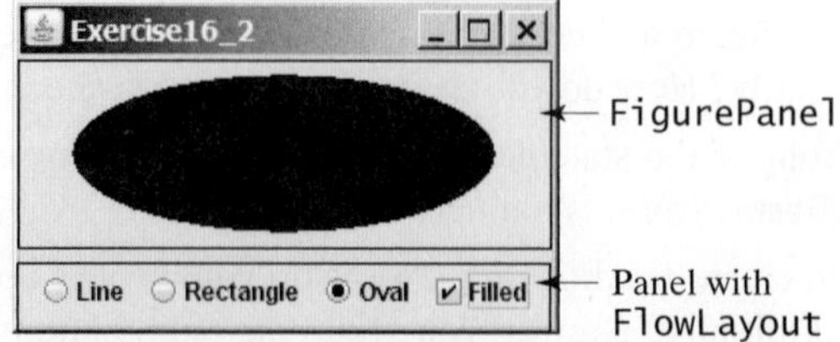

Figure 16.34 The program displays lines, rectangles, and ovals when you select a shape type.

whether it is filled in a check box. (*Hint*: Use the `FigurePanel` class introduced in §14.7 to display a figure.)

16.3** (*Traffic lights*) Write a program that simulates a traffic light. The program lets the user select one of three lights: red, yellow, or green. When a radio button is selected, the light is turned on, and only one light can be on at a time (see Figure 16.35). No light is on when the program starts.

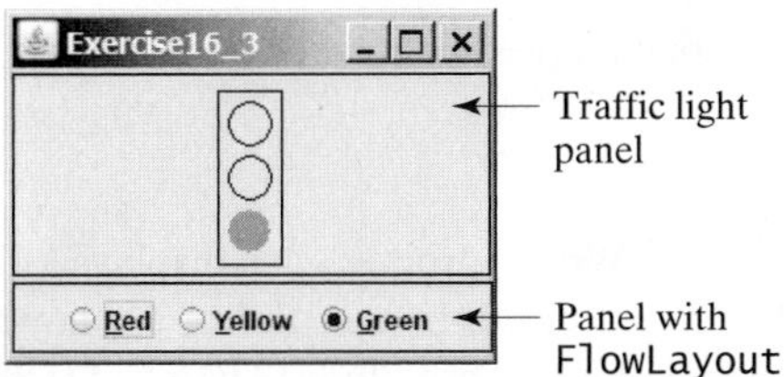

FIGURE 16.35 The radio buttons are grouped to let you select only one color in the group to control a traffic light.

Sections 16.6–16.10

16.4* (*Creating a simple calculator*) Write a program to perform add, subtract, multiply, and divide operations (see Figure 16.36).

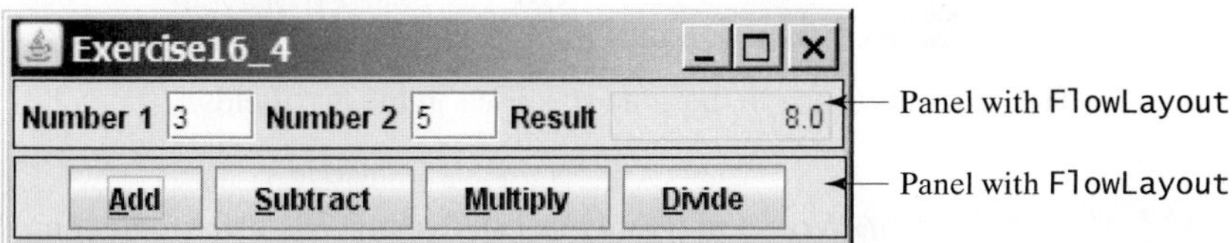

FIGURE 16.36 The program performs addition, subtraction, multiplication, and division on double numbers.

16.5* (*Creating a miles/kilometers converter*) Write a program that converts miles and kilometers, as shown in Figure 16.37. If you enter a value in the Mile text field and press the *Enter* key, the corresponding kilometer is displayed in the Kilometer text field. Likewise, if you enter a value in the Kilometer text field and press the *Enter* key, the corresponding mile is displayed in the Mile text field.

FIGURE 16.37 The program converts miles to kilometers, and vice versa.

16.6* (*Creating an investment value calculator*) Write a program that calculates the future value of an investment at a given interest rate for a specified number of years. The formula for the calculation is as follows:

```
futureValue = investmentAmount * (1 + monthlyInterestRate)^(years*12)
```

Use text fields for interest rate, investment amount, and years. Display the future amount in a text field when the user clicks the *Calculate* button, as shown in Figure 16.38.

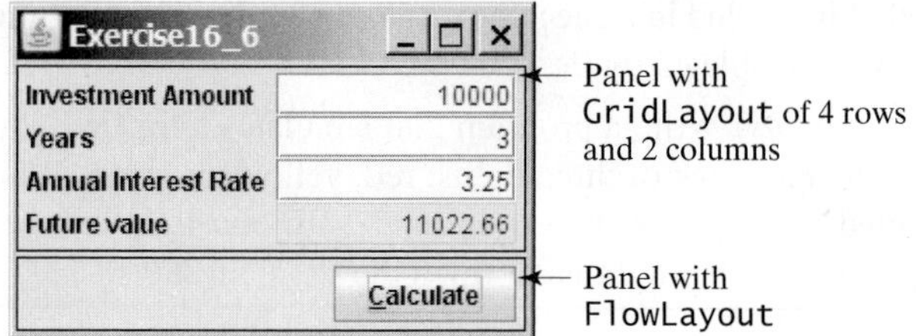

FIGURE 16.38 The user enters the investment amount, years, and interest rate to compute future value.

16.7* (*Setting clock time*) Write a program that displays a clock time and sets the clock time with the input from three text fields, as shown in Figure 16.39. Use the `StillClock` in §14.12, "Case Study: The `StillClock` Class."

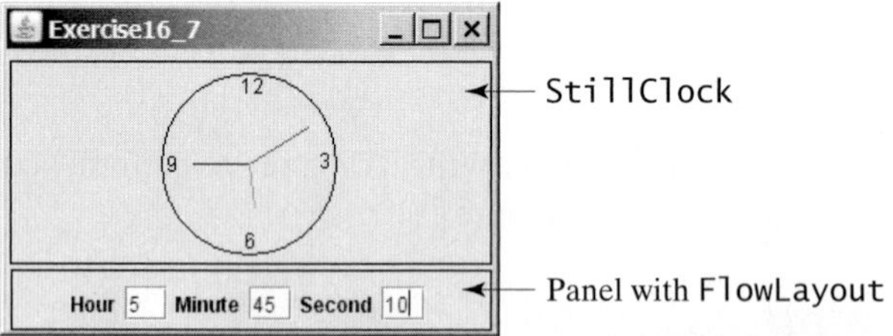

FIGURE 16.39 The program displays the time specified in the text fields.

16.8** (*Selecting a font*) Write a program that can dynamically change the font of a message to be displayed on a panel. The message can be displayed in bold and italic at the same time, or can be displayed in the center of the panel. You can select the font name or font size from combo boxes, as shown in Figure 16.40. The available font names can be obtained using `getAvailableFontFamilyNames()` in `GraphicsEnvironment` (§13.7, "The `Font` Class"). The combo box for font size is initialized with numbers from `1` to `100`.

FIGURE 16.40 You can dynamically set the font for the message.

16.9** (*Demonstrating `JLabel` properties*) Write a program to let the user dynamically set the properties `horizontalAlignment`, `verticalAlignment`, `horizontalTextAlignment`, and `verticalTextAlignment`, as shown in Figure 16.41.

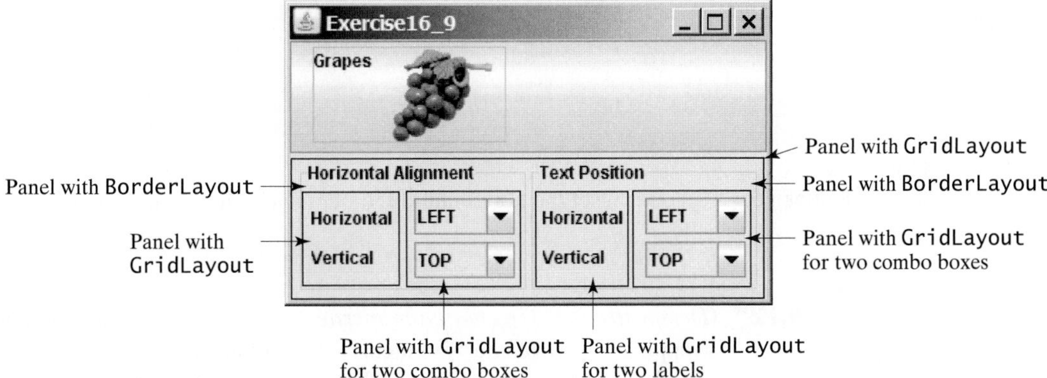

FIGURE 16.41 You can set the alignment and text-position properties of a button dynamically.

16.10* (*Adding new features into Listing 16.2, `ButtonDemo.java` incrementally*) Improve Listing 16.2 incrementally, as follows (see Figure 16.42):

1. Add a text field labeled `"Enter a new message"` in the same panel with the buttons. Upon typing a new message `in` the text field and pressing the Enter key, the new message is displayed in the message panel.
2. Add a combo box labeled `"Select an interval"` in the same panel with the buttons. The combo box enables the user to select a new interval for moving the message. The selection values range from `5` to `100` with interval `5`. The user can also type a new interval in the combo box.
3. Add three radio buttons that enable the user to select the foreground color for the message as `Red`, `Green`, and `Blue`. The radio buttons are grouped in a panel, and the panel is placed in the north of the frame's content pane.
4. Add three check boxes that enable the user to center the message and display it in italic or bold. Place the check boxes in the same panel with the radio buttons.
5. Add a border titled `"Message Panel"` on the message panel, add a border titled `"South Panel"` on the panel for buttons, and add a border titled `"North Panel"` on the panel for radio buttons and check boxes.

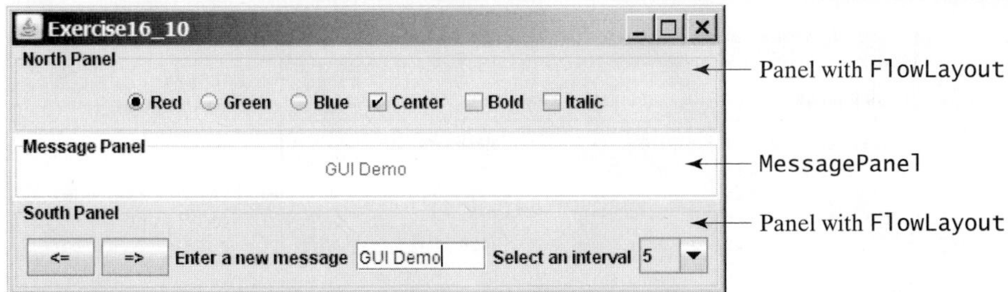

FIGURE 16.42 The program uses buttons, labels, text fields, combo boxes, radio buttons, check boxes, and borders.

16.11* (*Demonstrating `JTextField` properties*) Write a program that sets the horizontal-alignment and column-size properties of a text field dynamically, as shown in Figure 16.43.

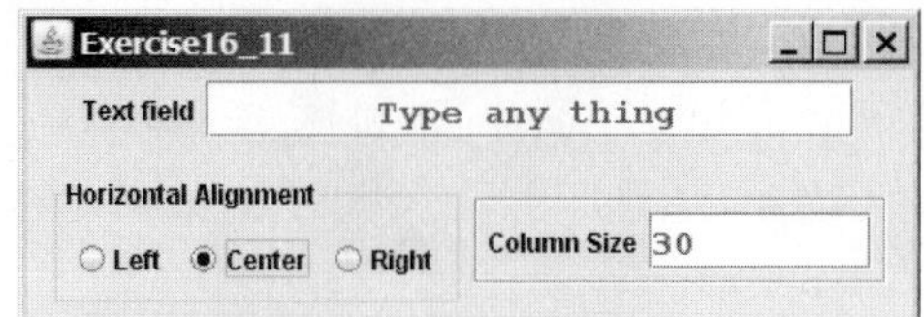

FIGURE 16.43 You can set the horizontal-alignment and column-size properties of a text field dynamically.

Video Note
Use text areas

16.12* (*Demonstrating `JTextArea` properties*) Write a program that demonstrates the wrapping styles of the text area. The program uses a check box to indicate whether the text area is wrapped. In the case where the text area is wrapped, you need to specify whether it is wrapped by characters or by words, as shown in Figure 16.44.

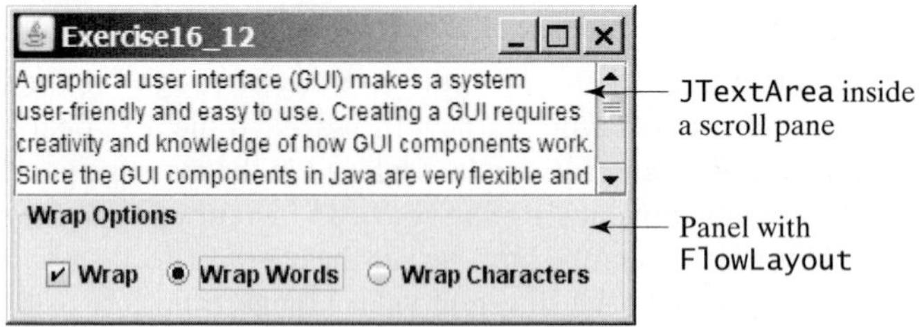

FIGURE 16.44 You can set the options to wrap a text area by characters or by words dynamically.

16.13* (*Comparing loans with various interest rates*) Rewrite Exercise 4.21 to create a user interface, as shown in Figure 16.45. Your program should let the user enter the loan amount and loan period in number of years from a text field, and should display the monthly and total payments for each interest rate starting from 5 percent to 8 percent, with increments of one-eighth, in a text area.

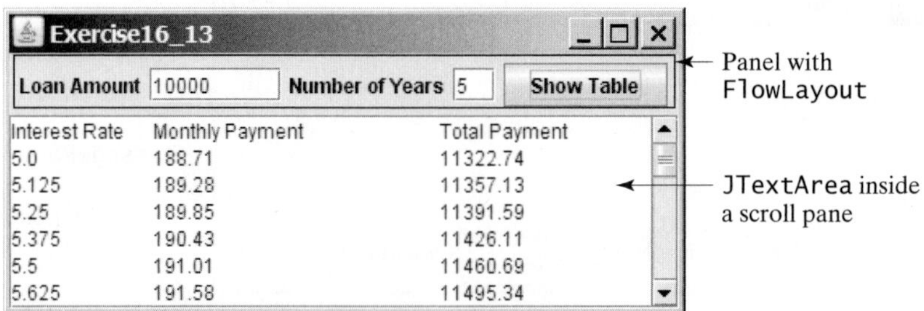

FIGURE 16.45 The program displays a table for monthly payments and total payments on a given loan based on various interest rates.

16.14* (*Using `JComboBox` and `JList`*) Write a program that demonstrates selecting items in a list. The program uses a combo box to specify a selection mode, as shown in Figure 16.46. When you select items, they are displayed in a label below the list.

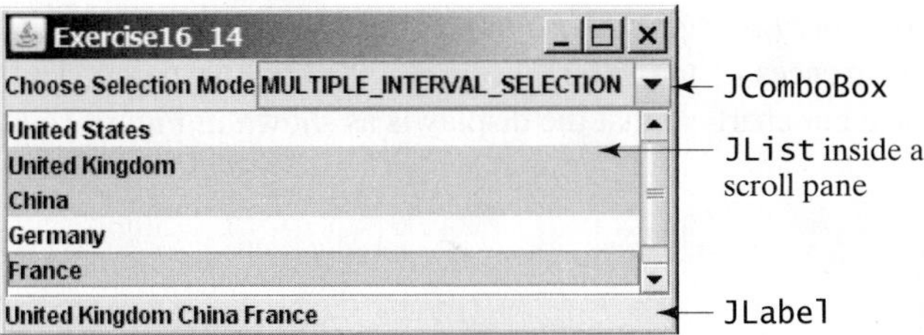

FIGURE 16.46 You can choose single selection, single-interval selection, or multiple-interval selection in a list.

Sections 16.11–16.13

16.15** (*Using `JScrollBar`*) Write a program that uses scroll bars to select the foreground color for a label, as shown in Figure 16.47. Three horizontal scroll bars are used for selecting the red, green, and blue components of the color. Use a title border on the panel that holds the scroll bars.

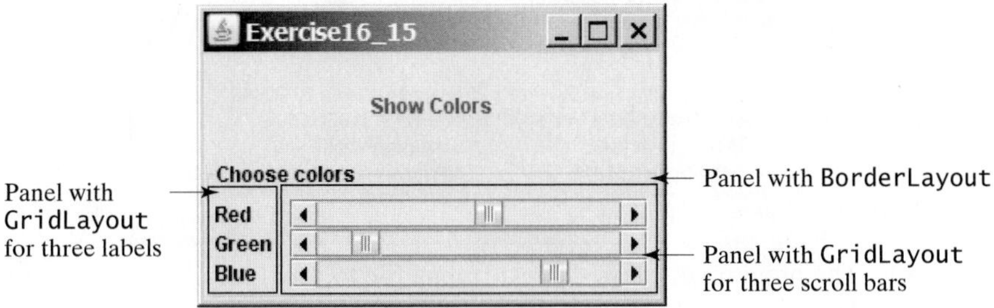

FIGURE 16.47 The foreground color changes in the label as you adjust the scroll bars.

16.16** (Using `JSlider`) Revise the preceding exercise using sliders.

16.17***(*Displaying a calendar*) Write a program that displays the calendar for the current month, as shown in Figure 16.48. Use labels, and set texts on the labels to display the calendar. Use the `GregorianCalendar` class in §11.3, "Example: `Calendar` and `GregorianCalendar`" to obtain the information about month, year, first day of the month, and number of days in the month.

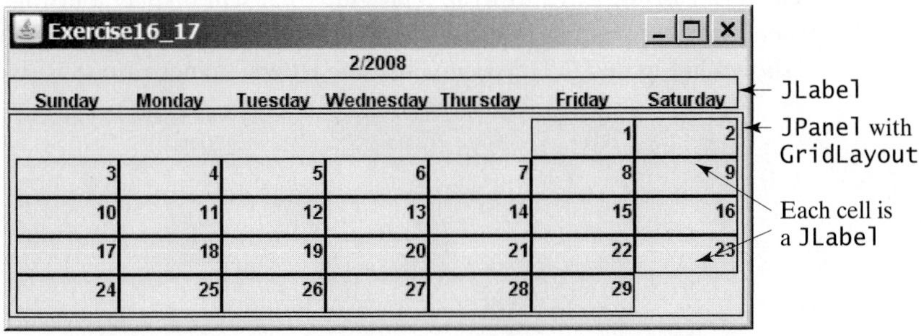

FIGURE 16.48 The program displays the calendar for the current month.

16.18* (*Revising Listing 16.12, MultipleWindowsDemo.java*) Instead of displaying the occurrences of the letters using the `Histogram` component in Listing 16.13, use a bar chart, so that the display is as shown in Figure 16.49.

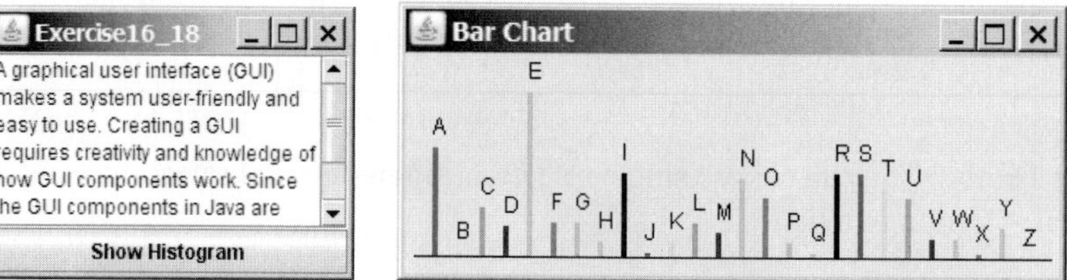

FIGURE 16.49 The number of occurrences of each letter is displayed in a bar chart.

The following exercises involing text I/O using Scanner

16.19** (*Text Viewer*) Write a program that displays a text file in a text area, as shown in Figure 16.50. The user enters a file name in a text field and clicks the *View* button; the file is then displayed in a text area.

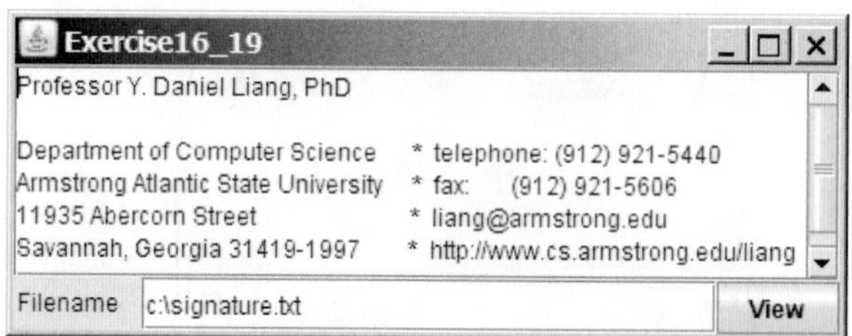

FIGURE 16.50 The program displays the text from a file to a text area.

16.20** (*Displaying country flag and flag description*) Listing 16.8, ComboBoxDemo.java, gives a program that lets users view a country's flag image and description by selecting the country from a combo box. The description is a string coded in the program. Rewrite the program to read the `text` description from a file. Suppose that the descriptions are stored in the file **description0.txt**, . . . , and **description8.txt** under the text directory for the nine countries Canada, China, Denmark, France, Germany, India, Norway, the United Kingdom, and the United States, in this order.

16.21** (*Creating a histogram for occurrences of letters*) In Listing 16.12, MultipleWindowsDemo.java, you developed a program that displays a histogram to show the occurrences of each letter in a text area. Reuse the `Histogram` class created in Listing 16.12 to write a program that will display a histogram on a panel. The histogram should show the occurrences of each letter in a text file, as shown in Figure 16.51. Assume that the letters are not case sensitive.

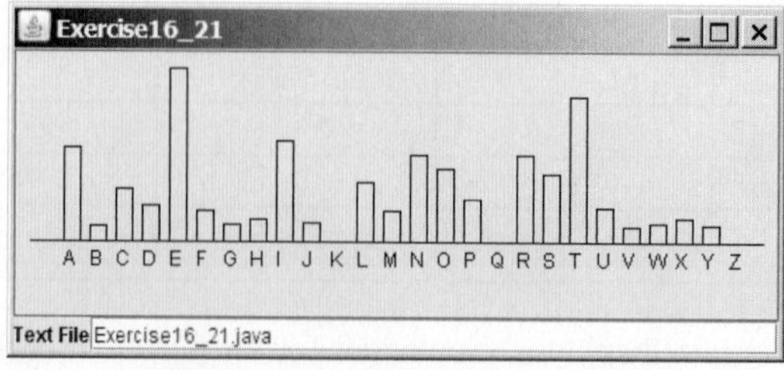

FIGURE 16.51 The program displays a histogram that shows the occurrences of each letter in the file.

- Place a panel that will display the histogram in the center of the frame.
- Place a label and a text field in a panel, and put the panel in the south side of the frame. The text file will be entered from this text field.
- Pressing the *Enter* key on the text field causes the program to count the occurrences of each letter and display the count in a histogram.

16.22** (*Slide show*) Exercise 15.13 developed slides show using images. Rewrite Exercise 15.13 to develop a slide show using text files. Suppose ten text files named `slide0.txt`, `slide1.txt`, ..., and `slide9.txt` are stored in the `text` directory. Each slide displays the text from one file. Each slide is shown for a second. The slides are displayed in order. When the last slide finishes, the first slide is redisplayed, and so on. Use a text area to display the slide.

CHAPTER 17

APPLETS AND MULTIMEDIA

Objectives

- To explain how the Web browser controls and executes applets (§17.2).
- To describe the `init`, `start`, `stop`, and `destroy` methods in the `Applet` class (§§17.2.1–17.2.4).
- To develop Swing applets using the `JApplet` class (§17.3).
- To embed applets in Web pages (§17.4).
- To run applets from the appletviewer and from Web browsers (§§17.4.1–17.4.2).
- To write a Java program that can run as both an application and an applet (§17.5).
- To pass string values to applets from HTML (§17.6).
- To locate resources (images and audio) using the `URL` class (§17.9).
- To play audio in any Java program (§17.10).

17.1 Introduction

When browsing the Web, often the graphical user interface and animation you see are developed by the use of Java. The programs used are called Java applets. Suppose you want to develop a Java applet for the Sudoku game, as shown in Figure 17.1. How do you write this program?

In this chapter, you will learn how to write Java applets, explore the relationship between applets and the Web browser, and discover the similarities and differences between applications and applets. You will also learn how to create multimedia Java applications and applets with images and audio.

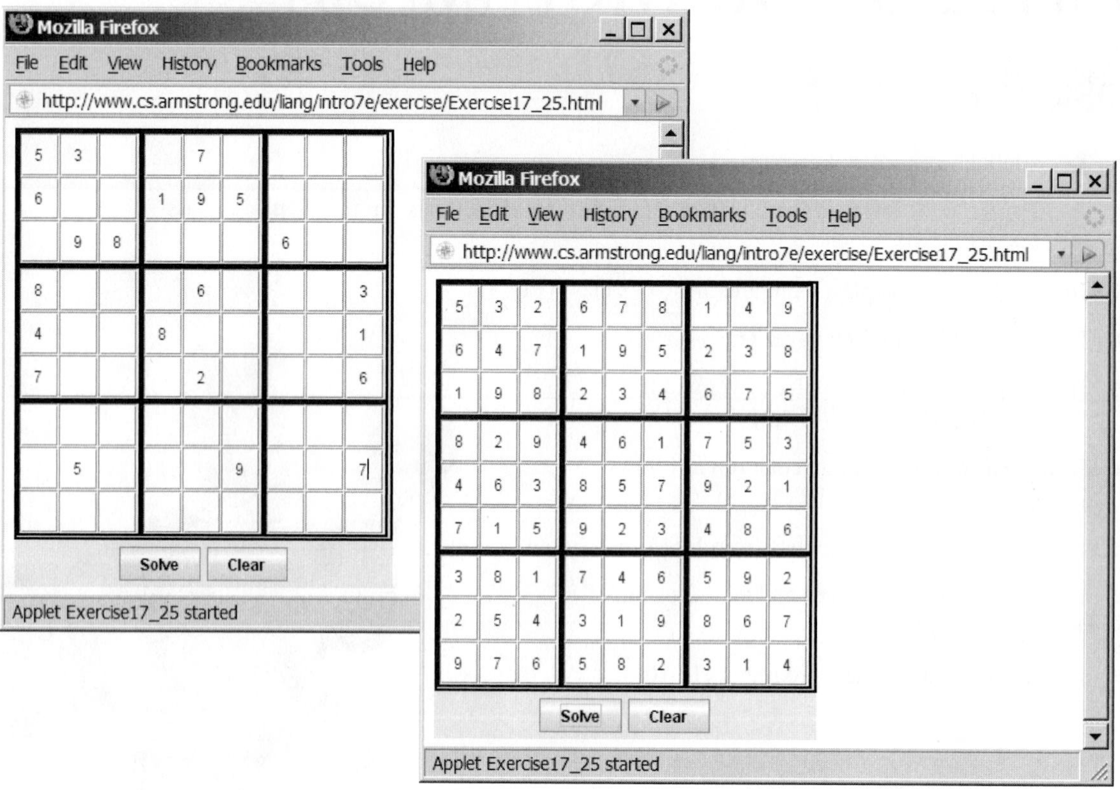

FIGURE 17.1 The Sudoku game is displayed in a Web browser.

17.2 The **Applet** Class

So far, you have used only Java applications. Everything you have learned about writing applications, however, applies also to writing applets. Applications and applets share many common programming features, although they differ slightly in some respects. For example, every application must have a `main` method, which is invoked by the Java interpreter. Java applets, on the other hand, do not need a `main` method. They run in the Web browser environment. Because applets are invoked from a Web page, Java provides special features that enable applets to run from a Web browser.

The `Applet` class provides the essential framework that enables applets to be run from a Web browser. While every Java application has a `main` method that is executed when the application starts, applets do not have a `main` method. Instead they depend on the browser to call the methods in the `Applet` class. Every applet is a subclass of `java.applet.Applet`, as outlined below:

subclass of **Applet**

```
public class MyApplet extends java.applet.Applet {
  ...
  /** The no-arg constructor is called by the browser when the Web
   * page containing this applet is initially loaded, or reloaded
```

```
   */
  public MyApplet() {
    ...
  }

  /** Called by the browser after the applet is loaded
   */
  public void init() {
    ...
  }

  /** Called by the browser after the init() method, or
   *  every time the Web page is visited
   */
  public void start() {
    ...
  }

  /** Called by the browser when the page containing this
   *  applet becomes inactive
   */
  public void stop() {
    ...
  }

  /** Called by the browser when the Web browser exits */
  public void destroy() {
    ...
  }

  /** Other methods if necessary... */
}
```

no-arg constructor required

When the applet is loaded, the Web browser creates an instance of the applet by invoking the applet's no-arg constructor. So the applet must have a no-arg constructor declared either explicitly or implicitly. The browser uses the `init`, `start`, `stop`, and `destroy` methods to control the applet. By default, these methods do nothing. To perform specific functions, they need to be modified in the user's applet so that the browser can call the code properly. Figure 17.2(a) shows how the browser calls these methods, and Figure 17.2(b) illustrates the flow of control of an applet using a statechart diagram.

no-arg constructor

17.2.1 The `init` Method

`init()`

The `init` method is invoked after the applet is created. If a subclass of `Applet` has an initialization to perform, it should override this method. The functions usually implemented in this method include setting up user-interface components, loading resources such as images and audio, and getting string parameter values from the `<applet>` tag in the HTML page.

17.2.2 The `start` Method

`start()`

The `start` method is invoked after the `init` method. It is also called when the user returns to the Web page containing the applet after surfing other pages.

A subclass of `Applet` overrides this method if it has any operation that needs to be performed whenever the Web page containing the applet is visited. An applet with animation, for example, might start the timer to resume animation.

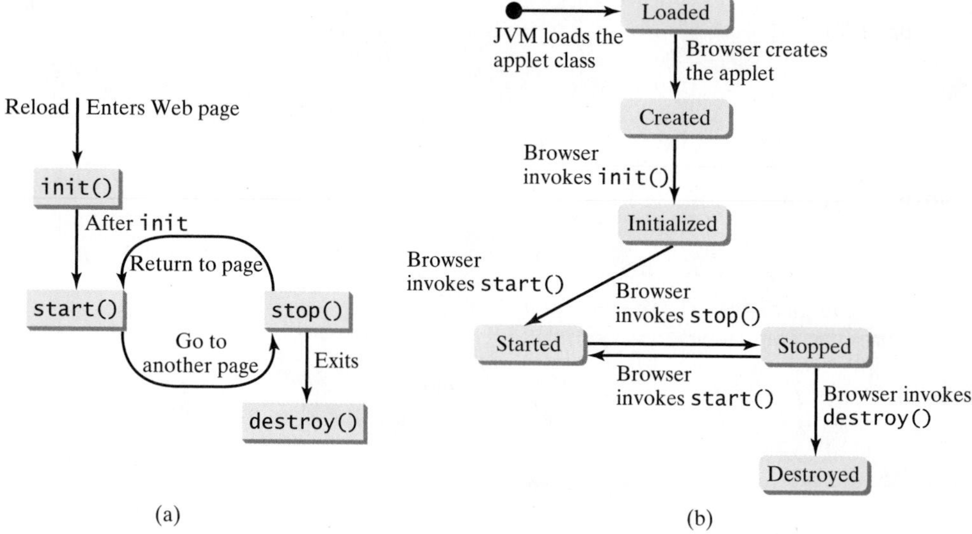

FIGURE 17.2 The Web browser uses the **init**, **start**, **stop**, and **destroy** methods to control the applet.

17.2.3 The stop Method

stop()

The **stop** method is the opposite of the **start** method. The **start** method is called when the user moves back to the page that contains the applet. The **stop** method is invoked when the user leaves the page.

A subclass of **Applet** overrides this method if it has any operation to be performed each time the Web page containing the applet is no longer visible. An applet with animation, for example, might stop the timer to pause animation.

17.2.4 The destroy Method

destroy()

The **destroy** method is invoked when the browser exits normally to inform the applet that it is no longer needed and should release any resources it has allocated. The **stop** method is always called before the **destroy** method.

A subclass of **Applet** overrides this method if it has any operation to be performed before it is destroyed. Usually, you won't need to override this method unless you wish to release specific resources that the applet created.

17.3 The JApplet Class

The **Applet** class is an AWT class and is not designed to work with Swing components. To use Swing components in Java applets, you need to create a Java applet that extends **javax.swing.JApplet**, which is a subclass of **java.applet.Applet**. **JApplet** inherits all the methods from the **Applet** class. In addition, it provides support for laying out Swing components.

To add a component to an applet, you add it to the applet's content pane, which is similar to adding a component to the content pane of a frame. By default, the content pane of **JApplet** uses **BorderLayout**. Here is an example of a simple applet that uses **JLabel** to display a message.

Video Note
First applet

```
// WelcomeApplet.java: Applet for displaying a message
import javax.swing.*;

public class WelcomeApplet extends JApplet {
  /** Initialize the applet */
```

```
  public void init() {
    add (new JLabel("Welcome to Java", JLabel.CENTER));
  }
}
```

add a label in applet

Note

The content pane delegation feature in JDK 1.5 allows you to invoke the **add** method from an applet to add components to the content pane of an applet. Strictly speaking, a component is added to an applet's content pane, but for simplicity we say that a component is added to an applet.

content pane delegation

You cannot run this applet standalone, because it does not have a **main** method. You have to create an HTML file with the applet tag that references the applet. When you write Java GUI applications, you must create a frame to hold graphical components, set the frame size, and make the frame visible. Applets are run from the Web browser. The Web browser automatically places the applet inside the frame and makes it visible. The following section shows how to create HTML files for applets.

Note

You may rewrite the **WelcomeApplet** by moving the code in the **init** method to the no-arg constructor, as follows:

alternative coding

```
// WelcomeApplet.java: Applet for displaying a message
import javax.swing.*;

public class WelcomeApplet extends JApplet {
  /** Construct the applet */
  public WelcomeApplet() {
    add(new JLabel("Welcome to Java", JLabel.CENTER));
  }
}
```

17.4 The HTML File and the <applet> Tag

HTML is a markup language that presents static documents on the Web. It uses tags to instruct the Web browser how to render a Web page and contains a tag called **<applet>** that incorporates applets into a Web page.

The following HTML file named WelcomeApplet.html invokes the **WelcomeApplet.class**:

```
<html>
  <head>
    <title>Welcome Java Applet</title>
  </head>
  <body>
    <applet
      code = "WelcomeApplet.class"
      width = 350
      height = 200>
    </applet>
  </body>
</html>
```

applet class

A *tag* is an instruction to the Web browser. The browser interprets the tag and decides how to display or otherwise treat the subsequent contents of the HTML document. Tags are enclosed inside brackets. The first word in a tag, called the *tag name*, describes tag functions. A tag can have additional attributes, sometimes with values after an equals sign, which further define the tag's action. For example, in the preceding HTML file, **<applet>** is the tag name, and **code**, **width**, and **height** are attributes. The **width** and **height** attributes specify the rectangular viewing area of the applet.

Most tags have a *start tag* and a corresponding *end tag*. The tag has a specific effect on the region between the start tag and the end tag. For example, `<applet...>...</applet>` tells the browser to display an applet. An end tag is always the start tag's name preceded by a slash.

HTML tag

An HTML document begins with the `<html>` tag, which declares that the document is written in HTML. Each document has two parts, a *head* and a *body*, defined by `<head>` and `<body>` tags, respectively. The head part contains the document title, including the `<title>` tag and other information the browser can use when rendering the document, and the body part contains the actual contents of the document. The header is optional. For more information, refer to Supplement V.A, "HTML and XHTML Tutorial."

<applet> tag

The complete syntax of the `<applet>` tag is as follows:

<param> tag

```
<applet
  [codebase = applet_url]
  code = classfilename.class
  width = applet_viewing_width_in_pixels
  height = applet_viewing_height_in_pixels
  [archive = archivefile]
  [vspace = vertical_margin]
  [hspace = horizontal_margin]
  [align = applet_alignment]
  [alt = alternative_text]
>
<param name = param_name1 value = param_value1>
<param name = param_name2 value = param_value2>
...
<param name = param_name3 value = param_value3>
</applet>
```

The `code`, `width`, and `height` attributes are required; all the others are optional. The `<param>` tag is introduced in §17.6, "Passing Strings to Applets." The other attributes are explained below.

codebase attribute

- **codebase** specifies a base where your classes are loaded. If this attribute is not used, the Web browser loads the applet from the directory in which the HTML page is located. If your applet is located in a different directory from the HTML page, you must specify the `applet_url` for the browser to load the applet. This attribute enables you to load the class from anywhere on the Internet. The classes used by the applet are dynamically loaded when needed.

archive attribute

- **archive** instructs the browser to load an archive file that contains all the class files needed to run the applet. Archiving allows the Web browser to load all the classes from a single compressed file at one time, thus reducing loading time and improving performance. To create archives, see Supplement III.Q, "Packaging and Deploying Java Projects."
- **vspace** and **hspace** specify the size, in pixels, of the blank margin to pad around the applet vertically and horizontally.
- **align** specifies how the applet will be aligned in the browser. One of nine values is used: `left`, `right`, `top`, `texttop`, `middle`, `absmiddle`, `baseline`, `bottom`, or `absbottom`.
- **alt** specifies the text to be displayed in case the browser cannot run Java.

17.4.1 Viewing Applets Using the Applet Viewer Utility

appletviewer

You can test the applet using the applet viewer utility, which can be invoked from the DOS prompt using the **appletviewer** command from **c:\book**, as shown in Figure 17.3(a). Its output is shown in Figure 17.3(b).

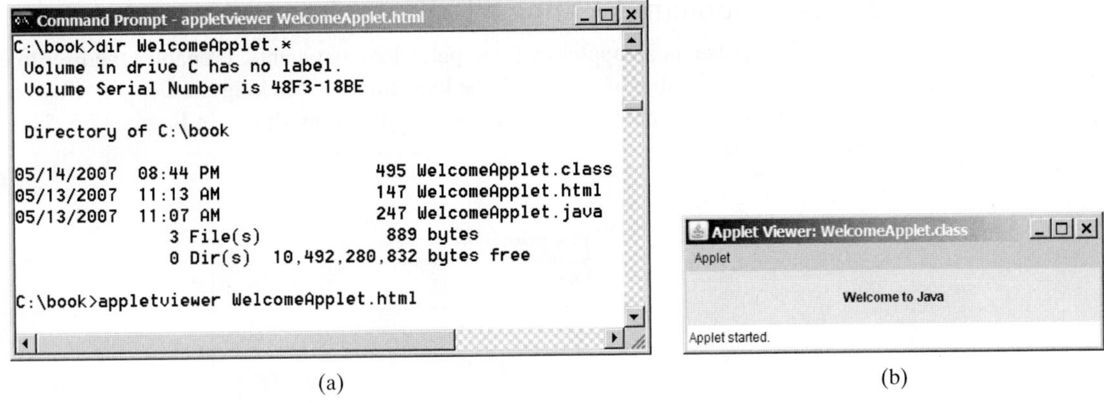

Figure 17.3 The appletviewer command runs a Java applet in the applet viewer utility.

17.4.2 Viewing Applets from a Web Browser

Applets are eventually displayed in a Web browser. Using the applet viewer, you do not need to start a Web browser. The applet viewer functions as a browser. It is convenient for testing applets during development. However, you should also test the applets from a Web browser before deploying them on a Web site. To display an applet from a Web browser, open the applet's HTML file (e.g., WelcomeApplet.html). Its output is shown in Figure 17.4.

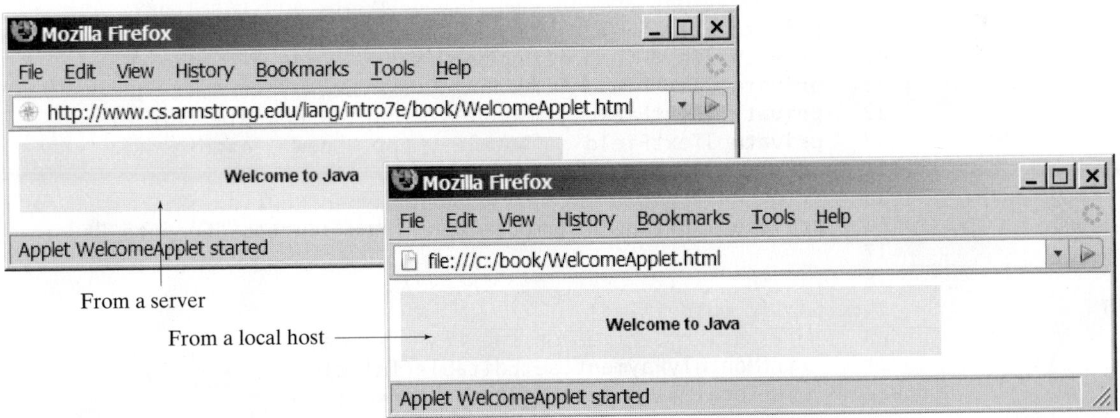

Figure 17.4 The WelcomeApplet program (from a Web server and from a local host) is displayed in a browser.

To make your applet accessible on the Web, you need to store the WelcomeApplet.class and WelcomeApplet.html on a Web server. You can view the applet from an appropriate URL. For example, I have uploaded these two files on Web server www.cs.armstrong.edu/. As shown in Figure 17.4, you can access the applet from www.cs.armstrong.edu/liang/intro7e/book/WelcomeApplet.html.

17.4.3 Problem: Creating a Loan Applet

This section presents an applet that computes loan payments. It enables the user to enter the interest rate, the number of years, and the loan amount. Clicking the *Compute Payment* button displays the monthly payment and the total payment, as shown in Figure 17.5. The applet is given in Listing 17.1.

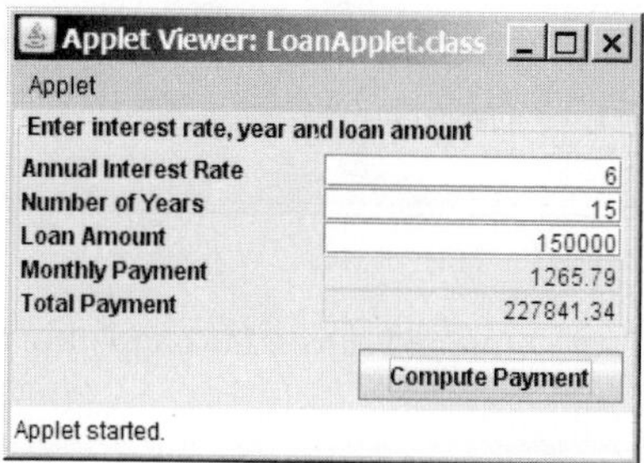

FIGURE 17.5 The applet computes the monthly payment and the total payment when provided with the interest rate, number of years, and loan amount.

LISTING 17.1 `LoanApplet.java`

create text fields

create a button

create UI

```
import java.awt.*;
import java.awt.event.*;
import javax.swing.*;
import javax.swing.border.TitledBorder;

public class LoanApplet extends JApplet {
  // Declare and create text fields for interest rate
  // year, loan amount, monthly payment, and total payment
  private JTextField jtfAnnualInterestRate = new JTextField();
  private JTextField jtfNumberOfYears = new JTextField();
  private JTextField jtfLoanAmount = new JTextField();
  private JTextField jtfMonthlyPayment = new JTextField();
  private JTextField jtfTotalPayment = new JTextField();

  // Declare and create a Compute Payment button
  private JButton jbtComputeLoan = new JButton("Compute Payment");

  /** Initialize user interface */
  public void init() {
    // Set properties on the text fields
    jtfMonthlyPayment.setEditable(false);
    jtfTotalPayment.setEditable(false);

    // Right align text fields
    jtfAnnualInterestRate.setHorizontalAlignment(JTextField.RIGHT);
    jtfNumberOfYears.setHorizontalAlignment(JTextField.RIGHT);
    jtfLoanAmount.setHorizontalAlignment(JTextField.RIGHT);
    jtfMonthlyPayment.setHorizontalAlignment(JTextField.RIGHT);
    jtfTotalPayment.setHorizontalAlignment(JTextField.RIGHT);

    // Panel p1 to hold labels and text fields
    JPanel p1 = new JPanel(new GridLayout(5, 2));
    p1.add(new JLabel("Annual Interest Rate"));
    p1.add(jtfAnnualInterestRate);
```

```
35     p1.add(new JLabel("Number of Years"));
36     p1.add(jtfNumberOfYears);
37     p1.add(new JLabel("Loan Amount"));
38     p1.add(jtfLoanAmount);
39     p1.add(new JLabel("Monthly Payment"));
40     p1.add(jtfMonthlyPayment);
41     p1.add(new JLabel("Total Payment"));
42     p1.add(jtfTotalPayment);
43     p1.setBorder(new
44       TitledBorder("Enter interest rate, year and loan amount"));
45
46     // Panel p2 to hold the button
47     JPanel p2 = new JPanel(new FlowLayout(FlowLayout.RIGHT));
48     p2.add(jbtComputeLoan);
49
50     // Add the components to the applet
51     add(p1, BorderLayout.CENTER);
52     add(p2, BorderLayout.SOUTH);
53
54     // Register listener
55     jbtComputeLoan.addActionListener(new ButtonListener());
56   }
57
58   /** Handle the Compute Payment button */
59   private class ButtonListener implements ActionListener {
60     public void actionPerformed(ActionEvent e) {
61       // Get values from text fields
62       double interest =
63         Double.parseDouble(jtfAnnualInterestRate.getText());
64       int year =
65         Integer.parseInt(jtfNumberOfYears.getText());
66       double loanAmount =
67         Double.parseDouble(jtfLoanAmount.getText());
68
69       // Create a loan object
70       Loan loan = new Loan(interest, year, loanAmount);
71
72       // Display monthly payment and total payment
73       jtfMonthlyPayment.setText(String.format("%.2f",
74         loan.getMonthlyPayment()));
75       jtfTotalPayment.setText(String.format("%.2f",
76         loan.getTotalPayment()));
77     }
78   }
79 }
```

titled border

add to applet

listener class

create Loan object

public applet

You need to use the **public** modifier (line 6) for the **LoanApplet**; otherwise, the Web browser cannot load it.

The **init** method initializes the user interface (lines 19–56). The program overrides this method to create user-interface components (labels, text fields, and a button), and places them in the applet.

The only event handled is the *Compute Payment* button. When this button is clicked, the **actionPerformed** method gets the interest rate, number of years, and loan amount from the text fields. It then creates a **Loan** object (line 70) to obtain the monthly payment and the total payment. Finally, it displays the monthly and total payments in their respective text fields. The **Loan** class is responsible for computing the payments. This class was introduced in Listing 9.2, Loan.java.

To run the applet, embed it in the HTML file, as shown in Listing 17.2.

Listing 17.2 LoanApplet.html

```
<!-- HTML code, this code is separated from the preceding Java code-->
<html>
  <head>
    <title>Loan Applet</title>
  </head>
  <body>
    This is a loan calculator. Enter your input for interest, year,
    and loan amount. Click the "Compute Payment" button, you will
    get the payment information. <p>
    <applet
      code = "LoanApplet.class"
      width = 300
      height = 150
      alt = "You must have a Java 2-enabled browser to view the applet">
    </applet>
  </body>
</html>
```

Applet demos

Tip

Many interesting applets are included in the JDK demo. To run them, change the directory to

```
c:\Program Files\Java\jdk1.6.0\demo\applets
```

Use the **dir** command to list the contents in the directory, as shown in Figure 17.6(a). Change to a subdirectory (e.g., using the command **cd Animator**). There are one or several .html files in that directory for executing applets (e.g., **example1.html**). In the command window, type the following to run the applet, as shown in Figure 17.6(b).

```
appletviewer example1.html
```

```
Command Prompt
Directory of C:\Program Files\Java\jdk1.6.0\demo\applets

12/14/2006  08:11 AM    <DIR>          .
12/14/2006  08:11 AM    <DIR>          ..
12/14/2006  08:11 AM    <DIR>          Animator
12/14/2006  08:11 AM    <DIR>          ArcTest
12/14/2006  08:11 AM    <DIR>          BarChart
12/14/2006  08:11 AM    <DIR>          Blink
12/14/2006  08:11 AM    <DIR>          CardTest
12/14/2006  08:11 AM    <DIR>          Clock
12/14/2006  08:11 AM    <DIR>          DitherTest
12/14/2006  08:11 AM    <DIR>          DrawTest
12/14/2006  08:11 AM    <DIR>          Fractal
12/14/2006  08:11 AM    <DIR>          GraphicsTest
12/14/2006  08:11 AM    <DIR>          GraphLayout
12/14/2006  08:11 AM    <DIR>          ImageMap
12/14/2006  08:11 AM    <DIR>          JumpingBox
12/14/2006  08:11 AM    <DIR>          MoleculeViewer
12/14/2006  08:11 AM    <DIR>          NervousText
12/14/2006  08:11 AM    <DIR>          SimpleGraph
12/14/2006  08:11 AM    <DIR>          SortDemo
12/14/2006  08:11 AM    <DIR>          SpreadSheet
12/14/2006  08:11 AM    <DIR>          TicTacToe
12/14/2006  08:11 AM    <DIR>          WireFrame
               0 File(s)              0 bytes
              22 Dir(s)  30,006,845,440 bytes free

C:\Program Files\Java\jdk1.6.0\demo\applets>
```

(a)

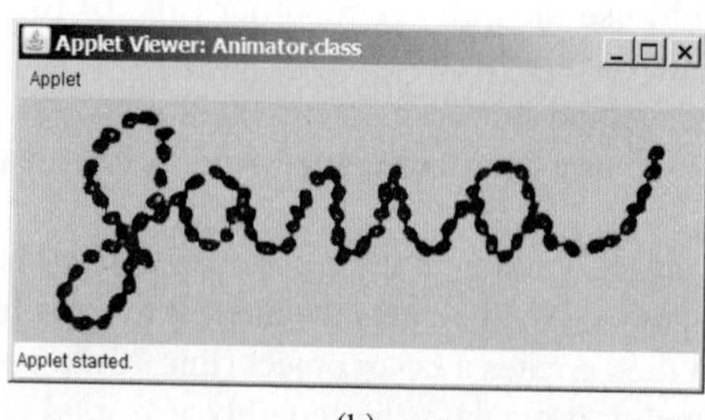

(b)

Figure 17.6 You can find applet examples in the JDK demo directory.

17.5 Enabling Applets to Run as Applications

Video Note
Run applets standalone

Despite some differences, the `JFrame` class and the `JApplet` class have a lot in common. Since they both are subclasses of the `Container` class, all their user-interface components, layout managers, and event-handling features are the same. Applications, however, are invoked from the static `main` method by the Java interpreter, and applets are run by the Web browser. The Web browser creates an instance of the applet using the applet's no-arg constructor and controls and executes the applet through the `init`, `start`, `stop`, and `destroy` methods.

For security reasons, the restrictions listed below are imposed on applets to prevent destructive programs from damaging the system on which the browser is running.

- Applets are not allowed to read from, or write to, the file system of the computer. Otherwise, they could damage the files and spread viruses.
- Applets are not allowed to run programs on the browser's computer. Otherwise, they might call destructive local programs and damage the local system on the user's computer.
- Applets are not allowed to establish connections between the user's computer and any other computer, except for the server where the applets are stored. This restriction prevents the applet from connecting the user's computer to another computer without the user's knowledge.

Note

trusted applet

A new security protocol was introduced in Java 2 to allow *trusted applets* to circumvent the security restrictions. See http://www.developer.com/java/ent/article.php/3303561 for detailed instructions on how to create trusted applets.

In general, an applet can be converted to an application without loss of functionality. An application can be converted to an applet as long as it does not violate the security restrictions imposed on applets. You can implement a `main` method in an applet to enable the applet to run as an application. This feature has both theoretical and practical implications. Theoretically, it blurs the difference between applets and applications. You can write a class that is both an applet and an application. From the standpoint of practicality, it is convenient to be able to run a program in two ways.

It is not difficult to write such programs on your own. Suppose you have an applet named `MyApplet`. To enable it to run as an application, all you need to do is add a `main` method in the applet with the implementation, as follows:

```
public static void main(String[] args) {
  // Create a frame
  JFrame frame = new JFrame("Applet is in the frame");          create frame

  // Create an instance of the applet
  MyApplet applet = new MyApplet();                               create applet

  // Add the applet to the frame
  frame.add(applet, BorderLayout.CENTER);                         add applet

  // Invoke init and start
  applet.init();                                                  init()
  applet.start();                                                 start()

  // Display the frame
  frame.setSize(300, 300);
  frame.setLocationRelativeTo(null); // Center the frame
  frame.setDefaultCloseOperation(JFrame.EXIT_ON_CLOSE);
  frame.setVisible(true);                                         show frame
}
```

You can revise the `LoanApplet` class in Listing 17.1 to enable `LoanApplet` to run standalone by adding a `main` method in Listing 17.3.

The `main` method creates a frame to hold an applet (line 12). When the applet is run from a Web browser, the Web browser invokes the `init` and `start` methods of the applet. When the applet is run standalone, you have to manually invoke the `init` and `start` methods in order to perform the operations in these methods.

LISTING 17.3 New LoanApplet.java With a **main** Method

code omitted

new main method

```
 1 import java.awt.*;
 2 import java.awt.event.*;
 3 import javax.swing.*;
 4 import javax.swing.border.TitledBorder;
 5
 6 public class LoanApplet extends JApplet {
 7   // Same code in Listing 17.1 from line 7 to line 78
 8   ...
 9
10   public static void main(String[] args) {
11     // Create a frame
12     JFrame frame = new JFrame("Applet is in the frame");
13
14     // Create an instance of the applet
15     LoanApplet applet = new LoanApplet();
16
17     // Add the applet to the frame
18     frame.add(applet, BorderLayout.CENTER);
19
20     // Invoke applet's init method
21     applet.init();
22
23     // Display the frame
24     frame.setSize(300, 300);
25     frame.setLocationRelativeTo(null); // Center the frame
26     frame.setDefaultCloseOperation(JFrame.EXIT_ON_CLOSE);
27     frame.setVisible(true);
28   }
29 }
```

17.6 Passing Strings to Applets

In §8.5, "Command-Line Arguments," you learned how to pass strings to Java applications from a command line. Strings are passed to the `main` method as an array of strings. When the application starts, the `main` method can use these strings. There is no `main` method in an applet, however, and applets are not run from the command line by the Java interpreter.

How, then, can applets accept arguments? In this section, you will learn how to pass strings to Java applets. To be passed to an applet, a parameter must be declared in the HTML file and must be read by the applet when it is initialized. Parameters are declared using the `<param>` tag. The `<param>` tag must be embedded in the `<applet>` tag and has no end tag. The syntax for the `<param>` tag is given below:

```
<param name = parametername value = stringvalue />
```

This tag specifies a parameter and its corresponding string value.

Note

No comma separates the parameter name from the parameter value in the HTML code. The HTML parameter names are not case sensitive.

Suppose you want to write an applet to display a message. The message is passed as a parameter. In addition, you want the message to be displayed at a specific location with x-coordinate and y-coordinate, which are passed as two parameters. The parameters and their values are listed in Table 17.1.

TABLE 17.1 Parameter Names and Values for the DisplayMessage Applet

Parameter Name	*Parameter Value*
MESSAGE	"Welcome to Java"
X	20
Y	30

The HTML source file is given in Listing 17.4:

LISTING 17.4 DisplayMessage.html

```
<html>
  <head>
    <title>Passing Strings to Java Applets</title>
  </head>
  <body>
    <p>This applet gets a message from the HTML
      page and displays it.</p>
    <applet
      code = "DisplayMessage.class"
      width = 200
      height = 50
      alt = "You must have a Java 2-enabled browser to view the
        applet"
    >
      <param name = MESSAGE value = "Welcome to Java" />
      <param name = X value = 20 />
      <param name = Y value = 30 />
    </applet>
  </body>
</html>
```

To read the parameter from the applet, use the following method defined in the Applet class:

```
public String getParameter(String parametername);
```

This returns the value of the specified parameter.

The applet is given in Listing 17.5. A sample run of the applet is shown in Figure 17.7.

LISTING 17.5 DisplayMessage.java

```
import javax.swing.*;

public class DisplayMessage extends JApplet {
```

getParameter

add to applet

```
 4   /** Initialize the applet */
 5   public void init() {
 6     // Get parameter values from the HTML file
 7     String message = getParameter("MESSAGE");
 8     int x = Integer.parseInt(getParameter("X"));
 9     int y = Integer.parseInt(getParameter("Y"));
10
11     // Create a message panel
12     MessagePanel messagePanel = new MessagePanel(message);
13     messagePanel.setXCoordinate(x);
14     messagePanel.setYCoordinate(y);
15
16     // Add the message panel to the applet
17     add(messagePanel);
18   }
19 }
```

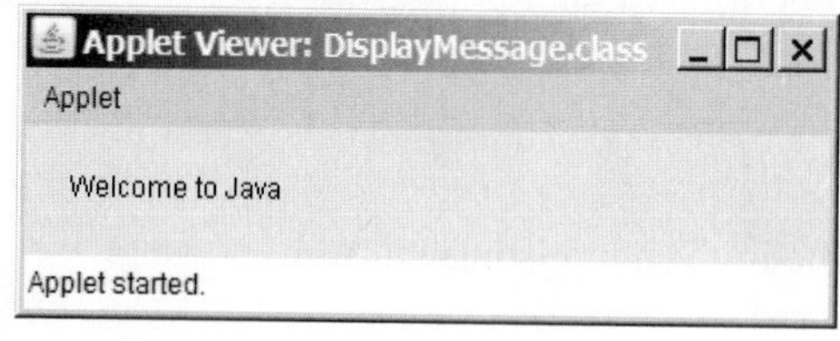

FIGURE 17.7 The applet displays the message `Welcome to Java` passed from the HTML page.

The program gets the parameter values from the HTML in the `init` method. The values are strings obtained using the `getParameter` method (lines 7–9). Because `x` and `y` are `int`, the program uses `Integer.parseInt(string)` to parse a digital string into an `int` value.

If you change *`Welcome to Java`* in the HTML file to *`Welcome to HTML`*, and reload the HTML file in the Web browser, you should see *`Welcome to HTML`* displayed. Similarly, the `x` and `y` values can be changed to display the message in a desired location.

Caution

The `Applet`'s `getParameter` method can be invoked only after an instance of the applet is created. Therefore, this method cannot be invoked in the constructor of the applet class. You should invoke it from the `init` method.

You can add a main method to enable this applet to run standalone. The applet takes the parameters from the HTML file when it runs as an applet and takes the parameters from the command line when it runs standalone. The program, as shown in Listing 17.6, is identical to `DisplayMessage` except for the addition of a new `main` method and of a variable named `isStandalone` to indicate whether it is running as an applet or as an application.

LISTING 17.6 `DisplayMessageApp.java`

```
import javax.swing.*;
import java.awt.Font;
import java.awt.BorderLayout;

public class DisplayMessageApp extends JApplet {
  private String message = "A default message"; // Message to display
```

```
  private int x = 20; // Default x-coordinate
  private int y = 20; // Default y-coordinate

  /** Determine if it is application */
  private boolean isStandalone = false;

  /** Initialize the applet */
  public void init() {
    if (!isStandalone) {
      // Get parameter values from the HTML file
      message = getParameter("MESSAGE");
      x = Integer.parseInt(getParameter("X"));
      y = Integer.parseInt(getParameter("Y"));
    }

    // Create a message panel
    MessagePanel messagePanel = new MessagePanel(message);
    messagePanel.setFont(new Font("SansSerif", Font.BOLD, 20));
    messagePanel.setXCoordinate(x);
    messagePanel.setYCoordinate(y);

    // Add the message panel to the applet
    add(messagePanel);
  }

  /** Main method to display a message
     @param args[0] x-coordinate
     @param args[1] y-coordinate
     @param args[2] message
    */
  public static void main(String[] args) {
    // Create a frame
    JFrame frame = new JFrame("DisplayMessageApp");

    // Create an instance of the applet
    DisplayMessageApp applet = new DisplayMessageApp();

    // It runs as an application
    applet.isStandalone = true;

    // Get parameters from the command line
    applet.getCommandLineParameters(args);

    // Add the applet instance to the frame
    frame.add(applet, BorderLayout.CENTER);

    // Invoke applet's init method
    applet.init();
    applet.start();

    // Display the frame
    frame.setSize(300, 300);
    frame.setLocationRelativeTo(null); // Center the frame
    frame.setDefaultCloseOperation(JFrame.EXIT_ON_CLOSE);
    frame.setVisible(true);
  }

  /** Get command-line parameters */
  private void getCommandLineParameters(String[] args) {
```

isStandalone

applet params

standalone

command params

```
66      // Check usage and get x, y and message
67      if (args.length != 3) {
68        System.out.println(
69          "Usage: java DisplayMessageApp x y message");
70        System.exit(0);
71      }
72      else {
73        x = Integer.parseInt(args[0]);
74        y = Integer.parseInt(args[1]);
75        message = args[2];
76      }
77    }
78  }
```

When you run the program as an applet, the `main` method is ignored. When you run it as an application, the `main` method is invoked. Sample runs of the program as an application and as an applet are shown in Figure 17.8.

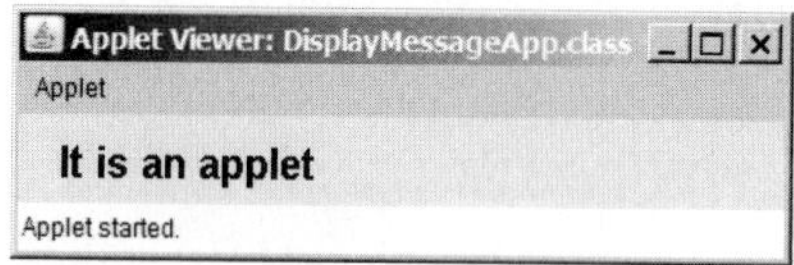

FIGURE 17.8 The `DisplayMessageApp` class can run as an application and as an applet.

The `main` method creates a `JFrame` object `frame` and creates a `JApplet` object `applet`, then places the applet `applet` into the frame `frame` and invokes its `init` method. The application runs just like an applet.

The `main` method sets `isStandalone true` (line 45) so that it does not attempt to retrieve HTML parameters when the `init` method is invoked.

The `setVisible(true)` method (line 61) is invoked *after* the components are added to the applet, and the applet is added to the frame to ensure that the components will be visible. Otherwise, the components are not shown when the frame starts.

omitting main method

Important Pedagogical Note

From now on, all the GUI examples will be created as applets with a `main` method. Thus you will be able to run the program either as an applet or as an application. For brevity, the `main` method is not listed in the text.

Video Note
TicTacToe

17.7 Case Study: TicTacToe

You have learned about objects, classes, arrays, class inheritance, GUI, event-driven programming, and applets from the many examples in this chapter and the preceding chapters. Now it is time to put what you have learned to work in developing comprehensive projects. In this section, you will develop a Java applet with which to play the popular game of TicTacToe.

Two players take turns marking an available cell in a 3×3 grid with their respective tokens (either X or O). When one player has placed three tokens in a horizontal, vertical, or diagonal row on the grid, the game is over and that player has won. A draw (no winner) occurs when all the cells on the grid have been filled with tokens and neither player has achieved a win. Figure 17.9 shows two representative sample runs of the example.

All the examples you have seen so far show simple behaviors that are easy to model with classes. The behavior of the TicTacToe game is somewhat more complex. To create classes that model the behavior, you need to study and understand the game.

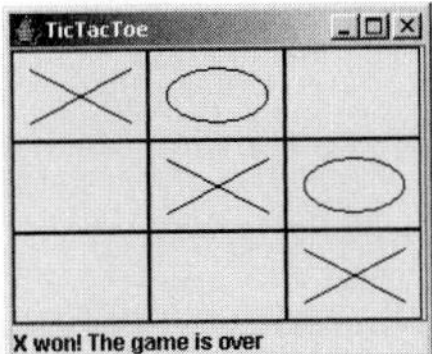

(a) The X player won the game

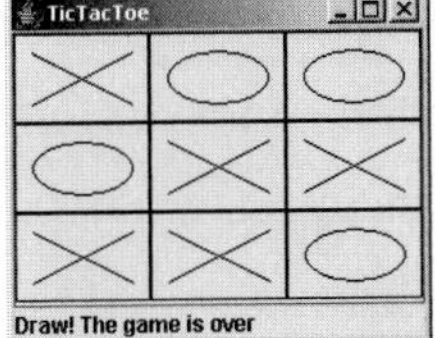

(b) Draw—no winners

FIGURE 17.9 Two players play a TicTacToe game.

Assume that all the cells are initially empty, and that the first player takes the X token, the second player the O token. To mark a cell, the player points the mouse to the cell and clicks it. If the cell is empty, the token (X or O) is displayed. If the cell is already filled, the player's action is ignored.

From the preceding description, it is obvious that a cell is a GUI object that handles the mouse-click event and displays tokens. Such an object could be either a button or a panel. Drawing on panels is more flexible than on buttons, because the token (X or O) can be drawn on a panel in any size, but on a button it can be displayed only as a text label. Therefore, a panel should be used to model a cell. How do you know the state of the cell (empty, X, or O)? You use a property named `token` of `char` type in the `Cell` class. The `Cell` class is responsible for drawing the token when an empty cell is clicked. So you need to write the code for listening to the `MouseEvent` and for painting the shapes for tokens X and O. The `Cell` class can be defined as shown in Figure 17.10.

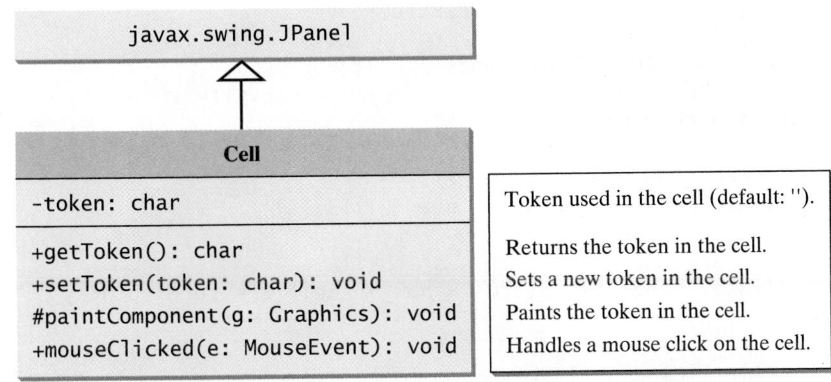

FIGURE 17.10 The `Cell` class paints the token on a cell.

The TicTacToe board consists of nine cells, declared using `new Cell[3][3]`. To determine which player's turn it is, you can introduce a variable named `whoseTurn` of `char` type. `whoseTurn` is initially X, then changes to O, and subsequently changes between X and O whenever a new cell is occupied. When the game is over, set `whoseTurn` to `' '`.

How do you know whether the game is over, whether there is a winner, and who the winner, if any, is? You can create a method named `isWon(char token)` to check whether a specified token has won and a method named `isFull()` to check whether all the cells are occupied.

Clearly, two classes emerge from the foregoing analysis. One is the `Cell` class, which handles operations for a single cell; and the other is the `TicTacToe` class, which plays the whole game and deals with all the cells. The relationship between these two classes is shown in Figure 17.11.

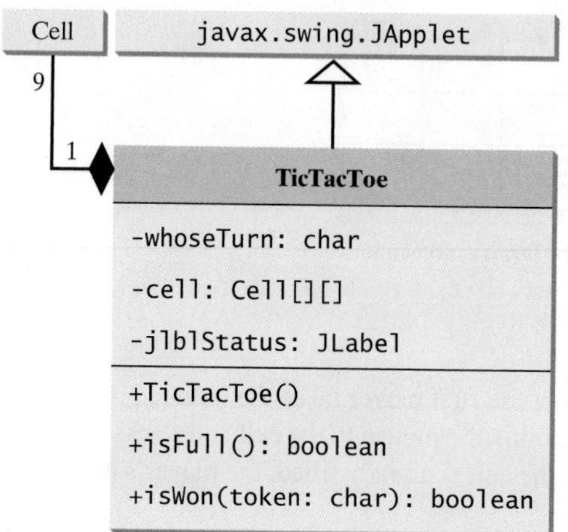

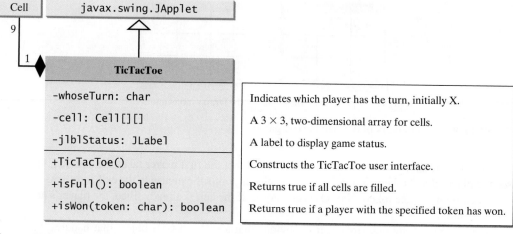

FIGURE 17.11 The TicTacToe class contains nine cells.

Since the Cell class is only to support the TicTacToe class, it can be defined as an inner class in TicTacToe. The complete program is given in Listing 17.7:

LISTING 17.7 TicTacToe.java

```
import java.awt.*;
import java.awt.event.*;
import javax.swing.*;
import javax.swing.border.LineBorder;

```

main class TicTacToe

```
public class TicTacToe extends JApplet {
  // Indicate which player has a turn; initially it is the X player
  private char whoseTurn = 'X';

  // Create and initialize cells
  private Cell[][] cells =  new Cell[3][3];

  // Create and initialize a status label
  private JLabel jlblStatus = new JLabel("X's turn to play");

  /** Initialize UI */
  public TicTacToe() {
    // Panel p to hold cells
    JPanel p = new JPanel(new GridLayout(3, 3, 0, 0));
    for (int i = 0; i < 3; i++)
      for (int j = 0; j < 3; j++)
        p.add(cells[i][j] = new Cell());

    // Set line borders on the cells panel and the status label
    p.setBorder(new LineBorder(Color.red, 1));
    jlblStatus.setBorder(new LineBorder(Color.yellow, 1));

    // Place the panel and the label to the applet
    add(p, BorderLayout.CENTER);
    add(jlblStatus, BorderLayout.SOUTH);
  }

  /** Determine if the cells are all occupied */
```

check isFull

```
  public boolean isFull() {
```

```
    for (int i = 0; i < 3; i++)
      for (int j = 0; j < 3; j++)
        if (cells[i][j].getToken() == ' ')
          return false;

    return true;
  }

  /** Determine if the player with the specified token wins */
  public boolean isWon(char token) {
    for (int i = 0; i < 3; i++)
      if ((cells[i][0].getToken() == token)
          && (cells[i][1].getToken() == token)
          && (cells[i][2].getToken() == token)) {
        return true;
      }

    for (int j = 0; j < 3; j++)
      if ((cells[0][j].getToken() ==  token)
          && (cells[1][j].getToken() == token)
          && (cells[2][j].getToken() == token)) {
        return true;
      }

    if ((cells[0][0].getToken() == token)
        && (cells[1][1].getToken() == token)
        && (cells[2][2].getToken() == token)) {
      return true;
    }

    if ((cells[0][2].getToken() == token)
        && (cells[1][1].getToken() == token)
        && (cells[2][0].getToken() == token)) {
      return true;
    }

    return false;
  }

  // An inner class for a cell
  public class Cell extends JPanel {
    // Token used for this cell
    private char token = ' ';

    public Cell() {
      setBorder(new LineBorder(Color.black, 1)); // Set cell's border
      addMouseListener(new MyMouseListener()); // Register listener
    }

    /** Return token */
    public char getToken() {
      return token;
    }

    /** Set a new token */
    public void setToken(char c) {
      token = c;
      repaint();
    }

```

check rows

check columns

check major diagonal

check subdiagonal

inner class Cell

register listener

paint cell

listener class

main method omitted

```
95      /** Paint the cell */
96      protected void paintComponent(Graphics g) {
97        super.paintComponent(g);
98
99        if (token == 'X') {
100         g.drawLine(10, 10, getWidth() - 10, getHeight() - 10);
101         g.drawLine(getWidth() - 10, 10, 10, getHeight() - 10);
102       }
103       else if (token == 'O') {
104         g.drawOval(10, 10, getWidth() - 20, getHeight() - 20);
105       }
106     }
107
108     private class MyMouseListener extends MouseAdapter {
109       /** Handle mouse click on a cell */
110       public void mouseClicked(MouseEvent e) {
111         // If cell is empty and game is not over
112         if (token == ' ' && whoseTurn != ' ') {
113           setToken(whoseTurn); // Set token in the cell
114
115           // Check game status
116           if (isWon(whoseTurn)) {
117             jlblStatus.setText(whoseTurn + " won! The game is over");
118             whoseTurn = ' '; // Game is over
119           }
120           else if (isFull()) {
121             jlblStatus.setText("Draw! The game is over");
122             whoseTurn = ' '; // Game is over
123           }
124           else {
125             // Change the turn
126             whoseTurn = (whoseTurn == 'X') ? 'O': 'X';
127             // Display whose turn
128             jlblStatus.setText(whoseTurn + "'s turn");
129           }
130         }
131       }
132     }
133   }
134 }
```

The **TicTacToe** class initializes the user interface with nine cells placed in a panel of **GridLayout** (lines 19–22). A label named **jlblStatus** is used to show the status of the game (line 14). The variable **whoseTurn** (line 8) is used to track the next type of token to be placed in a cell. The methods **isFull** (lines 34–41) and **isWon** (lines 44–72) are for checking the status of the game.

Since **Cell** is an inner class in **TicTacToe**, the variable (**whoseTurn**) and methods (**isFull** and **isWon**) defined in **TicTacToe** can be referenced from the **Cell** class. The inner class makes programs simple and concise. If **Cell** were not declared as an inner class of **TicTacToe**, you would have to pass an object of **TicTacToe** to **Cell** in order for the variables and methods in **TicTacToe** to be used in **Cell**. You will rewrite the program without using an inner class in Exercise 17.6.

The listener for **MouseEvent** is registered for the cell (line 81). If an empty cell is clicked and the game is not over, a token is set in the cell (line 113). If the game is over, **whoseTurn** is set to **' '** (lines 118, 122). Otherwise, **whoseTurn** is alternated to a new turn (line 126).

Tip

Use an incremental approach in developing and testing a Java project of this kind. The foregoing program can be divided into five steps:

incremental development and testing

1. Lay out the user interface and display a fixed token X on a cell.
2. Enable the cell to display a fixed token X upon a mouse click.
3. Coordinate between the two players so as to display tokens X and O alternately.
4. Check whether a player wins, or whether all the cells are occupied without a winner.
5. Implement displaying a message on the label upon each move by a player.

17.8 Case Study: Bouncing Ball

This section presents an applet that displays a ball bouncing in a panel. Use two buttons to suspend and resume the movement, and use a scroll bar to control the bouncing speed, as shown in Figure 17.12.

FIGURE 17.12 The ball's movement is controlled by the *Suspend* and *Resume* buttons and the scroll bar.

Here are the major steps to complete this example:

1. Create a subclass of `JPanel` named `Ball` to display a ball bouncing, as shown in Listing 17.8.
2. Create a subclass of `JPanel` named `BallControl` to contain the ball with a scroll bar and two control buttons *Suspend* and *Resume*, as shown in Listing 17.9.
3. Create an applet named `BounceBallApp` to contain an instance of `BallControl` and enable the applet to run standalone, as shown in Listing 17.10.

The relationship among these classes is shown in Figure 17.13.

LISTING 17.8 Ball.java

```
import javax.swing.Timer;
import java.awt.*;
import javax.swing.*;
import java.awt.event.*;

public class Ball extends JPanel {
  private int delay = 10;

  // Create a timer with delay 1000 ms
  private Timer timer = new Timer(delay, new TimerListener());

  private int x = 0; private int y = 0; // Current ball position
  private int radius = 5; // Ball radius
  private int dx = 2; // Increment on ball's x-coordinate
```

timer delay

create timer

start timer

timer listener

repaint ball

paint ball

```
15   private int dy = 2; // Increment on ball's y-coordinate
16
17   public Ball() {
18     timer.start();
19   }
20
21   private class TimerListener implements ActionListener {
22     /** Handle the action event */
23     public void actionPerformed(ActionEvent e) {
24       repaint();
25     }
26   }
27
28   protected void paintComponent(Graphics g) {
29     super.paintComponent(g);
30
31     g.setColor(Color.red);
32
33     // Check boundaries
34     if (x < radius) dx = Math.abs(dx);
35     if (x > getWidth() - radius) dx = -Math.abs(dx);
36     if (y < radius) dy = Math.abs(dy);
37     if (y > getHeight() - radius) dy = -Math.abs(dy);
38
39     // Adjust ball position
40     x += dx;
41     y += dy;
42     g.fillOval(x - radius, y - radius, radius * 2, radius * 2);
43   }
44
45   public void suspend() {
46     timer.stop(); // Suspend timer
47   }
48
49   public void resume() {
50     timer.start(); // Resume timer
51   }
52
53   public void setDelay(int delay) {
54     this.delay = delay;
55     timer.setDelay(delay);
56   }
57 }
```

Using `Timer` to control animation was introduced in §15.6, "Animation Using The `Timer` Class." `Ball` extends `JPanel` to display a moving ball. The timer listener implements `ActionListener` to listen for `ActionEvent` (line 21). Line 10 creates a `Timer` for a `Ball`. The timer is started in line 18 when a `Ball` is constructed. The timer fires an `ActionEvent` at a fixed rate. The listener responds in line 24 to repaint the ball to animate ball movement. The center of the ball is at (`x`, `y`), which changes to (`x + dx`, `y + dy`) on the next display (lines 40–41). The `suspend` and `resume` methods (lines 45–51) can be used to stop and start the timer. The `setDelay(int)` method (lines 53–56) sets a new delay.

LISTING 17.9 BallControl.java

```
import javax.swing.*;
import java.awt.event.*;
import java.awt.*;

```

```
 5 public class BallControl extends JPanel {
 6   private Ball ball = new Ball();
 7   private JButton jbtSuspend = new JButton("Suspend");
 8   private JButton jbtResume = new JButton("Resume");
 9   private JScrollBar jsbDelay = new JScrollBar();
10
11   public BallControl() {
12     // Group buttons in a panel
13     JPanel panel = new JPanel();
14     panel.add(jbtSuspend);
15     panel.add(jbtResume);
16
17     // Add ball and buttons to the panel
18     ball.setBorder(new javax.swing.border.LineBorder(Color.red));
19     jsbDelay.setOrientation(JScrollBar.HORIZONTAL);
20     ball.setDelay(jsbDelay.getMaximum());
21     setLayout(new BorderLayout());
22     add(jsbDelay, BorderLayout.NORTH);
23     add(ball, BorderLayout.CENTER);
24     add(panel, BorderLayout.SOUTH);
25
26     // Register listeners
27     jbtSuspend.addActionListener(new ActionListener() {
28       public void actionPerformed(ActionEvent e) {
29         ball.suspend();
30       }
31     });
32     jbtResume.addActionListener(new ActionListener() {
33       public void actionPerformed(ActionEvent e) {
34         ball.resume();
35       }
36     });
37     jsbDelay.addAdjustmentListener(new AdjustmentListener() {
38       public void adjustmentValueChanged(AdjustmentEvent e) {
39         ball.setDelay(jsbDelay.getMaximum() - e.getValue());
40       }
41     });
42   }
43 }
```

button

scroll bar

create UI

register listener

suspend

register listener

resume

register listener

new delay

The **BallControl** class extends **JPanel** to display the ball with a scroll bar and two control buttons. When the *Suspend* button is clicked, the ball's **suspend()** method is invoked to suspend the ball movement (line 29). When the *Resume* button is clicked, the ball's **resume()** method is invoked to resume the ball movement (line 34). The bouncing speed can be changed using the scroll bar.

LISTING 17.10 BounceBallApp.java

```
import java.awt.*;
import javax.swing.*;

public class BounceBallApp extends JApplet {
  public BounceBallApp() {
    add(new BallControl());
  }
}
```

add **BallControl**

main method omitted

The **BounceBallApp** class simply places an instance of **BallControl** in the applet. The **main** method is provided in the applet (not displayed in the listing for brevity) so that you can also run it standalone.

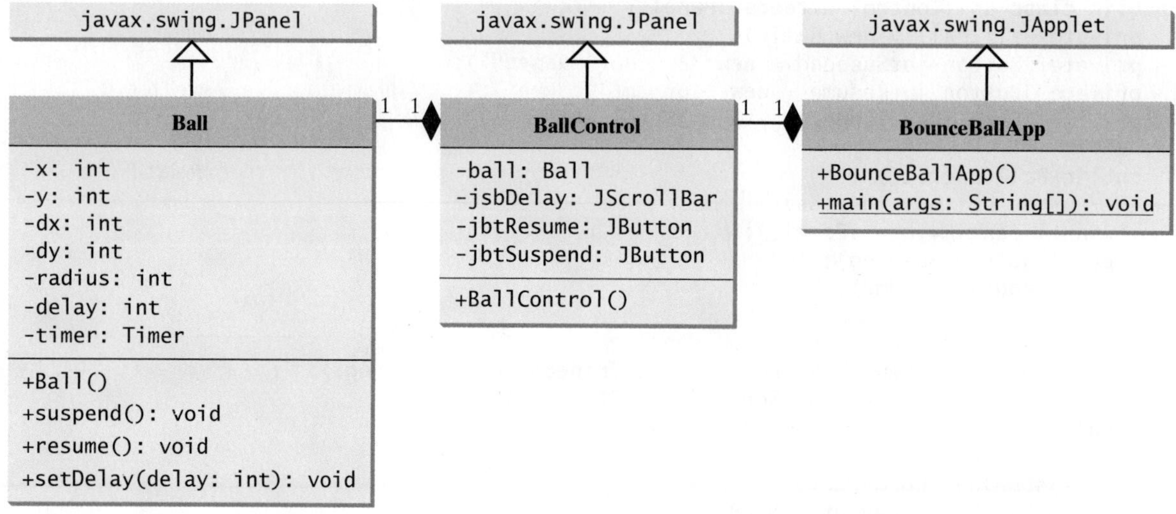

FIGURE 17.13 BounceBallApp contains BallControl, and BallControl contains Ball.

Video Note
Audio and image in applets and application

17.9 Locating Resources Using the **URL** Class

You have used the ImageIcon class to create an icon from an image file and used the setIcon method or the constructor to place the icon in a GUI component, such as a button or a label. For example, the following statements create an ImageIcon and set it on a JLabel object jlbl:

```
ImageIcon imageIcon = new ImageIcon("c:\\book\\image\\us.gif");
jlbl.setIcon(imageIcon);
```

This approach presents a problem. The file location is fixed, because it uses the absolute file path on the Windows platform. As a result, the program cannot run on other platforms and cannot run as an applet. Assume that image/us.gif is under the class directory. You can circumvent this problem by using a relative path as follows:

```
ImageIcon imageIcon = new ImageIcon("image/us.gif");
```

This works fine with Java applications on all platforms but not with Java applets, because applets cannot load local files. To enable it to work with both applications and applets, you need to locate the file using the URL class.

why URL class?

The java.net.URL class can be used to identify files (image, audio, text, etc.) on the Internet. In general, a URL (Uniform Resource Locator) is a pointer to a "resource" on the World Wide Web on a local machine or a remote host. A resource can be something as simple as a file or a directory.

A URL for a file can also be accessed by class code in a way that is independent of the location of the file, as long as the file is located in the class directory. Recall that the class directory is where the class (i.e., the .class file) is stored. For example, all the classes in this book are stored in c:\book. So the class directory is c:\book.

To obtain the URL of a file in the class directory, use

```
URL url = getClass().getResource(filename);
```

meta object

The getClass() method returns an instance of the java.lang.Class class. This instance is automatically created by the JVM when the class file is loaded into the memory. This instance, also known as a *meta object*, contains the information about the class file such as class name, constructors, methods, etc. You can obtain the URL of a file in the class path by invoking the `getResource(filename)` method on the meta object. For example, if the class file is in `c:\book`, the following statements create a URL for `c:\book\image\us.gif`.

```
Class metaObject = this.getClass(); // this. can be omitted
URL url = metaObject.getResource("image/us.gif");
```

You can now create an `ImageIcon` using

```
ImageIcon imageIcon = new ImageIcon(url);
```

Listing 17.11 gives the code that displays an image from `image/us.gif` in the class directory. The file `image/us.gif` is under the class directory, and its URL is obtained using the `getResource` method (line 5). A label with an image icon is created in line 6. The image icon is obtained from the URL.

LISTING 17.11 DisplayImageWithURL.java

```
1 import javax.swing.*;
2
3 public class DisplayImageWithURL extends JApplet {
4   public DisplayImageWithURL() {
5     java.net.URL url = this.getClass().getResource("image/us.gif");
6     add(new JLabel(new ImageIcon(url) ));
7   }
8 }
```

get image URL
create a label
main method omitted

If you replace the code in lines 5–6 with the following code,

```
add(new JLabel(new ImageIcon("image/us.gif")));
```

you can still run the program standalone, but not from a browser.

17.10 Playing Audio in Any Java Program

There are several formats for audio files. Java programs can play audio files in the WAV, AIFF, MIDI, AU, and RMF formats.

To play an audio file in Java (application or applet), first create an *audio clip object* for the file. The audio clip is created once and can be played repeatedly without reloading the file. To create an audio clip, use the static method `newAudioClip()` in the `java.applet.Applet` class:

```
AudioClip audioClip = Applet.newAudioClip(url);
```

Audio originally can be played only from Java applets. For this reason, the `AudioClip` interface is in the `java.applet` package. Since Java 2, audio can be played in any Java program.

The following statements, for example, create an `AudioClip` for the `beep.au` audio file in the class directory:

```
Class metaObject = this.getClass();
URL url = metaObject.getResource("beep.au");
AudioClip audioClip = Applet.newAudioClip(url);
```

To manipulate a sound for an audio clip, use the `play()`, `loop()`, and `stop()` methods in `java.applet.AudioClip`, as shown in Figure 17.14.

Listing 17.12 gives the code that displays the Danish flag and plays the Danish national anthem repeatedly. The image file `image/denmark.gif` and audio file `audio/denmark.mid` are stored under the class directory. Line 12 obtains the audio file URL. Line 13 creates an audio clip for the file. Line 14 repeatedly plays the audio.

«interface» *java.applet.AudioClip*	
+play()	Starts playing this audio clip. Each time this method is called, the clip is restarted from the beginning.
+loop()	Plays the clip repeatedly.
+stop()	Stops playing the clip.

FIGURE 17.14 The AudioClip interface provides the methods for playing sound.

LISTING 17.12 DisplayImagePlayAudio.java

get image URL
create a label
get audio URL
create an audio clip
play audio repeatedly
start audio
stop audio
main method omitted

```
1 import javax.swing.*;
2 import java.net.URL;
3 import java.applet.*;
4
5 public class DisplayImagePlayAudio extends JApplet {
6   private AudioClip audioClip;
7
8   public DisplayImagePlayAudio() {
9     URL urlForImage = getClass().getResource("image/denmark.gif");
10    add(new JLabel(new ImageIcon(urlForImage)));
11
12    URL urlForAudio = getClass().getResource("audio/denmark.mid");
13    audioClip = Applet.newAudioClip(urlForAudio);
14    audioClip.loop();
15  }
16
17  public void start() {
18    if (audioClip != null) audioClip.loop();
19  }
20
21  public void stop() {
22    if (audioClip != null) audioClip.stop();
23  }
24 }
```

The stop method (lines 21–23) stops the audio when the applet is not displayed, and the start method (lines 17–19) restarts the audio when the applet is redisplayed. Try to run this applet from a browser and observe the effect without the stop and start methods.

Run this program standalone from the main method and from a Web browser to test it. Recall that, for brevity, the main method in all applets in this text is not printed in the text.

17.11 Case Study: Multimedia Animations

This case study presents a multimedia animation with images and audio. The images are for seven national flags, named flag0.gif, flag1.gif, ..., flag6.gif for Denmark, Germany, China, India, Norway, U.K., and U.S. They are stored under the image directory in the class path. The audio consists of national anthems for these seven nations, named anthem0.mid, anthem1.mid, ..., and anthem6.mid. They are stored under the audio directory in the class path.

The program presents the nations, starting from the first one. For each nation, it displays its flag and plays its anthem. When the audio for a nation finishes, the next nation is presented, and so on. After the last nation is presented, the program starts to present all the nations again. You may suspend animation by clicking the *Suspend* button and resume it by clicking the *Resume* button, as shown in Figure 17.15. You can also directly select a nation from a combo box.

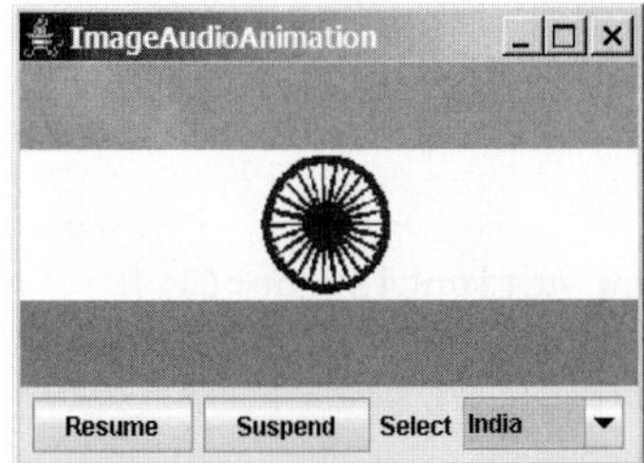

FIGURE 17.15 The applet displays a sequence of images and plays audio.

The program is given in Listing 17.13. A timer is created to control the animation (line 15). The timer delay for each presentation is the play time for the anthem. You can find the play time for an audio file using RealPlayer or Windows Media on Windows. The delay times are stored in an array named `delays` (lines 13–14). The delay time for the first audio file (the Danish anthem) is 48 seconds.

LISTING 17.13 ImageAudioAnimation.java

```
 1 import java.awt.*;
 2 import java.awt.event.*;
 3 import javax.swing.*;
 4 import java.applet.*;
 5
 6 public class ImageAudioAnimation extends JApplet {
 7   private final static int NUMBER_OF_NATIONS = 7;
 8   private int current = 0;
 9   private ImageIcon[] icons = new ImageIcon[NUMBER_OF_NATIONS];
10   private AudioClip[] audioClips = new AudioClip[NUMBER_OF_NATIONS];
11   private AudioClip currentAudioClip;
12
13   private int[] delays =
14     {48000, 54000, 59000, 54000, 59000, 31000, 68000};
15   private Timer timer = new Timer(delays[0], new TimerListener());
16
17   private JLabel jlblImageLabel = new JLabel();
18   private JButton jbtResume = new JButton("Resume");
19   private JButton jbtSuspend = new JButton("Suspend");
20   private JComboBox jcboNations = new JComboBox(new Object[]
21     {"Denmark", "Germany", "China", "India", "Norway", "UK", "US"});
22
23   public ImageAudioAnimation() {
24     // Load image icons and audio clips
25     for (int i = 0; i < NUMBER_OF_NATIONS; i++) {
26       icons[i] = new ImageIcon(getClass().getResource(
27         "image/flag" + i + ".gif"));
28       audioClips[i] = Applet.newAudioClip(
29         getClass().getResource("audio/anthem" + i + ".mid"));
30     }
31
32     JPanel panel = new JPanel();
33     panel.add(jbtResume);
34     panel.add(jbtSuspend);
35     panel.add(new JLabel("Select"));
36     panel.add(jcboNations);
37     add(jlblImageLabel, BorderLayout.CENTER);
38     add(panel, BorderLayout.SOUTH);
39
```

image icons (line 9)
audio clips (line 10)
current audio clip (line 11)
audio play time (line 13)
timer (line 15)
GUI components (line 17)
create icons (line 26)
create audio clips (line 28)
create UI (line 32)

register listener
start animation
register listener
stop animation
register listener
select a nation
present a nation
set a new delay
stop audio clip
main method omitted

```
40     jbtResume.addActionListener(new ActionListener() {
41       public void actionPerformed(ActionEvent e) {
42         start();
43       }
44     });
45     jbtSuspend.addActionListener(new ActionListener() {
46       public void actionPerformed(ActionEvent e) {
47         stop();
48       }
49     });
50     jcboNations.addActionListener(new ActionListener() {
51       public void actionPerformed(ActionEvent e) {
52         stop();
53         current = jcboNations.getSelectedIndex();
54         presentNation(current);
55         timer.start();
56       }
57     });
58
59     timer.start();
60     jlblImageLabel.setIcon(icons[0]);
61     jlblImageLabel.setHorizontalAlignment(JLabel.CENTER);
62     currentAudioClip = audioClips[0];
63     currentAudioClip.play();
64   }
65
66   private class TimerListener implements ActionListener {
67     public void actionPerformed(ActionEvent e) {
68       current = (current + 1) % NUMBER_OF_NATIONS;
69       presentNation(current);
70     }
71   }
72
73   private void presentNation(int index) {
74     jlblImageLabel.setIcon(icons[index]);
75     jcboNations.setSelectedIndex(index);
76     currentAudioClip = audioClips[index];
77     currentAudioClip.play();
78     timer.setDelay(delays[index]);
79   }
80
81   public void start() {
82     timer.start();
83     currentAudioClip.play();
84   }
85
86   public void stop() {
87     timer.stop();
88     currentAudioClip.stop();
89   }
90 }
```

A label is created in line 17 to display a flag image. An array of flag images for seven nations is created in lines 26–27. An array of audio clips is created in lines 28–29. Each audio clip is created for an audio file through the URL of the current class. The audio files are stored in the same directory with the applet class file.

The combo box for country names is created in lines 20–21. When a new country name in the combo box is selected, the current presentation is stopped and a new selected nation is presented (lines 52–55).

The presentNation(index) method (lines 73–79) presents a nation with the specified index. It sets a new image in the label (line 74), synchronizes with the combo box by setting the selected index (line 75), plays the new audio, and sets a new delay time (line 78).

The applet's start and stop methods are overridden to resume and suspend the animation (lines 81–89).

Key Terms

applet 558
HTML 561
.html or .htm 561
tag 561
archive 562

Chapter Summary

- The Web browser controls and executes applets through the init, start, stop, and destroy methods in the Applet class. Applets always extend the Applet class and implement these methods, if necessary.
- JApplet is a subclass of Applet. It should be used for developing Java applets with Swing components.
- The applet bytecode must be specified, using the <applet> tag in an HTML file to tell the Web browser where to find the applet. The applet can accept string parameters from HTML using the <param> tag.
- When an applet is loaded, the Web browser creates an instance of it by invoking its no-arg constructor. The init method is invoked after the applet is created. The start method is invoked after the init method. It is also called whenever the applet becomes active again after the page containing the applet is revisited. The stop method is invoked when the applet becomes inactive.
- The destroy method is invoked when the browser exits normally to inform the applet that it is no longer needed and should release any resources it has allocated. The stop method is always called before the destroy method.
- The procedures for writing applications and writing applets are very similar. An applet can easily be converted into an application, and vice versa. Moreover, an applet can be written with the additional capability of running as an application.
- You can pass arguments to an applet using the param attribute in the applet's tag in HTML. To retrieve the value of the parameter, invoke the getParameter(paramName) method.
- The Applet's getParameter method can be invoked only after an instance of the applet is created. Therefore, this method cannot be invoked in the constructor of the applet class. You should invoke this method from the init method.
- You learned how to incorporate images and audio in Java applications and applets. To load audio and images for Java applications and applets, you have to create a URL for the audio and image. You can create a URL from a file under the class directory or from an Internet source.
- To play an audio, create an audio clip from the URL for the audio source. You can use the AudioClip's play() method to play it once, the loop() method to play it repeatedly, and the stop() method to stop it.

REVIEW QUESTIONS

Sections 17.2–17.4

17.1 Is every applet an instance of `java.applet.Applet`? Is every applet an instance of `javax.swing.JApplet`?

17.2 Describe the `init()`, `start()`, `stop()`, and `destroy()` methods in the `Applet` class.

17.3 How do you add components to a `JApplet`? What is the default layout manager of the content pane of `JApplet`?

17.4 Why does the applet in (a) display nothing? Why does the applet in (b) have a runtime `NullPointerException` on the highlighted line?

```
import javax.swing.*;

public class WelcomeApplet extends JApplet {
  public void WelcomeApplet() {
    JLabel jlblMessage =
      new JLabel("It is Java");
  }
}
```

(a)

```
import javax.swing.*;

public class WelcomeApplet extends JApplet {
  private JLabel jlblMessage;

  public WelcomeApplet() {
    JLabel jlblMessage =
      new JLabel("It is Java");
  }

  public void init() {
    add(jlblMessage);
  }
}
```

(b)

Sections 17.5–17.6

17.5 Describe the `<applet>` HTML tag. How do you pass parameters to an applet?

17.6 Where is the `getParameter` method defined?

17.7 What is wrong if the `DisplayMessage` applet is revised as follows?

```
public class DisplayMessage extends JApplet {
  /** Initialize the applet */
  public DisplayMessage() {
    // Get parameter values from the HTML file
    String message = getParameter("MESSAGE");
    int x =
      Integer.parseInt(getParameter("X"));
    int y =
      Integer.parseInt(getParameter("Y"));

    // Create a message panel
    MessagePanel messagePanel =
      new MessagePanel(message);
    messagePanel.setXCoordinate(x);
    messagePanel.setYCoordinate(y);

    // Add the message panel to the applet
    getContentPane().add(messagePanel);
  }
}
```

(a) Revision 1

```
public class DisplayMessage extends JApplet {
  private String message;
  private int x;
  private int y;

  /** Initialize the applet */
  public void init() {
    // Get parameter values from the HTML file
    message = getParameter("MESSAGE");
    x = Integer.parseInt(getParameter("X"));
    y = Integer.parseInt(getParameter("Y"));
  }

  public DisplayMessage() {
    // Create a message panel
    MessagePanel messagePanel =
      new MessagePanel(message);
    messagePanel.setXCoordinate(x);
    messagePanel.setYCoordinate(y);

    // Add the message panel to the applet
    getContentPane().add(messagePanel);
  }
}
```

(b) Revision 2

17.8 What are the differences between applications and applets? How do you run an application, and how do you run an applet? Is the compilation process different for applications and applets? List some security restrictions on applets.

17.9 Can you place a frame in an applet?

17.10 Can you place an applet in a frame?

17.11 Delete `super.paintComponent(g)` on line 97 in TicTacToe.java in Listing 17.5 and run the program to see what happens.

Sections 17.8–17.9

17.12 How do you create a `URL` object for the file www.cs.armstrong.edu/liang/anthem/us.gif on the Internet? How do you create a `URL` object for the file image/us.gif in the class directory?

17.13 How do you create an `ImageIcon` from the file image/us.gif in the class directory? How do you create an `ImageIcon` from www.cs.armstrong.edu/liang/anthem/us.gif?

Section 17.10 Playing Audio

17.14 What types of audio files are used in Java?

17.15 How do you create an audio clip from a file anthem/us.mid in the class directory? How do you create an audio clip from www.cs.armstrong.edu/liang/anthem/us.mid?

17.16 How do you play, repeatedly play, and stop an audio clip?

Programming Exercises

Note:
For every applet in the exercise, add a main method to enable it to run standalone.

run standalone

Sections 17.2–17.4

17.1 (*Converting applications to applets*) Convert Listing 16.2, ButtonDemo.java, into an applet.

Sections 17.5–17.6

17.2* (*Passing strings to applets*) Rewrite Listing 17.5, DisplayMessage.java, to display a message with a standard color, font, and size. The `message`, `x`, `y`, `color`, `fontname`, and `fontsize` are parameters in the `<applet>` tag, as shown below:

```
<applet
  code = "Exercise17_2.class"
  width = 200
  height = 50
  alt = "You must have a Java-enabled browser to view the applet"
>
  <param name = MESSAGE value = "Welcome to Java" />
  <param name = X value = 40 />
  <param name = Y value = 50 />
  <param name = COLOR value = "red" />
  <param name = FONTNAME value = "Monospaced" />
  <param name = FONTSIZE value = 20 />
</applet>
```

17.3 (*Enabling applets to run standalone*) Rewrite the `LoanApplet` in Listing 17.1, LoanApplet.java, to enable it to run as an application as well as an applet.

17.4* (*Creating multiple windows from an applet*) Write an applet that contains two buttons called *Investment Calculator* and *Loan Calculator*. When you click *Investment*

Calculator, a frame appears in a new window for calculating future investment values. When you click *Loan Calculator*, a frame appears in a separate new window for computing loan payments (see Figure 17.16).

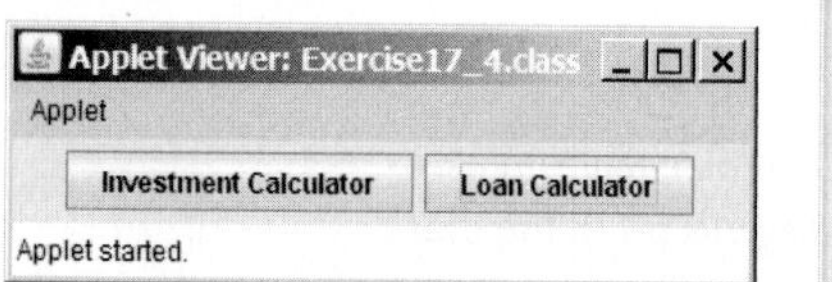

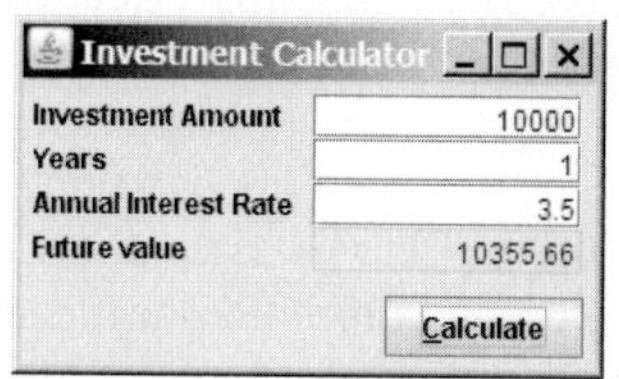

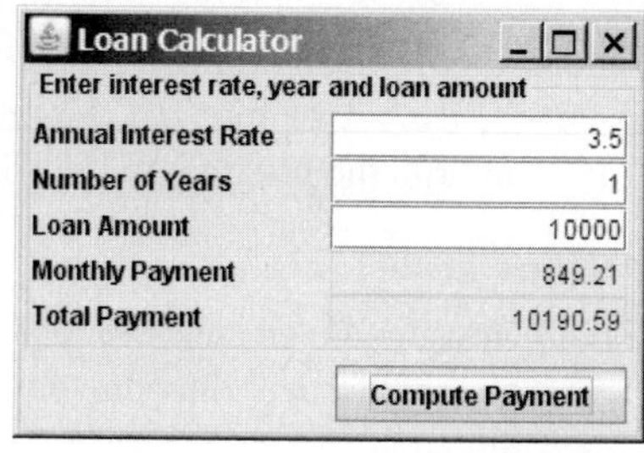

FIGURE 17.16 You can show frames in the applets.

17.5** (*Game: a clock learning tool*) Develop a clock applet to show a first-grade student how to read a clock. Modify Exercise 14.19 to display a detailed clock with an hour hand and minute hand in an applet, as shown in Figure 17.17(a). The hour and minute values are randomly generated. The hour is between `0` and `11`, and the minute is `0`, `15`, `30`, or `45`. Upon a mouse click, a new random time is displayed on the clock.

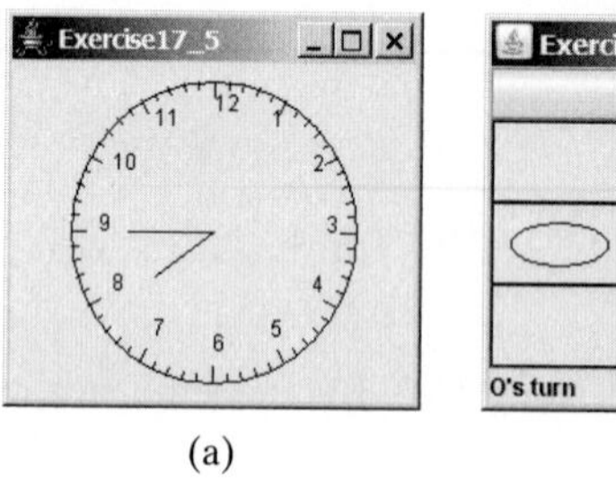

(a)

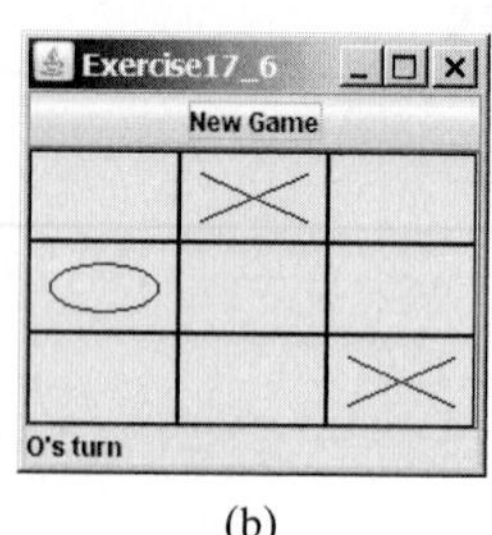

(b)

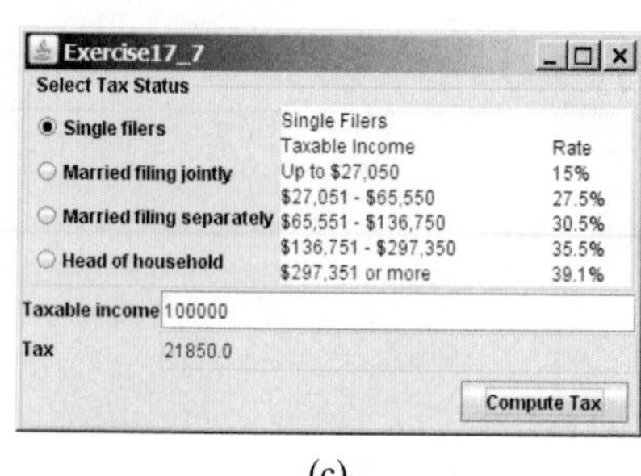

(c)

FIGURE 17.17 (a) Upon a mouse click on the clock, the clock time is randomly displayed. (b) The *New Game* button starts a new game. (c) The tax calculator computes the tax for the specified taxable income and tax status.

17.6** (*Game: TicTacToe*) Rewrite the program in §17.7, "Case Study: TicTacToe," with the following modifications:

- Declare `Cell` as a separate class rather than an inner class.
- Add a button named *New Game*, as shown in Figure 17.17(b). The *New Game* button starts a new game.

17.7** (*Financial application: tax calculator*) Create an applet to compute tax, as shown in Figure 17.17(c). The applet lets the user select the tax status and enter the taxable income to compute the tax based on the 2001 federal tax rates, as shown in Exercise 9.8.

17.8*** (*Creating a calculator*) Use various panels of `FlowLayout`, `GridLayout`, and `BorderLayout` to lay out the following calculator and to implement addition (+), subtraction (−), division (/), square root (`sqrt`), and modulus (%) functions (see Figure 17.18(a)).

FIGURE 17.18 (a) Exercise 17.8 is a Java implementation of a popular calculator. (b) Exercise 17.9 converts between decimal, hex, and binary numbers.

17.9* (*Converting numbers*) Write an applet that converts between decimal, hex, and binary numbers, as shown in Figure 17.18(b). When you enter a decimal value on the decimal value text field and press the Enter key, its corresponding hex and binary numbers are displayed in the other two text fields. Likewise, you can enter values in the other fields and convert them accordingly.

17.10** (*Repainting a partial area*) When you repaint the entire viewing area of a panel, sometimes only a tiny portion of the viewing area is changed. You can improve the performance by repainting only the affected area, but do not invoke `super.paintComponent(g)` when repainting the panel, because this will cause the entire viewing area to be cleared. Use this approach to write an applet to display the temperatures of each hour during the last 24 hours in a histogram. Suppose that temperatures between 50 and 90 degrees Fahrenheit are obtained randomly and are updated every hour. The temperature of the current hour needs to be redisplayed, while the others remain unchanged. Use a unique color to highlight the temperature for the current hour (see Figure 17.19(a)).

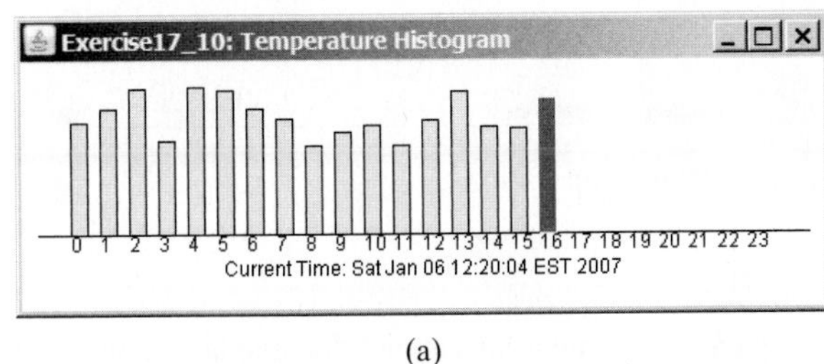

(a)

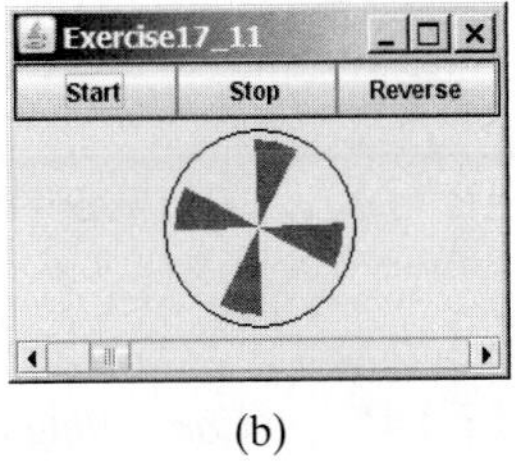

(b)

FIGURE 17.19 (a) The histogram displays the average temperature of every hour in the last 24 hours. (b) The program simulates a running fan.

17.11** (*Simulation: a running fan*) Write a Java applet that simulates a running fan, as shown in Figure 17.19(b). The buttons *Start*, *Stop*, and *Reverse* control the fan. The scrollbar controls the fan's speed. Create a class named `Fan`, a subclass of `JPanel`, to display the fan. This class also contains the methods to suspend and resume the fan, set its speed, and reverse its direction. Create a class named `FanControl` that contains a fan, and three buttons and a scroll bar to control the fan. Create a Java applet that contains an instance of `FanControl`.

17.12** (*Controlling a group of fans*) Write a Java applet that displays three fans in a group, with control buttons to start and stop all of them, as shown in Figure 17.20. Use the `FanControl` to control and display a single fan.

FIGURE 17.20 The program runs and controls a group of fans.

17.13*** (*Creating an elevator simulator*) Write an applet that simulates an elevator going up and down (see Figure 17.21). The buttons on the left indicate the floor where the passenger is now located. The passenger must click a button on the left to request that the elevator come to his or her floor. On entering the elevator, the passenger clicks a button on the right to request that it go to the specified floor.

FIGURE 17.21 The program simulates elevator operations.

Video Note
Control a group of clocks

17.14* (*Controlling a group of clocks*) Write a Java applet that displays three clocks in a group, with control buttons to start and stop all of them, as shown in Figure 17.22. Use the `ClockControl` to control and display a single clock.

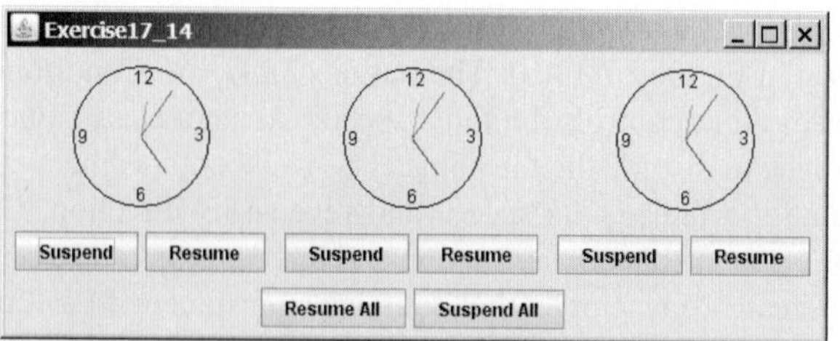

FIGURE 17.22 Three clocks run independently with individual control and group control.

Section 17.9 Displaying Images

17.15* (*Enlarging and shrinking an image*) Write an applet that will display a sequence of images from a single image file in different sizes. Initially, the viewing area for this image has a width of 300 and a height of 300. Your program should continuously shrink the viewing area by 1 in width and 1 in height until it reaches a width of 50 and a height of 50. At that point, the viewing area should continuously enlarge by 1 in width and 1 in height until it reaches a width of 300 and a height of 300. The viewing area should shrink and enlarge (alternately) to create animation for the single image.

17.16*** (*Simulating a stock ticker*) Write a Java applet that displays a stock index ticker (see Figure 17.23). The stock index information is passed from the `<param>` tag in the HTML file. Each index has four parameters: Index Name (e.g., S&P 500), Current Time (e.g., 15:54), the index from the previous day (e.g., 919.01), and Change (e.g., 4.54).

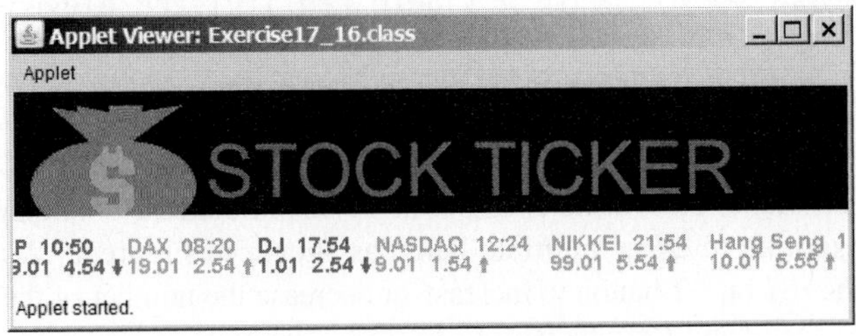

FIGURE 17.23 The program displays a stock index ticker.

Use at least five indexes, such as Dow Jones, S&P 500, NASDAQ, NIKKEI, and Gold & Silver Index. Display positive changes in green, and negative changes in red. The indexes move from right to left in the applet's viewing area. The applet freezes the ticker when the mouse button is pressed; it moves again when the mouse button is released.

17.17** (*Racing cars*) Write an applet that simulates four cars racing, as shown in Figure 17.24(a). You can set the speed for each car, with 1 being the highest.

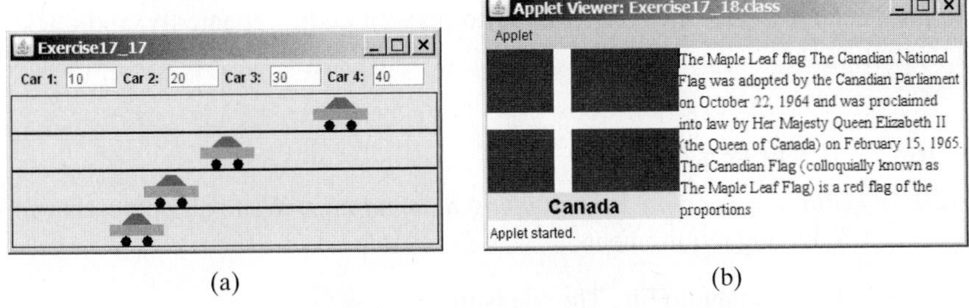

FIGURE 17.24 (a) You can set the speed for each car. (b) This applet shows each country's flag, name, and description, one after another, and reads the description that is currently shown.

17.18** (*Showing national flags*) Write an applet that introduces national flags, one after the other, by presenting each one's photo, name, and description (see Figure 17.24(b)) along with audio that reads the description.

Suppose your applet displays the flags of eight countries. Assume that the photo image files, named **flag0.gif**, **flag1.gif**, and so on, up to **flag7.gif**, are stored in a subdirectory named **image** in the applet's directory. The length of each audio is less than 10 seconds. Assume that the name and description of each country's flag are passed from the HTML using the parameters `name0`, `name1`, ..., `name7`, and `description0`, `description1`, ..., and `description7`. Pass the number of countries as an HTML parameter using `numberOfCountries`. Here is an example:

```
<param name="numberOfCountries" value=8>
<param name="name0" value="Canada">
<param name="description0" value=
"The Maple Leaf flag
The Canadian National Flag was adopted by the Canadian
Parliament on October 22, 1964 and was proclaimed into law
by Her Majesty Queen Elizabeth II (the Queen of Canada) on
February 15, 1965. The Canadian Flag (colloquially known
as The Maple Leaf Flag) is a red flag of the proportions
two by length and one by width, containing in its center a
white square, with a single red stylized eleven-point
maple leaf centered in the white square.">
```

Hint: Use the `DescriptionPanel` class to display the image, name, and the text. The `DescriptionPanel` class was introduced in Listing 16.6.

17.19*** (*Bouncing balls*) The example in §17.8 simulates a bouncing ball. Extend the example to allow multiple balls, as shown in Figure 17.25(a). You may use the *+1* or *−1* button to increase or decrease the number of the balls, and use the *Suspend* and *Resume* buttons to freeze the balls or resume bouncing.

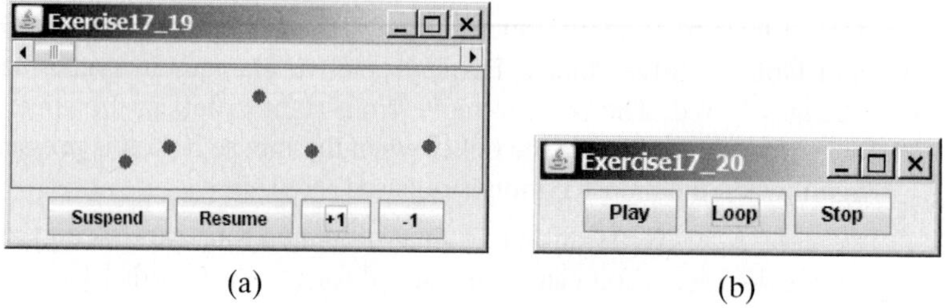

(a) (b)

FIGURE 17.25 (a) The applet allows you to add or remove bouncing balls. (b) Click *Play* to play an audio clip once, click *Loop* to play an audio repeatedly, and click *Stop* to terminate playing.

Section 17.12 Playing Audio

17.20* (*Playing, looping, and stopping a sound clip*) Write an applet that meets the following requirements:

- Get an audio file. The file is in the class directory.
- Place three buttons labeled *Play*, *Loop*, and *Stop*, as shown in Figure 17.25(b).
- If you click the *Play* button, the audio file is played once. If you click the *Loop* button, the audio file keeps playing repeatedly. If you click the *Stop* button, the playing stops.
- The applet can run as an application.

17.21** (*Creating an alarm clock*) Write an applet that will display a digital clock with a large display panel that shows hour, minute, and second. This clock should allow the user to set an alarm. Figure 17.26(a) shows an example of such a clock. To turn on the alarm, check the *Alarm* check box. To specify the alarm time, click the *Set alarm* button to display a new frame, as shown in Figure 17.26(b). You can set the alarm time in the frame.

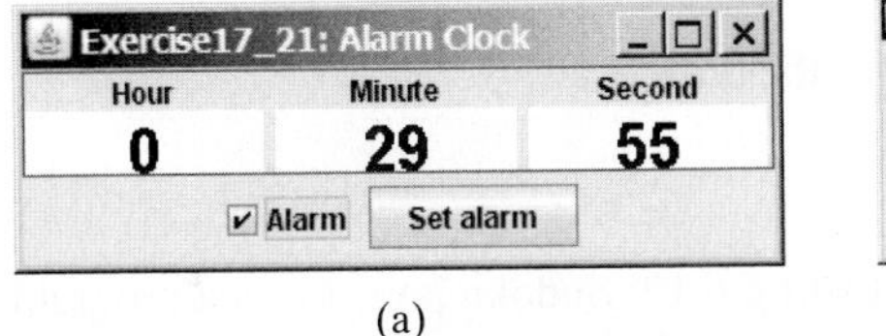

(a)

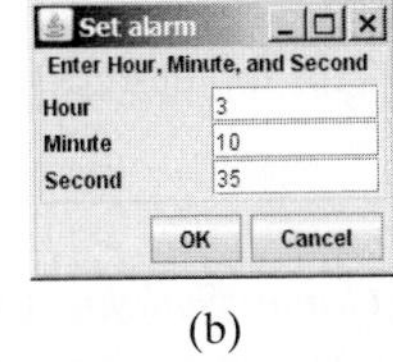

(b)

FIGURE 17.26 The program displays current hour, minute, and second, and enables you to set an alarm.

17.22** (*Creating an image animator with audio*) Create animation using the applet (see Figure 17.27) to meet the following requirements:

- Allow the user to specify the animation speed. The user can enter the speed in a text field.
- Get the number of frames and the image file-name prefix from the user. For example, if the user enters **n** for the number of frames and **L** for the image prefix, then the files are **L1**, **L2**, and so on, to **L*n***. Assume that the images are stored in the **image** directory, a subdirectory of the applet's directory.
- Allow the user to specify an audio file name. The audio file is stored in the same directory as the applet. The sound is played while the animation runs.

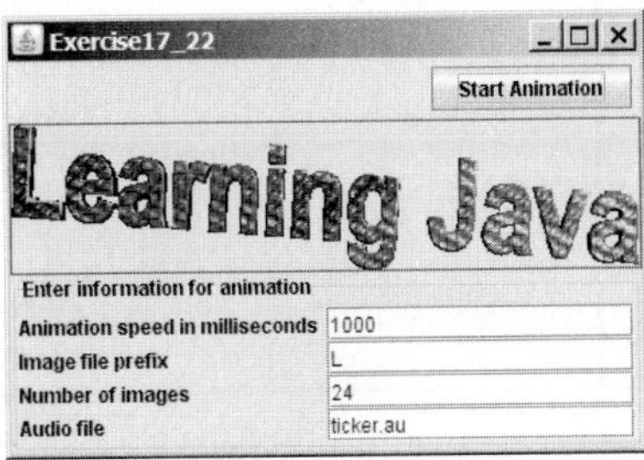

FIGURE 17.27 This applet lets the user select image files, audio file, and animation speed.

17.23** (*Simulation: raising flag and playing anthem*) Create an applet that displays a flag rising up, as shown in Figure 15.1. As the national flag rises, play the national anthem. (You may use a flag image and anthem audio file from Listing 17.13.)

17.24** (*Game: guessing birth dates*) Listing 3.8, GuessBirthDate.java, gives a program for guessing a birth date. Create an applet for guessing birth dates as shown in Figure 17.28. The applet prompts the user to check whether the date is in any of the five sets. The date is displayed in the text field upon clicking the *Guess Birth Date* button.

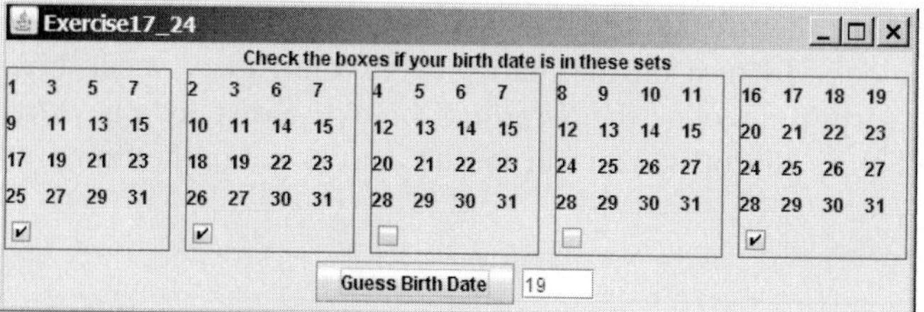

FIGURE 17.28 This applet guesses the birth dates.

17.25* ** (*Game: Sudoku*) Listing 6.12, Sudoku.java, gives a program that prompts the user to enter a Sudoku puzzle from the console. Write a program that lets the user enter the input from the text fields in an applet, as shown in Figure 17.1. Clicking the *Solve* button displays the result.

17.26* ** (*Game: Math quiz*) Listing 3.3, AdditionQuiz.java, and Listing 3.4, SubtractionQuiz.java, generate and grade Math quizzes. Write an applet that allows the user to select a question type and difficulty level, as shown in Figure 17.29(a). When the user clicks the *Start* button, the program begins to generate a question, after the user enters an answer with the *Enter* key, a new question is displayed. When the user clicks the *Start* button, the elapse time is displayed. The time is updated every second until the *Stop* button is clicked. The correct count is updated whenever a correct answer is made.

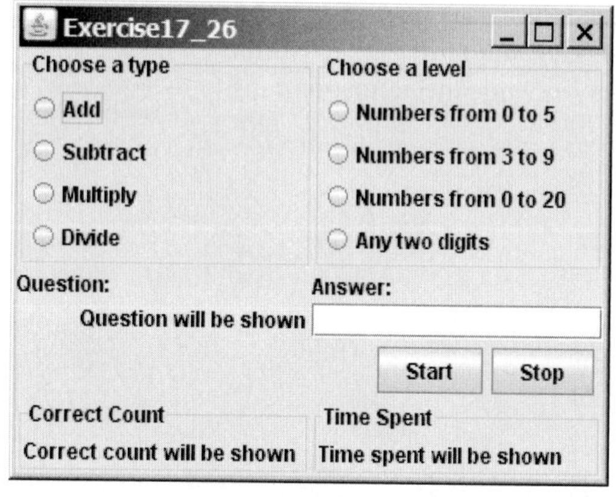

(a) Before a session starts

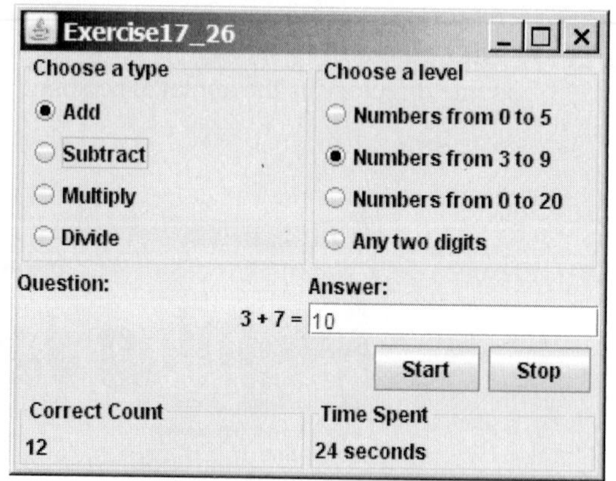

(b) After a session is started

FIGURE 17.29 The applet tests Math skills.

17.27* ** (*Simulation: traffic control*) Exercise 16.3 uses the radio buttons to change the traffic lights. Revise the program that simulates traffic control at an intersection, as shown in Figure 17.30. When the light turns red, the traffic flows vertically; when the light turns green, the traffic flows horizontally. The light changes automatically every one minute. Before the light changes to red from green, it first changes to yellow for a brief five seconds.

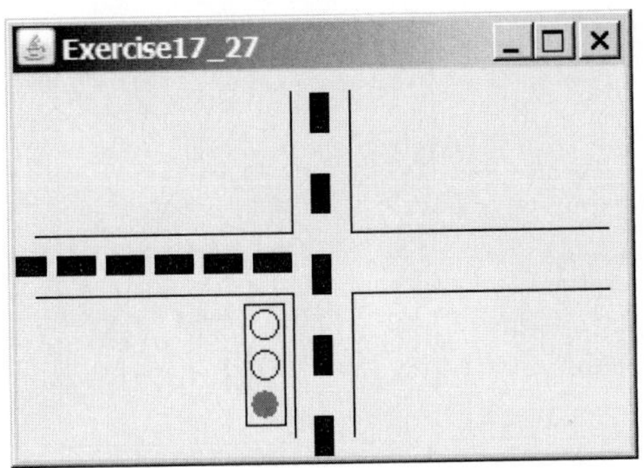

(a) The traffic flows vertically

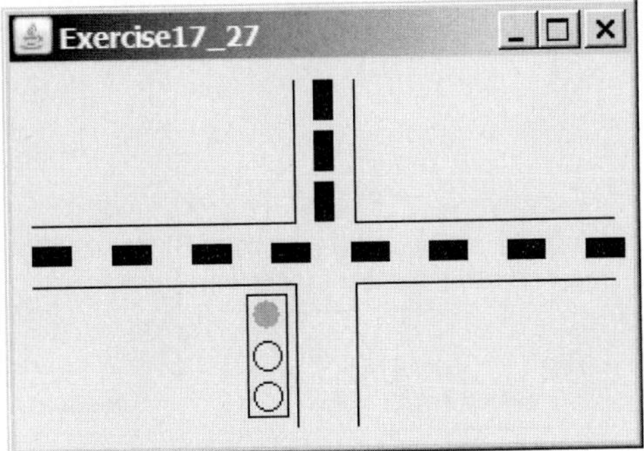

(b) The traffic flows horizontally

FIGURE 17.30 The applet simulates traffic control.

17.28** (*Geometry: two circles intersect?*) The `Circle2D` class was created in Exercise 9.11. Write an applet that enables the user to specify the location and size of the circles and displays whether the two circles intersect, as shown in Figure 17.31(a).

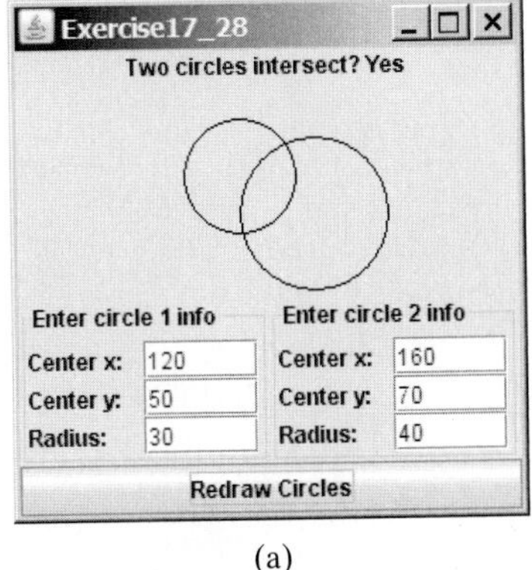

(a)

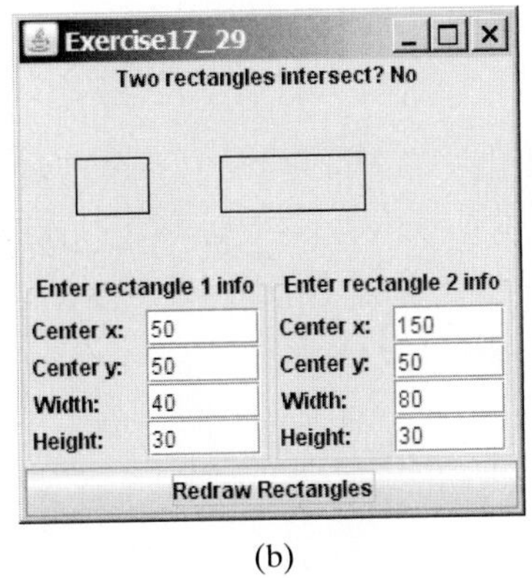

(b)

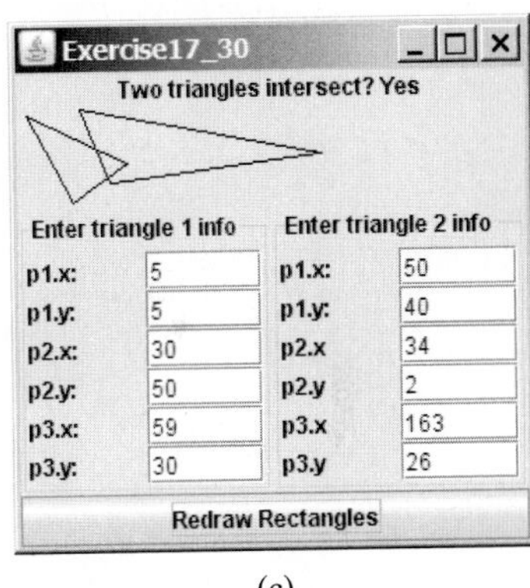

(c)

FIGURE 17.31 Check whether two circles, two rectangles, and two triangles are overlapping.

17.29** (*Geometry: two rectangles intersect?*) The `Rectangle2D` class was created in Exercise 9.12. Write an applet that enables the user to specify the location and size of the rectangles and displays whether the two rectangles intersect, as shown in Figure 17.31(b).

17.30** (*Geometry: two circles intersect?*) The `Triangle2D` class was created in Exercise 9.13. Write an applet that enables the user to specify the location of the two triangles and displays whether the two triangles intersect, as shown in Figure 17.31(c).

17.31*** (*Game: bean machine animation*) Write an applet that animates a bean machine introduced in Exercise 15.22. The applet lets you set the number of slots, as shown in Figure 17.32. Click *Start* to start or restart the animation and click *Stop* to stop.

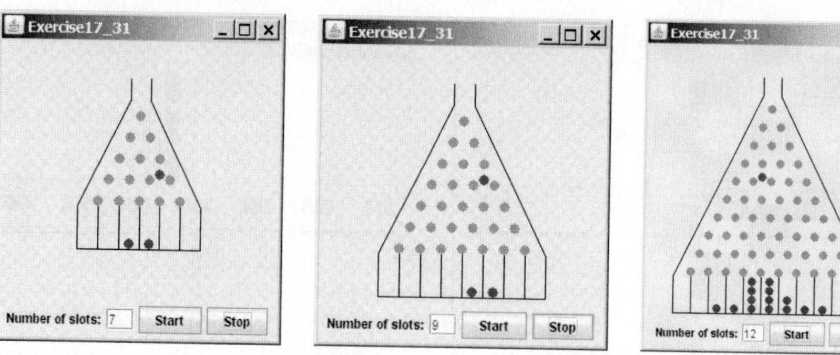

FIGURE 17.32 The applet controls a bean machine animation.

CHAPTER 18

EXCEPTION HANDLING

Objectives

- To get an overview of exceptions and exception handling (§18.2).
- To explore the advantages of using exception handling (§18.3).
- To distinguish exception types: `Error` (fatal) vs. `Exception` (nonfatal), and checked vs. unchecked (§18.4).
- To declare exceptions in a method header (§18.5.1).
- To throw exceptions in a method (§18.5.2).
- To write a `try-catch` block to handle exceptions (§18.5.3).
- To explain how an exception is propagated (§18.5.3).
- To use the `finally` clause in a `try-catch` block (§18.6).
- To use exceptions only for unexpected errors (§18.7).
- To rethrow exceptions in a `catch` block (§18.8).
- To create chained exceptions (§18.9).
- To declare custom exception classes (§18.10).

18.1 Introduction

When a program encounters a runtime error, it terminates abnormally. How can you handle the runtime error so that the program can continue to run or else terminate gracefully? This is the subject we will introduce in this chapter.

Video Note
Exception handling advantage

18.2 Exception-Handling Overview

To demonstrate exception handling, we begin with an example in Listing 18.1 that reads in two integers and displays their quotient.

LISTING 18.1 Quotient.java

```
import java.util.Scanner;

public class Quotient {
  public static void main(String[] args) {
    Scanner input = new Scanner(System.in);

    // Prompt the user to enter two integers
    System.out.print("Enter two integers: ");
    int number1 = input.nextInt();
    int number2 = input.nextInt();

    System.out.println(number1 + " / " + number2 + " is " +
      (number1 / number2 ));
  }
}
```

reads two integers

integer division

```
Enter two integers: 5 2 ↵Enter
5 / 2 is 2
```

```
Enter two integers: 3 0 ↵Enter
Exception in thread "main" java.lang.ArithmeticException: / by zero
          at Quotient.main(Quotient.java:11)
```

If you entered 0 for the second number, a runtime error would occur, because you cannot divide an integer by 0. (*Recall that a floating-point number divided by* 0 *does not raise an exception.*) A simple way to fix the error is to add an `if` statement to test the second number, as shown in Listing 18.2.

LISTING 18.2 QuotientWithIf.java

```
import java.util.Scanner;

public class QuotientWithIf {
  public static void main(String[] args) {
    Scanner input = new Scanner(System.in);

    // Prompt the user to enter two integers
    System.out.print("Enter two integers: ");
    int number1 = input.nextInt();
    int number2 = input.nextInt();

    if (number2 != 0)
```

reads two integers

test number2

```
      System.out.println(number1 + " / " + number2 + " is " +
        (number1 / number2));
    else
      System.out.println("Divisor cannot be zero ");
  }
}
```

```
Enter two integers: 5 0 ↵Enter
Divisor cannot be zero
```

Listing 18.2 can be rewritten using exception handling, as shown in Listing 18.3. Note that, since Listing 18.2 is simpler than Listing 18.3, you should not actually use exception handling in this situation. The purpose of Listing 18.3 is to give a simple example to demonstrate the concept of exception handling. Later you will see the practical advantages of using exception handling.

LISTING 18.3 QuotientWithException.java

```
 1 import java.util.Scanner;
 2
 3 public class QuotientWithException {
 4   public static void main(String[] args) {
 5     Scanner input = new Scanner(System.in);
 6
 7     // Prompt the user to enter two integers
 8     System.out.print("Enter two integers: ");
 9     int number1 = input.nextInt();
10     int number2 = input.nextInt();
11
12     try {
13       if (number2 == 0)
14         throw new ArithmeticException("Divisor cannot be zero");
15
16       System.out.println(number1 + " / " + number2 + " is " +
17         (number1 / number2));
18     }
19     catch (ArithmeticException ex) {
20       System.out.println("Exception: an integer " +
21         "cannot be divided by zero ");
22     }
23
24     System.out.println("Execution continues ...");
25   }
26 }
```

reads two integers

try block

catch block

```
Enter two integers: 5 3 ↵Enter
5 / 3 is 1
Execution continues ...
```

```
Enter two integers: 5 0 ↵Enter
Exception: an integer cannot be divided by zero
Execution continues ...
```

The program contains a **try** block and a **catch** block. The **try** block (lines 12–18) contains the code that is executed in normal circumstances. The **catch** block (lines 19–22)

contains the code that is executed when `number2` is `0`. In this event the program throws an exception by executing

`throw` statement

```
throw new ArithmeticException("Divisor cannot be zero");
```

exception
throwing exception

The value thrown, in this case `new ArithmeticException("Divisor cannot be zero")`, is called an *exception*. The execution of a throw statement is called *throwing an exception*. The exception is an object created from an exception class. In this case, the exception class is `java.lang.ArithmeticException`.

handle exception

When an exception is thrown, the normal execution flow is interrupted. As the name suggests, "throw exception" is to pass the exception from one place to another. The exception is caught by the `catch` block. The code in the `catch` block is executed to *handle the exception*. Afterward, the statement (line 23) after the `catch` block is executed.

The `throw` statement is analogous to a method call, but instead of calling a method, it calls a `catch` block. In this sense, a `catch` block is like a method definition with a parameter that matches the type of the value being thrown. Unlike a method, after executing the `catch` block, the program control does not return back to the `throw` statement; instead, it executes the next statement after the `catch` block.

The identifier `ex` in the catch block header

```
catch (ArithmeticException ex)
```

`catch` block parameter

acts very much like a parameter in a method. So this parameter is referred to as a `catch` block parameter. The type (e.g., `ArithmeticException`) preceding `ex` specifies what kind of exception the `catch` block can catch. Once the exception is caught, you can access the thrown value from this parameter in the body of a catch block.

In summary, a template for a `try-throw-catch` block may look like this:

```
try {
  Code to try;
  Throw an exception with a throw statement or
    from method if necessary;
  More code to try;
}
catch (type ex) {
  Code to process the exception;
}
```

An exception may be thrown directly using a `throw` statement in a `try` block, or from invoking a method that may throw an exception.

18.3 Exception-Handling Advantages

Listing 18.3 provides a simple example to demonstrate the concept of exception handling. This section uses methods to demonstrate the advantages of using exception handling.

Listing 18.4 rewrites Listing 18.3 to compute a quotient using a method.

LISTING 18.4 QuotientWithMethod.cpp

quotient method

```
import java.util.Scanner;

public class QuotientWithMethod {
  public static int quotient(int number1, int number2) {
    if (number2 == 0)
```

throw exception

reads two integers

try block

invoke method

catch block

```
6       throw new ArithmeticException("Divisor cannot be zero");
7
8     return number1 / number2;
9   }
10
11  public static void main(String[] args) {
12    Scanner input = new Scanner(System.in);
13
14    // Prompt the user to enter two integers
15    System.out.print("Enter two integers: ");
16    int number1 = input.nextInt();
17    int number2 = input.nextInt();
18
19    try {
20      int result = quotient(number1, number2);
21      System.out.println(number1 + " / " + number2 + " is "
22        + result);
23    }
24    catch (ArithmeticException ex) {
25      System.out.println("Exception: an integer " +
26        "cannot be divided by zero ");
27    }
28
29    System.out.println("Execution continues ...");
30  }
31 }
```

```
Enter two integers: 5 3 [Enter]
5 / 3 is 1
Execution continues ...
```

```
Enter two integers: 5 0 [Enter]
Exception: an integer cannot be divided by zero
Execution continues ...
```

Method `quotient` (lines 4–9) returns the quotient of two integers. If `number2` is `0`, it cannot return a value. So, an exception is thrown in line 6.

The main method invokes `quotient` (line 20). If the quotient method executes normally, it returns a value to the caller. If the `quotient` method encounters an exception, it throws the exception back to its caller. The caller's `catch` block handles the exception.

advantage

Now you see the *advantages* of using exception handling. It enables a method to throw an exception to its caller. Without this capability, a method must handle the exception or terminate the program.

18.4 Exception Types

The `catch` block parameter in the preceding section is of the `ArithmeticException` type. Are there any other types you can use? Yes. You can use the `Throwable` class or any subclass of `Throwable`. `ArithmeticException` is a subtype of `Throwable`.

The `Throwable` class is contained in the `java.lang` package, and subclasses of `Throwable` are contained in various packages. Errors related to GUI components are included in the `java.awt` package; numeric exceptions are included in the `java.lang` package, because they are related to the java.lang.Number class. You can create your own exception classes by extending Throwable or a subclass of Throwable. Figure 18.1 shows some of Java's predefined exception classes.

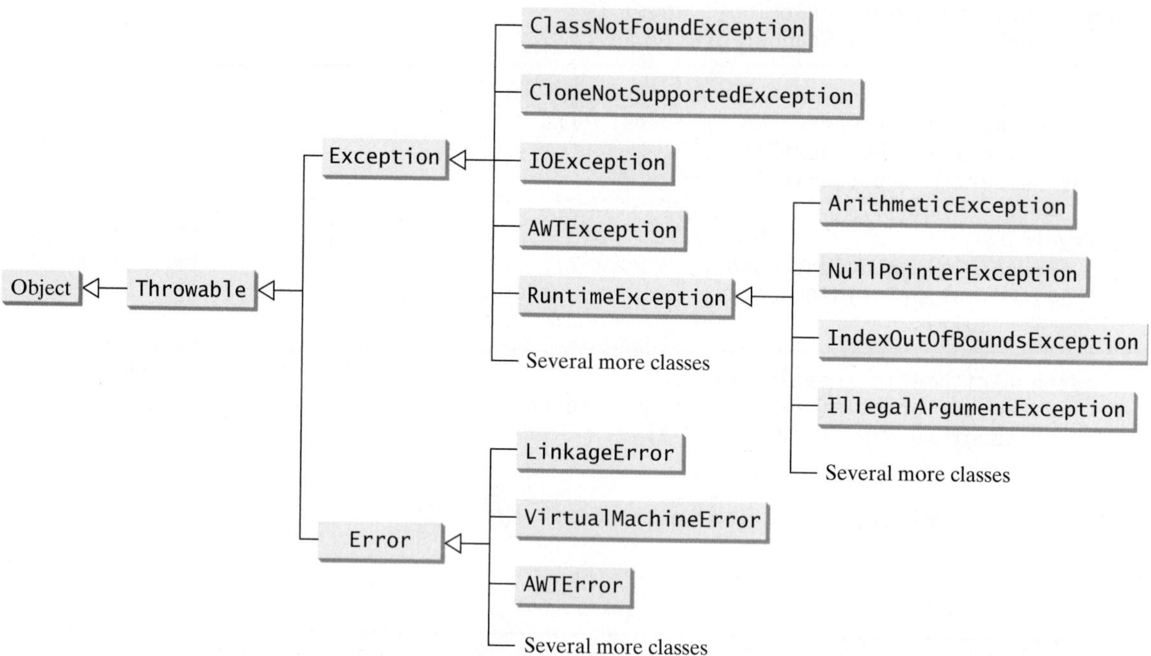

FIGURE 18.1 Exceptions thrown are instances of the classes shown in this diagram, or of subclasses of one of these classes.

Note

The class names Error, Exception, and RuntimeException are somewhat confusing. All three of these classes are exceptions, and all of the errors discussed here occur at runtime.

The exception classes can be classified into three major types: system errors, exceptions, and runtime exceptions.

system error

- *System errors* are thrown by the JVM and represented in the Error class. The Error class describes internal system errors. Such errors rarely occur. If one does, there is little you can do beyond notifying the user and trying to terminate the program gracefully. Examples of subclasses of Error are listed in Table 18.1.

exception

- *Exceptions* are represented in the Exception class, which describes errors caused by your program and by external circumstances. These errors can be caught and

TABLE 18.1 Examples of Subclasses of Error

Class	*Possible Reason for Exception*
LinkageError	A class has some dependency on another class, but the latter class has changed incompatibly after the compilation of the former class.
VirtualMachineError	The JVM is broken or has run out of the resources necessary for it to continue operating.
AWTError	A fatal error in the GUI runtime system.

handled by your program. Examples of subclasses of `Exception` are listed in Table 18.2.

TABLE 18.2 Examples of Subclasses of **`Exception`**

Class	*Possible Reason for Exception*
`ClassNotFoundException`	Attempt to use a class that does not exist. This exception would occur, for example, if you tried to run a nonexistent class using the **java** command, or if your program were composed of, say, three class files, only two of which could be found.
`CloneNotSupportedException`	Attempt to clone an object whose defining class does not implement the `Cloneable` interface. Cloning objects were introduced in Chapter 11, "Abstract Classes and Interfaces."
`IOException`	Related to input/output operations, such as invalid input, reading past the end of a file, and opening a nonexistent file. Examples of subclasses of `IOException` are `InterruptedIOException`, `EOFException` (EOF is short for End Of File), and `FileNotFoundException`.
`AWTException`	Exceptions in GUI components.

- *Runtime exceptions* are represented in the `RuntimeException` class, which describes programming errors, such as bad casting, accessing an out-of-bounds array, and numeric errors. Runtime exceptions are generally thrown by the JVM. Examples of subclasses are listed in Table 18.3. runtime exception

TABLE 18.3 Examples of Subclasses of **`RuntimeException`**

Class	*Possible Reason for Exception*
`ArithmeticException`	Dividing an integer by zero. Note that floating-point arithmetic does not throw exceptions. See Appendix E, "Special Floating-Point Values."
`NullPointerException`	Attempt to access an object through a `null` reference variable.
`IndexOutOfBoundsException`	Index to an array is out of range.
`IllegalArgumentException`	A method is passed an argument that is illegal or inappropriate.

`RuntimeException`, `Error`, and their subclasses are known as *unchecked exceptions*. All other exceptions are known as *checked exceptions*, meaning that the compiler forces the programmer to check and deal with them. unchecked exception checked exception

In most cases, unchecked exceptions reflect programming logic errors that are not recoverable. For example, a `NullPointerException` is thrown if you access an object through a reference variable before an object is assigned to it; an `IndexOutOfBoundsException` is thrown if you access an element in an array outside the bounds of the array. These are logic errors that should be corrected in the program. Unchecked exceptions can occur anywhere in a program. To avoid cumbersome overuse of try-catch blocks, Java does not mandate that you write code to catch or declare unchecked exceptions.

integer overflow/underflow

Caution

At present, Java does not throw integer overflow or underflow exceptions. The following statement adds `1` to the maximum integer.

```
int number = Integer.MAX_VALUE + 1;
System.out.println(number);
```

It displays `-2147483648`, which is logically incorrect. The cause of this problem is overflow; that is, the result exceeds the maximum for an `int` value.

A future version of Java may fix this problem by throwing an overflow exception.

`BigInteger`

Tip

For processing large integral values, use the `BigInteger` class, introduced in §11.12, "The `BigInteger` and `BigDecimal` Classes."

18.5 Understanding Exception Handling

Java's exception-handling model is based on three operations: *declaring an exception*, *throwing an exception*, and *catching an exception*, as shown in Figure 18.2.

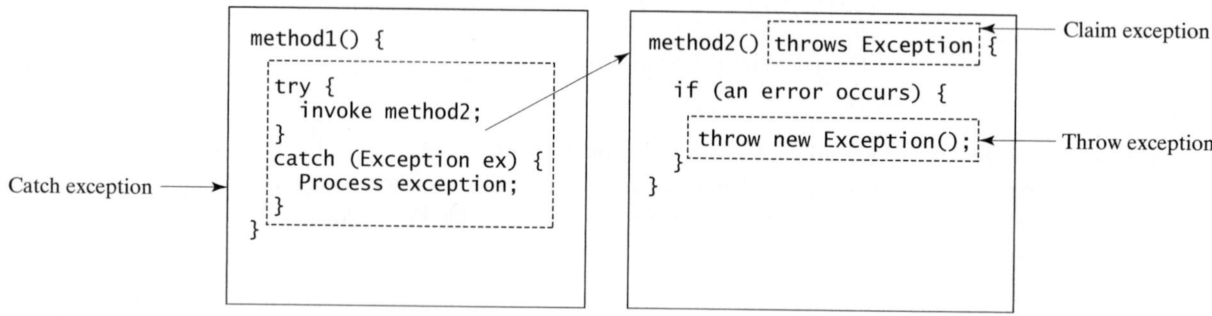

FIGURE 18.2 Exception handling in Java consists of declaring exceptions, throwing exceptions, and catching and processing exceptions.

18.5.1 Declaring Exceptions

declare exception

In Java, the statement currently being executed belongs to a method. The Java interpreter invokes the `main` method for a Java application, and the Web browser invokes the applet's no-arg constructor and then the `init` method for a Java applet. Every method must state the types of checked exceptions it might throw. This is known as *declaring exceptions*. Because system errors and runtime errors can happen to any code, Java does not require that you declare `Error` and `RuntimeException` (unchecked exceptions) explicitly in the method. However, all other exceptions thrown by the method must be explicitly declared in the method declaration so that the caller of the method is informed of the exception.

To declare an exception in a method, use the `throws` keyword in the method declaration, as in this example:

```
public void myMethod() throws IOException
```

The `throws` keyword indicates that `myMethod` might throw an `IOException`. If the method might throw multiple exceptions, add a list of the exceptions, separated by commas, after `throws`:

```
public void myMethod()
  throws Exception1, Exception2, ..., ExceptionN
```

Note

If a method does not declare exceptions in the superclass, you cannot override it to declare exceptions in the subclass.

18.5.2 Throwing Exceptions

A program that detects an error can create an instance of an appropriate exception type and throw it. This is known as *throwing an exception*. Here is an example: Suppose the program detects that an argument passed to the method violates the method contract (e.g., the argument must be nonnegative, but a negative argument is passed); the program can create an instance of `IllegalArgumentException` and throw it, as follows:

throw exception

```
IllegalArgumentException ex =
  new IllegalArgumentException("Wrong Argument");
throw ex;
```

Or, if you prefer, you can use the following:

```
throw new IllegalArgumentException("Wrong Argument");
```

Note

`IllegalArgumentException` is an exception class in the Java API. In general, each exception class in the Java API has at least two constructors: a no-arg constructor, and a constructor with a `String` argument that describes the exception. This argument is called the *exception message*, which can be obtained using `getMessage()`.

exception message

Tip

The keyword to declare an exception is `throws`, and the keyword to throw an exception is `throw`.

throws and **throw**

18.5.3 Catching Exceptions

You now know how to declare an exception and how to throw an exception. When an exception is thrown, it can be caught and handled in a try-catch block, as follows:

catch exception

```
try {
  statements;  // Statements that may throw exceptions
}
catch (Exception1 exVar1) {
  handler for exception1;
}
catch (Exception2 exVar2) {
  handler for exception2;
}
...
catch (ExceptionN exVar3) {
  handler for exceptionN;
}
```

If no exceptions arise during the execution of the `try` block, the `catch` blocks are skipped.

If one of the statements inside the `try` block throws an exception, Java skips the remaining statements in the try block and starts the process of finding the code to handle the exception. The code that handles the exception is called the *exception handler*; it is found by propagating the exception backward through a chain of method calls, starting from the current method. Each `catch` block is examined in turn, from first to last, to see whether the type of the exception object is an instance of the exception class in the `catch` block. If so, the exception object is assigned to the variable declared, and the code in the `catch`

exception handler

block is executed. If no handler is found, Java exits this method, passes the exception to the method that invoked the method, and continues the same process to find a handler. If no handler is found in the chain of methods being invoked, the program terminates and prints an error message on the console. The process of finding a handler is called *catching an exception*.

Suppose the `main` method invokes `method1`, `method1` invokes `method2`, `method2` invokes `method3`, and an exception occurs in `method3`, as shown in Figure 18.3. Consider the following scenario:

- If `method3` cannot handle the exception, `method3` is aborted and the control is returned to `method2`. If the exception type is `Exception3`, it is caught by the `catch` block for handling exception `ex3` in `method2`. `statement5` is skipped, and `statement6` is executed.

- If the exception type is `Exception2`, `method2` is aborted, the control is returned to `method1`, and the exception is caught by the `catch` block for handling exception `ex2` in `method1`. `statement3` is skipped, and `statement4` is executed.

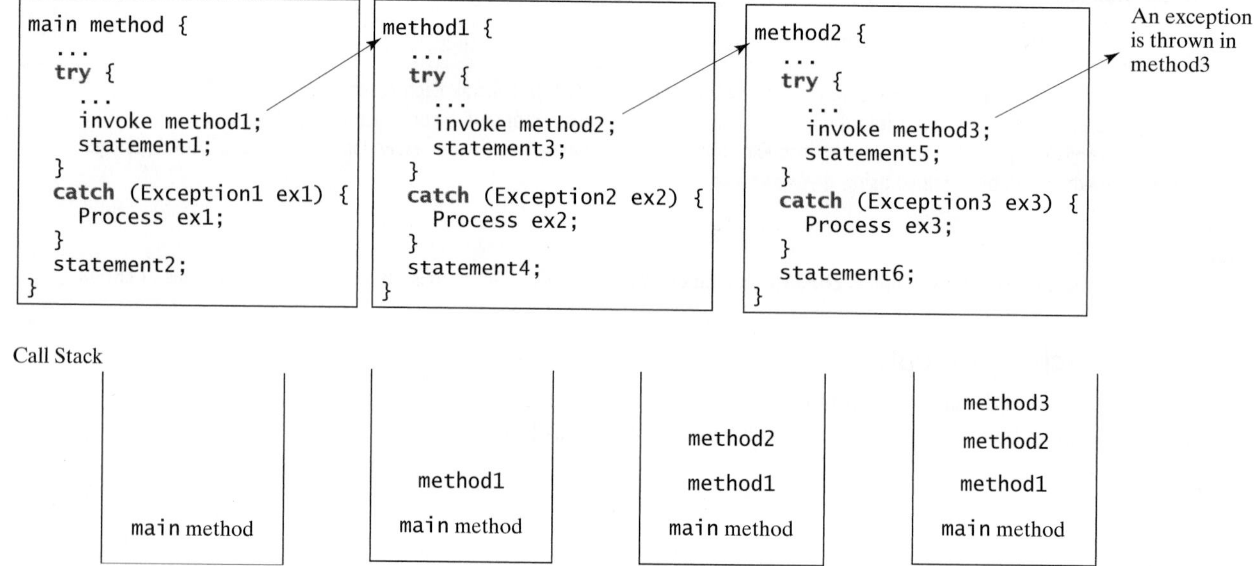

FIGURE 18.3 If an exception is not caught in the current method, it is passed to its caller. The process is repeated until the exception is caught or passed to the `main` method.

- If the exception type is `Exception1`, `method1` is aborted, the control is returned to the `main` method, and the exception is caught by the `catch` block for handling exception `ex1` in the `main` method. `statement1` is skipped, and `statement2` is executed.

- If the exception type is not `Exception1`, `Exception2`, or `Exception3`, the exception is not caught and the program terminates. `statement1` and `statement2` are not executed.

catch block

Note

Various exception classes can be derived from a common superclass. If a `catch` block catches exception objects of a superclass, it can catch all the exception objects of the subclasses of that superclass.

Note

The order in which exceptions are specified in **catch** blocks is important. A compilation error will result if a catch block for a superclass type appears before a catch block for a subclass type. For example, the ordering in (a) below is erroneous, because **RuntimeException** is a subclass of **Exception**. The correct ordering should be as shown in (b).

order of exception handlers

```
try {
  ...
}
catch (Exception ex) {
  ...
}
catch (RuntimeException ex) {
  ...
}
```

(a) Wrong order

```
try {
  ...
}
catch (RuntimeException ex) {
  ...
}
catch (Exception ex) {
  ...
}
```

(b) Correct order

Note

Java forces you to deal with checked exceptions. If a method declares a checked exception (i.e., an exception other than **Error** or **RuntimeException**), you must invoke it in a **try-catch** block or declare to throw the exception in the calling method. For example, suppose that method **p1** invokes method **p2** and **p2** may throw a checked exception (e.g., **IOException**); you have to write the code as shown in (a) or (b).

catch or declare checked exceptions

```
void p1() {
  try {
    p2();
  }
  catch (IOException ex) {
    ...
  }
}
```

(a) Catch exception

```
void p1() throws IOException {

  p2();

}
```

(b) Throw exception

18.5.4 Getting Information from Exceptions

An exception object contains valuable information about the exception. You may use the following instance methods in the **java.lang.Throwable** class to get information regarding the exception, as shown in Figure 18.4. The **printStackTrace()** method prints stack trace information on the console. The **getStackTrace()** method provides programmatic access to the stack trace information printed by **printStackTrace()**.

methods in **Throwable**

java.lang.Throwable	
+getMessage(): String	Returns the message of this object.
+toString(): String	Returns the concatenation of three strings: (1) the full name of the exception class; (2) ": " (a colon and a space); (3) the getMessage() method.
+printStackTrace(): void	Prints the Throwable object and its call stack trace information on the console.
+getStackTrace(): StackTraceElement[]	Returns an array of stack trace elements representing the stack trace pertaining to this throwable.

FIGURE 18.4 **Throwable** is the root class for all exception objects.

Listing 18.5 gives an example that uses the methods in `Throwable` to display exception information. Line 4 invokes the `sum` method to return the sum of all the elements in the array. There is an error in line 23 that causes the `ArrayIndexOutOfBoundsException`, a subclass of `IndexOutOfBoundsException`. This exception is caught in the try-catch block. Lines 7, 8, 9 display the stack trace, exception message, and exception object and message using the `printStackTrace()`, `getMessage()`, and `toString()` methods, as shown in Figure 18.5. Line 10 brings stack trace elements into an array. Each element represents a method call. You can obtain the method (line 12), class name (line 13), and exception line number (line 14) for each element.

LISTING 18.5 TestException.java

invoke sum

printStackTrace()
getMessage()
toString()

```
 1 public class TestException  {
 2   public static void main(String[] args) {
 3     try {
 4       System.out.println(sum(new int[] {1, 2, 3, 4, 5}) );
 5     }
 6     catch (Exception ex) {
 7       ex.printStackTrace();
 8       System.out.println("\n" + ex.getMessage());
 9       System.out.println("\n" + ex.toString());
10
11       System.out.println("\nTrace Info Obtained from getStackTrace");
12       StackTraceElement[] traceElements = ex.getStackTrace();
13       for (int i = 0; i < traceElements.length; i++) {
14         System.out.print("method " + traceElements[i].getMethodName());
15         System.out.print("(" + traceElements[i].getClassName() + ":");
16         System.out.println(traceElements[i].getLineNumber() + ")");
17       }
18     }
19   }
20
21   private static int sum(int[] list) {
22     int result = 0;
23     for (int i = 0; i <= list.length; i++)
24       result += list[i];
25     return result;
26   }
27 }
```

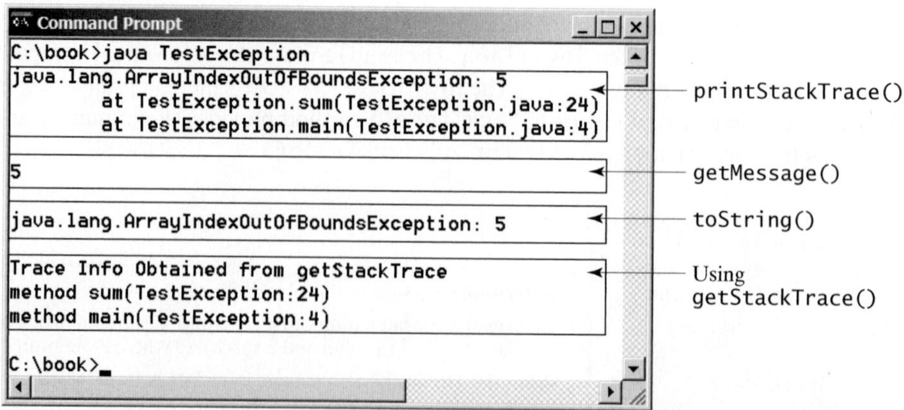

FIGURE 18.5 You can use the `printStackTrace()`, `getMessage()`, `toString()`, and `getStackTrace()` methods to obtain information from exception objects.

18.5.5 Example: Declaring, Throwing, and Catching Exceptions

This example demonstrates declaring, throwing, and catching exceptions by modifying the `setRadius` method in Listing 7.7, Circle3.java. The new `setRadius` method throws an exception if the radius is negative.

Rename the circle class given in Listing 18.6 as `CircleWithException`, which is the same as `Circle3` except that the `setRadius(double newRadius)` method throws an `IllegalArgumentException` if the argument `newRadius` is negative.

LISTING 18.6 CircleWithException.java

```
public class CircleWithException {
  /** The radius of the circle */
  private double radius;

  /** The number of the objects created */
  private static int numberOfObjects = 0;

  /** Construct a circle with radius 1 */
  public CircleWithException() {
    this(1.0);
  }

  /** Construct a circle with a specified radius */
  public CircleWithException(double newRadius) {
    setRadius(newRadius);
    numberOfObjects++;
  }

  /** Return radius */
  public double getRadius() {
    return radius;
  }

  /** Set a new radius */
  public void setRadius(double newRadius)
      throws IllegalArgumentException {
    if (newRadius >= 0)
      radius =  newRadius;
    else
      throw new IllegalArgumentException(
        "Radius cannot be negative");
  }

  /** Return numberOfObjects */
  public static int getNumberOfObjects() {
    return numberOfObjects;
  }

  /** Return the area of this circle */
  public double findArea() {
    return radius * radius * 3.14159;
  }
}
```

declare exception

throw exception

A test program that uses the new `Circle` class is given in Listing 18.7.

LISTING 18.7 TestCircleWithException.java

try

catch

```
1 public class TestCircleWithException {
2   /** Main method */
3   public static void main(String[] args) {
4     try {
5       CircleWithException c1 = new CircleWithException(5);
6       CircleWithException c2 = new CircleWithException(-5);
7       CircleWithException c3 = new CircleWithException(0);
8     }
9     catch (IllegalArgumentException ex) {
10      System.out.println(ex);
11    }
12
13    System.out.println("Number of objects created: " +
14      CircleWithException.getNumberOfObjects());
15  }
16 }
```

```
java.lang.IllegalArgumentException: Radius cannot be negative
Number of objects created: 1
```

The original `Circle3` class remains intact except that the class name is changed to `CircleWithException`, a new constructor `CircleWithException(newRadius)` is added, and the `setRadius` method now declares an exception and throws it if the radius is negative.

The `setRadius` method declares to throw `IllegalArgumentException` in the method declaration (lines 25–32 in CircleWithException.java). The `CircleWithException` class would still compile if the `throws IllegalArgumentException` clause were removed from the method declaration, since it is a subclass of `RuntimeException` and every method can throw `RuntimeException` (unchecked exception) regardless of whether it is declared in the method header.

The test program creates three `CircleWithException` objects, `c1`, `c2`, and `c3`, to test how to handle exceptions. Invoking `new CircleWithException(-5)` (line 5 in Listing 18.7) causes the `setRadius` method to be invoked, which throws an `IllegalArgumentException`, because the radius is negative. In the `catch` block, the type of the object `ex` is `IllegalArgumentException`, which matches the exception object thrown by the `setRadius` method. So, this exception is caught by the `catch` block.

The exception handler prints a short message, `ex.toString()` (line 10), about the exception, using `System.out.println(ex)`.

Note that the execution continues in the event of the exception. If the handlers had not caught the exception, the program would have abruptly terminated.

The test program would still compile if the `try` statement were not used, because the method throws an instance of `IllegalArgumentException`, a subclass of `RuntimeException` (unchecked exception). If a method throws an exception other than `RuntimeException` and `Error`, the method must be invoked within a `try-catch` block.

Note

multiple threads

As you will learn in Chapter 29, "Multithreading," Java supports multithreading. One program can have many threads. Methods are executed on threads. If an exception occurs on a thread, the thread is terminated if the exception is not caught. If a program has only one thread, an uncaught exception will cause the program to terminate. If a program has multiple threads, an uncaught exception will terminate only the thread where the exception occurred. However, since certain threads may rely on the terminated thread, terminating a thread may affect the rest of the program.

18.6 The **finally** Clause

Occasionally, you may want some code to be executed regardless of whether an exception occurs or is caught. Java has a `finally` clause that can be used to accomplish this objective. The syntax for the `finally` clause might look like this:

```
try {
  statements;
}
catch (TheException ex) {
  handling ex;
}
finally {
  finalStatements;
}
```

The code in the `finally` block is executed under all circumstances, regardless of whether an exception occurs in the `try` block or is caught. Consider three possible cases:

- If no exception arises in the `try` block, `finalStatements` is executed, and the next statement after the `try` statement is executed.
- If one of the statements causes an exception in the `try` block that is caught in a `catch` block, the other statements in the `try` block are skipped, the `catch` block is executed, and the `finally` clause is executed. If the `catch` block does not rethrow an exception, the next statement after the `try` statement is executed. If it does, the exception is passed to the caller of this method.
- If one of the statements causes an exception that is not caught in any `catch` block, the other statements in the `try` block are skipped, the `finally` clause is executed, and the exception is passed to the caller of this method.
- The `finally` block executes even if there is a `return` statement prior to reaching the `finally` block.

Note

The `catch` block may be omitted when the `finally` clause is used.

omitting catch block

A common use of the `finally` clause is in I/O programming. To ensure that a file is closed under all circumstances, you may place a file closing statement in the `finally` block, as shown in Listing 18.8.

LISTING 18.8 FinallyDemo.java

try

catch

finally

```
public class FinallyDemo {
  public static void main(String[] args) {
    java.io.PrintWriter output = null;

    try {
      // Create a file
      output = new java.io.PrintWriter("text.txt");

      // Write formatted output to the file
      output.println("Welcome to Java");
    }
    catch (java.io.IOException ex) {
      ex.printStackTrace();
    }
    finally {
```

```
16        // Close the file
17        if (output != null) output.close();
18      }
19    }
20  }
```

The statements in lines 7 and 10 may throw an `IOException`, so they are placed inside a `try` block. The statement `output.close()` closes the `PrintWriter` object output in the `finally` block. This statement is executed regardless of whether an exception occurs in the `try` block or is caught.

18.7 When to Use Exceptions

The `try` block contains the code that is executed in normal circumstances. The `catch` block contains the code that is executed in exceptional circumstances. Exception handling separates error-handling code from normal programming tasks, thus making programs easier to read and to modify. Be aware, however, that exception handling usually requires more time and resources, because it requires instantiating a new exception object, rolling back the call stack, and propagating the exception through the chain of methods invoked to search for the handler.

An exception occurs in a method. If you want the exception to be processed by its caller, you should create an exception object and throw it. If you can handle the exception in the method where it occurs, there is no need to throw or use exceptions.

In general, common exceptions that may occur in multiple classes in a project are candidates for exception classes. Simple errors that may occur in individual methods are best handled locally without throwing exceptions.

When should you use a `try-catch` block in the code? Use it when you have to deal with unexpected error conditions. Do not use a try-catch block to deal with simple, expected situations. For example, the following code

```
try {
  System.out.println(refVar.toString());
}
catch (NullPointerException ex) {
  System.out.println("refVar is null");
}
```

is better replaced by

```
if (refVar != null)
  System.out.println(refVar.toString());
else
  System.out.println("refVar is null");
```

Which situations are exceptional and which are expected is sometimes difficult to decide. The point is not to abuse exception handling as a way to deal with a simple logic test.

18.8 Rethrowing Exceptions

Java allows an exception handler to rethrow the exception if the handler cannot process the exception or simply wants to let its caller be notified of the exception. The syntax may look like this:

```
try {
  statements;
}
```

```
catch (TheException ex) {
  perform operations before exits;
  throw ex;
}
```

The statement **throw ex** rethrows the exception so that other handlers get a chance to process the exception **ex**.

18.9 Chained Exceptions

In the preceding section, the catch block rethrows the original exception. Sometimes, you may need to throw a new exception (with additional information) along with the original exception. This is called *chained exceptions*. Listing 18.9 illustrates how to create and throw chained exceptions.

LISTING 18.9 ChainedExceptionDemo.java

```
1 public class ChainedExceptionDemo {
2   public static void main(String[] args) {
3     try {
4       method1();
5     }
6     catch (Exception ex) {
7       ex.printStackTrace();
8     }
9   }
10
11   public static void method1() throws Exception {
12     try {
13       method2();
14     }
15     catch (Exception ex) {
16       throw new Exception("New info from method1", ex);
17     }
18   }
19
20   public static void method2() throws Exception {
21     throw new Exception("New info from method2");
22   }
23 }
```

stack trace

chained exception

throw exception

```
java.lang.Exception: New info from method1
        at ChainedExceptionDemo.method1(ChainedExceptionDemo.java:16)
        at ChainedExceptionDemo.main(ChainedExceptionDemo.java:4)
Caused by: java.lang.Exception: New info from method2
        at ChainedExceptionDemo.method2(ChainedExceptionDemo.java:21)
        at ChainedExceptionDemo.method1(ChainedExceptionDemo.java:13)
        ... 1 more
```

The **main** method invokes **method1** (line 4), **method1** invokes **method2** (line 13), and **method2** throws an exception (line 21). This exception is caught in the catch block in **method1** and is wrapped in a new exception in line 16. The new exception is thrown and caught in the catch block in the **main** method in line 4. The sample output shows the output from the **printStackTrace()** method in line 7. The new exception thrown from **method1** is displayed first, followed by the original exception thrown from **method2**.

Video Note
Create custom exception classes

18.10 Creating Custom Exception Classes

Java provides quite a few exception classes. Use them whenever possible instead of creating your own exception classes. However, if you run into a problem that cannot be adequately described by the predefined exception classes, you can create your own exception class, derived from `Exception` or from a subclass of `Exception`, such as `IOException`.

In Listing 18.6, CircleWithException.java, the `setRadius` method throws an exception if the radius is negative. Suppose you wish to pass the radius to the handler. In that case, you may create a custom exception class, as shown in Listing 18.10.

LISTING 18.10 `InvalidRadiusException.java`

extends **Exception**

```
1 public class InvalidRadiusException extends Exception {
2   private double radius;
3
4   /** Construct an exception */
5   public InvalidRadiusException(double radius) {
6     super("Invalid radius " + radius);
7     this.radius = radius;
8   }
9
10  /** Return the radius */
11  public double getRadius() {
12    return radius;
13  }
14 }
```

Exception constructors

This custom exception class extends `java.lang.Exception` (line 1). The `Exception` class extends `java.lang.Throwable`. All the methods (e.g., `getMessage()`, `toString()`, and `printStackTrace()`) in `Exception` are inherited from `Throwable`. The `Exception` class contains four constructors. Among them, the following two constructors are often used:

java.lang.Exception	
+Exception()	Constructs an exception with no message.
+Exception(message: String)	Constructs an exception with the specified message.

Line 6 invokes the superclass's constructor with a message. This message will be set in the exception object and can be obtained by invoking `getMessage()` on the object.

Tip

Most exception classes in the Java API contain two constructors: a no-arg constructor and a constructor with a message parameter.

To create an `InvalidRadiusException`, you have to pass a radius. So the `setRadius` method in Listing 18.6 can be modified as follows:

```
/** Set a new radius */
public void setRadius(double newRadius)
    throws InvalidRadiusException {
  if (newRadius >= 0)
    radius =  newRadius;
  else
    throw new InvalidRadiusException(newRadius);
}
```

The following code creates a circle object and sets its radius to -5.

```
try {
  CircleWithException1 c = new CircleWithException1(4);
  c.setRadius(-5);
}
catch (InvalidRadiusException ex) {
  System.out.println("The invalid radius is " + ex.getRadius());
}
```

Invoking `setRadius(-5)` throws an `InvalidRadiusException`, which is caught by the handler. The handler displays the radius in the exception object `ex`.

Tip

Can you declare a custom exception class by extending `RuntimeException`? Yes, but it is not a good way to go, because it makes your custom exception unchecked. It is better to make a custom exception checked so that the complier can force these exceptions to be caught in your program.

checked custom exception

Key Terms

chained exception 613
checked exception 603
declare exception 604
exception 600
exception propagation 605
throw exception 601
unchecked exception 603

Chapter Summary

- When an exception occurs, Java creates an object that contains the information for the exception. You can use the information to handle the exception.
- A Java exception is an instance of a class derived from `java.lang.Throwable`. Java provides a number of predefined exception classes, such as `Error`, `Exception`, `RuntimeException`, `ClassNotFoundException`, `NullPointerException`, and `ArithmeticException`. You can also define your own exception class by extending `Exception`.
- Exceptions occur during the execution of a method. `RuntimeException` and `Error` are unchecked exceptions; all other exceptions are checked.
- When declaring a method, you have to declare a checked exception if the method might throw it, thus telling the compiler what can go wrong.
- The keyword for declaring an exception is `throws`, and the keyword for throwing an exception is `throw`.
- To invoke the method that declares checked exceptions, you must enclose the method call in a `try` statement. When an exception occurs during the execution of the method, the `catch` block catches and handles the exception.
- If an exception is not caught in the current method, it is passed to its caller. The process is repeated until the exception is caught or passed to the `main` method.

- Various exception classes can be derived from a common superclass. If a **catch** block catches the exception objects of a superclass, it can also catch all the exception objects of the subclasses of that superclass.

- The order in which exceptions are specified in a **catch** block is important. A compilation error will result if you do not specify an exception object of a class before an exception object of the superclass of that class.

- When an exception occurs in a method, the method exits immediately if it does not catch the exception. If the method is required to perform some task before exiting, you can catch the exception in the method and then rethrow it to the real handler.

- The code in the **finally** block is executed under all circumstances, regardless of whether an exception occurs in the **try** block or is caught.

- Exception handling separates error-handling code from normal programming tasks, thus making programs easier to read and to modify.

- Exception handling should not be used to replace simple tests. You should test simple exceptions whenever possible, and reserve exception handling for dealing with situations that cannot be handled with **if** statements.

REVIEW QUESTIONS

Sections 18.1–18.13

18.1 Describe the Java **Throwable** class, its subclasses, and the types of exceptions. What **RunTimeException** will the following programs throw, if any?

```
public class Test {
  public static void main(String[] args) {
    System.out.println(1 / 0);
  }
}
```

(a)

```
public class Test {
  public static void main(String[] args) {
    int[] list = new int[5];
    System.out.println(list[5]);
  }
}
```

(b)

```
public class Test {
  public static void main(String[] args) {
    String s = "abc";
    System.out.println(s.charAt(3));
  }
}
```

(c)

```
public class Test {
  public static void main(String[] args) {
    Object o = new Object();
    String d = (String)o;
  }
}
```

(d)

```
public class Test {
  public static void main(String[] args) {
    Object o = null;
    System.out.println(o.toString());
  }
}
```

(e)

```
public class Test {
  public static void main(String[] args) {
    System.out.println(1.0 / 0);
  }
}
```

(f)

18.2 Show the output of the following code.

```
public class Test {
  public static void main(String[] args) {
    for (int i = 0; i < 2; i++) {
      System.out.print(i + " ");
      try {
        System.out.println(1 / 0);
      }
      catch (Exception ex) {
      }
    }
  }
}
```

(a)

```
public class Test {
  public static void main(String[] args) {
    try {
      for (int i = 0; i < 2; i++) {
        System.out.print(i + " ");
        System.out.println(1 / 0);
      }
    }
    catch (Exception ex) {
    }
  }
}
```

(b)

18.3 Point out the problem in the following code. Does the code throw any exceptions?

```
long value = Long.MAX_VALUE + 1;
System.out.println(value);
```

18.4 What is the purpose of declaring exceptions? How do you declare an exception, and where? Can you declare multiple exceptions in a method declaration?

18.5 What is a checked exception, and what is an unchecked exception?

18.6 How do you throw an exception? Can you throw multiple exceptions in one `throw` statement?

18.7 What is the keyword `throw` used for? What is the keyword `throws` used for?

18.8 What does the JVM do when an exception occurs? How do you catch an exception?

18.9 What is the printout of the following code?

```
public class Test {
  public static void main(String[] args) {
    try {
      int value = 30;
      if (value < 40)
        throw new Exception("value is too small");
    }
    catch (Exception ex) {
      System.out.println(ex.getMessage());
    }
    System.out.println("Continue after the catch block");
  }
}
```

What would be the printout if the line

```
int value = 30;
```

were changed to

```
int value = 50;
```

18.10 Suppose that `statement2` causes an exception in the following `try-catch` block:

```
try {
  statement1;
  statement2;
```

```
    statement3;
  }
  catch (Exception1 ex1) {
  }
  catch (Exception2 ex2) {
  }

  statement4;
```

Answer the following questions:

- Will statement3 be executed?
- If the exception is not caught, will statement4 be executed?
- If the exception is caught in the catch block, will statement4 be executed?
- If the exception is passed to the caller, will statement4 be executed?

18.11 What is displayed when the following program is run?

```
public class Test {
  public static void main(String[] args) {
    try {
      int[] list = new int[10];
      System.out.println("list[10] is " + list[10]);
    }
    catch (ArithmeticException ex) {
      System.out.println("ArithmeticException");
    }
    catch (RuntimeException ex) {
      System.out.println("RuntimeException");
    }
    catch (Exception ex) {
      System.out.println("Exception");
    }
  }
}
```

18.12 What is displayed when the following program is run?

```
public class Test {
  public static void main(String[] args) {
    try {
      method();
      System.out.println("After the method call");
    }
    catch (ArithmeticException ex) {
      System.out.println("ArithmeticException");
    }
    catch (RuntimeException ex) {
      System.out.println("RuntimeException");
    }
    catch (Exception e) {
      System.out.println("Exception");
    }
  }

  static void method() throws Exception {
    System.out.println(1 / 0);
  }
}
```

18.13 What is displayed when the following program is run?

```
public class Test {
  public static void main(String[] args) {
    try {
      method();
      System.out.println("After the method call");
    }
    catch (RuntimeException ex) {
      System.out.println("RuntimeException in main");
    }
    catch (Exception ex) {
      System.out.println("Exception in main");
    }
  }

  static void method() throws Exception {
    try {
      String s ="abc";
      System.out.println(s.charAt(3));
    }
    catch (RuntimeException ex) {
      System.out.println("RuntimeException in method()");
    }
    catch (Exception ex) {
      System.out.println("Exception in method()");
    }
  }
}
```

18.14 If an exception is not caught in a non-GUI application, what will happen? If an exception is not caught in a GUI application, what will happen?

18.15 What does the method `printStackTrace` do?

18.16 Does the presence of a `try-catch` block impose overhead when no exception occurs?

18.17 Correct a compilation error in the following code:

```
public void m(int value) {
  if (value < 40)
    throw new Exception("value is too small");
}
```

Sections 18.4–18.7

18.18 Suppose that `statement2` causes an exception in the following statement:

```
try {
  statement1;
  statement2;
  statement3;
}
catch (Exception1 ex1) {
}
catch (Exception2 ex2) {
}
catch (Exception3 ex3) {
  throw ex3;
}
finally {
  statement4;
};
statement5;
```

Answer the following questions:

- Will statement5 be executed if the exception is not caught?
- If the exception is of type Exception3, will statement4 be executed, and will statement5 be executed?

18.19 Suppose the setRadius method throws the RadiusException declared in §18.7. What is displayed when the following program is run?

```
public class Test {
  public static void main(String[] args) {
    try {
      method();
      System.out.println("After the method call");
    }
    catch (RuntimeException ex) {
      System.out.println("RuntimeException in main");
    }
    catch (Exception ex) {
      System.out.println("Exception in main");
    }
  }

  static void method() throws Exception {
    try {
      Circle c1 = new Circle(1);
      c1.setRadius(-1);
      System.out.println(c1.getRadius());
    }
    catch (RuntimeException ex) {
      System.out.println("RuntimeException in method()");
    }
    catch (Exception ex) {
      System.out.println("Exception in method()");
      throw ex;
    }
  }
}
```

18.20 The following method checks whether a string is a numeric string:

```
public static boolean isNumeric(String token) {
  try {
    Double.parseDouble(token);
    return true;
  }
  catch (java.lang.NumberFormatException ex) {
    return false;
  }
}
```

Is it correct? Rewrite it without using exceptions.

Programming Exercises

Sections 18.2–18.4

18.1* (*NumberFormatException*) Listing 8.4, Calculator.java, is a simple command-line calculator. Note that the program terminates if any operand is nonnumeric. Write a program with an exception handler that deals with nonnumeric operands;

then write another program without using an exception handler to achieve the same objective. Your program should display a message that informs the user of the wrong operand type before exiting (see Figure 18.6).

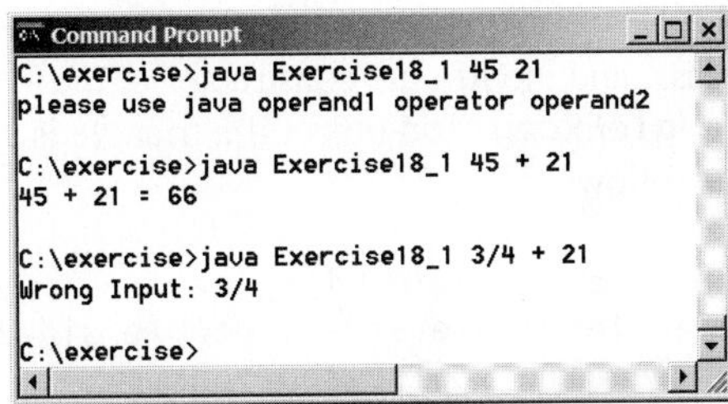

FIGURE 18.6 The program performs arithmetic operations and detects input errors.

18.2* (*`ArithmeticException` and `NumberFormatException`*) Write a program that creates a user interface to perform integer divisions, as shown in Figure 18.7. The user enters two numbers in the text fields, `Number 1` and `Number 2`. The division of `Number 1` and `Number 2` is displayed in the Result field when the Divide button is clicked. If `Number 1` or `Number 2` were not an integer, the program would throw a `NumberFormatException`. If `Number 2` were zero, the program would throw an `ArithmeticException`. Display the exception in a message dialog box, as shown in Figure 18.7.

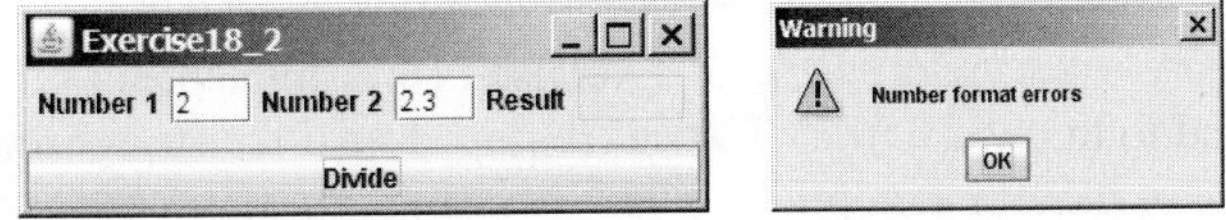

FIGURE 18.7 The program displays an error message in the dialog box if the number is not well formatted.

18.3* (*`ArrayIndexOutBoundsException`*) Write a program that meets the following requirements:

- Create an array with 100 randomly chosen integers.
- Create a text field to enter an array index and another text field to display the array element at the specified index (see Figure 18.8).
- Create a *Show Element* button to cause the array element to be displayed. If the specified index is out of bounds, display the message **Out of Bound**.

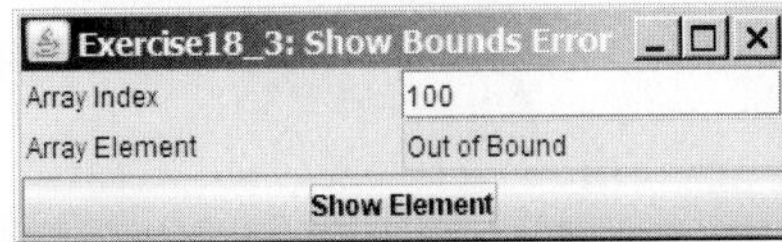

FIGURE 18.8 The program displays the array element at the specified index or displays the message **Out of Bound** if the index is out of bounds.

18.4* (*IllegalArgumentException*) Modify the `Loan` class in Listing 9.2 to throw `IllegalArgumentException` if the loan amount, interest rate, or number of years is less than or equal to zero.

18.5* (*IllegalTriangleException*) Exercise 10.1 defined the `Triangle` class with three sides. In a triangle, the sum of any two sides is greater than the other side. The `Triangle` class must adhere to this rule. Create the `IllegalTriangleException` class, and modify the constructor of the `Triangle` class to throw an `IllegalTriangleException` object if a triangle is created with sides that violate the rule, as follows:

```
/** Construct a triangle with the specified sides */
public Triangle(double side1, double side2, double side3)
  throws IllegalTriangleException {
  // Implement it
}
```

18.6* (*NumberFormatException*) Exercise 8.7 specifies the `parseHex(String hexString)` method, which converts a hex string into a decimal number. Implement the `parseHex` method to throw a `NumberFormatException` if the string is not a hex string.

18.7* (*NumberFormatException*) Exercise 8.8 specifies the `parseBinary(String binaryString)` method, which converts a binary string into a decimal number. Implement the `parseBinary` method to throw a `NumberFormatException` if the string is not a binary string.

Video Note
`HexFormatException`

18.8* (*HexFormatException*) Exercise 18.6 implements the `parseHex` method to throw a `NumberFormatException` if the string is not a hex string. Define a custom exception called `HexFormatException`. Implement the `parseHex` method to throw a `HexFormatException` if the string is not a hex string.

18.9* (*BinaryFormatException*) Exercise 18.7 implements the `parseBinary` method to throw a `BinaryFormatException` if the string is not a binary string. Define a custom exception called `BinaryFormatException`. Implement the `parseBinary` method to throw a `BinaryFormatException` if the string is not a binary string.

CHAPTER 19

BINARY I/O

Objectives

- To discover how I/O is processed in Java (§19.2).
- To distinguish between text I/O and binary I/O (§19.3).
- To read and write bytes using `FileInputStream` and `FileOutputStream` (§19.4.1).
- To filter data using base classes `FilterInputStream` / `FilterOutputStream` (§19.4.2).
- To read and write primitive values and strings using `DataInputStream`/ `DataOutputStream` (§19.4.3).
- To store and restore objects using `ObjectOutputStream` and `ObjectInputStream`, and to understand how objects are serialized and what kind of objects can be serialized (§19.6).
- To implement the `Serializable` interface to make objects serializable (§19.6.1).
- To serialize arrays (§19.6.2).
- To read and write files using the `RandomAccessFile` class (§19.7).

19.1 Introduction

text file
binary file

Data stored in a text file are represented in human-readable form. Data stored in a binary file are represented in binary form. You cannot read binary files. They are designed to be read by programs. For example, Java source programs are stored in text files and can be read by a text editor, but Java classes are stored in binary files and are read by the JVM. The advantage of binary files is that they are more efficient to process than text files.

Although it is not technically precise and correct, you can envision a text file as consisting of a sequence of characters and a binary file as consisting of a sequence of bits. For example, the decimal integer `199` is stored as the sequence of three characters, `'1'`, `'9'`, `'9'`, in a text file, and the same integer is stored as a `byte`-type value `C7` in a binary file, because decimal `199` equals hex `C7` ($199 = 12 \times 16^1 + 7$).

text I/O
binary I/O

Java offers many classes for performing file input and output. These can be categorized as *text I/O classes* and *binary I/O classes.* You learned how to read/write strings and numeric values from/to a text file using `Scanner` and `PrintWriter` in §8.7, "File Input and Output." This section introduces the classes for performing binary I/O.

19.2 How is I/O Handled in Java?

Recall that a `File` object encapsulates the properties of a file or a path, but does not contain the methods for reading/writing data from/to a file. In order to perform I/O, you need to create objects using appropriate Java I/O classes. The objects contain the methods for reading/writing data from/to a file. For example, to write text to a file named temp.txt, you may create an object using the `PrintWriter` class as follows:

```
PrintWriter output = new PrintWriter("temp.txt");
```

You can now invoke the `print` method from the object to write a string into the file. For example, the following statement writes `"Java 101"` to the file.

```
output.print("Java 101");
```

The next statement closes the file.

```
output.close();
```

There are many I/O classes for various purposes. In general, these can be classified as input classes and output classes. An input class contains the methods to read data, and an output class contains the methods to write data. `PrintWriter` is an example of an output class, and `Scanner` is an example of an input class. The following code creates an input object for the file **temp.txt** and reads data from the file.

```
Scanner input = new Scanner(new File("temp.txt"));
System.out.println(input.nextLine());
```

If **temp.txt** contains `"Java 101"`, `input.nextLine()` returns string `"Java 101"`.

Figure 19.1 illustrates Java I/O programming. An input object reads a stream of data from a file, and an output object writes a stream of data to a file. An input object is also called an *input stream* and an output object an *output stream.*

input stream
output stream

19.3 Text I/O vs. Binary I/O

Computers do not differentiate binary files and text files. All files are stored in binary format, and thus all files are essentially binary files. Text I/O is built upon binary I/O to provide a level of abstraction for character encoding and decoding, as shown in Figure 19.2(a). Encoding and decoding are automatically performed for text I/O. The JVM converts a Unicode

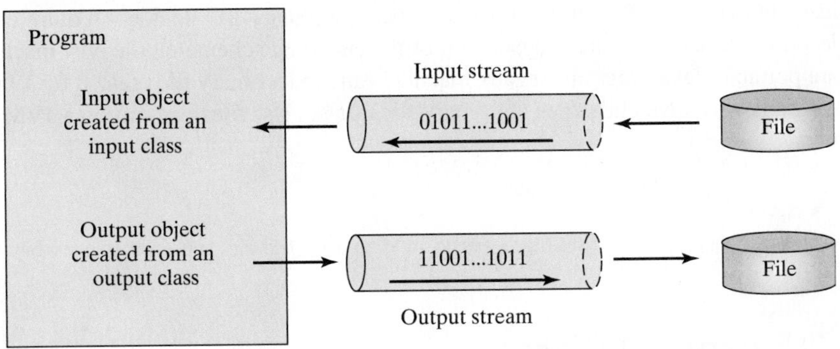

FIGURE 19.1 The program receives data through an input object and sends data through an output object.

to a file-specific encoding when writing a character and converts a file-specific encoding to a Unicode when reading a character. For example, suppose you write string `"199"` using text I/O to a file. Each character is written to the file. Since the Unicode for character `'1'` is `0x0031`, the Unicode `0x0031` is converted to a code that depends on the encoding scheme for the file. (Note that the prefix `0x` denotes a hex number.) In the United States, the default encoding for text files on Windows is ASCII. The ASCII code for character `'1'` is `49` (`0x31` in hex) and for character `'9'` is `57` (`0x39` in hex). So to write the characters `"199"`, three bytes, `0x31`, `0x39`, and `0x39`, are sent to the output, as shown in Figure 19.2(a).

Note

JDK 1.5 supports supplementary Unicode. For simplicity, however, this book considers only the original Unicode from `0` to `FFFF`.

supplementary Unicode

Binary I/O does not require conversions. If you write a numeric value to a file using binary I/O, the exact value in the memory is copied into the file. For example, a byte-type value `199` is represented as `0xC7` ($199 = 12 \times 16^1 + 7$) in the memory and appears exactly as `0xC7` in the file, as shown in Figure 19.2(b). When you read a byte using binary I/O, one byte value is read from the input.

In general, you should use text input to read a file created by a text editor or a text output program, and use binary input to read a file created by a Java binary output program.

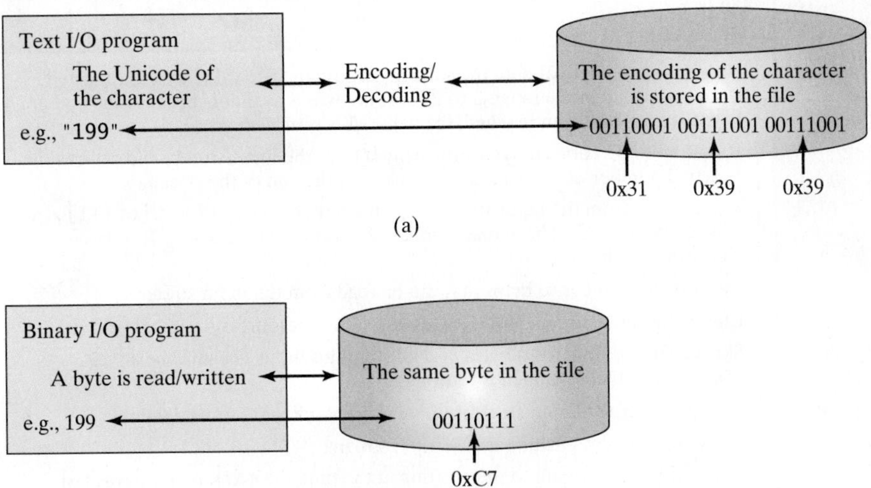

FIGURE 19.2 Text I/O requires encoding and decoding, whereas binary I/O does not.

Binary I/O is more efficient than text I/O, because binary I/O does not require encoding and decoding. Binary files are independent of the encoding scheme on the host machine and thus are portable. Java programs on any machine can read a binary file created by a Java program. This is why Java class files are binary files. Java class files can run on a JVM on any machine.

Note

.txt and .dat

For consistency, this book uses the extension `.txt` to name text files and `.dat` to name binary files.

19.4 Binary I/O Classes

The design of the Java I/O classes is a good example of applying inheritance, where common operations are generalized in superclasses, and subclasses provide specialized operations. Figure 19.3 lists some of the classes for performing binary I/O. `InputStream` is the root for binary input classes, and `OutputStream` is the root for binary output classes. Figures 19.4 and 19.5 list all the methods in `InputStream` and `OutputStream`.

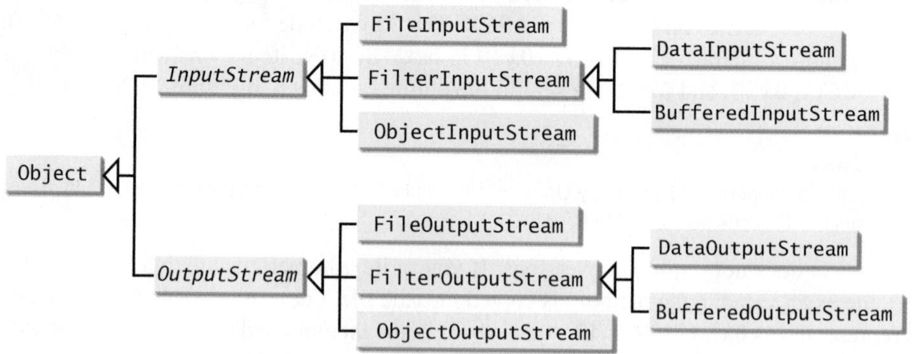

FIGURE 19.3 `InputStream`, `OutputStream`, and their subclasses are for binary I/O.

java.io.InputStream	
`+read(): int`	Reads the next byte of data from the input stream. The value byte is returned as an `int` value in the range `0` to `255`. If no byte is available because the end of the stream has been reached, the value –1 is returned.
`+read(b: byte[]): int`	Reads up to `b.length` bytes into array `b` from the input stream and returns the actual number of bytes read. Returns –1 at the end of the stream.
`+read(b: byte[], off: int, len: int): int`	Reads bytes from the input stream and stores them in `b[off]`, `b[off+1]`, . . ., `b[off+len-1]`. The actual number of bytes read is returned. Returns –1 at the end of the stream.
`+available(): int`	Returns the number of bytes that can be read from the input stream.
`+close(): void`	Closes this input stream and releases any system resources occupied with it.
`+skip(n: long): long`	Skips over and discards `n` bytes of data from this input stream. The actual number of bytes skipped is returned.
`+markSupported(): boolean`	Tests whether this input stream supports the `mark` and `reset` methods.
`+mark(readlimit: int): void`	Marks the current position in this input stream.
`+reset(): void`	Repositions this stream to the position at the time the `mark` method was last called on this stream.

FIGURE 19.4 The abstract `InputStream` class defines the methods for the input stream of bytes.

java.io.OutputStream	
+write(int b): void	Writes the specified byte to this output stream. The parameter `b` is an `int` value. `(byte)b` is written to the output stream.
+write(b: byte[]): void	Writes all the bytes in array `b` to the output stream.
+write(b: byte[], off: int, len: int): void	Writes `b[off]`, `b[off+1]`,. . ., `b[off+len-1]` into the output stream.
+close(): void	Closes this output stream and releases any system resources occupied by it.
+flush(): void	Flushes this output stream and forces any buffered output bytes to be written out.

FIGURE 19.5 The abstract `OutputStream` class defines the methods for the output stream of bytes.

Note

All the methods in the binary I/O classes are declared to throw `java.io.IOException` or a subclass of `java.io.IOException`.

throws IOException

19.4.1 `FileInputStream`/`FileOutputStream`

`FileInputStream`/`FileOutputStream` is for reading/writing bytes from/to files. All the methods in these classes are inherited from `InputStream` and `OutputStream`. `FileInputStream`/`FileOutputStream` does not introduce new methods. To construct a `FileInputStream`, use the following constructors, as shown in Figure 19.6:

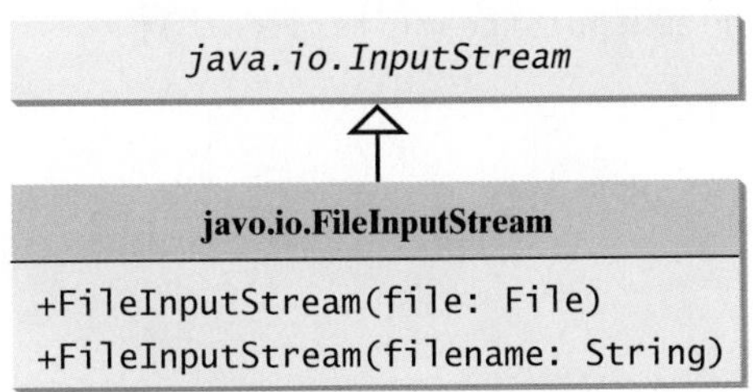

Creates a `FileInputStream` from a `File` object.
Creates a `FileInputStream` from a file name.

FIGURE 19.6 `FileInputStream` inputs stream of bytes from a file.

A `java.io.FileNotFoundException` will occur if you attempt to create a `FileInputStream` with a nonexistent file.

FileNotFoundException

To construct a `FileOutputStream`, use the constructors shown in Figure 19.7.

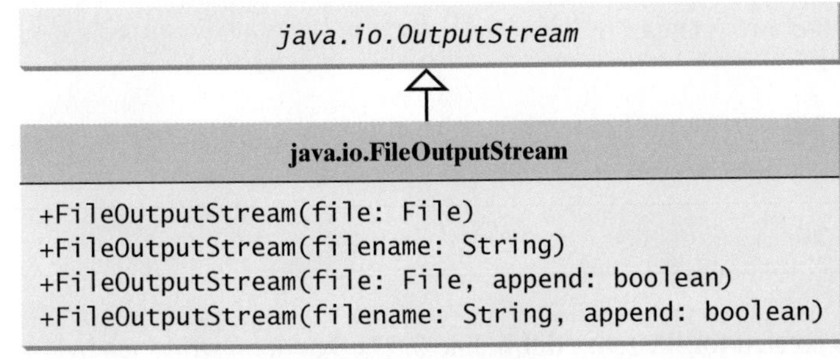

Creates a `FileOutputStream` from a `File` object.
Creates a `FileOutputStream` from a file name.
If `append` is true, data are appended to the existing file.
If `append` is true, data are appended to the existing file.

FIGURE 19.7 `FileOutputStream` outputs stream of bytes to a file.

If the file does not exist, a new file will be created. If the file already exists, the first two constructors will delete the current content of the file. To retain the current content and append new data into the file, use the last two constructors by passing `true` to the `append` parameter.

IOException

Almost all the methods in the I/O classes throw `java.io.IOException`. Therefore you have to declare `java.io.IOException` to throw in the method or place the code in a try-catch block, as shown below:

Declaring exception in the method

```
public static void main(String[] args)
    throws IOException {
  // Perform I/O operations
}
```

Using try-catch block

```
public static void main(String[] args) {
  try {
    // Perform I/O operations
  }
  catch (IOException ex) {
    ex.printStackTrace();
  }
}
```

Listing 19.1 uses binary I/O to write ten byte values from `1` to `10` to a file named **temp.dat** and reads them back from the file.

LISTING 19.1 TestFileStream.java

import
output stream
output
input stream
input

```
 1 import java.io.*;
 2
 3 public class TestFileStream {
 4   public static void main(String[] args) throws IOException {
 5     // Create an output stream to the file
 6     FileOutputStream output = new FileOutputStream("temp.dat");
 7
 8     // Output values to the file
 9     for (int i = 1; i <= 10; i++)
10       output.write(i);
11
12     // Close the output stream
13     output.close();
14
15     // Create an input stream for the file
16     FileInputStream input = new FileInputStream("temp.dat");
17
18     // Read values from the file
19     int value;
20     while ((value = input.read()) != -1)
21       System.out.print(value + " ");
22
23     // Close the output stream
24     input.close();
25   }
26 }
```

```
1 2 3 4 5 6 7 8 9 10
```

A `FileOutputStream` is created for file **temp.dat** in line 6. The `for` loop writes ten byte values into the file (lines 9–10). Invoking `write(i)` is the same as invoking `write((byte)i)`. Line 13 closes the output stream. Line 16 creates a `FileInputStream` for file **temp.dat**. Values are read from the file and displayed on the console in lines 19–21. The expression `((value = input.read()) != -1)` (line 20) reads a byte from `input.read()`, assigns it to `value`, and checks whether it is `-1`. The input value of `-1` signifies the end of a file.

end of a file

The file **temp.dat** created in this example is a binary file. It can be read from a Java program but not from a text editor, as shown in Figure 19.8.

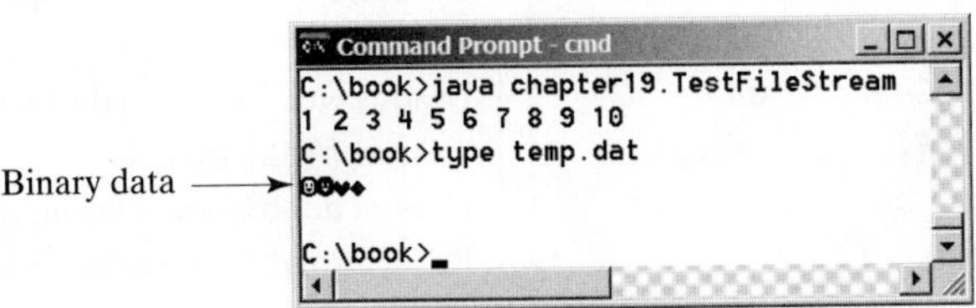

FIGURE 19.8 A binary file cannot be displayed in text mode.

Tip

close stream

When a stream is no longer needed, always close it using the `close()` method. Not closing streams may cause data corruption in the output file, or other programming errors.

Note

where is the file?

The root directory for the file is the classpath directory. For the example in this book, the root directory is **c:\book**. So the file **temp.dat** is located at **c:\book**. If you wish to place **temp.dat** in a specific directory, replace line 8 by

```
FileOutputStream output =
  new FileOutputStream("directory/temp.dat");
```

Note

appending to text file

An instance of `FileInputStream` can be used as an argument to construct a `Scanner`, and an instance of `FileOutputStream` can be used as an argument to construct a `PrintWriter`. You can create a `PrintWriter` to append text into a file using

```
new PrintWriter(new FileOutputStream("temp.txt", true));
```

If **temp.txt** does not exist, it is created. If **temp.txt** already exists, new data are appended to the file.

19.4.2 `FilterInputStream/FilterOutputStream`

Filter streams are streams that filter bytes for some purpose. The basic byte input stream provides a read method that can be used only for reading bytes. If you want to read integers, doubles, or strings, you need a filter class to wrap the byte input stream. Using a filter class enables you to read integers, doubles, and strings instead of bytes and characters. `FilterInputStream` and `FilterOutputStream` are the base classes for filtering data. When you need to process primitive numeric types, use `DataInputStream` and `DataOutputStream` to filter bytes.

19.4.3 `DataInputStream/DataOutputStream`

`DataInputStream` reads bytes from the stream and converts them into appropriate primitive type values or strings. `DataOutputStream` converts primitive type values or strings into bytes and outputs the bytes to the stream.

`DataInputStream` extends `FilterInputStream` and implements the `DataInput` interface, as shown in Figure 19.9. `DataOutputStream` extends `FilterOutputStream` and implements the `DataOutput` interface, as shown in Figure 19.10.

`DataInputStream` implements the methods defined in the `DataInput` interface to read primitive data type values and strings. `DataOutputStream` implements the methods defined in the `DataOutput` interface to write primitive data type values and strings. Primitive values

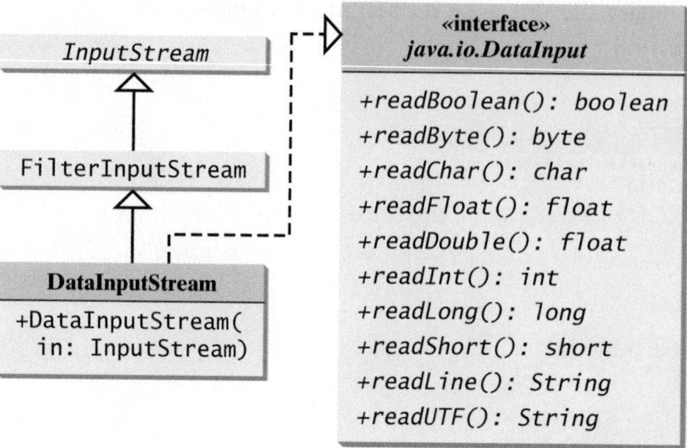

FIGURE 19.9 `DataInputStream` filters an input stream of bytes into primitive data type values and strings.

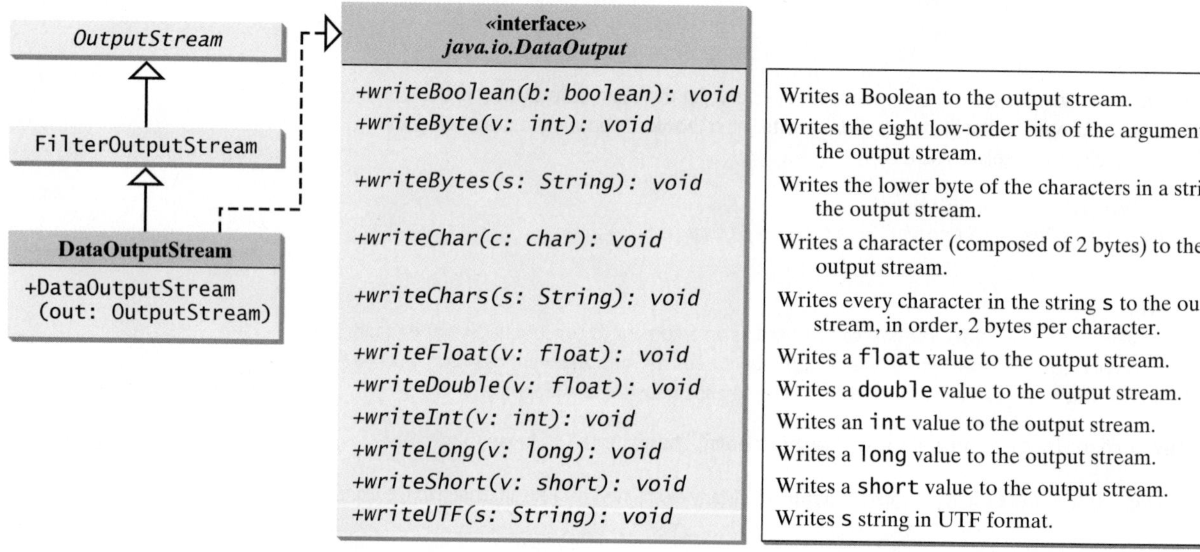

FIGURE 19.10 `DataOutputStream` enables you to write primitive data type values and strings into an output stream.

are copied from memory to the output without any conversions. Characters in a string may be written in several ways, as discussed in the next section.

Characters and Strings in Binary I/O

A Unicode consists of two bytes. The `writeChar(char c)` method writes the Unicode of character `c` to the output. The `writeChars(String s)` method writes the Unicode for each character in the string `s` to the output. The `writeBytes(String s)` method writes the lower byte of the Unicode for each character in the string `s` to the output. The high byte of the Unicode is discarded. The `writeBytes` method is suitable for strings that consist of ASCII characters, since an ASCII code is stored only in the lower byte of a Unicode. If a string consists of non-ASCII characters, you have to use the `writeChars` method to write the string.

The `writeUTF(String s)` method writes two bytes of length information to the output stream, followed by the `modified UTF-8` representation of every character in the string s. UTF-8 is a coding scheme that allows systems to operate with both ASCII and Unicode. Most operating systems use ASCII. Java uses Unicode. The ASCII character set is a subset of the Unicode character set. Since most applications need only the ASCII character set, it is a waste to represent an 8-bit ASCII character as a 16-bit Unicode character. The modified UTF-8 scheme stores a character using one, two, or three bytes. Characters are coded in one byte if their code is less than or equal to 0x7F, in two bytes if their code is greater than 0x7F and less than or equal to 0x7FF, in three bytes if their code is greater than 0x7FF.

UTF-8 scheme

The initial bits of a UTF-8 character indicate whether a character is stored in one byte, two bytes, or three bytes. If the first bit is 0, it is a one-byte character. If the first bits are 110, it is the first byte of a two-byte sequence. If the first bits are 1110, it is the first byte of a three-byte sequence. The information that indicates the number of characters in a string is stored in the first two bytes preceding the UTF-8 characters. For example, writeUTF("ABCDEF") actually writes eight bytes (i.e., 00 06 41 42 43 44 45 46) to the file, because the first two bytes store the number of characters in the string.

The writeUTF(String s) method converts a string into a series of bytes in the UTF-8 format and writes them into a binary stream. The readUTF() method reads a string that has been written using the writeUTF method.

The UTF-8 format has the advantage of saving a byte for each ASCII character, because a Unicode character takes up two bytes and an ASCII character in UTF-8 only one byte. If most of the characters in a long string are regular ASCII characters, using UTF-8 is efficient.

Using DataInputStream/DataOutputStream

Data streams are used as wrappers on existing input and output streams to filter data in the original stream. They are created using the following constructors (see Figure 19.9 and Figure 19.10):

```
public DataInputStream(InputStream instream)
public DataOutputStream(OutputStream outstream)
```

The statements given below create data streams. The first statement creates an input stream for file **in.dat**; the second statement creates an output stream for file **out.dat**.

```
DataInputStream input =
  new DataInputStream(new FileInputStream("in.dat"));
DataOutputStream ouput =
  new DataOutputStream(new FileOutputStream("out.dat"));
```

Listing 19.2 writes student names and scores to a file named **temp.dat** and reads the data back from the file.

LISTING 19.2 TestDataStream.java

```
import java.io.*;

public class TestDataStream {
  public static void main(String[] args) throws IOException {
    // Create an output stream for file temp.dat
    DataOutputStream output =
      new DataOutputStream(new FileOutputStream("temp.dat"));

    // Write student test scores to the file
    output.writeUTF("John");
    output.writeDouble(85.5);
    output.writeUTF("Jim");
    output.writeDouble(185.5);
    output.writeUTF("George");
    output.writeDouble(105.25);

    // Close output stream
    output.close();

```

output stream

output

close stream

input stream

input

```
20     // Create an input stream for file temp.dat
21     DataInputStream input =
22       new DataInputStream(new FileInputStream("temp.dat"));
23
24     // Read student test scores from the file
25     System.out.println(input.readUTF() + " " + input.readDouble());
26     System.out.println(input.readUTF() + " " + input.readDouble());
27     System.out.println(input.readUTF() + " " + input.readDouble());
28   }
29 }
```

```
John 85.5
Jim 185.5
George 105.25
```

A **DataOutputStream** is created for file **temp.dat** in lines 6–7. Student names and scores are written to the file in lines 10–15. Line 18 closes the output stream. A **DataInputStream** is created for the same file in lines 21–22. Student names and scores are read back from the file and displayed on the console in lines 25–27.

DataInputStream and **DataOutputStream** read and write Java primitive type values and strings in a machine-independent fashion, thereby enabling you to write a data file on one machine and read it on another machine that has a different operating system or file structure. An application uses a data output stream to write data that can later be read by a program using a data input stream.

Caution

You have to read data in the same order and format in which they are stored. For example, since names are written in UTF-8 using **writeUTF**, you must read names using **readUTF**.

Tip

If you keep reading data at the end of a **DataInputStream**, an **EOFException** will occur. How, then, do you check the end of a file? Use **input.available()** to check it. **input.available() == 0** indicates the end of a file.

19.4.4 BufferedInputStream/BufferedOutputStream

BufferedInputStream/BufferedOutputStream can be used to speed up input and output by reducing the number of reads and writes. **BufferedInputStream/BufferedOutputStream** does not contain new methods. All the methods in **BufferedInputStream/BufferedOutputStream** are inherited from the **InputStream/OutputStream** classes. **BufferedInputStream/BufferedOutputStream** adds a buffer in the stream for storing bytes for efficient processing.

You may wrap a **BufferedInputStream/BufferedOutputStream** on any **InputStream/OutputStream** using the constructors shown in Figures 19.11 and 19.12.

If no buffer size is specified, the default size is **512** bytes. A buffered input stream reads as many data as possible into its buffer in a single read call. By contrast, a buffered output stream calls the write method only when its buffer fills up or when the **flush()** method is called.

You can improve the performance of the **TestDataStream** program in the preceding example by adding buffers in the stream in lines 6–7 and 21–22, as follows:

```
DataOutputStream output = new DataOutputStream(
  new BufferedOutputStream (new FileOutputStream("temp.dat")));

DataInputStream input = new DataInputStream(
  new BufferedInputStream (new FileInputStream("temp.dat")));
```

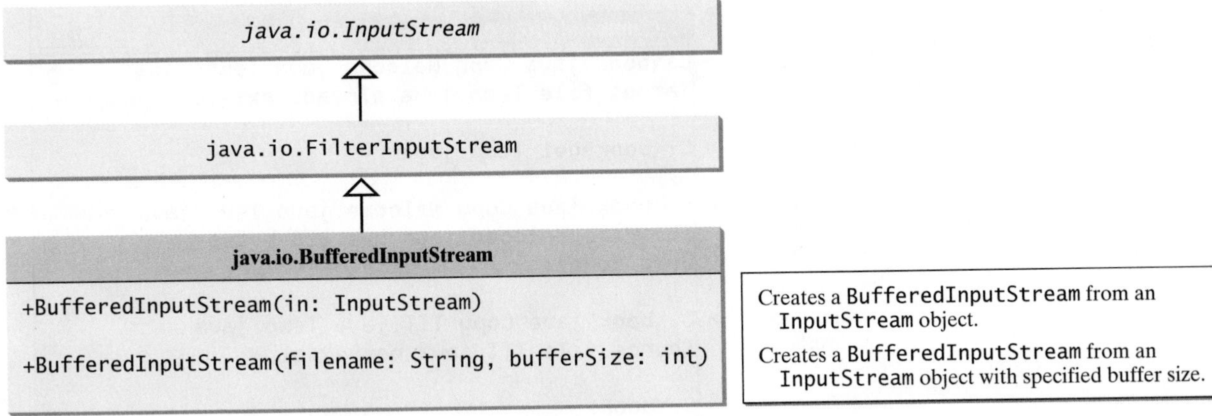

FIGURE 19.11 `BufferedInputStream` buffers input stream.

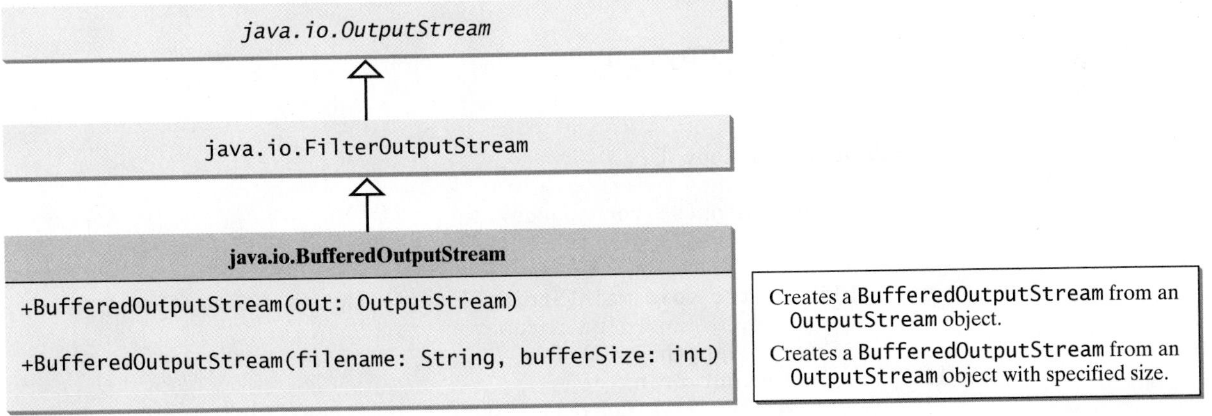

FIGURE 19.12 `BufferedOutputStream` buffers output stream.

Tip

You should always use buffered IO to speed up input and output. For small files, you may not notice performance improvements. However, for large files—over 100 MB—you will see substantial improvements using buffered IO.

19.5 Problem: Copying Files

Video Note
Copy file

This section develops a program that copies files. The user needs to provide a source file and a target file as command-line arguments using the following command:

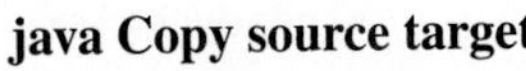

java Copy source target

The program copies a source file to a target file and displays the number of bytes in the file. If the source does not exist, tell the user that the file has not been found. If the target file already exists, tell the user that the file exists. A sample run of the program is shown in Figure 19.13.

To copy the contents from a source to a target file, it is appropriate to use a binary input stream to read bytes from the source file and a binary output stream to send bytes to the target file, regardless of the contents of the file. The source file and the target file are specified from the command line. Create an `InputFileStream` for the source file and an `OutputFileStream` for the target file. Use the `read()` method to read a byte from the input stream, and then use the `write(b)` method to write the byte to the output stream. Use `BufferedInputStream` and `BufferedOutputStream` to improve the performance. Listing 19.3 gives the solution to the problem.

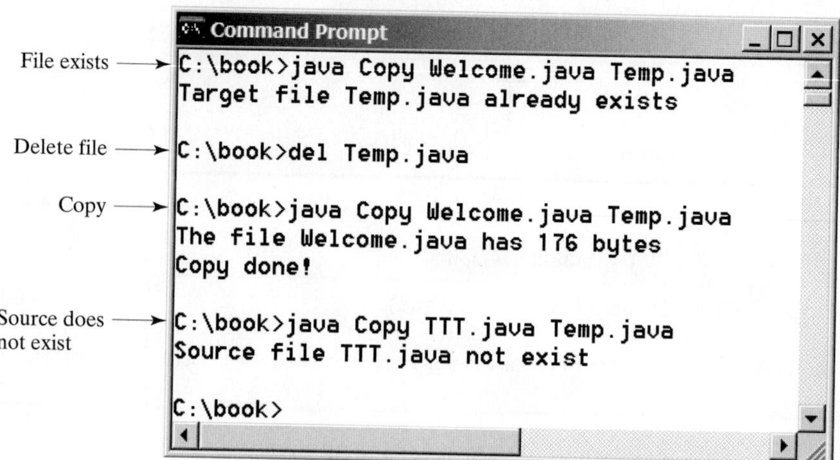

FIGURE 19.13 The program copies a file.

LISTING 19.3 Copy.java

```
import java.io.*;

public class Copy {
  /** Main method
     @param args[0] for sourcefile
     @param args[1] for target file
   */
  public static void main(String[] args) throws IOException {
    // Check command-line parameter usage
    if (args.length != 2) {
      System.out.println(
        "Usage: java CopyFile sourceFile targetfile");
      System.exit(0);
    }

    // Check if source file exists
    File sourceFile = new File(args[0]);
    if (!sourceFile.exists()) {
       System.out.println("Source file " + args[0] + " not exist");
       System.exit(0);
    }

    // Check if target file exists
    File targetFile = new File(args[1]);
    if (targetFile.exists()) {
      System.out.println("Target file " + args[1] + " already exists");
      System.exit(0);
    }

    // Create an input stream
    BufferedInputStream input =
      new BufferedInputStream(new FileInputStream(sourceFile));

    // Create an output stream
    BufferedOutputStream output =
      new BufferedOutputStream(new FileOutputStream(targetFile));

    // Display the file size
    System.out.println("The file " + args[0] + " has "+
```

check usage

source file

target file

input stream

output stream

```
40        input.available() + " bytes");
41
42      // Continuously read a byte from input and write it to output
43      int r;
44      while ((r = input.read()) != -1)
45        output.write((byte)r);
46
47      // Close streams
48      input.close();
49      output.close();
50
51      System.out.println("Copy done!");
52    }
53  }
```

read
write

close stream

- The program first checks whether the user has passed two required arguments from the command line in lines 10–14.
- The program uses the `File` class to check whether the source file and target file exist. If the source file does not exist (lines 18–21) or if the target file already exists, exit the program.
- An input stream is created using `BufferedInputStream` wrapped on `FileInputStream` in lines 31–32, and an output stream is created using `BufferedOutputStream` wrapped on `FileOutputStream` in lines 35–36.
- The `available()` method (line 40) defined in the `InputStream` class returns the number of bytes remaining in the input stream.
- The expression `((r = input.read()) != -1)` (line 44) reads a byte from `input.read()`, assigns it to `r`, and checks whether it is `-1`. The input value of `-1` signifies the end of a file. The program continuously reads bytes from the input stream and sends them to the output stream until all of the bytes have been read.

19.6 Object I/O

Video Note
Object I/O

`DataInputStream`/`DataOutputStream` enables you to perform I/O for primitive type values and strings. `ObjectInputStream`/`ObjectOutputStream` enables you to perform I/O for objects in addition to primitive type values and strings. Since `ObjectInputStream`/`ObjectOutputStream` contains all the functions of `DataInputStream`/`DataOutputStream`, you can replace `DataInputStream`/`DataOutputStream` completely with `ObjectInputStream`/`ObjectOutputStream`.

`ObjectInputStream` extends `InputStream` and implements `ObjectInput` and `ObjectStreamConstants`, as shown in Figure 19.14. `ObjectInput` is a subinterface of `DataInput`. `DataInput` is shown in Figure 19.9. `ObjectStreamConstants` contains the constants to support `ObjectInputStream`/`ObjectOutputStream`.

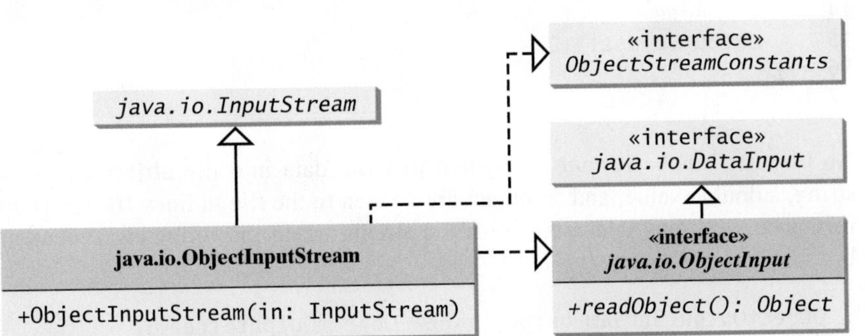

FIGURE 19.14 `ObjectInputStream` can read objects, primitive type values, and strings.

`ObjectOutputStream` extends `OutputStream` and implements `ObjectOutput` and `ObjectStreamConstants`, as shown in Figure 19.15. `ObjectOutput` is a subinterface of `DataOutput`. `DataOutput` is shown in Figure 19.10.

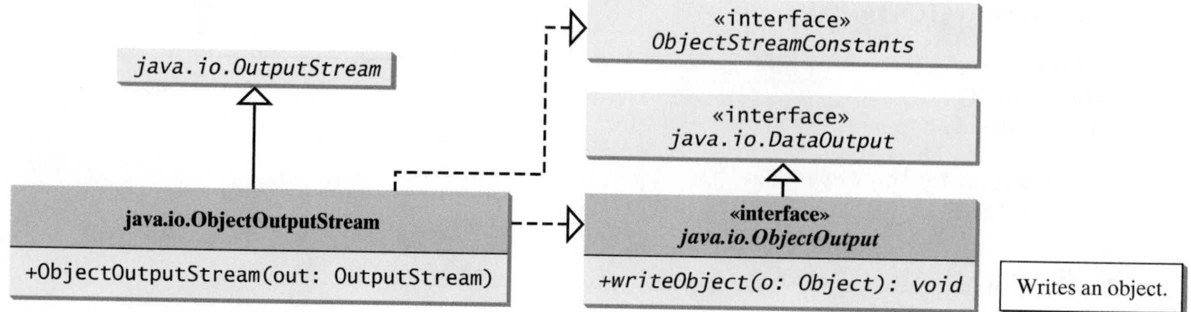

FIGURE 19.15 `ObjectOutputStream` can write objects, primitive type values, and strings.

You may wrap an `ObjectInputStream`/`ObjectOutputStream` on any `InputStream`/`OutputStream` using the following constructors:

```
// Create an ObjectInputStream
public ObjectInputStream(InputStream in)

// Create an ObjectOutputStream
public ObjectOutputStream(OutputStream out)
```

Listing 19.4 writes student names, scores, and current date to a file named **object.dat**.

LISTING 19.4 TestObjectOutputStream.java

output stream

output

```
 1 import java.io.*;
 2
 3 public class TestObjectOutputStream {
 4   public static void main(String[] args) throws IOException {
 5     // Create an output stream for file object.dat
 6     ObjectOutputStream output =
 7       new ObjectOutputStream(new FileOutputStream("object.dat"));
 8
 9     // Write a string, double value, and object to the file
10     output.writeUTF("John");
11     output.writeDouble(85.5);
12     output.writeObject(new java.util.Date());
13
14     // Close output stream
15     output.close();
16   }
17 }
```

An `ObjectOutputStream` is created to write data into file **object.dat** in lines 6–7. A string, a double value, and an object are written to the file in lines 10–12. To improve performance, you may add a buffer in the stream using the following statement to replace lines 6–7:

```
ObjectOutputStream output = new ObjectOutputStream(
  new BufferedOutputStream(new FileOutputStream("object.dat")));
```

Multiple objects or primitives can be written to the stream. The objects must be read back from the corresponding ObjectInputStream with the same types and in the same order as they were written. Java's safe casting should be used to get the desired type. Listing 19.5 reads data back from object.dat.

LISTING 19.5 TestObjectInputStream.java

```
 1 import java.io.*;
 2
 3 public class TestObjectInputStream {
 4   public static void main(String[] args)
 5     throws ClassNotFoundException, IOException {
 6     // Create an input stream for file object.dat
 7     ObjectInputStream input =
 8       new ObjectInputStream(new FileInputStream("object.dat"));
 9
10     // Write a string, double value, and object to the file
11     String name = input.readUTF();
12     double score = input.readDouble();
13     java.util.Date date = (java.util.Date)(input.readObject());
14     System.out.println(name + " " + score + " " + date);
15
16     // Close output stream
17     input.close();
18   }
19 }
```

input stream

input

```
John 85.5 Mon Jun 26 17:17:29 EDT 2006
```

The readObject() method may throw java.lang.ClassNotFoundException. The reason is that when the JVM restores an object, it first loads the class for the object if the class has not been loaded. Since ClassNotFoundException is a checked exception, the main method declares to throw it in line 5. An ObjectInputStream is created to read input from **object.dat** in lines 7–8. You have to read the data from the file in the same order and format as they were written to the file. A string, a double value, and an object are read in lines 11–13. Since readObject() returns an Object, it is cast into Date and assigned to a Date variable in line 13.

ClassNotFoundException

19.6.1 The Serializable Interface

Not every object can be written to an output stream. Objects that can be written to an object stream are said to be *serializable*. A serializable object is an instance of the java.io.Serializable interface, so the class of a serializable object must implement Serializable.

serializable

The Serializable interface is a marker interface. Since it has no methods, you don't need to add additional code in your class that implements Serializable. Implementing this interface enables the Java serialization mechanism to automate the process of storing objects and arrays.

To appreciate this automation feature and understand how an object is stored, consider what you otherwise need to do in order to store an object. Suppose you want to store a JButton object. To do this you need to store all the current values of the properties (e.g., color, font, text, alignment) in the object. Since JButton is a subclass of AbstractButton, the property values of AbstractButton have to be stored as well as the properties of all the superclasses of AbstractButton. If a property is of an object type (e.g., background of the Color type), storing it requires storing all the property values inside this object. As you can see, this is a very tedious process. Fortunately, you don't have to go through it manually. Java provides a built-in mechanism to automate the process of writing objects. This process is referred to as *object serialization*, which is implemented in ObjectOutputStream. In contrast, the process of reading objects is referred to as *object deserialization*, which is implemented in ObjectInputStream.

serialization
deserialization

Many classes in the Java API implement Serializable. The utility classes, such as java.util.Date, and all the Swing GUI component classes implement Serializable. Attempting to store an object that does not support the Serializable interface would cause a NotSerializableException.

NotSerializableException

When a serializable object is stored, the class of the object is encoded; this includes the class name and the signature of the class, the values of the object's instance variables, and the closure of any other objects referenced from the initial object. The values of the object's static variables are not stored.

Note

nonserializable fields

transient

If an object is an instance of Serializable but contains nonserializable instance data fields, can it be serialized? The answer is no. To enable the object to be serialized, mark these data fields with the transient keyword to tell the JVM to ignore them when writing the object to an object stream. Consider the following class:

```
public class Foo implements java.io.Serializable {
  private int v1;
  private static double v2;
  private transient A v3 = new A();
}

class A { } // A is not serializable
```

When an object of the Foo class is serialized, only variable v1 is serialized. Variable v2 is not serialized because it is a static variable, and variable v3 is not serialized because it is marked transient. If v3 were not marked transient, a java.io.NotSerializableException would occur.

Note

If an object is written to an object stream more than once, will it be stored in multiple copies? No, it will not. When an object is written for the first time, a serial number is created for it. The JVM writes the complete content of the object along with the serial number into the object stream. After the first time, only the serial number is stored if the same object is written again. When the objects are read back, their references are the same, since only one object is actually created in the memory.

duplicate objects

19.6.2 Serializing Arrays

An array is serializable if all its elements are serializable. An entire array can be saved using writeObject into a file and later can be restored using readObject. Listing 19.6 stores an array of five int values and an array of three strings, and reads them back to display on the console.

Listing 19.6 TestObjectStreamForArray.java

```
import java.io.*;

public class TestObjectStreamForArray {
  public static void main(String[] args)
      throws ClassNotFoundException, IOException {
    int[] numbers = {1, 2, 3, 4, 5};
    String[] strings = {"John", "Jim", "Jake"};

```

```
9       // Create an output stream for file array.dat
10      ObjectOutputStream output =
11        new ObjectOutputStream(new FileOutputStream("array.dat", true));
12
13      // Write arrays to the object output stream
14      output.writeObject(numbers);
15      output.writeObject(strings);
16
17      // Close the stream
18      output.close();
19
20      // Create an input stream for file array.dat
21      ObjectInputStream input =
22        new ObjectInputStream(new FileInputStream("array.dat"));
23
24      int[] newNumbers = (int[])(input.readObject());
25      String[] newStrings = (String[])(input.readObject());
26
27      // Display arrays
28      for (int i = 0; i < newNumbers.length; i++)
29        System.out.print(newNumbers[i] + " ");
30      System.out.println();
31
32      for (int i = 0; i < newStrings.length; i++)
33        System.out.print(newStrings[i] + " ");
34    }
35  }
```

output stream

store array

input stream

restore array

```
1 2 3 4 5
John Jim Jake
```

Lines 14–15 write two arrays into file **array.dat**. Lines 24–25 read three arrays back in the same order they were written. Since `readObject()` returns `Object`, casting is used to cast the objects into `int[]` and `String[]`.

19.7 Random Access Files

All of the streams you have used so far are known as *read-only* or *write-only* streams. The external files of these streams are *sequential* files that cannot be updated without creating a new file. It is often necessary to modify files or to insert new records into files. Java provides the `RandomAccessFile` class to allow a file to be read from and written to at random locations.

read-only
write-only
sequential

The `RandomAccessFile` class implements the `DataInput` and `DataOutput` interfaces, as shown in Figure 19.16. The `DataInput` interface shown in Figure 19.9 defines the methods (e.g., `readInt`, `readDouble`, `readChar`, `readBoolean`, `readUTF`) for reading primitive type values and strings, and the `DataOutput` interface shown in Figure 19.10 defines the methods (e.g., `writeInt`, `writeDouble`, `writeChar`, `writeBoolean`, `writeUTF`) for writing primitive type values and strings.

When creating a `RandomAccessFile`, you can specify one of two modes ("`r`" or "`rw`"). Mode "`r`" means that the stream is read-only, and mode "`rw`" indicates that the stream allows both read and write. For example, the following statement creates a new stream, `raf`, that allows the program to read from and write to the file **test.dat**:

```
RandomAccessFile raf = new RandomAccessFile("test.dat", "rw");
```

If **test.dat** already exists, `raf` is created to access it; if **test.dat** does not exist, a new file named **test.dat** is created, and `raf` is created to access the new file. The method `raf.length()`

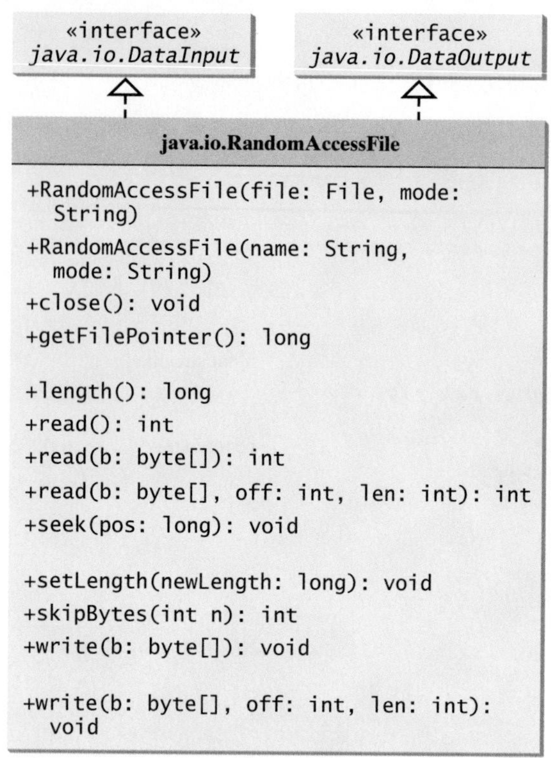

Creates a `RandomAccessFile` stream with the specified `File` object and mode.

Creates a `RandomAccessFile` stream with the specified file name, string, and mode.

Closes the stream and releases the resource associated with it.

Returns the offset, in bytes, from the beginning of the file to where the next `read` or `write` occurs.

Returns the length of this file.

Reads a byte of data from this file and returns –1 at the end of stream.

Reads up to `b.length` bytes of data from this file into an array of bytes.

Reads up to `len` bytes of data from this file into an array of bytes.

Sets the offset (in bytes specified in `pos`) from the beginning of the stream to where the next `read` or `write` occurs.

Sets a new length for this file.

Skips over `n` bytes of input.

Writes `b.length` bytes from the specified byte array to this file, starting at the current file pointer.

Writes `len` bytes from the specified byte array, starting at offset `off`, to this file.

FIGURE 19.16 `RandomAccessFile` implements the `DataInput` and `DataOutput` interfaces with additional methods to support random access.

returns the number of bytes in **test.dat** at any given time. If you append new data into the file, `raf.length()` increases.

Tip

Open the file with the `"r"` mode if the file is not intended to be modified. This prevents unintentional modification of the file.

file pointer

A random access file consists of a sequence of bytes. A special marker called a *file pointer* is positioned at one of these bytes. A read or write operation takes place at the location of the file pointer. When a file is opened, the file pointer is set at the beginning of the file. When you read or write data to the file, the file pointer moves forward to the next data item. For example, if you read an `int` value using `readInt()`, the JVM reads `4` bytes from the file pointer, and now the file pointer is `4` bytes ahead of the previous location, as shown in Figure 19.17.

For a `RandomAccessFile raf`, you can use the `raf.seek(position)` method to move the file pointer to a specified position. `raf.seek(0)` moves it to the beginning of the file, and

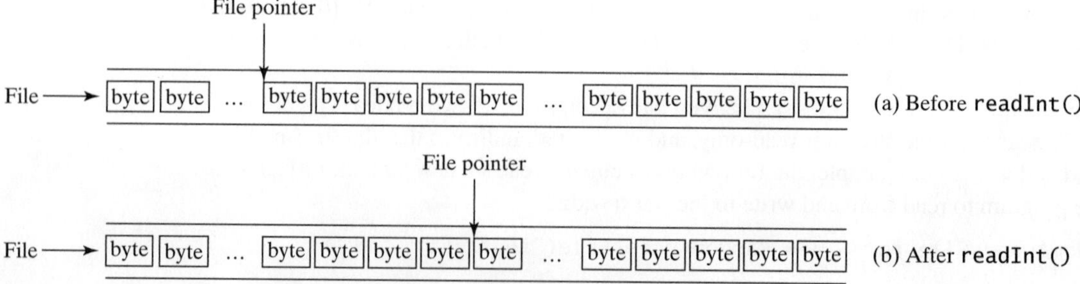

FIGURE 19.17 After reading an `int` value, the file pointer is moved `4` bytes ahead.

`raf.seek(raf.length())` moves it to the end of the file. Listing 19.7 demonstrates `RandomAccessFile`.

LISTING 19.7 TestRandomAccessFile.java

```java
import java.io.*;

public class TestRandomAccessFile {
  public static void main(String[] args) throws IOException {
    // Create a random access file
    RandomAccessFile inout = new RandomAccessFile("inout.dat", "rw");

    // Clear the file to destroy the old contents if exists
    inout.setLength(0);

    // Write new integers to the file
    for (int i = 0; i < 200; i++)
      inout.writeInt(i);

    // Display the current length of the file
    System.out.println("Current file length is " + inout.length());

    // Retrieve the first number
    inout.seek(0); // Move the file pointer to the beginning
    System.out.println("The first number is " + inout.readInt());

    // Retrieve the second number
    inout.seek(1 * 4); // Move the file pointer to the second number
    System.out.println("The second number is " + inout.readInt());

    // Retrieve the tenth number
    inout.seek(9 * 4); // Move the file pointer to the tenth number
    System.out.println("The tenth number is " + inout.readInt());

    // Modify the eleventh number
    inout.writeInt(555);

    // Append a new number
    inout.seek(inout.length()); // Move the file pointer to the end
    inout.writeInt(999);

    // Display the new length
    System.out.println("The new length is " + inout.length());

    // Retrieve the new eleventh number
    inout.seek(10 * 4); // Move the file pointer to the eleventh number
    System.out.println("The eleventh number is " + inout.readInt());

    inout.close();
  }
}
```

RandomAccessFile

empty file

write

move pointer

read

close file

```
Current file length is 800
The first number is 0
The second number is 1
The tenth number is 9
The new length is 804
The eleventh number is 555
```

A `RandomAccessFile` is created for the file named **inout.dat** with mode "`rw`" to allow both read and write operations in line 6.

`inout.setLength(0)` sets the length to `0` in line 9. This, in effect, destroys the old contents of the file.

The `for` loop writes `200 int` values from `0` to `199` into the file in lines 12–13. Since each `int` value takes `4` bytes, the total length of the file returned from `inout.length()` is now `800` (line 16), as shown in sample output.

Invoking `inout.seek(0)` in line 19 sets the file pointer to the beginning of the file. `inout.readInt()` reads the first value in line 20 and moves the file pointer to the next number. The second number is read in line 23.

`inout.seek(9 * 4)` (line 27) moves the file pointer to the tenth number. `inout.readInt()` reads the tenth number and moves the file pointer to the eleventh number in line 28. `inout.write(555)` writes a new eleventh number at the current position (line 31). The previous eleventh number is destroyed.

`inout.seek(inout.length())` moves the file pointer to the end of the file (line 34). `inout.writeInt(999)` writes a `999` to the file. Now the length of the file is increased by `4`, so `inout.length()` returns `804` (line 38).

`inout.seek(10 * 4)` moves the file pointer to the eleventh number in line 41. The new eleventh number, `555`, is displayed in line 42.

19.8 Problem: Creating an Address Book

Video Note
Address book

Now let us use `RandomAccessFile` to create a useful project for storing and viewing an address book. The user interface of the program is shown in Figure 19.18. The *Add* button stores a new address at the end of the file. The *First*, *Next*, *Previous*, and *Last* buttons retrieve the first, next, previous, and last addresses from the file, respectively.

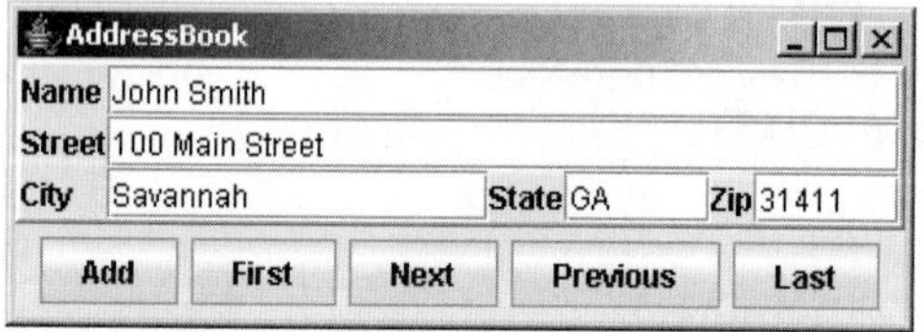

FIGURE 19.18 `AddressBook` stores and retrieves addresses from a file.

fixed-length record

Random access files are often used to process files of records. For convenience, fixed-length records are used in random access files so that a record can be located easily, as shown in Figure 19.19. A record consists of a fixed number of fields. A field can be a string or a primitive data type. A string in a fixed-length record has a maximum size. If a string is smaller than the maximum size, the rest of the string is padded with blanks.

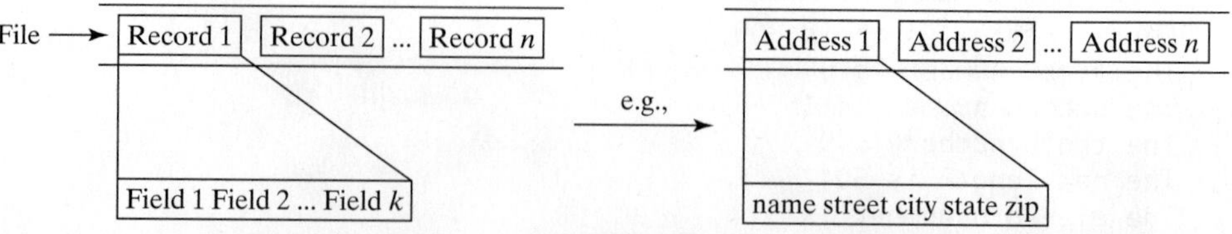

FIGURE 19.19 Random access files are often used to process files of fixed-length records.

Let **address.dat** be the file to store addresses. A `RandomAccessFile` for both read and write can be created using

```
RandomAccessFile raf = new RandomAccessFile("address.dat", "rw");
```

Let each address consist of a name (32 characters), street (32 characters), city (20 characters), state (2 characters), and zip (5 characters). If the actual size of a field (e.g., name) is less than the fixed maximum size, fill it with blank characters. If the actual size of a field is greater than the fixed maximum size, truncate the string. Thus the total size of an address is 32 + 32 + 20 + 2 + 5 = 91 characters. Since each character occupies two bytes, one address takes 2 * 91 = 182 bytes. After an address record is read, the file pointer is 182 bytes ahead of the previous file pointer.

For convenience, Listing 19.8 contains two methods for reading and writing a fixed-length string.

LISTING 19.8 `FixedLengthStringIO.java`

```
1 import java.io.*;
2
3 public class FixedLengthStringIO {
4   /** Read fixed number of characters from a DataInput stream */
5   public static String readFixedLengthString(int size,
6       DataInput in) throws IOException {
7     // Declare an array of characters
8     char[] chars = new char[size];
9
10    // Read fixed number of characters to the array
11    for (int i = 0; i < size; i++)
12      chars[i] = in.readChar();
13
14    return new String(chars);
15  }
16
17  /** Write fixed number of characters to a DataOutput stream */
18  public static void writeFixedLengthString(String s, int size,
19      DataOutput out) throws IOException {
20    char[] chars = new char[size];
21
22    // Fill an array of characters from the string
23    s.getChars(0, Math.min(s.length(), size), chars, 0);
24
25    // Fill in blank characters in the rest of the array
26    for (int i = Math.min(s.length(), size); i < chars.length; i++)
27      chars[i] = ' ';
28
29    // Create and write a new string padded with blank characters
30    out.writeChars(new String(chars));
31  }
32 }
```

read characters (line 12)

fill string (line 23)

fill blank (lines 26–27)

write string (line 30)

The `writeFixedLengthString(String s, int size, DataOutput out)` method writes a string in a fixed size to a `DataOutput` stream. If the string is longer than the specified size, it is truncated (line 23); if it is shorter than the specified size, blanks are padded into it (lines 26–27). In any case, a new fixed-length string is written to a specified output stream. Since `RandomAccessFile` implements `DataOutput`, this method can be used to write a string to a `RandomAccessFile`. For example, invoking `writeFixedLengthString("John", 2, raf)` actually writes "`Jo`" to the `RandomAccessFile raf`, since the size is 2. Invoking `writeFixedLengthString("John", 6, raf)` actually writes `"John  "` to the `RandomAccessFile raf`, since the size is 6.

The `readFixedLengthString(int size, InputOutput in)` method reads a fixed number of characters from an `InputStream` and returns as a string. Since `RandomAccessFile` implements `InputOutput`, this method can be used to read a string from a `writeFixedLengthString(String s, int size, DataOutput out)`.

The rest of the work can be summarized in the following steps:

1. Create the user interface.
2. Add a record to the file.
3. Read a record from the file.
4. Write the code to implement the button actions.

The program is shown in Listing 19.9.

LISTING 19.9 AddressBook.java

constant

raf

GUI component

open file

```
import java.io.*;
import java.awt.*;
import java.awt.event.*;
import javax.swing.*;
import javax.swing.border.*;

public class AddressBook extends JFrame {
  // Specify the size of five string fields in the record
  final static int NAME_SIZE = 32;
  final static int STREET_SIZE = 32;
  final static int CITY_SIZE = 20;
  final static int STATE_SIZE = 2;
  final static int ZIP_SIZE = 5;
  final static int RECORD_SIZE =
    (NAME_SIZE + STREET_SIZE + CITY_SIZE + STATE_SIZE + ZIP_SIZE);

  // Access address.dat using RandomAccessFile
  private RandomAccessFile raf;

  // Text fields
  private JTextField jtfName = new JTextField(NAME_SIZE);
  private JTextField jtfStreet = new JTextField(STREET_SIZE);
  private JTextField jtfCity = new JTextField(CITY_SIZE);
  private JTextField jtfState = new JTextField(STATE_SIZE);
  private JTextField jtfZip = new JTextField(ZIP_SIZE);

  // Buttons
  private JButton jbtAdd = new JButton("Add");
  private JButton jbtFirst = new JButton("First");
  private JButton jbtNext = new JButton("Next");
  private JButton jbtPrevious = new JButton("Previous");
  private JButton jbtLast = new JButton("Last");

  public AddressBook() {
    // Open or create a random access file
    try {
      raf = new RandomAccessFile("address.dat", "rw");
    }
    catch(IOException ex) {
      System.out.print("Error: " + ex);
      System.exit(0);
    }
```

create UI

```
    // Panel p1 for holding labels Name, Street, and City
    JPanel p1 = new JPanel();
    p1.setLayout(new GridLayout(3, 1));
    p1.add(new JLabel("Name"));
    p1.add(new JLabel("Street"));
    p1.add(new JLabel("City"));

    // Panel jpState for holding state
    JPanel jpState = new JPanel();
    jpState.setLayout(new BorderLayout());
    jpState.add(new JLabel("State"), BorderLayout.WEST);
    jpState.add(jtfState, BorderLayout.CENTER);

    // Panel jpZip for holding zip
    JPanel jpZip = new JPanel();
    jpZip.setLayout(new BorderLayout());
    jpZip.add(new JLabel("Zip"), BorderLayout.WEST);
    jpZip.add(jtfZip, BorderLayout.CENTER);

    // Panel p2 for holding jpState and jpZip
    JPanel p2 = new JPanel();
    p2.setLayout(new BorderLayout());
    p2.add(jpState, BorderLayout.WEST);
    p2.add(jpZip, BorderLayout.CENTER);

    // Panel p3 for holding jtfCity and p2
    JPanel p3 = new JPanel();
    p3.setLayout(new BorderLayout());
    p3.add(jtfCity, BorderLayout.CENTER);
    p3.add(p2, BorderLayout.EAST);

    // Panel p4 for holding jtfName, jtfStreet, and p3
    JPanel p4 = new JPanel();
    p4.setLayout(new GridLayout(3, 1));
    p4.add(jtfName);
    p4.add(jtfStreet);
    p4.add(p3);

    // Place p1 and p4 into jpAddress
    JPanel jpAddress = new JPanel(new BorderLayout());
    jpAddress.add(p1, BorderLayout.WEST);
    jpAddress.add(p4, BorderLayout.CENTER);

    // Set the panel with line border
    jpAddress.setBorder(new BevelBorder(BevelBorder.RAISED));

    // Add buttons to a panel
    JPanel jpButton = new JPanel();
    jpButton.add(jbtAdd);
    jpButton.add(jbtFirst);
    jpButton.add(jbtNext);
    jpButton.add(jbtPrevious);
    jpButton.add(jbtLast);

    // Add jpAddress and jpButton to the frame
    add(jpAddress, BorderLayout.CENTER);
    add(jpButton, BorderLayout.SOUTH);

```

register listener
add address
register listener
first record
register listener
next address
register listener
register listener
last address
first address

```
    jbtAdd.addActionListener(new ActionListener() {
      public void actionPerformed(ActionEvent e) {
        writeAddress();
      }
    });
    jbtFirst.addActionListener(new ActionListener() {
      public void actionPerformed(ActionEvent e) {
        try {
          if (raf.length() > 0) readAddress(0);
        }
        catch (IOException ex) {
          ex.printStackTrace();
        }
      }
    });
    jbtNext.addActionListener(new ActionListener() {
      public void actionPerformed(ActionEvent e) {
        try {
          long currentPosition = raf.getFilePointer();
          if (currentPosition < raf.length())
            readAddress(currentPosition);
        }
        catch (IOException ex) {
          ex.printStackTrace();
        }
      }
    });
    jbtPrevious.addActionListener(new ActionListener() {
      public void actionPerformed(ActionEvent e) {
        try {
          long currentPosition = raf.getFilePointer();
          if (currentPosition - 2 * RECORD_SIZE > 0)
            // Why 2 * 2 * RECORD_SIZE? See the follow-up remarks
            readAddress(currentPosition - 2 * 2 * RECORD_SIZE);
          else
            readAddress(0);
        }
        catch (IOException ex) {
          ex.printStackTrace();
        }
      }
    });
    jbtLast.addActionListener(new ActionListener() {
      public void actionPerformed(ActionEvent e) {
        try {
          long lastPosition = raf.length();
          if (lastPosition > 0)
            // Why 2 * RECORD_SIZE? See the follow-up remarks
            readAddress(lastPosition - 2 * RECORD_SIZE);
        }
        catch (IOException ex) {
          ex.printStackTrace();
        }
      }
    });

    // Display the first record if exists
    try {
      if (raf.length() > 0) readAddress(0);
    }
```

```
162     catch (IOException ex) {
163       ex.printStackTrace();
164     }
165   }
166
167   /** Write a record at the end of the file */
168   public void writeAddress() {
169     try {
170       raf.seek(raf.length());
171       FixedLengthStringIO.writeFixedLengthString(
172         jtfName.getText(), NAME_SIZE, raf);
173       FixedLengthStringIO.writeFixedLengthString(
174         jtfStreet.getText(), STREET_SIZE, raf);
175       FixedLengthStringIO.writeFixedLengthString(
176         jtfCity.getText(), CITY_SIZE, raf);
177       FixedLengthStringIO.writeFixedLengthString(
178         jtfState.getText(), STATE_SIZE, raf);
179       FixedLengthStringIO.writeFixedLengthString(
180         jtfZip.getText(), ZIP_SIZE, raf);
181     }
182     catch (IOException ex) {
183       ex.printStackTrace();
184     }
185   }
186
187   /** Read a record at the specified position */
188   public void readAddress(long position) throws IOException {
189     raf.seek(position);
190     String name = FixedLengthStringIO.readFixedLengthString(
191       NAME_SIZE, raf);
192     String street = FixedLengthStringIO.readFixedLengthString(
193       STREET_SIZE, raf);
194     String city = FixedLengthStringIO.readFixedLengthString(
195       CITY_SIZE, raf);
196     String state = FixedLengthStringIO.readFixedLengthString(
197       STATE_SIZE, raf);
198     String zip = FixedLengthStringIO.readFixedLengthString(
199       ZIP_SIZE, raf);
200
201     jtfName.setText(name);
202     jtfStreet.setText(street);
203     jtfCity.setText(city);
204     jtfState.setText(state);
205     jtfZip.setText(zip);
206   }
207
208   public static void main(String[] args) {
209     AddressBook frame = new AddressBook();
210     frame.pack();
211     frame.setTitle("AddressBook");
212     frame.setDefaultCloseOperation(JFrame.EXIT_ON_CLOSE);
213     frame.setVisible(true);
214   }
215 }
```

A random access file, **address.dat**, is created to store address information if the file does not yet exist (line 37). If it already exists, the file is opened. A random file object, `raf`, is used for both write and read operations. The size of each field in the record is fixed and therefore defined as a constant in lines 9–15.

The user interface is created in lines 44–100. The listeners are registered in lines 102–156. When the program starts, it displays the first record, if it exists, in lines 159–164.

The `writeAddress()` method sets the file pointer to the end of the file (line 170) and writes a new record to the file (lines 171–180).

The `readAddress()` method sets the file pointer at the specified position (line 189) and reads a record from the file (lines 190–199). The record is displayed in lines 201–205.

To add a record, you need to collect the address information from the user interface and write the address into the file (line 104).

The code to process button events is implemented in lines 102–156. For the *First* button, read the record from position `0` (line 110). For the *Next* button, read the record from the current file pointer (line 122). When a record is read, the file pointer is moved `2 * RECORD_SIZE` number of bytes ahead of the previous file pointer. For the *Previous* button, you need to display the record prior to the one being displayed now. You have to move the file pointer two records before the current file pointer (line 135). For the *Last* button, read the record from the position at `raf.length() - 2 * RECORD_SIZE`.

Key Terms

binary I/O 624
deserialization 638
file pointer 640
random access file 639
sequential access file 639
serialization 638
stream 624
text I/O 624

Chapter Summary

- I/O can be classified into text I/O and binary I/O. Text I/O interprets data in sequences of characters. Binary I/O interprets data as raw binary values. How text is stored in a file depends on the encoding scheme for the file. Java automatically performs encoding and decoding for text I/O.

- The `InputStream` and `OutputStream` classes are the roots of all binary I/O classes. `FileInputStream/FileOutputStream` associates a file for binary input/output. `BufferedInputStream/BufferedOutputStream` can be used to wrap on any binary I/O stream to improve performance. `DataInputStream/DataOutputStream` can be used to read/write primitive values and strings.

- `ObjectInputStream/ObjectOutputStream` can be used to read/write objects in addition to primitive values and strings. To enable object serialization, the object's defining class must implement the `java.io.Serializable` marker interface.

- The `RandomAccessFile` class enables you to read and write data to a file. You can open a file with the "`r`" mode to indicate that it is read-only, or with the "`rw`" mode to indicate that it is updateable. Since the `RandomAccessFile` class implements `DataInput` and `DataOutput` interfaces, many methods in `RandomAccessFile` are the same as those in `DataInputStream` and `DataOutputStream`.

Review Questions

Sections 19.1–19.2

19.1 What is a text file, and what is a binary file? Can you view a text file or a binary file using a text editor?

19.2 How do you read or write data in Java? What is a stream?

Section 19.3 Text I/O vs. Binary I/O

19.3 What are the differences between text I/O and binary I/O?

19.4 How is a Java character represented in the memory, and how is a character represented in a text file?

19.5 If you write string "ABC" to an ASCII text file, what values are stored in the file?

19.6 If you write string "100" to an ASCII text file, what values are stored in the file? If you write a numeric byte-type value 100 using binary I/O, what values are stored in the file?

19.7 What is the encoding scheme for representing a character in a Java program? By default, what is the encoding scheme for a text file on Windows?

Section 19.4 Binary I/O Classes

19.8 Why do you have to declare to throw `IOException` in the method or use a try-catch block to handle `IOException` for Java IO programs?

19.9 Why should you always close streams?

19.10 `InputStream` reads bytes. Why does the `read()` method return an `int` instead of a `byte`? Find the abstract methods in `InputStream` and `OutputStream`.

19.11 Does `FileInputStream`/`FileOutputStream` introduce any new methods? How do you create a `FileInputStream`/`FileOutputStream`?

19.12 What will happen if you attempt to create an input stream on a nonexistent file? What will happen if you attempt to create an output stream on an existing file? Can you append data to an existing file?

19.13 How do you append data to an existing text file using `java.io.PrintWriter`?

19.14 Suppose `input` is a `DataInputStream`, and `input.available()` returns `100`. After invoking `read()`, what is `input.available()`? After invoking `readInt()`, what is `input.available()`? After invoking `readChar()`, what is `input.available()`? After invoking `readDouble()`, what is `input.available()`?

19.15 What is written to a file using `writeByte(91)` on a `FileOutputStream`?

19.16 How do you check the end of a file in a binary input stream (`FileInputStream`, `DataInputStream`)?

19.17 What is wrong in the following code?

```
import java.io.*;

public class Test {
  public static void main(String[] args) {
    try {
      FileInputStream fis = new FileInputStream("test.dat");
    }
```

```
      catch (IOException ex) {
        ex.printStackTrace();
      }
      catch (FileNotFoundException ex) {
        ex.printStackTrace();
      }
    }
  }
```

19.18 Suppose you run the program on Windows using the default ASCII encoding. After the program is finished, how many bytes are in the file **t.txt**? Show the contents of each byte.

```
public class Test {
  public static void main(String[] args) throws
      java.io.IOException {
    java.io.PrintWriter output = new
      java.io.PrintWriter("t.txt");
    output.printf("%s", "1234");
    output.printf("%s", "5678");
    output.close();
  }
}
```

19.19 After the program is finished, how many bytes are in the file **t.dat**? Show the contents of each byte.

```
import java.io.*;

public class Test {
  public static void main(String[] args) throws IOException {
    DataOutputStream output = new DataOutputStream(
      new FileOutputStream("t.dat"));
    output.writeInt(1234);
    output.writeInt(5678);
    output.close();
  }
}
```

19.20 For each of the following statements on a `DataOutputStream out`, how many bytes are sent to the output?

```
output.writeChar('A');
output.writeChars("BC");
output.writeUTF("DEF");
```

19.21 What are the advantages of using buffered streams? Are the following statements correct?

```
BufferedInputStream input1 =
  new BufferedInputStream(new FileInputStream("t.dat"));

DataInputStream input2 = new DataInputStream(
  new BufferedInputStream(new FileInputStream("t.dat")));

ObjectInputStream input3 = new ObjectInputStream(
  new BufferedInputStream(new FileInputStream("t.dat")));
```

Section 19.6 Object I/O

19.22 What types of objects can be stored using the `ObjectOutputStream`? What is the method for writing an object? What is the method for reading an object? What is the return type of the method that reads an object from `ObjectInputStream`?

19.23 If you serialize two objects of the same type, will they take the same amount of space?

19.24 Is it true that any instance of `java.io.Serializable` can be successfully serialized? Are the static variables in an object serialized? How do you mark an instance variable not to be serialized?

19.25 Can you write an array to an `ObjectOutputStream`?

19.26 Is it true that `DataInputStream`/`DataOutputStream` can always be replaced by `ObjectInputStream`/`ObjectOutputStream`?

19.27 What will happen when you attempt to run the following code?

```
import java.io.*;

public class Test {
  public static void main(String[] args) throws IOException {
    ObjectOutputStream output =
      new ObjectOutputStream(new FileOutputStream("object.dat"));

    output.writeObject(new A());
  }
}

class A implements Serializable {
  B b = new B();
}

class B {
}
```

Section 19.7 Random Access Files

19.28 Can `RandomAccessFile` streams read and write a data file created by `DataOutputStream`? Can `RandomAccessFile` streams read and write objects?

19.29 Create a `RandomAccessFile` stream for the file **address.dat** to allow the updating of student information in the file. Create a `DataOutputStream` for the file **address.dat**. Explain the differences between these two statements.

19.30 What happens if the file **test.dat** does not exist when you attempt to compile and run the following code?

```
import java.io.*;

public class Test {
  public static void main(String[] args) {
    try {
      RandomAccessFile raf =
        new RandomAccessFile("test.dat", "r");
      int i = raf.readInt();
    }
    catch (IOException ex) {
      System.out.println("IO exception");
    }
  }
}
```

Programming Exercises

Section 19.3 Text I/O vs. Binary I/O

19.1* (*Creating a text file*) Write a program to create a file named **Exercise19_1.txt** if it does not exist. Append new data to it. Write 100 integers created randomly into the file using text I/O. Integers are separated by a space.

Section 19.4 Binary I/O Classes

19.2* (*Creating a binary data file*) Write a program to create a file named **Exercise19_2.dat** if it does not exist. Append new data to it. Write 100 integers created randomly into the file using binary I/O.

19.3* (*Summing all the integers in a binary data file*) Suppose a binary data file named **Exercise19_3.dat** has been created using `writeInt(int)` in `DataOutputStream`. The file contains an unspecified number of integers. Write a program to find the sum of integers.

19.4* (*Converting a text file into UTF*) Write a program that reads lines of characters from a text and writes each line as a UTF-8 string into a binary file. Display the sizes of the text file and the binary file. Use the following command to run the program:

java Exercise19_4 Welcome.java Welcome.utf

Section 19.6 Object I/O

19.5* (*Storing objects and arrays into a file*) Write a program that stores an array of five `int` values `1`, `2`, `3`, `4` and `5`, a `Date` object for current time, and a `double` value `5.5` into the file named **Exercise19_5.dat**.

19.6* (*Storing* Loan *objects*) The `Loan` class, in Listing 9.2, does not implement `Serializable`. Rewrite the `Loan` class to implement `Serializable`. Write a program that creates five `Loan` objects and stores them in a file named **Exercise19_6.dat**.

19.7* (*Restoring objects from a file*) Suppose a file named **Exercise19_7.dat** has been created using the `ObjectOutputStream`. The file contains `Loan` objects. The `Loan` class, in Listing 9.2, does not implement `Serializable`. Rewrite the `Loan` class to implement `Serializable`. Write a program that reads the `Loan` objects from the file and computes the total loan amount. Suppose you don't know how many `Loan` objects are in the file. Use `EOFException` to end the loop.

Section 19.7 Random Access Files

19.8* (*Updating count*) Suppose you want to track how many times a program has been executed. You may store an `int` to count the file. Increase the count by `1` each time this program is executed. Let the program be **Exercise19_8** and store the count in **Exercise19_8.dat**.

19.9** (*Updating address*) Modify `AddressBook` in Listing 19.9, AddressBook.java, to add an *Update* button, as shown in Figure 19.20, to enable the user to modify an address that is being displayed.

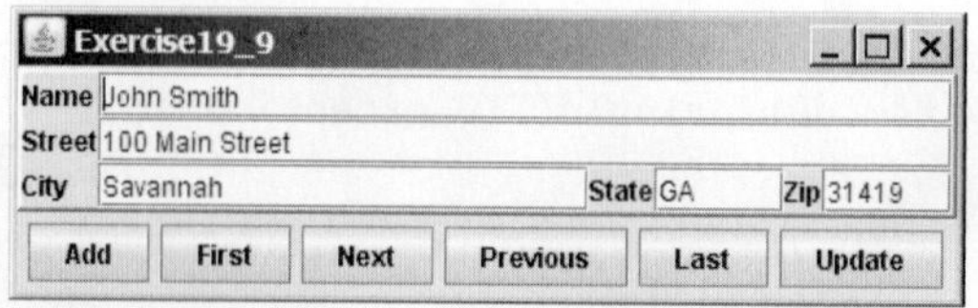

FIGURE 19.20 You can update the address record that is currently displayed.

Comprehensive

19.10* (*Splitting files*) Suppose you wish to back up a huge file (e.g., a 10-GB AVI file) to a CD-R. You can achieve it by splitting the file into smaller pieces and backing up these pieces separately. Write a utility program that splits a large file into smaller ones using the following command:

Video Note
Split a large file

java Exercise19_10 SourceFile numberOfPieces

The command creates files SourceFile.1, SourceFile.2, . . . , SourceFile.n, where `n` is `numberOfPieces` and the output files are about the same size.

19.11** (*Splitting files GUI*) Rewrite Exercise 19.10 with a GUI, as shown in Figure 19.21(a).

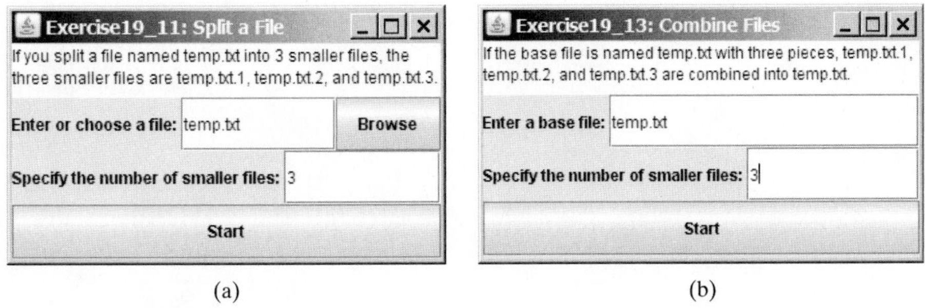

FIGURE 19.21 (a) The program splits a file. (b) The program combines files into a new file.

19.12* (*Combining files*) Write a utility program that combines the files together into a new file using the following command:

java Exercise19_12 SourceFile1 . . . SoureFilen TargetFile

The command combines SourceFile1, . . . , and SourceFilen into TargetFile.

19.13* (*Combining files GUI*) Rewrite Exercise 19.12 with a GUI, as shown in Figure 19.21(b).

19.14 (*Encrypting files*) Encode the file by adding `5` to every byte in the file. Write a program that prompts the user to enter an input file name and an output file name and saves the encrypted version of the input file to the output file.

19.15 (*Decrypting files*) Suppose a file is encrypted using the scheme in Exercise 19.14. Write a program to decode an encrypted file. Your program should prompt the user to enter an input file name and an output file name and should save the unencrypted version of the input file to the output file.

CHAPTER 20

RECURSION

Objectives

- To describe what a recursive method is and the benefits of using recursion (§20.1).
- To develop recursive methods for recursive mathematical functions (§§20.2–20.3).
- To explain how recursive method calls are handled in a call stack (§§20.2–20.3).
- To use an overloaded helper method to derive a recursive method (§20.5).
- To solve selection sort using recursion (§20.5.1).
- To solve binary search using recursion (§20.5.2).
- To get the directory size using recursion (§20.6).
- To solve the Towers of Hanoi problem using recursion (§20.7).
- To draw fractals using recursion (§20.8).
- To solve the Eight Queens problem (§20.9).
- To discover the relationship and difference between recursion and iteration (§20.10).

20.1 Introduction

search word problem

Suppose you want to find all the files under a directory that contain a particular word. How do you solve this problem? There are several ways to do so. An intuitive and effective solution is to use recursion by searching the files in the subdirectories recursively.

Eight Queens problem

The classic Eight Queens puzzle is to place eight queens on a chessboard such that no two can attack each other (i.e., no two queens are on the same row, same column, or same diagonal), as shown in Figure 20.1. How do you write a program to solve this problem? A good approach is to use recursion.

FIGURE 20.1 The Eight Queens problem can be solved using recursion.

recursive method

To use recursion is to program using *recursive methods*—methods that directly or indirectly invoke themselves. Recursion is a useful programming technique. In some cases, it enables you to develop a natural, straightforward, simple solution to an otherwise difficult problem. This chapter introduces the concepts and techniques of recursive programming and illustrates by examples how to "think recursively."

20.2 Problem: Computing Factorials

Many mathematical functions are defined using recursion. We begin with a simple example that illustrates recursion. The factorial of a number n can be recursively defined as follows:

```
0! = 1;
n! = n × (n - 1) × ... × 2 × 1 = n × (n - 1)!; n > 0
```

How do you find n! for a given n? To find 1! is easy, because you know that 0! is 1, and 1! is 1×0!. Assuming that you know (n - 1)!, you can obtain n! immediately using n × (n - 1)!. Thus, the problem of computing n! is reduced to computing (n - 1)!. When computing (n - 1)!, you can apply the same idea recursively until n is reduced to 0.

Let factorial(n) be the method for computing n!. If you call the method with n = 0, it immediately returns the result. The method knows how to solve the simplest case, which is referred to as the *base case* or the *stopping condition*. If you call the method with n > 0, it reduces the problem into a subproblem for computing the factorial of n - 1. The subproblem is essentially the same as the original problem, but is simpler or smaller. Because the subproblem has the same property as the original, you can call the method with a different argument, which is referred to as a *recursive call*.

base case or stopping condition

recursive call

The recursive algorithm for computing factorial(n) can be simply described as follows:

```
if (n == 0)
  return 1;
else
  return n * factorial(n - 1);
```

A recursive call can result in many more recursive calls, because the method keeps on dividing a subproblem into new subproblems. For a recursive method to terminate, the problem must eventually be reduced to a stopping case, at which point the method returns a result to its caller. The caller then performs a computation and returns the result to its own caller. This process continues until the result is passed back to the original caller. The original problem can now be solved by multiplying `n` by the result of `factorial(n - 1)`.

Listing 20.1 gives a complete program that prompts the user to enter a nonnegative integer and displays the factorial for the number.

LISTING 20.1 ComputeFactorial.java

```
 1 import java.util.Scanner;
 2 
 3 public class ComputeFactorial {
 4   /** Main method */
 5   public static void main(String[] args) {
 6     // Create a Scanner
 7     Scanner input = new Scanner(System.in);
 8     System.out.print("Enter a nonnegative integer: ");
 9     int n =input.nextInt();
10 
11     // Display factorial
12     System.out.println("Factorial of " + n + " is " + factorial(n));
13   }
14 
15   /** Return the factorial for a specified number */
16   public static long factorial(int n) {
17     if (n == 0) // Base case
18       return 1;
19     else
20       return n * factorial(n - 1); // Recursive call
21   }
22 }
```

base case

recursion

```
Enter a nonnegative integer: 4
Factorial of 4 is 24
```

```
Enter a nonnegative integer: 10
Factorial of 10 is 3628800
```

The `factorial` method (lines 16–21) is essentially a direct translation of the recursive mathematical definition for the factorial into Java code. The call to `factorial` is recursive because it calls itself. The parameter passed to `factorial` is decremented until it reaches the base case of `0`.

Figure 20.2 illustrates the execution of the recursive calls, starting with `n = 4`. The use of stack space for recursive calls is shown in Figure 20.3.

Caution

If recursion does not reduce the problem in a manner that allows it to eventually converge into the base case, *infinite recursion* can occur. For example, suppose you mistakenly write the `factorial` method as follows:

infinite recursion

```
public static long factorial(int n) {
  return n * factorial(n - 1);
}
```

The method runs infinitely and causes a `StackOverflowError`.

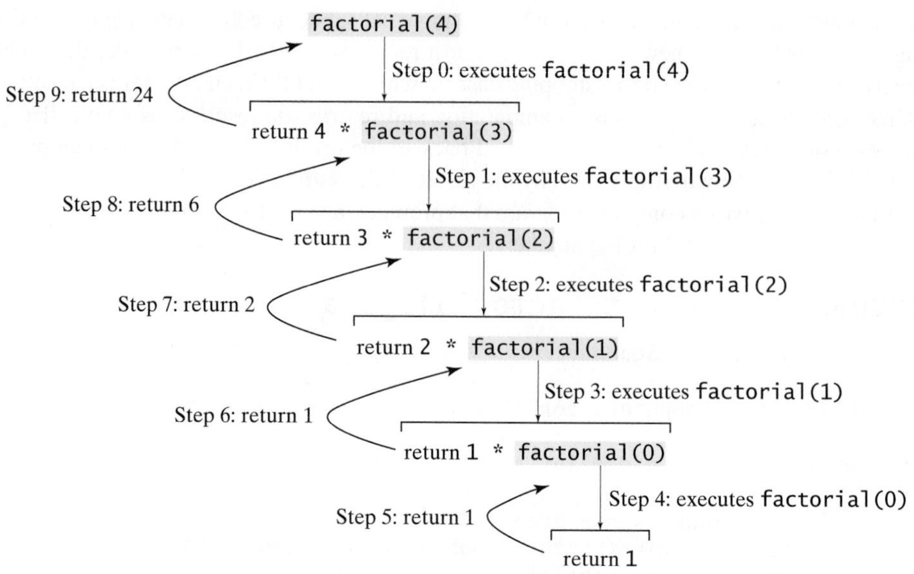

FIGURE 20.2 Invoking `factorial(4)` spawns recursive calls to `factorial`.

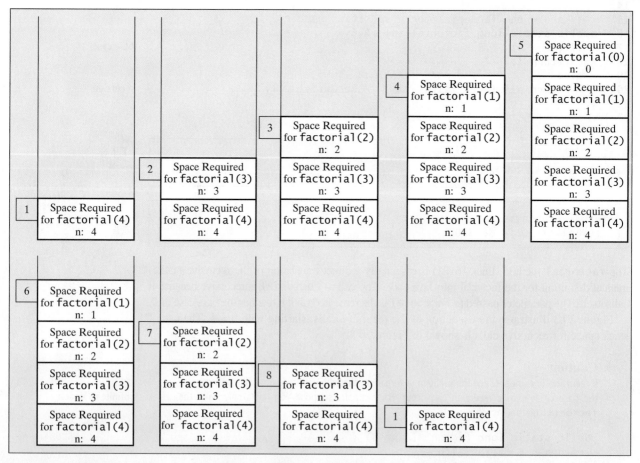

FIGURE 20.3 When `factorial(4)` is being executed, the `factorial` method is called recursively, causing memory space to dynamically change.

Pedagogical Note

It is simpler and more efficient to implement the `factorial` method using a loop. However, we use the recursive `factorial` method here to demonstrate the concept of recursion. Later in this chapter, we will present some problems that are inherently recursive and are difficult to solve without using recursion.

20.3 Problem: Computing Fibonacci Numbers

The `factorial` method in the preceding section could easily be rewritten without using recursion. In some cases, however, using recursion enables you to give a natural, straightforward, simple solution to a program that would otherwise be difficult to solve. Consider the well-known Fibonacci series problem:

The series:	0	1	1	2	3	5	8	13	21	34	55	89 ...
indices:	0	1	2	3	4	5	6	7	8	9	10	11

The Fibonacci series begins with `0` and `1`, and each subsequent number is the sum of the preceding two. The series can be recursively defined as follows:

```
fib(0) = 0;
fib(1) = 1;
fib(index) = fib(index - 2) + fib(index - 1); index >= 2
```

The Fibonacci series was named for Leonardo Fibonacci, a medieval mathematician, who originated it to model the growth of the rabbit population. It can be applied in numeric optimization and in various other areas.

How do you find `fib(index)` for a given `index`? It is easy to find `fib(2)`, because you know `fib(0)` and `fib(1)`. Assuming that you know `fib(index - 2)` and `fib(index - 1)`, you can obtain `fib(index)` immediately. Thus, the problem of computing `fib(index)` is reduced to computing `fib(index - 2)` and `fib(index - 1)`. When computing `fib(index - 2)` and `fib(index - 1)`, you apply the idea recursively until `index` is reduced to `0` or `1`.

The base case is `index = 0` or `index = 1`. If you call the method with `index = 0` or `index = 1`, it immediately returns the result. If you call the method with `index >= 2`, it divides the problem into two subproblems for computing `fib(index - 1)` and `fib(index - 2)` using recursive calls. The recursive algorithm for computing `fib(index)` can be simply described as follows:

```
if (index == 0)
  return 0;
else if (index == 1)
  return 1;
else
  return fib(index - 1) + fib(index - 2);
```

Listing 20.2 gives a complete program that prompts the user to enter an index and computes the Fibonacci number for the index.

LISTING 20.2 ComputeFibonacci.java

```
import java.util.Scanner;

public class ComputeFibonacci {
  /** Main method */
  public static void main(String args[]) {
    // Create a Scanner
    Scanner input = new Scanner(System.in);
```

```
    System.out.print("Enter an index for the Fibonacci number: ");
    int index = input.nextInt();

    // Find and display the Fibonacci number
    System.out.println(
      "Fibonacci number at index " + index + " is " + fib(index));
  }

  /** The method for finding the Fibonacci number */
  public static long fib(long index) {
    if (index == 0) // Base case
      return 0;
    else if (index == 1) // Base case
      return 1;
    else  // Reduction and recursive calls
      return fib(index - 1) + fib(index - 2);
  }
}
```

base case

base case

recursion

```
Enter an index for the Fibonacci number: 1
Fibonacci number at index 1 is 1
```

```
Enter an index for the Fibonacci number: 6 ↵Enter
Fibonacci number at index 6 is 8
```

```
Enter an index for the Fibonacci number: 7 ↵Enter
Fibonacci number at index 7 is 13
```

The program does not show the considerable amount of work done behind the scenes by the computer. Figure 20.4, however, shows successive recursive calls for evaluating `fib(4)`. The original method, `fib(4)`, makes two recursive calls, `fib(3)` and `fib(2)`, and then returns `fib(3) + fib(2)`. But in what order are these methods called? In Java, operands are

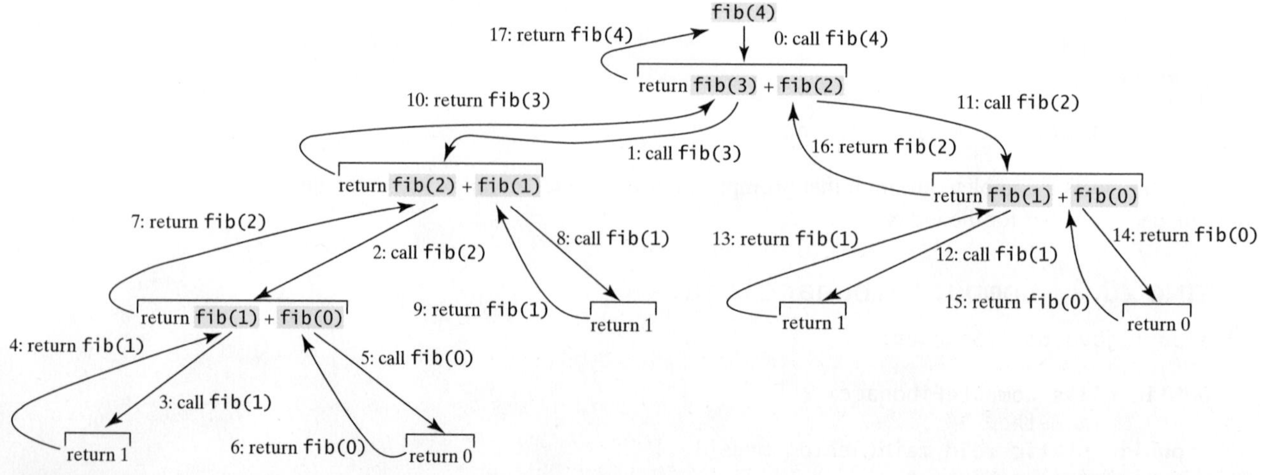

FIGURE 20.4 Invoking `fib(4)` spawns recursive calls to `fib`.

evaluated from left to right. fib(2) is called after fib(3) is completely evaluated. The labels in Figure 20.4 show the order in which methods are called.

As shown in Figure 20.4, there are many duplicated recursive calls. For instance, fib(2) is called twice, fib(1) is called three times, and fib(0) is called twice. In general, computing fib(index) requires roughly twice as many recursive calls as are needed for computing fib(index - 1). As you try larger index values, the number of calls substantially increases.

Besides the large number of recursive calls, the computer requires more time and space to run recursive methods.

Pedagogical Note

The recursive implementation of the fib method is very simple and straightforward, but not efficient. See Exercise 20.2 for an efficient solution using loops. Though it is not practical, the recursive fib method is a good example of how to write recursive methods.

20.4 Problem Solving Using Recursion

The preceding sections presented two classic recursion examples. All recursive methods have the following characteristics: recursion characteristics

- The method is implemented using an if-else or a switch statement that leads to different cases. if-else
- One or more base cases (the simplest case) are used to stop recursion. base cases
- Every recursive call reduces the original problem, bringing it increasingly closer to a base case until it becomes that case. reduction

In general, to solve a problem using recursion, you break it into subproblems. Each subproblem is almost the same as the original problem but smaller in size. You can apply the same approach to each subproblem to solve it recursively.

Let us consider the simple problem of printing a message n times. You can break the problem into two subproblems: one is to print the message one time and the other is to print it n - 1 times. The second problem is the same as the original problem but smaller in size. The base case for the problem is n == 0. You can solve this problem using recursion as follows:

```
public static void nPrintln(String message, int times) {
  if (times >= 1) {
    System.out.println(message);
    nPrintln(message, times - 1);
  } // The base case is times == 0
}
```

recursive call

Note that the fib method in the preceding example returns a value to its caller, but the nPrintln method is void and does not return a value to its caller.

If you *think recursively*, you can use recursion to solve many of the problems presented in earlier chapters of this book. Consider the palindrome problem in Listing 8.1. Recall that a string is a palindrome if it reads the same from the left and from the right. For example, mom and dad are palindromes, but uncle and aunt are not. The problem to check whether a string is a palindrome can be divided into two subproblems: think recursively

- Check whether the first character and the last character of the string are equal.
- Ignore the two end characters and check whether the rest of the substring is a palindrome.

The second subproblem is the same as the original problem but smaller in size. There are two base cases: (1) the two end characters are not same; (2) the string size is 0 or 1. In case 1, the string is not a palindrome; and in case 2, the string is a palindrome. The recursive method for this problem can be implemented as shown in Listing 20.3.

LISTING 20.3 RecursivePalindromeUsingSubstring.java

method header
base case
base case
recursive call

```
1 public class RecursivePalindromeUsingSubstring {
2   public static boolean isPalindrome(String s) {
3     if (s.length() <= 1) // Base case
4       return true;
5     else if (s.charAt(0) != s.charAt(s.length() - 1)) // Base case
6       return false;
7     else
8       return isPalindrome(s.substring(1, s.length() - 1));
9   }
10
11  public static void main(String[] args) {
12    System.out.println("Is moon a palindrome? "
13      + isPalindrome("moon"));
14    System.out.println("Is noon a palindrome? "
15      + isPalindrome("noon"));
16    System.out.println("Is a a palindrome? " + isPalindrome("a"));
17    System.out.println("Is aba a palindrome? " +
18      isPalindrome("aba"));
19    System.out.println("Is ab a palindrome? " + isPalindrome("ab"));
20  }
21 }
```

```
Is moon a palindrome? false
Is noon a palindrome? true
Is a a palindrome? true
Is aba a palindrome? true
Is ab a palindrome? false
```

The `substring` method in line 8 creates a new string that is the same as the original string except without the first and last characters in the original string. Checking whether a string is a palindrome is equivalent to checking whether the substring is a palindrome if the two end characters in the original string are the same.

20.5 Recursive Helper Methods

The preceding recursive `isPalindrome` method is not efficient, because it creates a new string for every recursive call. To avoid creating new strings, you can use the low and high indices to indicate the range of the substring. These two indices must be passed to the recursive method. Since the original method is `isPalindrome(String s)`, you have to create a new method `isPalindrome(String s, int low, int high)` to accept additional information on the string, as shown in Listing 20.4.

LISTING 20.4 RecursivePalindrome.java

helper method
base case
base case

```
public class RecursivePalindrome {
  public static boolean isPalindrome(String s) {
    return isPalindrome(s, 0, s.length() - 1);
  }

  public static boolean isPalindrome(String s, int low, int high) {
    if (high <= low) // Base case
      return true;
    else if (s.charAt(low) != s.charAt(high)) // Base case
      return false;
```

```
    else
      return isPalindrome(s, low + 1, high - 1);
  }

  public static void main(String[] args) {
    System.out.println("Is moon a palindrome? "
      + isPalindrome("moon"));
    System.out.println("Is noon a palindrome? "
      + isPalindrome("noon"));
    System.out.println("Is a a palindrome? " + isPalindrome("a"));
    System.out.println("Is aba a palindrome? " +
      isPalindrome("aba"));
    System.out.println("Is ab a palindrome? " + isPalindrome("ab"));
  }
}
```

Two overloaded `isPalindrome` methods are declared. The first, `isPalindrome(String s)`, checks whether a string is a palindrome, and the second, `isPalindrome(String s, int low, int high)`, checks whether a substring `s(low..high)` is a palindrome. The first method passes the string `s` with `low = 0` and `high = s.length() - 1` to the second method. The second method can be invoked recursively to check a palindrome in an ever-shrinking substring. It is a common design technique in recursive programming to declare a second method that receives additional parameters. Such a method is known as a *recursive helper method*.

recursive helper method

Helper methods are very useful in designing recursive solutions for problems involving strings and arrays. The sections that follow give two more examples.

20.5.1 Selection Sort

Selection sort was introduced in §6.8.1, "Selection Sort." Recall that it finds the largest number in the list and places it last. It then finds the largest number remaining and places it next to last, and so on until the list contains only a single number. The problem can be divided into two subproblems:

- Find the largest number in the list and swap it with the last number.
- Ignore the last number and sort the remaining smaller list recursively.

The base case is that the list contains only one number. Listing 20.5 gives the recursive sort method.

LISTING 20.5 RecursiveSelectionSort.java

helper method

base case

```
public class RecursiveSelectionSort {
  public static void sort(double[] list) {
    sort(list, list.length - 1);
  }

  public static void sort(double[] list, int high) {
    if (high > 0) {
      // Find the largest number and its index
      int indexOfMax = 0;
      double max = list[0];
      for (int i = 1; i <= high; i++) {
        if (list[i] > max) {
          max = list[i];
          indexOfMax = i;
        }
      }

```

recursive call

```
            // Swap the largest with the last number in the list
            list[indexOfMax] = list[high];
            list[high] = max;

            // Sort the remaining list
            sort(list, high - 1);
        }
    }
}
```

Two overloaded **sort** methods are declared. The first method, **sort(double[] list)**, sorts an array in **list[0..list.length - 1]** and the second method **sort(double[] list, int high)** sorts an array in **list[0..high]**. The second method can be invoked recursively to sort an ever-shrinking subarray.

20.5.2 Binary Search

Video Note
Binary search

Binary search was introduced in §6.7.2. For binary search to work, the elements in the array must already be ordered. The binary search first compares the key with the element in the middle of the array. Consider the following three cases:

- Case 1: If the key is less than the middle element, recursively search the key in the first half of the array.
- Case 2: If the key is equal to the middle element, the search ends with a match.
- Case 3: If the key is greater than the middle element, recursively search the key in the second half of the array.

Case 1 and Case 3 reduce the search to a smaller list. Case 2 is a base case when there is a match. Another base case is that the search is exhausted without a match. Listing 20.6 gives a clear, simple solution for the binary search problem using recursion.

LISTING 20.6 Recursive Binary Search Method

helper method
base case
recursive call
base case
recursive call

```
public class RecursiveBinarySearch {
  public static int recursiveBinarySearch(int[] list, int key) {
    int low = 0;
    int high = list.length - 1;
    return recursiveBinarySearch(list, key, low, high);
  }

  public static int recursiveBinarySearch(int[] list, int key,
      int low, int high) {
    if (low > high)  // The list has been exhausted without a match
      return -low - 1;

    int mid = (low + high) / 2;
    if (key < list[mid])
      return recursiveBinarySearch(list, key, low, mid - 1);
    else if (key == list[mid])
      return mid;
    else
      return recursiveBinarySearch(list, key, mid + 1, high);
  }
}
```

The first method finds a key in the whole list. The second method finds a key in the list with index from **low** to **high**.

The first `binarySearch` method passes the initial array with `low = 0` and `high = list.length - 1` to the second `binarySearch` method. The second method is invoked recursively to find the key in an ever-shrinking subarray.

20.6 Problem: Finding the Directory Size

Video Note
Directory size

The preceding examples can easily be solved without using recursion. This section presents a problem that is difficult to solve without using recursion. The problem is to find the size of a directory. The size of a directory is the sum of the sizes of all files in the directory. A directory d may contain subdirectories. Suppose a directory contains files $f_1, f_2, \ldots, f_m$, and subdirectories $d_1, d_2, \ldots, d_n$, as shown in Figure 20.5.

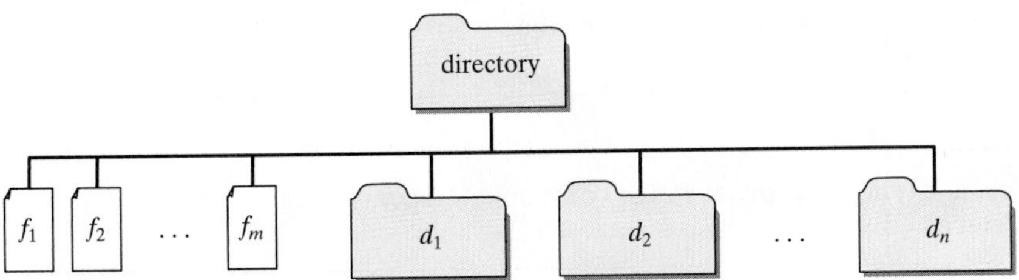

FIGURE 20.5 A directory contains files and subdirectories.

The size of the directory can be defined recursively as follows:

$$size(d) = size(f_1) + size(f_2) + \cdots + size(f_m) + size(d_1) + size(d_2) + \cdots + size(d_n)$$

The `File` class, introduced in §8.6, can be used to represent a file or a directory and obtain the properties for files and directories. Two methods in the `File` class are useful for this problem:

- The `length()` method returns the size of a file.
- The `listFiles()` method returns an array of `File` objects under a directory.

Listing 20.7 gives a program that prompts the user to enter a directory or a file and displays its size.

LISTING 20.7 `DirectorySize.java`

```
import java.io.File;
import java.util.Scanner;

public class DirectorySize {
  public static void main(String[] args) {
    // Prompt the user to enter a directory or a file
    System.out.print("Enter a directory or a file: ");
    Scanner input = new Scanner(System.in);
    String directory = input.nextLine();

    // Display the size
    System.out.println(getSize(new File(directory)) + " bytes");
  }

  public static long getSize(File file) {
    long size = 0; // Store the total size of all files

    if (file.isDirectory()) {
      File[] files =file.listFiles(); // All files and subdirectories
```

invoke method

`getSize` method

is directory?

all subitems

recursive call

base case

```
20      for (int i = 0; i < files.length; i++) {
21        size += getSize(files[i]); // Recursive call
22      }
23    }
24    else { // Base case
25      size += file.length();
26    }
27
28    return size;
29  }
30 }
```

```
Enter a directory or a file: c:\book [Enter]
48619631 bytes
```

```
Enter a directory or a file: c:\book\Welcome.java [Enter]
172 bytes
```

```
Enter a directory or a file: c:\book\NonExistentFile [Enter]
0 bytes
```

If the `file` object represents a directory (line 18), each subitem (file or subdirectory) in the directory is recursively invoked to obtain its size (line 21). If the `file` object represents a file (line 24), the file size is obtained (line 25).

What happens if an incorrect or a nonexistent directory is entered? The program will detect that it is not a directory and invoke `file.length()` (line 25), which returns `0`. So, in this case, the `getSize` method will return `0`.

testing base cases

Tip

To avoid mistakes, it is a good practice to test base cases. For example, you should trace the program for an input of file, an empty directory, a nonexistent directory, and a nonexistent file.

20.7 Problem: Tower of Hanoi

The Tower of Hanoi problem is a classic recursion example. The problem can be solved easily using recursion, but is difficult to solve otherwise.

The problem involves moving a specified number of disks of distinct sizes from one tower to another while observing the following rules:

- There are n disks labeled 1, 2, 3, . . . , n, and three towers labeled A, B, and C.
- No disk can be on top of a smaller disk at any time.
- All the disks are initially placed on tower A.
- Only one disk can be moved at a time, and it must be the top disk on the tower.

The objective of the problem is to move all the disks from A to B with the assistance of C. For example, if you have three disks, the steps to move all of the disks from A to B are shown in Figure 20.6.

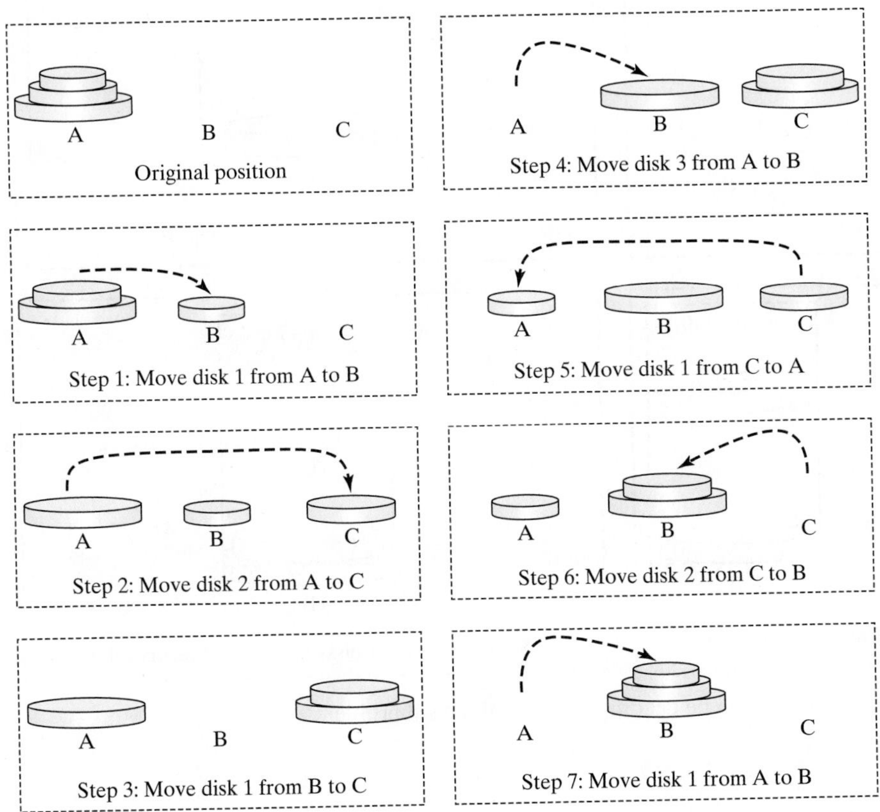

FIGURE 20.6 The goal of the Towers of Hanoi problem is to move disks from tower A to tower B without breaking the rules.

Note

The Towers of Hanoi is a classic computer-science problem, to which many Web sites are devoted. One of them worth seeing is www.cut-the-knot.com/recurrence/hanoi.html.

In the case of three disks, you can find the solution manually. For a larger number of disks, however—even for four—the problem is quite complex. Fortunately, the problem has an inherently recursive nature, which leads to a straightforward recursive solution.

The base case for the problem is `n = 1`. If `n == 1`, you could simply move the disk from A to B. When `n > 1`, you could split the original problem into three subproblems and solve them sequentially.

1. Move the first `n - 1` disks from A to C with the assistance of tower B, as shown in Step 1 in Figure 20.7.
2. Move disk `n` from A to B, as shown in Step 2 in Figure 20.7.
3. Move `n - 1` disks from C to B with the assistance of tower A, as shown in Step 3 in Figure 20.7.

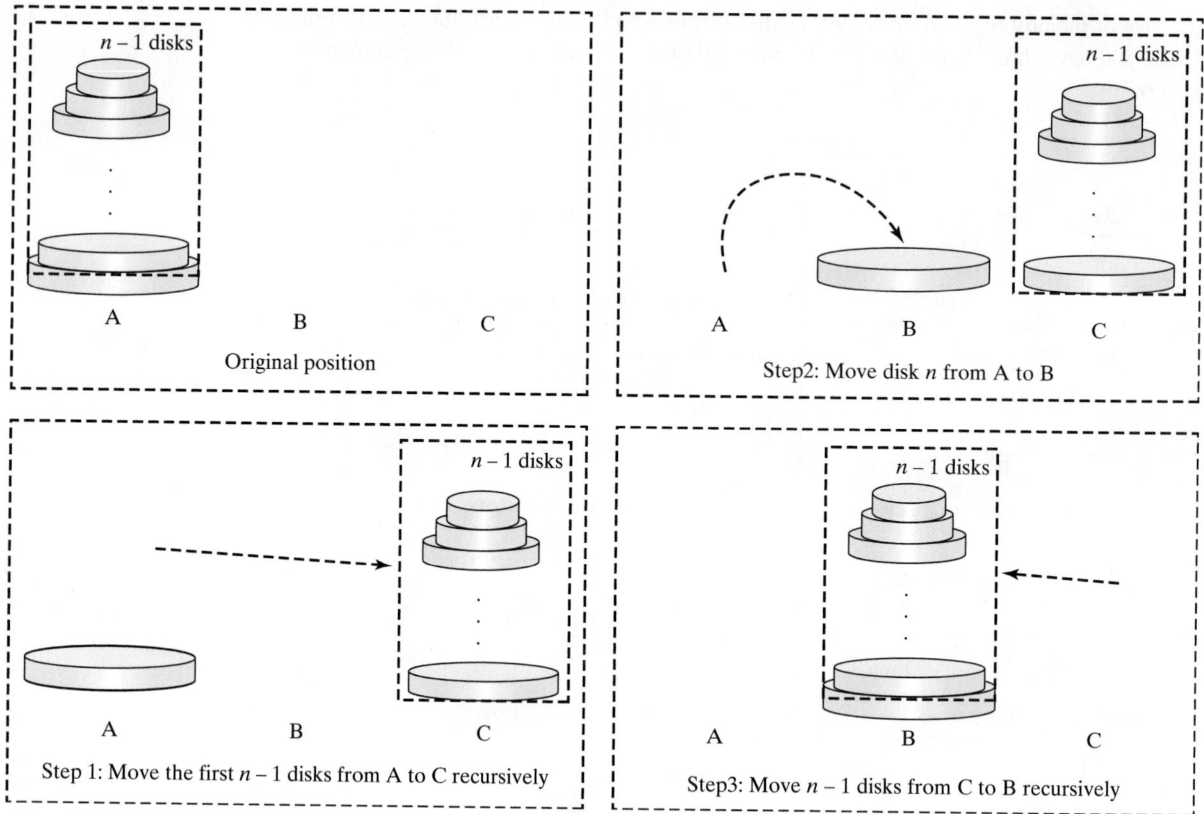

FIGURE 20.7 The Towers of Hanoi problem can be decomposed into three subproblems.

The following method moves *n* disks from the `fromTower` to the `toTower` with the assistance of the `auxTower`:

```
void moveDisks(int n, char fromTower, char toTower, char auxTower)
```

The algorithm for the method can be described as follows:

```
if (n == 1) // Stopping condition
  Move disk 1 from the fromTower to the toTower;
else {
  moveDisks(n - 1, fromTower, auxTower, toTower);
  Move disk n from the fromTower to the toTower;
  moveDisks(n - 1, auxTower, toTower, fromTower);
}
```

Listing 20.8 gives a program that prompts the user to enter the number of disks and invokes the recursive method `moveDisks` to display the solution for moving the disks.

LISTING 20.8 TowersOfHanoi.java

```
import java.util.Scanner;

public class TowersOfHanoi {
```

```
  /** Main method */
  public static void main(String[] args) {
    // Create a Scanner
    Scanner input = new Scanner(System.in);
    System.out.print("Enter number of disks: ");
    int n = input.nextInt();

    // Find the solution recursively
    System.out.println("The moves are:");
    moveDisks(n, 'A', 'B', 'C');
  }

  /** The method for finding the solution to move n disks
      from fromTower to toTower with auxTower */
  public static void moveDisks(int n, char fromTower,
      char toTower, char auxTower) {
    if (n == 1) // Stopping condition
      System.out.println("Move disk " + n + " from " +
        fromTower + " to " + toTower);
    else {
      moveDisks(n - 1, fromTower, auxTower, toTower);
      System.out.println("Move disk " + n + " from " +
        fromTower + " to " + toTower);
      moveDisks(n - 1, auxTower, toTower, fromTower);
    }
  }
}
```

base case

recursion

recursion

```
Enter number of disks: 4 ↵Enter
The moves are:
Move disk 1 from A to C
Move disk 2 from A to B
Move disk 1 from C to B
Move disk 3 from A to C
Move disk 1 from B to A
Move disk 2 from B to C
Move disk 1 from A to C
Move disk 4 from A to B
Move disk 1 from C to B
Move disk 2 from C to A
Move disk 1 from B to A
Move disk 3 from C to B
Move disk 1 from A to C
Move disk 2 from A to B
Move disk 1 from C to B
```

This problem is inherently recursive. Using recursion makes it possible to find a natural, simple solution. It would be difficult to solve the problem without using recursion.

Consider tracing the program for n = 3. The successive recursive calls are shown in Figure 20.8. As you can see, writing the program is easier than tracing the recursive calls. The system uses stacks to trace the calls behind the scenes. To some extent, recursion provides a level of abstraction that hides iterations and other details from the user.

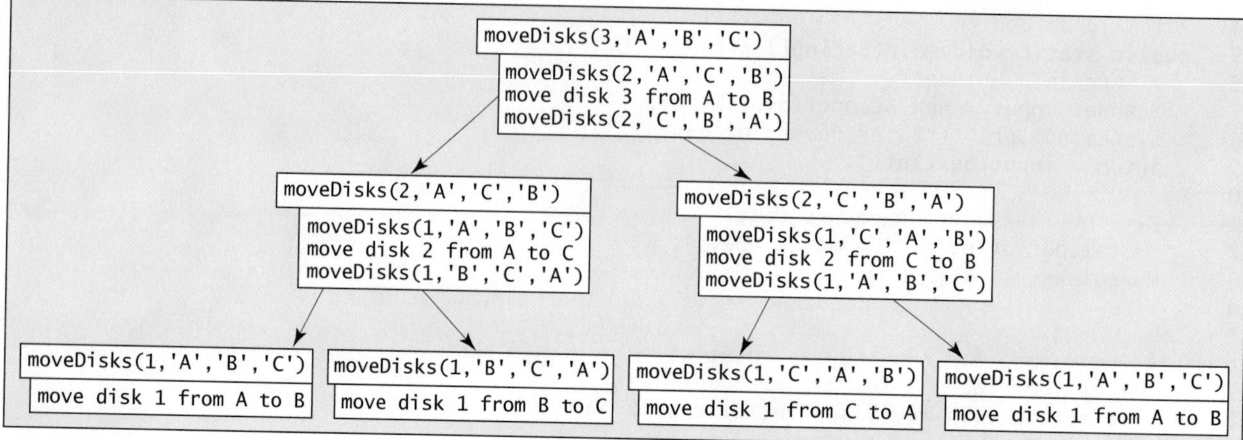

FIGURE 20.8 Invoking `moveDisks(3, 'A', 'B', 'C')` spawns calls to `moveDisks` recursively.

Video Note
Fractal (Sierpinski triangle)

20.8 Problem: Fractals

A *fractal* is a geometrical figure, but unlike triangles, circles, and rectangles, fractals can be divided into parts, each of which is a reduced-size copy of the whole. There are many interesting examples of fractals. This section introduces a simple fractal, the *Sierpinski triangle*, named after a famous Polish mathematician.

A Sierpinski triangle is created as follows:

1. Begin with an equilateral triangle, which is considered to be a Sierpinski fractal of order (or level) 0, as shown in Figure 20.9(a).
2. Connect the midpoints of the sides of the triangle of order 0 to create a Sierpinski triangle of order 1 (Figure 20.9(b)).

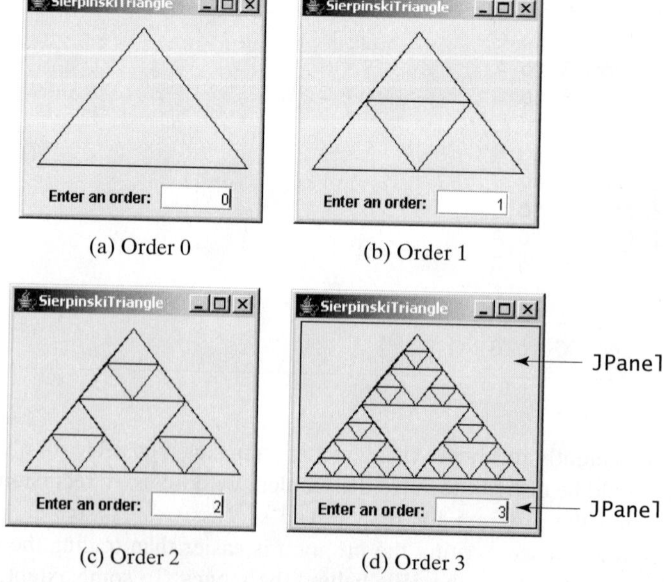

(a) Order 0 (b) Order 1

(c) Order 2 (d) Order 3

FIGURE 20.9 A Sierpinski triangle is a pattern of triangles.

3. Leave the center triangle intact. Connect the midpoints of the sides of the three other triangles to create a Sierpinski triangle of order 2 (Figure 20.9(c)).

4. You can repeat the same process recursively to create a Sierpinski triangle of order 3, 4, . . ., and so on (Figure 20.9(d)).

The problem is inherently recursive. How do you develop a recursive solution for it? Consider the base case when the order is 0. It is easy to draw a Sierpinski triangle of order 0. How do you draw a Sierpinski triangle of order 1? The problem can be reduced to drawing three Sierpinski triangles of order 0. How do you draw a Sierpinski triangle of order 2? The problem can be reduced to drawing three Sierpinski triangles of order 1. So the problem of drawing a Sierpinski triangle of order *n* can be reduced to drawing three Sierpinski triangles of order *n* - 1.

Listing 20.9 gives a Java applet that displays a Sierpinski triangle of any order, as shown in Figure 20.8. You can enter an order in a text field to display a Sierpinski triangle of the specified order.

LISTING 20.9 SierpinskiTriangle.java

```
import javax.swing.*;
import java.awt.*;
import java.awt.event.*;

public class SierpinskiTriangle extends JApplet {
  private JTextField jtfOrder = new JTextField(5); // To hold order
  private SierpinskiTrianglePanel trianglePanel =
    new SierpinskiTrianglePanel(); // To display the pattern

  public SierpinskiTriangle() {
    // Panel to hold label, text field, and a button
    JPanel panel = new JPanel();
    panel.add(new JLabel("Enter an order: "));
    panel.add(jtfOrder);
    jtfOrder.setHorizontalAlignment(SwingConstants.RIGHT);

    // Add a Sierpinski Triangle panel to the applet
    add(trianglePanel);
    add(panel, BorderLayout.SOUTH);

    // Register a listener
    jtfOrder.addActionListener(new ActionListener() {
      public void actionPerformed(ActionEvent e) {
        trianglePanel.setOrder(Integer.parseInt(jtfOrder.getText()));
      }
    });
  }

  static class SierpinskiTrianglePanel extends JPanel {
    private int order = 0;

    /** Set a new order */
    public void setOrder(int order) {
      this.order = order;
      repaint();
    }

```

listener

set a new order

```
38     protected void paintComponent(Graphics g) {
39       super.paintComponent(g);
40
41       // Select three points in proportion to the panel size
```

three initial points

```
42       Point p1 = new Point(getWidth() / 2, 10);
43       Point p2 = new Point(10, getHeight() - 10);
44       Point p3 = new Point(getWidth() - 10, getHeight() - 10);
45
46       displayTriangles(g, order, p1, p2, p3);
47     }
48
49     private static void displayTriangles(Graphics g, int order,
50         Point p1, Point p2, Point p3) {
51       if (order >= 0) {
52         // Draw a triangle to connect three points
```

draw a triangle

```
53         g.drawLine(p1.x, p1.y, p2.x, p2.y);
54         g.drawLine(p1.x, p1.y, p3.x, p3.y);
55         g.drawLine(p2.x, p2.y, p3.x, p3.y);
56
57         // Get three midpints in the triangle
58         Point midBetweenP1P2 = midpoint(p1, p2);
59         Point midBetweenP2P3 = midpoint(p2, p3);
60         Point midBetweenP3P1 = midpoint(p3, p1);
61
62         // Recursively display three triangles
```

top subtriangle

```
63         displayTriangles(g, order - 1,
64           p1, midBetweenP1P2, midBetweenP3P1);
```

left subtriangle

```
65         displayTriangles(g, order - 1,
66           midBetweenP1P2, p2, midBetweenP2P3);
```

right subtriangle

```
67         displayTriangles(g, order - 1,
68           midBetweenP3P1, midBetweenP2P3, p3);
69       }
70     }
71
72     private static Point midpoint(Point p1, Point p2) {
73       return new Point((p1.x + p2.x) / 2, (p1.y + p2.y) / 2);
74     }
75   }
```

main method omitted

```
76 }
```

The initial triangle has three points set in proportion to the panel size (lines 42–44). The **displayTriangles(g, order, p1, p2, p3)** method performs the following tasks if **order** >= **0**:

1. Display a triangle to connect three points **p1**, **p2**, and **p3** in lines 53–55.

2. Obtain a midpoint between **p1** and **p2** (line 58), a midpoint between **p2** and **p3** (line 59), and a midpoint between **p3** and **p1** (line 60), as shown in Figure 20.10.

3. Recursively invoke **displayTriangles** with a reduced order to display three smaller triangles (lines 63–68).

A Sierpinski triangle is displayed in a **SierpinskiTrianglePanel**. The **order** property in the inner class **SierpinskiTrianglePanel** specifies the order for the Sierpinski triangle. The **Point** class, introduced in §15.4, "Mouse Events," represents a point on a component. The **midpoint(Point p1, Point p2)** method returns the midpoint between **p1** and **p2** (lines 72–74).

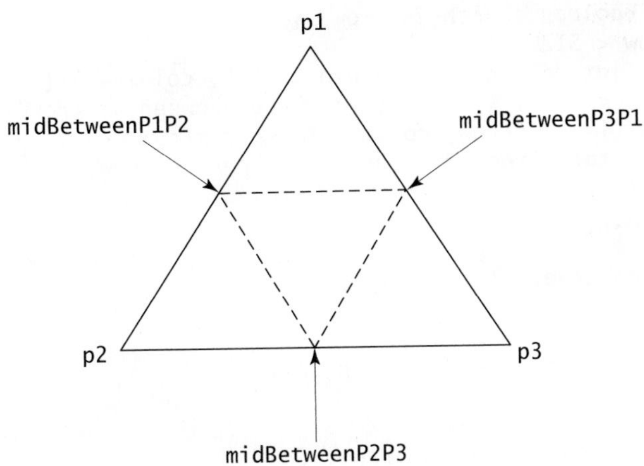

FIGURE 20.10 Three small triangles are created.

20.9 Problem: Eight Queens

This section gives a recursive solution to the Eight Queens problem presented at the beginning of this chapter. The task is to find a solution to place a queen in each row on a chessboard such that no two queens can attack each other. You may use a two-dimensional array to represent a chess board. However, since each row can have only one queen, it is sufficient to use a one-dimensional array to denote the position of the queen in the row. So, you may declare array **queens** as follows:

```
int[] queens = new int[8];
```

Assign `j` to **queens[i]** to denote that a queen is placed in row `i` and column `j`. Figure 20.11(a) shows the contents of array **queens** for the chessboard in Figure 20.11(b).

Listing 20.10 gives the program that displays a solution for the Eight Queens problem.

LISTING 20.10 `EightQueens.java`

```
import java.awt.*;
import javax.swing.*;

public class EightQueens extends JApplet {
  public static final int SIZE = 8; // The size of the chess board
  private int[] queens = new int[SIZE]; // Queen positions

  public EightQueens() {
    search(0); // Search for a solution from row 0
    add(new ChessBoard(), BorderLayout.CENTER);
  }

  /** Check if a queen can be placed at row i and column j */
  private boolean isValid(int row, int column) {
    for (int i = 1; i <= row; i++)
      if (queens[row - i] == column // Check column
        || queens[row - i] == column - i // Check upper left diagonal
        || queens[row - i] == column + i) // Check upright diagonal
        return false; // There is a conflict
    return true; // No conflict
  }

  /** Search for a solution starting from a specified row */
```

search for solution

check if valid

search this row
search columns
search next row
found
main method omitted

```java
  private boolean search(int row) {
    if (row < SIZE) {
      for (int column = 0; column < SIZE; column++) {
        queens[row] = column; // Place a queen at (row, column)
        if (isValid(row, column) && search(row + 1))
          return true; // Found, thus return true to exit the loop
      }
    }
    else {
      return true; // A solution found
    }

    return false; // No solution
  }

  class ChessBoard extends JPanel {
    private Image queenImage =
      new ImageIcon("image/queen.jpg").getImage();

    ChessBoard() {
      this.setBorder(BorderFactory.createLineBorder(Color.BLACK, 2));
    }

    protected void paintComponent(Graphics g) {
      super.paintComponent(g);

      // Paint the queens
      for (int i = 0; i < SIZE; i++) {
        int j = queens[i]; // The position of the queen in row i
        g.drawImage(queenImage, j * getWidth() / SIZE,
          i * getHeight() / SIZE, getWidth() / SIZE,
          getHeight() / SIZE, this);
      }

      // Draw the horizontal and vertical lines
      for (int i = 1; i < SIZE; i++) {
        g.drawLine(0, i * getHeight() / SIZE,
          getWidth(), i * getHeight() / SIZE);
        g.drawLine(i * getWidth() / SIZE, 0,
          i * getWidth() / SIZE, getHeight());
      }
    }
  }
}
```

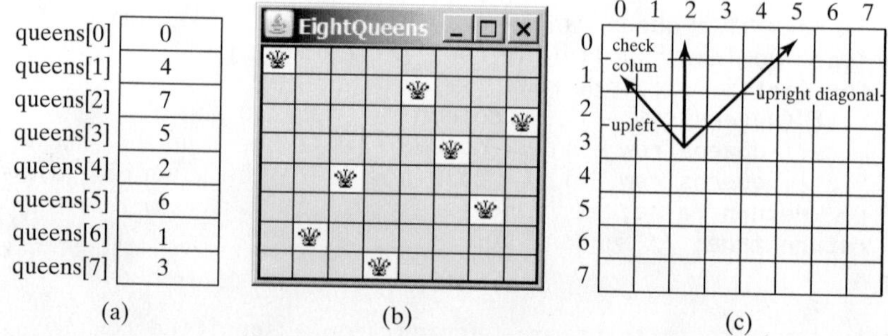

FIGURE 20.11 `queens[i]` denotes the position of the queen in row `i`.

The program invokes search(0) (line 9) to start a search for a solution at row 0, which recursively invokes search(1), search(2), . . . , and search(7) (line 26).

The search(row) method checks whether a queen can be placed in column 0, 1, 2, . . . , and 7 in a for loop (line 26). Place a queen in the column (line 25). If the placement is valid, recursively search for the next row (line 28). If search is successful, return true (line 29) to exit the for loop. In this case, there is no need to look for the next column in the row.

The isValid(row, column) method checks whether placing a queen at the specified position causes a conflict with the queens placed before this row. It ensures that no queen is placed in the same column (line 16), no queen is placed in the upper left diagonal (line 17), and no queen is placed in the upper right diagonal (line 18), as shown in Figure 20.11(c).

20.10 Recursion versus Iteration

Recursion is an alternative form of program control. It is essentially repetition without a loop control. When you use loops, you specify a loop body. The repetition of the loop body is controlled by the loop-control structure. In recursion, the method itself is called repeatedly. A selection statement must be used to control whether to call the method recursively or not.

recursion overhead

Recursion bears substantial overhead. Each time the program calls a method, the system must assign space for all of the method's local variables and parameters. This can consume considerable memory and requires extra time to manage the additional space.

recursion advantages

Any problem that can be solved recursively can be solved nonrecursively with iterations. Recursion has some negative aspects: it uses up too much time and too much memory. Why, then, should you use it? In some cases, using recursion enables you to specify a clear, simple solution for an inherent recursive problem that would otherwise be difficult to obtain. Examples are the directory-size problem, the Towers of Hanoi problem, and the fractal problem, which are rather difficult to solve without using recursion.

recursion or iteration?

The decision whether to use recursion or iteration should be based on the nature of, and your understanding of, the problem you are trying to solve. The rule of thumb is to use whichever approach can best develop an intuitive solution that naturally mirrors the problem. If an iterative solution is obvious, use it. It will generally be more efficient than the recursive option.

Note

Your recursive program could run out of memory, causing a StackOverflowError.

StackOverflowError

Tip

If you are concerned about your program's performance, avoid using recursion, because it takes more time and consumes more memory than iteration.

performance concern

Key Terms

base case 656
infinite recursion 657
recursive method 656
recursive helper method 663
stopping condition 656

Chapter Summary

- A recursive method is one that directly or indirectly invokes itself. For a recursive method to terminate, there must be one or more base cases.
- Recursion is an alternative form of program control. It is essentially repetition without a loop control. It can be used to specify simple, clear solutions for inherently recursive problems that would otherwise be difficult to solve.

- Sometimes the original method needs to be modified to receive additional parameters in order to be invoked recursively. A recursive helper method can be declared for this purpose.
- Recursion bears substantial overhead. Each time the program calls a method, the system must assign space for all of the method's local variables and parameters. This can consume considerable memory and requires extra time to manage the additional space.

Review Questions

Sections 20.1–20.3

20.1 What is a recursive method? Describe the characteristics of recursive methods. What is an infinite recursion?

20.2 Write a recursive mathematical definition for computing 2^n for a positive integer n.

20.3 Write a recursive mathematical definition for computing x^n for a positive integer n and a real number x.

20.4 Write a recursive mathematical definition for computing $1 + 2 + 3 + \cdots + n$ for a positive integer.

20.5 How many times is the `factorial` method in Listing 20.1 invoked for `factorial(6)`?

20.6 How many times is the `fib` method in Listing 20.2 invoked for `fib(6)`?

Sections 20.4–20.6

20.7 Show the call stack for `isPalindrome("abcba")` using the methods declared in Listing 20.3 and Listing 20.4, respectively.

20.8 Show the call stack for `selectionSort(new double[]{2, 3, 5, 1})` using the method declared in Listing 20.5.

20.9 What is a recursive helper method?

Section 20.7 Towers of Hanoi

20.10 How many times is the `moveDisks` method in Listing 20.8 invoked for `moveDisks(5, 'A', 'B', 'C')`?

Section 20.9 Recursion versus Iteration

20.11 Which of the following statements are true?

- Any recursive method can be converted into a nonrecursive method.
- Recursive methods take more time and memory to execute than nonrecursive methods.
- Recursive methods are *always* simpler than nonrecursive methods.
- There is always a condition statement in a recursive method to check whether a base case is reached.

20.12 What is the cause for the stack overflow exception?

Comprehensive

20.13 Show the output of the following program:

```
public class Test {
  public static void main(String[] args) {
    System.out.println(
      "Sum is " + xMethod(5));
  }

  public static int xMethod(int n) {
    if (n == 1)
      return 1;
    else
      return n + xMethod(n - 1);
  }
}
```

```
public class Test {
  public static void main(String[] args) {
    xMethod(1234567);
  }

  public static void xMethod(int n) {
    if (n > 0) {
      System.out.print(n % 10);
      xMethod(n / 10);
    }
  }
}
```

20.14 Show the output of the following two programs:

```
public class Test {
  public static void main(String[] args) {
    xMethod(5);
  }

  public static void xMethod(int n) {
    if (n > 0) {
      System.out.print(n + " ");
      xMethod(n - 1);
    }
  }
}
```

```
public class Test {
  public static void main(String[] args) {
    xMethod(5);
  }

  public static void xMethod(int n) {
    if (n > 0) {
      xMethod(n - 1);
      System.out.print(n + " ");
    }
  }
}
```

20.15 What is wrong in the following method?

```
public class Test {
  public static void main(String[] args) {
    xMethod(1234567);
  }

  public static void xMethod(double n) {
    if (n != 0) {
      System.out.print(n);
      xMethod(n / 10);
    }
  }
}
```

```
public class Test {
  public static void main(String[] args) {
    Test test = new Test();
    System.out.println(test.toString());
  }

  public Test() {
    Test test = new Test();
  }
}
```

PROGRAMMING EXERCISES

Sections 20.2–20.3

20.1** (*Factorial*) Using the `BigInteger` class introduced in §11.12, you can find the factorial for a large number (e.g., `100!`). Write a program that prompts the user to enter an integer and displays its factorial. Implement the method using recursion.

20.2* (*Fibonacci numbers*) Rewrite the `fib` method in Listing 20.2 using iterations.

Hint: To compute `fib(n)` without recursion, you need to obtain `fib(n - 2)` and `fib(n - 1)` first. Let `f0` and `f1` denote the two previous Fibonacci numbers. The current Fibonacci number would then be `f0 + f1`. The algorithm can be described as follows:

```
f0 = 0; // For fib(0)
f1 = 1; // For fib(1)

for (int i = 1; i <= n; i++) {
  currentFib = f0 + f1;
  f0 = f1;
  f1 = currentFib;
}

// After the loop, currentFib is fib(n)
```

20.3* (*Computing greatest common divisor using recursion*) The `gcd(m, n)` can also be defined recursively as follows:

- If `m % n` is `0`, `gcd (m, n)` is `n`.
- Otherwise, `gcd(m, n)` is `gcd(n, m % n)`.

Write a recursive method to find the GCD. Write a test program that computes `gcd(24, 16)` and `gcd(255, 25)`.

20.4 (*Summing series*) Write a recursive method to compute the following series:

$$m(i) = 1 + \frac{1}{2} + \frac{1}{3} + \cdots + \frac{1}{i}$$

20.5 (*Summing series*) Write a recursive method to compute the following series:

$$m(i) = \frac{1}{3} + \frac{2}{5} + \frac{3}{7} + \frac{4}{9} + \frac{5}{11} + \frac{6}{13} + \cdots + \frac{i}{2i + 1}$$

20.6* (*Summing series*) Write a recursive method to compute the following series:

$$m(i) = \frac{1}{2} + \frac{2}{3} + \cdots + \frac{i}{i + 1}$$

20.7* (*Fibonacci series*) Modify Listing 20.2, ComputeFibonacci.java, so that the program finds the number of times the `fib` method is called.

(*Hint*: Use a static variable and increment it every time the method is called.)

Section 20.4 Problem Solving Using Recursion

20.8* (*Printing the digits in an integer reversely*) Write a recursive method that displays an `int` value reversely on the console using the following header:

```
public static void reverseDisplay(int value)
```

For example, `reverseDisplay(12345)` displays `54321`.

20.9* (*Printing the characters in a string reversely*) Write a recursive method that displays a string reversely on the console using the following header:

```
public static void reverseDisplay(String value)
```

For example, `reverseDisplay("abcd")` displays `dcba`.

20.10* (*Occurrences of a specified character in a string*) Write a recursive method that finds the number of occurrences of a specified letter in a string using the following method header.

```
public static int count(String str, char a)
```

For example, `count("Welcome", 'e')` returns `2`.

20.11* (*Summing the digits in an integer using recursion*) Write a recursive method that computes the sum of the digits in an integer. Use the following method header:

```
public static int sumDigits(long n)
```

For example, `sumDigits(234)` returns 2 + 3 + 4 = 9.

Section 20.5 Recursive Helper Methods

20.12** (*Printing the characters in a string reversely*) Rewrite Exercise 20.9 using a helper method to pass the substring high index to the method. The helper method header is:

```
public static void reverseDisplay(String value, int high)
```

20.13* (*Finding the largest number in an array*) Write a recursive method that returns the largest integer in an array.

20.14* (*Finding the number of uppercase letters in a string*) Write a recursive method to return the number of uppercase letters in a string.

20.15* (*Occurrences of a specified character in a string*) Rewrite Exercise 20.10 using a helper method to pass the substring high index to the method. The helper method header is:

```
public static int count(String str, char a, int high)
```

20.16* (*Finding the number of uppercase letters in an array*) Write a recursive method to return the number of uppercase letters in an array of characters. You need to declare the following two methods. The second one is a recursive helper method.

```
public static int count(char[] chars)
public static int count(char[] chars, int high)
```

20.17* (*Occurrences of a specified character in an array*) Write a recursive method that finds the number of occurrences of a specified character in an array. You need to declare the following two methods. The second one is a recursive helper method.

```
public static int count(char[] chars, char ch)
public static int count(char[] chars, char ch, int high)
```

Sections 20.6 Tower of Hanoi

20.18* (*Towers of Hanoi*) Modify Listing 20.8, TowersOfHanoi.java, so that the program finds the number of moves needed to move *n* disks from tower A to tower B.

(*Hint*: Use a static variable and increment it every time the method is called.)

20.19* (*Sierpinski triangle*) Revise Listing 20.9 to develop an applet that lets the user use the *Increase* and *Decrease* buttons to increase or decrease the current order by `1`, as shown in Figure 20.12(a). The initial order is `0`. If the current order is `0`, the *Decrease* button is ignored.

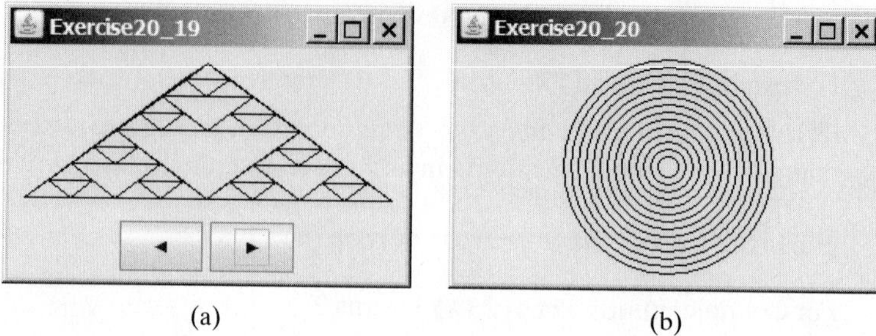

(a) (b)

FIGURE 20.12 (a) Exercise 20.19 uses the *Increase* and *Decrease* buttons to increase or decrease the current order by 1. (b) Exercise 20.10 draws ovals using a recursive method.

20.20* (*Displaying circles*) Write a Java applet that displays ovals, as shown in Figure 20.12(b). The ovals are centered in the panel. The gap between two adjacent ovals is 10 pixels, and the gap between the panel and the largest oval is also 10.

Comprehensive

20.21* (*Decimal to binary*) Write a recursive method that converts a decimal number into a binary number as a string. The method header is as follows:

```
public static String convertDecimalToBinary(int value)
```

20.22* (*Decimal to hex*) Write a recursive method that converts a decimal number into a hex number as a string. The method header is as follows:

```
public static String convertDecimalToHex(int value)
```

20.23* (*Binary to decimal*) Write a recursive method that parses a binary number as a string into a decimal integer. The method header is as follows:

```
public static int parseBinary(String binaryString)
```

20.24* (*Hex to decimal*) Write a recursive method that parses a hex number as a string into a decimal integer. The method header is as follows:

```
public static int parseHex(String hexString)
```

20.25** (*String permutation*) Write a recursive method to print all the permutations of a string. For example, for a string abc, the printout is

```
abc
acb
bac
bca
cab
cba
```

(*Hint*: Declare the following two methods. The second is a helper method.)

```
public static void displayPermuation(String s)
public static void displayPermuation(String s1, String s2)
```

The first method simply invokes `displayPermuation("", s)`. The second method uses a loop to move a character from `s2` to `s1` and recursively invoke it with a new `s1` and `s2`. The base case is that `s2` is empty and prints `s1` to the console.

20.26** (*Creating a maze*) Write an applet that will find a path in a maze, as shown in Figure 20.13(a). The applet should also run as an application. The maze is represented by an 8 × 8 board. The path must meet the following conditions:

- The path is between the upper-left corner cell and the lower-right corner cell in the maze.
- The applet enables the user to insert or remove a mark on a cell. A path consists of adjacent unmarked cells. Two cells are said to be adjacent if they are horizontal or vertical neighbors, but not if they are diagonal neighbors.
- The path does not contain cells that form a square. The path in Figure 20.13(b), for example, does not meet this condition. (The condition makes a path easy to identify on the board.)

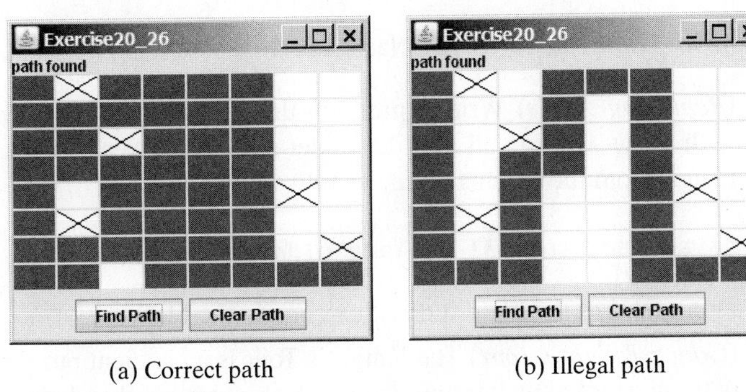

(a) Correct path (b) Illegal path

FIGURE 20.13 The program finds a path from the upper-left corner to the bottom-right corner.

20.27** (*Koch snowflake fractal*) The text presented the Sierpinski triangle fractal. In this exercise, you will write an applet to display another fractal, called the *Koch snowflake*, named after a famous Swedish mathematician. A Koch snowflake is created as follows:

1. Begin with an equilateral triangle, which is considered to be the Koch fractal of order (or level) `0`, as shown in Figure 20.14(a).
2. Divide each line in the shape into three equal line segments and draw an outward equilateral triangle with the middle line segment as the base to create a Koch fractal of order `1`, as shown in Figure 20.14(b).
3. Repeat step 2 to create a Koch fractal of order `2`, `3`,..., and so on, as shown in Figure 20.14(c).

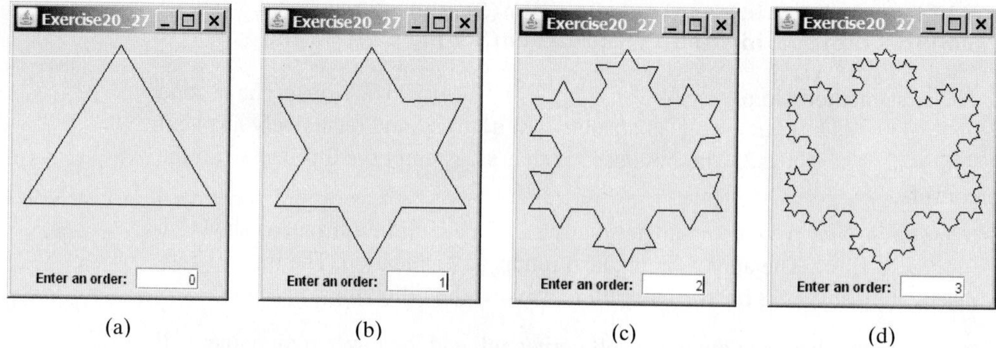

FIGURE 20.14 A Koch snowflake is a fractal starting with a triangle.

20.28** (*Nonrecursive directory size*) Rewrite Listing 20.7, DirectorySize.java, without using recursion.

20.29* (*Number of files in a directory*) Write a program that prompts the user to enter a directory and displays the number of the files in the directory.

Video Note
Search a string in a directory

20.30** (*Finding words*) Write a program that finds all occurrences of a word in all the files under a directory, recursively. Pass the parameters from the command line as follows:

```
java Exercise20_30 dirName word
```

20.31** (*Replacing words*) Write a program that replaces all occurrences of a word with a new word in all the files under a directory, recursively. Pass the parameters from the command line as follows:

```
java Exercise20_31 dirName oldWord newWord
```

Don't modify the file if it does not contain the oldWord.

20.32*** (*Game: Knight's Tour*) The Knight's Tour is an ancient puzzle. The objective is to move a knight, starting from any square on a chessboard, to every other square once, as shown in Figure 20.15(a). Note that the knight makes only L-shape moves (two spaces in one direction and one space in a perpendicular direction). As shown in Figure 20.15(b), the knight can move to eight squares. Write a program that displays the moves for the knight in an applet, as shown in Figure 20.15(b).

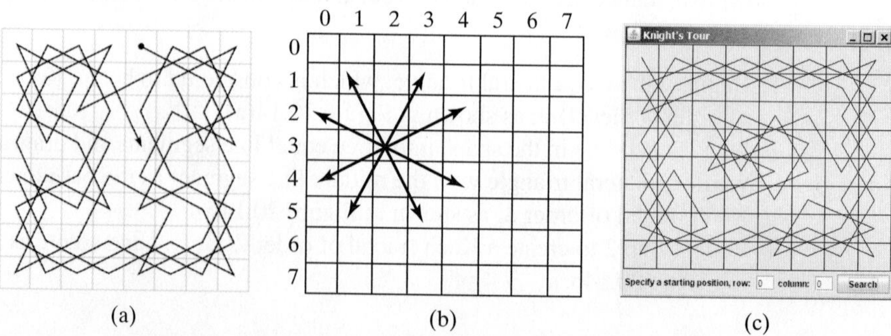

FIGURE 20.15 (a) A knight traverses all squares once. (b) A knight makes an L-shape move. (c) An applet displays a knight tour path.

(*Hint*: A brute-force approach for this problem is to move the knight from one square to another available square arbitrarily. Using such an approach, your program will take a long time to finish. A better approach is to employ some heuristics. A knight has two, three, four, six, or eight possible moves, depending on its location. Intuitively, you should attempt to move the knight to the least accessible squares first and leave those more accessible squares open, so there will be a better chance of success in the end of the search.)

20.33*** (*Game: Knight's Tour animation*) Write an applet for the Knight's Tour problem. Your applet should let the user move a knight to any starting square and click the *Solve* button to animate a knight moving along the path, as shown in Figure 20.16.

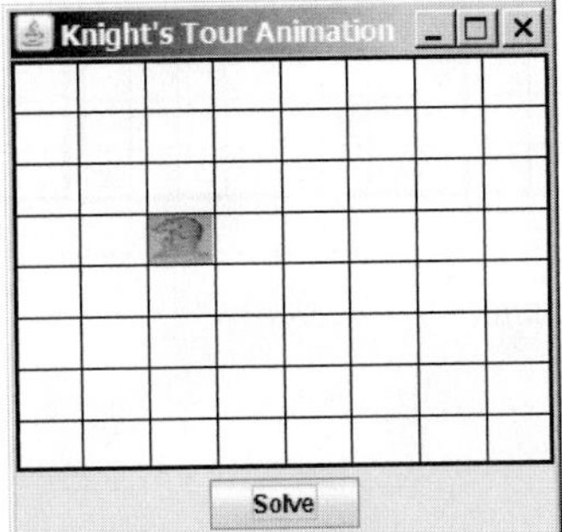

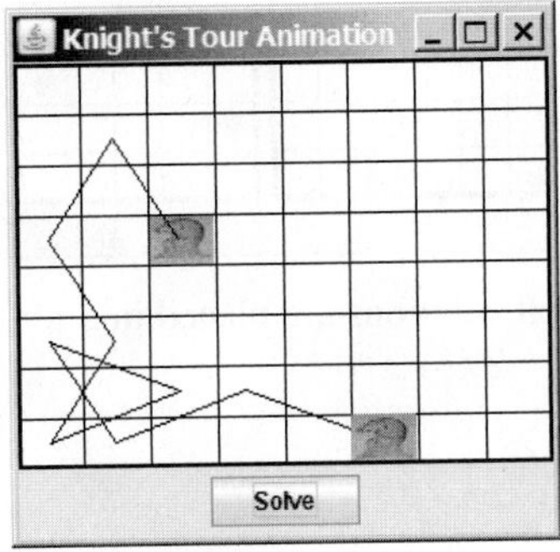

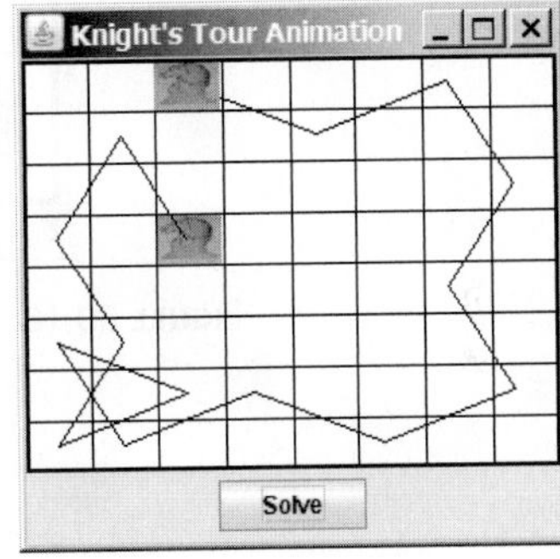

FIGURE 20.16 A knight traverses along the path.

20.34** (*Game: Sudoku*) Rewrite Listing 6.12, Sudoku.java, using recursion.

20.35** (*H-tree fractal*) An H-tree is a fractal defined as follows:

1. Begin with a letter H. The three lines of the H are of the same length, as shown in Figure 20.17(a).
2. The letter H has four endpoints. Draw an H centered at each of the four endpoints to an H-tree of order 1, as shown in Figure 20.17(b). These H's are half the size of the H that contains the four endpoints.
3. Repeat step 2 to create a H-tree of order 2, 3, . . . , and so on, as shown in Figure 20.17(c).

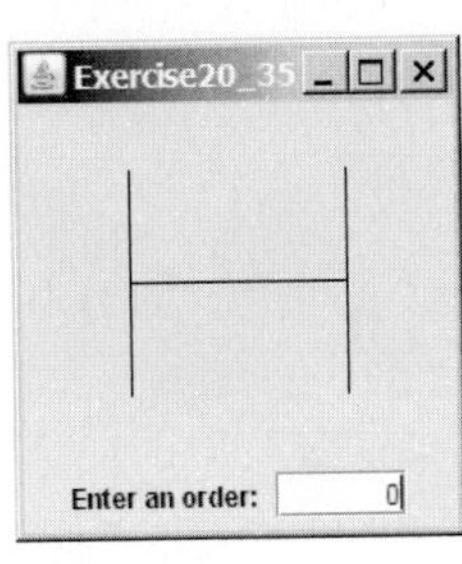

(a)

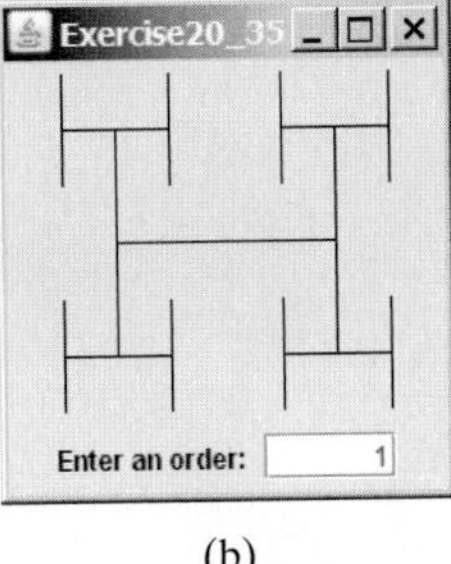

(b)

(c)

(d)

FIGURE 20.17 An H-tree is a fractal starting with three lines of equal length in an H-shape.

The H-tree is used in VLSI design as a clock distribution network for routing timing signals to all parts of a chip with equal propagation delays. Write an applet that draws an H-tree, as shown in Figure 20.17.

20.36*** (*Game: all Sudoku solutions*) Rewrite Exercise 20.34 to find all possible solutions to a Sudoku problem.

20.37*** (*Game: multiple Eight Queens solution*) Write an applet to display all possible solutions for the Eight Queens puzzle in a scroll pane, as shown in Figure 20.18. For each solution, put a label to denote the solution number.

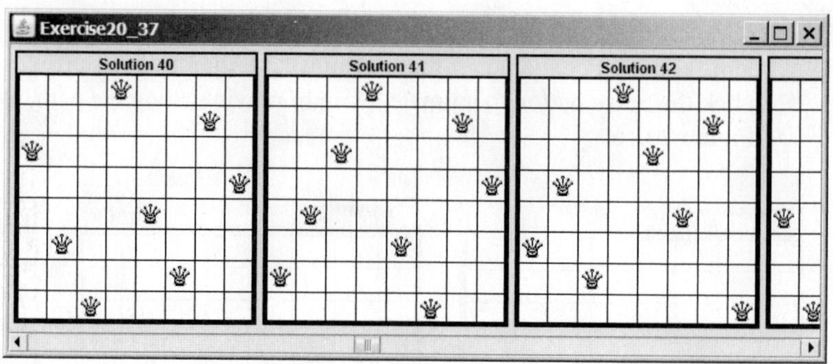

FIGURE 20.18 All solutions are placed in a scroll pane.

APPENDIXES

APPENDIX A

Java Keywords

The following fifty keywords are reserved for use by the Java language:

`abstract`	`double`	`int`	`super`
`assert`	`else`	`interface`	`switch`
`boolean`	`enum`	`long`	`synchronized`
`break`	`extends`	`native`	`this`
`byte`	`for`	`new`	`throw`
`case`	`final`	`package`	`throws`
`catch`	`finally`	`private`	`transient`
`char`	`float`	`protected`	`try`
`class`	`goto`	`public`	`void`
`const`	`if`	`return`	`volatile`
`continue`	`implements`	`short`	`while`
`default`	`import`	`static`	
`do`	`instanceof`	`strictfp`*	

The keywords **goto** and **const** are C++ keywords reserved, but not currently used, in Java. This enables Java compilers to identify them and to produce better error messages if they appear in Java programs.

The literal values `true`, `false`, and `null` are not keywords, just like literal value `100`. However, you cannot use them as identifiers, just as you cannot use `100` as an identifier.

assert is a keyword added in JDK 1.4 and **enum** is a keyword added in JDK 1.5.

---

*The **strictfp** keyword is a modifier for method or class to use strict floating-point calculations. Floating-point arithmetic can be executed in one of two modes: *strict* or *nonstrict*. The strict mode guarantees that the evaluation result is the same on all Java Virtual Machine implementations. The nonstrict mode allows intermediate results from calculations to be stored in an extended format different from the standard IEEE floating-point number format. The extended format is machine-dependent and enables code to be executed faster. However, when you execute the code using the nonstrict mode on different JVMs, you may not always get precisely the same results. By default, the nonstrict mode is used for floating-point calculations. To use the strict mode in a method or a class, add the **strictfp** keyword in the method or the class declaration. Strict floating-point may give you slightly better precision than nonstrict floating-point, but the distinction will only affect some applications. Strictness is not inherited; that is, the presence of **strictfp** on a class or interface declaration does not cause extended classes or interfaces to be strict.

Appendix B

The ASCII Character Set

Tables B.1 and B.2 show ASCII characters and their respective decimal and hexadecimal codes. The decimal or hexadecimal code of a character is a combination of its row index and column index. For example, in Table B.1, the letter A is at row 6 and column 5, so its decimal equivalent is 65; in Table B.2, letter A is at row 4 and column 1, so its hexadecimal equivalent is 41.

TABLE B.1 ASCII Character Set in the Decimal Index

	0	*1*	*2*	*3*	*4*	*5*	*6*	*7*	*8*	*9*
0	nul	soh	stx	etx	eot	enq	ack	bel	bs	ht
1	nl	vt	ff	cr	so	si	dle	dcl	dc2	dc3
2	dc4	nak	syn	etb	can	em	sub	esc	fs	gs
3	rs	us	sp	!	”	#	$	%	&	’
4	(	)	*	+	,	—	.	/	0	1
5	2	3	4	5	6	7	8	9	:	;
6	<	=	>	?	@	A	B	C	D	E
7	F	G	H	I	J	K	L	M	N	O
8	P	Q	R	S	T	U	V	W	X	Y
9	Z	[	\	]	∧	—	‘	a	b	c
10	d	e	f	g	h	i	j	k	l	m
11	n	o	p	q	r	s	t	u	v	w
12	x	y	z	{	|	}	~	del		

TABLE B.2 ASCII Character Set in the Hexadecimal Index

	0	*1*	*2*	*3*	*4*	*5*	*6*	*7*	*8*	*9*	*A*	*B*	*C*	*D*	*E*	*F*
0	nul	soh	stx	etx	eot	enq	ack	bel	bs	ht	nl	vt	ff	cr	so	si
1	dle	dcl	dc2	dc3	dc4	nak	syn	etb	can	em	sub	esc	fs	gs	rs	us
2	sp	!	”	#	$	%	&	’	(	)	*	+	,	—	.	/
3	0	1	2	3	4	5	6	7	8	9	:	;	<	=	>	?
4	@	A	B	C	D	E	F	G	H	I	J	K	L	M	N	O
5	P	Q	R	S	T	U	V	W	X	Y	Z	[	\	]	∧	—
6	‘	a	b	c	d	e	f	g	h	i	j	k	l	m	n	o
7	p	q	r	s	t	u	v	w	x	y	z	{	|	}	~	del

APPENDIX C

Operator Precedence Chart

The operators are shown in decreasing order of precedence from top to bottom. Operators in the same group have the same precedence, and their associativity is shown in the table.

Operator	*Name*	*Associativity*
`()`	Parentheses	Left to right
`()`	Function call	Left to right
`[]`	Array subscript	Left to right
`.`	Object member access	Left to right
`++`	Postincrement	Right to left
`--`	Postdecrement	Right to left
`++`	Preincrement	Right to left
`--`	Predecrement	Right to left
`+`	Unary plus	Right to left
`-`	Unary minus	Right to left
`!`	Unary logical negation	Right to left
`(type)`	Unary casting	Right to left
`new`	Creating object	Right to left
`*`	Multiplication	Left to right
`/`	Division	Left to right
`%`	Remainder	Left to right
`+`	Addition	Left to right
`-`	Subtraction	Left to right
`<<`	Left shift	Left to right
`>>`	Right shift with sign extension	Left to right
`>>>`	Right shift with zero extension	Left to right
`<`	Less than	Left to right
`<=`	Less than or equal to	Left to right
`>`	Greater than	Left to right
`>=`	Greater than or equal to	Left to right
`instanceof`	Checking object type	Left to right

Operator	*Name*	*Associativity*
`==`	Equal comparison	Left to right
`!=`	Not equal	Left to right
`&`	(Unconditional AND)	Left to right
`^`	(Exclusive OR)	Left to right
`|`	(Unconditional OR)	Left to right
`&&`	Conditional AND	Left to right
`||`	Conditional OR	Left to right
`?:`	Ternary condition	Right to left
`=`	Assignment	Right to left
`+=`	Addition assignment	Right to left
`-=`	Subtraction assignment	Right to left
`*=`	Multiplication assignment	Right to left
`/=`	Division assignment	Right to left
`%=`	Remainder assignment	Right to left

Appendix D

Java Modifiers

Modifiers are used on classes and class members (constructors, methods, data, and class-level blocks), but the final modifier can also be used on local variables in a method. A modifier that can be applied to a class is called a *class modifier*. A modifier that can be applied to a method is called a *method modifier*. A modifier that can be applied to a data field is called a *data modifier*. A modifier that can be applied to a class-level block is called a block modifier. The following table gives a summary of the Java modifiers.

Modifier	*class*	*constructor*	*method*	*data*	*block*	*Explanation*
(default)*	√	√	√	√	√	A class, constructor, method, or data field is visible in this package.
public	√	√	√	√		A class, constructor, method, or data field is visible to all the programs in any package.
private		√	√	√		A constructor, method or data field is only visible in this class.
protected		√	√	√		A constructor, method or data field is visible in this package and in subclasses of this class in any package.
static			√	√	√	Define a class method, or a class data field or a static initialization block.
final	√		√	√		A final class cannot be extended. A final method cannot be modified in a subclass. A final data field is a constant.
abstract	√		√			An abstract class must be extended. An abstract method must be implemented in a concrete subclass.
native			√			A native method indicates that the method is implemented using a language other than Java.

*Default access has no modifier associated with it. For example: **`class Test {}`**

Modifier	*class*	*constructor*	*method*	*data*	*block*	*Explanation*
`synchronized`			√		√	Only one thread at a time can execute this method.
`strictfp`	√	√				Use strict floating-point calculations to guarantee that the evaluation result is the same on all JVMs.
`transient`				√		Mark a nonserializable instance data field.

Appendix E

Special Floating-Point Values

Dividing an integer by zero is invalid and throws ArithmeticException, but dividing a floating-point value by zero does not cause an exception. Floating-point arithmetic can overflow to infinity if the result of the operation is too large for a double or a float, or underflow to zero if the result is too small for a double or a float. Java provides the special floating-point values POSITIVE_INFINITY, NEGATIVE_INFINITY, and NaN (Not a Number) to denote these results. These values are defined as special constants in the Float class and the Double class.

If a positive floating-point number is divided by zero, the result is POSITIVE_INFINITY. If a negative floating-point number is divided by zero, the result is NEGATIVE_INFINITY. If a floating-point zero is divided by zero, the result is NaN, which means that the result is undefined mathematically. The string representation of these three values are Infinity, -Infinity, and NaN. For example,

```
System.out.print(1.0 / 0); // Print Infinity
System.out.print(-1.0 / 0); // Print -Infinity
System.out.print(0.0 / 0); // Print NaN
```

These special values can also be used as operands in computations. For example, a number divided by POSITIVE_INFINITY yields a positive zero. Table E.1 summarizes various combinations of the /, *, %, +, and - operators.

TABLE E.1 Special Floating-Point Values

x	*y*	*x/y*	*x*y*	*x%y*	*x + y*	*x − y*
Finite	± 0.0	± ∞	± 0.0	NaN	Finite	Finite
Finite	± ∞	± 0.0	± 0.0	x	± ∞	∞
± 0.0	± 0.0	NaN	± 0.0	NaN	± 0.0	± 0.0
± ∞	Finite	± ∞	± 0.0	NaN	± ∞	± ∞
± ∞	± ∞	NaN	± 0.0	NaN	± ∞	∞
± 0.0	± ∞	± 0.0	NaN	± 0.0	± ∞	± 0.0
NaN	Any	NaN	NaN	NaN	NaN	NaN
Any	NaN	NaN	NaN	NaN	NaN	NaN

Note

If one of the operands is NaN, the result is NaN.

INDEX